Statistics Canada

Standards Division

North American Industry Classification System - NAICS Canada

2007

March 2007

Catalogue no. 12-501-XIE
ISBN 0-662-44519-8

Catalogue no. 12-501-XPE
ISBN 0-660-19682-4

Frequency: Occasional

Ottawa

Cette publication est disponible en français sur demande (n° 12-501-XIF au catalogue).

Note of appreciation

Canada owes the success of its statistical system to a long-standing partnership between Statistics Canada, the citizens of Canada, its businesses, governments and other institutions. Accurate and timely statistical information could not be produced without their continued cooperation and goodwill.

Foreword

This volume represents the second revision to the North American Industry Classification System. The first revision, NAICS Canada 2002, was published in April 2003. The original classification, NAICS Canada 1997, was published in March 1998. This is a minor revision to the classification.

The greatest change introduced by this revision is within the telecommunications area of the Information and Cultural Industries sector. The updates made to this sector reflect the rapid changes in the structure of these industries, including the merging of activities. Numerous updates were also made to this sector in the 2002 revision of the classification.

Overall, 18 new 6-digit classes have been added in this revision, and 18 old 6-digit classes have been deleted. There has also been some movement of activities between ongoing classes. With two exceptions, all revisions occur within sector boundaries.

In addition, other changes have also been made. These include revisions to class titles, example titles, industry definitions, and to the introduction to this manual.

The Instituto Nacional de Estadística, Geografía e Informática (INEGI) of Mexico, Statistics Canada, and the United States Office of Management and Budget, through its Economic Classification Policy Committee, have jointly developed this revision. This revision is scheduled to go into effect for reference year 2007 in Canada and the United States, and 2009 in Mexico. NAICS was developed to provide a consistent framework for the collection, analysis, and dissemination of industrial statistics used by government policy analysts, by academics and researchers, by the business community, and by the public. These latest revisions were made to account for and better reflect the structure of our rapidly changing economies.

Preface

Statistics Canada, Mexico's Instituto Nacional de Estadística, Geografía e Informática (INEGI), and the Economic Classification Policy Committee (ECPC) of the United States acting on behalf of the Office of Management and Budget, have developed this revision to the North American Industry Classification System as part of a five-year revision cycle intended to ensure that the classification continues to reflect the rapidly changing structure of our economies. In this revision, the Information and Cultural Industries sector has been further updated to take into account the rapid changes within this sector, including the merging of activities.

The most significant changes to the Information and Cultural Industries sector in NAICS 2007 are the merging of Internet Publishing and Broadcasting and Web Search Portals, the merging of Internet Service Providers and Data Processing, Hosting, and Related Services and the merging of Telecommunications Resellers and Other Telecommunications.

Overall, 18 6-digit classes have been added to NAICS Canada 2007. These classes cover activities that were previously embedded in other classes. The new classes are: 111994, Maple Syrup and Products Production; 326196, Plastic Window and Door Manufacturing; 419110, Business-to-Business Electronic Markets; 419120, Wholesale Trade Agents and Brokers; 454111, Internet Shopping; 454112, Electronic Auctions; 454113, Mail-Order Houses; 454311, Heating Oil Dealers; 454312, Liquefied Petroleum Gas (Bottled Gas) Dealers; 454319, Other Fuel Dealers; 519130, Internet Publishing and Broadcasting, and Web Search Portals; 531211, Real Estate Agents; 531212, Offices of Real Estate Brokers; 711511 Independent Artists, Visual Arts; 711512, Independent Actors, Comedians and Performers; 711513, Independent Writers and Authors; 712115, History and Science Museums; and 712119, Other Museums.

Eighteen old 6-digit classes have also been deleted from NAICS Canada 2007. These classes covered activities which are now embedded in other classes. The deleted classes are NAICS 2002: 419110, Farm Product Agents and Brokers, 419120, Petroleum Product Agents and Brokers; 419130, Food, Beverage and Tobacco Agents and Brokers; 419140, Personal and Household Goods Agents and Brokers; 419150, Motor Vehicle and Parts Agents and Brokers; 419160, Building Material and Supplies Agents and Brokers; 419170, Machinery, Equipment and Supplies Agents and Brokers; 419190, Other Wholesale Agents and Brokers; 454110, Electronic Shopping and Mail-Order Houses; 454310, Fuel Dealers; 516110, Internet Publishing and Broadcasting; 517310, Telecommunications Resellers; 518111, Internet Service Providers; 518112, Web Search Portals; 526920, Mortgage Investment Funds; 531210, Offices of Real Estate Agents and Brokers; 711510, Independent Artists, Writers and Performers; and 712119, Museums (except Art Museums and Galleries).

There has also been some movement of activities between ongoing classes. For example, sweet potato and yam farming has been moved from 111219, Other Vegetable (except Potato) and Melon Farming to 111211, Potato Farming.

With two exceptions, all NAICS 2007 revisions occur within sector boundaries. The exceptions are: Real Estate Investment Trusts (REITs), which move from sector 52, Finance and Insurance to sector 53, Real Estate and Rental and Leasing; and Executive Search Consulting Services, which move from sector 54, Professional, Scientific and Technical Services to sector 56, Administrative and Support, Waste Management and Remediation Services.

In addition, other changes, which do not affect the structure of the classification, have also been made. These include revisions to class titles, to example titles, to industry definitions, and to the introduction to this manual.

Preface to the 2002 edition

Statistics Canada, Mexico's Instituto Nacional de Estadística, Geografía e Informática (INEGI), and the Economic Classification Policy Committee (ECPC) of the United States acting on behalf of the Office of Management and Budget, have developed this revision to the North American Industry Classification System as part of a five-year revision cycle intended to ensure that the classification continues to reflect the rapidly changing structure of our economies. In this revision, the Construction sector has been harmonized across the three countries, which had not been achieved in NAICS 1997, and the Information and Cultural Industries sector has been updated to take into account new industries arising from the emergence of the Internet.

The most significant change to the Construction sector in NAICS 2002 is that five-digit comparability has been achieved for all areas of Construction, except one industry group (2381, Foundation, Structure, and Building Exterior Contractors). Also included is an increase from two to three subsectors and distribution of management of construction projects throughout the construction industries. Other changes include movement of Land Subdivision and Land Development within the Heavy and Civil Engineering Construction subsector, and the construction of structures, such as sewage treatment plants and water treatment plants, within the Utility System Construction industry group.

The most significant change to Information and Cultural Industries Sector in NAICS 2002 is the inclusion of new industries that have recently appeared in the economy due to the rapid expansion of the Internet. These include the creation of a new subsector for Internet Publishing and Broadcasting, and the creation of industries for Internet service providers and web search portals.

Preface to the 1997 edition

Statistics Canada, Mexico's Instituto Nacional de Estadística, Geografía e Informática (INEGI), and the Economic Classification Policy Committee (ECPC) of the United States acting on behalf of the Office of Management and Budget, have created a common classification system to replace the existing classification of each country, the Standard Industrial Classification (1980) of Canada, the Mexican Classification of Activities and Products (1994), and the Standard Industrial Classification (1987) of the United States.

The North American Industry Classification System (NAICS) is unique among industry classifications in that it is constructed within a single conceptual framework. Economic units that have similar production processes are classified in the same industry, and the lines drawn between industries demarcate, to the extent practicable, differences in production processes. This supply-based, or production-oriented, economic concept was adopted for NAICS because an industry classification system is a framework for collecting and publishing information on both inputs and outputs, for statistical uses that require that inputs and outputs be used together and be classified consistently. Examples of such uses include measuring productivity, unit labour costs, and the capital intensity of production, estimating employment-output relationships, constructing input-output tables, and other uses that imply the analysis of production relationships in the economy. The classification concept for NAICS will produce data that facilitate such analyses.

In the design of NAICS, attention was given to developing production-oriented classifications for (a) new and emerging industries, (b) service industries in general, and (c) industries engaged in the production of advanced technologies. These special emphases are embodied in the particular features of NAICS, discussed below. These same areas of special emphasis account for many of the differences between the structure of NAICS and the structures of industry classification systems in use elsewhere. NAICS provides enhanced industry comparability among the three NAFTA trading partners, while also increasing compatibility with the two-digit level of the International Standard Industrial Classification (ISIC Rev.3) of the United Nations.

NAICS divides the economy into twenty sectors. Industries within these sectors are grouped according to the production criterion. Though the goods/services distinction is not explicitly reflected in the structure of NAICS, five sectors are largely goods-producing and fifteen are entirely services-producing industries.

A new feature of NAICS is the creation of an Information sector that groups industries that primarily create and disseminate products subject to copyright. The NAICS Information sector brings together those activities that transform information into a commodity that is produced and distributed, and activities that provide the means for distributing those products, other than through traditional wholesale-retail distribution channels. A few of the new and important industries in this sector include: software publishing; database and directory publishing; satellite telecommunications; paging, cellular and other wireless telecommunications; and on-line and other information services. Also included in the Information sector are newspaper, book, and periodical publishers (formerly included in manufacturing); motion picture and sound recording industries; libraries; and other information services.

Another feature of NAICS is a sector for Professional, Scientific and Technical Services, which comprises establishments engaged in activities where human capital is the major input. The industries within this sector are each defined by the expertise and training of the service provider. The sector includes such industries as offices of lawyers; engineering services; architectural services; advertising agencies; and interior design services. Thirty-five NAICS industries comprise this sector, many of which are now recognized for the first time.

A new sector for Arts, Entertainment and Recreation greatly expands the number of industries providing services in these three areas.

Another new sector, Health Care and Social Assistance, recognizes the merging of the boundaries of health care and social assistance. The industries in this new sector are arranged in an order that reflects the range and extent of health care and social assistance provided. Some new industries are family planning centres, out-patient mental health and substance abuse centres, and community care facilities for the elderly.

In the Manufacturing sector, an important new subsector, Computer and Electronic Product Manufacturing, brings together industries producing electronic products and their components. The manufacture of computers, communications equipment, and semiconductors, for example, are grouped into the same subsector because of the inherent technological similarities of their production processes, and the likelihood that these technologies will continue to converge in the future. An important change is that reproduction of packaged software is placed in this sector, rather than in the services sector, because the reproduction of packaged software is a manufacturing process, and the product moves through the wholesale and retail distribution systems like any other manufactured product. NAICS acknowledges the importance of these electronic industries, their rapid growth over the past several years and the likelihood that these industries will, in the future, become even more important in the economies of the three North American countries.

This NAICS structure reflects the levels at which data comparability was agreed upon by the three statistical agencies. The boundaries of all the sectors of NAICS have been delineated. In most sectors, NAICS provides for compatibility at the industry (five-digit) level; however, for real estate; utilities; finance and insurance; and for three of the four subsectors in other services (except public administration), three-country compatibility will occur either at the industry group (four-digit) or subsector (three-digit) levels. For these sectors, differences in the economies of the three countries prevent full compatibility at the NAICS industry level. For retail trade, wholesale trade, construction, and public administration, the three countries' statistical agencies have agreed, at this time, only on the boundaries of the sector (two-digit level). Below the agreed upon level of compatibility, each country may add additional detailed industries, as necessary to meet national needs, provided that this additional detail aggregates to the NAICS level.

The new classification will be adopted by Canada in their annual surveys of economic statistics for reference year 1997 and by Mexico and the United States in their economic censuses for reference years 1998 and 1997, respectively.

Acknowledgements

The second revision of the North American Industry Classification System (NAICS) required the time, energy and co-operation of numerous people and organizations in three countries: Canada, Mexico and the United States. The work that has been accomplished is a testament to the individual and collective willingness of many persons and organizations in government, business and the private sector to contribute to its development.

In Canada, NAICS was revised under the guidance of Alice Born, Director of Standards Division, and Paul Johanis, former Director of Standards Division. NAICS Canada could not have been revised without input from the subject matter divisions of Statistics Canada, federal and provincial government departments and agencies; business and trade associations, and economic analysts, the contribution of all of whom is gratefully acknowledged.

NAICS Canada 2007 is published by Standards Division. The publication was prepared by A. (Tony) Malfara under the supervision of Alice Born and John Crysdale. Special thanks go to Guy Auger, JoAnn Casey, Leonardo De Socio, Sylvain Lafleur, Jeff Leonard, France McDougall and Michael Pedersen of Standards Division, to Stuart Pursey of Business Survey Methods Division, and to Stanley Moran of Systems Development Division.

Table of Contents

Introduction   **1**

Classification Structure   **11**

Descriptions   **59**
   11 Agriculture, Forestry, Fishing and Hunting   61
   21 Mining, Quarrying, and Oil and Gas Extraction   81
   22 Utilities   93
   23 Construction   96
   31-33 Manufacturing 118
   41 Wholesale Trade 280
   44-45 Retail Trade 323
   48-49 Transportation and Warehousing 354
   51 Information and Cultural Industries 378
   52 Finance and Insurance 399
   53 Real Estate and Rental and Leasing 417
   54 Professional, Scientific and Technical Services 428
   55 Management of Companies and Enterprises 449
   56 Administrative and Support, Waste Management and Remediation Services 450
   61 Educational Services 466
   62 Health Care and Social Assistance 473
   71 Arts, Entertainment and Recreation 489
   72 Accommodation and Food Services 506
   81 Other Services (except Public Administration) 514
   91 Public Administration 533

Concordance Tables   **547**
   NAICS 2007 to NAICS 2002 553
   NAICS 2002 to NAICS 2007 559

Short Titles   **565**

Alphabetical Index   **599**

Introduction

Introduction

NAICS

The North American Industry Classification System (NAICS) is an industry classification system developed by the statistical agencies of Canada, Mexico and the United States. Created against the background of the North American Free Trade Agreement, it is designed to provide common definitions of the industrial structure of the three countries and a common statistical framework to facilitate the analysis of the three economies. NAICS is based on supply-side or production-oriented principles, to ensure that industrial data, classified to NAICS, are suitable for the analysis of production-related issues such as industrial performance.

Economic statistics describe the behaviour and activities of economic transactors and of the transactions that take place among them. The economic transactors for which NAICS is designed are businesses and other organizations engaged in the production of goods and services. They include farms, incorporated and unincorporated business and government business enterprises. They also include government institutions and agencies engaged in the production of marketed and non-marketed services, as well as organizations such as professional associations and unions and charitable or non-profit organizations and the employees of households.

NAICS is a comprehensive system encompassing all economic activities. It has a hierarchical structure. At the highest level, it divides the economy into 20 sectors. At lower levels, it further distinguishes the different economic activities in which businesses are engaged.

NAICS is designed for the compilation of production statistics and, therefore, for the classification of data relating to establishments. It takes into account the specialization of activities generally found at the level of the producing units of businesses. The criteria used to group establishments into industries in NAICS are similarity of input structures, labour skills and production processes.

NAICS can also be used for classifying companies and enterprises. However, when NAICS is used in this way, the following caveat applies: NAICS has not been specially designed to take account of the wide range of vertically- or horizontally-integrated activities of large and complex, multi-establishment companies and enterprises. Hence, there will be a few large and complex companies and enterprises whose activities may be spread over the different sectors of NAICS, in such a way that classifying them to one sector will misrepresent the range of their activities. However, in general, a larger proportion of the activities of each complex company and enterprise is more likely to fall within the sector, subsector and industry group levels of the classification than within the industry levels. Hence, the higher levels of the classification are more suitable for the classification of companies and enterprises than are the lower levels. It should also be kept in mind that when businesses are composed of establishments belonging to different NAICS industries, their company- and enterprise-level data will show a different industrial distribution, when classified to NAICS, than will their establishment-level data, and the data will not be directly comparable.

While NAICS is designed for the classification of units engaged in market and non-market production, as defined by the System of National Accounts, it can also be used to classify own-account production, such as the unpaid work of households.

NAICS Canada has been designed for statistical purposes. Government departments and agencies and other users that use it for administrative, legislative and other non-statistical purposes are responsible for interpreting the classification for the purpose or purposes for which they use it.

Structure and Coding System of NAICS and NAICS Canada

NAICS is the agreed-upon common framework for the production of comparable industry statistics by the statistical agencies of the three countries, Canada, Mexico and the United States. Its hierarchical structure is composed of sectors (two-digit codes), subsectors (three-digit codes), industry groups (four-digit codes), and industries (five-digit codes).

NAICS agreements define the boundaries of the twenty sectors into which the classification divides the economies of the three countries. Although, typically, agreement has been reached that comparable data will be made available for Canada, Mexico and the United States up to the five-digit industry level of NAICS, differences in the organization of production in the economies of the three countries necessitated certain exceptions. For certain of the sectors, subsectors and industry groups, three-country agreement was reached only on their boundaries rather than on detailed industry structures.

NAICS agreements permit each country to create industries below the NAICS industry level to meet national needs. Canada and the US have established the same or comparable national industries where possible.

The numbering system that has been adopted is a six-digit code, of which the first five digits are used to describe the NAICS levels that will be used by the three countries to produce comparable data. The first two digits designate the sector, the third digit designates the subsector, the fourth digit designates the industry group and the fifth digit designates the industry. The sixth digit is used to designate national industries.

In general, the use of the same code across the three countries indicates that the class is comparable, even if the title is not identical because of differences in the use of language.

NAICS with Canadian detail is designated NAICS Canada. Mexico and the United States produce NAICS with their own six-digit detail, which publish as Sistema de Clasificación Industrial de América del Norte (SCIAN) México and the North American Industry Classification System (NAICS) United States.

Comparability among the three countries is indicated by superscript abbreviations at the end of industry titles in the classification structure and descriptions chapters of NAICS Canada 2007. A superscript "CAN" ([CAN]) indicates a Canadian industry, "MEX" ([MEX]) indicates that Canadian and Mexican industries are comparable, and "US" ([US]) indicates that Canadian and United States industries are comparable. When no superscript appears, the Canadian, Mexican and United States industries are comparable.

NAICS Canada 2007 consists of 20 sectors, 102 subsectors, 324 industry groups, 718 industries and 928 national industries, and replaces NAICS Canada 2002. Concordances showing the relationship between the changed sectors of these two versions of NAICS Canada are shown in the concordance tables chapter of this manual.

Historical Background

Over the years, Statistics Canada has developed and used a number of industrial classification systems. In 1948, the first Canadian Standard Industrial Classification (SIC) was developed. This was done to meet the government's need to establish a more comprehensive and fully-integrated system of economic reporting, in support of the key objectives of its post-war reconstruction programme outlined in the 1945 White Paper (on Employment and Income). The 1948 SIC brought together different industry descriptions in use at the time, each of which was applied to data about different aspects of the economy based on different definitions. It facilitated data comparability, by providing a framework of common concepts, terminology and groupings of industries. The introduction to the 1948 SIC manual stated that it was designed for the classification of the establishment but a precise definition was not provided.

In the major revision of the SIC in 1960, the importance of the need for a standard unit of observation was emphasized by the provision of a standard definition of the establishment. The variables needed to assemble the "basic industrial statistics" required for the analysis of the different sectors of the economy were specified and the establishment became the smallest unit capable of reporting that set of variables. The 1970 revision updated the industry groupings to reflect changes in the industrial structure of the economy.

The 1980 revision of the SIC was again a major one. This revision more directly linked the SIC to the System of National Accounts (SNA). It specified the universe of production to be as defined for the production accounts of the SNA. It drew a picture of all the variables that needed to be collected from or allocated to the establishment, in order to calculate value added by establishment for the Input Output accounts and Real Domestic Product by industry. It gave more emphasis to the role of "ancillary" activities in the collection of an integrated system of economic statistics and emphasized the difference between technical and ancillary activities and the role of ancillary units in accounting for total production. By using available statistics, it more explicitly used measures of specialization and coverage to delineate manufacturing industries.

It recommended the use of the 1980 SIC for the classification of establishments and the compilation of production statistics.

In 1980 a separate classification, the Canadian Standard Industrial Classification for Companies and Enterprises, was produced for the compilation of financial statistics related to companies and enterprises. This classification took account of vertically-integrated companies and enterprises and created special classes for them at the lowest level of the classification. The higher levels of the classification cut across the traditional groupings of industrial classifications based on separating primary, secondary and tertiary activities in the economy and created sector groupings that drew together single and vertically-integrated companies and enterprises engaged in the production of similar product groups.

It was customary to revise the SIC at ten-year intervals; however, by 1990 not all the economic statistics programs of Statistics Canada had implemented the 1980 SIC. It was decided to postpone the revision and to take into account the statistical needs of the Free Trade Agreement signed in January 1994. The needs were met by developing NAICS, an industrial classification common to Canada, Mexico and the United States. The first version, NAICS Canada 1997, was released in March 1998.

NAICS was revised for 2002 to achieve increased comparability among the three countries in selected areas and to identify additional industries for new and emerging activities. To that end, the construction sector was revised and comparability achieved, for the most part, at the NAICS industry (five-digit) level. Industries were created for Internet services providers and web search portals, and Internet publishing and broadcasting.

Changes to Canadian and world economies continue to impact on classification systems. NAICS has been revised for 2007 to reflect these changes. In particular, the Information and Cultural Industries sector has once again been updated. The updates take into account the rapid changes within this area, including the merging of activities. As a result, Internet publishing and broadcasting and web search portals have been combined, as have Internet service providers and data processing, hosting, and related services. Telecommunications resellers and other telecommunications have also been merged.

The Conceptual Framework of NAICS

NAICS is based on a production-oriented, or supply-based conceptual framework in that establishments are grouped into industries according to similarity in the production processes used to produce goods and services. A production-oriented industry classification system ensures that statistical agencies in the three countries can produce information on inputs and outputs, industrial performance, productivity, unit labour costs, employment, and other statistics that reflect structural changes occurring in the three economies.

The activity of an establishment can be described in terms of what is produced, namely the type of goods and services produced, or how they are produced, namely, the raw material and service inputs used and the process of production or skills and technology used.

To create industries, establishments can be grouped using the criterion of similarity of output or the criterion of similarity of inputs, processes, skills and technology used. The various versions of the Canadian SIC and of the International Standard Industrial Classification of All Economic Activities (ISIC) of the United Nations have all used mixed criteria to create the industries of the classification.

NAICS is based on a single production-oriented concept. Producing units are grouped into industries according to similarities in their production processes. The boundaries between industries demarcate, in principle, differences in production processes and production technologies. This means that, in the language of economics, producing units within an industry have similar production functions that differ from those of producing units in other industries.

It is possible to view the production process as consisting of two dimensions, industries and products. The unit of observation of the industrial classification for the production of industrial statistics is the producing unit or the establishment, and the industrial classification is primarily a grouping of producing units, not products. Groupings of producing units permit the collection of industrial statistics that bring together information about the inputs and outputs of establishments. Because establishments each produce a number of products, in different combinations, using different technologies, it is hardly possible to bring together and group all the establishments producing a particular product. It is more useful to use a production-oriented approach to bring together, into industries, establishments with common input structures, and to compile data on their product outputs. This permits the compilation of comprehensive data on the total output of each product by industry and across all industries. The needs of analysts to study market shares and the demand for products can more effectively be met by compiling data relating to the products produced by industries and using a product classification based on demand-oriented criteria to group products by markets served.

The Development of NAICS

NAICS was developed by Statistics Canada, Mexico's Instituto Nacional de Estadística, Geografía e Informática (INEGI) and the Economic Classification Policy Committee (ECPC) of the Office of Management and Budget (OMB).

The three countries agreed upon the conceptual framework of the new system and the principles upon which NAICS was to be developed.

1. NAICS would be based on a production-oriented or supply-based conceptual framework. This means that producing units using similar production processes would be grouped together in NAICS.

2. Special attention would be given to developing production-oriented classifications for (a) new and emerging industries (b) services industries in general and (c) industries engaged in the production of advanced technologies.

3. Time-series continuity would be maintained to the extent possible. However, changes in the economy and proposals from data users would be considered. In addition, in order to create a common system for all three countries, adjustments would be made where the United States, Canada and Mexico had incompatible definitions.

4. In the interest of a wider range of international comparisons, the three countries would strive for greater compatibility with the International Standard Industrial Classification of All Economic Activities (ISIC Revision 3) by minimising the extent to which the lowest levels of NAICS crossed the boundaries of the 2-digit level of ISIC Revision 3.

To help with the development of NAICS, a user committee meeting was called in November 1994 and extensive consultation was undertaken in Canada with federal and provincial government departments and agencies, business and trade associations, economic analysts and the advisory committees of Statistics Canada.

A co-ordinating committee and subcommittees, which covered agriculture, mining and manufacturing, construction, distribution networks (retail and wholesale trade, transportation, communications and utilities), finance, insurance and real estate, business and personal services and health, social assistance and public administration, were responsible for developing the proposed structure of NAICS, in co-operation with representatives from INEGI and the statistical agencies of the US. Proposals from all three countries concerning individual industries were considered for acceptance, if the proposed industry was based on the production-oriented concept of the system. The structure of NAICS was developed in a series of three-country meetings and formally accepted by the senior representatives of the ECPC, INEGI and Statistics Canada.

The final structure of NAICS was accepted by the heads of Statistics Canada, INEGI and the Office of Management and Budget of the United States on December 10, 1996.

Statistical Units

Businesses have an operating structure and also a legal structure. They define and register themselves in terms of legal units for the ownership of assets. The legal structure forms the legal base of the business. Businesses usually submit corporate tax returns to government revenue authorities for the units that comprise its legal structure. A business derives its autonomy from the common ownership and control of its resources regardless of the number of legal units under which it registers them.

Though in the case of most businesses the legal and operating structures of the business coincide, particularly when the business is comprised of a single legal and operating entity, this is not always the case. In addition, accounting practices differ from business to business and the entities for which economic and financial data are available may represent yet another view of the business. It therefore becomes necessary to delineate the statistical structure of businesses and to define statistical units or the unit of observation about which economic data will be compiled and classified. This is done by a process known as profiling. Businesses are consulted about their legal and operating structures and their accounting practices. A four-tier statistical structure is then delineated. The standardized model developed at Statistics Canada for business surveys consists of a four-level hierarchy of business units. The levels comprise the location, the establishment, the company and the enterprise.

Definitions of Statistical Units

At the lowest level of the operating structure of businesses are producing units, such as the mill, plant, factory, farm, mine, warehouse, store, airline terminal or movie theatre. The **location**, as a statistical unit, is defined as a producing unit at a single geographical location at which or from which economic activity is conducted and for which, at a minimum, employment data are available. Locations may also be referred to as cost centres or as revenue centres, based on the availability of accounting information about them.

The establishment is the level at which all accounting data required to measure production are available. The **establishment**, as a statistical unit, is defined as the most homogeneous unit of production for which the business maintains accounting records from which it is possible to assemble all the data elements required to compile the full structure of the gross value of production (total sales or shipments, and inventories), the cost of materials and services, and labour and capital used in production. Provided that the necessary accounts are available, the statistical structure replicates the operating structure of the business. In delineating the establishment, however, producing units may be grouped. An establishment comprises at least one location but it can also be composed of many. Establishments may also be referred to as profit centres.

There are a number of special cases for delineating establishments. In situations in which accounting records can provide all the data needed to identify a separate establishment for each distinct activity being undertaken from the same premises, particularly if they are activities belonging to different industries, two separate establishments may be delineated. An example would be the case of restaurants or shops in a hotel. In such cases, each activity is delineated as a separate establishment, provided that: no one industry description in the classification includes such combined activities; all the data required to define an establishment are available for each activity; and output and employment are significant for both activities. In the areas of construction, transportation and communication, activities tend to be dispersed. The individual sites, projects, fields, networks, lines or systems of such activities are not normally treated as establishments. The establishment is represented by those relatively permanent main or branch offices, terminals, or stations that are either (1) directly responsible for supervising such activities or (2) the base from which personnel operate to carry out these activities. Units producing goods for further processing by other establishments within the enterprise are treated as separate establishments, provided that they are a profit centre or a cost centre for which, at a minimum, transfer prices and the quantity of goods transferred for further processing can be reported by the business.

The company is the level at which operating profit can be measured. The **company**, as a statistical unit, is defined as the lowest level organizational unit for which income and expenditure accounts and balance sheets are maintained from which operating profit and the rate of return on capital can be derived. An enterprise may consist of one or more companies. Companies may also be referred to as investment centres.

The enterprise is an autonomous unit for which a complete set of financial statements is available. The **enterprise**, as a statistical unit, is defined as a business unit that directs and controls the allocation of resources relating to its operations, and for which consolidated financial and balance sheet accounts are maintained. International transactions, an international investment position and a consolidated financial position for the unit can be derived from these consolidated accounts. The enterprise corresponds to an institutional unit engaged in economic activity as defined in the System of National Accounts 1993. The System of National Accounts defines an institutional unit as an economic entity that is capable, in its own right, of owning assets, incurring liabilities, and engaging in economic activities and in transactions with other entities. In the case of most small- and medium-sized businesses, the enterprise and the establishment are identical. Large and complex enterprises, however, consist of more than one establishment, which may belong to different NAICS industries.

Reporting Arrangements

Information required about a statistical unit, as defined above, may or may not be available from the unit itself. Particularly in the case of businesses with complex operating structures, reporting arrangements will have to be made with the business to collect the required data about the statistical unit or to attribute all production costs to the producing establishments. These arrangements will differ from one business to the next, depending upon their particular record keeping practices.

Determining the Industry Classification of a Statistical Unit

NAICS is principally a classification system for establishments and for the compilation of production statistics. An establishment is classified to an industry when its principal activity meets the definition for that industry. This is a straightforward determination for establishments engaged in a single activity, but where establishments are engaged in more than one activity, it is necessary to establish procedures for identifying its principal activity.

In cases where there is more than one activity, the determination of the largest share is based on value-added (value of outputs minus cost of inputs). The activity with the largest value-added is identified as the establishment's principal activity, and the establishment is classified to the industry corresponding to that activity. In practice, because of measurement issues, it is often necessary to use other variables – such as revenue or employment – as proxies for value-added.

The assignment of the industry code is performed at the 6-digit level of the classification. For example, if the value added within an establishment consists of 40% from manufacturing dishwashers (NAICS 335223, Major Kitchen Appliance Manufacturing), 30% from manufacturing airspeed instruments (NAICS 334511, Navigational and Guidance Instruments Manufacturing), and 30% from assembling clocks (NAICS 334512, Measuring, Medical and Controlling Devices Manufacturing), it will be classified to NAICS 335223, Major Kitchen Appliance Manufacturing. Coding to the more aggregate levels of the classification follows automatically. This is referred to as "bottom-up" industry coding.

In most cases, when an establishment is engaged in more than one activity, the activities are treated independently. However, in some cases, the activities are treated in combination. There are two types of combined activities that are given special attention in NAICS. They are vertical integration and joint production (horizontal integration). These combined activities have an economic basis and occur in both goods-producing and services-producing sectors. In some cases, there are efficiencies to be gained from combining certain activities in the same establishment. Some of these combinations occur so commonly or frequently that their combination can be treated as a third activity in its own right and explicitly classified in a specific industry.

One approach to classifying these activities would be to use the primary activity rule, that is, whichever activity is largest. However, the fundamental principle of NAICS is that establishments that employ the same production process should be classified in the same industry. If the premise that the combined activities correspond to a distinct third activity is accepted, then using the primary activity rule would place establishments performing the same combination of activities in different industries, thereby violating the production principle of NAICS. A second reason for NAICS recognizing combined activities is to improve the stability of establishment classification, both over time and among the various parties that implement the classification. An establishment should remain classified in the same industry unless its production process changes; and different parties should code the same establishment or type of establishment in the same way. A consistent treatment of establishments with combined activities is more likely if they are classified to a single industry.

Vertical integration involves consecutive stages of fabrication or production processes in which the output of one step is the input of the next. In general, establishments will be classified based on the final process in a vertically-integrated production environment, unless specifically identified as classified in another industry. For example, paper may be produced either by establishments that first produce pulp and then consume that pulp to produce paper or by those establishments producing paper from purchased pulp. NAICS specifies that both of these types of paper-producing processes should be classified in NAICS 32212, Paper Mills rather than in NAICS 32211, Pulp Mills. In other cases, NAICS specifies that vertically-integrated establishments be classified in the industry representing the first stage of the manufacturing process. For example, steel mills that make steel and also perform other activities such as producing steel castings are classified in NAICS 33111, Iron and Steel Mills and Ferro-Alloy Manufacturing, the first stage of the manufacturing process.

The joint production of goods or services represents the second type of combined activities. In some cases, these combined activities have been assigned to a specific NAICS industry. Most of these activities involve either the sale and repair of goods or the sale and rental of goods in the same establishment. For example, establishments that both engage in the sale of new cars and also provide repair services are coded to NAICS 44111, New Car Dealers; establishments that both sell automobile parts and repair automobiles are classified in NAICS 44131, Automotive Parts and Accessories Stores; and establishments that both sell and rent musical instruments are classified in NAICS 45114, Musical Instrument and Supplies Stores. In other cases, specific industries have been identified for these combined activities, such as NAICS 44711, Gasoline Stations with Convenience Stores.

In some complex businesses, there are units that exclusively produce services in support of other units within the same company or enterprise. Examples of such units are transportation units, central administrative units and head offices. Such units are known as ancillary units and are classified according to the NAICS code related to their own activity. This means that a warehouse providing storage facilities for its own company or enterprise will be classified as a warehouse. Similarly, a head office providing headquarters services for its own company or enterprise will be classified to the head office industry.

Companies are classified to NAICS by using the principle of assigning them to the industry of the establishment or group of establishments that account for the largest proportion of the value-added of the company. Enterprises are classified by using the principle of assigning them to the industry of the company or group of companies that account for the largest proportion of the value-added of the enterprise. It has been pointed out above that NAICS is not specially designed for the classification of companies and enterprises, particularly those with establishments in different NAICS sectors. In general, the higher levels of NAICS better represent the activities of diversified companies and enterprises engaged in many activities.

The Relationship of NAICS Canada and ISIC Revision 4[1]

Recognizing that economic statistics are substantially more useful if they are also internationally comparable, the Economic and Social Council of the United Nations (UN) adopted the original version of the International Standard Industrial Classification of All Economic Activities (ISIC) in 1948. Since then, ISIC has been revised in 1958, 1968, 1989, and, most recently, in 2006. This 2006 version of the classification is referred to as ISIC Revision 4. With these various revisions, the Council has recommended that member states adopt, as soon as possible, the latest version of the classification, with such modifications as necessary to meet national requirements, without disturbing the framework of the classification.

In accordance with these recommendations and mindful of the need to provide data classified to ISIC for purposes of international comparability, the statistical agencies of the three North American countries agreed that, in the original development of NAICS, they would strive to create industries that, at least, did not cross the two-digit boundaries of ISIC Revision 3. This minimal agreement was reached in the knowledge that a very detailed comparison would not be possible without considerably greater harmonization. The NAICS 2002 revisions were performed to meet those same objectives; and the NAICS 2007 revisions were also made using a similar approach—although in this case it was the ISIC Revision 4 that was providing the framework.

NAICS, like ISIC, was principally designed to provide a classification for grouping establishments based on the kind of activity in which they are primarily engaged. Whereas the main criteria employed in delineating the divisions, groups and classes of ISIC are: (a) the character of the goods and services produced; (b) the uses to which the goods and services are put; and (c) the inputs, the process and technology of production, it is the third criterion of ISIC that corresponds to the conceptual basis of NAICS. This makes it unique among industrial classifications in that it is based on a single criterion.

---

[1]See ISIC on United Nations Statistical Division web site at http://unstats.un.org/unsd/cr/registry/isic-4.asp

Convergence Project

In addition to working to maintain coherence between NAICS and ISIC, international efforts have also focused on moving towards greater coherence between NAICS, ISIC and the Statistical Classification of Economic Activities in the European Community (NACE, Nomenclature statistique des activités économiques dans la Communauté européenne). In June 2000, a working group was assigned to study the potential for greater convergence between NACE and NAICS under an agreement signed by the heads of the statistical agencies of Canada, the European Union, and the United States. One output of the project was a convergence scenario, assuming a possible common top structure for NACE and NAICS, which was then discussed during an extensive consultation phase with stakeholders in the participating countries. The outcome of those consultations showed that, despite the benefits, there was insufficient support for the scenario. The overriding argument was that the number of necessary changes and associated implementation costs were too high. As a result, the new focus of the convergence work became a "better concordance" scenario, which addressed lower structure detail and concept issues. The suggested changes have resulted in classifications with much more comparable building blocks, allowing for data conversion at different levels of the classification while still maintaining different structures.

A comparison between the ISIC Revision 4 sections and NAICS 2007 sectors shows that of the 21 ISIC sections, 14 have good or better comparability, 3 have mixed comparability, and 4 have poor comparability or comparison is not possible. Because of the similarity between NACE and ISIC, comparability between NACE and NAICS was also significantly improved as the result of this project.

Classification Structure

Classification Structure

The Classification Structure displays the codes and titles of the sectors, subsectors, industry groups, industry, and national industries of NAICS Canada. In general, comparable sectors, subsectors, industry groups, industries carry the same code in NAICS Canada, NAICS Mexico and NAICS United States.

The superscript symbols at the end of NAICS class titles used to signify comparability are:

Symbol   **Explanation**

CAN   Canadian industry only
MEX   Canadian and Mexican industries are comparable
US   Canadian and United States industries are comparable
[Blank]   [No superscript symbol] Canadian, Mexican and United States industries are comparable.

11 Agriculture, Forestry, Fishing and Hunting

111 Crop Production

1111 Oilseed and Grain Farming

11111	Soybean Farming
111110	Soybean Farming
11112	Oilseed (except Soybean) Farming
111120	Oilseed (except Soybean) Farming US
11113	Dry Pea and Bean Farming
111130	Dry Pea and Bean Farming US
11114	Wheat Farming
111140	Wheat Farming
11115	Corn Farming
111150	Corn Farming US
11116	Rice Farming
111160	Rice Farming
11119	Other Grain Farming
111190	Other Grain Farming CAN

1112 Vegetable and Melon Farming

11121	Vegetable and Melon Farming
111211	Potato Farming US
111219	Other Vegetable (except Potato) and Melon Farming US

1113 Fruit and Tree Nut Farming

11131	Orange Groves
111310	Orange Groves
11132	Citrus (except Orange) Groves
111320	Citrus (except Orange) Groves US
11133	Non-Citrus Fruit and Tree Nut Farming
111330	Non-Citrus Fruit and Tree Nut Farming CAN

1114 Greenhouse, Nursery and Floriculture Production

11141	Food Crops Grown Under Cover
111411	Mushroom Production US
111419	Other Food Crops Grown Under Cover US
11142	Nursery and Floriculture Production
111421	Nursery and Tree Production US
111422	Floriculture Production US

1119 Other Crop Farming

11191	Tobacco Farming
111910	Tobacco Farming
11192	Cotton Farming
111920	Cotton Farming
11193	Sugar Cane Farming
111930	Sugar Cane Farming
11194	Hay Farming
111940	Hay Farming US
11199	All Other Crop Farming
111993	Fruit and Vegetable Combination Farming CAN
111994	Maple Syrup and Products Production CAN
111999	All Other Miscellaneous Crop Farming CAN

112 Animal Production

1121 Cattle Ranching and Farming

11211	Beef Cattle Ranching and Farming, including Feedlots

	112110	Beef Cattle Ranching and Farming, including Feedlots ^{CAN}
	11212	Dairy Cattle and Milk Production
	112120	Dairy Cattle and Milk Production

1122 Hog and Pig Farming

11221	Hog and Pig Farming
112210	Hog and Pig Farming ^{US}

1123 Poultry and Egg Production

11231	Chicken Egg Production
112310	Chicken Egg Production ^{US}
11232	Broiler and Other Meat-Type Chicken Production
112320	Broiler and Other Meat-Type Chicken Production
11233	Turkey Production
112330	Turkey Production
11234	Poultry Hatcheries
112340	Poultry Hatcheries
11239	Other Poultry Production
112391	Combination Poultry and Egg Production ^{CAN}
112399	All Other Poultry Production ^{CAN}

1124 Sheep and Goat Farming

11241	Sheep Farming
112410	Sheep Farming ^{US}
11242	Goat Farming
112420	Goat Farming

1125 Aquaculture

11251	Aquaculture
112510	Aquaculture ^{CAN}

1129 Other Animal Production

11291	Apiculture
112910	Apiculture
11292	Horse and Other Equine Production
112920	Horse and Other Equine Production
11293	Fur-Bearing Animal and Rabbit Production
112930	Fur-Bearing Animal and Rabbit Production
11299	All Other Animal Production
112991	Animal Combination Farming ^{CAN}
112999	All Other Miscellaneous Animal Production ^{CAN}

113 Forestry and Logging

1131 Timber Tract Operations

11311	Timber Tract Operations
113110	Timber Tract Operations

1132 Forest Nurseries and Gathering of Forest Products

11321	Forest Nurseries and Gathering of Forest Products
113210	Forest Nurseries and Gathering of Forest Products ^{US}

1133 Logging

11331	Logging
113311	Logging (except Contract) ^{CAN}
113312	Contract Logging ^{CAN}

114 Fishing, Hunting and Trapping

1141 Fishing

11411	Fishing
114113	Salt Water Fishing [CAN]
114114	Inland Fishing [CAN]

1142 Hunting and Trapping

11421	Hunting and Trapping
114210	Hunting and Trapping

115 Support Activities for Agriculture and Forestry

1151 Support Activities for Crop Production

11511	Support Activities for Crop Production
115110	Support Activities for Crop Production [CAN]

1152 Support Activities for Animal Production

11521	Support Activities for Animal Production
115210	Support Activities for Animal Production

1153 Support Activities for Forestry

11531	Support Activities for Forestry
115310	Support Activities for Forestry

21 Mining, Quarrying, and Oil and Gas Extraction

211 Oil and Gas Extraction

2111 Oil and Gas Extraction

21111	Oil and Gas Extraction
211113	Conventional Oil and Gas Extraction [CAN]
211114	Non-Conventional Oil Extraction [CAN]

212 Mining and Quarrying (except Oil and Gas)

2121 Coal Mining

21211	Coal Mining
212114	Bituminous Coal Mining [CAN]
212115	Subbituminous Coal Mining [CAN]
212116	Lignite Coal Mining [CAN]

2122 Metal Ore Mining

21221	Iron Ore Mining
212210	Iron Ore Mining
21222	Gold and Silver Ore Mining
212220	Gold and Silver Ore Mining [CAN]
21223	Copper, Nickel, Lead and Zinc Ore Mining
212231	Lead-Zinc Ore Mining [US]
212232	Nickel-Copper Ore Mining [CAN]
212233	Copper-Zinc Ore Mining [CAN]
21229	Other Metal Ore Mining
212291	Uranium Ore Mining [US]
212299	All Other Metal Ore Mining [US]

2123 Non-Metallic Mineral Mining and Quarrying

21231	Stone Mining and Quarrying
212314	Granite Mining and Quarrying [CAN]
212315	Limestone Mining and Quarrying [CAN]
212316	Marble Mining and Quarrying [CAN]
212317	Sandstone Mining and Quarrying [CAN]

	21232	Sand, Gravel, Clay, and Ceramic and Refractory Minerals Mining and Quarrying
	212323	Sand and Gravel Mining and Quarrying CAN
	212326	Shale, Clay and Refractory Mineral Mining and Quarrying CAN
	21239	Other Non-Metallic Mineral Mining and Quarrying
	212392	Diamond Mining CAN
	212393	Salt Mining CAN
	212394	Asbestos Mining CAN
	212395	Gypsum Mining CAN
	212396	Potash Mining CAN
	212397	Peat Extraction CAN
	212398	All Other Non-Metallic Mineral Mining and Quarrying CAN

213 Support Activities for Mining and Oil and Gas Extraction

2131 Support Activities for Mining and Oil and Gas Extraction

21311	Support Activities for Mining and Oil and Gas Extraction
213111	Oil and Gas Contract Drilling
213117	Contract Drilling (except Oil and Gas) CAN
213118	Services to Oil and Gas Extraction CAN
213119	Other Support Activities for Mining CAN

22 Utilities

221 Utilities US

2211 Electric Power Generation, Transmission and Distribution

22111	Electric Power Generation US
221111	Hydro-Electric Power Generation US
221112	Fossil-Fuel Electric Power Generation US
221113	Nuclear Electric Power Generation US
221119	Other Electric Power Generation US
22112	Electric Power Transmission, Control and Distribution US
221121	Electric Bulk Power Transmission and Control US
221122	Electric Power Distribution US

2212 Natural Gas Distribution US

22121	Natural Gas Distribution US
221210	Natural Gas Distribution US

2213 Water, Sewage and Other Systems US

22131	Water Supply and Irrigation Systems US
221310	Water Supply and Irrigation Systems US
22132	Sewage Treatment Facilities US
221320	Sewage Treatment Facilities US
22133	Steam and Air-Conditioning Supply US
221330	Steam and Air-Conditioning Supply US

23 Construction

236 Construction of Buildings

2361 Residential Building Construction

23611	Residential Building Construction
236110	Residential Building Construction CAN

2362 Non-residential Building Construction

23621	Industrial Building and Structure Construction
236210	Industrial Building and Structure Construction US

	23622	Commercial and Institutional Building Construction
	236220	Commercial and Institutional Building Construction US

237   Heavy and Civil Engineering Construction

2371   Utility System Construction

23711	Water and Sewer Line and Related Structures Construction
237110	Water and Sewer Line and Related Structures Construction US
23712	Oil and Gas Pipeline and Related Structures Construction
237120	Oil and Gas Pipeline and Related Structures Construction US
23713	Power and Communication Line and Related Structures Construction
237130	Power and Communication Line and Related Structures Construction US

2372   Land Subdivision

23721	Land Subdivision
237210	Land Subdivision US

2373   Highway, Street and Bridge Construction

23731	Highway, Street and Bridge Construction
237310	Highway, Street and Bridge Construction US

2379   Other Heavy and Civil Engineering Construction

23799	Other Heavy and Civil Engineering Construction
237990	Other Heavy and Civil Engineering Construction US

238   Specialty Trade Contractors

2381   Foundation, Structure, and Building Exterior Contractors

23811	Poured Concrete Foundation and Structure Contractors
238110	Poured Concrete Foundation and Structure Contractors
23812	Structural Steel and Precast Concrete Contractors
238120	Structural Steel and Precast Concrete Contractors US
23813	Framing Contractors US
238130	Framing Contractors US
23814	Masonry Contractors US
238140	Masonry Contractors US
23815	Glass and Glazing Contractors US
238150	Glass and Glazing Contractors US
23816	Roofing Contractors US
238160	Roofing Contractors US
23817	Siding Contractors US
238170	Siding Contractors US
23819	Other Foundation, Structure and Building Exterior Contractors US
238190	Other Foundation, Structure and Building Exterior Contractors US

2382   Building Equipment Contractors

23821	Electrical Contractors and Other Wiring Installation Contractors
238210	Electrical Contractors and Other Wiring Installation Contractors
23822	Plumbing, Heating and Air-Conditioning Contractors
238220	Plumbing, Heating and Air-Conditioning Contractors US
23829	Other Building Equipment Contractors
238291	Elevator and Escalator Installation Contractors CAN
238299	All Other Building Equipment Contractors CAN

2383   Building Finishing Contractors

23831	Drywall and Insulation Contractors
238310	Drywall and Insulation Contractors US
23832	Painting and Wall Covering Contractors
238320	Painting and Wall Covering Contractors

	23833	Flooring Contractors
	238330	Flooring Contractors
	23834	Tile and Terrazzo Contractors
	238340	Tile and Terrazzo Contractors
	23835	Finish Carpentry Contractors
	238350	Finish Carpentry Contractors
	23839	Other Building Finishing Contractors
	238390	Other Building Finishing Contractors

2389   Other Specialty Trade Contractors

	23891	Site Preparation Contractors
	238910	Site Preparation Contractors
	23899	All Other Specialty Trade Contractors
	238990	All Other Specialty Trade Contractors [US]

31-33   Manufacturing

311   Food Manufacturing

3111   Animal Food Manufacturing

31111	Animal Food Manufacturing
311111	Dog and Cat Food Manufacturing [US]
311119	Other Animal Food Manufacturing [US]

3112   Grain and Oilseed Milling

31121	Flour Milling and Malt Manufacturing
311211	Flour Milling [US]
311214	Rice Milling and Malt Manufacturing [CAN]
31122	Starch and Vegetable Fat and Oil Manufacturing
311221	Wet Corn Milling [US]
311224	Oilseed Processing [CAN]
311225	Fat and Oil Refining and Blending [US]
31123	Breakfast Cereal Manufacturing
311230	Breakfast Cereal Manufacturing

3113   Sugar and Confectionery Product Manufacturing

31131	Sugar Manufacturing
311310	Sugar Manufacturing [CAN]
31132	Chocolate and Confectionery Manufacturing from Cacao Beans
311320	Chocolate and Confectionery Manufacturing from Cacao Beans
31133	Confectionery Manufacturing from Purchased Chocolate
311330	Confectionery Manufacturing from Purchased Chocolate
31134	Non-Chocolate Confectionery Manufacturing
311340	Non-Chocolate Confectionery Manufacturing

3114   Fruit and Vegetable Preserving and Specialty Food Manufacturing

31141	Frozen Food Manufacturing
311410	Frozen Food Manufacturing [CAN]
31142	Fruit and Vegetable Canning, Pickling and Drying
311420	Fruit and Vegetable Canning, Pickling and Drying [CAN]

3115   Dairy Product Manufacturing

31151	Dairy Product (except Frozen) Manufacturing
311511	Fluid Milk Manufacturing [US]
311515	Butter, Cheese, and Dry and Condensed Dairy Product Manufacturing [CAN]
31152	Ice Cream and Frozen Dessert Manufacturing
311520	Ice Cream and Frozen Dessert Manufacturing

3116   Meat Product Manufacturing

	31161	Animal Slaughtering and Processing
	311611	Animal (except Poultry) Slaughtering US
	311614	Rendering and Meat Processing from Carcasses CAN
	311615	Poultry Processing US

3117   Seafood Product Preparation and Packaging

31171	Seafood Product Preparation and Packaging
311710	Seafood Product Preparation and Packaging MEX

3118   Bakeries and Tortilla Manufacturing

31181	Bread and Bakery Product Manufacturing
311811	Retail Bakeries US
311814	Commercial Bakeries and Frozen Bakery Product Manufacturing CAN
31182	Cookie, Cracker and Pasta Manufacturing
311821	Cookie and Cracker Manufacturing US
311822	Flour Mixes and Dough Manufacturing from Purchased Flour US
311823	Dry Pasta Manufacturing US
31183	Tortilla Manufacturing
311830	Tortilla Manufacturing

3119   Other Food Manufacturing

31191	Snack Food Manufacturing
311911	Roasted Nut and Peanut Butter Manufacturing US
311919	Other Snack Food Manufacturing US
31192	Coffee and Tea Manufacturing
311920	Coffee and Tea Manufacturing US
31193	Flavouring Syrup and Concentrate Manufacturing
311930	Flavouring Syrup and Concentrate Manufacturing
31194	Seasoning and Dressing Manufacturing
311940	Seasoning and Dressing Manufacturing MEX
31199	All Other Food Manufacturing
311990	All Other Food Manufacturing CAN

312   Beverage and Tobacco Product Manufacturing

3121   Beverage Manufacturing

31211	Soft Drink and Ice Manufacturing
312110	Soft Drink and Ice Manufacturing CAN
31212	Breweries
312120	Breweries
31213	Wineries
312130	Wineries US
31214	Distilleries
312140	Distilleries US

3122   Tobacco Manufacturing

31221	Tobacco Stemming and Redrying
312210	Tobacco Stemming and Redrying
31222	Tobacco Product Manufacturing
312220	Tobacco Product Manufacturing CAN

313   Textile Mills

3131   Fibre, Yarn and Thread Mills

31311	Fibre, Yarn and Thread Mills
313110	Fibre, Yarn and Thread Mills CAN

3132   Fabric Mills

31321	Broad-Woven Fabric Mills

313210	Broad-Woven Fabric Mills	
31322	Narrow Fabric Mills and Schiffli Machine Embroidery	
313220	Narrow Fabric Mills and Schiffli Machine Embroidery [MEX]	
31323	Nonwoven Fabric Mills	
313230	Nonwoven Fabric Mills	
31324	Knit Fabric Mills	
313240	Knit Fabric Mills [MEX]	

3133 Textile and Fabric Finishing and Fabric Coating

31331	Textile and Fabric Finishing
313310	Textile and Fabric Finishing [CAN]
31332	Fabric Coating
313320	Fabric Coating

314 Textile Product Mills

3141 Textile Furnishings Mills

31411	Carpet and Rug Mills
314110	Carpet and Rug Mills
31412	Curtain and Linen Mills
314120	Curtain and Linen Mills [MEX]

3149 Other Textile Product Mills

31491	Textile Bag and Canvas Mills
314910	Textile Bag and Canvas Mills [CAN]
31499	All Other Textile Product Mills
314990	All Other Textile Product Mills [CAN]

315 Clothing Manufacturing

3151 Clothing Knitting Mills

31511	Hosiery and Sock Mills
315110	Hosiery and Sock Mills [MEX]
31519	Other Clothing Knitting Mills
315190	Other Clothing Knitting Mills [CAN]

3152 Cut and Sew Clothing Manufacturing

31521	Cut and Sew Clothing Contracting [US]
315210	Cut and Sew Clothing Contracting [CAN]
31522	Men's and Boys' Cut and Sew Clothing Manufacturing [US]
315221	Men's and Boys' Cut and Sew Underwear and Nightwear Manufacturing [US]
315222	Men's and Boys' Cut and Sew Suit, Coat and Overcoat Manufacturing [US]
315226	Men's and Boys' Cut and Sew Shirt Manufacturing [CAN]
315227	Men's and Boys' Cut and Sew Trouser, Slack and Jean Manufacturing [CAN]
315229	Other Men's and Boys' Cut and Sew Clothing Manufacturing [CAN]
31523	Women's and Girls' Cut and Sew Clothing Manufacturing [US]
315231	Women's and Girls' Cut and Sew Lingerie, Loungewear and Nightwear Manufacturing [US]
315232	Women's and Girls' Cut and Sew Blouse and Shirt Manufacturing [US]
315233	Women's and Girls' Cut and Sew Dress Manufacturing [US]
315234	Women's and Girls' Cut and Sew Suit, Coat, Tailored Jacket and Skirt Manufacturing [US]
315239	Other Women's and Girls' Cut and Sew Clothing Manufacturing [US]
31529	Other Cut and Sew Clothing Manufacturing [US]
315291	Infants' Cut and Sew Clothing Manufacturing [US]
315292	Fur and Leather Clothing Manufacturing [US]
315299	All Other Cut and Sew Clothing Manufacturing [US]

3159   **Clothing Accessories and Other Clothing Manufacturing**

       31599   Clothing Accessories and Other Clothing Manufacturing

       315990   Clothing Accessories and Other Clothing Manufacturing CAN

316   **Leather and Allied Product Manufacturing**

3161   **Leather and Hide Tanning and Finishing**

       31611   Leather and Hide Tanning and Finishing

       316110   Leather and Hide Tanning and Finishing

3162   **Footwear Manufacturing**

       31621   Footwear Manufacturing

       316210   Footwear Manufacturing CAN

3169   **Other Leather and Allied Product Manufacturing**

       31699   Other Leather and Allied Product Manufacturing

       316990   Other Leather and Allied Product Manufacturing CAN

321   **Wood Product Manufacturing**

3211   **Sawmills and Wood Preservation**

       32111   Sawmills and Wood Preservation

       321111   Sawmills (except Shingle and Shake Mills) MEX

       321112   Shingle and Shake Mills MEX

       321114   Wood Preservation US

3212   **Veneer, Plywood and Engineered Wood Product Manufacturing**

       32121   Veneer, Plywood and Engineered Wood Product Manufacturing

       321211   Hardwood Veneer and Plywood Mills US

       321212   Softwood Veneer and Plywood Mills US

       321215   Structural Wood Product Manufacturing CAN

       321216   Particle Board and Fibreboard Mills CAN

       321217   Waferboard Mills CAN

3219   **Other Wood Product Manufacturing**

       32191   Millwork

       321911   Wood Window and Door Manufacturing US

       321919   Other Millwork CAN

       32192   Wood Container and Pallet Manufacturing

       321920   Wood Container and Pallet Manufacturing

       32199   All Other Wood Product Manufacturing

       321991   Manufactured (Mobile) Home Manufacturing US

       321992   Prefabricated Wood Building Manufacturing US

       321999   All Other Miscellaneous Wood Product Manufacturing US

322   **Paper Manufacturing**

3221   **Pulp, Paper and Paperboard Mills**

       32211   Pulp Mills

       322111   Mechanical Pulp Mills CAN

       322112   Chemical Pulp Mills CAN

       32212   Paper Mills

       322121   Paper (except Newsprint) Mills US

       322122   Newsprint Mills US

       32213   Paperboard Mills

       322130   Paperboard Mills US

3222   **Converted Paper Product Manufacturing**

       32221   Paperboard Container Manufacturing

322211	Corrugated and Solid Fibre Box Manufacturing [US]
322212	Folding Paperboard Box Manufacturing [US]
322219	Other Paperboard Container Manufacturing [CAN]
32222	Paper Bag and Coated and Treated Paper Manufacturing
322220	Paper Bag and Coated and Treated Paper Manufacturing [MEX]
32223	Stationery Product Manufacturing
322230	Stationery Product Manufacturing [MEX]
32229	Other Converted Paper Product Manufacturing
322291	Sanitary Paper Product Manufacturing [US]
322299	All Other Converted Paper Product Manufacturing [US]

323   Printing and Related Support Activities

3231   Printing and Related Support Activities

32311	Printing
323113	Commercial Screen Printing [US]
323114	Quick Printing [US]
323115	Digital Printing [US]
323116	Manifold Business Forms Printing [US]
323119	Other Printing [CAN]
32312	Support Activities for Printing
323120	Support Activities for Printing [MEX]

324   Petroleum and Coal Product Manufacturing

3241   Petroleum and Coal Product Manufacturing

32411	Petroleum Refineries
324110	Petroleum Refineries
32412	Asphalt Paving, Roofing and Saturated Materials Manufacturing
324121	Asphalt Paving Mixture and Block Manufacturing [US]
324122	Asphalt Shingle and Coating Material Manufacturing [US]
32419	Other Petroleum and Coal Product Manufacturing
324190	Other Petroleum and Coal Product Manufacturing [CAN]

325   Chemical Manufacturing

3251   Basic Chemical Manufacturing

32511	Petrochemical Manufacturing
325110	Petrochemical Manufacturing
32512	Industrial Gas Manufacturing
325120	Industrial Gas Manufacturing
32513	Synthetic Dye and Pigment Manufacturing
325130	Synthetic Dye and Pigment Manufacturing [MEX]
32518	Other Basic Inorganic Chemical Manufacturing
325181	Alkali and Chlorine Manufacturing [US]
325189	All Other Basic Inorganic Chemical Manufacturing [CAN]
32519	Other Basic Organic Chemical Manufacturing
325190	Other Basic Organic Chemical Manufacturing [MEX]

3252   Resin, Synthetic Rubber, and Artificial and Synthetic Fibres and Filaments Manufacturing

32521	Resin and Synthetic Rubber Manufacturing
325210	Resin and Synthetic Rubber Manufacturing [CAN]
32522	Artificial and Synthetic Fibres and Filaments Manufacturing
325220	Artificial and Synthetic Fibres and Filaments Manufacturing [MEX]

3253   Pesticide, Fertilizer and Other Agricultural Chemical Manufacturing

32531	Fertilizer Manufacturing

325313	Chemical Fertilizer (except Potash) Manufacturing [CAN]
325314	Mixed Fertilizer Manufacturing [US]
32532	Pesticide and Other Agricultural Chemical Manufacturing
325320	Pesticide and Other Agricultural Chemical Manufacturing

3254   Pharmaceutical and Medicine Manufacturing

32541	Pharmaceutical and Medicine Manufacturing
325410	Pharmaceutical and Medicine Manufacturing [CAN]

3255   Paint, Coating and Adhesive Manufacturing

32551	Paint and Coating Manufacturing
325510	Paint and Coating Manufacturing
32552	Adhesive Manufacturing
325520	Adhesive Manufacturing

3256   Soap, Cleaning Compound and Toilet Preparation Manufacturing

32561	Soap and Cleaning Compound Manufacturing
325610	Soap and Cleaning Compound Manufacturing [MEX]
32562	Toilet Preparation Manufacturing
325620	Toilet Preparation Manufacturing

3259   Other Chemical Product Manufacturing

32591	Printing Ink Manufacturing
325910	Printing Ink Manufacturing
32592	Explosives Manufacturing
325920	Explosives Manufacturing
32599	All Other Chemical Product Manufacturing
325991	Custom Compounding of Purchased Resins [US]
325999	All Other Miscellaneous Chemical Product Manufacturing [CAN]

326   Plastics and Rubber Products Manufacturing

3261   Plastic Product Manufacturing

32611	Plastic Packaging Materials and Unlaminated Film and Sheet Manufacturing
326111	Plastic Bag and Pouch Manufacturing [US]
326114	Plastic Film and Sheet Manufacturing [CAN]
32612	Plastic Pipe, Pipe Fitting, and Unlaminated Profile Shape Manufacturing
326121	Unlaminated Plastic Profile Shape Manufacturing [US]
326122	Plastic Pipe and Pipe Fitting Manufacturing [US]
32613	Laminated Plastic Plate, Sheet (except Packaging), and Shape Manufacturing
326130	Laminated Plastic Plate, Sheet (except Packaging), and Shape Manufacturing
32614	Polystyrene Foam Product Manufacturing
326140	Polystyrene Foam Product Manufacturing
32615	Urethane and Other Foam Product (except Polystyrene) Manufacturing
326150	Urethane and Other Foam Product (except Polystyrene) Manufacturing
32616	Plastic Bottle Manufacturing
326160	Plastic Bottle Manufacturing
32619	Other Plastic Product Manufacturing
326191	Plastic Plumbing Fixture Manufacturing [US]
326193	Motor Vehicle Plastic Parts Manufacturing [CAN]
326196	Plastic Window and Door Manufacturing [CAN]
326198	All Other Plastic Product Manufacturing [CAN]

3262   Rubber Product Manufacturing

32621	Tire Manufacturing
326210	Tire Manufacturing [CAN]
32622	Rubber and Plastic Hose and Belting Manufacturing
326220	Rubber and Plastic Hose and Belting Manufacturing

| 32629 | Other Rubber Product Manufacturing |
| 326290 | Other Rubber Product Manufacturing MEX |

327 Non-Metallic Mineral Product Manufacturing

3271 Clay Product and Refractory Manufacturing

32711	Pottery, Ceramics and Plumbing Fixture Manufacturing
327110	Pottery, Ceramics and Plumbing Fixture Manufacturing CAN
32712	Clay Building Material and Refractory Manufacturing
327120	Clay Building Material and Refractory Manufacturing CAN

3272 Glass and Glass Product Manufacturing

32721	Glass and Glass Product Manufacturing
327214	Glass Manufacturing CAN
327215	Glass Product Manufacturing from Purchased Glass US

3273 Cement and Concrete Product Manufacturing

32731	Cement Manufacturing
327310	Cement Manufacturing
32732	Ready-Mix Concrete Manufacturing
327320	Ready-Mix Concrete Manufacturing
32733	Concrete Pipe, Brick and Block Manufacturing
327330	Concrete Pipe, Brick and Block Manufacturing MEX
32739	Other Concrete Product Manufacturing
327390	Other Concrete Product Manufacturing US

3274 Lime and Gypsum Product Manufacturing

32741	Lime Manufacturing
327410	Lime Manufacturing
32742	Gypsum Product Manufacturing
327420	Gypsum Product Manufacturing

3279 Other Non-Metallic Mineral Product Manufacturing

32791	Abrasive Product Manufacturing
327910	Abrasive Product Manufacturing
32799	All Other Non-Metallic Mineral Product Manufacturing
327990	All Other Non-Metallic Mineral Product Manufacturing CAN

331 Primary Metal Manufacturing

3311 Iron and Steel Mills and Ferro-Alloy Manufacturing

| 33111 | Iron and Steel Mills and Ferro-Alloy Manufacturing |
| 331110 | Iron and Steel Mills and Ferro-Alloy Manufacturing CAN |

3312 Steel Product Manufacturing from Purchased Steel

33121	Iron and Steel Pipes and Tubes Manufacturing from Purchased Steel
331210	Iron and Steel Pipes and Tubes Manufacturing from Purchased Steel
33122	Rolling and Drawing of Purchased Steel
331221	Cold-Rolled Steel Shape Manufacturing US
331222	Steel Wire Drawing US

3313 Alumina and Aluminum Production and Processing

33131	Alumina and Aluminum Production and Processing
331313	Primary Production of Alumina and Aluminum CAN
331317	Aluminum Rolling, Drawing, Extruding and Alloying CAN

3314 Non-Ferrous Metal (except Aluminum) Production and Processing

| 33141 | Non-Ferrous Metal (except Aluminum) Smelting and Refining |
| 331410 | Non-Ferrous Metal (except Aluminum) Smelting and Refining CAN |

33142	Copper Rolling, Drawing, Extruding and Alloying	
331420	Copper Rolling, Drawing, Extruding and Alloying MEX	
33149	Non-Ferrous Metal (except Copper and Aluminum) Rolling, Drawing, Extruding and Alloying	
331490	Non-Ferrous Metal (except Copper and Aluminum) Rolling, Drawing, Extruding and Alloying CAN	

3315 Foundries

33151	Ferrous Metal Foundries
331511	Iron Foundries US
331514	Steel Foundries CAN
33152	Non-Ferrous Metal Foundries
331523	Non-Ferrous Die-Casting Foundries CAN
331529	Non-Ferrous Foundries (except Die-Casting) CAN

332 Fabricated Metal Product Manufacturing

3321 Forging and Stamping

33211	Forging and Stamping
332113	Forging CAN
332118	Stamping CAN

3322 Cutlery and Hand Tool Manufacturing

33221	Cutlery and Hand Tool Manufacturing
332210	Cutlery and Hand Tool Manufacturing CAN

3323 Architectural and Structural Metals Manufacturing

33231	Plate Work and Fabricated Structural Product Manufacturing
332311	Prefabricated Metal Building and Component Manufacturing US
332314	Concrete Reinforcing Bar Manufacturing CAN
332319	Other Plate Work and Fabricated Structural Product Manufacturing CAN
33232	Ornamental and Architectural Metal Product Manufacturing
332321	Metal Window and Door Manufacturing US
332329	Other Ornamental and Architectural Metal Product Manufacturing CAN

3324 Boiler, Tank and Shipping Container Manufacturing

33241	Power Boiler and Heat Exchanger Manufacturing
332410	Power Boiler and Heat Exchanger Manufacturing
33242	Metal Tank (Heavy Gauge) Manufacturing
332420	Metal Tank (Heavy Gauge) Manufacturing
33243	Metal Can, Box and Other Metal Container (Light Gauge) Manufacturing
332431	Metal Can Manufacturing US
332439	Other Metal Container Manufacturing US

3325 Hardware Manufacturing

33251	Hardware Manufacturing
332510	Hardware Manufacturing

3326 Spring and Wire Product Manufacturing

33261	Spring and Wire Product Manufacturing
332611	Spring (Heavy Gauge) Manufacturing US
332619	Other Fabricated Wire Product Manufacturing CAN

3327 Machine Shops, Turned Product, and Screw, Nut and Bolt Manufacturing

33271	Machine Shops
332710	Machine Shops
33272	Turned Product and Screw, Nut and Bolt Manufacturing
332720	Turned Product and Screw, Nut and Bolt Manufacturing MEX

3328 **Coating, Engraving, Heat Treating and Allied Activities**

33281   Coating, Engraving, Heat Treating and Allied Activities
332810   Coating, Engraving, Heat Treating and Allied Activities MEX

3329 **Other Fabricated Metal Product Manufacturing**

33291   Metal Valve Manufacturing
332910   Metal Valve Manufacturing MEX
33299   All Other Fabricated Metal Product Manufacturing
332991   Ball and Roller Bearing Manufacturing
332999   All Other Miscellaneous Fabricated Metal Product Manufacturing MEX

333 **Machinery Manufacturing**

3331 **Agricultural, Construction and Mining Machinery Manufacturing**

33311   Agricultural Implement Manufacturing
333110   Agricultural Implement Manufacturing CAN
33312   Construction Machinery Manufacturing
333120   Construction Machinery Manufacturing
33313   Mining and Oil and Gas Field Machinery Manufacturing
333130   Mining and Oil and Gas Field Machinery Manufacturing MEX

3332 **Industrial Machinery Manufacturing**

33321   Sawmill and Woodworking Machinery Manufacturing
333210   Sawmill and Woodworking Machinery Manufacturing
33322   Rubber and Plastics Industry Machinery Manufacturing
333220   Rubber and Plastics Industry Machinery Manufacturing
33329   Other Industrial Machinery Manufacturing
333291   Paper Industry Machinery Manufacturing US
333299   All Other Industrial Machinery Manufacturing CAN

3333 **Commercial and Service Industry Machinery Manufacturing**

33331   Commercial and Service Industry Machinery Manufacturing
333310   Commercial and Service Industry Machinery Manufacturing CAN

3334 **Ventilation, Heating, Air-Conditioning and Commercial Refrigeration Equipment Manufacturing**

33341   Ventilation, Heating, Air-Conditioning and Commercial Refrigeration Equipment Manufacturing
333413   Industrial and Commercial Fan and Blower and Air Purification Equipment Manufacturing CAN
333416   Heating Equipment and Commercial Refrigeration Equipment Manufacturing CAN

3335 **Metalworking Machinery Manufacturing**

33351   Metalworking Machinery Manufacturing
333511   Industrial Mould Manufacturing US
333519   Other Metalworking Machinery Manufacturing CAN

3336 **Engine, Turbine and Power Transmission Equipment Manufacturing**

33361   Engine, Turbine and Power Transmission Equipment Manufacturing
333611   Turbine and Turbine Generator Set Unit Manufacturing US
333619   Other Engine and Power Transmission Equipment Manufacturing CAN

3339 **Other General-Purpose Machinery Manufacturing**

33391   Pump and Compressor Manufacturing
333910   Pump and Compressor Manufacturing CAN
33392   Material Handling Equipment Manufacturing
333920   Material Handling Equipment Manufacturing MEX
33399   All Other General-Purpose Machinery Manufacturing

333990   All Other General-Purpose Machinery Manufacturing ^{CAN}

334   Computer and Electronic Product Manufacturing

   3341   Computer and Peripheral Equipment Manufacturing

      33411   Computer and Peripheral Equipment Manufacturing
      334110   Computer and Peripheral Equipment Manufacturing ^{MEX}

   3342   Communications Equipment Manufacturing

      33421   Telephone Apparatus Manufacturing
      334210   Telephone Apparatus Manufacturing
      33422   Radio and Television Broadcasting and Wireless Communications Equipment Manufacturing
      334220   Radio and Television Broadcasting and Wireless Communications Equipment Manufacturing
      33429   Other Communications Equipment Manufacturing
      334290   Other Communications Equipment Manufacturing

   3343   Audio and Video Equipment Manufacturing

      33431   Audio and Video Equipment Manufacturing
      334310   Audio and Video Equipment Manufacturing

   3344   Semiconductor and Other Electronic Component Manufacturing

      33441   Semiconductor and Other Electronic Component Manufacturing
      334410   Semiconductor and Other Electronic Component Manufacturing ^{MEX}

   3345   Navigational, Measuring, Medical and Control Instruments Manufacturing

      33451   Navigational, Measuring, Medical and Control Instruments Manufacturing
      334511   Navigational and Guidance Instruments Manufacturing ^{US}
      334512   Measuring, Medical and Controlling Devices Manufacturing ^{CAN}

   3346   Manufacturing and Reproducing Magnetic and Optical Media

      33461   Manufacturing and Reproducing Magnetic and Optical Media
      334610   Manufacturing and Reproducing Magnetic and Optical Media ^{MEX}

335   Electrical Equipment, Appliance and Component Manufacturing

   3351   Electric Lighting Equipment Manufacturing

      33511   Electric Lamp Bulb and Parts Manufacturing
      335110   Electric Lamp Bulb and Parts Manufacturing
      33512   Lighting Fixture Manufacturing
      335120   Lighting Fixture Manufacturing ^{CAN}

   3352   Household Appliance Manufacturing

      33521   Small Electrical Appliance Manufacturing
      335210   Small Electrical Appliance Manufacturing ^{MEX}
      33522   Major Appliance Manufacturing
      335223   Major Kitchen Appliance Manufacturing ^{CAN}
      335229   Other Major Appliance Manufacturing ^{CAN}

   3353   Electrical Equipment Manufacturing

      33531   Electrical Equipment Manufacturing
      335311   Power, Distribution and Specialty Transformers Manufacturing ^{US}
      335312   Motor and Generator Manufacturing ^{US}
      335315   Switchgear and Switchboard, and Relay and Industrial Control Apparatus Manufacturing ^{CAN}

   3359   Other Electrical Equipment and Component Manufacturing

      33591   Battery Manufacturing

335910	Battery Manufacturing CAN
33592	Communication and Energy Wire and Cable Manufacturing
335920	Communication and Energy Wire and Cable Manufacturing CAN
33593	Wiring Device Manufacturing
335930	Wiring Device Manufacturing CAN
33599	All Other Electrical Equipment and Component Manufacturing
335990	All Other Electrical Equipment and Component Manufacturing CAN

336   Transportation Equipment Manufacturing

3361   Motor Vehicle Manufacturing

33611	Automobile and Light-Duty Motor Vehicle Manufacturing
336110	Automobile and Light-Duty Motor Vehicle Manufacturing MEX
33612	Heavy-Duty Truck Manufacturing
336120	Heavy-Duty Truck Manufacturing

3362   Motor Vehicle Body and Trailer Manufacturing

33621	Motor Vehicle Body and Trailer Manufacturing
336211	Motor Vehicle Body Manufacturing US
336212	Truck Trailer Manufacturing US
336215	Motor Home, Travel Trailer and Camper Manufacturing CAN

3363   Motor Vehicle Parts Manufacturing

33631	Motor Vehicle Gasoline Engine and Engine Parts Manufacturing
336310	Motor Vehicle Gasoline Engine and Engine Parts Manufacturing MEX
33632	Motor Vehicle Electrical and Electronic Equipment Manufacturing
336320	Motor Vehicle Electrical and Electronic Equipment Manufacturing MEX
33633	Motor Vehicle Steering and Suspension Components (except Spring) Manufacturing
336330	Motor Vehicle Steering and Suspension Components (except Spring) Manufacturing
33634	Motor Vehicle Brake System Manufacturing
336340	Motor Vehicle Brake System Manufacturing
33635	Motor Vehicle Transmission and Power Train Parts Manufacturing
336350	Motor Vehicle Transmission and Power Train Parts Manufacturing
33636	Motor Vehicle Seating and Interior Trim Manufacturing
336360	Motor Vehicle Seating and Interior Trim Manufacturing
33637	Motor Vehicle Metal Stamping
336370	Motor Vehicle Metal Stamping
33639	Other Motor Vehicle Parts Manufacturing
336390	Other Motor Vehicle Parts Manufacturing MEX

3364   Aerospace Product and Parts Manufacturing

| 33641 | Aerospace Product and Parts Manufacturing |
| 336410 | Aerospace Product and Parts Manufacturing MEX |

3365   Railroad Rolling Stock Manufacturing

| 33651 | Railroad Rolling Stock Manufacturing |
| 336510 | Railroad Rolling Stock Manufacturing |

3366   Ship and Boat Building

33661	Ship and Boat Building
336611	Ship Building and Repairing US
336612	Boat Building US

3369   Other Transportation Equipment Manufacturing

| 33699 | Other Transportation Equipment Manufacturing |
| 336990 | Other Transportation Equipment Manufacturing CAN |

337   Furniture and Related Product Manufacturing

3371   Household and Institutional Furniture and Kitchen Cabinet Manufacturing

33711	Wood Kitchen Cabinet and Counter Top Manufacturing
337110	Wood Kitchen Cabinet and Counter Top Manufacturing
33712	Household and Institutional Furniture Manufacturing
337121	Upholstered Household Furniture Manufacturing US
337123	Other Wood Household Furniture Manufacturing CAN
337126	Household Furniture (except Wood and Upholstered) Manufacturing CAN
337127	Institutional Furniture Manufacturing US

3372   Office Furniture (including Fixtures) Manufacturing

33721	Office Furniture (including Fixtures) Manufacturing
337213	Wood Office Furniture, including Custom Architectural Woodwork, Manufacturing CAN
337214	Office Furniture (except Wood) Manufacturing US
337215	Showcase, Partition, Shelving and Locker Manufacturing US

3379   Other Furniture-Related Product Manufacturing

33791	Mattress Manufacturing
337910	Mattress Manufacturing
33792	Blind and Shade Manufacturing
337920	Blind and Shade Manufacturing

339   Miscellaneous Manufacturing

3391   Medical Equipment and Supplies Manufacturing

33911	Medical Equipment and Supplies Manufacturing
339110	Medical Equipment and Supplies Manufacturing CAN

3399   Other Miscellaneous Manufacturing

33991	Jewellery and Silverware Manufacturing
339910	Jewellery and Silverware Manufacturing CAN
33992	Sporting and Athletic Goods Manufacturing
339920	Sporting and Athletic Goods Manufacturing
33993	Doll, Toy and Game Manufacturing
339930	Doll, Toy and Game Manufacturing MEX
33994	Office Supplies (except Paper) Manufacturing
339940	Office Supplies (except Paper) Manufacturing MEX
33995	Sign Manufacturing
339950	Sign Manufacturing
33999	All Other Miscellaneous Manufacturing
339990	All Other Miscellaneous Manufacturing CAN

41   Wholesale Trade

411   Farm Product Wholesaler-Distributors CAN

4111   Farm Product Wholesaler-Distributors CAN

41111	Live Animal Wholesaler-Distributors CAN
411110	Live Animal Wholesaler-Distributors CAN
41112	Oilseed and Grain Wholesaler-Distributors CAN
411120	Oilseed and Grain Wholesaler-Distributors CAN
41113	Nursery Stock and Plant Wholesaler-Distributors CAN
411130	Nursery Stock and Plant Wholesaler-Distributors CAN
41119	Other Farm Product Wholesaler-Distributors CAN
411190	Other Farm Product Wholesaler-Distributors CAN

412   Petroleum Product Wholesaler-Distributors CAN

4121   **Petroleum Product Wholesaler-Distributors** CAN

    41211   Petroleum Product Wholesaler-Distributors CAN
    412110   Petroleum Product Wholesaler-Distributors CAN

413   **Food, Beverage and Tobacco Wholesaler-Distributors** CAN

4131   **Food Wholesaler-Distributors** CAN

    41311   General-Line Food Wholesaler-Distributors CAN
    413110   General-Line Food Wholesaler-Distributors CAN
    41312   Dairy and Milk Products Wholesaler-Distributors CAN
    413120   Dairy and Milk Products Wholesaler-Distributors CAN
    41313   Poultry and Egg Wholesaler-Distributors CAN
    413130   Poultry and Egg Wholesaler-Distributors CAN
    41314   Fish and Seafood Product Wholesaler-Distributors CAN
    413140   Fish and Seafood Product Wholesaler-Distributors CAN
    41315   Fresh Fruit and Vegetable Wholesaler-Distributors CAN
    413150   Fresh Fruit and Vegetable Wholesaler-Distributors CAN
    41316   Red Meat and Meat Product Wholesaler-Distributors CAN
    413160   Red Meat and Meat Product Wholesaler-Distributors CAN
    41319   Other Specialty-Line Food Wholesaler-Distributors CAN
    413190   Other Specialty-Line Food Wholesaler-Distributors CAN

4132   **Beverage Wholesaler-Distributors** CAN

    41321   Non-Alcoholic Beverage Wholesaler-Distributors CAN
    413210   Non-Alcoholic Beverage Wholesaler-Distributors CAN
    41322   Alcoholic Beverage Wholesaler-Distributors CAN
    413220   Alcoholic Beverage Wholesaler-Distributors CAN

4133   **Cigarette and Tobacco Product Wholesaler-Distributors** CAN

    41331   Cigarette and Tobacco Product Wholesaler-Distributors CAN
    413310   Cigarette and Tobacco Product Wholesaler-Distributors CAN

414   **Personal and Household Goods Wholesaler-Distributors** CAN

4141   **Textile, Clothing and Footwear Wholesaler-Distributors** CAN

    41411   Clothing and Clothing Accessories Wholesaler-Distributors CAN
    414110   Clothing and Clothing Accessories Wholesaler-Distributors CAN
    41412   Footwear Wholesaler-Distributors CAN
    414120   Footwear Wholesaler-Distributors CAN
    41413   Piece Goods, Notions and Other Dry Goods Wholesaler-Distributors CAN
    414130   Piece Goods, Notions and Other Dry Goods Wholesaler-Distributors CAN

4142   **Home Entertainment Equipment and Household Appliance Wholesaler-Distributors** CAN

    41421   Home Entertainment Equipment Wholesaler-Distributors CAN
    414210   Home Entertainment Equipment Wholesaler-Distributors CAN
    41422   Household Appliance Wholesaler-Distributors CAN
    414220   Household Appliance Wholesaler-Distributors CAN

4143   **Home Furnishings Wholesaler-Distributors** CAN

    41431   China, Glassware, Crockery and Pottery Wholesaler-Distributors CAN
    414310   China, Glassware, Crockery and Pottery Wholesaler-Distributors CAN
    41432   Floor Covering Wholesaler-Distributors CAN
    414320   Floor Covering Wholesaler-Distributors CAN
    41433   Linen, Drapery and Other Textile Furnishings Wholesaler-Distributors CAN
    414330   Linen, Drapery and Other Textile Furnishings Wholesaler-Distributors CAN
    41439   Other Home Furnishings Wholesaler-Distributors CAN
    414390   Other Home Furnishings Wholesaler-Distributors CAN

4144   **Personal Goods Wholesaler-Distributors** CAN

41441   Jewellery and Watch Wholesaler-Distributors CAN
414410   Jewellery and Watch Wholesaler-Distributors CAN
41442   Book, Periodical and Newspaper Wholesaler-Distributors CAN
414420   Book, Periodical and Newspaper Wholesaler-Distributors CAN
41443   Photographic Equipment and Supplies Wholesaler-Distributors CAN
414430   Photographic Equipment and Supplies Wholesaler-Distributors CAN
41444   Sound Recording Wholesalers CAN
414440   Sound Recording Wholesalers CAN
41445   Video Cassette Wholesalers CAN
414450   Video Cassette Wholesalers CAN
41446   Toy and Hobby Goods Wholesaler-Distributors CAN
414460   Toy and Hobby Goods Wholesaler-Distributors CAN
41447   Amusement and Sporting Goods Wholesaler-Distributors CAN
414470   Amusement and Sporting Goods Wholesaler-Distributors CAN

4145   **Pharmaceuticals, Toiletries, Cosmetics and Sundries Wholesaler-Distributors** CAN

41451   Pharmaceuticals and Pharmacy Supplies Wholesaler-Distributors CAN
414510   Pharmaceuticals and Pharmacy Supplies Wholesaler-Distributors CAN
41452   Toiletries, Cosmetics and Sundries Wholesaler-Distributors CAN
414520   Toiletries, Cosmetics and Sundries Wholesaler-Distributors CAN

415   **Motor Vehicle and Parts Wholesaler-Distributors** CAN

4151   **Motor Vehicle Wholesaler-Distributors** CAN

41511   New and Used Automobile and Light-Duty Truck Wholesaler-Distributors CAN
415110   New and Used Automobile and Light-Duty Truck Wholesaler-Distributors CAN
41512   Truck, Truck Tractor and Bus Wholesaler-Distributors CAN
415120   Truck, Truck Tractor and Bus Wholesaler-Distributors CAN
41519   Recreational and Other Motor Vehicles Wholesaler-Distributors CAN
415190   Recreational and Other Motor Vehicles Wholesaler-Distributors CAN

4152   **New Motor Vehicle Parts and Accessories Wholesaler-Distributors** CAN

41521   Tire Wholesaler-Distributors CAN
415210   Tire Wholesaler-Distributors CAN
41529   Other New Motor Vehicle Parts and Accessories Wholesaler-Distributors CAN
415290   Other New Motor Vehicle Parts and Accessories Wholesaler-Distributors CAN

4153   **Used Motor Vehicle Parts and Accessories Wholesaler-Distributors** CAN

41531   Used Motor Vehicle Parts and Accessories Wholesaler-Distributors CAN
415310   Used Motor Vehicle Parts and Accessories Wholesaler-Distributors CAN

416   **Building Material and Supplies Wholesaler-Distributors** CAN

4161   **Electrical, Plumbing, Heating and Air-Conditioning Equipment and Supplies Wholesaler-Distributors** CAN

41611   Electrical Wiring and Construction Supplies Wholesaler-Distributors CAN
416110   Electrical Wiring and Construction Supplies Wholesaler-Distributors CAN
41612   Plumbing, Heating and Air-Conditioning Equipment and Supplies Wholesaler-Distributors CAN
416120   Plumbing, Heating and Air-Conditioning Equipment and Supplies Wholesaler-Distributors CAN

4162   **Metal Service Centres** CAN

41621   Metal Service Centres CAN
416210   Metal Service Centres CAN

4163   **Lumber, Millwork, Hardware and Other Building Supplies Wholesaler-Distributors** ^{CAN}

41631   General-Line Building Supplies Wholesaler-Distributors ^{CAN}
416310   General-Line Building Supplies Wholesaler-Distributors ^{CAN}
41632   Lumber, Plywood and Millwork Wholesaler-Distributors ^{CAN}
416320   Lumber, Plywood and Millwork Wholesaler-Distributors ^{CAN}
41633   Hardware Wholesaler-Distributors ^{CAN}
416330   Hardware Wholesaler-Distributors ^{CAN}
41634   Paint, Glass and Wallpaper Wholesaler-Distributors ^{CAN}
416340   Paint, Glass and Wallpaper Wholesaler-Distributors ^{CAN}
41639   Other Specialty-Line Building Supplies Wholesaler-Distributors ^{CAN}
416390   Other Specialty-Line Building Supplies Wholesaler-Distributors ^{CAN}

417   **Machinery, Equipment and Supplies Wholesaler-Distributors** ^{CAN}

4171   **Farm, Lawn and Garden Machinery and Equipment Wholesaler-Distributors** ^{CAN}

41711   Farm, Lawn and Garden Machinery and Equipment Wholesaler-Distributors ^{CAN}
417110   Farm, Lawn and Garden Machinery and Equipment Wholesaler-Distributors ^{CAN}

4172   **Construction, Forestry, Mining, and Industrial Machinery, Equipment and Supplies Wholesaler-Distributors** ^{CAN}

41721   Construction and Forestry Machinery, Equipment and Supplies Wholesaler-Distributors ^{CAN}
417210   Construction and Forestry Machinery, Equipment and Supplies Wholesaler-Distributors ^{CAN}
41722   Mining and Oil and Gas Well Machinery, Equipment and Supplies Wholesaler-Distributors ^{CAN}
417220   Mining and Oil and Gas Well Machinery, Equipment and Supplies Wholesaler-Distributors ^{CAN}
41723   Industrial Machinery, Equipment and Supplies Wholesaler-Distributors ^{CAN}
417230   Industrial Machinery, Equipment and Supplies Wholesaler-Distributors ^{CAN}

4173   **Computer and Communications Equipment and Supplies Wholesaler-Distributors** ^{CAN}

41731   Computer, Computer Peripheral and Pre-Packaged Software Wholesaler-Distributors ^{CAN}
417310   Computer, Computer Peripheral and Pre-Packaged Software Wholesaler-Distributors ^{CAN}
41732   Electronic Components, Navigational and Communications Equipment and Supplies Wholesaler-Distributors ^{CAN}
417320   Electronic Components, Navigational and Communications Equipment and Supplies Wholesaler-Distributors ^{CAN}

4179   **Other Machinery, Equipment and Supplies Wholesaler-Distributors** ^{CAN}

41791   Office and Store Machinery and Equipment Wholesaler-Distributors ^{CAN}
417910   Office and Store Machinery and Equipment Wholesaler-Distributors ^{CAN}
41792   Service Establishment Machinery, Equipment and Supplies Wholesaler-Distributors ^{CAN}
417920   Service Establishment Machinery, Equipment and Supplies Wholesaler-Distributors ^{CAN}
41793   Professional Machinery, Equipment and Supplies Wholesaler-Distributors ^{CAN}
417930   Professional Machinery, Equipment and Supplies Wholesaler-Distributors ^{CAN}
41799   All Other Machinery, Equipment and Supplies Wholesaler-Distributors ^{CAN}
417990   All Other Machinery, Equipment and Supplies Wholesaler-Distributors ^{CAN}

418   **Miscellaneous Wholesaler-Distributors** ^{CAN}

4181   **Recyclable Material Wholesaler-Distributors** ^{CAN}

41811   Recyclable Metal Wholesaler-Distributors ^{CAN}

	418110	Recyclable Metal Wholesaler-Distributors CAN
	41812	Recyclable Paper and Paperboard Wholesaler-Distributors CAN
	418120	Recyclable Paper and Paperboard Wholesaler-Distributors CAN
	41819	Other Recyclable Material Wholesaler-Distributors CAN
	418190	Other Recyclable Material Wholesaler-Distributors CAN

4182 Paper, Paper Product and Disposable Plastic Product Wholesaler-Distributors CAN

	41821	Stationery and Office Supplies Wholesaler-Distributors CAN
	418210	Stationery and Office Supplies Wholesaler-Distributors CAN
	41822	Other Paper and Disposable Plastic Product Wholesaler-Distributors CAN
	418220	Other Paper and Disposable Plastic Product Wholesaler-Distributors CAN

4183 Agricultural Supplies Wholesaler-Distributors CAN

	41831	Agricultural Feed Wholesaler-Distributors CAN
	418310	Agricultural Feed Wholesaler-Distributors CAN
	41832	Seed Wholesaler-Distributors CAN
	418320	Seed Wholesaler-Distributors CAN
	41839	Agricultural Chemical and Other Farm Supplies Wholesaler-Distributors CAN
	418390	Agricultural Chemical and Other Farm Supplies Wholesaler-Distributors CAN

4184 Chemical (except Agricultural) and Allied Product Wholesaler-Distributors CAN

	41841	Chemical (except Agricultural) and Allied Product Wholesaler-Distributors CAN
	418410	Chemical (except Agricultural) and Allied Product Wholesaler-Distributors CAN

4189 Other Miscellaneous Wholesaler-Distributors CAN

	41891	Log and Wood Chip Wholesaler-Distributors CAN
	418910	Log and Wood Chip Wholesaler-Distributors CAN
	41892	Mineral, Ore and Precious Metal Wholesaler-Distributors CAN
	418920	Mineral, Ore and Precious Metal Wholesaler-Distributors CAN
	41893	Second-Hand Goods (except Machinery and Automotive) Wholesaler-Distributors CAN
	418930	Second-Hand Goods (except Machinery and Automotive) Wholesaler-Distributors CAN
	41899	All Other Wholesaler-Distributors CAN
	418990	All Other Wholesaler-Distributors CAN

419 Wholesale Electronic Markets, and Agents and Brokers US

4191 Wholesale Electronic Markets, and Agents and Brokers US

	41911	Business-to-Business Electronic Markets US
	419110	Business-to-Business Electronic Markets US
	41912	Wholesale Trade Agents and Brokers US
	419120	Wholesale Trade Agents and Brokers US

44-45 Retail Trade

441 Motor Vehicle and Parts Dealers US

4411 Automobile Dealers US

	44111	New Car Dealers US
	441110	New Car Dealers US
	44112	Used Car Dealers US
	441120	Used Car Dealers US

4412 Other Motor Vehicle Dealers US

	44121	Recreational Vehicle Dealers US
	441210	Recreational Vehicle Dealers US

| 44122 | Motorcycle, Boat and Other Motor Vehicle Dealers ^{US} |

44122   Motorcycle, Boat and Other Motor Vehicle Dealers ^{US}
441220   Motorcycle, Boat and Other Motor Vehicle Dealers ^{CAN}

4413   Automotive Parts, Accessories and Tire Stores ^{US}

44131   Automotive Parts and Accessories Stores ^{US}
441310   Automotive Parts and Accessories Stores ^{US}
44132   Tire Dealers ^{US}
441320   Tire Dealers ^{US}

442   Furniture and Home Furnishings Stores ^{US}

4421   Furniture Stores ^{US}

44211   Furniture Stores ^{US}
442110   Furniture Stores ^{US}

4422   Home Furnishings Stores ^{US}

44221   Floor Covering Stores ^{US}
442210   Floor Covering Stores ^{US}
44229   Other Home Furnishings Stores ^{US}
442291   Window Treatment Stores ^{US}
442292   Print and Picture Frame Stores ^{CAN}
442298   All Other Home Furnishings Stores ^{CAN}

443   Electronics and Appliance Stores ^{US}

4431   Electronics and Appliance Stores ^{US}

44311   Appliance, Television and Other Electronics Stores ^{US}
443110   Appliance, Television and Other Electronics Stores ^{CAN}
44312   Computer and Software Stores ^{US}
443120   Computer and Software Stores ^{US}
44313   Camera and Photographic Supplies Stores ^{US}
443130   Camera and Photographic Supplies Stores ^{US}

444   Building Material and Garden Equipment and Supplies Dealers ^{US}

4441   Building Material and Supplies Dealers ^{US}

44411   Home Centres ^{US}
444110   Home Centres ^{US}
44412   Paint and Wallpaper Stores ^{US}
444120   Paint and Wallpaper Stores ^{US}
44413   Hardware Stores ^{US}
444130   Hardware Stores ^{US}
44419   Other Building Material Dealers ^{US}
444190   Other Building Material Dealers ^{US}

4442   Lawn and Garden Equipment and Supplies Stores ^{US}

44421   Outdoor Power Equipment Stores ^{US}
444210   Outdoor Power Equipment Stores ^{US}
44422   Nursery Stores and Garden Centres ^{US}
444220   Nursery Stores and Garden Centres ^{US}

445   Food and Beverage Stores ^{US}

4451   Grocery Stores ^{US}

44511   Supermarkets and Other Grocery (except Convenience) Stores ^{US}
445110   Supermarkets and Other Grocery (except Convenience) Stores ^{US}
44512   Convenience Stores ^{US}
445120   Convenience Stores ^{US}

4452 **Specialty Food Stores** US

44521	Meat Markets US
445210	Meat Markets US
44522	Fish and Seafood Markets US
445220	Fish and Seafood Markets US
44523	Fruit and Vegetable Markets US
445230	Fruit and Vegetable Markets US
44529	Other Specialty Food Stores US
445291	Baked Goods Stores US
445292	Confectionery and Nut Stores US
445299	All Other Specialty Food Stores US

4453 **Beer, Wine and Liquor Stores** US

44531	Beer, Wine and Liquor Stores US
445310	Beer, Wine and Liquor Stores US

446 **Health and Personal Care Stores** US

4461 **Health and Personal Care Stores** US

44611	Pharmacies and Drug Stores US
446110	Pharmacies and Drug Stores US
44612	Cosmetics, Beauty Supplies and Perfume Stores US
446120	Cosmetics, Beauty Supplies and Perfume Stores US
44613	Optical Goods Stores US
446130	Optical Goods Stores US
44619	Other Health and Personal Care Stores US
446191	Food (Health) Supplement Stores US
446199	All Other Health and Personal Care Stores US

447 **Gasoline Stations** US

4471 **Gasoline Stations** US

44711	Gasoline Stations with Convenience Stores US
447110	Gasoline Stations with Convenience Stores US
44719	Other Gasoline Stations US
447190	Other Gasoline Stations US

448 **Clothing and Clothing Accessories Stores** US

4481 **Clothing Stores** US

44811	Men's Clothing Stores US
448110	Men's Clothing Stores US
44812	Women's Clothing Stores US
448120	Women's Clothing Stores US
44813	Children's and Infants' Clothing Stores US
448130	Children's and Infants' Clothing Stores US
44814	Family Clothing Stores US
448140	Family Clothing Stores US
44815	Clothing Accessories Stores US
448150	Clothing Accessories Stores US
44819	Other Clothing Stores US
448191	Fur Stores CAN
448199	All Other Clothing Stores CAN

4482 **Shoe Stores** US

44821	Shoe Stores US
448210	Shoe Stores US

4483   **Jewellery, Luggage and Leather Goods Stores** US

    44831   Jewellery Stores US
    448310   Jewellery Stores US
    44832   Luggage and Leather Goods Stores US
    448320   Luggage and Leather Goods Stores US

451   **Sporting Goods, Hobby, Book and Music Stores** US

4511   **Sporting Goods, Hobby and Musical Instrument Stores** US

    45111   Sporting Goods Stores US
    451110   Sporting Goods Stores US
    45112   Hobby, Toy and Game Stores US
    451120   Hobby, Toy and Game Stores US
    45113   Sewing, Needlework and Piece Goods Stores US
    451130   Sewing, Needlework and Piece Goods Stores US
    45114   Musical Instrument and Supplies Stores US
    451140   Musical Instrument and Supplies Stores US

4512   **Book, Periodical and Music Stores** US

    45121   Book Stores and News Dealers US
    451210   Book Stores and News Dealers CAN
    45122   Pre-Recorded Tape, Compact Disc and Record Stores US
    451220   Pre-Recorded Tape, Compact Disc and Record Stores US

452   **General Merchandise Stores** US

4521   **Department Stores** US

    45211   Department Stores US
    452110   Department Stores CAN

4529   **Other General Merchandise Stores** US

    45291   Warehouse Clubs and Superstores US
    452910   Warehouse Clubs and Superstores US
    45299   All Other General Merchandise Stores US
    452991   Home and Auto Supplies Stores CAN
    452999   All Other Miscellaneous General Merchandise Stores CAN

453   **Miscellaneous Store Retailers** US

4531   **Florists** US

    45311   Florists US
    453110   Florists US

4532   **Office Supplies, Stationery and Gift Stores** US

    45321   Office Supplies and Stationery Stores US
    453210   Office Supplies and Stationery Stores US
    45322   Gift, Novelty and Souvenir Stores US
    453220   Gift, Novelty and Souvenir Stores US

4533   **Used Merchandise Stores** US

    45331   Used Merchandise Stores US
    453310   Used Merchandise Stores US

4539   **Other Miscellaneous Store Retailers** US

    45391   Pet and Pet Supplies Stores US
    453910   Pet and Pet Supplies Stores US
    45392   Art Dealers US
    453920   Art Dealers US
    45393   Mobile Home Dealers US

	453930	Mobile Home Dealers US
	45399	All Other Miscellaneous Store Retailers US
	453992	Beer and Wine-Making Supplies Stores CAN
	453999	All Other Miscellaneous Store Retailers (except Beer and Wine-Making Supplies Stores) CAN

454   Non-Store Retailers US

4541   Electronic Shopping and Mail-Order Houses US

45411	Electronic Shopping and Mail-Order Houses US
454111	Internet Shopping US
454112	Electronic Auctions US
454113	Mail-Order Houses US

4542   Vending Machine Operators US

45421	Vending Machine Operators US
454210	Vending Machine Operators US

4543   Direct Selling Establishments US

45431	Fuel Dealers US
454311	Heating Oil Dealers US
454312	Liquefied Petroleum Gas (Bottled Gas) Dealers US
454319	Other Fuel Dealers US
45439	Other Direct Selling Establishments US
454390	Other Direct Selling Establishments US

48-49   Transportation and Warehousing

481   Air Transportation

4811   Scheduled Air Transportation

48111	Scheduled Air Transportation
481110	Scheduled Air Transportation CAN

4812   Non-Scheduled Air Transportation

48121	Non-Scheduled Air Transportation
481214	Non-Scheduled Chartered Air Transportation CAN
481215	Non-Scheduled Specialty Flying Services CAN

482   Rail Transportation

4821   Rail Transportation

48211	Rail Transportation
482112	Short-Haul Freight Rail Transportation US
482113	Mainline Freight Rail Transportation CAN
482114	Passenger Rail Transportation CAN

483   Water Transportation

4831   Deep Sea, Coastal and Great Lakes Water Transportation

48311	Deep Sea, Coastal and Great Lakes Water Transportation
483115	Deep Sea, Coastal and Great Lakes Water Transportation (except by Ferries) CAN
483116	Deep Sea, Coastal and Great Lakes Water Transportation by Ferries CAN

4832   Inland Water Transportation

48321	Inland Water Transportation
483213	Inland Water Transportation (except by Ferries) CAN
483214	Inland Water Transportation by Ferries CAN

484   **Truck Transportation**

     4841   **General Freight Trucking**

         48411   General Freight Trucking, Local
         484110   General Freight Trucking, Local [US]
         48412   General Freight Trucking, Long Distance
         484121   General Freight Trucking, Long Distance, Truck-Load [US]
         484122   General Freight Trucking, Long Distance, Less Than Truck-Load [US]

     4842   **Specialized Freight Trucking**

         48421   Used Household and Office Goods Moving
         484210   Used Household and Office Goods Moving
         48422   Specialized Freight (except Used Goods) Trucking, Local
         484221   Bulk Liquids Trucking, Local [CAN]
         484222   Dry Bulk Materials Trucking, Local [CAN]
         484223   Forest Products Trucking, Local [CAN]
         484229   Other Specialized Freight (except Used Goods) Trucking, Local [CAN]
         48423   Specialized Freight (except Used Goods) Trucking, Long Distance
         484231   Bulk Liquids Trucking, Long Distance [CAN]
         484232   Dry Bulk Materials Trucking, Long Distance [CAN]
         484233   Forest Products Trucking, Long Distance [CAN]
         484239   Other Specialized Freight (except Used Goods) Trucking, Long Distance [CAN]

485   **Transit and Ground Passenger Transportation**

     4851   **Urban Transit Systems**

         48511   Urban Transit Systems
         485110   Urban Transit Systems [CAN]

     4852   **Interurban and Rural Bus Transportation**

         48521   Interurban and Rural Bus Transportation
         485210   Interurban and Rural Bus Transportation

     4853   **Taxi and Limousine Service**

         48531   Taxi Service
         485310   Taxi Service [US]
         48532   Limousine Service
         485320   Limousine Service

     4854   **School and Employee Bus Transportation**

         48541   School and Employee Bus Transportation
         485410   School and Employee Bus Transportation

     4855   **Charter Bus Industry**

         48551   Charter Bus Industry
         485510   Charter Bus Industry

     4859   **Other Transit and Ground Passenger Transportation**

         48599   Other Transit and Ground Passenger Transportation
         485990   Other Transit and Ground Passenger Transportation [CAN]

486   **Pipeline Transportation**

     4861   **Pipeline Transportation of Crude Oil**

         48611   Pipeline Transportation of Crude Oil
         486110   Pipeline Transportation of Crude Oil

     4862   **Pipeline Transportation of Natural Gas**

         48621   Pipeline Transportation of Natural Gas
         486210   Pipeline Transportation of Natural Gas

4869   Other Pipeline Transportation

48691	Pipeline Transportation of Refined Petroleum Products
486910	Pipeline Transportation of Refined Petroleum Products
48699	All Other Pipeline Transportation
486990	All Other Pipeline Transportation

487   Scenic and Sightseeing Transportation

4871   Scenic and Sightseeing Transportation, Land

48711	Scenic and Sightseeing Transportation, Land
487110	Scenic and Sightseeing Transportation, Land

4872   Scenic and Sightseeing Transportation, Water

48721	Scenic and Sightseeing Transportation, Water
487210	Scenic and Sightseeing Transportation, Water

4879   Scenic and Sightseeing Transportation, Other

48799	Scenic and Sightseeing Transportation, Other
487990	Scenic and Sightseeing Transportation, Other

488   Support Activities for Transportation

4881   Support Activities for Air Transportation

48811	Airport Operations
488111	Air Traffic Control
488119	Other Airport Operations US
48819	Other Support Activities for Air Transportation
488190	Other Support Activities for Air Transportation

4882   Support Activities for Rail Transportation

48821	Support Activities for Rail Transportation
488210	Support Activities for Rail Transportation

4883   Support Activities for Water Transportation

48831	Port and Harbour Operations
488310	Port and Harbour Operations
48832	Marine Cargo Handling
488320	Marine Cargo Handling
48833	Navigational Services to Shipping
488331	Marine Salvage Services CAN
488332	Ship Piloting Services CAN
488339	Other Navigational Services to Shipping CAN
48839	Other Support Activities for Water Transportation
488390	Other Support Activities for Water Transportation

4884   Support Activities for Road Transportation

48841	Motor Vehicle Towing
488410	Motor Vehicle Towing
48849	Other Support Activities for Road Transportation
488490	Other Support Activities for Road Transportation US

4885   Freight Transportation Arrangement

48851	Freight Transportation Arrangement
488511	Marine Shipping Agencies CAN
488519	Other Freight Transportation Arrangement CAN

4889   Other Support Activities for Transportation

48899	Other Support Activities for Transportation
488990	Other Support Activities for Transportation MEX

491   Postal Service

    4911   Postal Service
       49111   Postal Service
       491110   Postal Service

492   Couriers and Messengers

    4921   Couriers
       49211   Couriers
       492110   Couriers

    4922   Local Messengers and Local Delivery
       49221   Local Messengers and Local Delivery
       492210   Local Messengers and Local Delivery

493   Warehousing and Storage

    4931   Warehousing and Storage
       49311   General Warehousing and Storage
       493110   General Warehousing and Storage [US]
       49312   Refrigerated Warehousing and Storage
       493120   Refrigerated Warehousing and Storage
       49313   Farm Product Warehousing and Storage
       493130   Farm Product Warehousing and Storage
       49319   Other Warehousing and Storage
       493190   Other Warehousing and Storage

51   Information and Cultural Industries

511   Publishing Industries (except Internet)

    5111   Newspaper, Periodical, Book and Directory Publishers
       51111   Newspaper Publishers
       511110   Newspaper Publishers [US]
       51112   Periodical Publishers
       511120   Periodical Publishers [US]
       51113   Book Publishers
       511130   Book Publishers [US]
       51114   Directory and Mailing List Publishers
       511140   Directory and Mailing List Publishers [US]
       51119   Other Publishers
       511190   Other Publishers [CAN]

    5112   Software Publishers
       51121   Software Publishers
       511210   Software Publishers

512   Motion Picture and Sound Recording Industries

    5121   Motion Picture and Video Industries
       51211   Motion Picture and Video Production
       512110   Motion Picture and Video Production [US]
       51212   Motion Picture and Video Distribution
       512120   Motion Picture and Video Distribution
       51213   Motion Picture and Video Exhibition
       512130   Motion Picture and Video Exhibition [MEX]
       51219   Post-Production and Other Motion Picture and Video Industries
       512190   Post-Production and Other Motion Picture and Video Industries [MEX]

5122   Sound Recording Industries

51221	Record Production
512210	Record Production
51222	Integrated Record Production/Distribution
512220	Integrated Record Production/Distribution
51223	Music Publishers
512230	Music Publishers
51224	Sound Recording Studios
512240	Sound Recording Studios
51229	Other Sound Recording Industries
512290	Other Sound Recording Industries

515   Broadcasting (except Internet)

5151   Radio and Television Broadcasting

51511	Radio Broadcasting
515110	Radio Broadcasting [MEX]
51512	Television Broadcasting
515120	Television Broadcasting

5152   Pay and Specialty Television

51521	Pay and Specialty Television
515210	Pay and Specialty Television

517   Telecommunications

5171   Wired Telecommunications Carriers

51711	Wired Telecommunications Carriers
517111	Wired Telecommunications Carriers (except Cable) [CAN]
517112	Cable and Other Program Distribution [CAN]

5172   Wireless Telecommunications Carriers (except Satellite)

51721	Wireless Telecommunications Carriers (except Satellite)
517210	Wireless Telecommunications Carriers (except Satellite) [MEX]

5174   Satellite Telecommunications

51741	Satellite Telecommunications
517410	Satellite Telecommunications

5179   Other Telecommunications

51791	Other Telecommunications
517910	Other Telecommunications

518   Data Processing, Hosting, and Related Services

5182   Data Processing, Hosting, and Related Services

51821	Data Processing, Hosting, and Related Services
518210	Data Processing, Hosting, and Related Services

519   Other Information Services

5191   Other Information Services

51911	News Syndicates
519110	News Syndicates
51912	Libraries and Archives
519121	Libraries [CAN]
519122	Archives [CAN]
51913	Internet Publishing and Broadcasting, and Web Search Portals
519130	Internet Publishing and Broadcasting, and Web Search Portals

51919	All Other Information Services
519190	All Other Information Services

52   Finance and Insurance

521   Monetary Authorities - Central Bank

5211   Monetary Authorities - Central Bank

52111	Monetary Authorities - Central Bank
521110	Monetary Authorities - Central Bank

522   Credit Intermediation and Related Activities

5221   Depository Credit Intermediation ^{US}

52211	Banking ^{CAN}
522111	Personal and Commercial Banking Industry ^{CAN}
522112	Corporate and Institutional Banking Industry ^{CAN}
52213	Local Credit Unions ^{US}
522130	Local Credit Unions ^{US}
52219	Other Depository Credit Intermediation ^{US}
522190	Other Depository Credit Intermediation ^{US}

5222   Non-Depository Credit Intermediation ^{US}

52221	Credit Card Issuing ^{US}
522210	Credit Card Issuing ^{US}
52222	Sales Financing ^{US}
522220	Sales Financing ^{US}
52229	Other Non-Depository Credit Intermediation ^{US}
522291	Consumer Lending ^{US}
522299	All Other Non-Depository Credit Intermediation ^{CAN}

5223   Activities Related to Credit Intermediation ^{US}

52231	Mortgage and Non-mortgage Loan Brokers ^{US}
522310	Mortgage and Non-mortgage Loan Brokers ^{US}
52232	Financial Transactions Processing, Reserve and Clearing House Activities ^{US}
522321	Central Credit Unions ^{CAN}
522329	Other Financial Transactions Processing and Clearing House Activities ^{CAN}
52239	Other Activities Related to Credit Intermediation ^{US}
522390	Other Activities Related to Credit Intermediation ^{US}

523   Securities, Commodity Contracts, and Other Financial Investment and Related Activities

5231   Securities and Commodity Contracts Intermediation and Brokerage

52311	Investment Banking and Securities Dealing ^{US}
523110	Investment Banking and Securities Dealing ^{US}
52312	Securities Brokerage ^{US}
523120	Securities Brokerage ^{US}
52313	Commodity Contracts Dealing ^{US}
523130	Commodity Contracts Dealing ^{US}
52314	Commodity Contracts Brokerage ^{US}
523140	Commodity Contracts Brokerage ^{US}

5232   Securities and Commodity Exchanges

52321	Securities and Commodity Exchanges
523210	Securities and Commodity Exchanges

5239   Other Financial Investment Activities

52391	Miscellaneous Intermediation ^{US}
523910	Miscellaneous Intermediation ^{US}

		52392	Portfolio Management [US]
		523920	Portfolio Management [US]
		52393	Investment Advice [US]
		523930	Investment Advice [US]
		52399	All Other Financial Investment Activities [US]
		523990	All Other Financial Investment Activities [CAN]

524   **Insurance Carriers and Related Activities**

     5241   **Insurance Carriers**

52411	Direct Life, Health and Medical Insurance Carriers [US]
524111	Direct Individual Life, Health and Medical Insurance Carriers [CAN]
524112	Direct Group Life, Health and Medical Insurance Carriers [CAN]
52412	Direct Insurance (except Life, Health and Medical) Carriers [US]
524121	Direct General Property and Casualty Insurance Carriers [CAN]
524122	Direct, Private, Automobile Insurance Carriers [CAN]
524123	Direct, Public, Automobile Insurance Carriers [CAN]
524124	Direct Property Insurance Carriers [CAN]
524125	Direct Liability Insurance Carriers [CAN]
524129	Other Direct Insurance (except Life, Health and Medical) Carriers [CAN]
52413	Reinsurance Carriers [US]
524131	Life Reinsurance Carriers [CAN]
524132	Accident and Sickness Reinsurance Carriers [CAN]
524133	Automobile Reinsurance Carriers [CAN]
524134	Property Reinsurance Carriers [CAN]
524135	Liability Reinsurance Carriers [CAN]
524139	General and Other Reinsurance Carriers [CAN]

     5242   **Agencies, Brokerages and Other Insurance Related Activities**

52421	Insurance Agencies and Brokerages [US]
524210	Insurance Agencies and Brokerages [US]
52429	Other Insurance Related Activities [US]
524291	Claims Adjusters [US]
524299	All Other Insurance Related Activities [CAN]

526   **Funds and Other Financial Vehicles** [CAN]

     5261   **Pension Funds** [CAN]

52611	Pension Funds [CAN]
526111	Trusteed Pension Funds [CAN]
526112	Non-Trusteed Pension Funds [CAN]

     5269   **Other Funds and Financial Vehicles** [CAN]

52691	Open-End Investment Funds [CAN]
526911	Equity Funds - Canadian [CAN]
526912	Equity Funds - Foreign [CAN]
526913	Mortgage Funds [CAN]
526914	Money Market Funds [CAN]
526915	Bond and Income / Dividend Funds - Canadian [CAN]
526916	Bond and Income / Dividend Funds - Foreign [CAN]
526917	Balanced Funds / Asset Allocation Funds [CAN]
526919	Other Open-Ended Funds [CAN]
52693	Segregated (except Pension) Funds [CAN]
526930	Segregated (except Pension) Funds [CAN]
52698	All Other Funds and Financial Vehicles [CAN]
526981	Securitization Vehicles [CAN]
526989	All Other Miscellaneous Funds and Financial Vehicles [CAN]

53   Real Estate and Rental and Leasing

531   Real Estate

5311   Lessors of Real Estate

53111   Lessors of Residential Buildings and Dwellings [US]

531111   Lessors of Residential Buildings and Dwellings (except Social Housing Projects) [CAN]

531112   Lessors of Social Housing Projects [CAN]

53112   Lessors of Non-Residential Buildings (except Mini-Warehouses) [US]

531120   Lessors of Non-Residential Buildings (except Mini-Warehouses) [US]

53113   Self-Storage Mini-Warehouses [US]

531130   Self-Storage Mini-Warehouses [US]

53119   Lessors of Other Real Estate Property [US]

531190   Lessors of Other Real Estate Property [US]

5312   Offices of Real Estate Agents and Brokers

53121   Offices of Real Estate Agents and Brokers

531211   Real Estate Agents [CAN]

531212   Offices of Real Estate Brokers [CAN]

5313   Activities Related to Real Estate

53131   Real Estate Property Managers [US]

531310   Real Estate Property Managers [CAN]

53132   Offices of Real Estate Appraisers [US]

531320   Offices of Real Estate Appraisers [US]

53139   Other Activities Related to Real Estate [US]

531390   Other Activities Related to Real Estate [US]

532   Rental and Leasing Services

5321   Automotive Equipment Rental and Leasing

53211   Passenger Car Rental and Leasing

532111   Passenger Car Rental [US]

532112   Passenger Car Leasing [US]

53212   Truck, Utility Trailer and RV (Recreational Vehicle) Rental and Leasing

532120   Truck, Utility Trailer and RV (Recreational Vehicle) Rental and Leasing [US]

5322   Consumer Goods Rental

53221   Consumer Electronics and Appliance Rental

532210   Consumer Electronics and Appliance Rental

53222   Formal Wear and Costume Rental

532220   Formal Wear and Costume Rental

53223   Video Tape and Disc Rental

532230   Video Tape and Disc Rental

53229   Other Consumer Goods Rental

532290   Other Consumer Goods Rental [CAN]

5323   General Rental Centres

53231   General Rental Centres

532310   General Rental Centres

5324   Commercial and Industrial Machinery and Equipment Rental and Leasing

53241   Construction, Transportation, Mining, and Forestry Machinery and Equipment Rental and Leasing

532410   Construction, Transportation, Mining, and Forestry Machinery and Equipment Rental and Leasing [CAN]

53242   Office Machinery and Equipment Rental and Leasing

532420   Office Machinery and Equipment Rental and Leasing

53249   Other Commercial and Industrial Machinery and Equipment Rental and Leasing

532490   Other Commercial and Industrial Machinery and Equipment Rental and Leasing US

533   Lessors of Non-Financial Intangible Assets (Except Copyrighted Works)

5331   Lessors of Non-Financial Intangible Assets (Except Copyrighted Works)

53311   Lessors of Non-Financial Intangible Assets (Except Copyrighted Works)

533110   Lessors of Non-Financial Intangible Assets (Except Copyrighted Works)

54   Professional, Scientific and Technical Services

541   Professional, Scientific and Technical Services

5411   Legal Services

54111   Offices of Lawyers

541110   Offices of Lawyers

54112   Offices of Notaries

541120   Offices of Notaries

54119   Other Legal Services

541190   Other Legal Services MEX

5412   Accounting, Tax Preparation, Bookkeeping and Payroll Services

54121   Accounting, Tax Preparation, Bookkeeping and Payroll Services

541212   Offices of Accountants CAN

541213   Tax Preparation Services US

541215   Bookkeeping, Payroll and Related Services CAN

5413   Architectural, Engineering and Related Services

54131   Architectural Services

541310   Architectural Services

54132   Landscape Architectural Services

541320   Landscape Architectural Services

54133   Engineering Services

541330   Engineering Services

54134   Drafting Services

541340   Drafting Services

54135   Building Inspection Services

541350   Building Inspection Services

54136   Geophysical Surveying and Mapping Services

541360   Geophysical Surveying and Mapping Services

54137   Surveying and Mapping (except Geophysical) Services

541370   Surveying and Mapping (except Geophysical) Services

54138   Testing Laboratories

541380   Testing Laboratories

5414   Specialized Design Services

54141   Interior Design Services

541410   Interior Design Services

54142   Industrial Design Services

541420   Industrial Design Services

54143   Graphic Design Services

541430   Graphic Design Services

54149   Other Specialized Design Services

541490   Other Specialized Design Services

5415   Computer Systems Design and Related Services

54151   Computer Systems Design and Related Services

	541510	Computer Systems Design and Related Services [MEX]
5416		**Management, Scientific and Technical Consulting Services**
	54161	Management Consulting Services
	541611	Administrative Management and General Management Consulting Services [US]
	541612	Human Resources Consulting Services [US]
	541619	Other Management Consulting Services [CAN]
	54162	Environmental Consulting Services
	541620	Environmental Consulting Services
	54169	Other Scientific and Technical Consulting Services
	541690	Other Scientific and Technical Consulting Services
5417		**Scientific Research and Development Services**
	54171	Research and Development in the Physical, Engineering and Life Sciences
	541710	Research and Development in the Physical, Engineering and Life Sciences [CAN]
	54172	Research and Development in the Social Sciences and Humanities
	541720	Research and Development in the Social Sciences and Humanities [US]
5418		**Advertising, Public Relations, and Related Services**
	54181	Advertising Agencies
	541810	Advertising Agencies
	54182	Public Relations Services
	541820	Public Relations Services
	54183	Media Buying Agencies
	541830	Media Buying Agencies
	54184	Media Representatives
	541840	Media Representatives
	54185	Display Advertising
	541850	Display Advertising
	54186	Direct Mail Advertising
	541860	Direct Mail Advertising
	54187	Advertising Material Distribution Services
	541870	Advertising Material Distribution Services
	54189	Other Services Related to Advertising
	541891	Specialty Advertising Distributors [CAN]
	541899	All Other Services Related to Advertising [CAN]
5419		**Other Professional, Scientific and Technical Services**
	54191	Marketing Research and Public Opinion Polling
	541910	Marketing Research and Public Opinion Polling
	54192	Photographic Services
	541920	Photographic Services [MEX]
	54193	Translation and Interpretation Services
	541930	Translation and Interpretation Services
	54194	Veterinary Services
	541940	Veterinary Services [US]
	54199	All Other Professional, Scientific and Technical Services
	541990	All Other Professional, Scientific and Technical Services

55   Management of Companies and Enterprises

551   **Management of Companies and Enterprises**

5511		**Management of Companies and Enterprises**
	55111	Management of Companies and Enterprises
	551113	Holding Companies [CAN]
	551114	Head Offices [US]

56   Administrative and Support, Waste Management and Remediation Services

561   Administrative and Support Services

5611   Office Administrative Services

56111   Office Administrative Services
561110   Office Administrative Services

5612   Facilities Support Services

56121   Facilities Support Services
561210   Facilities Support Services

5613   Employment Services

56131   Employment Placement Agencies and Executive Search Services
561310   Employment Placement Agencies and Executive Search Services
56132   Temporary Help Services
561320   Temporary Help Services
56133   Professional Employer Organizations
561330   Professional Employer Organizations

5614   Business Support Services

56141   Document Preparation Services
561410   Document Preparation Services
56142   Telephone Call Centres
561420   Telephone Call Centres CAN
56143   Business Service Centres
561430   Business Service Centres CAN
56144   Collection Agencies
561440   Collection Agencies
56145   Credit Bureaus
561450   Credit Bureaus
56149   Other Business Support Services
561490   Other Business Support Services MEX

5615   Travel Arrangement and Reservation Services

56151   Travel Agencies
561510   Travel Agencies
56152   Tour Operators
561520   Tour Operators
56159   Other Travel Arrangement and Reservation Services
561590   Other Travel Arrangement and Reservation Services MEX

5616   Investigation and Security Services

56161   Investigation, Guard and Armoured Car Services
561611   Investigation Services US
561612   Security Guard and Patrol Services US
561613   Armoured Car Services US
56162   Security Systems Services
561621   Security Systems Services (except Locksmiths) US
561622   Locksmiths US

5617   Services to Buildings and Dwellings

56171   Exterminating and Pest Control Services
561710   Exterminating and Pest Control Services
56172   Janitorial Services
561721   Window Cleaning Services CAN
561722   Janitorial Services (except Window Cleaning) CAN
56173   Landscaping Services
561730   Landscaping Services

56174	Carpet and Upholstery Cleaning Services
561740	Carpet and Upholstery Cleaning Services
56179	Other Services to Buildings and Dwellings
561791	Duct and Chimney Cleaning Services ^{CAN}
561799	All Other Services to Buildings and Dwellings ^{CAN}

5619   Other Support Services

56191	Packaging and Labelling Services
561910	Packaging and Labelling Services
56192	Convention and Trade Show Organizers
561920	Convention and Trade Show Organizers
56199	All Other Support Services
561990	All Other Support Services

562   Waste Management and Remediation Services

5621   Waste Collection ^{US}

| 56211 | Waste Collection ^{US} |
| 562110 | Waste Collection ^{CAN} |

5622   Waste Treatment and Disposal ^{US}

| 56221 | Waste Treatment and Disposal ^{US} |
| 562210 | Waste Treatment and Disposal ^{CAN} |

5629   Remediation and Other Waste Management Services ^{US}

56291	Remediation Services ^{US}
562910	Remediation Services ^{US}
56292	Material Recovery Facilities ^{US}
562920	Material Recovery Facilities ^{US}
56299	All Other Waste Management Services ^{US}
562990	All Other Waste Management Services ^{CAN}

61   Educational Services

611   Educational Services

6111   Elementary and Secondary Schools

| 61111 | Elementary and Secondary Schools ^{US} |
| 611110 | Elementary and Secondary Schools ^{US} |

6112   Community Colleges and C.E.G.E.P.s

| 61121 | Community Colleges and C.E.G.E.P.s |
| 611210 | Community Colleges and C.E.G.E.P.s ^{US} |

6113   Universities

| 61131 | Universities |
| 611310 | Universities ^{US} |

6114   Business Schools and Computer and Management Training

61141	Business and Secretarial Schools
611410	Business and Secretarial Schools ^{US}
61142	Computer Training
611420	Computer Training ^{US}
61143	Professional and Management Development Training
611430	Professional and Management Development Training ^{US}

6115   Technical and Trade Schools

| 61151 | Technical and Trade Schools |
| 611510 | Technical and Trade Schools ^{CAN} |

6116   Other Schools and Instruction

61161   Fine Arts Schools
611610   Fine Arts Schools US
61162   Athletic Instruction
611620   Athletic Instruction US
61163   Language Schools
611630   Language Schools US
61169   All Other Schools and Instruction
611690   All Other Schools and Instruction CAN

6117   Educational Support Services

61171   Educational Support Services
611710   Educational Support Services

62   Health Care and Social Assistance

621   Ambulatory Health Care Services

6211   Offices of Physicians

62111   Offices of Physicians
621110   Offices of Physicians CAN

6212   Offices of Dentists

62121   Offices of Dentists
621210   Offices of Dentists US

6213   Offices of Other Health Practitioners

62131   Offices of Chiropractors
621310   Offices of Chiropractors US
62132   Offices of Optometrists
621320   Offices of Optometrists
62133   Offices of Mental Health Practitioners (except Physicians)
621330   Offices of Mental Health Practitioners (except Physicians) US
62134   Offices of Physical, Occupational, and Speech Therapists and Audiologists
621340   Offices of Physical, Occupational, and Speech Therapists and Audiologists US
62139   Offices of All Other Health Practitioners
621390   Offices of All Other Health Practitioners CAN

6214   Out-Patient Care Centres

62141   Family Planning Centres
621410   Family Planning Centres US
62142   Out-Patient Mental Health and Substance Abuse Centres
621420   Out-Patient Mental Health and Substance Abuse Centres US
62149   Other Out-Patient Care Centres
621494   Community Health Centres CAN
621499   All Other Out-Patient Care Centres CAN

6215   Medical and Diagnostic Laboratories

62151   Medical and Diagnostic Laboratories
621510   Medical and Diagnostic Laboratories CAN

6216   Home Health Care Services

62161   Home Health Care Services
621610   Home Health Care Services

6219   Other Ambulatory Health Care Services

62191   Ambulance Services
621911   Ambulance (except Air Ambulance) Services CAN
621912   Air Ambulance Services CAN

| 62199 | All Other Ambulatory Health Care Services |
| 621990 | All Other Ambulatory Health Care Services ^{CAN} |

622   Hospitals

6221   General Medical and Surgical Hospitals

62211	General Medical and Surgical Hospitals
622111	General (except Paediatric) Hospitals ^{CAN}
622112	Paediatric Hospitals ^{CAN}

6222   Psychiatric and Substance Abuse Hospitals

| 62221 | Psychiatric and Substance Abuse Hospitals |
| 622210 | Psychiatric and Substance Abuse Hospitals ^{US} |

6223   Specialty (except Psychiatric and Substance Abuse) Hospitals

| 62231 | Specialty (except Psychiatric and Substance Abuse) Hospitals |
| 622310 | Specialty (except Psychiatric and Substance Abuse) Hospitals ^{US} |

623   Nursing and Residential Care Facilities

6231   Nursing Care Facilities

| 62311 | Nursing Care Facilities |
| 623110 | Nursing Care Facilities ^{US} |

6232   Residential Developmental Handicap, Mental Health and Substance Abuse Facilities

62321	Residential Developmental Handicap Facilities
623210	Residential Developmental Handicap Facilities ^{US}
62322	Residential Mental Health and Substance Abuse Facilities
623221	Residential Substance Abuse Facilities ^{CAN}
623222	Homes for the Psychiatrically Disabled ^{CAN}

6233   Community Care Facilities for the Elderly

| 62331 | Community Care Facilities for the Elderly |
| 623310 | Community Care Facilities for the Elderly ^{CAN} |

6239   Other Residential Care Facilities

62399	Other Residential Care Facilities
623991	Transition Homes for Women ^{CAN}
623992	Homes for Emotionally Disturbed Children ^{CAN}
623993	Homes for the Physically Handicapped or Disabled ^{CAN}
623999	All Other Residential Care Facilities ^{CAN}

624   Social Assistance

6241   Individual and Family Services

62411	Child and Youth Services
624110	Child and Youth Services ^{US}
62412	Services for the Elderly and Persons with Disabilities
624120	Services for the Elderly and Persons with Disabilities ^{US}
62419	Other Individual and Family Services
624190	Other Individual and Family Services ^{US}

6242   Community Food and Housing, and Emergency and Other Relief Services

62421	Community Food Services
624210	Community Food Services ^{US}
62422	Community Housing Services
624220	Community Housing Services ^{CAN}
62423	Emergency and Other Relief Services
624230	Emergency and Other Relief Services ^{US}

6243   Vocational Rehabilitation Services

62431   Vocational Rehabilitation Services
624310   Vocational Rehabilitation Services US

6244   Child Day-Care Services

62441   Child Day-Care Services
624410   Child Day-Care Services US

71   Arts, Entertainment and Recreation

711   Performing Arts, Spectator Sports and Related Industries

7111   Performing Arts Companies

71111   Theatre Companies and Dinner Theatres
711111   Theatre (except Musical) Companies CAN
711112   Musical Theatre and Opera Companies CAN
71112   Dance Companies
711120   Dance Companies US
71113   Musical Groups and Artists
711130   Musical Groups and Artists US
71119   Other Performing Arts Companies
711190   Other Performing Arts Companies US

7112   Spectator Sports

71121   Spectator Sports
711211   Sports Teams and Clubs US
711213   Horse Race Tracks CAN
711218   Other Spectator Sports CAN

7113   Promoters (Presenters) of Performing Arts, Sports and Similar Events

71131   Promoters (Presenters) of Performing Arts, Sports and Similar Events with Facilities
711311   Live Theatres and Other Performing Arts Presenters with Facilities CAN
711319   Sports Stadiums and Other Presenters with Facilities CAN
71132   Promoters (Presenters) of Performing Arts, Sports and Similar Events without Facilities
711321   Performing Arts Promoters (Presenters) without Facilities CAN
711322   Festivals without Facilities CAN
711329   Sports Presenters and Other Presenters without Facilities CAN

7114   Agents and Managers for Artists, Athletes, Entertainers and Other Public Figures

71141   Agents and Managers for Artists, Athletes, Entertainers and Other Public Figures
711410   Agents and Managers for Artists, Athletes, Entertainers and Other Public Figures

7115   Independent Artists, Writers and Performers

71151   Independent Artists, Writers and Performers
711511   Independent Artists, Visual Arts CAN
711512   Independent Actors, Comedians and Performers CAN
711513   Independent Writers and Authors CAN

712   Heritage Institutions

7121   Heritage Institutions

71211   Museums
712111   Non-Commercial Art Museums and Galleries CAN
712115   History and Science Museums CAN
712119   Other Museums CAN

71212	Historic and Heritage Sites
712120	Historic and Heritage Sites
71213	Zoos and Botanical Gardens
712130	Zoos and Botanical Gardens US
71219	Nature Parks and Other Similar Institutions
712190	Nature Parks and Other Similar Institutions

713   Amusement, Gambling and Recreation Industries

7131   Amusement Parks and Arcades

71311	Amusement and Theme Parks
713110	Amusement and Theme Parks US
71312	Amusement Arcades
713120	Amusement Arcades

7132   Gambling Industries

71321	Casinos (except Casino Hotels)
713210	Casinos (except Casino Hotels)
71329	Other Gambling Industries
713291	Lotteries MEX
713299	All Other Gambling Industries MEX

7139   Other Amusement and Recreation Industries

71391	Golf Courses and Country Clubs
713910	Golf Courses and Country Clubs
71392	Skiing Facilities
713920	Skiing Facilities
71393	Marinas
713930	Marinas
71394	Fitness and Recreational Sports Centres
713940	Fitness and Recreational Sports Centres US
71395	Bowling Centres
713950	Bowling Centres
71399	All Other Amusement and Recreation Industries
713990	All Other Amusement and Recreation Industries US

72   Accommodation and Food Services

721   Accommodation Services

7211   Traveller Accommodation

72111	Hotels (except Casino Hotels) and Motels
721111	Hotels CAN
721112	Motor Hotels CAN
721113	Resorts CAN
721114	Motels CAN
72112	Casino Hotels
721120	Casino Hotels
72119	Other Traveller Accommodation
721191	Bed and Breakfast US
721192	Housekeeping Cottages and Cabins CAN
721198	All Other Traveller Accommodation CAN

7212   RV (Recreational Vehicle) Parks and Recreational Camps

72121	RV (Recreational Vehicle) Parks and Recreational Camps
721211	RV (Recreational Vehicle) Parks and Campgrounds US
721212	Hunting and Fishing Camps CAN
721213	Recreational (except Hunting and Fishing) and Vacation Camps CAN

7213   **Rooming and Boarding Houses**

72131   Rooming and Boarding Houses
721310   Rooming and Boarding Houses ^{US}

722   **Food Services and Drinking Places**

7221   **Full-Service Restaurants**

72211   Full-Service Restaurants
722110   Full-Service Restaurants ^{US}

7222   **Limited-Service Eating Places**

72221   Limited-Service Eating Places
722210   Limited-Service Eating Places ^{CAN}

7223   **Special Food Services**

72231   Food Service Contractors
722310   Food Service Contractors
72232   Caterers
722320   Caterers
72233   Mobile Food Services
722330   Mobile Food Services

7224   **Drinking Places (Alcoholic Beverages)**

72241   Drinking Places (Alcoholic Beverages)
722410   Drinking Places (Alcoholic Beverages) ^{US}

81   Other Services (except Public Administration)

811   **Repair and Maintenance**

8111   **Automotive Repair and Maintenance**

81111   Automotive Mechanical and Electrical Repair and Maintenance
811111   General Automotive Repair ^{US}
811112   Automotive Exhaust System Repair ^{US}
811119   Other Automotive Mechanical and Electrical Repair and Maintenance ^{CAN}
81112   Automotive Body, Paint, Interior and Glass Repair
811121   Automotive Body, Paint and Interior Repair and Maintenance ^{US}
811122   Automotive Glass Replacement Shops ^{US}
81119   Other Automotive Repair and Maintenance
811192   Car Washes ^{US}
811199   All Other Automotive Repair and Maintenance ^{CAN}

8112   **Electronic and Precision Equipment Repair and Maintenance**

81121   Electronic and Precision Equipment Repair and Maintenance
811210   Electronic and Precision Equipment Repair and Maintenance ^{CAN}

8113   **Commercial and Industrial Machinery and Equipment (except Automotive and Electronic) Repair and Maintenance**

81131   Commercial and Industrial Machinery and Equipment (except Automotive and Electronic) Repair and Maintenance
811310   Commercial and Industrial Machinery and Equipment (except Automotive and Electronic) Repair and Maintenance ^{US}

8114   **Personal and Household Goods Repair and Maintenance**

81141   Home and Garden Equipment and Appliance Repair and Maintenance
811411   Home and Garden Equipment Repair and Maintenance ^{US}
811412   Appliance Repair and Maintenance ^{US}
81142   Reupholstery and Furniture Repair
811420   Reupholstery and Furniture Repair

81143		Footwear and Leather Goods Repair
	811430	Footwear and Leather Goods Repair
81149		Other Personal and Household Goods Repair and Maintenance
	811490	Other Personal and Household Goods Repair and Maintenance US

812   Personal and Laundry Services

8121   Personal Care Services US

81211   Hair Care and Esthetic Services US
812114   Barber Shops CAN
812115   Beauty Salons CAN
812116   Unisex Hair Salons CAN
81219   Other Personal Care Services US
812190   Other Personal Care Services CAN

8122   Funeral Services US

81221   Funeral Homes US
812210   Funeral Homes US
81222   Cemeteries and Crematoria US
812220   Cemeteries and Crematoria US

8123   Dry Cleaning and Laundry Services US

81231   Coin-Operated Laundries and Dry Cleaners US
812310   Coin-Operated Laundries and Dry Cleaners US
81232   Dry Cleaning and Laundry Services (except Coin-Operated) US
812320   Dry Cleaning and Laundry Services (except Coin-Operated) US
81233   Linen and Uniform Supply US
812330   Linen and Uniform Supply CAN

8129   Other Personal Services US

81291   Pet Care (except Veterinary) Services US
812910   Pet Care (except Veterinary) Services US
81292   Photo Finishing Services US
812921   Photo Finishing Laboratories (except One-Hour) US
812922   One-Hour Photo Finishing US
81293   Parking Lots and Garages US
812930   Parking Lots and Garages US
81299   All Other Personal Services US
812990   All Other Personal Services US

813   Religious, Grant-Making, Civic, and Professional and Similar Organizations

8131   Religious Organizations US

81311   Religious Organizations US
813110   Religious Organizations US

8132   Grant-Making and Giving Services US

81321   Grant-Making and Giving Services US
813210   Grant-Making and Giving Services CAN

8133   Social Advocacy Organizations US

81331   Social Advocacy Organizations US
813310   Social Advocacy Organizations CAN

8134   Civic and Social Organizations US

81341   Civic and Social Organizations US
813410   Civic and Social Organizations US

8139   Business, Professional, Labour and Other Membership Organizations US

81391	Business Associations [US]
813910	Business Associations [US]
81392	Professional Organizations [US]
813920	Professional Organizations [US]
81393	Labour Organizations [US]
813930	Labour Organizations [US]
81394	Political Organizations [US]
813940	Political Organizations [US]
81399	Other Membership Organizations [US]
813990	Other Membership Organizations [US]

814   Private Households

    8141   Private Households

| 81411 | Private Households |
| 814110 | Private Households |

91   Public Administration

911   Federal Government Public Administration [CAN]

    9111   Defence Services [CAN]

| 91111 | Defence Services [CAN] |
| 911110 | Defence Services [CAN] |

    9112   Federal Protective Services [CAN]

91121	Federal Courts of Law [CAN]
911210	Federal Courts of Law [CAN]
91122	Federal Correctional Services [CAN]
911220	Federal Correctional Services [CAN]
91123	Federal Police Services [CAN]
911230	Federal Police Services [CAN]
91124	Federal Regulatory Services [CAN]
911240	Federal Regulatory Services [CAN]
91129	Other Federal Protective Services [CAN]
911290	Other Federal Protective Services [CAN]

    9113   Federal Labour, Employment and Immigration Services [CAN]

91131	Federal Labour and Employment Services [CAN]
911310	Federal Labour and Employment Services [CAN]
91132	Immigration Services [CAN]
911320	Immigration Services [CAN]
91139	Other Federal Labour, Employment and Immigration Services [CAN]
911390	Other Federal Labour, Employment and Immigration Services [CAN]

    9114   Foreign Affairs and International Assistance [CAN]

91141	Foreign Affairs [CAN]
911410	Foreign Affairs [CAN]
91142	International Assistance [CAN]
911420	International Assistance [CAN]

    9119   Other Federal Government Public Administration [CAN]

| 91191 | Other Federal Government Public Administration [CAN] |
| 911910 | Other Federal Government Public Administration [CAN] |

912   Provincial and Territorial Public Administration [CAN]

    9121   Provincial Protective Services [CAN]

| 91211 | Provincial Courts of Law [CAN] |

	912110	Provincial Courts of Law CAN
	91212	Provincial Correctional Services CAN
	912120	Provincial Correctional Services CAN
	91213	Provincial Police Services CAN
	912130	Provincial Police Services CAN
	91214	Provincial Fire-Fighting Services CAN
	912140	Provincial Fire-Fighting Services CAN
	91215	Provincial Regulatory Services CAN
	912150	Provincial Regulatory Services CAN
	91219	Other Provincial Protective Services CAN
	912190	Other Provincial Protective Services CAN

9122   **Provincial Labour and Employment Services** CAN

	91221	Provincial Labour and Employment Services CAN
	912210	Provincial Labour and Employment Services CAN

9129   **Other Provincial and Territorial Public Administration** CAN

	91291	Other Provincial and Territorial Public Administration CAN
	912910	Other Provincial and Territorial Public Administration CAN

913   **Local, Municipal and Regional Public Administration** CAN

9131   **Municipal Protective Services** CAN

	91311	Municipal Courts of Law CAN
	913110	Municipal Courts of Law CAN
	91312	Municipal Correctional Services CAN
	913120	Municipal Correctional Services CAN
	91313	Municipal Police Services CAN
	913130	Municipal Police Services CAN
	91314	Municipal Fire-Fighting Services CAN
	913140	Municipal Fire-Fighting Services CAN
	91315	Municipal Regulatory Services CAN
	913150	Municipal Regulatory Services CAN
	91319	Other Municipal Protective Services CAN
	913190	Other Municipal Protective Services CAN

9139   **Other Local, Municipal and Regional Public Administration** CAN

	91391	Other Local, Municipal and Regional Public Administration CAN
	913910	Other Local, Municipal and Regional Public Administration CAN

914   **Aboriginal Public Administration** CAN

9141   **Aboriginal Public Administration** CAN

	91411	Aboriginal Public Administration CAN
	914110	Aboriginal Public Administration CAN

919   **International and Other Extra-Territorial Public Administration** CAN

9191   **International and Other Extra-Territorial Public Administration** CAN

	91911	International and Other Extra-Territorial Public Administration CAN
	919110	International and Other Extra-Territorial Public Administration CAN

Descriptions

11 Agriculture, Forestry, Fishing and Hunting

This sector comprises establishments primarily engaged in growing crops, raising animals, harvesting timber, harvesting fish and other animals from their natural habitats and providing related support activities.

Establishments primarily engaged in agricultural research or that supply veterinary services are not included in this sector.

111 Crop Production

This subsector comprises establishments, such as farms, orchards, groves, greenhouses and nurseries, primarily engaged in growing crops, plants, vines, trees and their seeds (excluding those engaged in forestry operations). Industries have been created taking into account input factors, such as suitable land, climatic conditions, type of equipment, and the amount and type of labour required. The production process is typically completed when the raw product or commodity grown reaches the "farm gate" for market, that is, at the point of first sale or price determination. Establishments in these industries may use traditional crop production methods, employ modified or improved crop inputs, or engage in organic crop production.

An establishment is classified to a NAICS industry or a national level industry within this subsector provided that fifty percent or more of the establishment's agricultural production consists of the crops of the industry. Establishments with fifty percent or more crop production and with no one product or family of products of an industry accounting for fifty percent of the production are treated as combination crop farms and classified to 11199, All Other Crop Farming, except for establishments with fifty percent or more in the production of oilseeds and grain, which are classified to 11119, Other Grain Farming.

1111 Oilseed and Grain Farming

This industry group comprises establishments primarily engaged in growing oilseeds and grains. Establishments primarily engaged in producing seeds are classified in the appropriate crop industry.

11111 Soybean Farming

This industry comprises establishments primarily engaged in growing soybeans.

Example Activities
- Soya bean (soybean) farming
- Soybeans (soya beans), growing

111110 Soybean Farming

See industry description for 11111, above.

11112 Oilseed (except Soybean) Farming

This industry comprises establishments primarily engaged in growing fibrous plants that produce oilseeds.

Example Activities
- Canola (rapeseed) farming
- Flaxseed farming
- Linseed (flaxseed), growing
- Mixed oilseeds (except Soybean), farming
- Mustard seed farming
- Safflower farming
- Sunflower farming

111120 Oilseed (except Soybean) Farming US

See industry description for 11112, above.

11113 Dry Pea and Bean Farming

This industry comprises establishments primarily engaged in growing dry peas, beans and lentils.

Exclusion(s): Establishments primarily engaged in:
- growing fresh green beans and peas (11121, Vegetable and Melon Farming).

Example Activities
- Bean farming (field crop)
- Cowpea farming, dry
- Dry field beans, growing
- Dry field peas, growing
- Dry peas, beans, and lentils, farming
- Faba beans, growing
- Field pea (dry) growing
- Legume (forage) farming
- Lentils farming, dry
- Pea farming (field crop)
- Pulses, dry, growing

111130 Dry Pea and Bean Farming US

See industry description for 11113, above.

11114 Wheat Farming

This industry comprises establishments primarily engaged in growing wheat.

Example Activities
- Durum wheat, growing
- Grain farming, wheat
- Spring wheat, growing
- Wheat farming
- Wheat, spring, winter and durum, growing
- Winter wheat, growing

111140 Wheat Farming

See industry description for 11114, above.

11115 Corn Farming

This industry comprises establishments primarily engaged in growing corn.

Exclusion(s): Establishments primarily engaged in:
- growing sweet corn (11121, Vegetable and Melon Farming).

Example Activities
- Corn farming (except sweet corn)
- Corn for fodder, growing
- Corn for popping, growing
- Corn for silage, growing
- Grain corn farming

111150 Corn Farming US

See industry description for 11115, above.

11116 Rice Farming

This industry comprises establishments primarily engaged in growing rice, except wild rice.

Exclusion(s): Establishments primarily engaged in:
- growing wild rice (11119, Other Grain Farming).

Example Activity
- Rice (except wild rice) farming

111160 Rice Farming

See industry description for 11116, above.

11119 Other Grain Farming

This industry comprises establishments, not classified to any other industry, primarily engaged in growing grains. Farms primarily engaged in growing a combination of oilseeds and grains are also included.

Exclusion(s): Establishments primarily engaged in:
- growing wheat (11114, Wheat Farming);
- growing corn, except sweet corn (11115, Corn Farming);
- growing rice, except wild rice (11116, Rice Farming); and
- growing sweet corn (11121, Vegetable and Melon Farming).

Example Activities
- Barley farming
- Buckwheat farming
- Canary seed farming
- Feed grain farms
- Grain farms (except wheat, rice, corn and soybeans)
- Millet, growing
- Milo farming
- Oat farming
- Oil seed and grain farming, combination
- Rye, growing
- Small grains (except wheat), growing
- Wild rice, farming

111190 Other Grain Farming CAN

See industry description for 11119, above.

1112 Vegetable and Melon Farming

See industry description for 11121, below.

11121 Vegetable and Melon Farming

This industry comprises establishments primarily engaged in growing vegetables and melons. Establishments primarily engaged in producing vegetable and melon seeds and vegetable and melon bedding plants are also included in this industry.

Exclusion(s): Establishments primarily engaged in:
- growing corn, except sweet corn (11115, Corn Farming); and
- growing vegetables and melons under glass or protective cover (11141, Food Crops Grown Under Cover).

111211 Potato Farming US

This Canadian industry comprises establishments primarily engaged in growing potatoes, yams and seed potatoes.

Example Activities
- Potato farming
- Potato farms, sweet
- Seed potatoes, growing
- Sweet potato farming
- Yam farming

111219 Other Vegetable (except Potato) and Melon Farming US

This Canadian industry comprises establishments, not classified to any other Canadian industry, primarily engaged in growing vegetables and melons. Establishments primarily engaged in producing vegetable and melon seeds, except seed potatoes, and vegetable and melon bedding plants are also included in this industry.

Example Activities

- Asparagus farming
- Bean farms (except dry beans)
- Bean growing, snap (wax and green)
- Cantaloup farms
- Corn, sweet, growing
- Lettuce farming
- Market gardening
- Melon farming
- Mixed vegetables growing
- Pepper farming (e.g., bell, chilli, green, hot, red, sweet)
- Rutabaga farming
- Sweet corn farming
- Truck farming
- Vegetable bedding plants, growing of
- Vegetable crops, growing
- Vegetable farming (except field crops)
- Vegetable seed growing
- Watermelon farming

1113 Fruit and Tree Nut Farming

This industry group comprises establishments primarily engaged in growing fruit and nuts.

11131 Orange Groves

This industry comprises establishments primarily engaged in growing oranges.

Example Activity

- Orange groves and farms

111310 Orange Groves

See industry description for 11131, above.

11132 Citrus (except Orange) Groves

This industry comprises establishments primarily engaged in growing citrus fruit, except oranges.

Example Activities

- Grapefruit groves and farms
- Lemon groves and farms
- Lime groves and farms

111320 Citrus (except Orange) Groves US

See industry description for 11132, above.

11133 Non-Citrus Fruit and Tree Nut Farming

This industry comprises establishments primarily engaged in growing tree nuts and non-citrus fruit.

Exclusion(s): Establishments primarily engaged in:

- harvesting berries and nuts from native and non-cultivated plants (11321, Forest Nurseries and Gathering of Forest Products).

Example Activities
- Apple orchards
- Berry farming
- Cranberry bogs
- Fruit farming
- Fruit orchard operating
- Grapes (vineyards)

- Peach orchards and farms
- Small fruit farming
- Strawberries, growing
- Tree fruit farming
- Tree nut groves and farms
- Vineyards

111330 Non-Citrus Fruit and Tree Nut Farming CAN

See industry description for 11133, above.

1114 Greenhouse, Nursery and Floriculture Production

This industry group comprises establishments primarily engaged in growing crops of any kind under cover, growing nursery crops and growing flowers. "Under cover" includes in greenhouses, cold frames, cloth houses, and lath houses. The crops grown are removed at various stages of maturity.

11141 Food Crops Grown Under Cover

This industry comprises establishments primarily engaged in growing food crops under glass or protective cover.

Exclusion(s): Establishments primarily engaged in:
- growing vegetable and melon bedding plants, not under protective cover (11121, Vegetable and Melon Farming); and
- raising both aquatic animals and plants in integrated growing operations, aquaponics (11251, Aquaculture).

111411 Mushroom Production US

This Canadian industry comprises establishments primarily engaged in growing mushrooms under cover.

Example Activities
- Mushroom cellars
- Mushroom farming

- Mushroom houses
- Mushroom spawn, production of

111419 Other Food Crops Grown Under Cover US

This Canadian industry comprises establishments, not classified to any other Canadian industry, primarily engaged in growing food crops under glass or protective cover.

Example Activities
- Food crops (except mushrooms) grown under cover
- Greenhouse tomatoes, growing
- Greenhouses for growing food crops
- Herb farming, grown under cover

- Hydroponic crops, grown under cover
- Market gardening, greenhouse
- Seaweed, grown under cover
- Truffles farming, grown under cover
- Vegetable farming, grown under cover

11142 Nursery and Floriculture Production

This industry comprises establishments primarily engaged in growing, under cover or in open fields, nursery and floriculture products, such as nursery stock, shrubbery, cut flowers, flower seeds, potted flowering and foliage plants, flower bedding plants, ornamental plants, or some combination of these, and propagating materials, for example, plugs, cuttings, and tissue cultures. The growing of short rotation woody crops, such as cut Christmas trees and cottonwoods for pulpwood, that have a typical growth cycle of ten years or less, are also included in this industry.

> *Exclusion(s): Establishments primarily engaged in:*
> - growing vegetable and melon bedding plants (11121, Vegetable and Melon Farming);
> - the operation of timber tracts that have a growth cycle of greater than ten years (11311, Timber Tract Operations);
> - growing seedling trees for reforestation (11321, Forest Nurseries and Gathering of Forest Products); and
> - retailing nursery, tree stock and floriculture products primarily purchased from others (44422, Nursery Stores and Garden Centres).

111421 Nursery and Tree Production US

This Canadian industry comprises establishments primarily engaged in growing, under cover or in open fields, nursery products and trees, and short rotation woody crops, for pulp and tree stock, that have a typical growth cycle of ten years or less.

> *Exclusion(s): Establishments primarily engaged in:*
> - the operation of timber tracts that have a growth cycle of greater than ten years (113110, Timber Tract Operations); and
> - retailing nursery, tree stock, and floriculture products primarily purchased from others (444220, Nursery Stores and Garden Centres).

Example Activities
- Bedding plants, nursery grown
- Christmas tree farming
- Fruit trees, nursery stock, growing
- Nursery (tree and plant)
- Nursery plant stock, growing
- Nursery stock, growing of
- Ornamental plant growing
- Ornamental shrubs, nursery grown
- Plant nursery
- Rose bushes, growing
- Shrub nursery, ornamental, growing
- Turf (sod) farming

111422 Floriculture Production US

This Canadian industry comprises establishments primarily engaged in growing, under cover or in open fields, floriculture products and propagating materials.

> *Exclusion(s): Establishments primarily engaged in:*
> - retailing floriculture products primarily purchased from others (444220, Nursery Stores and Garden Centres).

Example Activities
- Flower bulb growing, greenhouse
- Flower growing, greenhouse
- Flower nursery
- Flower seed production
- Greenhouses, growing of floral products
- Holly growing
- Tropical foliage and green plants, greenhouse grown

1119 Other Crop Farming

This industry group comprises establishments, not classified to any other industry group, primarily engaged in growing crops, such as tobacco, peanuts, sugarbeets, cotton, sugar-cane, hay, agave, herbs and spices, mint, hops, and hay and grass seeds. Combination crop farming and the gathering of maple sap are included in this industry group.

11191 Tobacco Farming

This industry comprises establishments primarily engaged in growing tobacco.

Example Activity
- Tobacco farming

111910 Tobacco Farming

See industry description for 11191, above.

11192 Cotton Farming

This industry comprises establishments primarily engaged in growing cotton.

Example Activity
- Cotton farming

111920 Cotton Farming

See industry description for 11192, above.

11193 Sugar Cane Farming

This industry comprises establishments primarily engaged in growing sugar-cane.

Example Activity
- Sugar cane farming

111930 Sugar Cane Farming

See industry description for 11193, above.

11194 Hay Farming

This industry comprises establishments primarily engaged in growing hay, grasses and mixed hay.

Exclusion(s): Establishments primarily engaged in:
- growing grain hay or forage/silage production (1111, Oilseed and Grain Farming); and
- growing grass and hay seeds (11199, All Other Crop Farming).

Example Activities
- Alfalfa hay farming
- Clover hay farming
- Forage crops (except corn for grain), farming
- Hay farming

111940 Hay Farming ^{US}

See industry description for 11194, above.

11199 All Other Crop Farming

This industry comprises establishments, not classified to any other industry, primarily engaged in growing crops, such as peanuts, sugarbeets, agave, hay and grass seeds, herbs and spices, mint, hops and algae, and gathering tea and maple sap. Establishments primarily engaged in general crop farming or combination crop farming, such as combination fruit and vegetable farming, are also included in this industry.

Exclusion(s): Establishments primarily engaged in:
- growing wheat, corn, rice, soybeans, and other grains and oilseeds (1111, Oilseed and Grain Farming);
- growing a combination of oilseeds and grains (11119, Other Grain Farming);
- growing vegetables and melons (11121, Vegetable and Melon Farming);
- growing tree nuts and fruit (1113, Fruit and Tree Nut Farming);
- growing greenhouse, nursery and floriculture products (1114, Greenhouse, Nursery and Floriculture Production);
- growing tobacco (11191, Tobacco Farming);
- growing cotton (11192, Cotton Farming);
- growing sugar cane (11193, Sugar Cane Farming);
- growing hay (11194, Hay Farming); and
- manufacturing artificially flavoured maple syrup products (31199, All Other Food Manufacturing).

111993 Fruit and Vegetable Combination Farming ^{CAN}

This Canadian industry comprises establishments primarily engaged in growing a combination of fruit and vegetables.

Exclusion(s): Establishments primarily engaged in:
- growing vegetables and melons (11121, Vegetable and Melon Farming).

Example Activities
- Fruit and vegetable farming, combination
- Small fruit and vegetable farming, combination
- Tree fruit and vegetable farming, combination

111994 Maple Syrup and Products Production ^{CAN}

This Canadian industry comprises establishments primarily engaged in gathering maple sap and producing maple products. Establishments primarily engaged in producing maple products in plants are also included.

Exclusion(s): Establishments primarily engaged in:
- manufacturing artificially flavoured maple syrup products (31199, All Other Food Manufacturing).

Example Activities
- Maple products production, central facility
- Maple sap, gathering of
- Maple sugar bush, operating
- Maple syrup and products production

111999 All Other Miscellaneous Crop Farming ^{CAN}

This Canadian industry comprises establishments, not classified to any other Canadian industry, primarily engaged in growing crops. Establishments primarily engaged in general crop farming or combination crop farming (except combination fruit and vegetable farming), are also included in this Canadian industry.

Exclusion(s): Establishments primarily engaged in:
- growing wheat, corn, rice, soybeans, and other grains and oilseeds (1111, Oilseed and Grain Farming);
- growing a combination of oilseeds and grains (11119, Other Grain Farming);
- growing tree nuts and fruit (1113, Fruit and Tree Nut Farming);
- growing greenhouse, nursery and floriculture products (1114, Greenhouse, Nursery and Floriculture Production);
- growing tobacco (11191, Tobacco Farming);
- growing cotton (11192, Cotton Farming);
- growing sugar cane (11193, Sugar Cane Farming); and
- growing hay (11194, Hay Farming).

Example Activities

- Beet, sugar, farming
- Combination field crop farming
- Crop and animal combination farming (primarily crop)
- Crop and livestock combination farm (primarily crop)
- Crop farms, general
- Field crop combination farm (except grain and oil seeds)
- Ginseng farming, except greenhouse grown
- Grass seed farming
- Hop, growing
- Mint farming, except greenhouse grown
- Peanut farming
- Sugar beet farming
- Tobacco, corn and beans growing, combination

112 Animal Production

This subsector comprises establishments, such as ranches, farms and feedlots, primarily engaged in raising animals, producing animal products and fattening animals. Industries have been created taking into account input factors such as suitable grazing or pasture land, specialized buildings, type of equipment, and the amount and type of labour required. An establishment is classified to a NAICS industry or a national level industry within this subsector provided that fifty percent or more of the establishment's agricultural production consists of the products of that industry. Establishments with fifty percent or more animal production and with no one product or family of products of an industry accounting for fifty percent of the production are treated as combination animal farms and classified to 11299, All Other Animal Production.

1121 Cattle Ranching and Farming

This industry group comprises establishments primarily engaged in raising, milking and fattening cattle.

11211 Beef Cattle Ranching and Farming, including Feedlots

This industry comprises establishments primarily engaged in raising and fattening cattle. The raising of cattle for dairy herd replacements is also included in this industry.

Exclusion(s): Establishments primarily engaged in:
- milking dairy cattle (11212, Dairy Cattle and Milk Production).

Example Activities
- Beef cattle feedlots
- Beef cattle ranching
- Cattle feedlot operations
- Dairy heifer replacement production
- Feedlot, beef cattle

112110 Beef Cattle Ranching and Farming, including Feedlots CAN

See industry description for 11211, above.

11212 Dairy Cattle and Milk Production

This industry comprises establishments primarily engaged in milking dairy cattle.

Exclusion(s): Establishments primarily engaged in:
- raising dairy herd replacements (11211, Beef Cattle Ranching and Farming, including Feedlots);
- raising, feeding or fattening cattle (11211, Beef Cattle Ranching and Farming, including Feedlots); and
- milking goats (11242, Goat Farming).

Example Activities
- Cream, fluid, raw, producing
- Dairy cows and milk, producing
- Dairy farming
- Farm, dairy
- Fluid cream, raw, producing
- Milk, fluid, raw, producing

112120 Dairy Cattle and Milk Production

See industry description for 11212, above.

1122 Hog and Pig Farming

See industry description for 11221, below.

11221 Hog and Pig Farming

This industry comprises establishments primarily engaged in raising hogs and pigs.

Example Activities
- Boar raising, domestic
- Farrow to finish hog farm
- Hog feedlot
- Hog raising
- Pig farming
- Raising hogs
- Swine farm
- Swine farrow to finish (farming)
- Weanling (feeder) pigs, raising

112210 Hog and Pig Farming US

See industry description for 11221, above.

1123 Poultry and Egg Production

This industry group comprises establishments primarily engaged in breeding, hatching and raising poultry for meat or egg production.

11231 Chicken Egg Production

This industry comprises establishments primarily engaged in raising chickens for the production of eggs, including hatching eggs.

Example Activities
- Chicken egg farming
- Egg farms, chicken
- Started pullet farms

112310 Chicken Egg Production US

See industry description for 11231, above.

11232 Broiler and Other Meat-Type Chicken Production

This industry comprises establishments primarily engaged in raising chickens for the production of meat.

Example Activities
- Broiler chicken farming
- Capon farming
- Fryer chickens, raising

112320 Broiler and Other Meat-Type Chicken Production

See industry description for 11232, above.

11233 Turkey Production

This industry comprises establishments primarily engaged in raising turkeys.

Example Activities
- Combination turkey farm, meat and eggs
- Egg farms, turkey
- Farm, turkey
- Turkey egg production
- Turkey farming

112330 Turkey Production

See industry description for 11233, above.

11234 Poultry Hatcheries

This industry comprises establishments primarily engaged in hatching poultry of any kind.

Exclusion(s): Establishments primarily engaged in:
- raising aviary birds, such as parakeets, canaries and love birds (11299, All Other Animal Production).

Example Activities
- Chick hatchery service
- Egg hatcheries, poultry
- Poultry hatchery

112340 Poultry Hatcheries

See industry description for 11234, above.

11239 Other Poultry Production

This industry comprises establishments, not classified to any other industry, primarily engaged in raising poultry such as ducks, geese, pheasant, quail, ostriches and emus. Establishments primarily engaged in raising a combination of poultry for meat or egg production, classified in other industries with no one predominating, are also included in this industry.

Exclusion(s): Establishments primarily engaged in:
- raising chickens for egg production (11231, Chicken Egg Production);
- raising broilers and other meat-type chickens (11232, Broiler and Other Meat-Type Chicken Production);
- raising turkeys (11233, Turkey Production);
- hatching poultry of any kind (11234, Poultry Hatcheries); and
- raising aviary birds, such as parakeets, canaries and love birds (11299, All Other Animal Production).

112391 Combination Poultry and Egg Production CAN

This Canadian industry comprises establishments primarily engaged in raising any combination of poultry for meat or egg production, classified in other industries with no one predominating.

Exclusion(s): Establishments primarily engaged in:
- raising chickens for egg production (112310, Chicken Egg Production);
- raising broilers and other meat-type chickens (112320, Broiler and Other Meat-Type Chicken Production);
- raising turkeys (112330, Turkey Production);
- hatching poultry of any kind (112340, Poultry Hatcheries);
- raising all other poultry (112399, All Other Poultry Production); and
- raising aviary birds, such as parakeets, canaries and love birds (112999, All Other Miscellaneous Animal Production).

Example Activities
- Hatchery service and poultry production
- Poultry and egg farm
- Poultry combination farming
- Poultry production and hatchery service

112399 All Other Poultry Production ^{CAN}

This Canadian industry comprises establishments, not classified to any other industry, primarily engaged in raising poultry such as ducks, geese, pheasant, quail, ostriches and emus.

Exclusion(s): Establishments primarily engaged in:
- raising chickens for egg production (112310, Chicken Egg Production);
- raising broilers and other meat-type chickens (112320, Broiler and Other Meat-Type Chicken Production);
- raising turkeys (112330, Turkey Production);
- hatching poultry of any kind (112340, Poultry Hatcheries);
- combination poultry and egg production (112391, Combination Poultry and Egg Production); and
- raising aviary birds, such as parakeets, canaries and love birds (112999, All Other Miscellaneous Animal Production).

Example Activities
- Duck farming
- Egg farms, poultry (except chicken and turkey)
- Emu farming
- Geese farming
- Guinea fowl, raising
- Ostrich farming
- Pheasant farming
- Quail farming
- Squab farming

1124 Sheep and Goat Farming

This industry group comprises establishments primarily engaged in raising sheep and goats, and feeding or fattening lambs.

11241 Sheep Farming

This industry comprises establishments primarily engaged in raising sheep and lambs, and feeding or fattening lambs.

Example Activities
- Feedlots, lamb
- Lamb raising
- Raising sheep
- Sheep farming
- Wool production, farming

112410 Sheep Farming US

See industry description for 11241, above.

11242 Goat Farming

This industry comprises establishments primarily engaged in raising goats.

Example Activities
- Farm, goat
- Goat farming
- Goat's milk, raw fluid, producing
- Milk production, goat farm
- Mohair farming

112420 Goat Farming

See industry description for 11242, above.

1125 Aquaculture

See industry description for 11251, below.

11251 Aquaculture

This industry comprises establishments primarily engaged in farm-raising aquatic animals and plants. Establishments primarily engaged in raising both aquatic animals and plants in integrated growing operations, aquaponics, are also included. These activities can occur both in natural waters and in artificial aquatic impoundments and include the use of some form of intervention in the rearing or growing process to enhance production.

Exclusion(s): Establishments primarily engaged in:
- hydroponic crops, grown under cover (111419, Other Food Crops Grown Under Cover); and
- catching or taking fish and other aquatic animals from their natural habitats (11411, Fishing).

Example Activities
- Algae and seaweed farming
- Aquaculture, animal, freshwater
- Aquaculture, animal, salt water
- Aquaponics
- Crustacean farming
- Cultured pearl production
- Finfish farming
- Finfish hatcheries
- Fingerlings (hatchery fish), raising, fisheries service
- Fish farming
- Frog production, farm raising
- Mollusk production, farm raising
- Oyster production, farm raising
- Pearls, cultured, production of
- Shellfish, farming
- Turtle and other animal aquaculture

112510 Aquaculture CAN

See industry description for 11251, above.

1129 Other Animal Production

This industry group comprises establishments, not classified to any other industry group, primarily engaged in raising animals, such as bees, horses and other equines, rabbits and other fur-bearing animals, llamas, deer, worms, crickets, laboratory animals and companion animals, for example dogs, cats, pet birds and other pets. The production of animal products, such as honey and other bee products, are also included. Establishments primarily engaged in raising a combination of animals, classified in other industries with no one predominating, are also included in this industry group.

11291 Apiculture

This industry comprises establishments primarily engaged in raising bees, collecting and gathering honey, and performing other apiculture activities.

Example Activities
- Apiaries
- Beekeeping
- Honey and beeswax production
- Honey, natural, unprocessed, producing

112910 Apiculture

See industry description for 11291, above.

11292 Horse and Other Equine Production

This industry comprises establishments primarily engaged in raising horses, mules, donkeys and other equines.

Exclusion(s): Establishments primarily engaged in:
- boarding horses (11521, Support Activities for Animal Production).

Example Activities
- Equines, raising
- Horse ranching
- Mule production
- Pregnant mares' urine (pmu), producing

112920 Horse and Other Equine Production

See industry description for 11292, above.

11293 Fur-Bearing Animal and Rabbit Production

This industry comprises establishments primarily engaged in raising fur-bearing animals, including rabbits.

Exclusion(s): Establishments primarily engaged in:
- trapping or hunting wild fur-bearing animals (11421, Hunting and Trapping).

Example Activities
- Chinchilla production
- Commercial mink ranch
- Fox production
- Fur farming
- Fur-bearing animal production
- Fur-bearing animal skins (ranch raised), undressed, producing
- Game farm (fur-bearing animals)
- Mink production
- Muskrat farm
- Rabbit raising

112930 Fur-Bearing Animal and Rabbit Production

See industry description for 11293, above.

11299 All Other Animal Production

This industry comprises establishments, not classified to any other industry, primarily engaged in raising animals, such as llamas, bison, wild boar, deer, elk, worms, crickets, laboratory animals and companion animals, for example dogs, cats, pet birds and other pets. Establishments primarily engaged in raising a combination of animals, classified in other industries with no one predominating, are also included in this industry.

Exclusion(s): Establishments primarily engaged in:
- raising cattle (1121, Cattle Ranching and Farming);
- raising hogs and pigs (11221, Hog and Pig Farming);
- raising poultry (1123, Poultry and Egg Production);
- raising sheep and goats (1124, Sheep and Goat Farming);
- raising aquatic animals (11251, Aquaculture);
- raising bees (11291, Apiculture);
- raising horses and other equines (11292, Horse and Other Equine Production); and
- raising fur-bearing animals, including rabbits (11293, Fur-Bearing Animal and Rabbit Production).

112991 Animal Combination Farming CAN

This Canadian industry comprises establishments primarily engaged in raising a combination of animals, classified in other industries with no one predominating.

Example Activities
- Animal specialty combination farm
- Combination livestock farming
- Crop and animal farming, combination (primarily animal)
- Crop and livestock farming, combination (primarily livestock)
- Livestock and animal specialty farms, general
- Livestock and poultry combination farm
- Livestock combination farm
- Livestock combination feedlots
- Swine and poultry combination farms

112999 All Other Miscellaneous Animal Production CAN

This Canadian industry comprises establishments, not classified to any other Canadian industry, primarily engaged in raising animals.

Example Activities
- Aviaries (e.g., raising parakeet, canary, and love birds)
- Bird (song and pet) raising
- Bison production
- Cats, domestic, raising
- Deer farming
- Earthworm hatcheries
- Elk production
- Laboratory animal production (e.g., rats, mice, and guinea pigs)
- Llama production
- Pet animal, raising
- Wild boar, raising
- Worm production

113 Forestry and Logging

This subsector comprises establishments primarily engaged in growing and harvesting timber on a long production cycle (of ten years or more). Long production cycles use different production processes than short production cycles, which require more horticultural interventions prior to harvest, resulting in processes more similar to those found in the Crop Production subsector. Consequently, Christmas tree production and other production involving production cycles of less than ten years, are classified to the Crop Production subsector.

Industries in this subsector specialize in different stages of the production cycle. Reforestation requires production of seedlings in specialized nurseries. Timber production requires natural forests or suitable areas of land that are available for a long duration. The maturation time for timber depends upon the species of tree, the climatic conditions of the region, and the intended purpose of the timber. The harvesting of timber, except when done on an extremely small scale, requires specialized machinery unique to the industry. The gathering of forest products, such as gums, barks, balsam needles and Spanish moss, are also included in this subsector.

1131 Timber Tract Operations

See industry description for 11311, below.

11311 Timber Tract Operations

This industry comprises establishments primarily engaged in the operation of timber tracts, for the purpose of selling standing timber.

Exclusion(s): Establishments primarily engaged in:
- growing short rotation woody crops, such as Christmas trees and cottonwood for pulpwood, where the typical life cycle for growing and harvesting is ten years or less (11142, Nursery and Floriculture Production);
- cutting timber (11331, Logging); and
- holding timbered property as real property and not for the sale of timber (53119, Lessors of Other Real Estate Property).

Example Activities
- Forestry farms
- Timber crop operations
- Timber tracts operations

113110 Timber Tract Operations

See industry description for 11311, above.

1132 Forest Nurseries and Gathering of Forest Products

See industry description for 11321, below.

11321 Forest Nurseries and Gathering of Forest Products

This industry comprises establishments with two different production processes, those primarily engaged in growing trees for the purpose of reforestation, and those primarily engaged in gathering forest products.

Exclusion(s): Establishments primarily engaged in:
- gathering maple sap (11199, All Other Crop Farming).

Example Activities
- Balsam needles, gathering of
- Barks, gathering of
- Cone gathering service
- Forest nurseries
- Gathering of forest products (e.g., gums, barks, seeds)
- Gathering of wild mushrooms and truffles
- Ginseng, gathering of
- Gum (i.e., forest product) gathering
- Moss, gathering of
- Nurseries for reforestation
- Tree seeds gathering
- Wild berry picking
- Wild rice gathering

113210 Forest Nurseries and Gathering of Forest Products US

See industry description for 11321, above.

1133 Logging

See industry description for 11331, below.

11331 Logging

This industry comprises establishments primarily engaged in cutting timber, producing rough, round, hewn, or riven primary wood, and producing wood chips in the forest. Establishments primarily engaged in cutting and transporting timber are also included in this industry.

Exclusion(s): Establishments primarily engaged in:
- trucking timber (48422, Specialized Freight (except Used Goods) Trucking, Local, or 484233, Forest Products Trucking, Long Distance).

113311 Logging (except Contract) CAN

This Canadian industry comprises establishments primarily engaged in cutting timber, producing rough, round, hewn, or riven primary wood, and producing wood chips in the forest, on an own-account basis. Establishments primarily engaged in cutting and transporting timber are also included.

Exclusion(s): Establishments primarily engaged in:
- trucking timber (484223, Forest Products Trucking, Local, or 484233, Forest Products Trucking, Long Distance).

Example Activities
- Barking mill
- Bolts, wooden, cutting
- Booming, bunching, rafting, driving logs
- Chipping logs (in the forest)
- Christmas tree cutting
- Cutting cordwood, in the forest
- Felling trees (logging)
- Fuelwood cutting
- Log cutting (forest trees)
- Log grading, scaling, sorting
- Mine timbers, cutting
- Peeler logs, cutting
- Pickets and paling, round or split, cutting
- Piling, wood, untreated, cutting
- Pitprops, wooden, untreated, cutting
- Poles and pilings, wooden, untreated, cutting
- Poles, wood, untreated, cutting
- Posts, wood, hewn, round or split, producing
- Pulpwood logs, cutting
- Railroad ties, hewn, cutting
- Rossing mill
- Sawlogs, cutting
- Telephone and telegraph poles, logging
- Tie bolts, cutting
- Ties, railroad, hewn, producing
- Timbers, mine, hewn, producing
- Timbers, round mine, cutting
- Tree felling, bucking, cutting
- Veneer logs, logging
- Wood chips produced in the forest

113312 Contract Logging CAN

This Canadian industry comprises establishments primarily engaged in cutting timber, producing rough, round, hewn, or riven primary wood, and producing wood chips in the forest, on a fee or contract basis. Establishments primarily engaged in cutting and transporting timber are also included.

Exclusion(s): Establishments primarily engaged in:
- trucking timber (484223, Forest Products Trucking, Local, or 484233, Forest Products Trucking, Long Distance).

Example Activities
- Contract logging
- Logging contractor (felling, cutting, bucking)
- Pulpwood cutting, on contract
- Timber cutting, on contract
- Yarding, timber, on contract

114 Fishing, Hunting and Trapping

This subsector comprises establishments primarily engaged in harvesting fish and other wild animals from their natural habitats. These establishments are dependent upon a continued supply of the natural resource. The harvesting of fish is the predominant economic activity of this subsector and it usually requires specialized vessels that, by the nature of their size, configuration and equipment, are not suitable for any other type of production, such as transportation. Hunting and trapping utilize a wide variety of production processes and are classified in the same subsector as fishing because the availability of resources and the constraints imposed, such as conservation requirements and proper habitat maintenance, are similar.

> *Exclusion(s): Establishments primarily engaged in:*
> - raising animals in captivity or producing animal products, for eventual sale or gain in product value (112, Animal Production).

1141 Fishing

See industry description for 11411, below.

11411 Fishing

This industry comprises establishments primarily engaged in the commercial catching or taking of finfish, shellfish, and other marine animals from their natural habitats.

> *Exclusion(s): Establishments primarily engaged in:*
> - farm-raising finfish, shellfish or other marine animals within a confined space and under controlled feeding and harvesting conditions (11251, Aquaculture); and
> - the commercial catching or taking and processing of fresh fish, such as canning, freezing, etc., on the fishing vessel (31171, Seafood Product Preparation and Packaging).

114113 Salt Water Fishing ^{CAN}

This Canadian industry comprises establishments primarily engaged in catching all types of finfish, trapping or otherwise catching shellfish, and harvesting other sea products.

Example Activities
- Clams, digging of
- Commercial fishing, salt water
- Crabs, catching of
- Dulsing (gathering Irish moss)
- Fishing, salt water
- Inshore fishing, salt water
- Jigging (fishing), salt water
- Laver gathering
- Lobster catching
- Marine products harvesting, salt water
- Mussel fishing
- Otter trawling
- Oyster fishing
- Sea worm gathering
- Seal hunting
- Seaweed gathering (uncultivated)
- Shellfish, fishing, salt water
- Shrimp fishing
- Turtle fishing

114114 Inland Fishing ^{CAN}

This Canadian industry comprises establishments primarily engaged in catching or gathering freshwater species of finfish and shellfish, and harvesting other freshwater products.

Example Activities
- Bait catching, inland
- Commercial fishing, inland
- Frogs, catching of (not raised on farms)
- Inland fishing, freshwater
- Marine products harvesting, freshwater
- Prairie jigging, fishing
- Shellfish digging, freshwater

1142 Hunting and Trapping

See industry description for 11421, below.

11421 Hunting and Trapping

This industry comprises establishments primarily engaged in commercial hunting and trapping, and operating and managing commercial game preserves.

Exclusion(s): Establishments primarily engaged in:
- farm-raising rabbits and other fur-bearing animals (11293, Fur-Bearing Animal and Rabbit Production); and
- operating nature preserves (71219, Nature Parks and Other Similar Institutions).

Example Activities
- Animal trapping, wild, for zoo or game farm
- Hunting and trapping, wild animals for furs (except seals)
- Hunting carried on as a business enterprise
- Hunting preserves, operation of
- Trapping
- Trapping fur-bearing animals for furs
- Worm gathering

114210 Hunting and Trapping

See industry description for 11421, above.

115 Support Activities for Agriculture and Forestry

This subsector comprises establishments primarily engaged in providing support services that are essential to agricultural and forestry production.

1151 Support Activities for Crop Production

See industry description for 11511, below.

11511 Support Activities for Crop Production

This industry comprises establishments primarily engaged in providing support activities for growing crops.

Exclusion(s): Establishments primarily engaged in:
- providing support activities for forestry (11531, Support Activities for Forestry);
- providing water for irrigation (22131, Water Supply and Irrigation Systems);
- artificially drying and dehydrating fruits and vegetables (31142, Fruit and Vegetable Canning, Pickling and Drying);
- stemming and redrying tobacco (31221, Tobacco Stemming and Redrying);
- buying farm products, such as fruits or vegetables, for resale, other than to the general public for household consumption, and incidentally preparing them for market or further processing (41315, Fresh Fruit and Vegetable Wholesaler-Distributors); and
- providing landscaping and horticultural services, such as lawn care services and ornamental shrub and tree services (56173, Landscaping Services).

Example Activities
- Agricultural product sterilization service
- Cleaning service, grain
- Combining service, agricultural crop
- Crop harvesting service
- Crop spraying service, with or without fertilizing
- Farm labour contractors
- Farm management service (crop production)
- Farm produce packing service

- Farm product sorting, grading or packing service (for the grower)
- Fertilizer application service
- Fruit sorting, grading and packing service
- Harvesting service, agricultural crop and plant
- Hulling and shelling of nuts
- Irradiation of fruits and vegetables
- Lime spreading service, agricultural
- Orchard fruit picking, hand
- Planting crops
- Ploughing service, agricultural
- Seeding crops
- Soil preparation service
- Surgery on orchard trees and vines
- Thinning of crops, mechanical and chemical
- Threshing service, agricultural crop and plant
- Vineyard cultivation services

115110 Support Activities for Crop Production CAN

See industry description for 11511, above.

1152 Support Activities for Animal Production

See industry description for 11521, below.

11521 Support Activities for Animal Production

This industry comprises establishments primarily engaged in providing support activities related to raising livestock, including companion animals.

Example Activities
- Animal pedigree service
- Animal semen collection, production and storage services
- Breeding services, livestock
- Breeding services, pet and small animal
- Breeding services, poultry
- Cattle dehorning service
- Cattle registration service
- Cleaning poultry houses
- Farriers
- Horses, boarding (except racehorses)
- Horseshoeing
- Livestock breeding services
- Pet breeding services
- Poultry breeding services
- Sheep dipping and shearing
- Small animal breeding services
- Stud services, farm animal
- Training horses (except racehorses)

115210 Support Activities for Animal Production

See industry description for 11521, above.

1153 Support Activities for Forestry

See industry description for 11531, below.

11531 Support Activities for Forestry

This industry comprises establishments primarily engaged in performing particular support activities, related to harvesting timber.

Example Activities
- Cruising timber
- Forest fire fighting services
- Log hauling in the bush (i.e., within the logging limits)
- Pest control services, forestry
- Reforestation services
- Timber cruising
- Timber valuation

115310 Support Activities for Forestry

See industry description for 11531, above.

21 Mining, Quarrying, and Oil and Gas Extraction

This sector comprises establishments primarily engaged in extracting naturally occurring minerals. These can be solids, such as coal and ores; liquids, such as crude petroleum; and gases, such as natural gas. The term "mining" is used in the broad sense to include quarrying, well operations, milling (for example, crushing, screening, washing, or flotation) and other preparation customarily done at the mine site, or as a part of mining activity. Establishments engaged in exploration for minerals, development of mineral properties and mining operations are included in this sector. Establishments performing similar activities, on a contract or fee basis, are also included.

211 Oil and Gas Extraction

This subsector comprises establishments primarily engaged in operating oil and gas field properties. Such activities may include exploration for crude petroleum and natural gas; drilling, completing and equipping wells; operating separators, emulsion breakers, desilting equipment and field gathering lines for crude petroleum; and all other activities in the preparation of oil and gas up to the point of shipment from the producing property. This subsector includes the production of oil, the mining and extraction of oil from oil shale and oil sands, and the production of gas and hydrocarbon liquids, through gasification, liquefaction and pyrolysis of coal at the mine site.

2111 Oil and Gas Extraction

See industry description for 21111, below.

21111 Oil and Gas Extraction

This industry comprises establishments primarily engaged in operating oil and gas field properties. Such activities may include exploration for crude petroleum and natural gas; drilling, completing and equipping wells; operating separators, emulsion breakers, desilting equipment and field gathering lines for crude petroleum; and all other activities in the preparation of oil and gas up to the point of shipment from the producing property. This industry includes the production of oil, the mining and extraction of oil from oil shale and oil sands, and the production of gas and hydrocarbon liquids, through gasification, liquefaction and pyrolysis of coal at the mine site.

Exclusion(s): Establishments primarily engaged in:
- performing oil field services for operators, on a contract or fee basis (21311, Support Activities for Mining and Oil and Gas Extraction);
- recovering liquefied petroleum gases incidental to petroleum refining (32411, Petroleum Refineries); and
- recovering helium from natural gas (32512, Industrial Gas Manufacturing).

211113 Conventional Oil and Gas Extraction CAN

This Canadian industry comprises establishments primarily engaged in the exploration for, and/or production of, petroleum or natural gas from wells in which the hydrocarbons will initially flow or can be produced using normal pumping techniques.

Exclusion(s): Establishments primarily engaged in:
- producing crude oil from surface shales or tar sands or from reservoirs in which the hydrocarbons are semisolids and conventional production methods are not possible (211114, Non-Conventional Oil Extraction);
- performing oil field services for operators, on a contract or fee basis (213118, Services to Oil and Gas Extraction); and
- recovering liquefied petroleum gases incidental to petroleum refining (324110, Petroleum Refineries).

Example Activities
- Coal gasification at the mine site
- Coal pyrolysis at the mine site
- Condensate, cycle, natural gas production
- Crude oil, conventional production, mining
- Crude oil, conventional, secondary recovering
- Crude oil, conventional, waterflood recovering
- Fractionating natural gas liquids
- Gas well, natural
- Liquefied petroleum gases (LPG) natural
- Natural gas cleaning plant
- Natural gas from oil shale or sand
- Natural gas liquids production
- Natural gas liquids recovering, mining
- Natural gas pumping, mining
- Natural gas washing and scrubbing, mining
- Natural sour gas processing, mining
- Petroleum (oil) well, crude, conventional
- Petroleum production, crude, conventional
- Propane (natural) production
- Well, natural gas

211114 Non-Conventional Oil Extraction ^{CAN}

This Canadian industry comprises establishments primarily engaged in producing crude oil from surface shales or tar sands or from reservoirs in which the hydrocarbons are semisolids and conventional production methods are not possible.

Exclusion(s): Establishments primarily engaged in:
- the exploration for, and/or production of, petroleum or natural gas from wells in which the hydrocarbons will initially flow or can be produced using normal pumping techniques (211113, Conventional Oil and Gas Extraction);
- performing oil field services for operators, on a contract or fee basis (213118, Services to Oil and Gas Extraction); and
- recovering liquefied petroleum gases incidental to petroleum refining (324110, Petroleum Refineries).

Example Activities
- Bitumen production, extraction by mining
- Bitumen production, in-situ extraction
- Bituminous sand and oil shale digging
- Heavy crude oil extracting
- Heavy oil in place, solution gas drive recovering
- Heavy oil, thermal in situ recovering
- Oil sand mining
- Petroleum, from shale or sand, production
- Sand, oil, mining
- Shale, oil, mining
- Tar sand mining for oil extraction

212 Mining and Quarrying (except Oil and Gas)

This subsector comprises establishments primarily engaged in mining, beneficiating or otherwise preparing metallic and non-metallic minerals, including coal.

Exclusion(s): Establishments primarily engaged in:
- providing support services, on a contract or fee basis, required for the mining and quarrying of minerals (21311, Support Activities for Mining and Oil and Gas Extraction).

2121 Coal Mining

See industry description for 21211, below.

21211 Coal Mining

This industry comprises establishments primarily engaged in mining bituminous coal, anthracite and lignite by underground mining, and auger mining, strip mining, culm bank mining and other surface mining. Mining operations and preparation plants (also known as cleaning plants and washeries), whether or not such plants are operated in conjunction with mine sites, are included.

Exclusion(s): Establishments primarily engaged in:
- producing coal fuel briquettes and packaged fuel (32419, Other Petroleum and Coal Product Manufacturing).

212114 Bituminous Coal Mining CAN

This Canadian industry comprises establishments primarily engaged in mining bituminous coal. Mining operations and preparation plants (also known as cleaning plants and washeries), whether or not such plants are operated in conjunction with mine sites, are included.

Exclusion(s): Establishments primarily engaged in:
- producing coal fuel briquettes and packaged fuel (324190, Other Petroleum and Coal Product Manufacturing).

Example Activities
- Anthracite mining
- Bituminous coal washeries
- Bituminous coal, mining
- Breaking, washing, grading, bituminous coal (contract)
- Coal mining, bituminous
- Colliery, bituminous coal
- Culm bank recovery, anthracite (except on a contract basis)
- Preparation plants, bituminous coal
- Strip mining, bituminous coal (except on a contract basis)
- Thermal coal, bituminous, mining
- Washeries, anthracite

212115 Subbituminous Coal Mining CAN

This Canadian industry comprises establishments primarily engaged in mining subbituminous coal. Mining operations and preparation plants (also known as cleaning plants and washeries), whether or not such plants are operated in conjunction with mine sites, are included.

Exclusion(s): Establishments primarily engaged in:
- producing coal fuel briquettes and packaged fuel (324190, Other Petroleum and Coal Product Manufacturing).

Example Activities
- Breaking, washing, grading, subbituminous coal
- Colliery, subbituminous coal
- Semibituminous coal mining
- Subbituminous coal mining

212116 Lignite Coal Mining CAN

This Canadian industry comprises establishments primarily engaged in mining lignite coal. Mining operations and preparation plants (also known as cleaning plants and washeries), whether or not such plants are operated in conjunction with mine sites, are included.

Exclusion(s): Establishments primarily engaged in:
- producing coal fuel briquettes and packaged fuel (324190, Other Petroleum and Coal Product Manufacturing).

Example Activities
- Brown coal mining
- Colliery, lignite coal
- Lignite mining

2122 Metal Ore Mining

This industry group comprises establishments primarily engaged in mining metallic minerals (ores). Also included are establishments engaged in ore dressing and beneficiating operations, whether performed at mills operated in conjunction with the mines served or at mills, such as custom mills, operated separately. These include mills that crush, grind, wash, dry, sinter, calcine or leach ore, or perform gravity separation or flotation operations.

21221 Iron Ore Mining

This industry comprises establishments primarily engaged in mining, beneficiating or otherwise preparing iron ores, and manganiferous ores valued chiefly for their iron content. Establishments engaged in the production of sinter and other agglomerates, except those associated with blast furnace operations, are included.

Exclusion(s): Establishments primarily engaged in:
- operating blast furnaces to produce pig iron from iron ore (33111, Iron and Steel Mills and Ferro-Alloy Manufacturing).

Example Activities
- Ilmenite, hematite, ore, mining
- Iron agglomerate and pellet production
- Iron ore dressing (beneficiation) plants
- Iron ore milling
- Iron ore mining
- Limonite mining
- Magnetite ore mining
- Manganiferous ore valued for iron content, mining
- Sintering iron ore produced at the mine
- Taconite mining

212210 Iron Ore Mining

See industry description for 21221, above.

21222 Gold and Silver Ore Mining

This industry comprises establishments primarily engaged in mining, beneficiating or otherwise preparing ores valued chiefly for their gold and/or silver content.

Example Activities
- Gold bullion production at mine site
- Gold mine, hydraulic
- Gold ore mining
- Gold quartz ore mining
- Gold, gravity concentrating
- Silver bullion, produced at mine site
- Silver ore milling
- Silver ores mining

212220 Gold and Silver Ore Mining CAN

See industry description for 21222, above.

21223 Copper, Nickel, Lead and Zinc Ore Mining

This industry comprises establishments primarily engaged in mining, beneficiating or otherwise preparing ores valued chiefly for their copper, nickel, lead or zinc content.

212231 Lead-Zinc Ore Mining US

This Canadian industry comprises establishments primarily engaged in mining, beneficiating or otherwise preparing lead ores, zinc ores or lead-zinc ores.

Example Activities
- Blende (zinc) mining
- Calamine mining
- Cerusite mining
- Galena mining
- Lead ore milling
- Lead ore mining
- Lead, zinc, ore, beneficiating
- Lead-zinc ore milling
- Lead-zinc ore mining
- Mining lead-zinc bearing ores
- Smithsonite mining
- Sphalerite ore mining
- Willemite mining
- Zinc ore, mining

212232 Nickel-Copper Ore Mining CAN

This Canadian industry comprises establishments primarily engaged in mining, beneficiating or otherwise preparing nickel and/or nickel-copper ores.

Exclusion(s): Establishments primarily engaged in:
- mining copper ores combined with zinc or any mineral other than nickel (212233, Copper-Zinc Ore Mining).

Example Activities
- Nickel ore dressing and beneficiating
- Nickel ore milling
- Nickel ore mining
- Nickel-copper ore mining

212233 Copper-Zinc Ore Mining CAN

This Canadian industry comprises establishments primarily engaged in mining, beneficiating or otherwise preparing copper and/or copper-zinc ores. Establishments engaged in the recovery of copper concentrates by the precipitation and leaching of copper ore are also included.

Exclusion(s): Establishments primarily engaged in:
- mining nickel-copper ores (212232, Nickel-Copper Ore Mining); and
- the recovery of refined copper by leaching copper concentrates (331410, Non-Ferrous Metal (except Aluminum) Smelting and Refining).

Example Activities
- Chalcocite mining
- Chalcopyrite mining
- Copper ore dressing and beneficiating
- Copper ore grinding
- Copper ore milling
- Copper ore, mining
- Copper-zinc ore mining
- Cuprite ore mining
- Mining copper bearing ores

21229 Other Metal Ore Mining

This industry comprises establishments, not classified to any other industry, primarily engaged in mining, beneficiating or otherwise preparing metallic ores, such as uranium-radium-vanadium ores, molybdenum ores, antimony ores, columbium ores, illmenite ores, magnesium ores, tantalum ores and tungsten ores.

Exclusion(s): Establishments primarily engaged in:
- mining, beneficiating or otherwise preparing iron ores (21221, Iron Ore Mining);
- mining, beneficiating or otherwise preparing ores valued chiefly for their gold and/or silver content (21222, Gold and Silver Ore Mining); and
- mining, beneficiating or otherwise preparing ores valued chiefly for their copper, nickel, lead or zinc content (21223, Copper, Nickel, Lead and Zinc Ore Mining).

212291 Uranium Ore Mining US

This Canadian industry comprises establishments primarily engaged in mining, beneficiating or otherwise preparing uranium-radium-vanadium ores.

Exclusion(s): Establishments primarily engaged in:
- mining, beneficiating or otherwise preparing molybdenum ores, antimony ores, columbium ores, ilmenite ores, magnesium ores, tantalum ores and tungsten ores (212299, All Other Metal Ore Mining).

Example Activities
- Carnotite mining
- Leaching of uranium or radium ore at mine site
- Pitchblende mining
- Radioactive ore mining
- Radium bearing ore milling
- Radium ore mining
- Tyuyamunite mining
- Uraninite (pitchblende) mining
- Uranium ore milling
- Vanadium ore mining
- Yttrium ore mining

212299 All Other Metal Ore Mining US

This Canadian industry comprises establishments, not classified to any other Canadian industry, primarily engaged in mining, beneficiating or otherwise preparing metallic ores.

Exclusion(s): Establishments primarily engaged in:
- mining, beneficiating or otherwise preparing uranium-radium-vanadium ores (212291, Uranium Ore Mining).

Example Activities
- Aluminum ore mining
- Antimony ore mining
- Chromite mining
- Chromite ore milling
- Chromium ore mining
- Cobalt ore dressing and beneficiating
- Cobalt ore milling
- Cobalt ore mining
- Columbite mining
- Columbium ores mining
- Ferberite mining
- Huebnerite mining
- Ilmenite ore mining
- Magnesium ore mining
- Manganese ore dressing and beneficiating
- Manganese ore mining
- Manganite mining
- Mercury ore mining
- Mining molybdenum bearing ores
- Molybdenum ore mining
- Monazite mining
- Palladium ore mining
- Psilomelane mining
- Pyrolusite mining
- Quicksilver (mercury) ore mining
- Rare-earths ore mining
- Rhodium mining
- Rhodochrosite mining

- Ruthenium ore mining
- Scheelite ore mining
- Tantalum ore dressing and beneficiating
- Tantalum ore mining
- Thorium ore mining
- Tin ore mining

- Titanium ore mining
- Tungsten ore dressing and beneficiating
- Tungsten ore mining
- Wolframite mining
- Wulfenite mining
- Zirconium ore mining

2123 Non-Metallic Mineral Mining and Quarrying

This industry group comprises establishments primarily engaged in mining or quarrying non-metallic minerals, except coal. Primary preparation plants, such as those engaged in crushing, grinding and washing, are included.

Exclusion(s): Establishments primarily engaged in:
- manufacturing brick and other structural clay products (32712, Clay Building Material and Refractory Manufacturing);
- manufacturing cement (32731, Cement Manufacturing);
- manufacturing lime (32741, Lime Manufacturing); and
- cutting and finishing stone and stone products (32799, All Other Non-Metallic Mineral Product Manufacturing).

21231 Stone Mining and Quarrying

This industry comprises establishments primarily engaged in mining or quarrying dimension stone, rough blocks or slabs of stone, and crushed and broken stone.

212314 Granite Mining and Quarrying CAN

This Canadian industry comprises establishments primarily engaged in mining or quarrying dimension granite, rough blocks or slabs of granite, and crushed and broken granite, including related rocks.

Example Activities
- Building stone, granite, rough, mining
- Dimensional stone, granite, rough, mining
- Diorite, quarrying
- Gneiss, quarrying
- Granite quarry

- Granite, crushed and broken stone, quarrying
- Greenstone, dimension, quarrying
- Syenite (except nepheline), quarrying

212315 Limestone Mining and Quarrying CAN

This Canadian industry comprises establishments primarily engaged in mining or quarrying dimension limestone, rough blocks or slabs of limestone, and crushed and broken limestone, including related rocks. Establishments engaged in the grinding or pulverizing of limestone are also included.

Exclusion(s): Establishments primarily engaged in:
- producing lime (327410, Lime Manufacturing).

Example Activities
- Agricultural limestone, ground
- Building stone, limestone, rough, mining
- Calcareous tufa, dimension, quarrying
- Calcium limestone, crude, mining
- Cement rock, quarrying
- Chalk mine or quarry
- Chalk, ground or otherwise treated, mining

- Chemical and metallurgical stone, limestone, crude, mining
- Dolomite (limestone), crude, quarrying
- Flux stone, limestone, crude, mining
- Limestone quarry
- Sedimentary rock quarry
- Stone quarrying, limestone
- Travertine, quarrying

212316 Marble Mining and Quarrying ^{CAN}

This Canadian industry comprises establishments primarily engaged in mining or quarrying dimension marble, rough blocks or slabs of marble, and crushed and broken marble. Establishments engaged in mining or quarrying slate are also included.

Example Activities
- Argillite, dimension, quarrying
- Basalt, crushed and broken stone, quarrying
- Basalt, dimension, quarrying
- Bluestone, dimension, quarrying
- Chemical and metallurgical stone, marble, rough, mining
- Diabase, crushed and broken stone, quarrying
- Diabase, quarrying
- Dolomitic marble, crushed and broken stone, quarrying
- Flagstone mining
- Gabbro, crushed and broken stone, quarrying
- Gabbro, quarrying
- Marble quarry
- Monumental and ornamental stone, marble, rough, mining
- Onyx marble, crushed and broken stone, quarrying
- Onyx marble, dimension-quarrying
- Riprap (except limestone and granite), quarrying
- Slate, quarrying
- Volcanic rock, quarrying

212317 Sandstone Mining and Quarrying ^{CAN}

This Canadian industry comprises establishments primarily engaged in mining or quarrying dimension sandstone, rough blocks or slabs of sandstone, and crushed and broken sandstone.

Example Activities
- Ganister, quarrying
- Grits, crushed and broken stone mining
- Quartzite, crushed and broken stone, quarrying
- Quartzite, quarrying
- Sandstone quarry

21232 Sand, Gravel, Clay, and Ceramic and Refractory Minerals Mining and Quarrying

This industry comprises establishments primarily engaged in operating sand and gravel pits, including dredging for sand and gravel; mining or quarrying shale; and mining, beneficiating or otherwise preparing kaolin or ball clay, including china clay, paper and slip clays, and other clays and refractory minerals.

212323 Sand and Gravel Mining and Quarrying ^{CAN}

This Canadian industry comprises establishments primarily engaged in operating sand and gravel pits, including dredging for sand and gravel, and washing, screening or otherwise preparing sand and gravel.

Example Activities
- Abrasive sand mining
- Fill dirt pits
- Filtration sand mining
- Foundry sand mining
- Gravel pit
- Industrial sand mining
- Sand pit or quarry
- Silica sand, mining

212326 Shale, Clay and Refractory Mineral Mining and Quarrying ^{CAN}

This Canadian industry comprises establishments primarily engaged in mining or quarrying shale and mining, beneficiating or otherwise preparing kaolin or ball clay and other clays and refractory minerals. Mines operated in conjunction with plants that manufacture cement, brick or other structural clay products, or pottery and related products, are included in this Canadian industry when separate reports are not available.

Exclusion(s): Establishments primarily engaged in:
- grinding, pulverizing or otherwise treating ceramic minerals, not in conjunction with mining or quarrying operations (327110, Pottery, Ceramics and Plumbing Fixture Manufacturing); and
- grinding, pulverizing or otherwise treating clay and refractory minerals, not in conjunction with mining or quarrying operations (327120, Clay Building Material and Refractory Manufacturing).

Example Activities
- Andalusite mining
- Aplite mining
- Ball clay mining
- Bentonite mining
- Brucite mining
- Burley mining
- Clay pits
- Conglomerate mine or quarry
- Cornwall stone mining
- Cyanite mining
- Diaspore mining
- Dumortierite mining
- Feldspar mining
- Fire clay mining
- Fuller's earth mining
- Kaolin mining
- Kyanite mining
- Magnesite mining
- Nepheline syenite quarrying
- Olivine (nongem) mining
- Paper clay mining
- Pinite mining
- Plastic fire clay mining
- Rubber clay mining
- Shale quarry
- Sillimanite mining
- Slip clay mining
- Stoneware clay mining
- Topaz (nongem) mining

21239 Other Non-Metallic Mineral Mining and Quarrying

This industry comprises establishments, not classified to any other industry, primarily engaged in mining, beneficiating or otherwise preparing non-metallic minerals, such as asbestos, gypsum and potash, and extracting peat.

Exclusion(s): Establishments primarily engaged in:
- mining or quarrying dimension stone (21231, Stone Mining and Quarrying);
- mining or quarrying shale and mining, beneficiating, or otherwise preparing clays and refractory minerals (21232, Sand, Gravel, Clay, and Ceramic and Refractory Minerals Mining and Quarrying);
- operating sand and gravel pits and dredging for sand and gravel (21232, Sand, Gravel, Clay, and Ceramic and Refractory Minerals Mining and Quarrying); and
- the production of phosphoric acid, superphosphates or other manufactured phosphate compounds or chemicals (32531, Fertilizer Manufacturing).

212392 Diamond Mining CAN

This Canadian industry comprises establishments primarily engaged in mining diamonds of industrial or gem quality.

Example Activity
- Diamond mining

212393 Salt Mining CAN

This Canadian industry comprises establishments primarily engaged in mining rock salt or in the recovery of salt from brine wells.

Example Activities
- Processing of salt at the mine site
- Refining salt at the mine site
- Rock salt mining
- Rock salt processing at the mine site
- Salt brining (deposit extraction)
- Salt mining, common
- Salt refining at the mine site

212394 Asbestos Mining CAN

This Canadian industry comprises establishments primarily engaged in mining, beneficiating or otherwise preparing asbestos.

Example Activities
- Amosite, milled fibre, mining
- Asbestos mining
- Chrysotile fibre, milling
- Crocidolite, milled fibre, mining

212395 Gypsum Mining CAN

This Canadian industry comprises establishments primarily engaged in mining, beneficiating or otherwise preparing gypsum.

Example Activities
- Alabaster (gypsum) mining
- Anhydrite mining
- Gypsite mining
- Hydrous calcium sulphate (gypsum) mining
- Mining gypsum
- Selenite mining

212396 Potash Mining CAN

This Canadian industry comprises establishments primarily engaged in mining, beneficiating or otherwise preparing potash.

Example Activities
- Muriate of potash, mining
- Potash mining and/or beneficiating
- Potash screening and pulverizing, mining
- Potassium chloride (i.e., potash), mining and/or beneficiating

212397 Peat Extraction CAN

This Canadian industry comprises establishments primarily engaged in extracting and processing peat.

Example Activities
- Peat bog
- Peat mining
- Peat moss digging or harvesting
- Peat moss harvesting, extraction, cutting
- Peat, fuel, mining
- Screening peat
- Sedge peat mining
- Shredding peat mining

212398 All Other Non-Metallic Mineral Mining and Quarrying CAN

This Canadian industry comprises establishments, not classified to any other Canadian industry, primarily engaged in mining, beneficiating or otherwise preparing non-metallic minerals.

Exclusion(s): Establishments primarily engaged in:

- mining or quarrying dimension stone (21231, Stone Mining and Quarrying);
- operating sand and gravel pits and dredging for sand and gravel (212323, Sand and Gravel Mining and Quarrying);
- mining or quarrying shale and mining, beneficiating or otherwise preparing clays and refractory minerals (212326, Shale, Clay and Refractory Mineral Mining and Quarrying);
- mining diamonds of industrial or gem quality (212392, Diamond Mining);
- mining salt or in the recovery of salt from brine wells (212393, Salt Mining);
- mining, beneficiating or otherwise preparing asbestos (212394, Asbestos Mining);
- mining, beneficiating or otherwise preparing gypsum (212395, Gypsum Mining);
- mining, beneficiating or otherwise preparing potash (212396, Potash Mining); and
- extracting and processing peat (212397, Peat Extraction).

Example Activities

- Actinolite mine
- Agate mining
- Alunite mining
- Amblygonite mining
- Amethyst mining
- Apatite mining
- Barium ore mining
- Black lead mine
- Borax mining
- Brimstone mining
- Celestite concentrate, mining
- Colemanite mining
- Corundum mining
- Diatomaceous earth mining
- Diatomite mining
- Earth, coloured, mine
- Epsomite, mining
- Fluorspar mining
- Gem stone mining
- Gilsonite mining
- Glauber's salt, mining
- Greensand mining
- Hydrous sodium sulphate (Glauber's salt), mining
- Iceland spar (i.e., optical grade calcite), mining
- Kernite mining
- Lepidolite mining
- Lithium mineral mining
- Magnesium sulphate mine
- Meerschaum mining or quarrying
- Mica mining
- Muscovite mining
- Ocher mining
- Ozokerite mining
- Perlite mining
- Phosphate rock mining
- Pozzolana (volcanic ash), mining
- Precious stones mining
- Probertite mining
- Pumicite mining
- Pyrites mining
- Pyrophyllite mining
- Quartz crystal mining (pure)
- Scoria mining
- Semiprecious stones mining
- Sienna mining
- Soda ash mining
- Sodium compounds, natural (except common salt) mining
- Strontianite mining
- Sulphur, ground or otherwise treated
- Talc mining
- Trona mining
- Turquoise mining
- Ulexite mining
- Umber mining
- Vermiculite mining
- Withrite mining or quarrying
- Wurtzilite mining

213 Support Activities for Mining and Oil and Gas Extraction

See industry description for 21311, below.

2131 Support Activities for Mining and Oil and Gas Extraction

See industry description for 21311, below.

21311 Support Activities for Mining and Oil and Gas Extraction

This industry comprises establishments primarily engaged in providing support services, on a contract or fee basis, required for the mining and quarrying of minerals and for the extraction of oil and gas. Establishments engaged in the exploration for minerals, other than oil or gas, are included. Exploration includes traditional prospecting methods, such as taking ore samples and making geological observations at prospective sites.

Exclusion(s): Establishments primarily engaged in:
- performing geophysical surveying services for minerals, on a contract or fee basis (54136, Geophysical Surveying and Mapping Services).

213111 Oil and Gas Contract Drilling

This Canadian industry comprises establishments primarily engaged in drilling wells for oil or gas field operations, for others, on a contract or fee basis.

Example Activities
- Directional drilling of oil and gas wells, on a contract basis
- Gas well drilling, on a contract basis
- Oil well drilling, on contract basis
- Redrilling oil and gas wells, on a contract basis
- Troubleshooting, natural gas and oil well

213117 Contract Drilling (except Oil and Gas) CAN

This Canadian industry comprises establishments primarily engaged in diamond, test, prospect and other types of drilling, for minerals, other than oil and gas.

Example Activities
- Boring test holes for non-metallic minerals mining (except fuels), on contract basis
- Contract diamond drilling, metallic minerals
- Drilling services for non-metallic minerals mining (except fuels), on a contract basis
- Iron ore mine diamond drilling, contract services
- Metal mining, prospect drilling for, on a contract basis
- Prospect drilling for metal mining, on a contract basis
- Prospect drilling for non-metallic minerals (except fuels), on contract basis
- Test drilling for metal mining, on a contract basis
- Test drilling for non-metallic minerals mining (except fuels), on a contract basis

213118 Services to Oil and Gas Extraction CAN

This Canadian industry comprises establishments primarily engaged in performing oil and gas field services, except contract drilling, for others, on a contract or fee basis.

Exclusion(s): Establishments primarily engaged in:
- performing exploration for oil or gas, other than geophysical (21111, Oil and Gas Extraction); and
- contract drilling for oil and gas (213111, Oil and Gas Contract Drilling).

Example Activities
- Acidizing wells, on a contract basis
- Bailing wells, on a contract basis
- Building oil and gas well foundations on site, on a contract basis
- Cementing oil and gas well casings, on a contract basis
- Chemically treating wells, on a contract basis
- Cleaning out (e.g., bailing out, steam and swabbing) oil and gas wells, on a contract basis
- Contract battery operators
- Cutting casings, tubes and rods, oil field

- Drilling water intake wells, on a contract basis
- Erecting lease tank, oil and gas field, on a contract basis
- Excavating slush pits and cellars, on a contract basis
- Fire-fighting service, other than forestry or public
- Gas compressing (natural gas) at the fields, on a contract basis
- Gas well surveying, contract services (except seismographic)
- Oil well logging, on a contract basis
- Perforating well casings, on a contract basis
- Pumping of oil and gas wells, on a contract basis

- Servicing oil and gas wells, on a contract basis
- Shot-hole drilling service, oil and gas field, on a contract basis
- Slush pits and cellars, excavation of, on a contract basis
- Swabbing wells, on a contract basis
- Thawing and cleaning wellheads in oil fields
- Water intake well drilling, on a contract basis
- Well foundation building, at oil and gas wells, on a contract basis
- Well pumping, oil and gas, on a contract basis
- Wells, cleaning out, bailing, swabbing, oil field

213119 Other Support Activities for Mining CAN

This Canadian industry comprises establishments, not classified to any other Canadian industry, primarily engaged in performing mining services, for others, on a contract or fee basis. Establishments engaged in the exploration for minerals are included. Such exploration is often accomplished using purchased services of specialty businesses, such as contract drilling services to obtain core samples.

Exclusion(s): Establishments primarily engaged in:
- performing geophysical surveying services for oil and gas, on a contract or fee basis (541360, Geophysical Surveying and Mapping Services).

Example Activities
- Draining or pumping of mines, on a contract basis
- Overburden removal, mines, on a contract basis

- Stripping services, coal and lignite, on a contract basis
- Tunnelling, coal and lignite mining, on a contract basis

22 Utilities

This sector comprises establishments primarily engaged in operating electric, gas and water utilities. These establishments generate, transmit, control and distribute electric power; distribute natural gas; treat and distribute water; operate sewer systems and sewage treatment facilities; and provide related services, generally through a permanent infrastructure of lines, pipes and treatment and processing facilities.

221 Utilities US

See industry description for 22, above.

2211 Electric Power Generation, Transmission and Distribution

This industry group comprises establishments primarily engaged in the generation of bulk electric power, transmission from generating facilities to distribution centres, and/or distribution to end users.

22111 Electric Power Generation ^{US}

This industry comprises establishments primarily engaged in the generation of bulk electric power, by hydro-electric, fossil fuel, nuclear or other processes.

Exclusion(s): Establishments primarily engaged in:
- transmitting and/or distributing electric power (22112, Electric Power Transmission, Control and Distribution);
- manufacturing batteries for the production of electricity (33591, Battery Manufacturing);
- operating incinerators that generate electricity (56221, Waste Treatment and Disposal); and
- concurrent generation of steam and electricity, co-generation (classified according to the primary activity of the establishment operated).

221111 Hydro-Electric Power Generation ^{US}

This Canadian industry comprises establishments primarily engaged in the generation of electricity using hydro-electric generation processes. Establishments that use pumped hydro storage generation processes are included.

Example Activities
- Electric power generation, hydroelectric
- Hydroelectric power generation

221112 Fossil-Fuel Electric Power Generation ^{US}

This Canadian industry comprises establishments primarily engaged in the generation of electricity using fossil fuels (coal, gas, oil) in internal combustion or combustion-turbine conventional steam processes.

Example Activities
- Electric power generation, fossil fuel
- Generation of electricity using fossil fuels

221113 Nuclear Electric Power Generation ^{US}

This Canadian industry comprises establishments primarily engaged in the generation of electric power using nuclear-powered generating plants.

Exclusion(s): Establishments primarily engaged in:
- operating nuclear research reactors (541710, Research and Development in the Physical, Engineering and Life Sciences).

Example Activities
- Electric power generation, nuclear
- Nuclear electric power generation

221119 Other Electric Power Generation ^{US}

This Canadian industry comprises establishments, not classified to any other Canadian industry, primarily engaged in the generation of electricity, such as wind, solar or tidal power generation.

Example Activities
- Compressed air electric power generation
- Electric power generation (except hydro, fossil fuel or nuclear)
- Geothermal electric power generation
- Solar electric power generation
- Tidal electric power generation
- Wind electric power generation

22112 Electric Power Transmission, Control and Distribution ᵁˢ

This industry comprises establishments primarily engaged in the transmission, distribution or control of electric power.

Exclusion(s): Establishments primarily engaged in:
- the generation of electric power (22111, Electric Power Generation).

221121 Electric Bulk Power Transmission and Control ᵁˢ

This Canadian industry comprises establishments primarily engaged in the transmission of electric power from the generating source to the distribution centre, or in transmission and distribution. The transmission system includes transmission lines and the transformer stations that are integral to transmission. The control of electric power, which includes arranging, facilitating or co-ordinating the transmission of electric power between or among electric utilities, is included.

Example Activities
- Electric power control (e.g., arranging transmission between utilities)
- Electric power transmission systems
- Transmission of electric power

221122 Electric Power Distribution ᵁˢ

This Canadian industry comprises establishments primarily engaged in the distribution of electric power to the individual user or consumer. The electric power distribution system includes distribution lines and transformer stations integral to power distribution, as well as any dedicated generating stations. Electric power brokers and agents, that arrange the sale of electricity over power distribution systems operated by others, are included.

Example Activities
- Distribution of electric power
- Electric power distribution systems

2212 Natural Gas Distribution ᵁˢ

See industry description for 22121, below.

22121 Natural Gas Distribution ᵁˢ

This industry comprises establishments primarily engaged in the distribution of natural or synthetic gas to the ultimate consumers through a system of mains. Gas marketers or brokers, that arrange the sale of natural gas over distribution systems operated by others, are included.

Example Activities
- Gas, natural, distribution
- Liquefied petroleum gas (LPG), distribution through mains
- Natural gas brokers
- Natural gas distribution
- Natural gas distribution systems
- Synthetic gas distribution

221210 Natural Gas Distribution ᵁˢ

See industry description for 22121, above.

2213 Water, Sewage and Other Systems ᵁˢ

This industry group comprises establishments primarily engaged in operating water, sewage and related systems.

22131 Water Supply and Irrigation Systems US

This industry comprises establishments primarily engaged in operating water collection, treatment and distribution systems for domestic and industrial needs. Establishments primarily engaged in operating irrigation systems are included.

Example Activities
- Filtration plant, water, municipal
- Irrigation system operation
- Water collection, treatment and distribution systems
- Water distribution for irrigation
- Water filtration plant, operation

221310 Water Supply and Irrigation Systems US

See industry description for 22131, above.

22132 Sewage Treatment Facilities US

This industry comprises establishments primarily engaged in operating sewer systems and sewage treatment facilities that collect, treat and dispose of waste.

Exclusion(s): Establishments primarily engaged in:
- operating waste treatment or disposal facilities, except sewer systems and sewage treatment facilities (56221, Waste Treatment and Disposal).

Example Activities
- Sewage treatment plant operation
- Sewer system, operation

221320 Sewage Treatment Facilities US

See industry description for 22132, above.

22133 Steam and Air-Conditioning Supply US

This industry comprises establishments primarily engaged in the production and/or distribution of steam and heated or cooled air.

Example Activities
- Heating plant
- Steam generation plant

221330 Steam and Air-Conditioning Supply US

See industry description for 22133, above.

23 Construction

This sector comprises establishments primarily engaged in constructing, repairing and renovating buildings and engineering works, and in subdividing and developing land. These establishments may operate on their own account or under contract to other establishments or property owners. They may produce complete projects or just parts of projects. Establishments often subcontract some or all of the work involved in a project, or work together in joint ventures. Establishments may produce new construction, or undertake repairs and renovations to existing structures.

A construction establishment may be the only establishment of an enterprise, or one of several establishments of an integrated real estate enterprise engaged in the land assembly, development, financing, building and sale of large projects.

There are substantial differences in the types of equipment, work force skills, and other inputs required by establishments in this sector. To highlight these differences and variations in the underlying production functions, this sector is divided into three subsectors. Establishments are distinguished initially between those that undertake projects that require several different construction activities (known as trades) to be performed, and establishments that specialize in one trade.

The former are classified in Subsectors 236, Construction of Buildings and 237, Heavy and Civil Engineering Construction, depending upon whether they are primarily engaged in the construction of buildings or in heavy construction and civil engineering projects. Establishments in these subsectors complete projects using their own labour force, by subcontracting, usually to trade contractors, or a combination of own account and subcontracting activities. Establishments classified in these subsectors are known by a variety of designations, such as general contractor, design-builder, speculative builder, operative builder and construction manager. The designation depends on the scope of the projects they undertake, the degree of responsibility and risk that they assume, the type of structure that they produce, and whether they work on contract for an owner or on their own account.

General contractors typically work under contract to a client (the owner of the land and the building or structure to be constructed), and undertake projects that require several specialized construction activities to be performed. Often the general contractor will subcontract some of the specialized tasks to other establishments.

Design-builders are similar to general contractors. However, in a design-build project a single contract is signed with the owner that makes the contractor responsible for providing the architectural and engineering designs. The design-builder therefore is responsible for the design of the project as well as its construction.

Construction establishments that build on their own account, for sale to others, are known as speculative builders, operative builders or merchant builders. They are most often engaged in the construction of residential buildings.

Construction managers provide oversight and scheduling services to the owner, for the most part during the actual construction process. This type of service is sometimes referred to as agency construction management, to distinguish it from a type of general contracting known as at-risk construction management. On the other hand, project management, which is a turnkey-type service involving the entire project, including feasibility studies, the arranging of financing, and the management of the contract bidding and selection process, is classified in 54133, Engineering Services when it is the primary activity of an establishment.

Establishments that specialize in one particular construction activity, or trade, are generally classified in Subsector 238, Specialty Trade Contractors. However, in order to conform to the generally accepted distinctions made by construction businesses themselves, some types of specialized establishments involved in road building and civil engineering are classified in Subsector 237, Heavy and Civil Engineering Construction.

Subsector 238, Specialty Trade Contractors, comprises establishments engaged in trade activities generally needed in the construction of buildings and structures, such as masonry, painting, or electrical work. Specialty trade contractors usually work under contract to another construction establishment but, especially in renovation and repair construction, they may contract directly with the owner of the property.

A significant amount of construction work is performed by enterprises that are primarily engaged in some business other than construction, for these enterprises' own use, using employees and equipment of the enterprise. This activity is not included in the construction sector unless the construction work performed is the primary activity of a separate establishment of the enterprise. However, if separate establishments do exist, they are classified in the construction sector.

Exclusion(s): Establishments primarily engaged in:
- manufacturing and installing building equipment, such as power boilers; manufacturing pre-fabricated buildings (31-33, Manufacturing);
- operating highways, streets and bridges (48-49, Transportation and Warehousing);
- project management services, when it is a primary activity (54133, Engineering Services); and
- maintenance of rights of way for power, communication and pipe lines; and cleaning building exteriors, after construction (56, Administrative and Support, Waste Management and Remediation Services).

236 Construction of Buildings

This subsector comprises establishments primarily engaged in the construction of buildings. Buildings are distinguished by their primary function, such as residential, commercial and industrial. Establishments may produce new construction, or undertake additions, alterations, or maintenance and repairs to existing structures. The on-site assembly of precast, panellized, and prefabricated buildings and construction of temporary buildings are included in this subsector. Part or all of the production work for which the establishments in this sector have responsibility may be subcontracted to other construction establishments - usually specialty trade contractors.

2361 Residential Building Construction

See industry description for 23611, below.

23611 Residential Building Construction

This industry comprises establishments primarily engaged in the construction or remodelling and renovation of single-family and multi-family residential buildings. Included in this industry are residential housing general contractors, operative builders and remodellers of residential structures, residential project construction management firms, and residential design-build firms.

Exclusion(s): Establishments primarily engaged in:
- performing specialized construction work on houses and other residential buildings, generally on a subcontract basis (238, Specialty Trade Contractors);
- performing manufactured (mobile) home set-up and tie-down work (23899, All Other Specialty Trade Contractors); and
- constructing and leasing residential buildings on their own account (53111, Lessors of Residential Buildings and Dwellings).

Example Activities
- Additions, alterations and renovations, residential buildings
- Additions, alterations and renovations, residential buildings, by operative builders
- Apartment building, construction
- Building construction, residential
- Condominiums, multifamily, construction, by general contractors
- Construction management, residential buildings
- Cottages, construction
- Fire and flood damage clean-up
- Fire and flood restoration of single-family houses, by general contractors
- Handyman construction services, residential buildings
- High-rise apartments, construction, by general contractors
- Home builders, operative
- Home improvement (e.g., additions, remodelling, renovations), single-family, by operative builders
- House construction
- House construction, by merchant builders
- Log home, construction
- Merchant builders (i.e., building on own land, for sale), residential
- Modular housing assembly and installation on site, construction
- Multifamily building construction, by general contractors

- Operative builders (i.e., building on own land, for sale), residential
- Remodelling and renovating single-family houses
- Renovation, residential, general contractor
- Residential house construction
- Time-share condominiums, construction, by operative builders

236110 Residential Building Construction CAN

See industry description for 23611, above.

2362 Non-residential Building Construction

This industry group comprises establishments primarily engaged in the construction (including new work, additions and major alterations) of industrial, commercial and institutional buildings. This industry group includes non-residential general contractors, non-residential operative builders, non-residential design-build firms, and non-residential construction management firms.

23621 Industrial Building and Structure Construction

This industry comprises establishments primarily engaged in the construction (including new work, additions and major alterations) of industrial buildings (except warehouses). The construction of selected additional structures, whose production processes are similar to those for industrial buildings (e.g., incinerators, cement plants, blast furnaces, and similar non-building structures), is included in this industry. Included in this industry are industrial building general contractors, industrial building operative builders, industry building design-build firms, and industrial building construction management firms.

Exclusion(s): Establishments primarily engaged in:
- constructing warehouses (23622, Commercial and Institutional Building Construction);
- constructing water treatment plants, sewage treatment plants, and pumping stations for water and sewer systems (23711, Water and Sewer Line and Related Structures Construction);
- constructing oil refineries and petrochemical plants (23712, Oil and Gas Pipeline and Related Structures Construction);
- constructing power generation plants (except hydroelectric) (23713, Power and Communication Line and Related Structures Construction); and
- performing specialized construction work on industrial buildings, generally on a subcontract basis (238, Specialty Trade Contractors).

Example Activities
- Additions, alterations and renovations, industrial buildings
- Aluminum plant construction, general contractors
- Assembly plant construction
- Blast furnaces, construction
- Cement plants, construction
- Construction management, industrial buildings and structures
- Factories, construction
- Garbage disposal plants, construction
- Handyman construction services, industrial buildings
- Industrial building construction, general contractors
- Industrial incinerator construction, general contractors
- Materials recovery facilities, construction
- Mine loading and discharge station, construction
- Operative builders (i.e., building on own land, for sale), industrial buildings
- Ore milling and metal processing plants, construction
- Refuse disposal plants, construction

236210 Industrial Building and Structure Construction US

See industry description for 23621, above.

23622 Commercial and Institutional Building Construction

This industry comprises establishments primarily engaged in the construction (including new work, additions and major alterations) of commercial and institutional buildings and related structures, such as stadiums, grain elevators, and indoor swimming pools. This industry includes establishments responsible for the on-site assembly of modular or prefabricated commercial and institutional buildings. Included in this industry are commercial and institutional building general contractors, commercial and institutional building operative builders, commercial and institutional building design-build firms, and commercial and institutional building construction management firms.

Exclusion(s): Establishments primarily engaged in:
- constructing structures that are integral parts of utility systems (e.g., storage tanks, pumping stations) or are used to produce products for these systems (e.g., power plants, refineries) (2371, Utility System Construction);
- performing specialized construction work on commercial and institutional buildings generally on a subcontract basis (238, Specialty Trade Contractors); and
- constructing buildings on their own account for rent or lease (5311, Lessors of Real Estate).

Example Activities
- Additions, alterations and renovations, commercial and institutional buildings, by general contractors
- Additions, alterations and renovations, commercial and institutional buildings, by operative builders
- Additions, alterations and renovations, hotels and motels
- Additions, alterations and renovations, industrial warehouses
- Airport building construction
- Animal shelter and clinic construction
- Arena, construction
- Athletic courts, indoor, construction
- Broadcasting stations, construction
- Bus shelter construction
- Bush depots and camps, construction
- Casino construction
- Cinemas, construction
- Construction management, commercial and institutional buildings
- Farm buildings (except dwellings), construction
- Handyman construction services, commercial and institutional buildings
- Hangars, aeroplane, construction
- Hotel, construction
- Ice rink, indoor, construction
- Institutional buildings, construction
- Office buildings and complexes, construction
- Prison construction
- Public warehouse construction
- Radio and television broadcast studio construction
- Restaurants, construction
- Shopping centres and complexes, construction
- Shopping mall construction
- Speculative builders (i.e., building on own land, for sale), commercial and institutional buildings
- Swimming pool construction (indoor)
- Television station construction
- Tennis courts, indoor, construction
- Warehouse (e.g., commercial, industrial, manufacturing, public or private) construction

236220 Commercial and Institutional Building Construction US

See industry description for 23622, above.

237 Heavy and Civil Engineering Construction

This subsector comprises establishments whose primary activity is the construction of entire engineering projects (e.g., highways and dams), and specialty trade contractors, whose primary activity is the production of a specific component for such projects. Establishments may produce new construction, or undertake additions, alterations, or maintenance and repairs to existing structures and works. Establishments in this subsector are classified based on the types of structures that they construct.

Specialty trade contractors in this subsector generally provide specialized services of a type related to heavy and civil engineering construction projects and not normally performed on buildings or building related projects. For example, specialized equipment is needed to paint lines on highways. This equipment is not normally used in building applications so the activity is classified in this subsector. Traffic signal installation, while specific to highways, uses much of the same skills and equipment that are needed for electrical work in building projects and is therefore classified in Subsector 238, Specialty Trade Contractors.

Construction projects involving water resources (e.g., dredging and land drainage) and projects involving open space improvement (e.g., parks and trails) are included in this subsector. Establishments whose primary activity is the subdivision of land into individual building lots usually perform various additional site-improvement activities (e.g., road building and utility line installation) and are included in this subsector.

Exclusion(s): Establishments primarily engaged in:
- construction activities normally performed on buildings or building related projects (238, Specialty Trade Contractors).

2371 Utility System Construction

This industry group comprises establishments primarily engaged in the construction of distribution lines and related buildings and structures for utilities (i.e., water, sewer, petroleum, gas, power, and communication). All structures (including buildings) that are integral parts of utility systems (e.g., storage tanks, pumping stations, power plants, and refineries) are included in this industry group.

23711 Water and Sewer Line and Related Structures Construction

This industry comprises establishments primarily engaged in the construction of water and sewer lines, mains, pumping stations, treatment plants and storage tanks. The work performed may include new work, reconstruction, rehabilitation, and repairs. Specialized trade activities related to water and sewer line and related structures construction are included. The construction of structures (including buildings) that are integral parts of water and sewer networks (e.g., storage tanks, pumping stations, water treatment plants, and sewage treatment plants) is included in this industry.

Exclusion(s): Establishments primarily engaged in:
- constructing water intake wells in oil and gas fields (213118, Services to Oil and Gas Extraction); and
- constructing marine facilities (e.g., ports), flood control structures, dams, or hydroelectric power generation facilities (23799, Other Heavy and Civil Engineering Construction).

Example Activities
- Aqueduct construction, general contractors
- Capping of water wells
- Construction management, water and sewage treatment plants
- Construction management, water and sewer lines and related structures
- Distribution line, sewer and water, construction
- Filtration plant, construction
- Lagoons, sewage treatment construction
- Pumping stations, water, construction
- Reservoir construction, general contractors
- Sanitary sewers, construction
- Sewage collection and disposal line construction
- Sewage treatment and disposal plants, construction
- Storm sewers, construction
- Utility line (i.e., sewer and water), construction
- Water desalination plant construction
- Water main line construction, general contractors
- Water mains and hydrants, construction
- Water treatment plant construction
- Water well drilling (except water intake wells in oil and gas fields)
- Water well pumps and well piping systems, installation

237110 Water and Sewer Line and Related Structures Construction ^{US}

See industry description for 23711, above.

23712 Oil and Gas Pipeline and Related Structures Construction

This industry comprises establishments primarily engaged in the construction of oil and gas lines, mains, refineries, and storage tanks. The work performed may include new work, reconstruction, rehabilitation, and repairs. Specialized trade activities related to oil and gas pipeline and related structures construction are included. The construction of structures (including buildings) that are integral parts of oil and gas networks (e.g., storage tanks, pumping stations, and refineries) is included in this industry.

Exclusion(s): Establishments primarily engaged in:
- building chemical plants (except petrochemical) and similar process or batch facilities (23621, Industrial Building and Structure Construction).

Example Activities
- Compressor, metering and pumping stations, gas and oil, construction
- Construction management, oil and gas pipelines and related structures
- Construction management, oil refineries and petrochemical complexes
- Gas mains, construction
- Natural gas processing plants, construction
- Oil and gas field distribution line construction
- Petroleum refineries, construction
- Pipeline rehabilitation contractors
- Pipeline wrapping construction contractors
- Pipelines, oil and gas, construction
- Storage tanks, natural gas or oil, construction

237120 Oil and Gas Pipeline and Related Structures Construction ^{US}

See industry description for 23712, above.

23713 Power and Communication Line and Related Structures Construction

This industry comprises establishments primarily engaged in the construction of power lines and towers, power plants (except hydroelectric generating facilities), and radio, television, and telecommunications transmitting/receiving towers. The work performed may include new work, reconstruction, rehabilitation, and repairs. Specialized trade activities related to power and communication line and related structures construction are included. The construction of structures (including buildings) that are integral parts of power and communication networks (e.g., transmitting towers, substations, and power plants) is included.

Exclusion(s): Establishments primarily engaged in:
- constructing broadcast studios and similar non-residential buildings (23622, Commercial and Institutional Building Construction);
- constructing hydroelectric generating facilities (23799, Other Heavy and Civil Engineering Construction);
- performing electrical work within buildings (23821, Electrical Contractors and Other Wiring Installation Contractors);
- line slashing or cutting (except maintenance) (23891, Site Preparation Contractors);
- installing and maintaining telecommunication lines by telecommunication companies (517, Telecommunications);
- tree and brush trimming for overhead utility lines (56173, Landscaping Services); and
- locating underground utility lines prior to digging (56199, All Other Support Services).

Example Activities

- Alternative energy (e.g., geothermal, ocean wave, solar and wind) structure construction
- Cellular phone towers, construction
- Co-generation plant construction
- Communication towers, construction
- Construction management, power and communication lines and related structures
- Electric power transmission lines and towers, construction
- Electricity generating plant (except hydroelectric) construction
- Fibre-optic cable transmission lines, construction
- Microwave relay towers, construction
- Nuclear power plants, construction
- Satellite receiving stations, construction
- Telephone line stringing
- Thermal power plants, construction
- Towers, power distribution and communication, construction
- Transformer stations and substations, electric power, construction
- Underground cable (e.g., cable television, electricity, and telephone) laying
- Utility line (e.g., communication and electric power), construction
- Wind energy equipment, construction

237130 Power and Communication Line and Related Structures Construction ^{US}

See industry description for 23713, above.

2372 Land Subdivision

See industry description for 23721, below.

23721 Land Subdivision

This industry comprises establishments primarily engaged in servicing raw land and subdividing real property into lots, for subsequent sale to builders. Land subdivision precedes building activity. The building sites created by land subdivision may be residential lots, commercial tracts or industrial parks.

Servicing of raw land entails some physical improvements, such as land clearing or excavation work for the installation of roads and utility lines. While the extent of work varies from project to project, the establishments classified in this industry are primarily engaged in subdivision activity that includes physical improvement of the land. Establishments that perform only the legal subdivision of land are not included in this industry.

Exclusion(s): Establishments primarily engaged in:
- legal subdivision of land without land preparation, classified elsewhere in the classification based on the primary activity of the establishment;
- constructing buildings, for sale, on lots they subdivide (236, Construction of Buildings);
- installing utilities on a subcontract basis for land subdividers (2371, Utility System Construction);
- installing roads on a subcontract basis for land subdividers (23731, Highway, Street and Bridge Construction);
- preparing land owned by others for building construction (23891, Site Preparation Contractors);
- constructing buildings, for rent or own use, on lots they subdivide (5311, Lessors of Real Estate); and
- operating cemeteries and crematoria (81222, Cemeteries and Crematoria).

Example Activities

- Building lot subdividing, land development
- Land (except cemeteries) subdividers
- Land servicing (hydro, sewer and water), land development
- Land subdivision and development
- Real property (except cemeteries) subdivision
- Servicing of raw land for subsequent sale
- Subdividing and servicing land owned by others

237210 Land Subdivision US

See industry description for 23721, above.

2373 Highway, Street and Bridge Construction

See industry description for 23731, below.

23731 Highway, Street and Bridge Construction

This industry comprises establishments primarily engaged in the construction of highways (including elevated), streets, roads, airport runways, public sidewalks, or bridges. The work performed may include new work, reconstruction, rehabilitation, and repairs. Specialized trade activities related to highway, street, and bridge construction (i.e., installing guardrails on highways) are included.

Exclusion(s): Establishments primarily engaged in:
- constructing tunnels (23799, Other Heavy and Civil Engineering Construction);
- highway lighting and signal installation (23821, Electrical Contractors and Other Wiring Installation Contractors);
- painting bridges (23832, Painting and Wall Covering Contractors); and
- constructing parking lots and private driveways and sidewalks, or erecting billboards (23899, All Other Specialty Trade Contractors).

Example Activities
- Abutment construction
- Airport runway construction, general contractors
- Asphalt paving (e.g., roads, public sidewalks, streets), contractors
- Bridge approaches, construction
- Bridge decking construction
- Bridge, construction
- Causeway, construction
- Concrete paving (i.e., highways, roads, streets, public sidewalks)
- Construction management, highway, road, street and bridge
- Culverts (highway, road and street) construction
- Curbs and street gutters, highway, road and street, construction
- Grading for highways, roads, streets and airport runways
- Guardrail construction on highways
- Highway grading
- Highway line painting
- Painting lines on highways
- Painting traffic lanes or parking lots
- Pavement, highways, roads, streets, bridges or airport runways, construction
- Repairing highways, roads, streets, bridges or airport runways
- Resurfacing highways, roads, streets, bridges or airport runways
- Sign erection (i.e., highway, street) contractors
- Sign erection, highway, road, street and bridge
- Surfacing highways, roads, streets, bridges or airport runways
- Tarring roads

237310 Highway, Street and Bridge Construction US

See industry description for 23731, above.

2379 Other Heavy and Civil Engineering Construction

See industry description for 23799, below.

23799 Other Heavy and Civil Engineering Construction

This industry comprises establishments, not classified to any other industry, primarily engaged in constructing heavy and civil engineering works. The work performed may include new work, reconstruction, rehabilitation, and repairs. Specialized trade activities related to these engineering and civil construction projects (such as marine pile driving) are included. Construction projects involving water resources (e.g., dredging and land drainage), development of marine facilities, and open space recreational construction projects (e.g., parks and trails) are included in this industry.

Exclusion(s): Establishments primarily engaged in:
- constructing water mains, sewers, and related structures (23711, Water and Sewer Line and Related Structures Construction);
- constructing oil and gas pipelines and related structures (23712, Oil and Gas Pipeline and Related Structures Construction);
- constructing power and communication transmission lines and related structures (23713, Power and Communication Line and Related Structures Construction);
- constructing highways, streets, and bridges (23731, Highway, Street and Bridge Construction); and
- trenching (except underwater) (23891, Site Preparation Contractors).

Example Activities
- Anchored earth retention contractors
- Athletic field construction, general contractors
- Breakwater construction, general contractors
- Bulkhead wall construction
- Caissons (i.e., marine or pneumatic structures), construction
- Cofferdams, construction
- Construction management, dams
- Construction management, marine structures
- Construction management, mass transit
- Construction management, miscellaneous heavy and civil engineering construction
- Construction management, outdoor recreation facilities
- Construction management, tunnels
- Dam construction, general contractors
- Dikes and other flood control structures, construction
- Dock and pier construction
- Drainage canals and ditches, construction
- Drainage project construction
- Dredging, canals, channels, waterways and ditches
- Drive-in movie facility construction
- Earth retention system construction
- Farm drainage tile installation
- Flood control project construction
- Gabion installations
- Generating station, construction (hydro)
- Golf course construction, general contractors
- Harbour construction, general contractors
- Horizontal drilling (e.g., cable, pipeline, sewer installation)
- Hydroelectric generating stations, construction
- Ice rink (except indoor) construction
- Jetty construction, general contractors
- Land drainage contractor
- Levee construction, general contractors
- Light rail system construction
- Lock and waterway construction, general contractors
- Marine construction, general contractors
- Mass transit, construction
- Microtunneling contractors
- Monorail construction
- Nuclear waste disposal site construction
- Outdoor recreation facilities, construction
- Pile driving, marine
- Pipe-jacking contractors
- Playground construction
- Port facilities construction
- Railway construction (track, roadbed, trestles, signals, interlockers)
- Recreation areas (open space), construction
- Recreational vehicle park construction
- Retaining walls, anchored (e.g., with piles, soil nails, tieback anchors), construction
- Revetment construction
- Rock removal, underwater, contractor
- Sediment control system construction
- Shipping channel construction
- Ski tow erection, general contractors
- Sports fields and facilities, construction
- Streetcar line construction
- Subway construction
- Subway construction, general contractors
- Swimming pools, outdoor nonresidential-type, construction
- Tennis court construction (outdoor), general contractors
- Timber removal underwater, general contractors
- Trenching, underwater
- Tunnel, construction
- Wharves, construction

237990 Other Heavy and Civil Engineering Construction US

See industry description for 23799, above.

238 Specialty Trade Contractors

This subsector comprises establishments primarily engaged in trade activities generally needed in the construction of buildings and structures, such as masonry, painting, or electrical work. The work performed may include new work, additions, alterations, maintenance, and repairs. Specialty trade contractors usually work under contract to general contractors or operative builders to carry out a component of an overall project. However, they may contract directly with the owner of the property, especially in renovation and repair construction.

Not all specialized trade activities are classified in this subsector. In order to conform to the generally accepted distinctions made by construction businesses themselves, some types of specialized establishments involved in heavy and civil engineering construction are classified in Subsector 237, Heavy and Civil Engineering Construction.

Usually most of the work is carried out at the construction site. Some trade contractors operate shops in which they carry out job-specific prefabrication and other work. However, establishments that manufacture structural components such as steel and pre-cast concrete, or that manufacture building equipment such as boilers and elevators, are classified in Sector 31-33, Manufacturing even if they install these goods themselves.

The specialized activities classified in this subsector range from the initial site preparation for new construction, through the construction of building foundations and structures, the installation of building equipment and systems, to the finishing of buildings and other structures.

> *Exclusion(s): Establishments primarily engaged in:*
> - providing specialized services of a type related to heavy and civil engineering construction, and not normally performed on buildings or building-related projects (237, Heavy and Civil Engineering Construction); and
> - selling construction materials (41, Wholesale Trade, or 44-45, Retail Trade).

2381 Foundation, Structure, and Building Exterior Contractors

This industry group comprises establishments primarily engaged in the specialty trades needed to complete the basic structure (i.e., foundation, frame, and shell) of buildings. The work performed may include new work, additions, alterations, maintenance, and repairs.

23811 Poured Concrete Foundation and Structure Contractors

This industry comprises establishments primarily engaged in pouring and finishing concrete foundations and structural elements. This industry also includes establishments performing grout and shotcrete work. The work performed may include new work, additions, alterations, maintenance, and repairs.

> *Exclusion(s): Establishments primarily engaged in:*
> - constructing or paving streets, highways, and public sidewalks (23731, Highway, Street and Bridge Construction);
> - erecting and dismantling forms for poured concrete (23819, Other Foundation, Structure and Building Exterior Contractors);
> - concrete sealing, coating, waterproofing, or dampproofing (23839, Other Building Finishing Contractors); and
> - paving residential driveways, commercial parking lots, and other private parking (23899, All Other Specialty Trade Contractors).

Example Activities
- Cement finishing
- Chimneys, concrete, construction
- Concrete footing and foundation contractors
- Concrete pumping (placement)
- Concrete resurfacing
- Footings and foundation contractor

- Foundations of buildings, poured concrete, contractors
- Gunite work on construction projects
- Mud-jacking contractors
- Retaining walls, poured concrete, construction
- Shotcrete contractors

238110 Poured Concrete Foundation and Structure Contractors

See industry description for 23811, above.

23812 Structural Steel and Precast Concrete Contractors

This industry comprises establishments primarily engaged in: (1) erecting and assembling structural parts made from steel or precast concrete (e.g., steel beams, structural steel components, and similar products of precast concrete); and/or (2) assembling and installing other steel construction products (e.g., steel rods, bars, rebar, mesh, and cages) to reinforce poured-in-place concrete. The work performed may include new work, additions, alterations, maintenance, and repairs.

Exclusion(s): Establishments primarily engaged in:
- pouring concrete at the construction site for building foundations or structural elements (23811, Poured Concrete Foundation and Structure Contractors).

Example Activities
- Balconies, precast, concrete, installation
- Concrete products, structural precast or prestressed, installation
- Concrete reinforcement placement, contractors
- Curtain wall, precast concrete, installation
- Metal storage tank erection
- Pre-stressed concrete beams, slabs or other components, installation

- Rebars (deformed steel bars for concrete reinforcement), installation
- Reinforcing rods, bars, mesh and cage, installation
- Reinforcing steel contractors
- Siding, precast concrete, installation
- Stairs, precast concrete, installation
- Structural steel erection, contractors

238120 Structural Steel and Precast Concrete Contractors [US]

See industry description for 23812, above.

23813 Framing Contractors [US]

This industry comprises establishments primarily engaged in structural framing and sheathing using materials other than structural steel or concrete. The work performed may include new work, additions, alterations, maintenance, and repairs.

Exclusion(s): Establishments primarily engaged in:
- installing structural steel framing or precast concrete framing (23812, Structural Steel and Precast Concrete Contractors);
- constructing brick, block, stone foundations (23814, Masonry Contractors); and
- finish carpentry (23835, Finish Carpentry Contractors).

Example Activities
- Building framing (except structural steel)
- Foundations, building, of wood, contractors
- Framing contractor
- Permanent wood foundations, installation
- Post frame contractors
- Prefabricated wood trusses and other building wood-frame components, installation
- Sheathing (house, building, structure), wood, construction
- Steel framing (except structural) contractors
- Stud walls, wood or steel, installation
- Wood frame components, installation

238130 Framing Contractors US

See industry description for 23813, above.

23814 Masonry Contractors US

This industry comprises establishments primarily engaged in masonry work, stone setting, brick laying, and other stone work. The work performed may include new work, additions, alterations, maintenance, and repairs.

Exclusion(s): Establishments primarily engaged in:
- erecting the basic structure of buildings by pouring concrete (23811, Poured Concrete Foundation and Structure Contractors);
- interior marble, granite and slate work (23834, Tile and Terrazzo Contractors); and
- laying precast stones or bricks for patios, sidewalks, and driveways; or paving residential driveways, commercial parking lots and other private parking (23899, All Other Specialty Trade Contractors).

Example Activities
- Blocklaying
- Bricklaying, contractors
- Cement block laying
- Field stone, installation
- Glass block laying
- Glass unit (i.e., glass block) masonry
- Masonry pointing, cleaning or caulking
- Retaining wall construction, block, stone, or brick, contractors
- Slate (i.e., exterior work), contractors
- Tuck pointing, contractors

238140 Masonry Contractors US

See industry description for 23814, above.

23815 Glass and Glazing Contractors US

This industry comprises establishments primarily engaged in installing glass panes in prepared openings (i.e., glazing work) and other glass work for buildings. The work performed may include new work, additions, alterations, maintenance, and repairs.

Exclusion(s): Establishments primarily engaged in:
- installing prefabricated window units (23835, Finish Carpentry Contractors); and
- the replacement, repair, and/or tinting of automotive glass (811122, Automotive Glass Replacement Shops).

Example Activities
- Curtain wall, glass, installation
- Glass cladding installation
- Glass installation (except automotive), contractors
- Glass partitions, installation
- Glass tinting, construction
- Glazing work, contractors
- Hermetically sealed window units, commercial type, installation
- Stained glass, installation

238150 Glass and Glazing Contractors US

See industry description for 23815, above.

23816 Roofing Contractors US

This industry comprises establishments primarily engaged in roofing. This industry also includes establishments treating roofs (i.e., spraying, painting, or coating) and installing skylights. The work performed may include new work, additions, alterations, maintenance, and repairs.

Exclusion(s): Establishments primarily engaged in:
- installing roof trusses and sheathing attached to trusses (23813, Framing Contractors); and
- installing downspouts, gutters, fascia, and soffits (23817, Siding Contractors).

Example Activities
- Asphalt roof shingles, installation
- Copper roofing, installation
- Corrugated metal roofing, installation
- Low slope roofing installation
- Low slope roofing installation (cold or hot apply)
- Painting, spraying or coating of roofs
- Roof membrane, installation
- Sheet metal roofing, installation
- Skylights, installation
- Solar reflecting coatings, application onto roofs
- Steep slope roofing installation
- Treating roofs (by spraying, painting or coating)

238160 Roofing Contractors US

See industry description for 23816, above.

23817 Siding Contractors US

This industry comprises establishments primarily engaged in installing siding of wood, aluminium, vinyl or other exterior finish material (except brick, stone, stucco, or curtain wall). This industry also includes establishments installing eavestroughs, gutters and downspouts. The work performed may include new work, additions, alterations, maintenance, and repairs.

Exclusion(s): Establishments primarily engaged in:
- installing brick, stone, or stucco building exterior finish materials (23814, Masonry Contractors);
- installing curtain wall (23819, Other Foundation, Structure and Building Exterior Contractors); and
- installing sheet metal duct work (23822, Plumbing, Heating and Air-Conditioning Contractors).

Example Activities
- Aluminum siding, installation
- Down spout and gutter, installation, contractors
- Eavestroughing, contractors
- Fascia and soffit, metal and plastic, installation
- Flashing, metal, installation
- Gutter installation, contractors
- Gutters, seamless roof, formed and installed on-site
- Ice apron, roof, installation
- Siding (aluminum, steel, asbestos, cement, plastic, hardboard), installation
- Siding, contractors (installation and repair)
- Vinyl siding, soffit and fascia, installation
- Wood siding, installation

238170 Siding Contractors US

See industry description for 23817, above.

23819 Other Foundation, Structure and Building Exterior Contractors US

This industry comprises establishments, not classified to any other industry, primarily engaged in foundation, structure and building exterior trades work. The work performed may include new work, additions, alterations, maintenance, and repairs.

Exclusion(s): Establishments primarily engaged in:
- poured concrete foundation and structure work (23811, Poured Concrete Foundation and Structure Contractors);
- erecting and assembling structural parts made from steel or precast concrete (23812, Structural Steel and Precast Concrete Contractors);
- framing buildings (23813, Framing Contractors);
- masonry work (23814, Masonry Contractors);
- glass and glazing work (23815, Glass and Glazing Contractors);
- installing or repairing roofs (23816, Roofing Contractors); and
- installing siding (23817, Siding Contractors).

Example Activities
- Awning installation
- Balconies, metal, installation
- Cathodic protection, installation
- Curtain wall (except glass and precast concrete) installation, contractors
- Epoxy application, contractors
- False work construction
- Fireproofing buildings, contractors
- Ornamental metal work, installation, contractors
- Shutters, installation
- Store front frames, metal, installation
- Welding contractors, operating at site of construction

238190 Other Foundation, Structure and Building Exterior Contractors US

See industry description for 23819, above.

2382 Building Equipment Contractors

This industry group comprises establishments primarily engaged in installing or servicing equipment that forms part of a building mechanical system (e.g., electricity, water, heating, and cooling). The work performed may include new work, additions, alterations, or maintenance and repairs. Contractors installing specialized building equipment, such as elevators, escalators, service station equipment, and central vacuum cleaning systems are also included.

23821 Electrical Contractors and Other Wiring Installation Contractors

This industry comprises establishments primarily engaged in installing and servicing electrical wiring and equipment. Electrical contractors included in this industry may include both the parts and labour when performing work. Electrical contractors may perform new work, additions, alterations, maintenance, and repairs.

Exclusion(s): Establishments primarily engaged in:
- constructing power and communication transmission lines (23713, Power and Communication Line and Related Structures Construction);
- installing and maintaining telecommunications lines by telecommunications companies (517, Telecommunications); and
- burglar and fire alarm installation combined with sales, maintenance, or monitoring services (561621, Security Systems Services (except Locksmiths)).

Example Activities

- Airport runway lighting contractors
- Building automation systems, contractors
- Cable splicing, electrical, contractors
- Cable television hookup, contractors
- Computer and network cable installation
- Electric power control panels and outlets, installation
- Electrical wiring contractors
- Electronic containment fencing for pets, installation
- Environmental control systems, central, installation
- Fibre-optic cable (except transmission lines), installation
- Fire alarm systems, installation
- Highway lighting and electrical signal construction, contractors

- Highway, street and bridge lighting systems and electrical signal installation
- Home automation system installation
- Home theatre installation
- Intercommunication systems, installation
- Lighting systems, electric, installation
- Low voltage electrical work
- Private driveway or parking area lighting contractors
- Security and fire systems, installation only
- Snow melting cable, electric, installation
- Sound equipment installation
- Surveillance systems, installation only
- Telephone and telephone equipment installation, contractors
- Traffic signal installation
- Tunnel lighting contractors

238210 Electrical Contractors and Other Wiring Installation Contractors

See industry description for 23821, above.

23822 Plumbing, Heating and Air-Conditioning Contractors

This industry comprises establishments primarily engaged in installing and servicing plumbing, heating, and air-conditioning equipment. Contractors in this industry may provide both parts and labour when performing work. The work performed may include new work, additions, alterations, maintenance, and repairs.

Exclusion(s): Establishments primarily engaged in:
- installing electrical controls for HVAC systems (23821, Electrical Contractors and Other Wiring Installation Contractors); and
- duct cleaning (561791, Duct and Chimney Cleaning Services).

Example Activities

- Air system balancing and testing, contractors
- Air-conditioning systems, installation or repair
- Bathroom plumbing fixtures and sanitary ware, installation
- Boiler chipping, cleaning and scaling
- Central air-conditioning equipment, installation
- Central cooling equipment and piping, installation
- Central heating equipment and piping, installation
- Chilled water systems, installation
- Commercial refrigeration systems, installation
- Cooling towers, installation
- Diffusers, grilles, air registers, installation

- Dry heating equipment and controls, installation (except electric baseboard)
- Duct work (e.g., heating, cooling, exhaust, dust collection), installation
- Dust collecting equipment installation, contractors
- Fire sprinkler systems, installation
- Fireplace installations (except masonry)
- Fireplace, natural gas, installation
- Furnace conversion from one fuel to another
- Furnace humidifiers and filters, installation
- Furnace installations and repairs
- Heating contractors
- Heating, ventilation and air-conditioning (HVAC) contractors
- HVAC (heating, ventilation and air-conditioning) contractors
- Hydronic heating systems, installation

- Industrial process piping installation
- Lawn sprinkler system installation, contractors
- Natural gas piping, installation
- Plumbers
- Plumbing fixtures, installation
- Process piping, installation
- Radiant floor heating equipment, installation
- Scrubbers (i.e., for air-purification) installation

- Snow melting systems (hot water or glycol), installation
- Sprinkler systems, lawn and garden, installation
- Sump pump installation and servicing, contractors
- Water heater installation
- Water softeners, installation
- Water system balancing and testing, contractors

238220 Plumbing, Heating and Air-Conditioning Contractors US

See industry description for 23822, above.

23829 Other Building Equipment Contractors

This industry comprises establishments, not classified to any other industry, primarily engaged in installing or servicing building equipment. The work performed may include new work, additions, alterations, maintenance, and repairs.

238291 Elevator and Escalator Installation Contractors CAN

This Canadian industry comprises establishments primarily engaged in installing or servicing elevators and escalators, moving sidewalks and similar conveying equipment in buildings. The work performed may include new work, additions, alterations, maintenance, and repairs.

Example Activities
- Elevator installation, contractors
- Escalators installation, contractors

- Moving sidewalks, installation and repair

238299 All Other Building Equipment Contractors CAN

This Canadian industry comprises establishments, not classified to any other Canadian industry, primarily engaged in installing or servicing building equipment. The work performed may include new work, additions, alterations, maintenance, and repairs. Some important examples of work done by these establishments are boiler and pipe installation, dismantling large-scale machinery and equipment, and installation of built-in vacuum cleaning systems.

Exclusion(s): Establishments primarily engaged in:
- manufacturing of industrial equipment with incidental installation (31-33, Manufacturing); and
- repair and maintenance of commercial refrigeration equipment or production (81131, Commercial and Industrial Machinery and Equipment (except Automotive and Electronic) Repair and Maintenance).

Example Activities
- Antennas, household, installation and service
- ATM (automated teller machine) installation
- Automated and revolving door installation
- Automated and revolving doors, installation
- Automated teller machine installation
- Automatic gate (e.g., garage, parking lot), installation
- Boiler and pipe, insulation of, contractors

- Boiler covering
- Church bells and tower clocks, installation
- Commercial-type door installation
- Dismantling large-scale machinery and equipment
- Dumb-waiter installation
- Garage door, industrial type, installation
- Hoisting and placement (only) of large-scale apparatus

- Incinerator installation, small, contractors
- Insulation of pipes and boilers, contractors
- Lightning rods and conductors, installation
- Machine rigging, contractors
- Mechanical equipment insulation
- Motor vehicle garage and service station mechanical equipment (e.g., gasoline pumps, hoists), installation

- Overhead door installation, commercial
- Power boilers, purchased, erection
- Revolving doors, installation, contractors
- Rigging large-scale equipment
- Rubber doors, installation
- Vacuum cleaning systems, built-in, contractors
- Vehicle lifts, installation

2383 Building Finishing Contractors

This industry group comprises establishments primarily engaged in the specialty trades needed to finish buildings. The work performed may include new work, additions, alterations, or maintenance and repairs.

23831 Drywall and Insulation Contractors

This industry comprises establishments primarily engaged in drywall, plaster work, and building insulation work. Plaster work includes applying plain or ornamental plaster, and installation of lath to receive plaster. The work performed may include new work, additions, alterations, maintenance, and repairs.

Exclusion(s): Establishments primarily engaged in:
- applying stucco (23814, Masonry Contractors); and
- insulating pipes and boilers (238299, All Other Building Equipment Contractors).

Example Activities
- Acoustical foam, sound barrier, installation
- Blown-in insulation (e.g., vermiculite, cellulose), installation
- Building insulation contractors
- Ceiling tiles, installation
- Drop ceiling installation
- Drywall hanging
- Drywall, finishing (taping, sanding, stippling)
- Drywall, installation
- Exterior insulation finish systems, installation
- Fabric wall systems, noise insulating, installation

- Finishing drywall contractors
- Fresco work (i.e., decorative plaster finishing) contractors
- Gypsum wallboard, installation
- Insulation work contractors
- Panel or rigid board insulation, installing
- Plastering (i.e., ornamental, plain), contractors
- Polystyrene insulating, installation
- Soundproofing contractors
- Styrofoam insulating, installation
- Suspended ceilings, installation
- Taping and finishing drywall, contractors
- Wall cavities and attic space, insulating

238310 Drywall and Insulation Contractors US

See industry description for 23831, above.

23832 Painting and Wall Covering Contractors

This industry comprises establishments primarily engaged in painting, paperhanging and decorating in buildings and painting heavy (engineering) structures. Paint or paper stripping, including sandblasting when it is an incidental part of surface preparation by paint and wall covering contractors, is included in this industry. The work performed may include new work, additions, alterations, maintenance, and repairs.

Exclusion(s): Establishments primarily engaged in:
- painting lines on highways, streets, and parking lots (23731, Highway, Street and Bridge Construction);
- roof painting (23816, Roofing Contractors);
- installing wood panelling (23835, Finish Carpentry Contractors); and
- sandblasting building exteriors (23899, All Other Specialty Trade Contractors).

Example Activities
- Bridges and structures, painting
- Heavy machinery painting
- House painting, contractors
- Paint and wallpaper stripping (removal), contractors

- Rustproofing contractor, buildings and structures (except automotive)
- Sand blasting and painting (non-masonry surfaces)
- Wall covering or removal contractors
- Wallpaper stripping (removal)

238320 Painting and Wall Covering Contractors

See industry description for 23832, above.

23833 Flooring Contractors

This industry comprises establishments primarily engaged in the installation of resilient floor tile, carpeting, linoleum, and hardwood flooring. The work performed may include new work, additions, alterations, maintenance, and repairs.

Exclusion(s): Establishments primarily engaged in:
- laying concrete flooring (23811, Poured Concrete Foundation and Structure Contractors);
- installing stone or ceramic floor tile (23834, Tile and Terrazzo Contractors); and
- retailing and installing carpet and other flooring products, except stone or ceramic tile (44221, Floor Covering Stores).

Example Activities
- Carpet installation and repair
- Computer flooring installation
- Fireproof flooring construction, contractors
- Floor laying, scraping, finishing, and refinishing, contractors
- Floor tile and sheets, composition, installation

- Hardwood flooring, installation
- Resurfacing hardwood floors
- Vinyl floor tile and sheet installation, contractors
- Wood floor finishing (e.g., coating, sanding)

238330 Flooring Contractors

See industry description for 23833, above.

23834 Tile and Terrazzo Contractors

This industry comprises establishments primarily engaged in setting and installing ceramic tile, stone (interior only), and mosaic and/or mixing marble particles and cement to make terrazzo at the job site. The work performed may include new work, additions, alterations, maintenance, and repairs.

Exclusion(s): Establishments primarily engaged in:
- exterior marble, granite, and slate work (23814, Masonry Contractors); and
- manufacturing precast terrazzo products (32739, Other Concrete Product Manufacturing).

Example Activities
- Ceramic tile, installation
- Mantel work (stone) installation
- Mantel, marble or stone, installation

- Marble, granite and slate work (interior), contractors
- Stone flooring, installation
- Terrazzo, pouring, setting and finishing

238340 Tile and Terrazzo Contractors

See industry description for 23834, above.

23835 Finish Carpentry Contractors

This industry comprises establishments primarily engaged in finish carpentry work. The work performed may include new work, additions, alterations, maintenance, and repairs.

Exclusion(s): Establishments primarily engaged in:
- framing (23813, Framing Contractors);
- installing skylights (23816, Roofing Contractors); and
- building custom kitchen and bath cabinets (except free standing) in a shop (33711, Wood Kitchen Cabinet and Counter Top Manufacturing).

Example Activities
- Built-in wood cabinets constructed on site
- Cabinet work performed at the construction site
- Carpentry work (except framing)
- Door and window frames, construction
- Garage door, wooden, installation
- Garage doors, residential type, installation
- Hermetically sealed glass for window units, installation
- Kitchen cabinets and counters, prefabricated wood, installation only

- Millwork installation
- Moulding or trim, wood or plastic, installation
- Overhead door installation, residential
- Panelling installation
- Prefabricated door and window installation
- Prefabricated kitchen and bath cabinet, residential-type, installation
- Shelving, wood, constructed on site
- Stairways, wood, installation

238350 Finish Carpentry Contractors

See industry description for 23835, above.

23839 Other Building Finishing Contractors

This industry comprises establishments, not classified to any other industry, primarily engaged in building finishing trade work. The work performed may include new work, additions, alterations, or maintenance and repairs.

Exclusion(s): Establishments primarily engaged in:
- installing drywall, plaster or insulation (23831, Drywall and Insulation Contractors);
- installing or removing paint or wall coverings (23832, Painting and Wall Covering Contractors);
- installing or repairing wood floors, resilient flooring, and carpet (23833, Flooring Contractors);
- setting tile or performing terrazzo work (23834, Tile and Terrazzo Contractors); and
- finish carpentry (23835, Finish Carpentry Contractors).

Example Activities
- Bath tub refinishing, contractors
- Bath tub refinishing, on site
- Bleachers, installation
- Building fixtures and fittings (except mechanical equipment), installation
- Ceilings, metal, erection and repair, contractors
- Closet organizer system installation
- Concrete coating, glazing or sealing
- Countertop and cabinet, metal (except residential-type), installation
- Drapery track hardware installation
- Fabricating metal cabinets or countertops on site
- Lead lining walls for x-ray room, contractor
- Metal partitions (e.g., office, washroom), installation
- Modular furniture system attachment and installation
- Panels, metal, installation
- Shelving, metal, constructed on site
- Spectator seating installation, contractors
- Trade show exhibit installation and dismantling
- Ventilated wire shelving (i.e., closet organizing-type) installation
- Vibration isolation contractor
- Weatherstripping installation
- Window shades and blinds installation, contractors

238390 Other Building Finishing Contractors

See industry description for 23839, above.

2389 Other Specialty Trade Contractors

This industry group comprises establishments, not classified to any other industry, primarily engaged in site preparation activities and other specialized trade activities such as crane rental with operator, fence installation, sandblasting building exteriors and steeplejack work. The work performed may include new work, additions, alterations, maintenance, and repairs.

23891 Site Preparation Contractors

This industry comprises establishments primarily engaged in site preparation activities, such as excavating and grading, demolition of buildings and other structures, and septic system installation. Earth moving and land clearing for all types of sites, except mine site overburden removal, is included in this industry. Establishments primarily engaged in construction equipment rental with operator (except cranes) are also included.

Exclusion(s): Establishments primarily engaged in:
- dismantling tanks in oil fields (213118, Services to Oil and Gas Extraction);
- drilling oil and gas field water intake wells (213118, Services to Oil and Gas Extraction);
- overburden removal (213119, Other Support Activities for Mining);
- earth retention or underwater trenching (23799, Other Heavy and Civil Engineering Construction);
- crane rental with operator (23899, All Other Specialty Trade Contractors);
- construction equipment rental without an operator (53241, Construction, Transportation, Mining, and Forestry Machinery and Equipment Rental and Leasing);
- tree and brush trimming for overhead utility lines (56173, Landscaping Services); and
- nuclear power plant decommissioning and environmental remediation work, such as the removal of underground steel tanks for hazardous materials (56291, Remediation Services).

Example Activities
- Blast hole drilling (except mining)
- Blasting, building demolition
- Building demolition
- Cesspool construction, contractors
- Concrete breaking and cutting for demolition
- Construction equipment (except crane) rental with operator
- Cutting of rights-of-way contractor
- Demolishing buildings and structures
- Digging foundations
- Dirt moving, for construction

- Dismantling of engineering structures (e.g., oil storage tanks)
- Drilled pier (i.e., for building foundations) contractors
- Drilled shaft (i.e., drilled building foundations), construction
- Equipment rental with operator (except cranes)
- Excavating contractors
- Excavating, earthmoving or land clearing, agricultural
- Excavating, earthmoving or land clearing, mining (except mine site overburden removal)
- Excavating, earthmoving, or land clearing contractors
- Foundation drilling contractors

- Grading, construction site
- House demolishing contractors
- House moving, contractors
- Hydrodemolition (i.e., demolition with pressurized water), contractor
- Land clearing, contractors
- Land levelling, irrigation, contractors
- Pile driving, contractors
- Piling (i.e., bored, cast-in-place, drilled), building foundation, contractors
- Power, communication and pipe lines, rights of way clearance (except maintenance)
- Rights of way, cutting (except maintenance)
- Septic tanks and weeping tile, installation
- Trenching, construction site
- Underground tank (except hazardous material) removal

238910 Site Preparation Contractors

See industry description for 23891, above.

23899 All Other Specialty Trade Contractors

This industry comprises establishments, not classified to any other industry, primarily engaged in specialized construction trades. The work performed may include new work, additions, alterations, maintenance, and repairs.

Exclusion(s): Establishments primarily engaged in:
- paving public highways, streets, and roads (23731, Highway, Street and Bridge Construction);
- foundation, structure, and building exterior work (2381, Foundation, Structure, and Building Exterior Contractors);
- installing, repairing, or maintaining building mechanical systems (2382, Building Equipment Contractors);
- finishing buildings (2383, Building Finishing Contractors);
- construction equipment rental with an operator (except cranes) or preparing land for building construction (23891, Site Preparation Contractors);
- construction equipment rental without an operator (53241, Construction, Transportation, Mining, and Forestry Machinery and Equipment Rental and Leasing);
- radon testing (54138, Testing Laboratories);
- power washing and other building exterior cleaning (except sandblasting) (56179, Other Services to Buildings and Dwellings); and
- environmental remediation work, such as asbestos abatement (56291, Remediation Services).

Example Activities
- Artificial turf, installation
- Boat lift installation
- Brick driveway contractors
- Brick pavers (e.g., driveways, patios and sidewalks), installation
- Cable splicing service, non-electrical, contractors
- Chain link fences, installing

- Cleaning new buildings interior after construction
- Concrete work, private driveways, sidewalks and parking areas, contractors
- Construction elevator, erection and dismantling
- Crane rental with operator
- Curbs and gutters, concrete, residential, installation

- Fencing for highway, installation
- Mobile home set-up contractor
- Mobile home site set up and tie down, contractors
- Outdoor residential-type swimming pool construction
- Parking lot and driveway, asphalt resurfacing
- Patio construction
- Patio construction, concrete, contractors
- Pavers, brick (e.g., driveways, patios and sidewalks), installation
- Paving (asphalt), residential driveways and commercial parking lots
- Radon mitigation contractors

- Safety net systems, erecting and dismantling
- Sand blasting building exteriors
- Scaffolds, erecting and dismantling
- Shoring, construction
- Signs on buildings, erection
- Statues, erection
- Steeplejack work
- Streets, interlocking brick (i.e., not mortared), installation
- Swimming pool construction (residential)
- Swimming pool screen enclosures, construction
- Tank lining contractors
- Turf, artificial, installation
- Underpinning, construction

238990 All Other Specialty Trade Contractors US

See industry description for 23899, above.

31-33 Manufacturing

This sector comprises establishments primarily engaged in the physical or chemical transformation of materials or substances into new products. These products may be finished, in the sense that they are ready to be used or consumed, or semi-finished, in the sense of becoming a raw material for an establishment to use in further manufacturing. Related activities, such as the assembly of the component parts of manufactured goods; the blending of materials; and the finishing of manufactured products by dyeing, heat-treating, plating and similar operations are also treated as manufacturing activities. Manufacturing establishments are known by a variety of trade designations, such as plants, factories or mills.

Manufacturing establishments may own the materials which they transform or they may transform materials owned by other establishments. Manufacturing may take place in factories or in workers' homes, using either machinery or hand tools.

Certain activities involving the transformation of goods are classified in other sectors. Some examples are post-harvest activities of agricultural establishments, such as crop drying; logging; the beneficiating of mineral ores; the production of structures by construction establishments; and various activities conducted by retailers, such as meat cutting and the assembly of products such as bicycles and computers.

311 Food Manufacturing

This subsector comprises establishments primarily engaged in producing food for human or animal consumption.

Exclusion(s): Establishments primarily engaged in:
- manufacturing beverages or tobacco (312, Beverage and Tobacco Product Manufacturing).

3111 Animal Food Manufacturing

See industry description for 31111, below.

31111 Animal Food Manufacturing

This industry comprises establishments primarily engaged in manufacturing food and feed for animals, including pets.

Exclusion(s): Establishments primarily engaged in:
- slaughtering animals for feed (31161, Animal Slaughtering and Processing); and
- manufacturing hormones or other pharmaceutical products for use in animal feed (32541, Pharmaceutical and Medicine Manufacturing).

311111 Dog and Cat Food Manufacturing US

This Canadian industry comprises establishments primarily engaged in manufacturing dog and cat food.

Exclusion(s): Establishments primarily engaged in:
- slaughtering animals for feed (311611, Animal (except Poultry) Slaughtering); and
- slaughtering poultry for dog and cat food (311615, Poultry Processing).

Example Activities
- Cat food, made from purchased meat and poultry
- Dog and cat food, manufacturing
- Dog food, made from purchased meat and poultry
- Feed supplements, dog and cat, manufacturing
- Mineral feed supplements, dog and cat, manufacturing
- Pet food, dog and cat, manufacturing

311119 Other Animal Food Manufacturing US

This Canadian industry comprises establishments, not classified to any other Canadian industry, primarily engaged in manufacturing animal food.

Exclusion(s): Establishments primarily engaged in:
- manufacturing hormones or other pharmaceutical products for use in animal feed (325410, Pharmaceutical and Medicine Manufacturing).

Example Activities
- Animal feed, prepared (except dogs and cats), manufacturing
- Bird food, prepared, manufacturing
- Complete feed, livestock, manufacturing
- Feed premixes, animal (except dogs and cats), manufacturing
- Feed supplements, animal (except cat and dog), manufacturing
- Feed, prepared for animals (except dogs and cats), manufacturing
- Feed, specialty (e.g., for mice, guinea pig, mink), manufacturing
- Grain mills, animal feed
- Hay, cubed, manufacturing
- Livestock feeds, supplements, concentrates and premixes, manufacturing
- Micro and macro premixes, livestock, manufacturing
- Mineral feed supplements for animals (except dogs and cats), manufacturing
- Pet food (except dogs and cats), manufacturing
- Poultry feeds, supplements, concentrates and premixes, manufacturing
- Swine feeds, supplements, concentrates and premixes, manufacturing

3112 Grain and Oilseed Milling

This industry group comprises establishments primarily engaged in milling grains and oilseeds; refining and blending fats and oils; and making breakfast cereal products.

Exclusion(s): Establishments primarily engaged in:
- milling grain to make animal feed (3111, Animal Food Manufacturing).

31121 Flour Milling and Malt Manufacturing

This industry comprises establishments primarily engaged in grinding grains or vegetables; milling, cleaning and polishing rice; or manufacturing malt. Integrated mills, which grind grain and further process the milling products into such products as prepared flour mixes or doughs, are included.

Exclusion(s): Establishments primarily engaged in:
- milling grain to make animal feed (31111, Animal Food Manufacturing);
- crushing oilseeds or wet-milling corn (31122, Starch and Vegetable Fat and Oil Manufacturing);
- milling grain to make breakfast cereals (31123, Breakfast Cereal Manufacturing);
- manufacturing prepared flour mixes or doughs from purchased flour (31182, Cookie, Cracker and Pasta Manufacturing);
- mixing purchased rice with other dried ingredients (31199, All Other Food Manufacturing); and
- brewing malt beverages (31212, Breweries).

311211 Flour Milling US

This Canadian industry comprises establishments primarily engaged in grinding grains, fruits or vegetables, except rice. Integrated mills, which grind grain and further process the milling products into such products as prepared flour mixes or doughs, are included.

Exclusion(s): Establishments primarily engaged in:
- milling grain to make animal feed (31111, Animal Food Manufacturing);
- milling rice (311214, Rice Milling and Malt Manufacturing);
- wet-milling corn and other vegetables (311221, Wet Corn Milling);
- crushing oilseeds (311224, Oilseed Processing);
- milling grain to make breakfast cereals (311230, Breakfast Cereal Manufacturing); and
- manufacturing prepared flour mixes or doughs from purchased flour (311822, Flour Mixes and Dough Manufacturing from Purchased Flour).

Example Activities
- Bran, shorts and other products of milling grain (except rice)
- Cereal grain flour, manufacturing
- Corn flour, manufacturing
- Doughs, prepared, made in flour mills
- Flour mills, cereal grain (except rice, breakfast cereal and feed mills)
- Flour mixes (e.g., pancake, cake, biscuit, doughnut), made in flour mills
- Flour, cereal grain (except rice), made in flour mills
- Flour, vegetable and fruit, manufacturing
- Fruit flour, meal and powders, manufacturing
- Grain mills (except rice, breakfast cereal and animal feed)
- Vegetable flour, manufacturing

311214 Rice Milling and Malt Manufacturing CAN

This Canadian industry comprises establishments primarily engaged in milling rice; cleaning and polishing rice; manufacturing rice flour or meal; or manufacturing malt from barley, rye or other grains.

Exclusion(s): Establishments primarily engaged in:
- manufacturing malt extract (311940, Seasoning and Dressing Manufacturing);
- mixing rice with other dried ingredients (311990, All Other Food Manufacturing); and
- brewing malt beverages (312120, Breweries).

Example Activities
- Flour, malt, manufacturing
- Flour, rice, manufacturing
- Grain mills, rice
- Malt, manufacturing
- Rice brans, flour and meal, manufacturing
- Rice cleaning and polishing
- Rice malt, manufacturing
- Rice milling
- Rice mixes, made in rice mills

31122 Starch and Vegetable Fat and Oil Manufacturing

This industry comprises establishments primarily engaged in wet-milling corn and vegetables; crushing oilseeds and tree nuts and extracting oils; or processing or blending purchased fats and oils.

Exclusion(s): Establishments primarily engaged in:
- grinding flour and edible meal from grains and vegetables (31121, Flour Milling and Malt Manufacturing);
- manufacturing butter (31151, Dairy Product (except Frozen) Manufacturing);
- manufacturing lard (31161, Animal Slaughtering and Processing);
- processing marine fats and oils (31171, Seafood Product Preparation and Packaging);
- manufacturing table syrups from corn syrup, and starch-based dessert powders (31199, All Other Food Manufacturing); and
- manufacturing ethyl alcohol by the wet-mill process (32519, Other Basic Organic Chemical Manufacturing).

311221 Wet Corn Milling US

This Canadian industry comprises establishments primarily engaged in wet-milling corn and other vegetables. Establishments primarily engaged in manufacturing starch are included.

Exclusion(s): Establishments primarily engaged in:
- reducing maple sap to maple syrup (111999, All Other Miscellaneous Crop Farming);
- grinding (dry-milling) corn (311211, Flour Milling);
- manufacturing table syrups from corn syrup; and starch-based dessert powders (311990, All Other Food Manufacturing); and
- manufacturing ethyl alcohol by the wet-mill process (325190, Other Basic Organic Chemical Manufacturing).

Example Activities
- Cooking oil, made by wet-milling corn
- Corn gluten feed, manufacturing
- Corn gluten meal, manufacturing
- Corn oil, crude and refined, made by wet-milling corn
- Corn starch, manufacturing
- Corn sweeteners (e.g., dextrose, fructose, glucose), made by wet-milling corn
- Corn syrup, made by wet-milling corn
- Dextrose, made by wet-milling corn
- Feed, corn gluten, manufacturing
- Fructose, made by wet-milling corn
- Glucose, made by wet-milling corn
- Gluten feed, flour and meal, made by wet-milling corn
- Gluten, manufacturing
- Grain starches, manufacturing
- HFCS (high fructose corn syrup), manufacturing
- Margarine and other corn oils, made by wet-milling corn
- Meal, corn oil, made by wet-milling corn
- Oil, corn, crude and refined, made by wet-milling corn
- Potato starch, manufacturing
- Rice starch, manufacturing
- Starches (except laundry), manufacturing
- Syrup, corn, made by wet-milling
- Vegetable starches, manufacturing
- Wet-milling corn and other vegetables

311224 Oilseed Processing CAN

This Canadian industry comprises establishments primarily engaged in crushing oilseeds and tree nuts and extracting oils. Both edible and inedible products may be produced.

Exclusion(s): Establishments primarily engaged in:
- manufacturing corn oil by wet corn milling (311221, Wet Corn Milling); and
- processing purchased vegetable oils (311225, Fat and Oil Refining and Blending).

Example Activities

- Canola oil, cake and meal, made in crushing mills
- Cooking oil, made in oilseed crushing mills
- Fats and oils, made in oilseed crushing mills
- Linseed oil, cake and meal, made in crushing mills
- Margarine, cooking oil and similar oil and fat products, made in oilseed crushing mills
- Oil, vegetable, made in oilseed crushing mills
- Oilseed crushing mills
- Olive oil, made in crushing mills
- Peanut oil, cake and meal, made in crushing mills

- Rapeseed oil, made in crushing mills
- Shortening, made in oilseed crushing mills
- Soybean crushing mills
- Soybean oil, cake and meal, made in crushing mills
- Sunflower seed oil, cake and meal, made in crushing mills
- Tree nut oils (e.g., tung, walnut), made in crushing mills
- Vegetable oils, made in oilseed crushing mills
- Walnut oil (except artists' materials), made in crushing mills

311225 Fat and Oil Refining and Blending US

This Canadian industry comprises establishments primarily engaged in manufacturing fats and oils by processing crude or partially refined oils, for example to deodorize them; or blending purchased fats and oils. Both edible and inedible products may be produced. Both animal and vegetable fats and oils may be used.

Exclusion(s): Establishments primarily engaged in:
- manufacturing corn oil by wet corn milling (311221, Wet Corn Milling);
- manufacturing vegetable fats and oils by crushing oilseeds (311224, Oilseed Processing);
- manufacturing butter (311515, Butter, Cheese, and Dry and Condensed Dairy Product Manufacturing);
- manufacturing lard (311614, Rendering and Meat Processing from Carcasses); and
- processing marine fats and oils (311710, Seafood Product Preparation and Packaging).

Example Activities

- Blending purchased fats and oils
- Cooking oil, made from purchased fats and oils
- Fats and oils, made from purchased fats and oils
- Hydrogenating purchased oils
- Lecithin, made from purchased oils
- Linseed oil, made from purchased oils
- Margarine (including imitation), made from purchased fats and oils

- Margarine-butter blend, made from purchased fats and oils
- Oils, cooking, made from purchased fats and oils
- Re-refining purchased fats and oils
- Shortening, made from purchased fats and oils
- Tree nut oils (e.g., tung, walnut), made from purchased oils
- Vegetable cooking and table oils, made from purchased oils

31123 Breakfast Cereal Manufacturing

This industry comprises establishments primarily engaged in manufacturing breakfast cereal foods.

Exclusion(s): Establishments primarily engaged in:
- manufacturing chocolate-coated granola and breakfast bars (31133, Confectionery Manufacturing from Purchased Chocolate); and
- manufacturing granola and breakfast bars, except chocolate-coated (31134, Non-Chocolate Confectionery Manufacturing).

Example Activities
- Breakfast cereals made in flour mills
- Breakfast cereals, manufacturing
- Corn breakfast foods, manufacturing
- Infants' cereals, dry, manufacturing
- Ready-to-serve breakfast cereal foods, manufacturing
- Rice breakfast foods, manufacturing

311230 Breakfast Cereal Manufacturing

See industry description for 31123, above.

3113 Sugar and Confectionery Product Manufacturing

This industry group comprises establishments primarily engaged in manufacturing sugar and confectionery products.

31131 Sugar Manufacturing

This industry comprises establishments primarily engaged in manufacturing raw sugar, sugar syrup and refined sugar from sugar cane, raw cane sugar or sugar beets.

Exclusion(s): Establishments primarily engaged in:
- reducing maple sap to maple syrup (11199, All Other Crop Farming);
- manufacturing corn sweeteners (31122, Starch and Vegetable Fat and Oil Manufacturing);
- manufacturing table syrups from corn syrup; manufacturing starch-based dessert powders; and pasteurizing honey (31199, All Other Food Manufacturing); and
- manufacturing artificial sweeteners, such as aspartame and saccharine (32519, Other Basic Organic Chemical Manufacturing).

Example Activities
- Beet sugar refining
- Cane sugar refining
- Confectioners' sugar, manufacturing
- Granulated sugar, manufacturing
- Invert sugar, manufacturing
- Molasses, manufacturing
- Sugar, manufacturing
- Syrup, sugar, manufacturing

311310 Sugar Manufacturing CAN

See industry description for 31131, above.

31132 Chocolate and Confectionery Manufacturing from Cacao Beans

This industry comprises establishments primarily engaged in shelling, roasting and grinding cacao beans into chocolate cacao products and chocolate confectionery.

Exclusion(s): Establishments primarily engaged in:
- manufacturing chocolate and chocolate confectionery from purchased chocolate (31133, Confectionery Manufacturing from Purchased Chocolate); and
- manufacturing non-chocolate confectionery (31134, Non-Chocolate Confectionery Manufacturing).

Example Activities
- Cacao beans, shelling, roasting and grinding
- Candy bars, chocolate (including chocolate-covered), made from cacao beans
- Candy, chocolate, made from cacao beans
- Chocolate (e.g., coatings, instant, liquor, syrup), made from cacao beans
- Chocolate bars, made from cacao beans
- Chocolate confectionery, made from cacao beans
- Cocoa (e.g., instant, mix, powdered), made from cacao beans

- Confectionery, chocolate, made from cacao beans
- Fudge, chocolate, made from cacao beans
- Nuts, chocolate-covered, made from cacao beans
- Syrup, chocolate, made from cacao beans

311320 Chocolate and Confectionery Manufacturing from Cacao Beans

See industry description for 31132, above.

31133 Confectionery Manufacturing from Purchased Chocolate

This industry comprises establishments primarily engaged in manufacturing chocolate confectionery from purchased chocolate.

Exclusion(s): Establishments primarily engaged in:
- manufacturing chocolate confectionery from cacao beans (31132, Chocolate and Confectionery Manufacturing from Cacao Beans); and
- manufacturing non-chocolate confectionery (31134, Non-Chocolate Confectionery Manufacturing).

Example Activities
- Candy bars, chocolate (including chocolate-covered), made from purchased chocolate
- Candy stores, chocolate candy made on the premises, not for immediate consumption
- Candy, chocolate, made from purchased chocolate
- Chocolate (e.g., coatings, instant, liquor, syrup), made from purchased chocolate
- Chocolate bars, made from purchased chocolate
- Chocolate confectionery, made from purchased chocolate
- Chocolate-covered granola bars, made from purchased chocolate
- Cocoa powder drink, made from purchased chocolate
- Drinks, chocolate instant, made from purchased chocolate
- Fudge, chocolate, made from purchased chocolate
- Nuts, chocolate-covered, made from purchased chocolate
- Syrup, chocolate, made from purchased chocolate

311330 Confectionery Manufacturing from Purchased Chocolate

See industry description for 31133, above.

31134 Non-Chocolate Confectionery Manufacturing

This industry comprises establishments primarily engaged in manufacturing non-chocolate confectionery.

Exclusion(s): Establishments primarily engaged in:
- manufacturing chocolate confectionery from cacao beans (31132, Chocolate and Confectionery Manufacturing from Cacao Beans);
- manufacturing chocolate confectionery from purchased chocolate (31133, Confectionery Manufacturing from Purchased Chocolate); and
- roasting, salting, drying, cooking or canning nuts and seeds (31191, Snack Food Manufacturing).

Example Activities
- Candied fruits and fruit peel, manufacturing
- Candy (except chocolate), manufacturing
- Candy bars (except chocolate), manufacturing
- Candy stores (except chocolate), candy made on the premises, not for immediate consumption
- Chewing gum, manufacturing

- Confectionery, non-chocolate, manufacturing
- Corn confections (i.e., candy-coated), manufacturing
- Cough drops (except medicated), manufacturing
- Fruit peel products (e.g., candied, glazed, crystallized), manufacturing
- Fruits (e.g., candied, glazed, crystallized), manufacturing
- Fudge (except chocolate), manufacturing
- Granola bars and clusters (except chocolate-coated), manufacturing
- Gum, chewing, manufacturing
- Marshmallows, manufacturing
- Nuts, covered (except chocolate covered), manufacturing
- Popcorn balls and other candy-covered popcorn products, manufacturing
- Synthetic chocolate, manufacturing
- Toffee, manufacturing

311340 Non-Chocolate Confectionery Manufacturing

See industry description for 31134, above.

3114 Fruit and Vegetable Preserving and Specialty Food Manufacturing

This industry group comprises establishments primarily engaged in manufacturing frozen fruits and vegetables; frozen entrées and side dishes of several ingredients, except seafood; and fruits and vegetables preserved by pickling, canning, dehydrating and similar processes.

Exclusion(s): Establishments primarily engaged in:
- manufacturing frozen, canned or dried dairy products (3115, Dairy Product Manufacturing);
- manufacturing frozen, canned or dried meat products (3116, Meat Product Manufacturing);
- manufacturing frozen, canned or dried seafood products (3117, Seafood Product Preparation and Packaging);
- manufacturing frozen or canned bakery products (3118, Bakeries and Tortilla Manufacturing);
- mixing purchased dehydrated potatoes, rice, pasta and other ingredients; freezing, canning or dehydrating eggs; or canning puddings; (3119, Other Food Manufacturing); and
- manufacturing canned fruit-flavoured drinks (3121, Beverage Manufacturing).

31141 Frozen Food Manufacturing

This industry comprises establishments primarily engaged in manufacturing frozen fruits and vegetables; and frozen dinners and side dishes of several ingredients, except seafood.

Exclusion(s): Establishments primarily engaged in:
- freeze-drying fruits and vegetables (31142, Fruit and Vegetable Canning, Pickling and Drying);
- manufacturing frozen dairy products (31152, Ice Cream and Frozen Dessert Manufacturing);
- manufacturing frozen meat products (31161, Animal Slaughtering and Processing);
- manufacturing frozen seafood products (31171, Seafood Product Preparation and Packaging);
- manufacturing frozen bakery products (31181, Bread and Bakery Product Manufacturing);
- manufacturing frozen doughs, made from purchased flour (31182, Cookie, Cracker and Pasta Manufacturing); and
- freezing eggs; (31199, All Other Food Manufacturing).

Example Activities
- Blast freezing, on a contract basis
- Concentrates, frozen fruit and vegetable juice, manufacturing
- Dinners, frozen (except seafood-based), manufacturing
- French fries, frozen, pre-cooked, manufacturing
- French toast, frozen, manufacturing
- Frozen dinners (except seafood-based), manufacturing
- Frozen food entrées (except seafood-based), manufacturing
- Frozen fruit and vegetable processing

- Frozen fruits, fruit juices and vegetables, manufacturing
- Frozen pot pies, manufacturing
- Frozen side dishes (except seafood-based), manufacturing
- Frozen soups (except seafood), manufacturing
- Fruit juice concentrates, frozen, manufacturing

- Fruits, frozen, manufacturing
- Pizza, frozen, manufacturing
- Quick freezing of fruit and vegetables
- Soups, frozen (except seafood), manufacturing
- Vegetable juice concentrates, frozen, manufacturing
- Vegetables, frozen, manufacturing

311410 Frozen Food Manufacturing ^{CAN}

See industry description for 31141, above.

31142 Fruit and Vegetable Canning, Pickling and Drying

This industry comprises establishments primarily engaged in preserving fruits and vegetables by canning, pickling, brining and dehydrating (including freeze-drying). Canning uses heat sterilization; pickling uses vinegar solutions and brining uses salt solutions. Establishments primarily engaged in manufacturing mixtures of dried ingredients, such as soup mixes and salad dressing mixes, are included provided they dehydrate at least one of the ingredients.

Exclusion(s): Establishments primarily engaged in:
- manufacturing canned dairy products (31151, Dairy Product (except Frozen) Manufacturing);
- manufacturing canned meat products (31161, Animal Slaughtering and Processing);
- manufacturing canned seafood products, including soups (31171, Seafood Product Preparation and Packaging);
- mixing purchased dehydrated potatoes, rice, pasta and other ingredients; canning or dehydrating eggs; or canning puddings; (31199, All Other Food Manufacturing); and
- manufacturing canned fruit-flavoured drinks (31211, Soft Drink and Ice Manufacturing).

Example Activities
- Baby foods (including meats), canning
- Baked beans, canning
- Beans, baked, canning
- Bouillon, canning
- Bouillon, made in dehydration plants
- Brining of fruits and vegetables
- Canning fruits and vegetables
- Canning soups (except seafood)
- Dehydrating fruits and vegetables
- Dried fruits and vegetables, manufacturing
- Freeze-drying fruits and vegetables
- Fruit juices, canning
- Fruit juices, fresh, manufacturing
- Fruit, brining
- Fruit, canning
- Fruit, dehydrating (except sun drying)
- Fruit, pickling
- Infant and junior food, canning
- Jam, manufacturing
- Jelly and jam, manufacturing
- Juice, fruit or vegetable, canned, manufacturing

- Juice, fruit or vegetable, fresh, manufacturing
- Ketchup, manufacturing
- Marmalade, manufacturing
- Meat bouillon, made in dehydration plants
- Meat, baby food, canning
- Pasta-based products, canning
- Pickles, manufacturing
- Pickling fruits and vegetables
- Pork and beans, canning
- Potato products (e.g., flakes, granules), dehydrating
- Potatoes, canning
- Preserves, jams and jellies, manufacturing
- Raisins, made in dehydration plants
- Relishes, canning
- Salad dressing mixes, dry, made in dehydration plants
- Salsa, canning
- Sauce mixes, dry, made in dehydration plants
- Sauces, tomato-based, canning

- Sauerkraut, manufacturing
- Soup mixes, made in dehydration plants
- Soups (except seafood), canning
- Spaghetti sauce, canning
- Sulphured fruit and vegetables, manufacturing
- Tomato juice, manufacturing

- Tomato paste, manufacturing
- Vegetable juices, canning
- Vegetables, brining
- Vegetables, canning
- Vegetables, dehydrating
- Vegetables, pickling
- Vegetables, sulphured, manufacturing

311420 Fruit and Vegetable Canning, Pickling and Drying CAN

See industry description for 31142, above.

3115 Dairy Product Manufacturing

This industry group comprises establishments primarily engaged in manufacturing dairy products. Establishments primarily engaged in manufacturing substitute products are included.

31151 Dairy Product (except Frozen) Manufacturing

This industry comprises establishments primarily engaged in manufacturing dairy products, except frozen. Establishments primarily engaged in manufacturing substitute products are included.

Exclusion(s): Establishments primarily engaged in:
- manufacturing margarine or margarine-butter blends (31122, Starch and Vegetable Fat and Oil Manufacturing);
- manufacturing ice cream, frozen yogurt and other frozen dairy desserts (31152, Ice Cream and Frozen Dessert Manufacturing); and
- manufacturing cheese-based salad dressings (31194, Seasoning and Dressing Manufacturing).

311511 Fluid Milk Manufacturing US

This Canadian industry comprises establishments primarily engaged in manufacturing milk and processed milk products. Establishments primarily engaged in manufacturing substitute products are included.

Exclusion(s): Establishments primarily engaged in:
- manufacturing frozen whipped toppings (311410, Frozen Food Manufacturing);
- manufacturing dry mix whipped toppings and canned milk (311515, Butter, Cheese, and Dry and Condensed Dairy Product Manufacturing); and
- manufacturing ice cream, frozen yogurt and other frozen dairy desserts (311520, Ice Cream and Frozen Dessert Manufacturing).

Example Activities
- Acidophilus milk, manufacturing
- Buttermilk, manufacturing
- Cheese, cottage, manufacturing
- Chocolate milk, manufacturing
- Cottage cheese, manufacturing
- Cream, manufacturing
- Cream, sour, manufacturing
- Dairy, fluid milk
- Dips, sour-cream based, manufacturing
- Drinks, chocolate milk, manufacturing
- Eggnog, fresh, non-alcoholic, manufacturing
- Fluid milk substitutes, manufacturing
- Fluid milk, processing

- Milk processing (e.g., bottling, homogenizing, pasteurizing, vitaminizing)
- Milk substitutes, manufacturing
- Milk, acidophilus, manufacturing
- Milk, fluid (except canned), manufacturing
- Milk-based drinks (except dietary), manufacturing
- Non-dairy creamers, liquid, manufacturing
- Sour cream, manufacturing
- Whipped toppings (except frozen or dry mix), manufacturing
- Whipping cream, manufacturing
- Yogurt (except frozen), manufacturing

311515 Butter, Cheese, and Dry and Condensed Dairy Product Manufacturing CAN

This Canadian industry comprises establishments primarily engaged in manufacturing butter, cheese, and dry and condensed dairy products. Establishments primarily engaged in manufacturing substitute products are included.

Exclusion(s): Establishments primarily engaged in:
- manufacturing margarine or margarine-butter blends (311225, Fat and Oil Refining and Blending);
- manufacturing cottage cheese (311511, Fluid Milk Manufacturing); and
- manufacturing cheese-based salad dressings (311940, Seasoning and Dressing Manufacturing).

Example Activities
- Anhydrous butterfat, manufacturing
- Animal feed, dry milk products for, manufacturing
- Baby formula, fresh, processed and bottled, manufacturing
- Butter, creamery and whey, manufacturing
- Butter, manufacturing
- Cheese (except cottage cheese), manufacturing
- Cheese spreads, manufacturing
- Cheese, imitation or substitute, manufacturing
- Cheese, natural (except cottage cheese), manufacturing
- Cheese, processed, manufacturing
- Condensed, evaporated or powdered milk, manufacturing
- Cream, dried and powdered, manufacturing
- Creamery butter, manufacturing
- Curds, cheese, manufacturing
- Dairy products (except fluid milk)
- Dehydrated milk, manufacturing
- Dietary drinks, dairy and non-dairy base, manufacturing
- Dips, cheese-based, manufacturing
- Eggnog, canned, non-alcoholic, manufacturing
- Evaporated milk, manufacturing
- Ice cream mix, manufacturing
- Infants' formulas, manufacturing
- Lactose, manufacturing
- Milk, concentrated, condensed, dried, evaporated or powdered, manufacturing
- Milk, UHT (ultra-high temperature), manufacturing
- Milk-based drinks, dietary, manufacturing
- Non-dairy creamers, dry, manufacturing
- Powdered milk, manufacturing
- Processed cheese, manufacturing
- Spreads, cheese, manufacturing
- UHT (ultra-high temperature) milk, manufacturing
- Whey butter, manufacturing
- Whey, condensed, dried, evaporated and powdered, manufacturing
- Whey, raw, liquid, manufacturing
- Whipped topping, dry mix, manufacturing

31152 Ice Cream and Frozen Dessert Manufacturing

This industry comprises establishments primarily engaged in manufacturing ice cream and other frozen desserts.

Exclusion(s): Establishments primarily engaged in:
- manufacturing frozen bakery products (31181, Bread and Bakery Product Manufacturing).

Example Activities
- Custard, frozen, manufacturing
- Desserts, frozen (except bakery), manufacturing
- Frozen desserts (except bakery), manufacturing
- Fruit pops, frozen, manufacturing
- Ice cream specialties, manufacturing
- Ice cream, manufacturing
- Ice milk specialties, manufacturing
- Ice milk, manufacturing
- Ices, flavoured sherbets, manufacturing
- Juice pops, frozen, manufacturing
- Pops, dessert, frozen (i.e., flavoured ice, fruit, pudding and gelatin), manufacturing
- Sherbets, manufacturing
- Tofu frozen desserts, manufacturing
- Yogurt, frozen, manufacturing

311520 Ice Cream and Frozen Dessert Manufacturing

See industry description for 31152, above.

3116 Meat Product Manufacturing

This industry group comprises establishments primarily engaged in manufacturing meat products.

31161 Animal Slaughtering and Processing

This industry comprises establishments primarily engaged in slaughtering animals, including poultry; preparing processed meats and meat by-products; or rendering animal fat, bones and meat scraps.

Exclusion(s): Establishments primarily engaged in:
- producing animal feed from purchased meat products (31111, Animal Food Manufacturing);
- processing or blending purchased animal fats and oils (31122, Starch and Vegetable Fat and Oil Manufacturing);
- manufacturing frozen preparations of meat, poultry and other ingredients, such as frozen dinners (31141, Frozen Food Manufacturing);
- manufacturing preparations, except frozen or fresh, of meat, poultry and other ingredients, such as baby food and pork and beans (31142, Fruit and Vegetable Canning, Pickling and Drying); and
- manufacturing fresh preparations of meat, poultry and other ingredients, such as pizza and egg rolls (31199, All Other Food Manufacturing).

311611 Animal (except Poultry) Slaughtering US

This Canadian industry comprises establishments primarily engaged in slaughtering animals, except poultry and small game. Establishments that slaughter animals and then prepare meat products are included.

Exclusion(s): Establishments primarily engaged in:
- rendering animal fat, bones and meat scraps, or processing purchased meat carcasses (311614, Rendering and Meat Processing from Carcasses); and
- slaughtering poultry and small game (311615, Poultry Processing).

Example Activities
- Abattoirs
- Animal fats (except poultry and small game), produced in slaughtering plants
- Animal feed, slaughtering animals (except poultry and small game) for
- Bacon, slab and sliced, produced in slaughtering plants
- Beef carcasses, half-carcasses, primal and sub-primal cuts, produced in slaughtering plants
- Boxed meat (except poultry and small game), produced in slaughtering plants
- Canned meats (except poultry and small game), produced in slaughtering plants
- Custom slaughtering (except poultry and small game)
- Feed, animal, slaughtering animals (except poultry and small game) for
- Frozen meat and meat products (except poultry and small game), produced in slaughtering plants
- Hams (except poultry), produced in slaughtering plants
- Hides and skins, produced in slaughtering plants
- Horse meat, produced in slaughtering plants
- Lamb carcasses, half-carcasses, primal and sub-primal cuts, produced in slaughtering plants
- Lard, produced in slaughtering plants
- Luncheon meat (except poultry), produced in slaughtering plants
- Meat, cured or smoked (except poultry and small game), produced in slaughtering plants
- Meat, fresh, chilled or frozen (except poultry and small game), produced in slaughtering plants
- Pork carcasses, half-carcasses, primal and sub-primal cuts, produced in slaughtering plants

- Sausages and similar products, produced in slaughtering plants
- Slaughterhouses (except poultry and small game)
- Tallow, produced in slaughtering plants
- Variety meats (i.e., edible organs), produced in slaughtering plants

- Veal carcasses, half-carcasses, primal and sub-primal cuts, produced in slaughtering plants
- Weiners, sausages, luncheon meats and other prepared meat products (except poultry), produced in slaughtering plants

311614 Rendering and Meat Processing from Carcasses CAN

This Canadian industry comprises establishments primarily engaged in rendering animal fat, bones and meat scraps; or preparing meat and meat by-products from carcasses. Establishments known as boxed meat plants, primarily engaged in assembly-line cutting and packing of purchased carcasses, are included.

Exclusion(s): Establishments primarily engaged in:
- producing dog and cat food from purchased meat (311111, Dog and Cat Food Manufacturing);
- producing animal feed, except dog and cat food, from purchased meat (311119, Other Animal Food Manufacturing);
- processing or blending purchased animal fats and oils (311225, Fat and Oil Refining and Blending);
- manufacturing frozen preparations of meat and other ingredients, such as frozen dinners (311410, Frozen Food Manufacturing);
- manufacturing preparations, except frozen or fresh, of meat and other ingredients, such as baby food and pork and beans (311420, Fruit and Vegetable Canning, Pickling and Drying);
- manufacturing fresh preparations of meat, poultry and other ingredients, such as pizza and egg rolls (311990, All Other Food Manufacturing); and
- cutting and packing of purchased meat, except boxed meat cut on an assembly-line basis (413160, Red Meat and Meat Product Wholesaler-Distributors).

Example Activities
- Animal fats, rendering
- Animal feed, processing dead stock or carrion for
- Animal oil, rendering
- Bacon, slab and sliced, made from purchased meat
- Beef, primal and sub-primal cuts, made from purchased meat
- Boxed meat (except poultry), made by assembly-line cutting of purchased meat
- Canning meat (except poultry, small game, pet food, baby food), from purchased meat
- Corned meats, made from purchased meat
- Cured meats (e.g., brined, dried, salted), made from purchased meat
- Fats, animal, rendering
- Feed, animal, processing dead stock or carrion for
- Frozen meats (except poultry, small game, pet food and baby food), made from purchased meat
- Ham, preserved (except poultry), made from purchased meat
- Hot dogs (except poultry), made from purchased meat
- Lamb, primal and sub-primal cuts, made from purchased meat

- Luncheon meat (except poultry), made from purchased meat
- Meat and bone meal, and tankage, processed in rendering plants
- Meat canning (except poultry, small game, pet food, baby food), from purchased meat
- Meat curing, drying, salting, smoking or pickling, made from purchased meat
- Oil, animal, rendering
- Pork, primal and sub-primal cuts, made from purchased meat
- Poultry fat, rendering
- Rendering plants
- Salami, made from purchased meat
- Sausages and similar cased products, made from purchased meat
- Stearin, animal, rendering
- Tallow, produced in rendering plants
- Tourtière meat pies, frozen, made from purchased meat
- Veal, primal and sub-primal cuts, made from purchased meat
- Weiners, sausages, luncheon meats and other processed meat products (except poultry and small game), made from purchased meat

311615 Poultry Processing US

This Canadian industry comprises establishments primarily engaged in slaughtering poultry and small game or preparing processed poultry and small game meat and meat by-products.

Exclusion(s): Establishments primarily engaged in:
- producing dog and cat food from poultry products (311111, Dog and Cat Food Manufacturing);
- manufacturing frozen preparations of poultry and other ingredients, such as frozen dinners (311410, Frozen Food Manufacturing);
- manufacturing preparations, except frozen or fresh, of poultry and other ingredients, such as baby food (311420, Fruit and Vegetable Canning, Pickling and Drying); and
- manufacturing fresh preparations of poultry and other ingredients, such as fresh pot pies (311990, All Other Food Manufacturing).

Example Activities
- Canning poultry (except baby and pet food)
- Chicken processing, fresh, frozen, canned or cooked (except baby or pet food)
- Chickens, slaughtering and dressing
- Ducks, slaughtering and dressing
- Game, small, slaughtering and dressing
- Geese slaughtering and dressing
- Ham, poultry, manufacturing
- Hot dogs, poultry, manufacturing
- Luncheon meat, poultry, manufacturing
- Meat canning, poultry (except baby and pet food)
- Meat products (e.g., hot dogs, luncheon meats, sausages), made from a combination of poultry and other meats
- Poultry (e.g., canned, cooked, fresh, frozen) processing (except baby or pet food)
- Poultry slaughtering, dressing and packing
- Rabbits, slaughtering and dressing
- Small game, slaughtering and dressing
- Turkeys, slaughtering and dressing

3117 Seafood Product Preparation and Packaging

See industry description for 31171, below.

31171 Seafood Product Preparation and Packaging

This industry comprises establishments primarily engaged in canning seafood, including soup; smoking, salting and drying seafood; preparing fresh fish by removing heads, fins, scales, bones and entrails; shucking and packing fresh shellfish; processing marine fats and oils; and freezing seafood. Establishments known as "floating factory ships", that are engaged in shipboard processing of seafood, are included.

Example Activities
- Canning fish, crustaceans and molluscs
- Chowders, fish and seafood, canning
- Chowders, fish and seafood, frozen, manufacturing
- Chowders, fish and seafood, manufacturing
- Cod liver oil extraction (crude)
- Curing fish and seafood
- Dinners, frozen, seafood-based, manufacturing
- Drying fish and seafood
- Fish and marine animal oils, manufacturing
- Fish and seafood chowder, canning
- Fish egg bait, canning
- Fish freezing (e.g., blocks, fillets, ready-to-serve products)
- Fish meal, manufacturing
- Fish, canned and cured, manufacturing
- Fish, curing, drying, pickling, salting and smoking
- Fish, fresh or frozen, manufacturing
- Floating factory ships, seafood-processing
- Freezing fish (e.g., blocks, fillets, ready-to-serve products)
- Frozen seafood products, manufacturing
- Lobster cannery
- Marine fats, oils and meal, manufacturing
- Oil, fish and marine animal, manufacturing
- Roe, fish, processing
- Salmon cannery
- Seafood and seafood products, canning

- Seafood and seafood products, curing
- Seafood and seafood products, fresh prepared, manufacturing
- Seafood and seafood products, frozen, manufacturing
- Seafood dinners (e.g., fish and chips), frozen, manufacturing
- Seafood, fresh, chilled or frozen, manufacturing
- Seaweed processing (e.g., dulse)
- Ships, floating seafood-processing factory
- Shucking and packing fresh shellfish
- Soup, fish and seafood, canning
- Soup, fish and seafood, frozen, manufacturing

311710 Seafood Product Preparation and Packaging MEX

See industry description for 31171, above.

3118 Bakeries and Tortilla Manufacturing

This industry group comprises establishments primarily engaged in manufacturing baked goods. Establishments primarily engaged in manufacturing bakery products, for retail sale, but not for immediate consumption, are included.

31181 Bread and Bakery Product Manufacturing

This industry comprises establishments primarily engaged in manufacturing bakery products, except cookies and crackers. Establishments classified in this industry may sell to commercial or retail customers, for consumption off the premises.

Exclusion(s): Establishments primarily engaged in:
- manufacturing cookies and crackers (31182, Cookie, Cracker and Pasta Manufacturing);
- selling bakery products, not manufactured on the premises, not for immediate consumption; or made from prepared doughs, for retail sale (44529, Other Specialty Food Stores); and
- selling bakery products for immediate consumption, e.g. food court outlets, fast food outlets (72221, Limited-Service Eating Places).

311811 Retail Bakeries US

This Canadian industry comprises establishments primarily engaged in manufacturing bakery products, for retail sale, but not for immediate consumption. Establishments in this industry make bakery products from flour, not from prepared doughs.

Exclusion(s): Establishments primarily engaged in:
- manufacturing bakery products, other than for retail sale (311814, Commercial Bakeries and Frozen Bakery Product Manufacturing);
- selling bakery products, not manufactured on the premises, not for immediate consumption; or made from prepared doughs, for retail sale (445291, Baked Goods Stores); and
- selling bakery products, for immediate consumption, e.g. food court outlets, fast food outlets (722210, Limited-Service Eating Places).

Example Activity
- Bakeries with baking from flour on the premises, for retail sale but not immediate consumption

311814 Commercial Bakeries and Frozen Bakery Product Manufacturing CAN

This Canadian industry comprises establishments primarily engaged in manufacturing bakery products, other than for retail sale. Establishments primarily engaged in manufacturing frozen baked products are included.

Exclusion(s): Establishments primarily engaged in:
- manufacturing bakery products, for retail sale, not for immediate consumption (311811, Retail Bakeries);
- selling bakery products, not manufactured on the premises, not for immediate consumption; or made from prepared doughs, for retail sale (445291, Baked Goods Stores); and
- selling bakery products, for immediate consumption (722210, Limited-Service Eating Places).

Example Activities
- Bagels, made in commercial bakeries
- Bakery products, frozen (e.g., cakes, doughnuts, pastries), made in commercial bakeries
- Bakery products, partially cooked, not frozen, made in commercial bakeries
- Biscuits, bread-type, made in commercial bakeries
- Bread and bread-type rolls, made in commercial bakeries
- Buns, bread-type (e.g., hamburger, hot dog), made in commercial bakeries
- Croissants, baking, made in commercial bakeries

- Croutons and bread crumbs, made in commercial bakeries
- Desserts, frozen bakery, manufacturing
- Doughnuts, made in commercial bakeries
- Frozen bakery products, manufacturing
- Frozen bread and bread-type rolls, made in commercial bakeries
- Pastries (e.g., Danish, French), made in commercial bakeries
- Pies, dessert type (except ice cream), manufacturing
- Pretzels, soft, made in commercial bakeries
- Unleavened bread, made in commercial bakeries

31182 Cookie, Cracker and Pasta Manufacturing

This industry comprises establishments primarily engaged in manufacturing cookies and crackers; preparing flour mixes and dough from purchased flour; and manufacturing dry pasta.

Exclusion(s): Establishments primarily engaged in:
- grinding flour and preparing flour mixes or dough (31121, Flour Milling and Malt Manufacturing);
- manufacturing canned pasta specialties (31142, Fruit and Vegetable Canning, Pickling and Drying); and
- manufacturing fresh pasta (31199, All Other Food Manufacturing).

311821 Cookie and Cracker Manufacturing US

This Canadian industry comprises establishments primarily engaged in manufacturing cookies, crackers, biscuits and similar products.

Example Activities
- Bakery products, dry (e.g., biscuits, cookies, crackers), manufacturing
- Biscuits, dry, manufacturing
- Cookies, manufacturing

- Crackers (e.g., graham, soda), manufacturing
- Graham wafers, manufacturing
- Ice cream cones and wafers, manufacturing
- Soda crackers, manufacturing

311822 Flour Mixes and Dough Manufacturing from Purchased Flour US

This Canadian industry comprises establishments primarily engaged in manufacturing prepared flour mixes or dough from purchased flour.

Exclusion(s): Establishments primarily engaged in:
- grinding flour and preparing flour mixes or dough (311211, Flour Milling).

Example Activities

- Batters, prepared, made from purchased flour
- Biscuit mixes and doughs, made from purchased flour
- Bread and bread-type roll mixes, made from purchased flour
- Cake mixes, made from purchased flour
- Cookie dough, made from purchased flour
- Dough, refrigerated or frozen, made from purchased flour
- Flour mixes (e.g., biscuit, cake, doughnut, pancake), made from purchased flour
- Flour, blended or self-rising, made from purchased flour
- Frozen doughs, made from purchased flour
- Mixes, flour (e.g., biscuit, cake, doughnut, pancake), made from purchased flour
- Pancake mixes, made from purchased flour
- Pastries, uncooked, made from purchased flour
- Pastry mixes, prepared, made from purchased flour
- Pie crust shells, uncooked, made from purchased flour
- Pizza doughs, made from purchased flour

311823 Dry Pasta Manufacturing US

This Canadian industry comprises establishments primarily engaged in manufacturing dry pasta.

Exclusion(s): Establishments primarily engaged in:
- manufacturing frozen pasta dinners (311410, Frozen Food Manufacturing);
- manufacturing canned pasta products (311420, Fruit and Vegetable Canning, Pickling and Drying); and
- manufacturing fresh pasta, or mixes of purchased dry pasta and other ingredients (311990, All Other Food Manufacturing).

Example Activities

- Dry pasta, manufacturing
- Egg noodles, dry, manufacturing
- Macaroni, dry, manufacturing
- Noodles, dry, manufacturing
- Pasta mixes, made in dry pasta plants
- Pasta, dry, manufacturing
- Spaghetti, dry, manufacturing

31183 Tortilla Manufacturing

This industry comprises establishments primarily engaged in manufacturing tortillas.

Exclusion(s): Establishments primarily engaged in:
- manufacturing frozen tortillas (31141, Frozen Food Manufacturing);
- manufacturing canned tortillas (31142, Fruit and Vegetable Canning, Pickling and Drying); and
- manufacturing tortilla chips (31191, Snack Food Manufacturing).

Example Activity
- Tortillas, manufacturing

311830 Tortilla Manufacturing

See industry description for 31183, above.

3119 Other Food Manufacturing

This industry group comprises establishments, not classified to any other industry group, primarily engaged in manufacturing food.

31191 Snack Food Manufacturing

This industry comprises establishments primarily engaged in salting, roasting, drying, cooking or canning nuts; processing grains or seeds into snacks; manufacturing peanut butter; or manufacturing potato chips, corn chips, popped popcorn, hard pretzels, pork rinds and similar snacks.

Exclusion(s): Establishments primarily engaged in:
- manufacturing chocolate-coated nuts from cacao beans (31132, Chocolate and Confectionery Manufacturing from Cacao Beans);
- manufacturing chocolate-coated nuts from purchased chocolate (31133, Confectionery Manufacturing from Purchased Chocolate);
- manufacturing candy-coated nuts and candy-covered popcorn (31134, Non-Chocolate Confectionery Manufacturing);
- manufacturing cookies and crackers (31182, Cookie, Cracker and Pasta Manufacturing); and
- manufacturing corn for popping (31199, All Other Food Manufacturing).

311911 Roasted Nut and Peanut Butter Manufacturing US

This Canadian industry comprises establishments primarily engaged in salting, roasting, drying, cooking or canning nuts; processing grains or seeds into snacks; or manufacturing peanut butter.

Exclusion(s): Establishments primarily engaged in:
- processing grains and seeds for animal consumption (311119, Other Animal Food Manufacturing);
- manufacturing chocolate-coated nuts from cacao beans (311320, Chocolate and Confectionery Manufacturing from Cacao Beans);
- manufacturing chocolate-coated nuts from purchased chocolate (311330, Confectionery Manufacturing from Purchased Chocolate); and
- manufacturing candy-coated nuts (311340, Non-Chocolate Confectionery Manufacturing).

Example Activities
- Butter, peanut, manufacturing
- Canned nuts, manufacturing
- Nuts, kernels and seeds, roasting and processing
- Nuts, salted, roasted, cooked or canned, manufacturing
- Peanut butter blended with jelly, manufacturing
- Peanut butter, manufacturing
- Roasted nuts and seeds, manufacturing
- Seeds, snack (e.g., canned, cooked, roasted, salted), manufacturing

311919 Other Snack Food Manufacturing US

This Canadian industry comprises establishments, not classified to any other Canadian industry, primarily engaged in manufacturing snack foods.

Exclusion(s): Establishments primarily engaged in:
- manufacturing candy-covered popcorn (311340, Non-Chocolate Confectionery Manufacturing);
- manufacturing cookies and crackers (311821, Cookie and Cracker Manufacturing);
- salting, roasting, drying, cooking or canning nuts and seeds (311911, Roasted Nut and Peanut Butter Manufacturing); and
- manufacturing corn for popping (311990, All Other Food Manufacturing).

Example Activities
- Cheese curls and puffs, manufacturing
- Corn chips and related corn snacks, manufacturing
- Popcorn, popped (except candy-covered), manufacturing
- Pork rinds, manufacturing
- Potato chips, manufacturing
- Pretzels (except soft), manufacturing
- Tortilla chips, manufacturing

31192 Coffee and Tea Manufacturing

This industry comprises establishments primarily engaged in roasting coffee; manufacturing coffee and tea extracts and concentrates, including instant and freeze dried; blending tea; or manufacturing herbal tea. Establishments primarily engaged in manufacturing coffee and tea substitutes are included.

Exclusion(s): Establishments primarily engaged in:
- bottling and canning iced tea or coffee (31211, Soft Drink and Ice Manufacturing).

Example Activities
- Coffee extracts, manufacturing
- Coffee flavourings and syrups (i.e., made from coffee), manufacturing
- Coffee roasting
- Coffee substitutes, manufacturing
- Coffee, blended, manufacturing
- Coffee, instant and freeze-dried, manufacturing
- Extracts, essences and preparations, coffee, manufacturing
- Extracts, essences and preparations, tea, manufacturing
- Freeze-dried coffee, manufacturing
- Herbal tea, manufacturing
- Instant coffee, manufacturing
- Instant tea, manufacturing
- Roasting coffee
- Tea blending
- Tea, herbal, manufacturing

311920 Coffee and Tea Manufacturing US

See industry description for 31192, above.

31193 Flavouring Syrup and Concentrate Manufacturing

This industry comprises establishments primarily engaged in manufacturing soft drink concentrates and syrup, and related products for soda fountain use or for making soft drinks.

Exclusion(s): Establishments primarily engaged in:
- reducing maple sap to maple syrup (11199, All Other Crop Farming);
- manufacturing chocolate syrup from cacao beans (31132, Chocolate and Confectionery Manufacturing from Cacao Beans);
- manufacturing chocolate syrup from purchased chocolate (31133, Confectionery Manufacturing from Purchased Chocolate);
- manufacturing flavouring extracts (31194, Seasoning and Dressing Manufacturing);
- manufacturing powdered drink mixes (except coffee, tea and chocolate); and table syrup from corn syrup (31199, All Other Food Manufacturing); and
- manufacturing soft drinks (31211, Soft Drink and Ice Manufacturing).

Example Activities
- Beverage bases, manufacturing
- Concentrates, drink (except frozen fruit juice), manufacturing
- Concentrates, flavouring (except coffee-based), manufacturing
- Flavouring concentrates (except coffee-based), manufacturing
- Flavouring pastes, powders and syrups, for soft drinks, manufacturing
- Fruit syrups, flavouring, manufacturing
- Soda fountain syrups, manufacturing
- Soft drink concentrates (i.e., syrup), manufacturing
- Syrup, beverage, manufacturing
- Syrup, flavouring (except coffee-based), manufacturing

311930 Flavouring Syrup and Concentrate Manufacturing

See industry description for 31193, above.

31194 Seasoning and Dressing Manufacturing

This industry comprises establishments primarily engaged in manufacturing dressings and seasonings.

Exclusion(s): Establishments primarily engaged in:
- manufacturing ketchup and other tomato-based sauces; canning gravy; manufacturing bouillon and dry salad dressing mixes by dehydrating ingredients (31142, Fruit and Vegetable Canning, Pickling and Drying);
- manufacturing flavouring syrups (31193, Flavouring Syrup and Concentrate Manufacturing); and
- manufacturing industrial salts (32599, All Other Chemical Product Manufacturing).

Example Activities
- Cheese-based salad dressings, manufacturing
- Cider vinegar, manufacturing
- Cider, non-alcoholic, manufacturing
- Colourings, natural food, manufacturing
- Dips (except cheese and sour cream-based), manufacturing
- Extracts, food (except coffee, meat), manufacturing
- Flavouring extracts (except coffee), manufacturing
- Food colourings, natural, manufacturing
- Fruit extracts (except coffee), manufacturing
- Gravy mixes, dry, manufacturing
- Horseradish, prepared sauce, manufacturing
- Malt extract, manufacturing
- Mayonnaise, manufacturing
- Mustard, prepared, manufacturing
- Pepper (i.e., spice), manufacturing
- Salad dressing mixes, dry, manufacturing
- Salad dressings, manufacturing
- Salt, substitute, manufacturing
- Sandwich spreads, manufacturing
- Sauce mixes, dry, manufacturing
- Sauces (except tomato-based, gravy), manufacturing
- Seasoning salt, manufacturing
- Soy sauce, manufacturing
- Spice grinding and blending
- Table salt, manufacturing
- Vinegar, manufacturing
- Worcestershire sauce, manufacturing

311940 Seasoning and Dressing Manufacturing ᴹᴱˣ

See industry description for 31194, above.

31199 All Other Food Manufacturing

This industry comprises establishments, not classified to any other industry, primarily engaged in manufacturing food. Establishments primarily engaged in manufacturing and packaging for individual resale, perishable prepared foods such as salads, fresh pizza, fresh pasta, and peeled or cut vegetables, are included.

Example Activities
- Baking powder, manufacturing
- Box lunches, for sale off premises, manufacturing
- Carrots, fresh (i.e., cut, peeled, polished or sliced), manufacturing
- Coconut, desiccated and shredded, manufacturing
- Cole slaw, fresh, manufacturing
- Coleslaw, fresh, manufacturing
- Corn for popping, manufacturing
- Corn syrups, made from purchased sweeteners
- Desserts, ready-to-mix, manufacturing
- Drink powder mixes (except chocolate, coffee, milk-based, tea), manufacturing
- Egg substitutes, manufacturing
- Eggs, processed, manufacturing
- Fillings, cake or pie (except fruit, meat, vegetable), manufacturing
- Food, prepared, perishable, packaged for individual resale
- Gelatin dessert preparations, manufacturing
- Gravy (except dry mix), manufacturing
- Honey processing
- Jelly powders, manufacturing
- Pasta mixes, made from purchased dried ingredients

- Pasta, fresh, manufacturing
- Pizza, fresh, manufacturing
- Popcorn (except popped), manufacturing
- Potato mixes, made from purchased dried ingredients
- Potatoes, fresh (i.e., cut, peeled, polished or sliced), manufacturing
- Powdered drink mixes (except chocolate, coffee, milk-based, tea), manufacturing
- Powders, baking, manufacturing
- Prepared meals, perishable, packaged for individual resale
- Rice mixes, made from purchased dried ingredients

- Salads, fresh or refrigerated, manufacturing
- Sandwiches, fresh (i.e., assembled and packaged for the wholesale market), manufacturing
- Soup mixes, dry, made from purchased dry ingredients
- Sweetening syrups (except pure maple), made from purchased sweeteners
- Syrups, table, artificially flavoured, manufacturing
- Tofu (i.e., bean curd) (except frozen desserts), manufacturing
- Vegetables, fresh (i.e., cut, peeled, polished or sliced), manufacturing
- Yeast, manufacturing

311990 All Other Food Manufacturing CAN

See industry description for 31199, above.

312 Beverage and Tobacco Product Manufacturing

This subsector comprises establishments primarily engaged in manufacturing beverages and tobacco products.

3121 Beverage Manufacturing

This industry group comprises establishments primarily engaged in manufacturing beverages.

Exclusion(s): Establishments primarily engaged in:
- canning fruit and vegetable juices; freezing juices and drinks (3114, Fruit and Vegetable Preserving and Specialty Food Manufacturing);
- manufacturing milk-based drinks (3115, Dairy Product Manufacturing); and
- manufacturing soft drink bases or fruit syrups for flavouring; coffee and tea, except ready-to-drink; powdered drink mixes; and non-alcoholic cider (3119, Other Food Manufacturing).

31211 Soft Drink and Ice Manufacturing

This industry comprises establishments primarily engaged in manufacturing soft drinks, ice or bottled water, including that which is naturally carbonated. Water-bottling establishments in this industry purify the water before bottling it.

Exclusion(s): Establishments primarily engaged in:
- freezing juices and drinks (31141, Frozen Food Manufacturing);
- canning fruit and vegetable juices (31142, Fruit and Vegetable Canning, Pickling and Drying);
- manufacturing milk-based drinks (31151, Dairy Product (except Frozen) Manufacturing);
- manufacturing coffee and tea, except ready-to-drink (31192, Coffee and Tea Manufacturing);
- manufacturing soft drink bases or fruit syrups for flavouring (31193, Flavouring Syrup and Concentrate Manufacturing);
- manufacturing non-alcoholic cider (31194, Seasoning and Dressing Manufacturing);
- manufacturing non-alcoholic beer (31212, Breweries);
- manufacturing non-alcoholic wine (31213, Wineries);
- manufacturing dry ice (32512, Industrial Gas Manufacturing); and
- bottling water without purification (41321, Non-Alcoholic Beverage Wholesaler-Distributors).

Example Activities
- Block ice, manufacturing
- Bottling flavoured water
- Carbonated soda, manufacturing
- Carbonated soft drinks, manufacturing
- Coffee, iced, manufacturing
- Drinks, fruit (except juice), manufacturing
- Fruit drinks (except juice), manufacturing
- Ice (except dry ice), manufacturing
- Iced tea, manufacturing
- Mineral waters, purifying and bottling
- Naturally carbonated water, purifying and bottling
- Pop, soda, manufacturing
- Soda, carbonated, manufacturing
- Soft drinks, manufacturing
- Spring waters, purifying and bottling
- Tea, iced, manufacturing
- Water, artificially carbonated, manufacturing
- Water, naturally carbonated, purifying and bottling
- Water, purifying and bottling

312110 Soft Drink and Ice Manufacturing CAN

See industry description for 31211, above.

31212 Breweries

This industry comprises establishments primarily engaged in brewing beer, ale, malt liquors and non-alcoholic beer.

Exclusion(s): Establishments primarily engaged in:
- manufacturing malt (31121, Flour Milling and Malt Manufacturing); and
- bottling purchased malt beverages (41322, Alcoholic Beverage Wholesaler-Distributors).

Example Activities
- Ale, brewing
- Beer, brewing
- Breweries
- Lager, brewing
- Non-alcoholic beer, brewing
- Porter, brewing
- Stout, brewing

312120 Breweries

See industry description for 31212, above.

31213 Wineries

This industry comprises establishments primarily engaged in manufacturing wine or brandy, from grapes or other fruit. Establishments primarily engaged in growing grapes and manufacturing wine; manufacturing wine from purchased grapes and other fruit; blending wines; or distilling brandy are included.

Exclusion(s): Establishments primarily engaged in:
- bottling purchased wine (41322, Alcoholic Beverage Wholesaler-Distributors).

Example Activities
- Blending wines
- Brandy, distilling
- Champagne-method sparkling wines, manufacturing
- Cider, alcoholic, manufacturing
- Distilling brandy
- Fruit brandy, distilling
- Grape growing and making wine
- Non-alcoholic wine, manufacturing
- Sparkling wines, manufacturing
- Wine (grape, berry or other fruit), manufacturing
- Wine coolers, manufacturing
- Wineries

312130 Wineries US

See industry description for 31213, above.

31214 Distilleries

This industry comprises establishments primarily engaged in distilling liquor, except brandy; blending liquor; or blending and mixing liquor and other ingredients.

Exclusion(s): Establishments primarily engaged in:
- manufacturing brandy (31213, Wineries);
- manufacturing non-potable ethanol (ethyl alcohol) (32519, Other Basic Organic Chemical Manufacturing); and
- bottling purchased liquor (41322, Alcoholic Beverage Wholesaler-Distributors).

Example Activities
- Alcoholic beverages (except brandy), distilling
- Blending distilled beverages (except brandy)
- Cordials, alcoholic, manufacturing
- Distilleries
- Distilling alcoholic beverages (except brandy)
- Eggnog, alcoholic, manufacturing
- Ethyl alcohol, potable, manufacturing
- Grain alcohol, beverage purposes, manufacturing
- Liqueurs, manufacturing
- Liquor-based coolers, manufacturing
- Liquors, distilling and blending (except brandy)
- Mixed drinks, alcoholic, manufacturing
- Rum, manufacturing
- Vodka, manufacturing
- Whisky, manufacturing

312140 Distilleries US

See industry description for 31214, above.

3122 Tobacco Manufacturing

This industry group comprises establishments primarily engaged in manufacturing tobacco products.

31221 Tobacco Stemming and Redrying

This industry comprises establishments primarily engaged in stemming or redrying tobacco. These establishments perform the final sorting, grading, redrying, treating and packing of tobacco leaf, and they typically age the tobacco.

Example Activities
- Leaf tobacco processing and aging
- Tobacco leaf processing and aging
- Tobacco stemming and redrying

312210 Tobacco Stemming and Redrying

See industry description for 31221, above.

31222 Tobacco Product Manufacturing

This industry comprises establishments primarily engaged in manufacturing cigarettes and other tobacco products.

Exclusion(s): Establishments primarily engaged in:
- stemming and redrying tobacco (31221, Tobacco Stemming and Redrying).

Example Activities
- Cigarette tobacco, prepared, manufacturing
- Cigarettes, manufacturing
- Cigars, manufacturing
- Imitation tobacco cigarettes, manufacturing
- Pipe tobacco, prepared, manufacturing
- Snuff, manufacturing
- Tobacco products (e.g., chewing, smoking, snuff), manufacturing

312220 Tobacco Product Manufacturing ^{CAN}

See industry description for 31222, above.

313 Textile Mills

This subsector comprises establishments primarily engaged in manufacturing yarn or textile fabrics, or finishing yarn, textile fabrics or clothing. Establishments primarily engaged in manufacturing both fabrics and textile products, except knitted clothing, are included.

Exclusion(s): Establishments primarily engaged in:
- manufacturing textile products, except clothing, from purchased fabric (314, Textile Product Mills); and
- manufacturing clothing (315, Clothing Manufacturing).

3131 Fibre, Yarn and Thread Mills

See industry description for 31311, below.

31311 Fibre, Yarn and Thread Mills

This industry comprises establishments primarily engaged in spinning yarn from fibres; texturing, throwing or twisting man-made fibre filaments or purchased yarns; or manufacturing thread for sewing, crocheting, embroidery, tatting and similar uses.

Exclusion(s): Establishments primarily engaged in:
- finishing yarn or thread (31331, Textile and Fabric Finishing);
- manufacturing artificial and synthetic fibres and filaments (32522, Artificial and Synthetic Fibres and Filaments Manufacturing); and
- manufacturing glass fibres (32721, Glass and Glass Product Manufacturing).

Example Activities
- Animal fibre yarn, spooling, twisting or winding purchased yarn
- Beaming wool yarn
- Beaming yarn
- Carpet and rug yarn, spinning
- Cotton spun yarn, manufacturing
- Crochet spun yarns (e.g., cotton, man-made fibre, silk, wool), made from purchased fibre
- Embroidery spun yarns (e.g., cotton, man-made fibre, silk, wool), made from purchased fibres
- Hemp bags and ropes, made in spinning mills
- Knitting and crochet thread, manufacturing
- Knitting yarn (e.g., cotton, man-made fibre, silk, wool), made in spinning mills
- Paper yarn, manufacturing
- Sewing thread, manufacturing
- Spinning carpet and rug yarns from purchased fibre
- Spinning yarns from purchased fibre
- Spooling yarn
- Texturizing purchased monofilament yarn
- Thread mills
- Throwing purchased man-made fibres and yarns
- Throwing, twisting and winding purchased yarn
- Winding, spooling, beaming and rewinding purchased yarn
- Wool yarn, spinning
- Yarn spinning mills
- Yarn, throwing, twisting and winding of purchased yarn

313110 Fibre, Yarn and Thread Mills CAN

See industry description for 31311, above.

3132 Fabric Mills

This industry group comprises establishments primarily engaged in manufacturing textile fabrics. Establishments classified in this industry group may finish the fabrics that they manufacture. Establishments primarily engaged in manufacturing both fabrics and textile products, except knitted clothing, are included.

Exclusion(s): Establishments primarily engaged in:
- finishing textile fabrics; and coating fabrics (3133, Textile and Fabric Finishing and Fabric Coating); and
- manufacturing tire cord fabric (3149, Other Textile Product Mills).

31321 Broad-Woven Fabric Mills

This industry comprises establishments primarily engaged in weaving broad fabrics. Establishments classified in this industry may finish the fabrics that they weave. Establishments primarily engaged in manufacturing textile products from broad-woven fabrics made in the same establishment are included.

Exclusion(s): Establishments primarily engaged in:
- knitting fabrics (31324, Knit Fabric Mills); and
- manufacturing tire cord fabric (31499, All Other Textile Product Mills).

Example Activities
- Blankets and bedspreads, made in weaving mills
- Broad-woven (more than 30 cm/12 in. wide) fabrics (except rugs, tire fabrics), weaving
- Elastic fabrics, broad-woven, weaving
- Fabrics (except rugs, tire fabrics), broad-woven, weaving
- Fabrics, broad-woven, natural hard fibres (e.g., linen, jute, hemp, ramie), weaving
- Glass fabrics, broad-woven, weaving
- Hand weaving fabrics (more than 30 cm/12 in.) in width
- Linen fabrics, broad-woven, weaving
- Man-made fabrics, broad-woven, weaving
- Natural hard fibre fabrics (e.g., linen, jute, hemp, ramie), broad-woven, weaving
- Sheets and pillow cases, made in broad-woven fabric mills
- Textile broad-woven fabrics mills
- Textile products (except clothing), made in broad fabric weaving mills
- Weaving and finishing of broad-woven fabrics (except rugs, tire fabric)
- Weaving broad-woven fabrics (except rugs, tire fabric)
- Weaving broad-woven felts
- Wool fabrics, broad-woven, weaving
- Wool felts, broad-woven, weaving

313210 Broad-Woven Fabric Mills

See industry description for 31321, above.

31322 Narrow Fabric Mills and Schiffli Machine Embroidery

This industry comprises establishments primarily engaged in weaving or braiding narrow fabrics; or manufacturing embroideries with Schiffli machines. Establishments classified in this industry may finish the fabrics that they manufacture. Establishments primarily engaged in manufacturing fabric-covered elastic thread, yarn and cord are included.

Exclusion(s): Establishments primarily engaged in:
- embroidering textile products (31499, All Other Textile Product Mills).

Example Activities

- Braiding narrow fabrics
- Cords and braids, narrow woven, manufacturing
- Elastic thread, yarn and cord, fabric-covered, manufacturing
- Embroideries, Schiffli machine, manufacturing
- Fabrics, narrow woven (i.e., 30 cm/12 in. or less in width), weaving
- Fibreglass fabric, narrow woven (i.e., 30 cm/12 in. or less in width), weaving
- Glass fabric, narrow woven (i.e., 30 cm/12 in. or less in width), weaving
- Hand weaving narrow fabrics (i.e., 30 cm/12 in. or less in width)
- Labels, weaving
- Laces (e.g., shoe), textile, manufacturing
- Man-made fibre fabric, narrow woven (i.e., 30 cm/12 in. or less in width), weaving
- Narrow fabrics (i.e., 30 cm/12 in. or less in width), weaving
- Paper fabric, narrow woven (i.e., 30 cm/12 in. or less in width), weaving
- Ribbons, made in narrow woven fabric mills
- Rubber thread and yarns, fabric-covered, manufacturing
- Schiffli machine embroideries, manufacturing
- Textile mills, narrow woven fabric
- Textile products (except clothing), made in narrow woven fabric mills
- Thread, elastic, fabric-covered, manufacturing
- Trimmings, made in narrow fabric weaving mills
- Weaving narrow fabrics
- Wool fabric, narrow woven (i.e., 30 cm/12 in. or less in width), weaving
- Yarn, elastic, fabric-covered, manufacturing
- Zipper tape, weaving

313220 Narrow Fabric Mills and Schiffli Machine Embroidery MEX

See industry description for 31322, above.

31323 Nonwoven Fabric Mills

This industry comprises establishments primarily engaged in manufacturing nonwoven fabrics, by bonding and/or interlocking fibres. Mechanical, chemical, thermal and solvent methods, and combinations thereof, are used. Establishments classified in this industry may finish the fabrics that they manufacture.

Exclusion(s): Establishments primarily engaged in:
- manufacturing woven felts or papermakers' felts (31321, Broad-Woven Fabric Mills).

Example Activities

- Carpet paddings, nonwoven, manufacturing
- Fabrics, nonwoven, manufacturing
- Felts, nonwoven, manufacturing
- Nonwoven fabrics, manufacturing
- Nonwoven felts, manufacturing
- Padding and wadding, nonwoven fabric, manufacturing
- Ribbons, made in nonwoven fabric mills

313230 Nonwoven Fabric Mills

See industry description for 31323, above.

31324 Knit Fabric Mills

This industry comprises establishments primarily engaged in knitting fabrics, on both circular (weft fabric) and flat-bed (warp fabric) machines. Establishments primarily engaged in manufacturing double and single knits, warp knits and interlock knits; manufacturing special construction fabrics by the Malimo, Arachne and similar processes; manufacturing knit lace; and making textile products in knitting mills are included. Establishments classified in this industry may finish the fabrics that they knit.

Example Activities

- Bags and bagging fabrics, made in knitting mills
- Bedspreads and bed sets, made in knitting mills
- Curtains, made in knitting mills
- Fabrics, lace, made in lace mills
- Fabrics, made in knitting mills
- Hand knitting
- Knitting fabric
- Lace, manufacturing
- Netting, made in knitting mills
- Pile fabrics, weft knit, made in knitting mills
- Towels and washcloths, made in knitting mills

313240 Knit Fabric Mills ᴹᴱˣ

See industry description for 31324, above.

3133 Textile and Fabric Finishing and Fabric Coating

This industry group comprises establishments primarily engaged in finishing yarn and thread, textile fabrics, textile products (except carpets and rugs), and clothing; and manufacturing coated or laminated fabrics.

Exclusion(s): Establishments primarily engaged in:
- finishing carpets and rugs (3141, Textile Furnishings Mills);
- embroidering textile products and clothing (3149, Other Textile Product Mills);
- knitting and finishing clothing in the same establishment (3151, Clothing Knitting Mills);
- manufacturing (cut-and-sew) and finishing clothing in the same establishment (3152, Cut and Sew Clothing Manufacturing);
- fur dressing and dyeing (3161, Leather and Hide Tanning and Finishing); and
- printing on articles of clothing, not made in the same establishment (3231, Printing and Related Support Activities).

31331 Textile and Fabric Finishing

This industry comprises establishments primarily engaged in finishing yarn and thread, textile fabrics, textile products (except carpets and rugs), and clothing, not made in the same establishment. Finishing operations include bleaching; dyeing; printing fabrics (roller, screen, flock, plisse); chemical finishing for water repellency, fire resistance and mildew proofing; and mechanical finishing, such as preshrinking, calendering, napping and stone-washing. Establishments, known as converters, primarily engaged in buying fabric in the grey and having it finished by contractors, are included.

Exclusion(s): Establishments primarily engaged in:
- coating, rubberizing, varnishing or waxing fabrics (31332, Fabric Coating);
- finishing carpets and rugs (31411, Carpet and Rug Mills);
- embroidering textile products and clothing (31499, All Other Textile Product Mills);
- knitting and finishing hosiery and socks, in the same establishment (31511, Hosiery and Sock Mills);
- knitting and finishing clothing, except hosiery and socks, in the same establishment (31519, Other Clothing Knitting Mills);
- manufacturing and finishing men's and boys' cut-and-sew clothing, in the same establishment (31522, Men's and Boys' Cut and Sew Clothing Manufacturing);
- manufacturing and finishing women's and girls' cut-and-sew clothing, in the same establishment (31523, Women's and Girls' Cut and Sew Clothing Manufacturing);
- manufacturing and finishing other cut-and-sew clothing, in the same establishment (31529, Other Cut and Sew Clothing Manufacturing);
- fur dressing and dyeing (31611, Leather and Hide Tanning and Finishing); and
- printing on clothing (323113, Commercial Screen Printing).

Example Activities

- Batik work (hand painting on textile fabrics)
- Bleaching textile fibres, thread, yarn or fabrics
- Bleaching textile products (including clothing)
- Burling and mending fabrics, for the trade
- Calendering textile fabrics or textile products (including clothing)
- Carbonizing textile fibres
- Carding textile fibres
- Chemical finishing (e.g., for fire, mildew, water resistance) of textile fabrics, for the trade
- Combing textile fibres
- Dyeing clothing
- Dyeing textile products, for the trade
- Dyeing textile raw stock, fibres, thread, yarn or fabrics
- Embossing textile products (including clothing)
- Finishing clothing
- Finishing purchased fabrics
- Finishing textile fabrics
- Flock printing of textile fabrics
- Hair, animal (except horse), preparation (e.g., dressing, heckling, teasing, willowing)
- Hosiery dyeing and finishing
- Knit fabrics, dyeing or finishing
- Mechanical finishing of clothing
- Mercerizing textile fibres and fabrics
- Mildew proofing textile fabrics and products
- Napping textile fabrics
- Preparing textile fibres for spinning
- Preshrinking textile fabrics and clothing
- Printed fabrics, made from purchased fabric
- Printing on narrow fabrics
- Printing on textile fabrics
- Scouring and combing textile fibres
- Shrinking textile fabrics and products (including clothing)
- Sponging textile fabrics
- Sponging textiles for tailors and dressmakers
- Stone washing textile fabrics and clothing, for the trade
- Sueding textile fabrics
- Teaseling textile fabrics
- Textile products finishing
- Thread bleaching, dyeing and finishing
- Yarn bleaching, dyeing and finishing

313310 Textile and Fabric Finishing ^{CAN}

See industry description for 31331, above.

31332 Fabric Coating

This industry comprises establishments primarily engaged in manufacturing coated or laminated fabrics; and in finishing textile fabrics or clothing by coating, laminating, rubberizing, varnishing, waxing or similar processes.

Example Activities

- Impregnating and coating of fabrics
- Laminating purchased textile fabrics
- Leather, artificial, made from purchased fabric
- Metallizing textile fabrics
- Oiling (i.e., waterproofing) purchased textiles and clothing
- Raincoats, oiling (i.e., waterproofing)
- Rubberizing fabrics and clothing
- Tapes, varnished and coated (except magnetic), made from purchased fabric
- Varnishing textile fabrics and clothing
- Waterproofing clothing
- Waterproofing fabrics, for the trade
- Waxing fabrics and clothing

313320 Fabric Coating

See industry description for 31332, above.

314 Textile Product Mills

This subsector comprises establishments primarily engaged in manufacturing textile products, except clothing.

Exclusion(s): Establishments primarily engaged in:
- manufacturing yarn or textile fabrics, or finishing yarn or fabrics, or manufacturing both fabrics and textile products (313, Textile Mills); and
- manufacturing clothing (315, Clothing Manufacturing).

3141 Textile Furnishings Mills

This industry group comprises establishments primarily engaged in manufacturing carpets and rugs, and curtains and linens.

31411 Carpet and Rug Mills

This industry comprises establishments primarily engaged in manufacturing carpets and rugs, including tufted, woven and needle-punched; or in finishing carpets and rugs.

Exclusion(s): Establishments primarily engaged in:
- manufacturing rugs from purchased carpet material; binding rugs (31499, All Other Textile Product Mills); and
- manufacturing rubber mats and matting, such as bath and door (32629, Other Rubber Product Manufacturing).

Example Activities
- Bath mats and bath sets, made in carpet mills
- Carpets and rugs, made from textile materials
- Carpets, rugs and mats, of textile materials, weaving or knitting
- Door mats, all materials (except entirely of rubber or plastic), manufacturing
- Finishing (e.g., dyeing) rugs and carpets
- Floor coverings, textile, weaving or knitting
- Mats and matting, made from textile materials

314110 Carpet and Rug Mills

See industry description for 31411, above.

31412 Curtain and Linen Mills

This industry comprises establishments primarily engaged in manufacturing curtains, draperies, linens and other home furnishings, from purchased materials.

Exclusion(s): Establishments primarily engaged in:
- manufacturing canvas exterior shades and awnings (31491, Textile Bag and Canvas Mills);
- manufacturing electric blankets (335210, Small Electrical Appliance Manufacturing); and
- manufacturing blinds and shades (33792, Blind and Shade Manufacturing).

Example Activities
- Bedspreads and bed sets, made from purchased fabric
- Blankets (except electric), made from purchased fabrics or felts
- Comforters, made from purchased fabric
- Curtains and draperies, window, made from purchased fabrics
- Cushions (except carpet or spring), made from purchased fabrics
- Draperies, made from purchased fabrics or sheet goods
- Napkins, made from purchased fabrics
- Pads and protectors (e.g., ironing board, mattress, table), made from purchased fabrics or felts
- Pillow cases, made from purchased fabrics
- Quilts, made from purchased materials
- Sheets and pillow cases, made from purchased fabrics

- Shower and bath curtains, all materials, made from purchased fabrics or sheet goods
- Tablecloths (except paper), made from purchased materials
- Towels and washcloths, made from purchased fabrics

314120 Curtain and Linen Mills MEX

See industry description for 31412, above.

3149 Other Textile Product Mills

This industry group comprises establishments, not classified to any other industry group, primarily engaged in manufacturing textile products.

31491 Textile Bag and Canvas Mills

This industry comprises establishments primarily engaged in manufacturing textile bags, such as shipping and other industrial bags; or products from canvas or canvas substitutes, such as tarpaulins and tents.

Exclusion(s): Establishments primarily engaged in:
- manufacturing hemp bags in integrated hemp mills (31311, Fibre, Yarn and Thread Mills).

Example Activities
- Awnings and canopies, outdoor, made from purchased fabrics
- Bags, plastic, made from purchased woven plastics
- Bags, textile, made from purchased woven or knitted materials
- Canvas products, made from purchased canvas or canvas substitutes
- Drop cloths, canvas, made from purchased fabric
- Duffel bags, canvas, manufacturing
- Flour bags, made from purchased woven or knitted materials
- Laundry bags, made from purchased woven or knitted materials
- Seed bags, made from purchased woven or knitted materials
- Shades, outdoor, made from purchased fabrics
- Shipping bags, made from purchased woven or knitted materials
- Tarpaulins, made from purchased fabrics
- Tents, made from purchased fabrics

314910 Textile Bag and Canvas Mills CAN

See industry description for 31491, above.

31499 All Other Textile Product Mills

This industry comprises establishments, not classified to any other industry, primarily engaged in manufacturing textile products. Establishments primarily engaged in garneting textile waste or other textile recycling; or embroidering textile products, including clothing, whether or not on a contract basis, are included.

Exclusion(s): Establishments primarily engaged in:
- manufacturing wire cable and rope (332619, Other Fabricated Wire Product Manufacturing).

Example Activities
- Appliquéing on textile products (except clothing)
- Appliquéing, on clothing owned by others
- Badges, fabric, manufacturing
- Bags, sleeping, manufacturing
- Banners, made from purchased fabric
- Bath mats and bath sets, made from purchased carpet

- Batts and batting (except nonwoven fabrics), manufacturing
- Belting, made from purchased fabric
- Binder and baler twine, manufacturing
- Binding carpets and rugs for the trade
- Bindings, bias, made from purchased fabric
- Bows, made from purchased fabrics
- Carpets and rugs, made from purchased fabric
- Cord (except tire, wire), manufacturing
- Cord for reinforcing rubber tires, industrial belting and fuel cells, manufacturing
- Cotton batting (except nonwoven batting), manufacturing
- Diapers (except disposable), made from purchased fabrics
- Dust cloths, made from purchased fabrics
- Embroidering on clothing owned by others
- Embroidering on textile products, for the trade
- Fabrics for reinforcing rubber tires, industrial belting and fuel cells, manufacturing
- Fishing line, natural or man-made fibres, manufacturing
- Fishing nets and seines, made in cordage or twine mills
- Flags, textile (e.g., banners, bunting, emblems, pennants), made from purchased fabrics
- Garnetting of textile waste and rags
- Glass tire cord and tire cord fabrics, manufacturing
- Lace, burnt-out, manufacturing
- Luggage linings, manufacturing
- Mouse pads (textile material laminated to a foam backing), manufacturing
- Padding and wadding (except nonwoven fabric), manufacturing
- Parachutes, manufacturing
- Pleating and hemstitching of made-up textile articles (except clothing)
- Quilting of textiles
- Rope (except wire rope), manufacturing
- Sleeping bags, manufacturing
- String, manufacturing
- Textile waste, processing
- Tire cord and fabric, of all materials, manufacturing
- Twine (except paper), manufacturing
- Upholstery filling, textile (except nonwoven fabric), manufacturing
- Waste, textile, processing of
- Weatherstripping made from purchased textiles

314990 All Other Textile Product Mills CAN

See industry description for 31499, above.

315 Clothing Manufacturing

This subsector comprises establishments primarily engaged in manufacturing clothing.

Exclusion(s): Establishments primarily engaged in:
- finishing clothing not made in the same establishment (313, Textile Mills);
- embroidering clothing not made in the same establishment (314, Textile Product Mills);
- printing on articles of clothing not made in the same establishment (323, Printing and Related Support Activities); and
- manufacturing safety clothing (339, Miscellaneous Manufacturing).

3151 Clothing Knitting Mills

This industry group comprises establishments primarily engaged in knitting clothing from yarn; or manufacturing clothing from knit fabrics made in the same establishment. Establishments classified in this industry group may finish the clothing that they knit.

Exclusion(s): Establishments primarily engaged in:
- finishing clothing not made in the same establishment (3133, Textile and Fabric Finishing and Fabric Coating); and
- manufacturing clothing from knit fabrics not produced in the same establishment (3152, Cut and Sew Clothing Manufacturing).

31511 Hosiery and Sock Mills

This industry comprises establishments primarily engaged in knitting hosiery for men, women and children. Establishments classified in this industry may finish the clothing that they knit.

Example Activities

- Anklets, hosiery or socks, knitting
- Athletic socks, knitting
- Hosiery mill
- Knitting hosiery and socks
- Leg warmers, manufacturing
- Nylons, sheer, women's, misses' and girls' full-length and knee-length, knitting
- Panty hose, manufacturing
- Socks, knitting
- Stockings, manufacturing
- Tights, knitting

315110 Hosiery and Sock Mills ᴹᴱˣ

See industry description for 31511, above.

31519 Other Clothing Knitting Mills

This industry comprises establishments, not classified to any other industry, primarily engaged in knitting clothing. Establishments classified in this industry may finish the clothing that they knit.

Exclusion(s): Establishments primarily engaged in:
- knitting hosiery and socks (31511, Hosiery and Sock Mills).

Example Activities

- Athletic clothing, men's and boys', made in knitting mills
- Athletic clothing, women's and girls', made in knitting mills
- Bathing suits, made in knitting mills
- Bathrobes, made in knitting mills
- Beachwear, made in knitting mills
- Body stockings, made in knitting mills
- Caps, made in knitting mills
- Dresses, hand-knit, manufacturing
- Dresses, made in knitting mills
- Girdles and other foundation garments, made in knitting mills
- Gloves, knit, made in knitting mills
- Hats, made in knitting mills
- Housecoats, made in knitting mills
- Jerseys, made in knitting mills
- Jogging suits, made in knitting mills
- Leotards, made in knitting mills
- Mens' and boys suits and jackets, made in knitting mills
- Neckties, made in knitting mills
- Nightwear, made in knitting mills
- Outerwear, made in knitting mills
- Panties, made in knitting mills
- Pants, outerwear, made in knitting mills
- Polo shirts, made in knitting mills
- Pyjamas, made in knitting mills
- Scarves, made in knitting mills
- Shawls, made in knitting mills
- Shirts, outerwear, men's and boys', made in knitting mills
- Shirts, underwear, made in knitting mills
- Shorts, underwear, men's and boys', made in knitting mills
- Ski suits, made in knitting mills
- Slacks, made in knitting mills
- Snow suits, made in knitting mills
- Suits, made in knitting mills
- Sweat suits, made in knitting mills
- Sweaters, knitting on a contract basis
- Sweaters, made in knitting mills
- Swimsuits, made in knitting mills
- Tank tops, men's and boys', made in knitting mills
- Tank tops, women's and girls', made in knitting mills
- Tennis shirts, men's and boys', made in knitting mills
- Ties, made in knitting mills
- Trousers, made in knitting mills
- T-shirts, men's and boys', made in knitting mills
- T-shirts, women's and girls', made in knitting mills
- Tuques, made in knitting mills

- Underwear, men's and boys', made in knitting mills
- Underwear, women's and girls', made in knitting mills
- Warm-up suits, made in knitting mills

315190 Other Clothing Knitting Mills CAN

See industry description for 31519, above.

3152 Cut and Sew Clothing Manufacturing

This industry group comprises establishments primarily engaged in manufacturing clothing from fabric made in other establishments.

Exclusion(s): Establishments primarily engaged in:
- manufacturing clothing from woven fabric made in the same establishment (3132, Fabric Mills);
- finishing clothing not made in the same establishment (3133, Textile and Fabric Finishing and Fabric Coating);
- manufacturing clothing from knit fabric made in the same establishment (3151, Clothing Knitting Mills); and
- printing on articles of clothing not made in the same establishment (3231, Printing and Related Support Activities).

31521 Cut and Sew Clothing Contracting US

This industry comprises establishments primarily engaged in manufacturing clothing from materials owned by others. These establishments are commonly referred to as contractors. This industry is limited to contract establishments that perform cutting and sewing operations, such as sewing arms to shirt bodies.

Exclusion(s): Establishments primarily engaged in:
- finishing clothing, on a contract basis (31331, Textile and Fabric Finishing);
- embroidering clothing, on a contract basis (31499, All Other Textile Product Mills);
- knitting hosiery and socks, on a contract basis (31511, Hosiery and Sock Mills);
- knitting clothing, except hosiery and socks, on a contract basis (31519, Other Clothing Knitting Mills);
- manufacturing men's and boys' clothing by cutting and sewing purchased fabric (31522, Men's and Boys' Cut and Sew Clothing Manufacturing);
- manufacturing women's and girls' clothing by cutting and sewing purchased fabric (31523, Women's and Girls' Cut and Sew Clothing Manufacturing); and
- printing on articles of clothing, on a contract basis (32311, Printing).

Example Activities
- Buttonholing and button covering, on clothing owned by others
- Children's clothing contractors
- Clothing contractors, cut-and-sew operations, on materials owned by others
- Clothing contractors, men's and boys' clothing
- Clothing contractors, women's, girls' and infants' clothing
- Fur clothing, cut and sewn from materials owned by others

315210 Cut and Sew Clothing Contracting CAN

See industry description for 31521, above.

31522 Men's and Boys' Cut and Sew Clothing Manufacturing US

This industry comprises establishments primarily engaged in manufacturing men's and boys' clothing from purchased fabric. Clothing jobbers, who perform entrepreneurial functions involved in clothing manufacture, such as buying raw materials, designing and preparing samples, arranging for clothing to be made from their materials, and marketing the finished apparel, are included.

Exclusion(s): Establishments primarily engaged in:
- knitting men's and boys' hosiery and socks from yarn (31511, Hosiery and Sock Mills);
- knitting men's and boys' clothing, except hosiery and socks, from yarn (31519, Other Clothing Knitting Mills);
- manufacturing men's and boys' clothing from materials owned by others (31521, Cut and Sew Clothing Contracting); and
- manufacturing men's and boys' fur and leather clothing (31529, Other Cut and Sew Clothing Manufacturing).

315221 Men's and Boys' Cut and Sew Underwear and Nightwear Manufacturing ᵁˢ

This Canadian industry comprises establishments primarily engaged in manufacturing men's and boys' underwear and nightwear from purchased fabric.

Exclusion(s): Establishments primarily engaged in:
- knitting underwear and nightwear from yarn (315190, Other Clothing Knitting Mills); and
- manufacturing men's and boys' underwear and nightwear from materials owned by others (315210, Cut and Sew Clothing Contracting).

Example Activities
- Pyjamas, men's and boys', cut and sewn from purchased fabric
- Underwear, men's and boys', cut and sewn from purchased fabric

315222 Men's and Boys' Cut and Sew Suit, Coat and Overcoat Manufacturing ᵁˢ

This Canadian industry comprises establishments primarily engaged in manufacturing men's and boys' suits, coats and overcoats from purchased fabric. Establishments known as tailors, primarily engaged in producing men's and boys' clothing for retail sale, are included.

Exclusion(s): Establishments primarily engaged in:
- knitting suits, coats and overcoats from yarn (315190, Other Clothing Knitting Mills);
- manufacturing men's and boys' suits, coats and overcoats from materials owned by others (315210, Cut and Sew Clothing Contracting);
- manufacturing men's and boys' non-tailored coats and jackets, such as ski jackets, ski suits and windbreakers (315229, Other Men's and Boys' Cut and Sew Clothing Manufacturing); and
- manufacturing fur and leather suits, coats and overcoats (315292, Fur and Leather Clothing Manufacturing).

Example Activities
- Custom tailors, men's and boys'
- Jackets, tailored (except fur, leather, sheepskin-lined), men's and boys', cut and sewn from purchased fabric
- Overcoats, tailored, men's and boys', cut and sewn from purchased fabric
- Suits, tailored, men's and boys', cut and sewn from purchased fabric
- Tuxedos, cut and sewn from purchased fabric
- Uniforms, dress (e.g., fire fighter, military, police), men's and boys', cut and sewn from purchased fabric

315226 Men's and Boys' Cut and Sew Shirt Manufacturing ᶜᴬᴺ

This Canadian industry comprises establishments primarily engaged in manufacturing men's and boys' shirts from purchased fabric. Some important products of this Canadian industry are tailored shirts and T-shirts.

Exclusion(s): Establishments primarily engaged in:
- knitting shirts from yarn (315190, Other Clothing Knitting Mills); and
- manufacturing men's and boys' shirts from materials owned by others (315210, Cut and Sew Clothing Contracting).

Example Activities
- Shirts, outerwear (except washable service type), men's and boys', cut and sewn from purchased fabric
- T-shirts, outerwear, men's and boys', cut and sewn from purchased fabric

315227 Men's and Boys' Cut and Sew Trouser, Slack and Jean Manufacturing ^{CAN}

This Canadian industry comprises establishments primarily engaged in manufacturing men's and boys' trousers, slacks and jeans from purchased fabric.

Exclusion(s): Establishments primarily engaged in:
- knitting trousers and slacks from yarn (315190, Other Clothing Knitting Mills);
- manufacturing men's and boys' trousers, slacks and jeans from materials owned by others (315210, Cut and Sew Clothing Contracting); and
- manufacturing leather trousers and slacks, (315292, Fur and Leather Clothing Manufacturing).

Example Activities
- Jeans, men's and boys', cut and sewn from purchased fabric
- Trousers, men's and boys', cut and sewn from purchased fabric

315229 Other Men's and Boys' Cut and Sew Clothing Manufacturing ^{CAN}

This Canadian industry comprises establishments, not classified to any other Canadian industry, primarily engaged in manufacturing men's and boys' clothing from purchased fabric.

Exclusion(s): Establishments primarily engaged in:
- knitting men's and boys' hosiery and socks from yarn (315110, Hosiery and Sock Mills);
- knitting men's and boys' sweaters and swimwear from yarn (315190, Other Clothing Knitting Mills);
- manufacturing men's and boys' clothing from materials owned by others (315210, Cut and Sew Clothing Contracting);
- manufacturing fur and leather clothing (315292, Fur and Leather Clothing Manufacturing); and
- manufacturing men's and women's athletic uniforms (315299, All Other Cut and Sew Clothing Manufacturing).

Example Activities
- Bathing suits, men's and boys', cut and sewn from purchased fabric
- Hunting coats and vests, men's and boys', cut and sewn from purchased fabric
- Non-tailored coats and jackets, men's and boys' (e.g., ski suits, windbreakers), manufacturing
- Pants, washable service type, men's and boys', cut and sewn from purchased fabric
- Shorts (e.g., Bermuda, Jamaica, gym), men's and boys', cut and sewn from purchased fabric
- Ski pants, men's and boys', cut and sewn from purchased fabric
- Ski suits, men's and boys', cut and sewn from purchased fabric
- Snow suits, men's and boys', cut and sewn from purchased fabric
- Snowmobile suits, men's and boys', cut and sewn from purchased fabric
- Sports clothing (except team uniforms), non-tailored, men's and boys', cut and sewn from purchased fabric
- Sweaters, men's and boys', cut and sewn from purchased fabric

- Uniforms, non-tailored, washable service type, men's, cut and sewn from purchased fabric
- Washable service apparel (e.g., barbers', hospital, professional), men's and boys', cut and sewn from purchased fabric
- Windbreakers (except leather), men's and boys', cut and sewn from purchased fabric
- Work shirts, men's and boys', cut and sewn from purchased fabric

31523 Women's and Girls' Cut and Sew Clothing Manufacturing US

This industry comprises establishments primarily engaged in manufacturing women's and girls' clothing from purchased fabric. Clothing jobbers, who perform entrepreneurial functions involved in clothing manufacture, such as buying raw materials, designing and preparing samples, arranging for clothing to be made from their materials, and marketing the finished apparel, are included.

Exclusion(s): Establishments primarily engaged in:
- knitting women's and girls' hosiery and socks from yarn (31511, Hosiery and Sock Mills);
- knitting women's and girls' clothing, except hosiery and socks, from yarn (31519, Other Clothing Knitting Mills);
- manufacturing women's and girls' clothing from materials owned by others (31521, Cut and Sew Clothing Contracting); and
- manufacturing women's and girls' fur and leather clothing (31529, Other Cut and Sew Clothing Manufacturing).

315231 Women's and Girls' Cut and Sew Lingerie, Loungewear and Nightwear Manufacturing US

This Canadian industry comprises establishments primarily engaged in manufacturing women's and girls' lingerie, loungewear and nightwear from purchased fabric.

Exclusion(s): Establishments primarily engaged in:
- knitting lingerie, loungewear and nightwear from yarn (315190, Other Clothing Knitting Mills); and
- manufacturing women's and girls' lingerie, loungewear and nightwear from materials owned by others (315210, Cut and Sew Clothing Contracting).

Example Activities
- Brassieres, cut and sewn from purchased fabric
- Foundation garments, women's, misses' and girls', cut and sewn from purchased fabric
- Girdles, women's, misses' and girls', cut and sewn from purchased fabric
- Lingerie, women's, misses' and girls', cut and sewn from purchased fabric
- Nightgowns, women's, misses' and girls', cut and sewn from purchased fabric
- Pyjamas, women's, misses' and girls', cut and sewn from purchased fabric
- Slips, women's, misses' and girls', cut and sewn from purchased fabric
- T-shirts, underwear, women's, misses' and girls', cut and sewn from purchased fabric
- Underwear, women's, misses' and girls', cut and sewn from purchased fabric

315232 Women's and Girls' Cut and Sew Blouse and Shirt Manufacturing US

This Canadian industry comprises establishments primarily engaged in manufacturing women's and girls' blouses and shirts from purchased fabric.

Exclusion(s): Establishments primarily engaged in:
- knitting blouses and shirts from yarn (315190, Other Clothing Knitting Mills);
- manufacturing women's and girls' blouses and shirts from materials owned by others (315210, Cut and Sew Clothing Contracting); and
- manufacturing women's and girls' sweat suits and sweat pants, from purchased fabric (315239, Other Women's and Girls' Cut and Sew Clothing Manufacturing).

Example Activities
- Blouses, women's, misses' and girls', cut and sewn from purchased fabric
- Shirts, outerwear, women's, misses' and girls', cut and sewn from purchased fabric
- Sweat shirts, women's, misses' and girls', cut and sewn from purchased fabric
- Tank tops, outerwear, women's, misses' and girls', cut and sewn from purchased fabric
- T-shirts, outerwear, women's, misses' and girls', cut and sewn from purchased fabric

315233 Women's and Girls' Cut and Sew Dress Manufacturing US

This Canadian industry comprises establishments primarily engaged in manufacturing women's and girls' dresses from purchased fabric. Establishments known as dressmakers, primarily engaged in producing women's and girls' clothing for retail sale, are included.

Exclusion(s): Establishments primarily engaged in:
- knitting dresses from yarn (315190, Other Clothing Knitting Mills);
- manufacturing dresses from materials owned by others (315210, Cut and Sew Clothing Contracting); and
- manufacturing leather dresses (315292, Fur and Leather Clothing Manufacturing).

Example Activities
- Dresses, women's, misses' and girls', cut and sewn from purchased fabric
- Dressmakers' shops, custom
- Paper dresses, women's, misses' and girls', cut and sewn from purchased fabric

315234 Women's and Girls' Cut and Sew Suit, Coat, Tailored Jacket and Skirt Manufacturing US

This Canadian industry comprises establishments primarily engaged in manufacturing women's and girls' suits, coats, tailored jackets and skirts from purchased fabric.

Exclusion(s): Establishments primarily engaged in:
- knitting suits, coats, tailored jackets and skirts from yarn (315190, Other Clothing Knitting Mills);
- manufacturing women's and girls' suits, coats, tailored jackets and skirts from materials owned by others (315210, Cut and Sew Clothing Contracting); and
- manufacturing fur and leather suits, coats, tailored jackets and skirts (315292, Fur and Leather Clothing Manufacturing).

Example Activities
- Coats, tailored (except fur, leather), women's, misses' and girls', cut and sewn from purchased fabric
- Jackets, tailored (except fur, leather, sheepskin-lined), women's, misses' and girls', cut and sewn from purchased fabric
- Overcoats (except fur, leather), women's, misses' and girls', cut and sewn from purchased fabric
- Pantsuits, women's, misses' and girls', cut and sewn from purchased fabric

- Skirts (except leather, tennis), women's, misses' and girls', cut and sewn from purchased fabric
- Suits, tailored, women's, misses' and girls', cut and sewn from purchased fabric

- Uniforms, dress, tailored (e.g., firefighter, military, police), women's and misses', cut and sewn from purchased fabric

315239 Other Women's and Girls' Cut and Sew Clothing Manufacturing US

This Canadian industry comprises establishments, not classified to any other Canadian industry, primarily engaged in manufacturing women's and girls' clothing from purchased fabric.

Exclusion(s): Establishments primarily engaged in:
- knitting women's and girls' hosiery and socks from yarn (315110, Hosiery and Sock Mills);
- knitting women's and girls' sweaters and swimwear from yarn (315190, Other Clothing Knitting Mills);
- manufacturing women's and girls' clothing from materials owned by others (315210, Cut and Sew Clothing Contracting);
- manufacturing leather clothing (315292, Fur and Leather Clothing Manufacturing); and
- manufacturing men's and women's athletic uniforms (315299, All Other Cut and Sew Clothing Manufacturing).

Example Activities
- Bathing suits, women's, misses' and girls', cut and sewn from purchased fabric
- Coats, non-tailored service apparel (e.g., laboratory, mechanics', medical), women's, misses' and girls', cut and sewn from purchased fabric
- Coveralls, work, women's, misses' and girls', cut and sewn from purchased fabric
- Culottes, women's, misses', and girls', cut and sewn from purchased fabric
- Jeans, women's, misses' and girls', cut and sewn from purchased fabric
- Jogging suits, women's, misses' and girls', cut and sewn from purchased fabric
- Leotards, women's, misses' and girls', cut and sewn from purchased fabric
- Occupational clothing, women's, misses' and girls', cut and sewn from purchased fabric
- Pants, women's, misses' and girls', cut and sewn from purchased fabric
- Shorts, outerwear, women's, misses' and girls', cut and sewn from purchased fabric
- Ski suits, jackets and pants, women's, misses' and girls', cut and sewn from purchased fabric
- Slacks, women's, misses' and girls', cut and sewn from purchased fabric
- Snowsuits, women's, misses' and girls', cut and sewn from purchased fabric
- Suits, non-tailored (e.g., jogging, snow, warm-up), women's, misses' and girls', cut and sewn from purchased fabric
- Sweat suits and pants, women's, misses' and girls', cut and sewn from purchased fabric
- Sweaters, women's, misses' and girls', cut and sewn from purchased fabric
- Swimsuits, women's, misses' and girls', cut and sewn from purchased fabric
- Uniforms, washable service apparel (e.g., maids', nurses', waitresses'), women's, misses' and girls', made from purchased fabric
- Washable service apparel (e.g., maids', nurses', waitresses'), women's, misses' and girls', cut and sewn from purchased fabric
- Windbreakers (except leather), women's, misses' and girls', cut and sewn from purchased fabric

31529 Other Cut and Sew Clothing Manufacturing US

This industry comprises establishments, not classified to any other industry, primarily engaged in manufacturing clothing from purchased fabric.

315291 Infants' Cut and Sew Clothing Manufacturing US

This Canadian industry comprises establishments primarily engaged in manufacturing infants' clothing from purchased fabric. For the purposes of classification, the term "infants'" clothing refers to articles for young children of a body height not exceeding 86 centimetres, or Canadian sizes less than 2X.

Exclusion(s): Establishments primarily engaged in:
- knitting infants' clothing from yarn (315190, Other Clothing Knitting Mills); and
- manufacturing infants' clothing from materials owned by others (315210, Cut and Sew Clothing Contracting).

Example Activity
- Infants' clothing, cut and sewn from purchased fabric

315292 Fur and Leather Clothing Manufacturing US

This Canadian industry comprises establishments primarily engaged in manufacturing fur and leather clothing.

Exclusion(s): Establishments primarily engaged in:
- manufacturing leather gloves (315990, Clothing Accessories and Other Clothing Manufacturing); and
- manufacturing leather safety and protective clothing (339110, Medical Equipment and Supplies Manufacturing).

Example Activities
- Clothing, fur, manufacturing
- Clothing, leather or sheepskin-lined, manufacturing
- Coats (including tailored), leather or sheepskin-lined, manufacturing
- Coats, fur, manufacturing
- Fur clothing (e.g., capes, coats, hats, jackets, neckpieces), manufacturing
- Hats, fur, manufacturing
- Jackets, leather (except welders') or sheepskin-lined, manufacturing
- Leather clothing (e.g., capes, coats, hats, jackets), manufacturing
- Leatherette clothing, manufacturing
- Pants, leather, manufacturing
- Sheepskin linings, manufacturing
- Trimmings, fur, manufacturing
- Vests, leather, fur or sheepskin-lined, manufacturing
- Windbreakers, leather, men's and boys', manufacturing

315299 All Other Cut and Sew Clothing Manufacturing US

This Canadian industry comprises establishments, not classified to any other Canadian industry, primarily engaged in manufacturing clothing from purchased fabric.

Example Activities
- Academic caps and gowns, cut and sewn from purchased fabric
- Athletic uniforms, cut and sewn from purchased fabric
- Baseball uniforms, cut and sewn from purchased fabric
- Basketball uniforms, cut and sewn from purchased fabric
- Capes, waterproof (e.g., plastics, rubber, similar materials), cut and sewn from purchased fabric
- Clerical vestments, cut and sewn from purchased fabric
- Clothing, waterproof, cut and sewn from purchased fabric
- Costumes (e.g., lodge, masquerade, theatrical), cut and sewn from purchased fabric
- Gowns, hospital, surgical and patient, cut and sewn from purchased fabric
- Halloween costumes, cut and sewn from purchased fabric

- Ponchos and similar waterproof raincoats, cut and sewn from purchased fabric
- Raincoats, waterproof (except infants'), cut and sewn from purchased fabric
- Sports clothing, team uniforms, cut and sewn from purchased fabric

- Team athletic uniforms, cut and sewn from purchased fabric
- Uniform shirts, team athletic, cut and sewn from purchased fabric
- Uniforms, team athletic, cut and sewn from purchased fabric

3159 Clothing Accessories and Other Clothing Manufacturing

See industry description for 31599, below.

31599 Clothing Accessories and Other Clothing Manufacturing

This industry comprises establishments, not classified to any other industry, primarily engaged in manufacturing clothing or clothing accessories.

Exclusion(s): Establishments primarily engaged in:
- manufacturing gloves from knit fabric made in the same establishment (31519, Other Clothing Knitting Mills);
- manufacturing fur and leather hats and caps (315292, Fur and Leather Clothing Manufacturing);
- manufacturing safety gloves (33911, Medical Equipment and Supplies Manufacturing); and
- manufacturing sports gloves (33992, Sporting and Athletic Goods Manufacturing).

Example Activities
- Apparel findings and trimmings, made from purchased fabric
- Aprons, household, made from purchased fabric
- Aprons, work (except rubberized and plastics), made from purchased fabric
- Baseball caps, manufacturing
- Belts, apparel (e.g., fabric, leather, vinyl), made from purchased material
- Caps and hats (except fur, leather), made from purchased fabric
- Fur mittens, manufacturing
- Glove linings (except fur), manufacturing
- Gloves and mittens (except athletic, metal, rubber), made from purchased fabric
- Handkerchiefs (except paper), made from purchased fabric

- Hats (except fur, leather), made from purchased fabric
- Leather gloves and mittens (except athletic), manufacturing
- Linings (e.g., coat, dress, millinery, necktie, suit), made from purchased fabric
- Millinery, made from purchased fabric
- Neckwear, made from purchased fabric
- Scarves, made from purchased fabric
- Shawls, made from purchased fabric
- Shoulder pads (e.g., coats, suits), made from purchased fabric
- Suspenders, made from purchased fabric
- Tuques, made from purchased fabric
- Uniform hats and caps (except protective head gear), made from purchased fabric
- Work gloves, leather, manufacturing

315990 Clothing Accessories and Other Clothing Manufacturing CAN

See industry description for 31599, above.

316 Leather and Allied Product Manufacturing

This subsector comprises establishments primarily engaged in manufacturing leather and allied products.

Exclusion(s): Establishments primarily engaged in:
- manufacturing leather clothing (315, Clothing Manufacturing).

3161 Leather and Hide Tanning and Finishing

See industry description for 31611, below.

31611 Leather and Hide Tanning and Finishing

This industry comprises establishments primarily engaged in tanning, currying, colouring and finishing hides and skins into leather. Leather converters, who buy hides and skins and have them processed into leather by others, on a contract basis, are included. Establishments primarily engaged in dressing and dyeing fur are also included.

Example Activities
- Dyeing furs
- Fur dressing and dyeing
- Hides, tanning, currying, dressing and finishing
- Leather tanning, currying and finishing
- Leather, manufacturing
- Tanneries, leather, manufacturing

316110 Leather and Hide Tanning and Finishing

See industry description for 31611, above.

3162 Footwear Manufacturing

See industry description for 31621, below.

31621 Footwear Manufacturing

This industry comprises establishments primarily engaged in manufacturing footwear, of any material.

Exclusion(s): Establishments primarily engaged in:
- manufacturing orthopedic extension shoes (33911, Medical Equipment and Supplies Manufacturing); and
- manufacturing skates, ice or roller, boots assembled with blades or rollers (33992, Sporting and Athletic Goods Manufacturing).

Example Activities
- Athletic shoes, manufacturing
- Boots, manufacturing
- Children's footwear (except orthopedic extension shoes), manufacturing
- Footwear (except orthopedic extension shoes), manufacturing
- Golf shoes, manufacturing
- Infant's footwear (except orthopedic extension shoes), manufacturing
- Leather footwear, manufacturing
- Men's footwear (except orthopedic extension shoes), manufacturing
- Orthopedic shoes (except extension shoes), men's, manufacturing
- Running shoes, manufacturing
- Shoes, manufacturing
- Skate boots, without blades or wheels, manufacturing
- Slippers, manufacturing
- Women's footwear (except orthopedic extension shoes), manufacturing
- Work boots and shoes, manufacturing

316210 Footwear Manufacturing CAN

See industry description for 31621, above.

3169 Other Leather and Allied Product Manufacturing

See industry description for 31699, below.

31699 Other Leather and Allied Product Manufacturing

This industry comprises establishments, not classified to any other industry, primarily engaged in manufacturing leather and allied products. Some important products of this industry are luggage, handbags, purses, and small articles normally carried on the person or in a handbag, such as billfolds, key cases and coin purses of leather or other materials, except precious metal.

Exclusion(s): Establishments primarily engaged in:
- manufacturing leather clothing (31529, Other Cut and Sew Clothing Manufacturing);
- manufacturing leather gloves and belts (31599, Clothing Accessories and Other Clothing Manufacturing); and
- manufacturing small articles normally carried on the person or in a handbag, such as billfolds, key cases and coin purses, of precious metal (33991, Jewellery and Silverware Manufacturing).

Example Activities
- Attaché cases, all materials, manufacturing
- Belting for machinery, leather, manufacturing
- Billfolds, all materials, manufacturing
- Boot and shoe cut stock, leather, manufacturing
- Boot and shoe findings, all materials, manufacturing
- Briefcases, all materials, manufacturing
- Burnt leather goods, manufacturing
- Handbags, manufacturing
- Harnesses and harness parts, leather, manufacturing
- Key cases (except metal), manufacturing
- Leather cut stock, boot and shoe, manufacturing
- Leather goods, small personal (e.g., coin purses, eyeglass cases, key cases), manufacturing
- Luggage, all materials, manufacturing
- Musical instrument cases, all materials, manufacturing
- Portfolios, manufacturing
- Purses (except precious metal), manufacturing
- Saddles and parts, leather, manufacturing
- Suitcases, all materials, manufacturing
- Vanity cases, leather, manufacturing
- Wallets (except metal), manufacturing

316990 Other Leather and Allied Product Manufacturing CAN

See industry description for 31699, above.

321 Wood Product Manufacturing

This subsector comprises establishments primarily engaged in manufacturing products from wood. There are three industry groups in this subsector, comprising establishments engaged in sawing logs into lumber and similar products, or preserving these products; making products that improve the natural characteristics of wood, by making veneers, plywood, reconstituted wood panel products or engineered wood assemblies; and making a diverse range of wood products, such as millwork.

Exclusion(s): Establishments primarily engaged in:
- logging; and chipping logs in the field (113, Forestry and Logging);
- manufacturing wood pulp, paper and paper products (322, Paper Manufacturing);
- manufacturing wood kitchen cabinets and counters, and bathroom vanities (337, Furniture and Related Product Manufacturing); and
- manufacturing wood signs and coffins (339, Miscellaneous Manufacturing).

3211 Sawmills and Wood Preservation

See industry description for 32111, below.

32111 Sawmills and Wood Preservation

This industry comprises establishments primarily engaged in manufacturing boards, dimension lumber, timber, poles and ties from logs and bolts. These establishments produce lumber that may be rough, or dressed by a planing machine to achieve smoothness and uniformity of size, but is generally not further worked or shaped. Establishments that preserve wood are also included.

Exclusion(s): Establishments primarily engaged in:
- chipping logs in the field (11331, Logging);
- manufacturing glued-laminated timber, nailed-laminated lumber beams, parallel strand lumber, laminated veneer lumber, fingerjoined lumber, and similar products (32121, Veneer, Plywood and Engineered Wood Product Manufacturing);
- peeling or slicing logs to make veneer (32121, Veneer, Plywood and Engineered Wood Product Manufacturing); and
- planing purchased lumber or working lumber further than dressed (32191, Millwork).

321111 Sawmills (except Shingle and Shake Mills) MEX

This Canadian industry comprises establishments primarily engaged in manufacturing boards, dimension lumber, timber, poles and ties, and siding, from logs and bolts. These establishments produce lumber that may be rough, or dressed by a planing machine to achieve smoothness and uniformity of size, but (except in the case of siding) is generally not further worked or shaped.

Example Activities
- Chipping logs (except in the forest)
- Dimension lumber (e.g., 2x4), made from logs or bolts
- Lath, made from logs or bolts
- Lumber (i.e., rough, dressed), made from logs or bolts
- Lumber, hardwood dimension (e.g., 2x4), made from logs or bolts
- Lumber, softwood dimension (e.g., 2x4), made from logs or bolts
- Sawdust and shavings, made from logs or bolts (i.e., in a sawmill)
- Sawmills
- Siding, dressed lumber, manufacturing
- Snow fence lath, made from logs or bolts
- Ties, railroad, made from logs or bolts
- Timber, made from logs or bolts
- Wood chips, made in sawmills

321112 Shingle and Shake Mills MEX

This Canadian industry comprises establishments primarily engaged in sawing blocks of wood to produce shingles or splitting blocks of wood to produce shakes.

Example Activities
- Shakes (i.e., hand split shingles), manufacturing
- Shingle mills, wood

321114 Wood Preservation US

This Canadian industry comprises establishments primarily engaged in treating lumber, plywood, poles and similar wood products, produced in other establishments, with preservatives to prevent decay and to protect against fire and insects. Establishments primarily engaged in cutting to size and treating poles, pilings, posts and similar roundwood products are included. Pressure treating is the most common method used. Some common preservatives are water-borne inorganic compounds, such as chromated copper arsenate and creosote.

Example Activities
- Creosoting of wood
- Lumber, treating with creosote or other preservatives
- Piles, foundation and marine construction, treating
- Plywood, treating with creosote or other preservatives
- Pressure treated plywood, made from purchased plywood

- Railroad ties (i.e., bridge, cross, switch), wood, treating
- Treating wood products with creosote or other preservatives

- Wood products, treating with creosote or other preservatives

3212 Veneer, Plywood and Engineered Wood Product Manufacturing

See industry description for 32121, below.

32121 Veneer, Plywood and Engineered Wood Product Manufacturing

This industry comprises establishments primarily engaged in manufacturing softwood and hardwood veneer and plywood; structural wood members, except lumber; and reconstituted wood panel products. Veneer is produced as a thin sheet of wood of uniform thickness by peeling or slicing logs. Plywood is produced by gluing and compressing together, three or more sheets of veneer, with the grain of alternate sheets usually laid crosswise. Structural wood members are made by laminating, joining and assembling wood components according to specified engineering design criteria. Reconstituted wood panel products are produced by processes involving pressure, adhesives and binders. The laminated products produced in this industry may have layers of materials other than wood.

Exclusion(s): Establishments primarily engaged in:
- manufacturing solid wood structural members, such as dimension lumber and timber; and preserving purchased plywood (32111, Sawmills and Wood Preservation);
- manufacturing containers, such as fruit baskets and boxes, from veneer made in the same establishment (32192, Wood Container and Pallet Manufacturing); and
- manufacturing gypsum board (32742, Gypsum Product Manufacturing).

321211 Hardwood Veneer and Plywood Mills US

This Canadian industry comprises establishments primarily engaged in manufacturing hardwood veneer and plywood.

Exclusion(s): Establishments primarily engaged in:
- preserving purchased plywood (321114, Wood Preservation).

Example Activities
- Panels, hardwood plywood, manufacturing
- Plywood mills, hardwood

- Veneer mills, hardwood

321212 Softwood Veneer and Plywood Mills US

This Canadian industry comprises establishments primarily engaged in manufacturing softwood veneer and plywood.

Exclusion(s): Establishments primarily engaged in:
- preserving purchased plywood (321114, Wood Preservation).

Example Activities
- Panels, softwood plywood, manufacturing
- Plywood mills, softwood

- Veneer mills, softwood

321215 Structural Wood Product Manufacturing ^{CAN}

This Canadian industry comprises establishments primarily engaged in manufacturing structural wood members, other than solid dimension lumber and timber.

Exclusion(s): Establishments primarily engaged in:
- fabricating structural wood members at construction sites (23, Construction); and
- manufacturing solid wood structural members, such as dimension lumber and timber (321111, Sawmills (except Shingle and Shake Mills)).

Example Activities
- Arches, glued-laminated or pre-engineered wood, manufacturing
- Beams, glued-laminated or pre-engineered wood, manufacturing
- Finger jointed lumber, manufacturing
- Glued-laminated timber (glulam), manufacturing
- I-joists, wood, manufacturing
- Laminated veneer lumber (LVL), manufacturing
- Lumber, parallel strand, manufacturing
- Nailed-laminated lumber beams, manufacturing
- Parallel strand lumber (PSL), manufacturing
- Prefabricated wood trusses, manufacturing
- Roof trusses, wood, manufacturing
- Structural wood members, prefabricated (e.g., arches, trusses, I-joists and parallel chord ceilings), manufacturing
- Timber, structural, glued-laminated or pre-engineered wood, manufacturing
- Trusses, wood, roof or floor, manufacturing

321216 Particle Board and Fibreboard Mills ^{CAN}

This Canadian industry comprises establishments primarily engaged in manufacturing particle board and fibreboard. Particle board is made from wood particles, which are often the residue from other wood processing operations, combined under heat and pressure with a water resistant binder. Fibreboard is made from wood fibres, bonded together completely or partially by the lignin in the wood.

Example Activities
- Fibreboard, manufacturing
- Hardboard, manufacturing
- Insulation board, cellular fibre or hard pressed wood, manufacturing
- MDF (medium density fibreboard), manufacturing
- Medium density fibreboard (MDF), manufacturing
- Particle board, manufacturing

321217 Waferboard Mills ^{CAN}

This Canadian industry comprises establishments primarily engaged in manufacturing waferboard and oriented strandboard (OSB). These products are made from wafers or strands of wood such as aspen, poplar or southern yellow pine, combined with a waterproof binder, and bonded together by heat and pressure.

Example Activities
- Oriented strandboard (OSB), manufacturing
- OSB (oriented strandboard), manufacturing
- Strandboard, oriented, manufacturing
- Waferboard, manufacturing

3219 Other Wood Product Manufacturing

This industry group comprises establishments, not classified to any other industry group, primarily engaged in manufacturing wood products.

Exclusion(s): Establishments primarily engaged in:
- manufacturing wood kitchen cabinets and counters, and bathroom vanities (3371, Household and Institutional Furniture and Kitchen Cabinet Manufacturing); and
- manufacturing wood signs and coffins (3399, Other Miscellaneous Manufacturing).

32191 Millwork

This industry comprises establishments primarily engaged in millwork. These establishments generally use woodworking machinery, such as jointers, planers, lathes and routers, to shape wood. Establishments primarily engaged in seasoning and planing purchased lumber are included. Wood millwork products may be covered with another material, such as plastic.

Exclusion(s): Establishments primarily engaged in:
- carpentry, including installing prefabricated windows, doors and stairs in buildings (23, Construction); and
- manufacturing dressed lumber from logs (32111, Sawmills and Wood Preservation).

321911 Wood Window and Door Manufacturing ^{US}

This Canadian industry comprises establishments primarily engaged in manufacturing wood doors and frames, and wood window units and frames, including those covered with metal or plastic.

Exclusion(s): Establishments primarily engaged in:
- installing prefabricated windows and doors in buildings (23, Construction);
- manufacturing plastic windows and doors (326196, Plastic Window and Door Manufacturing); and
- manufacturing metal windows and doors (332321, Metal Window and Door Manufacturing).

Example Activities
- Door frames and sash, wood and covered wood, manufacturing
- Door units, prehung, wood and covered wood, manufacturing
- Doors, wood and covered wood, manufacturing
- Frames, door and window, wood, manufacturing
- Garage doors, wood, manufacturing
- Shutters, door and window, wood and covered wood, manufacturing
- Window frames and sash, wood and covered wood, manufacturing
- Window units, wood and covered wood, manufacturing
- Wood door frames and sash, manufacturing
- Wood window frames and sash, manufacturing

321919 Other Millwork ^{CAN}

This Canadian industry comprises establishments, not classified to any other Canadian industry, primarily engaged in millwork. These establishments generally use woodworking machinery, such as jointers, planers, lathes and routers, to shape wood. Establishments primarily engaged in seasoning and planing purchased lumber are included. Wood millwork products may be covered with another material, such as plastic.

Exclusion(s): Establishments primarily engaged in:
- carpentry, including installing prefabricated stairs in buildings (23, Construction); and
- manufacturing dressed lumber from logs (32111, Sawmills and Wood Preservation).

Example Activities
- Baseboards, floor, wood, manufacturing
- Flooring, wood, manufacturing
- Furniture dimension stock, unfinished wood, manufacturing
- Ladder rounds or rungs, hardwood, manufacturing
- Lumber, dimension, made by resawing purchased lumber
- Mantels, wood, manufacturing
- Mouldings, wood, manufacturing
- Ornamental woodwork (e.g., cornices, mantels), manufacturing
- Parquet flooring, hardwood (assembled), manufacturing
- Planing mills (i.e., dressing purchased rough lumber)
- Planing purchased lumber
- Softwood flooring, manufacturing
- Stair railings, wood, manufacturing
- Stairs, prefabricated wood, manufacturing

- Stairwork (e.g., newel posts, railings, staircases, stairs), wood, manufacturing
- Tongue and groove lumber, made by resawing purchased lumber
- Wood flooring, manufacturing

- Wood squares, unfinished blanks, manufacturing
- Woodwork, interior and ornamental (e.g., windows, doors, sash, mantels), manufacturing

32192 Wood Container and Pallet Manufacturing

This industry comprises establishments primarily engaged in manufacturing wood containers, container parts (shook) ready for assembly, cooper's products and parts, and pallets.

Example Activities
- Barrels, wood, coopered, manufacturing
- Baskets, wood (e.g., round stave, veneer), manufacturing
- Box shook, manufacturing
- Boxes, wood, manufacturing
- Buckets, wood, manufacturing
- Container parts (shook) ready for assembly, manufacturing
- Containers (e.g., fruit baskets, boxes), made from veneer made in the same establishment
- Containers, wood, manufacturing
- Cooperage stock (e.g., heading, hoops, staves), manufacturing

- Cooperage, manufacturing
- Crates, wood, manufacturing
- Fruit containers (e.g., baskets, boxes, crates), wood, manufacturing
- Pallets, wood or wood and metal combination, manufacturing
- Shipping cases and drums, wood, wirebound, manufacturing
- Skids and pallets, wood or wood and metal combination, manufacturing
- Veneer, manufacturing and converting into containers (e.g., fruit baskets, boxes)

321920 Wood Container and Pallet Manufacturing

See industry description for 32192, above.

32199 All Other Wood Product Manufacturing

This industry comprises establishments, not classified to any other industry, primarily engaged in manufacturing wood products.

321991 Manufactured (Mobile) Home Manufacturing US

This Canadian industry comprises establishments primarily engaged in manufacturing mobile homes and non-residential mobile buildings. These units are portable structures built on a chassis equipped with wheels, but not designed for multiple or continuous movement, and are designed to be connected to sewage and water utilities.

Exclusion(s): Establishments primarily engaged in:
- manufacturing motor homes or recreational travel trailers (336215, Motor Home, Travel Trailer and Camper Manufacturing).

Example Activities
- Classroom buildings, manufactured portables, manufacturing
- Construction site buildings, manufactured portables, manufacturing

- Houses, prefabricated mobile homes, manufacturing
- Mobile buildings for commercial use, manufacturing
- Mobile homes, manufacturing

321992 Prefabricated Wood Building Manufacturing US

This Canadian industry comprises establishments primarily engaged in manufacturing prefabricated or pre-cut wood buildings, sections and panels. All buildings that are made away from the construction site, either in sections, complete units, or in components for on-site erection, are included. Establishments primarily engaged in manufacturing log cabins and log houses are included.

Exclusion(s): Establishments primarily engaged in:
- constructing wood frame buildings on site (23, Construction).

Example Activities
- Buildings, prefabricated or pre-cut, wood frame, manufacturing
- Cottages, prefabricated, wood frame, manufacturing
- Houses, prefabricated (except mobile homes), wood frame, manufacturing
- Log cabins, prefabricated wood, manufacturing
- Modular buildings, prefabricated, wood frame, manufacturing
- Panels for prefabricated wood buildings, manufacturing
- Prefabricated wood buildings, manufacturing

321999 All Other Miscellaneous Wood Product Manufacturing US

This Canadian industry comprises establishments, not classified to any other Canadian industry, primarily engaged in manufacturing wood products.

Example Activities
- Bearings, wood, manufacturing
- Bowls, wood, turned and shaped, manufacturing
- Broom handles, manufacturing
- Bungs, wood, manufacturing
- Burnt wood articles, manufacturing
- Clothes hangers, wood, manufacturing
- Clothes-drying frames, wood, manufacturing
- Clothespins, wood, manufacturing
- Cork products (except gaskets), manufacturing
- Excelsior (e.g., pads, wrappers), wood, manufacturing
- Fencing, prefabricated sections, wood, manufacturing
- Fencing, wood (except rough pickets, poles and rails), manufacturing
- Flagpoles, wood, manufacturing
- Flour, wood, manufacturing
- Handles (e.g., broom, brush, mop, hand tool), wood, manufacturing
- Hangers, garment, wood, manufacturing
- Kiln drying of lumber
- Kitchenware (e.g., utensils, rolling pins), wood, manufacturing
- Ladders, wood, manufacturing
- Lumber, kiln drying
- Paddles, wood, manufacturing
- Poles (e.g., clothesline, flag, tent), wood, manufacturing
- Reels, wood, manufacturing
- Stakes, surveyors', wood, manufacturing
- Tableware, wood, manufacturing
- Tool handles, turned and shaped wood, manufacturing
- Toothpicks, wood, manufacturing
- Trophy bases, wood, manufacturing
- Utensils, wood, manufacturing
- Wall-mounted hat and coat racks, wood, manufacturing

322 Paper Manufacturing

This subsector comprises establishments primarily engaged in manufacturing pulp, paper and paper products. The manufacture of pulp involves separating the cellulose fibres from other impurities in wood, used paper or other fibre sources. The manufacture of paper involves matting these fibres into a sheet. Converted paper products are produced from paper and other materials by various cutting and shaping techniques.

3221 Pulp, Paper and Paperboard Mills

This industry group comprises establishments primarily engaged in manufacturing pulp, paper or paperboard. Establishments that manufacture pulp, paper or paperboard, either alone or in combination with paper converting, are included.

Exclusion(s): Establishments primarily engaged in:
- manufacturing paper or paperboard products from purchased paper or paperboard (3222, Converted Paper Product Manufacturing).

32211 Pulp Mills

This industry comprises establishments primarily engaged in manufacturing pulp from any material, by any process. These establishments sell or transfer the pulp to separate paper-making establishments; they do not make it into paper themselves. Establishments that process waste paper into pulp ("de-inking plants") are included.

Exclusion(s): Establishments primarily engaged in:
- manufacturing pulp and making paper (32212, Paper Mills); and
- manufacturing pulp and making paperboard (32213, Paperboard Mills).

322111 Mechanical Pulp Mills ^{CAN}

This Canadian industry comprises establishments primarily engaged in manufacturing pulp from any material, using mechanical or semi-chemical methods. Some important products of this Canadian industry are mechanical pulp (sometimes called "groundwood" pulp), thermo-mechanical pulp (TMP) and semi-chemical pulp.

Exclusion(s): Establishments primarily engaged in:
- manufacturing pulp and making paper, except newsprint (322121, Paper (except Newsprint) Mills);
- manufacturing pulp and making newsprint (322122, Newsprint Mills); and
- manufacturing pulp and making paperboard (322130, Paperboard Mills).

Example Activities
- Groundwood pulp, manufacturing
- Mechanical wood pulp, manufacturing
- Pulp mills, mechanical or semi-chemical, not making paper or paperboard
- Semi-chemical wood pulp, manufacturing
- Thermo-mechanical wood pulp (TMP), manufacturing
- Wood pulp, mechanical or semi-chemical, manufacturing

322112 Chemical Pulp Mills ^{CAN}

This Canadian industry comprises establishments primarily engaged in manufacturing pulp from any material, using chemical methods. "Kraft" pulp is chemical pulp obtained from the sulphate or soda processes. Establishments that process waste paper into pulp are included.

Exclusion(s): Establishments primarily engaged in:
- manufacturing pulp and making paper, except newsprint (322121, Paper (except Newsprint) Mills);
- manufacturing pulp and making newsprint (322122, Newsprint Mills); and
- manufacturing pulp and making paperboard (322130, Paperboard Mills).

Example Activities
- Chemical wood pulp, manufacturing
- De-inking recovered paper
- Pulp mills, chemical, not making paper or paperboard
- Recycling paper (i.e., making pulp from waste and scrap paper)
- Wood pulp, chemical, manufacturing

32212 Paper Mills

This industry comprises establishments primarily engaged in manufacturing paper, other than paperboard. Establishments that manufacture paper in combination with pulp manufacture or paper converting, are included.

Exclusion(s): Establishments primarily engaged in:
- manufacturing pulp, but not making any paper or paperboard (32211, Pulp Mills);
- converting purchased paper into paperboard containers (32221, Paperboard Container Manufacturing);
- converting purchased paper and paperboard into paper bags and coated and treated paper products (32222, Paper Bag and Coated and Treated Paper Manufacturing); and
- converting purchased paper and paperboard into paper products other than paperboard containers, paper bags and coated and treated paper products (32229, Other Converted Paper Product Manufacturing).

322121 Paper (except Newsprint) Mills US

This Canadian industry comprises establishments primarily engaged in manufacturing paper, other than newsprint and paperboard. Establishments that manufacture paper (except newsprint) in combination with pulp manufacture or paper converting, are included.

Example Activities
- Asphalt paper, made in paper mills
- Building paper stock, manufacturing
- Coated paper, made in paper mills
- Diapers, disposable, made in paper mills
- Facial tissues, made in paper mills
- Fine paper stock, manufacturing
- Groundwood paper, coated, made in paper mills
- Kraft paper stock, manufacturing
- Looseleaf fillers and paper, made in paper mills
- Office paper (e.g., computer printer, photocopy, plain paper), made in paper mills
- Paper (except newsprint and uncoated groundwood) mills
- Paper (except newsprint and uncoated groundwood) products, made in paper mills
- Paper (except newsprint and uncoated groundwood) stock for conversion into paper products, manufacturing
- Paper (except newsprint and uncoated groundwood), coated, laminated or treated, made in paper mills
- Paper (except newsprint and uncoated groundwood), manufacturing
- Pulp and paper (except newsprint and uncoated groundwood) combined, manufacturing
- Sanitary paper products, made in paper mills
- Sanitary paper stock (e.g., for making towels, serviettes, tampons), manufacturing
- Tissue paper stock, manufacturing

322122 Newsprint Mills US

This Canadian industry comprises establishments primarily engaged in manufacturing newsprint, including groundwood printing paper. Establishments that manufacture newsprint in combination with pulp manufacture, are included.

Example Activities
- Groundwood paper, uncoated, made in paper mills
- Newsprint mills
- Newsprint stock, manufacturing
- Paper, newsprint, manufacturing
- Paper, uncoated groundwood, manufacturing
- Pulp and newsprint (including uncoated groundwood) combined, manufacturing
- Uncoated groundwood paper mills

32213 Paperboard Mills

This industry comprises establishments primarily engaged in manufacturing paperboard. Establishments that manufacture paperboard in combination with pulp manufacture or paperboard converting, are included.

Exclusion(s): Establishments primarily engaged in:
- manufacturing particle board, fibreboard, waferboard and similar reconstituted wood board products (32121, Veneer, Plywood and Engineered Wood Product Manufacturing); and
- manufacturing building paper (32212, Paper Mills).

Example Activities
- Boxboard paperboard stock, manufacturing
- Cardboard stock, manufacturing
- Coated, laminated or treated paperboard, made in paperboard mills
- Containers (e.g., boxes), made in paperboard mills
- Corrugated boxes, made in paperboard mills
- Corrugating medium, manufacturing
- Milk carton board, made in paperboard mills
- Paperboard mills
- Paperboard products (e.g., containers), made in paperboard mills
- Pulp and paperboard combined, manufacturing
- Stationery products, made in paperboard mills

322130 Paperboard Mills US

See industry description for 32213, above.

3222 Converted Paper Product Manufacturing

This industry group comprises establishments primarily engaged in manufacturing paper products from purchased paper and paperboard.

Exclusion(s): Establishments primarily engaged in:
- manufacturing paper or paperboard, and converting it into paper or paperboard products (3221, Pulp, Paper and Paperboard Mills).

32221 Paperboard Container Manufacturing

This industry comprises establishments primarily engaged in manufacturing paperboard containers, such as setup paperboard boxes, corrugated boxes, fibre boxes, cans and drums, and sanitary food containers, from purchased paperboard. These establishments use corrugating and cutting machinery to form paperboard into containers.

Exclusion(s): Establishments primarily engaged in:
- manufacturing paperboard and converting it into containers (32213, Paperboard Mills).

322211 Corrugated and Solid Fibre Box Manufacturing US

This Canadian industry comprises establishments primarily engaged in manufacturing corrugated and solid fibre boxes and related products, such as corrugated sheets, from purchased paperboard.

Exclusion(s): Establishments primarily engaged in:
- manufacturing paperboard and converting it into corrugated and fibre boxes (322130, Paperboard Mills).

Example Activities

- Boxes, corrugated, made from purchased paper or paperboard
- Boxes, shipping, laminated, made from purchased paper or paperboard
- Boxes, solid fibre, made from purchased paper or paperboard
- Containers, corrugated and solid fibreboard, made from purchased paper or paperboard
- Corrugated and solid fibreboard pads, made from purchased paper or paperboard
- Corrugated boxes, made from purchased paper or paperboard
- Corrugated paper, made from purchased paper or paperboard
- Folding boxes, corrugated, made from purchased paper or paperboard
- Pads, corrugated and solid fibreboard, made from purchased paper or paperboard
- Pallets, corrugated and solid fibre, made from purchased paper or paperboard
- Paper, corrugated, made from purchased paper or paperboard
- Partitions, corrugated and solid fibre, made from purchased paper or paperboard
- Set-up boxes, corrugated, made from purchased paper or paperboard
- Shipping containers, made from purchased paperboard
- Solid fibre boxes, made from purchased paper or paperboard

322212 Folding Paperboard Box Manufacturing US

This Canadian industry comprises establishments primarily engaged in manufacturing folding paperboard boxes, from purchased paperboard.

Exclusion(s): Establishments primarily engaged in:
- manufacturing paperboard and converting it into folding boxes (322130, Paperboard Mills); and
- manufacturing milk cartons (322219, Other Paperboard Container Manufacturing).

Example Activities

- Boxes, folding (except corrugated), made from purchased paperboard
- Cartons, folding (except milk), made from purchased paperboard
- Folding boxes (except corrugated), made from purchased paperboard
- Folding containers (except corrugated), made from purchased paperboard
- Food containers, sanitary, folding, made from purchased paperboard
- Sanitary food containers, folding, made from purchased paperboard
- Shoe boxes, folding, made from purchased paperboard

322219 Other Paperboard Container Manufacturing CAN

This Canadian industry comprises establishments, not classified to any other Canadian industry, primarily engaged in manufacturing paperboard containers, such as setup paperboard boxes, fibre cans and drums, and sanitary food containers, from purchased paperboard.

Exclusion(s): Establishments primarily engaged in:
- manufacturing paperboard and converting it into containers other than corrugated, solid fibre and folding boxes (322130, Paperboard Mills).

Example Activities

- Boxes (except corrugated), set-up (i.e., not shipped flat), made from purchased paperboard
- Boxes, sanitary food (except folding), made from purchased paper or paperboard
- Cans, fibre (i.e., fibre body, ends of any material), made from purchased paperboard
- Cartons, milk, made from purchased paper or paperboard

- Composite cans (i.e., foil-fibre and other combinations), made from purchased paperboard
- Cones (e.g., winding yarn, string, ribbons, cloth), fibre, made from purchased paperboard
- Containers, food, sanitary (except folding), made from purchased paper or paperboard
- Cores, fibre (i.e., fibre body, ends of any material), made from purchased paperboard
- Dishes, paper, made from purchased paper or paperboard
- Drums, fibre (i.e., fibre body, ends of any material), made from purchased paperboard
- Fibre cans and drums (i.e., fibre body, ends of any material), made from purchased paperboard
- Fibre spools, reels and blocks, made from purchased paperboard
- Fibre tubes, made from purchased paperboard
- Food containers, sanitary (except folding), made from purchased paper or paperboard
- Mailing cases and tubes, paper fibre (i.e., fibre body, ends of any material), made from purchased paperboard
- Milk cartons, made from purchased paper or paperboard
- Paper cups, made from purchased paper or paperboard
- Paper dishes (e.g., cups, plates), made from purchased paper or paperboard
- Paper plates, made from purchased paper or paperboard
- Reels, fibre, made from purchased paperboard
- Sanitary food containers (except folding), made from purchased paper or paperboard
- Set-up (i.e., not shipped flat) boxes (except corrugated), made from purchased paperboard
- Shoe boxes, set-up, made from purchased paperboard
- Spools, fibre, made from purchased paperboard
- Straws, drinking, made from purchased paper or paperboard
- Textile reels and bobbins, fibre, made from purchased paperboard
- Tubes, fibre, made from purchased paperboard
- Vulcanized fibre products, made from purchased paperboard
- Wastebaskets, fibre, made from purchased paperboard

32222 Paper Bag and Coated and Treated Paper Manufacturing

This industry comprises establishments primarily engaged in manufacturing paper bags, and coated and treated paper and paperboard products, from purchased paper and other flexible film materials. The products produced in this industry may be made from a single layer; or from several layers laminated together. The laminated products may consist entirely of materials other than paper, such as plastic film and aluminum foil.

Exclusion(s): Establishments primarily engaged in:
- manufacturing textile bags (31491, Textile Bag and Canvas Mills);
- manufacturing paper and converting it into paper bags and coated and treated paper products (32212, Paper Mills);
- manufacturing sensitized photographic and blueprint paper (32599, All Other Chemical Product Manufacturing);
- manufacturing plastic bags, either single- or multi-web, entirely of plastic (32611, Plastic Packaging Materials and Unlaminated Film and Sheet Manufacturing);
- manufacturing aluminum foil (331317, Aluminum Rolling, Drawing, Extruding and Alloying);
- manufacturing metal foil containers, such as aluminum pie plates (332999, All Other Miscellaneous Fabricated Metal Product Manufacturing);
- manufacturing medical adhesive tape and plasters (33911, Medical Equipment and Supplies Manufacturing); and
- manufacturing carbon paper (33994, Office Supplies (except Paper) Manufacturing).

Example Activities

- Adhesive tape (except medical), made from purchased materials
- Aluminum foil bags, made from purchased foil
- Aluminum foil laminates, made from purchased foil
- Bags (except plastics only), made by laminating or coating combinations of purchased foil, paper and plastics
- Bags, coated paper, made from purchased paper
- Bags, foil, made from purchased foil
- Bags, multiwall, made from purchased uncoated paper
- Bags, uncoated paper, made from purchased paper
- Book paper, coated, made from purchased paper
- Cardboard, laminated or surface coated, made from purchased paperboard
- Cellophane adhesive tape, made from purchased materials
- Chipboard, laminated or surface-coated, made from purchased paperboard
- Coated and treated paper products, made from purchased paper
- Coated board, made from purchased paperboard
- Coating purchased paper for non-packaging applications (except photosensitive paper)
- Coating purchased paper for packaging applications
- Duct tape, made from purchased materials
- Flexible packaging sheet materials (except foil-paper laminates), made by coating or laminating purchased paper
- Flexible packaging sheet materials, made by laminating purchased foil
- Foil bags, made from purchased foil
- Foil laminates, made from purchased foil
- Foil sheet, laminating purchased, for packaging applications
- Gift wrap, laminated, made from purchased paper
- Gold and silver foil laminates, made from purchased foil
- Grocers' bags and sacks, made from purchased uncoated paper
- Gummed paper products (e.g., labels, sheets, tapes), made from purchased paper
- Labels, gummed, made from purchased paper
- Laminating purchased foil sheets for flexible packaging applications
- Laminating purchased paper for non-packaging applications
- Laminating purchased paper for packaging applications
- Laminating purchased paperboard
- Leatherboard (i.e., paperboard-based), made from purchased paperboard
- Masking tape, made from purchased paper
- Milk carton board stock, made from purchased paperboard
- Multiwall shipping sacks, made from purchased uncoated paper
- Paper bags, coated, made from purchased paper
- Paper bags, uncoated, made from purchased paper
- Paper, coated (except photographic and carbon), made from purchased paper
- Paper, laminated, made from purchased paper
- Paper, sensitized (except photographic), made from purchased paper
- Paperboard, pasted, lined, laminated or surface coated, made from purchased paperboard
- Pressure sensitive paper and tape (except medical), made from purchased materials
- Sacks, multiwall, made from purchased uncoated paper
- Tapes (e.g., cellophane, masking, pressure sensitive), gummed, made from purchased paper or other materials
- Wallpaper, made from purchased paper or other materials
- Waxed paper, made from purchased paper

322220 Paper Bag and Coated and Treated Paper Manufacturing MEX

See industry description for 32222, above.

32223 Stationery Product Manufacturing

This industry comprises establishments primarily engaged in manufacturing paper stationery products, used for writing, filing and similar applications.

Exclusion(s): Establishments primarily engaged in:
- manufacturing paper and converting it into stationery products (32212, Paper Mills);
- manufacturing paperboard and converting it into stationery products (32213, Paperboard Mills); and
- manufacturing carbon paper and non-paper office supplies (33994, Office Supplies (except Paper) Manufacturing).

Example Activities
- Business machine paper, cut sheet, made from purchased paper
- Cards, die-cut office supply (e.g., index, library, time recording), made from purchased paper or paperboard
- Cash register tapes, made from purchased paper
- Die-cut paper products for office use, made from purchased paper or paperboard
- Envelopes (i.e., mailing, stationery), made from any material
- Exercise books and pads, made from purchased paper
- File folders (e.g., accordion, expanding, hanging, manila), made from purchased paper or paperboard
- Index and other die-cut cards, made from purchased cardboard
- Letters, die-cut, made from purchased cardboard
- Looseleaf fillers and paper, made from purchased paper
- Office paper (e.g., computer printer, photocopy, plain paper), cut sheet, made from purchased paper
- Office supplies, die-cut, made from purchased paper or paperboard
- Pads, desk, made from purchased paper
- Paper office supplies, made from purchased paper
- Paper products, die-cut office supplies, made from purchased paper or paperboard
- Rolls (e.g., adding machine, calculator, cash register), made from purchased paper
- Stationery, made from purchased paper
- Tablets and pads, made from purchased newsprint
- Tapes (e.g., adding machine, calculator, cash register), made from purchased paper
- Writing paper, cut sheet, made from purchased paper

322230 Stationery Product Manufacturing ᴹᴱˣ

See industry description for 32223, above.

32229 Other Converted Paper Product Manufacturing

This industry comprises establishments, not classified to any other industry, primarily engaged in manufacturing paper products from purchased paper and paperboard.

Exclusion(s): Establishments primarily engaged in:
- manufacturing paper and converting it into paper products (32212, Paper Mills); and
- manufacturing paperboard and converting it into paperboard products (32213, Paperboard Mills).

322291 Sanitary Paper Product Manufacturing ᵁˢ

This Canadian industry comprises establishments primarily engaged in manufacturing converted paper products from purchased sanitary paper stock. Establishments primarily engaged in manufacturing disposable sanitary products, such as tampons, from textile materials are included.

Exclusion(s): Establishments primarily engaged in:
- manufacturing sanitary paper and converting it into paper products (322121, Paper (except Newsprint) Mills).

Example Activities

- Diapers, disposable, made from purchased paper or textile wadding
- Facial tissues, made from purchased paper
- Napkins, sanitary, made from purchased paper stock
- Paper napkins (i.e., table), made from purchased paper
- Sanitary napkins and tampons, made from purchased paper
- Sanitary products, made from purchased sanitary paper stock
- Serviettes, paper, made from purchased paper
- Tablecloths, paper, made from purchased paper
- Tampons, sanitary, made from purchased paper
- Toilet paper, made from purchased paper
- Towels, paper, made from purchased paper

322299 All Other Converted Paper Product Manufacturing US

This Canadian industry comprises establishments, not classified to any other Canadian industry, primarily engaged in manufacturing converted paper products, from purchased paper. Establishments primarily engaged in manufacturing moulded pulp products, such as egg cartons, are included.

Exclusion(s): Establishments primarily engaged in:
- manufacturing paper, except newsprint, and converting it into paper products (322121, Paper (except Newsprint) Mills); and
- manufacturing paperboard and converting it into paper products (322130, Paperboard Mills).

Example Activities

- Cards, die-cut (except office supplies), made from purchased paper or paperboard
- Cartons, egg, moulded pulp, manufacturing
- Cigarette paper, made from purchased paper
- Confetti, made from purchased paper
- Crepe paper, made from purchased paper
- Cups, moulded pulp, manufacturing
- Die-cut paper products (except office supplies), made from purchased paper or paperboard
- Dishes, made from moulded pulp
- Doilies, paper, made from purchased paper
- Egg cartons, moulded pulp, manufacturing
- Filters, paper, made from purchased paper
- Florists' pots, moulded pulp, manufacturing
- Food containers, made from moulded pulp
- Food trays, moulded pulp, manufacturing
- Hats, made from purchased paper
- Insulating batts, fills or blankets, made from purchased paper
- Moulded pulp products (e.g., egg cartons, food containers, food trays), manufacturing
- Novelties, paper, manufacturing
- Paper novelties, manufacturing
- Paper products (except office supplies), die-cut, from purchased paper or paperboard
- Paperboard backs for blister or skin packages, made from purchased paper or paperboard
- Photograph folders, mats and mounts, manufacturing
- Plates, moulded pulp, manufacturing
- Pulp products, moulded, manufacturing
- Trays, moulded pulp, manufacturing

323 Printing and Related Support Activities

See industry description for 3231, below.

3231 Printing and Related Support Activities

This industry group comprises establishments primarily engaged in printing and providing related support activities.

Exclusion(s): Establishments primarily engaged in:
- printing on textile fabrics (3133, Textile and Fabric Finishing and Fabric Coating);
- publishing, or printing and publishing (5111, Newspaper, Periodical, Book and Directory Publishers); and
- printing using simple electrostatic printers, such as office-type photocopiers (5614, Business Support Services).

32311 Printing

This industry comprises establishments primarily engaged in printing.

Exclusion(s): Establishments primarily engaged in:
- printing on textile fabrics (31331, Textile and Fabric Finishing);
- publishing, or printing and publishing newspapers (51111, Newspaper Publishers);
- publishing, or printing and publishing periodicals (51112, Periodical Publishers);
- publishing, or printing and publishing books and pamphlets (51113, Book Publishers);
- publishing, or printing and publishing directories, including telephone (51114, Directory and Mailing List Publishers);
- publishing, or printing and publishing calendars, art and greeting cards (51119, Other Publishers); and
- printing using simple electrostatic printers, such as office-type photocopiers (56143, Business Service Centres).

323113 Commercial Screen Printing US

This Canadian industry comprises establishments primarily engaged in commercial printing using silk-screen printing equipment. Establishments in this Canadian industry typically have a pre-press capability, for example, to cut stencils. Typically, these establishments print on clothing; or produce paper documents of a graphical nature, such as pictures and large-format sign-type lettering.

Exclusion(s): Establishments primarily engaged in:
- silk-screen printing on textile fabrics (313310, Textile and Fabric Finishing).

Example Activities
- Art works, screen printing without publishing
- Clothing (e.g., caps, T-shirts), screen printing
- Glass, screen printing, for the trade
- Job printing, screen (except on textile fabrics)
- Posters, screen printing without publishing
- Print shops, screen (except on textile fabrics)
- Printing on clothing (e.g., caps, T-shirts)
- Printing on textile products (e.g., napkins, placemats, towels), own account
- Printing, screen (except on textile fabrics)
- Screen printing (except on textile fabrics)
- Screen printing on clothing, for the trade
- Screen printing paper documents (e.g., pictures, large-format banners), without publishing
- Screen printing T-shirts, for the trade

323114 Quick Printing US

This Canadian industry comprises establishments primarily engaged in commercial printing using small offset printers and/or non-impact printers. Establishments in this Canadian industry typically have a pre-press capability.

Exclusion(s): Establishments primarily engaged in:
- printing using simple electrostatic printers, such as office-type photocopiers (561430, Business Service Centres).

Example Activity
- Printing, quick (except photocopy service)

323115 Digital Printing ᵁˢ

This Canadian industry comprises establishments primarily engaged in digital printing. These establishments use computer-controlled non-impact (electrostatic, ink jet, spray jet) printing equipment. The image to be printed is input to the printer as a computer file (not simply scanned in and digitized by the printer itself). Establishments in this Canadian industry typically have extensive pre-press operations, including specialized scanners and colour-separation equipment. Typically, these establishments print documents of a high-resolution, graphical nature.

Exclusion(s): Establishments primarily engaged in:
- printing using simple electrostatic printers, such as office-type photocopiers (561430, Business Service Centres).

Example Activities
- Digital printing (e.g., billboards, other large format graphical materials)
- Digital printing (e.g., graphics, high resolution)
- Print shops, digital
- Printing, digital (e.g., billboards, other large format graphical materials)
- Printing, digital (e.g., graphics, high resolution)

323116 Manifold Business Forms Printing ᵁˢ

This Canadian industry comprises establishments primarily engaged in printing manifold business forms.

Example Activities
- Books, sales, manifold, printing
- Business forms, manifold, printing
- Cheque books and refills, printing
- Computer forms, manifold or continuous (except paper simply lined), printing
- Forms, business, manifold, printing
- Manifold business forms, printing
- Printing manifold business forms
- Sales books, manifold, printing
- Unit set forms (e.g., manifold credit card slips), printing

323119 Other Printing ᶜᴬᴺ

This Canadian industry comprises establishments, not classified to any other Canadian industry, primarily engaged in printing.

Example Activities
- Address lists, printing without publishing
- Advertising material (e.g., coupons, flyers), printing without publishing
- Albums (e.g., photo, scrap), manufacturing
- Almanacs, printing without publishing
- Appointment books and refills, manufacturing
- Art works, printing (except screen) without publishing
- Atlases, printing without publishing
- Bank notes, printing
- Binders, looseleaf, manufacturing
- Blankbooks and refills, manufacturing
- Books, printing without publishing
- Business forms (except manifold), printing without publishing
- Calendars, printing without publishing
- Cards (e.g., business, greeting, playing, postcards, trading), printing without publishing
- Catalogues of collections (e.g., museum), printing without publishing
- Catalogues, printing without publishing
- Certificates (e.g., bond, stock), printing without publishing
- Comic books, printing without publishing

- Credit and identification card imprinting, embossing and encoding
- Dictionaries, printing without publishing
- Directories, printing without publishing
- Encyclopedias, printing without publishing
- Fiction books, printing without publishing
- Flexographic printing (except manifold business forms, textile fabrics), without publishing
- Globe covers and maps, printing without publishing
- Gravure printing (except manifold business forms, textile fabrics), without publishing
- Greeting cards (e.g., birthday, holiday, sympathy), printing without publishing
- Guides, street map, printing without publishing
- Guides, travel books, printing without publishing
- Intaglio printing
- Job printing, lithographic (except quick)
- Job printing, offset (except quick)
- Journals and magazines, trade, printing without publishing
- Journals, scholarly, printing without publishing
- Labels, printing on a job-order basis
- Letterpress printing
- Lithographic printing (except manifold business forms, quick printing, textile fabrics), without publishing
- Looseleaf binders and devices, manufacturing
- Magazines and periodicals, printing without publishing
- Maps, printing without publishing
- Music books, printing without publishing
- Music, sheet, printing without publishing
- Newspapers, printing without publishing
- Nonfiction books, printing without publishing
- Offset printing (except manifold business forms, quick printing, textile fabrics), without publishing
- Pamphlets, printing without publishing
- Patterns and plans, printing without publishing
- Periodicals, printing without publishing
- Photo albums and refills, manufacturing
- Playing cards, printing without publishing
- Postage stamps, printing without publishing
- Postcards, printing without publishing
- Posters, printing (except quick, digital) without publishing
- Printing, books, without publishing
- Printing, flexographic (except manifold business forms, textile fabrics)
- Printing, gravure (except manifold business forms, textile fabrics), without publishing
- Printing, letterpress (except manifold business forms, textile fabrics)
- Printing, lithographic (except manifold business forms, quick, textile fabrics)
- Printing, offset (except manifold business forms, quick, textile fabrics)
- Programs, for sporting events, printing without publishing
- Religious books, printing without publishing
- Rotogravure printing
- Schedules (e.g., radio, television, transportation), printing without publishing
- School books, printing without publishing
- Scrapbooks and refills, manufacturing
- Sheet music, printing without publishing
- Signs and notices, paper, printing (except quick, digital) without publishing
- Stationery, printing (except quick) on a job-order basis
- Stock and bond certificates, printing without publishing
- Technical manuals and papers (books), printing without publishing
- Telephone directories, printing without publishing
- Textbooks, printing without publishing
- Time planners/organizers and refills, manufacturing
- Travel guide books, printing without publishing

32312 Support Activities for Printing

This industry comprises establishments primarily engaged in providing support services to commercial printers, such as pre-press and bindery work.

Example Activities

- Binderies (i.e., bookbinding shops)
- Book gilding, bronzing, edging, deckling, embossing and gold stamping, for the trade
- Book repairing
- Bookbinding, without printing
- Colour separation services, for the printing trade
- Electronic prepress services for the printing trade
- Electrotype plate preparation services
- Embossing plate preparation services
- Engraving printing plates, for the printing trades
- Flexographic plate preparation services
- Gravure plates and cylinders preparation services
- Imagesetting services, pre-press
- Letterpress plate preparation services
- Lithographic plate preparation services
- Offset plate preparation services
- Pamphlets and magazines, binding without printing

- Photocomposition services, for the printing trades
- Photoengraving plate preparation services
- Platemaking, for the printing trades
- Postpress services (e.g., bevelling, binding, bronzing, edging, foil stamping), on printed products
- Prepress printing services (e.g., colour separation, imagesetting, photocomposition, typesetting)
- Printing plate preparation services
- Printing postpress services (e.g., bevelling, binding, bronzing, edging, foil stamping)
- Printing prepress services (e.g., colour separation, imagesetting, photocomposition, typesetting)
- Repairing books
- Rotogravure printing plates and cylinders preparation services
- Samples and displays mounting
- Screens for printing, preparation services
- Trade binding services
- Typesetting (i.e., computer-controlled, hand, machine), for the printing trade

323120 Support Activities for Printing MEX

See industry description for 32312, above.

324 Petroleum and Coal Product Manufacturing

This subsector comprises establishments primarily engaged in transforming crude petroleum and coal into intermediate and end products. The dominant process is petroleum refining, which separates crude petroleum into components or fractions through such techniques as cracking and distillation.

Exclusion(s): Establishments primarily engaged in:
- manufacturing chemicals and chemical preparations from refined petroleum and coal products (325, Chemical Manufacturing).

3241 Petroleum and Coal Product Manufacturing

See industry description for 324, above.

32411 Petroleum Refineries

This industry comprises establishments primarily engaged in refining crude petroleum. Petroleum refining involves the transformation of crude oil by such processes as cracking and distillation.

Exclusion(s): Establishments primarily engaged in:
- producing natural gasoline from natural gas (21111, Oil and Gas Extraction);
- manufacturing asphalt paving and roofing materials from refined petroleum products (32412, Asphalt Paving, Roofing and Saturated Materials Manufacturing);
- blending and compounding lubricating oils and greases from refined petroleum products (32419, Other Petroleum and Coal Product Manufacturing); and
- manufacturing petrochemicals from petroleum feedstocks (32511, Petrochemical Manufacturing).

Example Activities

- Aliphatic (i.e., acyclic) chemicals, made in petroleum refineries
- Alkylates, made in petroleum refineries
- Asphalt and asphaltic materials, made in petroleum refineries
- Asphalt paving mixtures, made in petroleum refineries
- Aviation fuels, made in petroleum refineries
- Benzene, made in petroleum refineries
- Coke, petroleum, made in petroleum refineries
- Crude oil, refining
- Cyclic aromatic hydrocarbons, made in petroleum refineries
- Diesel fuels, made in petroleum refineries
- Ethylene, made in petroleum refineries
- Fuel oils, made in petroleum refineries
- Gasoline, made in petroleum refineries
- Greases, lubricating, made in petroleum refineries
- Heating oils, made in petroleum refineries
- Hydraulic fluids, made in petroleum refineries
- Jet fuels, made in petroleum refineries
- Kerosene, made in petroleum refineries
- Liquefied petroleum gases (LPG), made in petroleum refineries
- Lubricating oils and greases, made in petroleum refineries
- Naphtha, made in petroleum refineries
- Naphthalene, made in petroleum refineries
- Oil (i.e., petroleum) refineries
- Oils (e.g., fuel, lubricating and illuminating), made in petroleum refineries
- Petrochemical feedstocks, made in petroleum refineries
- Petrochemicals, made in petroleum refineries
- Petroleum jelly, made in petroleum refineries
- Petroleum refineries
- Propane gases, made in petroleum refineries
- Refineries, petroleum
- Toluene, made in petroleum refineries
- Waxes, petroleum, made in petroleum refineries
- Xylene, made in petroleum refineries

324110 Petroleum Refineries

See industry description for 32411, above.

32412 Asphalt Paving, Roofing and Saturated Materials Manufacturing

This industry comprises establishments primarily engaged in manufacturing asphalt paving materials; manufacturing roofing rolls, sheets and shingles, by saturating mats and felts with purchased asphalt or bituminous materials; and manufacturing roofing cements and coatings.

324121 Asphalt Paving Mixture and Block Manufacturing US

This Canadian industry comprises establishments primarily engaged in manufacturing asphalt paving mixtures and blocks, from purchased asphalt, bituminous materials or coal tar.

Example Activities

- Asphalt paving blocks, made from purchased asphaltic materials
- Asphalt paving mixtures, made from purchased asphaltic materials
- Blocks, asphalt paving, made from purchased asphaltic materials
- Coal tar paving materials, made from purchased coal tar
- Paving blocks and mixtures, made from purchased asphaltic materials
- Tar and asphalt paving mixtures, made from purchased asphaltic materials

324122 Asphalt Shingle and Coating Material Manufacturing US

This Canadian industry comprises establishments primarily engaged in manufacturing roofing rolls, sheets and shingles, by saturating mats and felts with purchased asphalt or bituminous materials; and manufacturing roofing cements and coatings.

Exclusion(s): Establishments primarily engaged in:
- manufacturing asphalt shingles and tar paper, from paper made in the same establishment (32212, Paper Mills).

Example Activities
- Asphalt roofing coatings, made from purchased asphaltic materials
- Asphalt saturated mats and felts, made from purchased asphaltic materials and paper
- Asphalt shingles, made from purchased asphaltic materials.
- Asphalt siding, made from purchased asphaltic materials
- Cements, asphalt roofing, made from purchased asphaltic materials
- Roofing felts, made from purchased asphaltic materials
- Shingles, made from purchased asphaltic materials
- Siding, made from purchased asphaltic materials
- Tar paper, made from purchased asphaltic materials and paper
- Tar roofing cements and coating, made from purchased asphaltic materials
- Undercoating for motor vehicles, made from purchased asphaltic materials

32419 Other Petroleum and Coal Product Manufacturing

This industry comprises establishments, not classified to any other industry, primarily engaged in manufacturing petroleum and coal products. Establishments primarily engaged in re-refining used products are included.

Example Activities
- Briquettes, petroleum, made from refined petroleum
- Calcining petroleum coke from refined petroleum
- Coal tar crudes, produced in coke ovens
- Coke oven products (e.g., coke, gases, tars), made in coke oven establishments
- Coke ovens
- Cutting oils, made from refined petroleum
- Fireplace logs, made from refined petroleum or coal
- Fuel briquettes or boulets, made from refined petroleum
- Greases, petroleum lubricating, made from refined petroleum
- Grinding oils, petroleum, made from refined petroleum
- Hydraulic fluids, petroleum, made from refined petroleum
- Lubricating oils and greases, petroleum, made from refined petroleum
- Petroleum jelly, made from refined petroleum
- Petroleum waxes, made from refined petroleum
- Recycling (i.e., re-refining) used motor oils
- Re-refining used petroleum lubricating oils
- Tar, made in coke ovens
- Transmission fluids, petroleum, made from refined petroleum
- Waxes, petroleum, made from refined petroleum

324190 Other Petroleum and Coal Product Manufacturing CAN

See industry description for 32419, above.

325 Chemical Manufacturing

This subsector comprises establishments primarily engaged in manufacturing chemicals and chemical preparations, from organic and inorganic raw materials.

Exclusion(s): Establishments primarily engaged in:
- field processing of crude petroleum and natural gas (211, Oil and Gas Extraction);
- beneficiating mineral ores (212, Mining and Quarrying (except Oil and Gas));
- processing crude petroleum and coal (324, Petroleum and Coal Product Manufacturing); and
- smelting and refining ores and concentrates (331, Primary Metal Manufacturing).

3251 Basic Chemical Manufacturing

This industry group comprises establishments primarily engaged in manufacturing chemicals, using basic processes such as thermal cracking and distillation. Chemicals produced in this industry group are usually separate chemical elements or separate chemically-defined compounds.

32511 Petrochemical Manufacturing

This industry comprises establishments primarily engaged in converting feedstocks derived from petroleum, or from petroleum and natural gas liquids, into petrochemicals. Some important processes used in petrochemical manufacturing include steam cracking and steam reforming. For the purpose of defining this industry, petrochemicals consist of acyclic (aliphatic) hydrocarbons and cyclic aromatic hydrocarbons.

Exclusion(s): Establishments primarily engaged in:
- refining crude petroleum into petrochemicals (32411, Petroleum Refineries);
- manufacturing acetylene (32512, Industrial Gas Manufacturing);
- converting petrochemicals into other basic chemicals (32519, Other Basic Organic Chemical Manufacturing); and
- manufacturing plastics resins and synthetic rubber (32521, Resin and Synthetic Rubber Manufacturing).

Example Activities
- Acyclic hydrocarbons (except acetylene), made from refined petroleum or natural gas liquids
- Aromatic cyclic hydrocarbons, made from refined petroleum or natural gas liquids
- Benzene, made from refined petroleum or natural gas liquids
- Butadiene, made from refined petroleum or natural gas liquids
- Butane, made from refined petroleum or natural gas liquids
- Butylene (butene), made from refined petroleum or natural gas liquids
- Cumene, made from refined petroleum or natural gas liquids
- Cyclic aromatic hydrocarbons, made from refined petroleum or natural gas liquids
- Ethane, made from refined petroleum or natural gas liquids
- Ethylbenzene, made from refined petroleum or natural gas liquids
- Ethylene (ethene), made from refined petroleum or natural gas liquids
- Heptane, made from refined petroleum or natural gas liquids
- Heptene, made from refined petroleum or natural gas liquids
- Hexane, made from refined petroleum or natural gas liquids
- Isobutene, made from refined petroleum or natural gas liquids
- Isoprene, made from refined petroleum or natural gas liquids
- Naphthalene, made from refined petroleum or natural gas liquids
- Nonene, made from refined petroleum or natural gas liquids
- Olefins (alkenes), made from refined petroleum or natural gas liquids
- Paraffins (alkanes), made from refined petroleum or natural gas liquids
- Pentane, made from refined petroleum or natural gas liquids
- Pentene, made from refined petroleum or natural gas liquids
- Petrochemicals, made from refined petroleum or natural gas liquids
- Propylene (propene), made from refined petroleum or natural gas liquids
- Styrene, made from refined petroleum or natural gas liquids
- Toluene, made from refined petroleum or natural gas liquids
- Xylene, made from refined petroleum or natural gas liquids

325110 Petrochemical Manufacturing

See industry description for 32511, above.

32512 Industrial Gas Manufacturing

This industry comprises establishments primarily engaged in manufacturing industrial organic and inorganic gases in compressed, liquid and solid forms.

Example Activities
- Acetylene, manufacturing
- Air, liquid, manufacturing
- Argon, manufacturing
- Carbon dioxide, manufacturing
- Dry ice (i.e., solid carbon dioxide), manufacturing
- Fluorocarbon gases, manufacturing
- Gases, industrial (i.e., compressed, liquefied, solid), manufacturing
- Helium, manufacturing
- Hydrogen, manufacturing
- Ice, dry (i.e., solid carbon dioxide), manufacturing
- Neon, manufacturing
- Nitrogen, manufacturing
- Nitrous oxide, manufacturing
- Oxygen, manufacturing

325120 Industrial Gas Manufacturing

See industry description for 32512, above.

32513 Synthetic Dye and Pigment Manufacturing

This industry comprises establishments primarily engaged in manufacturing synthetic organic and inorganic dyes, pigments, lakes and toners.

Exclusion(s): Establishments primarily engaged in:
- manufacturing carbon, bone and lamp black (32518, Other Basic Inorganic Chemical Manufacturing);
- manufacturing wood or coal tar distillation products used as dyeing materials (32519, Other Basic Organic Chemical Manufacturing);
- manufacturing paint (32551, Paint and Coating Manufacturing);
- manufacturing printing ink (32591, Printing Ink Manufacturing); and
- manufacturing toners for photocopiers, laser printers and similar electrostatic printing devices (32599, All Other Chemical Product Manufacturing).

Example Activities
- Antimony based pigments, manufacturing
- Azine dyes, manufacturing
- Azo dyes, manufacturing
- Barytes based pigments, manufacturing
- Black pigments (except carbon, bone and lamp black), manufacturing
- Ceramic colours, manufacturing
- Chrome pigments (i.e., chrome green, chrome orange, chrome yellow), manufacturing
- Colour lakes and toners (i.e., organic pigments), manufacturing
- Colour pigments, inorganic (except bone, carbon and lamp black), manufacturing
- Colour pigments, organic (except animal black, bone black), manufacturing
- Copper based pigments, manufacturing
- Direct dyes, manufacturing
- Disperse dyes, manufacturing
- Dyes, inorganic and synthetic organic, manufacturing
- Ferric oxide pigments, manufacturing
- Fluorescent dyes, manufacturing
- Food colouring, synthetic, manufacturing
- Inorganic pigments (except bone, carbon and lamp black), manufacturing
- Iron based pigments, manufacturing
- Lakes (i.e., organic pigments), manufacturing
- Lead pigments, manufacturing
- Litharge, manufacturing
- Lithopone, manufacturing

- Metallic pigments, inorganic, manufacturing
- Organic pigments, dyes, lakes and toners, manufacturing
- Pearl essence pigment, synthetic, manufacturing
- Pigments (except animal black, bone black), organic, manufacturing
- Pigments (except bone, carbon and lamp black), inorganic, manufacturing
- Stains, biological, manufacturing
- Titanium based pigments, manufacturing
- Toners (except electrostatic, photographic), manufacturing
- White extender pigments (e.g., barytes, blanc fixé, whiting), manufacturing
- Zinc based pigments, manufacturing

325130 Synthetic Dye and Pigment Manufacturing MEX

See industry description for 32513, above.

32518 Other Basic Inorganic Chemical Manufacturing

This industry comprises establishments, not classified to any other industry, primarily engaged in manufacturing basic inorganic chemicals.

Exclusion(s): Establishments primarily engaged in:
- manufacturing nitrogenous and phosphoric fertilizers (32531, Fertilizer Manufacturing);
- manufacturing inorganic insecticidal, herbicidal and fungicidal preparations (32532, Pesticide and Other Agricultural Chemical Manufacturing);
- manufacturing photographic chemicals (32599, All Other Chemical Product Manufacturing); and
- manufacturing alumina (33131, Alumina and Aluminum Production and Processing).

325181 Alkali and Chlorine Manufacturing US

This Canadian industry comprises establishments primarily engaged in manufacturing alkalies and chlorine.

Exclusion(s): Establishments primarily engaged in:
- mining and preparing alkalies (212396, Potash Mining);
- manufacturing industrial bleaches (325189, All Other Basic Inorganic Chemical Manufacturing);
- manufacturing household bleaches (325610, Soap and Cleaning Compound Manufacturing); and
- manufacturing chlorine preparations for swimming pools (325999, All Other Miscellaneous Chemical Product Manufacturing).

Example Activities
- Alkalis, manufacturing
- Caustic potash (i.e., potassium hydroxide), manufacturing
- Caustic soda (i.e., sodium hydroxide), manufacturing
- Chlorine, manufacturing
- Disodium carbonate (i.e., soda ash), manufacturing
- Potassium carbonate, manufacturing
- Potassium hydroxide (i.e., caustic potash), manufacturing
- Sal soda (i.e., washing soda), manufacturing
- Soda ash (i.e., disodium carbonate), manufacturing
- Sodium bicarbonate (i.e., baking soda), manufacturing
- Sodium carbonate (i.e., soda ash), manufacturing
- Sodium hydroxide (i.e., caustic soda), manufacturing

325189 All Other Basic Inorganic Chemical Manufacturing CAN

This Canadian industry comprises establishments, not classified to any other Canadian industry, primarily engaged in manufacturing inorganic chemicals.

Example Activities

- Aluminum compounds, not specified elsewhere by process, manufacturing
- Alums (e.g., aluminum ammonium sulphate, aluminum potassium sulphate), manufacturing
- Ammonium chloride, manufacturing
- Ammonium compounds, not specified elsewhere by process, manufacturing
- Arsenic compounds, not specified elsewhere by process, manufacturing
- Barium compounds, not specified elsewhere by process, manufacturing
- Bleaching agents, inorganic, manufacturing
- Bone black, manufacturing
- Boron compounds, not specified elsewhere by process, manufacturing
- Calcium hypochlorite, manufacturing
- Calcium inorganic compounds, not specified elsewhere by process, manufacturing
- Carbides (e.g., boron, calcium, silicon, tungsten), manufacturing
- Carbon black, manufacturing
- Carbon inorganic compounds, not specified elsewhere by process, manufacturing
- Cesium and cesium compounds, not specified elsewhere by process, manufacturing
- Chlorine compounds, not specified elsewhere by process, manufacturing
- Chromium compounds, not specified elsewhere by process, manufacturing
- Cobalt compounds, not specified elsewhere by process, manufacturing
- Copper compounds, not specified elsewhere by process, manufacturing
- Copper sulphate, manufacturing
- Fluorine, manufacturing
- Fuel propellants, solid inorganic, not specified elsewhere by process, manufacturing
- Heavy water (i.e., deuterium oxide), manufacturing
- Hydrazine, manufacturing
- Hydrochloric acid, manufacturing
- Hydrogen peroxide, manufacturing
- Iodine, crude or resublimed, manufacturing
- Iron compounds, not specified elsewhere by process, manufacturing
- Isotopes, radioactive, manufacturing
- Lamp black, manufacturing
- Lithium compounds, not specified elsewhere by process, manufacturing
- Magnesium compounds, not specified elsewhere by process, manufacturing
- Manganese dioxide, manufacturing
- Mercury compounds, not specified elsewhere by process, manufacturing
- Nickel compounds, not specified elsewhere by process, manufacturing
- Nuclear fuel scrap reprocessing
- Nuclear fuels, inorganic, manufacturing
- Oleum (i.e., fuming sulphuric acid), manufacturing
- Peroxides, inorganic, manufacturing
- Phosphorus compounds, not specified elsewhere by process, manufacturing
- Potassium inorganic compounds, not specified elsewhere by process, manufacturing
- Potassium salts, manufacturing
- Potassium sulphate, manufacturing
- Radioactive elements, manufacturing
- Radioactive isotopes, manufacturing
- Rare earth compounds, not specified elsewhere by process, manufacturing
- Selenium compounds, not specified elsewhere by process, manufacturing
- Silver compounds, not specified elsewhere by process, manufacturing
- Sodium chlorate, manufacturing
- Sodium hypochlorite, manufacturing
- Sodium inorganic compounds, not specified elsewhere by process, manufacturing
- Sodium phosphate, manufacturing
- Sodium silicate, manufacturing
- Sodium sulphate, manufacturing
- Strontium compounds, not specified elsewhere by process, manufacturing
- Sulphides and sulphites, manufacturing
- Sulphur and sulphur compounds, not specified elsewhere by process, manufacturing
- Sulphur dioxide, manufacturing
- Sulphur, recovering or refining (except from sour natural gas)
- Sulphuric acid, manufacturing
- Tin compounds, not specified elsewhere by process, manufacturing
- Titanium dioxide, manufacturing
- Tungsten compounds, not specified elsewhere by process, manufacturing
- Uranium compounds, not specified elsewhere by process, manufacturing
- Uranium oxide, manufacturing
- Uranium, enriched, manufacturing
- Zinc compounds, not specified elsewhere by process, manufacturing
- Zinc oxide, manufacturing

32519 Other Basic Organic Chemical Manufacturing

This industry comprises establishments, not classified to any other industry, primarily engaged in manufacturing basic organic chemicals. Establishments primarily engaged in coal tar distillation, the distillation of wood products or the manufacture of ethanol (ethyl alcohol) for non-beverage use are included. The main products of this class are vinyl chloride, methanol, alicyclic hydrocarbon, ethylene glycol, fatty acids and esters.

Exclusion(s): Establishments primarily engaged in:
- converting crude petroleum (32411, Petroleum Refineries);
- operating coke ovens (32419, Other Petroleum and Coal Product Manufacturing);
- converting petroleum or natural gas liquid feedstocks into petrochemicals (32511, Petrochemical Manufacturing);
- manufacturing synthetic rubber (32521, Resin and Synthetic Rubber Manufacturing); and
- manufacturing urea (32531, Fertilizer Manufacturing).

Example Activities
- Accelerators (i.e., basic synthetic chemicals), manufacturing
- Acetates, not specified elsewhere by process, manufacturing
- Acetic acid, manufacturing
- Acids, fatty (e.g., margaric, oleic, stearic), manufacturing
- Acids, organic, not specified elsewhere by process, manufacturing
- Adipic acid, manufacturing
- Alcohol, ethyl (ethanol), non-potable, manufacturing
- Alcohol, methyl (methanol), manufacturing
- Aldehydes, manufacturing
- Alginates (e.g., calcium, potassium, sodium), manufacturing
- Azobenzene, manufacturing
- Benzaldehyde, manufacturing
- Bleaching agents, organic, manufacturing
- Briquettes, charcoal, manufacturing
- Calcium organic compounds, not specified elsewhere by process, manufacturing
- Caprolactam, manufacturing
- Carbon organic compounds, not specified elsewhere by process, manufacturing
- Carbon tetrachloride, manufacturing
- Charcoal (except activated), manufacturing
- Citrates, not specified elsewhere by process, manufacturing
- Coal tar distillates, manufacturing
- Creosote, made by distillation of coal tar
- Creosote, made by distillation of wood tar
- Cresols, made by distillation of coal tar
- Cresylic acids, made from refined petroleum or natural gas
- Cyclic crudes, made by distillation of coal tar
- Cycloterpenes, manufacturing
- Diphenylamine, manufacturing
- Dyeing and tanning extracts, natural, manufacturing
- Dyes, natural, manufacturing
- Enzyme proteins (i.e., basic synthetic chemicals) (except pharmaceutical use), manufacturing
- Essential oils, synthetic, manufacturing
- Esters, not specified elsewhere by process, manufacturing
- Ethanol (ethyl alcohol), non-potable, made by the wet-mill process
- Ethyl alcohol (ethanol), non-potable, manufacturing
- Ethylene dichloride (dichloroethane), manufacturing
- Ethylene glycol, manufacturing
- Ethylene oxide, manufacturing
- Extracts, natural dyeing and tanning, manufacturing
- Fatty acid esters and amines, manufacturing
- Fatty acids (e.g., margaric, oleic, stearic), manufacturing
- Fatty alcohols, manufacturing
- Flavouring materials (i.e., basic synthetic chemicals such as coumarin), manufacturing
- Formaldehyde, manufacturing
- Fuel propellants, solid organic, not specified elsewhere by process, manufacturing
- Gum and wood chemicals, manufacturing
- Halogenated hydrocarbon (except aromatics) derivatives, manufacturing
- Heterocyclic chemicals, not specified elsewhere by process, manufacturing
- Isocyanates, manufacturing
- Isopropyl alcohol, manufacturing
- Ketone compounds, not specified elsewhere by process, manufacturing

- Methanol (methyl alcohol), natural, manufacturing
- Methanol (methyl alcohol), synthetic, manufacturing
- Methyl alcohol (methanol), natural, manufacturing
- Methyl alcohol (methanol), synthetic, manufacturing
- Naphtha, made by distillation of coal tar
- Naphthalene, made by distillation of coal tar
- Naphthalene, made from refined petroleum or natural gas
- Naval stores, gum or wood, manufacturing
- Nitrated hydrocarbon derivatives, manufacturing
- Nitrosated hydrocarbon derivatives, manufacturing
- Oils, made by distillation of coal tar
- Oils, wood, made by distillation of wood
- Oleic acid (red oil), manufacturing
- Organo-inorganic compounds, manufacturing
- Oxalates (e.g., ammonium oxalate, ethyl oxalate, sodium oxalate), manufacturing
- Oxalic acid, manufacturing
- Perfume materials (i.e., basic synthetic chemicals such as terpineol), manufacturing
- Peroxides, organic, manufacturing
- Phenol, manufacturing
- Phthalic anhydride, manufacturing
- Pinene, manufacturing
- Pitch, made by distillation of coal tar
- Pitch, wood, manufacturing
- Plasticizers (i.e., basic synthetic chemicals), manufacturing
- Potassium organic compounds, not specified elsewhere by process, manufacturing
- Pyroligneous acids, manufacturing
- Rosin, made by distillation of pine gum or pine wood
- Silicone (except resins), manufacturing
- Sodium organic compounds, not specified elsewhere by process, manufacturing
- Sulphonated derivatives, manufacturing
- Synthetic sweeteners (i.e., sweetening agents), manufacturing
- Tall oil (except skimmings), manufacturing
- Tannic acid (i.e., tannins), manufacturing
- Tanning extracts and materials, natural, manufacturing
- Tar and tar oils, made by distillation of wood
- Toluidines, manufacturing
- Turpentine, made by distillation of pine gum or pine wood
- Vinyl acetate (except resins), manufacturing
- Vinyl chloride (chloroethylene), manufacturing
- Wood distillates, manufacturing
- Wood oils, manufacturing

325190 Other Basic Organic Chemical Manufacturing MEX

See industry description for 32519, above.

3252 Resin, Synthetic Rubber, and Artificial and Synthetic Fibres and Filaments Manufacturing

This industry group comprises establishments primarily engaged in manufacturing polymers such as resins, synthetic rubber, and textile fibres and filaments. Polymerization of monomers into polymers, for example of styrene into polystyrene, is the basic process.

32521 Resin and Synthetic Rubber Manufacturing

This industry comprises establishments primarily engaged in manufacturing synthetic resins, plastics materials and synthetic rubber from basic organic chemicals.

Exclusion(s): Establishments primarily engaged in:
- manufacturing rubber processing chemicals and plasticizers, whether separate chemical elements or compounds (32519, Other Basic Organic Chemical Manufacturing);
- manufacturing plastics adhesives (32552, Adhesive Manufacturing);
- manufacturing rubber processing chemicals and plasticizers except from separate chemical elements or compounds; custom compounding of resins produced elsewhere (32599, All Other Chemical Product Manufacturing); and
- processing rubber into intermediate or final products (3262, Rubber Product Manufacturing).

Example Activities

- Acetal resins, manufacturing
- Acrylate rubber, manufacturing
- Acrylic resins, manufacturing
- Acrylonitrile-butadiene-styrene (ABS) resins, manufacturing
- Alkyd resins, manufacturing
- Amino resins, manufacturing
- Butadiene rubber (i.e., polybutadiene), manufacturing
- Butyl rubber, manufacturing
- Chloroprene rubber, manufacturing
- Coal tar resins, manufacturing
- Elastomers (except synthetic rubber), manufacturing
- Elastomers, synthetic rubber, manufacturing
- Epoxy resins, manufacturing
- Ethylene-propylene rubber, manufacturing
- Ethylene-vinyl acetate resins, manufacturing
- Fluoro-polymer resins, manufacturing
- Ion exchange resins, manufacturing
- Ionomer resins, manufacturing
- Isobutylene polymer resins, manufacturing
- Latex rubber, synthetic, manufacturing
- Lignin plastics, manufacturing
- Melamine resins, manufacturing
- Neoprene, manufacturing
- Nitrile rubber, manufacturing
- Nitrocellulose (i.e., pyroxylin) resins, manufacturing
- Nylon resins, manufacturing
- Phenolic resins, manufacturing
- Plastics and synthetic resins, regenerating, precipitating and coagulating
- Polyamide resins, manufacturing
- Polyester resins, manufacturing
- Polyethylene resins, manufacturing
- Polyethylene rubber, manufacturing
- Polyethylene terephathalate (PET) resins, manufacturing
- Polyisobutylene resins, manufacturing
- Polyisobutylene rubber, manufacturing
- Polypropylene resins, manufacturing
- Polystyrene resins, manufacturing
- Polysulfide rubber, manufacturing
- Polyurethane resins, manufacturing
- Polyvinyl alcohol resins, manufacturing
- Polyvinyl chloride (PVC) resins, manufacturing
- Polyvinyl resins, manufacturing
- Propylene resins, manufacturing
- Protein plastics, manufacturing
- Resins, plastics (except custom compounding purchased resins), manufacturing
- Rosin (i.e., modified resins), manufacturing
- Rubber, synthetic, manufacturing
- Silicone resins, manufacturing
- Silicone rubber, manufacturing
- Styrene resins, manufacturing
- Synthetic rubber (i.e., vulcanizable elastomers), manufacturing
- Thermoplastic resins and plastics materials, manufacturing
- Thermosetting plastics resins, manufacturing
- Thermosetting vulcanizable elastomers, manufacturing
- Urea resins, manufacturing
- Urethane rubber, manufacturing
- Vinyl resins, manufacturing
- Vinylidene resins, manufacturing

325210 Resin and Synthetic Rubber Manufacturing CAN

See industry description for 32521, above.

32522 Artificial and Synthetic Fibres and Filaments Manufacturing

This industry comprises establishments primarily engaged in manufacturing artificial and synthetic fibres and filaments in the form of monofilament, filament yarn, staple or tow. Artificial fibres are made from organic polymers derived from natural raw materials, mainly cellulose. Synthetic fibres are generally derived from petrochemicals. Establishments that both manufacture and texture fibres are included.

Exclusion(s): Establishments primarily engaged in:
- texturizing artificial and synthetic fibres and filaments produced elsewhere (31311, Fibre, Yarn and Thread Mills); and
- manufacturing glass fibres (32721, Glass and Glass Product Manufacturing).

Example Activities

- Acetate fibres and filaments, manufacturing
- Alginate fibres, manufacturing
- Artificial fibres and filaments, manufacturing
- Cellophane film or sheet, manufacturing
- Cellulosic fibres and filaments, manufacturing
- Cellulosic staple fibres, manufacturing
- Fibres and filaments, artificial, manufacturing
- Fibres and filaments, cellulosic, manufacturing and texturizing
- Fibres and filaments, synthetic, manufacturing
- Filament yarn, man-made, manufacturing
- Man-made fibres and filaments, manufacturing
- Nylon fibres and filaments, manufacturing
- Polyester fibres and filaments, manufacturing
- Polyethylene terephathalate (PET) fibres and filaments, manufacturing
- Polyolefin fibres and filaments, manufacturing
- Protein fibres and filaments, manufacturing
- Rayon fibres and filaments, manufacturing
- Throwing cellulosic yarn, made in the same establishment
- Throwing non-cellulosic yarn, made in the same establishment
- Yarn, monofilament, man-made, manufacturing
- Yarn, monofilament, man-made, manufacturing and texturizing

325220 Artificial and Synthetic Fibres and Filaments Manufacturing MEX

See industry description for 32522, above.

3253 Pesticide, Fertilizer and Other Agricultural Chemical Manufacturing

This industry group comprises establishments primarily engaged in manufacturing agricultural chemicals, including nitrogenous and phosphoric fertilizer materials; mixed fertilizers; and agricultural and household pest control chemicals.

32531 Fertilizer Manufacturing

This industry comprises establishments primarily engaged in manufacturing nitrogenous or phosphoric fertilizer materials and mixing these ingredients into fertilizers; and in purchasing ingredients and mixing them into fertilizers. Establishments engaged in the manufacture of phosphoric acid, urea, ammonia and nitric acid, whether or not for use as a fertilizer material, are included.

Exclusion(s): Establishments primarily engaged in:
- mining potash (212396, Potash Mining); and
- manufacturing agricultural lime products (32741, Lime Manufacturing).

325313 Chemical Fertilizer (except Potash) Manufacturing CAN

This Canadian industry comprises establishments primarily engaged in manufacturing nitrogenous and phosphoric fertilizer materials and mixing these ingredients with other ingredients into fertilizers. Establishments producing natural organic fertilizers and mixtures (except compost) are included. Establishments engaged in the manufacture of phosphoric acid, urea, ammonia and nitric acid, whether or not for use as a fertilizer material, are also included.

Exclusion(s): Establishments primarily engaged in:
- mining potash (212396, Potash Mining).

Example Activities

- Ammonia (i.e., anhydrous or ammonium hydroxyde), manufacturing
- Ammonium nitrate, manufacturing
- Ammonium phosphates, manufacturing
- Ammonium sulphate, manufacturing
- Anhydrous ammonia, manufacturing

- Fertilizer materials, nitrogenous and phosphatic, manufacturing
- Fertilizers, mixed, made in plants producing nitrogenous or phosphatic fertilizer materials
- Fertilizers, natural organic (except compost), manufacturing
- Nitric acid, manufacturing

- Nitrogenous fertilizer materials, manufacturing
- Phosphatic fertilizer materials, manufacturing
- Phosphoric acid, manufacturing
- Superphosphates, manufacturing
- Urea, manufacturing

325314 Mixed Fertilizer Manufacturing US

This Canadian industry comprises establishments primarily engaged in mixing ingredients produced elsewhere into fertilizers.

Example Activities
- Compost, manufacturing
- Fertilizers, mixed, made in plants not manufacturing fertilizer materials
- Mixing purchased fertilizer materials
- Nitrogenous fertilizers, made by mixing purchased materials

- Phosphatic fertilizers, made by mixing purchased materials
- Potassic fertilizers, made by mixing purchased materials
- Potting soil, manufacturing

32532 Pesticide and Other Agricultural Chemical Manufacturing

This industry comprises establishments primarily engaged in manufacturing agricultural chemicals, except fertilizers. Establishments engaged in manufacturing household pest control products are included.

Exclusion(s): Establishments primarily engaged in:
- manufacturing basic chemicals requiring further processing or formulation before use as agriculture chemicals (3251, Basic Chemical Manufacturing); and
- manufacturing agricultural lime products (32741, Lime Manufacturing).

Example Activities
- Exterminating chemical products (e.g., fungicides, insecticides, pesticides), manufacturing
- Fungicides, manufacturing
- Herbicides, manufacturing
- Insecticides, manufacturing
- Nicotine insecticides, manufacturing

- Pesticides, manufacturing
- Plant growth regulators, manufacturing
- Rodenticides, manufacturing
- Soil conditioning preparations, manufacturing
- Tick powder or spray, manufacturing

325320 Pesticide and Other Agricultural Chemical Manufacturing

See industry description for 32532, above.

3254 Pharmaceutical and Medicine Manufacturing

See industry description for 32541, below.

32541 Pharmaceutical and Medicine Manufacturing

This industry comprises establishments primarily engaged in manufacturing drugs, medicines and related products for human or animal use. Establishments in this industry may undertake one or more of several processes, including basic processes, such as chemical synthesis, fermentation, distillation and solvent extraction; grading, grinding and milling; and packaging in forms suitable for internal and external use, such as tablets, vials, ampoules and ointments.

Exclusion(s): Establishments primarily engaged in:
- manufacturing food supplements and food substitutes (classified in the industry of the specified product).

Example Activities
- Acetylsalicylic acid, manufacturing
- Agar culture media, manufacturing
- Agar-agar grinding, manufacturing
- Amphetamines, uncompounded, manufacturing
- Analgesic preparations, manufacturing
- Anesthetic preparations, manufacturing
- Anesthetics, uncompounded, manufacturing
- Antibacterial preparations, manufacturing
- Antibiotics (including veterinary), manufacturing
- Antihistamine preparations, manufacturing
- Antiseptic preparations, manufacturing
- Bacterial vaccines, manufacturing
- Barbiturate preparations, manufacturing
- Barbiturates, uncompounded, manufacturing
- Birth control pills, manufacturing
- Blood derivatives, manufacturing
- Blood glucose test kits, manufacturing
- Cardiac preparations, manufacturing
- Cephalosporin, uncompounded, manufacturing
- Cold remedies, manufacturing
- Contact lens solutions, manufacturing
- Contraceptive preparations, manufacturing
- Cortisone, uncompounded, manufacturing
- Cough medicines, manufacturing
- Culture media, manufacturing
- Diagnostic biological preparations, manufacturing
- Diagnostic substances, in-vitro, manufacturing
- Digestive system preparations, manufacturing
- Digitoxin, uncompounded, manufacturing
- Diuretic preparations, manufacturing
- Endocrine products, uncompounded, manufacturing
- Enzyme proteins (i.e., basic synthetic chemicals), pharmaceutical use, manufacturing
- Eye and ear preparations, manufacturing
- Fish liver oils, medicinal, uncompounded, manufacturing
- Glandular derivatives, uncompounded, manufacturing
- Glandular medicinal preparations, manufacturing
- Glycosides, uncompounded, manufacturing
- Grinding and milling botanicals (i.e., for medicinal use)
- Hematology in-vivo diagnostic substances, manufacturing
- Hematology products (except diagnostic substances), manufacturing
- Herb grinding and milling (i.e., for medicinal use)
- HIV test kits, manufacturing
- Hormone in-vitro diagnostic substances, manufacturing
- Hormones and derivatives, uncompounded, manufacturing
- Insulin preparations, manufacturing
- Insulin, uncompounded, manufacturing
- In-vitro diagnostic substances, manufacturing
- In-vivo diagnostic substances, manufacturing
- Laxative preparations, manufacturing
- Medicinal chemicals, uncompounded, manufacturing
- Nicotine and derivatives (i.e., basic chemicals), manufacturing
- Nuclear medicine (e.g., radioactive isotopes) preparations, manufacturing
- Nutraceuticals, botanical based, manufacturing
- Oils, vegetable and animal, medicinal, uncompounded, manufacturing
- Opium and opium derivatives (i.e., basic chemicals), manufacturing
- Oral contraceptive preparations, manufacturing
- Patent medicine preparations, manufacturing
- Penicillin preparations, manufacturing
- Penicillin, uncompounded, manufacturing
- Pharmaceutical preparations (e.g., capsules, liniments, ointments, tablets), manufacturing

- Pituitary gland derivatives, uncompounded, manufacturing
- Pregnancy test kits, manufacturing
- Radioactive in-vivo diagnostic substances, manufacturing
- Salicylic acid, medicinal, uncompounded, manufacturing
- Sedative preparations, manufacturing
- Sodium chloride pharmaceutical preparations, manufacturing
- Steroids, uncompounded, manufacturing
- Sulpha drugs, uncompounded, manufacturing

- Tetracycline, uncompounded, manufacturing
- Toxoids (e.g., diphtheria, tetanus), manufacturing
- Tranquilizers preparations, manufacturing
- Vaccines (i.e., bacterial, virus), manufacturing
- Vegetable alkaloids (e.g., caffeine, codeine, morphine, nicotine), basic chemicals, manufacturing
- Veterinary medicinal preparations, manufacturing
- Water decontamination or purification tablets, manufacturing

325410 Pharmaceutical and Medicine Manufacturing CAN

See industry description for 32541, above.

3255 Paint, Coating and Adhesive Manufacturing

This industry group comprises establishments primarily engaged in manufacturing paints, coatings and adhesives.

32551 Paint and Coating Manufacturing

This industry comprises establishments primarily engaged in mixing pigments, solvents and binders into paints, stains and other coatings; and manufacturing related products.

Exclusion(s): Establishments primarily engaged in:
- manufacturing synthetic organic and inorganic dyes, pigments, lakes and toners (32513, Synthetic Dye and Pigment Manufacturing);
- manufacturing turpentine (32519, Other Basic Organic Chemical Manufacturing);
- manufacturing caulking compounds (32552, Adhesive Manufacturing); and
- manufacturing artists' paints (33994, Office Supplies (except Paper) Manufacturing).

Example Activities
- Architectural coatings (i.e., paint), manufacturing
- Driers, paint and varnish, manufacturing
- Enamel paints, manufacturing
- Fillers, wood (e.g., dry, liquid, paste), manufacturing
- Frit, manufacturing
- Glass frit, manufacturing
- Glaziers' putty, manufacturing
- Lacquers, manufacturing
- Latex paints (i.e., water-based), manufacturing
- Oil-based paints, manufacturing
- Oil-based stains, manufacturing
- Paint and varnish removers, manufacturing
- Paint thinner and reducer preparations, manufacturing

- Paintbrush cleaners, manufacturing
- Paints (except artists'), manufacturing
- Paints, emulsion (i.e., latex paint), manufacturing
- Paints, oil and alkyd vehicle, manufacturing
- Plastic wood fillers, manufacturing
- Polyurethane coatings, manufacturing
- Primers, paint, manufacturing
- Putty, glaziers', manufacturing
- Shellac, manufacturing
- Stains (except biological), manufacturing
- Varnish removers, manufacturing
- Varnishes, manufacturing
- Water repellent coatings for wood, concrete and masonry, manufacturing
- Wood fillers, manufacturing
- Wood stains, manufacturing

325510 Paint and Coating Manufacturing

See industry description for 32551, above.

32552 Adhesive Manufacturing

This industry comprises establishments primarily engaged in manufacturing glue, adhesives and related products.

Exclusion(s): Establishments primarily engaged in:
- manufacturing roofing cement (32412, Asphalt Paving, Roofing and Saturated Materials Manufacturing); and
- manufacturing gypsum-based caulking compounds, joint compounds and patching plaster (32742, Gypsum Product Manufacturing).

Example Activities
- Adhesives (except asphalt, dental, gypsum-based), manufacturing
- Caulking compounds (except gypsum-based), manufacturing
- Cement, rubber, manufacturing
- Construction adhesives (except asphalt, gypsum-based), manufacturing
- Epoxy adhesives, manufacturing
- Glue (except dental), manufacturing
- Joint compounds (except gypsum-based), manufacturing
- Mucilage adhesives, manufacturing
- Pastes, adhesive, manufacturing
- Pipe sealing compounds, manufacturing
- Plastics-based adhesives, manufacturing
- Putty, plumbers', manufacturing
- Rubber cement, manufacturing
- Sealing compounds for pipe threads and joints, manufacturing
- Starch glues, manufacturing

325520 Adhesive Manufacturing

See industry description for 32552, above.

3256 Soap, Cleaning Compound and Toilet Preparation Manufacturing

This industry group comprises establishments primarily engaged in manufacturing soap and other cleaning compounds and toilet preparations.

32561 Soap and Cleaning Compound Manufacturing

This industry comprises establishments primarily engaged in manufacturing soap and other cleaning compounds.

Exclusion(s): Establishments primarily engaged in:
- manufacturing industrial bleaches (32518, Other Basic Inorganic Chemical Manufacturing); and
- manufacturing shampoos and shaving preparations (32562, Toilet Preparation Manufacturing).

Example Activities
- Air fresheners, manufacturing
- Ammonia, household type, manufacturing
- Assistants, textile and leather finishing, manufacturing
- Automobile polishes and cleaners, manufacturing
- Bleaches, formulated for household use, manufacturing
- Brass polishes, manufacturing
- Cleaners, household type (e.g., oven, toilet bowl, window), manufacturing
- Cleaning and polishing preparations, manufacturing
- Cloths, dusting and polishing, chemically treated, manufacturing
- Dentifrices, manufacturing

- Deodorants (except personal), manufacturing
- Detergents (e.g., dishwashing, industrial, laundry), manufacturing
- Dishwasher detergents, manufacturing
- Disinfectants, household type and industrial, manufacturing
- Drain pipe cleaners, manufacturing
- Drycleaning preparations, manufacturing
- Dusting cloths, chemically treated, manufacturing
- Emulsifiers (i.e., surface active agents), manufacturing
- Fabric softeners, manufacturing
- Finishing agents, textile and leather, manufacturing
- Floor polishes and waxes, manufacturing
- Furniture polishes and waxes, manufacturing
- Hand soaps (e.g., hard, liquid, soft), manufacturing
- Laundry bleaches, formulated for household use, manufacturing
- Laundry soap, chips and powder, manufacturing
- Leather finishing assistants, manufacturing
- Metal polishes (i.e., tarnish removers), manufacturing
- Mordants, manufacturing
- Oils, soluble (i.e., textile finishing assistants), manufacturing

- Oven cleaners, manufacturing
- Penetrants, manufacturing
- Polishes (e.g., automobile, furniture, metal, shoe), manufacturing
- Polishing preparations, manufacturing
- Recycling drycleaning fluids
- Rug cleaning preparations, manufacturing
- Rust removers, manufacturing
- Scouring cleansers (e.g., pastes, powders), manufacturing
- Shoe polishes and cleaners, manufacturing
- Silver polishes, manufacturing
- Soaps (e.g., bar, chip, powder), manufacturing
- Spot removers (except laundry presoaks), manufacturing
- Starches, laundry, manufacturing
- Surface active agents, manufacturing
- Textile finishing assistants, manufacturing
- Textile scouring agents, manufacturing
- Toilet bowl cleaners, manufacturing
- Toothpastes, gels and tooth powders, manufacturing
- Tub and tile cleaning preparations, manufacturing
- Waxes, polishing (e.g., floor, furniture), manufacturing
- Wetting agents, manufacturing
- Window cleaning preparations, manufacturing

325610 Soap and Cleaning Compound Manufacturing MEX

See industry description for 32561, above.

32562 Toilet Preparation Manufacturing

This industry comprises establishments primarily engaged in preparing, blending and compounding toilet preparations.

Exclusion(s): Establishments primarily engaged in:
- manufacturing toothpaste (32561, Soap and Cleaning Compound Manufacturing).

Example Activities
- After-shave preparations, manufacturing
- Anti-perspirants, personal, manufacturing
- Bath salts, manufacturing
- Colognes, manufacturing
- Cosmetic creams, lotions and oils, manufacturing
- Dental floss, manufacturing
- Deodorants, personal, manufacturing
- Depilatory preparations, manufacturing

- Dyes, hair, manufacturing
- Eye make-up (e.g., eye shadow, eyebrow pencils, mascara), manufacturing
- Face creams (e.g., cleansing, moisturizing), manufacturing
- Foundations (i.e., make-up), manufacturing
- Hair preparations (e.g., conditioners, dyes, rinses, shampoos), manufacturing
- Lipsticks, manufacturing

- Make-up (i.e., cosmetics), manufacturing
- Nail polish removers, manufacturing
- Nail polishes, manufacturing
- Perfumes, manufacturing
- Permanent wave preparations, manufacturing
- Powder (e.g., baby, body, face, talcum, toilet), manufacturing
- Rouge, cosmetic, manufacturing
- Shampoos and conditioners, hair, manufacturing

- Shaving preparations (e.g., creams, gels, lotions, powders), manufacturing
- Sunscreen lotions and oils, manufacturing
- Suntan lotions and oils, manufacturing
- Talcum powders, manufacturing
- Tints, dyes and rinses, hair, manufacturing
- Toilet preparations (e.g., cosmetics, deodorants, perfumes), manufacturing
- Towelettes, premoistened, manufacturing

325620 Toilet Preparation Manufacturing

See industry description for 32562, above.

3259 Other Chemical Product Manufacturing

This industry group comprises establishments, not classified to any other industry group, primarily engaged in manufacturing chemical products.

32591 Printing Ink Manufacturing

This industry comprises establishments primarily engaged in manufacturing printing inks and ink jet inks, whether black or coloured. Establishments engaged in the manufacture of ink jet cartridges are included.

Exclusion(s): Establishments primarily engaged in:
- manufacturing toners for photocopiers, laser printers and similar electrostatic printing devices (32599, All Other Chemical Product Manufacturing);
- manufacturing writing, drawing and stamping ink (32599, All Other Chemical Product Manufacturing); and
- recycling ink jet cartridges (81121, Electronic and Precision Equipment Repair and Maintenance).

Example Activities
- Inkjet cartridges, manufacturing
- Inkjet inks, manufacturing
- Inks, printing, manufacturing

- Printing inks, manufacturing
- Screen process inks, manufacturing
- Stencil inks, manufacturing

325910 Printing Ink Manufacturing

See industry description for 32591, above.

32592 Explosives Manufacturing

This industry comprises establishments primarily engaged in manufacturing explosive preparations, detonators for explosives, and explosive devices, except ammunition.

Exclusion(s): Establishments primarily engaged in:
- manufacturing pyrotechnics (32599, All Other Chemical Product Manufacturing); and
- manufacturing ammunition and detonators for ammunition (33299, All Other Fabricated Metal Product Manufacturing).

Example Activities
- Azides explosive materials, manufacturing
- Blasting accessories (e.g., blasting caps, fuses, ignitors, squibbs), manufacturing
- Blasting powders, manufacturing
- Caps, blasting and detonating, manufacturing
- Detonators (except ammunition), manufacturing
- Dynamite, manufacturing
- Explosives, manufacturing
- Fuses, detonating and safety, manufacturing
- Gunpowder, manufacturing
- Nitroglycerin explosive materials, manufacturing
- TNT (trinitrotoluene), manufacturing
- Trinitrotoluene (TNT), manufacturing

325920 Explosives Manufacturing

See industry description for 32592, above.

32599 All Other Chemical Product Manufacturing

This industry comprises establishments, not classified to any other industry, primarily engaged in manufacturing chemical products.

325991 Custom Compounding of Purchased Resins US

This Canadian industry comprises establishments primarily engaged in the custom mixing and blending of purchased plastics resins; and compounding plastics resins from recycled plastics products.

Exclusion(s): Establishments primarily engaged in:
- manufacturing synthetic resins from basic organic chemicals (325210, Resin and Synthetic Rubber Manufacturing).

Example Activities
- Compounding plastics resins from recycled materials
- Custom compounding of purchased resins
- Plastics resins, compounding from recycled materials
- Plastics resins, custom compounding of purchased

325999 All Other Miscellaneous Chemical Product Manufacturing CAN

This Canadian industry comprises establishments, not classified to any other Canadian industry, primarily engaged in manufacturing chemical products.

Example Activities
- Activated carbon and charcoal, manufacturing
- Activated clays, earths and other mineral products, manufacturing
- Additive preparations for gasoline (e.g., anti-knock preparations, detergents, gum inhibitors), manufacturing
- Aerosol can filling, on a job order or contract basis
- Aerosol packaging services
- Antifreeze preparations, manufacturing
- Anti-scaling compounds, manufacturing
- Carbon, activated, manufacturing
- Cat litter (clay based), manufacturing
- Charcoal, activated, manufacturing
- Computer printer toner cartridges, manufacturing
- Concrete additive preparations (e.g., curing, hardening), manufacturing
- Crankcase additive preparations, manufacturing
- Degreasing preparations for machinery parts, manufacturing
- Deicing preparations, manufacturing
- Distilled water, manufacturing
- Drawing inks, manufacturing
- Drilling mud compounds, conditioners and additives (except bentonites), manufacturing

- Dye preparations, clothing, household type, manufacturing
- Embalming fluids, manufacturing
- Engine degreasers, manufacturing
- Essential oils, natural, manufacturing
- Film, sensitized (e.g., camera, motion picture, X-ray), manufacturing
- Fire extinguisher chemical preparations, manufacturing
- Fire retardant chemical preparations, manufacturing
- Fireworks, manufacturing
- Flares, manufacturing
- Fluxes (e.g., brazing, galvanizing, soldering, welding), manufacturing
- Foundry core oil, wash and wax, manufacturing
- Gelatin capsules, empty, manufacturing
- Greases, synthetic lubricating, manufacturing
- Hydraulic fluids, synthetic, manufacturing
- Incense, manufacturing
- Inhibitors (e.g., corrosion, oxidation, polymerization), manufacturing
- Inks, drawing, stamp pad and writing, manufacturing
- Insulating oils, manufacturing
- Lighter fluids (e.g., charcoal, cigarette), manufacturing
- Lubricating oils and greases, synthetic, manufacturing
- Matches and match books, manufacturing
- Motion picture film, manufacturing
- Motor oils, synthetic, manufacturing
- Napalm, manufacturing
- Oil additive preparations, manufacturing
- Oils (e.g., cutting, lubricating), synthetic, manufacturing
- Oils, essential, manufacturing
- Paper, photographic sensitized, manufacturing

- Photographic chemicals, manufacturing
- Photographic film, cloth, paper and plate, sensitized, manufacturing
- Photomasks, manufacturing
- Plasticizers, preparations, manufacturing
- Pyrotechnics (e.g., flares, flashlight bombs, signals), manufacturing
- Radiator additive preparations, manufacturing
- Recycling services for degreasing solvents (e.g., engine, machine part)
- Retarders (e.g., flameproofing agents, mildewing agents), manufacturing
- Rubber processing preparations (e.g., accelerators, stabilizers), manufacturing
- Rust preventative preparations, manufacturing
- Solvents recovery service, on a contract or fee basis
- Stabilizers, chemical preparations, manufacturing
- Sugar substitutes (i.e., synthetic sweeteners blended with other ingredients), made from purchased synthetic sweeteners
- Swimming pool chemical preparations, manufacturing
- Toner cartridges, manufacturing
- Toner cartridges, rebuilding
- Toners (i.e., for photocopiers, laser printers and similar electrostatic printing devices), manufacturing
- Toners (i.e., photographic), manufacturing
- Transmission fluids, synthetic, manufacturing
- Water treatment chemical preparations, manufacturing
- Water, distilled, manufacturing
- Writing inks, manufacturing
- X-ray films and plates, sensitized, manufacturing

326 Plastics and Rubber Products Manufacturing

This subsector comprises establishments primarily engaged in making goods by processing raw rubber and plastics materials. Rubber- and plastics-based activities are combined in the same subsector because the technical properties of these polymers are related.

Generally, establishments classified in this subsector manufacture products made of just one material, rubber or plastics, with the major exception of tire manufacturing.

Exclusion(s): Establishments primarily engaged in:
- manufacturing synthetic resins from basic organic chemicals (325210, Resin and Synthetic Rubber Manufacturing); and
- compounding plastics resins from recycled materials (32599, All Other Chemical Product Manufacturing).

3261 Plastic Product Manufacturing

This industry group comprises establishments primarily engaged in manufacturing intermediate or final products from plastics resins, using such processes as compression moulding, extrusion moulding, injection moulding, blow moulding and casting. The production process in most of these industries is such that a wide variety of products can be produced. The plastics resins used by these establishments may be new or recycled.

Exclusion(s): Establishments primarily engaged in:
- manufacturing laminated film, sheet and bags of plastic combined with other materials (3222, Converted Paper Product Manufacturing); and
- manufacturing plastic hose and belting (3262, Rubber Product Manufacturing).

32611 Plastic Packaging Materials and Unlaminated Film and Sheet Manufacturing

This industry comprises establishments primarily engaged in converting plastic resins into unsupported plastic films, sheets and bags and those that form, coat or laminate unsupported plastic films and sheets into unsupported plastic bags.

Exclusion(s): Establishments primarily engaged in:
- manufacturing plastic blister and bubble packaging (32619, Other Plastic Product Manufacturing).

326111 Plastic Bag and Pouch Manufacturing ᵁˢ

This Canadian industry comprises establishments primarily engaged in converting plastics resins into unsupported plastic bags and those that only form, coat or laminate plastic or cellulose films and sheets into unsupported plastic bags. Establishments that manufacture bags and print on them are included.

Exclusion(s): Establishments primarily engaged in:
- manufacturing bags of plastic coated or laminated with other materials (322220, Paper Bag and Coated and Treated Paper Manufacturing).

Example Activities
- Bags, plastics film, single or multi-wall, manufacturing
- Plastics film bags, single or multi-wall, manufactured and printed in the same establishment
- Plastics film bags, single or multi-wall, manufacturing

326114 Plastic Film and Sheet Manufacturing ᶜᴬᴺ

This Canadian industry comprises establishments primarily engaged in converting plastics resins into unsupported plastic film and sheet.

Exclusion(s): Establishments primarily engaged in:
- manufacturing film or sheet of plastic coated or laminated with other materials (322220, Paper Bag and Coated and Treated Paper Manufacturing); and
- manufacturing laminated plastic sheets (326130, Laminated Plastic Plate, Sheet (except Packaging), and Shape Manufacturing).

Example Activities

- Acrylic film and unlaminated sheet, manufacturing
- Film, plastics, manufacturing
- Film, plastics, packaging, manufacturing
- Packaging film, plastics, single or multi-web, manufacturing
- Photographic, micrographic and X-ray plastics sheet and film (except sensitized), manufacturing
- Plastics film and unlaminated sheet, manufacturing

- Polyester film and unlaminated sheet, manufacturing
- Polyethylene film and unlaminated sheet, manufacturing
- Polypropylene film and unlaminated sheet, manufacturing
- Sheet, plastics, unlaminated, manufacturing
- Vinyl and vinyl copolymer film and unlaminated sheet, manufacturing
- Window sheeting, unlaminated plastics, manufacturing

32612 Plastic Pipe, Pipe Fitting, and Unlaminated Profile Shape Manufacturing

This industry comprises establishments primarily engaged in manufacturing unsupported plastic profile shapes or plastic pipes and pipe fittings.

Exclusion(s): Establishments primarily engaged in:
- manufacturing plastic plumbing fixtures (32619, Other Plastic Product Manufacturing);
- manufacturing plastic hose (32622, Rubber and Plastic Hose and Belting Manufacturing); and
- manufacturing non-current-carrying plastic conduit (33593, Wiring Device Manufacturing).

326121 Unlaminated Plastic Profile Shape Manufacturing ᵁˢ

This Canadian industry comprises establishments primarily engaged in converting plastics resins into unsupported plastic profile shapes, except films, sheets and bags.

Exclusion(s): Establishments primarily engaged in:
- manufacturing unsupported plastic bags (326111, Plastic Bag and Pouch Manufacturing);
- manufacturing unsupported plastic films and sheets (326114, Plastic Film and Sheet Manufacturing); and
- manufacturing rigid plastic pipe and tubing (326122, Plastic Pipe and Pipe Fitting Manufacturing).

Example Activities

- Casings, sausage, plastics, manufacturing
- Lay flat tubing, plastics, manufacturing
- Profile shapes (e.g., rod, tube), non-rigid plastics, manufacturing

- Sausage casings, plastics, manufacturing
- Tube, non-rigid plastics, manufacturing

326122 Plastic Pipe and Pipe Fitting Manufacturing ᵁˢ

This Canadian industry comprises establishments primarily engaged in converting plastics resins into plastic pipes and pipe fittings.

Exclusion(s): Establishments primarily engaged in:
- manufacturing unsupported plastic tubing (326121, Unlaminated Plastic Profile Shape Manufacturing);
- manufacturing plastic plumbing fixtures (326191, Plastic Plumbing Fixture Manufacturing);
- manufacturing plastic hose (326220, Rubber and Plastic Hose and Belting Manufacturing); and
- manufacturing non-current-carrying plastic conduit (335930, Wiring Device Manufacturing).

Example Activities

- Fittings and unions, rigid plastics pipe, manufacturing
- Pipe fittings, rigid plastics, manufacturing
- Pipe, rigid plastics, manufacturing

32613 Laminated Plastic Plate, Sheet (except Packaging), and Shape Manufacturing

This industry comprises establishments primarily engaged in laminating plastic profile shapes, such as plates, sheets and rods. The lamination process generally involves bonding or impregnating profiles with plastics resins and compressing them under heat.

Exclusion(s): Establishments primarily engaged in:
- manufacturing unsupported laminated plastic film, sheets and bags (32611, Plastic Packaging Materials and Unlaminated Film and Sheet Manufacturing).

Example Activities

- Laminated plastics plate, rod and sheet, manufacturing
- Plate, laminated plastics, manufacturing
- Profile shapes (e.g., plate, rod, sheet), laminated plastics, manufacturing
- Rod, laminated plastics, manufacturing
- Sheet, laminated plastics, manufacturing
- Window sheeting, laminated plastics, manufacturing

326130 Laminated Plastic Plate, Sheet (except Packaging), and Shape Manufacturing

See industry description for 32613, above.

32614 Polystyrene Foam Product Manufacturing

This industry comprises establishments primarily engaged in converting polystyrene resins into foam products.

Example Activities

- Coolers or ice chests, polystyrene foam, manufacturing
- Dinnerware, polystyrene foam, manufacturing
- Expanded polystyrene products, manufacturing
- Foam polystyrene products, manufacturing
- Food containers, polystyrene foam, manufacturing
- Ice chests or coolers, polystyrene foam, manufacturing
- Insulation and cushioning, polystyrene foam, manufacturing
- Polystyrene foam packaging, manufacturing
- Profile shapes, polystyrene foam, manufacturing
- Sheet (i.e., board), polystyrene foam insulation, manufacturing
- Shipping pads and shaped cushioning, polystyrene foam, manufacturing
- Thermal insulation, polystyrene foam, manufacturing

326140 Polystyrene Foam Product Manufacturing

See industry description for 32614, above.

32615 Urethane and Other Foam Product (except Polystyrene) Manufacturing

This industry comprises establishments primarily engaged in converting plastics resins, other than polystyrene, into foam products.

Example Activities

- Cushion blocks, foam plastics (except polystyrene), manufacturing
- Expanded plastics (except polystyrene) products, manufacturing
- Foam plastics products (except polystyrene), manufacturing
- Food containers, foam plastics (except polystyrene), manufacturing
- Ice chests or coolers, foam plastics (except polystyrene), manufacturing
- Insulation and cushioning, foam plastics (except polystyrene), manufacturing
- Packaging, foam plastics (except polystyrene), manufacturing
- Polyurethane foam products, manufacturing
- Seat cushions, foam plastics (except polystyrene), manufacturing
- Shipping pads and shaped cushioning, foam plastics (except polystyrene), manufacturing
- Underlay, carpet and rug, foam plastics (except polystyrene), manufacturing

326150 Urethane and Other Foam Product (except Polystyrene) Manufacturing

See industry description for 32615, above.

32616 Plastic Bottle Manufacturing

This industry comprises establishments primarily engaged in blow moulding or casting plastic bottles.

Exclusion(s): Establishments primarily engaged in:
- manufacturing plastic containers, except bottles (32619, Other Plastic Product Manufacturing).

Example Activity
- Bottles, plastics, manufacturing

326160 Plastic Bottle Manufacturing

See industry description for 32616, above.

32619 Other Plastic Product Manufacturing

This industry comprises establishments, not classified to any other industry, primarily engaged in manufacturing plastic products.

326191 Plastic Plumbing Fixture Manufacturing US

This Canadian industry comprises establishments primarily engaged in manufacturing plastic plumbing fixtures.

Exclusion(s): Establishments primarily engaged in:
- manufacturing plastic pipes and pipe fittings (326122, Plastic Pipe and Pipe Fitting Manufacturing).

Example Activities
- Bathroom fixtures, plastics, manufacturing
- Bathtubs, plastics, manufacturing
- Chemical toilets, plastics, manufacturing
- Cultured marble plumbing fixtures, manufacturing
- Flush tanks, plastics, manufacturing
- Hot tubs, plastics or fibreglass, manufacturing
- Laundry tubs, plastics, manufacturing
- Plumbing fixtures (e.g., shower stalls, toilets, urinals), plastics or fibreglass, manufacturing
- Portable toilets, plastics, manufacturing
- Shower stalls, plastics or fibreglass, manufacturing
- Sinks, plastics, manufacturing
- Toilet fixtures, plastics, manufacturing
- Urinals, plastics, manufacturing

326193 Motor Vehicle Plastic Parts Manufacturing ^{CAN}

This Canadian industry comprises establishments primarily engaged in manufacturing plastic parts for motor vehicles. These parts are produced by basic plastics processes, such as moulding and extrusion, without further fabrication or assembly.

Exclusion(s): Establishments primarily engaged in:
- manufacturing motor vehicle parts by further fabrication of plastic components (33639, Other Motor Vehicle Parts Manufacturing).

Example Activities
- Bumper components, motor vehicle, plastics, manufacturing
- Fibreglass automobile body skins, manufacturing
- Hardware, plastics, motor vehicle, manufacturing
- Lenses, plastics, motor vehicle, manufacturing
- Motor vehicle mouldings and extrusions, plastics, manufacturing
- Plastics extrusions and mouldings, for making automobile parts, manufacturing
- Trim, motor vehicle, plastic mouldings and extrusions, manufacturing

326196 Plastic Window and Door Manufacturing ^{CAN}

This Canadian industry comprises establishments primarily engaged in manufacturing plastic doors and windows.

Exclusion(s): Establishments primarily engaged in:
- manufacturing plastic covered wood windows and doors (321911, Wood Window and Door Manufacturing).

Example Activities
- Doors and door frames, plastics, manufacturing
- Plastic window and door manufacturing
- Vinyl window and door manufacturing
- Window and door manufacturing, plastic or fibreglass
- Windows and window frames, plastics, manufacturing

326198 All Other Plastic Product Manufacturing ^{CAN}

This Canadian industry comprises establishments, not classified to any other Canadian industry, primarily engaged in manufacturing plastic products.

Example Activities
- Awnings, rigid plastic or fibreglass, manufacturing
- Badges, plastics, manufacturing
- Balloons, plastics, manufacturing
- Bathroom and toilet accessories, plastics, manufacturing
- Boats, inflatable plastics, manufacturing
- Bolts, nuts and rivets, plastics, manufacturing
- Bottle caps and lids, plastics, manufacturing
- Building materials (e.g., fascia, panels, siding, soffits), plastics, manufacturing
- Closures, plastics, manufacturing
- Clothes hangers, plastics, manufacturing
- Clothes pins, plastics, manufacturing
- Combs, plastics, manufacturing
- Containers, plastics (except foam, bottles and bags), manufacturing
- Coolers or ice chests, plastics (except foam), manufacturing
- Credit and identification card stock, plastics, manufacturing
- Cultured marble products (except plumbing fixtures), manufacturing
- Cups, plastics (except foam), manufacturing
- Dinnerware, plastics (except foam), manufacturing
- Door mats, plastics, manufacturing

- Drums, plastics (i.e., containers), manufacturing
- Floor coverings, resilient, manufacturing
- Floor tiles (i.e., linoleum, rubber, vinyl), manufacturing
- Flower pots, plastics, manufacturing
- Footwear parts (e.g., heels, soles), plastics, manufacturing
- Fourdrinier wires, plastics, manufacturing
- Garbage containers (except bags), plastics, manufacturing
- Gutters and down spouts, plastics, manufacturing
- Hardware (except motor vehicle), plastics, manufacturing
- Ice chests or coolers, plastics (except foam), manufacturing
- Identification card stock, plastics, manufacturing
- Kitchen utensils, plastic, manufacturing
- Lamp shades, plastics, manufacturing
- Lens blanks, optical and ophthalmic, plastics, manufacturing

- Life rafts, inflatable plastics, manufacturing
- Linoleum floor coverings, manufacturing
- Mattresses, air, plastics, manufacturing
- Nuts, bolts and rivets, plastics, manufacturing
- Packaging, plastics (e.g., blister, bubble), manufacturing
- Resilient floor coverings (e.g., sheet, tile), manufacturing
- Shoe parts (e.g., heels, soles), plastics, manufacturing
- Siding, plastics, manufacturing
- Sponges, plastics, manufacturing
- Swimming pool covers and liners, plastic, manufacturing
- Tableware, plastics (except foam), manufacturing
- Tanks, storage, plastic or fibreglass, manufacturing
- Tiles, floor (i.e., linoleum, vinyl, rubber), manufacturing
- Watch crystals, plastics, manufacturing
- Windshields, plastics, manufacturing

3262 Rubber Product Manufacturing

This industry group comprises establishments primarily engaged in processing natural, synthetic or reclaimed rubber materials into intermediate or final products using such processes as vulcanizing, cementing, moulding, extruding and lathe-cutting.

32621 Tire Manufacturing

This industry comprises establishments primarily engaged in manufacturing tires and inner tubes from natural and synthetic rubber; and retreading or rebuilding tires.

Exclusion(s): Establishments primarily engaged in:
- manufacturing synthetic rubber (32521, Resin and Synthetic Rubber Manufacturing);
- retailing and repairing tires (44132, Tire Dealers); and
- repairing tires (81119, Other Automotive Repair and Maintenance).

Example Activities
- Aircraft tires, manufacturing
- Camelback (i.e., retreading materials), manufacturing
- Inner tubes, manufacturing
- Motor vehicle tires, manufacturing
- Rebuilding tires
- Retreading materials, tire, manufacturing

- Retreading tires
- Tire retreading, recapping or rebuilding
- Tires (e.g., pneumatic, semi-pneumatic, solid rubber), manufacturing
- Tread rubber (i.e., camelback), manufacturing
- Tubes, inner, manufacturing

326210 Tire Manufacturing CAN

See industry description for 32621, above.

32622 Rubber and Plastic Hose and Belting Manufacturing

This industry comprises establishments primarily engaged in manufacturing rubber and plastic hose (reinforced) and belting from natural and synthetic rubber and/or plastics resins.

Exclusion(s): Establishments primarily engaged in:
- manufacturing plastic tubing and pipe (32612, Plastic Pipe, Pipe Fitting, and Unlaminated Profile Shape Manufacturing); and
- manufacturing rubber tubing (32629, Other Rubber Product Manufacturing).

Example Activities
- Belting, rubber (e.g., conveyor, elevator, transmission), manufacturing
- Conveyor belts, rubber, manufacturing
- Fan belts, rubber or plastics, manufacturing
- Garden hose, rubber or plastics, manufacturing
- Hose, reinforced, made from purchased plastics
- Hose, reinforced, made from purchased rubber
- Hose, rubberized fabric, manufacturing
- Hydraulic hose (without fittings), rubber or plastics, manufacturing
- Motor vehicle belts and hoses, rubber or plastics, manufacturing
- Pneumatic hose, without fittings, rubber or plastic, manufacturing
- Radiator and heater hoses, rubber, manufacturing
- Transmission belts, rubber, manufacturing
- V-belts, plastics, manufacturing
- V-belts, rubber, manufacturing

326220 Rubber and Plastic Hose and Belting Manufacturing

See industry description for 32622, above.

32629 Other Rubber Product Manufacturing

This industry comprises establishments, not classified to any other industry, primarily engaged in manufacturing rubber products.

Exclusion(s): Establishments primarily engaged in:
- rubberizing fabric (31332, Fabric Coating).

Example Activities
- Balloons, rubber, manufacturing
- Birth control devices (i.e., diaphragms, prophylactics), rubber, manufacturing
- Bottles, rubber, manufacturing
- Combs, rubber, manufacturing
- Condoms, manufacturing
- Diaphragms (i.e., birth control devices), rubber, manufacturing
- Dinghies, inflatable rubber, manufacturing
- Erasers, rubber, or rubber and abrasive combined, manufacturing
- Floor mats (e.g., bath, door), rubber, manufacturing
- Footwear parts (e.g., heels, soles, soling strips), rubber, manufacturing
- Hard rubber products, not specified elsewhere by process, manufacturing
- Heels, shoe, rubber, manufacturing
- Hot water bottles, rubber, manufacturing
- Inflatable rubber rafts (non-recreative), manufacturing
- Inflatable rubber swimming pool rafts and similar flotation devices, manufacturing
- Jar rings, rubber, manufacturing
- Latex foam rubber, manufacturing
- Life rafts, inflatable rubber, manufacturing
- Mats and matting, rubber, manufacturing
- Mattresses, air, rubber, manufacturing
- Mechanical rubber goods (i.e, extruded, lathe-cut, moulded), manufacturing
- Nipples and teething rings, rubber, manufacturing
- Pipe, hard rubber, manufacturing
- Prophylactics, rubber, manufacturing
- Reclaiming rubber from waste or scrap

- Roofing (i.e., single-ply rubber membrane), manufacturing
- Rubber bands, manufacturing
- Rubber goods, mechanical (i.e, extruded, lathe-cut, moulded), manufacturing
- Stair treads, rubber, manufacturing
- Thread, rubber (except fabric covered), manufacturing
- Tubing, rubber, manufacturing
- Weatherstripping, rubber, manufacturing

326290 Other Rubber Product Manufacturing ^{MEX}

See industry description for 32629, above.

327 Non-Metallic Mineral Product Manufacturing

This subsector comprises establishments primarily engaged in manufacturing non-metallic mineral products. These establishments cut, grind, shape and finish granite, marble, limestone, slate and other stone; mix non-metallic minerals with chemicals and other additives; and heat non-metallic mineral preparations to make products, such as bricks, refractories, ceramic products, cement and glass.

Exclusion(s): Establishments primarily engaged in:
- beneficiating non-metallic minerals (212, Mining and Quarrying (except Oil and Gas)).

3271 Clay Product and Refractory Manufacturing

This industry group comprises establishments primarily engaged in manufacturing pottery, ceramic and structural clay products.

32711 Pottery, Ceramics and Plumbing Fixture Manufacturing

This industry comprises establishments primarily engaged in shaping, moulding, glazing and firing pottery, ceramics and plumbing fixtures. These products may be made of clay or other materials with similar properties. Establishments that fire and decorate white china (whiteware) for the trade are included.

Example Activities
- Ashtrays, pottery, manufacturing
- Bathroom accessories, vitreous china and earthenware, manufacturing
- Ceramic insulators, manufacturing
- China tableware, vitreous, manufacturing
- Clay and ceramic statuary, manufacturing
- Cooking ware, china, earthenware, pottery or stoneware, manufacturing
- Decalcomania on china and glass, for the trade
- Dishes, pottery, manufacturing
- Drinking fountains, vitreous china, non-refrigerated, manufacturing
- Earthenware table and kitchen articles, manufacturing
- Electrical insulators, porcelain, manufacturing
- Filtering media, pottery, manufacturing
- Flower pots, red earthenware, manufacturing
- Garden pottery, manufacturing
- Insulators, electrical porcelain, manufacturing
- Kitchenware, china, earthenware, pottery or stoneware, manufacturing
- Magnets, permanent, ceramic or ferrite, manufacturing
- Plumbing fixtures, vitreous china, manufacturing
- Porcelain parts, electrical and electronic devices, moulded, manufacturing
- Porcelain, chemical, manufacturing
- Pottery products, manufacturing
- Sinks, vitreous china, manufacturing
- Spark plug insulators, porcelain, manufacturing
- Statuary, clay and ceramic, manufacturing
- Table articles, earthenware, manufacturing
- Table articles, vitreous china, manufacturing
- Tanks, flush, vitreous china, manufacturing
- Toilet fixtures, vitreous china, manufacturing
- Vases, pottery (e.g., china, earthenware and stoneware), manufacturing

327110 Pottery, Ceramics and Plumbing Fixture Manufacturing CAN

See industry description for 32711, above.

32712 Clay Building Material and Refractory Manufacturing

This industry comprises establishments primarily engaged in shaping, moulding, baking, burning and hardening building materials and refractories. These products may be made of clay or other materials with similar properties.

Example Activities

- Aluminous refractory cement, manufacturing
- Brick (i.e., common face, glazed, vitrified, hollow), clay, manufacturing
- Brick, clay refractory, manufacturing
- Brick, nonclay (e.g., chrome, magnesite, silica) refractory, manufacturing
- Cement, refractory, manufacturing
- Ceramic tile, floor and wall, manufacturing
- Clay brick, manufacturing
- Conduit, vitrified clay, manufacturing
- Coping, wall, clay, manufacturing
- Drain tile, clay, manufacturing
- Fire brick, clay refractories, manufacturing
- Floor tile, ceramic, manufacturing
- Flue lining, clay, manufacturing
- Kiln furniture, clay, manufacturing
- Liner brick and plates, vitrified clay, manufacturing
- Magnesia refractory cement, manufacturing
- Mortars, refractory, manufacturing
- Mosaic tile, ceramic, manufacturing
- Paving brick, clay, manufacturing
- Refractories (e.g., block, brick, mortar, tile), manufacturing
- Refractory cement and mortar, manufacturing
- Roofing tile, clay, manufacturing
- Sewer pipe and fittings, clay, manufacturing
- Structural clay tile, manufacturing
- Tile, ceramic wall and floor, manufacturing
- Tile, clay refractory, manufacturing
- Tile, clay, structural, manufacturing
- Tile, roofing and drain, clay, manufacturing
- Tile, sewer, clay, manufacturing
- Wall tile, ceramic, manufacturing

327120 Clay Building Material and Refractory Manufacturing CAN

See industry description for 32712, above.

3272 Glass and Glass Product Manufacturing

See industry description for 32721, below.

32721 Glass and Glass Product Manufacturing

This industry comprises establishments primarily engaged in manufacturing glass and glass products.

Exclusion(s): Establishments primarily engaged in:
- manufacturing windows (32191, Millwork);
- manufacturing fibreglass insulation (32799, All Other Non-Metallic Mineral Product Manufacturing);
- manufacturing optical fibre cable, made of individually sheathed strands (33592, Communication and Energy Wire and Cable Manufacturing); and
- manufacturing fibreglass boats (33661, Ship and Boat Building).

327214 Glass Manufacturing CAN

This Canadian industry comprises establishments primarily engaged in making glass from sand and cullet. These establishments may also make glass products. Establishments primarily engaged in manufacturing unsheathed optical fibres, and bundles and cables made of unsheathed fibres, are included.

Exclusion(s): Establishments primarily engaged in:
- manufacturing optical fibre cable, made of individually sheathed glass strands (335920, Communication and Energy Wire and Cable Manufacturing).

Example Activities
- Ashtrays, glass, made in glass-making plants
- Blanks for electric light bulbs, glass, made in glass-making plants
- Blanks, ophthalmic lens and optical glass, made in glass-making plants
- Blocks, glass, made in glass-making plants
- Bottles (i.e., bottling, canning, packaging), made in glass-making plants
- Brick, glass, made in glass-making plants
- Christmas tree ornaments, glass, made in glass-making plants
- Containers for packaging, bottling and canning, made in glass-making plants
- Cooking ware (e.g., pots, baking pans), made in glass-making plants
- Flat glass (e.g., float, plate), made in glass-making plants
- Glass blocks and bricks, made in glass-making plants
- Glass packaging containers, made in glass-making plants
- Glass products (except packaging containers), made in glass-making plants
- Glass yarn, made in glass-making plants
- Glass, automotive, made in glass-making plants
- Glass, plate, made in glass-making plants
- Glassware for industrial, scientific and technical use, made in glass-making plants
- Glassware for lighting fixtures, made in glass-making plants
- Insulating glass, sealed units, made in glass-making plants
- Lens blanks, optical and ophthalmic, made in glass-making plants
- Optical fibres, strands, bundles and cables, unsheathed, made in glass-making plants
- Safety glass (including motor vehicle), made in glass-making plants
- Stained glass and stained glass products, made in glass-making plants
- Yarn, fibreglass, made in glass-making plants

327215 Glass Product Manufacturing from Purchased Glass US

This Canadian industry comprises establishments primarily engaged in remelting, pressing, blowing or otherwise shaping purchased glass. Establishments primarily engaged in blowing glass by hand are included.

Example Activities
- Aquariums, made from purchased glass
- Blanks, ophthalmic lens and optical glass, made from purchased glass
- Containers for packaging, bottling and canning, made from purchased glass
- Doors, unframed glass, made from purchased glass
- Furniture tops, glass (e.g., bevelled, cut, polished), made from purchased glass
- Glass blanks for electric light bulbs, made from purchased glass
- Glass packaging containers, made from purchased glass
- Glass products, made from purchased glass
- Glass, automotive, made from purchased glass
- Glassware for industrial, scientific and technical use, made from purchased glass
- Glassware for lighting fixtures, made from purchased glass
- Glassware, cut and engraved, made from purchased glass
- Hand blowing purchased glass
- Insulating glass, sealed units, made from purchased glass
- Laminated glass, made from purchased glass
- Lamp shades, made from purchased glass
- Lens blanks, optical and ophthalmic, made from purchased glass
- Mirrors, framed or unframed, made from purchased glass
- Optical fibres, strands, bundles and cables, unsheathed, made from purchased glass
- Safety glass (including motor vehicle), made from purchased glass
- Stained glass and stained glass products, made from purchased glass
- Watch crystals, made from purchased glass

3273 Cement and Concrete Product Manufacturing

This industry group comprises establishments primarily engaged in manufacturing hydraulic cement, ready-mix concrete, concrete bricks, pipes and blocks, and other concrete products.

32731 Cement Manufacturing

This industry comprises establishments primarily engaged in the production of clinker and subsequent grinding of clinker using either dry or wet production processes.

Exclusion(s): Establishments primarily engaged in:
- manufacturing refractory cements (32712, Clay Building Material and Refractory Manufacturing).

Example Activities
- Cement (e.g., hydraulic, masonry, portland, pozzolana), manufacturing
- Hydraulic cement, manufacturing
- Masonry cement, manufacturing
- Natural (i.e., calcined earth) cement, manufacturing
- Portland cement, manufacturing

327310 Cement Manufacturing

See industry description for 32731, above.

32732 Ready-Mix Concrete Manufacturing

This industry comprises establishments primarily engaged in mixing together water, cement, sand, gravel or crushed stone to make concrete, and delivering it to a purchaser in a plastic or unhardened state.

Exclusion(s): Establishments primarily engaged in:
- mixing concrete, or pouring ready-mix concrete, at a construction site (23811, Poured Concrete Foundation and Structure Contractors); and
- manufacturing dry-batched ready-mix concrete (32731, Cement Manufacturing).

Example Activities
- Central-mixed concrete, manufacturing
- Concrete batch plants (including temporary)
- Ready-mixed concrete manufacturing and distribution
- Transit-mixed concrete, manufacturing

327320 Ready-Mix Concrete Manufacturing

See industry description for 32732, above.

32733 Concrete Pipe, Brick and Block Manufacturing

This industry comprises establishments primarily engaged in manufacturing concrete pipe, brick and block from a mixture of cement, water and aggregate.

Example Activities
- Architectural block, concrete (e.g., fluted, screen, split, slump, ground face), manufacturing
- Blocks, concrete and cinder, manufacturing
- Bricks, concrete, manufacturing
- Cinder (i.e., clinker) block, concrete, manufacturing
- Concrete blocks, bricks and pipe, precast, manufacturing
- Culvert pipe, concrete, manufacturing
- Patio blocks, concrete, manufacturing
- Paving blocks, concrete, manufacturing
- Pipe, concrete, manufacturing

- Precast concrete blocks and bricks, manufacturing
- Precast concrete pipe, manufacturing
- Prestressed concrete pipe, manufacturing
- Sewer pipe, concrete, manufacturing

327330 Concrete Pipe, Brick and Block Manufacturing MEX

See industry description for 32733, above.

32739 Other Concrete Product Manufacturing

This industry comprises establishments, not classified to any other industry, primarily engaged in manufacturing concrete products.

Example Activities
- Architectural wall panels, precast concrete, manufacturing
- Catch basin covers, concrete, manufacturing
- Concrete furniture (e.g., benches, tables), manufacturing
- Concrete products, precast (except block, brick, pipe), manufacturing
- Concrete tanks, manufacturing
- Floor slabs, precast concrete, manufacturing
- Furniture, concrete (e.g., benches, tables), manufacturing
- Girders and beams, prestressed concrete, manufacturing
- Joists, girders and beams, prestressed concrete, manufacturing
- Lintels, concrete, manufacturing
- Monuments and tombstones, concrete, manufacturing
- Ornaments, concrete lawn and garden, manufacturing
- Poles, concrete, manufacturing
- Posts, concrete, manufacturing
- Precast concrete products (except block, brick, pipe), manufacturing
- Prestressed concrete products (except block, brick, pipe), manufacturing
- Roofing tile, concrete, manufacturing
- Stairs, steps and landings, prefabricated concrete, manufacturing
- Storage tanks, concrete, manufacturing
- Terrazzo products, precast (except block, brick and pipe), manufacturing
- Ties, concrete railroad, manufacturing

327390 Other Concrete Product Manufacturing US

See industry description for 32739, above.

3274 Lime and Gypsum Product Manufacturing

This industry group comprises establishments primarily engaged in manufacturing lime and gypsum products.

32741 Lime Manufacturing

This industry comprises establishments primarily engaged in manufacturing quicklime, hydrated lime and dead-burned dolomite by crushing, screening and roasting limestone, dolomite shells or other sources of calcium carbonate.

Example Activities
- Agricultural lime, manufacturing
- Calcium hydroxide (i.e., hydrated lime), manufacturing
- Calcium oxide (i.e., quicklime), manufacturing
- Dolomite, dead-burned, manufacturing
- Hydrated lime (i.e., calcium hydroxide), manufacturing
- Lime, manufacturing
- Quicklime (i.e., calcium oxide), manufacturing

327410 Lime Manufacturing

See industry description for 32741, above.

32742 Gypsum Product Manufacturing

This industry comprises establishments primarily engaged in manufacturing products composed wholly or chiefly of gypsum.

Example Activities

- Art goods (e.g., gypsum, plaster of Paris), manufacturing
- Board, gypsum, manufacturing
- Cement, Keene's (i.e., tiling plaster), manufacturing
- Drywall cement and panels, gypsum-based, manufacturing
- Ecclesiastical statuary, gypsum, manufacturing
- Gypsum building products, manufacturing
- Joint compounds, gypsum-based, manufacturing
- Keene's cement, manufacturing
- Lath, gypsum, manufacturing
- Ornamental and architectural plaster work (e.g., columns, mantels, mouldings), manufacturing
- Plaster of Paris, manufacturing
- Plaster, gypsum, manufacturing
- Wallboard, gypsum, manufacturing

327420 Gypsum Product Manufacturing

See industry description for 32742, above.

3279 Other Non-Metallic Mineral Product Manufacturing

This industry group comprises establishments, not classified to any other industry group, primarily engaged in manufacturing non-metallic mineral products.

32791 Abrasive Product Manufacturing

This industry comprises establishments primarily engaged in manufacturing abrasive grinding wheels, abrasive-coated materials and other abrasive products.

Exclusion(s): Establishments primarily engaged in:
- manufacturing metallic scouring sponges and soap-impregnated scouring pads (33299, All Other Fabricated Metal Product Manufacturing).

Example Activities

- Abrasive products, manufacturing
- Artificial corundum, manufacturing
- Buffing and polishing wheels, abrasive and nonabrasive, manufacturing
- Cloth (e.g., aluminum oxide, emery, garnet, silicon carbide), abrasive-coated, manufacturing
- Diamond dressing wheels, manufacturing
- Grinding balls, ceramic, manufacturing
- Paper (e.g., aluminum oxide, emery, garnet, silicon carbide) abrasive-coated, manufacturing
- Polishing wheels, manufacturing
- Sandpaper, manufacturing
- Silicon carbide abrasives, manufacturing
- Steel shot abrasives, manufacturing
- Wheels, abrasive, manufacturing
- Wheels, polishing and grinding, manufacturing

327910 Abrasive Product Manufacturing

See industry description for 32791, above.

32799 All Other Non-Metallic Mineral Product Manufacturing

This industry comprises establishments, not classified to any other industry, primarily engaged in manufacturing non-metallic mineral products.

Exclusion(s): Establishments primarily engaged in:
- manufacturing asbestos brake and clutch linings (33634, Motor Vehicle Brake System Manufacturing); and
- manufacturing asbestos gaskets and gasket materials (33999, All Other Miscellaneous Manufacturing).

Example Activities
- Bricks and blocks, sand-lime, manufacturing
- Concrete, dry mixture, manufacturing
- Dimension stone dressing and manufacturing
- Dimension stone for buildings, manufacturing
- Dry mix concrete, manufacturing
- Ecclesiastical statuary, stone, manufacturing
- Fibreglass insulation products, manufacturing
- Fuller's earth, processing beyond beneficiating
- Furniture, cut stone (i.e., benches, tables, church), manufacturing
- Insulating batts, fills or blankets, fibreglass, manufacturing
- Insulation, mineral wool, manufacturing
- Kaolin, processing beyond beneficiating
- Mica products, manufacturing
- Mineral wool insulation materials, manufacturing
- Mineral wool products (e.g., board, insulation, tile), manufacturing
- Monuments and tombstones, cut stone (except finishing or lettering to order only), manufacturing
- Peat pots, manufacturing
- Statuary, marble, manufacturing
- Stone, cut products (e.g., blocks, statuary), manufacturing
- Stucco and stucco products, manufacturing
- Synthetic stones, for gem stones and industrial use, manufacturing
- Tile, acoustical, mineral wool, manufacturing
- Vermiculite, exfoliated, manufacturing

327990 All Other Non-Metallic Mineral Product Manufacturing CAN

See industry description for 32799, above.

331 Primary Metal Manufacturing

This subsector comprises establishments primarily engaged in smelting and refining ferrous and non-ferrous metals from ore, pig or scrap in blast or electric furnaces. Metal alloys are made with the introduction of other chemical elements. The output of smelting and refining, usually in ingot form, is used in rolling and drawing operations to produce sheet, strip, bars, rods and wire, and in molten form to produce castings and other basic metal products.

Exclusion(s): Establishments primarily engaged in:
- manufacturing metal forgings or stampings (332, Fabricated Metal Product Manufacturing).

3311 Iron and Steel Mills and Ferro-Alloy Manufacturing

See industry description for 33111, below.

33111 Iron and Steel Mills and Ferro-Alloy Manufacturing

This industry comprises establishments primarily engaged in smelting iron ore and steel scrap to produce pig iron in molten or solid form; converting pig iron into steel by the removal, through combustion in furnaces, of the carbon in the iron. These establishments may cast ingots only, or also produce iron and steel basic shapes, such as plates, sheets, strips, rods and bars, and other fabricated products. Electric arc furnace mini-mills are included. Establishments primarily engaged in producing ferro-alloys are also included.

Exclusion(s): Establishments primarily engaged in:
- operating coke ovens (32419, Other Petroleum and Coal Product Manufacturing);
- manufacturing iron and steel pipe and tube, from purchased metal (33121, Iron and Steel Pipes and Tubes Manufacturing from Purchased Steel); and
- manufacturing iron and steel basic shapes by cold-rolling purchased metal, or drawing wire from purchased bars, rod or wire (33122, Rolling and Drawing of Purchased Steel).

Example Activities
- Bars, iron or steel, made in steel mills
- Blast furnaces
- Cold rolled steel shapes (e.g., bar, plate, rod, sheet, strip), made in steel mills
- Direct reduction of iron ore
- Drawing iron or steel wire in steel mills
- Electric arc furnace steel mills
- Electrometallurgical ferro-alloys, manufacturing
- Ferro-alloys, manufacturing
- Forgings, iron or steel, made in steel mills
- Hot-rolled iron and steel products, made in steel mills
- Ingot, made in steel mills
- Iron ore recovery from open hearth slag
- Iron, pig, manufacturing
- Mini-mills, steel
- Pig iron, manufacturing
- Pipe, iron or steel, made in steel mills
- Reclaiming iron and steel scrap from slag
- Spiegeleisen ferro-alloys, manufacturing
- Steel mills
- Steel products (e.g., bar, plate, rod, sheet, structural shapes), made in steel mills
- Steel, manufacturing
- Strip, galvanized iron or steel, made in steel mills
- Strip, iron or steel, made in steel mills
- Superalloys, iron or steel, made in steel mills
- Tube, iron or steel, made in steel mills
- Wire products, iron or steel, made in steel mills

331110 Iron and Steel Mills and Ferro-Alloy Manufacturing CAN

See industry description for 33111, above.

3312 Steel Product Manufacturing from Purchased Steel

This industry group comprises establishments primarily engaged in manufacturing iron and steel pipe and tube, drawing steel wire, and rolling steel shapes, from purchased steel.

33121 Iron and Steel Pipes and Tubes Manufacturing from Purchased Steel

This industry comprises establishments primarily engaged in the production of welded or seamless iron and steel pipes and tubes, and heavy, rivetted steel pipes, from purchased steel.

Example Activities
- Line pipe for oil or gas, made from purchased steel
- Pipe (e.g., heavy riveted, lock joint, seamless, welded), made from purchased iron or steel
- Steel pipe and tubing, made from purchased steel
- Tube (e.g., heavy riveted, lock joint, seamless, welded), made from purchased iron or steel

331210 Iron and Steel Pipes and Tubes Manufacturing from Purchased Steel

See industry description for 33121, above.

33122 Rolling and Drawing of Purchased Steel

This industry comprises establishments primarily engaged in drawing wire or rolling sheets, strips and bars from purchased iron or steel.

Exclusion(s): Establishments primarily engaged in:
- manufacturing wire products from wire drawn in other establishments (33261, Spring and Wire Product Manufacturing).

331221 Cold-Rolled Steel Shape Manufacturing ᵁˢ

This Canadian industry comprises establishments primarily engaged in cold-rolling steel bars, sheets, strips and other steel shapes, from purchased steel. Establishments primarily engaged in re-heating purchased steel, and hot-rolling steel shapes, are also included.

Exclusion(s): Establishments primarily engaged in:
- manufacturing steel shapes from steel made in the same establishment (331110, Iron and Steel Mills and Ferro-Alloy Manufacturing).

Example Activities
- Cold-rolled steel shapes (e.g., bar, plate, rod, sheet, strip), made from purchased steel
- Hot-rolling purchased steel
- Iron basic shapes (except pipe, tube or wire), made from purchased iron
- Rolled steel products, made from purchased steel
- Steel basic shapes (except pipe, tube or wire), made from purchased steel
- Wire, flat, rolled strip, made from purchased iron or steel

331222 Steel Wire Drawing ᵁˢ

This Canadian industry comprises establishments primarily engaged in drawing purchased iron or steel rods, bars or wire through a die, to produce wire. Establishments primarily engaged in drawing steel wire and manufacturing wire products are included.

Exclusion(s): Establishments primarily engaged in:
- manufacturing ferrous wire from iron or steel produced in the same establishment (331110, Iron and Steel Mills and Ferro-Alloy Manufacturing);
- drawing aluminum wire (331317, Aluminum Rolling, Drawing, Extruding and Alloying);
- drawing copper wire (331420, Copper Rolling, Drawing, Extruding and Alloying);
- drawing non-ferrous wire, except copper and aluminum (331490, Non-Ferrous Metal (except Copper and Aluminum) Rolling, Drawing, Extruding and Alloying); and
- manufacturing non-insulated wire products from wire drawn in other establishments (332619, Other Fabricated Wire Product Manufacturing).

Example Activities
- Barbed and twisted wire, made in wire drawing plants
- Cable, iron or steel, insulated or armoured, made in wire drawing plants
- Chain link fencing, iron or steel, made in wire drawing plants
- Drawing wire from purchased iron or steel
- Drawing wire from purchased iron or steel and fabricating wire products
- Nails, iron or steel, made in wire drawing plants
- Paper clips, iron or steel, made in wire drawing plants
- Staples, iron or steel, made in wire drawing plants
- Wire garment hangers, iron or steel, made in wire drawing plants
- Wire products, iron or steel, made in wire drawing plants
- Wire, iron or steel (e.g., armoured, bare or insulated), made in wire drawing plants
- Wire, iron or steel, electric, made in wire drawing plants

3313 Alumina and Aluminum Production and Processing

See industry description for 33131, below.

33131 Alumina and Aluminum Production and Processing

This industry comprises establishments primarily engaged in extracting alumina generally from bauxite ore; producing aluminum from alumina; refining aluminum by any process; and rolling, drawing, casting, extruding and alloying aluminum and aluminum-based alloy basic shapes.

Exclusion(s): Establishments primarily engaged in:
- pouring non-ferrous molten metal into moulds, or under pressure into dies, to form castings (33152, Non-Ferrous Metal Foundries).

331313 Primary Production of Alumina and Aluminum CAN

This Canadian industry comprises establishments primarily engaged in extracting alumina generally from bauxite or producing aluminum from alumina. Establishments engaged in secondary activities, such as rolling, drawing , casting or extruding basic shapes, from aluminum produced in the same establishment, are included.

Exclusion(s): Establishments primarily engaged in:
- rolling, drawing, extruding or alloying purchased aluminum (331317, Aluminum Rolling, Drawing, Extruding and Alloying).

Example Activities
- Alumina (aluminum oxide), refining from bauxite
- Aluminum basic shapes (e.g., bar, ingot, rod, sheet), made in primary aluminum plants
- Aluminum ingot and other primary production shapes, made in primary aluminum plants
- Aluminum, producing from bauxite or alumina
- Ingot, primary aluminum, manufacturing
- Primary smelting of aluminum

331317 Aluminum Rolling, Drawing, Extruding and Alloying CAN

This Canadian industry comprises establishments primarily engaged in rolling purchased aluminum ingots; further hot- or cold-rolling to produce sheet, plate or foil; drawing aluminum alloys into products such as beverage cans and wire; extruding basic shapes; and alloying or re-alloying aluminum or aluminum alloys. Establishments primarily engaged in drawing aluminum wire, whether or not the establishment further works the wire by such operations as insulating it, are included. Establishments primarily engaged in recovering aluminum from scrap are also included.

Exclusion(s): Establishments primarily engaged in:
- rolling, drawing, extruding or alloying aluminum produced in the same establishment (331313, Primary Production of Alumina and Aluminum).

Example Activities
- Aluminum alloys, made from purchased metals
- Aluminum basic shapes (e.g., bar, ingot, rod, sheet), made from purchased aluminum
- Aluminum billet, made from purchased aluminum
- Aluminum foil, made by flat rolling purchased aluminum
- Aluminum ingot, made from purchased aluminum
- Aluminum wire and cable, made from purchased aluminum
- Aluminum, recovering from scrap or dross
- Bar, made from purchased aluminum
- Energy wire or cable, made in aluminum wire drawing plants

- Foil, aluminum, made by flat rolling purchased aluminum
- Ingot, made by rolling purchased aluminum
- Mesh, wire, made in aluminum wire drawing plants
- Molten aluminum, made from purchased aluminum
- Nails, made in aluminum wire drawing plants
- Pipe, aluminum, made from purchased aluminum
- Rod, made from purchased aluminum
- Scrap and dross aluminum, refining into ingot
- Sheet, aluminum, made by flat rolling purchased aluminum
- Structural shapes, made from purchased aluminum
- Wire cloth, made in aluminum wire drawing plants
- Wire products, made in aluminum wire drawing plants
- Wire screening, made in aluminum wire drawing plants
- Wire, aluminum, made in wire drawing plants
- Wire, armoured, made in aluminum wire drawing plants
- Wire, bare, made in aluminum wire drawing plants
- Wire, insulated, made in aluminum wire drawing plants

3314 Non-Ferrous Metal (except Aluminum) Production and Processing

This industry group comprises establishments primarily engaged in smelting, refining, rolling, drawing, extruding and alloying non-ferrous metal, except aluminum.

Exclusion(s): Establishments primarily engaged in:
- smelting, refining, rolling, drawing, extruding and alloying aluminum (3313, Alumina and Aluminum Production and Processing).

33141 Non-Ferrous Metal (except Aluminum) Smelting and Refining

This industry comprises establishments primarily engaged in smelting non-ferrous metals, except aluminum, from ores; and refining these metals by electrolytic or other processes. Establishments engaged in secondary activities, such as rolling or extruding basic shapes, from metal produced in the same establishment, are included.

Exclusion(s): Establishments primarily engaged in:
- producing bullion at a mine site (21222, Gold and Silver Ore Mining);
- aluminum smelting and refining (33131, Alumina and Aluminum Production and Processing);
- rolling, drawing, extruding and alloying purchased copper (33142, Copper Rolling, Drawing, Extruding and Alloying); and
- rolling, drawing, extruding and alloying purchased non-ferrous metals, except aluminum and copper (33149, Non-Ferrous Metal (except Copper and Aluminum) Rolling, Drawing, Extruding and Alloying).

Example Activities
- Antimony smelting and primary refining
- Beryllium smelting and primary refining
- Bismuth smelting and primary refining
- Cadmium smelting and primary refining
- Chromium smelting and primary refining
- Cobalt smelting and primary refining
- Copper alloys, made in primary copper smelting and refining mills
- Copper shapes (e.g., bar, billet, ingot, plate, sheet), made in primary copper smelting and refining mills
- Copper smelting and primary refining
- Germanium smelting and primary refining
- Gold smelting and primary refining
- Iridium smelting and primary refining
- Lead smelting and primary refining
- Magnesium smelting and primary refining
- Nickel smelting and primary refining
- Niobium smelting and primary refining
- Non-ferrous alloys, made in primary smelting and refining mills (except aluminum)

- Non-ferrous metals (except aluminum), smelting and primary refining
- Platinum smelting and primary refining
- Precious metals smelting and primary refining
- Primary refining of non-ferrous metals (except aluminum)
- Rhenium smelting and primary refining
- Selenium smelting and primary refining
- Silver smelting and primary refining

- Smelting of non-ferrous metals (except aluminum), primary
- Tantalum smelting and primary refining
- Tellurium smelting and primary refining
- Tin smelting and primary refining
- Titanium smelting and primary refining
- Tungsten smelting and primary refining
- Uranium smelting and primary refining
- Zinc smelting and primary refining
- Zirconium smelting and primary refining

331410 Non-Ferrous Metal (except Aluminum) Smelting and Refining [CAN]

See industry description for 33141, above.

33142 Copper Rolling, Drawing, Extruding and Alloying

This industry comprises establishments primarily engaged in rolling, drawing, extruding and re-alloying copper, brass, bronze and other copper-based alloys, to produce products such as plates, sheets, strips, bars, wire and tubing, and specialty alloys. Establishments primarily engaged in drawing copper wire (whether or not the establishment further works the wire by such operations as insulating it); and in recovering copper from scrap, are included.

Exclusion(s): Establishments primarily engaged in:
- manufacturing copper and copper alloy products in a smelter or refinery (33141, Non-Ferrous Metal (except Aluminum) Smelting and Refining);
- casting copper (33152, Non-Ferrous Metal Foundries); and
- insulating purchased copper wire and cable (33592, Communication and Energy Wire and Cable Manufacturing).

Example Activities
- Alloying purchased copper
- Brass products, made by rolling, drawing, extruding or alloying purchased metal
- Bronze products, made by rolling, drawing, extruding or alloying purchased metal
- Coaxial cable, made in copper wire drawing plants
- Copper alloys (e.g., brass, bronze), made from purchased metals and copper-based alloys
- Copper and copper alloy shapes (e.g., bar, ingot, rod, sheet), made from purchased metal or scrap
- Copper powder, paste and flakes, made from purchased copper
- Copper products, made by rolling, drawing, extruding or alloying purchased metal
- Copper refining, secondary (i.e., from purchased metal or scrap)

- Copper rolling, drawing and extruding
- Electric cable and wire, copper, made in wire drawing plants
- Foil, copper and copper alloy, made by rolling purchased metal or scrap
- Pipe, copper and copper alloy, made from purchased metal or scrap
- Powder, made from purchased copper
- Refining copper, secondary (i.e., of purchased metal or scrap)
- Strip, copper and copper alloy, made from purchased metal or scrap
- Tubing, copper and copper alloy, made from purchased metal or scrap
- Wire products, made in copper wire drawing plants
- Wire, copper and copper alloy, made in wire drawing plants

331420 Copper Rolling, Drawing, Extruding and Alloying [MEX]

See industry description for 33142, above.

33149 Non-Ferrous Metal (except Copper and Aluminum) Rolling, Drawing, Extruding and Alloying

This industry comprises establishments, not classified to any other industry, primarily engaged in rolling, drawing, extruding and re-alloying non-ferrous metals, to produce products such as plates, sheets, strips, bars, wire and tubing, and specialty alloys. Establishments primarily engaged in drawing wire of these metals are included (whether or not the establishment further works the wire by such operations as insulating it); and in recovering these metals from scrap, are included.

Exclusion(s): Establishments primarily engaged in:
- manufacturing non-ferrous metal (except aluminum) products in a smelter or refinery (33141, Non-Ferrous Metal (except Aluminum) Smelting and Refining); and
- insulating purchased wire and cable (33592, Communication and Energy Wire and Cable Manufacturing).

Example Activities
- Alloying purchased non-ferrous metals (except aluminum, copper)
- Alloying purchased precious metals
- Gold foil and leaf, made by rolling purchased metal or scrap
- Gold rolling and drawing, purchased metal or scrap
- Lead rolling, drawing or extruding, purchased metal or scrap
- Magnesium rolling, drawing or extruding, purchased metal or scrap
- Nails, made in non-ferrous (except aluminum, copper) wire drawing plants
- Nickel and nickel alloy bar, sheet, strip and tubing, made from purchased metal or scrap
- Nickel rolling, drawing and extruding, purchased metal or scrap
- Non-ferrous alloys (except aluminum, copper), made from purchased metals
- Non-ferrous metal (except aluminum, copper) powder, paste and flakes, made from purchased metals
- Paste, non-ferrous metal (except aluminum, copper), made from purchased metals
- Powder, non-ferrous metal (except aluminum, copper), made from purchased metals
- Rolling, drawing and extruding purchased non-ferrous metal (except aluminum, copper)
- Secondary refining (i.e, of purchased metal and scrap), precious metals
- Silver rolling, drawing or extruding, purchased metal or scrap
- Superalloys, non-ferrous based, made from purchased metals or scrap
- Tin rolling, drawing or extruding, purchased metal or scrap
- Tubing, made from purchased non-ferrous (except aluminum, copper) metal or scrap
- Wire, non-ferrous metal (except aluminum, copper), made in wire drawing plants
- Zinc rolling, drawing and extruding, purchased metal or scrap

331490 Non-Ferrous Metal (except Copper and Aluminum) Rolling, Drawing, Extruding and Alloying CAN

See industry description for 33149, above.

3315 Foundries

This industry group comprises establishments primarily engaged in pouring molten metal into moulds or dies to form castings.

Exclusion(s): Establishments primarily engaged in:
- forging and stamping metal (3321, Forging and Stamping).

33151 Ferrous Metal Foundries

This industry comprises establishments primarily engaged in pouring molten iron or steel into moulds to produce castings. These establishments generally operate on a job order basis, manufacturing castings for sale or transfer to other establishments.

Exclusion(s): Establishments primarily engaged in:
- producing iron and steel castings and further fabricating them, such as by machining and assembling (classified in the industry of the specified product).

331511 Iron Foundries ^{US}

This Canadian industry comprises establishments primarily engaged in pouring molten pig iron or alloy irons, into moulds to manufacture castings.

Example Activities
- Castings, unfinished, iron (e.g. ductile, grey, malleable, semisteel), manufacturing
- Castings, unfinished, semisteel, manufacturing
- Engine block castings, iron, unfinished, manufacturing
- Foundries, iron (i.e., ductile, grey, malleable, semisteel)
- Grey iron foundries
- Grinding balls, cast iron, manufacturing
- Hydrants, unfinished iron castings, manufacturing
- Iron foundries
- Manhole covers, cast iron, manufacturing
- Moulds for casting steel ingots, manufacturing
- Moulds, steel ingot, industrial, manufacturing
- Pipe and fittings, cast iron (e.g., soil, pressure), manufacturing
- Rolling mill rolls, iron, manufacturing
- Sewer pipe, cast iron, manufacturing

331514 Steel Foundries ^{CAN}

This Canadian industry comprises establishments primarily engaged in pouring molten steel into investment moulds or full moulds to manufacture steel castings.

Example Activities
- Castings, unfinished, steel, manufacturing
- Foundries, steel
- Investment castings, steel, unfinished, manufacturing
- Rolling mill rolls, steel, manufacturing
- Steel foundries

33152 Non-Ferrous Metal Foundries

This industry comprises establishments primarily engaged in pouring non-ferrous molten metal into moulds, or under pressure into dies, to form castings.

331523 Non-Ferrous Die-Casting Foundries ^{CAN}

This Canadian industry comprises establishments primarily engaged in introducing molten, non-ferrous metal, such as aluminum, copper or zinc, under high pressure, into a metal mould or die to manufacture castings.

Exclusion(s): Establishments primarily engaged in:
- manufacturing non-ferrous castings without using high pressure (331529, Non-Ferrous Foundries (except Die-Casting)).

Example Activities
- Copper die-casting foundries
- Die-castings, aluminum, unfinished, manufacturing
- Die-castings, non-ferrous metals, unfinished, manufacturing
- Foundries, die-casting, non-ferrous metals
- Nickel die-castings, unfinished, manufacturing
- Non-ferrous metal die-casting foundries

331529 Non-Ferrous Foundries (except Die-Casting) CAN

This Canadian industry comprises establishments, not classified to any other Canadian industry, primarily engaged in pouring non-ferrous molten metal, such as aluminum, copper or zinc, into moulds, without using high pressure, to manufacture castings.

Exclusion(s): Establishments primarily engaged in:
- manufacturing non-ferrous castings using high pressure (331523, Non-Ferrous Die-Casting Foundries).

Example Activities
- Aluminum foundries (except die-castings)
- Castings (except die-castings), aluminum, unfinished, manufacturing
- Castings (except die-castings), copper, unfinished, manufacturing
- Castings (except die-castings), non-ferrous metals, unfinished, manufacturing
- Foundries, aluminum (except die-castings)
- Foundries, non-ferrous metal (except die-castings)
- Investment castings, non-ferrous metals, unfinished, manufacturing
- Nickel castings (except die-castings), unfinished, manufacturing
- Non-ferrous metal castings (except die-castings), manufacturing
- Permanent mould castings, non-ferrous metals, unfinished, manufacturing
- Sand castings, non-ferrous metals, unfinished, manufacturing

332 Fabricated Metal Product Manufacturing

This subsector comprises establishments primarily engaged in forging, stamping, forming, turning and joining processes to produce ferrous and non-ferrous metal products, such as cutlery and hand tools, architectural and structural metal products, boilers, tanks and shipping containers, hardware, spring and wire products, turned products, and bolts, nuts and screws.

Exclusion(s): Establishments primarily engaged in:
- manufacturing metal products by rolling, drawing, extruding, alloying or casting (331, Primary Metal Manufacturing).

3321 Forging and Stamping

See industry description for 33211, below.

33211 Forging and Stamping

This industry comprises establishments primarily engaged in shaping hot metal by forging to produce a part near its final size and shape; or pressing and cutting sheet metal stock to form stampings. These establishments generally operate on a job or order basis, manufacturing metal stampings or forgings for sale to others or for inter-plant transfer. These establishments may surface-finish the forgings and stampings produced, by such activities as deburring and grinding, but they do not further process them.

Exclusion(s): Establishments primarily engaged in:
- making forgings or stampings, and then further processing them, for example by machining (classified according to the particular product or process).

332113 Forging CAN

This Canadian industry comprises establishments primarily engaged in hot forming metal using hammers or presses to forge parts. The forging process involves the use of dies to draw out or increase the length of a part, squeezing the part to reduce its length and increase its cross section, or piercing the part to create a cavity. Forging techniques include hammer, drop, press, upset, roll and hydraulic forging. These establishments may surface-finish the forgings produced, by such activities as deburring and grinding, but they do not further process them.

Example Activities

- Aluminum forgings, unfinished, made from purchased aluminum
- Automotive forgings, unfinished, made from purchased metal
- Cold forgings, unfinished, made from purchased metal
- Copper forgings, unfinished, made from purchased copper
- Drop forgings, unfinished, made from purchased metal
- Engine and turbine forgings, unfinished, made from purchased metal
- Ferrous forgings, unfinished, made from purchased iron or steel
- Forgings, ferrous, unfinished, made from purchased iron or steel

- Forgings, non-ferrous, unfinished, made from purchased non-ferrous metal
- Hammer forgings, unfinished, made from purchased metal
- Hot forgings, unfinished, made from purchased metal
- Iron forgings, unfinished, made from purchased iron
- Press forgings, unfinished, made from purchased metal
- Steel forgings, unfinished, made from purchased steel
- Titanium forgings, unfinished, made from purchased titanium
- Upset forgings, unfinished, made from purchased metal

332118 Stamping ^{CAN}

This Canadian industry comprises establishments primarily engaged in using a press to form and cut sheet-metal stock in one or a series of operations. The operations can be done in a single press closing with a mated die, or with several press closings and multiple dies. The part involved may have holes, slots, notches or features formed in it and be cut to size and deburred, but is otherwise essentially completed by the stamping operation. Establishments primarily engaged in custom roll-forming, using the rotary motion of rolls with various profiles to bend metal, are included.

Exclusion(s): Establishments primarily engaged in:
- manufacturing motor vehicle stampings (336370, Motor Vehicle Metal Stamping).

Example Activities

- Bottle caps and tops, metal, stamping
- Closures, metal, stamping
- Crowns (e.g., bottle, can), metal, stamping
- Custom roll forming of metal products
- Gutters and down spouts, sheet metal, roll formed, manufacturing
- Lids, jar, metal, stamping

- Metal stampings (except automotive, cans, coins), unfinished, manufacturing
- Powder metallurgy products, manufactured on a job or order basis
- Roll forming of metal products
- Spinning unfinished metal products
- Stampings (except automotive, cans, coins), metal, unfinished, manufacturing

3322 Cutlery and Hand Tool Manufacturing

See industry description for 33221, below.

33221 Cutlery and Hand Tool Manufacturing

This industry comprises establishments primarily engaged in manufacturing cutlery and hand tools. Establishments primarily engaged in manufacturing files and other hand and edge tools for metalworking, woodworking and general maintenance are included.

Exclusion(s): Establishments primarily engaged in:
- manufacturing precious metal cutlery (33991, Jewellery and Silverware Manufacturing).

Example Activities

- Agricultural handtools (e.g., hay forks, hoes, rakes, spades), non-powered, manufacturing
- Axes, manufacturing
- Bits, edge tools, woodworking, manufacturing
- Blades, saw, all types, manufacturing
- Carpenters' handtools (except saws), non-powered, manufacturing
- Caulking guns, non-powered, manufacturing
- Chainsaw blades, manufacturing
- Chisels, manufacturing
- Clippers for animal use, non-powered, manufacturing
- Clippers, fingernail and toenail, manufacturing
- Clippers, hair, for human use, non-powered, manufacturing
- Cooking utensils, fabricated metal, manufacturing
- Cutlery, base metal plated with precious metal, manufacturing
- Cutlery, non-precious metal, manufacturing
- Cutters, glass, manufacturing
- Cutting dies (except metal cutting), manufacturing
- Dies, cutting (except metal cutting), manufacturing
- Drill bits, woodworking, manufacturing
- Drills, hand held, non-power, manufacturing
- Edge tools for woodworking (e.g., augers, bits, gimlets, countersinks), non-powered manufacturing
- Enamelled metal cooking utensils, manufacturing
- Files and rasps, hand held, manufacturing
- Flatware (cutlery), base metal plated with precious metal, manufacturing
- Flatware (cutlery), non-precious metal, manufacturing
- Forks, handtools (e.g., garden, hay, manure, stone), manufacturing
- Garden handtools, non-powered, manufacturing
- Gear pullers, handtools, manufacturing
- Guns, caulking, non-powered, manufacturing
- Hair clippers, for human or animal use, non-powered, manufacturing
- Hammers, handtools, manufacturing
- Hand held edge tools, non-powered, manufacturing
- Hand saws, all non-powered types, manufacturing
- Hand tools, metal blade (e.g., putty knives, scrapers, screwdrivers), non-powered, manufacturing
- Hatchets, manufacturing
- Hedge shears and trimmers, non-electric, manufacturing
- Hoes, garden and masons' handtools, manufacturing
- Jacks (except hydraulic and pneumatic), manufacturing
- Jacks (screw and ratchet), motor vehicle, manufacturing
- Jewellers' handtools, non-powered, manufacturing
- Kitchen cutlery, base metal plated with precious metal, manufacturing
- Kitchen cutlery, non-precious metal, manufacturing
- Kitchen utensils (e.g., colanders, garlic presses, ice cream scoops, spatulas), fabricated metal, manufacturing
- Kitchen utensils (except cutting type), fabricated metal, manufacturing
- Knife blades, manufacturing
- Knives (e.g., hunting, pocket, table non-precious, table precious plated), manufacturing
- Knives, machine (except metal cutting), manufacturing
- Lawn and garden handtools, non-powered, manufacturing
- Lawn mowers, non-powered, manufacturing
- Levels, carpenters', manufacturing
- Machine knives (except metal cutting), manufacturing
- Machinists' precision measuring tools (except optical), manufacturing
- Masons' handtools, manufacturing
- Measuring tools, machinists' (except optical), manufacturing
- Mechanics' handtools, non-powered, manufacturing
- Mitre boxes, manufacturing
- Picks (i.e., hand tools), manufacturing
- Planes, hand held, non-powered, manufacturing
- Plated (with precious metal) cutlery, manufacturing
- Plated (with precious metal) flatware (cutlery), manufacturing

- Pliers, hand tool, manufacturing
- Pressure cookers, household type, manufacturing
- Putty knives, manufacturing
- Rakes, non-powered hand tool, manufacturing
- Ratchets, non-powered, manufacturing
- Razor blades, manufacturing
- Razors (except electric), manufacturing
- Rulers, metal, manufacturing
- Saw blades, all types, manufacturing
- Saws, hand, non-powered, manufacturing
- Scissors, non-powered, manufacturing
- Scoops, metal, hand (except kitchen), manufacturing
- Screwdrivers, non-powered, manufacturing
- Shears, non-powered, manufacturing
- Sockets and socket sets, manufacturing
- Soldering guns and irons, hand held (including electric), manufacturing
- Spoons, table, base metal plated with precious metal, manufacturing
- Spoons, table, non-precious metal, manufacturing
- Table cutlery, base metal plated with precious metal, manufacturing
- Table cutlery, non-precious metal, manufacturing
- Tape measures, metal, manufacturing
- Tinners' snips, manufacturing
- Tools, garden, hand held, non-powered, manufacturing
- Tools, hand held, metal blade (e.g., putty knives, scrapers, screwdrivers), non-powered, manufacturing
- Tools, hand held, non-powered (except kitchen type), manufacturing
- Tools, woodworking edge (e.g., augers, bits, countersinks), manufacturing
- Trimmers, hedge, non-electric, manufacturing
- Utensils, kitchen (e.g., spatulas, ice cream scoops, garlic presses, colanders), fabricated metal, manufacturing
- Vises (except machine attachments), manufacturing
- Wrenches, hand tools, non-powered, manufacturing

332210 Cutlery and Hand Tool Manufacturing CAN

See industry description for 33221, above.

3323 Architectural and Structural Metals Manufacturing

This industry group comprises establishments primarily engaged in fabricating metal products for structural or architectural purposes.

33231 Plate Work and Fabricated Structural Product Manufacturing

This industry comprises establishments primarily engaged in fabricating plate work and structural products by cutting, punching, bending, shaping and welding purchased steel plate.

332311 Prefabricated Metal Building and Component Manufacturing US

This Canadian industry comprises establishments primarily engaged in manufacturing prefabricated and pre-engineered metal buildings.

Exclusion(s): Establishments primarily engaged in:
- manufacturing prefabricated wood frame buildings (321992, Prefabricated Wood Building Manufacturing).

Example Activities
- Aircraft hangars, pre-engineered, metal, manufacturing
- Buildings, pre-engineered, metal, manufacturing
- Buildings, prefabricated, metal (except portable), manufacturing
- Buildings, prefabricated, metal, manufacturing
- Bus shelters, metal frame, manufacturing
- Farm buildings, prefabricated, metal, manufacturing

- Garden sheds, prefabricated, metal, manufacturing
- Grain storage buildings, metal, manufacturing
- Greenhouses, prefabricated, metal, manufacturing
- Panels, prefabricated, metal building, manufacturing
- Portable buildings, prefabricated, metal, manufacturing

- Pre-engineered metal buildings, manufacturing
- Prefabricated buildings, metal, manufacturing
- Sections for prefabricated metal buildings (except portable), manufacturing
- Silos, prefabricated metal, manufacturing
- Silos, prefabricated, metal, manufacturing and installation
- Utility buildings, prefabricated, metal, manufacturing

332314 Concrete Reinforcing Bar Manufacturing CAN

This Canadian industry comprises establishments primarily engaged in manufacturing assemblies and other fabrications of concrete reinforcing bars by cutting, bending, shaping purchased deformed reinforcing bar.

Example Activities

- Concrete reinforcing bar assemblies, manufacturing
- Rebar (deformed steel bars for concrete reinforcement), manufacturing

- Rebar (i.e., concrete reinforcing bar), manufacturing

332319 Other Plate Work and Fabricated Structural Product Manufacturing CAN

This Canadian industry comprises establishments, not classified to any other Canadian industry, primarily engaged in fabricating plate work and structural products by cutting, punching, bending, shaping and welding purchased steel plate. This work may be done according to custom or standard design, for factory or field assembly. These establishments may engage in both fabrication and installation.

Example Activities

- Barge sections, prefabricated, metal, manufacturing
- Boat sections, prefabricated, metal, manufacturing
- Bridge sections, prefabricated, metal, manufacturing
- Fabricated bar joists, manufacturing
- Fabricated metal plate work, manufacturing
- Girders for bridges and buildings, fabricated metal, manufacturing
- Joists, open web steel, long-span series, manufacturing

- Nuclear shielding, fabricated metal plate, manufacturing
- Radio and television tower sections, fabricated structural metal, manufacturing
- Railway bridge sections, prefabricated metal, manufacturing
- Ship sections, prefabricated metal, manufacturing
- Transmission towers and masts, prefabricated, manufacturing
- Tunnel lining, fabricated metal plate, manufacturing
- Weldments, manufacturing

33232 Ornamental and Architectural Metal Product Manufacturing

This industry comprises establishments primarily engaged in manufacturing doors, windows, and other ornamental and architectural metal products.

332321 Metal Window and Door Manufacturing US

This Canadian industry comprises establishments primarily engaged in manufacturing metal (typically steel or aluminum) doors and windows, sash, door and window frames, and screens, moulding and trim.

Exclusion(s): Establishments primarily engaged in:
- manufacturing wood windows and doors, whether or not metal-covered (321911, Wood Window and Door Manufacturing).

Example Activities
- Door frames and sash, metal, manufacturing
- Garage doors, metal, manufacturing
- Hermetically sealed window units, metal frame, manufacturing
- Insulated windows, hermetically sealed, metal frame, manufacturing
- Moulding and trim (except motor vehicle), metal, manufacturing

- Shutters, door and window, metal, manufacturing
- Skylights, metal frame, manufacturing
- Trim, metal, manufacturing
- Weather strip, metal, manufacturing
- Window screens, metal frame, manufacturing

332329 Other Ornamental and Architectural Metal Product Manufacturing CAN

This Canadian industry comprises establishments, not classified to any other Canadian industry, primarily engaged in manufacturing ornamental and architectural metal products.

Exclusion(s): Establishments primarily engaged in:
- manufacturing prefabricated metal buildings (332311, Prefabricated Metal Building and Component Manufacturing); and
- manufacturing fences and gates from purchased wire (332619, Other Fabricated Wire Product Manufacturing).

Example Activities
- Architectural metal work, manufacturing
- Ducts, sheet metal, manufacturing
- Eavestrough, sheet metal, manufacturing
- Fences and gates (except wire), metal, manufacturing
- Fire escapes, metal, manufacturing
- Flooring, open steel (i.e., grating), manufacturing
- Flooring, sheet metal, manufacturing
- Flumes, sheet metal, manufacturing
- Gates, metal (except wire), manufacturing
- Grillwork, ornamental metal, manufacturing
- Highway guardrails, sheet metal, manufacturing

- Joists, sheet metal, manufacturing
- Lamp posts, metal, manufacturing
- Livestock corrals, cattle holders and stalls, metal, manufacturing
- Ornamental metal work, manufacturing
- Pipe railings, metal, manufacturing
- Pipe, sheet metal, manufacturing
- Railings, metal, manufacturing
- Sheet metal work (except stamped), manufacturing
- Siding, sheet metal, manufacturing
- Stairs, metal, manufacturing
- Studs, sheet metal, manufacturing

3324 Boiler, Tank and Shipping Container Manufacturing

This industry group comprises establishments primarily engaged in cutting, forming and joining metal to manufacture products, such as power boilers, heat exchangers and tanks of heavy gauge metal, and cans, boxes and other light gauge metal containers.

33241 Power Boiler and Heat Exchanger Manufacturing

This industry comprises establishments primarily engaged in manufacturing power boilers and parts (including nuclear generated steam), and industrial heat exchangers, by the process of cutting, forming and joining metal plates, bars, sheets, pipe mill products and tubing, to custom or standard design, for factory or field assembly. These establishments may engage in both fabrication and installation.

Exclusion(s): Establishments primarily engaged in:
- erecting purchased boilers (23822, Plumbing, Heating and Air-Conditioning Contractors); and
- manufacturing cast iron sectional heating boilers (33341, Ventilation, Heating, Air-Conditioning and Commercial Refrigeration Equipment Manufacturing).

Example Activities
- Boilers, power, manufacturing
- Condensers, steam, manufacturing
- Exchangers, heat, manufacturing
- Heat exchangers, manufacturing
- Intercooler shells, manufacturing
- Marine power boilers, manufacturing
- Nuclear reactor control rod drive mechanisms, manufacturing
- Nuclear reactor steam supply systems, manufacturing
- Nuclear reactors, manufacturing
- Power boilers, manufacturing
- Reactors, nuclear, manufacturing

332410 Power Boiler and Heat Exchanger Manufacturing

See industry description for 33241, above.

33242 Metal Tank (Heavy Gauge) Manufacturing

This industry comprises establishments primarily engaged in cutting, forming and joining heavy gauge steel to manufacture tanks. Establishments primarily engaged in fabricating and erecting large storage tanks, which must be assembled at the site, are included.

Exclusion(s): Establishments primarily engaged in:
- manufacturing tanks for tank trucks (33621, Motor Vehicle Body and Trailer Manufacturing).

Example Activities
- Acetylene cylinders, manufacturing
- Bulk storage tanks, heavy gauge steel, manufacturing
- Cylinders, pressure, manufacturing
- Farm storage tanks, heavy gauge metal, manufacturing
- Fermentation tanks, heavy gauge metal, manufacturing
- Gas storage tanks, heavy gauge metal, manufacturing
- Liquefied petroleum gas (LPG) cylinders, manufacturing
- Nuclear waste casks, heavy gauge metal, manufacturing
- Oil storage tanks, heavy gauge metal, manufacturing
- Pots (e.g., annealing, melting, smelting), heavy gauge metal, manufacturing
- Septic tanks, heavy gauge metal, manufacturing
- Smelting pots and retorts, manufacturing
- Storage tanks, heavy gauge metal, manufacturing
- Tanks, heavy gauge metal, manufacturing
- Vacuum tanks, heavy gauge metal, manufacturing
- Vats, heavy gauge metal, manufacturing
- Water tanks, heavy gauge metal, manufacturing

332420 Metal Tank (Heavy Gauge) Manufacturing

See industry description for 33242, above.

33243 Metal Can, Box and Other Metal Container (Light Gauge) Manufacturing

This industry comprises establishments primarily engaged in forming light gauge metal to manufacture cans and other metal containers to store or transport products.

332431 Metal Can Manufacturing ^{US}

This Canadian industry comprises establishments primarily engaged in manufacturing metal cans or other containers, from purchased sheet metal (typically aluminum or chrome oxide-coated steel).

Exclusion(s): Establishments primarily engaged in:
- manufacturing metal shipping containers (332439, Other Metal Container Manufacturing).

Example Activities
- Aerosol cans, manufacturing
- Aluminum cans, manufacturing
- Can lids and ends, metal, manufacturing
- Cans, metal (e.g., food, beverage, aerosol), manufacturing
- Paint cans, metal, manufacturing
- Steel cans, manufacturing

332439 Other Metal Container Manufacturing ^{US}

This Canadian industry comprises establishments, not classified to any other Canadian industry, primarily engaged in manufacturing metal containers from light gauge sheet metal.

Exclusion(s): Establishments primarily engaged in:
- manufacturing metal cans, or pails, except shipping pails (332431, Metal Can Manufacturing); and
- reconditioning drums and shipping containers (811310, Commercial and Industrial Machinery and Equipment (except Automotive and Electronic) Repair and Maintenance).

Example Activities
- Air cargo containers, light gauge metal, manufacturing
- Bins (e.g., grain and feed storage), light gauge metal, manufacturing
- Bottles, vacuum, manufacturing
- Boxes, light gauge metal, manufacturing
- Collapsible tubes (e.g., toothpaste, glue), light gauge metal, manufacturing
- Containers, air cargo, light gauge metal, manufacturing
- Coolers and ice chests (except foam plastics), manufacturing
- Drums, light gauge metal, manufacturing
- Garbage or trash cans, light gauge metal, manufacturing
- Ice chests and coolers (except foam plastics), manufacturing
- Jugs, vacuum, light gauge metal, manufacturing
- Shipping barrels, drums, kegs and pails, light gauge metal, manufacturing
- Tool boxes, light gauge metal, manufacturing
- Vacuum bottles and jugs, manufacturing
- Vacuum bottles, light gauge metal, manufacturing
- Vats, light gauge metal, manufacturing

3325 Hardware Manufacturing

See industry description for 33251, below.

33251 Hardware Manufacturing

This industry comprises establishments primarily engaged in manufacturing metal hardware.

Example Activities
- Aircraft hardware, metal, manufacturing
- Automobile hardware, metal, manufacturing
- Builders' hardware, metal, manufacturing
- Door locks, manufacturing
- Door opening and closing devices (except electrical), manufacturing
- Furniture hardware, metal, manufacturing
- Hardware, metal, manufacturing
- Hinges, metal, manufacturing

- Key blanks, manufacturing
- Locks (except coin-operated and time), manufacturing
- Luggage hardware, metal, manufacturing

- Marine hardware, metal, manufacturing
- Motor vehicle hardware, metal, manufacturing

332510 Hardware Manufacturing

See industry description for 33251, above.

3326 Spring and Wire Product Manufacturing

See industry description for 33261, below.

33261 Spring and Wire Product Manufacturing

This industry comprises establishments primarily engaged in manufacturing wire products made from purchased wire.

Exclusion(s): Establishments primarily engaged in:
- drawing iron or steel wire (33111, Iron and Steel Mills and Ferro-Alloy Manufacturing);
- drawing aluminum wire (33131, Alumina and Aluminum Production and Processing);
- drawing copper wire (33142, Copper Rolling, Drawing, Extruding and Alloying);
- drawing non-ferrous wire, except copper and aluminum (33149, Non-Ferrous Metal (except Copper and Aluminum) Rolling, Drawing, Extruding and Alloying); and
- manufacturing electrical wire by insulating purchased wire (33592, Communication and Energy Wire and Cable Manufacturing).

332611 Spring (Heavy Gauge) Manufacturing US

This Canadian industry comprises establishments primarily engaged in manufacturing heavy gauge springs. These springs are typically used in machinery, motor vehicles and other transportation equipment.

Exclusion(s): Establishments primarily engaged in:
- manufacturing light gauge springs, such as upholstery springs (332619, Other Fabricated Wire Product Manufacturing);
- manufacturing precision springs, such as hairsprings, instrument springs and clock springs (334512, Measuring, Medical and Controlling Devices Manufacturing); and
- manufacturing valve springs for internal combustion engines (336310, Motor Vehicle Gasoline Engine and Engine Parts Manufacturing).

Example Activities
- Automobile suspension springs, manufacturing
- Coil springs, heavy gauge, manufacturing
- Disc and ring springs, heavy-gauge, manufacturing

- Flat springs, heavy gauge, manufacturing
- Helical springs, heavy gauge, manufacturing
- Leaf springs, manufacturing
- Springs, heavy-gauge, manufacturing
- Torsion bars (i.e., springs), manufacturing

332619 Other Fabricated Wire Product Manufacturing CAN

This Canadian industry comprises establishments, not classified to any other Canadian industry, primarily engaged in manufacturing wire products from purchased wire.

Exclusion(s): Establishments primarily engaged in:
- drawing iron or steel wire (331110, Iron and Steel Mills and Ferro-Alloy Manufacturing);
- drawing aluminum wire (331317, Aluminum Rolling, Drawing, Extruding and Alloying);
- drawing copper wire (331420, Copper Rolling, Drawing, Extruding and Alloying);
- drawing non-ferrous wire, except copper and aluminum (331490, Non-Ferrous Metal (except Copper and Aluminum) Rolling, Drawing, Extruding and Alloying); and
- manufacturing electrical wire by insulating purchased wire (335920, Communication and Energy Wire and Cable Manufacturing).

Example Activities
- Barbed wire, made from purchased wire
- Baskets, metal, made from purchased wire
- Brackets, made from purchased wire
- Brads, metal, made from purchased wire
- Cable, non-insulated wire, made from purchased wire
- Cages, made from purchased wire
- Chain link fencing and fence gates, made from purchased wire
- Chain, made from purchased wire
- Chain, welded, made from purchased wire
- Cloth, woven wire, made from purchased wire
- Coat hangers, made from purchased wire
- Coil springs, light gauge (except clock and watch), made from purchased wire
- Concrete reinforcing mesh, made from purchased wire
- Fabrics, woven wire, made from purchased wire
- Fencing and fence gates, made from purchased wire
- Flat springs, light gauge (except clock and watch), made from purchased wire
- Fourdrinier wire cloth, made from purchased wire
- Furniture springs, unassembled, made from purchased wire
- Garment hangers, made from purchased wire
- Helical springs, light gauge, made from purchased wire
- Mats and matting, made from purchased wire
- Mattress springs and spring units, made from purchased wire
- Mesh, made from purchased wire
- Nails, brads and staples, made from purchased wire
- Netting, woven wire, made from purchased wire
- Paper clips, made from purchased wire
- Partitions, made from purchased wire
- Racks, household type, made from purchased wire
- Reinforcing mesh, concrete, made from purchased wire
- Rope, wire, made from purchased wire
- Screening, woven, made from purchased wire
- Shelving, wire, made from purchased wire
- Springs and spring units (except clock and watch), light gauge, made from purchased wire
- Springs, precision (except clock and watch), manufacturing
- Staples, wire, made from purchased wire
- Stranded wire, uninsulated, made from purchased wire
- Tire chains, made from purchased wire
- Traps, animal and fish, made from purchased wire
- Upholstery springs and spring units, made from purchased wire
- Window screening, made from purchased wire
- Wire mesh, concrete reinforcing, made from purchased wire

3327 Machine Shops, Turned Product, and Screw, Nut and Bolt Manufacturing

This industry group comprises establishments primarily engaged in operating machine shops, which use machine tools, such as lathes and automatic screw machines, for turning, boring, threading or otherwise shaping metal, to manufacture parts, other than complete machines, for the trade. Shops that set up to do production runs of industrial fasteners, such as bolts, nuts and screws, are included.

33271 Machine Shops

This industry comprises establishments primarily engaged in operating machine tools, such as lathes (including computer numerically controlled), automatic screw machines, and machines for boring, grinding, milling and otherwise working metal, to produce machine parts and equipment, other than complete machines, for the trade. Machine shops providing custom and repair services are included.

Example Activities
- Chemical milling job shops
- Machine shops
- Machine shops providing custom and repair services
- Machining composite materials parts
- Machining plastic parts

332710 Machine Shops

See industry description for 33271, above.

33272 Turned Product and Screw, Nut and Bolt Manufacturing

This industry comprises establishments primarily engaged in turning, facing, forming, parting, boring, threading and knurling metal on machine tools or lathes with machine-held cutting tools, to manufacture precision turned products. Establishments primarily engaged in manufacturing metal fasteners, such as nuts, bolts, rivets and washers, are included.

Exclusion(s): Establishments primarily engaged in:
- manufacturing flat washers (33211, Forging and Stamping).

Example Activities
- Bolts, metal, manufacturing
- Cotter pins, metal, manufacturing
- Hook and eye latches, manufacturing
- Hooks (i.e., general purpose fasteners), metal, manufacturing
- Hose clamps, metal, manufacturing
- Nuts, metal, manufacturing
- Rivets, metal, manufacturing
- Screws, metal, manufacturing
- Spring washers, metal, manufacturing
- Toggle bolts, metal, manufacturing
- Washers, metal, manufacturing

332720 Turned Product and Screw, Nut and Bolt Manufacturing MEX

See industry description for 33272, above.

3328 Coating, Engraving, Heat Treating and Allied Activities

See industry description for 33281, below.

33281 Coating, Engraving, Heat Treating and Allied Activities

This industry comprises establishments primarily engaged in coating, engraving, heat treating and similarly processing metal. These activities often involve heating the metal, and the purpose is often to harden it. In general, the hardening of metal is included. Other activities of this industry include tempering, brazing, plating (including electroplating and re-chroming), polishing, sand-blasting and colouring metal and metal products. Establishments that perform these processes on other materials, such as plastics, in addition to metals, as well as establishments primarily engaged in plating with precious metal for the trade are included.

Exclusion(s): Establishments primarily engaged in:
- turning metal (33271, Machine Shops);
- etching and engraving jewellery and articles of precious metals (33991, Jewellery and Silverware Manufacturing); and
- fabricating, coating and engraving products (classified in the Manufacturing sector according to the product made).

Example Activities

- Brazing (i.e., hardening) metals and metal products, for the trade
- Buffing metals and metal products, for the trade
- Burning metals and metal products, for the trade
- Chasing metals and metal products (except printing plates), for the trade
- Coating metals and metal products, for the trade
- Coating products of metal combined with other materials, for the trade
- Colouring metals and metal products, for the trade
- Depolishing metals and metal products, for the trade
- Electroplating metals and metal products, for the trade
- Enamelling metals and metal products, for the trade
- Engraving metals and metal products (except printing plates, precious metal jewellery and flatware), for the trade
- Etching metals and metal products (except printing plates, precious metal jewellery and flatware), for the trade
- Galvanizing metals and metal products, for the trade
- Heat treating metals and metal products, for the trade
- Hot dip galvanizing metals and metal products, for the trade
- Lacquering metals and metal products, for the trade
- Painting metals and metal products, for the trade
- Plating metals and metal products, for the trade
- Polishing metals and metal products, for the trade
- Powder coating metals and metal products, for the trade
- Precious metal plating of metals and metal products, for the trade
- Rust proofing metals and metal products, for the trade
- Sandblasting metals and metal products, for the trade
- Teflon (TM) coating metals and metal products, for the trade
- Tempering metals and metal products, for the trade
- Varnishing metals and metal products, for the trade

332810 Coating, Engraving, Heat Treating and Allied Activities MEX

See industry description for 33281, above.

3329 Other Fabricated Metal Product Manufacturing

This industry group comprises establishments, not classified to any other industry group, primarily engaged in fabricating metal products.

33291 Metal Valve Manufacturing

This industry comprises establishments primarily engaged in casting and machining metal valves used to regulate the flow of fluids, liquids and gases, and related fixtures and fittings. Establishments primarily engaged in manufacturing hydraulic and pneumatic pipe and tube assemblies are included.

Exclusion(s): Establishments primarily engaged in:
- manufacturing internal combustion valves for diesel engines (33361, Engine, Turbine and Power Transmission Equipment Manufacturing); and
- manufacturing internal combustion valves for gasoline engines (33631, Motor Vehicle Gasoline Engine and Engine Parts Manufacturing).

Example Activities
- Aerosol valves, metal, manufacturing
- Cocks, drain, plumbing, manufacturing
- Drain cocks, plumbing, manufacturing
- Faucets, plumbing, manufacturing
- Fire hydrant valves, manufacturing
- Fire hydrants, complete, manufacturing
- Flanges and flange unions, pipe, metal, manufacturing
- Fluid power aircraft sub-assemblies, manufacturing
- Fluid power hose assemblies, manufacturing
- Fluid power valves and hose fittings, manufacturing
- Gas valves, industrial type, manufacturing
- Hose and tube assemblies, fluid power (i.e., hydraulic and pneumatic), manufacturing
- Hose nozzles and couplings, manufacturing
- Hydraulic aircraft sub-assemblies, manufacturing
- Hydraulic hose fittings, fluid power, manufacturing
- Hydraulic valves, fluid power, manufacturing
- Nuclear application valves, manufacturing
- Plumbing and heating inline valves (e.g., check, cut-off, stop), manufacturing
- Plumbing fittings and couplings (e.g., compression fittings, metal unions, metal elbows), manufacturing
- Plumbing fixture fittings and trim, all materials, manufacturing
- Pneumatic hose fittings, fluid power, manufacturing
- Pneumatic valves, fluid power, manufacturing
- Pressure control valves (except fluid power), industrial type, manufacturing
- Pressure control valves, fluid power, manufacturing
- Safety valves, industrial type, manufacturing
- Solenoid valves (except fluid power), industrial type, manufacturing
- Solenoid valves, fluid power, manufacturing
- Steam traps, industrial type, manufacturing
- Tire valves and parts, manufacturing
- Valves, for water works and municipal water systems, manufacturing
- Valves, hydraulic and pneumatic, fluid power, manufacturing
- Valves, industrial type (e.g., gate, globe, check, pop safety, relief), manufacturing
- Valves, inline plumbing and heating (e.g., check, cut-off, stop), manufacturing

332910 Metal Valve Manufacturing ^{MEX}

See industry description for 33291, above.

33299 All Other Fabricated Metal Product Manufacturing

This industry comprises establishments, not classified to any other industry, primarily engaged in fabricating metal products.

332991 Ball and Roller Bearing Manufacturing

This Canadian industry comprises establishments primarily engaged in manufacturing ball and roller bearings, and parts, such as bearing races.

Exclusion(s): Establishments primarily engaged in:
- manufacturing plain bearings (333619, Other Engine and Power Transmission Equipment Manufacturing).

Example Activities
- Ball bearings and parts (including mounted), manufacturing
- Bearings, ball and roller, manufacturing
- Needle roller bearings, manufacturing
- Races, ball or roller bearing, manufacturing
- Roller bearings, manufacturing

332999 All Other Miscellaneous Fabricated Metal Product Manufacturing MEX

This Canadian industry comprises establishments, not classified to any other Canadian industry, primarily engaged in fabricating metal products.

Exclusion(s): Establishments primarily engaged in:
- manufacturing explosives, and detonators for explosives (325920, Explosives Manufacturing).

Example Activities
- Aluminum freezer foil, made from purchased foil
- Ammunition, manufacturing
- Badges, metal, manufacturing
- Buckles, shoe, metal, manufacturing
- Cartridges, ammunition, manufacturing
- Chests, fire or burglary resistive, metal, manufacturing
- Containers, foil (except bags), made from purchased foil
- Doors, safe and vault, metal, manufacturing
- Drain plugs, magnetic, metal, manufacturing
- Firearms, manufacturing
- Fireplace fixtures and equipment, manufacturing
- Flexible metal hose and tubing, manufacturing
- Foil containers (except bags), made from purchased metal foil
- Foil, made from purchased foil
- Gold foil and leaf, made from purchased foil
- Grenades, hand or projectile, manufacturing
- Guns, manufacturing
- Hose, flexible metal, manufacturing
- Ironing boards, metal, manufacturing
- Ladders, portable, metal, manufacturing
- Leaf, metal, manufacturing
- Ordnance, military, manufacturing
- Pallets, metal, manufacturing
- Patterns (except shoe), industrial, manufacturing
- Pipe and pipe fittings, made from purchased metal pipe
- Pipe couplings, made from purchased metal pipe
- Pipe fabricating (e.g., bending, cutting, threading), of purchased metal pipe
- Pipe fittings, made from purchased metal pipe
- Pistols (except toy), manufacturing
- Plumbing fixtures, metal, manufacturing
- Propellers, ship and boat, machined, manufacturing
- Revolvers, manufacturing
- Rifles (except toy), manufacturing
- Safe deposit boxes and chests, metal, manufacturing
- Safe doors and linings, metal, manufacturing
- Safes, metal, manufacturing
- Sanitary ware (e.g., bathtubs, lavatories, sinks), metal, manufacturing
- Shotguns, manufacturing
- Shower rods, metal, manufacturing
- Small arms (e.g., revolvers), manufacturing
- Soap-impregnated steel wool pads, manufacturing
- Sponges, scouring, metal, manufacturing
- Steel wool, manufacturing
- Stepladders, metal, manufacturing
- Thimbles, wire rope, manufacturing
- Trophies, precious plated metal, manufacturing
- Tubes, made from purchased metal pipe
- Tubing, flexible metal, manufacturing

333 Machinery Manufacturing

This subsector comprises establishments primarily engaged in manufacturing industrial and commercial machinery. These establishments assemble parts into components, subassemblies and complete machines. They may make the parts themselves, using general metal-working processes, or purchase them.

Establishments tend to specialize in producing machinery designed for particular applications, and this is reflected in the structure of the industry groups and industries. A broad distinction exists between general-purpose machinery, that is designed to be used in a variety of industrial applications, such as pumping or machining, and special-purpose machinery, that is designed to be used in a particular industry, such as agriculture or printing. The first three industry groups consist of establishments that produce special-purpose machinery. Establishments that produce general-purpose machinery are classified in the remaining industry groups.

Establishments primarily engaged in rebuilding machinery are included in the same industry as establishments manufacturing the particular type of new machinery. Unless otherwise specified, establishments primarily engaged in manufacturing parts, designed for use solely or principally with a particular machine, are classified in the same industry as establishments manufacturing that type of machinery.

3331 Agricultural, Construction and Mining Machinery Manufacturing

This industry group comprises establishments primarily engaged in manufacturing machinery designed for use in the agriculture, construction and mining industries.

33311 Agricultural Implement Manufacturing

This industry comprises establishments primarily engaged in manufacturing machinery for use in performing farm operations, such as the preparation and maintenance of soil; planting, harvesting or threshing; field spraying; and preparing crops for market; or for use in horticultural and residential lawn care. Establishments primarily engaged in manufacturing snowblowers are included.

Exclusion(s): Establishments primarily engaged in:
- manufacturing agricultural hand tools, such as manual shears and non-powered lawn mowers (33221, Cutlery and Hand Tool Manufacturing);
- manufacturing metal corrals, stalls and cattle holders (33232, Ornamental and Architectural Metal Product Manufacturing);
- manufacturing food manufacturing machinery, such as milk processing equipment (33329, Other Industrial Machinery Manufacturing); and
- manufacturing farm conveyors and farm elevators (33392, Material Handling Equipment Manufacturing).

Example Activities
- Attachments for powered lawn and garden equipment, manufacturing
- Balers, farm (e.g., hay, straw, cotton), manufacturing
- Cabs for agricultural machinery, manufacturing
- Carts, lawn and garden type, manufacturing
- Chicken brooders, manufacturing
- Combines, harvester-threshers, manufacturing
- Cream separators, farm type, manufacturing
- Crop driers, farm type, manufacturing
- Dusters, farm type, manufacturing
- Farm tractors and attachments, manufacturing
- Farm wagons, manufacturing
- Feed grinders (i.e., crushers and mixers), farm type, manufacturing
- Feed processing equipment, farm type, manufacturing
- Fertilizing machinery, farm type, manufacturing
- Grading, cleaning and sorting machinery, farm type, manufacturing
- Grass mowing equipment (except lawn and garden), manufacturing
- Harvesting machinery and equipment, manufacturing
- Haying machines, manufacturing
- Hedge trimmers, powered, manufacturing
- Hog feeding and watering equipment, manufacturing
- Incubators, poultry, manufacturing
- Lawn and garden machinery (e.g., hedge trimmers, lawn mowers, tractors), powered, manufacturing

- Lawn mowers (except agricultural type), powered, manufacturing
- Milking machines, manufacturing
- Planting machines, farm type, manufacturing
- Ploughs, farm type, manufacturing
- Poultry brooders, feeders and waterers, manufacturing
- Sheep shears, powered, manufacturing
- Snowblowers and throwers, residential type, manufacturing
- Sprayers and dusters, farm type, manufacturing
- Tillers, lawn and garden type, manufacturing
- Tractors and attachments, farm type, manufacturing
- Tractors and attachments, lawn and garden type, manufacturing
- Windmills, farm type, manufacturing

333110 Agricultural Implement Manufacturing CAN

See industry description for 33311, above.

33312 Construction Machinery Manufacturing

This industry comprises establishments primarily engaged in manufacturing heavy machinery and equipment of a type used primarily in the construction industry, such as crawler or rubber-tired tractors with bulldozer blade or ripper tooth attachments, front-end loaders, cranes, concrete mixers, power shovels and pavers. Machinery that can be used in both the construction and mining industries is treated as construction machinery. Establishments primarily engaged in manufacturing forestry machinery, such as tree harvesting and handling equipment, are also included.

Exclusion(s): Establishments primarily engaged in:
- manufacturing farm tractors (33311, Agricultural Implement Manufacturing);
- manufacturing mining and oil and gas field drilling equipment (33313, Mining and Oil and Gas Field Machinery Manufacturing);
- manufacturing industrial plant overhead travelling cranes, hoists, truck-type cranes and hoists, winches, aerial work platforms, and automotive wrecker hoists (33392, Material Handling Equipment Manufacturing); and
- manufacturing rail layers, ballast distributors and other railroad track-laying equipment (33651, Railroad Rolling Stock Manufacturing).

Example Activities
- Aggregate spreaders, manufacturing
- Backhoes, manufacturing
- Bits, rock drill, construction and surface mining type, manufacturing
- Buckets, excavating (e.g., clamshell, concrete, dragline, drag scraper, shovel), manufacturing
- Bulldozers, manufacturing
- Cabs for construction machinery, manufacturing
- Chippers, portable commercial (e.g., brush, limb and log), manufacturing
- Concrete finishing machinery, manufacturing
- Concrete gunning equipment, manufacturing
- Concrete mixing machinery, portable, manufacturing
- Construction machinery, manufacturing
- Construction tractors and attachments, manufacturing
- Cranes, construction type, manufacturing
- Draglines, crawlers, manufacturing
- Dredging machinery, manufacturing
- Grader attachments, elevating, manufacturing
- Graders, road, manufacturing
- Hammers, pneumatic, hand-operated, manufacturing
- Jackhammers, manufacturing
- Loaders, shovel, manufacturing
- Off-highway trucks, manufacturing
- Planers, bituminous, manufacturing
- Portable crushing, pulverizing and screening machinery, manufacturing
- Rock crushing machinery, portable, manufacturing
- Scrapers, construction type, manufacturing

- Shovel loaders, manufacturing
- Snowplough attachments (except lawn and garden type), manufacturing
- Surface mining machinery (except drilling), manufacturing
- Teeth, bucket and scarifier, manufacturing

- Tractors and attachments, construction type, manufacturing
- Tractors, crawler, manufacturing
- Tree harvesting equipment, manufacturing
- Trucks, off-highway, manufacturing

333120 Construction Machinery Manufacturing

See industry description for 33312, above.

33313 Mining and Oil and Gas Field Machinery Manufacturing

This industry comprises establishments primarily engaged in manufacturing mining and oil and gas field industry equipment.

Exclusion(s): Establishments primarily engaged in:
- manufacturing machinery with both construction and mining uses, including portable rock crushing machinery (33312, Construction Machinery Manufacturing);
- manufacturing coal and ore conveyors (33392, Material Handling Equipment Manufacturing);
- manufacturing underground mining locomotives (33651, Railroad Rolling Stock Manufacturing); and
- manufacturing offshore oil and gas well drilling and production platforms (33661, Ship and Boat Building).

Example Activities
- Bits, rock drill, oil and gas field type, manufacturing
- Bits, rock drill, underground mining type, manufacturing
- Cars, mining, manufacturing
- Coal breakers, cutters and pulverizers, manufacturing
- Crushing machinery, stationary, manufacturing
- Derricks, oil and gas field type, manufacturing
- Drilling equipment, oil and gas field type, manufacturing
- Drilling equipment, underground mining type, manufacturing
- Drilling rigs, manufacturing
- Drills, core, underground mining type, manufacturing
- Drills, rock, underground mining type, manufacturing

- Mineral beneficiating machinery, manufacturing
- Mining cars, manufacturing
- Mining, underground, machinery, manufacturing
- Oil and gas field drilling machinery and equipment (except offshore floating platforms), manufacturing
- Ore crushing, washing, screening and loading machinery, manufacturing
- Quarrying machinery and equipment, manufacturing
- Rock crushing machinery, stationary, manufacturing
- Rock drill bits, oil and gas field type, manufacturing
- Rock drill bits, underground mining type, manufacturing
- Underground mining machinery, manufacturing
- Water well drilling machinery, manufacturing

333130 Mining and Oil and Gas Field Machinery Manufacturing MEX

See industry description for 33313, above.

3332 Industrial Machinery Manufacturing

This industry group comprises establishments primarily engaged in manufacturing machinery designed for use in specific manufacturing industries.

33321 Sawmill and Woodworking Machinery Manufacturing

This industry comprises establishments primarily engaged in manufacturing machinery of a type used in processing logs or lumber.

Exclusion(s): Establishments primarily engaged in:
- manufacturing non-powered hand tools, such as planes and handsaws (33221, Cutlery and Hand Tool Manufacturing);
- manufacturing lumber and veneer drying machines (33329, Other Industrial Machinery Manufacturing); and
- manufacturing power-driven hand tools (33399, All Other General-Purpose Machinery Manufacturing).

Example Activities
- Bandsaws, woodworking type, manufacturing
- Circular saws, woodworking, stationary, manufacturing
- Drill presses, woodworking, manufacturing
- Jointers, woodworking, manufacturing
- Lathes, woodworking type, manufacturing
- Planers, woodworking type, stationary, manufacturing
- Presses for making composite wood (e.g., hardboard, fibreboard, plywood, particleboard), manufacturing
- Sanding machines, woodworking type, stationary, manufacturing
- Sawmill equipment, manufacturing
- Saws, bench and table, power, woodworking type, manufacturing
- Veneer and plywood forming machinery, manufacturing
- Woodworking machines (except hand-held), manufacturing

333210 Sawmill and Woodworking Machinery Manufacturing

See industry description for 33321, above.

33322 Rubber and Plastics Industry Machinery Manufacturing

This industry comprises establishments primarily engaged in manufacturing machinery used in processing rubber or plastics materials.

Exclusion(s): Establishments primarily engaged in:
- manufacturing industrial moulds for plastics and rubber working machinery (33351, Metalworking Machinery Manufacturing).

Example Activities
- Blow moulding machinery for plastics, manufacturing
- Calendering machinery for plastics, manufacturing
- Camelback (i.e., retreading material) machinery, manufacturing
- Compression moulding machinery for plastics, manufacturing
- Extruding machinery for plastics and rubber, manufacturing
- Granulating and pelletizing machinery for plastics, manufacturing
- Injection moulding machinery for plastics, manufacturing
- Plastics working machinery, manufacturing
- Rubber working machinery, manufacturing
- Thermoforming machinery for plastics, manufacturing
- Tire making machinery, manufacturing
- Tire recapping machinery, manufacturing
- Tire shredding machinery, manufacturing
- Vulcanizing machinery, manufacturing

333220 Rubber and Plastics Industry Machinery Manufacturing

See industry description for 33322, above.

33329 Other Industrial Machinery Manufacturing

This industry comprises establishments, not classified to any other industry, primarily engaged in manufacturing industrial machinery.

Exclusion(s): Establishments primarily engaged in:
- manufacturing commercial cooking and food warming equipment (33331, Commercial and Service Industry Machinery Manufacturing);
- manufacturing industrial refrigeration equipment (33341, Ventilation, Heating, Air-Conditioning and Commercial Refrigeration Equipment Manufacturing); and
- manufacturing food and beverage packaging machinery (33399, All Other General-Purpose Machinery Manufacturing).

333291 Paper Industry Machinery Manufacturing US

This Canadian industry comprises establishments primarily engaged in manufacturing paper-making machinery.

Example Activities
- Chippers (e.g., logs), stationary, manufacturing
- Envelope making machinery, manufacturing
- Fourdrinier machinery, manufacturing
- Paper and paperboard coating and finishing machinery, manufacturing
- Paper and paperboard converting machinery, manufacturing
- Paper and paperboard corrugating machinery, manufacturing
- Paper and paperboard cutting and folding machinery, manufacturing
- Paper and paperboard die-cutting and stamping machinery, manufacturing
- Paper bag making machinery, manufacturing
- Paper making machinery, manufacturing
- Paper stock preparation machinery, manufacturing
- Paperboard box making machinery, manufacturing
- Paperboard making machinery, manufacturing
- Pulp making machinery, manufacturing
- Pulp washers and thickeners, manufacturing
- Sandpaper making machinery, manufacturing

333299 All Other Industrial Machinery Manufacturing CAN

This Canadian industry comprises establishments, not classified to any other Canadian industry, primarily engaged in manufacturing industrial machinery.

Example Activities
- Bakery machinery and equipment, manufacturing
- Bindery machinery, manufacturing
- Bookbinding machinery, manufacturing
- Boot making and repairing machinery, manufacturing
- Braiding machinery, textile, manufacturing
- Bread slicing machinery, manufacturing
- Brewery machinery, manufacturing
- Buttonhole and eyelet machinery, manufacturing
- Calendering machinery for textiles, manufacturing
- Cheese processing machinery, manufacturing
- Chemical processing machinery and equipment, manufacturing
- Cigarette making machinery, manufacturing
- Circuit board making machinery, manufacturing
- Clayworking and tempering machinery, manufacturing

- Coffee roasting and grinding machinery (i.e., food manufacturing type), manufacturing
- Corn popping machinery (i.e., food manufacturing type), manufacturing
- Cream separators (except farm type), manufacturing
- Distillery equipment, beverage, manufacturing
- Distilling apparatus, laboratory type, manufacturing
- Distilling equipment (except beverage), manufacturing
- Dough mixing machinery (i.e., food manufacturing type), manufacturing
- Drawing machinery for textiles, manufacturing
- Drying kilns, lumber, manufacturing
- Drying machinery for textiles, manufacturing
- Extruding machinery, textile, manufacturing
- Finishing machinery, textile, manufacturing
- Fish and shellfish processing machinery, manufacturing
- Flexographic printing presses, manufacturing
- Flour mill machinery, manufacturing
- Food choppers, grinders, mixers and slicers (i.e., food manufacturing type), manufacturing
- Glass-making machinery (e.g., blowing, moulding, forming), manufacturing
- Gravure printing presses, manufacturing
- Homogenizing machinery, food, manufacturing
- Hosiery machinery, manufacturing
- Juice extractors, fruit and vegetable (i.e., food manufacturing type), manufacturing
- Kilns (i.e., cement, wood, chemical), manufacturing
- Knitting machinery, manufacturing
- Leather working machinery, manufacturing
- Letterpress printing presses, manufacturing
- Lithographic printing presses, manufacturing
- Looms, textile, manufacturing
- Lumber drying kilns, manufacturing
- Metal casting machinery, manufacturing
- Milk processing machinery (i.e., food manufacturing type), manufacturing
- Offset printing presses, manufacturing
- Oilseed crushing and extracting machinery, manufacturing
- Ovens, bakery, manufacturing

- Pasteurizing equipment (i.e., food manufacturing type), manufacturing
- Petroleum refining machinery, manufacturing
- Presses (i.e., food manufacturing type), manufacturing
- Presses, printing (except textile printing machinery), manufacturing
- Printing machinery for textiles, manufacturing
- Printing plate engraving machinery, manufacturing
- Printing presses (except textile printing machinery), manufacturing
- Semiconductor making machinery, manufacturing
- Sewing machines (including household type), manufacturing
- Sewing machines and attachments, household, manufacturing
- Sewing machines and attachments, industrial, manufacturing
- Shoe making and repairing machinery, manufacturing
- Sieves and screening equipment, chemical processing type, manufacturing
- Sieves and screening equipment, food manufacturing type, manufacturing
- Silk screen machinery for textiles, manufacturing
- Silver recovery equipment, electrolytic, manufacturing
- Slicing machinery (i.e., food manufacturing type), manufacturing
- Spindles for textile machinery, manufacturing
- Spinning machines, textile, manufacturing
- Spools for textile machinery, manufacturing
- Tannery machinery, manufacturing
- Textile finishing machinery (e.g., bleaching, dyeing, mercerizing), manufacturing
- Textile making machinery (except sewing machines), manufacturing
- Textile printing machinery, manufacturing
- Texturizing machinery for textiles, manufacturing
- Thread making machinery, manufacturing
- Tile making machinery (except kilns), manufacturing
- Tobacco processing machinery (except farm type), manufacturing
- Tufting machinery for textiles, manufacturing
- Typesetting machinery, manufacturing

- Vegetable oil processing machinery, manufacturing
- Veneer drying machinery, manufacturing
- Wafer processing equipment, semiconductor, manufacturing
- Warping machinery, manufacturing

- Weaving machinery, manufacturing
- Wire and cable insulating machinery, manufacturing
- Wood drying kilns, manufacturing
- Yarn texturizing machinery, manufacturing

3333 Commercial and Service Industry Machinery Manufacturing

See industry description for 33331, below.

33331 Commercial and Service Industry Machinery Manufacturing

This industry comprises establishments primarily engaged in manufacturing machinery for use in commercial and service industries.

Exclusion(s): Establishments primarily engaged in:
- manufacturing sensitized film, paper, cloth and plates; prepared photographic chemicals; and photocopier toner and toner cartridges (32599, All Other Chemical Product Manufacturing);
- manufacturing computer and peripheral equipment; point-of-sale machines and automatic teller machines (33411, Computer and Peripheral Equipment Manufacturing);
- manufacturing television and video cameras (33431, Audio and Video Equipment Manufacturing);
- manufacturing time clocks and other time-recording devices (33451, Navigational, Measuring, Medical and Control Instruments Manufacturing);
- manufacturing household appliances (3352, Household Appliance Manufacturing); and
- manufacturing pencil sharpeners, staplers and similar office supplies (33994, Office Supplies (except Paper) Manufacturing).

Example Activities
- Adding machines, electronic, manufacturing
- Adding machines, manufacturing
- Alignment equipment, motor vehicle wheel, manufacturing
- Balancing equipment, motor vehicle wheel, manufacturing
- Binoculars, manufacturing
- Calculators, manufacturing
- Camera lenses, manufacturing
- Cameras (except television, video and digital), manufacturing
- Car washing machinery, manufacturing
- Carnival and amusement park rides, manufacturing
- Carnival and amusement park shooting gallery machinery, manufacturing
- Carpet sweepers, mechanical, manufacturing
- Cash registers (except point-of-sale terminals), manufacturing
- Cash registers, electronic, manufacturing
- Central vacuuming systems, commercial type, manufacturing
- Change making machines, manufacturing

- Coffee makers, commercial type, manufacturing
- Cooking equipment, commercial type, manufacturing
- Currency counting machinery, manufacturing
- Developing equipment, photographic film, manufacturing
- Drycleaning equipment and machinery, manufacturing
- Dryers, laundry (except household type), manufacturing
- Enlargers, photographic, manufacturing
- Envelope stuffing, sealing and addressing machinery, manufacturing
- Flight simulators, manufacturing
- Hole punches (except hand operated), office type, manufacturing
- Incoming mail handling equipment (e.g., opening, sorting, scanning), manufacturing
- Laundry machinery and equipment (except household type), manufacturing
- Lens polishing (except ophthalmic)
- Lenses (except ophthalmic), manufacturing

- Letter folding, stuffing and sealing machines, manufacturing
- Light meters, photographic, manufacturing
- Mechanisms for coin-operated machines, manufacturing
- Microfiche equipment (e.g., cameras, projectors, readers), manufacturing
- Microfilm equipment (e.g., cameras, projectors, readers), manufacturing
- Microwave ovens, commercial type, manufacturing
- Ovens, commercial type, manufacturing
- Overhead projectors (except computer peripherals), manufacturing
- Photocopying machines, manufacturing
- Photographic equipment, coin operated, manufacturing
- Photographic film developing equipment, manufacturing
- Photographic lenses, manufacturing
- Postage meters, manufacturing
- Pressing machines (except household type), manufacturing
- Projection screens (i.e., motion picture, slide, overhead), manufacturing
- Ranges, commercial type, manufacturing
- Screens, projection (i.e., motion picture, slide, overhead), manufacturing
- Sewage treatment equipment, manufacturing
- Stoves, commercial type, manufacturing
- Teaching machines (e.g., flight simulators), manufacturing
- Trash and garbage compactors, commercial type, manufacturing
- Vacuum cleaners, industrial and commercial type, manufacturing
- Vending machines, manufacturing
- Voting machines, manufacturing
- Washing machines, laundry (except household type), manufacturing
- Water purification equipment, manufacturing
- Water softening equipment, manufacturing
- Water treatment equipment, manufacturing

333310 Commercial and Service Industry Machinery Manufacturing CAN

See industry description for 33331, above.

3334 Ventilation, Heating, Air-Conditioning and Commercial Refrigeration Equipment Manufacturing

See industry description for 33341, below.

33341 Ventilation, Heating, Air-Conditioning and Commercial Refrigeration Equipment Manufacturing

This industry comprises establishments primarily engaged in manufacturing ventilation, heating, air-conditioning and commercial refrigeration equipment.

Exclusion(s): Establishments primarily engaged in:
- manufacturing industrial, power and marine boilers (33241, Power Boiler and Heat Exchanger Manufacturing);
- manufacturing commercial cooking and food warming equipment (33331, Commercial and Service Industry Machinery Manufacturing);
- manufacturing industrial process furnaces and ovens (33399, All Other General-Purpose Machinery Manufacturing);
- manufacturing household fans (except attic), and portable electric space heaters, humidifiers and dehumidifiers (33521, Small Electrical Appliance Manufacturing);
- manufacturing household cooking stoves, ranges, refrigerators and freezers (33522, Major Appliance Manufacturing); and
- manufacturing motor vehicle air-conditioning systems and compressors (33639, Other Motor Vehicle Parts Manufacturing).

333413 Industrial and Commercial Fan and Blower and Air Purification Equipment Manufacturing ^{CAN}

This Canadian industry comprises establishments primarily engaged in manufacturing industrial and commercial blowers.

Exclusion(s): Establishments primarily engaged in:
- manufacturing household fans (except attic), and portable electric space heaters, humidifiers and dehumidifiers (335210, Small Electrical Appliance Manufacturing).

Example Activities
- Air purification equipment, stationary, manufacturing
- Air scrubbing systems, manufacturing
- Air washers (i.e., scrubbers), manufacturing
- Attic fans, manufacturing
- Dust and fume collecting equipment, manufacturing
- Electrostatic precipitation equipment, manufacturing

- Exhaust fans, industrial and commercial type, manufacturing
- Fans, industrial and commercial type, manufacturing
- Filters, furnace, manufacturing
- Furnace filters, manufacturing
- Ventilating fans, industrial and commercial type, manufacturing

333416 Heating Equipment and Commercial Refrigeration Equipment Manufacturing CAN

This Canadian industry comprises establishments primarily engaged in manufacturing electric and non-electric heating equipment, and commercial and industrial refrigeration equipment.

Exclusion(s): Establishments primarily engaged in:
- manufacturing industrial, power and marine boilers (332410, Power Boiler and Heat Exchanger Manufacturing);
- manufacturing commercial cooking and food-warming equipment (333310, Commercial and Service Industry Machinery Manufacturing);
- manufacturing blowers for warm-air heating equipment (333413, Industrial and Commercial Fan and Blower and Air Purification Equipment Manufacturing);
- manufacturing industrial process furnaces and ovens (333990, All Other General-Purpose Machinery Manufacturing);
- manufacturing household cooking stoves, ranges, refrigerators, freezers and water coolers (335223, Major Kitchen Appliance Manufacturing); and
- manufacturing motor vehicle air-conditioning systems and compressors (336390, Other Motor Vehicle Parts Manufacturing).

Example Activities
- Air-conditioning and warm air heating combination units, manufacturing
- Air-conditioning compressors (except motor vehicle), manufacturing
- Air-conditioning condensers and condensing units, manufacturing
- Air-conditioning equipment (except motor vehicle), manufacturing
- Air-conditioning units (e.g., window, travel trailer, motor home), manufacturing
- Baseboard heating units, manufacturing
- Beer cooling and dispensing equipment, manufacturing

- Boilers, heating, manufacturing
- Burners, heating, manufacturing
- Compressors, refrigeration and air-conditioning (except motor vehicle), manufacturing
- Coolers, refrigeration, manufacturing
- Coolers, water, manufacturing
- Cooling towers, manufacturing
- Counters and display cases, refrigerated, manufacturing
- Dehumidifiers (except portable), manufacturing
- Display cases, refrigerated, manufacturing

- Drinking fountains, refrigerated, manufacturing
- Evaporative condensers (i.e., heat transfer equipment), manufacturing
- Fireplace inserts (i.e., heat directing), manufacturing
- Fireplace logs, gas, manufacturing
- Fountains, refrigerated drinking, manufacturing
- Freezers, laboratory type, manufacturing
- Furnaces, manufacturing
- Gas space heaters, manufacturing
- Heat pumps, manufacturing
- Heaters, space (except portable electric), manufacturing
- Heaters, swimming pool, electric, manufacturing
- Heaters, swimming pool, manufacturing
- Heating and air-conditioning combination units, manufacturing
- Heating equipment, forced air, manufacturing
- Heating equipment, hot water (except hot water heaters), manufacturing
- Heating units, baseboard, manufacturing
- Humidifying equipment (except portable), manufacturing
- Ice making machinery, manufacturing
- Radiators (except motor vehicle, portable electric), manufacturing
- Refrigerated counters and display cases, manufacturing
- Refrigeration compressors, manufacturing
- Refrigeration equipment, industrial and commercial type, manufacturing
- Refrigeration units, truck type, manufacturing
- Snow making machinery, manufacturing
- Soda fountain cooling and dispensing equipment, manufacturing
- Solar energy heating equipment, manufacturing
- Space heaters (except portable electric), manufacturing
- Swimming pool heaters, manufacturing
- Unit heaters (except portable, electric), manufacturing
- Water coolers, manufacturing

3335 Metalworking Machinery Manufacturing

See industry description for 33351, below.

33351 Metalworking Machinery Manufacturing

This industry comprises establishments primarily engaged in manufacturing metal cutting and forming machine tools (except hand tools), and related products. The machine tools included in this industry are those not supported in the hands of an operator when in use. Establishments primarily engaged in manufacturing industrial moulds; tools, dies, jigs and fixtures; machine tool accessories and attachments; and rolls are included.

Exclusion(s): Establishments primarily engaged in:
- manufacturing cutting dies (except metal cutting), hand tools (except power-driven), precision measuring devices, and saw blades and handsaws (33221, Cutlery and Hand Tool Manufacturing);
- manufacturing machinery for cutting and forming wood (33321, Sawmill and Woodworking Machinery Manufacturing); and
- manufacturing power-driven hand tools, welding and soldering equipment, and industrial robots (33399, All Other General-Purpose Machinery Manufacturing).

333511 Industrial Mould Manufacturing US

This Canadian industry comprises establishments primarily engaged in casting and machining industrial metal moulds.

Exclusion(s): Establishments primarily engaged in:
- manufacturing moulds for heavy steel ingots (331511, Iron Foundries).

Example Activities

- Foundry casting moulds, manufacturing
- Industrial moulds (except steel ingots), manufacturing
- Metal moulds (e.g., for working plastics, rubber, glass), manufacturing
- Moulds (except steel ingots), industrial, manufacturing
- Moulds for forming materials (e.g., plastics, rubber, glass), manufacturing
- Moulds for metal casting (except steel ingots), manufacturing

333519 Other Metalworking Machinery Manufacturing ^{CAN}

This Canadian industry comprises establishments, not classified to any other Canadian industry, primarily engaged in manufacturing metal cutting and forming machine tools (except hand tools), and related products, except industrial moulds. The machine tools included in this industry are those not supported in the hands of an operator when in use. Establishments primarily engaged in manufacturing tools, dies, jigs and fixtures; machine tool accessories and attachments; and rolls are included.

Exclusion(s): Establishments primarily engaged in:
- manufacturing cutting dies (except metal cutting), hand tools (except power-driven), precision measuring devices, and saw blades and handsaws (332210, Cutlery and Hand Tool Manufacturing);
- manufacturing machinery for cutting and forming wood (333210, Sawmill and Woodworking Machinery Manufacturing);
- manufacturing moulds for die-casting and foundry casting, plaster working, rubber and plastics working, glass working and similar machinery (333511, Industrial Mould Manufacturing); and
- manufacturing power-driven hand tools, welding and soldering equipment, and industrial robots (333990, All Other General-Purpose Machinery Manufacturing).

Example Activities

- Assembly machines (e.g., rotary transfer, in-line transfer), manufacturing
- Automatic screw machines, manufacturing
- Bending and forming machines, metalworking, manufacturing
- Bits and knives, for metalworking lathes, planers and shapers, manufacturing
- Bits, drill, metalworking, manufacturing
- Broaching machines, metalworking, manufacturing
- Buffing and polishing machines, metalworking, manufacturing
- Can forming machines, metalworking, manufacturing
- Chemical milling machines, metalworking, manufacturing
- Coil winding and cutting machinery, metalworking, manufacturing
- Cold rolling mill machinery, metalworking, manufacturing
- Cradle assemblies machinery (i.e., wire making equipment), manufacturing
- Cutting dies, metalworking, manufacturing
- Deburring machines, metalworking, manufacturing
- Die-casting machines, metalworking, manufacturing
- Dies, metalworking (except threading), manufacturing
- Dies, thread cutting, manufacturing
- Drill bits, metalworking, manufacturing
- Drill presses, metalworking, manufacturing
- Drilling machines, metalworking, manufacturing
- Electro-chemical milling machines, metalworking, manufacturing
- Forging machinery and hammers, manufacturing
- Forming machines, metalworking, manufacturing
- Galvanizing machinery, manufacturing
- Gear cutting and finishing machines, metalworking, manufacturing
- Grinding machines, metalworking, manufacturing
- Honing and lapping machines, metalworking, manufacturing
- Jigs (e.g., inspection, gauging, checking), manufacturing
- Jigs and fixtures, for use with machine tools, manufacturing
- Knives and bits, for metalworking lathes, planers and shapers, manufacturing

- Laser boring, drilling and milling machines, metalworking, manufacturing
- Lathes, metal cutting, manufacturing
- Machine tool attachments and accessories, manufacturing
- Machine tools, metal forming, manufacturing
- Machine tools, rebuilding
- Metal cutting machine tools, manufacturing
- Metal forming machine tools, manufacturing
- Milling machines, metalworking, manufacturing
- Numerically controlled metal cutting machine tools, manufacturing
- Picklers and pickling machinery, metalworking, manufacturing
- Pipe and tube rolling mill machinery, metalworking, manufacturing
- Pipe cutting and threading machines, metalworking, manufacturing
- Polishing and buffing machines, metalworking, manufacturing
- Powder metallurgy forming presses, manufacturing
- Presses (e.g., punching, shearing, stamping), metal forming, manufacturing
- Presses, drill, metal cutting, manufacturing
- Punching machines, metalworking, manufacturing
- Rebuilding machine tools, metal cutting types
- Rebuilding machine tools, metal forming types
- Rolling mill machinery and equipment, metalworking, manufacturing
- Sawing machines, metalworking, manufacturing
- Saws, metal cutting (except hand held), manufacturing
- Spinning machines, metalworking, manufacturing
- Spring winding and forming machines, metalworking, manufacturing
- Stamping machines, metalworking, manufacturing
- Tools and accessories for machine tools, manufacturing
- Tube rolling mill machinery, metalworking, manufacturing
- Wire drawing machines, metalworking, manufacturing

3336 Engine, Turbine and Power Transmission Equipment Manufacturing

See industry description for 33361, below.

33361 Engine, Turbine and Power Transmission Equipment Manufacturing

This industry comprises establishments primarily engaged in manufacturing turbines and turbine generator sets; internal combustion engines (except automotive gasoline and aircraft); and speed changers, industrial high-speed drives and gears. Establishments primarily engaged in manufacturing wind- and solar-powered turbine generators and windmills for generating electric power are included.

Exclusion(s): Establishments primarily engaged in:
- manufacturing ball and roller bearings (33299, All Other Fabricated Metal Product Manufacturing);
- manufacturing electric power transmission and distribution, and electric motors, except outboard (33531, Electrical Equipment Manufacturing);
- manufacturing automotive engines (except diesel) (33631, Motor Vehicle Gasoline Engine and Engine Parts Manufacturing);
- manufacturing motor vehicle power transmission equipment (33635, Motor Vehicle Transmission and Power Train Parts Manufacturing); and
- manufacturing aircraft engines and power transmission equipment (33641, Aerospace Product and Parts Manufacturing).

333611 Turbine and Turbine Generator Set Unit Manufacturing US

This Canadian industry comprises establishments primarily engaged in manufacturing turbines and turbine generator sets.

Exclusion(s): Establishments primarily engaged in:
- manufacturing aircraft-type turbines (336410, Aerospace Product and Parts Manufacturing).

Example Activities

- Gas turbine generator set units, manufacturing
- Gas turbines (except aircraft type), manufacturing
- Generator sets, turbine (e.g., steam, gas, hydraulic), manufacturing
- Turbine generator set units, manufacturing
- Turbines (except aircraft type), manufacturing
- Water turbines, manufacturing
- Wind powered turbine-generator sets, manufacturing

333619 Other Engine and Power Transmission Equipment Manufacturing CAN

This Canadian industry comprises establishments, not classified to any other Canadian industry, primarily engaged in manufacturing engine and power transmission equipment.

Exclusion(s): Establishments primarily engaged in:

- manufacturing ball and roller bearings (332991, Ball and Roller Bearing Manufacturing);
- manufacturing electric power transmission and distribution equipment, and electric motors, except outboard (33531, Electrical Equipment Manufacturing);
- manufacturing automotive engines (except diesel) (336310, Motor Vehicle Gasoline Engine and Engine Parts Manufacturing); and
- manufacturing motor vehicle power transmission equipment (336350, Motor Vehicle Transmission and Power Train Parts Manufacturing).

Example Activities

- Bearings, plain (except internal combustion engines), manufacturing
- Brakes (except motor vehicle and electromagnetic industrial controls), manufacturing
- Bushings, plain (except internal combustion engine), manufacturing
- Chains, power transmission, manufacturing
- Clutches (except motor vehicle and electromagnetic industrial controls), manufacturing
- Couplings, mechanical power transmission, manufacturing
- Diesel and semi-diesel engines, manufacturing
- Diesel engine parts, not specified elsewhere by process, manufacturing
- Diesel engines, rebuilding
- Drive chains, bicycle and motorcycle, manufacturing
- Drives, high-speed industrial (except hydrostatic), manufacturing
- Engines, diesel and semi-diesel, manufacturing
- Engines, internal combustion (except aircraft and non-diesel automotive), manufacturing
- Engines, natural gas or propane (except automotive), manufacturing
- Gasoline engines (except aircraft and automotive), manufacturing
- Gearmotors (i.e., power transmission equipment), manufacturing
- Gears, power transmission (except motor vehicle and aircraft), manufacturing
- Internal combustion engines (except aircraft and non-diesel automotive), manufacturing
- Joints, universal (except motor vehicle and aircraft), manufacturing
- Locomotive diesel engines, manufacturing
- Motors, outboard, manufacturing
- Outboard motors, manufacturing
- Pulleys, power transmission, manufacturing
- Reducers, speed, manufacturing
- Semi-diesel engines, manufacturing
- Speed changers (i.e., power transmission equipment), manufacturing
- Speed reducers (i.e., power transmission equipment), manufacturing
- Sprockets, power transmission equipment, manufacturing
- Universal joints (except motor vehicle and aircraft), manufacturing

3339 Other General-Purpose Machinery Manufacturing

This industry group comprises establishments, not classified to any other industry group, primarily engaged in manufacturing machinery that is not designed for use in any specific industry.

33391 Pump and Compressor Manufacturing

This industry comprises establishments primarily engaged in manufacturing pumps, pumping equipment and compressors for general use.

Exclusion(s): Establishments primarily engaged in:
- manufacturing agricultural spraying and dusting equipment (33311, Agricultural Implement Manufacturing);
- manufacturing air-conditioning and refrigeration systems and compressors (except motor vehicle) (33341, Ventilation, Heating, Air-Conditioning and Commercial Refrigeration Equipment Manufacturing);
- manufacturing pneumatic pumps and motors for fluid power transmission (33399, All Other General-Purpose Machinery Manufacturing);
- manufacturing motor vehicle pumps (3363, Motor Vehicle Parts Manufacturing);
- manufacturing motor vehicle air-conditioning systems and compressors (33639, Other Motor Vehicle Parts Manufacturing); and
- manufacturing laboratory vacuum pumps (33911, Medical Equipment and Supplies Manufacturing).

Example Activities
- Air compressors, manufacturing
- Bicycle pumps, manufacturing
- Centrifugal pumps, manufacturing
- Compressors, general purpose air and gas, manufacturing
- Dispensing and measuring pumps (e.g., gasoline), manufacturing
- Gasoline measuring and dispensing pumps, manufacturing
- Oil well and oil field pumps, manufacturing
- Paint sprayers (i.e., compressor and spray gun units), manufacturing
- Pumps, industrial and commercial type, general purpose, manufacturing
- Pumps, measuring and dispensing (e.g., gasoline), manufacturing
- Pumps, oil well and oil field, manufacturing
- Pumps, sump or water, residential type, manufacturing
- Sprayers, manually-pumped units, general purpose type, manufacturing
- Sump pumps, residential type, manufacturing
- Vacuum pumps (except laboratory), manufacturing

333910 Pump and Compressor Manufacturing CAN

See industry description for 33391, above.

33392 Material Handling Equipment Manufacturing

This industry comprises establishments primarily engaged in manufacturing material handling equipment.

Exclusion(s): Establishments primarily engaged in:
- manufacturing farm-type wheeled tractors (33311, Agricultural Implement Manufacturing);
- manufacturing construction tractors and cranes (33312, Construction Machinery Manufacturing); and
- manufacturing motor vehicle trailers (33621, Motor Vehicle Body and Trailer Manufacturing).

Example Activities
- Aerial work platforms, manufacturing
- Aircraft loading hoists, manufacturing
- Automobile hoists (i.e., tow truck, wrecker), manufacturing
- Automobile lifts (i.e., service station and garage type), manufacturing
- Belt conveyor systems, manufacturing
- Block and tackle, manufacturing
- Boat lifts, manufacturing
- Buckets, elevators or conveyors, manufacturing
- Cabs for industrial trucks and tractors, manufacturing
- Carousel conveyors (e.g., luggage), manufacturing

- Carts for moving goods (e.g., laundry, industrial), manufacturing
- Conveyor systems, general industrial type, manufacturing
- Conveyors, farm type, manufacturing
- Cranes, industrial truck, manufacturing
- Cranes, overhead travelling, manufacturing
- Dollies, industrial, manufacturing
- Elevators, farm type, manufacturing
- Elevators, passenger and freight, manufacturing
- Escalators, passenger and freight, manufacturing
- Farm conveyors, manufacturing
- Farm elevators, manufacturing
- Forklift trucks, manufacturing
- Hoists, manufacturing
- Industrial truck cranes, manufacturing
- Industrial trucks and tractors (plant and warehouse), manufacturing
- Laundry carts, manufacturing
- Lowering devices, burial, manufacturing
- Mechanics' creepers, manufacturing
- Monorail systems (except passenger), manufacturing
- Overhead conveyors, manufacturing
- Overhead travelling cranes, manufacturing
- Pallet movers, manufacturing
- Pneumatic tube conveyors, manufacturing
- Ship cranes and derricks, manufacturing
- Stairways, moving, manufacturing
- Straddle carriers, mobile, manufacturing
- Tractors, industrial, manufacturing
- Trucks, industrial (plant and warehouse), manufacturing
- Walkways, moving, manufacturing
- Wheelbarrows, manufacturing
- Winches, manufacturing
- Wire rope hoists, manufacturing

333920 Material Handling Equipment Manufacturing MEX

See industry description for 33392, above.

33399 All Other General-Purpose Machinery Manufacturing

This industry comprises establishments, not classified to any other industry, primarily engaged in manufacturing machinery that is not designed for use in any specific industry.

Exclusion(s): Establishments primarily engaged in:
- manufacturing bakery ovens, and cement, wood and chemical kilns (33329, Other Industrial Machinery Manufacturing);
- manufacturing furnace filters (33341, Ventilation, Heating, Air-Conditioning and Commercial Refrigeration Equipment Manufacturing);
- manufacturing electric welding transformers (33531, Electrical Equipment Manufacturing); and
- manufacturing motor vehicle engine filters, and motor vehicle screw jacks (33639, Other Motor Vehicle Parts Manufacturing).

Example Activities
- Actuators, fluid power, manufacturing
- Arc-welding equipment, manufacturing
- Balances and scales, laboratory type, manufacturing
- Bathroom scales, manufacturing
- Battery-powered, hand held power tools, manufacturing
- Bottle washers, packaging machinery, manufacturing
- Bottling machinery (e.g., washing, sterilizing, filling, capping, labelling), manufacturing
- Bridge and gate lifting machinery, manufacturing
- Canning machinery, manufacturing
- Capping, sealing and lidding packaging machinery, manufacturing
- Carton filling machines, manufacturing
- Cartridge (i.e., powder) hand held power-driven tools, manufacturing
- Chain saws, hand held power-driven, manufacturing
- Circular saws, hand held power driven, manufacturing
- Coding, dating and imprinting packaging machinery, manufacturing
- Corded (i.e., electric-powered), hand held power tools, manufacturing

- Cremating ovens, manufacturing
- Cylinders, fluid power, manufacturing
- Dielectric industrial heating equipment, manufacturing
- Drills (except heavy construction, mining type), hand held power-driven, manufacturing
- Electrodes, welding, manufacturing
- Filters, industrial and general line (except for warm air furnaces and internal combustion engines), manufacturing
- Fire-fighting sprinklers, automatic systems, manufacturing
- Fluid power actuators, manufacturing
- Fluid power cylinders, manufacturing
- Fluid power motors, manufacturing
- Fluid power pumps, manufacturing
- Food packaging machinery, manufacturing
- Fuel cell-powered, hand held power tools, manufacturing
- Furnaces and ovens for drying and redrying, industrial process, manufacturing
- Furnaces, industrial process, manufacturing
- Gasoline-powered, hand held power tools, manufacturing
- Gate and bridge lifting machinery, manufacturing
- Guides, for hand held woodworking tool, manufacturing
- Hand tools, power-driven, manufacturing
- Heat treating ovens, industrial process type, manufacturing
- Hydraulic cylinders, fluid power, manufacturing
- Hydraulic pumps, fluid power, manufacturing
- Impact wrenches, hand held power-driven, manufacturing
- Incinerators, industrial process type, manufacturing
- Induction heating equipment, industrial process type, manufacturing
- Industrial scales, manufacturing
- Infrared ovens, industrial process type, manufacturing
- Jacks, hydraulic and pneumatic, manufacturing
- Jig saws, hand held power driven, manufacturing
- Kilns (except cement, chemical, wood), manufacturing
- Labelling (i.e., packaging machinery), manufacturing
- Laboratory furnaces, manufacturing
- Laboratory type equipment (e.g., furnaces, balances, centifruges), manufacturing
- Laser welding equipment, manufacturing
- Motor truck scales, manufacturing
- Motors, fluid power, manufacturing
- Ovens, industrial process type, manufacturing
- Packaging machinery, manufacturing
- Paint baking and drying ovens, manufacturing
- Paint spray guns, pneumatic, hand held power-driven, manufacturing
- Parcel post scales, manufacturing
- Plasma welding equipment, manufacturing
- Pneumatic cylinders, fluid power, manufacturing
- Pneumatic pumps, fluid power, manufacturing
- Pneumatic, hand held power tools, manufacturing
- Powder-actuated hand held power tools, manufacturing
- Power-driven hand tools, manufacturing
- Pumps, fluid power, manufacturing
- Resistance welding and cutting equipment, manufacturing
- Retail scales (e.g., butcher, delicatessen, produce), manufacturing
- Routers, hand held power-driven, manufacturing
- Sanders, hand held power-driven, manufacturing
- Saws, hand held power driven, manufacturing
- Screwdrivers and nut drivers, hand held power driven, manufacturing
- Seam welding equipment, manufacturing
- Sieves and screening equipment, general industrial type, manufacturing
- Smelting ovens, manufacturing
- Soldering equipment (except hand held), manufacturing
- Sprinkler systems, automatic fire, manufacturing
- Staplers and nailers, hand held power-driven, manufacturing
- Testing, weighing and inspecting packaging machinery, manufacturing
- Thermoform, blister and skin packaging machinery, manufacturing
- Tools, hand held power-driven, manufacturing
- Ultrasonic welding equipment, manufacturing

- Welding electrodes, manufacturing
- Welding equipment, manufacturing
- Welding wire or rod (i.e., coated or cored), manufacturing

333990 All Other General-Purpose Machinery Manufacturing ^{CAN}

See industry description for 33399, above.

334 Computer and Electronic Product Manufacturing

This subsector comprises establishments primarily engaged in manufacturing computers, computer peripheral equipment, communications equipment, and similar electronic products, as well as components for such products. The computer and electronic product manufacturing industries employ production processes that are characterized by the design and use of integrated circuits and the application of highly specialized miniaturization technologies.

3341 Computer and Peripheral Equipment Manufacturing

See industry description for 33411, below.

33411 Computer and Peripheral Equipment Manufacturing

This industry comprises establishments primarily engaged in manufacturing computers and computer peripheral equipment.

Computers can be digital, analogue or hybrid. The most common type, digital, are devices that can do all of the following: (1) store the processing program or programs and the data immediately necessary for the execution of the program; (2) be freely programmed in accordance with the requirements of the user; (3) perform arithmetical computations specified by the user; and (4) execute, without human intervention, a processing program that requires the computer to modify its execution, by logical decision, during the processing run. Analogue computers are capable of simulating mathematical models and comprise, at least, analogue, control and programming elements.

Peripherals are assemblies of components that are self-contained, but designed for use with computers. For purposes of classification, a peripheral must consist of more than a loaded circuit board. Peripheral equipment may be installed inside or outside the computer's housing. Important types of peripheral equipment are input-output devices, such as monitors, keyboards, mice and joysticks; storage devices, such as disk drives and CD-ROM readers; and printers. "Dumb" computer terminals, automated teller machines (ATM's), point-of-sale (POS) terminals and bar code scanners are treated as peripheral equipment.

Computers and peripheral equipment may be sold complete or in kits to be assembled by the purchaser.

Exclusion(s): Establishments primarily engaged in:
- manufacturing digital telecommunications switches, local area network and wide area network communications equipment, such as bridges, routers and gateways (33421, Telephone Apparatus Manufacturing);
- manufacturing audio speakers, for use in computer systems (33431, Audio and Video Equipment Manufacturing);
- manufacturing internal loaded printed circuit-board devices, such as sound, video, controller and network interface cards; personal computer modems, whether or not in an external housing; central processing units, memory chips and similar integrated circuits (33441, Semiconductor and Other Electronic Component Manufacturing);
- manufacturing magnetic and optical recording media (33461, Manufacturing and Reproducing Magnetic and Optical Media);
- retailing computers, assembled in the store (44312, Computer and Software Stores);
- manufacturing parts, such as casings, stampings, cable sets and switches, for computers and peripheral equipment (other manufacturing industries based on the associated production processes); and
- manufacturing machinery or equipment that incorporate electronic computers for operation or control purposes and embedded control applications (other manufacturing industries based on the classification of the complete machinery or equipment).

Example Activities
- Analog computers, manufacturing
- ATM's (automatic teller machines), manufacturing
- Automatic teller machines (ATM), manufacturing
- Bar code scanners, manufacturing
- CD-ROM drives, manufacturing
- Computer terminals, manufacturing
- Computers, manufacturing
- Digital cameras, manufacturing
- Digital computers, manufacturing
- Direct access storage devices, manufacturing
- Disk drives, computer, manufacturing
- DVD (digital video disc) drives, computer peripheral equipment, manufacturing
- Flat panel displays (i.e., complete units), computer peripheral equipment, manufacturing
- Hand-held computer (e.g., PDA's), manufacturing
- Joystick devices, manufacturing
- Keyboards, computer peripheral equipment, manufacturing
- Mainframe computers, manufacturing
- Microcomputers, manufacturing
- Minicomputers, manufacturing
- Monitors, computer peripheral equipment, manufacturing
- Mouse devices, computer peripheral equipment, manufacturing
- Optical readers and scanners, manufacturing
- Overhead projectors, computer peripheral-type, manufacturing
- Personal computers, manufacturing
- Pointing devices, computer peripheral equipment, manufacturing
- Point-of-sale (POS) terminals, manufacturing
- Printers, computer, manufacturing
- Storage devices, computer, manufacturing
- Tape storage units (e.g., drives, backups), computer peripheral equipment, manufacturing
- Terminals, computer, manufacturing

334110 Computer and Peripheral Equipment Manufacturing ᴹᴱˣ

See industry description for 33411, above.

3342 Communications Equipment Manufacturing

This industry group comprises establishments primarily engaged in manufacturing equipment used to move signals electronically over wires or through the air, such as telephone apparatus, radio and television broadcast equipment, and satellite communications equipment.

33421 Telephone Apparatus Manufacturing

This industry comprises establishments primarily engaged in manufacturing wired telephone and data communications equipment. These products may be stand-alone or board-level components of a larger system.

Exclusion(s): Establishments primarily engaged in:
- manufacturing cellular telephones; and microwave transmission equipment (33422, Radio and Television Broadcasting and Wireless Communications Equipment Manufacturing); and
- manufacturing internal and external computer modems, fax/modems and telephone transformers (33441, Semiconductor and Other Electronic Component Manufacturing).

Example Activities
- Cordless telephones (except cellular), manufacturing
- Facsimile equipment, stand-alone, manufacturing
- Local area network (LAN) communication equipment (e.g., bridges, gateways, routers), manufacturing
- Modems, carrier equipment, manufacturing
- PBX (private branch exchange) equipment, manufacturing
- Private branch exchange (PBX) equipment, manufacturing
- Switching equipment, telephone, manufacturing
- Telephone answering machines, manufacturing
- Telephone carrier line equipment, manufacturing
- Telephone carrier switching equipment, manufacturing
- Telephones (except cellular telephones), manufacturing
- Wide area network communications equipment (e.g., bridges, gateways, routers), manufacturing

334210 Telephone Apparatus Manufacturing

See industry description for 33421, above.

33422 Radio and Television Broadcasting and Wireless Communications Equipment Manufacturing

This industry comprises establishments primarily engaged in manufacturing radio and television broadcast and wireless communication equipment.

Exclusion(s): Establishments primarily engaged in:
- manufacturing wired and non-wired intercommunications equipment (intercoms) (33429, Other Communications Equipment Manufacturing); and
- manufacturing household audio and video equipment, such as television and radio receiving sets (33431, Audio and Video Equipment Manufacturing).

Example Activities
- Antennas, satellite, manufacturing
- Antennas, transmitting and communications, manufacturing
- Broadcast equipment (including studio), for radio and television, manufacturing
- Cable television transmission and receiving equipment, manufacturing
- CB (citizens' band) radios, manufacturing
- Cellular telephones, manufacturing
- Closed circuit television equipment, manufacturing
- GPS (global positioning system) equipment, manufacturing
- Pagers, manufacturing
- Space satellites, communications equipment, manufacturing

334220 Radio and Television Broadcasting and Wireless Communications Equipment Manufacturing

See industry description for 33422, above.

33429 Other Communications Equipment Manufacturing

This industry comprises establishments, not classified to any other industry, primarily engaged in manufacturing communications equipment.

Example Activities
- Alarm systems and equipment, manufacturing
- Fire detection and alarm systems, manufacturing
- Intercom systems and equipment, manufacturing
- Remote control units (e.g., garage door, television) manufacturing
- Smoke detectors, manufacturing
- Traffic signals, manufacturing

334290 Other Communications Equipment Manufacturing

See industry description for 33429, above.

3343 Audio and Video Equipment Manufacturing

See industry description for 33431, below.

33431 Audio and Video Equipment Manufacturing

This industry comprises establishments primarily engaged in manufacturing electronic audio and video equipment.

Exclusion(s): Establishments primarily engaged in:
- manufacturing photographic (still and motion picture) equipment (33331, Commercial and Service Industry Machinery Manufacturing); and
- manufacturing telephone answering machines (33421, Telephone Apparatus Manufacturing).

Example Activities
- Amplifiers (e.g., auto, home, musical instrument, public address), manufacturing
- Camcorders, manufacturing
- Clock radios, manufacturing
- Compact disc players (e.g., automotive, household-type), manufacturing
- DVD (digital video disc) players, manufacturing
- Home stereo systems, manufacturing
- Home theatre audio and video equipment, manufacturing
- Karaoke machines, manufacturing
- Microphones, manufacturing
- Public address systems and equipment, manufacturing
- Radio receiving sets, manufacturing
- Speaker systems, manufacturing
- Television (TV) sets, manufacturing
- TV (television) sets, manufacturing
- VCR (video cassette recorders), manufacturing
- Video cameras, household-type, manufacturing
- Video cassette recorders (VCR), manufacturing

334310 Audio and Video Equipment Manufacturing

See industry description for 33431, above.

3344 Semiconductor and Other Electronic Component Manufacturing

See industry description for 33441, below.

33441 Semiconductor and Other Electronic Component Manufacturing

This industry comprises establishments primarily engaged in manufacturing semiconductors and other electronic components.

The following activities involving printed circuit boards are undertaken in this industry: the production of the laminate material; the manufacture of the bare (rigid or flexible) printed circuit boards without mounted electronic components; and the loading of electronic components onto the boards.

Exclusion(s): Establishments primarily engaged in:
- manufacturing X-ray tubes (33451, Navigational, Measuring, Medical and Control Instruments Manufacturing);
- manufacturing wire and cable for electronic, computer and communications applications (33592, Communication and Energy Wire and Cable Manufacturing);
- manufacturing capacitors, rectifiers, surge suppressors and similar devices for electrical applications (33599, All Other Electrical Equipment and Component Manufacturing); and
- manufacturing finished products that incorporate loaded printed circuit boards (other manufacturing industries based on the classification of the final product).

Example Activities
- Capacitors, electronic, fixed and variable, manufacturing
- Chokes for electronic circuitry, manufacturing
- Circuit boards, printed, bare, manufacturing
- Connectors, electronic (e.g., coaxial, cylindrical, printed circuit, rack, panel), manufacturing
- CRT (cathode ray tubes), manufacturing
- Diodes, solid state (e.g., germanium, silicon), manufacturing
- Electron tubes, manufacturing
- Fibre optic connectors, manufacturing
- Inductors, electronic component type (e.g., chokes, coils, transformers), manufacturing
- Integrated microcircuits, manufacturing
- Integrated optical circuits (IOC), manufacturing
- LCD (liquid crystal display) unit screens, manufacturing
- LED's (light emitting diodes), manufacturing
- Loaded computer boards, manufacturing
- Memory boards, manufacturing
- Memory chips, semiconductor, manufacturing
- Microcontroller chips, manufacturing
- Microprocessor chips, manufacturing
- Modems, personal computer, manufacturing
- MOS (metal oxide silicon) devices, manufacturing
- Optoelectronic devices, manufacturing
- Personal computer modems, manufacturing
- Photonic integrated circuits (PIC), manufacturing
- Printed circuit boards, bare (i.e., without mounted electronic components), manufacturing
- Printed circuit laminates, manufacturing
- RAM (random access memory) chips, manufacturing
- Rectifiers, electronic component-type, manufacturing
- Resistors, electronic, manufacturing
- Semiconductor devices, manufacturing
- Silicon waveguides, manufacturing
- Solar cells, manufacturing
- Telephone and telegraph transformers, electronic component type, manufacturing
- Transformers, electronic component type, manufacturing
- Transistors, manufacturing
- Vacuum tubes, manufacturing
- Wafers (i.e., semiconductor devices), manufacturing

334410 Semiconductor and Other Electronic Component Manufacturing MEX

See industry description for 33441, above.

3345 Navigational, Measuring, Medical and Control Instruments Manufacturing

See industry description for 33451, below.

33451 Navigational, Measuring, Medical and Control Instruments Manufacturing

This industry comprises establishments primarily engaged in manufacturing navigational, measuring, medical and controlling devices.

334511 Navigational and Guidance Instruments Manufacturing US

This Canadian industry comprises establishments primarily engaged in manufacturing navigational and guidance equipment.

Exclusion(s): Establishments primarily engaged in:
- manufacturing global positioning system equipment (334220, Radio and Television Broadcasting and Wireless Communications Equipment Manufacturing); and
- manufacturing aircraft engine instruments, and meteorological systems and equipment (334512, Measuring, Medical and Controlling Devices Manufacturing).

Example Activities
- Aeronautical systems and instruments, manufacturing
- Air traffic control radar systems and equipment, manufacturing
- Airframe equipment instruments, manufacturing
- Airspeed instruments (aeronautical), manufacturing
- Cabin environment indicators, transmitters and sensors, manufacturing
- Compasses, gyroscopic and magnetic (except portable), manufacturing
- Electronic guidance systems and equipment, manufacturing
- Fish finders (i.e., sonar), manufacturing
- Flight and navigation sensors, transmitters and displays, manufacturing
- Gyroscopes, manufacturing
- HUD (heads-up display) systems, aeronautical, manufacturing
- Instruments, aeronautical, manufacturing
- Nautical systems and instruments, manufacturing
- Navigational instruments, electronic, manufacturing
- Navigational instruments, manufacturing
- Proximity warning (i.e., collision avoidance) equipment, manufacturing
- Radar detectors, manufacturing
- Radar systems and equipment, manufacturing
- Sonar systems and equipment, manufacturing
- Space vehicle guidance systems and equipment, manufacturing
- Speed, pitch and roll navigational instruments and systems, manufacturing
- Wheel position indicators and transmitters, aircraft, manufacturing

334512 Measuring, Medical and Controlling Devices Manufacturing CAN

This Canadian industry comprises establishments primarily engaged in manufacturing measuring, medical and controlling devices.

Exclusion(s): Establishments primarily engaged in:
- manufacturing optical instruments (333310, Commercial and Service Industry Machinery Manufacturing);
- manufacturing equipment for measuring and testing communications signals (3342, Communications Equipment Manufacturing);
- manufacturing instrument transformers, including portable (334410, Semiconductor and Other Electronic Component Manufacturing);
- manufacturing motor control switches and relays, including timing relays (335315, Switchgear and Switchboard, and Relay and Industrial Control Apparatus Manufacturing);
- manufacturing switches for appliances (335930, Wiring Device Manufacturing); and
- manufacturing medical thermometers and non-electrical medical and therapeutic apparatus (339110, Medical Equipment and Supplies Manufacturing).

Example Activities
- Aircraft engine instruments, manufacturing
- Automatic environmental controls and regulators (e.g., heating, air-conditioning, refrigeration), manufacturing
- Clocks, assembling
- Communication signal testing apparatus, manufacturing
- Computerized axial tomography (CT/CAT) scanners, manufacturing
- Controllers for process variables (e.g., electric, electronic, mechanical, pneumatic operation), manufacturing
- CT/CAT (computerized axial tomography), scanners, manufacturing
- Diagnostic equipment, electromedical, manufacturing
- Diagnostic equipment, MRI (magnetic resonance imaging), manufacturing
- Drafting instruments, manufacturing
- Electromedical apparatus and instruments, manufacturing
- Electromedical diagnostic equipment, manufacturing
- Electron tube test equipment, manufacturing
- Hearing aids, electronic, manufacturing
- Humidistats (e.g., duct, skeleton, wall), manufacturing
- Hydronic limit, pressure and temperature controls, manufacturing
- Ignition controls for gas appliances and furnaces, automatic, manufacturing
- Industrial process control instruments, manufacturing
- Instrument panels, assembling using gauges made in the same establishment
- Instruments for industrial process control, manufacturing
- Instruments for measuring electrical quantities, manufacturing
- Instruments, laboratory analysis type, manufacturing
- Irradiation equipment, manufacturing
- Laboratory analytical instruments (except optical), manufacturing
- Laboratory standards testing equipment (e.g., capacitance, electrical resistance, inductance), manufacturing
- Magnetic resonance imaging (MRI) devices, manufacturing
- Medical equipment, ultrasonic, manufacturing
- Medical radiation therapy equipment, manufacturing
- Meteorological instruments, manufacturing
- Meters (except electrical and industrial process control), manufacturing
- Meters, electrical (i.e, graphic recording, panelboard, pocket, portable), manufacturing
- Meters, industrial process control type, manufacturing
- MRI (magnetic resonance imaging) medical diagnostic equipment, manufacturing
- Nuclear radiation detection instruments, manufacturing
- Oscilloscopes, manufacturing
- PET (positron emission tomography) scanners, manufacturing
- Physical properties testing and inspection equipment, manufacturing
- Radiation detection and monitoring instruments, manufacturing
- Refractometers, manufacturing
- Refrigeration controls, residential and commercial type, manufacturing
- Soil testing and analysis instruments, manufacturing

- Surgical support systems (e.g., heart-lung machines) (except iron lungs), manufacturing
- Surveying instruments, manufacturing
- Temperature controls, automatic, residential and commercial type, manufacturing
- Temperature instruments (except glass and bimetal thermometers), industrial process type, manufacturing
- TENS (transcutaneous electrical nerve stimulators), manufacturing
- Thermocouples, manufacturing

- Thermostats (e.g., air-conditioning, appliance, comfort heating, refrigeration), manufacturing
- Totalizing fluid meters, manufacturing
- Watches and parts (except crystals), manufacturing
- Water quality monitoring and control systems, manufacturing
- X-ray apparatus and tubes (e.g., control, industrial, medical, research), manufacturing

3346 Manufacturing and Reproducing Magnetic and Optical Media

See industry description for 33461, below.

33461 Manufacturing and Reproducing Magnetic and Optical Media

This industry comprises establishments primarily engaged in manufacturing magnetic and optical media, and the mass reproduction of recordings on such media. The media include audio and video tapes, diskettes, hard disk media and CD-ROMs. The products of the industry are blank media; and software (shrink-wrapped), audio, video, and multimedia products recorded on these media.

Exclusion(s): Establishments primarily engaged in:
- designing, developing or publishing prepackaged software or documentation, and publishing and reproducing software in integrated facilities (51121, Software Publishers); and
- audio and video producing and publishing, including the production of masters or matrices of recordings, and publishing and reproducing audio, video and film materials in integrated facilities (512, Motion Picture and Sound Recording Industries).

Example Activities
- Audio tape, blank, manufacturing
- Blank tapes, audio and video, manufacturing
- Compact discs, pre-recorded audio, mass-reproducing
- Compact discs, recordable or re-writable, blank, manufacturing
- Diskettes, blank, manufacturing
- Floppy disks, blank, manufacturing
- Magnetic tapes, cassettes and disks, blank, manufacturing
- Mass reproduction of pre-packaged software
- Multimedia products, pre-recorded, mass-reproducing

- Optical recording media, blank, manufacturing
- Pre-recorded magnetic audio tapes and cassettes, mass-reproducing
- Shrink-wrapped computer software, mass-reproducing
- Tapes, magnetic recording (i.e., audio, data, video), blank, manufacturing
- Video cassettes, blank, manufacturing
- Video cassettes, pre-recorded, mass-reproducing
- Video game software cartridges, mass-reproducing
- Video tapes, blank, manufacturing

334610 Manufacturing and Reproducing Magnetic and Optical Media MEX

See industry description for 33461, above.

335 Electrical Equipment, Appliance and Component Manufacturing

This subsector comprises establishments primarily engaged in manufacturing products that generate, distribute and use electrical power.

3351 Electric Lighting Equipment Manufacturing

This industry group comprises establishments primarily engaged in manufacturing electric lamp bulbs and tubes and lighting fixtures.

33511 Electric Lamp Bulb and Parts Manufacturing

This industry comprises establishments primarily engaged in manufacturing all types of electric lamps (bulbs and tubes).

Example Activities
- Discharge lamps, high intensity (mercury, sodium, metal halide), manufacturing
- Filaments, for electric lamps, manufacturing
- Fluorescent tubes, manufacturing
- Halogen bulbs, manufacturing
- Health lamps, infra-red and ultra-violet-radiation, manufacturing
- Incandescent filament lamp bulbs, complete, manufacturing
- Light bulbs and tubes, electric, manufacturing
- Photographic bulbs, lamps and cubes, manufacturing
- Sealed beam lamps, manufacturing

335110 Electric Lamp Bulb and Parts Manufacturing

See industry description for 33511, above.

33512 Lighting Fixture Manufacturing

This industry comprises establishments primarily engaged in manufacturing lighting fixtures and lamps.

Exclusion(s): Establishments primarily engaged in:
- manufacturing lamp shades of materials other than textiles (32721, Glass and Glass Product Manufacturing);
- manufacturing lamp shades of materials other than textiles (32721, Glass and Glass Product Manufacturing, or 33299, All Other Fabricated Metal Product Manufacturing);
- manufacturing sealed-beam headlamps and other light bulbs for motor vehicles (33511, Electric Lamp Bulb and Parts Manufacturing); and
- manufacturing motor vehicle lighting fixtures (33632, Motor Vehicle Electrical and Electronic Equipment Manufacturing).

Example Activities
- Arc lighting fixtures, manufacturing
- Chandeliers, manufacturing
- Christmas tree lighting sets, electric, manufacturing
- Desk lamps, manufacturing
- Electric lighting fixtures, manufacturing
- Fixtures, electric lighting, manufacturing
- Flashlights, manufacturing
- Floor lamps, residential, manufacturing
- Fluorescent lighting fixtures, manufacturing
- Gas lighting fixtures, manufacturing
- Incandescent lighting fixtures, manufacturing
- Kerosene lamps, manufacturing
- Lamp shades (except glass, plastic), manufacturing
- Lighting fixtures, manufacturing
- Mantles, incandescent, manufacturing
- Searchlights, manufacturing
- Street lighting equipment, manufacturing
- Table lamps, manufacturing

335120 Lighting Fixture Manufacturing CAN

See industry description for 33512, above.

3352 Household Appliance Manufacturing

This industry group comprises establishments primarily engaged in manufacturing kitchen, bathroom and other household appliances.

33521 Small Electrical Appliance Manufacturing

This industry comprises establishments primarily engaged in manufacturing household and commercial electrical and other small appliances.

Exclusion(s): Establishments primarily engaged in:
- manufacturing household sewing machines (33329, Other Industrial Machinery Manufacturing); and
- manufacturing domestic water heaters (33522, Major Appliance Manufacturing).

Example Activities
- Appliances, small electrical, manufacturing
- Blankets, electric, manufacturing
- Blenders, food, electric, manufacturing
- Can openers, electric, domestic, manufacturing
- Coffee makers, household, electric, manufacturing
- Corn poppers, electric, manufacturing
- Fans, household, electric (except attic fans), manufacturing
- Food grinders, choppers and slicers, electric, domestic, manufacturing
- Fry pans, electric, manufacturing
- Hair clippers for human use, electric, manufacturing
- Hair styling equipment, domestic, electric, manufacturing
- Humidifiers, electric, portable, manufacturing
- Knives, electric, domestic, manufacturing
- Razors, electric, manufacturing
- Space heaters, portable, electric, manufacturing
- Toasters, electric (including sandwich toasters), manufacturing

335210 Small Electrical Appliance Manufacturing MEX

See industry description for 33521, above.

33522 Major Appliance Manufacturing

This industry comprises establishments primarily engaged in manufacturing electric and non-electric major household appliances and equipment.

335223 Major Kitchen Appliance Manufacturing CAN

This Canadian industry comprises establishments primarily engaged in manufacturing major electric and non-electric kitchen appliances and equipment.

Example Activities
- Dishwashers, household, electric, manufacturing
- Freezers, household, manufacturing
- Refrigerators, household, manufacturing
- Stoves, domestic, electric or non-electric, manufacturing

335229 Other Major Appliance Manufacturing CAN

This Canadian industry comprises establishments, not classified to any other Canadian industry, primarily engaged in manufacturing electric and non-electric major household appliances and equipment.

Exclusion(s): Establishments primarily engaged in:
- manufacturing domestic sewing machines (333299, All Other Industrial Machinery Manufacturing).

Example Activities

- Barbecues, gas, manufacturing
- Barbeque grills (charcoal), manufacturing
- Clothes dryers, domestic, manufacturing
- Garbage disposal units, household, manufacturing

- Gas barbecues, manufacturing
- Washing machines, household (including coin-operated), manufacturing
- Water heaters, household (including non-electric), manufacturing

3353 Electrical Equipment Manufacturing

See industry description for 33531, below.

33531 Electrical Equipment Manufacturing

This industry comprises establishments primarily engaged in manufacturing equipment that generates and distributes electrical power.

Exclusion(s): Establishments primarily engaged in:
- operating electric power generating plants (22111, Electric Power Generation);
- manufacturing electronic transformers (33441, Semiconductor and Other Electronic Component Manufacturing);
- manufacturing industrial process controls (33451, Navigational, Measuring, Medical and Control Instruments Manufacturing); and
- manufacturing automotive electrical equipment (33632, Motor Vehicle Electrical and Electronic Equipment Manufacturing).

335311 Power, Distribution and Specialty Transformers Manufacturing US

This Canadian industry comprises establishments primarily engaged in manufacturing power, distribution, instrument and specialty transformers.

Exclusion(s): Establishments primarily engaged in:
- manufacturing electronic transformers (334410, Semiconductor and Other Electronic Component Manufacturing).

Example Activities

- Distribution transformers, manufacturing
- Instrument transformers (except portable), manufacturing

- Power transformers, manufacturing

335312 Motor and Generator Manufacturing US

This Canadian industry comprises establishments primarily engaged in manufacturing electric motors and generators.

Exclusion(s): Establishments primarily engaged in:
- manufacturing automotive electrical equipment, such as starters, generators and alternators (336320, Motor Vehicle Electrical and Electronic Equipment Manufacturing).

Example Activities

- Armature rewinding, remanufacturing
- Armatures, manufacturing
- Coils, for motors and generators, manufacturing
- Commutators, electric motor, manufacturing
- Electric motors, manufacturing

- Industrial electrical motor rebuilding
- Motors, electric (except starting motors), manufacturing
- Rebuilding motors, electric, other than automotive
- Storage battery chargers, engine generator type, manufacturing

335315 Switchgear and Switchboard, and Relay and Industrial Control Apparatus Manufacturing CAN

This Canadian industry comprises establishments primarily engaged in manufacturing electrical switchgear and protective equipment.

Exclusion(s): Establishments primarily engaged in:
- manufacturing industrial process control instruments (334512, Measuring, Medical and Controlling Devices Manufacturing).

Example Activities
- Circuit breakers, power, manufacturing
- Control panels, electric power distribution, manufacturing
- Cubicles (i.e., electric switchboard equipment), manufacturing
- Electromagnetic clutches and brakes, manufacturing
- Electromagnets, manufacturing
- Fuse mountings, electric power, manufacturing
- Fuses, electric, manufacturing
- Instrument relays, all types, manufacturing
- Metering panels, electric, manufacturing
- Power switching equipment, manufacturing
- Relays, electrical, manufacturing
- Switchboards and parts, power, manufacturing
- Switches, electric power (except snap, push button, tumbler and solenoid), manufacturing
- Switchgear and switchgear accessories, manufacturing

3359 Other Electrical Equipment and Component Manufacturing

This industry group comprises establishments, not classified to any other industry group, primarily engaged in manufacturing electrical power storage and transmission devices, and accessories for carrying current.

33591 Battery Manufacturing

This industry comprises establishments primarily engaged in manufacturing primary batteries and secondary storage or accumulator batteries and parts thereof.

Example Activities
- Accumulator batteries and parts, manufacturing
- Alkaline batteries, manufacturing
- Batteries, primary, dry or wet, manufacturing
- Batteries, storage, manufacturing
- Flashlight batteries, manufacturing
- Hearing aid batteries, manufacturing
- Nickel cadmium storage batteries, manufacturing

335910 Battery Manufacturing CAN

See industry description for 33591, above.

33592 Communication and Energy Wire and Cable Manufacturing

This industry comprises establishments primarily engaged in insulating communications and energy wire and cable, made from purchased non-ferrous wire and optical fibres.

Exclusion(s): Establishments primarily engaged in:
- manufacturing unsheathed optical fibres, bundles and cables (32721, Glass and Glass Product Manufacturing);
- drawing and insulating wire of own manufacture (331, Primary Metal Manufacturing); and
- manufacturing uninsulated wire products (33261, Spring and Wire Product Manufacturing).

Example Activities

- Building wire and cable, electric, insulated, manufacturing
- Coaxial cable, non-ferrous, manufacturing
- Fibre-optic cable, made from purchased strand (data transmission), manufacturing

- Insulated wire and cable, made from purchased wire
- Magnet wire, insulated, manufacturing
- Power cables, electric, manufacturing
- Telephone wire and cable, insulated, manufacturing

335920 Communication and Energy Wire and Cable Manufacturing ^{CAN}

See industry description for 33592, above.

33593 Wiring Device Manufacturing

This industry comprises establishments primarily engaged in manufacturing current and non-current carrying wiring devices.

Exclusion(s): Establishments primarily engaged in:
- manufacturing electric cable and wire made in wire drawing plants (331, Primary Metal Manufacturing); and
- manufacturing electric cable and wire made from purchased wire (33592, Communication and Energy Wire and Cable Manufacturing).

Example Activities

- Conduits and fittings, electrical, manufacturing
- Connectors and terminals for electrical devices, manufacturing
- Face plates (wiring devices), manufacturing
- Junction boxes and covers, electrical, manufacturing

- Outlet boxes (electric wiring devices), manufacturing
- Outlet receptacles, electrical, manufacturing
- Pole line hardware, manufacturing
- Switch boxes, electric, manufacturing
- Switches for electric wiring (e.g., snap, tumbler, pressure, pushbutton), manufacturing

335930 Wiring Device Manufacturing ^{CAN}

See industry description for 33593, above.

33599 All Other Electrical Equipment and Component Manufacturing

This industry comprises establishments, not classified to any other industry, primarily engaged in manufacturing electrical equipment and components.

Exclusion(s): Establishments primarily engaged in:
- manufacturing electronic capacitors (33441, Semiconductor and Other Electronic Component Manufacturing).

Example Activities

- Battery chargers, manufacturing
- Capacitors (except electronic), fixed and variable, manufacturing
- Carbon specialties for electrical use, manufacturing
- Chimes, electric, manufacturing
- Door opening and closing devices, electrical, manufacturing
- Electric fence chargers, manufacturing

- Electrodes, carbon, graphite, manufacturing
- Fuel cells, electrochemical generators, manufacturing
- Power capacitors, manufacturing
- Rectifiers (electrical apparatus), manufacturing
- Ultrasonic cleaning equipment (except medical and dental), manufacturing

335990 All Other Electrical Equipment and Component Manufacturing ^{CAN}

See industry description for 33599, above.

336 Transportation Equipment Manufacturing

This subsector comprises establishments primarily engaged in manufacturing equipment for transporting people and goods. The industry groups are based on the various modes of transport - road, rail, air and water. Three industry groups are based on road transportation equipment - for complete vehicles, for body and trailer manufacture and for parts.

Establishments primarily engaged in rebuilding equipment and parts are included in the same industry as establishments manufacturing new products.

Exclusion(s): Establishments primarily engaged in:
- manufacturing equipment designed for moving materials and goods on industrial sites, construction sites, in logging camps and other off-highway locations (333, Machinery Manufacturing).

3361 Motor Vehicle Manufacturing

This industry group comprises establishments primarily engaged in manufacturing motor vehicles. Establishments that manufacture chassis and then assemble complete motor vehicles (including truck cab and chassis assemblies) and those that only manufacture motor vehicle chassis are both classified in this industry group.

Exclusion(s): Establishments primarily engaged in:
- manufacturing motor vehicles on purchased chassis or purchased truck cab and chassis assemblies (3362, Motor Vehicle Body and Trailer Manufacturing).

33611 Automobile and Light-Duty Motor Vehicle Manufacturing

This industry comprises establishments primarily engaged in manufacturing light-duty vehicles and their chassis, for highway use. The manufacture of electric cars for highway use is included.

Exclusion(s): Establishments primarily engaged in:
- manufacturing kit cars (33621, Motor Vehicle Body and Trailer Manufacturing).

Example Activities
- Assembly plants, passenger car and light duty motor vehicles, on chassis of own manufacture
- Automobiles, assembling on chassis of own manufacture
- Cab and chassis assemblies, light trucks and vans, manufacturing
- Chassis, automobile, light truck and sport utility, manufacturing
- Electric automobiles for highway use, manufacturing
- Mini-vans, assembling on chassis of own manufacture
- Motor homes, self-contained, mounted on light duty truck chassis of own manufacture
- Pick-up trucks, light duty, assembling on chassis of own manufacture
- Sport utility vehicles assembling on chassis of own manufacture
- Trucks, light duty, assembling on chassis of own manufacture
- Vans, commercial and passenger, light duty, assembling on chassis of own manufacture

336110 Automobile and Light-Duty Motor Vehicle Manufacturing ^{MEX}

See industry description for 33611, above.

33612 Heavy-Duty Truck Manufacturing

This industry comprises establishments primarily engaged in manufacturing heavy-duty vehicles and heavy-duty vehicle chassis, for highway use.

Exclusion(s): Establishments primarily engaged in:
- manufacturing heavy-duty vehicles on purchased chassis (33621, Motor Vehicle Body and Trailer Manufacturing); and
- manufacturing military armoured vehicles (33699, Other Transportation Equipment Manufacturing).

Example Activities
- Buses, passenger (except trackless trolley), assembling on chassis of own manufacture
- Cab and chassis assemblies, heavy-duty trucks, manufacturing
- Chassis, heavy truck, with or without cabs, manufacturing
- Fire-fighting trucks (e.g., ladder, pumper), assembling on chassis of own manufacture
- Garbage trucks, assembling on chassis of own manufacture
- Heavy trucks, assembling on chassis of own manufacture
- Highway maintenance motor vehicles (e.g., road oilers, sanders), assembling on chassis of own manufacture
- Highway tractors (i.e., for semi-trailers), assembling on chassis of own manufacture
- Motor homes, self-contained, mounted on heavy truck chassis of own manufacture
- Special purpose highway vehicles (e.g., firefighting vehicles), assembling on chassis of own manufacture
- Street-cleaning motor vehicles (e.g., street flushers, sprinklers, sweepers), assembling on chassis of own manufacture
- Tractors, truck, for highway use, assembled on chassis of own manufacture
- Truck tractors for highway use, assembling on chassis of own manufacture
- Trucks, heavy (except off-highway), assembling on chassis of own manufacture

336120 Heavy-Duty Truck Manufacturing

See industry description for 33612, above.

3362 Motor Vehicle Body and Trailer Manufacturing

See industry description for 33621, below.

33621 Motor Vehicle Body and Trailer Manufacturing

This industry comprises establishments primarily engaged in manufacturing motor vehicle bodies and cabs, truck trailers and non-commercial trailers. The bodies and cabs may be sold as such, or assembled on purchased chassis.

Exclusion(s): Establishments primarily engaged in:
- manufacturing trucks and bus bodies on chassis made in the same establishment (33612, Heavy-Duty Truck Manufacturing).

336211 Motor Vehicle Body Manufacturing US

This Canadian industry comprises establishments primarily engaged in manufacturing truck, bus, and other motor vehicle bodies. These establishments purchase the chassis or semi-complete vehicle and manufacture the rest of the body, thereby completing the vehicle, or manufacture bodies and cabs for sale separately. The manufacture of specialty vehicles is included in this Canadian industry, when made from purchased chassis. These may be manufactured on heavy-duty chassis, such as street-sweepers and fire-fighting vehicles, or on light-duty chassis, such as stretch limousines, ambulances and kit cars.

Exclusion(s): Establishments primarily engaged in:
- manufacturing motor vehicle bodies on chassis made in the same establishment (336120, Heavy-Duty Truck Manufacturing).

Example Activities

- Ambulances, assembling on purchased chassis
- Automobile bodies, passenger car, manufacturing
- Boxes, truck (e.g., dump, cargo, utility, van), assembled on purchased chassis
- Cars in kit form, manufacturing
- Dump truck lifting mechanisms, manufacturing
- Fifth wheel assemblies, manufacturing
- Fire-fighting trucks (e.g., ladder, pumper), assembling on purchased chassis

- Kit car bodies, manufacturing
- School buses, assembling on purchased chassis
- Special purpose highway vehicle (e.g., fire-fighting vehicles) bodies, manufacturing
- Special purpose highway vehicles (e.g., fire-fighting vehicles), assembling on purchased chassis
- Stretch limousines, assembling on purchased chassis
- Truck bodies and cabs, manufacturing

336212 Truck Trailer Manufacturing US

This Canadian industry comprises establishments primarily engaged in manufacturing truck trailers and truck trailer chassis.

Exclusion(s): Establishments primarily engaged in:
- manufacturing utility, light-truck, travel and other non-commercial trailers (336215, Motor Home, Travel Trailer and Camper Manufacturing).

Example Activities

- Automobile transporter trailers, multi-car, manufacturing
- Car transporter trailers, multi-car, manufacturing
- Dump trailers, manufacturing

- Flatbed trailers, commercial, manufacturing
- Logging trailers, manufacturing
- Tank trailers, liquid and dry bulk, manufacturing

336215 Motor Home, Travel Trailer and Camper Manufacturing CAN

This Canadian industry comprises establishments primarily engaged in manufacturing non-commercial trailers.

Exclusion(s): Establishments primarily engaged in:
- manufacturing mobile homes (large homes designed to be towed to a permanent location and anchored) (321991, Manufactured (Mobile) Home Manufacturing);
- manufacturing commercial car trailers (336212, Truck Trailer Manufacturing); and
- customizing van interiors, other than on a factory basis (811121, Automotive Body, Paint and Interior Repair and Maintenance).

Example Activities

- Boat transporter trailers, single-unit, manufacturing
- Camping trailers and chassis, manufacturing
- Caps for pickup trucks, manufacturing
- Homes, motor, self-contained, assembling on purchased chassis
- Motor homes, self-contained, assembling on purchased chassis

- Recreational vehicles (RV), self-contained, manufacturing
- Travel trailers, recreational, manufacturing
- Truck campers (i.e., slide-in campers), manufacturing
- Utility trailers, manufacturing

3363 Motor Vehicle Parts Manufacturing

This industry group comprises establishments primarily engaged in manufacturing motor vehicle parts, including engines. Establishments that rebuild motor vehicle parts are included in this industry group, in the same industry as the manufacture of new parts.

Exclusion(s): Establishments primarily engaged in:
- manufacturing motor vehicle plastic parts (32619, Other Plastic Product Manufacturing);
- manufacturing rubber and plastic hose and belts (32622, Rubber and Plastic Hose and Belting Manufacturing);
- manufacturing motor vehicle hardware (33251, Hardware Manufacturing);
- manufacturing motor vehicle coil and leaf springs (33261, Spring and Wire Product Manufacturing); and
- manufacturing diesel engines and parts for motor vehicles (33361, Engine, Turbine and Power Transmission Equipment Manufacturing).

33631 Motor Vehicle Gasoline Engine and Engine Parts Manufacturing

This industry comprises establishments primarily engaged in manufacturing and rebuilding motor vehicle gasoline engines and engine parts, whether or not for vehicular use.

Exclusion(s): Establishments primarily engaged in:
- manufacturing diesel engines and parts for motor vehicles (33361, Engine, Turbine and Power Transmission Equipment Manufacturing);
- manufacturing electrical fuel pumps (33632, Motor Vehicle Electrical and Electronic Equipment Manufacturing); and
- manufacturing transmission and power train equipment (33635, Motor Vehicle Transmission and Power Train Parts Manufacturing).

Example Activities
- Bearings (e.g., camshaft, crankshaft, connecting rod), automotive and truck gasoline engine, manufacturing
- Carburetors, all types, manufacturing
- Crankshaft assemblies, automotive and truck gasoline engine, manufacturing
- Cylinder heads, automotive and truck gasoline engine, manufacturing
- Engines and parts (except diesel), automotive and truck, manufacturing
- Flywheels and ring gears, automotive and truck gasoline engine, manufacturing
- Fuel injection systems and parts, automotive and truck gasoline engine, manufacturing
- Fuel pumps, mechanical, automotive and truck gasoline engine, manufacturing
- Gasoline engine parts, automotive and truck, manufacturing
- Gasoline engines, automotive and truck, manufacturing
- Internal combustion gasoline engines, automotive and truck, manufacturing
- Manifolds (i.e., intake and exhaust), automotive and truck gasoline engine, manufacturing
- Oil pumps, mechanical, automotive and truck gasoline engine, manufacturing
- Pistons and piston rings, manufacturing
- Rebuilding automotive and truck gasoline engines
- Rings, piston, manufacturing
- Timing gears and chains, automotive and truck gasoline engine, manufacturing
- Valves, engine, intake and exhaust, manufacturing

336310 Motor Vehicle Gasoline Engine and Engine Parts Manufacturing ᴹᴱˣ

See industry description for 33631, above.

33632 Motor Vehicle Electrical and Electronic Equipment Manufacturing

This industry comprises establishments primarily engaged in manufacturing and rebuilding electrical and electronic equipment for motor vehicles and internal combustion engines.

Exclusion(s): Establishments primarily engaged in:
- manufacturing sealed-beam lamps (33511, Electric Lamp Bulb and Parts Manufacturing); and
- manufacturing batteries (33591, Battery Manufacturing).

Example Activities
- Aircraft lighting fixtures, manufacturing
- Alternators and generators, for internal combustion engines, manufacturing
- Automotive harness and ignition wiring sets, manufacturing
- Automotive lighting fixtures, manufacturing
- Bicycle light fixtures, manufacturing
- Coils, ignition, internal combustion engine, manufacturing
- Cruise control mechanisms, electronic, automotive, truck and bus, manufacturing
- Distributors for internal combustion engines, manufacturing
- Electronic control modules, motor vehicle, manufacturing
- Electronic sensors (e.g., air bag, brake, fuel, exhaust), manufacturing
- Fuel pumps, electric, automotive, truck and bus, manufacturing
- Ignition points and condensers, for internal combustion engines, manufacturing
- Ignition wiring harness, for internal combustion engines, manufacturing
- Instrument control panels (i.e., assembling purchased gauges), automotive, truck and bus, manufacturing
- Keyless entry systems, automotive, truck and bus, manufacturing
- Lighting fixtures, vehicular, manufacturing
- Locomotive and railroad car light fixtures, manufacturing
- Motors, starter, for internal combustion engines, manufacturing
- Rebuilding motor vehicle electrical equipment (e.g., alternators, generators and distributors)
- Spark plugs, for internal combustion engines, manufacturing
- Vehicular lighting fixtures, manufacturing
- Windshield wiper systems, automotive, truck and bus, manufacturing
- Wiring harness and ignition sets, for internal combustion engines, manufacturing

336320 Motor Vehicle Electrical and Electronic Equipment Manufacturing ᴹᴱˣ

See industry description for 33632, above.

33633 Motor Vehicle Steering and Suspension Components (except Spring) Manufacturing

This industry comprises establishments primarily engaged in manufacturing motor vehicle steering mechanisms and suspension components, except springs. The rebuilding, on a factory basis, of rack and pinion steering assemblies is included.

Exclusion(s): Establishments primarily engaged in:
- manufacturing motor vehicle coil and leaf springs (33261, Spring and Wire Product Manufacturing).

Example Activities
- Automotive, truck and bus steering assemblies and parts, manufacturing
- Automotive, truck and bus suspension assemblies and parts (except springs), manufacturing
- Ball joints, motor vehicle, manufacturing
- McPherson struts, manufacturing
- Power steering pumps, manufacturing
- Power steering pumps, rebuilding on a factory basis
- Rack and pinion steering assemblies, rebuilding on factory basis
- Shock absorbers, automotive, truck and bus, manufacturing
- Tie rods, tie rod ends and assemblies, manufacturing

336330 Motor Vehicle Steering and Suspension Components (except Spring) Manufacturing

See industry description for 33633, above.

33634 Motor Vehicle Brake System Manufacturing

This industry comprises establishments primarily engaged in manufacturing motor vehicle brake systems and related components.

Example Activities
- Brake cylinders, master and wheel, automotive, truck and bus, manufacturing
- Brake drums, automotive, truck and bus, manufacturing
- Brake shoe relining, on a factory basis
- Vacuum brake boosters, automotive, truck and bus, manufacturing

336340 Motor Vehicle Brake System Manufacturing

See industry description for 33634, above.

33635 Motor Vehicle Transmission and Power Train Parts Manufacturing

This industry comprises establishments primarily engaged in manufacturing and rebuilding motor vehicle transmission and power train parts.

Example Activities
- Assembly line rebuilding of automotive, truck and bus transmissions
- Axle assemblies, differential and rear, automotive, truck and bus, manufacturing
- Clutch assemblies, automotive, truck and bus, manufacturing
- Clutch assemblies, automotive, truck and bus, rebuilding
- Gears (i.e., crown, pinion, spider), automotive, truck and bus, manufacturing
- Joints, universal, automotive, truck and bus, manufacturing
- Pressure and clutch plate assemblies, automotive, truck and bus, manufacturing
- Torque converters, automotive, truck and bus, manufacturing
- Transaxles, automotive, truck and bus, manufacturing
- Transmissions and parts, automotive, truck and bus, manufacturing
- Universal joints, automotive, truck and bus, manufacturing

336350 Motor Vehicle Transmission and Power Train Parts Manufacturing

See industry description for 33635, above.

33636 Motor Vehicle Seating and Interior Trim Manufacturing

This industry comprises establishments primarily engaged in manufacturing motor vehicle fabric accessories and trimmings, seat belts and safety straps, and seats for transportation equipment of all kinds.

Example Activities
- Aircraft seats, manufacturing
- Automobile trimmings, textile, manufacturing
- Cushions, motor vehicle, manufacturing
- Motor vehicle interior systems (e.g., headliners, panels, seats, trim), manufacturing
- Motor vehicle seats, manufacturing
- Motor vehicle trimmings, fabric, manufacturing

- Seat belts, motor vehicle and aircraft, manufacturing
- Seating for buses, railway cars and aircraft, manufacturing
- Transportation equipment seating, manufacturing
- Visor assemblies, motor vehicle, manufacturing

336360 Motor Vehicle Seating and Interior Trim Manufacturing

See industry description for 33636, above.

33637 Motor Vehicle Metal Stamping

This industry comprises establishments primarily engaged in manufacturing motor vehicle metal stampings. Establishments in this industry perform the stamping operation, and incidental operations such as removing burrs and other stamping defects, but do not further work the stamping into a final product.

Exclusion(s): Establishments primarily engaged in:
- manufacturing metal stampings, except motor vehicle (33211, Forging and Stamping); and
- further processing automotive stampings into a final product (3363, Motor Vehicle Parts Manufacturing).

Example Activities
- Automotive metal stampings (e.g., body parts, fenders, hub caps, tops, trim), manufacturing
- Firewall, motor vehicle, metal, stamping
- Floor pans, motor vehicle, metal, stamping
- Motor vehicle metal stampings (e.g., body parts, fenders, hub caps, tops, trim), manufacturing
- Mouldings and trim, motor vehicle, metal, stamping
- Quarter panels, motor vehicle, metal, stamping
- Rocker panels, motor vehicle, metal, stamping
- Stamping metal, motor vehicle body parts
- Wheel centres and trim, motor vehicle, metal, stamping

336370 Motor Vehicle Metal Stamping

See industry description for 33637, above.

33639 Other Motor Vehicle Parts Manufacturing

This industry comprises establishments, not classified to any other industry, primarily engaged in manufacturing motor vehicle parts and accessories.

Example Activities
- Air bag assemblies, manufacturing
- Air-conditioners, motor vehicle, manufacturing
- Bumpers and bumperettes, assembled, automotive, truck and bus, manufacturing
- Catalytic converters, engine exhaust, automotive, truck and bus, manufacturing
- Compressors, motor vehicle air-conditioning, manufacturing
- Convertible tops, for automobiles, manufacturing
- Exhaust systems and parts, automotive, truck and bus, manufacturing
- Filters (e.g., air, engine oil, fuel), internal combustion engine, manufacturing
- Luggage racks, car top, manufacturing
- Motor vehicle air-conditioning systems and compressors, manufacturing
- Mufflers and resonators, automotive, truck and bus, manufacturing
- Racks (e.g., bicycle, luggage, ski, tire), automotive, truck and bus, manufacturing
- Radiators and cores, automotive, truck and bus, manufacturing
- Thermostats, automotive, truck and bus, manufacturing

- Wheels (i.e., rims), automotive, truck and bus, manufacturing
- Windshield wiper blades and refills, manufacturing

336390 Other Motor Vehicle Parts Manufacturing ᴹᴱˣ

See industry description for 33639, above.

3364 Aerospace Product and Parts Manufacturing

See industry description for 33641, below.

33641 Aerospace Product and Parts Manufacturing

This industry comprises establishments primarily engaged in manufacturing aircraft, missiles, space vehicles and their engines, propulsion units, auxiliary equipment, and parts thereof. The development and production of prototypes is classified in this industry, as is the factory overhaul and conversion of aircraft and propulsion systems.

Exclusion(s): Establishments primarily engaged in:
- manufacturing aircraft fluid power subassemblies (33291, Metal Valve Manufacturing);
- manufacturing fluid power pumps (33399, All Other General-Purpose Machinery Manufacturing);
- manufacturing communications satellites (33422, Radio and Television Broadcasting and Wireless Communications Equipment Manufacturing);
- manufacturing aeronautical instruments (33451, Navigational, Measuring, Medical and Control Instruments Manufacturing);
- manufacturing aircraft intake and exhaust valves and pistons (33631, Motor Vehicle Gasoline Engine and Engine Parts Manufacturing);
- manufacturing aircraft lighting fixtures (33632, Motor Vehicle Electrical and Electronic Equipment Manufacturing);
- manufacturing aircraft seating (33636, Motor Vehicle Seating and Interior Trim Manufacturing);
- manufacturing aircraft internal combustion engine filters (33639, Other Motor Vehicle Parts Manufacturing);
- repairing aircraft, except on a factory basis (48819, Other Support Activities for Air Transportation); and
- performing research and development on aircraft, but not producing prototypes (54171, Research and Development in the Physical, Engineering and Life Sciences).

Example Activities
- Aircraft assemblies, subassemblies and parts, manufacturing
- Aircraft conversions (i.e., major modifications to systems or equipment)
- Aircraft engines and engine parts (except carburetors, pistons, piston rings, valves), manufacturing
- Aircraft fuselage, wing, tail and similar assemblies, manufacturing
- Aircraft rebuilding (i.e., restoration to original design specifications)
- Aircraft, manufacturing
- Developing and producing prototypes for aerospace products
- Engines and engine parts (except carburetors, pistons, piston rings, valves), aircraft, manufacturing
- Guided missile and space vehicle engines, manufacturing
- Guided missiles and space vehicles, manufacturing
- Guided missiles, complete, assembling
- Helicopters, manufacturing
- Propellers, aircraft, manufacturing
- Rockets (guided missiles), space and military, complete, manufacturing
- Space vehicle propulsion units, manufacturing
- Space vehicles parts, manufacturing
- Stabilizers, aircraft, manufacturing
- Tail assemblies and parts (empennage), aircraft, manufacturing
- Universal joints, aircraft, manufacturing
- Wing assemblies and parts, aircraft, manufacturing

336410 Aerospace Product and Parts Manufacturing ᴹᴱˣ

See industry description for 33641, above.

3365 Railroad Rolling Stock Manufacturing

See industry description for 33651, below.

33651 Railroad Rolling Stock Manufacturing

This industry comprises establishments primarily engaged in manufacturing and rebuilding locomotives and railroad cars, of any type or gauge, including frames and parts. The manufacture of rapid transit cars and special-purpose self-propelled railroad equipment, such as rail layers, ballast distributors, rail-tamping equipment and other railway track maintenance equipment is included in this industry.

Exclusion(s): Establishments primarily engaged in:
- manufacturing mining rail cars (33313, Mining and Oil and Gas Field Machinery Manufacturing);
- manufacturing diesel engines and parts for locomotives (33361, Engine, Turbine and Power Transmission Equipment Manufacturing);
- manufacturing locomotive fuel lubricating or cooling medium pumps (33391, Pump and Compressor Manufacturing); and
- activities of repair shops that are part of a railroad or local transit network (48821, Support Activities for Rail Transportation).

Example Activities
- Diesel-electric locomotives, manufacturing
- Locomotives, manufacturing
- Mining locomotives and parts, manufacturing
- Rail laying and tamping equipment, manufacturing
- Railroad cars, self-propelled, manufacturing
- Railroad track equipment (e.g., rail layers, ballast distributors), manufacturing
- Rapid transit cars and equipment, manufacturing
- Subway cars, manufacturing

336510 Railroad Rolling Stock Manufacturing

See industry description for 33651, above.

3366 Ship and Boat Building

See industry description for 33661, below.

33661 Ship and Boat Building

This industry comprises establishments primarily engaged in operating a shipyard or manufacturing boats. Shipyards are fixed facilities with dry docks and fabrication equipment capable of building a ship, defined as water-craft suitable or intended for other than personal or recreational use. Boats are defined as water-craft suitable or intended for personal or recreational use. The activities of shipyards include the construction of ships, their repair, conversion and alteration, the production of prefabricated ship sections and barge sections, and specialized services, such as ship scaling, when performed at the shipyard.

Exclusion(s): Establishments primarily engaged in:
- ship painting, carpentry work, and electrical wiring installation (238, Specialty Trade Contractors);
- manufacturing prefabricated metal ship, boat and barge sections, not at a shipyard or boatyard (33231, Plate Work and Fabricated Structural Product Manufacturing); and
- ship repair, not at a shipyard (48839, Other Support Activities for Water Transportation).

336611 Ship Building and Repairing US

This Canadian industry comprises establishments primarily engaged in operating a shipyard. Shipyards are fixed facilities with dry docks and fabrication equipment capable of building a ship, defined as water-craft suitable or intended for other than personal or recreational use. The activities of shipyards include the construction of ships, their repair, conversion and alteration, the production of prefabricated ship sections and barge sections, and specialized services, such as ship scaling, when performed at the shipyard.

Exclusion(s): Establishments primarily engaged in:
- ship painting, carpentry work and electrical wiring installation (238, Specialty Trade Contractors);
- manufacturing prefabricated metal ship, boat and barge sections, not at a shipyard (332319, Other Plate Work and Fabricated Structural Product Manufacturing); and
- ship repairing, not at a shipyard (488390, Other Support Activities for Water Transportation).

Example Activities
- Barges, building
- Drilling and production platforms, floating, oil and gas, building
- Fishing boats, commercial, building
- Hydrofoil vessels, building and repairing in shipyards
- Ship repair, done in a shipyard
- Ships (i.e., not suitable or intended for personal use), manufacturing
- Shipyard (i.e., facility capable of building ships)

336612 Boat Building US

This Canadian industry comprises establishments primarily engaged in manufacturing boats. Boats are defined as water-craft suitable or intended for personal or recreational use.

Exclusion(s): Establishments primarily engaged in:
- manufacturing rubber boats and life rafts, except rigid hull inflatable boats (32629, Other Rubber Product Manufacturing); and
- manufacturing prefabricated metal boat sections, not at a boatyard (332319, Other Plate Work and Fabricated Structural Product Manufacturing).

Example Activities
- Boats (i.e., suitable or intended personal use), manufacturing
- Canoes and kayaks, manufacturing
- Canoes, manufacturing
- Fibreglass boats, building
- Fishing boats (i.e., suitable or intended personal use), building
- Houseboats, building
- Hydrofoil vessels, recreational type, manufacturing
- Rigid hull inflatable boats
- Underwater ROV (remotely operated vehicle), manufacturing
- Yachts, building, not done in shipyards

3369 Other Transportation Equipment Manufacturing

See industry description for 33699, below.

33699 Other Transportation Equipment Manufacturing

This industry comprises establishments, not classified to any other industry, primarily engaged in manufacturing transportation equipment and parts.

Exclusion(s): Establishments primarily engaged in:
- manufacturing wheelbarrows and push-carts (33392, Material Handling Equipment Manufacturing);
- manufacturing wheelchairs (33911, Medical Equipment and Supplies Manufacturing); and
- manufacturing children's tricycles (33993, Doll, Toy and Game Manufacturing).

Example Activities
- All-terrain vehicles (ATVs), wheeled or tracked, manufacturing
- Animal-drawn vehicles and parts, manufacturing
- Armoured military vehicles and parts (except tanks), manufacturing
- Bicycles and parts, manufacturing
- Carriages, horse-drawn, manufacturing
- Carts, horse-drawn, manufacturing
- Go-carts (except children's), manufacturing
- Golf carts, powered, manufacturing
- Military armoured vehicles, manufacturing
- Motorcycles and parts, manufacturing
- Off-highway tracked vehicles (except construction), manufacturing
- Personal watercraft, manufacturing
- Race cars, manufacturing
- Snowmobiles and parts, manufacturing
- Tanks, military (including factory rebuilding), manufacturing
- Tricycles, adults', metal, manufacturing
- Tricycles, children's, metal, manufacturing
- Wagons, horse-drawn, manufacturing
- Weapons, self-propelled, manufacturing

336990 Other Transportation Equipment Manufacturing CAN

See industry description for 33699, above.

337 Furniture and Related Product Manufacturing

This subsector comprises establishments primarily engaged in manufacturing furniture and related products. The processes used in the manufacture of furniture are standard methods of forming materials and assembling components, including cutting, moulding and laminating. The design of the article, for both aesthetic and functional qualities, is an important aspect of the production process. Design services may be performed by the furniture establishment's own work force or may be purchased from industrial designers. Furniture is classified based on the application for which it is designed. For example, an upholstered sofa is treated as household furniture, although it may also be used in hotels or offices.

Furniture is also classified according to the component material from which it is made. Furniture made from more than one material is classified based on the material used in the frame, or if there is no frame, the predominant component material. Upholstered household furniture is classified as such, without regard to the frame material.

Furniture may be produced on a stock or custom basis and may be shipped assembled or unassembled (knock-down). Establishments primarily engaged in manufacturing furniture frames and parts are included.

Exclusion(s): Establishments primarily engaged in:
- manufacturing furniture hardware (332, Fabricated Metal Product Manufacturing);
- manufacturing seating for transportation equipment (336, Transportation Equipment Manufacturing);
- manufacturing laboratory and hospital furniture (339, Miscellaneous Manufacturing); and
- repairing, refinishing and reupholstering furniture (811, Repair and Maintenance).

3371 Household and Institutional Furniture and Kitchen Cabinet Manufacturing

This industry group comprises establishments primarily engaged in manufacturing furniture designed for use in households; institutions such as schools, churches, restaurants and other public buildings; and wood kitchen cabinets, bathroom vanities, and counters.

33711 Wood Kitchen Cabinet and Counter Top Manufacturing

This industry comprises establishments primarily engaged in manufacturing wood kitchen cabinets, bathroom vanities, and counters, designed for permanent installation.

Example Activities
- Bathroom vanities, wood, manufacturing
- Counter tops, wood, manufacturing
- Kitchen cabinets (except free standing), wood, manufacturing
- Kitchen cabinets and counters, prefabricated wood, manufacturing and installation combined
- Table or counter tops (e.g., kitchen, bathroom, bar), plastic laminated, manufacturing
- Vanities, bathroom, wood, manufacturing

337110 Wood Kitchen Cabinet and Counter Top Manufacturing

See industry description for 33711, above.

33712 Household and Institutional Furniture Manufacturing

This industry comprises establishments primarily engaged in manufacturing furniture designed for use in households, and institutions such as schools, churches, restaurants and other public buildings.

337121 Upholstered Household Furniture Manufacturing US

This Canadian industry comprises establishments primarily engaged in manufacturing upholstered household furniture.

Example Activities
- Chairs, household, upholstered, manufacturing
- Chesterfields, manufacturing
- Convertible sofas, manufacturing
- Cushions, spring, manufacturing
- Furniture, household, upholstered, manufacturing
- Reclining chairs, household, upholstered, manufacturing
- Sofas (including sofa beds), manufacturing
- Spring cushions, manufacturing

337123 Other Wood Household Furniture Manufacturing CAN

This Canadian industry comprises establishments primarily engaged in manufacturing wood furniture designed for household use, except upholstered. Such furniture may be used in buildings other than private dwellings, for example in hotel rooms.

Exclusion(s): Establishments primarily engaged in:
- manufacturing wood kitchen cabinets and bathroom vanities designed for permanent installation (337110, Wood Kitchen Cabinet and Counter Top Manufacturing); and
- manufacturing upholstered household furniture (337121, Upholstered Household Furniture Manufacturing).

Example Activities
- Bedroom furniture, wood, manufacturing
- Bookcases, wood, household, manufacturing
- Cabinets, sewing machine, wood, manufacturing
- Cabinets, wood household (e.g., radio, television, stereo, sewing machine), manufacturing
- Cedar chests, manufacturing
- Chairs, wood household (except upholstered), manufacturing
- Chests, cedar, manufacturing
- Coffee tables, wood, manufacturing
- Cribs, wood, manufacturing
- Dining room furniture, wood, manufacturing
- Furniture, wood household, made to individual order
- Furniture, wood household, porch, lawn, garden and beach, manufacturing
- Furniture, wood household, unassembled or knock-down, manufacturing

- Furniture, wood household, unfinished, manufacturing
- Garden furniture, wood, manufacturing
- Headboards, wood, manufacturing
- Kitchen furniture, wood, manufacturing
- Living room furniture, wood, manufacturing
- Microwave cabinets, free standing, wood, manufacturing
- Vanity dressers, manufacturing

337126 Household Furniture (except Wood and Upholstered) Manufacturing ^{CAN}

This Canadian industry comprises establishments primarily engaged in manufacturing household furniture, except wood or upholstered.

Example Activities
- Baby seats for automobiles, manufacturing
- Beds, household, metal, manufacturing
- Brass furniture, manufacturing
- Cabinets (free standing), metal, manufacturing
- Cabinets, kitchen, free standing, metal or plastic, manufacturing
- Cane chairs, manufacturing
- Card table and chair sets, metal, manufacturing
- Furniture, household, glass, manufacturing
- Furniture, household, metal, manufacturing
- Furniture, household, plastics (including fibreglass), manufacturing
- Furniture, household, rattan, reed, malacca, fibre, willow and wicker, manufacturing
- Household furniture (except wooden and upholstered), manufacturing
- Rattan furniture, manufacturing
- Stools, household (except wood), manufacturing
- Wicker and reed furniture, manufacturing
- Wrought iron furniture, manufacturing

337127 Institutional Furniture Manufacturing ^{US}

This Canadian industry comprises establishments primarily engaged in manufacturing furniture designed for use in institutions such as schools, churches, restaurants and other public buildings. Establishments primarily engaged in manufacturing factory furniture, such as work benches and tool stands, are included.

Exclusion(s): Establishments primarily engaged in:
- manufacturing specialised hospital and/or dental furniture (339110, Medical Equipment and Supplies Manufacturing).

Example Activities
- Altars (except stone and concrete), manufacturing
- Assembly hall furniture, manufacturing
- Benches, public buildings, manufacturing
- Cafeteria furniture, manufacturing
- Chairs, hydraulic, barber and beauty shop, manufacturing
- Chairs, portable folding, manufacturing
- Church furniture, manufacturing
- Draughting tables (without attachments), manufacturing
- Factory furniture (e.g., stools, work benches, tool stands, cabinets), manufacturing
- Furniture, institutional, church, public building, manufacturing
- Furniture, laboratory (e.g., cabinets, benches, tables, stools), manufacturing
- Hotel furniture, manufacturing
- Laboratory furniture (e.g., cabinets, benches, tables, stools), manufacturing
- Motel furniture, manufacturing
- Public building furniture, manufacturing
- Restaurant furniture, manufacturing
- School furniture, manufacturing
- Store furniture, manufacturing
- Theatre furniture, manufacturing

3372 Office Furniture (including Fixtures) Manufacturing

See industry description for 33721, below.

33721 Office Furniture (including Fixtures) Manufacturing

This industry comprises establishments primarily engaged in manufacturing furniture designed for office use, such as office chairs and desks; and office and store fixtures, such as showcases. Establishments primarily engaged in manufacturing furniture parts and frames, for all types of furniture, are also included,

337213 Wood Office Furniture, including Custom Architectural Woodwork, Manufacturing CAN

This Canadian industry comprises establishments primarily engaged in manufacturing wood furniture designed for office use, such as office chairs and desks. Establishments primarily engaged in manufacturing custom designed interiors consisting of architectural woodwork and fixtures, primarily utilizing wood, are included.

Example Activities

- Bookcases, wood office, manufacturing
- Cabinets, wood office, manufacturing
- Chairs, wood office, manufacturing
- Custom-designed office interiors (i.e., furniture, architectural woodwork and fixtures), manufacturing
- Desks, wood office, manufacturing
- Filing boxes, cabinets and cases, wood office, manufacturing
- Furniture, wood office, padded, upholstered or plain, manufacturing
- Modular furniture systems, wood office, manufacturing
- Office furniture, wood, padded, upholstered, or plain, manufacturing
- Panel furniture systems, wood office, manufacturing
- Visible record equipment (e.g., filing cabinets, boxes), wood, manufacturing

337214 Office Furniture (except Wood) Manufacturing US

This Canadian industry comprises establishments primarily engaged in manufacturing non-wood furniture designed for office use, such as office chairs and desks.

Example Activities

- Bookcases, office (except wood), manufacturing
- Cabinets, office (except wood), manufacturing
- Chairs, office (except wood), manufacturing
- Desks, office (except wood), manufacturing
- Filing boxes, cabinets and cases, office (except wood), manufacturing
- Furniture, office (except wood), manufacturing
- Modular furniture systems, office (except wood), manufacturing
- Office furniture (except wood), manufacturing
- Stools, rotating, office (except wood), manufacturing
- Tables, office (except wood), manufacturing

337215 Showcase, Partition, Shelving and Locker Manufacturing US

This Canadian industry comprises establishments primarily engaged in manufacturing fixtures for office, store and similar applications, such as display cases, shelving and lockers. Establishments primarily engaged in manufacturing furniture parts and frames, for all types of furniture, are also included,

Exclusion(s): Establishments primarily engaged in:
- manufacturing refrigerated cabinets, showcases and display cases (333416, Heating Equipment and Commercial Refrigeration Equipment Manufacturing).

Example Activities

- Display cases and fixtures (except refrigerated), manufacturing
- Fixtures, office and store, manufacturing
- Furniture frames, manufacturing
- Furniture parts and components, manufacturing
- Lockers (except refrigerated), manufacturing
- Partitions, freestanding, prefabricated, manufacturing
- Partitions, prefabricated (modular or free-standing), manufacturing
- Point of purchase display racks, wire, manufacturing
- Postal service lock boxes, manufacturing
- Shelving, office and store, manufacturing
- Showcases (except refrigerated), manufacturing
- Stands, merchandise display, manufacturing
- Stands, merchandise display, wire, manufacturing
- Wire display racks, manufacturing

3379 Other Furniture-Related Product Manufacturing

This industry group comprises establishments, not classified to any other industry group, primarily engaged in manufacturing furniture-related products.

Exclusion(s): Establishments primarily engaged in:
- manufacturing furniture hardware (3325, Hardware Manufacturing);
- manufacturing safes and vaults (3329, Other Fabricated Metal Product Manufacturing); and
- repairing, refinishing and reupholstering furniture (8114, Personal and Household Goods Repair and Maintenance).

33791 Mattress Manufacturing

This industry comprises establishments primarily engaged in manufacturing mattresses and related products.

Exclusion(s): Establishments primarily engaged in:
- manufacturing individual wire springs (33261, Spring and Wire Product Manufacturing).

Example Activities

- Box springs, assembled, manufacturing
- Foam plastic mattress, manufacturing
- Foam rubber mattress, manufacturing
- Mattresses and springs, manufacturing
- Springs, assembled, bed and box, manufacturing

337910 Mattress Manufacturing

See industry description for 33791, above.

33792 Blind and Shade Manufacturing

This industry comprises establishments primarily engaged in manufacturing blinds and shades, and related fixtures, for interior use.

Exclusion(s): Establishments primarily engaged in:
- manufacturing curtains (31412, Curtain and Linen Mills); and
- manufacturing canvas exterior shades and awnings (31491, Textile Bag and Canvas Mills).

Example Activities

- Bamboo shades and blinds, manufacturing
- Blinds, venetian, manufacturing
- Blinds, vertical, manufacturing
- Curtain rods, poles and fixtures, manufacturing
- Venetian blinds (wood), manufacturing
- Vertical blinds, manufacturing

337920 Blind and Shade Manufacturing

See industry description for 33792, above.

339 Miscellaneous Manufacturing

This subsector comprises establishments, not classified to any other subsector, primarily engaged in manufacturing activities. These establishments manufacture a diverse range of products, such as medical equipment and supplies, jewellery, sporting goods, toys and office supplies.

3391 Medical Equipment and Supplies Manufacturing

See industry description for 33911, below.

33911 Medical Equipment and Supplies Manufacturing

This industry comprises establishments primarily engaged in manufacturing medical equipment and supplies. Establishments primarily engaged in grinding eyeglasses and hard contact lenses to prescription, on a factory basis, are included.

Exclusion(s): Establishments primarily engaged in:
- manufacturing moulded plastic lens blanks (32619, Other Plastic Product Manufacturing);
- manufacturing moulded glass lens blanks (32721, Glass and Glass Product Manufacturing);
- manufacturing laboratory instruments, x-ray apparatus, and electro-medical apparatus, such as hearing aids (33451, Navigational, Measuring, Medical and Control Instruments Manufacturing); and
- retailing prescription eyeglasses and contact lenses made on the premises (44613, Optical Goods Stores).

Example Activities
- Abrasive points, wheels and disks, dental, manufacturing
- Adhesive tape, medical, manufacturing
- Bandages and dressings, surgical and orthopedic, manufacturing
- Blood transfusion equipment, manufacturing
- Bridges, custom made in dental laboratories
- Catheters, manufacturing
- Contact lenses, manufacturing
- Cotton and cotton balls, absorbent, manufacturing
- Dental chairs, manufacturing
- Dental equipment and instruments, manufacturing
- Dental furniture, manufacturing
- Dental glues and cements, manufacturing
- Dental laboratories
- Dental wax, manufacturing
- Denture materials, manufacturing
- Dentures, custom made in dental laboratories
- Ear stoppers (noise protectors), manufacturing
- Eyeglass frames and parts, manufacturing
- Eyeglasses, lenses and frames, manufacturing
- First-aid equipment and supplies, manufacturing
- Furniture, hospital (e.g., hospital beds, operating room furniture), manufacturing
- Gauze, surgical, made from purchased fabric
- Gloves (e.g., surgeons', electricians', household), rubber, manufacturing
- Glue, dental, manufacturing
- Gut sutures, surgical, manufacturing
- Hard hats manufacturing
- Hospital furniture (e.g., hospital beds, operating room furniture), manufacturing
- Hypodermic needles and syringes, manufacturing
- Lens grinding, ophthalmic (except in retail stores)
- Life preservers, inflatable, manufacturing
- Lifejackets, plastics, manufacturing
- Magnifiers, vision correcting type, manufacturing
- Magnifying glasses, manufacturing
- Medical and related instruments, apparatus and equipment (except electro-medical), manufacturing
- Ophthalmic instruments and apparatus (except laser surgery), manufacturing

- Orthodontic appliances, custom made in dental laboratories
- Orthopedic devices and materials, manufacturing
- Orthopedic extension shoes, manufacturing
- Personal safety devices, not specified elsewhere, manufacturing
- Prosthetic devices, manufacturing
- Protective industrial clothing, manufacturing
- Radiation shielding aprons, gloves and sheeting, manufacturing
- Respiratory protection equipment, personal, manufacturing
- Safety appliances and equipment, personal, manufacturing

- Safety clothing, manufacturing
- Shoes, orthopedic extension, manufacturing
- Splints, manufacturing
- Sunglasses, manufacturing
- Supports, orthopedic (e.g., abdominal, ankle, arch, kneecap), manufacturing
- Surgical bandages (including medicated), manufacturing
- Sutures, manufacturing
- Syringes, hypodermic, manufacturing
- Tape, medical adhesive, manufacturing
- Teeth, custom made in dental laboratories
- Ultrasonic dental equipment, manufacturing
- Ultrasonic medical cleaning equipment, manufacturing
- Wheelchairs, manufacturing

339110 Medical Equipment and Supplies Manufacturing ^{CAN}

See industry description for 33911, above.

3399 Other Miscellaneous Manufacturing

This industry group comprises establishments, not classified to any other industry group, primarily engaged in manufacturing activities.

33991 Jewellery and Silverware Manufacturing

This industry comprises establishments primarily engaged in manufacturing, engraving, chasing or etching jewellery, novelties or precious metal flatware, and other plated ware; stamping coins; cutting, slabbing, tumbling, carving, engraving, polishing or faceting precious or semiprecious stones and gems; recutting, repolishing and setting gem stones; or drilling, sawing, and peeling cultured and costume pearls. Establishments primarily engaged in manufacturing pewter jewellery or flatware are included.

Exclusion(s): Establishments primarily engaged in:
- manufacturing personal goods, except metal, carried on or about the person, such as compacts and vanity cases (31699, Other Leather and Allied Product Manufacturing);
- manufacturing synthetic stones or gem stones (32799, All Other Non-Metallic Mineral Product Manufacturing);
- manufacturing non-precious metal cutlery and flatware (33221, Cutlery and Hand Tool Manufacturing);
- engraving, chasing or etching non-precious metal flatware and other plated ware (33281, Coating, Engraving, Heat Treating and Allied Activities); and
- manufacturing non-precious metal plated ware (except cutlery and flatware) (33299, All Other Fabricated Metal Product Manufacturing).

Example Activities
- Costume jewellery (including imitation stones and pearls), manufacturing
- Cutlery, precious metal (except plated), manufacturing
- Engraving, chasing or etching precious metal flatware
- Flatware, precious metal (except plated), manufacturing

- Industrial diamonds, cut and polished, manufacturing
- Jewellers' findings, manufacturing
- Jewellery and silverware, metal embossing for the trade
- Jewellery engraving, chasing or etching for the trade

- Jewellery polishing for the trade, manufacturing
- Jewellery, made of precious metal or precious or semiprecious stones, manufacturing
- Lapidary work
- Medals, precious or semi-precious metal, manufacturing
- Minting of coins
- Pearls, drilling, sawing, or peeling of, manufacturing

- Pewter ware, manufacturing
- Precious stones, cutting and polishing
- Rings, jewellery, manufacturing
- Table cutlery, precious metal (except plated), manufacturing
- Table flatware, precious metal (except plated), manufacturing
- Trophies, precious metal (except plated), manufacturing

339910 Jewellery and Silverware Manufacturing CAN

See industry description for 33991, above.

33992 Sporting and Athletic Goods Manufacturing

This industry comprises establishments primarily engaged in manufacturing sporting and athletic goods, except clothing and footwear.

Exclusion(s): Establishments primarily engaged in:
- manufacturing team uniforms (31529, Other Cut and Sew Clothing Manufacturing);
- manufacturing gloves, except sport (31599, Clothing Accessories and Other Clothing Manufacturing);
- manufacturing athletic footwear (31621, Footwear Manufacturing);
- manufacturing small arms and small arms ammunition (33299, All Other Fabricated Metal Product Manufacturing); and
- manufacturing bicycles (33699, Other Transportation Equipment Manufacturing).

Example Activities
- Athletic and sporting goods (except clothing, firearms and ammunition), manufacturing
- Baseball equipment, manufacturing
- Basketball equipment, manufacturing
- Billiard, pool and snooker equipment, manufacturing
- Exercising machines, manufacturing
- Fishing tackle, manufacturing
- Football equipment, manufacturing
- Gloves, sport and athletic (e.g., boxing, baseball, racquetball, handball), manufacturing
- Golf equipment, manufacturing
- Gymnasium and playground equipment, manufacturing
- Hockey equipment (e.g., pants, pads, shinguards), manufacturing
- Ice skates, manufacturing
- Pigeons, clay (targets), manufacturing

- Pool balls, cues, cue tips and tables, manufacturing
- Rackets and frames, sports (e.g., tennis, badminton, squash, racquetball, lacrosse), manufacturing
- Roller skates, manufacturing
- Sailboards, manufacturing
- Skates, ice (boots and blades assembled), manufacturing
- Skates, roller (boots and wheels assembled), manufacturing
- Ski boots, manufacturing
- Skis, manufacturing
- Snowshoes, manufacturing
- Sticks, sports (e.g., hockey, lacrosse), manufacturing
- Swimming pools, prefabricated, manufacturing
- Tennis equipment, manufacturing

339920 Sporting and Athletic Goods Manufacturing

See industry description for 33992, above.

33993 Doll, Toy and Game Manufacturing

This industry comprises establishments primarily engaged in manufacturing dolls, toys and games.

Exclusion(s): Establishments primarily engaged in:
- manufacturing electronic video game cartridges and reproducing video game software (33461, Manufacturing and Reproducing Magnetic and Optical Media);
- manufacturing bicycles and adults' tricycles (33699, Other Transportation Equipment Manufacturing);
- manufacturing sporting and athletic goods (33992, Sporting and Athletic Goods Manufacturing); and
- manufacturing coin-operated game machines (33999, All Other Miscellaneous Manufacturing).

Example Activities
- Airplane models, toy and hobby, manufacturing
- Baby carriages or strollers, manufacturing
- Balls, rubber (except athletic equipment), manufacturing
- Chessmen and chessboards, manufacturing
- Dolls (including parts and accessories), manufacturing
- Electronic toys and games, manufacturing
- Games (except amusement park and playground), manufacturing
- Handicraft supplies, manufacturing
- Kites, manufacturing
- Model kits, manufacturing
- Stuffed toys (including animals), manufacturing
- Toys, electric (including parts), manufacturing
- Tricycles, children's toy, manufacturing
- Vehicles (except bicycles), children's, manufacturing

339930 Doll, Toy and Game Manufacturing ᴹᴱˣ

See industry description for 33993, above.

33994 Office Supplies (except Paper) Manufacturing

This industry comprises establishments primarily engaged in manufacturing office supplies, except paper.

Exclusion(s): Establishments primarily engaged in:
- manufacturing paper office supplies (32223, Stationery Product Manufacturing);
- manufacturing manifold business forms, blankbooks and loose-leaf binders (32311, Printing);
- manufacturing writing, drawing and India inks (32599, All Other Chemical Product Manufacturing);
- manufacturing rubber erasers (32629, Other Rubber Product Manufacturing); and
- manufacturing drafting tables and boards (33712, Household and Institutional Furniture Manufacturing).

Example Activities
- Artists' supplies (except paper), manufacturing
- Ball point pens, manufacturing
- Blackboards, framed, manufacturing
- Brushes, artists', manufacturing
- Bulletin boards, of metal, manufacturing
- Carbon paper, manufacturing
- Chalk (e.g., carpenters', blackboard, marking, artists', tailors'), manufacturing
- Clay, modelling, manufacturing
- Colours, artists', manufacturing
- Crayons, manufacturing
- Felt tip markers, manufacturing
- Fountain pens, manufacturing
- Hand stamps, stencils and brands, manufacturing
- Hole punches, hand operated, manufacturing
- Inked ribbons, manufacturing
- Marker boards (i.e., whiteboards), manufacturing
- Modelling clay, manufacturing
- Paints, artists', manufacturing
- Palettes, artists', manufacturing
- Paper, carbon, manufacturing
- Pen refills and cartridges, manufacturing

- Pencil leads, manufacturing
- Pencil sharpeners, manufacturing
- Pencils, lead and mechanical, manufacturing
- Pens and pen parts (e.g., fountain, stylographic, ballpoint), manufacturing
- Pens, manufacturing
- Ribbons, inked (e.g., typewriter, adding machine, cash register), manufacturing

- Rubber stamps, manufacturing
- Stamping devices, hand operated, manufacturing
- Stamps, hand (e.g., time, date, postmark, cancelling, shoe and textile marking), manufacturing
- Staplers, office, manufacturing

339940 Office Supplies (except Paper) Manufacturing MEX

See industry description for 33994, above.

33995 Sign Manufacturing

This industry comprises establishments primarily engaged in manufacturing signs and related displays, of all materials except paper and paperboard.

Exclusion(s): Establishments primarily engaged in:
- printing advertising specialties, and printing paper and paperboard signs and notices (32311, Printing); and
- sign painting and lettering (54189, Other Services Related to Advertising).

Example Activities
- Electric backlight signs, manufacturing
- Electrical signs and advertising displays, manufacturing
- Letters and numerals (except wood and paper), for signs, manufacturing

- Neon signs, manufacturing
- Scoreboards, electric, manufacturing
- Signs and signboards, non-electric, of wood, manufacturing

339950 Sign Manufacturing

See industry description for 33995, above.

33999 All Other Miscellaneous Manufacturing

This industry comprises establishments, not classified to any other industry, primarily engaged in manufacturing activities.

Exclusion(s): Establishments primarily engaged in:
- manufacturing wood products, such as burnt wood articles (32199, All Other Wood Product Manufacturing);
- manufacturing plastic products, such as lamp shades, combs and hair curlers (32619, Other Plastic Product Manufacturing);
- manufacturing glass products, such as lamp shades and non-electric Christmas tree ornaments (32721, Glass and Glass Product Manufacturing); and
- manufacturing metal products, such as combs and hair curlers (33299, All Other Fabricated Metal Product Manufacturing).

Example Activities
- Artificial Christmas trees, manufacturing
- Artificial flower arrangements, assembling from purchased components
- Bone novelties, manufacturing

- Brooms, manufacturing
- Brushes, household and industrial, manufacturing
- Buckles and buckle parts, manufacturing

- Burial caskets, manufacturing
- Buttons, apparel, manufacturing
- Candles, manufacturing
- Canes (except orthopedic), manufacturing
- Caskets (burial), metal and wood, manufacturing
- Christmas tree ornaments (except electrical and glass), manufacturing
- Christmas trees, artificial, manufacturing
- Cigarette holders, manufacturing
- Coffins, wood or metal, manufacturing
- Coin-operated amusement machine (except juke boxes), manufacturing
- Coin-operated gambling machines, manufacturing
- Coin-operated photograph machines, manufacturing
- Feathers, preparing for use in clothing and textile products
- Fire extinguishers, portable, manufacturing
- Flowers, artificial (except glass or plastic), manufacturing
- Frames, mirror and picture, all materials, manufacturing
- Games, coin-operated, manufacturing
- Gaskets, manufacturing

- Hair nets, made from purchased netting
- Hair pieces (e.g., wigs, toupees, wiglets), manufacturing
- Lighters, cigar and cigarette (except precious metal and motor vehicle), manufacturing
- Mops, floor and dust, manufacturing
- Music boxes, manufacturing
- Musical instruments, manufacturing
- Needles and pins, sewing, manufacturing
- Novelties, not specified elsewhere by process, manufacturing
- Pianos, manufacturing
- Pinball machines, coin-operated, manufacturing
- Pipes, smoker's, manufacturing
- Potpourri, manufacturing
- Safety pins, manufacturing
- Shell novelties, manufacturing
- Tooth brushes (except electric), manufacturing
- Trees and plants, artificial, manufacturing
- Umbrellas, manufacturing
- Wax figures (i.e., manikins), manufacturing
- Wigs, wiglets, toupees, hair pieces, manufacturing
- Zippers (i.e., slide fasteners), manufacturing

339990 All Other Miscellaneous Manufacturing CAN

See industry description for 33999, above.

41 Wholesale Trade

This sector comprises establishments primarily engaged in wholesaling merchandise and providing related logistics, marketing and support services. The wholesaling process is generally an intermediate step in the distribution of merchandise; many wholesalers are therefore organized to sell merchandise in large quantities to retailers, and business and institutional clients. However, some wholesalers, in particular those that supply non-consumer capital goods, sell merchandise in single units to final users.

This sector recognizes two main types of wholesalers, that is, wholesale merchants and wholesale agents and brokers.

Wholesale Merchants

Wholesale merchants buy and sell merchandise on their own account, that is, they take title to the goods they sell. They generally operate from warehouse or office locations and they may ship from their own inventory or arrange for the shipment of goods directly from the supplier to the client. In addition to the sale of goods, they may provide, or arrange for the provision of, logistics, marketing and support services, such as packaging and labelling, inventory management, shipping, handling of warranty claims, in-store or co-op promotions, and product training. Dealers of machinery and equipment, such as dealers of farm machinery and heavy-duty trucks, also fall within this category.

Wholesale merchants are known by a variety of trade designations depending on their relationship with suppliers or customers, or the distribution method they employ. Examples include wholesale merchants, wholesale distributors, drop shippers, rack-jobbers, import-export merchants, buying groups, dealer-owned cooperatives and banner wholesalers.

The first eight subsectors of wholesale trade comprise wholesale merchants. The grouping of these establishments into industry groups and industries is based on the merchandise line or lines supplied by the wholesaler.

Wholesale Agents and Brokers

Wholesale agents and brokers buy and sell merchandise owned by others on a fee or commission basis. They do not take title to the goods they buy or sell, and they generally operate at or from an office location.

Wholesale agents and brokers are known by a variety of trade designations including import-export agents, wholesale commission agents, wholesale brokers, and manufacturer's representatives and agents.

411 Farm Product Wholesaler-Distributors CAN

See industry description for 4111, below.

4111 Farm Product Wholesaler-Distributors CAN

This industry group comprises establishments primarily engaged in wholesaling livestock, grain and other farm products.

41111 Live Animal Wholesaler-Distributors CAN

This industry comprises establishments primarily engaged in wholesaling live animals.

> *Exclusion(s): Establishments primarily engaged in:*
> - wholesaling fresh, cured or frozen (unpackaged) fish (41314, Fish and Seafood Product Wholesaler-Distributors).

> *Example Activities*
> - Auctioning livestock, with own facilities
> - Bait, live, wholesale
> - Bees, wholesale
> - Cattle drovers (dealer)
> - Farm animals, live, wholesale
> - Fish, live, wholesale
> - Fish, tropical, wholesale
> - Live bait, wholesale
> - Livestock auctioning, with own facilities
> - Livestock, wholesale
> - Pet animals, wholesale
> - Worms, wholesale

411110 Live Animal Wholesaler-Distributors CAN

See industry description for 41111, above.

41112 Oilseed and Grain Wholesaler-Distributors CAN

This industry comprises establishments primarily engaged in wholesaling oilseeds and grains. Establishments operating grain elevators other than primary storage, are included.

> *Exclusion(s): Establishments primarily engaged in:*
> - wholesaling hay, processed seeds, grain used as fodder, and animal feeds (41831, Agricultural Feed Wholesaler-Distributors); and
> - wholesaling seeds for field crops, flowers and plants, garden seeds and grass seeds (41832, Seed Wholesaler-Distributors).

Example Activities
- Beans, dry, wholesale
- Grain merchant, wholesale
- Grain, wholesale
- Oilseeds, wholesale

- Peas, dry, wholesale
- Rice, unpolished, wholesale
- Soybeans, wholesale
- Wheat, wholesale

411120 Oilseed and Grain Wholesaler-Distributors CAN

See industry description for 41112, above.

41113 Nursery Stock and Plant Wholesaler-Distributors CAN

This industry comprises establishments primarily engaged in wholesaling nursery stock and plants.

Example Activities
- Flowers and florists' supplies, wholesale
- Nursery stock, wholesale

- Ornamental plants and flowers, wholesale
- Trees, bushes and plants, wholesale

411130 Nursery Stock and Plant Wholesaler-Distributors CAN

See industry description for 41113, above.

41119 Other Farm Product Wholesaler-Distributors CAN

This industry comprises establishments, not classified to any other industry, primarily engaged in wholesaling crude, unprocessed farm products.

Exclusion(s): Establishments primarily engaged in:
- wholesaling cured tobacco (41331, Cigarette and Tobacco Product Wholesaler-Distributors).

Example Activities
- Animal hair, wholesale
- Auctioneers, tobacco, wholesale
- Cocoa beans, wholesale
- Feathers, unprocessed, wholesale
- Fibres, vegetable, wholesale
- Hides and skins, raw, wholesale
- Importers, raw wool, wholesale
- Milk, raw, wholesale
- Nuts and seeds, unshelled, wholesale

- Raw leaf tobacco, wholesale
- Raw sugar, wholesale
- Semen, bovine, wholesale
- Silk, raw, wholesale
- Skins, raw, wholesale
- Tobacco auctioning, wholesale
- Vegetable and fruit, crude, unprocessed, wholesale
- Wool, raw, wholesale

411190 Other Farm Product Wholesaler-Distributors CAN

See industry description for 41119, above.

412 Petroleum Product Wholesaler-Distributors CAN

See industry description for 41211, below.

4121 Petroleum Product Wholesaler-Distributors CAN

See industry description for 41211, below.

41211 Petroleum Product Wholesaler-Distributors CAN

This industry comprises establishments primarily engaged in wholesaling crude oil, liquefied petroleum gases, heating oil and other refined petroleum products.

Exclusion(s): Establishments primarily engaged in:
- retailing motor fuels, lubricating oils and greases (4471, Gasoline Stations);
- retailing heating oil, liquefied petroleum (LP) gas and other fuels, via direct selling (45431, Fuel Dealers); and
- lubricating motor vehicles (81119, Other Automotive Repair and Maintenance).

Example Activities
- Aircraft fuelling services, wholesale
- Bulk tank station, wholesale
- Crude oil, wholesale
- Fuel oil dealers, wholesale
- Gasoline, wholesale
- Liquefied petroleum gases, wholesale
- Lubricating oils and greases, wholesale
- Petroleum bulk station, wholesale
- Refined petroleum products, wholesale

412110 Petroleum Product Wholesaler-Distributors CAN

See industry description for 41211, above.

413 Food, Beverage and Tobacco Wholesaler-Distributors CAN

This subsector comprises establishments primarily engaged in wholesaling food products, beverages and tobacco products.

4131 Food Wholesaler-Distributors CAN

This industry group comprises establishments primarily engaged in wholesaling processed milk and other dairy products, poultry and eggs, fish and seafood products, fresh fruit and vegetables, red meat and meat products, bread and other bakery products, processed rice, flour, flour mixes, prepared cereal foods and spices.

41311 General-Line Food Wholesaler-Distributors CAN

This industry comprises establishments primarily engaged in wholesaling a general line of food products.

Example Activity
- Groceries, general line, wholesale

413110 General-Line Food Wholesaler-Distributors CAN

See industry description for 41311, above.

41312 Dairy and Milk Products Wholesaler-Distributors CAN

This industry comprises establishments primarily engaged in wholesaling processed milk and other dairy products.

Exclusion(s): Establishments primarily engaged in:
- wholesaling dried and canned dairy products (41319, Other Specialty-Line Food Wholesaler-Distributors).

Example Activities
- Bottling (not pasteurizing) fresh milk and cream
- Butter, wholesale
- Cheese, wholesale
- Dairy products, processed (except canned), wholesale
- Frozen dairy products, wholesale
- Ice cream and ices, wholesale
- Ice cream, wholesale
- Milk, processed, wholesale
- Yogurt, wholesale

413120 Dairy and Milk Products Wholesaler-Distributors CAN

See industry description for 41312, above.

41313 Poultry and Egg Wholesaler-Distributors CAN

This industry comprises establishments primarily engaged in wholesaling dressed poultry and eggs.

Exclusion(s): Establishments primarily engaged in:
- wholesaling live poultry (41111, Live Animal Wholesaler-Distributors); and
- wholesaling packaged frozen poultry (41319, Other Specialty-Line Food Wholesaler-Distributors).

Example Activities
- Chickens, dressed, wholesale
- Eggs, wholesale
- Geese, dressed, wholesale
- Poultry products, wholesale
- Poultry, dressed, wholesale
- Turkeys, dressed, wholesale

413130 Poultry and Egg Wholesaler-Distributors CAN

See industry description for 41313, above.

41314 Fish and Seafood Product Wholesaler-Distributors CAN

This industry comprises establishments primarily engaged in wholesaling fresh, cured or frozen fish and seafood products, except packaged.

Exclusion(s): Establishments primarily engaged in:
- wholesaling packaged frozen fish and seafood or canned sea products (41319, Other Specialty-Line Food Wholesaler-Distributors).

Example Activities
- Crustaceans and molluscs, wholesale
- Fish, cured, wholesale
- Fish, fresh, wholesale
- Fish, frozen (except packaged), wholesale
- Fresh fish, wholesale
- Lobsters, fresh or frozen (except frozen packaged), wholesale
- Oysters, fresh or frozen (except frozen packaged), wholesale
- Seafood, dressed, wholesale
- Seafood, frozen (except packaged), wholesale

413140 Fish and Seafood Product Wholesaler-Distributors CAN

See industry description for 41314, above.

41315 Fresh Fruit and Vegetable Wholesaler-Distributors CAN

This industry comprises establishments primarily engaged in cleaning, sorting, repackaging and wholesaling fresh fruit and vegetables. These establishments typically supply retailers.

Exclusion(s): Establishments primarily engaged in:
- buying and reselling unprocessed fruit and vegetables (41119, Other Farm Product Wholesaler-Distributors); and
- wholesaling packaged frozen, and canned fruit and vegetables (41319, Other Specialty-Line Food Wholesaler-Distributors).

Example Activities
- Banana ripening for the trade, wholesale
- Fruit, fresh, cleaning, sorting and repackaging, on contract for wholesalers
- Fruits, fresh, wholesale
- Packing house, fruit, fresh, wholesale
- Vegetable packing shed, wholesale
- Vegetables, fresh, wholesale

413150 Fresh Fruit and Vegetable Wholesaler-Distributors ^{CAN}

See industry description for 41315, above.

41316 Red Meat and Meat Product Wholesaler-Distributors ^{CAN}

This industry comprises establishments primarily engaged in wholesaling fresh, frozen (except frozen packaged), cured and cooked meats.

Exclusion(s): Establishments primarily engaged in:
- cutting purchased carcasses and selling boxed beef (31161, Animal Slaughtering and Processing); and
- wholesaling packaged frozen meats or canned meats (41319, Other Specialty-Line Food Wholesaler-Distributors).

Example Activities
- Cooked meats (except canned), wholesale
- Cured meat (except canned), wholesale
- Frozen meat (except packaged), wholesale
- Lard, wholesale
- Meat carcasses, wholesale
- Meat preparations (except canned), wholesale
- Meats, fresh, wholesale
- Sausage casings, wholesale

413160 Red Meat and Meat Product Wholesaler-Distributors ^{CAN}

See industry description for 41316, above.

41319 Other Specialty-Line Food Wholesaler-Distributors ^{CAN}

This industry comprises establishments, not classified to any other industry, primarily engaged in wholesaling specialized lines of food, including canned foods and packaged frozen foods.

Example Activities
- Baby foods, canned, wholesale
- Bakery products, wholesale
- Breakfast cereals, wholesale
- Candy, wholesale
- Canned foods, wholesale
- Coffee, wholesale
- Confectionery, wholesale
- Dairy products, canned or dried, wholesale
- Dietary foods, canned, wholesale
- Dinners, frozen, wholesale
- Flavouring extract (except for fountain use), wholesale
- Frozen foods, packaged, wholesale
- Fruit concentrates and syrups, fountain, wholesale
- Fruit juices, wholesale
- Fruit preparations, wholesale
- Gelatin, edible, wholesale
- Health food, wholesale
- Honey, processed, wholesale
- Jams, jellies and marmalades, wholesale
- Junior foods, canned, wholesale
- Malt, wholesale
- Meats, packaged frozen, wholesale
- Nuts and seeds, edible, processed, wholesale
- Pastries, wholesale
- Pastry, quick-frozen, packaged, wholesale
- Pickles, preserves, jellies, jams and sauces, wholesale
- Poultry, packaged frozen, wholesale
- Puddings, dessert, wholesale
- Rice, polished, wholesale
- Sandwiches, wholesale
- Seafood, packaged frozen, wholesale
- Soups, wholesale
- Spices, wholesale
- Sugar, refined, wholesale
- Tea, wholesale

413190 Other Specialty-Line Food Wholesaler-Distributors CAN

See industry description for 41319, above.

4132 Beverage Wholesaler-Distributors CAN

This industry group comprises establishments primarily engaged in wholesaling alcoholic and non-alcoholic beverages.

Exclusion(s): Establishments primarily engaged in:
- wholesaling fruit juices (41319, Other Specialty-Line Food Wholesaler-Distributors).

41321 Non-Alcoholic Beverage Wholesaler-Distributors CAN

This industry comprises establishments primarily engaged in wholesaling non-alcoholic beverages.

Exclusion(s): Establishments primarily engaged in:
- wholesaling fruit juices (41319, Other Specialty-Line Food Wholesaler-Distributors).

Example Activities
- Apple cider (less than 2.5% alcohol), wholesale
- Beverage concentrates, wholesale
- Carbonated beverages, wholesale
- Distribution of water in bottles
- Mineral and spring waters, wholesale
- Soft drinks, wholesale

413210 Non-Alcoholic Beverage Wholesaler-Distributors CAN

See industry description for 41321, above.

41322 Alcoholic Beverage Wholesaler-Distributors CAN

This industry comprises establishments primarily engaged in wholesaling alcoholic beverages.

Example Activities
- Alcoholic beverages, wholesale
- Beers, wholesale
- Bottled wines and liquors, wholesale
- Coolers (2.5% or greater alcohol content), wholesale
- Distilled spirits, wholesale
- Hard cider, wholesale
- Importers of wines and spirits for embassies
- Liquor, wholesale
- Wine coolers, alcoholic, wholesale
- Wines, wholesale

413220 Alcoholic Beverage Wholesaler-Distributors CAN

See industry description for 41322, above.

4133 Cigarette and Tobacco Product Wholesaler-Distributors CAN

See industry description for 41331, below.

41331 Cigarette and Tobacco Product Wholesaler-Distributors CAN

This industry comprises establishments primarily engaged in wholesaling cured tobacco and tobacco products.

Exclusion(s): Establishments primarily engaged in:
- wholesaling raw leaf tobacco (41119, Other Farm Product Wholesaler-Distributors).

Example Activities
- Chewing tobacco, wholesale
- Cigars, cigarettes and cut tobacco, wholesale
- Pipe tobacco, wholesale
- Snuff (powdered tobacco), wholesale
- Tobacco, cured or processed, wholesale

413310 Cigarette and Tobacco Product Wholesaler-Distributors CAN

See industry description for 41331, above.

414 Personal and Household Goods Wholesaler-Distributors CAN

This subsector comprises establishments primarily engaged in wholesaling textiles, clothing, footwear, home entertainment equipment, household appliances, home furnishings, personal articles, pharmaceuticals, toiletries, cosmetics and sundries.

4141 Textile, Clothing and Footwear Wholesaler-Distributors CAN

This industry group comprises establishments primarily engaged in wholesaling textiles, clothing, clothing accessories, footwear, piece goods, notions and other dry goods.

41411 Clothing and Clothing Accessories Wholesaler-Distributors CAN

This industry comprises establishments primarily engaged in wholesaling clothing and clothing accessories for adults and children.

Example Activities
- Athletic clothing, wholesale
- Beachwear, wholesale
- Beachwear, women's and misses', wholesale
- Bulletproof vests, wholesale
- Caps, women's and children's, wholesale
- Children's clothing, wholesale
- Clothing accessories, wholesale
- Clothing accessories, women's, misses' and children's, wholesale
- Clothing, men's and boys', wholesale
- Diapers (except paper), wholesale
- Dresses, wholesale
- Family clothing wholesale
- Fine or dress clothing, men's and boys', wholesale
- Foundation garments, women's and misses', wholesale
- Fur clothing, wholesale
- Furnishings (except shoes), women's, girls' and infants', wholesale
- Furs, dressed, wholesale
- Gloves, women's, misses' and children's, wholesale
- Handbags and pocketbooks, wholesale
- Hats, women's, misses' and girls', wholesale
- Hosiery, women's, misses' and children's, wholesale
- Infants' clothing, wholesale
- Knit wear, wholesale
- Leather and sheep-lined clothing, women's and children's, wholesale
- Lingerie, wholesale
- Men's and boys' clothing and furnishings, wholesale
- Men's clothing and furnishings, wholesale
- Millinery, wholesale
- Neckwear, women's, misses' and children's, wholesale
- Outerwear, men's and boys', wholesale
- Outerwear, women's, children's, and infants', wholesale
- Purses, women's and misses', wholesale
- Robes and gowns, women's and children's, wholesale
- Scarves and neckwear, women's, misses' and children's, wholesale
- Sleepwear, men's and boys', wholesale
- Sleepwear, women's, misses' and children's, wholesale
- Sportswear, women's and children's, wholesale
- Suits, men's and boys', wholesale
- Underwear, men's and boys', wholesale
- Underwear, women's, misses' and children's, wholesale
- Uniforms and work clothing, wholesale
- Uniforms, men's and boys', wholesale
- Uniforms, women's and children's, wholesale
- Unisex clothing, wholesale
- Women's clothing wholesale

414110 Clothing and Clothing Accessories Wholesaler-Distributors CAN

See industry description for 41411, above.

41412 Footwear Wholesaler-Distributors CAN

This industry comprises establishments primarily engaged in wholesaling footwear.

Example Activities
- Athletic footwear, wholesale
- Footwear, wholesale
- Overshoes, wholesale
- Plastic footwear, wholesale
- Rubber footwear, wholesale
- Shoes, wholesale
- Slippers (footwear), wholesale
- Waterproof footwear, wholesale

414120 Footwear Wholesaler-Distributors CAN

See industry description for 41412, above.

41413 Piece Goods, Notions and Other Dry Goods Wholesaler-Distributors CAN

This industry comprises establishments primarily engaged in wholesaling piece goods, notions and other "dry goods".

Exclusion(s): Establishments primarily engaged in:
- wholesaling household linens and draperies (41433, Linen, Drapery and Other Textile Furnishings Wholesaler-Distributors).

Example Activities
- Apparel trimmings, wholesale
- Automobile fabrics, wholesale
- Braided material, piece goods, wholesale
- Broad-woven fabrics, wholesale
- Buttons, wholesale
- Cheesecloth, woven, wholesale
- Clothing fasteners, wholesale
- Drapery material, wholesale
- Dry goods, wholesale
- Fabric, textile, wholesale
- Industrial yarn, wholesale
- Jute fabrics, piece goods, wholesale
- Knitting yarns, wholesale
- Labels, woven, wholesale
- Lace fabrics, wholesale
- Linen piece goods, woven, wholesale
- Millinery supplies, wholesale
- Narrow fabrics, wholesale
- Notions, wholesale
- Patterns, clothing, wholesale
- Piece goods, textile, wholesale
- Rayon piece goods, wholesale
- Shoulder pads, wholesale
- Silk piece goods, wholesale
- Textile piece goods, wholesale
- Thread, wholesale
- Warp knit fabrics, wholesale
- Weft knit fabrics, wholesale
- Yard goods, textile, wholesale
- Yarn and thread, wholesale
- Zippers, wholesale

414130 Piece Goods, Notions and Other Dry Goods Wholesaler-Distributors CAN

See industry description for 41413, above.

4142 Home Entertainment Equipment and Household Appliance Wholesaler-Distributors CAN

This industry group comprises establishments primarily engaged in wholesaling home entertainment equipment and household electrical and electronic appliances and parts.

Exclusion(s): Establishments primarily engaged in:
- wholesaling office furniture, machinery and equipment (41791, Office and Store Machinery and Equipment Wholesaler-Distributors); and
- wholesaling professional machinery and equipment (41793, Professional Machinery, Equipment and Supplies Wholesaler-Distributors).

41421 Home Entertainment Equipment Wholesaler-Distributors ^{CAN}

This industry comprises establishments primarily engaged in wholesaling new home entertainment equipment and related parts.

Exclusion(s): Establishments primarily engaged in:
- wholesaling computers and pre-packaged software (41731, Computer, Computer Peripheral and Pre-Packaged Software Wholesaler-Distributors); and
- wholesaling used entertainment equipment and parts (41893, Second-Hand Goods (except Machinery and Automotive) Wholesaler-Distributors).

Example Activities
- Amplifiers, speakers and related sound equipment, wholesale
- Audio system sales, wholesale
- Cassette player, recorder, portable, wholesale
- Electronic TV games, wholesale
- Games, video, wholesale
- Radios, household-type, wholesale
- Sound systems, domestic, wholesale
- Television sets, wholesale
- Video disc players, wholesale
- Video recorder, domestic, wholesale

414210 Home Entertainment Equipment Wholesaler-Distributors ^{CAN}

See industry description for 41421, above.

41422 Household Appliance Wholesaler-Distributors ^{CAN}

This industry comprises establishments primarily engaged in wholesaling large and small, new, electric, household appliances

Exclusion(s): Establishments primarily engaged in:
- wholesaling gas appliances (41612, Plumbing, Heating and Air-Conditioning Equipment and Supplies Wholesaler-Distributors); and
- wholesaling restaurant and hotel equipment (417920, Service Establishment Machinery, Equipment and Supplies Wholesaler-Distributors).

Example Activities
- Air-conditioners, electric, window-type, wholesale
- Answering machines, telephone, wholesale
- Appliances, beauty care, electric, wholesale
- Beauty care appliances, electric, wholesale
- Clocks, electric, wholesale
- Electric appliances, household, wholesale
- Fans, electric, domestic, wholesale
- Humidifiers and dehumidifiers, portable, wholesale
- Kitchen appliances (e.g., toasters, kettles, ironers), electric, wholesale
- Microwave ovens, household, wholesale
- Personal care appliances (e.g., hair dryers, razors, toothbrushes), electric, wholesale
- Refrigerators, electric, domestic, wholesale
- Sewing machines, electric, domestic, wholesale
- Smoke detectors, household, wholesale
- Stoves, electric, domestic, wholesale
- Vacuum cleaners, electric, domestic, wholesale
- Vacuum cleaners, household, wholesale
- Washing machines, electric, domestic, wholesale

414220 Household Appliance Wholesaler-Distributors ^{CAN}

See industry description for 41422, above.

4143 Home Furnishings Wholesaler-Distributors ^{CAN}

This industry group comprises establishments primarily engaged in wholesaling home furnishings, such as furniture, china, glassware, crockery and pottery, floor coverings, linens and draperies.

41431 China, Glassware, Crockery and Pottery Wholesaler-Distributors ^{CAN}

This industry comprises establishments primarily engaged in wholesaling household china, glassware, crockery and pottery, including ceramic kitchenware and tableware.

Exclusion(s): Establishments primarily engaged in:
- wholesaling cutlery other than precious metal (41439, Other Home Furnishings Wholesaler-Distributors);
- wholesaling precious metal cutlery (41441, Jewellery and Watch Wholesaler-Distributors); and
- wholesaling restaurant and hotel goods (41792, Service Establishment Machinery, Equipment and Supplies Wholesaler-Distributors).

Example Activities
- Ceramic goods, household, wholesale
- Chinaware, household, wholesale
- Household china and glassware, wholesale
- Household crockery and pottery, wholesale
- Pottery, household, wholesale
- Tableware, ceramic, wholesale

414310 China, Glassware, Crockery and Pottery Wholesaler-Distributors ^{CAN}

See industry description for 41431, above.

41432 Floor Covering Wholesaler-Distributors ^{CAN}

This industry comprises establishments primarily engaged in wholesaling floor coverings.

Exclusion(s): Establishments primarily engaged in:
- wholesaling hardwood flooring (41632, Lumber, Plywood and Millwork Wholesaler-Distributors).

Example Activities
- Carpet and carpet supplies, wholesale
- Carpets, wholesale
- Floor coverings, carpets, rugs and other, wholesale
- Floor tiles (except ceramic), wholesale
- Linoleum floor covering, wholesale
- Tile carpets, wholesale

414320 Floor Covering Wholesaler-Distributors ^{CAN}

See industry description for 41432, above.

41433 Linen, Drapery and Other Textile Furnishings Wholesaler-Distributors ^{CAN}

This industry comprises establishments primarily engaged in wholesaling household linens, draperies and other textile home furnishings, including bedding.

Example Activities
- Bath mats and bathroom sets, wholesale
- Bed coverings, wholesale
- Bedding, wholesale
- Curtains, wholesale
- Cushions and pillows, wholesale
- Draperies, wholesale
- Household linens, wholesale
- Table linens, wholesale
- Tapestries, household furnishings, wholesale

414330 Linen, Drapery and Other Textile Furnishings Wholesaler-Distributors CAN

See industry description for 41433, above.

41439 Other Home Furnishings Wholesaler-Distributors CAN

This industry comprises establishments, not classified to any other industry, primarily engaged in wholesaling furniture and other home furnishings, such as window accessories, blinds, pictures and picture frames, mirrors and decorative ware. Establishments primarily engaged in wholesaling a combination of home furnishings with none predominating are also included.

Exclusion(s): Establishments primarily engaged in:
- wholesaling china and glassware, kitchen and tableware (41431, China, Glassware, Crockery and Pottery Wholesaler-Distributors);
- wholesaling carpets and other floor coverings (41432, Floor Covering Wholesaler-Distributors); and
- wholesaling bedding, draperies and other textile furnishings (41433, Linen, Drapery and Other Textile Furnishings Wholesaler-Distributors).

Example Activities
- Art and decorative ware, household, wholesale
- Bamboo furniture, wholesale
- Baskets, boxes, cans and bags, household, wholesale
- Bedroom furniture, wholesale
- Blinds, window, wholesale
- Box springs and mattresses, wholesale
- Cutlery, household, wholesale
- Decorative window accessories, wholesale
- Dining room furniture, wholesale
- Food preparation and storage utensils, household, wholesale
- Frames and pictures, wholesale
- Furnishings, household, wholesale
- Furniture, household, office, restaurant and public building, wholesale
- Furniture, household, wholesale
- Household furniture, wholesale
- Kitchen utensils, household, wholesale
- Lawn furniture, wholesale
- Mattresses and box springs, wholesale
- Mirrors (except automotive), wholesale
- Patio furniture, wholesale
- Public building furniture, wholesale
- Storage and food preparation utensils, household, wholesale
- Wall decorations, household, wholesale
- Window shades and blinds, wholesale

414390 Other Home Furnishings Wholesaler-Distributors CAN

See industry description for 41439, above.

4144 Personal Goods Wholesaler-Distributors CAN

This industry group comprises establishments primarily engaged in wholesaling personal articles, such as jewellery, watches, books, periodicals, newspapers, photographic equipment and supplies, sound recordings, video cassettes, toys, hobby goods, and amusement and sporting goods.

41441 Jewellery and Watch Wholesaler-Distributors CAN

This industry comprises establishments primarily engaged in wholesaling jewellery, watches, silverware, table flatware, hollowware, and cutlery of precious metal.

Exclusion(s): Establishments primarily engaged in:
- wholesaling non-precious metal cutlery (41633, Hardware Wholesaler-Distributors); and
- repairing jewellery and watches (81149, Other Personal and Household Goods Repair and Maintenance).

Example Activities

- Clocks, mechanical, wholesale
- Coins, wholesale
- Diamonds (gems), wholesale
- Diamonds, jewellery, wholesale
- Gem stones, wholesale
- Hollowware, table, sterling and silverplate, wholesale
- Imitation stones and pearls, jewellery, wholesale
- Jewellers' findings, precious metal, wholesale
- Jewellery, wholesale
- Silverware and plated ware, wholesale
- Stones, precious, wholesale
- Table flatware and hollowware, sterling and silverplate, wholesale
- Watches, wholesale

414410 Jewellery and Watch Wholesaler-Distributors CAN

See industry description for 41441, above.

41442 Book, Periodical and Newspaper Wholesaler-Distributors CAN

This industry comprises establishments primarily engaged in wholesaling books, periodicals and newspapers, including textbooks, dictionaries and encyclopaedias.

Example Activities

- Books and pamphlets, wholesale
- Fiction books, wholesale
- Magazines, wholesale
- Maps, wholesale
- Newspapers, wholesale
- Pocket books, wholesale
- Textbooks, wholesale

414420 Book, Periodical and Newspaper Wholesaler-Distributors CAN

See industry description for 41442, above.

41443 Photographic Equipment and Supplies Wholesaler-Distributors CAN

This industry comprises establishments primarily engaged in wholesaling photographic equipment and supplies.

Example Activities

- Cameras, equipment and supplies, wholesale
- Chemicals, photographic, wholesale
- Dark room apparatus, wholesale
- Developing apparatus, photographic, wholesale
- Enlarging equipment, photographic, wholesale
- Film developing and finishing equipment, wholesale
- Film, photographic, wholesale
- Home movie cameras, equipment and supplies, wholesale
- Photofinishing equipment, wholesale
- Photographic cameras, projectors, equipment and supplies, wholesale
- Photographic chemicals, wholesale
- Photographic film and plates, wholesale
- Photographic paper and cloth, wholesale
- Processing and finishing equipment, photographic, wholesale
- Projection equipment (e.g., motion picture, slide), photographic, wholesale

414430 Photographic Equipment and Supplies Wholesaler-Distributors CAN

See industry description for 41443, above.

41444 Sound Recording Wholesalers CAN

This industry comprises establishments primarily engaged in wholesaling sound recordings in any format, including cassette and CD. These establishments engage in buy-and-sell distribution, including the distribution of imported CDs and cassettes, and they may be known as "rack-jobbers" or "one-stop" distributors.

Exclusion(s): Establishments primarily engaged in:
- wholesaling music videos (41445, Video Cassette Wholesalers); and
- releasing, promoting and distributing sound recordings from masters produced by the establishment or bought, leased or licensed from another establishment (51222, Integrated Record Production/Distribution).

Example Activities
- Cassettes or tapes, music, wholesale
- Compact disc (CD's), music, wholesale
- Phonograph records, wholesale
- Tapes or cassettes, music, wholesale

414440 Sound Recording Wholesalers CAN

See industry description for 41444, above.

41445 Video Cassette Wholesalers CAN

This industry comprises establishments primarily engaged in wholesaling pre-recorded video cassettes.

Exclusion(s): Establishments primarily engaged in:
- wholesaling blank video cassettes (41791, Office and Store Machinery and Equipment Wholesaler-Distributors).

Example Activities
- Movies, video, wholesale
- Tapes, video, recorded, wholesale
- Video tapes, recorded, wholesale

414450 Video Cassette Wholesalers CAN

See industry description for 41445, above.

41446 Toy and Hobby Goods Wholesaler-Distributors CAN

This industry comprises establishments primarily engaged in wholesaling toys and hobby goods.

Exclusion(s): Establishments primarily engaged in:
- wholesaling video games (41421, Home Entertainment Equipment Wholesaler-Distributors).

Example Activities
- Board games, wholesale
- Craft kits, wholesale
- Dolls, wholesale
- Fireworks, wholesale
- Handicraft and hobbycraft kits, wholesale
- Hobbycraft kits, wholesale
- Puzzles, wholesale
- Science kits or sets, wholesale
- Toys, wholesale

414460 Toy and Hobby Goods Wholesaler-Distributors CAN

See industry description for 41446, above.

41447 Amusement and Sporting Goods Wholesaler-Distributors CAN

This industry comprises establishments primarily engaged in wholesaling amusement and sporting goods.

Exclusion(s): Establishments primarily engaged in:
- wholesaling snowmobiles, tent trailers, motorized bicycles and pleasure boats (41519, Recreational and Other Motor Vehicles Wholesaler-Distributors).

Example Activities

- Ammunition and firearms, sporting, wholesale
- Amusement and sporting goods, wholesale
- Athletic and sporting goods, wholesale
- Bicycle tires and tubes, wholesale
- Bicycles (except motorized), wholesale
- Camping equipment, wholesale
- Firearms and ammunition, wholesale

- Fitness equipment, wholesale
- Gymnasium equipment, wholesale
- Sails and tents, wholesale
- Sporting goods, wholesale
- Swimming pools and equipment, wholesale
- Tennis equipment and supplies, wholesale
- Vehicles, children's, wholesale

414470 Amusement and Sporting Goods Wholesaler-Distributors ^{CAN}

See industry description for 41447, above.

4145 Pharmaceuticals, Toiletries, Cosmetics and Sundries Wholesaler-Distributors ^{CAN}

This industry group comprises establishments primarily engaged in wholesaling proprietary and patent medicines, cosmetics, toiletries and druggists' sundries.

41451 Pharmaceuticals and Pharmacy Supplies Wholesaler-Distributors ^{CAN}

This industry comprises establishments primarily engaged in wholesaling ethical drugs and/or proprietary drugs and pharmacy supplies.

Example Activities

- Antiseptic preparations, wholesale
- Bacteriological medicines, wholesale
- Biological medicines, wholesale
- Dermatological medicines, wholesale
- Ethical drugs, wholesale
- Hematinic medicines, wholesale
- Hormonal medicines, wholesale

- Medicinals and botanicals, wholesale
- Patent medicines, wholesale
- Pharmaceutical preparations, wholesale
- Prescription medicines, wholesale
- Proprietary (patent) medicines, wholesale
- Radioactive pharmaceutical isotopes, wholesale

414510 Pharmaceuticals and Pharmacy Supplies Wholesaler-Distributors ^{CAN}

See industry description for 41451, above.

41452 Toiletries, Cosmetics and Sundries Wholesaler-Distributors ^{CAN}

This industry comprises establishments primarily engaged in wholesaling toiletries, cosmetics and druggists' sundries.

Exclusion(s): Establishments primarily engaged in:
- wholesaling laundry soap, detergents and cleansers (41841, Chemical (except Agricultural) and Allied Product Wholesaler-Distributors).

Example Activities

- Bandages, dressings and gauzes, wholesale
- Bath oils and salts, wholesale
- Beauty preparations, wholesale
- Body care preparations, wholesale
- Cosmetics, wholesale
- Dental care preparations, wholesale
- Druggists' sundries, wholesale
- First-aid supplies, wholesale

- Hair care products, wholesale
- Hygiene products, oral, wholesale
- Medical glass, wholesale
- Medicinal herbs, non-prescription, wholesale
- Perfumes and fragrances, wholesale
- Razors and blades, non-electric, wholesale
- Sanitary products, personal, wholesale

- Shampoo, hair, wholesale
- Soap, toilet, wholesale
- Toilet waters and colognes, wholesale
- Toiletries, wholesale
- Toothbrushes (except electric), wholesale
- Toothpaste, wholesale

414520 Toiletries, Cosmetics and Sundries Wholesaler-Distributors CAN

See industry description for 41452, above.

415 Motor Vehicle and Parts Wholesaler-Distributors CAN

This subsector comprises establishments primarily engaged in wholesaling motor vehicles, parts and accessories, including tires.

4151 Motor Vehicle Wholesaler-Distributors CAN

This industry group comprises establishments primarily engaged in wholesaling new and used automobiles, trucks, truck trailers, buses and recreational vehicles.

41511 New and Used Automobile and Light-Duty Truck Wholesaler-Distributors CAN

This industry comprises establishments primarily engaged in wholesaling new and used automobiles and light-duty trucks, sport utility vehicles and mini-vans.

Exclusion(s): Establishments primarily engaged in:
- wholesaling new and used heavy-duty trucks, truck tractors and buses (41512, Truck, Truck Tractor and Bus Wholesaler-Distributors).

Example Activities
- Auctioneers, automobile, with own facilities, not open to the general public
- Automobile auctioneers, with own facilities, not open to the general public
- Automobiles, new and used, wholesale
- Used cars, wholesale

415110 New and Used Automobile and Light-Duty Truck Wholesaler-Distributors CAN

See industry description for 41511, above.

41512 Truck, Truck Tractor and Bus Wholesaler-Distributors CAN

This industry comprises establishments primarily engaged in wholesaling new and used heavy-duty trucks, truck tractors and buses.

Exclusion(s): Establishments primarily engaged in:
- wholesaling new and used automobiles and light-duty trucks, sport utility vehicles and mini-vans (41511, New and Used Automobile and Light-Duty Truck Wholesaler-Distributors); and
- repairing trucks, truck tractors and trailers, and buses (8111, Automotive Repair and Maintenance).

Example Activities
- Buses, wholesale
- Buses, wholesale and repair
- Motor coaches, wholesale
- School buses, wholesale
- School buses, wholesale and repair
- Truck tractors, road, wholesale
- Truck tractors, road, wholesale and repair
- Trucks and buses, wholesale
- Trucks and buses, wholesale and repair

415120 Truck, Truck Tractor and Bus Wholesaler-Distributors ^{CAN}

See industry description for 41512, above.

41519 Recreational and Other Motor Vehicles Wholesaler-Distributors ^{CAN}

This industry comprises establishments, not classified to any other industry, primarily engaged in wholesaling recreational motor vehicles and camper trailers.

Exclusion(s): Establishments primarily engaged in:
- wholesaling pleasure boats (41799, All Other Machinery, Equipment and Supplies Wholesaler-Distributors); and
- wholesaling mobile homes (house trailers) (41899, All Other Wholesaler-Distributors).

Example Activities
- All terrain vehicles (ATVs), wholesale
- All terrain vehicles (ATVs), wholesale and repair
- Bodies, automotive, wholesale
- Campers, motor vehicle, wholesale
- Campers, motor vehicle, wholesale and repair
- Go-carts, wholesale
- Go-carts, wholesale and repair
- Motor homes, wholesale
- Motor homes, wholesale and repair
- Motor scooters, wholesale
- Motor scooters, wholesale and repair
- Motorcycles, wholesale
- Motorcycles, wholesale and repair
- Recreational vehicles, wholesale
- Recreational vehicles, wholesale and repair
- Snowmobiles, wholesale
- Snowmobiles, wholesale and repair
- Trailers for passenger automobiles, wholesale
- Trailers for passenger automobiles, wholesale and repair
- Trailers for trucks, new and used, wholesale
- Trailers for trucks, new and used, wholesale and repair
- Travel trailers (e.g., tent trailers), wholesale
- Travel trailers (e.g., tent trailers), wholesale and repair
- Vehicles, recreational and special purpose, wholesale

415190 Recreational and Other Motor Vehicles Wholesaler-Distributors ^{CAN}

See industry description for 41519, above.

4152 New Motor Vehicle Parts and Accessories Wholesaler-Distributors ^{CAN}

This industry group comprises establishments primarily engaged in wholesaling new and rebuilt motor vehicle parts and accessories.

41521 Tire Wholesaler-Distributors ^{CAN}

This industry comprises establishments primarily engaged in wholesaling tires and tubes for all vehicles.

Exclusion(s): Establishments primarily engaged in:
- rebuilding tires (32621, Tire Manufacturing).

Example Activities
- Automobile tires and tubes, wholesale
- Motor vehicle tires and tubes, wholesale
- Repair materials, tire and tube, wholesale
- Tires and tubes, wholesale
- Tires, used (except scrap), wholesale
- Truck tires and tubes, wholesale

415210 Tire Wholesaler-Distributors CAN

See industry description for 41521, above.

41529 Other New Motor Vehicle Parts and Accessories Wholesaler-Distributors CAN

This industry comprises establishments, not classified to any other industry, primarily engaged in wholesaling new and rebuilt automotive parts and accessories, auto body and upholsterers' supplies, and automotive chemicals.

Example Activities

- Auto body shop supplies, wholesale
- Automotive accessories, new, wholesale
- Automotive air-conditioners, new, wholesale
- Automotive chemicals, wholesale
- Automotive engines, new, wholesale
- Automotive parts, new, wholesale
- Batteries, automotive, new, wholesale
- Body compounds, automotive, wholesale
- Chemicals, automotive, wholesale
- Fuel additives, wholesale
- Glass, automobile, wholesale
- Motor vehicle parts and accessories, new, wholesale
- Motor vehicle sound systems, new, wholesale
- Oil additives, wholesale
- Radios and tape decks, motor vehicle, new, wholesale
- Refrigeration units, motor vehicle, sales and service
- Snowmobile engines, wholesale
- Sound systems, motor vehicle, new, wholesale
- Wheels, motor vehicle, new, wholesale

415290 Other New Motor Vehicle Parts and Accessories Wholesaler-Distributors CAN

See industry description for 41529, above.

4153 Used Motor Vehicle Parts and Accessories Wholesaler-Distributors CAN

See industry description for 41531, below.

41531 Used Motor Vehicle Parts and Accessories Wholesaler-Distributors CAN

This industry comprises establishments primarily engaged in dismantling automobiles and wholesaling used automotive parts and accessories. These establishments also typically sell dismantled automobiles to metal scrap dealers.

Exclusion(s): Establishments primarily engaged in:
- rebuilding automotive engines on a factory basis (33631, Motor Vehicle Gasoline Engine and Engine Parts Manufacturing);
- rebuilding transmissions on a factory basis (33635, Motor Vehicle Transmission and Power Train Parts Manufacturing);
- crushing automobiles for scrap metal recycling (41811, Recyclable Metal Wholesaler-Distributors); and
- repairing and replacing transmissions (81111, Automotive Mechanical and Electrical Repair and Maintenance).

Example Activities
- Automobile parts, used, wholesale
- Motor vehicle dismantling

415310 Used Motor Vehicle Parts and Accessories Wholesaler-Distributors CAN

See industry description for 41531, above.

416 Building Material and Supplies Wholesaler-Distributors CAN

This subsector comprises establishments primarily engaged in wholesaling electrical, plumbing, heating and air-conditioning equipment and supplies, metal and metal products, lumber, millwork, hardware and other building supplies.

4161 Electrical, Plumbing, Heating and Air-Conditioning Equipment and Supplies Wholesaler-Distributors CAN

This industry group comprises establishments primarily engaged in wholesaling electrical construction supplies, and plumbing, heating and air-conditioning equipment and supplies.

41611 Electrical Wiring and Construction Supplies Wholesaler-Distributors CAN

This industry comprises establishments primarily engaged in wholesaling electrical wiring supplies and electrical construction material. Wholesalers of electrical generation and transmission equipment, such as transformers, motors, generators and powerhouse equipment, are also included.

Example Activities

- Alarm signal systems, wholesale
- Bus bars and trolley ducts, wholesale
- Circuit breakers, wholesale
- Coaxial cable, wholesale
- Conduit electric wire and cable, wholesale
- Conduits and raceways, wholesale
- Construction materials, electrical, interior and exterior, wholesale
- Demand meters, wholesale
- Distribution transformers, wholesale
- Electric construction material, wholesale
- Electric lamps and lighting fixtures, parts and accessories, wholesale
- Electric transformers, wholesale
- Electrical construction materials, wholesale
- Electrical wiring supplies and electrical construction materials, wholesale
- Flashlights, wholesale
- Fuses and accessories, wholesale
- Generators, electrical, wholesale
- Insect control devices, electric, wholesale
- Insulated wire and cable, annunciator, building and power, wholesale
- Insulators, electrical, wholesale
- Lamps, floor, boudoir, desk, wholesale
- Light bulbs, electric, wholesale
- Lighting fixtures, residential, commercial and industrial, wholesale
- Measuring and testing equipment, electrical (except automotive), wholesale
- Panelboards, electrical distribution, wholesale
- Pole line hardware, wholesale
- Power house equipment, electrical, wholesale
- Power transmission equipment, electric, wholesale
- Receptacles, electrical, wholesale
- Relays, wholesale
- Signalling equipment, electrical, wholesale
- Street lighting equipment, wholesale
- Switchboards, electrical distribution, wholesale
- Switchgear and protective equipment, electrical, wholesale
- Testing and measuring equipment, electrical (except automotive), wholesale
- Transformers, electric, wholesale
- Voltage regulators (except motor vehicle), wholesale
- Wire, insulated, wholesale
- Wiring devices and related electrical supplies, wholesale

416110 Electrical Wiring and Construction Supplies Wholesaler-Distributors CAN

See industry description for 41611, above.

41612 Plumbing, Heating and Air-Conditioning Equipment and Supplies Wholesaler-Distributors CAN

This industry comprises establishments primarily engaged in wholesaling plumbing, heating and air-conditioning equipment and supplies.

Exclusion(s): Establishments primarily engaged in:
- wholesaling window-type air-conditioners (41422, Household Appliance Wholesaler-Distributors); and
- retailing plumbing fixtures and supplies (44419, Other Building Material Dealers).

Example Activities
- Air-conditioning equipment (except window type units), wholesale
- Baseboard heaters, electric, non-portable, wholesale
- Bath tubs and sinks, wholesale
- Boilers (e.g., heating, hot water, power, steam), wholesale
- Compressors, air-conditioning, wholesale
- Condensing units, air-conditioning, wholesale
- Drinking fountains, non-refrigerated, wholesale
- Dust collecting equipment, wholesale
- Electric furnaces, wholesale
- Exhaust and air-moving equipment, wholesale
- Fireplaces, metal, wholesale
- Fixtures, plumbing, wholesale
- Furnaces and heaters, wholesale
- Gas and oil heating equipment, wholesale
- Gas appliances and supplies, wholesale
- Heat pumps, wholesale
- Heating and cooking equipment, non-electric, wholesale
- Hot water heaters, oil and gas, wholesale
- Humidifiers and dehumidifiers (except portable), wholesale
- Laundry tubs, wholesale
- Oil and gas heating equipment, wholesale
- Plumbers' brass goods, fittings and valves, wholesale
- Plumbing and heating equipment and supplies, wholesale
- Plumbing supplies, wholesale
- Pumps, electrical (except industrial), wholesale
- Radiators, heating equipment, wholesale
- Ranges (except electric), wholesale
- Ranges, stoves and furnaces (except electric), wholesale
- Refrigerators, gas, domestic, wholesale
- Sanitary ware, wholesale
- Sauna equipment, wholesale
- Solar heating panels and equipment, wholesale
- Sprinkler systems, wholesale
- Steam fittings, heating equipment, wholesale
- Tanks and bowls, toilet, wholesale
- Valves and fittings, plumbers', wholesale
- Ventilating equipment and supplies, wholesale
- Warm air heating and cooling equipment, wholesale
- Water heaters, electric, wholesale
- Water meters, wholesale
- Water softeners, wholesale

416120 Plumbing, Heating and Air-Conditioning Equipment and Supplies Wholesaler-Distributors CAN

See industry description for 41612, above.

4162 Metal Service Centres CAN

See industry description for 41621, below.

41621 Metal Service Centres CAN

This industry comprises establishments primarily engaged in wholesaling metals and metal products. These establishments may also cut, bend or otherwise prepare metals to customer specification.

Exclusion(s): Establishments primarily engaged in:
- wholesaling electrical wire (41611, Electrical Wiring and Construction Supplies Wholesaler-Distributors); and
- wholesaling metal ores and concentrates (41892, Mineral, Ore and Precious Metal Wholesaler-Distributors).

Example Activities

- Aluminum and aluminum alloy, primary forms and basic shapes, wholesale
- Aluminum bars, rods, ingots, sheets, pipes, plates, wholesale
- Angles, rods and bars, steel, wholesale
- Anode metal, wholesale
- Architectural metal work, wholesale
- Bar joists, fabricated, wholesale
- Bars, rods and angles, steel, wholesale
- Blooms, billets, slabs and other semi-finished shapes, wholesale
- Cable and rope, wire, steel, wholesale
- Carbon and alloy steels, primary forms and structural shapes, wholesale
- Castings and forgings, iron and steel products, wholesale
- Concrete forms, steel, wholesale
- Concrete reinforcing bars, wholesale
- Copper and copper alloy, primary forms and basic shapes, wholesale
- Copper architectural and structural metal products, wholesale
- Copper sheets, plates, bars, rods, pipes, wholesale
- Ferroalloys, wholesale
- Forgings and castings, iron and steel products, wholesale
- Grinding balls, cast or forged, wholesale
- Ingots (except precious), wholesale
- Ingots, non-ferrous metals, wholesale
- Iron and steel in primary forms and shapes, wholesale
- Iron and steel wire, wholesale
- Iron and steel, rough cast, wholesale
- Lead and zinc fabricated basic products, wholesale
- Lead primary forms and basic shapes, wholesale
- Mercury, wholesale
- Nickel and nickel alloy, primary forms and basic shapes, wholesale
- Ornamental iron and steel products, wholesale
- Pig and other primary iron, wholesale
- Pipes and tubes, metal, wholesale
- Plate, sheet and strip, steel, wholesale
- Primary forms and basic shapes, non-ferrous metal, wholesale
- Rails and accessories, metal, wholesale
- Reinforcement mesh, wire, wholesale
- Reinforcing rods, steel, wholesale
- Rods, bars and angles, steel, wholesale
- Rope, wire (except insulated), wholesale
- Sheet piling, steel, wholesale
- Sheets, galvanized or other coated, wholesale
- Sheets, metal, wholesale
- Springs, general purpose, steel, wholesale
- Stainless steel fabricated products, wholesale
- Steel strapping, wholesale
- Steel tubing, wholesale
- Structural shapes and plates, wholesale
- Terneplate, wholesale
- Tin plate, wholesale
- Tubing, metal, wholesale
- Wire rods, wholesale
- Wire screening, wholesale

416210 Metal Service Centres CAN

See industry description for 41621, above.

4163 Lumber, Millwork, Hardware and Other Building Supplies Wholesaler-Distributors CAN

This industry group comprises establishments primarily engaged in wholesaling lumber and millwork, paint, glass, wallpaper, hardware and other building supplies.

Exclusion(s): Establishments primarily engaged in:
- wholesaling logs and wood chips (41891, Log and Wood Chip Wholesaler-Distributors).

41631 General-Line Building Supplies Wholesaler-Distributors CAN

This industry comprises establishments primarily engaged in wholesaling a broad range of building supplies, such as lumber, hardware, plumbing and electrical supplies, paint, glass and other construction supplies.

Exclusion(s): Establishments primarily engaged in:
- retailing a general line of home repair and improvement materials and supplies (44411, Home Centres).

Example Activities
- Combinations of lumber and building materials, wholesale
- Timber and building materials, combinations of, wholesale

416310 General-Line Building Supplies Wholesaler-Distributors CAN

See industry description for 41631, above.

41632 Lumber, Plywood and Millwork Wholesaler-Distributors CAN

This industry comprises establishments primarily engaged in wholesaling rough and dressed lumber, plywood, and other millwork products.

Exclusion(s): Establishments primarily engaged in:
- retailing lumber, plywood and millwork (44419, Other Building Material Dealers).

Example Activities
- Custom millwork and woodwork, wholesale
- Doors and windows, wooden, wholesale
- Fencing, wood, wholesale
- Flooring, wooden, wholesale
- Frames, door and window, wooden, wholesale
- Lumber and planing mill products, wholesale
- Lumber, rough or dressed, wholesale
- Millwork products, wholesale
- Moulding, wooden, wholesale
- Panels, plywood, overlaid or prefinished, wholesale
- Planing mill products, wholesale
- Plywood, wholesale
- Roofing materials, wood, wholesale
- Sash, door, planing mill products, wholesale
- Shaped or turned wood products, wholesale
- Shingles and shakes, wooden, wholesale
- Siding, wood, wholesale
- Stairs, wooden, wholesale
- Turned or shaped wood products, wholesale
- Veneer, wholesale
- Wallboard, wooden, wholesale
- Wood siding, wholesale

416320 Lumber, Plywood and Millwork Wholesaler-Distributors CAN

See industry description for 41632, above.

41633 Hardware Wholesaler-Distributors CAN

This industry comprises establishments primarily engaged in wholesaling hardware and tradesmen's tools.

Example Activities
- Appliance hardware, wholesale
- Auto mechanics' tools, wholesale
- Bolts, nuts, rivets, screws and other fasteners, wholesale
- Builders' hardware, wholesale
- Carpenters' tools, wholesale
- Chain, metal, wholesale
- Chainsaws, wholesale
- Fasteners, hardware, wholesale
- Furniture and cabinet hardware and fittings, wholesale
- Handtools (except automotive and machinists' precision), wholesale
- Hardware purchasing, packaging and selling to retailers
- Hardware, wholesale
- Hinges and butts, wholesale
- Ladders, wholesale
- Locks and related materials, wholesale

- Luggage and trunk fittings, wholesale
- Marine and rigging hardware, wholesale
- Nuts, bolts, rivets, screws and other fasteners, wholesale
- Plumbers' tools and equipment, wholesale
- Power handtools, wholesale
- Shelf hardware, wholesale
- Tinware, wholesale
- Tools, carpenters', mechanics', plumbers' and other trades, wholesale

416330 Hardware Wholesaler-Distributors CAN

See industry description for 41633, above.

41634 Paint, Glass and Wallpaper Wholesaler-Distributors CAN

This industry comprises establishments primarily engaged in wholesaling paints and varnishes, glass, wallpaper and building decorators' supplies.

Example Activities

- Colours and pigments, wholesale
- Decorative wall coverings, wholesale
- Flat glass, wholesale
- Glass, float and plate, wholesale
- Lacquers, wholesale
- Metallic paints, wholesale
- Paint materials and supplies, wholesale
- Paint, glass and wallpaper, wholesale
- Paints, wholesale
- Pigments and colours, wholesale
- Shellacs, wholesale
- Turpentine and resin, wholesale
- Varnishes, stains, lacquers and shellacs, wholesale
- Wall coverings (e.g., fabric, plastic), wholesale
- Wallpaper, wholesale

416340 Paint, Glass and Wallpaper Wholesaler-Distributors CAN

See industry description for 41634, above.

41639 Other Specialty-Line Building Supplies Wholesaler-Distributors CAN

This industry comprises establishments, not classified to any other industry, primarily engaged in wholesaling specialized lines of building supplies.

Exclusion(s): Establishments primarily engaged in:
- retailing specialty lines of building supplies (44419, Other Building Material Dealers).

Example Activities

- Aggregate, wholesale
- Air ducts, sheet metal, wholesale
- Asphalt roofing materials, wholesale
- Awnings (except canvas), wholesale
- Brick, tile, cement, wholesale
- Building stone, wholesale
- Caulking materials, wholesale
- Cement, brick, tile, wholesale
- Ceramic construction materials (except refractory), wholesale
- Ceramic wall and floor tile, wholesale
- Concrete and cinder block, wholesale
- Concrete building products, wholesale
- Concrete mixtures, wholesale
- Conduit and pipe, concrete, wholesale
- Cottages, prefabricated, wholesale
- Counter tops and kitchen cabinets, wholesale
- Crushed stone, wholesale
- Drywall and plaster supplies, wholesale
- Eavestroughing, wholesale
- Fence and accessories, wire, wholesale
- Fencing and accessories, wire, wholesale
- Fibreglass insulation materials, wholesale
- Gates and accessories, wire, wholesale
- Gravel, wholesale
- Insulation materials, wholesale
- Kitchen cabinets, built in, wholesale
- Limestone, wholesale
- Marble building stone, wholesale

- Masonry bricks, blocks, tile and stone, builders' supply, wholesale
- Masons' materials, wholesale
- Metal buildings, wholesale
- Metal siding and roofing materials, wholesale
- Mineral wool insulation materials, wholesale
- Paving mixtures, wholesale
- Plaster and drywall supplies, wholesale
- Prefabricated buildings, wholesale
- Prefabricated cottages, wholesale
- Prefabricated homes, wholesale
- Roofing materials, dealers (except wooden)
- Sand, gravel and cement, builders' supply, wholesale
- Septic tanks (except concrete), wholesale
- Sheet metal roofing materials, wholesale
- Shingles (except wood), wholesale
- Siding, metal, wholesale
- Slate and slate products, wholesale
- Sound proofing materials, wholesale
- Stone, building, wholesale
- Stone, crushed or broken, wholesale
- Structural assemblies, prefabricated, wood, wholesale
- Stucco, wholesale
- Tile, clay or other ceramic (except refractory), wholesale
- Trim, sheet metal, wholesale
- Windows and doors (except wooden), wholesale
- Wire fences, gates and accessories, wholesale

416390 Other Specialty-Line Building Supplies Wholesaler-Distributors CAN

See industry description for 41639, above.

417 Machinery, Equipment and Supplies Wholesaler-Distributors CAN

This subsector comprises establishments primarily engaged in wholesaling farm, lawn and garden machinery and equipment; construction, forestry, mining and industrial machinery, equipment and supplies; computers and communication equipment and supplies; and other machinery, equipment and supplies.

4171 Farm, Lawn and Garden Machinery and Equipment Wholesaler-Distributors CAN

See industry description for 41711, below.

41711 Farm, Lawn and Garden Machinery and Equipment Wholesaler-Distributors CAN

This industry comprises establishments primarily engaged in wholesaling new or used farm, lawn and garden machinery, equipment and parts.

Exclusion(s): Establishments primarily engaged in:
- retailing lawn and garden equipment (44421, Outdoor Power Equipment Stores);
- repairing farm machinery and equipment (81131, Commercial and Industrial Machinery and Equipment (except Automotive and Electronic) Repair and Maintenance); and
- repairing lawn and garden machinery and equipment (81141, Home and Garden Equipment and Appliance Repair and Maintenance).

Example Activities
- Agricultural implement, wholesale
- Agricultural implement, wholesale and repair
- Agricultural machinery and equipment, wholesale
- Agricultural machinery and equipment, wholesale and repair
- Auctioning farm machinery, from own facilities
- Barn machinery and equipment (including elevating), wholesale
- Barn machinery and equipment (including elevating), wholesale and repair
- Combines, wholesale
- Crop preparation machinery (e.g., cleaning, drying, conditioning), wholesale
- Cultivators, seeders, spreaders, farm, wholesale

- Dairy farm machinery and equipment, wholesale
- Farm machinery and equipment, wholesale
- Farm machinery and equipment, wholesale and repair
- Garden and lawn tractors, wholesale
- Garden and lawn tractors, wholesale and repair
- Harrows, ploughs and tillers, farm and garden, wholesale
- Harvesting machinery and equipment, wholesale
- Haying machinery, wholesale
- Irrigation equipment, wholesale
- Irrigation equipment, wholesale and repair

- Land preparation machinery, agricultural, wholesale
- Planting machinery and equipment, wholesale
- Ploughs, harrows and tillers, farm and garden, wholesale
- Ploughs, harrows and tillers, farm and garden, wholesale and repair
- Poultry equipment, wholesale
- Sprayers and dusters, farm, wholesale
- Tractors (farm), new or used, wholesale
- Tractors (farm), new or used, wholesale and repair
- Wind machines (frost protection equipment), wholesale
- Wind machines (frost protection equipment), wholesale and repair

417110 Farm, Lawn and Garden Machinery and Equipment Wholesaler-Distributors
CAN

See industry description for 41711, above.

4172 Construction, Forestry, Mining, and Industrial Machinery, Equipment and Supplies Wholesaler-Distributors CAN

This industry group comprises establishments primarily engaged in wholesaling construction, forestry, mining and industrial machinery, equipment and supplies.

41721 Construction and Forestry Machinery, Equipment and Supplies Wholesaler-Distributors CAN

This industry comprises establishments primarily engaged in wholesaling new and used construction and forestry machinery, equipment and parts.

Exclusion(s): Establishments primarily engaged in:
- repairing construction and forestry machinery and equipment (81131, Commercial and Industrial Machinery and Equipment (except Automotive and Electronic) Repair and Maintenance).

Example Activities
- Asphalt mixing and laying machinery, wholesale
- Asphalt mixing and laying machinery, wholesale and repair
- Concrete mixing plant machinery, wholesale
- Concrete mixing plant machinery, wholesale and repair
- Construction machinery and equipment, wholesale
- Construction machinery and equipment, wholesale and repair
- Cranes, construction, wholesale
- Crawler tractors, construction, wholesale
- Crawler tractors, construction, wholesale and repair

- Crushing, pulverizing and screening machinery for construction, wholesale
- Drainage and tile laying machinery, wholesale
- Dredges and draglines (except ships), wholesale
- Excavating machinery and equipment, wholesale
- Excavating machinery and equipment, wholesale and repair
- Forestry equipment, wholesale
- Forestry equipment, wholesale and repair
- Fork lift trucks for logs, wholesale
- Fork lift trucks for logs, wholesale and repair
- Front-end loaders, wholesale

- Front-end loaders, wholesale and repair
- Graders, wholesale
- Graders, wholesale and repair
- Logging machinery and equipment, wholesale
- Logging machinery and equipment, wholesale and repair
- Quarrying machinery and equipment, wholesale
- Road construction and maintenance machinery, wholesale
- Road construction and maintenance machinery, wholesale and repair

- Rock drilling machinery and equipment, wholesale
- Scaffolding, dismantable, wholesale
- Sweepers and snow removal equipment, wholesale
- Sweepers and snow removal equipment, wholesale and repair
- Tracklaying equipment, wholesale
- Tracklaying equipment, wholesale and repair
- Tractors, construction, wholesale
- Tractors, construction, wholesale and repair

417210 Construction and Forestry Machinery, Equipment and Supplies Wholesaler-Distributors CAN

See industry description for 41721, above.

41722 Mining and Oil and Gas Well Machinery, Equipment and Supplies Wholesaler-Distributors CAN

This industry comprises establishments primarily engaged in wholesaling new and used mining, oil and gas well equipment, and petroleum refinery machinery, equipment, supplies and parts.

Exclusion(s): Establishments primarily engaged in:
- wholesaling quarrying and rock drilling equipment (41721, Construction and Forestry Machinery, Equipment and Supplies Wholesaler-Distributors); and
- repairing mining and oil and gas well machinery and equipment (81131, Commercial and Industrial Machinery and Equipment (except Automotive and Electronic) Repair and Maintenance).

Example Activities
- Agitators, crushers and classifiers, mine, wholesale
- Agitators, crushers and classifiers, mine, wholesale and repair
- Ball, rod and pebble mill machinery, wholesale
- Floating roof seals for oil and gas storage tanks, wholesale
- Floating roof seals for oil and gas storage tanks, wholesale and repair
- Flotation machinery, ore dressing, wholesale
- Mineral beneficiation machinery, wholesale
- Mineral beneficiation machinery, wholesale and repair
- Mining machinery, wholesale
- Mining machinery, wholesale and repair
- Natural gas field production equipment, wholesale

- Oil refining machinery and equipment, wholesale
- Oil refining machinery and equipment, wholesale and repair
- Oil well machinery and equipment, wholesale
- Oil well machinery and equipment, wholesale and repair
- Oil well supply houses, wholesale
- Ore dressing machinery, wholesale
- Ore dressing machinery, wholesale and repair
- Petroleum production machinery and equipment, wholesale
- Petroleum production machinery and equipment, wholesale and repair
- Vibrating and screening equipment, mine, wholesale

417220 Mining and Oil and Gas Well Machinery, Equipment and Supplies Wholesaler-Distributors CAN

See industry description for 41722, above.

41723 Industrial Machinery, Equipment and Supplies Wholesaler-Distributors ^{CAN}

This industry comprises establishments primarily engaged in wholesaling new and used industrial machinery.

Exclusion(s): Establishments primarily engaged in:
- wholesaling electric generators and transmission equipment (41611, Electrical Wiring and Construction Supplies Wholesaler-Distributors); and
- repairing industrial machinery, equipment and supplies (81131, Commercial and Industrial Machinery and Equipment (except Automotive and Electronic) Repair and Maintenance).

Example Activities
- Abrasives, wholesale
- Bakery machinery, equipment and supplies, wholesale
- Bakery machinery, equipment and supplies, wholesale and repair
- Batteries, storage, industrial, wholesale
- Bearings, wholesale
- Belting, hose and packing, industrial, wholesale
- Boilers, power (industrial), wholesale
- Bort, wholesale
- Bottles, glass or plastic, wholesale
- Cans for fruits and vegetables, wholesale
- Cement making machinery, wholesale
- Chemical industries machinery, equipment and supplies, wholesale
- Chemical industries machinery, equipment and supplies, wholesale and repair
- Citrus processing machinery, wholesale
- Compressors and vacuum pumps, wholesale
- Compressors and vacuum pumps, wholesale and repair
- Controlling instruments and accessories, wholesale
- Controlling instruments and accessories, wholesale and repair
- Conveyor systems, wholesale
- Cranes, industrial, wholesale
- Crowns and closures, metal, wholesale
- Crushing machinery and equipment, industrial, wholesale
- Derricks, wholesale
- Diamonds, industrial, natural and crude, wholesale
- Drums, new and reconditioned, wholesale
- Elevating machinery and equipment (except farm), wholesale
- Elevating machinery and equipment (except farm), wholesale and repair
- Elevators, wholesale
- Fans, industrial, wholesale
- Food product manufacturing machinery, wholesale
- Foundry machinery and equipment, wholesale
- Gaskets, wholesale
- Heat exchange equipment, industrial, wholesale
- Heat exchange equipment, industrial, wholesale and repair
- Hoisting machinery and equipment, wholesale (except construction and forestry)
- Hose, belting and packing, industrial, wholesale
- Indicating instruments and accessories, wholesale
- Industrial equipment, wholesale
- Industrial furnaces, kilns and ovens, wholesale and repair
- Industrial machinery, equipment and supplies, wholesale
- Industrial machinery, equipment and supplies, wholesale and repair
- Industrial sewing thread, wholesale
- Ink, printer's, wholesale
- Jigs, wholesale
- Lapidary equipment, wholesale
- Lift trucks, wholesale
- Machine tools and accessories, wholesale
- Machinery and equipment, industrial (except farm and electrical), wholesale
- Manufacturing industry machinery and equipment, wholesale
- Manufacturing industry machinery and equipment, wholesale and repair
- Materials handling equipment, wholesale and repair
- Mechanical and power transmission equipment, wholesale
- Mechanical and power transmission equipment, wholesale and repair
- Metalworking machinery, wholesale

- Milk products manufacturing machinery and equipment, wholesale
- Packing machinery and equipment, wholesale
- Packing machinery and equipment, wholesale and repair
- Paint spray equipment, industrial, wholesale
- Paper manufacturing machinery, wholesale
- Pistons and valves, industrial, wholesale
- Plastic and rubber industries machinery, equipment and supplies, wholesale
- Power house equipment (except electrical), wholesale
- Power house equipment (except electrical), wholesale and repair
- Power plant machinery, wholesale
- Power plant machinery, wholesale and repair
- Power transmission equipment, mechanical, wholesale
- Precision tools, machinists', wholesale
- Printing and lithographing industries machinery, wholesale
- Printing and lithographing industries machinery, wholesale and repair
- Printing trades machinery and equipment, wholesale
- Pulp and paper industry machinery, wholesale
- Pulverizing machinery and equipment, industrial, wholesale
- Pumps and pumping equipment, wholesale
- Recapping machinery, for tires, wholesale
- Rubber and plastic industries machinery, equipment and supplies, wholesale

- Sawmill and woodworking machinery, equipment and supplies, wholesale
- Screening machinery and equipment, industrial, wholesale
- Seals, gaskets and packing, wholesale
- Sewing machines, industrial, wholesale
- Sewing machines, industrial, wholesale and repair
- Smelting machinery and equipment, wholesale
- Stackers, industrial, wholesale
- Textile machinery and equipment, wholesale
- Threading tools, wholesale
- Tools, machinists' precision, wholesale
- Tractors, industrial, wholesale
- Tractors, industrial, wholesale and repair
- Trailers, industrial, wholesale
- Transportation equipment industries, machinery, equipment and supplies, wholesale
- Vacuum pumps and compressors, wholesale
- Valves and fittings (except plumbers'), wholesale
- Warehouse trucks and supplies, wholesale
- Warehouse trucks and supplies, wholesale and repair
- Welding electrodes and wire, wholesale
- Welding machinery and equipment, wholesale
- Welding machinery and equipment, wholesale and repair
- Woodworking and sawmill, machinery, equipment and supplies, wholesale

417230 Industrial Machinery, Equipment and Supplies Wholesaler-Distributors CAN

See industry description for 41723, above.

4173 Computer and Communications Equipment and Supplies Wholesaler-Distributors CAN

See industry description for 41731, below.

41731 Computer, Computer Peripheral and Pre-Packaged Software Wholesaler-Distributors CAN

This industry comprises establishments primarily engaged in wholesaling new and used computers, computer peripherals and pre-packaged computer software.

Exclusion(s): Establishments primarily engaged in:
- retailing new computers, computer peripherals, pre-packaged software, game software and related products (44312, Computer and Software Stores);
- designing, developing and publishing, or publishing only, computer software products (51121, Software Publishers); and
- repairing computers (81121, Electronic and Precision Equipment Repair and Maintenance).

Example Activities
- Computer software, packaged, wholesale
- Computer terminals, wholesale
- Computers and peripheral equipment, wholesale
- Computers and peripheral equipment, wholesale and repair
- Disk drives, wholesale
- Electronic controllers, modems and related devices, wholesale
- Home computers, wholesale
- Home computers, wholesale and repair
- Peripheral equipment, computer, wholesale

417310 Computer, Computer Peripheral and Pre-Packaged Software Wholesaler-Distributors CAN

See industry description for 41731, above.

41732 Electronic Components, Navigational and Communications Equipment and Supplies Wholesaler-Distributors CAN

This industry comprises establishments primarily engaged in wholesaling new and used electronic components, navigational and communications equipment and supplies. Establishments primarily engaged in wholesaling telephones, intercoms, pagers and public address systems are included.

Exclusion(s): Establishments primarily engaged in:
- wholesaling computer and related equipment (41731, Computer, Computer Peripheral and Pre-Packaged Software Wholesaler-Distributors).

Example Activities
- Alarm and signal systems and devices, electronic (except household smoke detectors), wholesale
- Alarm and signal systems and devices, electronic (except household smoke detectors), wholesale and repair
- Amateur radio communications equipment, wholesale
- Capacitors, electronic, wholesale
- Cathode ray picture tubes, wholesale
- Cellular telephone, wholesale
- Citizens' band radios, wholesale
- Citizens' band radios, wholesale and repair
- Communication equipment, electronic, wholesale
- Communication equipment, electronic, wholesale and repair
- Condensers, electronic, wholesale
- Connectors, electronic, wholesale
- Diodes, wholesale
- Electronic aircraft instruments, wholesale
- Electronic aircraft instruments, wholesale and repair
- Electronic coils and transformers, wholesale
- Electronic communications equipment, wholesale
- Electronic navigational equipment and devices, wholesale
- Electronic navigational equipment and devices, wholesale and repair
- Electronic tubes (e.g., receiving, transmitting, industrial), wholesale
- Intercommunication equipment, electronic, wholesale
- Modems, wholesale
- Navigational equipment and devices, electronic, wholesale
- Navigational equipment and devices, electronic, wholesale and repair
- Public address equipment, wholesale
- Radar equipment, wholesale
- Radio communications equipment, wholesale

- Radio communications equipment, wholesale and repair
- Radio receiving and transmitting tubes, wholesale
- Rectifiers, electronic, wholesale
- Replacement parts, electronic, wholesale
- Resistors, electronic, wholesale
- Semiconductor devices, wholesale
- Signal systems and alarm devices, electronic (except household smoke detection), wholesale

- Sonar equipment, wholesale
- Sonar equipment, wholesale and repair
- Telephone equipment and apparatus, wholesale
- Telephone equipment and apparatus, wholesale and repair
- Transistors, wholesale
- Transmitters, wholesale
- Tubes, electronic (e.g., receiving, transmitting, industrial), wholesale

417320 Electronic Components, Navigational and Communications Equipment and Supplies Wholesaler-Distributors CAN

See industry description for 41732, above.

4179 Other Machinery, Equipment and Supplies Wholesaler-Distributors CAN

This industry group comprises establishments primarily engaged in wholesaling office, store, service industry, professional and other machinery, equipment and supplies.

41791 Office and Store Machinery and Equipment Wholesaler-Distributors CAN

This industry comprises establishments primarily engaged in wholesaling new and used office and store machinery and equipment furniture and fixtures

Exclusion(s): Establishments primarily engaged in:
- wholesaling computers and other data processing machines (41731, Computer, Computer Peripheral and Pre-Packaged Software Wholesaler-Distributors);
- wholesaling stationery and office supplies (41821, Stationery and Office Supplies Wholesaler-Distributors); and
- retailing new office furniture (44211, Furniture Stores).

Example Activities
- Business machines, wholesale
- Business machines, wholesale and repair
- Commercial cooling and refrigeration equipment and supplies, wholesale
- Commercial cooling and refrigeration equipment and supplies, wholesale and repair
- Coolers, beverage and drinking water, mechanical, wholesale
- Coolers, beverage and drinking water, mechanical, wholesale and repair
- Desk calculators (including electric and electronic), wholesale
- Dictating machines, wholesale
- Display cases and fixtures, for office and store, wholesale
- Display cases and fixtures, for office and store, wholesale and repair
- Drinking fountains, refrigerated, wholesale
- Duplicating machines, wholesale

- Facsimile machinery, sales and service, wholesale
- Fixtures, refrigerated, wholesale
- Furniture and fixtures, office and store, wholesale
- Furniture and fixtures, office and store, wholesale and repair
- Ice making machines, wholesale
- Ice making machines, wholesale and repair
- Machines, commercial (except electronic computers), wholesale
- Machines, office, wholesale
- Mail handling machines, wholesale
- Mail handling machines, wholesale and repair
- Mannequins, wholesale
- Microfilm equipment and supplies, wholesale
- Office furniture, wholesale
- Office furniture, wholesale and repair

- Office machines and equipment (except electronic data processing equipment), wholesale
- Office machines and equipment (except electronic data processing equipment), wholesale and repair
- Partitions, wholesale
- Photocopy machines, wholesale
- Photocopy machines, wholesale and repair
- Refrigeration and cooling equipment and supplies, commercial, wholesale

- Scales, wholesale
- Shelving, office and store, wholesale
- Show cases, refrigerated, wholesale
- Soda fountain fixtures, refrigerated, wholesale
- Store equipment (except furniture), wholesale
- Typewriters, wholesale
- Vaults and safes, wholesale
- Vaults and safes, wholesale and repair

417910 Office and Store Machinery and Equipment Wholesaler-Distributors CAN

See industry description for 41791, above.

41792 Service Establishment Machinery, Equipment and Supplies Wholesaler-Distributors CAN

This industry comprises establishments primarily engaged in wholesaling new and used service establishment machinery and equipment.

Exclusion(s): Establishments primarily engaged in:
- wholesaling domestic washing machines and dryers (41422, Household Appliance Wholesaler-Distributors); and
- wholesaling supplies such as soaps and detergents (41841, Chemical (except Agricultural) and Allied Product Wholesaler-Distributors).

Example Activities
- Bar furniture, wholesale
- Barber shop equipment and supplies, wholesale
- Beauty parlour equipment and supplies, wholesale
- Beauty parlour equipment and supplies, wholesale and repair
- Boot and shoe cut stock and findings, wholesale
- Cafeteria furniture, wholesale
- Carwash equipment and supplies, wholesale
- Caskets, burial, wholesale
- Coin-operated game machines, wholesale
- Concrete burial vaults and boxes, wholesale
- Cooking equipment, commercial, wholesale
- Cutlery, commercial and industrial, wholesale
- Dishwashing equipment, commercial, wholesale
- Drycleaning plant equipment and supplies, wholesale
- Drycleaning plant equipment and supplies, wholesale and repair
- Food warming equipment, commercial, wholesale
- Food warming equipment, commercial, wholesale and repair
- Funeral equipment and morticians' goods, wholesale
- Game machines, coin-operated, wholesale
- Hotel and restaurant equipment and supplies, wholesale
- Hotel and restaurant equipment and supplies, wholesale and repair
- Janitorial machinery and equipment, wholesale
- Janitors' supplies, wholesale
- Kitchen utensils, commercial, wholesale
- Laundry machinery and equipment, wholesale
- Laundry machinery and equipment, wholesale and repair
- Locksmith equipment and supplies, wholesale
- Merchandising machines, automatic, wholesale
- Merchandising machines, automatic, wholesale and repair
- Morticians' goods, wholesale
- Motion picture studio and theatre equipment, wholesale

- Motion picture studio and theatre equipment, wholesale and repair
- Neon signs, wholesale
- Phonographs, coin-operated, wholesale
- Restaurant and hotel equipment, wholesale
- Restaurant and hotel equipment, wholesale and repair
- Service industries machinery and equipment, wholesale
- Shoe repair equipment and supplies, wholesale
- Signs, electrical, wholesale
- Soda fountain fixtures (except refrigerated), wholesale
- Soles, shoe, wholesale

- Tailors' supplies, wholesale
- Theatre equipment and supplies (including projection equipment), wholesale
- Theatre equipment and supplies (including projection equipment), wholesale and repair
- Theatre projection equipment, wholesale
- Theatre seats, wholesale
- Upholsterers' equipment and supplies, wholesale
- Upholstery filling and padding, wholesale
- Vending machines, wholesale
- Vending machines, wholesale and repair
- Water softening equipment, commercial, wholesale
- Water sterilization equipment, wholesale

417920 Service Establishment Machinery, Equipment and Supplies Wholesaler-Distributors CAN

See industry description for 41792, above.

41793 Professional Machinery, Equipment and Supplies Wholesaler-Distributors CAN

This industry comprises establishments primarily engaged in wholesaling new and used professional machinery and equipment.

Exclusion(s): Establishments primarily engaged in:
- wholesaling school textbooks (41442, Book, Periodical and Newspaper Wholesaler-Distributors);
- wholesaling pharmaceuticals and pharmacy supplies (41451, Pharmaceuticals and Pharmacy Supplies Wholesaler-Distributors); and
- wholesaling school stationery (41821, Stationery and Office Supplies Wholesaler-Distributors).

Example Activities
- Analytical instruments (e.g., photometers, spectrographs, chromatographic), wholesale
- Architects' equipment and supplies, wholesale
- Architects' equipment and supplies, wholesale and repair
- Artificial limbs, wholesale
- Artist equipment and supplies, wholesale
- Artist equipment and supplies, wholesale and repair
- Barometers, wholesale
- Beds, hospital, wholesale
- Binoculars, wholesale
- Ceramic equipment, greenware and supplies, wholesale
- Church pews, wholesale
- Contact lenses, wholesale
- Dental equipment and supplies, wholesale
- Dental equipment and supplies, wholesale and repair
- Desks (including school), wholesale

- Diagnostic equipment, medical, wholesale
- Drafting instruments, wholesale
- Electromedical equipment, wholesale
- Engineering instruments, equipment and supplies, wholesale
- Engineering instruments, equipment and supplies, wholesale and repair
- Eyeglasses, wholesale
- Frames, ophthalmic, wholesale
- Gas detecting equipment and supplies, wholesale
- Hearing aids, wholesale
- Hospital equipment and supplies, wholesale
- Hospital equipment and supplies, wholesale and repair
- Industrial safety devices (e.g., first-aid kits, face and eye masks), wholesale
- Instruments, professional, wholesale
- Laboratory instruments and apparatus, wholesale

- Laboratory instruments and apparatus, wholesale and repair
- Measuring and measuring-controlling instruments, professional, wholesale
- Medical, surgical, hospital equipment, wholesale
- Optical goods (except cameras), wholesale
- Optical goods (except cameras), wholesale and repair
- Optometric equipment and supplies, wholesale
- Orthopaedic equipment and supplies, wholesale
- Ostomy supplies, wholesale
- Patient monitoring equipment, wholesale
- Physicians' equipment and supplies, wholesale
- Physicians' equipment and supplies, wholesale and repair
- Professional machinery, equipment and supplies, wholesale

- Professional machinery, equipment and supplies, wholesale and repair
- School classroom equipment and supplies (except stationery), wholesale
- School classroom equipment and supplies (except stationery), wholesale and repair
- Scientific instruments and apparatus, wholesale
- Scientific instruments and apparatus, wholesale and repair
- Surgical and medical instruments, wholesale
- Teaching machines (except computers), electronic, wholesale
- Therapeutic beds, wholesale
- Therapy equipment, wholesale
- Thermometers, wholesale
- Timing instruments, wholesale
- Veterinarians' equipment and supplies, wholesale
- X-ray machines and related equipment and supplies, wholesale

417930 Professional Machinery, Equipment and Supplies Wholesaler-Distributors CAN

See industry description for 41793, above.

41799 All Other Machinery, Equipment and Supplies Wholesaler-Distributors CAN

This industry comprises establishments, not classified to any other industry, primarily engaged in wholesaling new and used machinery, equipment and supplies; or a combination of goods classified to other industries in this industry group, with none predominating. Wholesalers of aircraft and non-electronic aircraft equipment, fishing and pleasure boats, playground and amusement park equipment, engines (except motor vehicle), and locomotives are included.

Exclusion(s): Establishments primarily engaged in:
- wholesaling motor vehicles and parts (415, Motor Vehicle and Parts Wholesaler-Distributors).

Example Activities
- Aircraft and aeronautical equipment (except electronic), wholesale and repair
- Aircraft and parts, wholesale
- Aircraft engines and engine parts, wholesale
- Aircraft instruments, electric, wholesale
- Aircraft, wholesale
- Aircraft, wholesale and repair
- Amusement park equipment, wholesale
- Amusement park equipment, wholesale and repair
- Automobile engine testing equipment, electrical, wholesale
- Automobile service station equipment, wholesale
- Boats, pleasure (e.g., canoes, motorboats, sailboats), wholesale

- Boats, pleasure (e.g., canoes, motorboats, sailboats), wholesale and repair
- Carnival equipment, wholesale
- Diesel engines and engine parts, industrial, wholesale
- Diesel engines and engine parts, industrial, wholesale and repair
- Engine testing equipment, automobile, electrical, wholesale
- Engines (except motor vehicle), wholesale
- Engines and turbines, marine, wholesale
- Equipment parts for railroads, aircraft, ships and boats, wholesale
- Equipment parts for railroads, aircraft, ships and boats, wholesale and repair
- Filling station equipment, wholesale

- Fire-fighting equipment, wholesale
- Fire-fighting equipment, wholesale and repair
- Garage equipment, wholesale
- Garage equipment, wholesale and repair
- Golf carts, self-propelled, wholesale
- Locomotives, wholesale
- Machinery, equipment and parts for railroad locomotives, aircraft, ships and boats, wholesale
- Marine propulsion machinery and equipment, wholesale
- Motorboats, wholesale
- Outboard motors, wholesale
- Outboard motors, wholesale and repair
- Playground equipment, wholesale
- Pumps, measuring and dispensing, gasoline and oil, wholesale
- Railroad equipment and supplies, wholesale
- Railroad equipment and supplies, wholesale and repair
- Railroad locomotive machinery and equipment parts, wholesale
- Sailboat, wholesale
- Service station equipment and supplies, wholesale
- Service station equipment and supplies, wholesale and repair
- Ships, wholesale
- Ships, wholesale and repair
- Tanks and tank components, wholesale
- Transportation equipment and supplies (except motor vehicles), wholesale
- Transportation equipment and supplies (except motor vehicles), wholesale and repair
- Yacht sales, wholesale

417990 All Other Machinery, Equipment and Supplies Wholesaler-Distributors CAN

See industry description for 41799, above.

418 Miscellaneous Wholesaler-Distributors CAN

This subsector comprises establishments, not classified to any other subsector, primarily engaged in wholesaling merchandise, such as recyclable materials, paper, paper products and disposable plastic products, agricultural supplies, chemicals and allied products, logs and wood chips, minerals, ores and precious metals, and second-hand goods (except machinery and automotive).

Exclusion(s): Establishments primarily engaged in:
- wholesaling used automotive parts and accessories (415, Motor Vehicle and Parts Wholesaler-Distributors); and
- wholesaling used machinery (417, Machinery, Equipment and Supplies Wholesaler-Distributors).

4181 Recyclable Material Wholesaler-Distributors CAN

This industry group comprises establishments primarily engaged in wholesaling recyclable metals, paper and paperboard, and other recyclable materials.

Exclusion(s): Establishments primarily engaged in:
- operating facilities in which recyclable materials are removed from waste, or mixed recyclable materials are sorted into distinct categories and prepared for shipment (56292, Material Recovery Facilities).

41811 Recyclable Metal Wholesaler-Distributors CAN

This industry comprises establishments primarily engaged in buying, breaking up, sorting and selling ferrous and non-ferrous scrap metal, including automobiles for scrap.

Example Activities
- Automotive wrecking for scrap, wholesale
- Dismantling machinery for scrap
- Dismantling ships
- Iron and steel scrap, wholesale
- Marine wrecking, ships for scrap
- Metal waste and scrap, wholesale
- Non-ferrous metals scrap, wholesale
- Wreckers, auto, wholesale

418110 Recyclable Metal Wholesaler-Distributors ^{CAN}

See industry description for 41811, above.

41812 Recyclable Paper and Paperboard Wholesaler-Distributors ^{CAN}

This industry comprises establishments primarily engaged in buying, breaking up, sorting and selling used newspaper, paperboard and other papers.

Example Activities
- Baling and grading waste paper
- Grading and baling waste paper, wholesale
- Recyclable paper, wholesale
- Recyclable paperboard, wholesale

418120 Recyclable Paper and Paperboard Wholesaler-Distributors ^{CAN}

See industry description for 41812, above.

41819 Other Recyclable Material Wholesaler-Distributors ^{CAN}

This industry comprises establishments, not classified to any other industry, primarily engaged in buying, breaking up, sorting, grinding, shredding and selling recyclable materials, such as plastic, glass, textiles, liquids and sludges.

Exclusion(s): Establishments primarily engaged in:
- manufacturing intermediate or finished products from recycled materials (31-33, Manufacturing); and
- compounding plastics resins from recycled plastic products (32599, All Other Chemical Product Manufacturing).

Example Activities
- Bottles, waste, wholesale
- Glass scrap, wholesale
- Grinding into flakes used plastic milk jugs and similar plastic containers
- Liquid waste recovery (collection only)
- Oil, waste, wholesale
- Rags, paper, rubber and bottles (scrap), wholesale
- Recycling empty bottles
- Rubber waste, wholesale
- Shredding rubber tires for rubber and metal content
- Textile waste, wholesale
- Waste oil collection
- Waste rags, wholesale

418190 Other Recyclable Material Wholesaler-Distributors ^{CAN}

See industry description for 41819, above.

4182 Paper, Paper Product and Disposable Plastic Product Wholesaler-Distributors ^{CAN}

This industry group comprises establishments primarily engaged in wholesaling newsprint, stationery and office supplies, other paper and paper products, and disposable plastic products.

Exclusion(s): Establishments primarily engaged in:
- buying, breaking up, sorting and selling recycled newspaper, paperboard and other papers (41812, Recyclable Paper and Paperboard Wholesaler-Distributors).

41821 Stationery and Office Supplies Wholesaler-Distributors CAN

This industry comprises establishments primarily engaged in wholesaling stationery and office supplies.

Exclusion(s): Establishments primarily engaged in:
- wholesaling office furniture (41791, Office and Store Machinery and Equipment Wholesaler-Distributors); and
- wholesaling school classroom equipment and supplies (41793, Professional Machinery, Equipment and Supplies Wholesaler-Distributors).

Example Activities
- Albums (photo) and scrapbooks, wholesale
- Blankbooks, wholesale
- Business forms, wholesale
- Carbon paper, wholesale
- Commercial stationers (not printers), wholesale
- Desk accessories, office supply, wholesale
- Envelopes, paper, wholesale
- File folders, tabs and accessories, wholesale
- Greeting cards, wholesale
- Ink, paste and solvent, office supply, wholesale
- Inked ribbons, wholesale
- Looseleaf binders, wholesale
- Manifold business forms, wholesale
- Marking devices, pens and pencils, wholesale
- Office supplies (except furniture, machines), wholesale
- Pressure sensitive tape, wholesale
- School supplies (except furniture and fixtures), wholesale
- Stationery and stationery supplies, wholesale

418210 Stationery and Office Supplies Wholesaler-Distributors CAN

See industry description for 41821, above.

41822 Other Paper and Disposable Plastic Product Wholesaler-Distributors CAN

This industry comprises establishments primarily engaged in wholesaling paper and disposable household products, such as facial tissues and toilet paper, waxed paper, paper towels and napkins, plastic wrap, disposable cups, plates, cutlery, food trays and containers of plastic and other paper and disposable plastic products; or a combination of products classified to other industries in this industry group, with none predominating.

Example Activities
- Bags, paper and disposable plastics, wholesale
- Bags, paper and plastic, wholesale
- Boxes, paperboard and disposable plastics, wholesale
- Closures, paper and disposable plastics, wholesale
- Containers, paper and disposable plastics, wholesale
- Corrugated and solid fibre boxes, wholesale
- Cups, paper and disposable plastics, wholesale
- Dishes, paper and disposable plastics, wholesale
- Eating utensils, forks, knives, spoons - disposable plastics, wholesale
- Facial tissue paper, wholesale
- Fibre cans and drums, wholesale
- Fine papers (except stationery), wholesale
- Foam plastic food trays, wholesale
- Folding paperboard boxes, wholesale
- Gummed kraft paper, wholesale
- Moulded pulp products, wholesale
- Newsprint, wholesale
- Paper cups, dishes, napkins, towels and patterns, wholesale
- Paperboard and products (except office supplies), wholesale
- Patterns, paper, wholesale
- Pressed and moulded pulp goods, wholesale
- Printing paper, wholesale
- Sanitary paper products, wholesale
- Shipping supplies, paper and disposable plastics (e.g., cartons, gummed tapes), wholesale
- Tissue paper, toilet and facial, wholesale

418220 Other Paper and Disposable Plastic Product Wholesaler-Distributors ^{CAN}

See industry description for 41822, above.

4183 Agricultural Supplies Wholesaler-Distributors ^{CAN}

This industry group comprises establishments primarily engaged in wholesaling agricultural feeds, seeds and processed seeds, agricultural chemicals and other farm supplies.

41831 Agricultural Feed Wholesaler-Distributors ^{CAN}

This industry comprises establishments primarily engaged in wholesaling animal feed. Wholesalers of pet food are also included.

Exclusion(s): Establishments primarily engaged in:
- wholesaling grain for human consumption (41112, Oilseed and Grain Wholesaler-Distributors); and
- wholesaling seed grain (41832, Seed Wholesaler-Distributors).

Example Activities
- Alfalfa, wholesale
- Dog and cat food, wholesale
- Feed additives, animal, wholesale
- Feed grains, wholesale
- Feeds, animal, wholesale
- Hay and fodder, wholesale
- Livestock feeds, prepared, wholesale
- Pet food, wholesale
- Poultry feeds, prepared, wholesale
- Vegetable cake and meal, wholesale

418310 Agricultural Feed Wholesaler-Distributors ^{CAN}

See industry description for 41831, above.

41832 Seed Wholesaler-Distributors ^{CAN}

This industry comprises establishments primarily engaged in wholesaling seeds for field crops, flowers and plants, garden seeds and grass seeds.

Exclusion(s): Establishments primarily engaged in:
- cleaning grain or seeds for the grower (11511, Support Activities for Crop Production).

Example Activities
- Bulbs, flower and field, wholesale
- Field crop seeds, wholesale
- Flower and field bulbs, wholesale
- Flower seeds, bulk and packaged, wholesale
- Seeds (e.g., field, garden, flower), wholesale
- Seeds, farm and garden, wholesale
- Vegetable seeds, bulk and packaged, wholesale

418320 Seed Wholesaler-Distributors ^{CAN}

See industry description for 41832, above.

41839 Agricultural Chemical and Other Farm Supplies Wholesaler-Distributors ^{CAN}

This industry comprises establishments, not classified to any other industry, primarily engaged in wholesaling agricultural chemicals, such as fertilizers, herbicides, pesticides and farm supplies; or a combination of goods classified to other industries in this industry group, with none predominating.

Example Activities

- Agricultural chemical dusts and sprays, wholesale
- Agricultural limestone, wholesale
- Beekeeping supplies, wholesale
- Chemical fertilizers, wholesale
- Disinfectants, agricultural, wholesale
- Fertilizer and fertilizer materials, wholesale
- Fly and animal sprays, wholesale
- Fumigants, wholesale

- Fungicides, wholesale
- Herbicides, wholesale
- Insecticides, wholesale
- Lawn care chemical products, wholesale
- Orchard care chemicals, wholesale
- Pesticides, agricultural, wholesale
- Rodenticides, wholesale
- Sterilizing compounds and disinfectants, agricultural, wholesale

418390 Agricultural Chemical and Other Farm Supplies Wholesaler-Distributors ^{CAN}

See industry description for 41839, above.

4184 Chemical (except Agricultural) and Allied Product Wholesaler-Distributors ^{CAN}

See industry description for 41841, below.

41841 Chemical (except Agricultural) and Allied Product Wholesaler-Distributors ^{CAN}

This industry comprises establishments primarily engaged in wholesaling industrial and household chemicals, cleaning compounds and preparations, plastics resins, plastic basic forms and shapes, and industrial gases.

Exclusion(s): Establishments primarily engaged in:
- wholesaling refined petroleum products (41211, Petroleum Product Wholesaler-Distributors);
- wholesaling fireworks (41446, Toy and Hobby Goods Wholesaler-Distributors);
- wholesaling ammunition (41447, Amusement and Sporting Goods Wholesaler-Distributors);
- wholesaling agricultural chemicals (41839, Agricultural Chemical and Other Farm Supplies Wholesaler-Distributors); and
- retailing heating oil, liquefied petroleum (LP) gas and other fuels via direct selling (45431, Fuel Dealers).

Example Activities

- Alcohol, industrial, wholesale
- Alkalies, wholesale
- Ammonia (except fertilizer material), wholesale
- Bleaches, wholesale
- Bleaching compounds, wholesale
- Carbon black, wholesale
- Caustic soda, wholesale
- Chemicals, industrial and household, wholesale
- Chlorine, wholesale
- Cleaning compounds and preparations, wholesale
- Cleansers, soaps, detergents, wholesale
- Coal tar products, primary and intermediate, wholesale
- Compound catalysts, industrial, wholesale
- Compressed and liquefied gases (except petroleum gases), wholesale
- Concrete additives, wholesale

- Deodorants (except personal), wholesale
- Detergents, wholesale
- Detonators and fuses, wholesale
- Disinfectants, wholesale
- Dry cleaning solvents and chemicals, wholesale
- Dry ice, wholesale
- Dyestuffs, wholesale
- Essential oils, wholesale
- Explosives, all kinds (except ammunition and fireworks), wholesale
- Fire extinguisher preparations, wholesale
- Floor cleaning compounds, wholesale
- Gases, compressed and liquefied (except liquefied petroleum gas), wholesale
- Glue, wholesale
- Gum and wood chemicals, wholesale
- Industrial chemicals, wholesale
- Industrial gases, wholesale
- Laundry soap, chips and powder, wholesale

- Linseed oil, wholesale
- Man-made fibres, wholesale
- Metal working compounds, wholesale
- Organic chemicals, synthetic, wholesale
- Plasticizers and stabilizers, wholesale
- Plastics basic shapes, wholesale
- Plastics materials, wholesale
- Plastics resins, wholesale
- Plastics sheet and rods, wholesale
- Polishes (e.g., furniture, automobile, metal, shoe), wholesale
- Polishing preparations, wholesale
- Resins, plastics, wholesale
- Resins, synthetic (except rubber), wholesale

- Rug cleaning compounds, wholesale
- Rustproofing chemicals, wholesale
- Salts, industrial, wholesale
- Sanitation preparations, wholesale
- Scouring cleansers, wholesale
- Sealants, wholesale
- Stabilizers and plasticizers, wholesale
- Sulphur, wholesale
- Sulphuric acid, wholesale
- Surface active agents, wholesale
- Synthetic rubber, wholesale
- Textile chemicals, wholesale
- Waxes, wholesale
- Wood treating preparations, wholesale

418410 Chemical (except Agricultural) and Allied Product Wholesaler-Distributors CAN

See industry description for 41841, above.

4189 Other Miscellaneous Wholesaler-Distributors CAN

This industry group comprises establishments, not classified to any other industry group, primarily engaged in wholesaling logs, wood chips, minerals, ores and concentrates, precious metals, second-hand goods and other products.

41891 Log and Wood Chip Wholesaler-Distributors CAN

This industry comprises establishments primarily engaged in wholesaling logs and bolts, wood chips and other unprocessed forest products.

Exclusion(s): Establishments primarily engaged in:
- wholesaling fuel wood (41899, All Other Wholesaler-Distributors).

Example Activities
- Bolts and logs, wholesale
- Logs and bolts, wholesale
- Poles and pilings, wooden, untreated, wholesale
- Posts, logs, hewn ties and poles, wholesale

- Pulpwood, wholesale
- Roundwood, wholesale
- Timber products, rough, wholesale
- Wood chips, wholesale

418910 Log and Wood Chip Wholesaler-Distributors CAN

See industry description for 41891, above.

41892 Mineral, Ore and Precious Metal Wholesaler-Distributors CAN

This industry comprises establishments primarily engaged in wholesaling minerals, ores and concentrates, and precious metals.

Example Activities
- Ferrous ores and concentrates, wholesale
- Gold ore, wholesale
- Metal concentrates and ores (ferrous), wholesale
- Non-ferrous ores and concentrates, wholesale

- Precious metals and alloys, primary forms and basic shapes, wholesale
- Silver ore, wholesale
- Zinc ore, wholesale

418920 Mineral, Ore and Precious Metal Wholesaler-Distributors ^{CAN}

See industry description for 41892, above.

41893 Second-Hand Goods (except Machinery and Automotive) Wholesaler-Distributors ^{CAN}

This industry comprises establishments primarily engaged in wholesaling second-hand goods.

Exclusion(s): Establishments primarily engaged in:
- wholesaling used motor vehicles (4151, Motor Vehicle Wholesaler-Distributors); and
- wholesaling used machinery (417, Machinery, Equipment and Supplies Wholesaler-Distributors).

Example Activities
- Book, second-hand, wholesale
- Clothing and furnishings, second hand, wholesale
- Furniture and fixtures, second hand, wholesale
- Second hand goods (except machinery and motor vehicles), wholesale

418930 Second-Hand Goods (except Machinery and Automotive) Wholesaler-Distributors ^{CAN}

See industry description for 41893, above.

41899 All Other Wholesaler-Distributors ^{CAN}

This industry comprises establishments, not classified to any other industry, primarily engaged in wholesaling a single line of products; and establishments primarily engaged in wholesaling a diversified line of merchandise, where no line is sufficiently important to constitute a primary activity.

Example Activities
- Artificial flowers, wholesale
- Baskets, reed, rattan, willow and wood, wholesale
- Brooms, brushes and mops, wholesale
- Brushes, industrial, wholesale
- Charcoal, wholesale
- Church supplies (except silverware and plated ware), wholesale
- Coal and coke dealers, wholesale
- Cordwood, wholesale
- Cork, wholesale
- Curios, wholesale
- Fish oil, wholesale
- Flowers, artificial, wholesale
- Foam rubber, wholesale
- Fuel, coal and coke, wholesale
- Fuelwood, wholesale
- Gas lighting fixtures, wholesale
- Gifts and novelties, wholesale
- Glassware, novelty, wholesale
- Greases, animal and vegetable, wholesale
- Ice, manufactured or natural, wholesale
- Leather and cut stock, wholesale
- Leather goods (except footwear), wholesale
- Lighters, cigar and cigarette, wholesale
- Luggage, wholesale
- Mobile homes, wholesale
- Monuments and grave markers, wholesale
- Musical instruments, accessories and supplies, wholesale
- Novelties, wholesale
- Oils and greases, animal or vegetable, wholesale
- Outfitter (ship chandler)
- Pet supplies (except pet food), wholesale
- Plastics foam, wholesale
- Portrait, wholesale
- Religious supplies, wholesale
- Rope, binder twine and string, wholesale
- Saddlery, wholesale
- Sawdust, wholesale
- Sheet music, wholesale
- Ship chandlers, wholesale
- Smokers' supplies, wholesale
- Sponges, wholesale
- Stamps, for collectors, wholesale
- Statuary, wholesale
- Taxidermy supplies, wholesale

- Tombstones, wholesale
- Top soil or potting soil, wholesale
- Wholesalers of coal and coke

- Wigs and hairpieces, wholesale
- Wood pulp, wholesale

418990 All Other Wholesaler-Distributors CAN

See industry description for 41899, above.

419 Wholesale Electronic Markets, and Agents and Brokers US

This subsector comprises establishments primarily engaged in buying and/or selling products, owned by others, and generally receiving a fee or a commission for the service. These establishments may be known as business-to-business electronic markets, commission merchants, import agents or brokers, export agents or brokers, manufacturers' agents, purchasing agents, selling agents, and they may deal in any type of product. These establishments bring together sellers and buyers or undertake commercial transactions on behalf of a principal, without taking title of the goods bought or sold.

Exclusion(s): Establishments primarily engaged in:
- bringing together buyers and sellers of goods using the Internet in a business-to-consumer or consumer-to-consumer environment (45411, Electronic Shopping and Mail-Order Houses);
- operating as shipping agents (48851, Freight Transportation Arrangement);
- trading commodities and commodity futures, which are usually listed on a commodity exchange (5231, Securities and Commodity Contracts Intermediation and Brokerage);
- buying and selling insurance, on a commission basis (52421, Insurance Agencies and Brokerages);
- buying and selling real estate, on a commission basis (53121, Offices of Real Estate Agents and Brokers); and
- buying and selling goods on own account using a combination of electronic and traditional methods (classified according to the merchandise line or lines sold by the merchant wholesaler-distributor).

4191 Wholesale Electronic Markets, and Agents and Brokers US

See industry description for 419, above.

41911 Business-to-Business Electronic Markets US

This industry comprises business-to-business wholesale electronic markets bringing together buyers and sellers of goods using the Internet or other electronic means and generally receiving a commission or fee for the service. Business-to-business wholesale electronic markets facilitate wholesale transactions without taking title of the goods bought or sold. Establishments primarily engaged in facilitating business-to-business sales of new and used merchandise on an auction basis using the Internet are also included.

Exclusion(s): Establishments primarily engaged in:
- bringing together buyers and sellers of goods using the Internet in a business-to-consumer or consumer-to-consumer environment (45411, Electronic Shopping and Mail-Order Houses); and
- acting as merchant wholesalers and bringing together buyers and sellers of goods using the Internet or a combination of electronic and traditional methods (classified according to the merchandise line or lines sold by the merchant wholesaler-distributor).

Example Activities
- B2B electronic auctions
- B2B wholesale electronic markets
- Business-to-business electronic markets, wholesale trade
- Computers and peripheral equipment, business to business (B2B) electronic markets, wholesale

- Floor coverings, carpets, rugs and other, business to business (B2B) electronic markets, wholesale
- Groceries, general line, business to business (B2B) electronic markets, wholesale
- Household appliance, business to business (B2B) electronic markets, wholesale

- Household china and glassware, business to business (B2B) electronic markets, wholesale
- Linen, drapery and other textile furnishings, business to business (B2B) electronic markets, wholesale
- Nursery stock and plant, business to business (B2B) electronic markets, wholesale
- Petroleum product, business to business (B2B) electronic markets, wholesale

- Poultry and egg, business to business (B2B) electronic markets, wholesale
- Red meat and meat product, fresh, business to business (B2B) electronic markets, wholesale
- Wine and spirits, business to business (B2B) electronic markets, wholesale

419110 Business-to-Business Electronic Markets US

See industry description for 41911, above.

41912 Wholesale Trade Agents and Brokers US

This industry comprises establishments primarily engaged in buying and/or selling products, owned by others, on a commission basis. These establishments may be known as commission merchants, import agents or brokers, export agents or brokers, manufacturers' agents, purchasing agents, selling agents, and they may deal in any type of product. These establishments usually bring sellers and buyers together or undertake commercial transactions on behalf of a principal, without taking title of the goods bought or sold.

Exclusion(s): Establishments primarily engaged in:
- acting as agents and brokers and wholesaling products, owned by others, using the Internet or other electronic means (41911, Business-to-Business Electronic Markets);
- shipping agents (48851, Freight Transportation Arrangement);
- trading commodities and commodity futures, which are usually listed on a commodity exchange (5231, Securities and Commodity Contracts Intermediation and Brokerage);
- buying and selling insurance, on a commission basis (52421, Insurance Agencies and Brokerages);
- buying and selling real estate for others, on a fee or commission basis (53121, Offices of Real Estate Agents and Brokers); and
- wholesaling merchandise on own account, merchant wholesaler-distributors (classified according to the merchandise line or lines sold by the merchant wholesaler-distributor).

Example Activities
- Agents and brokers, wholesale trade
- Agricultural supplies, wholesale agents and brokers
- Alcoholic beverages, wholesale agents and brokers
- Amusement and sporting goods, wholesale agents and brokers
- Apparel, wholesale agents and brokers
- Automobiles, wholesale agents and brokers
- Book, periodical and newspaper, wholesale agents and brokers
- Chemicals (except agricultural), wholesale agents and brokers
- China, glassware, crockery and pottery, wholesale agents and brokers
- Coal brokers, wholesale
- Commission agency, general, wholesale
- Commission salesman, representing several products of companies

- Computer and related machinery and equipment, wholesale agents and brokers
- Confectionery, wholesale agents and brokers
- Construction and forestry machinery and equipment, wholesale agents and brokers
- Dairy products, wholesale agents and brokers
- Drugs, wholesale agents and brokers
- Dry goods, wholesale agents and brokers
- Electrical wiring supplies and electrical construction materials, wholesale agents and brokers
- Farm machinery and equipment, wholesale agents and brokers
- Ferrous and non-ferrous metal ores and concentrates, combined, wholesale agents and brokers
- Ferrous and non-ferrous metals, combination, wholesale agents and brokers

- Fish and seafood, wholesale agents and brokers
- Floor coverings, wholesale agents and brokers
- Food, wholesale agents and brokers
- Footwear, wholesale agents and brokers
- Fresh fruits and vegetables, wholesale agents and brokers
- Frozen packaged food, wholesale agents and brokers
- General line building material, wholesale agents and brokers
- General line of food, wholesale agents and brokers
- General line of merchandise, wholesale agents and brokers
- Grain, wholesale agents and brokers
- Hardware, wholesale agents and brokers
- Home electronics, wholesale agents and brokers
- Household appliances and home electronics, wholesale agents and brokers
- Household furnishings, wholesale agents and brokers
- Household furniture, wholesale agents and brokers
- Import-export agents and brokers, wholesale trade
- Industrial machinery and equipment, wholesale agents and brokers
- Iron and steel primary forms and structural shapes, agents and brokers
- Jewellery and watch, wholesale agents and brokers
- Linens, draperies and other textile furnishings, wholesale agents and brokers
- Livestock, wholesale agents and brokers
- Logs and wood chips, wholesale agents and brokers
- Lumber, plywood and millwork, wholesale agents and brokers
- Meat and meat products, wholesale agents and brokers
- Men's clothing, wholesale agents and brokers
- Metal and metal products (except ores), wholesale agents and brokers

- Mining machinery and equipment, wholesale agents and brokers
- Motor vehicles (except automobiles, trucks and buses), wholesale agents and brokers
- New and rebuilt auto parts, wholesale agents and brokers
- Newsprint, wholesale agents and brokers
- Non-alcoholic beverages, wholesale agents and brokers
- Office and store machinery and equipment, wholesale agents and brokers
- Paint, glass and wallpaper, wholesale agents and brokers
- Paper and paper products, wholesale agents and brokers
- Photographic equipment and supplies, wholesale agents and brokers
- Plumbing, heating and air-conditioning equipment, wholesale agents and brokers
- Poultry and eggs, wholesale agents and brokers
- Produce brokers, wholesale
- Professional machinery and equipment, wholesale agents and brokers
- Purchasing agents, wholesale trade
- Recycled materials (except auto parts), wholesale agents and brokers
- Second-hand goods (except machinery and auto parts), wholesale agents and brokers
- Seeds, wholesale agents and brokers
- Service machinery and equipment, wholesale agents and brokers
- Stationery and office supplies, wholesale agents and brokers
- Timber brokers, wholesale
- Tires, wholesale agents and brokers
- Tobacco products, wholesale agents and brokers
- Toys and hobby goods, wholesale agents and brokers
- Trailers, wholesale agents and brokers
- Trucks and buses, wholesale agents and brokers
- Used (recycled) auto parts, wholesale agents and brokers
- Wheat brokers, wholesale
- Women's and children outerwear, wholesale agents and brokers

419120 Wholesale Trade Agents and Brokers US

See industry description for 41912, above.

44-45 Retail Trade

The retail trade sector comprises establishments primarily engaged in retailing merchandise, generally without transformation, and rendering services incidental to the sale of merchandise.

The retailing process is the final step in the distribution of merchandise; retailers are therefore organized to sell merchandise in small quantities to the general public. This sector comprises two main types of retailers, that is, store and non-store retailers. Their main characteristics are described below.

Store Retailers

Store retailers operate fixed point-of-sale locations, located and designed to attract a high volume of walk-in customers. In general, retail stores have extensive displays of merchandise and use mass-media advertising to attract customers. They typically sell merchandise to the general public for personal or household consumption, but some also serve business and institutional clients. These include establishments such as office supplies stores, computer and software stores, gasoline stations, building material dealers, plumbing supplies stores and electrical supplies stores.

In addition to selling merchandise, some types of store retailers are also engaged in the provision of after-sales services, such as repair and installation. For example, new automobile dealers, electronic and appliance stores and musical instrument and supplies stores often provide repair services, while floor covering stores and window treatment stores often provide installation services. As a general rule, establishments engaged in retailing merchandise and providing after sales services are classified in this sector.

Catalogue sales showrooms, gasoline service stations, and mobile home dealers are treated as store retailers.

Non-Store Retailers

Non-store retailers, like store retailers, are organized to serve the general public, but their retailing methods differ. The establishments of this subsector reach customers and market merchandise with methods such as the broadcasting of infomercials, the broadcasting and publishing of direct-response advertising, the publishing of traditional and electronic catalogues, door-to-door solicitation, in-home demonstration, temporary displaying of merchandise (stalls) and distribution by vending machines.

The methods of transaction and delivery of merchandise vary by type of non-store retailers. For example, non-store retailers that reach their customers using information technologies can receive payment at the time of purchase or at the time of delivery, and the delivery of the merchandise may be done by the retailer or by a third party, such as the post office or a courier. In contrast, non-store retailers that reach their customers by door-to-door solicitation, in-home demonstration, temporary displaying of merchandise (stalls) and vending machines typically receive payment and deliver the merchandise to the customer at the time of the purchase.

The non-store retailers subsector also includes establishments engaged in the home delivery of products. This includes home heating oil dealers and newspaper delivery companies.

441 Motor Vehicle and Parts Dealers US

This subsector comprises establishments primarily engaged in retailing motor vehicles and providing complementary services, and retailing motor vehicle parts and accessories. The establishments of this subsector are generally specialized in the retailing of particular types of vehicles or in the retailing of particular types of parts and accessories.

> *Exclusion(s): Establishments primarily engaged in:*
> - heavy-duty truck sales (41, Wholesale Trade).

4411 Automobile Dealers ^{US}

This industry group comprises establishments primarily engaged in retailing new and used automobiles, sport utility vehicles, and light-duty trucks and vans, including mini-vans.

Exclusion(s): Establishments primarily engaged in:
- RV, watercraft, motorcycle and snowmobile retailing (4412, Other Motor Vehicle Dealers).

44111 New Car Dealers ^{US}

This industry comprises establishments primarily engaged in retailing new automobiles, sport utility vehicles, and light-duty trucks and vans, including mini-vans, to final consumers or to automobile lessors. These establishments also typically retail used cars, replacement parts and accessories, and provide repair services.

Exclusion(s): Establishments primarily engaged in:
- used car retailing (44112, Used Car Dealers); and
- providing automotive repair services, without retailing motor vehicles (8111, Automotive Repair and Maintenance).

Example Activities
- Automobiles, new, retail
- Dealers in automobiles, new, retail

441110 New Car Dealers ^{US}

See industry description for 44111, above.

44112 Used Car Dealers ^{US}

This industry comprises establishments primarily engaged in retailing used automobiles, sport utility vehicles, and light-duty trucks and vans, including mini-vans.

Exclusion(s): Establishments primarily engaged in:
- retailing new and used automobiles, sport utility vehicles, and light-duty trucks and vans, including mini-vans (44111, New Car Dealers); and
- providing automotive repair services, without retailing motor vehicles (8111, Automotive Repair and Maintenance).

Example Activities
- Antique autos, retail
- Automobiles, used, retail
- Dealers in automobiles, used, retail
- Motor vehicle dealers, used, retail
- Used automobiles, retail

441120 Used Car Dealers ^{US}

See industry description for 44112, above.

4412 Other Motor Vehicle Dealers ^{US}

This industry group comprises establishments primarily engaged in retailing new and used vehicles, except automobiles, sport utility vehicles, and light-duty trucks and vans, including mini-vans. Establishments engaged in the retailing of motor homes, recreational trailers, campers, motorcycles, recreational watercraft, snowmobiles, off-road all-terrain vehicles, utility trailers and aircraft are included.

44121 Recreational Vehicle Dealers ^{US}

This industry comprises establishments primarily engaged in retailing new and used RVs, such as motor homes, recreational trailers and campers. These establishments also typically retail replacement parts and accessories, and provide repair services.

Exclusion(s): Establishments primarily engaged in:
- retailing utility trailers (44122, Motorcycle, Boat and Other Motor Vehicle Dealers); and
- retailing new and used manufactured (mobile) homes (45393, Mobile Home Dealers).

Example Activities
- Motor home dealers, retail
- Parts for recreational vehicles, retail
- Recreational vehicle dealers, retail
- Travel trailers, retail

441210 Recreational Vehicle Dealers US

See industry description for 44121, above.

44122 Motorcycle, Boat and Other Motor Vehicle Dealers US

This industry comprises establishments primarily engaged in retailing new and used motorcycles, watercraft and other vehicles, such as snowmobiles, off-road all-terrain vehicles, utility trailers, and aircraft. These establishments also typically retail replacement parts and accessories, and provide repair services.

Example Activities
- Aircraft dealers, retail
- All terrain vehicles (ATV's), retail
- Boat dealers, retail
- Golf carts, powered, retail
- Marine supply dealers, retail
- Motor bicycles, retail
- Motorcycle dealers, retail
- Outboard motor dealers, retail
- Snowmobiles, retail
- Utility trailers, retail
- Watercraft, retail

441220 Motorcycle, Boat and Other Motor Vehicle Dealers CAN

See industry description for 44122, above.

4413 Automotive Parts, Accessories and Tire Stores US

This industry group comprises establishments primarily engaged in retailing automotive parts and accessories.

44131 Automotive Parts and Accessories Stores US

This industry comprises establishments primarily engaged in retailing new, rebuilt and used automotive parts and accessories; both retailing automotive parts and accessories and repairing automobiles; and retailing automotive accessories that generally require installation.

Exclusion(s): Establishments primarily engaged in:
- selling used auto parts from a non-retail location, commonly known as automobile recyclers (41531, Used Motor Vehicle Parts and Accessories Wholesaler-Distributors);
- tire retailing (44132, Tire Dealers); and
- repairing and replacing automotive parts, such as transmissions, mufflers, brake linings and glass (81111, Automotive Mechanical and Electrical Repair and Maintenance).

Example Activities
- Air-conditioning equipment, automobile, sale and installation, retail
- Automobile accessory dealers, retail
- Automotive accessories and parts, second-hand, retail store
- Automotive parts and accessories stores selling primarily to other businesses but open to the public
- Battery dealers, automobile, retail
- Sound systems, motor vehicle, retail
- Speed shops, retail
- Used automotive parts, retail

441310 Automotive Parts and Accessories Stores US

See industry description for 44131, above.

44132 Tire Dealers US

This industry comprises establishments primarily engaged in retailing tires and tubes. These establishments also typically provide complementary services, such as tire mounting and wheel balancing and aligning.

Example Activities
- Retailing and repairing tires
- Tire stores selling primarily to other businesses but also selling to household consumers
- Tires (new or used), retail

441320 Tire Dealers US

See industry description for 44132, above.

442 Furniture and Home Furnishings Stores US

This subsector comprises establishments primarily engaged in retailing new furniture and home furnishings. These establishments usually operate from showrooms and many offer interior decorating services in addition to the sale of products.

Exclusion(s): Establishments primarily engaged in:
- used furniture and home furnishings retailing (45331, Used Merchandise Stores); and
- retailing furniture and home furnishings by means of electronic shopping, mail-order or direct sale (454, Non-Store Retailers).

4421 Furniture Stores US

See industry description for 44211, below.

44211 Furniture Stores US

This industry comprises establishments primarily engaged in retailing new household and office furniture. These establishments may also retail major appliances, home electronics, home furnishings and floor coverings, and may provide interior decorating services.

Exclusion(s): Establishments primarily engaged in:
- retailing custom furniture made on the premises (337, Furniture and Related Product Manufacturing);
- retailing office furniture, office equipment and supplies (45321, Office Supplies and Stationery Stores); and
- retailing used household furniture (45331, Used Merchandise Stores).

Example Activities
- Appliances and furniture, household, retail (primarily furniture)
- Household furniture and appliances, retail (primarily furniture)
- Household furniture stores
- Mattress stores (including custom made), retail
- Office furniture store selling primarily to other businesses but also selling to household consumers
- Outdoor furniture, household, retail
- Waterbeds-retail

442110 Furniture Stores US

See industry description for 44211, above.

4422 Home Furnishings Stores US

This industry group comprises establishments primarily engaged in retailing home furnishings, such as floor coverings, window treatments, kitchen and tableware, bedding and linens, lamps and shades, bathroom accessories, and pictures and picture frames.

44221 Floor Covering Stores US

This industry comprises establishments primarily engaged in retailing new floor coverings, such as rugs and carpets, vinyl floor coverings, wood floor coverings, and floor tiles, except ceramic. These establishments also typically provide installation and repair services.

Exclusion(s): Establishments primarily engaged in:
- installing, but not retailing, floor coverings (23833, Flooring Contractors, or 23834, Tile and Terrazzo Contractors); and
- retailing ceramic tiles only or hardwood flooring only (44419, Other Building Material Dealers).

Example Activities
- Asphalt flooring, installation combined with selling
- Carpet stores, retail
- Floor covering store selling primarily to other businesses but also selling to household consumers
- Floor tile and sheets, installation combined with selling
- Floor tile stores, retail (except ceramic tiles only and hardwood flooring only)
- Hardwood flooring, installation combined with selling
- Linoleum, installation combined with selling
- Resilient floor tiles or sheets (e.g., linoleum, rubber, vinyl), installation combined with selling
- Rug stores, retail
- Wood flooring, installation combined with selling

442210 Floor Covering Stores US

See industry description for 44221, above.

44229 Other Home Furnishings Stores US

This industry comprises establishments, not classified to any other industry, primarily engaged in retailing new home furnishings, such as window treatments, kitchen and tableware, bedding and linens, brooms and brushes, lamps and shades, and prints and picture frames.

Exclusion(s): Establishments primarily engaged in:
- new furniture retailing (44211, Furniture Stores);
- retailing floor coverings (44221, Floor Covering Stores); and
- providing interior decorating services, but not retailing home furnishings (54141, Interior Design Services).

442291 Window Treatment Stores US

This Canadian industry comprises establishments primarily engaged in retailing ready-made and custom draperies, blinds and shades.

Example Activities
- Curtains and draperies, household, new, retail
- Drapery stores, retail
- Venetian blind shops, retail
- Vertical blinds, retail

442292 Print and Picture Frame Stores CAN

This Canadian industry comprises establishments primarily engaged in retailing posters, prints and ready-made frames, and in custom framing, mounting and laminating. These establishments may also retail a limited number of original works of art.

Exclusion(s): Establishments primarily engaged in:
- retailing original and limited edition art works, including native art and art carvings (453920, Art Dealers).

Example Activities
- Custom framing, mounting, and laminating pictures, retail store
- Custom picture frame, retail store
- Picture frames, retail
- Posters and prints, retail

442298 All Other Home Furnishings Stores CAN

This Canadian industry comprises establishments, not classified to any other Canadian industry, primarily engaged in retailing new home furnishings.

Example Activities
- Bath boutique
- Bedding (sheets, blankets, spreads and pillows), retail
- China and glassware stores
- Cutlery stores, retail
- Enamelware stores, retail
- Fireplace accessories, retail
- Fireplace stores, retail
- Glassware stores, retail
- Home furnishing stores
- Housewares stores, retail
- Kitchenware stores, retail
- Lamps and lighting fixtures, electric, retail
- Linen shops, retail
- Mirrors, retail
- Pottery stores, retail
- Table and floor lamps, retail
- Woodburning stoves, retail

443 Electronics and Appliance Stores US

This subsector comprises establishments primarily engaged in retailing household appliances, home audio and video equipment, cameras, computers and related goods. These establishments may also retail replacement parts and provide repair services.

Exclusion(s): Establishments primarily engaged in:
- retailing used household appliances, home audio and video equipment, cameras, computers and related goods (45331, Used Merchandise Stores); and
- retailing household appliances, home audio and video equipment, cameras, computers and related goods by means of electronic shopping, mail-order or direct sale (454, Non-Store Retailers).

4431 Electronics and Appliance Stores US

This industry group comprises establishments primarily engaged in retailing household appliances, home audio and video equipment, cameras, computers and related goods. These establishments may also retail replacement parts and provide repair services.

44311 Appliance, Television and Other Electronics Stores ^{US}

This industry comprises establishments primarily engaged in retailing new household appliances, home audio and video equipment, and other electronic products. These establishments may also retail used electronics and appliances, provide repair services, and retail computers and computer software.

Exclusion(s): Establishments primarily engaged in:
- computer, computer peripheral equipment and software retailing (44312, Computer and Software Stores);
- electronic toy retailing (45112, Hobby, Toy and Game Stores);
- retailing used household appliances (45331, Used Merchandise Stores); and
- repairing, without retailing, televisions or other electronic products (81121, Electronic and Precision Equipment Repair and Maintenance).

Example Activities
- Air-conditioning room units, self-contained, retail
- Antenna stores, household, retail
- Appliance, radio, television and stereo stores, retail
- Built-in vacuum systems, retail
- Cellular plans and/or phone stores (authorized agents)
- Consumer electronic equipment stores, retail
- Electric household appliances, retail
- Electric razor shops, retail
- Freezers, household, retail
- Garbage disposers, electric, retail
- Gas household appliance stores, retail
- Hair driers, household, retail
- Home security equipment, retail
- Household appliance stores, electric or gas, retail
- Kitchens, complete (sinks, cabinets), retail
- Personal care appliance store
- Ranges, gas and electric, retail
- Refrigerators and related electric and gas appliances, retail
- Satellite ground station receivers, retail
- Sewing machine stores, retail
- Smoke detectors, retail
- Stereo equipment, retail
- Telephone stores, retail
- Television, radio and stereo stores
- Television, radio, stereo and appliances stores
- Two-way radios, home or auto, retail
- Vacuum cleaner stores, retail
- Video camera stores, retail
- Video recorders, retail

443110 Appliance, Television and Other Electronics Stores ^{CAN}

See industry description for 44311, above.

44312 Computer and Software Stores ^{US}

This industry comprises establishments primarily engaged in retailing new computers, computer peripherals, pre-packaged software, game software and related products. These establishments may also retail used computer equipment and replacement parts and accessories, and provide repair services.

Exclusion(s): Establishments primarily engaged in:
- retailing electronic toys, such as television (TV) games and hand-held games (45112, Hobby, Toy and Game Stores); and
- repairing, without retailing, computers (81121, Electronic and Precision Equipment Repair and Maintenance).

Example Activities
- Computer equipment and supplies sales, retail
- Computer hardware and software, retail
- Computer software games stores
- Computer software stores, retail
- Peripheral equipment, computer stores, retail
- Personal computers sales and service

443120 Computer and Software Stores US

See industry description for 44312, above.

44313 Camera and Photographic Supplies Stores US

This industry comprises establishments primarily engaged in retailing new cameras, photographic equipment and photographic supplies. These establishments may also retail used cameras and photographic equipment, and replacement parts and accessories, and provide repair and film developing services.

Exclusion(s): Establishments primarily engaged in:
- video camera retailing (44311, Appliance, Television and Other Electronics Stores);
- repairing, without retailing, photographic equipment (81121, Electronic and Precision Equipment Repair and Maintenance); and
- commercially developing film and photographic prints; one-hour film developing (81292, Photo Finishing Services).

Example Activities
- Camera shops, photographic, retail
- Film and photographic supplies, retail
- Photographic camera parts and accessories, retail
- Photographic equipment, retail
- Photographic film and plates (unexposed), retail
- Photographic supply stores, retail

443130 Camera and Photographic Supplies Stores US

See industry description for 44313, above.

444 Building Material and Garden Equipment and Supplies Dealers US

This subsector comprises establishments primarily engaged in retailing a specialized or general line of building and home improvement materials, lawn and garden equipment and supplies, outdoor power equipment, and nursery and garden products.

Exclusion(s): Establishments primarily engaged in:
- retailing used building and home improvement materials, and lawn, garden and outdoor power equipment (45331, Used Merchandise Stores); and
- retailing building and home improvement materials, and lawn, garden and outdoor power equipment by means of electronic shopping, mail-order or direct sale (454, Non-Store Retailers).

4441 Building Material and Supplies Dealers US

This industry group comprises establishments primarily engaged in retailing building materials, hardware, paint, wallpaper and related supplies.

44411 Home Centres US

This industry comprises establishments primarily engaged in retailing a general line of home repair and improvement materials and supplies, such as lumber, doors and windows, plumbing goods, electrical goods, floor coverings, tools, housewares, hardware, paint and wallpaper, and lawn and garden equipment and supplies. The merchandise lines are normally arranged in separate sections. These establishments may provide installation and repair services for the merchandise they retail.

Example Activity
- Home centre (building supplies)

444110 Home Centres US

See industry description for 44411, above.

44412 Paint and Wallpaper Stores US

This industry comprises establishments primarily engaged in retailing paint, wallpaper and related supplies.

Example Activities
- Paint and paint supply stores, retail
- Paint and wallpaper store selling primarily to businesses but also selling to household consumers
- Wallcovering stores, retail

444120 Paint and Wallpaper Stores US

See industry description for 44412, above.

44413 Hardware Stores US

This industry comprises establishments, known as hardware stores, primarily engaged in retailing a general line of basic hardware items, such as tools and builders' hardware. These establishments may sell additional product lines, such as paint, housewares and garden supplies, that are not normally arranged in separate departments.

Example Activities
- Builders' hardware, retail
- Carpenters' tools, retail
- Door locks and lock sets, retail
- Furniture and cabinet fittings, retail
- Handtools, retail
- Hardware stores, retail
- Power driven hand tools, retail

444130 Hardware Stores US

See industry description for 44413, above.

44419 Other Building Material Dealers US

This industry comprises establishments primarily engaged in retailing specialized lines of building materials. These establishments may provide installation services in addition to retailing.

Exclusion(s): Establishments primarily engaged in:
- retailing a general line of home repair and improvement materials and supplies (44411, Home Centres);
- paint and wallpaper retailing (44412, Paint and Wallpaper Stores); and
- retailing a general line of hardware items (44413, Hardware Stores).

Example Activities
- Aluminum doors and screens, retail
- Brick and tile dealers, retail
- Cabinets, kitchen (to be installed), retail
- Concrete and cinder block dealers, retail
- Electrical supplies stores selling primarily to other business but also selling to household consumers
- Electrical supplies, retail
- Fencing dealers, retail
- Garage doors, retail (wood)
- Glass stores, retail
- Lumber and planing mill product dealers, retail
- Plumbing supplies stores selling primarily to other businesses but also selling to household consumers

- Plumbing supplies, retail
- Prefabricated house and building dealers, retail
- Retailers of ceramic floor and wall tiles

- Roofing material dealers, retail
- Sales of aluminum doors and installation
- Tile and brick dealers, retail

444190 Other Building Material Dealers US

See industry description for 44419, above.

4442 Lawn and Garden Equipment and Supplies Stores US

This industry group comprises establishments primarily engaged in retailing lawn and garden equipment and supplies.

44421 Outdoor Power Equipment Stores US

This industry comprises establishments primarily engaged in retailing outdoor power equipment. These establishments also retail replacement parts and may provide repair services.

Exclusion(s): Establishments primarily engaged in:
- repairing, without retailing, outdoor power equipment (81141, Home and Garden Equipment and Appliance Repair and Maintenance).

Example Activities
- Garden and lawn tractor stores selling primarily to other businesses but open to the general public
- Garden and lawn tractor stores, retail

- Generators, electric, portable, retail
- Hedge trimmers, power, retail
- Lawn blower/vacuum, retail
- Snowblowers and lawn-mowers, retail

444210 Outdoor Power Equipment Stores US

See industry description for 44421, above.

44422 Nursery Stores and Garden Centres US

This industry comprises establishments primarily engaged in retailing nursery and garden products, such as trees, shrubs, plants, seeds, bulbs and sod, that are predominantly grown elsewhere. These establishments may provide landscaping services.

Exclusion(s): Establishments primarily engaged in:
- growing and retailing nursery stock (11142, Nursery and Floriculture Production);
- wholesaling new or used farm, lawn and garden machinery, equipment and parts (41711, Farm, Lawn and Garden Machinery and Equipment Wholesaler-Distributors); and
- providing landscaping services (56173, Landscaping Services).

Example Activities
- Agricultural supplies stores selling primarily to other business but also selling to household consumers
- Bedding plants, retail
- Garden centre, retail, flowers and plants
- Garden supplies and tools, retail
- Insecticides and weed killers, retail
- Lawn and garden ornaments, retail

- Lawn and garden supplies, retail
- Nursery and garden centres selling primarily to other businesses but also selling to household consumers
- Nursery stock, seeds and bulbs, retail
- Seeds, bulbs, and nursery stock, retail
- Shrubs and trees, ornamental, retail (except nurseries)
- Sod, retail

444220 Nursery Stores and Garden Centres US

See industry description for 44422, above.

445 Food and Beverage Stores US

This subsector comprises establishments primarily engaged in retailing a general or specialized line of food or beverage products.

Exclusion(s): Establishments primarily engaged in:
- retailing a general or specialized line of food or beverage products by means of electronic shopping, mail-order or direct sale (454, Non-Store Retailers).

4451 Grocery Stores US

This industry group comprises establishments primarily engaged in retailing a general line of food products.

44511 Supermarkets and Other Grocery (except Convenience) Stores US

This industry comprises establishments, known as supermarkets and grocery stores, primarily engaged in retailing a general line of food, such as canned, dry and frozen foods; fresh fruits and vegetables; fresh and prepared meats; fish, poultry, dairy products, baked products and snack foods. These establishments also typically retail a range of non-food household products, such as household paper products, toiletries and non-prescription drugs.

Exclusion(s): Establishments primarily engaged in:
- retailing a limited line of food and convenience items (44512, Convenience Stores);
- retailing prescription drugs in a supermarket, on a concession basis (44611, Pharmacies and Drug Stores); and
- retailing a general line of food products as well as a general line of non-food products (45291, Warehouse Clubs and Superstores).

Example Activities
- Food freezer plan, groceries (except direct sellers)
- Food markets, retail
- Food store, groceries, retail
- Grocery stores, with or without fresh meat, retail
- Supermarkets, grocery, retail

445110 Supermarkets and Other Grocery (except Convenience) Stores US

See industry description for 44511, above.

44512 Convenience Stores US

This industry comprises establishments, known as convenience stores, primarily engaged in retailing a limited line of convenience items that generally includes milk, bread, soft drinks, snacks, tobacco products, newspapers and magazines. These establishments may retail a limited line of canned goods, dairy products, household paper and cleaning products, as well as alcoholic beverages, and provide related services, such as lottery ticket sales and video rental.

Exclusion(s):
- convenience stores that sell gasoline (44711, Gasoline Stations with Convenience Stores).

Example Activities
- Confectionery stores, convenience
- Variety and convenience store

445120 Convenience Stores US

See industry description for 44512, above.

4452 Specialty Food Stores US

This industry group comprises establishments primarily engaged in retailing specialized lines of food products.

44521 Meat Markets US

This industry comprises establishments primarily engaged in retailing fresh, frozen, or cured meats and poultry. Delicatessens primarily engaged in retailing fresh meat are included.

Example Activities
- Butcher shops, retail
- Freezer provisioners (meat only), retail store
- Meat market, retail (store)
- Poultry dealers, retail
- Retail meat market

445210 Meat Markets US

See industry description for 44521, above.

44522 Fish and Seafood Markets US

This industry comprises establishments primarily engaged in retailing fresh, frozen, or cured fish and seafood products.

Example Activities
- Fish markets, retail
- Seafood markets, retail

445220 Fish and Seafood Markets US

See industry description for 44522, above.

44523 Fruit and Vegetable Markets US

This industry comprises establishments primarily engaged in retailing fresh fruits and vegetables.

Exclusion(s): Establishments primarily engaged in:
- growing vegetables and fruits and selling them at roadside stands (11121, Vegetable and Melon Farming, or 1113, Fruit and Tree Nut Farming).

Example Activities
- Fruit and vegetable stores, retail
- Vegetable and fruit stands, retail
- Vegetables and fruit, fresh, retail store

445230 Fruit and Vegetable Markets US

See industry description for 44523, above.

44529 Other Specialty Food Stores US

This industry comprises establishments, not classified to any other industry, primarily engaged in retailing specialty foods. Dairy product stores, baked goods stores, and candy, nut and confectionery stores are included.

Exclusion(s): Establishments primarily engaged in:
- retailing candy and confectionery products made on premises, not for immediate consumption (3113, Sugar and Confectionery Product Manufacturing);
- retailing goods baked on the premises, not for immediate consumption (31181, Bread and Bakery Product Manufacturing); and
- retailing food for immediate consumption (e.g., donut and bagel shops) (722, Food Services and Drinking Places).

445291 Baked Goods Stores US

This Canadian industry comprises establishments primarily engaged in retailing baked goods not baked on the premises, and not for immediate consumption.

Exclusion(s): Establishments primarily engaged in:
- retailing goods baked on premises, not for immediate consumption (31181, Bread and Bakery Product Manufacturing); and
- retailing baked goods for immediate consumption whether or not baked on the premises, (722210, Limited-Service Eating Places).

Example Activities
- Bagel stores, without baking on the premises, retail
- Bakeries without baking on the premises, retail
- Pastry shops, without baking on the premises, retail
- Pretzel stores and stands, without baking on the premises, retail

445292 Confectionery and Nut Stores US

This Canadian industry comprises establishments primarily engaged in retailing candy and other confections, nuts and popcorn.

Exclusion(s): Establishments primarily engaged in:
- retailing confectionery goods and nuts made on premises, not for immediate consumption (3113, Sugar and Confectionery Product Manufacturing).

Example Activities
- Candy stores, retail
- Nut shops, retail
- Popcorn stands, retail

445299 All Other Specialty Food Stores US

This Canadian industry comprises establishments, not classified to any other Canadian industry, primarily engaged in retailing specialty foods.

Exclusion(s): Establishments primarily engaged in:
- preparing and serving snack items for immediate consumption (722210, Limited-Service Eating Places).

Example Activities
- Beverages, soft drink, retail
- Cheese stores, retail
- Coffee stores, retail
- Dietary foods, retail
- Honey, retail
- Ice cream (i.e., packaged) stores, retail
- Milk and other dairy products specialty stores
- Mineral water, retail
- Spice and herb stores, retail
- Tea and coffee, retail

4453 Beer, Wine and Liquor Stores US

See industry description for 44531, below.

44531 Beer, Wine and Liquor Stores US

This industry comprises establishments primarily engaged in retailing packaged alcoholic beverages, such as beer, wine and liquor.

Exclusion(s): Establishments primarily engaged in:
- retailing convenience items as well as alcoholic beverages (44512, Convenience Stores);
- retailing beer and wine-making supplies (45399, All Other Miscellaneous Store Retailers); and
- providing prepared drinks for immediate consumption on the premises (72241, Drinking Places (Alcoholic Beverages)).

Example Activities
- Beer stores, retail
- Distilled spirits, retail
- Duty free liquor shops
- Liquor stores, retail
- Wine stores, retail

445310 Beer, Wine and Liquor Stores US

See industry description for 44531, above.

446 Health and Personal Care Stores US

This subsector comprises establishments primarily engaged in retailing health and personal care products. Drug stores and pharmacies, cosmetics, beauty supplies and perfume stores, optical goods stores, food (health) supplement stores and health appliance stores are included.

Exclusion(s): Establishments primarily engaged in:
- retailing health and personal care products by means of electronic shopping, mail-order or direct sale (454, Non-Store Retailers).

4461 Health and Personal Care Stores US

See industry description for 446, above.

44611 Pharmacies and Drug Stores US

This industry comprises establishments, known as pharmacies and drug stores, primarily engaged in retailing prescription or non-prescription drugs and medicines. These establishments also typically retail snacks, cosmetics, personal hygiene products, greeting cards and stationery, and health aids, and may also retail confectionery, tobacco products, novelties and giftware, and cameras and photographic supplies.

Exclusion(s): Establishments primarily engaged in:
- retailing food supplement products, such as vitamins, nutrition supplements and body enhancing supplements (44619, Other Health and Personal Care Stores).

Example Activities
- Apothecaries, retail
- Dispensary, retail
- Drug store
- Drug sundries, retail

- Patent medicines, retail
- Pharmaceuticals, retail
- Pharmacies, retail
- Proprietary medicines, retail

446110 Pharmacies and Drug Stores US

See industry description for 44611, above.

44612 Cosmetics, Beauty Supplies and Perfume Stores US

This industry comprises establishments primarily engaged in retailing cosmetics, perfumes, toiletries and personal grooming products.

Example Activities
- Beauty supplies retail
- Beauty supplies stores selling primarily to other businesses but also selling to household consumers

- Perfume and cosmetics, retail
- Toilet preparations, retail

446120 Cosmetics, Beauty Supplies and Perfume Stores US

See industry description for 44612, above.

44613 Optical Goods Stores US

This industry comprises establishments primarily engaged in retailing and fitting prescription eyeglasses and contact lenses. These establishments may or may not grind lenses to order on the premises. Establishments primarily engaged in retailing non-prescription sunglasses are also included.

Exclusion(s): Establishments primarily engaged in:
- lens grinding without retailing (33911, Medical Equipment and Supplies Manufacturing); and
- operating a private or group practice of optometry (62132, Offices of Optometrists).

Example Activities
- Contact lenses, retail
- Eyeglasses, spectacles and frames, retail
- Lens grinding, ophthalmic, in retail stores
- Optical goods stores, retail

- Opticians, retail
- Prescription eyeglasses and contact lenses made on the premises, retail
- Spectacle and eyeglass accessories, retail

446130 Optical Goods Stores US

See industry description for 44613, above.

44619 Other Health and Personal Care Stores US

This industry comprises establishments, not classified to any other industry, primarily engaged in retailing health and personal care items. Establishments primarily engaged in retailing health and personal care items, such as vitamin supplements, hearing aids, and medical equipment and supplies are included.

446191 Food (Health) Supplement Stores US

This Canadian industry comprises establishments primarily engaged in retailing food supplement products, such as vitamins, nutrition supplements and body enhancing supplements. These establishments may also retail a limited line of health food products.

Exclusion(s): Establishments primarily engaged in:
- retailing organic foods, such as fruits and vegetables, dairy products, and cereals and grains (445, Food and Beverage Stores); and
- retailing prescription and non-prescription drugs (446110, Pharmacies and Drug Stores).

Example Activities
- Body enhancing supplements, retail
- Food (i.e., health) supplements, retail
- Nutrition supplements, retail

446199 All Other Health and Personal Care Stores US

This Canadian industry comprises establishments, not classified to any other Canadian industry, primarily engaged in retailing specialized lines of health and personal care merchandise. These establishments may provide fitting services in addition to retailing.

Exclusion(s): Establishments primarily engaged in:
- retailing prescription or non-prescription drugs and medicines (446110, Pharmacies and Drug Stores); and
- retailing food supplement products (446191, Food (Health) Supplement Stores).

Example Activities
- Artificial limb stores, retail
- Health appliance stores
- Health appliance stores selling primarily to other businesses but also selling to household consumers
- Hearing aids, retail
- Orthopaedic aids, retail
- Orthopedic and artificial limb stores, retail
- Oxygen tent sales and medical gas supplying, retail store

447 Gasoline Stations US

This subsector comprises establishments primarily engaged in retailing motor fuels, whether or not the gasoline station is operated in conjunction with a convenience store, repair garage, restaurant or other type of operation. Establishments that operate gasoline stations on behalf of their owners and receive a commission on the sale of fuels are also included.

4471 Gasoline Stations US

See industry description for 447, above.

44711 Gasoline Stations with Convenience Stores US

This industry comprises establishments primarily engaged in retailing automotive fuels combined with the retail sale of a limited line of merchandise, such as milk, bread, soft drinks and snacks in a convenience store setting. Establishments that operate such establishments on behalf of their owners are also included.

Example Activity
- Gasoline station with convenience store

447110 Gasoline Stations with Convenience Stores US

See industry description for 44711, above.

44719 Other Gasoline Stations US

This industry comprises establishments, not classified to any other industry, primarily engaged in retailing gasoline, diesel fuel and automotive oils, whether or not the gasoline station is operated in conjunction with a repair garage, restaurant or other type of operation. Establishments that operate such establishments on behalf of their owners are also included.

Exclusion(s): Establishments primarily engaged in:
- operating gasoline stations combined with convenience stores (44711, Gasoline Stations with Convenience Stores).

Example Activities
- Gasoline service stations
- Marine service stations, retail
- Self-serve gasoline stations
- Service station (gasoline, lubricating oils and greases), retail
- Truck stops

447190 Other Gasoline Stations US

See industry description for 44719, above.

448 Clothing and Clothing Accessories Stores US

This subsector comprises establishments primarily engaged in retailing clothing and clothing accessories.

Exclusion(s): Establishments primarily engaged in:
- retailing used clothing and clothing accessories (45331, Used Merchandise Stores); and
- retailing clothing and clothing accessories by means of electronic shopping, mail-order or direct sale (454, Non-Store Retailers).

4481 Clothing Stores US

This industry group comprises establishments primarily engaged in retailing new, ready-to-wear clothing.

44811 Men's Clothing Stores US

This industry comprises establishments primarily engaged in retailing a general line of new, men's and boys', ready-to-wear clothing. These establishments may also provide alterations on the garments they sell.

Exclusion(s): Establishments primarily engaged in:
- retailing men's custom clothing made on the premises (3152, Cut and Sew Clothing Manufacturing);
- retailing ready-to-wear clothing for both genders and all age groups (44814, Family Clothing Stores);
- retailing men's and boys' clothing accessories (44815, Clothing Accessories Stores); and
- retailing a specialized line of apparel, such as raincoats, leather coats, fur apparel and swimwear (44819, Other Clothing Stores).

Example Activities
- Clothing stores, men's and boys', retail
- Haberdashery stores, retail
- Men's clothing stores

448110 Men's Clothing Stores US

See industry description for 44811, above.

44812 Women's Clothing Stores US

This industry comprises establishments primarily engaged in retailing a general line of new, women's, ready-to-wear clothing, including maternity wear.

Exclusion(s): Establishments primarily engaged in:
- retailing women's custom clothing made on the premises (3152, Cut and Sew Clothing Manufacturing);
- retailing ready-to-wear clothing for both genders and all age groups (44814, Family Clothing Stores);
- retailing women's clothing accessories (44815, Clothing Accessories Stores); and
- retailing a specialized line of clothing, such as bridal gowns, raincoats, leather apparel, fur clothing and swimwear (44819, Other Clothing Stores).

Example Activities
- Apparel, women's, retail
- Ladies clothing, retail
- Maternity shops, retail
- Women's clothing, stores

448120 Women's Clothing Stores US

See industry description for 44812, above.

44813 Children's and Infants' Clothing Stores US

This industry comprises establishments primarily engaged in retailing a general line of new, children's and infants', ready-to-wear clothing.

Exclusion(s): Establishments primarily engaged in:
- retailing ready-to-wear clothing for both genders and all age groups (44814, Family Clothing Stores); and
- retailing children's and infants' clothing accessories (44815, Clothing Accessories Stores).

Example Activities
- Children's clothing stores, retail
- Dresses, children's, retail
- Infants and toddlers clothing, retail
- Infants' wear stores, retail
- Toddlers clothing, retail

448130 Children's and Infants' Clothing Stores US

See industry description for 44813, above.

44814 Family Clothing Stores US

This industry comprises establishments primarily engaged in retailing a general line of new, ready-to-wear clothing for men, women and children, without specializing in sales for an individual gender or age group.

Exclusion(s): Establishments primarily engaged in:
- retailing new, men's and boys', ready-to-wear clothing (44811, Men's Clothing Stores);
- retailing new, women's, ready-to-wear clothing (44812, Women's Clothing Stores);
- retailing children's and infants', ready-to-wear clothing (44813, Children's and Infants' Clothing Stores); and
- retailing specialized clothing, such as raincoats, bridal gowns, leather apparel, fur clothing and swimwear (44819, Other Clothing Stores).

Example Activities
- Family clothing stores, retail
- Jeans stores, retail
- Unisex clothing stores, retail
- Western wear retail

448140 Family Clothing Stores US

See industry description for 44814, above.

44815 Clothing Accessories Stores US

This industry comprises establishments primarily engaged in retailing a single or general line of new clothing accessories.

Example Activities

- Apparel accessory stores, retail
- Belts, apparel, custom, retail
- Body belts, leather, retail
- Costume accessories (e.g., handbags, costume jewellery, gloves), retail
- Costume jewellery stores, retail
- Handbags and pocketbooks, retail
- Hats and caps, retail

- Hosiery stores, retail
- Millinery stores, retail
- Neckwear, apparel, retail
- Personal leather goods, retail
- Purses and bags, leather, retail
- Tie shops, retail
- Umbrella stores, retail
- Wallets and billfolds, leather, retail

448150 Clothing Accessories Stores US

See industry description for 44815, above.

44819 Other Clothing Stores US

This industry comprises establishments, not classified to any other industry, primarily engaged in retailing specialized lines of new clothing.

448191 Fur Stores CAN

This Canadian industry comprises establishments primarily engaged in retailing ready-to-wear or custom-made fur apparel.

Example Activities

- Fur apparel made to custom order, retail

- Fur shops, retail

448199 All Other Clothing Stores CAN

This Canadian industry comprises establishments, not classified to any other Canadian industry, primarily engaged in retailing specialized lines of new clothing.

Exclusion(s): Establishments primarily engaged in:

- retailing custom clothing and accessories made on the premises (315, Clothing Manufacturing);
- retailing a general line of men's and boys', ready-to-wear clothing (448110, Men's Clothing Stores);
- maternity wear retailing (448120, Women's Clothing Stores);
- retailing a general line of children's and infants' ready-to-wear clothing (448130, Children's and Infants' Clothing Stores);
- retailing ready-to-wear clothing for both genders and all age groups (448140, Family Clothing Stores); and
- retailing athletic uniforms (451110, Sporting Goods Stores).

Example Activities

- Athletic clothing (except uniforms), retail
- Beachwear, men's and boys', retail
- Bridal shops (except custom dressmakers), retail

- Dress shops, retail
- Foundation garments, retail
- Leather (including suede) clothing stores
- Lingerie stores, retail

- Raincoat stores, retail
- Riding apparel stores, retail
- Sports apparel stores, retail

- Swimwear stores, retail
- Tee shirts, custom printed, retail
- Uniforms and work clothing, retail

4482 Shoe Stores US

See industry description for 44821, below.

44821 Shoe Stores US

This industry comprises establishments primarily engaged in retailing all types of new footwear. These establishments may also retail shoe-care products.

Example Activities
- Athletic footwear, retail
- Boots and shoes, retail
- Children's and infants' shoes, retail
- Custom made orthopaedic shoes, retail

- Family shoe store, retail
- Footwear stores, retail
- Ladies' shoes, retail
- Retail shoe store

448210 Shoe Stores US

See industry description for 44821, above.

4483 Jewellery, Luggage and Leather Goods Stores US

This industry group comprises establishments primarily engaged in retailing jewellery, luggage and leather goods, and clothing accessories, such as hats, gloves, handbags, ties and belts.

44831 Jewellery Stores US

This industry comprises establishments primarily engaged in retailing jewellery, sterling and plated silverware, and watches and clocks. These establishments may provide services such as cutting and mounting stones and jewellery repair.

Exclusion(s): Establishments primarily engaged in:
- retailing costume jewellery (44815, Clothing Accessories Stores).

Example Activities
- Clocks and watches, retail
- Custom jewellery, retail
- Flatware and hollow ware, precious metal, retail
- Gem stones, rough, retail
- Holloware, precious metal, retail

- Jewellery store
- Jewellery, precious stones and precious metals (including custom made), retail
- Silverware and plated ware, retail
- Watches and clocks, retail

448310 Jewellery Stores US

See industry description for 44831, above.

44832 Luggage and Leather Goods Stores US

This industry comprises establishments primarily engaged in retailing luggage, briefcases, trunks and related products, and establishments engaged in retailing a line of leather items.

Exclusion(s): Establishments primarily engaged in:
- retailing a single or general line of leather and non-leather clothing accessories (44815, Clothing Accessories Stores); and
- retailing leather coats and other leather clothing articles (44819, Other Clothing Stores).

Example Activities
- Luggage and leather good stores, retail
- Luggage and travelling cases, retail
- Trunks, storage or travel, retail

448320 Luggage and Leather Goods Stores US

See industry description for 44832, above.

451 Sporting Goods, Hobby, Book and Music Stores US

This subsector comprises establishments primarily engaged in retailing sporting goods, games and toys, sewing supplies, fabrics, patterns, yarns and other needlework accessories, musical instruments, books and other reading materials, and audio and video recordings.

Exclusion(s): Establishments primarily engaged in:
- retailing used sporting goods, hobby goods, books, musical instruments, and audio and video recordings (45331, Used Merchandise Stores); and
- retailing sporting goods, hobby goods, books, musical instruments, and audio and video recordings by means of electronic shopping, mail-order or direct sale (454, Non-Store Retailers).

4511 Sporting Goods, Hobby and Musical Instrument Stores US

This industry group comprises establishments primarily engaged in retailing new sporting goods, games and toys, and musical instruments.

45111 Sporting Goods Stores US

This industry comprises establishments primarily engaged in retailing new sporting goods. These establishments may also retail used sporting goods, and provide repair services.

Exclusion(s): Establishments primarily engaged in:
- camper and camping trailer retailing (44121, Recreational Vehicle Dealers);
- snowmobile, motorized bicycle and motorized golf cart retailing (44122, Motorcycle, Boat and Other Motor Vehicle Dealers);
- athletic shoe retailing (44821, Shoe Stores); and
- repairing or servicing, without selling, sporting goods (81149, Other Personal and Household Goods Repair and Maintenance).

Example Activities
- Archery equipment, retail
- Backpacking, hiking and mountaineering equipment, retail
- Bait and tackle shops, retail
- Baseball equipment, retail
- Bicycle and bicycle parts dealers (except motorized), retail
- Bowling equipment and supplies, retail
- Camping equipment (except tent trailers), retail
- Exercise and fitness equipment, retail
- Firearms and ammunition, retail
- Fitness equipment, retail
- Golf goods and equipment, retail
- Gymnasium equipment, retail
- Hockey equipment, retail
- Hunting equipment, retail
- Playground equipment, retail
- Pool and billiard table stores, retail
- Riding goods and equipment, retail
- Skiing equipment, retail
- Skin diving and scuba equipment, retail
- Soccer equipment, retail
- Softball equipment, retail
- Sporting goods, equipment and supplies, retail
- Track and field equipment, retail
- Tricycles and parts, retail

451110 Sporting Goods Stores US

See industry description for 45111, above.

45112 Hobby, Toy and Game Stores US

This industry comprises establishments primarily engaged in retailing new toys, games, and hobby and craft supplies.

Exclusion(s): Establishments primarily engaged in:
- retailing software, including game software (44312, Computer and Software Stores); and
- retailing artists' supplies or collectors' items, such as coins, stamps, autographs and cards (45399, All Other Miscellaneous Store Retailers).

Example Activities
- Board games (amusement), retail
- Ceramic greenware and supplies, retail
- Ceramics supplies, retail
- Craft kits and supplies, retail
- Hobby kits, model, retail
- Lapidary supplies, retail
- Macramé supplies, retail
- Paint-by-number sets, retail
- Puzzles (game), retail
- Rug hooking supplies, retail
- Toy and game stores, retail
- Toy vehicles, children's, retail

451120 Hobby, Toy and Game Stores US

See industry description for 45112, above.

45113 Sewing, Needlework and Piece Goods Stores US

This industry comprises establishments primarily engaged in retailing new sewing supplies, fabrics, patterns, yarns and other needlework accessories. These stores may also retail sewing machines.

Exclusion(s): Establishments primarily engaged in:
- sewing machine retailing (44311, Appliance, Television and Other Electronics Stores).

Example Activities
- Fabric, upholstery, retail
- Knitting yarn and accessories, retail
- Needlework stores, retail
- Notions, sewing thread and needles, retail
- Quilting materials and supplies, retail
- Remnant stores, retail
- Sewing supplies, retail
- Textile piece goods, retail
- Upholstery fabric, retail
- Yard goods (textile fabric), retail

451130 Sewing, Needlework and Piece Goods Stores US

See industry description for 45113, above.

45114 Musical Instrument and Supplies Stores US

This industry comprises establishments primarily engaged in retailing new musical instruments, sheet music and related supplies. These establishments may also rent and repair musical instruments.

Exclusion(s): Establishments primarily engaged in:
- retailing musical recordings (45122, Pre-Recorded Tape, Compact Disc and Record Stores);
- renting, without retailing, musical instruments (53229, Other Consumer Goods Rental); and
- repairing, without retailing, musical instruments (81149, Other Personal and Household Goods Repair and Maintenance).

Example Activities
- Musical instrument amplifying equipment, retail
- Musical instrument stores, retail
- Pianos, retail
- Sheet music, retail

451140 Musical Instrument and Supplies Stores US

See industry description for 45114, above.

4512 Book, Periodical and Music Stores US

This industry group comprises establishments primarily engaged in retailing new books, newspapers, magazines, and audio and video recordings.

45121 Book Stores and News Dealers US

This industry comprises establishments primarily engaged in retailing new books, newspapers, magazines and other periodicals.

Exclusion(s): Establishments primarily engaged in:
- selling newspapers, magazines, and other periodicals via electronic shopping, mail-order or direct sale (454, Non-Store Retailers); and
- delivering newspapers to homes (45439, Other Direct Selling Establishments).

Example Activities
- Book stores
- Magazines and newspapers, retail
- Newspaper and magazine stores, retail

451210 Book Stores and News Dealers CAN

See industry description for 45121, above.

45122 Pre-Recorded Tape, Compact Disc and Record Stores US

This industry comprises establishments primarily engaged in retailing new audio and video recordings in any format or medium.

Exclusion(s): Establishments primarily engaged in:
- computer software retailing (44312, Computer and Software Stores); and
- retailing pre-recorded tapes, compact discs and records by mail-order (45411, Electronic Shopping and Mail-Order Houses).

Example Activities
- Cassettes and tapes, pre-recorded (audio), retail
- Disks, music and video, retail
- Records and tapes retail
- Tapes and cassettes, pre-recorded (audio), retail
- Video tape stores, retail

451220 Pre-Recorded Tape, Compact Disc and Record Stores US

See industry description for 45122, above.

452 General Merchandise Stores US

This subsector comprises establishments primarily engaged in retailing a general line of merchandise that may, or may not, include a general line of grocery items.

Exclusion(s): Establishments primarily engaged in:
- retailing a general line of building and home improvement materials (44411, Home Centres);
- retailing a general line of grocery items (44511, Supermarkets and Other Grocery (except Convenience) Stores);
- retailing a general line of used goods (45331, Used Merchandise Stores); and
- retailing a general line of goods by means of electronic shopping, mail-order, or direct sale (454, Non-Store Retailers).

4521 Department Stores US

See industry description for 45211, below.

45211 Department Stores US

This industry comprises establishments, known as department stores, primarily engaged in retailing a wide range of products, with each merchandise line constituting a separate department within the store. Selected departments may be operated by separate establishments, on a concession basis.

Exclusion(s):
- warehouse-style stores engaged in retailing a general line of grocery items in combination with a general line of non-grocery items (45291, Warehouse Clubs and Superstores).

Example Activities
- Department stores, retail
- Discount department stores

452110 Department Stores CAN

See industry description for 45211, above.

4529 Other General Merchandise Stores US

This industry group comprises establishments, not classified to any other industry group, primarily engaged in retailing goods in general merchandise stores.

45291 Warehouse Clubs and Superstores US

This industry comprises establishments, known as warehouse clubs, superstores or supercentres, primarily engaged in retailing a general line of grocery items in combination with a general line of non-grocery items, and typically selling grocery items in larger formats.

Exclusion(s): Establishments primarily engaged in:
- retailing a general line of grocery items (44511, Supermarkets and Other Grocery (except Convenience) Stores); and
- retailing a general line of merchandise in department stores (45211, Department Stores).

Example Activity
- Superstores (i.e. food and general merchandise), retail

452910 Warehouse Clubs and Superstores US

See industry description for 45291, above.

45299 All Other General Merchandise Stores US

This industry comprises establishments, not classified to any other industry, primarily engaged in retailing a general line of new merchandise. Establishments known as home and auto supplies stores, catalogue showrooms, agricultural co-op stores, variety stores and country general stores are included.

Exclusion(s): Establishments primarily engaged in:
- automotive parts retailing (44131, Automotive Parts and Accessories Stores); and
- retailing merchandise in catalogue showrooms, without stock (45411, Electronic Shopping and Mail-Order Houses).

452991 Home and Auto Supplies Stores ^{CAN}

This Canadian industry comprises establishments primarily engaged in retailing a general line of auto supplies, such as tires, batteries, parts and accessories, along with a general line of home supplies, such as hardware, housewares, small appliances, sporting goods, and lawn and garden equipment and supplies.

Example Activities
- Auto and home supplies, retail
- Home and auto supply stores

452999 All Other Miscellaneous General Merchandise Stores ^{CAN}

This Canadian industry comprises establishments, not classified to any other Canadian industry, primarily engaged in retailing a general line of new merchandise.

Exclusion(s): Establishments primarily engaged in:
- merchandise retailing in catalogue showrooms, without stock (454110,).

Example Activities
- Agricultural co-op stores (i.e., general stores, not primarily food)
- Catalogue sales showrooms (except mail order), retail
- General store (not primarily food)
- Variety stores, retail

453 Miscellaneous Store Retailers ^{US}

This subsector comprises establishments primarily engaged in retailing a specialized line of merchandise in other types of specialty stores. Florists, office supplies stores, stationery stores, gift, novelty and souvenir stores, used merchandise stores, pet and pet supplies stores, art dealers and manufactured (mobile) home dealers are included.

4531 Florists ^{US}

See industry description for 45311, below.

45311 Florists ^{US}

This industry comprises establishments primarily engaged in retailing cut flowers, floral arrangements, and potted plants purchased from others. These establishments typically prepare the arrangements they sell.

Exclusion(s): Establishments primarily engaged in:
- retailing flowers or nursery stock grown on the premises (11142, Nursery and Floriculture Production); and
- retailing trees, shrubs, plants, seeds, bulbs and sod grown elsewhere (44422, Nursery Stores and Garden Centres).

Example Activities
- Florist shops, retail
- Flowers, fresh, retail
- Plants and cut flowers, retail
- Retail florists

453110 Florists US

See industry description for 45311, above.

4532 Office Supplies, Stationery and Gift Stores US

This industry group comprises establishments primarily engaged in retailing new office supplies, stationery and gifts.

45321 Office Supplies and Stationery Stores US

This industry comprises establishments primarily engaged in retailing office supplies or a combination of office supplies, equipment and furniture. Establishments primarily engaged in retailing stationery and school supplies are also included.

> *Exclusion(s): Establishments primarily engaged in:*
> - office furniture retailing (44211, Furniture Stores);
> - typewriter retailing (44311, Appliance, Television and Other Electronics Stores);
> - computer retailing (44312, Computer and Software Stores); and
> - greeting card retailing (45322, Gift, Novelty and Souvenir Stores).

> *Example Activities*
> - Office and school supplies (except furniture), retail
> - Office supplies stores selling primarily to other businesses but also selling to household consumers
> - Stationery retail

453210 Office Supplies and Stationery Stores US

See industry description for 45321, above.

45322 Gift, Novelty and Souvenir Stores US

This industry comprises establishments primarily engaged in retailing new gifts, novelty merchandise, souvenirs, greeting cards, seasonal and holiday decorations, and curios. These establishments may also retail stationery.

> *Exclusion(s): Establishments primarily engaged in:*
> - stationery retailing (45321, Office Supplies and Stationery Stores).

> *Example Activities*
> - Artcraft, retail
> - Balloon shops, retail
> - Carvings and artcraft, retail
> - Ceramics, handicraft, retail
> - Ceramics, retail
> - Curio shops, retail
> - Decorations, seasonal and holiday, retail
> - Duty free shops, gifts
> - Gift shops, retail
> - Gift wrap supplies, retail
> - Gifts, novelties and souvenirs, retail
> - Greeting card shops, retail
> - Handicraft, retail
> - Joke shops
> - Novelty merchandise, retail
> - Souvenirs, retail

453220 Gift, Novelty and Souvenir Stores US

See industry description for 45322, above.

4533 Used Merchandise Stores US

See industry description for 45331, below.

45331 Used Merchandise Stores US

This industry comprises establishments primarily engaged in retailing used merchandise. Establishments primarily engaged in retailing antiques are also included.

Exclusion(s): Establishments primarily engaged in:
- used automobile retailing (44112, Used Car Dealers);
- used RV retailing (44121, Recreational Vehicle Dealers);
- used motorcycle and boat retailing (44122, Motorcycle, Boat and Other Motor Vehicle Dealers);
- used tire retailing (44132, Tire Dealers);
- used mobile home retailing (45393, Mobile Home Dealers);
- retailing a general line of used merchandise on an auction basis (45399, All Other Miscellaneous Store Retailers); and
- operating pawnshops (52229, Other Non-Depository Credit Intermediation).

Example Activities
- Antique home furnishings, retail
- Antiques, retail
- Appliances, used, retail
- Book stores, second-hand, retail
- Building materials, used, retail
- China and crockery, household, used retail
- Clothing stores, second-hand, retail
- Furniture stores, second-hand, retail
- Glassware and china, used, retail
- Musical instruments, used, retail
- Phonograph and phonograph record stores, second-hand, retail
- Rare book stores
- Second-hand book store, retail
- Second-hand merchandise, retail
- Used appliances, household, retail

453310 Used Merchandise Stores US

See industry description for 45331, above.

4539 Other Miscellaneous Store Retailers US

This industry group comprises establishments, not classified to any other industry group, primarily engaged in retailing new merchandise in other types of specialty stores.

45391 Pet and Pet Supplies Stores US

This industry comprises establishments primarily engaged in retailing pets, pet food and pet supplies. These establishments may also provide pet grooming services.

Exclusion(s): Establishments primarily engaged in:
- providing veterinary services (54194, Veterinary Services); and
- providing pet grooming and boarding services (81291, Pet Care (except Veterinary) Services).

Example Activities
- Animal foods, pet, retail
- Cages for pet animals, retail
- Fish tanks (for pets), retail
- Pet animal care equipment and supplies, retail
- Pet animals, retail
- Pet food stores, retail
- Pet shops, retail

453910 Pet and Pet Supplies Stores US

See industry description for 45391, above.

45392 Art Dealers ^{US}

This industry comprises establishments primarily engaged in retailing original and limited edition art works. Establishments primarily engaged in the exhibition of native art and art carvings for retail sale are also included.

Exclusion(s): Establishments primarily engaged in:
- retailing art reproductions (44229, Other Home Furnishings Stores); and
- operating non-commercial art galleries (71211, Museums).

Example Activities
- Art dealers, retail
- Oil paintings, original and prints, retail
- Pictures and art objects, retail

453920 Art Dealers ^{US}

See industry description for 45392, above.

45393 Mobile Home Dealers ^{US}

This industry comprises establishments primarily engaged in retailing new and used mobile homes, parts and equipment. These establishments may provide installation services in addition to retailing the homes.

Exclusion(s): Establishments primarily engaged in:
- motor home, camper and travel trailer retailing (44121, Recreational Vehicle Dealers); and
- retailing prefabricated buildings and kits (44419, Other Building Material Dealers).

Example Activities
- House trailer dealers, retail
- Mobile home dealers, retail
- Trailer, house, dealers, retail

453930 Mobile Home Dealers ^{US}

See industry description for 45393, above.

45399 All Other Miscellaneous Store Retailers ^{US}

This industry comprises establishments, not classified to any other industry, primarily engaged in retailing specialized lines of merchandise, such as tobacco and tobacco products; artists' supplies; collectors' items, such as coins, stamps, autographs and cards; beer and wine making supplies; swimming pool supplies and accessories; religious goods; and monuments and tombstones. Establishments primarily engaged in retailing a general line of new and used merchandise on an auction basis are also included.

Exclusion(s): Establishments primarily engaged in:
- auctioning new and used merchandise on a fee basis (56199, All Other Support Services).

453992 Beer and Wine-Making Supplies Stores ^{CAN}

This Canadian industry comprises establishments primarily engaged in retailing beer and wine-making supplies and equipment. These establishments may also provide access to on-premise beer and wine-making equipment.

Example Activities
- Sales of beer making supplies and use of brewing equipment
- Wine making supplies, retail

453999 All Other Miscellaneous Store Retailers (except Beer and Wine-Making Supplies Stores) CAN

This Canadian industry comprises establishments, not classified to any other Canadian industry, primarily engaged in retailing specialized lines of merchandise. Establishments primarily engaged in retailing a general line of new and used merchandise on an auction basis are also included.

Exclusion(s): Establishments primarily engaged in:
- new and used merchandise auctioning on a fee basis (561990, All Other Support Services).

Example Activities
- Architectural supplies, retail
- Artists' supplies, retail
- Auctioneering, with own facilities, open to the general public, retail
- Automobile auctioneers, with own facilities, open to the general public, retail
- Banner shops, retail
- Brooms and brushes, retail
- Cake decorating supplies, retail
- Candle shops, retail
- Church supplies, retail
- Cigar stores and stands, retail
- Coin and stamp dealing, retail
- Collectors' coins, retail
- Fireworks, retail
- Flag shops, retail
- Gravestones, finished, retail
- Hot-tubs and whirlpools, retail
- Lettering and designing of monuments, retail
- Numismatic supplies, retail
- Party supplies store, retail
- Philatelic supplies, retail
- Pipes and smokers' supplies, retail
- Religious goods stores (except books), retail
- Smoke shop
- Stamp collection sets, retail
- Swimming pools, retail
- Tobacco stores and stands
- Tombstones, retail
- Trophy shops, retail
- Water conditioning equipment, retail

454 Non-Store Retailers US

This subsector comprises establishments primarily engaged in retailing merchandise by non-store retail methods. The establishments of this subsector employ methods, such as broadcasting infomercials, broadcasting and publishing direct-response advertising, publishing traditional and electronic catalogues, door-to-door solicitation, in-home demonstration, temporary displaying of merchandise (temporary stands or stalls), distribution by vending machines, and using the Internet to reach their customers and market their merchandise. Establishments primarily engaged in the direct sale (i.e. non-store) of products such as home heating fuels and in newspaper delivery are also included.

4541 Electronic Shopping and Mail-Order Houses US

See industry description for 45411, below.

45411 Electronic Shopping and Mail-Order Houses US

This industry comprises establishments primarily engaged in retailing all types of merchandise using the electronic and print media to induce direct response by the customer. These establishments can employ methods, such as broadcasting infomercials, broadcasting and publishing direct-response advertising and publishing traditional or electronic catalogues, to display their merchandise and reach their customers. They can also provide sites facilitating consumer-to-consumer or business-to-consumer trade in new and used goods, on an auction basis, using the Internet. Transactions between these retailers and their customers typically require the use of information technology (telephone or computer network) and the delivery of merchandise is typically done by mail or courier. Establishments primarily engaged in retailing from catalogue showrooms, without stock, are also included.

454111 Internet Shopping US

This Canadian industry comprises establishments engaged in retailing all types of merchandise using the Internet.

Exclusion(s): Establishments primarily engaged in:
- retailing all types of merchandise using mail-order catalogues or television to generate clients and display merchandise (454113, Mail-Order Houses); and
- store retailing or a combination of store retailing and Internet retailing of merchandise in the same establishment (classified to the store portion of the activity).

Example Activity
- Merchandise retailing via Internet

454112 Electronic Auctions US

This Canadian industry comprises establishments engaged in providing sites for and facilitating consumer-to-consumer or business-to-consumer trade in new and used goods, on an auction basis, using the Internet. Establishments in this industry provide the electronic location for retail auctions, but do not take title to the goods being sold.

Exclusion(s): Establishments primarily engaged in:
- facilitating business-to-business sales of new and used merchandise on an auction basis using the Internet (41911, Business-to-Business Electronic Markets); and
- retailing a general line of new and used merchandise on an auction basis from physical auction sites or a combination of Internet auction and auction house sales in the same establishment (453999, All Other Miscellaneous Store Retailers (except Beer and Wine-Making Supplies Stores)).

Example Activity
- Auction, Internet retailing

454113 Mail-Order Houses US

This Canadian industry comprises establishments primarily engaged in retailing all types of merchandise using catalogues or television to display their merchandise and reach their clients. Included in this industry are establishments primarily engaged in retailing from catalogue showrooms of mail-order houses as well as establishments providing a combination of Internet and mail-order sales.

Exclusion(s): Establishments primarily engaged in:
- call centres providing telemarketing services for others (56142, Telephone Call Centres); and
- retailing merchandise using store and non-store methods at the same establishment (classified to the store portion of the activity).

Example Activities
- Book club, mail order
- Catalog (order taking) offices of mail order houses, retail
- Combined Internet and mail order sales
- Computer and peripheral equipment, mail order, retail
- Direct mail marketing operators, retail
- Magazines, mail order, retail
- Mail order houses, retail
- Mail order offices of department stores, retail
- Order taking offices of mail order houses, retail
- Record clubs, mail order, retail
- Television, mail order (home shopping), retail

4542 Vending Machine Operators US

See industry description for 45421, below.

45421 Vending Machine Operators US

This industry comprises establishments primarily engaged in owning, stocking and servicing vending machines designed to retail merchandise.

Exclusion(s): Establishments primarily engaged in:
- selling insurance policies through vending machines (524, Insurance Carriers and Related Activities);
- operating coin-operated amusement machines (71312, Amusement Arcades); and
- operating coin-operated gambling machines (71329, Other Gambling Industries).

Example Activities
- Coin-operated machines selling merchandise, retail
- Merchandising, automatic (sale of products through vending machines), retail
- Vending machine merchandise, non-store, retail

454210 Vending Machine Operators US

See industry description for 45421, above.

4543 Direct Selling Establishments US

This industry group comprises establishments primarily engaged in non-store retailing, except direct-response advertising and operating vending machines. These establishments use methods, such as home delivery, door-to-door solicitation, in-home demonstration and displaying of merchandise through temporary stalls or kiosks, to reach their customers and market their merchandise. Direct sales establishments may operate from an office and have incidental sales of items.

Exclusion(s): Establishments primarily engaged in:
- direct-response advertising (45411, Electronic Shopping and Mail-Order Houses).

45431 Fuel Dealers US

This industry comprises establishments primarily engaged in retailing heating oil, liquefied petroleum gas (LPG) and other fuels via direct selling.

454311 Heating Oil Dealers US

This Canadian industry comprises establishments primarily engaged in retailing heating oil via direct selling to the final consumer including both households and commercial businesses. Heating oil dealers may also provide furnace repair and maintenance services in addition to the primary activity of retailing and delivering oil.

Exclusion(s): Establishments primarily engaged in:
- installing oil burners without retailing home heating oil (23822, Plumbing, Heating and Air-Conditioning Contractors);
- operating heating oil bulk stations and terminals (41211, Petroleum Product Wholesaler-Distributors);
- retailing heating oil in combination with retailing non-related merchandise such as found in establishments usually referred to as agricultural co-ops (452999, All Other Miscellaneous General Merchandise Stores); and
- repairing oil burners (811411, Home and Garden Equipment Repair and Maintenance).

Example Activities
- Direct sale of heating oil (non-store, delivered to customer's premises)
- Fuel oil dealers, retail
- Home heating oil dealer, retail

454312 Liquefied Petroleum Gas (Bottled Gas) Dealers US

This Canadian industry comprises establishments primarily engaged in retailing liquefied petroleum gas (LPG) gas via direct selling.

Example Activities

- Liquefied petroleum gas (LPG), delivered to customers' premises, retail
- Propane dealer, retail
- Propane gas sales and distribution, retail

454319 Other Fuel Dealers US

This Canadian industry comprises establishments primarily engaged in retailing fuels (except liquefied petroleum gas and heating oil) via direct selling. Establishments retailing a combination of fuels including those previously listed, with none predominating, are also included.

Example Activities

- Coal dealers, retail
- Diesel fuel, delivered to customers' premises, retail
- Firewood dealers, retail
- Wood dealers, fuel, retail

45439 Other Direct Selling Establishments US

This industry comprises establishments, not classified to any other industry, primarily engaged in non-store retailing. These establishments use methods, such as door-to-door solicitation, in-home demonstration and temporary displaying of merchandise (stalls), to reach their customers and market their merchandise.

Exclusion(s): Establishments primarily engaged in:

- preparing and serving meals and snacks for immediate consumption from motorized vehicles catering a route or from non-motorized carts (72233, Mobile Food Services).

Example Activities

- Canvassers (door-to-door), headquarters for retail sale of merchandise
- Cosmetics, house-to-house or party-plan selling, retail
- Direct personal retailing operators, retail
- Direct selling of merchandise (door-to-door), retail
- Door-to-door retailing of merchandise, retail
- Fruit stand (temporary), road side, retail
- Home provisioners, frozen food service, direct seller, retail
- House-to-house selling of coffee, soda, beer, bottled water, or other products, retail
- Housewares, house-to-house, telephone or party plan selling, retail
- Hucksters, retail
- Ice dealers, retail, door-to-door
- Magazine subscription sales (except mail order), retail
- Newspaper distributor, newspaper boy, retail
- Non-store retailing, direct sales (door-to-door), retail
- Party plan merchandising, retail
- Telephone selling of merchandise (retailing by home solicitation)
- Water selling, home distribution, retail

454390 Other Direct Selling Establishments US

See industry description for 45439, above.

48-49 Transportation and Warehousing

This sector comprises establishments primarily engaged in transporting passengers and goods, warehousing and storing goods, and providing services to these establishments. The modes of transportation are road (trucking, transit and ground passenger), rail, water, air and pipeline. These are further subdivided according to the way in which businesses in each mode organize their establishments. National post office and courier establishments, which also transport goods, are included in this sector. Warehousing and storage establishments are subdivided according to the type of service and facility that is operated.

Many of the establishments in this sector are structured as networks, with activities, workers, and physical facilities distributed over an extensive geographic area.

Exclusion(s): Establishments primarily engaged in:
- renting and leasing transportation equipment without operator (532, Rental and Leasing Services).

481 Air Transportation

This subsector comprises establishments primarily engaged in for-hire, common-carrier transportation of people and/or goods using aircraft, such as airplanes and helicopters.

Exclusion(s): Establishments primarily engaged in:
- scenic or sightseeing air services (48799, Scenic and Sightseeing Transportation, Other); and
- air courier services (49211, Couriers).

4811 Scheduled Air Transportation

See industry description for 48111, below.

48111 Scheduled Air Transportation

This industry comprises establishments primarily engaged in transporting passengers and/or goods by aircraft, over regular routes and on regular schedules. Establishments in this industry have less flexibility with respect to choice of airports, hours of operation, load factors and similar operational characteristics than do establishments in 4812, Non-Scheduled Air Transportation.

Exclusion(s): Establishments primarily engaged in:
- non-scheduled air transport (4812, Non-Scheduled Air Transportation).

Example Activities
- Air cargo carriers (except air courier), scheduled
- Air freight transportation service, scheduled
- Air passenger carriers, scheduled
- Cargo carriers, air, scheduled
- Commuter air carriers, scheduled
- Helicopter carriers, passenger, scheduled
- Passenger air transportation, scheduled

481110 Scheduled Air Transportation CAN

See industry description for 48111, above.

4812 Non-Scheduled Air Transportation

See industry description for 48121, below.

48121 Non-Scheduled Air Transportation

This industry comprises establishments primarily engaged in the non-scheduled air transportation of passengers and/or goods. Establishments in this industry have more flexibility with respect to choice of airports, hours of operation, load factors and similar operational characteristics than do establishments in 4811, Scheduled Air Transportation. Establishments primarily engaged in providing specialty air transportation or flying services using small, general-purpose aircraft are included.

Exclusion(s): Establishments primarily engaged in:
- crop-dusting using specialized aircraft (11511, Support Activities for Crop Production);
- fighting forest fires using specialized water bombers (11531, Support Activities for Forestry);
- scheduled air transport (48111, Scheduled Air Transportation);
- specialized air sightseeing services (48799, Scenic and Sightseeing Transportation, Other);
- aerial gathering of geophysical data (54136, Geophysical Surveying and Mapping Services);
- providing aerial mapping services (54137, Surveying and Mapping (except Geophysical) Services);
- flight training, including all training for commercial pilots (61151, Technical and Trade Schools); and
- operating air ambulance services using specialized equipment (62191, Ambulance Services).

481214 Non-Scheduled Chartered Air Transportation CAN

This Canadian industry comprises establishments primarily engaged in the non-scheduled air transportation of passengers and/or goods by aircraft, at a toll per mile or per hour for the charter of the aircraft.

Exclusion(s): Establishments primarily engaged in:
- providing specialty flying services, with no service predominating (481215, Non-Scheduled Specialty Flying Services).

Example Activities
- Air cargo carriers (except air courier), non-scheduled
- Air passenger charter transportation service
- Cargo transportation, air, charter service
- Freight transportation, air, charter service
- Passenger transportation, air charter service

481215 Non-Scheduled Specialty Flying Services CAN

This Canadian industry comprises establishments primarily engaged in providing a combination of flying services, with no single service predominating. These establishments use small, general-purpose aircraft. The services performed may be specialized, such as aerial photography, aerial crop spraying, fighting forest fires, air ambulance, towing advertising banners, skywriting, and aerial traffic reporting, or general air transportation of passengers and goods.

Exclusion(s): Establishments primarily engaged in:
- crop-dusting using specialized aircraft (115110, Support Activities for Crop Production);
- fighting forest fires using specialized water bombers (115310, Support Activities for Forestry);
- non-scheduled chartered air transportation (481214, Non-Scheduled Chartered Air Transportation);
- specialized air sightseeing services (487990, Scenic and Sightseeing Transportation, Other);
- aerial gathering of geophysical data (541360, Geophysical Surveying and Mapping Services);
- providing aerial mapping services (541370, Surveying and Mapping (except Geophysical) Services);
- flight training, including all training for commercial pilots (611510, Technical and Trade Schools); and
- operating air ambulance services using specialized equipment (621912, Air Ambulance Services).

Example Activities
- Aerial advertising, using general purpose aircraft
- Aerial crop dusting, using general purpose aircraft
- Air taxi services
- Aviation clubs, providing air transportation services to the general public
- Sky writing, using general purpose aircraft
- Specialty flying services, using general purpose aircraft

482 Rail Transportation

See industry description for 48211, below.

4821 Rail Transportation

See industry description for 48211, below.

48211 Rail Transportation

This industry comprises establishments primarily engaged in operating railways. Establishments primarily engaged in the operation of long-haul or mainline railways, short-haul railways and passenger railways are included.

Exclusion(s): Establishments primarily engaged in:
- operating street railways and urban rapid transit (48511, Urban Transit Systems);
- operating tourist and scenic trains (48711, Scenic and Sightseeing Transportation, Land); and
- operating switching and terminal railways (48821, Support Activities for Rail Transportation).

482112 Short-Haul Freight Rail Transportation US

This Canadian industry comprises establishments primarily engaged in operating railways for the transport of goods on a rail line that does not comprise a rail network. A short-haul railway line usually takes goods from one or more points to a point on the larger transportation network, which is usually a mainline railway, but may be a trans-shipment point onto another transportation mode.

Exclusion(s): Establishments primarily engaged in:
- operating switching and terminal railways (488210, Support Activities for Rail Transportation).

Example Activities
- Belt line railways
- Freight railway, short-haul
- Logging railways
- Railway transportation, freight, short-haul
- Railways, belt line
- Railways, freight, short-haul
- Railways, logging

482113 Mainline Freight Rail Transportation CAN

This Canadian industry comprises establishments primarily engaged in operating railways for the transport of goods over a mainline rail network. A mainline rail network is a system that usually comprises one or more trunk lines, into which a network of branch lines feed. The branch lines may be part of the mainline establishment or may be separate establishments of short-haul freight railways.

Example Activities
- Freight railway, mainline
- Railways, freight, mainline

482114 Passenger Rail Transportation CAN

This Canadian industry comprises establishments primarily engaged in the railway transport of passengers.

Exclusion(s): Establishments primarily engaged in:
- operating street railways and urban rapid transit (485110, Urban Transit Systems); and
- operating same-day return tourist and scenic trains (487110, Scenic and Sightseeing Transportation, Land).

Example Activities
- Interurban passenger railways
- Passenger transportation services, railway
- Railways, passenger (except urban transit and scenic and sightseeing)

483 Water Transportation

This subsector comprises establishments primarily engaged in the water transportation of passengers and goods, using equipment designed for those purposes.

Exclusion(s): Establishments primarily engaged in:
- same-day return sightseeing trips and cruises (48721, Scenic and Sightseeing Transportation, Water).

4831 Deep Sea, Coastal and Great Lakes Water Transportation

See industry description for 48311, below.

48311 Deep Sea, Coastal and Great Lakes Water Transportation

This industry comprises establishments primarily engaged in deep sea, coastal and Great Lakes water transportation of freight and passengers. The St. Lawrence Seaway is considered to be part of the Great Lakes system. Establishments that operate ocean-going cruise ships are included.

> *Exclusion(s): Establishments primarily engaged in:*
> * inland water transport (48321, Inland Water Transportation).

483115 Deep Sea, Coastal and Great Lakes Water Transportation (except by Ferries) CAN

This Canadian industry comprises establishments primarily engaged in deep sea, coastal and Great Lakes water transportation of freight and passengers. The St. Lawrence Seaway is considered to be part of the Great Lakes system. Establishments that operate ocean-going cruise ships are included.

> *Example Activities*
> * Barge transport service, coastal
> * Chartering vessels with crew, deep sea, coastal and Great Lakes
> * Coastal shipping
> * Deep water transportation of freight (except by ferries)
> * Deep water transportation of passengers (except by ferries)
> * Great Lakes and St. Lawrence Seaway transportation (except by ferries)
> * Log rafting and towing, coastal
> * Supply vessels to drilling rigs

483116 Deep Sea, Coastal and Great Lakes Water Transportation by Ferries CAN

This Canadian industry comprises establishments primarily engaged in operating ferries for the transport of passengers and/or freight contained in self-propelled, motorized vehicles, in deep sea, coastal or Great Lakes waters.

> *Exclusion(s): Establishments primarily engaged in:*
> * operating inland, including harbour, ferries (483214, Inland Water Transportation by Ferries).

> *Example Activities*
> * Ferries, operating on coastal waters
> * Ferries, operating on the Great Lakes

4832 Inland Water Transportation

See industry description for 48321, below.

48321 Inland Water Transportation

This industry comprises establishments primarily engaged in the inland water transportation of freight and passengers. Transportation within harbours is included.

> *Exclusion(s): Establishments primarily engaged in:*
> * water transportation on the Great Lakes (48311, Deep Sea, Coastal and Great Lakes Water Transportation).

483213 Inland Water Transportation (except by Ferries) CAN

This Canadian industry comprises establishments primarily engaged in the inland water transportation of freight and passengers, except by ferries.

Example Activities
- Canal transportation
- Chartering vessels with crew, inland waters (except Great Lakes)
- Lake (except Great Lakes) transportation (except ferries)
- Log rafting and towing, inland waters (except Great Lakes)
- River freight transportation (except using the St. Lawrence Seaway)
- River passenger transportation (except ferries)
- Water taxi service, inland waterways

483214 Inland Water Transportation by Ferries ^{CAN}

This Canadian industry comprises establishments primarily engaged in operating inland ferries, including ferries operated in harbours.

Exclusion(s): Establishments primarily engaged in:
- operating coastal and Great Lakes ferries (483116, Deep Sea, Coastal and Great Lakes Water Transportation by Ferries).

Example Activities
- Ferries, operating on rivers or inland lakes (except Great Lakes)
- Harbour ferry service

484 Truck Transportation

This subsector comprises establishments primarily engaged in the truck transportation of goods. These establishments may carry general freight or specialized freight. Specialized freight comprises goods that, because of size, weight, shape or other inherent characteristics, require specialized equipment for transportation. Establishments may operate locally, that is within a metropolitan area and its hinterland, or over long distances, that is between metropolitan areas.

4841 General Freight Trucking

This industry group comprises establishments primarily engaged in the local or long distance trucking of general freight. General freight trucking does not require the use of specialized equipment. The trucks used can handle a wide variety of commodities. Freight is generally palletized, and generally carried in a box, container or van trailer.

48411 General Freight Trucking, Local

This industry comprises establishments primarily engaged in local general freight trucking. These establishments primarily provide trucking services within a metropolitan area and its hinterland.

Example Activities
- Container trucking service, local
- Contract bulk mail, truck transportation, local
- General freight trucking, local
- General trucking, local
- Local trucking service, general freight
- Non-specialized freight transport, local
- Transfer (trucking) service, general freight, local
- Truck transport service, general freight, local
- Trucking, general freight, local

484110 General Freight Trucking, Local US

See industry description for 48411, above.

48412 General Freight Trucking, Long Distance

This industry comprises establishments primarily engaged in long distance, general freight trucking. These establishments primarily provide trucking services between metropolitan areas.

484121 General Freight Trucking, Long Distance, Truck-Load US

This Canadian industry comprises establishments primarily engaged in long distance, general freight trucking of complete truck-loads. A truck-load shipment is generally devoted to the goods of a single shipper, taken directly from a point of origin to one or more destination points.

Example Activities
- Container trucking service, long-distance, truck-load
- Contract bulk mail, truck transportation, long-distance
- General freight trucking, long-distance, truck-load
- Motor freight carrier, general, long-distance, truckload
- Trucking, general freight, long-distance, truckload

484122 General Freight Trucking, Long Distance, Less Than Truck-Load US

This Canadian industry comprises establishments primarily engaged in long distance, general freight trucking of less than complete truck-loads. Less-than-truck-load carriers are characterized by the use of terminals to consolidate shipments, generally from several shippers, into a single truck for haulage between a load assembly terminal and a disassembly terminal, where the load is sorted and shipments are re-routed for delivery.

Example Activities
- General freight trucking, long-distance, less than truck-load
- Motor freight carrier, general, long-distance, less-than-truckload
- Trucking, general freight, long-distance, less than truckload

4842 Specialized Freight Trucking

This industry group comprises establishments primarily engaged in specialized freight trucking. These establishments transport articles that, because of size, weight, shape or other inherent characteristics, require specialized equipment for transportation. Some important types of specialized equipment are bulk tankers, dump trucks and trailers, refrigerated vans, and motor vehicle haulers. Establishments that transport used household and office goods are included.

Exclusion(s): Establishments primarily engaged in:
- local hauling of garbage (56211, Waste Collection).

48421 Used Household and Office Goods Moving

This industry comprises establishments primarily engaged in the trucking of used household and office goods, whether local or long distance. Establishments engaged in the transportation of used institutional equipment are included. Incidental storage activities may be carried out by these establishments, except for new furniture.

Example Activities
- Furniture moving, used
- Furniture, used, household, moving of
- Moving used goods, office or institutional
- Office furniture moving, used
- Trucking service, used goods, household, office or institutional
- Used uncrated goods, moving and storage
- Van lines, moving and storage service

484210 Used Household and Office Goods Moving

See industry description for 48421, above.

48422 Specialized Freight (except Used Goods) Trucking, Local

This industry comprises establishments primarily engaged in providing local trucking services using specialized equipment. Local trucking establishments provide trucking services within a metropolitan area.

484221 Bulk Liquids Trucking, Local CAN

This Canadian industry comprises establishments primarily engaged in the local trucking of bulk liquids. These establishments use tank trucks (which may be refrigerated) to transport goods such as milk, water, chemicals and petroleum products.

Example Activities
- Bulk liquid trucking service, local
- Liquid petroleum products trucking, local
- Milk hauling, local

484222 Dry Bulk Materials Trucking, Local CAN

This Canadian industry comprises establishments primarily engaged in the local trucking of dry bulk materials. These establishments use dump trucks and dump trailers, tank trucks, hopper trucks and similar vehicles to transport goods such as sand, gravel, snow, dry chemicals and ores.

Exclusion(s): Establishments primarily engaged in:
- local hauling of garbage (562110, Waste Collection).

Example Activities
- Construction rubble, hauling, local
- Dirt hauling, truck, local
- Dry bulk materials trucking (except local garbage hauling without disposal), local
- Dump trucking, local
- Grain trucking, local
- Gravel hauling, local
- Sand hauling, local

484223 Forest Products Trucking, Local CAN

This Canadian industry comprises establishments primarily engaged in the local trucking of forest products, including logs, wood chips and lumber.

Exclusion(s): Establishments primarily engaged in:
- trucking forest products in the bush (i.e., within logging limits) (115310, Support Activities for Forestry).

Example Activities
- Forest products trucking, local
- Log trucking, local (i.e., to the mill)
- Pulpwood trucking, local (i.e., to the mill)
- Timber trucking, local (i.e., to the mill)

484229 Other Specialized Freight (except Used Goods) Trucking, Local CAN

This Canadian industry comprises establishments, not classified to any other Canadian industry, primarily engaged in providing local trucking services, using specialized equipment.

Example Activities

- Agricultural products trucking, local
- Automobile carriers, local
- Boat hauling, by truck, local
- Farm products hauling, local
- Flat-bed trucking, local
- Freight transportation, using animal-drawn vehicle
- House moving, local (i.e., transportation only)
- Livestock trucking, local

- Mobile home towing service, local
- Refrigerated products trucking, local
- Rental of truck, with driver
- Snowmobile operation, freight
- Tracked vehicle freight transportation, local
- Transporting automobiles and other motor vehicles, local
- Transporting mobile homes, local
- Trucking, agricultural products, local
- Trucking, automobiles, local

48423 Specialized Freight (except Used Goods) Trucking, Long Distance

This industry comprises establishments primarily engaged in providing long distance trucking services using specialized equipment. Long distance trucking establishments provide trucking services between metropolitan areas.

484231 Bulk Liquids Trucking, Long Distance CAN

This Canadian industry comprises establishments primarily engaged in the long distance trucking of bulk liquids. These establishments use tank trucks (which may be refrigerated) to transport goods such as chemicals and petroleum products.

Example Activities

- Bulk liquids trucking, long-distance
- Liquid petroleum products trucking, long-distance

- Trucking bulk liquid, long-distance

484232 Dry Bulk Materials Trucking, Long Distance CAN

This Canadian industry comprises establishments primarily engaged in the long distance trucking of dry bulk materials. These establishments use dump trucks and dump trailers, tank trucks, hopper trucks and similar vehicles to transport goods such as sand, gravel, dry chemicals and ores.

Example Activities

- Dry bulk materials trucking, long-distance

- Grain hauling, long-distance

484233 Forest Products Trucking, Long Distance CAN

This Canadian industry comprises establishments primarily engaged in the long distance trucking of forest products, including logs, wood chips and lumber.

Example Activities

- Forest products trucking, long-distance

- Log trucking, long-distance

484239 Other Specialized Freight (except Used Goods) Trucking, Long Distance CAN

This Canadian industry comprises establishments, not classified to any other Canadian industry, primarily engaged in providing long distance trucking services, using specialized equipment. Some important truck types used by these establishments are refrigerated vans and motor vehicle haulers.

Example Activities
- Automobile carrier, trucking, long-distance
- Flat bed trucking, long-distance
- Hazardous materials trucking using specialized equipment, long-distance
- House moving, long distance (i.e., transportation only)
- Livestock hauling, long-distance
- Mobile home towing service, long-distance
- Refrigerated products trucking, long-distance
- Rubbish hauling without collection, long-distance
- Trucking, automobiles, long-distance
- Trucking, hazardous materials, using specialized equipment, long-distance
- Trucking, refrigerated, long-distance

485 Transit and Ground Passenger Transportation

This subsector comprises establishments primarily engaged in a variety of passenger transportation activities, using equipment designed for those purposes. These activities are distinguished based on process factors, such as whether routes are scheduled, run over fixed routes, and charged on a per-seat or per-vehicle basis.

Exclusion(s): Establishments primarily engaged in:
- passenger transportation associated with scenic or sightseeing activities (487, Scenic and Sightseeing Transportation).

4851 Urban Transit Systems

See industry description for 48511, below.

48511 Urban Transit Systems

This industry comprises establishments primarily engaged in operating local and suburban mass passenger transit systems. Such transportation may involve the use of one or more modes of transport including light rail, subways and streetcars, as well as buses. These establishments operate over fixed routes and schedules, and allow passengers to pay on a per-trip basis (whether or not they also use payment methods such as monthly passes).

Example Activities
- Bus line operation, local
- Bus service, urban and suburban
- Cable cars operation, commuter
- City bus service
- Combination bus, subway, and trolley system
- Commuter bus operation
- Commuter rail operation
- Electric street railway transportation
- Electrical railway operation, commuter
- Elevated railway operation
- Light rail systems
- Local and suburban transit systems, mixed mode
- Local bus service
- Monorail transport, urban
- Passenger transit systems, mixed mode
- Passenger transit systems, urban and suburban
- Rail transportation, commuter
- Railroads, commuter operation
- Street railway operation
- Tramway operation, commuter
- Transit system, operation of
- Trolley operation, commuter
- Urban and suburban passenger transit system operation
- Urban and suburban transit systems, mixed mode

485110 Urban Transit Systems CAN

See industry description for 48511, above.

4852 Interurban and Rural Bus Transportation

See industry description for 48521, below.

48521 Interurban and Rural Bus Transportation

This industry comprises establishments primarily engaged in providing passenger transportation, principally outside a single municipality and its suburban areas, primarily by bus. These establishments operate over fixed routes and schedules, and charge a per-trip fee.

> *Exclusion(s): Establishments primarily engaged in:*
> - operating chartered bus transportation (48551, Charter Bus Industry).

> *Example Activities*
> - Bus line operation, intercity
> - Bus line operation, interurban
> - Intercity bus line operation
> - Interurban bus line operation
> - Motor coach operation, interurban and rural
> - Rural bus service (except school bus)

485210 Interurban and Rural Bus Transportation

See industry description for 48521, above.

4853 Taxi and Limousine Service

This industry group comprises establishments primarily engaged in providing passenger transportation by taxi and limousine.

48531 Taxi Service

This industry comprises establishments primarily engaged in providing passenger transportation by taxi (that is, automobiles, except limousines), not operated on regular schedules or routes. Taxicab fleet owners and organizations that provide dispatch services are included, regardless of whether drivers are hired, rent their cabs or are otherwise compensated. Owner-operated taxicabs are included.

> *Example Activities*
> - Cab service (i.e., taxi)
> - Dispatch, taxicab, services
> - Taxicab fleet owners
> - Taxicab operation
> - Taxicab owner-operator
> - Taxicab service

485310 Taxi Service US

See industry description for 48531, above.

48532 Limousine Service

This industry comprises establishments primarily engaged in providing passenger transportation by limousine.

> *Exclusion(s): Establishments primarily engaged in:*
> - transporting passengers to or from hotels and airports or stations, using buses or vans (48599, Other Transit and Ground Passenger Transportation).

Example Activities
- Automobile rental with driver (except taxicab)
- Automobiles for hire with driver (except taxicab)
- Hearse rental with driver
- Limousine rental with driver
- Limousine service (except scheduled)

485320 Limousine Service

See industry description for 48532, above.

4854 School and Employee Bus Transportation

See industry description for 48541, below.

48541 School and Employee Bus Transportation

This industry comprises establishments primarily engaged in operating buses and other motor vehicles to transport pupils to and from school or employees to and from work. These establishments operate over fixed routes and schedules, but do not charge a per-trip fee.

Example Activities
- Bus operation, school
- Employee bus service
- School bus operator
- School bus service

485410 School and Employee Bus Transportation

See industry description for 48541, above.

4855 Charter Bus Industry

See industry description for 48551, below.

48551 Charter Bus Industry

This industry comprises establishments primarily engaged in providing charter bus services. These establishments do not operate over fixed routes and schedules, and rent the entire vehicle, rather than individual seats.

Exclusion(s): Establishments primarily engaged in:
- operating local sightseeing buses (48711, Scenic and Sightseeing Transportation, Land); and
- providing packaged tours involving bus transportation (56152, Tour Operators).

Example Activity
- Bus charter service

485510 Charter Bus Industry

See industry description for 48551, above.

4859 Other Transit and Ground Passenger Transportation

See industry description for 48599, below.

48599 Other Transit and Ground Passenger Transportation

This industry comprises establishments, not classified to any other industry, primarily engaged in providing shuttle services to airports and similar facilities, special needs transportation services and other transit and ground passenger transport. Shuttle services included in this industry are those that use vans and/or buses as a means of transport. They usually travel on fixed routes and service particular hotels or carriers. Special needs transportation establishments use conventional or specially converted vehicles to provide passenger transportation to the infirm, elderly or handicapped.

Example Activities
- Airport limousine service, scheduled
- Carpool operation
- Handicapped transportation services
- Limousine service to airports or stations, scheduled
- Paratransit transportation services
- Senior citizen transportation service
- Shuttle services (except employee bus)
- Special needs passenger transportation service
- Vanpool operation

485990 Other Transit and Ground Passenger Transportation ^{CAN}

See industry description for 48599, above.

486 Pipeline Transportation

This subsector comprises establishments primarily engaged in the transport of products by pipeline. The pipelines are designed to specifications for the transport of a particular product, such as crude oil, natural gas and refined petroleum products. Pipeline transportation includes integrated systems comprising various types of pipelines and ancillary facilities, such as pumping stations and incidental storage facilities.

Exclusion(s): Establishments primarily engaged in:
- operating gathering lines to transport crude oil or natural gas from wells to field processing plants (211, Oil and Gas Extraction); and
- operating bulk storage facilities incidental to a wholesaling activity (412, Petroleum Product Wholesaler-Distributors).

4861 Pipeline Transportation of Crude Oil

See industry description for 48611, below.

48611 Pipeline Transportation of Crude Oil

This industry comprises establishments primarily engaged in the pipeline transportation of crude oil.

Example Activities
- Booster pumping station, oil transport
- Crude oil pipeline service
- Pipeline transport, crude oil

486110 Pipeline Transportation of Crude Oil

See industry description for 48611, above.

4862 Pipeline Transportation of Natural Gas

See industry description for 48621, below.

48621 Pipeline Transportation of Natural Gas

This industry comprises establishments primarily engaged in the pipeline transportation of natural gas, from gas fields or processing plants to local distribution systems.

Example Activities
- Gas, natural, pipeline operation
- Natural gas pipeline service
- Pipeline transport service, natural gas

486210 Pipeline Transportation of Natural Gas

See industry description for 48621, above.

4869 Other Pipeline Transportation

This industry group comprises establishments, not classified to any other industry group, primarily engaged in pipeline transportation.

48691 Pipeline Transportation of Refined Petroleum Products

This industry comprises establishments primarily engaged in the pipeline transportation of refined petroleum products.

Example Activities
- Gasoline pipeline transport service
- Natural gas liquids, pipeline transport service
- Pipeline transport service, gasoline
- Pipeline transport service, natural gas liquids
- Pipelines transport service, refined petroleum products
- Refined petroleum products, pipeline transport service

486910 Pipeline Transportation of Refined Petroleum Products

See industry description for 48691, above.

48699 All Other Pipeline Transportation

This industry comprises establishments, not classified to any other industry, primarily engaged in pipeline transportation. Establishments engaged in the operation of slurry pipelines are included.

Example Activities
- Coal pipeline transport service
- Slurry pipeline transport service
- Water pipelines (long distance) without water treatment activities

486990 All Other Pipeline Transportation

See industry description for 48699, above.

487 Scenic and Sightseeing Transportation

This subsector comprises establishments primarily engaged in providing recreational transportation, such as sightseeing or dinner cruises, steam train excursions, horse-drawn sightseeing rides, air-boat rides or hot-air balloon rides. These establishments often use vintage or specialized transportation equipment. The services provided are local in nature, usually involving same-day return. Establishments that provide charter fishing services are included.

Exclusion(s): Establishments primarily engaged in:
- providing scenic and sightseeing services using airplanes, in combination with other specialty air transportation or flying services (481215, Non-Scheduled Specialty Flying Services); and
- providing sporting services, such as fishing guides, white-water rafting, pack trains and water-skiing (71399, All Other Amusement and Recreation Industries).

4871 Scenic and Sightseeing Transportation, Land

See industry description for 48711, below.

48711 Scenic and Sightseeing Transportation, Land

This industry comprises establishments primarily engaged in providing scenic and sightseeing transportation on land, such as steam train excursions and horse-drawn sightseeing rides.

Example Activities

- Buses, sightseeing, local, operation
- Cabs, horse drawn, sightseeing
- Calèche service, sightseeing
- Cog railways, scenic and sightseeing, operation
- Horse-drawn carriages, sightseeing
- Monorails, scenic and sightseeing
- Railroads, scenic and sightseeing, local

- Scenic and sightseeing bus transportation, local
- Scenic railroad, local, operation
- Sightseeing services, human-drawn vehicle
- Steam train excursions, local
- Tracked vehicle, passenger, sightseeing operation
- Tramways (except aerial), scenic and sightseeing
- Trolley operation, scenic and sightseeing

487110 Scenic and Sightseeing Transportation, Land

See industry description for 48711, above.

4872 Scenic and Sightseeing Transportation, Water

See industry description for 48721, below.

48721 Scenic and Sightseeing Transportation, Water

This industry comprises establishments primarily engaged in providing scenic and sightseeing transportation on water, such as sightseeing or dinner cruises or air-boat rides. These establishments often use vintage or specialized transportation equipment. The services provided are local in nature, usually involving same-day return. Establishments that provide charter fishing services are included.

Exclusion(s): Establishments primarily engaged in:
- providing sporting services, such as fishing guides, white-water rafting and water-skiing (71399, All Other Amusement and Recreation Industries).

Example Activities
- Airboats (i.e., swamp buggies) operation
- Boat charters, pleasure
- Boats, fishing charter, operation
- Charter fishing boats
- Charter yachts, with crew
- Dinner cruises

- Excursion boat operation
- Harbour sightseeing tours
- Hovercraft operation (sightseeing)
- Sightseeing boat operation
- Swamp buggy operations
- Whale watching excursions

487210 Scenic and Sightseeing Transportation, Water

See industry description for 48721, above.

4879 Scenic and Sightseeing Transportation, Other

See industry description for 48799, below.

48799 Scenic and Sightseeing Transportation, Other

This industry comprises establishments, not classified to any other industry, primarily engaged in providing scenic and sightseeing transportation. Some examples of these services are scenic helicopter rides and hot-air balloon rides.

Example Activities
- Aerial cable cars, sightseeing
- Aerial tramways, sightseeing or scenic
- Cable cars, scenic and sightseeing
- Glider rides operations
- Gondola (cablecar), sightseeing, operations
- Helicopter rides, scenic and sightseeing
- Hot air balloon rides
- Sightseeing helicopter operations

487990 Scenic and Sightseeing Transportation, Other

See industry description for 48799, above.

488 Support Activities for Transportation

This subsector comprises establishments primarily engaged in providing services to other transportation establishments. These services may be specific to a mode of transportation, or they may be multi-modal.

4881 Support Activities for Air Transportation

This industry group comprises establishments primarily engaged in providing specialized services to the air transport industry.

48811 Airport Operations

This industry comprises establishments primarily engaged in operating international, national and other civil airports. The activities involved in operating airports include renting hangar space, and providing air traffic control services, baggage handling, cargo handling and aircraft parking services. Public flying fields are included.

488111 Air Traffic Control

This Canadian industry comprises establishments primarily engaged in operating air traffic control services to promote the safe, orderly, and expeditious flow of air traffic.

Example Activity
- Air traffic control services

488119 Other Airport Operations US

This Canadian industry comprises establishments, not classified to any other Canadian industry, primarily engaged in operating civil airports.

Example Activities
- Air freight handling at airports
- Aircraft parking service
- Airport baggage handling
- Airport cargo handling services
- Airport hangar rental
- Airport operations
- Airport runway maintenance service
- Airport, civil, operation and maintenance
- Aviation club providing primarily flying field services to general public
- Fixed base operations
- Flying fields operation
- Hangar operation
- Loading service, aircraft

48819 Other Support Activities for Air Transportation

This industry comprises establishments, not classified to any other industry, primarily engaged in providing specialized services to the air transport industry. Some important activities are servicing aircraft, repairing and maintaining aircraft (except on a factory basis), and inspecting and testing aircraft.

Exclusion(s): Establishments primarily engaged in:
- repairing and maintaining aircraft on a factory basis (33641, Aerospace Product and Parts Manufacturing);
- providing janitorial and cleaning services for airlines (56172, Janitorial Services); and
- providing food catering services for airlines (72231, Food Service Contractors).

Example Activities
- Aircraft ferrying service
- Aircraft inspection service
- Aircraft maintenance service (except factory conversions and overhauls)
- Aircraft servicing and repairing (except factory conversions and overhauls)
- Aircraft servicing, at airports
- Aircraft testing services
- Aircraft upholstery repair

488190 Other Support Activities for Air Transportation

See industry description for 48819, above.

4882 Support Activities for Rail Transportation

See industry description for 48821, below.

48821 Support Activities for Rail Transportation

This industry comprises establishments primarily engaged in providing specialized services to the rail transport industry. Establishments engaged in the operation of railway terminals and stations, and the maintenance of railway rights-of-way and structures are included.

Example Activities
- Cleaning of freight cars
- Container loading or unloading service, railroad
- Freight car cleaning service
- Grain levelling and trimming service, in railroad cars
- Loading and unloading rail freight cars
- Locomotives and railroad cars, repair
- Maintenance of rights-of-way and structures, railway
- Railroad car repair (except factory rebuilding of rolling stock)
- Railroad switching services
- Railroad terminals, independent operation
- Railway maintenance services (i.e., rights-of-way, structures)
- Switching services, railroad

488210 Support Activities for Rail Transportation

See industry description for 48821, above.

4883 Support Activities for Water Transportation

This industry group comprises establishments primarily engaged in providing specialized services to the water transportation industry.

48831 Port and Harbour Operations

This industry comprises establishments primarily engaged in operating port and harbour facilities and services. Establishments engaged in the operation of lighthouses are included.

Example Activities

- Canal locks, operating
- Canal maintenance (except dredging)
- Canal operations
- Dock, marine, operation
- Harbour operation
- Lighthouse operation
- Maintenance of piers, docks, wharves
- Piers, docks and wharves, maintenance
- Piers, docks and wharves, operation
- Port facilities operation
- Seaway operation
- Waterfront terminal operation

488310 Port and Harbour Operations

See industry description for 48831, above.

48832 Marine Cargo Handling

This industry comprises establishments primarily engaged in providing stevedoring and other marine cargo handling services.

Example Activities

- Loading and unloading ships or boats
- Longshoremen service
- Marine cargo handling
- Ship hold cleaning
- Stevedoring service
- Unloading ships or boats

488320 Marine Cargo Handling

See industry description for 48832, above.

48833 Navigational Services to Shipping

This industry comprises establishments primarily engaged in providing navigational services to shipping. Important navigational services are pilotage, moorage and vessel traffic services. Establishments engaged in marine salvage are included.

Exclusion(s): Establishments primarily engaged in:
- operating lighthouses (48831, Port and Harbour Operations).

488331 Marine Salvage Services CAN

This Canadian industry comprises establishments primarily engaged in salvaging ships and their cargoes. Typical salvage situations include rescue towing, rescuing strandings and raising sunken vessels.

Example Activities

- Cargo salvaging, marine
- Marine salvaging service
- Ship salvaging

488332 Ship Piloting Services CAN

This Canadian industry comprises establishments primarily engaged in providing piloting service to ships when entering or leaving harbours or where required by law. The areas in which the services of a marine pilot are essential are generally referred to as pilotage waters.

Example Activities

- Piloting service, water transport
- Ship piloting service

488339 Other Navigational Services to Shipping CAN

This Canadian industry comprises establishments, not classified to any other Canadian industry, primarily engaged in providing navigational services to shipping.

Example Activities
- Docking and undocking marine vessel services
- Harbour navigational operations

- Marine vessel traffic reporting
- Radio beacon service, ship navigation
- Tugboat service, harbour operations

48839 Other Support Activities for Water Transportation

This industry comprises establishments, not classified to any other industry, primarily engaged in providing water transportation services. Establishments engaged in ship repair and maintenance (not done in a shipyard) and lighter operations are included.

Example Activities
- Cargo surveyors, marine
- Cargo, checkers, marine
- Drydocks, floating, for repairing ships and boats
- Lighter operation services
- Marine cargo checkers

- Marine surveyors, cargo
- Ship repair and maintenance, not in a shipyard
- Ship scaling services
- Surveyors, marine cargo

488390 Other Support Activities for Water Transportation

See industry description for 48839, above.

4884 Support Activities for Road Transportation

This industry group comprises establishments primarily engaged in providing specialized services to trucking establishments, bus operators and other establishments using the road network.

48841 Motor Vehicle Towing

This industry comprises establishments primarily engaged in towing motor vehicles. Establishments engaged in light and heavy towing services, both local and long distance, to the general public, commercial, transportation and other sectors, are included. These establishments may offer incidental services, such as tire repair, battery boosting and other emergency road services.

Example Activities
- Emergency road service, motor vehicle
- Motor vehicle towing service

- Towing service, motor vehicle
- Wrecker service (towing), motor vehicle

488410 Motor Vehicle Towing

See industry description for 48841, above.

48849 Other Support Activities for Road Transportation

This industry comprises establishments, not classified to any other industry, primarily engaged in providing services to trucking establishments, bus operators and other establishments using the road network. Establishments engaged in the operation of trucking terminals; inspection and weighing services connected with truck transportation; and the operation of toll roads, bridges and tunnels are included.

Example Activities

- Bridge, tunnel and highway operation
- Bus terminal operation, independent
- Cargo surveyors, truck transportation
- Commercial vehicle safety inspection, without repairs
- Flagging service (i.e., traffic control)
- Inspection or weighing service, truck transportation
- Pilot car services (i.e., wide load warning service)

- Snow clearing, highways and bridges, road transport service
- Snow removal, highway
- Street cleaning service
- Truck loading and unloading service
- Truck weighing station operation
- Trucking terminals, independent, with or without maintenance facilities

488490 Other Support Activities for Road Transportation ^{US}

See industry description for 48849, above.

4885 Freight Transportation Arrangement

See industry description for 48851, below.

48851 Freight Transportation Arrangement

This industry comprises establishments primarily engaged in acting as intermediaries between shippers and carriers. These establishments are usually referred to as freight forwarders, marine shipping agents or customs brokers. They may offer a combination of services, which may span transportation modes.

Exclusion(s): Establishments primarily engaged in:
- providing tariff and customs consultants services (54161, Management Consulting Services).

488511 Marine Shipping Agencies ^{CAN}

This Canadian industry comprises establishments primarily engaged in representing shipping lines, arranging for the taking on of cargo and performing other business transactions in port, on behalf of ship owners and charterers.

Exclusion(s): Establishments primarily engaged in:
- acting as intermediaries between shippers and carriers, involving more than one mode of transportation (488519, Other Freight Transportation Arrangement).

Example Activities
- Agents, shipping (marine)
- Marine shipping agency

488519 Other Freight Transportation Arrangement ^{CAN}

This Canadian industry comprises establishments, not classified to any other Canadian industry, primarily engaged in acting as intermediaries between shippers and carriers. These establishments are usually referred to as freight forwarders or customs brokers. They may offer a combination of services spanning transportation modes.

Exclusion(s): Establishments primarily engaged in:
- acting as intermediaries between shippers and carriers, involving only the marine mode of transportation (488511, Marine Shipping Agencies).

Example Activities
- Air cargo customs clearances, service
- Brokers, customs
- Brokers, shipping
- Customs brokers
- Freight forwarding service
- Shipping agents, freight forwarding
- Transportation brokers

4889 Other Support Activities for Transportation

See industry description for 48899, below.

48899 Other Support Activities for Transportation

This industry comprises establishments, not classified to any other industry, primarily engaged in providing specialized services to transportation establishments. Establishments engaged in packing, crating and otherwise preparing goods for transportation are included.

Exclusion(s): Establishments primarily engaged in:
- packaging and labelling services (56191, Packaging and Labelling Services).

Example Activities
- Arrangement of carpools and vanpools
- Automobile delivery service (drive-away)
- Crating goods for shipping
- Driving service (auto and truck delivery)
- Freight packing and crating
- Liquefaction and regasification of natural gas for purposes of transport at mine site
- Livestock feeding station service, livestock in transit
- Packing and crating service, transportable goods
- Pipeline terminal facilities independently operated
- Truck transportation brokers

488990 Other Support Activities for Transportation MEX

See industry description for 48899, above.

491 Postal Service

See industry description for 49111, below.

4911 Postal Service

See industry description for 49111, below.

49111 Postal Service

This industry comprises establishments primarily engaged in operating the postal service. Establishments of the Post Office, other than those primarily engaged in providing courier services, are classified in this industry, as well as establishments that carry on one or more functions of the postal service on a contract basis, except the delivery of mail in bulk.

Exclusion(s): Establishments primarily engaged in:
- the delivery of mail in bulk, on contract to the Post Office (481, Air Transportation, or 482, Rail Transportation, or 484, Truck Transportation);
- providing courier services, including separate courier establishments of the Post Office (49211, Couriers);
- delivering advertising material, door-to-door (54187, Advertising Material Distribution Services); and
- providing mail box services along with other business services (56143, Business Service Centres).

Example Activities
- Mail delivery, private (except air)
- Mail service, contract
- Post Office operations
- Postal service on a contract basis
- Rural mail carrier service

491110 Postal Service

See industry description for 49111, above.

492 Couriers and Messengers

This subsector comprises establishments primarily engaged in providing courier delivery services; or messenger and delivery services of small parcels within a single urban area.

4921 Couriers

See industry description for 49211, below.

49211 Couriers

This industry comprises establishments primarily engaged in providing air, surface or combined courier delivery services. Courier establishments of the Post Office are included.

> *Exclusion(s): Establishments primarily engaged in:*
> - providing local messenger and delivery services, including bicycle couriers (49221, Local Messengers and Local Delivery).

Example Activities
- Courier operation of Post Office
- Courier service
- Messenger service, courier
- Parcel delivery, private (except air)
- Parcel express service, courier

492110 Couriers

See industry description for 49211, above.

4922 Local Messengers and Local Delivery

See industry description for 49221, below.

49221 Local Messengers and Local Delivery

This industry comprises establishments primarily engaged in providing messenger and delivery services of small parcels within a single urban area. Establishments engaged in the delivery of letters and documents, such as legal documents, often by bicycle or on foot; and the delivery of small parcels, such as take-out restaurant meals, alcoholic beverages and groceries, on a fee basis, usually by small truck or van, are included.

Example Activities
- Bicycle messenger and delivery service
- Food delivery, for restaurants
- Liquor delivery services (dial-a-bottle)
- Local delivery service, small parcels

492210 Local Messengers and Local Delivery

See industry description for 49221, above.

493 Warehousing and Storage

See industry description for 4931, below.

4931 Warehousing and Storage

This industry group comprises establishments primarily engaged in operating general merchandise, refrigerated and other warehousing and storage facilities. These establishments provide facilities to store goods for customers. They do not take title to the goods they handle. These establishments take responsibility for storing the goods and keeping them secure. They may also provide a range of services, often referred to as logistics services, related to the distribution of a customer's goods. Logistics services can include labelling, breaking bulk, inventory control and management, light assembly, order entry and fulfillment, packaging, pick and pack, price marking and ticketing and transportation arrangement. However, establishments in this industry group always provide storage services in addition to any logistics services. Furthermore, the storage of goods must be more than incidental to the performance of a service such as price marking.

Both public and contract warehousing are included in this industry group. Public warehousing generally provides short-term storage, typically for less than thirty days. Contract warehousing generally involves a longer-term contract, often including the provision of logistical services and dedicated facilities.

Bonded warehousing and storage services, and warehouses located in free trade zones, are included in the industries of this industry group. However, storage services primarily associated with the provision of credit are not.

Exclusion(s): Establishments primarily engaged in:
- handling and distribution of goods, when the establishment takes title (41, Wholesale Trade);
- operating grain elevators, other than primarily storage (41112, Oilseed and Grain Wholesaler-Distributors);
- trucking of used goods (48421, Used Household and Office Goods Moving);
- pipeline distribution systems, whether or not incidental storage is provided (48621, Pipeline Transportation of Natural Gas, or 48691, Pipeline Transportation of Refined Petroleum Products);
- self-storage of goods, commonly known as mini-warehouses (53113, Self-Storage Mini-Warehouses);
- packaging and labelling services, whether or not incidental storage is provided (56191, Packaging and Labelling Services); and
- storing garments and furs for individuals (81232, Dry Cleaning and Laundry Services (except Coin-Operated)).

49311 General Warehousing and Storage

This industry comprises establishments primarily engaged in operating public and contract general merchandise warehousing and storage facilities. These establishments handle goods in containers, such as boxes, barrels and drums, using equipment such as fork lifts, pallets and racks. They are not specialized in the handling of a particular type of good.

Example Activities
- Bonded warehouse, general merchandise
- General warehousing and storage
- Public storage (except self storage)
- Warehousing, general

493110 General Warehousing and Storage US

See industry description for 49311, above.

49312 Refrigerated Warehousing and Storage

This industry comprises establishments primarily engaged in operating refrigerated warehousing and storage facilities. These establishments provide public and contract warehouse and storage services, using equipment designed to keep goods frozen or refrigerated. The services provided include blast freezing, tempering and modified atmosphere storage, in addition to the warehousing services typically provided by establishments in this industry group. Establishments engaged in the storage of furs for the trade are included.

Exclusion(s): Establishments primarily engaged in:
- storing garments and furs for individuals (81232, Dry Cleaning and Laundry Services (except Coin-Operated)).

Example Activities
- Bonded cold storage warehousing
- Cold storage locker service (except self storage)
- Fur storage service for the trade
- Refrigerated warehousing

493120 Refrigerated Warehousing and Storage

See industry description for 49312, above.

49313 Farm Product Warehousing and Storage

This industry comprises establishments primarily engaged in operating farm product warehousing and storage facilities, except refrigerated. Grain elevators primarily engaged in storage are included.

Exclusion(s): Establishments primarily engaged in:
- operating grain elevators, other than primarily storage (41112, Oilseed and Grain Wholesaler-Distributors); and
- operating refrigerated warehousing and storage facilities (49312, Refrigerated Warehousing and Storage).

Example Activities
- Bean cleaning and warehousing
- Farm product warehousing and storage, other than cold storage
- Grain elevators (storage only)
- Potato cellars
- Tobacco warehousing, storage
- Wool and mohair warehousing

493130 Farm Product Warehousing and Storage

See industry description for 49313, above.

49319 Other Warehousing and Storage

This industry comprises establishments, not classified to any other industry, primarily engaged in operating warehousing and storage facilities. These establishments operate facilities and equipment that are designed to handle a particular type of good, for example, dead automobile storage, petroleum storage caverns and whisky warehousing.

Example Activities
- Automobile dead storage
- Document storage and warehousing
- Furniture storage (without local trucking)
- Furniture storage service (used uncrated), household (without trucking)
- Household goods, warehousing and storage (without trucking)

- Lumber terminals, storage
- Natural gas storage
- Oil and gasoline storage caverns (for hire)
- Storage of natural gas

- Warehousing service, furniture and household goods (except used uncrated goods)
- Whisky warehousing

493190 Other Warehousing and Storage

See industry description for 49319, above.

51 Information and Cultural Industries

This sector comprises establishments primarily engaged in producing and distributing (except by wholesale and retail methods) information and cultural products. Establishments providing the means to transmit or distribute these products or providing access to equipment and expertise for processing data are also included.

The unique characteristics of information and cultural products, and of the processes involved in their production and distribution, distinguish this sector from the goods-producing and services-producing sectors.

The value of these products lies in their information, educational, cultural or entertainment content, not in the format in which they are distributed. Most of these products are protected from unlawful reproduction by copyright laws. Only those possessing the rights to these works are authorized to reproduce, alter, improve and distribute them. Acquiring and using these rights often involves significant costs.

The intangible nature of the content of information and cultural products allows for their distribution in various forms. For example, a movie can be shown at a movie theatre, on a television broadcast, through video on demand, or rented at a local video store; a sound recording can be aired on radio, embedded in multi-media products or sold at a record store; software can be bought at retail outlets or downloaded from an electronic bulletin board; a newspaper can be purchased at a newsstand or received on-line. In addition, improvements in information technology are revolutionizing the distribution of these products. The inclusion in this sector of telecommunications carriers and Internet access providers reflects the increasingly important role these establishments play in making these products accessible to the public.

The main components of this sector are the publishing industries (except exclusively on Internet), including software publishing, the motion picture and sound recording industries, the broadcasting industries (except exclusively on Internet), the telecommunications and related services industries (i.e., telephony, including VoIP; cable and satellite television distribution services; Internet access; telecommunications reselling services), data processing industries, and the other information services industries, including Internet publishing and broadcasting and web search portals. There are establishments engaged in culture-related activities that are classified in other sectors of NAICS. The most important are listed below.

Exclusion(s): Establishments primarily engaged in:
- duplicating information or cultural products in print form, or in the form of optical or magnetic media (31-33, Manufacturing);
- wholesaling information and cultural products such as newspapers, books, software, videocassettes, DVDs and sound recordings (41, Wholesale Trade);
- retailing information and cultural products such as newspapers, books, software and sound recordings (44-45, Retail Trade);
- design activities (54, Professional, Scientific and Technical Services);
- performing in artistic productions, and in creating artistic and cultural works or productions as independent individuals (71, Arts, Entertainment and Recreation);
- preserving and exhibiting objects, sites, and natural wonders of historical, cultural and/or educational value (71, Arts, Entertainment and Recreation); and
- producing live presentations that involve the performances of actors and actresses, singers, dancers, musical groups and artists, and other performing artists (71, Arts, Entertainment and Recreation).

511 Publishing Industries (except Internet)

This subsector comprises establishments primarily engaged in publishing newspapers, periodicals, books, databases, software and other works. These works are characterized by the intellectual creativity required in their development and are usually protected by copyright. Publishers distribute, or arrange for the distribution of copies of these works.

Publishing establishments may create the works in-house, or contract for, purchase, or compile works that were originally created by others. These works may be published in one or more formats including traditional print form, electronic and on-line. Publishers of "multimedia" products, such as interactive children's books, multimedia CD-ROM and digital video disk (DVD) reference books, and musical greeting cards are also included. Establishments in this subsector may print, reproduce or offer direct on-line access to the works themselves or they may arrange with others to carry out such functions.

Exclusion(s): Establishments primarily engaged in:
- publishing exclusively on the Internet (51913, Internet Publishing and Broadcasting, and Web Search Portals).

5111 Newspaper, Periodical, Book and Directory Publishers

This industry group comprises establishments primarily engaged in publishing (or publishing and printing) newspapers, periodicals, books, maps, directories, databases and other works, such as calendars, catalogues and greeting cards.

Exclusion(s): Establishments primarily engaged in:
- publishing software (51121, Software Publishers); and
- publishing music (51223, Music Publishers).

51111 Newspaper Publishers

This industry comprises establishments, known as newspaper publishers, primarily engaged in carrying out operations necessary for producing and distributing newspapers, including gathering news; writing news columns, feature stories and editorials; and selling and preparing advertisements. These establishments may publish newspapers in print or electronic form.

Exclusion(s): Establishments primarily engaged in:
- printing, but not publishing, newspapers (32311, Printing);
- supplying information, such as news, reports and pictures, to the news media (51911, News Syndicates);
- publishing newspapers exclusively on the Internet (51913, Internet Publishing and Broadcasting, and Web Search Portals); and
- selling media time or space for media owners (54184, Media Representatives).

Example Activities
- Newspapers, publishing (except exclusively on Internet)
- Newspapers, publishing and printing
- Publishers, newspaper (except exclusively on Internet)
- Publishers, newspaper, combined with printing

511110 Newspaper Publishers US

See industry description for 51111, above.

51112 Periodical Publishers

This industry comprises establishments, known as magazine or periodical publishers, primarily engaged in carrying out operations necessary for producing and distributing magazines and other periodicals, including gathering, writing, soliciting and editing articles, and preparing and selling advertisements. Periodicals are published at regular intervals, typically on a weekly, monthly or quarterly basis. These periodicals may be published in printed or electronic form.

Exclusion(s): Establishments primarily engaged in:
- printing, but not publishing, periodicals (32311, Printing);
- publishing newspapers (51111, Newspaper Publishers);
- publishing directories and databases (i.e., establishments known as publishers) (51114, Directory and Mailing List Publishers);
- publishing sheet music (51223, Music Publishers);
- publishing periodicals exclusively on the Internet (51913, Internet Publishing and Broadcasting, and Web Search Portals); and
- selling media time or space for media owners (54184, Media Representatives).

Example Activities
- Advertising periodicals, publishing (except exclusively on Internet)
- Agricultural magazines and periodicals, publishing (except exclusively on Internet)
- Comic books, publishing (except exclusively on Internet)
- Comic books, publishing and printing combined
- Financial magazines and periodicals, publishing (except exclusively on Internet)
- Financial magazines and periodicals, publishing and printing combined
- Juvenile magazines and periodicals, publishing (except exclusively on Internet)
- Magazine publishers, all formats, publishing (except exclusively on Internet)
- Magazines, publishing (except exclusively on Internet)
- Magazines, publishing and printing combined
- Newsletters, all formats, publishing (except exclusively on Internet)
- Periodicals, all formats, publishing and printing combined
- Periodicals, publishing (except exclusively on Internet)
- Professional magazines and periodicals, publishing and printing combined
- Publishers, periodicals, all formats (except exclusively on Internet)
- Religious magazines and periodicals, publisher (except exclusively on Internet)

- Scholarly journals, publishing (except exclusively on Internet)
- Scholastic magazines and periodicals, publishing and printing combined
- Technical magazines and periodicals, publishing (except exclusively on Internet)

- Television guides, publishing (except exclusively on Internet)
- Trade magazines and periodicals, publishing (except exclusively on Internet)

511120 Periodical Publishers US

See industry description for 51112, above.

51113 Book Publishers

This industry comprises establishments, known as book publishers, primarily engaged in carrying out various design, editing and marketing activities necessary for producing and distributing books of all kinds, such as text books; technical, scientific and professional books; and mass market paperback books. These books may be published in print, audio or electronic form.

Exclusion(s): Establishments primarily engaged in:
- printing, but not publishing, books (32311, Printing);
- direct selling, but not publishing, books, e.g. book clubs (4541, Electronic Shopping and Mail-Order Houses);
- publishing music books (51223, Music Publishers); and
- publishing books exclusively on the Internet (51913, Internet Publishing and Broadcasting, and Web Search Portals).

Example Activities
- Almanacs, publishing (except exclusively on Internet)
- Atlases, publishing (except exclusively on Internet)
- Books, all formats, printing and publishing combined
- Books, all formats, publishing (except exclusively on Internet)
- Dictionaries, publishing (except exclusively on Internet)
- Encyclopedias, publishing (except exclusively on Internet)
- Encyclopedias, publishing and printing combined
- Fiction books, publishing (except exclusively on Internet)
- Fiction books, publishing and printing combined
- Globe covers (maps), publishing (except exclusively on Internet)
- Guides, street, publishing and printing combined
- Maps, publishing (except exclusively on Internet)
- Non-fiction books, publishing (except exclusively on Internet)

- Non-fiction books, publishing and printing combined
- Professional books, publishing (except exclusively on Internet)
- Publishing, books (except exclusively on Internet)
- Publishing, maps, street guides and atlases (except exclusively on Internet)
- Religious books, publishers (except exclusively on Internet)
- Religious books, publishing and printing combined
- School textbooks, publishing (except exclusively on Internet)
- School textbooks, publishing and printing combined
- Street guide, publishers (except exclusively on Internet)
- Technical books, publishing (except exclusively on Internet)
- Travel guide books, publishing (except exclusively on Internet)
- Travel guide books, publishing and printing combined

511130 Book Publishers US

See industry description for 51113, above.

51114 Directory and Mailing List Publishers

This industry comprises establishments primarily engaged in publishing compilations and collections of information or facts that are logically organized to facilitate their use. These collections may be published in one or more formats, such as print or electronic form. Electronic versions may be provided directly to customers by the establishment, or offered through on-line services or third party vendors. The products are typically protected in their selection, arrangement and/or presentation.

Exclusion(s): Establishments primarily engaged in:
- printing, but not publishing, business directories, telephone books and similar products (32311, Printing);
- duplicating electronic media, such as CD-ROMs and DVDs (33461, Manufacturing and Reproducing Magnetic and Optical Media);
- publishing encyclopaedias (51113, Book Publishers);
- designing, developing and publishing computer software products (51121, Software Publishers);
- providing on-line access to databases developed by others (51913, Internet Publishing and Broadcasting, and Web Search Portals); and
- publishing directories and mailing lists exclusively on the Internet (51913, Internet Publishing and Broadcasting, and Web Search Portals).

Example Activities
- Address list compilers (except exclusively on Internet)
- Business directory, publishing (except exclusively on Internet)
- Business directory, publishing and printing combined
- Database publishing (except exclusively on Internet)
- Directories, publishing (except exclusively on Internet)
- Electronic database publishing (except exclusively on Internet)
- Mailing list compilers (except exclusively on Internet)
- Publishers, database (except exclusively on Internet)
- Telephone directories, publishing (except exclusively on Internet)
- Telephone directories, publishing and printing combined

511140 Directory and Mailing List Publishers US

See industry description for 51114, above.

51119 Other Publishers

This industry comprises establishments, not classified to any other industry, primarily engaged in publishing other works such as calendars, colouring books, greeting cards and posters.

Exclusion(s): Establishments primarily engaged in:
- publishing newspapers (51111, Newspaper Publishers);
- publishing magazines and periodicals (51112, Periodical Publishers);
- publishing books, maps and atlases (51113, Book Publishers);
- publishing directories and mailing lists (51114, Directory and Mailing List Publishers);
- publishing music (51223, Music Publishers); and
- publishing other works, such as calendars and greeting cards exclusively on the Internet (51913, Internet Publishing and Broadcasting, and Web Search Portals).

Example Activities
- Art prints, publishing (except exclusively on Internet)
- Calendars, publishing (except exclusively on Internet)
- Catalogues (i.e., mail order, store and merchandise), publishing (except exclusively on Internet)
- Colouring books, publishing (except exclusively on Internet)
- Diaries and time schedulers, publishers (except exclusively on Internet)
- Greeting cards, publishing (except exclusively on Internet)
- Racing forms, publishing (except exclusively on Internet)
- Yearbooks (i.e., high school, college, university), publishing (except exclusively on Internet)

511190 Other Publishers CAN

See industry description for 51119, above.

5112 Software Publishers

See industry description for 51121, below.

51121 Software Publishers

This industry comprises establishments primarily engaged in publishing computer software, usually for multiple clients and generally referred to as packaged software. Establishments in this industry carry out operations necessary for producing and distributing computer software, such as designing, providing documentation, assisting in installation and providing support services to software purchasers. These establishments may design and publish, or publish only.

Exclusion(s): Establishments primarily engaged in:
- mass duplication of software (33461, Manufacturing and Reproducing Magnetic and Optical Media);
- reselling packaged software (41731, Computer, Computer Peripheral and Pre-Packaged Software Wholesaler-Distributors, or 44312, Computer and Software Stores);
- providing access to software for clients from a central host site (51821, Data Processing, Hosting, and Related Services);
- publishing software exclusively on the Internet (51913, Internet Publishing and Broadcasting, and Web Search Portals); and
- custom designing software to meet the needs of specific users (54151, Computer Systems Design and Related Services).

Example Activities
- Computer software publishing (including designing and developing), packaged
- Computer software, all formats, packaged, publishers
- Games, computer software, packaged, publishers
- Publishers, packaged computer software, all formats

511210 Software Publishers

See industry description for 51121, above.

512 Motion Picture and Sound Recording Industries

This subsector comprises establishments primarily engaged in producing and distributing video and audio recordings or providing related services, such as post-production services, exhibition services, and motion picture processing and developing services. Sound recording studios are also included.

Exclusion(s): Establishments primarily engaged in:
- mass duplication of pre-recorded audio and video tapes, cassettes, diskettes, DVDs and CD-ROMs (33461, Manufacturing and Reproducing Magnetic and Optical Media);
- wholesaling sound recordings (41444, Sound Recording Wholesalers); and
- wholesaling pre-recorded video cassettes and DVDs (41445, Video Cassette Wholesalers).

5121 Motion Picture and Video Industries

This industry group comprises establishments primarily engaged in producing and/or distributing motion pictures, videos, television programs or commercials; exhibiting motion pictures or providing post-production and related services.

51211 Motion Picture and Video Production

This industry comprises establishments primarily engaged in producing, or producing and distributing, motion pictures, videos, television programs or commercials.

Exclusion(s): Establishments primarily engaged in:
- mass duplication of pre-recorded audio and video tapes, cassettes, diskettes, DVDs and CD-ROMs (33461, Manufacturing and Reproducing Magnetic and Optical Media);
- distributing film and video productions only (51212, Motion Picture and Video Distribution);
- providing post-production services, including motion picture laboratories (51219, Post-Production and Other Motion Picture and Video Industries); and
- videotaping special events (54192, Photographic Services).

Example Activities
- Animated film production
- Commercials, television, production
- Films, motion picture production
- Instructional film production
- Instructional video production
- Motion picture and video production
- Motion picture production
- Motion picture production and distribution
- Motion picture studios, producing motion pictures
- Music video production
- Programs producing, television
- Television commercial production
- Television show production
- Video production

512110 Motion Picture and Video Production US

See industry description for 51211, above.

51212 Motion Picture and Video Distribution

This industry comprises establishments primarily engaged in acquiring distribution rights and distributing film and video productions to motion picture theatres, television networks and stations, and other exhibitors.

Exclusion(s): Establishments primarily engaged in:
- mass duplication of pre-recorded audio and video tapes, cassettes, diskettes, DVDs and CD-ROMs (33461, Manufacturing and Reproducing Magnetic and Optical Media);
- wholesaling pre-recorded video cassettes and discs (41445, Video Cassette Wholesalers);
- retailing video cassettes and discs (45122, Pre-Recorded Tape, Compact Disc and Record Stores);
- both producing and distributing motion pictures and videos (51211, Motion Picture and Video Production);
- providing motion picture and video stock footage (via libraries) to producers, the media, multimedia and advertising industries (51219, Post-Production and Other Motion Picture and Video Industries);
- operating film and video archives whose primary purpose is preservation (51912, Libraries and Archives); and
- renting video cassettes and discs to the general public (53223, Video Tape and Disc Rental).

Example Activities

- Film distribution agencies
- Motion picture distributing
- Motion picture film distributors

- Tape distribution for television
- Television show syndicators
- Video productions, distributing

512120 Motion Picture and Video Distribution

See industry description for 51212, above.

51213 Motion Picture and Video Exhibition

This industry comprises establishments primarily engaged in exhibiting motion pictures. Establishments primarily engaged in providing occasional motion picture exhibition services, such as those provided during film festivals, are also included.

Example Activities

- Cinemas
- Drive-in theatres
- Festivals, film, with or without facilities
- Motion picture exhibition
- Motion picture exhibitors for airlines

- Motion picture theatres, drive-ins
- Motion picture theatres, indoor
- Outdoor theatres, motion pictures
- Theatres, motion picture, drive-in
- Theatres, motion picture, indoor

512130 Motion Picture and Video Exhibition MEX

See industry description for 51213, above.

51219 Post-Production and Other Motion Picture and Video Industries

This industry comprises establishments, not classified to any other industry, primarily engaged in providing post-production services and services to the motion picture and video industries, including specialized motion picture or video post-production services, such as editing, film/tape transferring, dubbing, subtitling, creating credits, closed captioning, and producing computer graphics, animation and special effects, as well as developing and processing motion picture films.

Exclusion(s): Establishments primarily engaged in:

- mass duplication of pre-recorded video cassettes and DVDs (33461, Manufacturing and Reproducing Magnetic and Optical Media);
- providing audio services for film, television, and video productions (51224, Sound Recording Studios);
- operating film and video archives whose primary purpose is preservation (51912, Libraries and Archives);
- renting wardrobes and costumes (53222, Formal Wear and Costume Rental);
- renting studio equipment (53249, Other Commercial and Industrial Machinery and Equipment Rental and Leasing); and
- casting actors and actresses with production companies (56131, Employment Placement Agencies and Executive Search Services).

Example Activities

- Closed captioning service, film or tape
- Developing and printing of commercial motion picture film
- Dubbing sound, motion picture
- Editing motion picture films or video
- Film and video transfer service

- Film or tape closed captioning
- Film processing laboratories, motion picture
- Libraries, motion picture film, stock footage
- Libraries, video tape, stock footage
- Motion picture (or video) editing services

- Motion picture and video post-production services
- Motion picture film library, stock footage
- Motion picture film processing, editing and titling
- Motion picture laboratories
- Motion picture or video titling or sub-titling
- Motion picture production special effects, post-production
- Motion picture stock footage, film libraries
- Post-production facilities
- Post-synchronization, sound dubbing

- Sound dubbing service, motion picture
- Special effects for motion picture, post production
- Stock footage, film libraries
- Tape transfer service
- Teleproduction services
- Television tape services (e.g., editing, transfers)
- Titling of motion picture film or video
- Video conversion services (i.e., between formats)
- Video post-production services

512190 Post-Production and Other Motion Picture and Video Industries ᴹᴱˣ

See industry description for 51219, above.

5122 Sound Recording Industries

This industry group comprises establishments primarily engaged in producing and distributing music recordings, publishing music, or providing sound recording and related services.

Exclusion(s):
- musical groups and artists (71113, Musical Groups and Artists);
- songwriters (711513, Independent Writers and Authors);

and establishments primarily engaged in:
- mass duplication of sound recordings (33461, Manufacturing and Reproducing Magnetic and Optical Media); and
- wholesaling sound recordings (41444, Sound Recording Wholesalers).

51221 Record Production

This industry comprises establishments primarily engaged in record production. These establishments contract with musical artists, and arrange and finance the production of original master recordings. Establishments in this industry hold the copyright to the master recording and derive most of their revenues from selling, leasing, and licensing master recordings. Establishments in this industry do not have their own duplication or distribution capabilities.

Exclusion(s):
- independent record producers hired on contract (711512, Independent Actors, Comedians and Performers);

and establishments primarily engaged in:
- mass duplication of sound recordings (33461, Manufacturing and Reproducing Magnetic and Optical Media);
- wholesaling (distribution of finished products, bought for resale, including imports) sound recordings (41444, Sound Recording Wholesalers);
- releasing, promoting and distributing sound recordings (51222, Integrated Record Production/Distribution);
- promoting and authorizing the use of musical works in various media (51223, Music Publishers);
- providing facilities and technical expertise for recording musical performances (51224, Sound Recording Studios); and
- managing artist careers (71141, Agents and Managers for Artists, Athletes, Entertainers and Other Public Figures).

Example Activities
- Production of master recordings, exclusive of distribution
- Publishing and reproducing audio materials in integrated facilities

- Record production (except independent record producers), without duplication or distribution
- Record production companies (producing only)

512210 Record Production

See industry description for 51221, above.

51222 Integrated Record Production/Distribution

This industry comprises establishments primarily engaged in releasing, promoting and distributing sound recordings. Establishments in this industry manufacture or arrange for the manufacture of recordings, such as audio tapes/cassettes and compact discs, and promote and distribute these products to wholesalers, retailers or directly to the public. These establishments produce master recordings themselves, or obtain reproduction and/or distribution rights to master recordings produced by record production companies or other integrated record companies.

Exclusion(s): Establishments primarily engaged in:
- mass duplication of sound recordings (33461, Manufacturing and Reproducing Magnetic and Optical Media);
- wholesaling (distribution of finished products, bought for resale, including imports) sound recordings (41444, Sound Recording Wholesalers);
- record production, including contracting with musical artists, arranging and financing the production of original master recordings, and marketing the reproduction rights (51221, Record Production); and
- providing facilities and technical expertise for recording musical performances (51224, Sound Recording Studios).

Example Activities
- Integrated record production and distribution
- Pre-recorded audio tapes and compact discs, integrated manufacture, release and distribution

- Record production and distribution combined
- Sound recordings, integrated production, reproduction, release and distribution

512220 Integrated Record Production/Distribution

See industry description for 51222, above.

51223 Music Publishers

This industry comprises establishments primarily engaged in acquiring and registering copyrights in musical compositions, in accordance with the law, and promoting and authorizing the use of these compositions in recordings, on radio and television, in motion pictures, live performances, print, multimedia or other media. Establishments in this industry represent the interests of songwriters or other owners of musical compositions in generating revenues from the use of such works, generally through licensing agreements. These establishments may own the copyright or act as administrator of the music copyrights on behalf of copyright owners.

Exclusion(s):
- songwriters who act as their own publishers (711513, Independent Writers and Authors).

Example Activities
- Music books (i.e., bound sheet music), publishing
- Music books (i.e., bound sheet music), publishing and printing combined
- Music copyright buying and licensing
- Music, publishing
- Music, publishing and printing combined
- Publishing music
- Sheet music, publishing
- Sheet music, publishing and printing combined
- Songs, publishing
- Songs, publishing and printing combined

512230 Music Publishers

See industry description for 51223, above.

51224 Sound Recording Studios

This industry comprises establishments primarily engaged in providing the facilities and technical expertise for recording musical performances. Establishments in this industry may also provide audio production or post-production services for producing master recordings, and audio services for film, television and video productions.

Exclusion(s): Establishments primarily engaged in:
- mass duplication of sound recordings (33461, Manufacturing and Reproducing Magnetic and Optical Media);
- record production, including contracting with musical artists, arranging and financing the production of original master recordings, and marketing the reproduction rights (51221, Record Production); and
- releasing, promoting and distributing sound recordings (51222, Integrated Record Production/Distribution).

Example Activities
- Audio recording post-production services
- Recording studios (except integrated record company)
- Recording studios, operating on a contract or fee basis
- Sound recording studio

512240 Sound Recording Studios

See industry description for 51224, above.

51229 Other Sound Recording Industries

This industry comprises establishments, not classified to any other industry, primarily engaged in providing sound recording services.

Exclusion(s): Establishments primarily engaged in:
- mass duplication of sound recordings (33461, Manufacturing and Reproducing Magnetic and Optical Media);
- wholesaling (distribution of finished products, bought for resale, including imports) sound recordings (41444, Sound Recording Wholesalers);
- record production, including contracting with musical artists, arranging and financing the production of original master recordings, and marketing the reproduction rights (51221, Record Production);
- releasing, promoting and distributing sound recordings (51222, Integrated Record Production/Distribution);
- promoting and authorizing the use of musical works in various media (51223, Music Publishers);
- providing facilities and technical expertise for recording musical performances (51224, Sound Recording Studios);
- organizing and promoting the presentation of performing arts productions (7113, Promoters (Presenters) of Performing Arts, Sports and Similar Events); and
- managing artist careers (71141, Agents and Managers for Artists, Athletes, Entertainers and Other Public Figures).

Example Activities
- Audio taping of meetings or conferences
- Recording of books on tape or disc (except publishing)
- Recording seminars and conferences, audio

512290 Other Sound Recording Industries

See industry description for 51229, above.

515 Broadcasting (except Internet)

This subsector comprises establishments primarily engaged in operating radio and television broadcasting studios and facilities.

Exclusion(s): Establishments primarily engaged in:
- operating telecommunications networks (517, Telecommunications); and
- broadcasting exclusively on the Internet (519, Other Information Services).

5151 Radio and Television Broadcasting

This industry group comprises establishments primarily engaged in operating broadcasting studios and facilities for the transmission of a variety of radio and television broadcasts, including entertainment, news, talk shows and other programs. These establishments produce, purchase and schedule programs; and generate revenues from the sale of air time to advertisers, from donations and subsidies, or from the sale of programs.

Exclusion(s): Establishments primarily engaged in:
- broadcasting television programs in a defined and limited format via operators of cable and satellite distribution systems (51521, Pay and Specialty Television);
- delivering programs to subscribers by cable or satellite systems (517112, Cable and Other Program Distribution); and
- broadcasting exclusively on the Internet (51913, Internet Publishing and Broadcasting, and Web Search Portals).

51511 Radio Broadcasting

This industry comprises establishments primarily engaged in operating broadcasting studios and facilities for the production and transmission of radio programs to its affiliates or the public. The radio broadcasts may include entertainment, news, talk shows and other programs.

Example Activities

- Broadcasting stations, radio
- Radio broadcasting network services

- Radio broadcasting stations
- Satellite radio networks

515110 Radio Broadcasting ᴹᴱˣ

See industry description for 51511, above.

51512 Television Broadcasting

This industry comprises establishments primarily engaged in operating broadcasting studios and facilities for the production, and over-the-air transmission to the public, of a variety of television programs. Programming may originate in their own studios, from an affiliated network or from external sources.

Exclusion(s): Establishments primarily engaged in:

- producing television programs without broadcasting (51211, Motion Picture and Video Production);
- broadcasting television programs in a defined and limited format via operators of cable or satellite distribution systems (51521, Pay and Specialty Television);
- delivering programs to subscribers by cable or satellite systems (517112, Cable and Other Program Distribution); and
- broadcasting television programs exclusively on the Internet (51913, Internet Publishing and Broadcasting, and Web Search Portals).

Example Activities

- Broadcasting networks, television
- Broadcasting stations, television
- Public broadcasting television

- Television broadcasting network services
- Television broadcasting stations

515120 Television Broadcasting

See industry description for 51512, above.

5152 Pay and Specialty Television

This industry group comprises establishments primarily engaged in broadcasting television programs, in a defined and limited format, via operators of cable and satellite distribution systems. The programming is delivered to subscribers by operators of cable or satellite distribution systems.

51521 Pay and Specialty Television

This industry comprises establishments primarily engaged in broadcasting television programs, in a defined and limited format, such as family and youth-oriented, news, feature films, music, health, sports, religion, weather, travel and educational programming. These establishments may produce programs in their own broadcasting studios or they may acquire programming from external sources. The programming is delivered to subscribers by operators of cable or satellite distribution systems.

Exclusion(s): Establishments primarily engaged in:

- producing programs for television without broadcasting (51211, Motion Picture and Video Production);
- delivering programs to subscribers by cable or satellite systems (517112, Cable and Other Program Distribution); and
- broadcasting television programs in a defined and limited format exclusively on the Internet (51913, Internet Publishing and Broadcasting, and Web Search Portals).

Example Activities
- Cable broadcasting networks
- Cable program broadcasting
- Cable television network
- Pay television

- Satellite television networks
- Specialty cable television (e.g., music, sports, news) networks
- Subscription television, network

515210 Pay and Specialty Television

See industry description for 51521, above.

517 Telecommunications

This subsector comprises establishments primarily engaged in providing telecommunications and/or video entertainment services over their own or leased networks, on a resale basis or over client-supplied high speed Internet connections. The establishments of this subsector are grouped into industries on the basis of the nature of services provided (fixed or mobile), the type of network used to deliver those services (wireline or wireless), and the business model they employ (facilities-based or resale).

Exclusion(s): Establishments primarily engaged in:
- the installation and maintenance of broadcasting and telecommunications systems by independent contractors (23, Construction); and
- offering limited Internet connectivity at establishments usually known as Internet cafés and a combination of other services such as facsimile services, training, rental of on-site personal computers for word processing, games rooms, or food services (56143, Business Service Centres, or 722, Food Services and Drinking Places).

5171 Wired Telecommunications Carriers

See industry description for 51711, below.

51711 Wired Telecommunications Carriers

This industry comprises establishments primarily engaged in providing telecommunications and/or video entertainment services to their customer premises over network facilities operated by them. The establishments of this industry can own a network, lease a network or combine leased and owned facilities and their networks can integrate various technologies.

517111 Wired Telecommunications Carriers (except Cable) CAN

This Canadian industry comprises establishments primarily engaged in providing telecommunications and video entertainment services primarily by copper twisted pair links to the network. Establishments in this industry are generally known as telephone companies, incumbent local exchange carriers (ILECs) and facilities based competitive service providers and they often provide a full range of telecommunication services to residential, business and wholesale customers. Establishments providing a similar range of services through a co-axial-based network are classified in 517112, Cable and Other Program Distribution.

Exclusion(s): Establishments primarily engaged in:
- installing and maintaining wired systems on contract (23821, Electrical Contractors and Other Wiring Installation Contractors);
- providing telecommunications and/or video entertainment services to mobile telecommunication devices over network facilities operated by them (51721, Wireless Telecommunications Carriers (except Satellite));
- providing access to satellite telecommunications facilities to telecommunications carriers and business users (51741, Satellite Telecommunications);
- providing telecommunications services to customer premises or mobile telecommunication devices over network facilities operated by others on a re-sale basis or over a high speed Internet connection provided by others (51791, Other Telecommunications);
- offering limited Internet connectivity at establishments usually known as Internet cafés and a combination of other services such as facsimile services, training, rental of on-site personal computers for word processing, games rooms, or food services (56143, Business Service Centres, or 722, Food Services and Drinking Places); and
- operating coin-operated pay telephones (81299, All Other Personal Services).

Example Activities
- Access-dependent VoIP services providers, facilities based, except wireless and cable
- Facilities-based competitive service providers
- Facilities-based telecommunication carrier, except wireless and cable operators
- Incumbent local exchange carriers (ILECs)
- Internet service providers (ISPs), facilities-based (except cable)
- Local telephone carrier, except wireless and cable operators
- Long-distance telephone carrier, facilities-based
- Telephone companies

517112 Cable and Other Program Distribution CAN

This Canadian industry comprises establishments primarily engaged in providing telecommunications and video entertainment on networks originally designed for the distribution of television channels. Establishments in this industry are generally known as cable, satellite and wireless cable television operators. They operate co-axial based distribution networks, satellite-based distribution networks and fixed wireless-based distribution networks and they primarily serve the residential market. The establishments of this industry can offer a range of telecommunications and video entertainment services or specialize in the latter. Establishments providing a similar range of services through a copper twisted pair based network are classified in 517111, Wired Telecommunications Carriers (except Cable).

Exclusion(s): Establishments primarily engaged in:

- installing and maintaining cable systems by independent contractors (23821, Electrical Contractors and Other Wiring Installation Contractors);
- broadcasting radio programs in a defined and limited format via operators of cable or satellite radio networks (51511, Radio Broadcasting);
- broadcasting television programs in a defined and limited format via operators of cable or satellite distribution systems (51521, Pay and Specialty Television);
- providing telecommunications and/or video entertainment services to mobile telecommunication devices over network facilities operated by them (51721, Wireless Telecommunications Carriers (except Satellite));
- providing access to satellite telecommunications facilities to telecommunications carriers and business users (51741, Satellite Telecommunications);
- providing telecommunications services to customer premises or mobile telecommunication devices over network facilities operated by others on a re-sale basis or over a high speed Internet connection provided by others (51791, Other Telecommunications); and
- offering limited Internet connectivity at establishments usually known as Internet cafés and a combination of other services such as facsimile services, training, rental of on-site personal computers for word processing, games rooms, or food services (56143, Business Service Centres, or 722, Food Services and Drinking Places).

Example Activities

- Cable program distribution operator
- Cable television providers
- Cablevision services
- Closed circuit television (CCTV) services
- Direct-to-home (DTH) satellite television service providers
- Internet service providers (ISPs), cable

- Managed VoIP services providers, cable
- Multichannel multipoint distribution services (MMDS)
- Multipoint distribution systems (MDS)
- Satellite television operators
- Television operation, closed circuit
- Wireless cable television operators

5172 Wireless Telecommunications Carriers (except Satellite)

See industry description for 51721, below.

51721 Wireless Telecommunications Carriers (except Satellite)

This industry comprises establishments primarily engaged in providing telecommunications and/or video entertainment services to mobile telecommunication devices over network facilities operated by them. The establishments of this industry can own a network, lease a network or combine leased and owned facilities.

Exclusion(s): Establishments primarily engaged in:

- providing fixed telecommunications or video entertainment services using fixed wireless facilities (51711, Wired Telecommunications Carriers);
- providing access to satellite telecommunications facilities to telecommunications carriers and business users (51741, Satellite Telecommunications); and
- providing telecommunications and/or video entertainment services to mobile telecommunication devices over network facilities operated by others (mobile virtual network operators) (51791, Other Telecommunications).

Example Activities

- Beeper (radio pager) communications carriers
- Cellular telephone services
- Mobile data services
- Mobile Internet service

- Mobile messaging service (text, picture, video)
- Mobile telephone communications carriers
- Paging services

- Personal communication services (PCS) (i.e., communications carriers)
- Personal mobile communications services
- Radio paging communications carriers
- Satellite telephone services
- Ship-to-shore broadcasting communications carriers

- Telecommunications carriers, cellular telephone
- Two-way paging communications carriers
- Wireless data communications carriers
- Wireless telephone communications carriers
- Wireless video service

517210 Wireless Telecommunications Carriers (except Satellite) MEX

See industry description for 51721, above.

5174 Satellite Telecommunications

See industry description for 51741, below.

51741 Satellite Telecommunications

This industry comprises establishments primarily engaged in providing mobile and fixed telecommunications services over satellite network facilities operated by them or by distributing the services of other satellite network operators. Establishments in this industry typically serve a business clientele (telecommunication carriers, private business networks, broadcasters) but can also provide services to individual customers that are beyond the reach of terrestrial networks (e.g. high speed Internet).

Exclusion(s): Establishments primarily engaged in:
- broadcasting radio or television programs by conventional means or over the Internet (515, Broadcasting (except Internet), or 51913, Internet Publishing and Broadcasting, and Web Search Portals);
- distributing radio programs on a subscription basis by satellite (51511, Radio Broadcasting);
- delivering television and radio programs to subscribers by a direct-to-home (DTH) satellite system (517112, Cable and Other Program Distribution); and
- delivering mobile personal communication services with low earth orbiting satellite technology (51721, Wireless Telecommunications Carriers (except Satellite)).

Example Activities
- Fixed-to-mobile satellite services
- Long-distance telephone, satellite-communications carriers
- Resellers, satellite telecommunications
- Satellite communication service

- Satellite communications carriers
- Satellite service resellers
- Telephone communications carriers, satellite
- VSAT (very small aperture terminal) services

517410 Satellite Telecommunications

See industry description for 51741, above.

5179 Other Telecommunications

See industry description for 51791, below.

51791 Other Telecommunications

This industry comprises establishments primarily engaged in providing telecommunications and/or video entertainment services over network facilities operated by others and establishments primarily engaged in operating telecommunications networks or providing telecommunication services not elsewhere classified.

Exclusion(s): Establishments primarily engaged in:
- providing telecommunications and/or video entertainment services to their customer premises over network facilities operated by them (51711, Wired Telecommunications Carriers);
- providing telecommunications and/or video entertainment services to mobile telecommunication devices over network facilities operated by them (51721, Wireless Telecommunications Carriers (except Satellite));
- providing mobile and fixed telecommunications services over satellite network facilities operated by them or by distributing the services of other satellite network operators (51741, Satellite Telecommunications); and
- providing expert advice in the field of information technology or in integrating communication and computer systems (54151, Computer Systems Design and Related Services).

Example Activities
- Information access services, on-line
- ISPs, independent
- ISPs, resale
- Long distance telecommunication resellers (except satellite)
- Long-distance telephone resellers (except satellite)
- Microwave communications resellers
- Mobile virtual network operators (MVNO)
- Non-facilities based ISPs
- Radar station operation
- Resellers, long-distance telephone communications (except satellite)
- Resellers, microwave communications
- Resellers, telephone communications (except satellite)
- Reselling dial-up or broadband ISP services
- Satellite earth stations facilities operators
- Satellite telemetry operation on a contract or fee basis
- Satellite terminal stations
- Satellite tracking stations
- Telecommunication resellers (except satellite)
- Telemetry and tracking system operation on a contract or fee basis
- Telephone communications resellers (except satellite)
- Tracking missiles by telemetry and photography on a contract basis
- VoIP services, access-independent (non-managed)

517910 Other Telecommunications

See industry description for 51791, above.

518 Data Processing, Hosting, and Related Services

This subsector comprises establishments primarily engaged in providing the infrastructure for data processing, hosting, and related services.

5182 Data Processing, Hosting, and Related Services

See industry description for 51821, below.

51821 Data Processing, Hosting, and Related Services

This industry comprises establishments primarily engaged in providing hosting or data processing services. Hosting establishments may provide specialized hosting activities, such as web hosting, video and audio streaming services, application hosting, application service provisioning, or may provide general time-share mainframe facilities to clients. Data processing establishments may provide complete processing and preparation of reports from data supplied by the customer; specialized services, such as automated data entry; or they may make data processing resources available to clients on an hourly or time-sharing basis.

Exclusion(s): Establishments primarily engaged in:
- processing financial transactions (52232, Financial Transactions Processing, Reserve and Clearing House Activities);
- computer facilities management (54151, Computer Systems Design and Related Services);
- providing data keying, text processing or desktop publishing (56141, Document Preparation Services); and
- providing access to microcomputers and office equipment from a retail location (56143, Business Service Centres).

Example Activities
- Application hosting
- Automatic data processing, computer services
- Computer input preparation services
- Computer processing
- Computer processing services
- Computer time, rental
- Computer time-sharing services
- Data entry services
- Data processing services
- Data processing, computer services
- Disk and diskette conversion services
- Input preparation services, computer
- Leasing of computer time
- Microfilm recording and imaging service
- Optical scanning data services
- Rental of computer time
- Service bureaus, computer
- Video and audio streaming services
- Web hosting

518210 Data Processing, Hosting, and Related Services

See industry description for 51821, above.

519 Other Information Services

See industry description for 5191, below.

5191 Other Information Services

This industry group comprises establishments, not classified to any other industry, primarily engaged in providing other information services. The main components are news syndicates, libraries and archives, and other information search services on a contract basis.

51911 News Syndicates

This industry comprises establishments primarily engaged in supplying information, such as news reports, articles, pictures and features to the news media.

Exclusion(s):
- independent correspondents and free-lance news journalists (711513, Independent Writers and Authors).

Example Activities
- Feature syndicate
- News agencies
- News feature syndicates
- News picture gathering and distributing service
- News reporting service
- News syndicates
- News ticker service
- Newspaper feature syndicate
- Press service (news syndicate)
- Syndicates, news
- Wire services, news

519110 News Syndicates

See industry description for 51911, above.

51912 Libraries and Archives

This industry comprises establishments primarily engaged in providing library or archive services. These establishments maintain collections of documents (such as books, journals, newspapers and music) and facilitate the use of such documents (regardless of their physical form and characteristics) as are required to meet the informational, research, educational or recreational needs of their users. They may also acquire, research, store, and make accessible to the public, original historical documents, photographs, maps, audio material, audio-visual material and other archival materials of historical interest. Cinematheques, videotheques and other film and video archives, whose primary purpose is the preservation of archival audio-visual material, are included. All or portions of these collections may be accessible electronically.

> *Exclusion(s): Establishments primarily engaged in:*
> - providing motion picture and video stock footage (via libraries) to producers, the media, multimedia and advertising industries (51219, Post-Production and Other Motion Picture and Video Industries).

519121 Libraries CAN

This Canadian industry comprises establishments primarily engaged in maintaining collections and facilitating the use of such documents (regardless of its physical form and characteristics) as are required to meet the informational, research, educational or recreational needs of their users.

> *Exclusion(s): Establishments primarily engaged in:*
> - retailing books (45121, Book Stores and News Dealers); and
> - providing motion picture and video stock footage (via libraries) to producers, the media, multimedia and advertising industries (51219, Post-Production and Other Motion Picture and Video Industries).

Example Activities
- Bookmobiles
- Circulating libraries
- Lending libraries
- Libraries (except motion picture and video tape stock footage)
- Public libraries
- Reference libraries

519122 Archives CAN

This Canadian industry comprises establishments primarily engaged in acquiring, researching, storing, and making accessible to the public, original historical documents, photographs, maps, audio or audio-visual material, and other archival materials of historical interest. Cinematheques, videotheques, and other film and video archives whose primary purpose is the preservation of archival audio-visual material, are included.

> *Exclusion(s): Establishments primarily engaged in:*
> - providing motion picture and video stock footage (via libraries) to producers, the media, multimedia and advertising industries (51219, Post-Production and Other Motion Picture and Video Industries).

Example Activities
- Archives
- Centres for documentation (i.e., archives)
- Cinematheques (film library)
- Film archives
- Music archives
- Photographic libraries, archives
- Video archives

51913 Internet Publishing and Broadcasting, and Web Search Portals

This industry comprises establishments exclusively engaged in publishing and/or broadcasting content on the Internet or operating web sites, known as web search portals, that use a search engine to generate and maintain extensive databases of Internet addresses and content in an easily searchable format. The Internet publishing and broadcasting establishments in this industry provide textual, audio, and/or video content of general or specific interest. These establishments do not provide traditional (non-Internet) versions of the content that they publish or broadcast. Establishments known as web search portals often provide additional Internet services, such as e-mail, connections to other web sites, auctions, news, and other limited content, and serve as a home base for Internet users.

Exclusion(s): Establishments primarily engaged in:
- retailing new and used goods using the Internet (44-45, Retail Trade);
- providing Internet publishing and other print or electronic editions; offering direct on-line access to information that they publish or compile (511, Publishing Industries (except Internet));
- publishing databases (51114, Directory and Mailing List Publishers);
- traditional or combined broadcasting (515, Broadcasting (except Internet));
- providing Internet access (Internet services providers (ISPs)) (517, Telecommunications);
- offering limited Internet connectivity at establishments usually known as Internet cafés and a combination of other services such as facsimile services, training, rental of on-site personal computers for word processing, games rooms, or food services (56143, Business Service Centres, or 722, Food Services and Drinking Places); and
- developing databases for the purpose of credit reporting (56145, Credit Bureaus).

Example Activities
- Directory publishing, Internet
- Internet book publishing
- Internet broadcasting
- Internet entertainment sites
- Internet game sites
- Internet newspaper publishing
- Internet periodical publishing

- Internet software publishing
- Newspapers, publishing (exclusively on Internet)
- Publishing, maps, street guides and atlases (exclusively on Internet)
- Technical books, publishing (exclusively on Internet)
- Web search portals

519130 Internet Publishing and Broadcasting, and Web Search Portals

See industry description for 51913, above.

51919 All Other Information Services

This industry comprises establishments, not classified to any other industry, primarily engaged in providing information services, including telephone-based information recordings and information search services on a contract basis.

Example Activities
- News clipping service
- Stock photo agencies

- Telephone-based information services
- Telephone-based recorded information services

519190 All Other Information Services

See industry description for 51919, above.

52 Finance and Insurance

This sector comprises establishments primarily engaged in financial transactions (that is, transactions involving the creation, liquidation, or change in ownership of financial assets) or in facilitating financial transactions. Included are:

● establishments that are primarily engaged in financial intermediation. They raise funds by taking deposits and/or issuing securities, and, in the process, incur liabilities, which they use to acquire financial assets by making loans and/or purchasing securities. Putting themselves at risk, they channel funds from lenders to borrowers and transform or repackage the funds with respect to maturity, scale and risk.

● establishments that are primarily engaged in the pooling of risk by underwriting annuities and insurance. They collect fees (insurance premiums or annuity considerations), build up reserves, invest those reserves and make contractual payments. Fees are based on the expected incidence of the insured risk and the expected return on investment.

● establishments that are primarily engaged in providing specialized services that facilitate or support financial intermediation, insurance and employee benefit programs.

In addition, establishments charged with monetary control - the monetary authorities - are included in this sector.

521 Monetary Authorities - Central Bank

See industry description for 5211, below.

5211 Monetary Authorities - Central Bank

This industry group comprises establishments primarily engaged in performing central banking functions, such as issuing currency (paper money); managing the nation's money supply and international reserves; overseeing payment, clearing and settlement systems; holding deposits that represent the reserves of other banks and institutions; and acting as fiscal agent for the federal government.

The institutional arrangements for performing these functions and for conducting monetary policy may differ among the countries. In Canada, these functions are performed by the Bank of Canada, in Mexico by the Bank of Mexico, and in the United States by the Federal Reserve Banks and their branches.

52111 Monetary Authorities - Central Bank

This industry comprises establishments primarily engaged in performing central banking functions, such as issuing currency (paper money); managing the nation's money supply and international reserves; overseeing payment, clearing and settlement systems; holding deposits that represent the reserves of other banks and institutions; and acting as fiscal agent for the federal government.

Example Activity
● Bank of Canada

521110 Monetary Authorities - Central Bank

See industry description for 52111, above.

522 Credit Intermediation and Related Activities

This subsector comprises establishments primarily engaged in lending funds raised from depositors or by issuing debt, and establishments that facilitate the lending of funds or issuance of credit by engaging in such activities as mortgage and loan brokerage, clearinghouse and reserve services, and cheque-cashing services.

5221 Depository Credit Intermediation US

This industry group comprises establishments primarily engaged in accepting deposits and lending funds. Deposits are the principal source of funds loaned.

52211 Banking CAN

This industry comprises establishments primarily engaged in accepting deposits and issuing loans. Examples of establishments in this industry are establishments of chartered banks, trust companies and deposit-accepting mortgage companies that are primarily engaged in accepting deposits and issuing loans.

Exclusion(s):
- local credit unions (52213, Local Credit Unions);
- provincial government savings establishments that channel deposits received to the government rather than lending them to customers (52219, Other Depository Credit Intermediation);

and establishments primarily engaged in:
- investment banking (52311, Investment Banking and Securities Dealing);
- buying and selling securities for others on a commission basis (52312, Securities Brokerage); and
- underwriting insurance (5241, Insurance Carriers).

522111 Personal and Commercial Banking Industry CAN

This Canadian industry comprises establishments primarily engaged in accepting deposits from, and issuing loans to, persons or small- and medium-sized businesses. Establishments of chartered banks, trust companies and deposit-accepting mortgage companies that are primarily engaged in these activities are included.

Exclusion(s):
- local credit unions (522130, Local Credit Unions); and
- provincial government savings establishments that channel deposits to the government rather than lending them to customers (522190, Other Depository Credit Intermediation).

Example Activities
- Bank branches, chartered, providing personal and commercial banking services
- Deposit-accepting mortgage companies (except co-operative)
- Establishments of chartered banks providing personal and commercial banking services
- Establishments of trust companies providing personal and commercial banking services
- Trust company branches, chartered, providing personal and commercial banking services

522112 Corporate and Institutional Banking Industry CAN

This Canadian industry comprises establishments primarily engaged in issuing loans to large businesses, governments or other large institutional clients, using funds primarily obtained from related personal and commercial banking establishments. Corporate and institutional banking establishments provide deposit and other services to their clients. Establishments of chartered banks that are primarily engaged in issuing loans to the above-mentioned clients are included.

Exclusion(s): Establishments primarily engaged in:
- investment banking (523110, Investment Banking and Securities Dealing).

Example Activities
- Bank branches, chartered, providing corporate and institutional banking services
- Corporate and institutional banking services
- Trust company branches, chartered, providing corporate and institutional banking services

52213 Local Credit Unions US

This industry comprises establishments of local credit unions and caisses populaires primarily engaged in accepting deposits from, and issuing loans to, members. Local credit unions raise funds from members through the sale of shares and the acceptance of deposits.

Example Activity
- Credit unions, local

522130 Local Credit Unions US

See industry description for 52213, above.

52219 Other Depository Credit Intermediation US

This industry comprises establishments, not classified to any other industry, primarily engaged in accepting deposits and making loans. Provincial government savings establishments that channel deposits to the government rather than lending them to customers are also included.

Example Activities
- Banks, private (i.e., unincorporated)
- Deposit-accepting mortgage companies, co-operative

522190 Other Depository Credit Intermediation US

See industry description for 52219, above.

5222 Non-Depository Credit Intermediation US

This industry group comprises establishments, both public (government-sponsored enterprises) and private, primarily engaged in extending credit or lending funds raised by credit market borrowing, such as by issuing commercial paper and other debt instruments, and by borrowing from other financial intermediaries.

52221 Credit Card Issuing US

This industry comprises establishments primarily engaged in providing credit sales services to business entities, such as retailers, and to consumers by providing the funds required in return for payment of the full balance or payments on an installment basis.

Example Activity
- Credit card companies

522210 Credit Card Issuing US

See industry description for 52221, above.

52222 Sales Financing US

This industry comprises establishments primarily engaged in sales financing. Establishments primarily engaged in providing financial leases or operating leases are also included if they are engaged in any sales financing.

Sales financing establishments lend money to consumers and businesses, for the purchase of goods and services, using a contractual installment sales agreement, often either directly from, or through arrangements with, dealers of the products. Examples of establishments in this industry are acceptance companies of motor vehicle manufacturers and heavy equipment manufacturers. Establishments engaged in the purchase of installment and credit card receivables, created as a result of retail sales to businesses and individuals, are included.

> *Exclusion(s): Establishments primarily engaged in:*
> * providing operating leases and financial leases if they are not engaged in any sales financing (532, Rental and Leasing Services).

> *Example Activities*
> * Acceptance companies
> * Automobile sales finance company
> * Conditional sales finance companies
> * Leasing, in combination with sales financing
> * Sales finance companies

522220 Sales Financing US

See industry description for 52222, above.

52229 Other Non-Depository Credit Intermediation US

This industry comprises establishments, not classified to any other industry, primarily engaged in making cash loans or granting credit to consumers and businesses through credit instruments other than credit cards, sales finance agreements, or financial leases. Examples of types of lending are consumer credit, real estate credit, international trade financing, secondary market financing, and other non-depository credit intermediation.

522291 Consumer Lending US

This Canadian industry comprises establishments primarily engaged in providing unsecured cash loans to consumers. However, some cash lending activities may be secured by a chattel mortgage enabling the lender to take possession of the chattel in case of default. Examples of establishments in this Canadian industry are consumer loan companies, personal finance companies and small loan companies.

> *Example Activities*
> * Mutual benefit associations (loan association)
> * Personal credit institutions
> * Personal loan companies

522299 All Other Non-Depository Credit Intermediation CAN

This Canadian industry comprises establishments, not classified to any other Canadian industry, primarily engaged in providing non-depository credit, such as real estate credit, international trade financing, short-term inventory credit and loans, working capital credit, and agricultural credit and loans. Examples of establishments in this industry are factoring companies, pawnshops, mortgage companies and government credit agencies that make direct loans or extend credit.

Example Activities
- Factoring companies
- Pawnbrokers

- Secondary market financing (i.e, buying, pooling and repackaging loans for sale to others)

5223 Activities Related to Credit Intermediation US

This industry group comprises establishments primarily engaged in providing services closely related to credit intermediation, but not acting as intermediaries.

52231 Mortgage and Non-mortgage Loan Brokers US

This industry comprises establishments primarily engaged in arranging mortgage or other loans for others on a commission or fee basis. These establishments ordinarily do not have any continuing relationship with either borrower or lender.

Exclusion(s): Establishments primarily engaged in:
- mortgage banking (52229, Other Non-Depository Credit Intermediation).

Example Activities
- Brokerages, loan
- Brokerages, mortgage
- Loan brokers' or agents' (i.e., independent) offices

- Mortgage brokerages
- Mortgage brokers' or agents' (i.e., independent) offices

522310 Mortgage and Non-mortgage Loan Brokers US

See industry description for 52231, above.

52232 Financial Transactions Processing, Reserve and Clearing House Activities US

This industry comprises establishments primarily engaged in providing financial transaction processing; reserve and overnight advance services; cheque or other financial instrument clearing house services; credit card processing; and electronic financial payment services. Examples of establishments in this industry are central credit unions, automated clearing houses and electronic financial payment services.

Exclusion(s): Establishments primarily engaged in:
- data processing (51821, Data Processing, Hosting, and Related Services); and
- cheque clearing and other transaction processing of the central bank (52111, Monetary Authorities - Central Bank).

522321 Central Credit Unions CAN

This Canadian industry comprises establishments of centrals, regionals, leagues and federations primarily engaged in providing financial transaction processing; reserve and overnight advances services; cheque or other financial instrument clearing house services; credit card processing; electronic financial payment services; and in accepting deposits from, and issuing loans to, members.

Exclusion(s): Establishments primarily engaged in:
- data processing (51821, Data Processing, Hosting, and Related Services);
- cheque clearing and other transaction processing of the central bank (52111, Monetary Authorities - Central Bank);
- automated clearinghouses (522329, Other Financial Transactions Processing and Clearing House Activities);
- cheque validation service (522329, Other Financial Transactions Processing and Clearing House Activities); and
- electronic funds transfer networks (including switching (ATM's)) (522329, Other Financial Transactions Processing and Clearing House Activities).

Example Activities
- Caisses populaires, federation, league or regional (i.e., central clearing house services)
- Credit unions, central, regional or league (i.e., central clearing house services)

522329 Other Financial Transactions Processing and Clearing House Activities CAN

This Canadian industry comprises establishments primarily engaged in providing cheque or other financial instrument clearing house services; credit card processing; and electronic financial payment services. Examples of establishments in this industry are automated clearing houses and electronic financial payment services.

Exclusion(s): Establishments primarily engaged in:
- data processing (51821, Data Processing, Hosting, and Related Services); and
- cheque clearing and other transaction processing of the central bank (52111, Monetary Authorities - Central Bank).

Example Activities
- ATM network providers
- Automated clearing houses, bank or cheque (except central bank)
- Cheque clearing services (except central bank)
- Cheque validation services
- Clearing house associations (i.e., bank or cheque)
- Credit card processing services
- Electronic funds transfer services
- Financial transactions processing (except central bank)

52239 Other Activities Related to Credit Intermediation US

This industry comprises establishments, not classified to any other industry, primarily engaged in facilitating credit intermediation, such as cheque-cashing, money order issuance, traveller's cheque issuance and servicing loans originated by others.

Exclusion(s):
- foreign currency exchange dealers (52313, Commodity Contracts Dealing).

Example Activities
- Cheque cashing services
- Money order issuance services
- Travellers' cheque issuance services

522390 Other Activities Related to Credit Intermediation US

See industry description for 52239, above.

523 Securities, Commodity Contracts, and Other Financial Investment and Related Activities

This subsector comprises establishments primarily engaged in putting capital at risk in the process of underwriting securities issues or in making markets for securities and commodities; acting as intermediaries between buyers and sellers of securities; providing securities and commodity exchange services (furnishing space, marketplaces, and often facilities for the purpose of facilitating the buying and selling of stocks, stock options, bonds or commodity contracts); facilitating the marketing of financial contracts; asset management (managing portfolios of securities); and providing investment advice, trust, fiduciary, custody and other investment services.

5231 Securities and Commodity Contracts Intermediation and Brokerage

This industry group comprises establishments primarily engaged in putting capital at risk in the process of underwriting securities issues or in making markets for securities, and acting as intermediaries between buyers and sellers of securities.

52311 Investment Banking and Securities Dealing US

This industry comprises establishments primarily engaged in acting as principals (investors who buy or sell on their own account), generally on a spread basis, in originating, underwriting and/or distributing issues of securities of businesses, governments and institutions. Establishments primarily engaged in making markets (dealing or trading) in securities are included.

Exclusion(s): Establishments primarily engaged in:
- buying or selling securities for others on a commission basis (52312, Securities Brokerage).

Example Activities
- Banking, investment
- Government bond underwriters
- Investment banking
- Securities distributing (i.e., acting as a principal in dealing securities to investors)
- Securities originating (i.e., acting as a principal in dealing new securities to investors)
- Securities underwriters
- Underwriters, securities

523110 Investment Banking and Securities Dealing US

See industry description for 52311, above.

52312 Securities Brokerage US

This industry comprises establishments primarily engaged in buying or selling securities for others on a commission basis.

Exclusion(s): Establishments primarily engaged in:
- securities dealing and underwriting (52311, Investment Banking and Securities Dealing).

Example Activities
- Brokerages, stock
- Brokers, securities
- Stock brokers, offices

523120 Securities Brokerage US

See industry description for 52312, above.

52313 Commodity Contracts Dealing US

This industry comprises establishments primarily engaged in buying and selling spot or future contracts, such as commodities, foreign currency or futures options.

Exclusion(s): Establishments primarily engaged in:
- buying and selling physical commodities for resale to other than the general public (41, Wholesale Trade).

Example Activities
- Commodity contract trading companies (i.e., acting as a principal in dealing commodities to investors)
- Commodity contracts dealing (i.e., acting as a principal in dealing commodities to investors)
- Foreign currency exchange dealing (i.e., acting as a principal in dealing commodities to investors)
- Foreign currency exchange services (i.e., selling to the public)
- Futures commodity contracts dealing (i.e., acting as a principal in dealing commodities to investors)

523130 Commodity Contracts Dealing US

See industry description for 52313, above.

52314 Commodity Contracts Brokerage US

This industry comprises establishments primarily engaged in buying and selling commodity contracts and futures contracts for others on a commission basis.

Exclusion(s): Establishments primarily engaged in:
- buying and selling physical commodities for resale to other than the general public (41, Wholesale Trade).

Example Activities
- Brokerages, commodity contract
- Brokers, commodity contracts, offices
- Commodity contracts floor brokers
- Commodity contracts options brokers

523140 Commodity Contracts Brokerage US

See industry description for 52314, above.

5232 Securities and Commodity Exchanges

See industry description for 52321, below.

52321 Securities and Commodity Exchanges

This industry comprises establishments primarily engaged in providing marketplaces and mechanisms for the purpose of facilitating the buying and selling of stocks, stock options, bonds or commodity contracts. The establishments in this industry do not buy, sell, own or set the prices of the traded securities and/or commodities.

Example Activities
- Commodity contract exchanges
- Exchanges, commodity contract
- Exchanges, securities
- Futures commodity contract exchanges
- Grain exchanges
- Securities exchanges
- Stock exchanges
- Stock or commodities options exchanges

523210 Securities and Commodity Exchanges

See industry description for 52321, above.

5239 Other Financial Investment Activities

This industry group comprises establishments, not classified to any other industry group, primarily engaged in managing portfolios of securities and providing investment advice, trust, fiduciary, custody and other investment services.

52391 Miscellaneous Intermediation US

This industry comprises establishments primarily engaged in acting as principals in the buying and selling of financial contracts, other than securities or commodity contracts, generally on a spread basis. Principals are investors that buy or sell for their own account.

Example Activities
- Investment clubs
- Oil royalty dealing (i.e., acting as principals)

- Syndicates, investment
- Venture capital companies

523910 Miscellaneous Intermediation US

See industry description for 52391, above.

52392 Portfolio Management US

This industry comprises establishments primarily engaged in managing the portfolio assets of others on a fee or commission basis. These establishments have the authority to make investment decisions, with fees usually based on the size and/or overall performance of the portfolio. Examples of establishments in this industry are pension fund managers and mutual fund managers.

Exclusion(s): Establishments primarily engaged in:
- buying and selling securities on a transaction fee basis (52312, Securities Brokerage).

Example Activities
- Mutual fund management companies

- Pension funds, management

523920 Portfolio Management US

See industry description for 52392, above.

52393 Investment Advice US

This industry comprises establishments primarily engaged in providing investment advice to others on a fee basis, provided that they do not also have the authority to execute trades. Establishments in this industry may communicate their advice both directly to their clients and via printed or electronic media as part of a subscription service. Establishments providing financial planning advice, investment counseling and investment research are included.

Exclusion(s):
- establishments providing investment advice in conjunction with their primary activity, such as portfolio management, or the sale of stocks, bonds, annuities and real estate (classified according to their primary activity).

Example Activities
- Certified financial planner services, customized, fees paid by clients
- Financial investment advice services, customized, fees paid by clients

- Financial planning services, customized, fees paid by clients
- Investment advice counselling services, customized, fees paid by clients

523930 Investment Advice US

See industry description for 52393, above.

52399 All Other Financial Investment Activities US

This industry comprises establishments, not classified to any other industry, primarily engaged in providing, on a contract or fee basis, miscellaneous financial investment services, such as trust, fiduciary and custody services, and other investment services. Establishments, such as note brokers, oil and gas lease brokers and stock transfer agents, are included.

Example Activities

- Clearinghouses (i.e., commodities or securities)
- Escrow agencies (except real estate)
- Exchange clearinghouses, commodity or security
- Fiduciary agencies (except real estate)

- Personal investment trusts, administration by trust companies
- Quotation services, securities
- Securities transfer agencies
- Trust companies, nondepository
- Trusts administration
- Trusts administration, personal investment

523990 All Other Financial Investment Activities ^{CAN}

This Canadian industry comprises establishments, not classified to any other Canadian industry, primarily engaged in providing, on a fee or contract basis, miscellaneous financial investment services.

524 Insurance Carriers and Related Activities

This subsector comprises establishments primarily engaged in underwriting annuities and insurance policies, reinsurance, and the retailing of insurance and the provision of related services to policy holders. Industries are defined in terms of the type of risk being insured against, such as death, loss of employment due to age or disability, and property damage. Establishments that pool risk invest premiums to build up a portfolio of financial assets to be used against future claims. Contributions and premiums are set on the basis of actuarial calculations of probable payouts based on risk factors from experience tables and expected investment returns on reserves.

5241 Insurance Carriers

This industry group comprises establishments primarily engaged in underwriting annuities and insurance policies, and reinsurance. The establishments of this group invest premiums to build up a portfolio of financial assets to be used against future claims. Contributions and premiums are set on the basis of actuarial calculations of reserves. Direct insurance carriers that are primarily engaged in underwriting annuities and insurance policies directly to policy holders, and reinsurance carriers that are primarily engaged in assuming all or part of the risk associated with existing insurance policies originally underwritten by other insurance carriers, are included. Industries are defined in terms of the type of risk against which the policy holders are being insured, such as death, loss of employment due to age or disability, and property damage.

52411 Direct Life, Health and Medical Insurance Carriers ^{US}

This industry comprises establishments primarily engaged in underwriting annuities and life insurance, accidental death and dismemberment insurance, disability income insurance and insurance for hospital, medical, dental, vision and other health services, directly to policyholders.

Exclusion(s):
- government establishments providing health insurance (91291, Other Provincial and Territorial Public Administration);

and establishments primarily engaged in:
- reinsuring life, health and medical insurance (52413, Reinsurance Carriers).

524111 Direct Individual Life, Health and Medical Insurance Carriers ^{CAN}

This Canadian industry comprises establishments primarily engaged in underwriting annuities and life insurance, accidental death and dismemberment insurance, disability income insurance and insurance for hospital, medical, dental, vision and other health services, directly to individual policyholders.

Exclusion(s):
- government establishments providing health insurance (91291, Other Provincial and Territorial Public Administration);

and establishments primarily engaged in:
- reinsuring life insurance (524131, Life Reinsurance Carriers); and
- reinsuring health insurance (524132, Accident and Sickness Reinsurance Carriers).

Example Activities
- Direct individual health insurance carriers
- Direct individual life and pension insurance carriers

524112 Direct Group Life, Health and Medical Insurance Carriers CAN

This Canadian industry comprises establishments primarily engaged in underwriting annuities and life insurance, accidental death and dismemberment insurance, disability income insurance and insurance for hospital, medical, dental, vision and other health services, directly to group policyholders.

Exclusion(s):
- government establishments providing health insurance (91291, Other Provincial and Territorial Public Administration);

and establishments primarily engaged in:
- reinsuring life insurance (524131, Life Reinsurance Carriers); and
- reinsuring health insurance (524132, Accident and Sickness Reinsurance Carriers).

Example Activities
- Direct group health insurance carriers
- Direct group life and pension insurance carriers

52412 Direct Insurance (except Life, Health and Medical) Carriers US

This industry comprises establishments primarily engaged in underwriting all types of insurance (other than life, health or medical), directly to policyholders. Examples of establishments in this industry are automobile, property and liability insurance carriers.

Exclusion(s): Establishments primarily engaged in:
- reinsurance (52413, Reinsurance Carriers).

524121 Direct General Property and Casualty Insurance Carriers CAN

This Canadian industry comprises establishments engaged only in underwriting a combination of automobile insurance, property insurance and liability insurance, directly to policyholders, with no one of the three types accounting for more than 70 percent of the nominal output. Nominal output is measured as premiums less claims plus investment income.

Exclusion(s): Establishments primarily engaged in:
- reinsuring general and other insurance (524139, General and Other Reinsurance Carriers).

Example Activity
- Direct property and casualty insurance carriers (combination of policies)

524122 Direct, Private, Automobile Insurance Carriers CAN

This Canadian industry comprises private establishments in which more than 70 percent of nominal output is derived from underwriting automobile insurance directly to policyholders. Nominal output is measured as premiums less claims plus investment income.

Automobile insurance is often provided in a package which includes liability insurance and vehicle loss or damage insurance. Automobile insurance includes insurance for private and commercial vehicles.

Exclusion(s):
- government-owned establishments engaged in underwriting automobile insurance (524123, Direct, Public, Automobile Insurance Carriers);

and establishments primarily engaged in:
- reinsuring automobile insurance (524133, Automobile Reinsurance Carriers).

Example Activity
- Direct private, automobile insurance carriers

524123 Direct, Public, Automobile Insurance Carriers CAN

This Canadian industry comprises government-owned establishments engaged in underwriting automobile insurance directly to policyholders.

Exclusion(s):
- private establishments engaged in underwriting a combination of automobile, property and liability insurance (524121, Direct General Property and Casualty Insurance Carriers);
- private establishments specialized in underwriting automobile insurance (524122, Direct, Private, Automobile Insurance Carriers);

and establishments primarily engaged in:
- reinsuring automobile insurance (524133, Automobile Reinsurance Carriers).

Example Activity
- Government owned automobile insurance carriers

524124 Direct Property Insurance Carriers CAN

This Canadian industry comprises establishments in which more than 70 per cent of nominal output is derived from underwriting property insurance directly to policyholders. Nominal output is measured as premiums less claims plus investment income.

Property insurance provides protection for losses to buildings and contents. It may be provided in a package with related types of protection, such as personal liability for homeowners and tenants, business-interruption insurance and temporary accommodation costs. Property insurance includes personal and commercial insurance.

Exclusion(s): Establishments primarily engaged in:
- reinsuring property insurance (524134, Property Reinsurance Carriers).

Example Activities
- Burglary and theft insurance
- Fire and theft insurance
- Fire insurance underwriters
- Property damage insurance

524125 Direct Liability Insurance Carriers CAN

This Canadian industry comprises establishments in which more than 70 percent of nominal output is derived from underwriting liability insurance directly to policyholders. Nominal output is measured as premiums less claims plus investment income.

Liability insurance provides protection for legal liability to others for injury, death or damage to property which may arise in the course of carrying out occupational or personal activities. Examples of liability insurance are product liability insurance, professional malpractice insurance and directors' liability insurance.

Example Activity
- Direct liability insurance carriers

524129 Other Direct Insurance (except Life, Health and Medical) Carriers CAN

This Canadian industry comprises establishments, not classified to any other Canadian industry, primarily engaged in underwriting insurance, other than life, health or medical, such as boiler and machinery insurance, surety insurance, fidelity insurance and marine and aircraft insurance, directly to policyholders.

Boiler and machinery insurance provides protection against losses resulting from faulty or malfunctioning machinery, including damage to the insured equipment as well as surrounding buildings and equipment. Surety insurance guarantees that an individual or company will complete work that it has promised to do. Fidelity insurance or fidelity bonds protect organizations against dishonest or fraudulent acts of their employees. Marine and aircraft insurance provides protection for losses to vessels, cargo and liability to passengers.

Establishments primarily engaged in underwriting title insurance, guaranteeing loans and insuring deposits and shares in depository institutions, or providing workers' compensation insurance are included.

Exclusion(s): Establishments primarily engaged in:
- general and other reinsurance (524139, General and Other Reinsurance Carriers).

Example Activities
- Aircraft insurance
- Bank deposit insurance
- Boiler insurance
- Deposit or share insurance
- Fidelity insurance
- Machinery and equipment insurance
- Marine insurance
- Workmen's compensation, insurance

52413 Reinsurance Carriers US

This industry comprises establishments primarily engaged in assuming all or part of the risk associated with any type of insurance policy originally underwritten by other insurance carriers.

Exclusion(s): Establishments primarily engaged in:
- underwriting insurance directly to policyholders (52411, Direct Life, Health and Medical Insurance Carriers, or 52412, Direct Insurance (except Life, Health and Medical) Carriers).

524131 Life Reinsurance Carriers CAN

This Canadian industry comprises establishments in which more than 70 percent of nominal output is derived from assuming all or part of the risk associated with individual and group annuities and policies for life insurance, accidental death and dismemberment insurance, and disability income insurance originally underwritten by other insurance carriers. Nominal output is measured as premiums less claims plus investment income.

Example Activities
- Life reinsurance
- Reinsurance carriers, life

524132 Accident and Sickness Reinsurance Carriers CAN

This Canadian industry comprises establishments in which more than 70 percent of nominal output is derived from assuming all or part of the risk associated with insurance policies for hospital, medical, dental, vision and other health services originally underwritten by other insurance carriers. Nominal output is measured as premiums less claims plus investment income.

Example Activities
- Health reinsurance underwriters
- Reinsurance carriers, accident and health

524133 Automobile Reinsurance Carriers CAN

This Canadian industry comprises establishments in which more than 70 percent of nominal output is derived from assuming all or part of the risk associated with automobile insurance policies originally underwritten by other insurance carriers. Nominal output is measured as premiums less claims plus investment income.

Example Activity
- Automobile reinsurance carriers

524134 Property Reinsurance Carriers CAN

This Canadian industry comprises establishments in which more than 70 percent of nominal output is derived from assuming all or part of the risk associated with property insurance policies originally underwritten by other insurance carriers. Nominal output is measured as premiums less claims plus investment income.

Property insurance provides protection for losses to buildings and contents.

Example Activity
- Property reinsurance carriers

524135 Liability Reinsurance Carriers CAN

This Canadian industry comprises establishments in which more than 70 per cent of nominal output is derived from assuming all or part of the risk associated with liability insurance policies originally underwritten by other insurance carriers. Nominal output is measured as premiums less claims plus investment income.

Liability insurance provides protection for legal liability to others for injury, death or damage to property which may arise in the course of carrying out occupational or personal activities. Examples of liability insurance are product liability insurance, professional malpractice insurance and directors' liability insurance.

Example Activity
- Liability reinsurance carriers

524139 General and Other Reinsurance Carriers CAN

This Canadian industry comprises establishments, not classified to any other Canadian industry, primarily engaged in assuming all or part of the risk associated with insurance policies originally underwritten by other insurance carriers.

Example Activity
- Non-specialized reinsurance carriers

5242 Agencies, Brokerages and Other Insurance Related Activities

This industry group comprises establishments primarily engaged in selling insurance or providing services related to insurance.

52421 Insurance Agencies and Brokerages US

This industry comprises establishments primarily engaged in selling insurance and pension products. The staff of these agencies and brokerages are not employed by the insurance carriers they represent.

Exclusion(s):
- insurance agencies with staff employed by the carriers they represent (5241, Insurance Carriers).

Example Activities
- General insurance agency
- General insurance broker
- Insurance agents and brokers

524210 Insurance Agencies and Brokerages US

See industry description for 52421, above.

52429 Other Insurance Related Activities US

This industry comprises establishments, not classified to any other industry, primarily engaged in providing, on a contract or fee basis, services related to providing insurance, such as claims administration and adjusting. The staff of these establishments are not employed by the insurance carriers they represent.

Exclusion(s): Establishments primarily engaged in:
- third-party portfolio management of funds' assets (52392, Portfolio Management).

524291 Claims Adjusters US

This Canadian industry comprises establishments primarily engaged in investigating, appraising and settling insurance claims on a contract or fee basis.

Example Activities
- Appraisal of damaged cars, by independent adjusters
- Insurance claim adjusters

524299 All Other Insurance Related Activities CAN

This Canadian industry comprises establishments, not classified to any other Canadian industry, primarily engaged in providing, on a contract or fee basis, insurance services other than claims adjusting, such as claims processing, utilization review and other administrative services to insurance carriers, employee benefit plans and self-insurance funds.

Exclusion(s):
- consulting actuaries (541612, Human Resources Consulting Services);

and establishments primarily engaged in:
- third-party portfolio management of funds' assets (523920, Portfolio Management).

Example Activities
- Health insurance coverage consulting service
- Insurance advisory services
- Insurance consultants
- Insurance educational services
- Insurance information bureaus

- Insurance inspection and investigation (except claims investigation), services
- Insurance professional standards services
- Insurance rate making services

- Medical insurance claims, processing of, contract or fee basis
- Pension and retirement plan consultants

526 Funds and Other Financial Vehicles CAN

This subsector comprises funds, trusts and other financial vehicles organized to hold portfolio assets for the benefit of others, such as unit holders, beneficiaries of pension funds, and investors. These entities earn interest, dividends and other property income, but have little or no employment and no revenue from the sale of services.

5261 Pension Funds CAN

See industry description for 52611, below.

52611 Pension Funds CAN

This class comprises funds containing net assets set aside for the purpose of meeting retirement benefit payments of the pension plan, when they become due. Pension funds may or may not have separate legal identities and may or may not have trustees. A pension plan is a reporting entity separate from a sponsor and the plan participants that, by any arrangement (contractual or otherwise), establishes a program to provide retirement income to employees. This class includes pension plans of all types, regardless of whether the fund is registered as a separate legal identity or is administered by trustees.

526111 Trusteed Pension Funds CAN

This Canadian class comprises funds where contributions to provide pension benefits are deposited with a trustee who is responsible for the receipt, disbursement and investment of the funds. The trust is a fiduciary relationship in which individuals (at least three) or a trust company hold title to the assets of the fund in accordance with a written trust agreement for the benefit of the plan members.

Example Activity
- Trusteed pension funds

526112 Non-Trusteed Pension Funds CAN

This Canadian class comprises funds where contributions to provide pension benefits are funded through a contract for insurance with an authorized life insurance company or a corporate pension fund society or an arrangement administered by the Government of Canada or by any one of the provincial governments.

Example Activities
- Pension funds, not trusteed

- Segregated pension funds, of life insurance carriers

5269 Other Funds and Financial Vehicles CAN

This group comprises portfolios of specialized or diversified securities and other investments held on behalf of unit holders, shareholders or investors.

Exclusion(s):
- pension funds (52611, Pension Funds).

52691 Open-End Investment Funds ^{CAN}

This class comprises funds primarily engaged in investing in a specialized (except real estate) or a diversified portfolio of securities and other investments on behalf of their shareholders/unit holders. Shares are offered in an initial public offering, after which additional shares are offered continuously. Shares are redeemed at the market price, as determined by the net asset value.

526911 Equity Funds - Canadian ^{CAN}

This Canadian class comprises funds primarily engaged in investing in common shares of Canadian companies with the objective being investment appreciation or growth.

Example Activity
- Equity funds, Canadian

526912 Equity Funds - Foreign ^{CAN}

This Canadian class comprises funds primarily engaged in investing common shares of foreign companies with the objective being investment appreciation or growth.

Example Activity
- Equity funds, foreign

526913 Mortgage Funds ^{CAN}

This Canadian class comprises funds primarily engaged in investing in mortgages on property with the objective being interest income.

Example Activity
- Mortgage funds

526914 Money Market Funds ^{CAN}

This Canadian class comprises funds primarily engaged in investing in money market instruments, short term investments, such as treasury bills, government or government guaranteed debt, or commercial paper with the objective being income from the change in short term interest rates. The investment may be in Canadian or foreign instruments.

Example Activity
- Money market funds

526915 Bond and Income / Dividend Funds - Canadian ^{CAN}

This Canadian class comprises funds primarily engaged in investing in a portfolio of Canadian debt issues or preferred and/or common shares of Canadian companies with the objective being interest and/or dividend income.

Example Activity
- Bond and income / Dividend funds, Canadian

526916 Bond and Income / Dividend Funds - Foreign ^{CAN}

This Canadian class comprises funds primarily engaged in investing in a portfolio of foreign debt issues or preferred and/or common shares of foreign companies with the objective being interest and/or dividend income.

Example Activity
- Bond and income / Dividend funds, foreign

526917 Balanced Funds / Asset Allocation Funds CAN

This Canadian class comprises funds primarily engaged in investing in a portfolio that will include equity investments, fixed income investments and money market securities. The blend will depend on the fund as well as stock and bond trends, the objective being a balance of income and capital appreciation.

Example Activity
- Balanced funds / Asset allocation funds

526919 Other Open-Ended Funds CAN

This Canadian class comprises other open-end funds, not classified to other classes, which invest in futures, precious metals, hedge funds and others.

Example Activity
- Other open-ended funds

52693 Segregated (except Pension) Funds CAN

This class comprises funds that are separate investment accounts established by life insurers under the provisions of the Canadian and British Insurance Companies Act, or the corresponding sections of the Foreign Insurance Companies Act or a provincial act. Setting up of these funds allows life insurers' policyholders to invest in funds that are not subject to the investment restriction in effect on the insurers' portfolio as contained in the insurance act.

Example Activity
- Segregated funds (except pension), of life insurance carriers

526930 Segregated (except Pension) Funds CAN

See industry description for 52693, above.

52698 All Other Funds and Financial Vehicles CAN

This class comprises funds and financial vehicles, not classified to any other class, such as special purpose trusts, closed-end funds and securitization vehicles.

526981 Securitization Vehicles CAN

This Canadian class comprises special purpose financial vehicles organized for the acquisition of pools of receivables and the issuance of marketable fixed-income securities. These receivables are generally loans made to persons and/or businesses, such as credit card receivables, automobile and equipment loans and leases, and residential and commercial mortgages. These securities are broadly referred to as asset-backed securities.

Exclusion(s): Establishments primarily engaged in:
- the factoring of receivables (522299, All Other Non-Depository Credit Intermediation).

Example Activity
- Securitization vehicles (fund)

526989 All Other Miscellaneous Funds and Financial Vehicles ^{CAN}

This Canadian class comprises funds and financial vehicles, not classified to any other Canadian class, such as special purpose trusts or closed-end funds.

Exclusion(s): Establishments primarily engaged in:
- Equity Real Estate Investment Trusts (REITs) that are primarily engaged in leasing buildings, dwellings, or other real estate property to others (classified in Industry Group 5311, Lessors of Real Estate based on primary type of real estate property leased).

Example Activities
- Agency fund
- Foundation funds
- Mortgage investment funds
- Union trust funds
- Vacation funds for employees

53 Real Estate and Rental and Leasing

This sector comprises establishments primarily engaged in renting, leasing or otherwise allowing the use of tangible or intangible assets. Establishments primarily engaged in managing real estate for others; selling, renting and/or buying of real estate for others; and appraising real estate, are also included.

531 Real Estate

This subsector comprises establishments primarily engaged in renting and leasing real estate, managing real estate for others, acting as intermediaries in the sale and/or rental of real estate, and appraising real estate.

Exclusion(s): Establishments primarily engaged in:
- the construction and development of buildings (23, Construction);
- the acquisition, assembly, subdivision into lots and servicing of raw land for subsequent sale to builders (23721, Land Subdivision); and
- providing short-term lodging for travellers, vacationers and others (721, Accommodation Services).

5311 Lessors of Real Estate

This industry group comprises establishments primarily engaged in renting and leasing real estate properties. These establishments may operate (rent, lease, administer and maintain) their properties on own account, or they may subcontract the operation to a third party. This industry group also includes establishments that lease real estate from others, and sublease it to others.

Exclusion(s): Establishments primarily engaged in:
- Real Estate Investment Trusts, primarily investing in mortgages or construction loans (526989, All Other Miscellaneous Funds and Financial Vehicles); and
- real estate property management on behalf of property owners (53131, Real Estate Property Managers).

53111 Lessors of Residential Buildings and Dwellings US

This industry comprises establishments primarily engaged in renting and leasing residential buildings and dwellings, such as apartments, single family homes and semi-detached or row houses. These establishments may operate (lease, administer and maintain) their properties on own account, or they may subcontract the operation to a third party, and they may provide additional services, such as security, maintenance, parking, and snow and trash removal.

Exclusion(s): Establishments primarily engaged in:
- managing residential buildings on behalf of their owners (53131, Real Estate Property Managers).

531111 Lessors of Residential Buildings and Dwellings (except Social Housing Projects) CAN

This Canadian industry comprises establishments primarily engaged in renting and leasing residential buildings and dwellings, except social housing projects. These establishments may operate (lease, administer and maintain) their properties on own account, or they may subcontract the operation to a third party, and they may provide additional services, such as security, maintenance, parking, and snow and trash removal.

Example Activities
- Flats or apartments, operators
- Operators of apartment buildings
- Real Estate Investment Trusts (REIT's), operating residential buildings, except social housing
- Residential hotels, operators of

531112 Lessors of Social Housing Projects CAN

This Canadian industry comprises establishments primarily engaged in renting and leasing residential buildings and dwellings provided to low-income earners. These establishments are typically operated or funded by non-profit government entities, but they may also be operated by private, non-profit housing corporations.

Exclusion(s): Establishments primarily engaged in:
- operating short stay emergency housing facilities (624220, Community Housing Services).

Example Activities
- Housing for low income elderly
- Social housing projects, operators of

53112 Lessors of Non-Residential Buildings (except Mini-Warehouses) US

This industry comprises establishments primarily engaged in owning, or owning and operating, non-residential buildings. These establishments may operate (lease, administer and maintain) their properties on own account, or they may subcontract the operation to a third party, and they may provide additional services, such as security, maintenance, parking, and snow and trash removal.

Exclusion(s):
- warehouses engaged in goods handling activities (4931, Warehousing and Storage);
- self-storage mini-warehouses (53113, Self-Storage Mini-Warehouses); and
- non-residential property managers (53131, Real Estate Property Managers).

Example Activities
- Auditorium rental or leasing
- Banquet halls or rooms, without own catering staff, rental
- Commercial and industrial buildings, operators of
- Concert hall operation, real estate operation
- Convention facilities, rental only

- Flea market space renting
- Halls, reception, rental
- Leasing non-residential buildings
- Meeting hall operating
- Non-residential buildings, operators
- Office building rental or leasing

- Operators of commercial and industrial buildings
- Real Estate Investment Trusts (REIT's), operating non-residential buildings (except mini-warehouses)
- Shopping centres, property operation only
- Stadium operating

531120 Lessors of Non-Residential Buildings (except Mini-Warehouses) US

See industry description for 53112, above.

53113 Self-Storage Mini-Warehouses US

This industry comprises establishments primarily engaged in renting or leasing space for self-storage. These establishments provide secure space (rooms, compartments, lockers, containers or outdoor space) where clients can store and retrieve their goods.

Exclusion(s): Establishments primarily engaged in:
- providing warehousing services that include the handling of client's goods (4931, Warehousing and Storage); and
- providing coin-operated locker services (812990, All Other Personal Services).

Example Activities
- Cold storage locker rental (self storage)
- Miniwarehouse rental or leasing

- Real Estate Investment Trusts (REIT's), operating self-storage mini-warehouses
- Warehousing, self-storage

531130 Self-Storage Mini-Warehouses US

See industry description for 53113, above.

53119 Lessors of Other Real Estate Property US

This industry comprises establishments, not classified to any other industry, primarily engaged in renting and leasing real estate other than buildings.

Example Activities
- Agricultural property rental
- Industrial park developing and operating
- Lessors of railroad property
- Mining property leasing
- Mobile home park operating
- Mobile home sites, operators of

- Oil and gas rights, leasing (if lessors)
- Operators of "permanent" trailer sites
- Public utility property, lessors of
- Railroad property, lessor of
- Real Estate Investment Trusts (REIT's), operating real estate other than buildings

531190 Lessors of Other Real Estate Property US

See industry description for 53119, above.

5312 Offices of Real Estate Agents and Brokers

See industry description for 53121, below.

53121 Offices of Real Estate Agents and Brokers

This industry comprises establishments primarily engaged in renting, buying and selling real estate for others, on a fee or commission basis. These establishments assist vendors by advertising and listing properties and conducting open houses for prospective buyers, assist prospective buyers by selecting, visiting and making purchase offers. They may also rent or lease properties on behalf of clients.

531211 Real Estate Agents CAN

This Canadian industry comprises establishments, known as independent real estate sales persons that are licensed to participate in the activities of buying and selling real estate for others, on a fee or commission basis. These establishments assist vendors by advertising and listing properties and conducting open houses for prospective buyers, assist prospective buyers by selecting, visiting and making purchase offers. They may also rent or lease properties on behalf of clients. Real estate agents are obligated by contract to represent real estate brokers and can be identified by various names such as sales representatives, sales associates and associate brokers. This category also includes brokers that are acting in the capacity of independent real estate sales persons.

Example Activity
- Sales agents, real estate

531212 Offices of Real Estate Brokers CAN

This Canadian industry comprises establishments that are licensed or registered as real estate brokers where the primary activity is renting, buying and selling real estate for others, on a fee or commission basis. Brokers may also assist vendors by advertising and listing properties, conducting open houses for prospective buyers, and assist prospective buyers by selecting, visiting and making purchase offers.

Exclusion(s):
- brokers that are acting in the capacity of independent real estate sales persons (531211, Real Estate Agents);

and establishments primarily engaged in:
- providing real estate consulting services (53139, Other Activities Related to Real Estate).

Example Activities
- Brokers of manufactured homes, on site
- Brokers, real estate
- Real estate agencies
- Real estate brokers
- Real estate sales and brokerage services
- Realtor
- Realty company

5313 Activities Related to Real Estate

This industry group comprises establishments primarily engaged in activities related to real estate, such as real estate property management, real estate appraising and real estate listing.

53131 Real Estate Property Managers US

This industry comprises establishments primarily engaged in managing real estate properties on behalf of property owners (on a contract or fee basis). These establishments are engaged in administrative and co-ordination activities, such as the negotiation and approval of lease agreements, the collection of rental payments, the administration of contracts for property services (for example, cleaning, maintenance and security) and the preparation of accounting statements.

Exclusion(s):
- associations or corporations of dwelling owners engaged in the management of properties on behalf of dues-paying members, such as condominium owners' associations (81399, Other Membership Organizations).

Example Activities
- Condominium management
- Cooperative apartment manager
- Housing authorities, operating (managers)
- Managers of commercial real estate
- Managers of residential real estate
- Property management, non residential
- Real estate management

531310 Real Estate Property Managers CAN

See industry description for 53131, above.

53132 Offices of Real Estate Appraisers US

This industry comprises establishments primarily engaged in appraising the value of real estate and preparing appraisal reports for creditors, insurance companies, courts, buyers, sellers or auctioneers.

Example Activities
- Appraisal services, real estate
- Evaluation services (real estate)

531320 Offices of Real Estate Appraisers US

See industry description for 53132, above.

53139 Other Activities Related to Real Estate US

This industry comprises establishments, not classified to any other industry, primarily engaged in providing real estate related services.

Exclusion(s):
- offices of notaries (54112, Offices of Notaries); and
- title search offices (54119, Other Legal Services).

Example Activities
- Escrow agents, real estate
- Listing service, real estate
- Multiple listing services, real estate
- Real estate advisory services
- Rental accommodation referral service

531390 Other Activities Related to Real Estate US

See industry description for 53139, above.

532 Rental and Leasing Services

This subsector comprises establishments primarily engaged in renting or leasing tangible goods, such as automobiles, computers, consumer goods, and industrial machinery and equipment, to customers in return for a periodic payment.

The subsector includes two main types of establishments:

• those that are engaged in renting consumer goods and equipment; and

• those that are engaged in leasing machinery and equipment of the kind often used for business operations.

The first type typically operates from a retail-like or store-front facility and maintains inventories of goods that are rented for short periods of time.

The latter type typically does not operate from retail-like locations or maintain inventories, and offers longer-term leases. These establishments work directly with clients by providing or arranging financing to enable them to acquire the use of equipment on a lease basis; or they work with equipment vendors or dealers to support the marketing of equipment to their customers under lease arrangements. Equipment lessors generally structure lease contracts to meet the specialized needs of their clients and use their remarketing expertise to find other users for previously leased equipment. Establishments that provide operating and financial leases are included in this subsector.

Exclusion(s): Establishments primarily engaged in:
- renting or leasing intangibles or intellectual property (51, Information and Cultural Industries, or 533, Lessors of Non-Financial Intangible Assets (Except Copyrighted Works), or 54, Professional, Scientific and Technical Services, or 71, Arts, Entertainment and Recreation);
- leasing and providing loans to buyers of goods and equipment, or to vendors and dealers to finance their inventories (52222, Sales Financing);
- leasing real property (531, Real Estate);
- employee leasing services (56133, Professional Employer Organizations); and
- renting or leasing equipment with operators (classified in various subsectors of NAICS depending on the nature of the service provided).

5321 Automotive Equipment Rental and Leasing

This industry group comprises establishments primarily engaged in renting or leasing vehicles, such as passenger cars, passenger vans, trucks, truck tractors, buses, semi-trailers, utility trailers and RVs (recreational vehicles), without drivers. These establishments generally operate from a retail-like facility, some offer only short-term rental, others only longer-term leases, and some provide both type of services.

53211 Passenger Car Rental and Leasing

This industry comprises establishments primarily engaged in renting or leasing passenger cars without drivers. Examples of establishments in this industry are car rental agencies and passenger car lessors.

Exclusion(s): Establishments primarily engaged in:
- retailing passenger cars through sales or lease arrangements (4411, Automobile Dealers);
- renting or leasing passenger cars, hearses, with drivers (4853, Taxi and Limousine Service); and
- leasing and providing loans to buyers of goods and equipment, or to vendors and dealers to finance their inventories (52222, Sales Financing).

532111 Passenger Car Rental ᵁˢ

This Canadian industry comprises establishments primarily engaged in renting passenger cars without drivers, generally for short periods of time.

Exclusion(s): Establishments primarily engaged in:
- renting or leasing passenger cars, hearses, with drivers (4853, Taxi and Limousine Service); and
- leasing passenger cars without drivers, generally for long periods of time (532112, Passenger Car Leasing).

Example Activities
- Car rental agency
- Hearse rental, without drivers
- Hearses and limousines, rental without drivers
- Limousine rental, without driver
- Passenger car rental, without driver

532112 Passenger Car Leasing ᵁˢ

This Canadian industry comprises establishments primarily engaged in leasing passenger cars without drivers, generally for long periods of time.

Exclusion(s): Establishments primarily engaged in:
- retailing passenger cars through sales or lease arrangements (4411, Automobile Dealers);
- renting or leasing passenger cars, hearses, with drivers (4853, Taxi and Limousine Service);
- leasing and providing loans to buyers of goods and equipment, or to vendors and dealers to finance their inventories (522220, Sales Financing); and
- renting passenger cars without drivers generally for short periods of time (532111, Passenger Car Rental).

Example Activities
- Automotive leasing
- Passenger car leasing (except finance leasing), without drivers

53212 Truck, Utility Trailer and RV (Recreational Vehicle) Rental and Leasing

This industry comprises establishments primarily engaged in renting or leasing trucks, truck tractors, buses, semi-trailers, utility trailers and RVs (recreational vehicles), without drivers.

Exclusion(s): Establishments primarily engaged in:
- retailing vehicles commonly referred to as RVs through sales or lease arrangements (44121, Recreational Vehicle Dealers);
- leasing and providing loans to buyers of goods and equipment, or to vendors and dealers to finance their inventories (52222, Sales Financing);
- renting or leasing mobile home sites (53119, Lessors of Other Real Estate Property);
- renting recreational goods, such as pleasure boats, canoes, motorcycles, mopeds or bicycles (53229, Other Consumer Goods Rental); and
- renting or leasing industrial trucks, such as forklifts, materials handling equipment, farm tractors and other industrial equipment (53249, Other Commercial and Industrial Machinery and Equipment Rental and Leasing).

Example Activities
- Bus rental, without driver
- Motor home rental
- Recreational trailer rental
- Rental of trailers
- Renting travel, camping, or recreational trailers
- Tractor rental (truck), without drivers
- Truck rental (except industrial), without drivers
- Utility trailer rental

532120 Truck, Utility Trailer and RV (Recreational Vehicle) Rental and Leasing US

See industry description for 53212, above.

5322 Consumer Goods Rental

This industry group comprises establishments primarily engaged in renting or leasing personal and household goods. These establishments generally provide short-term rental, although, in some instances, the goods may be leased for longer periods of time. These establishments often operate from a retail-like or store-front facility.

53221 Consumer Electronics and Appliance Rental

This industry comprises establishments primarily engaged in renting consumer electronics and appliances.

Exclusion(s): Establishments primarily engaged in:
- renting household furniture or party and banquet supplies (53229, Other Consumer Goods Rental); and
- leasing or renting computers (53242, Office Machinery and Equipment Rental and Leasing).

Example Activities
- Appliance rental and leasing
- Rental of consumer audio-visual equipment (including rent-to-own)
- Television rental and leasing
- Video recorder and player rental and leasing
- Washers and dryers, rental

532210 Consumer Electronics and Appliance Rental

See industry description for 53221, above.

53222 Formal Wear and Costume Rental

This industry comprises establishments primarily engaged in renting formal wear, costumes (including theatrical) and other clothing.

Exclusion(s): Establishments primarily engaged in:
- laundering and renting uniforms and other work apparel (81233, Linen and Uniform Supply).

Example Activities
- Clothing, rental of
- Formal wear rental
- Rental of clothing or costumes
- Theatrical costume rental
- Wardrobe rental for motion picture film production

532220 Formal Wear and Costume Rental

See industry description for 53222, above.

53223 Video Tape and Disc Rental

This industry comprises establishments primarily engaged in renting pre-recorded video tapes and discs to the general public.

Exclusion(s): Establishments primarily engaged in:
- retailing pre-recorded video tapes and discs (45122, Pre-Recorded Tape, Compact Disc and Record Stores);
- distributing motion pictures and videos to movie theatres and other distributors (51212, Motion Picture and Video Distribution); and
- renting video recorders and players (53221, Consumer Electronics and Appliance Rental).

Example Activities
- Home video movie rental
- Video cassette rental
- Video disk rental to the general public
- Video rental

532230 Video Tape and Disc Rental

See industry description for 53223, above.

53229 Other Consumer Goods Rental

This industry comprises establishments, not classified to any other industry, primarily engaged in renting consumer goods.

Exclusion(s): Establishments primarily engaged in:
- retailing and renting musical instruments (45114, Musical Instrument and Supplies Stores);
- renting consumer electronics and appliances (53221, Consumer Electronics and Appliance Rental);
- formal wear and costume rental (53222, Formal Wear and Costume Rental);
- renting pre-recorded video tapes (53223, Video Tape and Disc Rental);
- renting a general line of products such as lawn and garden equipment, home repair tools, and party and banquet equipment (53231, General Rental Centres); and
- renting commercial and industrial medical equipment (53249, Other Commercial and Industrial Machinery and Equipment Rental and Leasing).

Example Activities
- Beach chairs and accessories, rental
- Bicycle rental
- Boat rental, pleasure
- Exercise (physical fitness) equipment rental
- Garden equipment rental
- Home health equipment, rental
- Household furniture rental
- Invalid supplies rental and leasing, consumer
- Motorcycles and motor-scooters, rental and leasing
- Musical instrument rental
- Party supplies rental and leasing
- Pleasure boats rental
- Recreation and sports equipment rental
- Rental of dishes, silverware, tables and banquet accessories
- Rental of golf carts
- Rodeo animal rental
- Ski equipment rental
- Sporting goods rental
- Sports and recreation equipment rental
- Toy library (i.e., renting toys)
- Yachts rental

532290 Other Consumer Goods Rental ^{CAN}

See industry description for 53229, above.

5323 General Rental Centres

See industry description for 53231, below.

53231 General Rental Centres

This industry comprises establishments primarily engaged in renting a range of consumer, commercial and industrial equipment. These establishments typically operate from conveniently located facilities in which they maintain inventories of goods and equipment that are rented for short periods of time. The type of equipment that these establishments provide often includes, but is not limited to, contractors' and builders' tools and equipment, home repair tools, lawn and garden equipment, moving equipment and supplies, and party and banquet equipment and supplies.

Exclusion(s): Establishments primarily engaged in:
- renting personal and household goods (5322, Consumer Goods Rental);
- renting party and banquet supplies (53229, Other Consumer Goods Rental); and
- renting and leasing heavy construction equipment, without operator (53241, Construction, Transportation, Mining, and Forestry Machinery and Equipment Rental and Leasing).

Example Activities
- General rental centres
- Rental of floor waxing and sanding machines
- Rental of tools, consumer
- Rent-all centres

532310 General Rental Centres

See industry description for 53231, above.

5324 Commercial and Industrial Machinery and Equipment Rental and Leasing

This industry group comprises establishments primarily engaged in renting or leasing commercial and industrial machinery and equipment, without operator. The types of establishments included in this industry group are generally involved in providing capital/investment-type equipment that clients use in their business operations. These establishments typically serve businesses and do not generally operate a retail-like or store-front facility.

53241 Construction, Transportation, Mining, and Forestry Machinery and Equipment Rental and Leasing

This industry comprises establishments primarily engaged in renting or leasing heavy machinery without operators.

Exclusion(s): Establishments primarily engaged in:
- renting or leasing heavy equipment for forestry, with operator (11531, Support Activities for Forestry);
- renting or leasing heavy equipment for mining, with operator (21311, Support Activities for Mining and Oil and Gas Extraction);
- renting or leasing heavy construction equipment, with operators (2389, Other Specialty Trade Contractors);
- renting or leasing air, rail, highway and water transportation equipment, with operators (48-49, Transportation and Warehousing);
- leasing and providing loans to buyers of goods and equipment, or to vendors and dealers to finance their inventories (52222, Sales Financing);
- renting or leasing automobiles or trucks without operators (5321, Automotive Equipment Rental and Leasing); and
- renting pleasure boats (53229, Other Consumer Goods Rental).

Example Activities
- Airplane rental and leasing
- Bareboat (vessel) chartering
- Bulldozer rental and leasing (without operator)
- Chartering of commercial boats without operator
- Construction equipment, heavy, rental and leasing (without operator)
- Construction machinery, rental (without operator)
- Crane rental and leasing (without operator)
- Earth moving equipment rental and leasing (without operator)
- Financial leasing of construction, mining and forestry machinery
- Mining machinery and equipment, rental
- Oil field equipment rental and leasing
- Railway car leasing (except financial)
- Rental of oil field equipment (without operator)
- Rental of scaffolding (including mobile platforms)
- Rentals, heavy machinery and equipment (except construction with operator)

532410 Construction, Transportation, Mining, and Forestry Machinery and Equipment Rental and Leasing CAN

See industry description for 53241, above.

53242 Office Machinery and Equipment Rental and Leasing

This industry comprises establishments primarily engaged in renting or leasing office machinery and equipment.

Exclusion(s): Establishments primarily engaged in:
- leasing and providing loans to buyers of goods and equipment, or to vendors and dealers to finance their inventories (52222, Sales Financing);
- renting consumer electronics and appliances (53221, Consumer Electronics and Appliance Rental); and
- renting or leasing residential furniture (53229, Other Consumer Goods Rental).

Example Activities
- Business machines, rental (except computers)
- Computer peripheral equipment, rental and leasing
- Duplicating machine rental
- Office furniture rental
- Rental of business machines (not manufacturing)
- Rental service, computer

532420 Office Machinery and Equipment Rental and Leasing

See industry description for 53242, above.

53249 Other Commercial and Industrial Machinery and Equipment Rental and Leasing

This industry comprises establishments, not classified to any other industry, primarily engaged in renting or leasing commercial and industrial machinery and equipment.

Exclusion(s): Establishments primarily engaged in:
- renting or leasing agricultural machinery and equipment, with operators (115, Support Activities for Agriculture and Forestry);
- leasing and providing loans to buyers of goods and equipment, or to vendors and dealers to finance their inventories (52222, Sales Financing);
- renting home furniture (53229, Other Consumer Goods Rental);
- renting or leasing heavy equipment without operators (53241, Construction, Transportation, Mining, and Forestry Machinery and Equipment Rental and Leasing); and
- renting or leasing office machinery and equipment (53242, Office Machinery and Equipment Rental and Leasing).

Example Activities
- Agricultural machinery and equipment rental
- Commercial equipment rental (except coin-operated)
- Farm equipment rental or leasing
- Industrial machinery and equipment, rental and leasing
- Industrial truck rental and leasing
- Leasing of industrial machinery and equipment
- Materials handling machinery and equipment, rental
- Medical equipment rental and leasing, commercial and industrial
- Metalworking machinery and equipment rental
- Motion picture equipment rental
- Painting equipment rental
- Public address system rental
- Rental agency, theatrical equipment (except costumes)
- Rental and sales of public address systems
- Rental of industrial machinery and equipment
- Sawmill machinery rental service
- Sound and lighting equipment rental
- Studio property rental for motion picture film production
- Textile machinery rental or leasing
- Theatrical equipment (except costumes), rental
- Vending machines, rental only
- Welding equipment, rental
- Woodworking machinery and equipment rental

532490 Other Commercial and Industrial Machinery and Equipment Rental and Leasing US

See industry description for 53249, above.

533 Lessors of Non-Financial Intangible Assets (Except Copyrighted Works)

See industry description for 53311, below.

5331 Lessors of Non-Financial Intangible Assets (Except Copyrighted Works)

See industry description for 53311, below.

53311 Lessors of Non-Financial Intangible Assets (Except Copyrighted Works)

This industry comprises establishments primarily engaged in holding non-financial intangible assets such as patents, trademarks, brand names, and/or franchise agreements, and allowing others to use or reproduce those assets for a fee.

Exclusion(s): Establishments primarily engaged in:
- the creation, production, reproduction and/or distribution of artistic and literary works subject to copyright, such as newspapers, periodicals, books, databases, software and multimedia products, film and videos, and musical works (51, Information and Cultural Industries, or 71, Arts, Entertainment and Recreation);
- leasing real property (5311, Lessors of Real Estate); and
- leasing equipment and goods (532, Rental and Leasing Services).

Example Activities
- Brand-name owners
- Franchises, selling or licensing
- Intellectual property holders, except copyright
- Inventors, self-employed
- Oil royalty holders
- Patent buying and licensing
- Patent holders
- Trademark holders
- Trademark lessors
- Trademark owners

533110 Lessors of Non-Financial Intangible Assets (Except Copyrighted Works)

See industry description for 53311, above.

54 Professional, Scientific and Technical Services

This sector comprises establishments primarily engaged in activities in which human capital is the major input. These establishments make available the knowledge and skills of their employees, often on an assignment basis. The individual industries of this sector are defined on the basis of the particular expertise and training of the service provider.

The main components of this sector are legal services industries, accounting and related services industries, architectural, engineering and related services industries, surveying and mapping services industries, design services industries, management, scientific and technical consulting services industries, scientific research and development services industries, and advertising services industries.

The distinguishing feature of this sector is the fact that most of the industries grouped in it have production processes that are almost wholly dependent on worker skills. In most of these industries, equipment and materials are not of major importance. Thus, the establishments classified in this sector sell expertise. Much of the expertise requires a university or college education, though not in every case.

Establishments primarily engaged in providing instruction and training in a wide variety of subjects and those primarily engaged in providing health care by diagnosis and treatment are not included in this sector.

541 Professional, Scientific and Technical Services

See industry description for 54, above.

5411 Legal Services

This industry group comprises establishments primarily engaged in providing legal and paralegal services. Examples of establishments in this industry group are offices of lawyers, offices of notaries and offices of paralegals.

54111 Offices of Lawyers

This industry comprises offices of legal practitioners, known as lawyers, barristers and solicitors, primarily engaged in the practice of law. Establishments in this industry may provide expertise in a range of, or specific area of law, such as criminal law, corporate law, real estate law, family and estate law, and intellectual property law.

Exclusion(s):
- offices of notaries (54112, Offices of Notaries); and
- offices of legal and paralegal practitioners, except offices of lawyers and notaries (54119, Other Legal Services).

Example Activities
- Attorneys, private practice
- Barrister and solicitor, private practice
- Counsellors at law, private practice
- Law offices
- Lawyers, private practice
- Legal aid services
- Patent attorneys, private practice

541110 Offices of Lawyers

See industry description for 54111, above.

54112 Offices of Notaries

This industry comprises establishments, except offices of lawyers, primarily engaged in drafting and approving legal documents, such as real estate transactions, wills and contracts, and in receiving, indexing and storing such documents.

Exclusion(s):
- offices of legal and paralegal practitioners, except offices of lawyers and notaries (54119, Other Legal Services); and
- offices of notaries public engaged in activities, such as administering oaths and taking affidavits and depositions, and witnessing and certifying signatures on documents, but not empowered to draw up and approve legal documents and contracts (54119, Other Legal Services).

Example Activity
- Notary services (Québec)

541120 Offices of Notaries

See industry description for 54112, above.

54119 Other Legal Services

This industry comprises establishments of legal practitioners, not classified to any other industry, primarily engaged in providing legal and paralegal services.

Exclusion(s):
- offices of lawyers (54111, Offices of Lawyers); and
- offices of notaries (54112, Offices of Notaries).

Example Activities
- Bailiff services
- Immigration consultant
- Land and/or title search, service
- Notaries public, private practice (outside Québec)
- Paralegal services
- Patent agent services (i.e., patent filing and searching services)
- Process server
- Real estate title searching and consulting
- Settlement offices, real estate
- Title abstract companies, real estate
- Title search companies, real estate

541190 Other Legal Services MEX

See industry description for 54119, above.

5412 Accounting, Tax Preparation, Bookkeeping and Payroll Services

See industry description for 54121, below.

54121 Accounting, Tax Preparation, Bookkeeping and Payroll Services

This industry comprises establishments primarily engaged in auditing accounting records; designing accounting systems; preparing financial statements; developing budgets; preparing tax returns; processing payrolls; bookkeeping; and billing.

541212 Offices of Accountants CAN

This Canadian industry comprises establishments primarily engaged in providing a range of accounting services, such as the preparation of financial statements, the preparation of management accounting reports, the review and auditing of accounting records, the development of budgets, the design of accounting systems, and the provision of advice on matters related to accounting. These establishments may also provide related services, such as bookkeeping services, tax return preparation services, payroll services, management consulting services and insolvency services.

Exclusion(s): Establishments primarily engaged in:
- providing tax return preparation services, without also providing accounting or auditing services (541213, Tax Preparation Services); and
- providing bookkeeping, billing and payroll processing services, without also providing accounting or auditing services (541215, Bookkeeping, Payroll and Related Services).

Example Activities
- Accountant, professional
- Accounting services, professional
- Certified accountants' offices
- Public accountants, offices of
- Registered industrial accountants' offices

541213 Tax Preparation Services US

This Canadian industry comprises establishments primarily engaged in providing only tax return preparation services. These establishments do not provide accounting, bookkeeping, billing or payroll processing services.

Exclusion(s): Establishments primarily engaged in:
- providing a range of accounting services (541212, Offices of Accountants).

Example Activities
- Income tax return preparation services without accounting, auditing, or bookkeeping services
- Tax return preparation services (without accounting, auditing, or bookkeeping services)

541215 Bookkeeping, Payroll and Related Services CAN

This Canadian industry comprises establishments primarily engaged in providing bookkeeping, billing or payroll processing services. These establishments do not provide accounting services, such as the preparation of financial statements, the preparation of management accounting reports, and the review and auditing of accounting records.

Exclusion(s): Establishments primarily engaged in:
- providing a range of accounting services (541212, Offices of Accountants); and
- providing tax return preparation services, without also providing accounting or auditing services (541213, Tax Preparation Services).

Example Activities
- Billing and bookkeeping services
- Billing services
- Bookkeepers, offices of
- Bookkeeping services
- Payroll processing services
- Talent payment services

5413 Architectural, Engineering and Related Services

This industry group comprises establishments primarily engaged in providing architectural, engineering and related services, such as structure design, drafting, building inspection, landscape design, surveying and mapping, laboratory and on-site testing, and interior, industrial, graphic and other specialized design services.

54131 Architectural Services

This industry comprises establishments primarily engaged in planning and designing the construction of residential, institutional, leisure, commercial and industrial buildings and other structures by applying knowledge of design, construction procedures, zoning regulations, building codes and building materials.

Exclusion(s): Establishments primarily engaged in:
- both the design and construction of buildings, highways or other structures (23, Construction);
- managing construction projects (236, Construction of Buildings, or 237, Heavy and Civil Engineering Construction); and
- planning and designing landscapes (54132, Landscape Architectural Services).

Example Activities
- Architects (except landscape), offices of
- Architectural design services (except landscape)
- Buildings and structures, architectural design

541310 Architectural Services

See industry description for 54131, above.

54132 Landscape Architectural Services

This industry comprises establishments primarily engaged in planning, designing and administering the development of land areas for projects such as parks and other recreational areas, airports, highways, hospitals, schools, land subdivisions, and commercial, industrial and residential areas by applying knowledge of land characteristics, location of buildings and structures, use of land areas, and design of landscape projects.

Exclusion(s): Establishments primarily engaged in:
- operating retail nursery and garden centres that also provide landscape consulting and design services (44422, Nursery Stores and Garden Centres); and
- designing, installing and maintaining the materials specified in the design as part of an integrated service (56173, Landscaping Services).

Example Activities
- Architects, landscape, offices of
- City planning services (except engineers)
- Garden planning services
- Golf course design services
- Industrial development planning service (i.e., urban planning)
- Land use planning services
- Landscape architectural services
- Landscape planning services
- Ski area planning services
- Town planners, offices of
- Urban planning services

541320 Landscape Architectural Services

See industry description for 54132, above.

54133 Engineering Services

This industry comprises establishments primarily engaged in applying principles of engineering in the design, development and utilization of machines, materials, instruments, structures, processes and systems. The assignments undertaken by these establishments may involve any of the following activities: the provision of advice, the preparation of feasibility studies, the preparation of preliminary and final plans and designs, the provision of technical services during the construction or installation phase, the inspection and evaluation of engineering projects, and related services.

Exclusion(s): Establishments primarily engaged in:
- both the design and construction of buildings, highways and other structures (23, Construction);
- managing construction projects (236, Construction of Buildings, or 237, Heavy and Civil Engineering Construction);
- gathering, interpreting and mapping geophysical data (54136, Geophysical Surveying and Mapping Services);
- providing engineering surveying services (54137, Surveying and Mapping (except Geophysical) Services);
- creating and developing designs and specifications that optimize the function, value and appearance of products (54142, Industrial Design Services);
- planning and designing computer systems that integrate existing hardware, packaged or custom software and communication technologies (54151, Computer Systems Design and Related Services); and
- providing advice and assistance to others on environmental issues, such as the control of environmental contamination from pollutants, toxic substances and hazardous materials (54162, Environmental Consulting Services).

Example Activities

- Acoustical engineering consulting services
- Boat engineering designing services
- Chemical engineering services
- Civil engineering services
- Combustion and heating engineering consultants
- Construction engineering services
- Consulting engineering services
- Electrical and electronic engineering services
- Engineering consulting services
- Engineering design services
- Engineers, private practice
- Environmental engineering services

- Environmental engineers
- Erosion control engineering services
- Geological engineering services
- Geophysical engineering services
- Industrial engineering services
- Logging engineering services
- Marine engineering services
- Mechanical engineering services
- Mining engineering services
- Office of engineers
- Petroleum engineering services
- Traffic consultants, engineering services

541330 Engineering Services

See industry description for 54133, above.

54134 Drafting Services

This industry comprises establishments primarily engaged in drawing detailed layouts, plans and illustrations of buildings, structures, systems or components from engineering and architectural specifications.

Example Activities

- Blueprint drafting services
- Drafting services

- Draftsmen, offices of

541340 Drafting Services

See industry description for 54134, above.

54135 Building Inspection Services

This industry comprises establishments primarily engaged in providing building inspection services. These establishments typically evaluate all aspects of the building structure and component systems and prepare a report on the physical condition of the property, generally for buyers or others involved in real estate transactions.

Exclusion(s): Establishments primarily engaged in:

- inspecting buildings for hazardous materials (54162, Environmental Consulting Services);
- inspecting buildings for termites and other pests (56171, Exterminating and Pest Control Services); and
- conducting inspections and enforcing public building codes (91, Public Administration).

Example Activities

- Building inspection services

- Home inspection services

541350 Building Inspection Services

See industry description for 54135, above.

54136 Geophysical Surveying and Mapping Services

This industry comprises establishments primarily engaged in gathering, interpreting and mapping geophysical data. These establishments often specialize in locating and measuring the extent of subsurface resources, such as oil, gas and minerals, but they may also conduct surveys for engineering purposes. A variety of surveying techniques are used, including seismic, magnetic, gravity, electrical and electromagnetic, radioactive and remote sensing, depending on the purpose of the survey.

Exclusion(s): Establishments primarily engaged in:
- geophysical surveying activities in combination with other exploration activities (21311, Support Activities for Mining and Oil and Gas Extraction).

Example Activities
- Electrical geophysical surveying services
- Electromagnetic geophysical surveying services
- Geological surveying services
- Geophysical surveying for non metallic minerals, services

- Gravimetric surveying services, geophysical
- Oceanic surveying, geophysical
- Oil gas field seismographic surveys
- Seismic drilling
- Seismic geophysical surveying services

541360 Geophysical Surveying and Mapping Services

See industry description for 54136, above.

54137 Surveying and Mapping (except Geophysical) Services

This industry comprises establishments primarily engaged in providing surveying and mapping services of the surface of the earth, including the sea floor. These services may include surveying and mapping of areas above or below the surface of the earth, such as the creation of view easements or segregating rights in parcels of land by creating underground utility easements. Examples of activities in this industry are cadastral and topographic surveying and mapping services; control surveying services, such as geodesy and Global Positioning System (GPS) surveying; cartographic surveying services, including photogrammetric mapping; geographic information system (GIS) base mapping and quality control services; and geospatial mapping services.

Exclusion(s): Establishments primarily engaged in:
- publishing atlases and maps (51113, Book Publishers);
- developing and/or publishing GIS software (51121, Software Publishers); and
- providing geophysical surveying and mapping services (54136, Geophysical Surveying and Mapping Services).

Example Activities
- Aerial surveying (except geophysical), using specialized equipment
- Cadastral surveying services
- Cartographic surveying services
- Geographic Information System (GIS), base mapping services
- Geospatial mapping services
- Hydrographic mapping services

- Land surveying services (except geophysical)
- Mapmaking (except geophysical) services
- Oceanic surveying (except geophysical) services
- Photogrammetric mapping services
- Production of topographic materials and maps
- Surveying services (except geophysical)

541370 Surveying and Mapping (except Geophysical) Services

See industry description for 54137, above.

54138 Testing Laboratories

This industry comprises establishments primarily engaged in providing physical, chemical and other analytical testing services. The testing activities may occur in a laboratory or on-site.

Exclusion(s): Establishments primarily engaged in:
- performing laboratory testing for the veterinary profession (54194, Veterinary Services);
- performing clinical laboratory testing for the medical profession (62151, Medical and Diagnostic Laboratories); and
- auto emissions testing (81119, Other Automotive Repair and Maintenance).

Example Activities
- Assaying services
- Automobile proving and testing ground
- Biological testing (except clinical and veterinary)
- Calibration and certification testing services
- Electrical testing laboratory
- Environmental laboratory testing services
- Film badge testing services
- Fire Insurance Underwriters' Laboratories
- Food testing laboratory
- Forensic laboratories (except medical)
- Geotechnical testing laboratory
- Hydrostatic testing laboratories
- Industrial testing laboratories
- Laboratories, product testing
- Laboratory testing service (except clinical and veterinary)
- Laboratory, food testing
- Mechanical testing, laboratories
- Metallurgical testing laboratories
- Non destructive testing services
- Pollution testing service (except automotive emissions testing)
- Product testing services
- Radiation testing services
- Radiographic testing services
- Radon testing services
- Seed testing laboratories
- Soil testing services
- Testing laboratory (except medical or dental)
- Thermal testing, laboratories
- Vibration testing services
- X-ray inspection service

541380 Testing Laboratories

See industry description for 54138, above.

5414 Specialized Design Services

This industry group comprises establishments primarily engaged in providing specialized design services, except architectural, engineering and computer systems design.

54141 Interior Design Services

This industry comprises establishments primarily engaged in planning, designing and administering projects in interior spaces to meet the physical and aesthetic needs of people, taking into consideration building codes, health and safety regulations, traffic patterns and floor planning, mechanical and electrical needs, and interior fittings and furniture. Interior designers and interior design consultants work in areas such as hospitality design, health care design, institutional design, commercial and corporate design and residential design. This industry also includes interior decorating consultants engaged exclusively in providing aesthetic services associated with interior spaces.

Exclusion(s): Establishments primarily engaged in:
- selling furniture and furnishings at retail or wholesale locations that also provide interior design or decorating services (41, Wholesale Trade, or 44-45, Retail Trade).

Example Activities
- Consulting services and consultants, interior design
- Decorators, interior, consulting service
- Designers, interior, offices of
- Interior decorating consulting service
- Interior design services
- Layouts-office, factory (designers, interior)

541410 Interior Design Services

See industry description for 54141, above.

54142 Industrial Design Services

This industry comprises establishments primarily engaged in creating and developing designs and specifications that optimize the function, value and appearance of products. These services can include the determination of the materials, construction, mechanisms, shape, colour, and surface finishes of the product, taking into consideration human needs, safety, market appeal and efficiency in production, distribution, use and maintenance.

Exclusion(s): Establishments primarily engaged in:
- designing, subcontracting the manufacturing and marketing of products (31-33, Manufacturing);
- applying principles of engineering in the design, development and utilization of machines, materials, instruments, structures, processes and systems (54133, Engineering Services); and
- designing clothing, shoes and jewellery (54149, Other Specialized Design Services).

Example Activities
- Automobile industrial design services
- Furniture design services
- Industrial design consulting services
- Industrial design services
- Modelling services (for scale models)
- Package design (industrial) services

541420 Industrial Design Services

See industry description for 54142, above.

54143 Graphic Design Services

This industry comprises establishments primarily engaged in planning, designing and managing the production of visual communication, so as to convey specific messages or concepts, clarify complex information or project visual identities. These services can include the design of printed materials, packaging, video screen displays, advertising, signage systems and corporate identification.

Exclusion(s): Establishments primarily engaged in:
- printing (32311, Printing);
- publishing newspapers, periodicals, books, databases, software and related works (511, Publishing Industries (except Internet));
- producing animated films (51211, Motion Picture and Video Production);
- providing advice concerning marketing strategies (54161, Management Consulting Services);
- creating and placing advertising campaigns in media (54181, Advertising Agencies);
- purchasing advertising time or space from media owners and reselling it directly to advertising agencies or advertisers (54183, Media Buying Agencies);
- creating and/or placing public display advertising material (54185, Display Advertising);
- providing photography services (54192, Photographic Services); and
- creating cartoons and visual art (711511, Independent Artists, Visual Arts).

Example Activities
- Art studios, commercial
- Artists, graphic, independent
- Artists, independent medical
- Commercial art services
- Commercial artists, independent
- Commercial illustrators, independent
- Communication, design consultants
- Graphic arts and related design
- Graphic design services
- Illustrators, commercial
- Medical illustration services
- Silk screen design service
- Studios, commercial art

541430 Graphic Design Services

See industry description for 54143, above.

54149 Other Specialized Design Services

This industry comprises establishments, not classified to any other industry, primarily engaged in providing professional design services.

Exclusion(s): Establishments primarily engaged in:
- providing architectural design services (54131, Architectural Services);
- providing landscape architectural design services (54132, Landscape Architectural Services);
- providing engineering design services (54133, Engineering Services);
- providing interior design services (54141, Interior Design Services);
- providing industrial design services (54142, Industrial Design Services);
- providing graphic design services (54143, Graphic Design Services); and
- providing computer systems design services (54151, Computer Systems Design and Related Services).

Example Activities
- Clothing design services
- Costume design services (except independent designers)
- Fashion design services
- Fashion designer, service of
- Floats, design services
- Jewellery design services
- Set design, theatrical (except independent)
- Shoe design services
- Textile design services

541490 Other Specialized Design Services

See industry description for 54149, above.

5415 Computer Systems Design and Related Services

See industry description for 54151, below.

54151 Computer Systems Design and Related Services

This industry comprises establishments primarily engaged in providing expertise in the field of information technologies through one or more activities, such as writing, modifying, testing and supporting software to meet the needs of a particular customer, including the creation of Internet home pages; planning and designing computer systems that integrate hardware, software and communication technologies; on-site management and operation of clients' computer and data processing facilities; providing advice in the field of information technologies; and other professional and technical computer-related services.

Exclusion(s): Establishments primarily engaged in:
- retailing computer hardware and software and providing support services (44312, Computer and Software Stores);
- publishing packaged software (51121, Software Publishers); and
- providing data processing services (51821, Data Processing, Hosting, and Related Services).

Example Activities
- Application software programming services, custom
- CAD/CAM systems services
- CAE (computer-aided engineering) systems services
- Computer consulting services
- Computer disaster recovery services
- Computer facilities management services
- Computer hardware consulting services
- Computer programming services, custom

- Computer programs or systems software development, custom
- Computer software consulting services
- Computer software programming services, custom
- Computer software systems analysis and design, custom
- Computer systems analysis and design services
- Computer systems design consulting services
- Computer systems integrators
- Computer-aided design (CAD) systems services
- Computer-aided engineering (CAE) systems services
- Data processing facilities management services
- Design and system analysis, computer services (software)
- Facilities management services, computer
- Facilities support services, computer

- Information management system design services, computer
- Internet page design services, custom
- Local area network (LAN) systems integrators
- Management information systems design consulting services
- Office automation, computer systems integration
- Programming services, computer, custom
- Requirements analysis, computer hardware
- Software installation services
- Software programming, custom
- Software systems analysis and design, custom
- Systems analysis and design, computer services (software)
- Systems analysis and design, computer software
- Systems engineering (system integration)
- Systems integration, computer
- Web page developing

541510 Computer Systems Design and Related Services MEX

See industry description for 54151, above.

5416 Management, Scientific and Technical Consulting Services

This industry group comprises establishments primarily engaged in providing expert advice and assistance to other organizations on management, environmental, scientific and technical issues.

> *Exclusion(s): Establishments primarily engaged in:*
> - providing expert advice and assistance to other organizations on architectural and engineering issues (5413, Architectural, Engineering and Related Services);
> - providing expert advice and assistance to other organizations on interior, industrial and graphic design issues (5414, Specialized Design Services); and
> - providing expert advice and assistance to other organizations on information technology issues (5415, Computer Systems Design and Related Services).

54161 Management Consulting Services

This industry comprises establishments primarily engaged in providing advice and assistance to other organizations on management issues, such as strategic and organizational planning; financial planning and budgeting; marketing objectives and policies; human resource policies, practices and planning; and production scheduling and control planning.

Exclusion(s): Establishments primarily engaged in:
- planning and designing industrial processes and systems (54133, Engineering Services);
- planning and designing computer systems (54151, Computer Systems Design and Related Services);
- developing and implementing public relations plans (54182, Public Relations Services);
- developing and conducting marketing research or public opinion polling studies (54191, Marketing Research and Public Opinion Polling);
- providing office or general administrative services on a day-to-day basis (56111, Office Administrative Services); and
- providing professional and management development training (61143, Professional and Management Development Training).

541611 Administrative Management and General Management Consulting Services US

This Canadian industry comprises establishments primarily engaged in providing advice and assistance to other organizations on administrative management issues, such as financial planning and budgeting; equity and asset management; records management; office planning; strategic and organizational planning; site selection; new business start-up; and business process improvement. This Canadian industry also includes general management consultants that provide a full range of administrative; human resource; marketing; process, physical distribution and logistics; or other management consulting services to clients.

Exclusion(s): Establishments primarily engaged in:
- providing office or general administrative services on a day-to-day basis (561110, Office Administrative Services).

Example Activities
- Administrative management consultants
- Business start-up consulting services
- Financial management consulting services (except investment advice)
- General management consulting services
- Records management consulting services
- Reorganization consulting service
- Site selection consulting services
- Strategic planning consulting services

541612 Human Resources Consulting Services US

This Canadian industry comprises establishments primarily engaged in providing advice and assistance to other organizations on human resource management issues, such as human resource and personnel policies, practices and procedures; employee benefits planning, communication, and administration; compensation systems planning; wage and salary administration; and executive search and recruitment.

Exclusion(s): Establishments primarily engaged in:
- executive search consultants (56131, Employment Placement Agencies and Executive Search Services); and
- providing professional and management development training (61143, Professional and Management Development Training).

Example Activities
- Actuarial consulting services
- Benefit consulting services
- Compensation consulting services
- Consulting services, labour relations
- Consulting services, personnel management
- Employee assessment consulting services
- Employee compensation consulting services
- Human resource consulting services
- Labour relation consulting services
- Organization development consulting services
- Personnel management consulting services

541619 Other Management Consulting Services [CAN]

This Canadian industry comprises establishments, not classified to any other Canadian industry, primarily engaged in providing advice and assistance to other organizations on management issues.

Example Activities

- Auditors, freight rate
- Customer services management consulting services
- Customs consulting services
- Efficiency experts
- Freight rate consulting services
- Inventory planning and control management consulting services
- Logistics management consulting services
- Manufacturing operations improvement consulting services
- Materials management consulting services
- New product development consulting services
- Operations research consulting services
- Physical distribution consulting services
- Production planning and control consulting services
- Productivity improvement consulting services
- Sales management consulting services
- Tariff consulting services
- Telecommunications management consulting services

54162 Environmental Consulting Services

This industry comprises establishments primarily engaged in providing advice and assistance to other organizations on environmental issues, such as the control of environmental contamination from pollutants, toxic substances and hazardous materials. These establishments identify problems, measure and evaluate risks, and recommend solutions. They employ a multi-disciplined staff of scientists, engineers and other technicians, with expertise in areas such as air and water quality, asbestos contamination, remediation and environmental law. Examples of establishments in this industry are environmental consultants, sanitation consultants and site remediation consultants.

Exclusion(s): Establishments primarily engaged in:
- providing environmental engineering services (54133, Engineering Services); and
- environmental remediation (56291, Remediation Services).

Example Activities
- Environmental consulting services
- Sanitation consulting services
- Site remediation consulting services

541620 Environmental Consulting Services

See industry description for 54162, above.

54169 Other Scientific and Technical Consulting Services

This industry comprises establishments, not classified to any other industry, primarily engaged in providing advice and assistance to other organizations on scientific and technical issues.

Example Activities

- Agricultural consulting (technical) services
- Agrology consulting services
- Agronomy consulting services
- Economic consulting services
- Energy consulting services
- Hydrology consulting services
- Livestock breeding consulting services
- Motion picture consulting services
- Nuclear energy consulting services
- Occupational health and safety consulting services
- Physics consulting services
- Safety consulting services

541690 Other Scientific and Technical Consulting Services

See industry description for 54169, above.

5417 Scientific Research and Development Services

This industry group comprises establishments primarily engaged in conducting original investigation, undertaken on a systematic basis to gain new knowledge (research), and in the application of research findings or other scientific knowledge for the creation of new or significantly improved products or processes (experimental development). The industries within this industry group are defined on the basis of the domain of research; that is, on the scientific expertise of the establishment.

54171 Research and Development in the Physical, Engineering and Life Sciences

This industry comprises establishments primarily engaged in conducting research and experimental development in the physical engineering and life sciences, including electronics, computers, chemistry, oceanography, geology, mathematics, physics, environmental, medicine, health, biology, botany, biotechnology, agriculture, fisheries, forestry, pharmacy, veterinary and other allied subjects.

Exclusion(s):
- research and development on aerospace equipment undertaken by establishments belonging to enterprises manufacturing such equipment (33641, Aerospace Product and Parts Manufacturing);
- physical, chemical or other analytical testing services (54138, Testing Laboratories);
- performing laboratory testing for the veterinary profession (54194, Veterinary Services); and
- performing clinical laboratory testing for the medical profession (62151, Medical and Diagnostic Laboratories).

Example Activities
- Agriculture research and development laboratories
- Bacteriological research and development laboratories
- Biotechnology research and development laboratories
- Botany research and development laboratories
- Cancer research laboratories
- Cerebral palsy research laboratories
- Chemical research and development laboratories
- Computer research and development laboratories
- Dental research and development laboratories
- Development of computer and related technology (hardware)
- Electronic research and development laboratories
- Engineering research and development laboratories
- Entomological research and development laboratories
- Environmental research and development laboratories
- Farms, experimental
- Fisheries research and development laboratories
- Food research and development laboratories
- Forestry research and development laboratories
- Genetics research and development laboratories
- Geology research and development laboratories
- Health research and development laboratories
- Horticulture research and development
- Industrial research and development laboratories (except testing)
- Life sciences research and development laboratories
- Mathematics research and development services
- Medical research and development laboratories
- Observatories, astronomical
- Oceanographic research and development laboratories
- Physical science research and development laboratories
- Research and development laboratories or services, engineering

- Research and development laboratories or services, life sciences
- Research and development laboratories or services, physical sciences
- Veterinary research and development laboratories

541710 Research and Development in the Physical, Engineering and Life Sciences CAN

See industry description for 54171, above.

54172 Research and Development in the Social Sciences and Humanities

This industry comprises establishments primarily engaged in conducting research and analyses in education, sociology, psychology, language, economics, law, and other social sciences and humanities.

Exclusion(s): Establishments primarily engaged in:
- marketing research (54191, Marketing Research and Public Opinion Polling).

Example Activities
- Archeological research and development services
- Archeological sites, excavations
- Behavioural research and development services
- Business research and development services
- Cognitive research and development services
- Demographic research and development services
- Economic research and development services
- Education research and development services
- Humanities research and development services
- Language research and development services
- Learning disability research and development services
- Psychology research and development services
- Social science research and development services
- Sociological research and development services

541720 Research and Development in the Social Sciences and Humanities US

See industry description for 54172, above.

5418 Advertising, Public Relations, and Related Services

This industry group comprises establishments primarily engaged in creating mass-media advertising or public relation campaigns; placing advertising in media for advertisers or advertising agencies; selling media time or space to advertisers or advertising agencies for media owners; creating and implementing indoor or outdoor display advertising campaigns; creating and implementing direct mail advertising campaigns; delivering (except by mail) advertising materials or samples; creating and implementing specialty advertising campaigns; providing related services, such as sign painting and lettering, welcoming services and window trimming services.

54181 Advertising Agencies

This industry comprises establishments primarily engaged in creating advertising campaigns and placing such advertising in periodicals and newspapers, on radio and television, or with other media. These establishments are organized to provide a full range of services (through in-house capabilities or subcontracting), including advice, creative services, account management, media planning and buying, and production of advertising material.

Exclusion(s): Establishments primarily engaged in:
- conceptualizing and producing graphic designs, but not placing the advertising with media (54143, Graphic Design Services);
- providing marketing consulting services (54161, Management Consulting Services);
- purchasing advertising space from media outlets and reselling it to advertising agencies or individual companies directly (54183, Media Buying Agencies);
- selling media time or space for media owners (54184, Media Representatives);
- creating direct mail advertising campaigns (54186, Direct Mail Advertising); and
- writing advertising copy, but not placing the advertising with media (54189, Other Services Related to Advertising).

Example Activities
- Advertising agencies
- Advertising consultants (agencies)
- Full-service advertising agency
- Sales promotion campaign services

541810 Advertising Agencies

See industry description for 54181, above.

54182 Public Relations Services

This industry comprises establishments primarily engaged in creating and implementing public relation campaigns. These campaigns are designed to promote the interests and image of their clients.

Example Activities
- Lobbyists, offices of
- Political consultants, offices of
- Public relations agencies
- Public relations services
- Public relations, consultants, offices of

541820 Public Relations Services

See industry description for 54182, above.

54183 Media Buying Agencies

This industry comprises establishments primarily engaged in purchasing advertising time or space from media owners and reselling it directly to advertising agencies or advertisers.

Exclusion(s): Establishments primarily engaged in:
- creating and placing advertising campaigns in media (54181, Advertising Agencies); and
- selling time and space to advertisers for media owners (54184, Media Representatives).

Example Activity
- Media buying agencies

541830 Media Buying Agencies

See industry description for 54183, above.

54184 Media Representatives

This industry comprises establishments primarily engaged in selling media time or space for media owners.

Exclusion(s): Establishments primarily engaged in:
- creating and placing advertising campaigns in media (54181, Advertising Agencies); and
- purchasing advertising time or space from media owners and reselling it directly to advertising agencies or advertisers (54183, Media Buying Agencies).

Example Activities
- Advertising media representatives, offices of
- Advertising representatives, media, independent
- Advertising representatives, television or radio, independent
- Magazine advertising representatives, independent
- Media advertising representatives, independent
- Media advertising representatives, offices of

- Media representatives, independent
- Newspaper advertising representatives, independent
- Publishers' advertising representatives, independent
- Radio advertising representatives, independent
- Television advertising representatives, independent

541840 Media Representatives

See industry description for 54184, above.

54185 Display Advertising

This industry comprises establishments primarily engaged in creating public display advertising material, such as printed, painted, or electronic displays, and placing such displays on indoor or outdoor billboards and panels, on or within transit vehicles or facilities, in shopping mall displays, and on other display structures or sites.

Exclusion(s): Establishments primarily engaged in:
- erecting display boards (23, Construction); and
- manufacturing electrical, mechanical or plate signs, and point-of-sale advertising displays (33995, Sign Manufacturing).

Example Activities
- Advertising services, indoor or outdoor display
- Billboard display advertising services
- Billboard display agency
- Bus and subway card advertising services
- Bus card advertising services
- Display advertising services

- Display card advertising services
- Display installation services
- Indoor display advertising services
- Outdoor display advertising services
- Poster advertising services
- Store display advertising services
- Taxicab card advertising services

541850 Display Advertising

See industry description for 54185, above.

54186 Direct Mail Advertising

This industry comprises establishments primarily engaged in creating and designing direct mail advertising campaigns, and preparing advertising material for mailing or other direct distribution. These establishments may also compile, maintain, sell and rent mailing lists.

Exclusion(s): Establishments primarily engaged in:
- compiling and selling mailing lists, without also providing direct mail advertising services (51114, Directory and Mailing List Publishers);
- creating and placing advertising campaigns in media (54181, Advertising Agencies);
- the door-to-door distribution or delivery of advertising materials or samples (54187, Advertising Material Distribution Services); and
- distributing advertising specialties (54189, Other Services Related to Advertising).

Example Activities
- Advertising mailing services (i.e., preparing advertising material, such as coupons, flyers or samples, for mailing or other direct distribution)
- Coupon and sample packages, development of
- Direct mail advertising campaign services
- Sample and coupon packages, development of

541860 Direct Mail Advertising

See industry description for 54186, above.

54187 Advertising Material Distribution Services

This industry comprises establishments primarily engaged in the distribution or delivery, except by mail or electronic distribution, of advertising materials or samples.

Exclusion(s): Establishments primarily engaged in:
- providing direct mail advertising services (54186, Direct Mail Advertising); and
- distributing advertising specialties (54189, Other Services Related to Advertising).

Example Activities
- Advertising material (e.g., circulars, samples), direct distribution services
- Circular and handbill direct distribution services
- Coupon direct distribution services
- Directories, telephone, distribution on a contract or fee basis
- Door-to-door distribution of advertising material (e.g., circulars, samples)
- Flyer direct distribution services
- Handbill and circular direct distribution services
- Sample direct distribution services
- Telephone directory distribution services, door-to-door

541870 Advertising Material Distribution Services

See industry description for 54187, above.

54189 Other Services Related to Advertising

This industry comprises establishments, not classified to any other industry, primarily engaged in providing advertising related services, such as advertising specialties distribution; sign painting and lettering; welcoming services; window trimming services; and writing of advertising copy.

541891 Specialty Advertising Distributors CAN

This Canadian industry comprises establishments primarily engaged in creating, and organizing the production of, promotional messages applied to specialty advertising products, such as wearables, writing instruments, calendars, desk accessories, buttons, badges and stickers. These establishments act as intermediaries between clients (who distribute the products free-of-charge) and specialty advertising product suppliers.

Example Activities
- Advertising specialty distribution services (creating and organizing the production of specialty advertising products)
- Specialty advertising distribution services (creating and organizing the production of specialty advertising products)

541899 All Other Services Related to Advertising CAN

This Canadian industry comprises establishments, not classified to any other Canadian industry, primarily engaged in providing advertising related services.

Exclusion(s): Establishments primarily engaged in:
- creating and placing advertising campaigns in media (541810, Advertising Agencies);
- creating and implementing public relations campaigns (541820, Public Relations Services);
- purchasing advertising time or space from media owners and reselling it directly to advertising agencies or advertisers (541830, Media Buying Agencies);
- selling time and space to advertisers for media owners (541840, Media Representatives);
- creating and/or placing public display advertising material (541850, Display Advertising);
- providing direct mail advertising services (541860, Direct Mail Advertising); and
- the door-to-door distribution or delivery of advertising materials or samples (541870, Advertising Material Distribution Services).

Example Activities
- Demonstration services, merchandise
- Display lettering services
- Lettering services, door and window
- Mannequin decorating services
- Sign painting and lettering services
- Welcoming services (i.e., advertising services)
- Window dressing or trimming services

5419 Other Professional, Scientific and Technical Services

This industry group comprises establishments, not classified to any other industry group, primarily engaged in providing professional, scientific and technical services. Examples of establishments included in this industry group are marketing research and public opinion polling houses; photographic studios; translators and interpreters; and veterinary practices.

54191 Marketing Research and Public Opinion Polling

This industry comprises establishments primarily engaged in gathering, recording, tabulating, and presenting marketing and public opinion data.

Exclusion(s): Establishments primarily engaged in:
- providing advice on marketing strategies (54161, Management Consulting Services); and
- conducting fundamental and experimental research in economics, sociology, and related fields (54172, Research and Development in the Social Sciences and Humanities).

Example Activities
- Broadcast media rating services
- Market analysis or research services
- Opinion research services
- Political opinion polling services
- Public opinion polling services
- Public opinion research services
- Sampling services, statistical

541910 Marketing Research and Public Opinion Polling

See industry description for 54191, above.

54192 Photographic Services

This industry comprises establishments primarily engaged in providing still, video or computer photography services, including the video taping of special events. These establishments may specialize in a particular field of photography, such as aerial photography, commercial and industrial photography, portrait photography and special event photography.

Exclusion(s): Establishments primarily engaged in:
- producing commercial, institutional or educational films and videos (51211, Motion Picture and Video Production);
- developing motion picture films (51219, Post-Production and Other Motion Picture and Video Industries);
- supplying photographs to the news media (51911, News Syndicates);
- taking, developing and selling artistic photographs (711511, Independent Artists, Visual Arts);
- developing still photographs (81292, Photo Finishing Services); and
- supplying and servicing automatic photography machines in places of business operated by others (81299, All Other Personal Services).

Example Activities
- Aerial photography services (i.e., photographers specializing in aerial photography, except map making)
- Commercial photography services
- Medical photography services
- Passport photography services
- Photography studios
- Portrait photographers
- Portrait photography services
- Portrait photography studios
- School photography (i.e., portrait photography) services
- Video photography services, portrait
- Video taping services for special events
- Video taping services for weddings
- Wedding and portrait photography services

541920 Photographic Services MEX

See industry description for 54192, above.

54193 Translation and Interpretation Services

This industry comprises establishments primarily engaged in translating written material and interpreting speech from one language to another, and establishments primarily engaged in providing sign language services.

Exclusion(s): Establishments primarily engaged in:
- providing transcription services (56141, Document Preparation Services); and
- providing real-time closed captioning services (56149, Other Business Support Services).

Example Activities
- Interpreting services
- Language interpretation services
- Language sign services
- Language translation services
- Sign language services
- Speech interpretation services, language
- Translation services

541930 Translation and Interpretation Services

See industry description for 54193, above.

54194 Veterinary Services

This industry comprises establishments of licensed veterinary practitioners primarily engaged in the practice of veterinary medicine, dentistry, or surgery for animals. This industry also includes veterinary laboratories.

Exclusion(s): Establishments primarily engaged in:
- boarding horses (11521, Support Activities for Animal Production);
- veterinary research and development (54171, Research and Development in the Physical, Engineering and Life Sciences); and
- providing pet care services, except veterinary (81291, Pet Care (except Veterinary) Services).

Example Activities
- Animal hospitals
- Consulting and visiting services, veterinary
- Disease testing services, veterinary
- Herd inspecting and testing services, veterinary
- Hospitals, animal
- Pet hospitals
- Small animal veterinary services
- Surgeons, veterinary, offices of
- Surgery services, veterinary
- Testing laboratories, veterinary
- Veterinarians, offices of
- Veterinary clinics
- Veterinary practices
- Veterinary testing laboratories

541940 Veterinary Services US

See industry description for 54194, above.

54199 All Other Professional, Scientific and Technical Services

This industry comprises establishments, not classified to any other industry, primarily engaged in the provision of professional, scientific or technical services.

Exclusion(s): Establishments primarily engaged in:
- providing legal services (5411, Legal Services);
- providing accounting, tax preparation, bookkeeping and payroll services (5412, Accounting, Tax Preparation, Bookkeeping and Payroll Services);
- providing architectural, engineering and related services (5413, Architectural, Engineering and Related Services);
- providing specialized design services (5414, Specialized Design Services);
- providing computer systems design and related services (5415, Computer Systems Design and Related Services);
- providing management, scientific and technical consulting services (5416, Management, Scientific and Technical Consulting Services);
- providing scientific research and development services (5417, Scientific Research and Development Services);
- providing advertising and related services (5418, Advertising, Public Relations, and Related Services);
- providing marketing research and public opinion polling (54191, Marketing Research and Public Opinion Polling);
- providing photographic services (54192, Photographic Services);
- providing translation and interpretation services (54193, Translation and Interpretation Services); and
- providing veterinary services (54194, Veterinary Services).

Example Activities
- Appraising services (except insurance or real estate)
- Arbitration and conciliation service, non-government
- Bankruptcy trustees
- Consumer credit counselling services
- Credit repair services
- Estate assessment (i.e., appraisal) services
- Handwriting analysis services
- Marine surveyor (i.e., ship appraisal) services
- Meteorological services
- Patent broker services (i.e., patent marketing services)

- Patrolling (i.e., visual inspection) of electric transmission or gas lines
- Pipeline and power line inspection (i.e., visual inspection) services

- Receivership services
- Trustees, bankruptcy
- Weather forecasting services

541990 All Other Professional, Scientific and Technical Services

See industry description for 54199, above.

55 Management of Companies and Enterprises

This sector comprises establishments primarily engaged in managing companies and enterprises and/or holding the securities or financial assets of companies and enterprises, for the purpose of owning a controlling interest in them and/or influencing their management decisions. They may undertake the function of management, or they may entrust the function of financial management to portfolio managers.

551 Management of Companies and Enterprises

See industry description for 55111, below.

5511 Management of Companies and Enterprises

See industry description for 55111, below.

55111 Management of Companies and Enterprises

This industry comprises establishments primarily engaged in managing companies and enterprises and/or holding the securities or financial assets of companies and enterprises, for the purpose of owning a controlling interest in them and/or influencing their management decisions. They may undertake the function of management, or they may entrust the function of financial management to portfolio managers.

551113 Holding Companies CAN

This Canadian industry comprises establishments primarily engaged in holding the securities of (or other equity interests in) other businesses, for the purpose of exercising control, either directly or through subsidiaries, and/or influencing the management decisions of these businesses.

Exclusion(s): Establishments primarily engaged in:
- providing general management and/or administrative support services to the establishments of the businesses whose securities they hold (551114, Head Offices).

Example Activities
- Bank holding companies
- Holding management companies
- Investment holding companies (except banks)
- Management offices, subsidiary
- Personal holding companies (except banks)

551114 Head Offices US

This Canadian industry comprises establishments primarily engaged in providing general management and/or administrative support services to affiliated establishments.

Example Activity
- Head offices

56 Administrative and Support, Waste Management and Remediation Services

This sector comprises two different types of establishments: those primarily engaged in activities that support the day-to-day operations of other organizations; and those primarily engaged in waste management activities.

The first type of establishment is engaged in activities such as administration, hiring and placing personnel, preparing documents, taking orders from clients, collecting payments for claims, arranging travel, providing security and surveillance, cleaning buildings, and packaging and labelling products. These activities are often undertaken, in-house, by establishments found in many sectors of the economy. The establishments classified to this sector specialize in one or more of these activities and can therefore provide services to clients in a variety of industries and, in some cases, to households.

Waste management establishments are engaged in the collection, treatment and disposal of waste material, the operation of material recovery facilities, the remediation of polluted sites and the cleaning of septic tanks.

561 Administrative and Support Services

This subsector comprises establishments primarily engaged in activities that support the day-to-day operations of other organizations. This includes activities such as administration, hiring and placing personnel, preparing documents, taking orders from clients, collecting payments for claims, arranging travel, providing security and surveillance, cleaning buildings, and packaging and labelling products. These activities are often undertaken in-house by establishments found in many sectors of the economy, but the establishments of this subsector specialize in one or more of these activities and can therefore provide services to clients in a variety of industries and, in some cases, to households. The individual industries of this subsector are defined on the basis of the particular process in which they are engaged and the particular services they provide.

5611 Office Administrative Services

See industry description for 56111, below.

56111 Office Administrative Services

This industry comprises establishments primarily engaged in providing services to clients to administer, direct or coordinate a range of day-to-day business operations, such as financing, billing and record keeping; personnel; physical distribution; and other administrative and managerial activities. These establishments do not provide the operating staff to carry out the complete operations of a client's business.

Exclusion(s): Establishments primarily engaged in:
- providing farm management services (11, Agriculture, Forestry, Fishing and Hunting);
- providing construction management services (236, Construction of Buildings, or 237, Heavy and Civil Engineering Construction);
- providing computer facilities management services (54151, Computer Systems Design and Related Services);
- providing management advice (54161, Management Consulting Services);
- holding the securities or financial assets of companies and enterprises for the purpose of controlling them and influencing their management decisions, and/or managing (strategic decision-making aspects) companies and enterprises (55, Management of Companies and Enterprises); and
- providing both management and operating staff on contract for the complete operation of a client's establishment, such as a hotel, restaurant or hospital (classified according to the primary activity of the establishment operated).

Example Activities
- Administrative management services
- Business management services
- Executive management services
- Hotel management, operating staff not furnished (except complete operations of client business)
- Management service, operating staff not furnished (except complete operations of client business)
- Managing office of dentist, general
- Managing office of dentist, specialist
- Managing office of doctors
- Managing office of physicians and surgeons
- Motel management, operating staff not furnished (except complete operations of client business)
- Office administration services
- Office management services

561110 Office Administrative Services

See industry description for 56111, above.

5612 Facilities Support Services

See industry description for 56121, below.

56121 Facilities Support Services

This industry comprises establishments primarily engaged in providing a combination of services to support operations within a client's facilities. These establishments typically provide a combination of services, such as janitorial; maintenance; trash disposal; guard and security; mail routing and other logistical support; reception; laundry; and related services, to support operations within facilities. They provide operating staff to carry out these support activities, but are not involved with, or responsible for, the core business or activities of the client.

Exclusion(s): Establishments primarily engaged in:
- providing computer facilities management services (54151, Computer Systems Design and Related Services);
- providing both management and operating staff for the complete operation of a client's establishment, such as a hotel, restaurant or hospital (classified according to the primary activity of the establishment operated); and
- providing a single support service to clients, but not the range of services that establishments in this industry provide (classified according to the service provided).

Example Activities
- Base facilities management and support
- Correctional facilities, privately operated
- Facilities management (except computers)
- Facilities support services (except computer)
- Jails, privately operated

561210 Facilities Support Services

See industry description for 56121, above.

5613 Employment Services

This industry group comprises establishments primarily engaged in listing employment vacancies and selecting, referring and placing applicants in employment, either on a permanent or temporary basis; and establishments primarily engaged in supplying workers for limited periods of time to supplement the workforce of the client.

56131 Employment Placement Agencies and Executive Search Services

This industry comprises establishments primarily engaged in listing employment vacancies and selecting, referring and placing applicants in employment, either on a permanent or temporary basis. The individuals placed are not employees of the placement agencies.

Example Activities
- Babysitter, registries
- Casting agencies, motion picture or video
- Casting agencies, theatrical
- Casting bureau, motion picture or video
- Casting bureaus, theatrical
- Chauffeur registries
- Employment agencies (except theatrical and motion picture)
- Employment agencies, motion picture or video
- Employment agencies, radio or television
- Employment agencies, theatrical
- Employment placement agencies
- Employment registries
- Executive placement consulting services
- Executive search consulting services
- Film casting bureau
- Maid registries
- Model registries
- Motion picture casting bureau
- Nurses' registries
- Placement services, casting bureaus
- Placement services, employment agency
- Registries, employment (e.g., maid, nurses, teachers)
- Registries, nurses'
- Ship crew agencies
- Ship crew registries
- Teachers' registries
- Television employment agencies
- Theatrical employment agencies

561310 Employment Placement Agencies and Executive Search Services

See industry description for 56131, above.

56132 Temporary Help Services

This industry comprises establishments primarily engaged in supplying workers for limited periods of time to supplement the workforce of the client. The individuals provided are employees of the temporary help service establishment. These establishments do not provide direct supervision of their employees at the clients' work sites.

Exclusion(s): Establishments primarily engaged in:
- supplying farm labour (11511, Support Activities for Crop Production).

Example Activities

- General labour contractors (personnel suppliers)
- Help supply service
- Industrial personnel services (personnel suppliers)
- Labour pools (except farm labour)
- Lifeguard supply service
- Manpower pools
- Model supply services
- Office help supply service
- Office personnel services (personnel suppliers)
- Personnel pool services (personnel suppliers)
- Temporary employment services

561320 Temporary Help Services

See industry description for 56132, above.

56133 Professional Employer Organizations

This industry comprises establishments primarily engaged in providing human resources and human resource management services to clients. These establishments operate in a co-employment relationship with client businesses or organizations and are specialized in performing a wide range of human resource and personnel management duties, such as payroll accounting, payroll tax return preparation, benefits administration, recruiting, and managing labour relations. Professional employer establishments typically acquire and lease back some or all of the employees of their clients and serve as the employer of the leased employees for payroll, benefits and related purposes. Professional employer establishments exercise varying degrees of decision making relating to their human resource or personnel management role, but do not have management accountability for the work of their clients' operations with regard to strategic planning, output or profitability.

Exclusion(s): Establishments primarily engaged in:
- supplying workers for limited periods of time to supplement the work force of the client (56132, Temporary Help Services).

Example Activities

- Employee leasing service (providing permanent employees paid by supplying company but under the supervision of the hiring company)
- Labour leasing services (providing permanent employees paid by supplying company but under the supervision of the hiring company)
- Professional employer organizations
- Staff leasing services (providing permanent employees paid by supplying company but under the supervision of the hiring company)

561330 Professional Employer Organizations

See industry description for 56133, above.

5614 Business Support Services

This industry group comprises establishments primarily engaged in providing business support services, such as preparing documents, operating telephone call centres, operating business service centres, collecting unpaid claims, and providing credit information.

56141 Document Preparation Services

This industry comprises establishments primarily engaged in writing, editing or proofreading documents; providing word processing or desktop publishing services; and providing stenographic (except court or stenographic reporting), transcription and other secretarial services.

Exclusion(s): Establishments primarily engaged in:
- providing pre-press and post-press services in support of printing activities (32312, Support Activities for Printing);
- providing translation services (54193, Translation and Interpretation Services);
- reproducing documents (56143, Business Service Centres); and
- verbatim reporting and stenographic recording of live legal proceedings and transcribing subsequent recorded materials (56149, Other Business Support Services).

Example Activities
- Computer word processing
- Desktop publishing services
- Dictation services
- Document transcription services
- Editing service
- Proofreading service
- Radio transcription service
- Resume writing service
- Secretarial service
- Stenographic services (except court or stenographic reporting)
- Transcription services
- Typing services
- Word processing service

561410 Document Preparation Services

See industry description for 56141, above.

56142 Telephone Call Centres

This industry comprises establishments primarily engaged in receiving and/or making telephone calls for others. These establishments are engaged in activities such as soliciting or providing information; promoting products or services; taking orders; and raising funds for clients. This industry also includes establishments primarily engaged in answering telephone calls and relaying messages to clients; and establishments primarily engaged in providing voice mailbox services.

Exclusion(s): Establishments primarily engaged in:
- taking orders in offices of mail-order houses (454113, Mail-Order Houses);
- providing paging services (51721, Wireless Telecommunications Carriers (except Satellite));
- gathering, recording, tabulating, and presenting marketing and public opinion data (54191, Marketing Research and Public Opinion Polling); and
- organizing and conducting fund-raising campaigns for others (56149, Other Business Support Services).

Example Activities
- Answering services, telephone
- Floral wire service
- Message service, telephone answering
- Telemarketing bureaus
- Telemarketing service on a contract or fee basis
- Telephone answering services
- Telephone call centre
- Telephone message service
- Telephone solicitation service on a contract or fee basis
- Voice mail box services
- Wake up call services

561420 Telephone Call Centres CAN

See industry description for 56142, above.

56143 Business Service Centres

This industry comprises establishments, known as copy shops, establishments primarily engaged in providing mailbox rental and other postal and mailing services (except direct-mail advertising), and establishments that provide a range of office support services, such as mailing services, copying services, facsimile services, word processing services, on-site personal computer (PC) rental services and office product retailing.

Exclusion(s):
- commercial or quick printers (32311, Printing);

and establishments primarily engaged in:
- providing direct mail advertising services (54186, Direct Mail Advertising); and
- providing voice mailbox services (56142, Telephone Call Centres).

Example Activities
- Blueprinting services
- Business service centre
- Copy centres
- Copy shops
- Mail box centres, private
- Private mail box rental centres
- Private mail centres
- Reprographic services

561430 Business Service Centres CAN

See industry description for 56143, above.

56144 Collection Agencies

This industry comprises establishments primarily engaged in collecting payment for claims and remitting these payments to their clients.

Exclusion(s): Establishments primarily engaged in:
- purchasing accounts receivables and assuming the risk of collection and credit losses (522299, All Other Non-Depository Credit Intermediation).

Example Activities
- Accounts collection agencies
- Collecting delinquent accounts services
- Collection agency
- Debt collection services
- Tax collection services on a contract or fee basis

561440 Collection Agencies

See industry description for 56144, above.

56145 Credit Bureaus

This industry comprises establishments primarily engaged in compiling information, such as credit and employment histories on individuals and credit histories on businesses, and providing the information to financial institutions, retailers and others who have a need to evaluate the credit worthiness of these persons and businesses. This industry also includes establishments providing credit investigation services.

Example Activities
- Commercial credit reporting bureaus
- Consumer credit reporting bureaus
- Credit bureaus and agencies
- Credit investigation services
- Credit rating services
- Mercantile credit reporting bureaus

561450 Credit Bureaus

See industry description for 56145, above.

56149 Other Business Support Services

This industry comprises establishments, not classified to any other industry, primarily engaged in providing other business support services.

Exclusion(s): Establishments primarily engaged in:
- writing, editing and document preparation services (56141, Document Preparation Services);
- telephone answering or telemarketing services (56142, Telephone Call Centres);
- providing photocopying and mailbox services (56143, Business Service Centres);
- providing collection services (56144, Collection Agencies); and
- providing credit reporting services (56145, Credit Bureaus).

Example Activities
- Address bar coding services
- Automobile repossession services
- Closed captioning services, real-time (i.e., simultaneous)
- Court reporting services
- Fundraising service, on a contract or fee basis, for charitable organizations
- Mail consolidation services
- Presorting mail services
- Public stenography services
- Real time closed captioning (i.e., simultaneous)
- Repossession services
- Stenography services, public
- Stenotype reporting services

561490 Other Business Support Services MEX

See industry description for 56149, above.

5615 Travel Arrangement and Reservation Services

This industry group comprises establishments primarily engaged in travel arrangement and reservation services. Examples of establishments in this industry group are tourist and travel agencies; travel tour operators and wholesale operators; convention and visitors' bureaus; airline, bus, railroad and steamship ticket offices; sports and theatrical ticket offices; and airline, hotel and restaurant reservation offices.

56151 Travel Agencies

This industry comprises establishments primarily engaged in acting as agents for tour operators, transportation companies and accommodation establishments in selling travel, tour and accommodation services to the general public and commercial clients.

Exclusion(s): Establishments primarily engaged in:
- arranging, assembling and marketing packaged tours, generally through travel agencies (56152, Tour Operators);
- providing reservation services (56159, Other Travel Arrangement and Reservation Services); and
- providing tourist, hunting and fishing guide services (71399, All Other Amusement and Recreation Industries).

Example Activity
- Travel agencies

561510 Travel Agencies

See industry description for 56151, above.

56152 Tour Operators

This industry comprises establishments primarily engaged in arranging, assembling and marketing tours, generally through travel agencies.

Exclusion(s): Establishments primarily engaged in:
- conducting local scenic and sightseeing tours (487, Scenic and Sightseeing Transportation);
- providing access to outdoor adventure facilities and services without accommodation (71399, All Other Amusement and Recreation Industries);
- providing tourist, hunting and fishing guide services (71399, All Other Amusement and Recreation Industries);
- providing short-stay accommodation and/or food services (72, Accommodation and Food Services); and
- providing access to outdoor adventure facilities and services with accommodation (72121, RV (Recreational Vehicle) Parks and Recreational Camps).

Example Activities
- Tour operators
- Travel tour operators
- Travel tour services, tour operators
- Wholesale tour operators

561520 Tour Operators

See industry description for 56152, above.

56159 Other Travel Arrangement and Reservation Services

This industry comprises establishments primarily engaged in providing travel arrangement and reservation services, except travel agencies and tour operators.

Exclusion(s): Establishments primarily engaged in:
- arranging and assembling tours (56152, Tour Operators); and
- operating automobile clubs (81399, Other Membership Organizations).

Example Activities
- Airline reservation offices
- Airline ticket offices
- Automobile clubs, road and travel services
- Bus ticket offices
- Car rental reservations
- Condominium time share exchange services
- Convention and visitors bureaus
- Convention bureaus
- Cruise ship ticket offices
- Hotel reservation services
- Motor travel clubs
- Railroad ticket offices
- Reservation service (e.g., airline, car rental, hotel, restaurant)
- Sports ticket offices
- Theatrical ticket agencies
- Theatrical ticket offices
- Ticket agencies, amusement (except theatrical)
- Ticket agencies, sports
- Ticket agencies, theatrical
- Ticket agencies, transportation
- Ticket offices for foreign cruise ship companies
- Ticket sales agency
- Time share exchange services
- Tourist information bureaus
- Visitor bureaus
- Visitor information centres
- Welcome centres

561590 Other Travel Arrangement and Reservation Services MEX

See industry description for 56159, above.

5616 Investigation and Security Services

This industry group comprises establishments primarily engaged in providing investigation and detective services, guard and patrol services, armoured car services and security system services.

56161 Investigation, Guard and Armoured Car Services

This industry comprises establishments primarily engaged in providing investigation and detective services; providing guard and patrol services; and picking up and delivering money, receipts or other valuable items using personnel and equipment to protect such properties while in transit.

Exclusion(s): Establishments primarily engaged in:
- providing credit information services (56145, Credit Bureaus); and
- selling, installing, monitoring and maintaining security systems and devices (56162, Security Systems Services).

561611 Investigation Services US

This Canadian industry comprises establishments primarily engaged in providing investigation and detective services.

Exclusion(s): Establishments primarily engaged in:
- providing credit information services (561450, Credit Bureaus).

Example Activities
- Detective agencies
- Fingerprint services
- Investigation services (except credit)
- Lie detection service
- Missing person tracing service
- Polygraph service
- Private detectives services
- Private investigation services
- Skip tracers services

561612 Security Guard and Patrol Services US

This Canadian industry comprises establishments primarily engaged in providing guard and patrol services.

Exclusion(s): Establishments primarily engaged in:
- selling, installing, monitoring and maintaining security systems and devices, such as burglar and fire systems (56162, Security Systems Services).

Example Activities
- Body guard services
- Guard dog services
- Guard service
- Patrol services, security
- Personal protection services
- Security patrol service

561613 Armoured Car Services US

This Canadian industry comprises establishments primarily engaged in picking up and delivering money, receipts or other valuable items using personnel and equipment to protect such properties while in transit.

Example Activities
- Armoured car services
- Convoy guard services
- Transportation guard service

56162 Security Systems Services

This industry comprises establishments primarily engaged in remote monitoring of security alarm systems, such as burglar and fire alarms; and selling security systems, including locking devices, along with installation, maintenance or monitoring services.

Exclusion(s): Establishments primarily engaged in:
- selling security systems for buildings, without installation, maintenance or monitoring services (41, Wholesale Trade, or 44-45, Retail Trade);
- retailing motor vehicle security systems, with or without installation or maintenance services (44131, Automotive Parts and Accessories Stores); and
- providing key duplication services (81149, Other Personal and Household Goods Repair and Maintenance). ·

561621 Security Systems Services (except Locksmiths) US

This Canadian industry comprises establishments primarily engaged in remote monitoring of electronic security alarm systems, such as burglar and fire alarms; and selling security systems, along with installation, maintenance or monitoring services.

Exclusion(s): Establishments primarily engaged in:
- selling security systems for buildings without installation, repair or monitoring services (41, Wholesale Trade, or 44-45, Retail Trade); and
- retailing motor vehicle security systems, with or without installation or repair services (44131, Automotive Parts and Accessories Stores).

Example Activities
- Alarm system monitoring
- Alarm systems sale, combined with installation, maintenance or monitoring
- Burglar alarm sale, combined with installation, maintenance or monitoring
- Fire alarm sale, combined with installation, maintenance or monitoring
- Security system sale, combined with installation, maintenance or monitoring

561622 Locksmiths US

This Canadian industry comprises establishments primarily engaged in selling mechanical or electronic locking devices, safes and security vaults, along with installation, repair, rebuilding or adjusting services; and installing, repairing, rebuilding and adjusting mechanical or electronic locking devices, safes and security vaults.

Exclusion(s): Establishments primarily engaged in:
- selling security systems, such as locking devices, safes and vaults, without installation or maintenance services (41, Wholesale Trade, or 44-45, Retail Trade); and
- providing key duplication services (81149, Other Personal and Household Goods Repair and Maintenance).

Example Activities
- Locksmith services
- Locksmith services, with or without sales of locking devices, safes, and security vaults

5617 Services to Buildings and Dwellings

This industry group comprises establishments primarily engaged in exterminating and controlling insects, rodents and other pests, in and around buildings and other structures; cleaning building interiors and windows; landscaping installation, care and maintenance; cleaning and dyeing rugs, carpets and upholstery; and providing other services to buildings and dwellings.

56171 Exterminating and Pest Control Services

This industry comprises establishments primarily engaged in exterminating and controlling insects, rodents and other pests, in and around buildings and other structures.

Exclusion(s): Establishments primarily engaged in:
- providing pest control for agriculture or forestry (115, Support Activities for Agriculture and Forestry).

Example Activities
- Bird proofing
- Disinfecting service
- Extermination services
- Fumigation service
- Pest control services
- Termite control services

561710 Exterminating and Pest Control Services

See industry description for 56171, above.

56172 Janitorial Services

This industry comprises establishments primarily engaged in the exterior cleaning of windows or in cleaning building interiors.

561721 Window Cleaning Services CAN

This Canadian industry comprises establishments primarily engaged in the cleaning of windows.

Example Activity
- Window cleaning services

561722 Janitorial Services (except Window Cleaning) CAN

This Canadian industry comprises establishments primarily engaged in cleaning building interiors, and/or transportation equipment (aircraft, ships, rail cars) interiors.

Exclusion(s): Establishments primarily engaged in:
- cleaning chimneys (56179, Other Services to Buildings and Dwellings).

Example Activities
- Abattoir cleaning
- Aircraft janitorial services
- Building cleaning, janitorial services
- Cleaning of homes
- Cleaning offices
- Cleaning shopping centres
- Custodial services
- Deodorant servicing of rest rooms
- Housekeeping (i.e., cleaning service)
- Janitorial services
- Maid cleaning services
- Office cleaning service
- Residential cleaning services
- Rest room cleaning services
- Restaurant kitchen cleaning services
- Service station cleaning and degreasing service
- Washroom sanitation service

56173 Landscaping Services

This industry comprises establishments primarily engaged in providing landscape care and maintenance services and/or installing trees, shrubs, plants, lawns or gardens, and establishments engaged in these activities along with the construction (installation) of walkways, retaining walls, decks, fences, ponds and similar structures.

Exclusion(s): Establishments primarily engaged in:
- the construction (installation) of walkways, retaining walls, decks, fences, ponds and similar structures (23, Construction);
- retailing, installing and maintaining landscaping materials, such as trees, shrubs and plants (44422, Nursery Stores and Garden Centres); and
- planning and designing the development of land areas for projects such as parks and other recreational areas; airports; highways; hospitals; schools; land subdivisions; and commercial, industrial and residential areas (54132, Landscape Architectural Services).

Example Activities
- Arborist services
- Cemetery plot care services
- Garden maintenance services
- Landscape contractors
- Landscape services
- Lawn care services
- Lawn seeding services
- Lawn spraying services
- Line slash (rights-of-way) maintenance
- Maintenance of plants and shrubs in buildings
- Maintenance of rights-of-way (i.e., controlling vegetation)
- Power, communication and pipe lines, maintenance of rights of way
- Rights of way, cutting, maintenance
- Seasonal property maintenance services (i.e., snow ploughing in winter, landscaping during other seasons)
- Seeding lawns
- Sod laying services
- Tree removal services
- Tree surgery service
- Turf installation (except artificial)
- Weed control and fertilizing services (except for crops)

561730 Landscaping Services

See industry description for 56173, above.

56174 Carpet and Upholstery Cleaning Services

This industry comprises establishments primarily engaged in cleaning and dyeing rugs, carpets, and upholstery.

Exclusion(s): Establishments primarily engaged in:
- reupholstering and repairing furniture (81142, Reupholstery and Furniture Repair).

Example Activities
- Carpet and furniture cleaning on location, services
- Carpet cleaning services
- Furniture and carpet cleaning on location, services
- Mobile cleaning, carpets and rugs
- Rug cleaning services
- Upholstery cleaning services

561740 Carpet and Upholstery Cleaning Services

See industry description for 56174, above.

56179 Other Services to Buildings and Dwellings

This industry comprises establishments primarily engaged in providing services to buildings and dwellings.

561791 Duct and Chimney Cleaning Services ^{CAN}

This Canadian industry comprises establishments primarily engaged in providing duct and furnace cleaning services, and chimney cleaning services.

Example Activities

- Chimney cleaning services
- Chimney sweep services
- Duct cleaning services
- Ventilating ducts, cleaning services

561799 All Other Services to Buildings and Dwellings ^{CAN}

This Canadian industry comprises establishments, not classified to any other industry, primarily engaged in providing other services to buildings and dwellings, such as swimming pool cleaning and building exterior cleaning (except sandblasting).

Exclusion(s): Establishments primarily engaged in:

- sandblasting building exteriors (23, Construction);
- providing janitorial services or exterior window cleaning services (56172, Janitorial Services);
- providing care and maintenance of lawns (561730, Landscaping Services); and
- providing pest control for lawns (561730, Landscaping Services).

Example Activities

- Building exterior cleaning services (except sandblasting and window cleaning)
- Cedar (exterior) cleaning, preserving and repairing
- Cleaning building exteriors (except sand blasting and window cleaning)
- Cleaning swimming pools
- Drain cleaning services
- Gutter cleaning services
- Lighting maintenance service (i.e., bulb and fuse replacement and cleaning)
- Power cleaning paved areas (except streets)
- Power washing building exteriors
- Snow ploughing services, parking lots and driveways, not combined with any other service
- Steam cleaning of building exteriors
- Swimming pool cleaning and maintenance service

5619 Other Support Services

This industry group comprises establishments, not classified to any other industry group, primarily engaged in providing day-to-day support services.

56191 Packaging and Labelling Services

This industry comprises establishments primarily engaged in packaging client-owned materials. The packaging service may include the labelling or imprinting of the package.

Exclusion(s): Establishments primarily engaged in:

- mixing water and concentrate to produce soft drinks (31211, Soft Drink and Ice Manufacturing);
- packing and crating incidental to transportation (48899, Other Support Activities for Transportation); and
- providing warehousing services as well as packaging or other logistics services (4931, Warehousing and Storage).

Example Activities

- Blister packaging services
- Cosmetic kits, assembling and packaging
- Folding and refolding service, textiles and apparel
- Kit packaging services
- Labelling services
- Mounting merchandise on cards

- Packaging and labelling service (not packing and crating for transportation)
- Packaging services (except crating for transportation)

- Product sterilization and packaging service
- Shrink wrapping services
- Skin blister packaging services
- Textile folding and packaging services

561910 Packaging and Labelling Services

See industry description for 56191, above.

56192 Convention and Trade Show Organizers

This industry comprises establishments primarily engaged in organizing, promoting and supporting conventions and trade shows, whether or not they operate the facilities in which these events take place.

Exclusion(s): Establishments primarily engaged in:
- promoting and presenting artistic and sporting events (7113, Promoters (Presenters) of Performing Arts, Sports and Similar Events).

Example Activities
- Automobile shows, flower shows and home shows, promoters of
- Convention promoters

- Convention services
- Trade fairs promoters
- Trade show promoters

561920 Convention and Trade Show Organizers

See industry description for 56192, above.

56199 All Other Support Services

This industry comprises establishments, not classified to any other industry, primarily engaged in providing support services.

Exclusion(s): Establishments primarily engaged in:
- providing employment services (5613, Employment Services);
- providing business support services (5614, Business Support Services);
- providing travel arrangement and reservation services (5615, Travel Arrangement and Reservation Services);
- providing security and investigation services (5616, Investigation and Security Services);
- providing services to buildings and other structures (5617, Services to Buildings and Dwellings);
- packaging and labelling services (56191, Packaging and Labelling Services); and
- organizing convention and trade shows (56192, Convention and Trade Show Organizers).

Example Activities
- Auctioneering service, on a commission or fee basis, not done on own facilities (except currency and tobacco)
- Bartering services
- Bottle exchange
- Cloth, cutting to length, bolting, or winding for textile distributors
- Coin pick-up services, from parking meters
- Contract meter reading service, water
- Coupon redemption service (clearinghouses)
- Diving service on a fee or contract basis

- Electricity meter reading service, contract
- Floats, decoration of
- Gas meter reading service, contract
- Grading lumber services
- Inventory computing service
- Inventory taking service
- Meter reading services, contract
- Motor vehicle licences, issuer, private franchise
- Tape slitting for the trade (i.e., cutting plastic, leather, other materials into widths)

- Textile cutting service
- Water conditioning service
- Water meter reading service, contract

- Water softening and conditioning services
- Wood piling

561990 All Other Support Services

See industry description for 56199, above.

562 Waste Management and Remediation Services

This subsector comprises establishments primarily engaged in providing waste management services, such as waste collection, treatment and disposal services; environmental remediation services; and septic tank pumping services. Material recovery facilities are also included.

Exclusion(s):
- establishments that use recyclable materials as inputs to a manufacturing process (31-33, Manufacturing); and
- wholesalers of recyclable materials, including those engaged in the grinding of plastic or recovery of rubber from tires without further processing (4181, Recyclable Material Wholesaler-Distributors).

5621 Waste Collection US

See industry description for 56211, below.

56211 Waste Collection US

This industry comprises establishments primarily engaged in collecting and hauling non-hazardous or hazardous waste within a local area. Establishments engaged in hazardous waste collection may be responsible for treating and packaging the waste for transport. Waste transfer stations are also included.

Exclusion(s): Establishments primarily engaged in:
- the long distance transportation of waste without waste collection (48423, Specialized Freight (except Used Goods) Trucking, Long Distance).

Example Activities
- Ashes, collection
- Brush removal
- Dead stock removal services
- Dump trucking of non-hazardous construction rubble, with collection or disposal
- Garbage collection
- Garbage pick-up

- Hazardous waste collection
- Recyclable material, collection
- Refuse collection service
- Rubbish collection
- Trash collection
- Waste collection
- Waste collection, solid

562110 Waste Collection CAN

See industry description for 56211, above.

5622 Waste Treatment and Disposal US

See industry description for 56221, below.

56221 Waste Treatment and Disposal US

This industry comprises establishments primarily engaged in operating land fill sites, incinerators, or other treatment or disposal facilities for non-hazardous or hazardous waste. Establishments that integrate the collection, treatment and disposal of waste are also included.

Exclusion(s): Establishments primarily engaged in:
- composting (32531, Fertilizer Manufacturing).

Example Activities
- Ashes, collection and disposal of
- Compost dumps
- Disposal of dead stock, incinerator and combustor
- Garbage collection and disposal service
- Garbage disposal, incinerator and combustor
- Garbage disposal, landfill
- Garbage dump operation
- Hazardous waste material treatment and disposal sites
- Incinerator operation
- Landfill, garbage disposal
- Radioactive waste disposal service
- Refuse collection and disposal service
- Refuse disposal, incinerator and combustor
- Refuse disposal, landfill
- Sanitary landfill operation
- Sludge disposal sites
- Waste disposal, hazardous
- Waste disposal, solid, incinerator and combustor
- Waste disposal, solid, landfill
- Waste treatment, hazardous

562210 Waste Treatment and Disposal ^{CAN}

See industry description for 56221, above.

5629 Remediation and Other Waste Management Services ^{US}

This industry group comprises establishments, not classified to any other industry group, primarily engaged in waste management activities, such as the remediation and clean-up of contaminated sites, the operation of material recovery facilities, and the cleaning of septic tanks.

56291 Remediation Services ^{US}

This industry comprises establishments primarily engaged in the remediation and clean-up of contaminated buildings, mine sites, soil or ground water. Establishments primarily engaged in integrated mine site reclamation activities, such as soil remediation, waste water treatment, hazardous material removal, contouring of land and revegetation, are also included.

Exclusion(s): Establishments primarily engaged in:
- demolishing or dismantling buildings, and/or soil excavation (23891, Site Preparation Contractors); and
- developing remedial action plans (54162, Environmental Consulting Services).

Example Activities
- Asbestos removal contractors
- Contaminated site, remediation
- Environmental remediation services
- Integrated mine reclamation services
- Lead paint removal contractors
- Oil spill cleanup
- Site remediation
- Toxic material abatement services

562910 Remediation Services ^{US}

See industry description for 56291, above.

56292 Material Recovery Facilities ^{US}

This industry comprises establishments primarily engaged in operating facilities in which recyclable materials are removed from waste, or mixed recyclable materials are sorted into distinct categories and prepared for shipment.

Exclusion(s): Establishments primarily engaged in:
- the treatment and disposal of hazardous wastes, such as paints and used solvents (56221, Waste Treatment and Disposal).

Example Activities
- Materials recovery facility (i.e., sorting recyclable materials)
- Sorting, cleaning, and baling of commingled recyclable materials (except hazardous)
- Waste recovery facility

562920 Material Recovery Facilities US

See industry description for 56292, above.

56299 All Other Waste Management Services US

This industry comprises establishments, not classified to any other industry, primarily engaged in waste management activities.

Example Activities
- Beach maintenance and cleaning services
- Catch basin cleaning services
- Cesspool cleaning services
- Rental and pumping of portable toilets
- Renting of portable toilets
- Septic tank cleaning services
- Septic tank pumping services
- Sewer and storm basin cleanout services
- Sewer cleaning and rodding services
- Toilets, portable, rental, leasing and pumping

562990 All Other Waste Management Services CAN

See industry description for 56299, above.

61 Educational Services

This sector comprises establishments primarily engaged in providing instruction and training in a wide variety of subjects. This instruction and training is provided by specialized establishments, such as schools, colleges, universities and training centres. These establishments may be privately owned and operated, either for profit or not, or they may be publicly owned and operated. They may also offer food and accommodation services to their students.

Educational services are usually delivered by teachers who explain, tell, demonstrate, supervise and direct self-learning. Instruction is imparted in diverse settings, such as educational institutions, the workplace or the home (through correspondence, television or other means). The lessons can be adapted to the particular needs of the students, for example sign language can replace verbal language for teaching students with hearing impairments. All industries in the sector share this commonality of process, namely, labour inputs of teachers with the requisite subject matter expertise and teaching ability.

611 Educational Services

This subsector comprises establishments primarily engaged in providing instruction and training in a wide variety of subjects. This instruction and training is provided by specialized establishments, such as schools, colleges, universities and training centres.

The subsector is structured according to the level and type of educational services provided. Elementary and secondary schools, community colleges, Collèges d'enseignement général et professionnel (C.E.G.E.P.s) and universities correspond to a recognized series of formal levels of education designated by diplomas, associate degrees (and equivalent certificates) and degrees. The remaining industry groups are based on the type of instruction or training offered and the levels are not always as formally defined. The establishments are often highly specialized, many offering instruction in a very limited subject matter, for example ski lessons or one specific type of software.

Within the subsector, the level and types of training that are required of the instructors and teachers vary depending on the industry.

6111 Elementary and Secondary Schools

See industry description for 61111, below.

61111 Elementary and Secondary Schools US

This industry comprises establishments primarily engaged in providing academic courses that comprise a basic preparatory education, that is, kindergarten through 12th grade.

Exclusion(s): Establishments primarily engaged in:
- pre-school or pre-kindergarten education (62441, Child Day-Care Services).

Example Activities
- Academies, elementary or secondary
- Boarding schools, elementary or secondary
- Collegiate institutes, elementary or secondary
- Convent schools, elementary or secondary
- Elementary schools
- High schools
- Kindergartens
- Military academies, elementary or secondary
- Parochial schools, elementary or secondary
- Preparatory schools, elementary or secondary
- Primary schools
- Private schools, elementary or secondary
- School boards, elementary and secondary
- School, elementary
- Schools for the physically handicapped (elementary and secondary)
- Secondary schools

611110 Elementary and Secondary Schools US

See industry description for 61111, above.

6112 Community Colleges and C.E.G.E.P.s

See industry description for 61121, below.

61121 Community Colleges and C.E.G.E.P.s

This industry comprises establishments primarily engaged in providing academic, or academic and technical, courses and granting associate degrees, certificates or diplomas that are below the university level. The requirement for admission to an associate or equivalent degree program is at least a high school diploma or equivalent general academic training.

Example Activities
- Agriculture schools (non-university)
- C.E.G.E.P. (collège d'enseignement général et professionnel)
- College of applied arts and sciences
- College of fisheries
- College of general and vocational education
- College of trades and technology
- Community colleges
- E-learning, Community Colleges and C.E.G.E.P.s

- Engineering schools (non-university)
- Forest technology schools
- Institute of marine technology, post-secondary
- Land surveying institutes
- Marine engineering school, post-secondary

- Post-secondary or non-university educational
- Teachers' colleges
- Technical institute, post-secondary
- Technical school, post-secondary non-university

611210 Community Colleges and C.E.G.E.P.s US

See industry description for 61121, above.

6113 Universities

See industry description for 61131, below.

61131 Universities

This industry comprises establishments primarily engaged in providing academic courses and granting degrees at baccalaureate or graduate levels. The requirement for admission is at least a high school diploma or equivalent general academic training for baccalaureate programs, and often a baccalaureate degree for professional or graduate programs.

Example Activities
- Colleges (except junior)
- Conservatory of music, degree granting
- Degree-granting institutions
- Dentistry schools
- Law schools
- Medical schools

- Military training schools (university-degree granting)
- Professional schools (e.g., dental, engineering, law, medical)
- Theological colleges or seminary (degree-granting)
- Universities

611310 Universities US

See industry description for 61131, above.

6114 Business Schools and Computer and Management Training

This industry group comprises establishments primarily engaged in providing courses in office procedures and secretarial and stenographic skills; conducting training in all phases of computer activities, including computer programming, software packages, computerized business systems, computer electronics technology, computer operations and local area network management; and offering an array of short-duration courses and seminars for management and professional development.

61141 Business and Secretarial Schools

This industry comprises establishments primarily engaged in providing courses in office procedures and secretarial and stenographic skills and may offer courses in basic computer skills, word processing, spreadsheets, and desktop publishing. In addition, these establishments may offer classes such as office machine operation, reception, communications, and other skills designed for individuals pursuing a clerical or secretarial career, or a career in court reporting.

Exclusion(s): Establishments primarily engaged in:
- providing business education at the degree level (61131, Universities); and
- providing computer training (61142, Computer Training).

Example Activities
- Business schools (non-university)
- Commercial schools (non-university)
- Court reporting schools
- Secretarial schools

611410 Business and Secretarial Schools ^{US} 611410 Business and Secretarial Schools US

See industry description for 61141, above.

61142 Computer Training

This industry comprises establishments primarily engaged in conducting training in all phases of computer activities, including computer programming, software packages, computerized business systems, computer electronics technology, computer operations and local area network management. Instruction may be provided at the establishment's facilities or at an off-site location, including the client's own facilities.

Exclusion(s): Establishments primarily engaged in:
- computer wholesaling that includes computer training (41731, Computer, Computer Peripheral and Pre-Packaged Software Wholesaler-Distributors);
- computer retailing that includes computer training (44312, Computer and Software Stores); and
- providing training in computer repair and maintenance (61151, Technical and Trade Schools).

Example Activities
- Computer operator training
- Computer software training

611420 Computer Training US

See industry description for 61142, above.

61143 Professional and Management Development Training

This industry comprises establishments primarily engaged in providing an array of short-duration courses and seminars for management and professional development. Training may be provided directly to individuals or through employers' training programs. Career development and courses may be customized or modified to meet the special needs of customers. Instruction may be provided at the establishment's facilities or at an off-site location, including the client's own facilities.

Exclusion(s): Establishments primarily engaged in:
- providing human resource advisory services, but not providing training (54161, Management Consulting Services); and
- academic degree granting (61131, Universities).

Example Activity
- Professional and management development training

611430 Professional and Management Development Training US

See industry description for 61143, above.

6115 Technical and Trade Schools

See industry description for 61151, below.

61151 Technical and Trade Schools

This industry comprises establishments primarily engaged in providing vocational and technical training in a variety of technical subjects and trades. The training often leads to non-academic certification. Vocational correspondence schools are also included.

Exclusion(s): Establishments primarily engaged in:
- secondary school education with technical and trade instruction (61111, Elementary and Secondary Schools);
- registered nurses training at the associate degree level or equivalent (61121, Community Colleges and C.E.G.E.P.s);
- technical and trade instruction at the associate degree or equivalent level (61121, Community Colleges and C.E.G.E.P.s);
- registered nurses training at the degree level (61131, Universities);
- business and secretarial training (61141, Business and Secretarial Schools);
- computer training (61142, Computer Training); and
- professional and management development training (61143, Professional and Management Development Training).

Example Activities
- Banking schools (training in banking)
- Barbering schools
- Commercial art schools
- Computer repair training
- Construction equipment operation schools
- Cooking school
- Correspondence school (except elementary and secondary levels)
- Cosmetology schools
- Fire training school
- Flying school, civilian
- Forestry school
- Ground training service for air crew
- Homemaking school
- Industrial school, government (except corrective or reform school)
- Navigation and fisheries school
- Nurses' aides' school
- Nurses' schools, practical
- Nursing assistants' school
- Police schools
- Radio and television broadcasting schools
- Real estate schools
- Restaurant operation schools
- School of cooking
- School, hairdressing and beauty culture
- School, trade post-secondary
- Trade school post-secondary
- Truck driving schools
- Vocational apprenticeship training
- Vocational institute post-secondary

611510 Technical and Trade Schools CAN

See industry description for 61151, above.

6116 Other Schools and Instruction

This industry group comprises establishments primarily engaged in providing instruction in the fine arts; athletics and sports; languages; and other instruction (except academic, business, computer, management, and technical and trade instruction); and providing services, such as tutoring and exam preparation.

61161 Fine Arts Schools

This industry comprises establishments primarily engaged in providing instruction in the arts, including art (except commercial and graphic arts), dance, drama, music and photography (except commercial photography). Professional dance schools are also included.

Exclusion(s): Establishments primarily engaged in:
- providing high school education with fine arts instruction (61111, Elementary and Secondary Schools);
- fine arts instruction at the associate degree level (61121, Community Colleges and C.E.G.E.P.s);
- fine arts instruction at the degree level (61131, Universities); and
- commercial and graphic art and commercial photography instruction (61151, Technical and Trade Schools).

Example Activities

- Art schools (except commercial)
- Arts and crafts school
- Ballet schools
- College of art
- Conservatory of music (except degree-granting)
- Dance instruction
- Dance studios and schools
- Drama school
- Fine arts schools
- Handicrafts school
- Music teachers, own account
- Performing arts schools
- School, arts and crafts
- Schools of the dance (ballroom and popular)
- Sculpture teachers, own account
- Theatre arts school

611610 Fine Arts Schools US

See industry description for 61161, above.

61162 Athletic Instruction

This industry comprises establishments primarily engaged in providing instruction in athletic activities. Included are overnight and day sports instruction camps.

Exclusion(s): Establishments primarily engaged in:

- providing elementary or secondary education with sports instruction (61111, Elementary and Secondary Schools);
- sports instruction at the associate degree or equivalent level (61121, Community Colleges and C.E.G.E.P.s);
- sports instruction at the degree level (61131, Universities);
- operating sports and recreation facilities, in which athletic instruction is offered (7139, Other Amusement and Recreation Industries); and
- operating overnight recreational camps, in which athletic instruction is offered as an incidental activity (72121, RV (Recreational Vehicle) Parks and Recreational Camps).

Example Activities

- Aerobic dance instructors, independent
- Gymnastics instruction
- Hockey schools
- Independent sports instructors
- Judo and jiu-jitsu instruction
- Karate school
- Martial arts clubs
- Professional sports instructors for golf, skiing, swimming
- Riding academies and schools
- Schools and camps, sports instructional
- Scuba and skin diving instruction
- Skating instruction, ice or roller
- Skiing instruction
- Sports instructors, independent
- Sports instructors, professional (e.g., golf, skiing, swimming)
- Swimming instruction

611620 Athletic Instruction US

See industry description for 61162, above.

61163 Language Schools

This industry comprises establishments primarily engaged in providing courses in foreign language instruction. These establishments offer language instruction ranging from conversational skills for personal enrichment to intensive training courses for career or educational opportunities.

Exclusion(s): Establishments primarily engaged in:
- providing translation and interpretation services (54193, Translation and Interpretation Services);
- providing elementary or secondary education with language instruction (61111, Elementary and Secondary Schools);
- providing associate degree or equivalent education with language instruction (61121, Community Colleges and C.E.G.E.P.s); and
- providing degree-level education with language instruction (61131, Universities).

Example Activity
- Language schools

611630 Language Schools US

See industry description for 61163, above.

61169 All Other Schools and Instruction

This industry comprises establishments, not classified to any other industry, primarily engaged in providing instruction services.

Example Activities
- Automobile driving instruction
- Bible schools (except degree-granting)
- Charm schools
- Driver education, automobile
- Driving schools, automobile
- Personal development courses
- Public speaking schools
- Speed reading courses
- Survival schools
- Tutors, private

611690 All Other Schools and Instruction CAN

See industry description for 61169, above.

6117 Educational Support Services

See industry description for 61171, below.

61171 Educational Support Services

This industry comprises establishments primarily engaged in providing non-instructional services that support educational processes or systems.

Exclusion(s): Establishments primarily engaged in:
- job placement services (56131, Employment Placement Agencies and Executive Search Services); and
- job training for the unemployed, underemployed, physically disabled, and persons who have a job market disadvantage because of lack of education or job skills (62431, Vocational Rehabilitation Services).

Example Activities
- Child guidance centre, vocational
- Curriculum development, educational
- Educational counselling
- Educational testing services
- Student exchange programs
- Vocational counselling (except rehabilitation)

611710 Educational Support Services

See industry description for 61171, above.

62 Health Care and Social Assistance

This sector comprises establishments primarily engaged in providing health care by diagnosis and treatment, providing residential care for medical and social reasons, and providing social assistance, such as counselling, welfare, child protection, community housing and food services, vocational rehabilitation and child care, to those requiring such assistance.

621 Ambulatory Health Care Services

This subsector comprises establishments primarily engaged in providing health care services, directly or indirectly, to ambulatory patients. Health practitioners in this subsector provide out-patient services, in which the facilities and equipment are not usually the most significant part of the production process.

6211 Offices of Physicians

See industry description for 62111, below.

62111 Offices of Physicians

This industry comprises establishments of licensed physicians primarily engaged in the private or group practice of general or specialized medicine or surgery. Offices of physicians, especially walk-in centres that accept patients without appointment and that often have extended office hours, are sometimes called clinics or medical centres. These establishments must not be confused with other out-patient centres that are also referred to as clinics.

Example Activities
- Anesthesiologists, offices of
- Cardiologists' offices
- Dermatologists, offices of
- Doctors' clinics, general practice
- Family physicians, general practice
- Group practice, osteopaths
- Group practice, physicians
- Medical offices, specialist, physicians and surgeons
- Medical pathologists' offices
- Obstetricians' offices
- Ophthalmologists' offices
- Osteopaths' offices
- Paediatricians' offices
- Physicians' offices, general practice
- Plastic surgeons' offices
- Psychiatrists' offices
- Radiologists' offices
- Surgeons, offices of
- Urologists, offices of

621110 Offices of Physicians CAN

See industry description for 62111, above.

6212 Offices of Dentists

See industry description for 62121, below.

62121 Offices of Dentists

This industry comprises establishments of licensed dentists primarily engaged in the private or group practice of general or specialized dentistry or dental surgery. Offices of dentists, especially walk-in centres that accept patients without appointment and that often have extended office hours, are sometimes called clinics or dental centres.

Exclusion(s): Establishments primarily engaged in:
- denture, artificial teeth and orthodontic appliance making, made-to-order for dentists (33911, Medical Equipment and Supplies Manufacturing);
- impression taking and denture-fitting by denturists practising their profession independently (62139, Offices of All Other Health Practitioners); and
- teeth and gum cleaning by dental hygienists practising their profession independently (62139, Offices of All Other Health Practitioners).

Example Activities
- Dental clinic
- Dental surgeons, offices of
- Dentists, offices and clinics of
- Group practice, general dentist
- Orthodontists, offices of
- Periodontists, offices of
- Prosthodontists, offices of

621210 Offices of Dentists US

See industry description for 62121, above.

6213 Offices of Other Health Practitioners

This industry group comprises establishments of health practitioners, except physicians and dentists. Offices, especially walk-in centres that accept patients without appointment and that often have extended office hours, are sometimes called clinics or centres.

62131 Offices of Chiropractors

This industry comprises establishments primarily engaged in the private or group practice of chiropractic medicine. These practitioners provide diagnostic and therapeutic treatment of neuro-musculoskeletal and related disorders through the manipulation and adjustment of the spinal column and extremities.

Example Activities
- Chiropractic services
- Chiropractors, offices and clinics of

621310 Offices of Chiropractors US

See industry description for 62131, above.

62132 Offices of Optometrists

This industry comprises establishments primarily engaged in the private or group practice of optometry. These practitioners provide eye examinations to determine visual acuity or the presence of vision problems and to prescribe eyeglasses, contact lenses and eye exercises. They may also perform those services provided by an optician, such as selling and fitting prescription eyeglasses and contact lenses.

Exclusion(s): Establishments primarily engaged in:
- prescription eyeglass and contact lens selling and fitting (44613, Optical Goods Stores).

Example Activities
- Clinics of optometrists
- Optometrists, offices and clinics of

621320 Offices of Optometrists

See industry description for 62132, above.

62133 Offices of Mental Health Practitioners (except Physicians)

This industry comprises establishments primarily engaged in providing mental health services. Clinical psychologists, psychiatric social workers and other mental health practitioners, who do not hold a doctorate degree in medicine, are included.

Exclusion(s): Establishments primarily engaged in:
- providing treatment and diagnostic services by psychiatrists, psychoanalysts and psychotherapists having a doctorate degree in medicine (62111, Offices of Physicians).

Example Activities
- Psychiatric social workers, offices of
- Psychologists' offices
- Psychotherapists (except M.D.), offices of

621330 Offices of Mental Health Practitioners (except Physicians) US

See industry description for 62133, above.

62134 Offices of Physical, Occupational, and Speech Therapists and Audiologists

This industry comprises establishments primarily engaged in administering medically-prescribed physical therapy treatment; planning and administering educational, recreational and social activities designed to help patients with disabilities regain physical or mental functioning or to adapt to their disabilities; and diagnosing and treating speech, language or hearing problems.

Example Activities
- Audiologists, offices of
- Occupational therapists, offices of
- Physiotherapists' offices, private practice
- Speech pathologists, offices of
- Speech therapy clinics

621340 Offices of Physical, Occupational, and Speech Therapists and Audiologists US

See industry description for 62134, above.

62139 Offices of All Other Health Practitioners

This industry comprises establishments of health practitioners, not classified to any other industry, primarily engaged in providing health services.

Exclusion(s): Establishments primarily engaged in:
- general or specialized medicine or surgery (62111, Offices of Physicians);
- dentistry (62121, Offices of Dentists);
- chiropractic medicine (62131, Offices of Chiropractors);
- optometry (62132, Offices of Optometrists);
- mental health practising, except by physicians (62133, Offices of Mental Health Practitioners (except Physicians)); and
- physical, occupational, and speech therapy and audiology (62134, Offices of Physical, Occupational, and Speech Therapists and Audiologists).

Example Activities
- Acupuncturists' offices
- Chiropodists' offices
- Christian Science practitioners' offices
- Dental hygienists, offices of
- Denturists' offices
- Dieticians, offices of
- Herbalists, private practice

- Holistic medicine, practitioners' offices
- Midwives' offices
- Naturopaths' offices
- Nurses, registered and practical, offices of (except home health care services)
- Nutritionists, offices of
- Podiatrists, offices and clinics of
- Registered nurses' offices

621390 Offices of All Other Health Practitioners CAN

See industry description for 62139, above.

6214 Out-Patient Care Centres

This industry group comprises establishments, with medical staff, primarily engaged in general out-patient care, by providing the services of a variety of health practitioners within the same establishment, and specialized out-patient services.

62141 Family Planning Centres

This industry comprises establishments, with medical staff, primarily engaged in providing a range of family planning services, such as contraceptive services, genetic and prenatal counselling, voluntary sterilization, and therapeutic and medically-indicated termination of pregnancy, on an out-patient basis.

Example Activities
- Family planning counselling services

- Planned parenthood

621410 Family Planning Centres US

See industry description for 62141, above.

62142 Out-Patient Mental Health and Substance Abuse Centres

This industry comprises establishments, with medical staff, primarily engaged in providing out-patient services related to the diagnosis and treatment of mental health disorders, and alcohol and other substance abuse. These establishments may provide a counselling staff and information regarding a wide range of mental health and substance abuse issues.

Exclusion(s): Establishments primarily engaged in:
- the in-patient treatment of mental health and substance abuse illnesses with an emphasis on medical treatment and monitoring (62221, Psychiatric and Substance Abuse Hospitals); and
- the in-patient treatment of mental health and substance abuse illness with an emphasis on counselling rather than medical treatment (62322, Residential Mental Health and Substance Abuse Facilities).

Example Activities
- Outpatient mental health clinics
- Outpatient treatment clinics for alcoholism and drug addiction

- Rehabilitation clinics, out-patient

621420 Out-Patient Mental Health and Substance Abuse Centres ^{US}

See industry description for 62142, above.

62149 Other Out-Patient Care Centres

This industry comprises establishments, with medical staff, not classified to any other industry, primarily engaged in general out-patient care, which provides the services of a variety of health practitioners within the same establishment, and specialized out-patient services, such as dialysis. These establishments are often referred to as clinics or centres and must not be confused with the offices of health practitioners classified to other industries that are also referred to as clinics or centres.

Exclusion(s): Establishments primarily engaged in:
- general or specialized medicine or surgery (62111, Offices of Physicians);
- dentistry (62121, Offices of Dentists);
- chiropractic medicine (62131, Offices of Chiropractors);
- optometry (62132, Offices of Optometrists);
- mental health practising, except by physicians (62133, Offices of Mental Health Practitioners (except Physicians));
- physical, occupational, and speech therapy and audiology (62134, Offices of Physical, Occupational, and Speech Therapists and Audiologists);
- a range of family planning services, such as contraceptive services, genetic and prenatal counselling, voluntary sterilization, and therapeutic and medically-indicated termination of pregnancy, on an out-patient basis (62141, Family Planning Centres); and
- out-patient services related to the diagnosis and treatment of mental health disorders and alcohol and other substance abuse (62142, Out-Patient Mental Health and Substance Abuse Centres).

621494 Community Health Centres ^{CAN}

This Canadian industry comprises establishments, with medical staff, primarily engaged in general out-patient care, which provides the services of a variety of health practitioners within the same establishment. These establishments are often referred to as clinics or centres and must not be confused with the offices of health practitioners classified to other industries that are also referred to as clinics or centres.

Exclusion(s): Establishments primarily engaged in:
- general or specialized medicine or surgery (621110, Offices of Physicians);
- dentistry (621210, Offices of Dentists);
- chiropractic medicine (621310, Offices of Chiropractors);
- optometry (621320, Offices of Optometrists);
- mental health practising, except by physicians (621330, Offices of Mental Health Practitioners (except Physicians));
- physical, occupational, and speech therapy and audiology (621340, Offices of Physical, Occupational, and Speech Therapists and Audiologists);
- a range of family planning services, such as contraceptive services, genetic and prenatal counselling, voluntary sterilization, and therapeutic and medically-indicated termination of pregnancy, on an out-patient basis (621410, Family Planning Centres);
- out-patient services related to the diagnosis and treatment of mental health disorders and alcohol and other substance abuse (621420, Out-Patient Mental Health and Substance Abuse Centres); and
- specialized out-patient services, not classified to any other industry, such as dialysis (621499, All Other Out-Patient Care Centres).

Example Activities
- Community health centres, out-patient
- Public health clinics
- Regional health services centre

621499 All Other Out-Patient Care Centres CAN

This Canadian industry comprises establishments, with medical staff, not classified to any other Canadian industry, primarily engaged in providing specialized out-patient services, such as dialysis. These establishments are often referred to as clinics or centres and must not be confused with the offices of health practitioners classified to other industries that are also referred to as clinics or centres.

Exclusion(s): Establishments primarily engaged in:
- general or specialized medicine or surgery (621110, Offices of Physicians);
- dentistry (621210, Offices of Dentists);
- chiropractic medicine (621310, Offices of Chiropractors);
- optometry (621320, Offices of Optometrists);
- mental health practising, except by physicians (621330, Offices of Mental Health Practitioners (except Physicians));
- physical, occupational, and speech therapy and audiology (621340, Offices of Physical, Occupational, and Speech Therapists and Audiologists);
- a range of family planning services, such as contraceptive services, genetic and prenatal counselling, voluntary sterilization, and therapeutic and medically-indicated termination of pregnancy, on an out-patient basis (621410, Family Planning Centres);
- out-patient services related to the diagnosis and treatment of mental health disorders and alcohol and other substance abuse (621420, Out-Patient Mental Health and Substance Abuse Centres); and
- general out-patient care, which provides the services of a variety of health practitioners within the same establishment (621494, Community Health Centres).

Example Activities
- Hearing testing service
- Kidney dialysis centres
- Osteoporosis centres
- Physical examination service (except by physicians)
- Plasmapheresis centres
- Respiratory therapy clinics

6215 Medical and Diagnostic Laboratories

See industry description for 62151, below.

62151 Medical and Diagnostic Laboratories

This industry comprises establishments primarily engaged in providing analytic or diagnostic services. These services are generally provided to the medical profession, or to the patient on referral from a health practitioner.

Exclusion(s): Establishments primarily engaged in:
- grinding lens to prescription (optical laboratories) (33911, Medical Equipment and Supplies Manufacturing);
- making dentures, artificial teeth and orthodontic appliances (dental laboratories) (33911, Medical Equipment and Supplies Manufacturing); and
- making prescription orthopaedic or prosthetic appliances (orthopaedic laboratories) (33911, Medical Equipment and Supplies Manufacturing).

Example Activities
- Bacteriological laboratories, diagnostic
- Biological laboratories (not manufacturing facility)
- Dental laboratory, analysis and diagnostic
- Medical laboratories (clinical)
- Medical pathology laboratories
- X-ray laboratories, medical

621510 Medical and Diagnostic Laboratories ^{CAN}

See industry description for 62151, above.

6216 Home Health Care Services

See industry description for 62161, below.

62161 Home Health Care Services

This industry comprises establishments primarily engaged in providing skilled nursing services in the home, combined with a range of other home services, such as personal care services, homemaker and companion services, physical therapy, medical social services, counselling, occupational and vocational therapy, dietary and nutritional services, speech therapy, audiology, medical equipment and supplies, medications and intravenous therapy. Only establishments that provide nursing services in combination with the other services listed are included.

Exclusion(s): Establishments primarily engaged in:
- home health care product renting or leasing (53229, Other Consumer Goods Rental);
- physical, occupational, and speech therapy and audiology (62134, Offices of Physical, Occupational, and Speech Therapists and Audiologists);
- non-medical home care (62412, Services for the Elderly and Persons with Disabilities); and
- in-home health services provided by health practitioners primarily engaged in the independent practice of their profession (classified with the profession).

Example Activities
- Home health care services
- Home nursing services (except own-account-private practice)
- Home physiotherapy services (except own-account-private practice)

621610 Home Health Care Services

See industry description for 62161, above.

6219 Other Ambulatory Health Care Services

This industry group comprises establishments, not classified to any other industry group, primarily engaged in providing ambulatory health care services, such as ambulance services, blood banks, blood donor stations, organ banks, blood pressure screening services, hearing testing services and physical examination services, except by health practitioners.

62191 Ambulance Services

This industry comprises establishments primarily engaged in the ground or air transportation of patients and the provision of emergency medical care. The vehicles are equipped with life-saving equipment operated by trained personnel.

Exclusion(s): Establishments primarily engaged in:
- transporting the disabled or elderly, without medical care (48599, Other Transit and Ground Passenger Transportation).

621911 Ambulance (except Air Ambulance) Services ^{CAN}

This Canadian industry comprises establishments primarily engaged in the ground transportation of patients and the provision of emergency medical care. The vehicles are equipped with life-saving equipment operated by trained personnel.

Exclusion(s): Establishments primarily engaged in:
- transporting the disabled or elderly, without medical care (485990, Other Transit and Ground Passenger Transportation).

Example Activity
- Ambulance service, road

621912 Air Ambulance Services CAN

This Canadian industry comprises establishments primarily engaged in the air transportation of patients and the provision of emergency medical care. The vehicles are equipped with life-saving equipment operated by trained personnel.

Example Activity
- Ambulance services, air

62199 All Other Ambulatory Health Care Services

This industry comprises establishments, not classified to any other industry, primarily engaged in providing ambulatory health care services.

Example Activities
- Blood banks
- Blood donor stations
- Childbirth preparation classes
- Eye bank
- Sperm banks
- Stop smoking clinic

621990 All Other Ambulatory Health Care Services CAN

See industry description for 62199, above.

622 Hospitals

This subsector comprises establishments, licensed as hospitals, primarily engaged in providing medical, diagnostic and treatment services, and specialized accommodation services to in-patients. These establishments have an organized medical staff of physicians, nurses and other health professionals, technologists and technicians. Hospitals use specialized facilities and equipment that form a significant and integral part of the production process. Hospitals may also provide a wide variety of out-patient services as a secondary activity.

6221 General Medical and Surgical Hospitals

See industry description for 62211, below.

62211 General Medical and Surgical Hospitals

This industry comprises establishments, licensed as hospitals, primarily engaged in providing diagnostic and medical treatment to in-patients of any age with any of a wide variety of diseases or medical conditions. These establishments usually provide other services, such as out-patient services, diagnostic X-ray services, clinical laboratory services and pharmacy services.

622111 General (except Paediatric) Hospitals CAN

This Canadian industry comprises establishments, licensed as hospitals, primarily engaged in providing diagnostic and medical treatment to in-patients with any of a wide variety of diseases or medical conditions. These establishments usually provide other services, such as out-patient services, diagnostic X-ray services, clinical laboratory services and pharmacy services.

Example Activities

- General medical and surgical hospitals
- Hospitals, general medical and surgical
- Military hospital
- Veterans' hospital

622112 Paediatric Hospitals CAN

This Canadian industry comprises establishments, licensed as hospitals, primarily engaged in providing in-patient diagnostic and medical treatment to children with any of a wide variety of diseases or medical conditions. These establishments usually provide other services, such as out-patient services, diagnostic X-ray services, clinical laboratory services and pharmacy services.

Example Activities

- Children's hospitals
- Paediatric hospitals

6222 Psychiatric and Substance Abuse Hospitals

See industry description for 62221, below.

62221 Psychiatric and Substance Abuse Hospitals

This industry comprises establishments, licensed as hospitals, primarily engaged in providing diagnostic and medical treatment, and monitoring patients who suffer from mental illness or substance abuse disorders. The treatment often requires an extended stay in the hospital. These hospitals may provide other services, such as out-patient services and electroencephalograph services.

Exclusion(s): Establishments primarily engaged in:

- treatment of mental health and substance abuse illnesses on an exclusively out-patient basis (62142, Out-Patient Mental Health and Substance Abuse Centres);
- residential care for persons with developmental handicaps (62321, Residential Developmental Handicap Facilities); and
- in-patient treatment of mental health and substance abuse illness with an emphasis on counselling rather than medical treatment (62322, Residential Mental Health and Substance Abuse Facilities).

Example Activities

- Addiction hospitals
- Drug addiction rehabilitation hospitals
- Hospital for emotionally disturbed children
- Mental hospitals
- Psychiatric hospitals
- Rehabilitation hospitals, drug addiction and alcoholism

622210 Psychiatric and Substance Abuse Hospitals US

See industry description for 62221, above.

6223 Specialty (except Psychiatric and Substance Abuse) Hospitals

See industry description for 62231, below.

62231 Specialty (except Psychiatric and Substance Abuse) Hospitals

This industry comprises establishments, licensed as hospitals, primarily engaged in providing diagnostic and medical treatment to in-patients with a specific type of disease or medical condition, except psychiatric or substance abuse. Hospitals providing long-term care for the chronically ill and hospitals providing rehabilitation, restorative and adjustive services to physically-challenged or disabled people are included in this industry. Specialty hospitals may provide other services, such as out-patient services, diagnostic X-ray services, clinical laboratory services, physical therapy services, educational and vocational services, and psychological and social work services.

Exclusion(s): Establishments primarily engaged in:

- diagnostic and therapeutic in-patient services for a wide variety of diseases and medical conditions (62211, General Medical and Surgical Hospitals);
- diagnostic and treatment services for in-patients with psychiatric or substance abuse illnesses (62221, Psychiatric and Substance Abuse Hospitals);
- in-patient nursing and rehabilitative services to persons requiring convalescence (62311, Nursing Care Facilities); and
- residential care of persons with developmental handicaps (62321, Residential Developmental Handicap Facilities).

Example Activities

- Cancer hospital
- Chronic disease hospitals
- Convalescent hospitals
- Extended care hospitals
- Geriatric hospitals

- Hospitals, specialty (except psychiatric)
- Maternity hospitals
- Nursing stations
- Tuberculosis hospital

622310 Specialty (except Psychiatric and Substance Abuse) Hospitals US

See industry description for 62231, above.

623 Nursing and Residential Care Facilities

This subsector comprises establishments primarily engaged in providing residential care combined with either nursing, supervisory or other types of care as required by the residents. In this subsector, the facilities are a significant part of the production process and the care provided is a mix of health and social services, with the health component being largely nursing services.

6231 Nursing Care Facilities

See industry description for 62311, below.

62311 Nursing Care Facilities

This industry comprises establishments primarily engaged in providing in-patient nursing and rehabilitative services, and continuous personal care services. Individuals requiring nursing care usually require an extended stay in the care facility.

Exclusion(s): Establishments primarily engaged in:

- the services of psychiatric convalescent homes (62322, Residential Mental Health and Substance Abuse Facilities).

Example Activities

- Convalescent homes
- Domiciliary care with health care
- Extended care facilities

- Intermediate care facilities
- Nursing homes
- Personal care homes

623110 Nursing Care Facilities US

See industry description for 62311, above.

6232 Residential Developmental Handicap, Mental Health and Substance Abuse Facilities

This industry group comprises establishments primarily engaged in providing residential care to people with developmental handicaps, mental illnesses or substance abuse problems.

62321 Residential Developmental Handicap Facilities

This industry comprises establishments primarily engaged in providing residential care services for persons diagnosed with developmental handicaps. These facilities may provide some health care, though the focus is protective supervision, room, board and counselling. This care can be provided in a group home or institutional setting. Some institutions may be referred to as "hospitals" for the developmentally handicapped.

Exclusion(s): Establishments primarily engaged in:
- the treatment of mental health and substance abuse illnesses on an exclusively out-patient basis (62142, Out-Patient Mental Health and Substance Abuse Centres);
- in-patient treatment of mental health and substance abuse illnesses with an emphasis on medical treatment and monitoring (62221, Psychiatric and Substance Abuse Hospitals); and
- in-patient treatment of mental health and substance abuse illnesses with an emphasis on counselling rather than medical treatment (62322, Residential Mental Health and Substance Abuse Facilities).

Example Activity
- Homes for the developmentally handicapped

623210 Residential Developmental Handicap Facilities US

See industry description for 62321, above.

62322 Residential Mental Health and Substance Abuse Facilities

This industry comprises establishments primarily engaged in providing residential care and treatment for patients with mental health and substance abuse illnesses. These establishments provide room, board, supervision, counselling and other social services. Medical services may be available but they are incidental to the counselling, mental rehabilitation and support services offered. These establishments generally provide a wide range of social services in addition to counselling.

Exclusion(s): Establishments primarily engaged in:
- the treatment of mental health and substance abuse illnesses on an exclusively out-patient basis (62142, Out-Patient Mental Health and Substance Abuse Centres);
- in-patient treatment of mental health and substance abuse illnesses with an emphasis on medical treatment and monitoring (62221, Psychiatric and Substance Abuse Hospitals); and
- residential care for persons with developmental handicaps (62321, Residential Developmental Handicap Facilities).

623221 Residential Substance Abuse Facilities CAN

This Canadian industry comprises establishments primarily engaged in providing residential care and treatment for patients with substance abuse illnesses. These establishments provide room, board, supervision, counselling and other social services. Medical services may be available but they are incidental to the counselling, mental rehabilitation and support services offered. These establishments generally provide a wide range of social services in addition to counselling.

Example Activities
- Homes for alcoholics
- Homes for drug addicts

623222 Homes for the Psychiatrically Disabled CAN

This Canadian industry comprises establishments primarily engaged in providing residential care and treatment for patients with mental health illnesses. These establishments provide room, board, supervision, counselling and other social services. Medical services may be available but they are incidental to the counselling, mental rehabilitation and support services offered. These establishments generally provide a wide range of social services in addition to counselling.

Example Activities
- Homes for the mentally disabled
- Homes for the mentally handicapped

6233 Community Care Facilities for the Elderly

See industry description for 62331, below.

62331 Community Care Facilities for the Elderly

This industry comprises establishments primarily engaged in providing residential and personal care services for the elderly and persons who are unable to fully care for themselves or who do not desire to live independently. The care typically includes room, board, supervision and assistance in daily living by providing services such as housekeeping. In some instances these establishments provide skilled nursing care for residents in separate on-site facilities.

Exclusion(s): Establishments primarily engaged in:
- in-patient nursing and rehabilitative services (62311, Nursing Care Facilities).

Example Activities
- Aged nursing home
- Homes for the aged
- Old folks home
- Old soldiers' homes

623310 Community Care Facilities for the Elderly CAN

See industry description for 62331, above.

6239 Other Residential Care Facilities

See industry description for 62399, below.

62399 Other Residential Care Facilities

This industry comprises establishments, not classified to any other industry, primarily engaged in providing residential care, such as transition homes for women, homes for emotionally disturbed children, camps for delinquent youth, group foster homes, halfway group homes for delinquents and offenders, and orphanages.

Exclusion(s): Establishments primarily engaged in:
- the services of developmental handicap homes (62321, Residential Developmental Handicap Facilities);
- the services of continuing care retirement communities and homes for the elderly (62331, Community Care Facilities for the Elderly); and
- emergency shelter provision (62422, Community Housing Services).

623991 Transition Homes for Women CAN

This Canadian industry comprises establishments primarily engaged in providing extended residential care to women who have been victims of violence. These establishments provide room, board, protective supervision, counselling services and other social services.

Exclusion(s): Establishments primarily engaged in:
- providing emergency shelter of a short duration and without other services (62422, Community Housing Services).

Example Activities
- Homes for battered women
- Transition homes for women (except short stay)

623992 Homes for Emotionally Disturbed Children CAN

This Canadian industry comprises establishments primarily engaged in providing residential care to children with emotional problems. These establishments provide room, board and parental-type supervision, as well as additional specialized supervision and services required by these children.

Exclusion(s): Establishments primarily engaged in:
- room and board services with supervision of a parental nature only (623999, All Other Residential Care Facilities).

Example Activity
- Homes for emotionally disturbed children

623993 Homes for the Physically Handicapped or Disabled CAN

This Canadian industry comprises establishments primarily engaged in providing residential care and the appropriate supervision and services to ambulant residents with physical handicaps or disabilities, such as visual impairments.

Example Activities
- Homes for the blind
- Homes for the deaf
- Homes for the deaf or blind
- Homes for the physically disabled
- Homes for the physically handicapped

623999 All Other Residential Care Facilities CAN

This Canadian industry comprises establishments, not classified to any other Canadian industry, primarily engaged in providing residential care.

Example Activities
- Boys' towns
- Children's villages
- Group foster homes
- Halfway homes for delinquents and offenders
- Homes for children in need of protection
- Homes for single mothers
- Juvenile correctional homes
- Orphanages
- Self-help group homes for persons with social or personal problems

624 Social Assistance

This subsector comprises establishments primarily engaged in providing a wide variety of assistance services directly to their clients. These services do not include residential or accommodation services, except on a short-stay basis.

6241 Individual and Family Services

This industry group comprises establishments primarily engaged in providing non-residential social assistance services for individual and families.

62411 Child and Youth Services

This industry comprises establishments primarily engaged in providing non-residential social assistance services for children and youth.

Exclusion(s): Establishments primarily engaged in:
- providing day-care services for children (62441, Child Day-Care Services); and
- youth recreation services and provision of facilities (71394, Fitness and Recreational Sports Centres).

Example Activities
- Adoption services
- Aid to families with dependent children (AFDC)
- Big Brother services
- Big Sister services
- Child support services

- Children's aid services
- Family location services
- Friendship and counselling offered to young people
- Youth centres
- Youth self-help organizations

624110 Child and Youth Services US

See industry description for 62411, above.

62412 Services for the Elderly and Persons with Disabilities

This industry comprises establishments primarily engaged in providing non-residential social assistance services to improve the quality of life for the elderly, the developmentally handicapped or persons with disabilities. These establishments provide for the welfare of these individuals in such areas as day-care, non-medical home care, social activities, group support and companionship.

Exclusion(s): Establishments primarily engaged in:
- job training for persons with disabilities and the developmentally handicapped (62431, Vocational Rehabilitation Services).

Example Activities
- Adult day-care centres
- Day care centres, adult and handicapped
- Home care of elderly

- Home-maker services
- Senior citizen centres

624120 Services for the Elderly and Persons with Disabilities US

See industry description for 62412, above.

62419 Other Individual and Family Services

This industry comprises establishments, not classified to any other industry, primarily engaged in providing non-residential social assistance services for individual and families.

Exclusion(s): Establishments primarily engaged in:
- clinical psychological and psychiatric social counselling services (62133, Offices of Mental Health Practitioners (except Physicians));
- child and youth social assistance services, except day-care (62411, Child and Youth Services);
- social assistance services to the elderly and persons with disabilities (62412, Services for the Elderly and Persons with Disabilities); and
- day-care services for children (62441, Child Day-Care Services).

Example Activities
- Alcoholic and drug addiction self-help organizations
- Crisis intervention centres
- Friendship centre

- Marriage (family) counselling services
- Neighbourhood centres
- Offender rehabilitation agencies
- Offender self-help organizations

- Outreach programs
- Parenting services
- Rape crisis centres
- Refugee services

- Self-help action group
- Suicide crisis centre
- Telephone counselling service

624190 Other Individual and Family Services US

See industry description for 62419, above.

6242 Community Food and Housing, and Emergency and Other Relief Services

This industry group comprises establishments primarily engaged in the collection, preparation and delivery of food for the needy; providing short-term emergency shelter; and providing food, shelter, clothing, medical relief, resettlement and counselling to victims of domestic or international disasters or conflicts.

62421 Community Food Services

This industry comprises establishments primarily engaged in the collection, preparation and delivery of food for the needy. Establishments in this industry may also distribute clothing and blankets to the poor. These establishments may prepare and deliver meals to persons who, by reason of age, disability or illness, are unable to prepare meals for themselves; collect and distribute donated food; or prepare and provide meals at fixed or mobile locations.

Example Activities
- Community meals, social services
- Food banks
- Meal delivery programs

- Meals on wheels, social services
- Neighbourhood meal services
- Soup kitchen

624210 Community Food Services US

See industry description for 62421, above.

62422 Community Housing Services

This industry comprises establishments primarily engaged in providing short-term shelter for victims of domestic violence, sexual assault or child abuse; temporary residential shelter for the homeless, runaway youths, and patients and families caught in medical crisis; and transitional housing for low-income individuals and families. Volunteer housing repair organizations, that provide low-cost housing, in partnership with the homeowner who assists in construction or repair of a home, and that repair homes for elderly or disabled homeowners, are included in this industry.

Exclusion(s): Establishments primarily engaged in:
- providing extended residential care to women who have been victims of violence (62399, Other Residential Care Facilities).

Example Activity
- Community housing services

624220 Community Housing Services CAN

See industry description for 62422, above.

62423 Emergency and Other Relief Services

This industry comprises establishments primarily engaged in providing food, shelter, clothing, medical relief, resettlement and counselling to victims of domestic or international disasters.

Example Activity
- Emergency and other relief services

624230 Emergency and Other Relief Services US

See industry description for 62423, above.

6243 Vocational Rehabilitation Services

See industry description for 62431, below.

62431 Vocational Rehabilitation Services

This industry comprises establishments primarily engaged in providing vocational rehabilitation or habilitation services, such as job counselling, job training, and work experience, to unemployed and underemployed persons, persons with disabilities, and persons who have a job-market disadvantage because of lack of education, job skill or experience; and training and employment to mentally and physically handicapped persons in sheltered workshops.

Exclusion(s): Establishments primarily engaged in:
- vocational training in high schools (61111, Elementary and Secondary Schools);
- vocational training in technical and trade schools (61151, Technical and Trade Schools); and
- career and vocational counselling, except rehabilitative (61171, Educational Support Services).

Example Activities
- Community service employment training programs
- Handicapped workshop
- Rehabilitation counselling and training, vocational
- Sheltered workshops
- Vocational rehabilitation services

624310 Vocational Rehabilitation Services US

See industry description for 62431, above.

6244 Child Day-Care Services

See industry description for 62441, below.

62441 Child Day-Care Services

This industry comprises establishments primarily engaged in providing day-care services for infants or children. These establishments may care for older children when they are not in school and may also offer pre-kindergarten educational programs.

Exclusion(s): Establishments primarily engaged in:
- providing kindergarten education (61111, Elementary and Secondary Schools); and
- providing baby-sitting or nanny services (81411, Private Households).

Example Activities
- Child care centres
- Day-care centres, child
- Nursery school
- Pre-kindergarten (except when part of elementary school system)
- Pre-kindergarten care services (except when part of elementary school system)
- Preschool centres (except when part of elementary school system)

624410 Child Day-Care Services ^{US}

See industry description for 62441, above.

71 Arts, Entertainment and Recreation

This sector comprises establishments primarily engaged in operating facilities or providing services to meet the cultural, entertainment and recreational interests of their patrons. These establishments produce, promote or participate in live performances, events or exhibits intended for public viewing; provide the artistic, creative and technical skills necessary for the production of artistic products and live performances; preserve and exhibit objects and sites of historical, cultural or educational interest; and operate facilities or provide services that enable patrons to participate in sports or recreational activities or pursue amusement, hobbies and leisure-time interests.

There are establishments engaged in activities related to arts and recreation that are classified in other sectors of NAICS. The most important are listed below.

Exclusion(s):
- transportation establishments providing sightseeing and pleasure cruises (48-49, Transportation and Warehousing);
- motion picture theatres, libraries and archives, and publishers of newspapers, magazines, books, periodicals and computer software (51, Information and Cultural Industries);
- establishments that provide both accommodation and recreational facilities, such as hunting and fishing camps, resorts and casino hotels (721, Accommodation Services); and
- restaurants and night clubs that provide live entertainment in addition to the sale of food and beverages (722, Food Services and Drinking Places).

711 Performing Arts, Spectator Sports and Related Industries

This subsector comprises establishments primarily engaged in producing, or organizing and promoting, live presentations that involve the performances of actors and actresses, singers, dancers, musical groups and artists, athletes and other entertainers. This subsector also includes independent (free lance) entertainers and artists and the establishments that manage their careers. The classification recognizes four basic processes: producing events; organizing and promoting events; managing and representing entertainers; and providing the artistic, creative and technical skills necessary for the production of artistic products and live performances.

This subsector makes a clear distinction between performing arts companies and performing artists (independents). Although not unique to arts and entertainment, free-lancing is a particularly important phenomenon in this subsector; however, it is difficult to implement in the case of musical groups (companies) and artists, especially pop groups. These establishments tend to be more loosely organized and it can be difficult to distinguish companies from free lances. Therefore, this subsector includes one industry that covers both musical groups and musical artists.

7111 Performing Arts Companies

This industry group comprises establishments primarily engaged in producing live presentations that involve the performances of actors and actresses, singers, dancers, musical groups and artists, and other performing artists. Examples of establishments in this industry group are theatre companies, dance companies, musical groups and artists, circuses and ice-skating shows.

Exclusion(s):

- establishments primarily engaged in organizing and promoting, but not producing, such presentations, whether or not they operate their own facilities (7113, Promoters (Presenters) of Performing Arts, Sports and Similar Events); and
- independent performing artists (711512, Independent Actors, Comedians and Performers).

71111 Theatre Companies and Dinner Theatres

This industry comprises establishments primarily engaged in producing live presentations that involve the performances of actors and actresses, opera singers and other vocalists. Included are theatre companies that operate their own facilities, primarily for the staging of their own productions, as well as establishments, known as dinner theatres, engaged in producing live theatrical entertainment and in providing food and beverages for consumption on the premises. Examples of establishments in this industry are theatre companies, opera companies, musical theatre companies, community theatres, multidisciplinary theatres, puppet theatres, mime theatres and comedy troupes.

Exclusion(s):

- free lance musicians and vocalists (71113, Musical Groups and Artists);
- free lance producers and performing artists (711512, Independent Actors, Comedians and Performers);

and establishments primarily engaged in:

- organizing and promoting, but not producing, performing arts productions (7113, Promoters (Presenters) of Performing Arts, Sports and Similar Events); and
- providing food and beverages for consumption on the premises and that also present live entertainment, such as comedy clubs (except dinner theatres) (722, Food Services and Drinking Places).

711111 Theatre (except Musical) Companies CAN

This Canadian industry comprises establishments primarily engaged in producing live presentations that involve the performances of actors and actresses. Theatre companies that operate their own facilities, primarily for the staging of their own productions, are included.

Example Activities

- Burlesque companies
- Comedy troupes
- Community theatres
- Production of live theatrical entertainment
- Puppet theatres
- Repertory or stock companies, theatrical
- Road companies, theatrical
- Stock or repertory companies, theatrical

- Summer theatres (except theatre-dinner)
- Theatre companies
- Theatre production agencies
- Theatrical and other staged entertainment services
- Theatrical companies, amateur
- Theatrical production, live
- Theatrical road companies
- Vaudeville companies

711112 Musical Theatre and Opera Companies CAN

This Canadian industry comprises establishments primarily engaged in producing live presentations that involve the performances of actors and actresses, opera singers and other vocalists. Establishments, known as dinner theatres, engaged in producing live theatrical entertainment and in providing food and beverages for consumption on the premises, are included.

Example Activities
- Musical theatre companies
- Opera companies
- Theatre, musical

71112 Dance Companies

This industry comprises establishments primarily engaged in producing live presentations that involve the performances of dancers. Dance companies that operate their own facilities, primarily for the staging of their own production, are included.

Exclusion(s):
- free-lance producers and dancers (711512, Independent Actors, Comedians and Performers);

and establishments primarily engaged in:
- organizing and promoting, but not producing, dance productions (7113, Promoters (Presenters) of Performing Arts, Sports and Similar Events); and
- providing food and beverages for consumption on the premises and that also present live dance entertainment, such as exotic dance clubs (722, Food Services and Drinking Places).

Example Activities
- Ballet companies
- Ballet productions, live
- Classical dance companies
- Contemporary dance companies
- Dance companies
- Folk dance companies
- Interpretive dance companies
- Jazz dance companies
- Modern dance companies
- Tap dance companies

711120 Dance Companies ^{US}

See industry description for 71112, above.

71113 Musical Groups and Artists

This industry comprises establishments primarily engaged in producing live presentations that involve the performances of musicians and/or vocalists. Establishments in this industry may consist of groups or individual artists. Examples of establishments in this industry are chamber and symphony orchestras, country music groups, jazz music groups, and pop and rock music groups, as well as independent musicians and vocalists.

Exclusion(s):
- agents and managers for musical groups and artists (71141, Agents and Managers for Artists, Athletes, Entertainers and Other Public Figures);
- free lance producers (711512, Independent Actors, Comedians and Performers);

and establishments primarily engaged in:
- producing theatrical, musical and opera productions (71111, Theatre Companies and Dinner Theatres);
- organizing and promoting, but not producing, concerts and other musical performances (7113, Promoters (Presenters) of Performing Arts, Sports and Similar Events); and
- providing food and beverages for consumption on the premises and also presenting live musical entertainment, such as night clubs (722, Food Services and Drinking Places).

Example Activities

- Bands, musical
- Chamber music groups
- Choirs
- Concert artists, independent
- Country music groups
- Dance bands
- Drum and bugle corps (e.g., drill teams)
- Jazz music groups
- Music productions, live (except musical theatre production)

- Musical artists, independent
- Musical groups
- Musicians, independent
- Orchestras
- Popular music groups
- Rock music groups
- Soloists, musical, independent
- Symphony orchestras
- Vocalist, independent

711130 Musical Groups and Artists US

See industry description for 71113, above.

71119 Other Performing Arts Companies

This industry comprises establishments, not classified to any other industry, primarily engaged in producing live performing arts presentations.

Exclusion(s):

- musical groups and independent musicians and vocalists (71113, Musical Groups and Artists);
- freelance producers and independent performing artists (711512, Independent Actors, Comedians and Performers);

and establishments primarily engaged in:

- producing musicals, plays, operas, and puppet and mime shows (71111, Theatre Companies and Dinner Theatres);
- producing dance performances (71112, Dance Companies);
- organizing and promoting, but not producing, ice shows, circuses and other live performing arts presentations (7113, Promoters (Presenters) of Performing Arts, Sports and Similar Events); and
- providing food and beverages for consumption on the premises and also presenting live entertainment, such as comedy clubs (722, Food Services and Drinking Places).

Example Activities

- Carnivals, travelling show
- Circuses
- Ice skating companies (except theatrical)

- Ice skating shows (except theatrical)
- Magic shows

711190 Other Performing Arts Companies US

See industry description for 71119, above.

7112 Spectator Sports

See industry description for 71121, below.

71121 Spectator Sports

This industry comprises professional, semi-professional, or amateur sports clubs primarily engaged in presenting sporting events before an audience. These establishments may or may not operate the facility for presenting these events. Independent professional, semi-professional or amateur athletes (in their role of athletes), and operators of race tracks are also included.

Exclusion(s): Establishments primarily engaged in:
- promoting sports events and operating sports facilities, but not operating a sports club (71131, Promoters (Presenters) of Performing Arts, Sports and Similar Events with Facilities);
- promoting sports events, but not operating a sports facility or sports club (71132, Promoters (Presenters) of Performing Arts, Sports and Similar Events without Facilities);
- providing endorsement, speaking and similar services of independent athletes (711512, Independent Actors, Comedians and Performers);
- operating recreational sports and athletic clubs and leagues (71399, All Other Amusement and Recreation Industries); and
- operating amateur or professional sports associations and leagues (81399, Other Membership Organizations).

711211 Sports Teams and Clubs US

This Canadian industry comprises professional, semi-professional, or amateur sports clubs primarily engaged in presenting sporting events before an audience. These establishments may or may not operate the facility for presenting these events.

Exclusion(s): Establishments primarily engaged in:
- promoting sports events and operating sports facilities, but not operating a sports club (71131, Promoters (Presenters) of Performing Arts, Sports and Similar Events with Facilities);
- promoting sports events, but not operating a sports facility or sports club (71132, Promoters (Presenters) of Performing Arts, Sports and Similar Events without Facilities);
- operating recreational sports and athletic clubs and leagues (713990, All Other Amusement and Recreation Industries); and
- operating amateur or professional sports associations and leagues (813990, Other Membership Organizations).

Example Activities
- Amateur sports teams, spectator sports
- Baseball clubs, professional or semi-professional
- Basketball clubs, professional or semi-professional
- Football clubs, professional or semi-professional
- Hockey clubs, professional or semi-professional
- Ice hockey clubs, professional or semiprofessional
- Professional or semi-professional sports clubs
- Roller hockey clubs, professional or semi-professional
- Semiprofessional sports clubs
- Soccer clubs, professional or semi-professional
- Sports teams, professional or semi-professional

711213 Horse Race Tracks CAN

This Canadian industry comprises establishments primarily engaged in operating horse race tracks and presenting horse racing events.

Exclusion(s):
- operators of auto, dog, and other race tracks (711218, Other Spectator Sports).

Example Activities
- Harness drivers
- Harness race tracks
- Horse race tracks, operation of
- Horses, race, owners of
- Horses, racing stables
- Jockeys, horse racing
- Race horse training
- Racing stables, horse, operation of
- Stables, horse racing
- Thoroughbred race tracks
- Training race horses

711218 Other Spectator Sports ^{CAN}

This Canadian industry comprises establishments, not classified to any other Canadian industry, primarily engaged in operating race tracks and presenting racing events, other than horse race tracks and horse racing events. Independent athletes, such as golf professionals, professional boxers, tennis players and race car drivers, are also included.

Exclusion(s): Establishments primarily engaged in:
- operating horse race tracks and presenting horse races (711213, Horse Race Tracks);
- presenting racing events, but not operating a race track (71132, Promoters (Presenters) of Performing Arts, Sports and Similar Events without Facilities); and
- representing or managing the careers of sports figures (711410, Agents and Managers for Artists, Athletes, Entertainers and Other Public Figures).

Example Activities
- Athletes, independent, amateur
- Athletes, independent, professional (i.e., participating in sporting events)
- Automobile race tracks, operation of
- Automobile racing teams
- Boxers, independent, professional
- Drag strip, operation of
- Figure skaters, independent
- Golfers, independent, professional (i.e., participating in sporting events)
- Hockey scouts, independent
- Motorcycle race track operation
- Motorcycle racing teams
- Race car drivers and owners
- Race horse trainers
- Snowmobile race track operation
- Snowmobile racing teams
- Speedway operation
- Sports professionals, independent (i.e., participating in sporting events)
- Sports trainers, independent
- Stock car race track operation
- Stock car racing teams
- Tennis professionals, independent (i.e., participating in sporting events)

7113 Promoters (Presenters) of Performing Arts, Sports and Similar Events

This industry group comprises establishments primarily engaged in organizing and promoting performing arts productions, sports events and similar events, such as festivals. Establishments in this industry group may operate arenas, stadiums, theatres or other related facilities, or they may present these events in facilities operated by others.

Exclusion(s): Establishments primarily engaged in:
- producing live presentations that involve the performances of actors and actresses, singers, dancers, musical groups and artists, whether or not they operate their own facilities (7111, Performing Arts Companies); and
- operating professional, semi-professional or amateur sports teams that present sporting events to the public, whether or not they operate their own facilities (71121, Spectator Sports).

71131 Promoters (Presenters) of Performing Arts, Sports and Similar Events with Facilities

This industry comprises establishments primarily engaged in operating arts, sports and mixed-use facilities, and in organizing and promoting performing arts productions, sports events and similar events, such as festivals, held in these facilities. These establishments may also rent their facilities to other promoters.

Exclusion(s): Establishments primarily engaged in:
- owning and leasing stadiums, arenas, theatres, and other related facilities, but not producing or promoting live events held in these facilities (53112, Lessors of Non-Residential Buildings (except Mini-Warehouses));
- organizing convention and trade shows (56192, Convention and Trade Show Organizers);
- producing and promoting live theatre, dance, music or other performing arts presentations in their own facilities (7111, Performing Arts Companies);
- operating professional, semi-professional or amateur sports teams that operate their own facilities (71121, Spectator Sports);
- operating race tracks and presenting races (71121, Spectator Sports); and
- organizing and promoting performing arts productions, sports events, and similar events, such as festivals, in facilities managed and operated by others (71132, Promoters (Presenters) of Performing Arts, Sports and Similar Events without Facilities).

711311 Live Theatres and Other Performing Arts Presenters with Facilities CAN

This Canadian industry comprises establishments primarily engaged in operating live theatres and other arts facilities, and organizing and promoting performing arts productions held in these facilities. Theatre festivals with facilities are included.

Exclusion(s): Establishments primarily engaged in:
- promoting and presenting film festivals (512130, Motion Picture and Video Exhibition); and
- producing theatrical performances in their own facilities, including dinner theatres and theatre festivals (71111, Theatre Companies and Dinner Theatres).

Example Activities
- Arts events organizers, with facilities
- Arts festival promoters, with facilities
- Concert halls, promoting events
- Concert organizers, with facilities
- Dance festival promoters, with facilities
- Live arts centres, promoting events
- Live theatres, promoting events
- Music festival promoters, with facilities
- Performing arts centres, promoting events
- Presenters, arts events, with their own facilities
- Promoters of arts events, with facilities
- Theatre festival promoters, with facilities
- Theatre operators, promoting events

711319 Sports Stadiums and Other Presenters with Facilities CAN

This Canadian industry comprises establishments primarily engaged in operating sports stadiums and other sports facilities, and organizing and promoting sports events and/or similar events held in these facilities. Establishments primarily engaged in promoting and presenting sports tournaments, in their own facilities, are included.

Exclusion(s): Establishments primarily engaged in:
- operating sports teams that manage their own facilities (711211, Sports Teams and Clubs);
- operating horse race tracks (711213, Horse Race Tracks); and
- operating auto and other race tracks (711218, Other Spectator Sports).

Example Activities
- Arena operators, promoting events
- Fair organizers, agricultural, with facilities
- Horse show promoters, with facilities
- Promoters of sports events, with facilities
- Rodeo promoters, with facilities
- Sports arenas, promoting events
- Sports event promoters, with facilities
- Sports stadiums, promoting events
- Stadiums, promoting events
- Wrestling promoters, with facilities

71132 Promoters (Presenters) of Performing Arts, Sports and Similar Events without Facilities

This industry comprises establishments primarily engaged in organizing and promoting live performing arts productions, sports events, and similar events, such as festivals, in facilities operated by others.

Exclusion(s): Establishments primarily engaged in:
- organizing convention and trade shows (56192, Convention and Trade Show Organizers);
- producing live theatre, dance, music, or other theatrical presentations in facilities operated by others (7111, Performing Arts Companies);
- operating sports teams that present their own events (71121, Spectator Sports); and
- operating performing arts, sports, and mixed-use facilities and organizing and promoting events, such as festivals, held in these facilities (71131, Promoters (Presenters) of Performing Arts, Sports and Similar Events with Facilities).

711321 Performing Arts Promoters (Presenters) without Facilities ^{CAN}

This Canadian industry comprises establishments primarily engaged in organizing and promoting performing arts productions in facilities operated by others.

Exclusion(s): Establishments primarily engaged in:
- producing live theatre, dance, music or other theatrical presentations, in facilities operated by others (7111, Performing Arts Companies); and
- organizing and promoting arts festivals, without facilities, including theatrical and music festivals (711322, Festivals without Facilities).

Example Activities
- Arts events organizers, without facilities (except festivals)
- Arts presenters, without facilities (except festivals)
- Booking agencies, theatrical (except motion picture)
- Concert booking agencies
- Concert promoters, without facilities
- Theatrical booking agencies (except motion picture)
- Theatrical promoters, without facilities

711322 Festivals without Facilities ^{CAN}

This Canadian industry comprises establishments primarily engaged in organizing and promoting festivals in facilities operated by others.

Exclusion(s): Establishments primarily engaged in:
- organizing and promoting film festivals (51213, Motion Picture and Video Exhibition); and
- producing theatrical festivals in their own facilities (71111, Theatre Companies and Dinner Theatres).

Example Activities
- Agricultural fair promoters, without facilities
- Arts (except film) festival organizers, without facilities
- Arts (except film) festival promoters, without facilities
- Community festivals, without facilities
- Dance festival promoters, without facilities
- Ethnic festival promoters, without facilities
- Fair, agricultural, promoters, without facilities
- Festival of arts (except film) promoters, without facilities
- Heritage festivals promoters, without facilities
- Music festival promoters, without facilities

711329 Sports Presenters and Other Presenters without Facilities ^{CAN}

This Canadian industry comprises establishments, not classified to any other Canadian industry, primarily engaged in organizing and promoting sports and/or other events in facilities operated by others.

Exclusion(s):
- sports teams that present their own events (71121, Spectator Sports).

Example Activities
- Air show promoters, without facilities
- Boxing event promoters, without facilities
- Dog show promoters, without facilities
- Horse show promoters, without facilities
- Promoters, sports events, without facilities
- Rodeo promoters, without facilities
- Sports events organizers, without facilities
- Wrestling event promoters, without facilities

7114 Agents and Managers for Artists, Athletes, Entertainers and Other Public Figures

See industry description for 71141, below.

71141 Agents and Managers for Artists, Athletes, Entertainers and Other Public Figures

This industry comprises establishments primarily engaged in representing or managing creative and performing artists, sports figures, entertainers, and celebrities. These establishments represent their clients in contract negotiations, manage or organize the client's financial affairs, and generally promote the careers of their clients.

Exclusion(s): Establishments primarily engaged in:
- recruiting and placing models for clients, known as model registries (56131, Employment Placement Agencies and Executive Search Services); and
- supplying models to clients (56132, Temporary Help Services).

Example Activities
- Agents or managers for artists
- Agents or managers for authors
- Agents or managers for celebrities
- Agents or managers for entertainers
- Agents or managers for public figures
- Agents or managers for sports figures
- Agents, theatrical talent
- Literary agents
- Management agencies for artists, entertainers and other public figures
- Managers, artists
- Managers, entertainers
- Managers, sports figures
- Modelling agents
- Speakers' bureaus, agents or managers
- Sports agents
- Talent agencies
- Theatrical talent agents

711410 Agents and Managers for Artists, Athletes, Entertainers and Other Public Figures

See industry description for 71141, above.

7115 Independent Artists, Writers and Performers

See industry description for 71151, below.

71151 Independent Artists, Writers and Performers

This industry comprises independent individuals (free-lance) primarily engaged in performing in artistic productions, creating artistic and cultural works or productions, or providing technical expertise necessary for these productions. Independent celebrities, such as athletes, engaging in endorsement, speaking and similar services, are included.

Exclusion(s):
- agents and managers for artists and entertainers (71141, Agents and Managers for Artists, Athletes, Entertainers and Other Public Figures).

711511 Independent Artists, Visual Arts CAN

This Canadian industry comprises independent individuals (freelance) primarily engaged in creating artistic and cultural visual art works, or providing technical expertise necessary for these works.

Exclusion(s):
- artisans and crafts persons, other than visual artists (31-33, Manufacturing); and
- independent graphic designers (54143, Graphic Design Services).

Example Activities
- Art restorers, independent
- Artists (except commercial, medical and musical), independent
- Painters (i.e., artists), independent
- Photo journalist, independent
- Political cartoonists, independent
- Sculptors, independent
- Sketch artists, independent
- Taxidermists, independent

711512 Independent Actors, Comedians and Performers CAN

This Canadian industry comprises independent individuals (freelance) primarily engaged in performing in artistic and cultural productions, or providing technical expertise necessary for these works. Independent celebrities, such as athletes, engaged in endorsement, speaking and similar services are included, as are independent radio and television journalists.

Exclusion(s):
- independent musicians and vocalists (71113, Musical Groups and Artists).

Example Activities
- Actors, independent
- Actresses, independent
- Celebrity spokesperson, independent
- Choreographers, independent
- Comedians, independent
- Conductors, orchestra, independent
- Costume designers, theatrical, independent
- Director, film and video, independent
- Disc jockey, independent
- Journalists, radio and television, independent
- Lecturers, independent
- Lighting technicians, theatrical, independent
- Magicians, independent
- Models, independent
- Motion picture directors, independent
- Motion picture producers, independent
- Music arrangers, independent
- Record producers, independent
- Set designers, independent
- Speakers, independent
- Stage sets, erecting and dismantling
- Television producers, independent

711513 Independent Writers and Authors CAN

This Canadian industry comprises independent individuals (freelance) primarily engaged in creating artistic and cultural literary works, or providing technical expertise necessary for the production of these works. Independent print journalists are included.

Example Activities

- Authors, independent
- Freelance journalist
- Journalists, print, independent
- News correspondents, independent
- Newspaper columnists, independent

- Playwrights, independent
- Reporters, independent
- Script writers, independent
- Song writers, independent
- Writers, independent

712 Heritage Institutions

See industry description for 7121, below.

7121 Heritage Institutions

This industry group comprises establishments primarily engaged in preserving and exhibiting objects, sites and natural wonders of historical, cultural and educational value.

71211 Museums

This industry comprises establishments primarily engaged in acquiring, conserving, interpreting, and exhibiting permanent collections of objects of historical, cultural and educational value.

712111 Non-Commercial Art Museums and Galleries CAN

This Canadian industry comprises establishments primarily engaged in acquiring, researching, conserving, interpreting, and exhibiting art to the public. Art museums and art galleries with permanent collections are included.

Exclusion(s):

- commercial art galleries and art dealers who operate primarily for the sale of art objects (453920, Art Dealers).

Example Activities

- Art galleries (except retail)
- Art museums

- Galleries, art (except retail)
- Museums, art

712115 History and Science Museums CAN

This Canadian industry comprises establishments primarily engaged in acquiring, conserving, interpreting, exhibiting and making accessible to the public, objects of historical and cultural value.

Example Activities

- Human history museums
- Military museums

- Science and technology museums

712119 Other Museums CAN

This Canadian industry comprises establishments primarily engaged in the operation of exhibits, except non-commercial art museums and galleries, and history and science museums.

Example Activities

- Community museums
- Planetariums

- Sports hall of fame
- Wax museums

71212 Historic and Heritage Sites

This industry comprises establishments primarily engaged in maintaining, protecting and making accessible for public viewing, sites, buildings, forts or communities that illustrate events or persons of particular historical interest.

Example Activities

- Archaeological sites (i.e., public display)
- Battlefields
- Heritage villages
- Historic sites
- Historical forts
- Pioneer villages

712120 Historic and Heritage Sites

See industry description for 71212, above.

71213 Zoos and Botanical Gardens

This industry comprises establishments primarily engaged in constructing and maintaining displays of live plant and animal life for public viewing.

Example Activities

- Animal exhibits, live
- Animal safari park
- Aquariums
- Arboreta
- Aviaries (bird exhibit)
- Botanical gardens
- Conservatories, botanical
- Garden, zoological or botanical
- Parks, wild animal
- Petting zoos
- Reptile exhibits, live
- Zoological gardens
- Zoos

712130 Zoos and Botanical Gardens US

See industry description for 71213, above.

71219 Nature Parks and Other Similar Institutions

This industry comprises establishments, not classified to any other industry, primarily engaged in operating other heritage institutions. Establishments primarily engaged in operating, maintaining and protecting nature parks, nature reserves or conservation areas, are included.

Example Activities

- Bird sanctuaries
- Caverns
- Conservation areas
- National parks
- Natural wonders, tourist attractions
- Nature centres
- Nature parks
- Nature reserves
- Parks, nature
- Provincial parks
- Wildlife sanctuaries

712190 Nature Parks and Other Similar Institutions

See industry description for 71219, above.

713 Amusement, Gambling and Recreation Industries

This subsector comprises establishments primarily engaged in operating recreation, amusement and gambling facilities and services. Examples of establishments in this subsector are golf courses, skiing facilities, marinas, recreational sports and fitness centres, bowling centres, amusement parks, amusement arcades and parlours, casinos, bingo halls, operators of video gaming terminals and operators of lotteries.

There are establishments engaged in amusement, gambling and recreation activities in combination with other activities that are classified in other sectors of NAICS. The most important are listed below.

Exclusion(s):
- providers of sightseeing and pleasure cruises (487, Scenic and Sightseeing Transportation);
- horse race tracks (7112, Spectator Sports); and
- operators of resort hotels, casino hotels, and recreation and vacation camps (721, Accommodation Services).

7131 Amusement Parks and Arcades

This industry group comprises establishments primarily engaged in operating amusement parks, amusement arcades and parlours.

Exclusion(s): Establishments primarily engaged in:
- maintaining and operating coin-operated gaming devices, such as slot machines or video gambling terminals, in places of business operated by others (71329, Other Gambling Industries); and
- maintaining coin-operated amusement devices, such as juke boxes, pinball machines, and mechanical and video games, in places of business operated by others (71399, All Other Amusement and Recreation Industries).

71311 Amusement and Theme Parks

This industry comprises establishments, known as amusement or theme parks, primarily engaged in operating a variety of attractions, such as mechanical rides, water slides, games, shows and theme exhibits. These establishments may lease space to others on a concession basis.

Exclusion(s): Establishments primarily engaged in:
- maintaining coin-operated amusement devices (71312, Amusement Arcades);
- operating mechanical rides on a concession basis, or in the operation of travelling carnivals (71399, All Other Amusement and Recreation Industries); and
- operating refreshment stands on a concession basis (72221, Limited-Service Eating Places).

Example Activities
- Amusement parks (i.e., theme parks, water parks)
- Park, amusement (i.e., theme parks, water parks)
- Piers, amusement
- Theme parks, amusement
- Water parks, amusement

713110 Amusement and Theme Parks US

See industry description for 71311, above.

71312 Amusement Arcades

This industry comprises establishments primarily engaged in operating amusement arcades and parlours.

Exclusion(s): Establishments primarily engaged in:
- operating coin-operated gaming devices, such as slot machines or video gambling terminals, in places of business operated by others (71329, Other Gambling Industries);
- maintaining and operating coin-operated amusement devices, such as pinball machines and mechanical and video games, in places of business operated by others (71399, All Other Amusement and Recreation Industries); and
- operating billiard parlours (71399, All Other Amusement and Recreation Industries).

Example Activities
- Amusement arcades
- Amusement device (except gambling) parlours, coin-operated
- Arcades, amusement
- Family fun centres

- Indoor play areas
- Pinball arcades
- Video game arcades (except gambling machines)

713120 Amusement Arcades

See industry description for 71312, above.

7132 Gambling Industries

This industry group comprises establishments primarily engaged in operating gambling facilities, such as casinos, bingo halls and video gaming terminals; or providing gambling services, such as lotteries and off-track betting.

Exclusion(s): Establishments primarily engaged in:
- operating horse race tracks (7112, Spectator Sports);
- operating casino hotels (72112, Casino Hotels); and
- operating bars and restaurants with video gaming or other gambling machines on the premises (722, Food Services and Drinking Places).

71321 Casinos (except Casino Hotels)

This industry comprises establishments primarily engaged in operating gambling facilities that offer table wagering games along with other gambling activities, such as slot machines. These establishments often provide food and beverage services.

Exclusion(s): Establishments primarily engaged in:
- operating coin-operated gambling devices, such as slot machines and video gaming terminals, in places of business operated by others (71329, Other Gambling Industries);
- operating casino hotels (72112, Casino Hotels); and
- operating bars with video gaming or other gambling machines on the premises (72241, Drinking Places (Alcoholic Beverages)).

Example Activities
- Casinos (except casino hotels)
- Cruises, gambling

- Gambling cruises
- Riverboat casinos

713210 Casinos (except Casino Hotels)

See industry description for 71321, above.

71329 Other Gambling Industries

This industry comprises establishments, not classified to any other industry, primarily engaged in providing gambling services, such as lotteries, bingo games, off-track betting, and coin-operated gambling devices that are not operated in their own places of business.

Exclusion(s): Establishments primarily engaged in:
- operating race tracks or presenting live racing or sporting events (71121, Spectator Sports);
- operating coin-operated, non-gambling amusement devices (71312, Amusement Arcades);
- operating casinos (71321, Casinos (except Casino Hotels));
- operating casino hotels (72112, Casino Hotels); and
- operating bars with video gaming or other gambling machines on the premises (72241, Drinking Places (Alcoholic Beverages)).

713291 Lotteries MEX

This Canadian industry comprises establishments primarily engaged in organizing lotteries and selling lottery tickets through existing retail distribution channels or directly to consumers. Establishments owned or operated by governments are included.

Exclusion(s):
- stores that sell lottery tickets and a variety of food and convenience items (445120, Convenience Stores).

Example Activities
- Distributing lottery tickets
- Lotteries, operation of
- Lottery control boards (i.e., operating lottery)
- Lottery ticket sales agent (except retail stores)
- Lottery ticket vendors (except retail stores)

713299 All Other Gambling Industries MEX

This Canadian industry comprises establishments, not classified to any other Canadian industry, primarily engaged in providing gambling services.

Example Activities
- Bingo parlours
- Bookmakers
- Card rooms (e.g. poker rooms)
- Off-track betting parlours
- Slot machines parlours

7139 Other Amusement and Recreation Industries

This industry group comprises establishments, not classified to any other industry group, primarily engaged in operating outdoor or indoor facilities, or providing services that enable patrons to participate in sports and recreational activities. Examples of establishments in this industry group are golf courses, skiing facilities, marinas, recreational, sports and fitness centres, and bowling centres.

Exclusion(s):
- resorts in which recreational facilities are combined with hotel accommodation (72111, Hotels (except Casino Hotels) and Motels).

71391 Golf Courses and Country Clubs

This industry comprises establishments primarily engaged in operating golf courses and country clubs that operate golf courses along with dining facilities and other recreational facilities. These establishments often provide food and beverage services, equipment rental services and golf instruction services.

Exclusion(s): Establishments primarily engaged in:
- renting golf equipment, without provision of other services (53229, Other Consumer Goods Rental);
- operating curling clubs; and driving ranges and miniature golf courses (71399, All Other Amusement and Recreation Industries); and
- operating resorts in which recreational facilities are combined with hotel accommodation (72111, Hotels (except Casino Hotels) and Motels).

Example Activities
- Country clubs
- Golf and country clubs
- Golf clubs, membership
- Golf courses (except miniature), public

713910 Golf Courses and Country Clubs

See industry description for 71391, above.

71392 Skiing Facilities

This industry comprises establishments primarily engaged in operating downhill and cross-country skiing areas, and equipment, such as ski lifts and tows. These establishments often provide food and beverage services, equipment rental services and ski instruction services.

Exclusion(s): Establishments primarily engaged in:
- renting skiing equipment, without provision of other services (53229, Other Consumer Goods Rental); and
- operating resorts in which recreational facilities are combined with hotel accommodation (72111, Hotels (except Casino Hotels) and Motels).

Example Activities
- Alpine skiing facilities
- Cross country skiing facilities
- Downhill skiing facilities
- Ski lift and tow operation
- Ski resorts, without accommodations

713920 Skiing Facilities

See industry description for 71392, above.

71393 Marinas

This industry comprises establishments, known as marinas, primarily engaged in operating docking and storage facilities for pleasure-craft owners, with or without related activities, such as retailing fuel and marine supplies, and boat repair and maintenance, and rental services. Sailing clubs and yacht clubs that operate marinas are included.

Exclusion(s): Establishments primarily engaged in:
- retailing marine supplies (44122, Motorcycle, Boat and Other Motor Vehicle Dealers);
- retailing fuel for boats (44719, Other Gasoline Stations);
- renting pleasure boats (53229, Other Consumer Goods Rental); and
- operating resorts which include a marina facility (72111, Hotels (except Casino Hotels) and Motels).

Example Activities
- Boating clubs (i.e., operating marinas)
- Marinas
- Sailing clubs (i.e., operating marinas)
- Yacht clubs (i.e., operating marinas)

713930 Marinas

See industry description for 71393, above.

71394 Fitness and Recreational Sports Centres

This industry comprises establishments primarily engaged in operating health clubs and similar facilities featuring exercise and other active physical fitness conditioning, or recreational sports activities, such as swimming, skating or racquet sports.

Exclusion(s): Establishments primarily engaged in:
- operating health resorts and spas providing lodging (72111, Hotels (except Casino Hotels) and Motels); and
- helping their clients lose weight through the control or management of diet (81219, Other Personal Care Services).

Example Activities

- Aerobic dance centres
- Athletic clubs, physical fitness facilities
- Body building studios, physical fitness
- Exercise centres
- Fitness centres
- Gymnasiums
- Health club, physical fitness
- Health spas (without lodging), physical fitness
- Health studio, physical fitness
- Ice skating rinks
- Physical fitness centres
- Physical fitness studio
- Racquetball clubs
- Rinks, ice or roller skating
- Roller skating rinks
- Skating rinks, ice or roller
- Spas, fitness (without lodging)
- Sports clubs, physical fitness facilities
- Squash clubs
- Strength development centres
- Swimming pools
- Tennis clubs
- Wave pools
- Weight training centres

713940 Fitness and Recreational Sports Centres US

See industry description for 71394, above.

71395 Bowling Centres

This industry comprises establishments primarily engaged in operating bowling centres. These establishments often provide food and beverage services.

Exclusion(s): Establishments primarily engaged in:
- operating lawn bowling clubs (71394, Fitness and Recreational Sports Centres).

Example Activities
- Bowling alleys
- Bowling centres

713950 Bowling Centres

See industry description for 71395, above.

71399 All Other Amusement and Recreation Industries

This industry comprises establishments, not classified to any other industry, primarily engaged in operating recreation and amusement facilities and services, including providing tourist, hunting and fishing guide services. Establishments primarily engaged in maintaining coin-operated amusement devices, in businesses operated by others, are included.

Exclusion(s):
- independent sports professionals (71121, Spectator Sports);

and establishments primarily engaged in:
- providing sightseeing transportation (487, Scenic and Sightseeing Transportation);
- providing sports instruction (61, Educational Services);
- operating amusement facilities, such as amusement and theme parks, coin-operated amusement facilities, and coin-operated, non-gambling amusement devices (7131, Amusement Parks and Arcades); and
- operating gambling facilities or providing gambling services (7132, Gambling Industries).

Example Activities

- Amusement rides, concession operators
- Archery ranges
- Aviation club, recreation
- Ballrooms
- Baseball clubs, recreational
- Basketball clubs, recreational
- Bathing beaches
- Beaches, bathing
- Billiard parlours
- Bowling leagues or teams, recreational
- Boxing clubs, recreational
- Bridge clubs, recreational
- Canoe and kayak clubs, recreational
- Curling clubs
- Curling rinks
- Dance halls
- Fireworks display service
- Fishing guide services
- Fishing piers, operation of
- Football clubs, recreational
- Galleries, shooting
- Golf courses, miniature
- Golf driving ranges
- Golf practice ranges
- Guide services (i.e., fishing, hunting, tourist)
- Hockey clubs, recreational
- Horseback riding, recreational
- Hunting and fishing clubs, recreational
- Hunting guide services
- Juke box concession operators, in facilities operated by others
- Lawn bowling clubs
- Miniature golf courses
- Observation tower operation
- Outdoor adventure operations (e.g., white water rafting), without accommodation
- Pack trains (i.e., trail riding)
- Picnic grounds
- Pool halls
- Recreational sports teams and leagues
- Riding clubs, recreational
- Riding stables (except racing)
- River rafting, recreational
- Rowing clubs, recreational
- Sailing clubs, without marinas
- Shooting clubs, recreational
- Shooting ranges
- Soccer clubs, recreational
- Sports teams and leagues, recreational or youth
- Summer day camp
- Tourist guide services
- Trapshooting facilities, recreational
- Water slides, operation of
- White water rafting, recreational
- Yacht clubs, without marinas
- Youths sports leagues or teams

713990 All Other Amusement and Recreation Industries US

See industry description for 71399, above.

72 Accommodation and Food Services

This sector comprises establishments primarily engaged in providing short-term lodging and complementary services to travellers, vacationers and others, in facilities such as hotels, motor hotels, resorts, motels, casino hotels, bed and breakfast accommodation, housekeeping cottages and cabins, recreational vehicle parks and campgrounds, hunting and fishing camps, and various types of recreational and adventure camps. This sector also comprises establishments primarily engaged in preparing meals, snacks and beverages, to customer order, for immediate consumption on and off the premises.

721 Accommodation Services

This subsector comprises establishments primarily engaged in providing short-term lodging for travellers, vacationers and others. In addition to lodging, a range of other services may be provided. For example, many establishments have restaurants, while others have recreational facilities. Lodging establishments are classified in this subsector even if the provision of complementary services generates more revenues.

Establishments that operate lodging facilities primarily designed to accommodate outdoor enthusiasts, are also included in this subsector. These establishments are characterized by the type of accommodation and by the nature and the range of recreational facilities and activities provided to their clients.

Establishments that manage short-stay accommodation establishments, such as hotels and motels, on a contractual basis are classified in this subsector if they provide both management and operating staff. These establishments are classified according to the type of facility they manage.

7211 Traveller Accommodation

This industry group comprises establishments primarily engaged in providing short-term lodging in facilities such as hotels, motor hotels, resorts, motels, casino hotels, bed and breakfast homes, and housekeeping cottages and cabins. These establishments may offer food and beverage services, recreational services, conference rooms and convention services, laundry services, parking and other services.

72111 Hotels (except Casino Hotels) and Motels

This industry comprises establishments primarily engaged in providing short-term lodging in facilities known as hotels, motor hotels, resort hotels and motels. These establishments may offer food and beverage services, recreational services, conference rooms and convention services, laundry services, parking and other services.

Exclusion(s):
- establishments providing lodging with a casino on the premises (72112, Casino Hotels); and
- bed and breakfast, youth hostels, housekeeping cabins and cottages, and tourist homes (72119, Other Traveller Accommodation).

721111 Hotels CAN

This Canadian industry comprises establishments primarily engaged in providing short-term lodging in facilities known as hotels. These establishments provide suites or guest rooms within a multi-storey or high-rise structure, accessible from the interior only, and they generally offer guests a range of complementary services and amenities, such as food and beverage services, parking, laundry services, swimming pools and exercise rooms, and conference and convention facilities.

Exclusion(s):
- hotels that operate in a non-urban setting next to lakes, rivers, mountains or beaches, and that feature access to extensive indoor and/or outdoor leisure activities (721113, Resorts); and
- hotels with a casino on the premises (721120, Casino Hotels).

Example Activities
- Accommodation services, hotel
- Health spas (i.e., physical fitness facilities) with hotel accommodations
- Hotel lodging services (except apartment hotel)
- Hotel management services (i.e., providing management and operating staff to run hotel)
- Hotels (except casino hotels) with integrated health spa facilities
- Hotels (except residential)
- Inns, furnishing food and lodging
- Membership hotel
- Private hotels
- Sleeping car operation, contract service
- Sleeping car services not operated by railway company

721112 Motor Hotels CAN

This Canadian industry comprises establishments primarily engaged in providing short-term lodging in facilities known as motor hotels. These establishments are designed to accommodate clients travelling by motor vehicle and provide short-stay suites or guest rooms within a low-rise structure, characterized by ample, convenient parking areas, interior access to rooms, and their location along major roads. Limited complementary services and amenities may also be provided.

Exclusion(s):
- similar establishments that feature exterior access to rooms and parking areas adjacent to the room entrances (721114, Motels).

Example Activities
- Motor court
- Motor hotel

721113 Resorts CAN

This Canadian industry comprises establishments primarily engaged in providing short-term lodging in facilities known as resorts. These establishments feature extensive indoor and/or outdoor leisure activities on the premises on a year-round basis. Resorts are designed to accommodate vacationers and provide full-service suites and guest rooms, typically in a non-urban setting next to lakes, rivers or mountains. Establishments of this type often provide access to conference facilities.

Exclusion(s):
- establishments that provide accommodation services and access to a particular recreational activity on a seasonal basis (7139, Other Amusement and Recreation Industries); and
- establishments integrating accommodation and recreational services in camp-like facilities (72121, RV (Recreational Vehicle) Parks and Recreational Camps).

Example Activities
- Pleasure resort (summer hotel)
- Recreational hotels
- Resort hotel
- Resort management services (i.e., providing management and operating staff to run resort)
- Resorts with integrated health spa facilities
- Seasonal hotel
- Ski lodges and resorts

721114 Motels CAN

This Canadian industry comprises establishments primarily engaged in providing short-term lodging in facilities known as motels. These establishments are designed to accommodate clients travelling by motor vehicle, and provide short-stay suites or guest rooms, within a one or two-storey structure, characterized by exterior access to rooms and ample parking areas adjacent to the room entrances. Limited complementary services and amenities may also be provided.

Exclusion(s):
- similar establishments that feature interior access to rooms (721112, Motor Hotels).

Example Activities
- Accommodation services, motel
- Motel, accommodation services

72112 Casino Hotels

This industry comprises establishments primarily engaged in providing short-term lodging in hotel facilities with a casino on the premises. The casino operation includes table wagering games and may include other gambling activities, such as slot machines and sports betting. These establishments generally offer a range of services and amenities, such as food and beverage services, entertainment, valet parking, swimming pools, and conference and convention facilities.

Exclusion(s):
- stand-alone casinos (71321, Casinos (except Casino Hotels)); and
- hotels and motels that provide limited gambling activities, such as slot machines, without a casino on the premises (72111, Hotels (except Casino Hotels) and Motels).

Example Activity
- Casino hotels

721120 Casino Hotels

See industry description for 72112, above.

72119 Other Traveller Accommodation

This industry comprises establishments, not classified to any other industry, primarily engaged in providing short-term lodging.

Exclusion(s): Establishments primarily engaged in:
- providing short-term lodging in hotels without casinos (72111, Hotels (except Casino Hotels) and Motels); and
- providing short-term lodging in hotels with a casino on the premise (72112, Casino Hotels).

721191 Bed and Breakfast US

This Canadian industry comprises establishments primarily engaged in providing short-term lodging in facilities known as bed and breakfast homes. These establishments provide guest rooms in private homes or in small buildings converted for this use, and they often possess a unique or historic character. Bed and breakfast homes are characterized by a highly personalized service, and the inclusion, in the room rate, of a full breakfast, served by the owner or owner-supervised staff.

Example Activity
- Bed and breakfast, accommodations

721192 Housekeeping Cottages and Cabins CAN

This Canadian industry comprises establishments primarily engaged in providing short-term lodging in facilities known as housekeeping cottages and cabins. These establishments are designed to accommodate vacationers and may include access to private beaches and fishing.

Exclusion(s): Establishments primarily engaged in:
- operating hunting and fishing camps (721212, Hunting and Fishing Camps); and
- supplying accommodation with recreational activities organized around a particular theme (721213, Recreational (except Hunting and Fishing) and Vacation Camps).

Example Activities
- Accommodation services, tourist courts and cabins
- Housekeeping cottages and cabins
- Tourist cabins, accommodations
- Tourist courts, accommodations

721198 All Other Traveller Accommodation CAN

This Canadian industry comprises establishments, not classified to any other Canadian industry, primarily engaged in providing short-term lodging.

Example Activities
- Accommodation services, guest houses and tourist homes
- Tourist homes, accommodations
- Youth hostels, accommodations

7212 RV (Recreational Vehicle) Parks and Recreational Camps

See industry description for 72121, below.

72121 RV (Recreational Vehicle) Parks and Recreational Camps

This industry comprises establishments primarily engaged in operating recreational vehicle parks and campgrounds, hunting and fishing camps, and various types of vacation and adventure camps. These establishments cater to outdoor enthusiasts and are characterized by the type of accommodation and by the nature and the range of recreational facilities and activities provided to their clients.

Exclusion(s): Establishments primarily engaged in:
- operating residential mobile home sites (53119, Lessors of Other Real Estate Property);
- operating instructional camps, such as sports camps, fine arts camps and computer camps (61, Educational Services);
- operating recreational facilities without accommodation (713, Amusement, Gambling and Recreation Industries); and
- operating children's day camps, except instructional (71399, All Other Amusement and Recreation Industries).

721211 RV (Recreational Vehicle) Parks and Campgrounds US

This Canadian industry comprises establishments primarily engaged in operating serviced or unserviced sites to accommodate campers and their equipment, including tents, tent trailers, travel trailers and RVs (recreational vehicles). These establishments may provide access to facilities, such as washrooms, laundry rooms, recreation halls and facilities, and stores and snack bars.

Exclusion(s): Establishments primarily engaged in:
- operating residential mobile home sites (531190, Lessors of Other Real Estate Property); and
- operating recreational facilities without accommodation (713, Amusement, Gambling and Recreation Industries).

Example Activities
- Accommodation services, camping grounds and trailer parks
- Campground
- Campsites for transients
- Recreational vehicle parks
- Tourist camping park
- Tourist camps (campground)
- Travel trailer parks

721212 Hunting and Fishing Camps CAN

This Canadian industry comprises establishments primarily engaged in operating hunting and fishing camps. These establishments provide a range of services, such as access to outpost camps or housekeeping cabins, meals and guides, and they may also provide transportation to the facility, and sale of food, beverages, and hunting and fishing supplies.

Example Activities
- Fishing camps
- Hunting camps
- Outfitters (fishing and hunting)

721213 Recreational (except Hunting and Fishing) and Vacation Camps CAN

This Canadian industry comprises establishments primarily engaged in operating overnight recreational camps, such as children's camps, family vacation camps, and outdoor adventure retreats that offer trail riding, white-water rafting, hiking and similar activities. These establishments provide accommodation facilities, such as cabins and fixed camp sites, and other amenities, such as food services, recreational facilities and equipment, and organized recreational activities.

Exclusion(s): Establishments primarily engaged in:
- operating instructional camps, such as sports camps, fine arts camps and computer camps (61, Educational Services); and
- operating children's day camps, except instructional (713990, All Other Amusement and Recreation Industries).

Example Activities
- Boys' camps
- Camp, vacation, boys' or girls'
- Dude ranches
- Girls' camps
- Nudist camps
- Outdoor adventure retreats (with accommodation)
- Recreation camps (except fishing and hunting camps)
- Summer camps (except day and sports instructional)
- Tourist camp
- Vacation camps (except hunting and fishing camps)
- Wilderness camps (except hunting and fishing camps)

7213 Rooming and Boarding Houses

See industry description for 72131, below.

72131 Rooming and Boarding Houses

This industry comprises establishments primarily engaged in operating rooming and boarding houses and similar facilities. These establishments provide temporary or longer-term accommodation, which, for the period of occupancy, may serve as a principal residence. These establishments may also provide complementary services, such as housekeeping, meals and laundry services.

Example Activities
- Boarding houses
- Camp, residential, for farm or other workers
- Fraternity residential houses
- Furnished rooms, rental of
- Lodging houses operated by organizations for members only
- Lodging houses, private
- Residence, college (if separate establishment from college)
- Residential clubs
- Rooming houses
- Sorority residential houses
- Workers' camp or hostel (at work site)

721310 Rooming and Boarding Houses US

See industry description for 72131, above.

722 Food Services and Drinking Places

The subsector comprises establishments primarily engaged in preparing meals, snacks and beverages, to customer order, for immediate consumption on and off the premises. This subsector does not include food service activities that occur within establishments such as hotels, civic and social associations, amusement and recreation parks, and theatres. However, leased food-service locations in facilities such as hotels, shopping malls, airports and department stores are included. The industry groups within this subsector reflect the level and type of service provided.

Exclusion(s): Establishments primarily engaged in:
- preparing and/or delivering food for the needy (62421, Community Food Services).

7221 Full-Service Restaurants

See industry description for 72211, below.

72211 Full-Service Restaurants

This industry comprises establishments primarily engaged in providing food services to patrons who order and are served while seated and pay after eating. These establishments may sell alcoholic beverages, provide take-out services, operate a bar or present live entertainment, in addition to serving food and beverages.

Exclusion(s):
- food service establishments in which patrons order at a counter and pay before eating (72221, Limited-Service Eating Places);
- bars, taverns, pubs and night clubs (72241, Drinking Places (Alcoholic Beverages));

and establishments primarily engaged in:
- producing and presenting live theatrical productions and providing food and beverages for consumption on the premises (71111, Theatre Companies and Dinner Theatres).

Example Activities
- Diner
- Dining lounge
- Family restaurant
- Fine-dining restaurants
- Full-service restaurants

722110 Full-Service Restaurants US

See industry description for 72211, above.

7222 Limited-Service Eating Places

See industry description for 72221, below.

72221 Limited-Service Eating Places

This industry comprises establishments primarily engaged in providing foodservices to patrons who order or select items at a counter, food bar or cafeteria line (or order by telephone) and pay before eating. Food and drink are picked up for consumption on the premises or for take-out, or delivered to the customer's location. These establishments may offer a variety of food items or they may offer specialty snacks or non-alcoholic beverages.

Exclusion(s):
- food service establishments in which patrons order while seated and pay after eating, whether or not take-out services are provided (72211, Full-Service Restaurants); and
- food service establishments engaged in preparing and serving meals and snacks from motorized vehicles or non-motorized carts (72233, Mobile Food Services).

Example Activities
- Cafeterias, public
- Chinese take out restaurant
- Coffee shops (without food services)
- Doughnut shops
- Drive-in restaurants
- Fast food concession
- Fast food restaurants
- Fish and chips, take-out
- Food bars
- Food court

- Food, take-out services
- Hamburger stand
- Hot dog stands
- Ice cream parlour
- Limited-service restaurant
- Limited-service restaurant, licensed

- Oyster bar
- Pizza take out store
- Pizzerias, take-out, food service
- Refreshment stands
- Sandwich shop
- Take-out restaurant

722210 Limited-Service Eating Places CAN

See industry description for 72221, above.

7223 Special Food Services

This industry group comprises establishments primarily engaged in providing food services at the customer's location, at a location designated by the customer, or from a motorized vehicle or non-motorized cart.

72231 Food Service Contractors

This industry comprises establishments primarily engaged in supplying food services under contract for a specific period of time. Establishments providing food services to airlines, railways and institutions, as well as establishments that operate food concessions at sports and similar facilities, are included.

Exclusion(s):
- food vending machine operators (45421, Vending Machine Operators);
- event caterers (72232, Caterers); and
- mobile canteens (72233, Mobile Food Services).

Example Activities
- Cafeterias, industrial
- Caterers, industrial
- Catering food service, industrial

- Commissary restaurants
- Company cafeteria
- School cafeteria service

722310 Food Service Contractors

See industry description for 72231, above.

72232 Caterers

This industry comprises establishments primarily engaged in providing food services for events, such as graduation parties, wedding receptions and trade shows. These establishments generally have equipment and vehicles to transport meals and snacks to events and to prepare food at the event site. Caterers who own or manage permanent facilities in which they provide event-based food services are also included.

Exclusion(s): Establishments primarily engaged in:
- preparing and/or delivering food for the needy (62421, Community Food Services); and
- industrial caterers (72231, Food Service Contractors).

Example Activities
- Banquet halls, with own catering staff, doing outside catering
- Buffet catering, social

- Catering for dining room and banquets
- Social catering services (weddings, parties)

722320 Caterers

See industry description for 72232, above.

72233 Mobile Food Services

This industry comprises establishments primarily engaged in preparing and serving meals and snacks for immediate consumption from motorized vehicles or non-motorized carts.

Exclusion(s): Establishments primarily engaged in:
- selling fruit, vegetables and other non-prepared food items from mobile equipment (45439, Other Direct Selling Establishments); and
- selling a specialty snack, such as ice cream, frozen yogurt, cookies, popcorn or non-alcoholic beverages, from a permanent facility (72221, Limited-Service Eating Places).

Example Activities
- Chip wagon
- French fries, mobile
- Lunch wagon
- Mobile canteens, service
- Snack truck operation
- Street vendors, food

722330 Mobile Food Services

See industry description for 72233, above.

7224 Drinking Places (Alcoholic Beverages)

See industry description for 72241, below.

72241 Drinking Places (Alcoholic Beverages)

This industry comprises establishments, known as bars, taverns or drinking places, primarily engaged in preparing and serving alcoholic beverages for immediate consumption. These establishments may also provide limited food services.

Exclusion(s):
- civic or social organizations that operate a bar for their members (81341, Civic and Social Organizations).

Example Activities
- Bars (i.e., drinking places), alcoholic beverage
- Beer gardens
- Beer parlours
- Brasseries (beer gardens)
- Brew pub
- Cabarets (night clubs)
- Cocktail lounges
- Discotheques, alcoholic beverage
- Drinking places, alcoholic beverages
- Military messes (npf)
- Neighbourhood pub
- Night clubs
- Pubs
- Saloons (drinking places)
- Taverns

722410 Drinking Places (Alcoholic Beverages) US

See industry description for 72241, above.

81 Other Services (except Public Administration)

This sector comprises establishments, not classified to any other sector, primarily engaged in repairing, or performing general or routine maintenance, on motor vehicles, machinery, equipment and other products to ensure that they work efficiently; providing personal care services, funeral services, laundry services and other services to individuals, such as pet care services and photo finishing services; organizing and promoting religious activities; supporting various causes through grant-making, advocating (promoting) various social and political causes, and promoting and defending the interests of their members. Private households are also included.

811 Repair and Maintenance

This subsector comprises establishments primarily engaged in repairing and maintaining motor vehicles, machinery, equipment and other products. These establishments repair or perform general or routine maintenance on such products, to ensure that they work efficiently.

Exclusion(s): Establishments primarily engaged in:
- the repair of construction works or components (23, Construction);
- rebuilding machinery and equipment on a factory basis (31-33, Manufacturing);
- retailing and repair activities (e.g. automobile dealers) (44-45, Retail Trade);
- retailing gasoline and providing motor repair services (4471, Gasoline Stations); and
- repairing transportation equipment at airports, seaports and other transportation facilities (488, Support Activities for Transportation).

8111 Automotive Repair and Maintenance

This industry group comprises establishments primarily engaged in repairing and maintaining motor vehicles, such as cars, trucks, vans and commercial trailers.

81111 Automotive Mechanical and Electrical Repair and Maintenance

This industry comprises establishments primarily engaged in providing mechanical or electrical repair and maintenance services for motor vehicles, such as engine repair and maintenance, exhaust system replacement, transmission repair and electrical system repair.

Exclusion(s): Establishments primarily engaged in:
- retailing motor vehicles, parts and accessories, and providing repair services (441, Motor Vehicle and Parts Dealers); and
- retailing motor fuels and providing motor vehicle repair services (4471, Gasoline Stations).

811111 General Automotive Repair US

This Canadian industry comprises establishments primarily engaged in providing a range of mechanical and electrical repair and maintenance services for motor vehicles, such as engine repair and maintenance, exhaust system replacement, transmission repair and electrical system repair. Establishments specializing in engine repair and replacement are also included.

Exclusion(s): Establishments primarily engaged in:
- retailing motor vehicles, parts and accessories, and providing repair services (441, Motor Vehicle and Parts Dealers);
- retailing new and rebuilt motor vehicle parts and accessories and repairing automobiles (441310, Automotive Parts and Accessories Stores);
- retailing motor fuels (gasoline stations) and providing motor vehicle repair services (4471, Gasoline Stations);
- replacing exhaust systems in motor vehicles (811112, Automotive Exhaust System Repair);
- installing or repairing transmissions in motor vehicles (811119, Other Automotive Mechanical and Electrical Repair and Maintenance); and
- changing oil and lubricating chassis of cars and trucks (811199, All Other Automotive Repair and Maintenance).

Example Activities
- Automotive repair shops, general
- Diesel engine repair, automotive
- Engine repair, automotive
- Garages, general automotive repair and service

- Motor vehicle (except motorcycle), general repair service
- Repair shops, automotive, general

811112 Automotive Exhaust System Repair US

This Canadian industry comprises establishments primarily engaged in replacing and repairing exhaust systems in motor vehicles.

Example Activities
- Custom made exhaust systems, installation
- Exhaust system repair and replacement shops

- Motor vehicle exhaust systems replacement service
- Muffler replacement shop

811119 Other Automotive Mechanical and Electrical Repair and Maintenance CAN

This Canadian industry comprises establishments, not classified to any other Canadian industry, primarily engaged in providing specialized motor vehicle mechanical or electrical repair and maintenance.

Exclusion(s): Establishments primarily engaged in:
- providing a range of mechanical and electrical motor vehicle repair services (811111, General Automotive Repair); and
- replacing motor vehicle exhaust systems (811112, Automotive Exhaust System Repair).

Example Activities
- Air-conditioning installation and repair, motor vehicle
- Automotive brake repairing
- Automotive springs, rebuilding and repair
- Electrical repair shops, motor vehicle
- Front end alignment shops, motor vehicle
- Fuel injection service

- Fuel system conversion, automotive
- Fuel system repair, motor vehicle
- Ignition service, automotive
- Motor vehicle suspension shops
- Radiator repair shops, motor vehicle
- Transmission repair and replacement, motor vehicle

81112 Automotive Body, Paint, Interior and Glass Repair

This industry comprises establishments primarily engaged in repairing, customizing and painting motor vehicle bodies, repairing and customizing motor vehicle interiors, and installing and repairing motor vehicle glass. Establishments engaged in customizing automobile, truck and van interiors for the physically disabled or other customers with special requirements are included.

Exclusion(s): Establishments primarily engaged in:
- manufacturing motor vehicles and also customizing these vehicles (336, Transportation Equipment Manufacturing).

811121 Automotive Body, Paint and Interior Repair and Maintenance US

This Canadian industry comprises establishments primarily engaged in repairing, customizing and painting motor vehicle bodies, and repairing and customizing motor vehicle interiors.

Exclusion(s): Establishments primarily engaged in:
- manufacturing motor vehicles and converting vehicles on a factory basis (336, Transportation Equipment Manufacturing); and
- glass replacement and repair (811122, Automotive Glass Replacement Shops).

Example Activities

- Antique and classic automobile restoration
- Automotive upholstery and trim shops
- Collision repair, motor vehicle
- Frame repair shops, automotive
- Limousine, produced by custom conversion
- Paint and body shops, motor vehicle
- Plastic bumpers (auto), repair and installation
- Seat cover and auto upholstery shop
- Truck or trailer body repair

811122 Automotive Glass Replacement Shops US

This Canadian industry comprises establishments primarily engaged in replacing and repairing motor vehicle glass.

Example Activities

- Automotive glass replacement and repair service
- Motor vehicle glass replacement service
- Window tinting, automotive

81119 Other Automotive Repair and Maintenance

This industry comprises establishments, not classified to any other industry, primarily engaged in providing motor vehicle repair and maintenance. Examples of establishments in this industry are oil change and lubrication shops, car washes, motor vehicle detailers, tire repair shops, and rustproofing or undercoating shops.

Exclusion(s): Establishments primarily engaged in:
- tire retreading or recapping (32621, Tire Manufacturing);
- repairing and maintaining motor vehicle electrical and mechanical systems (81111, Automotive Mechanical and Electrical Repair and Maintenance); and
- repairing motor vehicle bodies, paint, interiors and glass (81112, Automotive Body, Paint, Interior and Glass Repair).

811192 Car Washes US

This Canadian industry comprises establishments primarily engaged in washing and cleaning motor vehicles.

Example Activities

- Auto detail shop
- Automobile washing and polishing
- Bus washing
- Car washes, self-service or automatic
- Mobile wash unit (trucks, autos)
- Truck washing
- Waxing and polishing, automotive

811199 All Other Automotive Repair and Maintenance CAN

This Canadian industry comprises establishments, not classified to any other Canadian industry, primarily engaged in providing motor vehicle repair and maintenance.

Exclusion(s): Establishments primarily engaged in:
- tire retreading or recapping (326210, Tire Manufacturing);
- performing a range of mechanical and electrical repairs or specializing in engine repair or replacement (811111, General Automotive Repair);
- repairing exhaust systems (811112, Automotive Exhaust System Repair);
- repairing transmissions (811119, Other Automotive Mechanical and Electrical Repair and Maintenance);
- repairing motor vehicle bodies and interiors (811121, Automotive Body, Paint and Interior Repair and Maintenance);
- repairing motor vehicle glass (811122, Automotive Glass Replacement Shops); and
- repairing air-conditioners, other than automotive (811412, Appliance Repair and Maintenance).

Example Activities
- Diagnostic centres, motor vehicle
- Emissions testing service, automotive, without repair
- Lubrication services, motor vehicles
- Motor vehicle emissions testing, without repairs
- Rustproofing service, automotive
- Tire repairing
- Undercoating service, automotive

8112 Electronic and Precision Equipment Repair and Maintenance

See industry description for 81121, below.

81121 Electronic and Precision Equipment Repair and Maintenance

This industry comprises establishments primarily engaged in repairing and maintaining electronic equipment and precision instruments.

Exclusion(s): Establishments primarily engaged in:
- rewinding armatures and rebuilding electric motors (33531, Electrical Equipment Manufacturing);
- retailing new electronics and also providing repair services (44311, Appliance, Television and Other Electronics Stores); and
- installing and repairing locks (56162, Security Systems Services).

Example Activities
- Aircraft electrical equipment repair (except radio)
- Aircraft flight instrument repair (except electrical)
- Automotive radio repair shops
- Binoculars and other optical goods repair
- Drafting instrument repair
- Electrical measuring instrument repair and calibration
- Electronic data processing equipment, maintenance
- Ink jet cartridges, recycling (i.e., cleaning and re-filling)
- Intercommunication equipment, commercial, repair
- Intercommunication equipment, household type, repair
- Maintenance and repair of computers and related equipment
- Medical equipment repair, electrical
- Meteorological instrument repair
- Microscopes, repair
- Nautical and navigational instrument, repair
- Photographic equipment, repairing
- Precision instrument repair
- Recycling (i.e., cleaning and re-filling) ink jet cartridges
- Repair and maintenance of computers and related equipment
- Repair of electronic equipment
- Repair of industrial process control equipment
- Repair of motion picture studio equipment
- Scientific instrument, repair
- Stereo equipment, repair service
- Surgical instrument repair
- Surveying instrument repair
- Television repair shops
- Typewriters and desk calculators, repair service

811210 Electronic and Precision Equipment Repair and Maintenance CAN

See industry description for 81121, above.

8113 Commercial and Industrial Machinery and Equipment (except Automotive and Electronic) Repair and Maintenance

See industry description for 81131, below.

81131 Commercial and Industrial Machinery and Equipment (except Automotive and Electronic) Repair and Maintenance

This industry comprises establishments primarily engaged in repairing and maintaining commercial and industrial machinery and equipment, except automotive and electronic.

Exclusion(s): Establishments primarily engaged in:
- rewinding armatures or rebuilding electric motors (33531, Electrical Equipment Manufacturing);
- repairing and overhauling aircraft at the factory (33641, Aerospace Product and Parts Manufacturing);
- repairing and overhauling railroad engines and cars at the factory (33651, Railroad Rolling Stock Manufacturing);
- repairing and overhauling ships at the shipyard (33661, Ship and Boat Building);
- repairing and servicing aircraft in a hangar (48819, Other Support Activities for Air Transportation);
- repairing and servicing railroad cars and engines in a railroad yard (48821, Support Activities for Rail Transportation); and
- repairing and overhauling ships at floating dry docks (48839, Other Support Activities for Water Transportation).

Example Activities
- Agricultural machinery and equipment repair and maintenance
- Boiler, power, repair shops (except manufacturing)
- Cleaning and reglazing of baking pans
- Cleaning grease and air filters, service of
- Construction machinery and equipment, repair
- Electrical generating and transmission equipment repair
- Fire extinguishers, servicing
- Forestry machinery and equipment repair
- Foundry machinery and equipment repair
- Industrial equipment and machinery, repair and maintenance
- Mending service, fish net
- Mining machinery and equipment, repair
- Motor repair, electric
- Paper making machinery repair
- Pneumatic controls, oil field equipment, repair
- Portable welding shop (mobile)
- Printing trade machinery repair
- Reconditioning metal drums and shipping containers
- Repair of electrical switchgear and control equipment
- Repair of industrial furnaces
- Repair of machine tools
- Repair of machinery for food, beverage and tobacco processing
- Repair of non-domestic cooling and refrigeration equipment
- Repair of paperboard making machinery
- Repair of pumps and compressors (except for refrigeration)
- Repair of rubber or plastic industry machinery
- Repair of taps and valves
- Repair of textile, apparel and leather production machinery
- Repairing pallets (except wooden)
- Shipping container (cargo) repair service
- Tanks, repairing (heavy gauge)
- Welding equipment, repair and maintenance
- Welding repair services (except construction)

811310 Commercial and Industrial Machinery and Equipment (except Automotive and Electronic) Repair and Maintenance US

See industry description for 81131, above.

8114 Personal and Household Goods Repair and Maintenance

This industry group comprises establishments primarily engaged in repairing and maintaining personal and household goods, such as home and garden equipment, appliances, furniture, footwear and leather goods, garments, watches, jewellery, musical instruments, bicycles and recreational boats.

81141 Home and Garden Equipment and Appliance Repair and Maintenance

This industry comprises establishments primarily engaged in repairing and maintaining home and garden equipment and household appliances. Establishments in this industry repair and maintain products such as lawnmowers, edgers, snow and leaf blowers, washing machines and clothes dryers, and refrigerators.

Exclusion(s): Establishments primarily engaged in:
- retailing appliances and also providing repair services (44311, Appliance, Television and Other Electronics Stores);
- retailing outdoor power equipment and also providing repair services (44421, Outdoor Power Equipment Stores); and
- repairing consumer electronics (81121, Electronic and Precision Equipment Repair and Maintenance).

811411 Home and Garden Equipment Repair and Maintenance US

This Canadian industry comprises establishments primarily engaged in repairing and maintaining home and garden equipment, without retail sales of new equipment.

Example Activities
- Electric tool repair
- Hedge and lawn trimmers, repair service (without retail sales of new equipment)
- Lawn and garden equipment, repair service (without retail sales of new equipment)
- Motor, outboard, repairs
- Power tools, repair (without retail sales of new equipment)
- Repair motors for boats (without retail sales of new equipment)
- Small gas engines, repair (without retail sales of new equipment)
- Snow- and leaf-blower, repair service (without retail sales of new equipment)

811412 Appliance Repair and Maintenance US

This Canadian industry comprises establishments primarily engaged in repairing and maintaining household appliances, without retail sales of new equipment.

Exclusion(s): Establishments primarily engaged in:
- retailing new appliances and also providing repair services (443110, Appliance, Television and Other Electronics Stores);
- repairing motor vehicle air-conditioning equipment (811199, All Other Automotive Repair and Maintenance);
- repairing consumer electronics (811210, Electronic and Precision Equipment Repair and Maintenance); and
- repairing commercial refrigeration equipment (811310, Commercial and Industrial Machinery and Equipment (except Automotive and Electronic) Repair and Maintenance).

Example Activities
- Air-conditioner repair, self-contained units (except automotive)
- Gas appliance repair service
- Household appliances repair service (without retail sales of new equipment)
- Household appliances, repair
- Refrigerator repair service, electric (without retail sales of new equipment)
- Sewing machine repair shops (without retail sales of new equipment)

81142 Reupholstery and Furniture Repair

This industry comprises establishments primarily engaged in reupholstering furniture, refinishing furniture, repairing furniture and restoring furniture, without retail sales of new equipment.

Exclusion(s): Establishments primarily engaged in:
- making furniture and cabinets on a custom basis (337, Furniture and Related Product Manufacturing);
- retailing upholstery materials (45113, Sewing, Needlework and Piece Goods Stores);
- restoring museum pieces (711511, Independent Artists, Visual Arts); and
- repairing motor vehicle interiors (81112, Automotive Body, Paint, Interior and Glass Repair).

Example Activities
- Antique furniture repair and restoration
- Furniture refinishing and repair shops
- Furniture repairing, cleaning, redecorating and remodelling shops
- Furniture reupholstering
- Furniture stripping and refinishing
- Furniture, household, repair shop
- Office chair reupholstering and upholstery repair
- Polishing of furniture
- Refinish office furniture
- Refinishing furniture
- Repairing furniture (without retail sales of new equipment)
- Restoration and repair of antique furniture
- Upholstery repair

811420 Reupholstery and Furniture Repair

See industry description for 81142, above.

81143 Footwear and Leather Goods Repair

This industry comprises establishments primarily engaged in repairing footwear and/or other leather or leather-like goods, such as handbags and briefcases.

Exclusion(s): Establishments primarily engaged in:
- retailing luggage and leather goods and also providing repair services (44832, Luggage and Leather Goods Stores).

Example Activities
- Boot and shoe repair shop
- Cobblers, own account
- Harness repair
- Leather goods repair shops
- Luggage repair shop
- Saddlery repair
- Shoe repair shops

811430 Footwear and Leather Goods Repair

See industry description for 81143, above.

81149 Other Personal and Household Goods Repair and Maintenance

This industry comprises establishments, not classified to any other industry, primarily engaged in repairing and maintaining personal and household goods, without retail sales of new equipment.

Exclusion(s): Establishments primarily engaged in:
- operating marinas and providing a range of other services, including boat cleaning and repair (71393, Marinas);
- repairing appliances (81141, Home and Garden Equipment and Appliance Repair and Maintenance);
- repairing home and garden equipment (81141, Home and Garden Equipment and Appliance Repair and Maintenance);
- reupholstering and repairing furniture (81142, Reupholstery and Furniture Repair);
- repairing footwear and leather goods (81143, Footwear and Leather Goods Repair); and
- dry cleaning combined with laundry and alteration of garments (81232, Dry Cleaning and Laundry Services (except Coin-Operated)).

Example Activities
- Awning repair shops
- Bicycles, repairing (without retail sales of new equipment)
- Bowling pins, refinishing or repair
- China firing and decorating to individual order
- Cutlery sharpening (without retail sales of new equipment)
- Electric razor repair (without retail sales of new equipment)
- Garment repair
- Gunsmith shops (without retail sales of new equipment)
- Jewellery engraving service
- Jewellery repair service (without retail sales of new equipment)
- Mattress renovating and repair shops (without retail sales of new equipment)
- Motorcycle repair service
- Musical instruments repairing and tuning (without retail sales of new equipment)
- Pearl restringing, for the trade
- Repairing golf clubs (without retail sales of new equipment)
- Repairing horse-drawn wagon
- Restoration and repair of antiques (except furniture and automobiles)
- Restringing tennis rackets (without retail sales of new equipment)
- Rug and carpet repair only
- Sharpening saws, lawn mowers, knives and scissors (without retail sales of new equipment)
- Silverware-cleaning, repairing and replating
- Skate sharpening
- Tennis rackets restringing
- Tent repair shops (without retail sales of new equipment)
- Tuning of pianos and organs (without retail sales of new equipment)
- Watch repair service (without retail sales of new equipment)
- Window shade repair shops (without retail sales of new equipment)

811490 Other Personal and Household Goods Repair and Maintenance US

See industry description for 81149, above.

812 Personal and Laundry Services

This subsector comprises establishments primarily engaged in providing personal care services, funeral services, laundry services and other services, such as pet care and photo finishing. Operators of parking facilities are also included.

Exclusion(s):
- establishments consisting of private households (81411, Private Households).

8121 Personal Care Services US

This industry group comprises establishments primarily engaged in providing personal care services, such as hair care and esthetic services, hair replacement and scalp treatment services, massage services, diet counselling services and ear piercing services.

81211 Hair Care and Esthetic Services US

This industry comprises establishments primarily engaged in cutting and styling hair, providing esthetic services such as manicures and pedicures, or in providing a combination of hair care and esthetic services.

812114 Barber Shops CAN

This Canadian industry comprises establishments primarily engaged in providing hair care services to men, including hair cutting and styling, and the trimming or shaving of beards and moustaches.

Exclusion(s):
- unisex hair salons (812116, Unisex Hair Salons); and
- hair replacement centres (812190, Other Personal Care Services).

Example Activities
- Barber shops
- Hair stylists, men's
- Men's hair stylist shop

812115 Beauty Salons CAN

This Canadian industry comprises establishments primarily engaged in providing hair care services to women, providing esthetic services such as manicures and pedicures, or a combination of these services.

Exclusion(s):
- cosmetician/esthetician schools (611690, All Other Schools and Instruction);
- practices of dermatologists (621110, Offices of Physicians);
- unisex hair salons (812116, Unisex Hair Salons); and
- hair removal and hair replacement studios (812190, Other Personal Care Services).

Example Activities
- Beauticians
- Beauty parlours
- Beauty shops or salons
- Hair stylists, women's
- Manicure and pedicure salons
- Nail salons
- Women's hair stylist shop

812116 Unisex Hair Salons CAN

This Canadian industry comprises establishments primarily engaged in cutting and styling men's or women's hair. Establishments that combine hair care services for men or women with esthetic services are also included.

Exclusion(s):
- barber shops and men's hair stylists (812114, Barber Shops); and
- hairdressing/beauty salons for women (812115, Beauty Salons).

Example Activities
- Barber and beauty shops, combined
- Unisex hair stylist shops

81219 Other Personal Care Services US

This industry comprises establishments, not classified to any other industry, primarily engaged in providing personal care services.

Exclusion(s):
- health clubs and similar facilities featuring exercise and other active physical fitness conditioning (71394, Fitness and Recreational Sports Centres).

Example Activities
- Bath houses
- Colour consultants
- Day spa
- Diet centres (non-medical)
- Ear piercing service
- Estheticians, services (i.e., hair removal)
- Hair removal (i.e., by electrolysis)
- Hair replacement service
- Hair weaving service
- Massage parlours
- Saunas
- Scalp treatment service
- Tanning salon
- Tattoo parlours
- Turkish baths
- Weight-reduction centres (non-medical)

812190 Other Personal Care Services CAN

See industry description for 81219, above.

8122 Funeral Services US

This industry group comprises establishments primarily engaged in preparing the dead for burial or interment, conducting funerals, operating sites or structures reserved for the interment of human or animal remains, and cremating the dead. Examples of establishments in this industry group are funeral homes, cemeteries and crematoria.

81221 Funeral Homes US

This industry comprises establishments primarily engaged in preparing the dead for burial or interment and conducting funerals.

Example Activities
- Funeral directors
- Funeral home services
- Funeral parlours
- Mortuaries
- Undertakers

812210 Funeral Homes US

See industry description for 81221, above.

81222 Cemeteries and Crematoria US

This industry comprises establishments primarily engaged in operating sites or structures reserved for the interment of human or animal remains, and cremating the dead.

Example Activities
- Cemetery
- Crematoria
- Mausoleum
- Memorial gardens (i.e., burial place)
- Pet cemeteries

812220 Cemeteries and Crematoria US

See industry description for 81222, above.

8123 Dry Cleaning and Laundry Services US

This industry group comprises establishments primarily engaged in providing self-service laundry and dry-cleaning facilities for public use; providing dry cleaning and laundering services; laundering and supplying laundered uniforms, linens and other fabric items; and providing other laundry services.

81231 Coin-Operated Laundries and Dry Cleaners US

This industry comprises establishments primarily engaged in providing self-service, coin-operated laundry and dry-cleaning facilities for public use.

Example Activities
- Coin-operated laundry and dry cleaning service
- Laundromat
- Self-service laundry and dry cleaning

812310 Coin-Operated Laundries and Dry Cleaners US

See industry description for 81231, above.

81232 Dry Cleaning and Laundry Services (except Coin-Operated) US

This industry comprises establishments primarily engaged in laundering, dry cleaning, and pressing apparel and linens of all types, including leather. These establishments may also provide clothing repair and alteration services. Laundry pick-up and delivery stations, operated independently from power laundries and dry-cleaning plants, and establishments primarily engaged in cleaning, repairing and storing fur garments are also included.

Exclusion(s): Establishments primarily engaged in:
- retailing fur garments, combined with cleaning, repairing or storing (44819, Other Clothing Stores);
- storing furs for the trade (49312, Refrigerated Warehousing and Storage);
- operating clothing alteration and repair shops (81149, Other Personal and Household Goods Repair and Maintenance);
- operating self-service laundry and dry-cleaning facilities (81231, Coin-Operated Laundries and Dry Cleaners); and
- supplying household or commercial linens (81233, Linen and Uniform Supply).

Example Activities
- Apparel pressing service, for the trade
- Bobtailers, laundry and dry cleaning
- Collecting and distributing agents, laundry and dry cleaning
- Dry cleaning agents, pick-up and delivery services
- Dry cleaning plants
- Fur garments, cleaning, repairing and storage
- Hand laundries
- Hat cleaning and blocking
- Laundry and drycleaning agents
- Power laundries (except coin operated)
- Power laundry and dry cleaning plants
- Valet service, cleaning and pressing clothing

812320 Dry Cleaning and Laundry Services (except Coin-Operated) US

See industry description for 81232, above.

81233 Linen and Uniform Supply US

This industry comprises establishments primarily engaged in supplying and laundering towels, napkins, table cloths, sheets, gowns, aprons, diapers and other linen items, for household or commercial use, typically on a contract basis. Establishments engaged in supplying and laundering commercial and industrial uniforms, laboratory coats, safety gloves, and flame and heat resistant clothing are also included.

Exclusion(s): Establishments primarily engaged in:
- renting formal wear and costumes (53222, Formal Wear and Costume Rental).

Example Activities
- Clean room apparel supply service
- Diaper supply service
- Flame and heat resistant clothing supply service
- Industrial launderers
- Linen supply service
- Mat and rug launders
- Overall supply service
- Radiation protective garments supply service

- Towel supply service
- Treated mops, dust cloths and tool covers, supply service
- Uniform supply service
- Work clothing supply services, industrial

812330 Linen and Uniform Supply ^{CAN}

See industry description for 81233, above.

8129 Other Personal Services ^{US}

This industry group comprises establishments, not classified to any other industry group, primarily engaged in providing personal services, such as pet care, photo finishing and parking services.

81291 Pet Care (except Veterinary) Services ^{US}

This industry comprises establishments primarily engaged in grooming and boarding pet animals.

Exclusion(s): Establishments primarily engaged in:
- breeding and raising pets (11521, Support Activities for Animal Production);
- operating animal hospitals (54194, Veterinary Services); and
- operating humane societies (81331, Social Advocacy Organizations).

Example Activities
- Animal shelters
- Boarding kennel service, pet
- Guard dog training
- Guide dog training
- Humane society (animal shelters)
- Kennels, pet boarding
- Obedience training services, pet
- Pet care (except veterinary), service
- Pet grooming services
- Pet sitting services
- Pet training services
- Training of pets, service

812910 Pet Care (except Veterinary) Services ^{US}

See industry description for 81291, above.

81292 Photo Finishing Services ^{US}

This industry comprises establishments primarily engaged in developing film and making photographic slides, prints, and enlargements

Exclusion(s):
- laboratories that process film for the motion picture industry (51219, Post-Production and Other Motion Picture and Video Industries).

812921 Photo Finishing Laboratories (except One-Hour) ^{US}

This Canadian industry comprises establishments, known as commercial and professional photo finishing laboratories, primarily engaged in developing film and making photographic slides, prints, and enlargements, on a large-scale basis, typically for commercial clients, and providing specialty services not normally available from one-hour photo finishing laboratories.

Exclusion(s):
- laboratories that process film for the motion picture industry (512190, Post-Production and Other Motion Picture and Video Industries).

Example Activities
- Developing and printing of films (except for the motion picture industry)
- Film processing (except for the motion picture industry), laboratories
- Photofinishing services (except one-hour)
- Photograph developing, printing and enlarging services (except one-hour)
- Photographic laboratories (except for the motion picture industry)
- Satellite photographs, processing

812922 One-Hour Photo Finishing US

This Canadian industry comprises establishments, known as one-hour photo finishers, primarily engaged in developing film and printing still photographs, for the public, through the use of automated photo finishing equipment located in shopping malls and other convenient locations. These establishments also typically retail photographic supplies.

Exclusion(s): Establishments primarily engaged in:
- providing access to coin-operated photo machines (812990, All Other Personal Services).

Example Activity
- Photofinishing services, one-hour

81293 Parking Lots and Garages US

This industry comprises establishments primarily engaged in operating parking lots and parking garages. These establishments provide temporary parking services for motor vehicles, usually on an hourly, daily, or monthly basis.

Exclusion(s): Establishments primarily engaged in:
- the dead storage of automobiles (49319, Other Warehousing and Storage).

Example Activities
- Automobile parking lots
- Parking garages
- Parking services, valet
- Valet parking services

812930 Parking Lots and Garages US

See industry description for 81293, above.

81299 All Other Personal Services US

This industry comprises establishments, not classified to any other industry, primarily engaged in providing personal services.

Exclusion(s):
- private households employing nannies or other domestics (81411, Private Households);

and establishments primarily engaged in:
- babysitting (child care) in own home (62441, Child Day-Care Services); and
- hair removal, hair replacement, massage, diet counselling, ear piercing, scalp treatments, skin treatments, sun tanning or tattooing (81219, Other Personal Care Services).

Example Activities
- Astrologers, own account
- Bail bonding services
- Balloon-o-gram, service
- Bootblack parlours
- Check room service
- Coin operated photo machine, operators

- Coin-operated service machine operation (i.e., scales, shoe shine, lockers, blood pressure)
- College clearinghouses
- Comfort station operation
- Consumer buying service
- Dating service
- Escort service, social
- Fortune tellers
- Genealogical investigation service
- House sitting services
- Marriage bureau
- Palm readers
- Party planning service
- Personal shopping service
- Phrenologists
- Porter service
- Psychic services
- Rest room operation
- Shoeshine service
- Shopping service
- Special occasion greeting service
- Wedding chapels (except churches)
- Wedding planning services

812990 All Other Personal Services US

See industry description for 81299, above.

813 Religious, Grant-Making, Civic, and Professional and Similar Organizations

This subsector comprises establishments primarily engaged in organizing and promoting religious activities; supporting various causes through grant-making; advocating (promoting) various social and political causes; and promoting and defending the interests of their members.

8131 Religious Organizations US

See industry description for 81311, below.

81311 Religious Organizations US

This industry comprises establishments primarily engaged in operating religious organizations for religious worship, training or study; administering an organized religion; or promoting religious activities.

Exclusion(s):
- used merchandise stores operated by religious organizations (45331, Used Merchandise Stores);
- publishing houses operated by religious organizations (511, Publishing Industries (except Internet));
- radio and television stations operated by religious organizations (515, Broadcasting (except Internet), or 51913, Internet Publishing and Broadcasting, and Web Search Portals);
- educational institutions operated by religious organizations (61, Educational Services);
- health and social service institutions operated by religious organizations (62, Health Care and Social Assistance); and
- bingos or casinos operated by religious organizations (7132, Gambling Industries).

Example Activities
- Bible societies
- Christian Science lecturers
- Churches
- Convents (except schools)
- Faith healers, religious organization
- Missions, religious organization
- Monasteries (except schools)
- Places of worship
- Reading rooms, promoting a religion
- Religious organizations
- Retreat houses, religious
- Roman Catholic church
- Shrines, religious
- Synagogues
- Temples, religious

813110 Religious Organizations US

See industry description for 81311, above.

8132 Grant-Making and Giving Services US

See industry description for 81321, below.

81321 Grant-Making and Giving Services US

This industry comprises establishments primarily engaged in awarding grants from trust funds, or in soliciting contributions on behalf of others, to support a wide range of health, educational, scientific, cultural and other social welfare activities.

Exclusion(s): Establishments primarily engaged in:
- managing trust investment activities, for others (52399, All Other Financial Investment Activities);
- health research (54171, Research and Development in the Physical, Engineering and Life Sciences);
- sponsoring commercial events or ventures (54189, Other Services Related to Advertising);
- raising funds on a contract or fee basis (56149, Other Business Support Services);
- advocating social causes or issues (81331, Social Advocacy Organizations);
- political fund-raising (81394, Political Organizations); and
- directly undertaking activities in support of health, educational and other social objectives, including those that raise funds on their own account (classified to the specific activity undertaken).

Example Activities
- Bursaries (scholarship trusts), management of
- Charitable trusts, awarding grants
- Conservation foundation
- Educational trusts, awarding grants
- Federated charities organizations
- Grant-making foundation
- Health awareness fundraising organization
- Health research fundraising organization
- Philanthropic trusts, awarding grants
- Scholarship trusts
- Trusts, charitable, awarding grants
- Trusts, educational, awarding grants
- Trusts, religious, awarding grants
- United fund councils
- Voluntary health organization

813210 Grant-Making and Giving Services CAN

See industry description for 81321, above.

8133 Social Advocacy Organizations US

See industry description for 81331, below.

81331 Social Advocacy Organizations US

This industry comprises establishments primarily engaged in promoting a particular social or political cause intended to benefit a broad or specific constituency. Organizations of this type may also solicit contributions or sell memberships to support their activities.

Example Activities
- Accident prevention association
- Advocacy groups
- Animal rights organizations
- Antipoverty advocacy organizations
- Associations for retired persons, advocacy
- Civil liberties groups
- Community action advocacy groups
- Conservation advocacy groups
- Developmentally handicap organizations
- Drug abuse prevention advocacy organizations
- Drunk driving prevention advocacy organizations
- Environmental advocacy groups
- Human rights advocacy organizations
- Humane society (advocacy group)
- Natural resource preservation organizations
- Neighbourhood development advocacy groups
- Peace advocacy groups
- Public interest groups (e.g., environment, conservation, human rights, wildlife)

- Public safety advocacy groups
- Social service advocacy organizations
- Taxpayers advocacy organizations
- Temperance organizations
- Tenant advocacy associations

- Veterans' rights associations
- Wildlife preservation advocacy organizations
- World peace and understanding advocacy groups

813310 Social Advocacy Organizations CAN

See industry description for 81331, above.

8134 Civic and Social Organizations US

See industry description for 81341, below.

81341 Civic and Social Organizations US

This industry comprises establishments primarily engaged in promoting the civic, social or other interests or purposes of their members. Establishments of this type may also operate bars and restaurants and provide other recreational services to members.

Exclusion(s): Establishments primarily engaged in:
- providing access to recreational facilities on a membership basis (7139, Other Amusement and Recreation Industries).

Example Activities
- Alumni associations
- Athletic associations
- Booster clubs
- Businessmen's clubs, civic and social
- Civic associations
- Community association
- Computer enthusiasts' clubs
- Ethnic associations
- Fraternal associations or lodges, social or civic
- Fraternal lodges

- Fraternal organization
- Girl guiding organization
- Historical clubs
- Membership associations, civic or social
- Parent-teachers associations
- Public speaking improvement clubs
- Retirement associations, social
- Scouting organization
- Senior citizens' club
- Social organization, civic and fraternal
- Students' associations

813410 Civic and Social Organizations US

See industry description for 81341, above.

8139 Business, Professional, Labour and Other Membership Organizations US

This industry group comprises establishments, not classified to any other industry group, primarily engaged in promoting the interests of their members. Examples of establishments in this industry group are business associations, professional membership organizations, labour organizations and political organizations.

81391 Business Associations US

This industry comprises establishments primarily engaged in promoting the business interests of their members. These establishments may conduct research on new products and services, publish newsletters, develop market statistics, or sponsor quality and certification standards.

Example Activities

- Animal breeders association
- Association for truckers
- Bankers' association
- Better business bureaus
- Board of trade
- Business associations
- Chambers of commerce
- Construction association
- Electrical manufacturers' association
- Equipment distributors' association
- Farm bureaus
- Federation of agriculture
- Freight shippers' association
- Funeral directors' association

- Growers' association
- Hospital associations
- Industrial associations
- Insurance association
- Junior Chambers of Commerce
- Manufacturers' associations
- Merchants' associations
- Mining associations
- Real estate boards
- Restaurant association
- Retailers' associations
- Trade associations
- Warehousing association
- Wholesalers' associations

813910 Business Associations US

See industry description for 81391, above.

81392 Professional Organizations US

This industry comprises establishments primarily engaged in advancing the professional interests of their members and the profession as a whole.

Example Activities

- Accountants' associations
- Architects' associations
- Bar associations
- Chiropractors' associations
- Dental examining board (national)
- Dentists' associations
- Dieticians' associations
- Educators' associations
- Engineers' associations
- Health care standards agencies
- Health professionals' associations
- Hospital administrators' associations
- Learned societies
- Medical associations

- Nurses' associations
- Ontario College of Pharmacy (licensing bureau)
- Optometrists' associations
- Peer review boards
- Personnel management associations
- Pharmacists' associations
- Professional associations
- Professional standards review boards
- Psychologists' associations
- Scientist membership associations
- Social workers' associations
- Standards review committees, professional
- Teacher associations (except bargaining)

813920 Professional Organizations US

See industry description for 81392, above.

81393 Labour Organizations US

This industry comprises establishments primarily engaged in the regulation of relations between employers and employees. These establishments negotiate with employers to improve the income and working conditions of their members.

Example Activities
- Employees' associations, for improvement of wages and working conditions
- Federation of labour
- Industrial labour unions
- Labour unions
- Trade unions
- Union organizations

813930 Labour Organizations US

See industry description for 81393, above.

81394 Political Organizations US

This industry comprises establishments primarily engaged in promoting the interests of national, provincial or local political parties or candidates. Political groups, organized to raise funds for a political party or individual candidates, are included.

Exclusion(s):
- establishments raising funds on a contract or fee basis (56149, Other Business Support Services).

Example Activities
- Campaign organizations, political
- Constituency associations, political party
- Local political organization
- Political Action Committees (PACs)
- Political campaign organizations
- Political organizations and clubs
- Political parties
- Riding association, political party

813940 Political Organizations US

See industry description for 81394, above.

81399 Other Membership Organizations US

This industry comprises establishments, not classified to any other industry, primarily engaged in promoting the interests of their members.

Example Activities
- Art councils
- Condominium owners' associations
- Property owners' association
- Sport leagues
- Tenant associations (except advocacy)

813990 Other Membership Organizations US

See industry description for 81399, above.

814 Private Households

See industry description for 81411, below.

8141 Private Households

See industry description for 81411, below.

81411 Private Households

This industry comprises private households engaged in employing workers, on or about the premises, in activities primarily concerned with the operation of the household. These private households may employ individuals such as cooks, maids and butlers, and outside workers, such as gardeners, caretakers and other maintenance workers. The services of individuals providing baby-sitting or nanny services are included.

Example Activities
- Babysitting (private households employing babysitters in their home)
- Baby-sitting in the child's home
- Domestic service (private households employing cooks, maids)
- Estates, private employing domestic personnel
- Household, private employing domestic personnel
- Live-in babysitter
- Live-in housekeeper
- Private households employing domestic personnel

814110 Private Households

See industry description for 81411, above.

91 Public Administration

This sector comprises establishments primarily engaged in activities of a governmental nature, that is, the enactment and judicial interpretation of laws and their pursuant regulations, and the administration of programs based on them. Legislative activities, taxation, national defence, public order and safety, immigration services, foreign affairs and international assistance, and the administration of government programs are activities that are purely governmental in nature.

Ownership is not a criterion for classification. Government owned establishments engaged in activities that are not governmental in nature are classified to the same industry as privately owned establishments engaged in similar activities.

Government establishments may engage in a combination of governmental and non-governmental activities. When separate records are not available to separate the activities that are not governmental in nature from those that are, the establishment is classified to this sector.

911 Federal Government Public Administration CAN

This subsector comprises establishments of the federal government primarily engaged in activities of a governmental nature, such as legislative activities, judicial activities, taxation, national defence, public order and safety, immigration services, foreign affairs and international assistance and the administration of government programs.

9111 Defence Services CAN

See industry description for 91111, below.

91111 Defence Services CAN

This industry comprises establishments of the Canadian Armed Forces and civilian agencies primarily engaged in providing defence services.

Example Activities
- Armed services
- Bases, military
- Civil defence services
- Defence research board, federal government
- Defence services, federal government
- Military bases and camps
- Military defence services
- Military messes (pf)
- Naval base
- Radar stations, defence

911110 Defence Services CAN

See industry description for 91111, above.

9112 Federal Protective Services CAN

This industry group comprises establishments of the federal government primarily engaged in providing services to ensure the security of persons and property. Protection includes measures to protect against negligence, exploitation and abuse.

91121 Federal Courts of Law CAN

This industry comprises establishments of the federal government primarily engaged in rendering judgements in, and interpretations of, the law, including the arbitration of civil actions. Appeal boards of federal jurisdiction are included.

Example Activities
- Administrative courts, federal government
- Chancery courts
- Court of appeal, federal government
- Courts of customs and patent appeals
- Exchequer court
- Federal court of law
- Supreme Court of Canada

911210 Federal Courts of Law CAN

See industry description for 91121, above.

91122 Federal Correctional Services CAN

This industry comprises establishments of the federal government primarily engaged in providing the incarceration and rehabilitation services of prisons and other detention establishments.

Example Activities
- Correctional services, federal government
- Detention centres, federal government
- Federal correctional services
- Parole services, federal government
- Penitentiary services, federal government

911220 Federal Correctional Services CAN

See industry description for 91122, above.

91123 Federal Police Services CAN

This industry comprises establishments of the federal government primarily engaged in maintaining law and order by means of operating police forces and services.

Exclusion(s): Establishments primarily engaged in:
- providing private police services (56161, Investigation, Guard and Armoured Car Services).

Example Activities
- Federal police services
- Royal Canadian Mounted Police

911230 Federal Police Services CAN

See industry description for 91123, above.

91124 Federal Regulatory Services CAN

This industry comprises establishments of the federal government primarily engaged in the general protection of individuals, singly or in groups, against negligence, exploitation or abuse.

Example Activities
- Federal regulatory services, general
- Occupational safety and health standards services, federal government
- Regulation and inspection of agricultural products
- Securities regulation commissions
- Work safety and health program administration, federal government

911240 Federal Regulatory Services CAN

See industry description for 91124, above.

91129 Other Federal Protective Services CAN

This industry comprises establishments of the federal government, not classified to any other industry, primarily engaged in dealing with major emergencies and catastrophes. Establishments primarily engaged in animal or pest control activities, or other federal protective services, are included.

Example Activities
- Animal quarantine service, federal government
- Emergency planning services, federal government
- Fishery inspection and protection services
- Fishery patrol service

911290 Other Federal Protective Services CAN

See industry description for 91129, above.

9113 Federal Labour, Employment and Immigration Services CAN

This industry group comprises establishments of the federal government primarily engaged in providing services for labour, employment, immigration, citizenship and the like.

91131 Federal Labour and Employment Services CAN

This industry comprises establishments of the federal government primarily engaged in labour market research and dealing in matters pertaining to employer-employee relations, including the promotion of improved working conditions and the provision of arbitration and conciliation services in collective bargaining.

Example Activities
- Arbitration services, federal government
- Conciliation and mediation services, federal government
- Employment services (placement counselling), federal government
- Industrial relations services, federal government
- Labour relations board, federal government
- Manpower program, federal (job placement)
- Mediation and conciliation services, federal

911310 Federal Labour and Employment Services CAN

See industry description for 91131, above.

91132 Immigration Services CAN

This industry comprises establishments of the federal government primarily engaged in promoting immigration, assisting immigrants and controlling the entry of individuals into the country.

Example Activities

- Deportation services
- Federal immigration services
- Immigration services, federal
- Refugee settlement, federal government
- Visitor admissions (tourists and temporary)

911320 Immigration Services CAN

See industry description for 91132, above.

91139 Other Federal Labour, Employment and Immigration Services CAN

This industry comprises establishments of federal government departments or agencies primarily engaged in activities that combine labour, employment and immigration services. Establishments primarily engaged in the registration of citizens and the promotion of citizen-oriented activities are included.

Example Activity

- Citizenship registration services, federal government

911390 Other Federal Labour, Employment and Immigration Services CAN

See industry description for 91139, above.

9114 Foreign Affairs and International Assistance CAN

See industry description for 91141, below.

91141 Foreign Affairs CAN

This industry comprises establishments of the federal government primarily engaged in promoting formal relations between the government of Canada and foreign countries.

Example Activities

- Consular service, federal government
- Diplomatic representation, federal
- Diplomatic services, federal government
- Embassies, federal government
- External affairs services, federal government
- International agency representation, federal
- International exchange services (scientific, academic), federal government
- Missions established in foreign countries, federal government
- Passport services
- State and official visits, organization of, federal government

911410 Foreign Affairs CAN

See industry description for 91141, above.

91142 International Assistance CAN

This industry comprises establishments of the federal government primarily engaged in economic development and improvement of social conditions in foreign countries.

Example Activities

- External aid services, federal government
- Food aid programs, federal government
- Foreign economic and social development services, federal government
- International development assistance, federal government

911420 International Assistance ^{CAN}

See industry description for 91142, above.

9119 Other Federal Government Public Administration ^{CAN}

See industry description for 91191, below.

91191 Other Federal Government Public Administration ^{CAN}

This industry comprises establishments of the federal government, not classified to any other industry, primarily engaged in executive and legislative activities; fiscal and related policies and the administration of the public debt; assessing, levying and collecting taxes; conducting relations with other governments; and the administration of programs.

Exclusion(s): Establishments primarily engaged in:
- railway operation (482, Rail Transportation);
- airport operation (48811, Airport Operations);
- port operation (48831, Port and Harbour Operations);
- archive or library operation (51912, Libraries and Archives);
- operating the Bank of Canada (52111, Monetary Authorities - Central Bank);
- operating schools and local school boards (61, Educational Services);
- hospital operation (622, Hospitals);
- residential care facility operation (623, Nursing and Residential Care Facilities); and
- museum and art gallery operation (71211, Museums).

Example Activities
- Agricultural extension services, federal government
- Air transport program, federal government
- Amateur sports program, federal government
- Arts and cultural programs, federal government
- Atomic Energy Commission (except inspection and defence)
- Auditor General's office, federal government
- Civil rights commissions, federal government
- Civil service commissions, federal government
- Commissioner of Official Languages, federal government
- Communications policy planning, federal government
- Conservation and stabilization agencies, federal government
- Conservation authority, federal government
- Consumer and corporate affairs, federal government
- Councils of economic advisers
- Criminal justice statistics centres, federal government
- Culture and arts support programs, federal
- Customs tariff, federal government
- Duty/tax collection on goods, federal government
- Economic and fiscal policy, federal government
- Economic development agencies, federal government
- Economic research programs to improve performance and competitiveness, federal government
- Education programs for Indians and Eskimos, federal government
- Electoral offices, federal government
- Environment policy, programs, federal government
- Export development programs, federal government
- Federal Communications Commission
- Federal-provincial relations, federal government
- Financial affairs, federal government
- General economics statistics agencies, federal government
- Governor General's office
- Health and medical care programs, federal government
- Housing programs, federal government
- Human Rights Commission, federal government
- Indian affairs program, federal government

- National science foundation
- Natural resource conservation programs, federal government
- Old age security program, federal government
- Parliament, federal government
- Performing arts program, federal government
- Prime Minister's office, federal government
- Privy Council office
- Public Service Commission, federal government
- Public Service Staff Relations Board, federal government
- Public works programs, federal government

- Recreation policy and planning, federal government
- Regional industrial development programs, federal government
- Revenue ministry, federal government
- Senate
- Social development services, federal government
- Space research and development, federal government
- Taxation, federal government
- Tourism promotion programs, federal government
- Treasury board secretariat, federal government
- Veterans' benefits program, federal government

911910 Other Federal Government Public Administration CAN

See industry description for 91191, above.

912 Provincial and Territorial Public Administration CAN

This subsector comprises establishments of provincial or territorial governments primarily engaged in activities of a governmental nature, such as legislative activities, judicial activities, taxation, public order and safety, and the administration of provincial or territorial government programs.

9121 Provincial Protective Services CAN

This industry group comprises establishments of provincial and territorial governments primarily engaged in providing services to ensure the security of persons and property. Protection includes measures to protect against negligence, exploitation and abuse.

91211 Provincial Courts of Law CAN

This industry comprises establishments of provincial and territorial governments primarily engaged in rendering judgements in, and interpretations of, the law, including the arbitration of civil actions. Appeal boards of provincial jurisdiction are included.

Example Activities
- Administrative courts, provincial government
- Appeal courts, provincial government
- County courts
- Court of law, provincial government
- Courts, civil law, provincial government

- Courts, criminal law, provincial government
- Family courts
- Probate courts
- Provincial courts of law
- Small claims court provincial government

912110 Provincial Courts of Law CAN

See industry description for 91211, above.

91212 Provincial Correctional Services CAN

This industry comprises establishments of provincial and territorial governments primarily engaged in providing the incarceration and rehabilitation services of jails, and operating other detention establishments.

Example Activities

- Correctional school, provincial government
- Detention centres, provincial government
- Industrial school, provincial government (reform school)
- Jails, provincial government
- Parole offices, provincial

- Penitentiaries, provincial government
- Provincial correctional services
- Reformatories, provincial government
- Rehabilitation services, provincial government (correctional)

912120 Provincial Correctional Services ^{CAN}

See industry description for 91212, above.

91213 Provincial Police Services ^{CAN}

This industry comprises establishments of provincial and territorial governments primarily engaged in maintaining law and order by means of operating police forces and services.

Exclusion(s): Establishments primarily engaged in:
- providing private police services (56161, Investigation, Guard and Armoured Car Services).

Example Activities
- Police forces, provincial government

- Provincial police services

912130 Provincial Police Services ^{CAN}

See industry description for 91213, above.

91214 Provincial Fire-Fighting Services ^{CAN}

This industry comprises establishments of provincial and territorial governments primarily engaged in the prevention, investigation and extinction of fires.

Example Activities
- Fire investigation service, provincial government
- Fire marshals office, provincial government

- Fire prevention programs, provincial government
- Fire-fighting services, provincial government

912140 Provincial Fire-Fighting Services ^{CAN}

See industry description for 91214, above.

91215 Provincial Regulatory Services ^{CAN}

This industry comprises establishments of provincial and territorial governments primarily engaged in the general protection of individuals, singly or in groups, against negligence, exploitation or abuse.

Example Activities
- Alcoholic beverage control boards, provincial government
- Occupational safety and health standards services, provincial government

- Regulatory services, general, provincial government
- Rent control agencies, provincial government

912150 Provincial Regulatory Services ^{CAN}

See industry description for 91215, above.

91219 Other Provincial Protective Services ^{CAN}

This industry comprises establishments of provincial and territorial governments, not classified to any other industry, primarily engaged in dealing with major emergencies and catastrophes. Establishments primarily engaged in animal or pest control activities, or other provincial protection services, are included.

Example Activities
- Emergency measures organizations, provincial government
- Emergency program services, provincial

912190 Other Provincial Protective Services ^{CAN}

See industry description for 91219, above.

9122 Provincial Labour and Employment Services ^{CAN}

See industry description for 91221, below.

91221 Provincial Labour and Employment Services ^{CAN}

This industry comprises establishments of provincial and territorial governments primarily engaged in labour market research and dealing in matters pertaining to employer-employee relations, including the promotion of improved working conditions and the provision of arbitration and conciliation services in collective bargaining.

Example Activities
- Arbitration services, provincial government
- Employment counselling service, provincial government
- Industrial relations services, provincial government
- Manpower employer services, provincial government
- Mediation and conciliation services, provincial government

912210 Provincial Labour and Employment Services ^{CAN}

See industry description for 91221, above.

9129 Other Provincial and Territorial Public Administration ^{CAN}

See industry description for 91291, below.

91291 Other Provincial and Territorial Public Administration ^{CAN}

This industry comprises establishments of provincial and territorial governments, not classified to any other industry, primarily engaged in executive and legislative activities; fiscal and related policies and the administration of the public debt; assessing, levying and collecting taxes; conducting relations with other governments; and the administration of provincial and territorial government programs.

Exclusion(s): Establishments primarily engaged in:

- electricity generation and distribution (2211, Electric Power Generation, Transmission and Distribution);
- water and sewer system operation (2213, Water, Sewage and Other Systems);
- railway operation (482, Rail Transportation);
- urban transit system operation (48511, Urban Transit Systems);
- airport operation (48811, Airport Operations);
- port operation (48831, Port and Harbour Operations);
- archive or library operation (51912, Libraries and Archives);
- garbage collection and disposal (562, Waste Management and Remediation Services);
- operating schools and local school boards (61, Educational Services);
- providing ambulatory health care services (621, Ambulatory Health Care Services);
- hospital operation (622, Hospitals);
- residential care facility operation (623, Nursing and Residential Care Facilities); and
- museum and art gallery operation (71211, Museums).

Example Activities

- Adult and recreational education programs, provincial government
- Agriculture and forestry programs, provincial government
- Auditor's office, provincial government
- Community social service programs, provincial government
- Consumer and corporate affairs, provincial government
- Cultural affairs programs, provincial government
- Electoral offices, provincial government
- Energy resources programs, provincial government
- Environmental control programs, provincial government
- Family welfare programs, provincial government
- Fisheries support programs, provincial government
- Game and inland fish agencies, provincial government
- General economics statistics agencies, provincial
- Health programs, provincial government
- Highway and transport programs, provincial government
- Hospital and medical insurance plans, provincial government
- Housing programs, provincial government
- Human Rights Commission, provincial government
- Interprovincial relations, provincial government
- Legislative assemblies, provincial government
- License plate issuer (government office), provincial government
- Lieutenant-Governor's office, provincial government
- Mineral resources programs, provincial government
- Motor vehicle license bureau, provincial government
- Municipal affairs, provincial government
- National Assembly, provincial government
- Official languages office, provincial government
- Ombudsman's office, provincial government
- Parks commission, provincial government
- Provincial-federal fiscal relations, provincial government
- Provincial-federal relations, provincial government
- Public health service programs, provincial government
- Public Service Commission, provincial government
- Public utility commissions, provincial government
- Public welfare assistance programs, provincial government
- Purchasing services, provincial government
- Revenue ministry, provincial government
- Sales tax collection, provincial government
- Small business support programs, provincial government
- Tourism development programs, provincial government
- Transportation and communications, provincial government
- Wildlife conservation programs, provincial government

912910 Other Provincial and Territorial Public Administration ^{CAN} CAN

See industry description for 91291, above.

913 Local, Municipal and Regional Public Administration ^{CAN} CAN

This subsector comprises establishments of local governments primarily engaged in activities of a governmental nature, such as legislative activities, taxation, public order and safety, and the administration of local government programs.

9131 Municipal Protective Services CAN

This industry group comprises establishments of local governments primarily engaged in providing services to ensure the security of persons and property. Protection includes measures to protect against negligence, exploitation and abuse.

91311 Municipal Courts of Law CAN

This industry comprises establishments of local governments primarily engaged in rendering judgements in, and interpretations of, the law including the arbitration of civil actions.

Example Activities
- City courts
- Court, municipal government

- Juvenile courts
- Municipal courts

913110 Municipal Courts of Law CAN

See industry description for 91311, above.

91312 Municipal Correctional Services CAN

This industry comprises establishments of local governments primarily engaged in providing incarceration and rehabilitation services of jails and other detention establishments.

Example Activities
- Detention centres, municipal/local

- Municipal correctional services

913120 Municipal Correctional Services CAN

See industry description for 91312, above.

91313 Municipal Police Services CAN

This industry comprises establishments of local governments primarily engaged in maintaining law and order by means of operating police forces and services.

Exclusion(s): Establishments primarily engaged in:
- providing private police services (56161, Investigation, Guard and Armoured Car Services).

Example Activities
- 911 emergency services
- Municipal police services

- Police force, municipal
- Urban community police force

913130 Municipal Police Services CAN

See industry description for 91313, above.

91314 Municipal Fire-Fighting Services CAN

This industry comprises establishments of local governments primarily engaged in the prevention, investigation and extinction of fires.

Example Activities
- Fire department, local government
- Fire investigating service, local government
- Municipal fire-fighting services
- Volunteer fire-fighter

913140 Municipal Fire-Fighting Services CAN

See industry description for 91314, above.

91315 Municipal Regulatory Services CAN

This industry comprises establishments of local governments primarily engaged in the general protection of individuals, singly or in groups, against negligence, exploitation or abuse.

Example Activities
- City solicitor
- Municipal regulatory services, general

913150 Municipal Regulatory Services CAN

See industry description for 91315, above.

91319 Other Municipal Protective Services CAN

This industry comprises establishments of local governments, not classified to any other industry, primarily engaged in dealing with major emergencies and catastrophes. Establishments primarily engaged in animal or pest control activities or other municipal protective services are included.

Example Activity
- Emergency measures organization services, local government

913190 Other Municipal Protective Services CAN

See industry description for 91319, above.

9139 Other Local, Municipal and Regional Public Administration CAN

See industry description for 91391, below.

91391 Other Local, Municipal and Regional Public Administration CAN

This industry comprises establishments of local governments, not classified to any other industry, primarily engaged in executive and legislative activities; planning, fiscal and related policies and the administration of the public debt; assessing, levying and collecting taxes; conducting relations with other governments; and the administration of local, municipal, and regional government programs.

Exclusion(s): Establishments primarily engaged in:
- electricity generation and distribution (2211, Electric Power Generation, Transmission and Distribution);
- water and sewer system operation (2213, Water, Sewage and Other Systems);
- railway operation (482, Rail Transportation);
- urban transit system operation (48511, Urban Transit Systems);
- airport operation (48811, Airport Operations);
- port operation (48831, Port and Harbour Operations);
- archive or library operation (51912, Libraries and Archives);
- garbage collection and disposal (562, Waste Management and Remediation Services);
- operating schools and local school boards (61, Educational Services);
- providing ambulatory health care services (621, Ambulatory Health Care Services);
- hospital operation (622, Hospitals);
- residential care facility operation (623, Nursing and Residential Care Facilities); and
- museum and art gallery operation (71211, Museums).

Example Activities
- City and town councils
- Community development agencies, local government
- Community health programs, local government
- Community social service programs, local government
- Housing programs, local government
- Mayor's office
- Municipal board/council
- Parks and recreation commission, municipal government
- Recreation programs, municipal administration
- Regional board/council, local government
- Tax collection, local administration
- Tourist information, local government
- Urban community council

913910 Other Local, Municipal and Regional Public Administration ^{CAN}

See industry description for 91391, above.

914 Aboriginal Public Administration ^{CAN}

See industry description for 91411, below.

9141 Aboriginal Public Administration ^{CAN}

See industry description for 91411, below.

91411 Aboriginal Public Administration ^{CAN}

This industry comprises establishments of aboriginal governments primarily engaged in providing to their constituents, a wide variety of government services that would otherwise be provided by federal, provincial or municipal levels of governments.

Example Activities
- Aboriginal administration, public
- Indian band or tribe council

914110 Aboriginal Public Administration ^{CAN}

See industry description for 91411, above.

919 International and Other Extra-Territorial Public Administration ^{CAN}

See industry description for 91911, below.

9191 International and Other Extra-Territorial Public Administration ^{CAN}

See industry description for 91911, below.

91911 International and Other Extra-Territorial Public Administration ^{CAN}

This industry comprises establishments of foreign governments in Canada, primarily engaged in governmental service activities, such as consular, diplomatic and legation activities.

Exclusion(s):
- Commonwealth and foreign establishments, engaged in activities such as air transportation, and cable and wireless services (classified to the appropriate industries).

Example Activities
- Consular service, foreign government in Canada
- Embassy, foreign governments in Canada
- Foreign government service, office in Canada
- International Monetary Fund, office in Canada
- Legation services, foreign government in Canada

919110 International and Other Extra-Territorial Public Administration ^{CAN}

See industry description for 91911, above.

Concordance Tables

Concordance Tables

Concordance Tables for NAICS Canada 2007

The concordance tables presented here for NAICS Canada 2007 show the relationship between NAICS 2002 and NAICS 2007 for those areas of the classification which have changed. Areas of the classification that have not changed are not covered by the tables presented here.

The first table shows the relationship of NAICS 2007 to NAICS 2002. It presents the concordance in the order of NAICS 2007, with the NAICS 2007 code shown on the left side of the table.

The second table shows the relationship of NAICS 2002 to NAICS 2007. It presents the concordance in the order of NAICS 2002, with the NAICS 2002 code shown on the left side of the table.

The tables are at the 6-digit level of NAICS Canada and have been constructed based on business activity descriptions that have been coded to both classifications. Links deemed to be insignificant have been omitted from these tables.

The two tables, taken together, provide a cross-reference of the relationship between the two classifications and provide information that is useful when converting data from one classification to the other.

How to Read the Concordance Tables

Below are examples illustrating types of situations found in these tables. The examples are taken from Tables 1 and 2.

Example 1: The NAICS 2002 and NAICS 2007 classes are identical, only the title has changed.

NAICS 2002	NAICS 2007	Explanatory Notes
238210, Electrical Contractors	238210, Electrical Contractors and Other Wiring Installation Contractors	

Example 2: A class in one classification is exactly equivalent to more than one class in the other classification.

NAICS 2007	NAICS 2002	Explanatory Notes
519130, Internet Publishing and Broadcasting and Web Search Portals	516110, Internet Publishing and Broadcasting	
	518112, Web Search Portals	

Example 3: A class in one classification is equivalent to part of a class in the other classification.

When the concordance relates one class on the left to only part of a class on the right, this partial relationship is denoted by an asterisk (*) against the code on the right.

The asterisk marked class will reappear in the table against all the other classes on the left to which it also partially relates.

Whenever an asterisk appears, there is an explanatory note. The note specifies the particular piece of the right-hand side class that is accounted for by the class on the left-hand side. In some cases, for brevity, the note begins with the word "Except". In those cases, the note is to be interpreted as indicating that all of the contents of the right-hand side class are accounted for by the left-hand side class, except for the particular piece that is specified, which is accounted for by one or more other left-hand side classes.

NAICS 2007	NAICS 2002	Explanatory Notes
339110, Medical Equipment and Supplies Manufacturing	339110*, Medical Equipment and Supplies Manufacturing	Except laboratory furniture, scales, balances, furnaces, ovens, centrifuges, distilling equipment and freezers

Example 4: A class in one classification is linked to more than one class in the other classification.

NAICS 2002	NAICS 2007	Explanatory Notes
518111, Internet Service Providers	517111*, Wired Telecommunications Carriers (except Cable)	Broadband Internet service providers, DSL
	517112*, Cable and Other Program Distribution	Broadband Internet service providers, cable
	517910*, Other Telecommunications	ISPs providing services via client-supplied telecommunications connections

Example 5: A class in one classification is linked to more than one class in the other classification, sometimes accounting for the entire class and sometimes only part of it.

NAICS 2002	NAICS 2007	Explanatory Notes
339110, Medical Equipment and Supplies Manufacturing	333299*, All Other Industrial Machinery Manufacturing	Laboratory distilling equipment
	333416*, Heating Equipment and Commercial Refrigeration Equipment Manufacturing	Laboratory freezers
	333990*, All Other General-Purpose Machinery Manufacturing	Laboratory furnaces and ovens, scales and balances, and centrifuges
	337127*, Institutional Furniture Manufacturing	Laboratory furniture (e.g., stools, tables, benches)
	339110, Medical Equipment and Supplies Manufacturing	

Users are cautioned that data coded to one classification cannot automatically be converted to the other with the help of these concordance tables.

Data can be automatically converted from the codes of one classification to the codes of the other for those classes that are identical. For the rest, in order to convert records relating to businesses or establishments from one classification to the other, it is necessary to know the principal activity of the business or establishment and to recode each one to the other classification with the help of the explanatory notes of the concordance or with the help of a detailed alphabetical index of activity descriptions coded to both classifications. A short index is provided in this manual; however, a much more detailed index of activity descriptions is available from:

Statistics Canada
Standards Division
Jean Talon Bldg., 12th Floor
170 Tunney's Pasture Driveway
Ottawa (Ontario)
K1A OT6
Tel.: 613-951-8576
Fax: 613-951-8578
E-mail: standards@statcan.ca
Website: www.statcan.ca

NAICS 2007 to NAICS 2002

NAICS 2007	NAICS 2002	Explanatory Notes
111211, Potato Farming	111211, Potato Farming	
	111219*, Other Vegetable (except Potato) and Melon Farming	Sweet potato and yam farming
111219, Other Vegetable (except Potato) and Melon Farming	111219*, Other Vegetable (except Potato) and Melon Farming	Except sweet potato and yam farming
111994, Maple Syrup and Products Production	111999*, All Other Miscellaneous Crop Farming	Maple syrup and products production
111999, All Other Miscellaneous Crop Farming	111999*, All Other Miscellaneous Crop Farming	Except maple syrup and products production; algae and sea weed farming
112510, Aquaculture	111999*, All Other Miscellaneous Crop Farming	Algae and sea weed farming
	112510, Animal Aquaculture	
238210, Electrical Contractors and Other Wiring Installation Contractors	238210, Electrical Contractors	
311515, Butter, Cheese, and Dry and Condensed Dairy Product Manufacturing	311515, Butter, Cheese, and Dry and Condensed Dairy Products Manufacturing	
314990, All Other Textile Product Mills	314990, All Other Textile Product Mills	
	315210*, Cut and Sew Clothing Contracting	Embroidery contractors
315210, Cut and Sew Clothing Contracting	315210*, Cut and Sew Clothing Contracting	Except embroidery contractors
324190, Other Petroleum and Coal Product Manufacturing	32419, Other Petroleum and Coal Products Manufacturing	
326111, Plastic Bag and Pouch Manufacturing	326111, Plastics Bag Manufacturing	
326121, Unlaminated Plastic Profile Shape Manufacturing	326121, Unlaminated Plastics Profile Shape Manufacturing	
326130, Laminated Plastic Plate, Sheet (except Packaging), and Shape Manufacturing	326130, Laminated Plastics Plate, Sheet (except Packaging), and Shape Manufacturing	
326196, Plastic Window and Door Manufacturing	326198*, All Other Plastic Product Manufacturing	Plastic window and door manufacturing

NAICS 2007	NAICS 2002	Explanatory Notes
326198, All Other Plastic Product Manufacturing	326198*, All Other Plastic Product Manufacturing	Except plastic window and door manufacturing; inflatable plastic boats manufacturing
326290, Other Rubber Product Manufacturing	326290*, Other Rubber Product Manufacturing	Except inflatable rubber boats manufacturing
332329, Other Ornamental and Architectural Metal Product Manufacturing	332329, Other Ornamental and Architectural Metal Products Manufacturing	
333299, All Other Industrial Machinery Manufacturing	333299, All Other Industrial Machinery Manufacturing	
	339110*, Medical Equipment and Supplies Manufacturing	Laboratory distilling equipment
333416, Heating Equipment and Commercial Refrigeration Equipment Manufacturing	333416, Heating Equipment and Commercial Refrigeration Equipment Manufacturing	
	339110*, Medical Equipment and Supplies Manufacturing	Laboratory freezers
333990, All Other General-Purpose Machinery Manufacturing	333990, All Other General-Purpose Machinery Manufacturing	
	339110*, Medical Equipment and Supplies Manufacturing	Laboratory furnaces and ovens, scales and balances, and centrifuges
336612, Boat Building	326198*, All Other Plastic Product Manufacturing	Inflatable plastic boats manufacturing
	326290*, Other Rubber Product Manufacturing	Inflatable rubber boats manufacturing
	336612, Boat Building	
337127, Institutional Furniture Manufacturing	337127, Institutional Furniture Manufacturing	
	339110*, Medical Equipment and Supplies Manufacturing	Laboratory furniture (e.g., stools, tables, benches)
339110, Medical Equipment and Supplies Manufacturing	339110*, Medical Equipment and Supplies Manufacturing	Except laboratory furniture, scales, balances, furnaces, ovens, centrifuges, distilling equipment and freezers
414390, Other Home Furnishings Wholesaler-Distributors	414390, Other Home Furnishings Wholesaler-Distributors	
	416330*, Hardware Wholesaler-Distributors	Household cutlery; pots and pans, wholesale

NAICS 2007	NAICS 2002	Explanatory Notes
416330, Hardware Wholesaler-Distributors	416330*, Hardware Wholesaler-Distributors	Except household cutlery; pots and pans, wholesale
419110, Business-to-Business Electronic Markets	419190*, Other Wholesale Agents and Brokers	Business-to-business (B2B) electronic markets, wholesale
419120, Wholesale Trade Agents and Brokers	419110, Farm Product Agents and Brokers	
	419120, Petroleum Product Agents and Brokers	
	419130, Food, Beverage and Tobacco Agents and Brokers	
	419140, Personal and Household Goods Agents and Brokers	
	419150, Motor Vehicle and Parts Agents and Brokers	
	419160, Building Material and Supplies Agents and Brokers	
	419170, Machinery, Equipment and Supplies Agents and Brokers	
	419190*, Other Wholesale Agents and Brokers	Except business-to-business (B2B) electronic markets, wholesale
454111, Internet Shopping	454110*, Electronic Shopping and Mail-Order Houses	Electronic shopping
454112, Electronic Auctions	454110*, Electronic Shopping and Mail-Order Houses	Electronic auctions
454113, Mail-Order Houses	454110*, Electronic Shopping and Mail-Order Houses	Mail-order houses
454311, Heating Oil Dealers	454310*, Fuel Dealers	Heating oil dealers
454312, Liquefied Petroleum Gas (Bottled Gas) Dealers	454310*, Fuel Dealers	Liquefied petroleum gas (bottled gas) dealers
454319, Other Fuel Dealers	454310*, Fuel Dealers	Other fuel dealers
517111, Wired Telecommunications Carriers (except Cable)	517110, Wired Telecommunications Carriers	
	518111*, Internet Service Providers	Broadband Internet service providers, DSL
517112, Cable and Other Program Distribution	517510, Cable and Other Program Distribution	

NAICS 2007	NAICS 2002	Explanatory Notes
	518111*, Internet Service Providers	Broadband Internet service providers, cable
517910, Other Telecommunications	517310, Telecommunications Resellers	
	517910, Other Telecommunications	
	518111*, Internet Service Providers	ISPs providing services via client-supplied telecommunications connections
519130, Internet Publishing and Broadcasting, and Web Search Portals	516110, Internet Publishing and Broadcasting	
	518112, Web Search Portals	
526989, All Other Miscellaneous Funds and Financial Vehicles	526920*, Mortgage Investment Funds	Except Real Estate Investment Trusts (REIT's)
	526989, All Other Miscellaneous Funds and Financial Vehicles	
531111, Lessors of Residential Buildings and Dwellings (except Social Housing Projects)	526920*, Mortgage Investment Funds	Real Estate Investment Trusts (REIT's), operating residential buildings, except social housing
	531111, Lessors of Residential Buildings and Dwellings (except Social Housing Projects)	
531120, Lessors of Non-Residential Buildings (except Mini-Warehouses)	526920*, Mortgage Investment Funds	Real Estate Investment Trusts (REIT's), operating non-residential buildings (except mini-warehouses)
	531120, Lessors of Non-Residential Buildings (except Mini-Warehouses)	
531130, Self-Storage Mini-Warehouses	526920*, Mortgage Investment Funds	Real Estate Investment Trusts (REIT's), operating self-storage mini-warehouses
	531130, Self-Storage Mini-Warehouses	
531190, Lessors of Other Real Estate Property	526920*, Mortgage Investment Funds	Real Estate Investment Trusts (REIT's), operating real estate other than buildings
	531190, Lessors of Other Real Estate Property	
531211, Real Estate Agents	531210*, Offices of Real Estate Agents and Brokers	Real estate agents
531212, Offices of Real Estate Brokers	531210*, Offices of Real Estate Agents and Brokers	Real estate brokers

NAICS 2007	NAICS 2002	Explanatory Notes
541612, Human Resources Consulting Services	541612*, Human Resource and Executive Search Consulting Services	Except executive search consulting services
561310, Employment Placement Agencies and Executive Search Services	541612*, Human Resource and Executive Search Consulting Services	Executive search consulting services
	561310, Employment Placement Agencies	
711511, Independent Artists, Visual Arts	711510*, Independent Artists, Writers and Performers	Independent visual arts artists
711512, Independent Actors, Comedians and Performers	711510*, Independent Artists, Writers and Performers	Independent actors, comedians and performers
711513, Independent Writers and Authors	711510*, Independent Artists, Writers and Performers	Independent writers and authors
712115, History and Science Museums	712119*, Museums (except Art Museums and Galleries)	History and science museums
712119, Other Museums	712119*, Museums (except Art Museums and Galleries)	Other museums n.e.c.
712190, Nature Parks and Other Similar Institutions	712190, Other Heritage Institutions	

NAICS 2002 to NAICS 2007

NAICS 2002	NAICS 2007	Explanatory Notes
111211, Potato Farming	111211*, Potato Farming	Except sweet potato and yam farming
111219, Other Vegetable (except Potato) and Melon Farming	111211*, Potato Farming	Sweet potato and yam farming
	111219, Other Vegetable (except Potato) and Melon Farming	
111999, All Other Miscellaneous Crop Farming	111994, Maple Syrup and Products Production	
	111999, All Other Miscellaneous Crop Farming	
	112510*, Aquaculture	Algae and sea weed farming
112510, Animal Aquaculture	112510*, Aquaculture	Except algae and sea weed farming
238210, Electrical Contractors	238210, Electrical Contractors and Other Wiring Installation Contractors	
311515, Butter, Cheese, and Dry and Condensed Dairy Products Manufacturing	311515, Butter, Cheese, and Dry and Condensed Dairy Product Manufacturing	
314990, All Other Textile Product Mills	314990*, All Other Textile Product Mills	Except embroidery contractors
315210, Cut and Sew Clothing Contracting	314990*, All Other Textile Product Mills	Embroidery contractors
	315210, Cut and Sew Clothing Contracting	
324190, Other Petroleum and Coal Products Manufacturing	32419, Other Petroleum and Coal Product Manufacturing	
326111, Plastics Bag Manufacturing	326111, Plastic Bag and Pouch Manufacturing	
326121, Unlaminated Plastics Profile Shape Manufacturing	326121, Unlaminated Plastic Profile Shape Manufacturing	
326130, Laminated Plastics Plate, Sheet (except Packaging), and Shape Manufacturing	326130, Laminated Plastic Plate, Sheet (except Packaging), and Shape Manufacturing	
326198, All Other Plastic Product Manufacturing	326196, Plastic Window and Door Manufacturing	

NAICS 2002	NAICS 2007	Explanatory Notes
	326198, All Other Plastic Product Manufacturing	
	336612*, Boat Building	Inflatable plastic boats manufacturing
326290, Other Rubber Product Manufacturing	326290, Other Rubber Product Manufacturing	
	336612*, Boat Building	Inflatable rubber boats manufacturing
332329, Other Ornamental and Architectural Metal Products Manufacturing	332329, Other Ornamental and Architectural Metal Product Manufacturing	
333299, All Other Industrial Machinery Manufacturing	333299*, All Other Industrial Machinery Manufacturing	Except laboratory distilling equipment
333416, Heating Equipment and Commercial Refrigeration Equipment Manufacturing	333416*, Heating Equipment and Commercial Refrigeration Equipment Manufacturing	Except laboratory freezers
333990, All Other General-Purpose Machinery Manufacturing	333990*, All Other General-Purpose Machinery Manufacturing	Except laboratory furnaces and ovens, scales and balances, and centrifuges
336612, Boat Building	336612*, Boat Building	Except inflatable rubber boats manufacturing, inflatable plastic boats manufacturing
337127, Institutional Furniture Manufacturing	337127*, Institutional Furniture Manufacturing	Except laboratory furniture (e.g., stools, tables, benches)
339110, Medical Equipment and Supplies Manufacturing	333299*, All Other Industrial Machinery Manufacturing	Laboratory distilling equipment
	333416*, Heating Equipment and Commercial Refrigeration Equipment Manufacturing	Laboratory freezers
	333990*, All Other General-Purpose Machinery Manufacturing	Laboratory furnaces and ovens, scales and balances, and centrifuges
	337127*, Institutional Furniture Manufacturing	Laboratory furniture (e.g., stools, tables, benches)
	339110, Medical Equipment and Supplies Manufacturing	
414390, Other Home Furnishings Wholesaler-Distributors	414390*, Other Home Furnishings Wholesaler-Distributors	Except household cutlery; pots and pans, wholesale
416330, Hardware Wholesaler-Distributors	414390*, Other Home Furnishings Wholesaler-Distributors	Household cutlery; pots and pans, wholesale

NAICS 2002	NAICS 2007	Explanatory Notes
	416330, Hardware Wholesaler-Distributors	
419110, Farm Product Agents and Brokers	419120*, Wholesale Trade Agents and Brokers	Farm products (other than livestock and grain), wholesale agents and brokers
419120, Petroleum Product Agents and Brokers	419120*, Wholesale Trade Agents and Brokers	Petroleum products, wholesale agents and brokers
419130, Food, Beverage and Tobacco Agents and Brokers	419120*, Wholesale Trade Agents and Brokers	Food, Beverage and Tobacco Agents and Brokers
419140, Personal and Household Goods Agents and Brokers	419120*, Wholesale Trade Agents and Brokers	Personal and Household Goods Agents and Brokers
419150, Motor Vehicle and Parts Agents and Brokers	419120*, Wholesale Trade Agents and Brokers	Motor vehicles and parts (except automobiles, trucks and buses), wholesale agents and brokers
419160, Building Material and Supplies Agents and Brokers	419120*, Wholesale Trade Agents and Brokers	Building Material and Supplies Agents and Brokers
419170, Machinery, Equipment and Supplies Agents and Brokers	419120*, Wholesale Trade Agents and Brokers	Machinery, equipment and supplies n.e.c., wholesale agents and brokers
419190, Other Wholesale Agents and Brokers	419110, Business-to-Business Electronic Markets	
	419120*, Wholesale Trade Agents and Brokers	Except business-to-business (B2B) electronic markets, wholesale
454110, Electronic Shopping and Mail-Order Houses	454111, Internet Shopping	
	454112, Electronic Auctions	
	454113, Mail-Order Houses	
454310, Fuel Dealers	454311, Heating Oil Dealers	
	454312, Liquefied Petroleum Gas (Bottled Gas) Dealers	
	454319, Other Fuel Dealers	
516110, Internet Publishing and Broadcasting	519130*, Internet Publishing and Broadcasting, and Web Search Portals	Internet Publishing and Broadcasting
517110, Wired Telecommunications Carriers	517111*, Wired Telecommunications Carriers (except Cable)	Except broadband Internet service providers, DSL
517310, Telecommunications Resellers	517910*, Other Telecommunications	Telecommunications Resellers

NAICS 2002	NAICS 2007	Explanatory Notes
517510, Cable and Other Program Distribution	517112*, Cable and Other Program Distribution	Except broadband Internet service providers, cable
517910, Other Telecommunications	517910*, Other Telecommunications	Other Telecommunications n.e.c.
518111, Internet Service Providers	517111*, Wired Telecommunications Carriers (except Cable)	Broadband Internet service providers, DSL
	517112*, Cable and Other Program Distribution	Broadband Internet service providers, cable
	517910*, Other Telecommunications	ISPs providing services via client-supplied telecommunications connections
518112, Web Search Portals	519130*, Internet Publishing and Broadcasting, and Web Search Portals	Web Search Portals
526920, Mortgage Investment Funds	526989*, All Other Miscellaneous Funds and Financial Vehicles	Except Real Estate Investment Trusts (REIT's)
	531111*, Lessors of Residential Buildings and Dwellings (except Social Housing Projects)	Real Estate Investment Trusts (REIT's), operating residential buildings, except social housing
	531120*, Lessors of Non-Residential Buildings (except Mini-Warehouses)	Real Estate Investment Trusts (REIT's), operating non-residential buildings (except mini-warehouses)
	531130*, Self-Storage Mini-Warehouses	Real Estate Investment Trusts (REIT's), operating self-storage mini-warehouses
	531190*, Lessors of Other Real Estate Property	Real Estate Investment Trustss (REIT's), operating real estate other than buildings
526989, All Other Miscellaneous Funds and Financial Vehicles	526989*, All Other Miscellaneous Funds and Financial Vehicles	Except Real Estate Investment Trusts (REIT's)
531111, Lessors of Residential Buildings and Dwellings (except Social Housing Projects)	531111*, Lessors of Residential Buildings and Dwellings (except Social Housing Projects)	Except Real Estate Investment Trusts (REIT's), operating residential buildings, except social housing
531120, Lessors of Non-Residential Buildings (except Mini-Warehouses)	531120*, Lessors of Non-Residential Buildings (except Mini-Warehouses)	Except Real Estate Investment Trusts (REIT's), operating non-residential buildings (except mini-warehouses)
531130, Self-Storage Mini-Warehouses	531130*, Self-Storage Mini-Warehouses	Except Real Estate Investment Trusts (REIT's), operating self-storage mini-warehouses
531190, Lessors of Other Real Estate Property	531190*, Lessors of Other Real Estate Property	Except Real Estate Investment Trusts (REIT's), operating real estate other than buildings

NAICS 2002	NAICS 2007	Explanatory Notes
531210, Offices of Real Estate Agents and Brokers	531211, Real Estate Agents	
	531212, Offices of Real Estate Brokers	
541612, Human Resource and Executive Search Consulting Services	541612, Human Resources Consulting Services	
	561310*, Employment Placement Agencies and Executive Search Services	Executive search consulting services
561310, Employment Placement Agencies	561310*, Employment Placement Agencies and Executive Search Services	Except executive search consulting services
711510, Independent Artists, Writers and Performers	711511, Independent Artists, Visual Arts	
	711512, Independent Actors, Comedians and Performers	
	711513, Independent Writers and Authors	
712119, Museums (except Art Museums and Galleries)	712115, History and Science Museums	
	712119, Other Museums	
712190, Other Heritage Institutions	712190, Nature Parks and Other Similar Institutions	

Short Titles

Short Titles

Standard Short Titles for NAICS Canada are shown below in numerical order. They have been created for use when space limitations preclude the use of the full title for the dissemination of data classified to NAICS Canada. The adoption of these titles is recommended in all cases when the full title cannot be used.

The standard short titles listed below have been limited to 45 spaces for English titles and 47 spaces for French titles. If the official full title falls within 45 spaces, it generally remains unchanged. (Some exceptions occur, such as "&" for "and" and "mfg" for "Manufacturing"). If it exceeds 45 spaces, standard abbreviations have been used.

When space limitations do not permit the use of the standard 45 English and 47 French spaces for short titles, users may have to reduce them further. In such cases, when data are disseminated, it should be mentioned that the short titles used differ from Statistics Canada's standard short titles, and an explanation of how the short titles differ from the standard should be provided.

It should be noted that these short titles produced for NAICS Canada may differ from the short titles produced for NAICS US and NAICS Mexico.

Abbreviations Used in the Short Titles

-A-

accessories	access.
activities	act.
administrative	admin.
agricultural	agr.
air-conditioning	AC
aluminum	Al
and	&
appliance	appl.
architectural	arch.
automotive	auto.

-B-

broadcasting	brdcst.

-C-

chemical	chem.
coin-operated	coin-op.
communications	com.
compact disc	CD
components	comp.
condensed	cond.
construction	con.
copper	Cu

-D-

database	DB
distribution	dist.

-E-

electric(al)	elect.
emergency	emerg.
employment	employ.
engineering	eng.
equipment	eqp.
establishment	est.
except	exc.
executive	exec.
extraction	extr.

-F-

fabricated	fab.
facilities	fac.
federal	fed.
financial	fin.
for	-

-G-

gasoline	gas.
general	gen.

-H-

household	hhld.

-I-

immigration	immig.
including	inc.
industrial	ind'l
industries	ind.
institutional	inst.
intermediation	intermed.
international	intl.

-J-

Jacket	jkt.

-L-

less than	<
less than truck-load	LTL
long distance	LDist.

-M-

machinery	mach.
made from purchased	mfp.
management	mgmt.
manufacturing	mfg.
materials	mtl.
membership	member.
mini-warehouses	mini-ware
miscellaneous	misc.
motor vehicle	MV

-N-

navigational	navig.
non-metallic	non-met.
non-residential	non-res.
not elsewhere classified	n.e.c.

-O-

of	-
operated	op.
organizations	orgs.
other	oth.

-P-

packaging	pack.
preparation	prep.
processing	process.
production	prod.
professional	prof.
provincial	prov.
psychiatric	psych.

-R-

recreational	rec.
recreational vehicle	RV
refrigeration	refrig.
religious	relig.
remediation	remed.
repair and maintenance	R&M
research and development	R&D
residential	res.

-S-

services	serv.
social	soc.

specialized	spec.
structural	struct.
supply	supp.
synthetic	synth.

-T-

technical	tech.
telecommunications	telecom.
territorial	terr.
transaction	transac.
transportation	trans.
treating	treat.
trucking	truck.

-V-

vacation	vac.
vegetable	veg.

-W-

wholesaler-distributor	whl.
without	w/o

11   Agriculture, Forestry, Fishing & Hunting

111   Crop Production

1111	Oilseed & Grain Farming
11111	Soybean Farming
111110	Soybean Farming
11112	Oilseed (exc. Soybean) Farming
111120	Oilseed (exc. Soybean) Farming
11113	Dry Pea & Bean Farming
111130	Dry Pea & Bean Farming
11114	Wheat Farming
111140	Wheat Farming
11115	Corn Farming
111150	Corn Farming
11116	Rice Farming
111160	Rice Farming
11119	Other Grain Farming
111190	Other Grain Farming
1112	Vegetable & Melon Farming
11121	Vegetable & Melon Farming
111211	Potato Farming
111219	Other Vegetable (exc. Potato) & Melon Farming
1113	Fruit & Tree Nut Farming
11131	Orange Groves
111310	Orange Groves
11132	Citrus (exc. Orange) Groves
111320	Citrus (exc. Orange) Groves
11133	Non-Citrus Fruit & Tree Nut Farming
111330	Non-Citrus Fruit & Tree Nut Farming
1114	Greenhouse, Nursery & Floriculture Production
11141	Food Crops Grown Under Cover
111411	Mushroom Production
111419	Other Food Crops Grown Under Cover
11142	Nursery & Floriculture Production
111421	Nursery & Tree Production
111422	Floriculture Production
1119	Other Crop Farming
11191	Tobacco Farming
111910	Tobacco Farming
11192	Cotton Farming
111920	Cotton Farming
11193	Sugar Cane Farming
111930	Sugar Cane Farming
11194	Hay Farming
111940	Hay Farming
11199	All Other Crop Farming
111993	Fruit & Vegetable Combination Farming
111994	Maple Syrup & Products Production
111999	All Other Misc. Crop Farming

112   Animal Production

1121	Cattle Ranching & Farming
11211	Beef Cattle Ranching & Farming, inc. Feedlots
112110	Beef Cattle Ranching & Farming, inc. Feedlots
11212	Dairy Cattle & Milk Production
112120	Dairy Cattle & Milk Production
1122	Hog & Pig Farming
11221	Hog & Pig Farming
112210	Hog & Pig Farming
1123	Poultry & Egg Production
11231	Chicken Egg Production
112310	Chicken Egg Production
11232	Broiler & Other Meat-Type Chicken Production
112320	Broiler & Other Meat-Type Chicken Production
11233	Turkey Production
112330	Turkey Production
11234	Poultry Hatcheries
112340	Poultry Hatcheries
11239	Other Poultry Production
112391	Combination Poultry & Egg Production
112399	All Other Poultry Production
1124	Sheep & Goat Farming
11241	Sheep Farming
112410	Sheep Farming
11242	Goat Farming
112420	Goat Farming
1125	Aquaculture
11251	Aquaculture
112510	Aquaculture
1129	Other Animal Production
11291	Apiculture
112910	Apiculture
11292	Horse & Other Equine Production
112920	Horse & Other Equine Production
11293	Fur-Bearing Animal & Rabbit Production
112930	Fur-Bearing Animal & Rabbit Production
11299	All Other Animal Production
112991	Animal Combination Farming
112999	All Other Misc. Animal Production

113   Forestry & Logging

1131	Timber Tract Operations
11311	Timber Tract Operations
113110	Timber Tract Operations
1132	Forest Nurseries & Gathering Forest Products

11321	Forest Nurseries & Gathering Forest Products
113210	Forest Nurseries & Gathering Forest Products
1133	Logging
11331	Logging
113311	Logging (exc. Contract)
113312	Contract Logging

114   Fishing, Hunting & Trapping

1141	Fishing
11411	Fishing
114113	Salt Water Fishing
114114	Inland Fishing
1142	Hunting & Trapping
11421	Hunting & Trapping
114210	Hunting & Trapping

115   Support Activities for Agriculture & Forestry

1151	Support Activities for Crop Production
11511	Support Activities for Crop Production
115110	Support Activities for Crop Production
1152	Support Activities for Animal Production
11521	Support Activities for Animal Production
115210	Support Activities for Animal Production
1153	Support Activities for Forestry
11531	Support Activities for Forestry
115310	Support Activities for Forestry

21   Mining, Quarrying & Oil & Gas Extraction

211   Oil & Gas Extraction

2111	Oil & Gas Extraction
21111	Oil & Gas Extraction
211113	Conventional Oil & Gas Extraction
211114	Non-Conventional Oil Extraction

212   Mining & Quarrying (exc. Oil & Gas)

2121	Coal Mining
21211	Coal Mining
212114	Bituminous Coal Mining
212115	Subbituminous Coal Mining

212116	Lignite Coal Mining
2122	Metal Ore Mining
21221	Iron Ore Mining
212210	Iron Ore Mining
21222	Gold & Silver Ore Mining
212220	Gold & Silver Ore Mining
21223	Copper, Nickel, Lead & Zinc Ore Mining
212231	Lead-Zinc Ore Mining
212232	Nickel-Copper Ore Mining
212233	Copper-Zinc Ore Mining
21229	Other Metal Ore Mining
212291	Uranium Ore Mining
212299	All Other Metal Ore Mining
2123	Non-Metallic Mineral Mining & Quarrying
21231	Stone Mining & Quarrying
212314	Granite Mining & Quarrying
212315	Limestone Mining & Quarrying
212316	Marble Mining & Quarrying
212317	Sandstone Mining & Quarrying
21232	Sand, Gravel, Clay, etc., Mining & Quarrying
212323	Sand & Gravel Mining & Quarrying
212326	Shale, Clay & Refractory Mining & Quarrying
21239	Other Non-Metallic Mineral Mining & Quarrying
212392	Diamond Mining
212393	Salt Mining
212394	Asbestos Mining
212395	Gypsum Mining
212396	Potash Mining
212397	Peat Extraction
212398	All Other Non-Met. Mineral Mining & Quarrying

213   Support Act. - Mining & Oil & Gas Extraction

2131	Support Act. - Mining & Oil & Gas Extraction
21311	Support Act. - Mining & Oil & Gas Extraction
213111	Oil & Gas Contract Drilling
213117	Contract Drilling (exc. Oil & Gas)
213118	Services to Oil & Gas Extraction
213119	Other Support Activities for Mining

22   Utilities

221   Utilities

2211	Electricity Generation, Transmission & Dist.

22111	Electric Power Generation
221111	Hydro-Electric Power Generation
221112	Fossil-Fuel Electric Power Generation
221113	Nuclear Electric Power Generation
221119	Other Electric Power Generation
22112	Electric Power Transmission, Control & Dist.
221121	Electric Bulk Power Transmission & Control
221122	Electric Power Distribution
2212	Natural Gas Distribution
22121	Natural Gas Distribution
221210	Natural Gas Distribution
2213	Water, Sewage & Other Systems
22131	Water Supply & Irrigation Systems
221310	Water Supply & Irrigation Systems
22132	Sewage Treatment Facilities
221320	Sewage Treatment Facilities
22133	Steam & Air-Conditioning Supply
221330	Steam & Air-Conditioning Supply

23 Construction

236 Construction of Buildings

2361	Residential Building Construction
23611	Residential Building Construction
236110	Residential Building Construction
2362	Non-residential Building Construction
23621	Industrial Building & Structure Construction
236210	Industrial Building & Structure Construction
23622	Commercial & Inst. Building Construction
236220	Commercial & Inst. Building Construction

237 Heavy and Civil Engineering Construction

2371	Utility System Construction
23711	Water & Sewer Line & Related Structures Con.
237110	Water & Sewer Line & Related Structures Con.
23712	Oil & Gas Pipeline & Related Struct. Con.
237120	Oil & Gas Pipeline & Related Struct. Con.
23713	Power & Com. Line & Related Structures Con.
237130	Power & Com. Line & Related Structures Con.

2372	Land Subdivision
23721	Land Subdivision
237210	Land Subdivision
2373	Highway, Street & Bridge Construction
23731	Highway, Street & Bridge Construction
237310	Highway, Street & Bridge Construction
2379	Other Heavy & Civil Engineering Construction
23799	Other Heavy & Civil Engineering Construction
237990	Other Heavy & Civil Engineering Construction

238 Specialty Trade Contractors

2381	Foundation, Structure & Related Contractors
23811	Poured Concrete Foundation Contractors
238110	Poured Concrete Foundation Contractors
23812	Struct. Steel & Precast Concrete Contractors
238120	Struct. Steel & Precast Concrete Contractors
23813	Framing Contractors
238130	Framing Contractors
23814	Masonry Contractors
238140	Masonry Contractors
23815	Glass & Glazing Contractors
238150	Glass & Glazing Contractors
23816	Roofing Contractors
238160	Roofing Contractors
23817	Siding Contractors
238170	Siding Contractors
23819	Other Foundation & Structure Contractors
238190	Other Foundation & Structure Contractors
2382	Building Equipment Contractors
23821	Electrical & Other Wiring Contractors
238210	Electrical & Other Wiring Contractors
23822	Plumbing, Heating & AC Contractors
238220	Plumbing, Heating & AC Contractors
23829	Other Building Equipment Contractors
238291	Elevator & Escalator Installation Contractors
238299	All Other Building Equipment Contractors
2383	Building Finishing Contractors
23831	Drywall & Insulation Contractors

238310	Drywall & Insulation Contractors
23832	Painting & Wall Covering Contractors
238320	Painting & Wall Covering Contractors
23833	Flooring Contractors
238330	Flooring Contractors
23834	Tile & Terrazzo Contractors
238340	Tile & Terrazzo Contractors
23835	Finish Carpentry Contractors
238350	Finish Carpentry Contractors
23839	Other Building Finishing Contractors
238390	Other Building Finishing Contractors
2389	Other Specialty Trade Contractors
23891	Site Preparation Contractors
238910	Site Preparation Contractors
23899	All Other Specialty Trade Contractors
238990	All Other Specialty Trade Contractors

31-33   Manufacturing

311   Food Mfg.

3111	Animal Food Mfg.
31111	Animal Food Mfg.
311111	Dog & Cat Food Mfg.
311119	Other Animal Food Mfg.
3112	Grain & Oilseed Milling
31121	Flour Milling & Malt Mfg.
311211	Flour Milling
311214	Rice Milling & Malt Mfg.
31122	Starch & Vegetable Fat & Oil Mfg.
311221	Wet Corn Milling
311224	Oilseed Processing
311225	Fat & Oil Refining & Blending
31123	Breakfast Cereal Mfg.
311230	Breakfast Cereal Mfg.
3113	Sugar & Confectionery Product Mfg.
31131	Sugar Mfg.
311310	Sugar Mfg.
31132	Chocolate & Confectionery Mfg. from Beans
311320	Chocolate & Confectionery Mfg. from Beans
31133	Confectionery Mfg. from Purchased Chocolate
311330	Confectionery Mfg. from Purchased Chocolate
31134	Non-Chocolate Confectionery Mfg.
311340	Non-Chocolate Confectionery Mfg.
3114	Fruit & Veg. Preserving & Specialty Food Mfg.
31141	Frozen Food Mfg.
311410	Frozen Food Mfg.
31142	Fruit & Vegetable Canning, Pickling & Drying
311420	Fruit & Vegetable Canning, Pickling & Drying

3115	Dairy Product Mfg.
31151	Dairy Product (exc. Frozen) Mfg.
311511	Fluid Milk Mfg.
311515	Butter, Cheese, Dry/Cond. Dairy Product Mfg.
31152	Ice Cream & Frozen Dessert Mfg.
311520	Ice Cream & Frozen Dessert Mfg.
3116	Meat Product Mfg.
31161	Animal Slaughtering & Processing
311611	Animal (exc. Poultry) Slaughtering
311614	Rendering & Meat Processing from Carcasses
311615	Poultry Processing
3117	Seafood Product Preparation & Packaging
31171	Seafood Product Preparation & Packaging
311710	Seafood Product Preparation & Packaging
3118	Bakeries & Tortilla Mfg.
31181	Bread & Bakery Product Mfg.
311811	Retail Bakeries
311814	Commercial Bakeries & Frozen Product Mfg.
31182	Cookie, Cracker & Pasta Mfg.
311821	Cookie & Cracker Mfg.
311822	Flour Mixes & Dough Mfg. from Purchased Flour
311823	Dry Pasta Mfg.
31183	Tortilla Mfg.
311830	Tortilla Mfg.
3119	Other Food Mfg.
31191	Snack Food Mfg.
311911	Roasted Nut & Peanut Butter Mfg.
311919	Other Snack Food Mfg.
31192	Coffee & Tea Mfg.
311920	Coffee & Tea Mfg.
31193	Flavouring Syrup & Concentrate Mfg.
311930	Flavouring Syrup & Concentrate Mfg.
31194	Seasoning & Dressing Mfg.
311940	Seasoning & Dressing Mfg.
31199	All Other Food Mfg.
311990	All Other Food Mfg.

312   Beverage & Tobacco Product Mfg.

3121	Beverage Mfg.
31211	Soft Drink & Ice Mfg.
312110	Soft Drink & Ice Mfg.
31212	Breweries
312120	Breweries
31213	Wineries
312130	Wineries
31214	Distilleries
312140	Distilleries
3122	Tobacco Mfg.

31221	Tobacco Stemming & Redrying
312210	Tobacco Stemming & Redrying
31222	Tobacco Product Mfg.
312220	Tobacco Product Mfg.

313   Textile Mills

3131	Fibre, Yarn & Thread Mills
31311	Fibre, Yarn & Thread Mills
313110	Fibre, Yarn & Thread Mills
3132	Fabric Mills
31321	Broad-Woven Fabric Mills
313210	Broad-Woven Fabric Mills
31322	Narrow Fabric Mills & Schiffli Embroidery
313220	Narrow Fabric Mills & Schiffli Embroidery
31323	Nonwoven Fabric Mills
313230	Nonwoven Fabric Mills
31324	Knit Fabric Mills
313240	Knit Fabric Mills
3133	Textile & Fabric Finishing & Fabric Coating
31331	Textile & Fabric Finishing
313310	Textile & Fabric Finishing
31332	Fabric Coating
313320	Fabric Coating

314   Textile Product Mills

3141	Textile Furnishings Mills
31411	Carpet & Rug Mills
314110	Carpet & Rug Mills
31412	Curtain & Linen Mills
314120	Curtain & Linen Mills
3149	Other Textile Product Mills
31491	Textile Bag & Canvas Mills
314910	Textile Bag & Canvas Mills
31499	All Other Textile Product Mills
314990	All Other Textile Product Mills

315   Clothing Mfg.

3151	Clothing Knitting Mills
31511	Hosiery & Sock Mills
315110	Hosiery & Sock Mills
31519	Other Clothing Knitting Mills
315190	Other Clothing Knitting Mills
3152	Cut & Sew Clothing Mfg.
31521	Cut & Sew Clothing Contracting
315210	Cut & Sew Clothing Contracting
31522	Men's & Boys' Cut & Sew Clothing Mfg.
315221	Men's & Boys' Underwear & Nightwear Mfg.

315222	Men's & Boys' Suit, Coat & Overcoat Mfg.
315226	Men's & Boys' Cut & Sew Shirt Mfg.
315227	Men's & Boys' Trouser, Slack & Jean Mfg.
315229	Other Men's & Boys' Cut & Sew Clothing Mfg.
31523	Women's & Girls' Cut & Sew Clothing Mfg.
315231	Women's & Girls' Lingerie & Nightwear Mfg.
315232	Women's & Girls' Blouse & Shirt Mfg.
315233	Women's & Girls' Cut & Sew Dress Mfg.
315234	Women's & Girls' Suit, Coat, Jkt., Skirt Mfg.
315239	Other Women's & Girls' Cut & Sew Clothing Mfg
31529	Other Cut & Sew Clothing Mfg.
315291	Infants' Cut & Sew Clothing Mfg.
315292	Fur & Leather Clothing Mfg.
315299	All Other Cut & Sew Clothing Mfg.
3159	Clothing Accessories & Other Clothing Mfg.
31599	Clothing Accessories & Other Clothing Mfg.
315990	Clothing Accessories & Other Clothing Mfg.

316   Leather & Allied Product Mfg.

3161	Leather & Hide Tanning & Finishing
31611	Leather & Hide Tanning & Finishing
316110	Leather & Hide Tanning & Finishing
3162	Footwear Mfg.
31621	Footwear Mfg.
316210	Footwear Mfg.
3169	Other Leather & Allied Product Mfg.
31699	Other Leather & Allied Product Mfg.
316990	Other Leather & Allied Product Mfg.

321   Wood Product Mfg.

3211	Sawmills & Wood Preservation
32111	Sawmills & Wood Preservation
321111	Sawmills (except Shingle & Shake Mills)
321112	Shingle & Shake Mills
321114	Wood Preservation
3212	Veneer, Plywood & Engineered Wood Product Mfg
32121	Veneer, Plywood & Engineered Wood Product Mfg
321211	Hardwood Veneer & Plywood Mills
321212	Softwood Veneer & Plywood Mills

321215	Structural Wood Product Mfg.
321216	Particle Board & Fibreboard Mills
321217	Waferboard Mills
3219	Other Wood Product Mfg.
32191	Millwork
321911	Wood Window & Door Mfg.
321919	Other Millwork
32192	Wood Container & Pallet Mfg.
321920	Wood Container & Pallet Mfg.
32199	All Other Wood Product Mfg.
321991	Manufactured (Mobile) Home Mfg.
321992	Prefabricated Wood Building Mfg.
321999	All Other Misc. Wood Product Mfg.

322   Paper Mfg.

3221	Pulp, Paper & Paperboard Mills
32211	Pulp Mills
322111	Mechanical Pulp Mills
322112	Chemical Pulp Mills
32212	Paper Mills
322121	Paper (except Newsprint) Mills
322122	Newsprint Mills
32213	Paperboard Mills
322130	Paperboard Mills
3222	Converted Paper Product Mfg.
32221	Paperboard Container Mfg.
322211	Corrugated & Solid Fibre Box Mfg.
322212	Folding Paperboard Box Mfg.
322219	Other Paperboard Container Mfg.
32222	Paper Bag & Coated & Treated Paper Mfg.
322220	Paper Bag & Coated & Treated Paper Mfg.
32223	Stationery Product Mfg.
322230	Stationery Product Mfg.
32229	Other Converted Paper Product Mfg.
322291	Sanitary Paper Product Mfg.
322299	All Other Converted Paper Product Mfg.

323   Printing & Related Support Activities

3231	Printing & Related Support Activities
32311	Printing
323113	Commercial Screen Printing
323114	Quick Printing
323115	Digital Printing
323116	Manifold Business Forms Printing
323119	Other Printing
32312	Support Activities for Printing
323120	Support Activities for Printing

324   Petroleum & Coal Product Mfg.

3241	Petroleum & Coal Product Mfg.
32411	Petroleum Refineries
324110	Petroleum Refineries
32412	Asphalt Product Mfg.
324121	Asphalt Paving Mixture & Block Mfg.
324122	Asphalt Shingle & Coating Material Mfg.
32419	Other Petroleum & Coal Product Mfg.
324190	Other Petroleum & Coal Product Mfg.

325   Chemical Mfg.

3251	Basic Chemical Mfg.
32511	Petrochemical Mfg.
325110	Petrochemical Mfg.
32512	Industrial Gas Mfg.
325120	Industrial Gas Mfg.
32513	Synthetic Dye & Pigment Mfg.
325130	Synthetic Dye & Pigment Mfg.
32518	Other Basic Inorganic Chemical Mfg.
325181	Alkali & Chlorine Mfg.
325189	All Other Basic Inorganic Chemical Mfg.
32519	Other Basic Organic Chemical Mfg.
325190	Other Basic Organic Chemical Mfg.
3252	Resin, Synth. Rubber, & Fibre & Filament Mfg.
32521	Resin & Synthetic Rubber Mfg.
325210	Resin & Synthetic Rubber Mfg.
32522	Artificial & Synthetic Fibres & Filaments Mfg
325220	Artificial & Synthetic Fibres & Filaments Mfg
3253	Pesticide, Fertilizer & Other Agr. Chem. Mfg.
32531	Fertilizer Mfg.
325313	Chemical Fertilizer (exc. Potash) Mfg.
325314	Mixed Fertilizer Mfg.
32532	Pesticide & Other Agricultural Chemical Mfg.
325320	Pesticide & Other Agricultural Chemical Mfg.
3254	Pharmaceutical & Medicine Mfg.
32541	Pharmaceutical & Medicine Mfg.
325410	Pharmaceutical & Medicine Mfg.
3255	Paint, Coating & Adhesive Mfg.
32551	Paint & Coating Mfg.
325510	Paint & Coating Mfg.
32552	Adhesive Mfg.
325520	Adhesive Mfg.
3256	Soap, Cleaning Compound & Toilet Prep. Mfg.
32561	Soap & Cleaning Compound Mfg.
325610	Soap & Cleaning Compound Mfg.
32562	Toilet Preparation Mfg.
325620	Toilet Preparation Mfg.

3259	Other Chemical Product Mfg.
32591	Printing Ink Mfg.
325910	Printing Ink Mfg.
32592	Explosives Mfg.
325920	Explosives Mfg.
32599	All Other Chemical Product Mfg.
325991	Custom Compounding of Purchased Resins
325999	All Other Misc. Chemical Product Mfg.

326 Plastics & Rubber Products Mfg.

3261	Plastic Product Mfg.
32611	Plastic Pack. Mtl. & Film, Sheet Mfg.
326111	Plastic Bag & Pouch Mfg.
326114	Unsupported Plastic Film & Sheet Mfg.
32612	Plastic Pipe & Unsupported Profile Shape Mfg.
326121	Unsupported Plastic Profile Shape Mfg.
326122	Plastic Pipe & Pipe Fitting Mfg.
32613	Laminated Plastic Plate, Sheet & Shape Mfg.
326130	Laminated Plastic Plate, Sheet & Shape Mfg.
32614	Polystyrene Foam Product Mfg.
326140	Polystyrene Foam Product Mfg.
32615	Urethane & Miscellaneous Foam Product Mfg.
326150	Urethane & Miscellaneous Foam Product Mfg.
32616	Plastic Bottle Mfg.
326160	Plastic Bottle Mfg.
32619	Other Plastic Product Mfg.
326191	Plastic Plumbing Fixture Mfg.
326193	Motor Vehicle Plastic Parts Mfg.
326196	Plastic Window & Door Manufacturing
326198	All Other Plastic Product Mfg.
3262	Rubber Product Mfg.
32621	Tire Mfg.
326210	Tire Mfg.
32622	Rubber & Plastic Hose & Belting Mfg.
326220	Rubber & Plastic Hose & Belting Mfg.
32629	Other Rubber Product Mfg.
326290	Other Rubber Product Mfg.

327 Non-Metallic Mineral Product Mfg.

3271	Clay Product & Refractory Mfg.
32711	Pottery, Ceramics & Plumbing Fixture Mfg.
327110	Pottery, Ceramics & Plumbing Fixture Mfg.
32712	Clay Building Material & Refractory Mfg.
327120	Clay Building Material & Refractory Mfg.
3272	Glass & Glass Product Mfg.
32721	Glass & Glass Product Mfg.
327214	Glass Mfg.
327215	Glass Product Mfg. from Purchased Glass
3273	Cement & Concrete Product Mfg.
32731	Cement Mfg.
327310	Cement Mfg.
32732	Ready-Mix Concrete Mfg.
327320	Ready-Mix Concrete Mfg.
32733	Concrete Pipe, Brick & Block Mfg.
327330	Concrete Pipe, Brick & Block Mfg.
32739	Other Concrete Product Mfg.
327390	Other Concrete Product Mfg.
3274	Lime & Gypsum Product Mfg.
32741	Lime Mfg.
327410	Lime Mfg.
32742	Gypsum Product Mfg.
327420	Gypsum Product Mfg.
3279	Other Non-Metallic Mineral Product Mfg.
32791	Abrasive Product Mfg.
327910	Abrasive Product Mfg.
32799	All Other Non-Metallic Mineral Product Mfg.
327990	All Other Non-Metallic Mineral Product Mfg.

331 Primary Metal Mfg.

3311	Iron & Steel Mills & Ferro-Alloy Mfg.
33111	Iron & Steel Mills & Ferro-Alloy Mfg.
331110	Iron & Steel Mills & Ferro-Alloy Mfg.
3312	Steel Product Mfg. from Purchased Steel
33121	Iron & Steel Pipes & Tubes Mfg.
331210	Iron & Steel Pipes & Tubes Mfg.
33122	Rolling & Drawing of Purchased Steel
331221	Cold-Rolled Steel Shape Mfg.
331222	Steel Wire Drawing
3313	Alumina & Aluminum Production & Processing
33131	Alumina & Aluminum Production & Processing
331313	Primary Production of Alumina & Aluminum
331317	Al Rolling, Drawing, Extruding & Alloying

3314	Non-Ferrous (exc. Al) Production & Processing
33141	Non-Ferrous (except Al) Smelting & Refining
331410	Non-Ferrous (except Al) Smelting & Refining
33142	Copper Rolling, Drawing, Extruding & Alloying
331420	Copper Rolling, Drawing, Extruding & Alloying
33149	Non-Ferrous (except Cu & Al) Secondary Proc.
331490	Non-Ferrous (except Cu & Al) Secondary Proc.
3315	Foundries
33151	Ferrous Metal Foundries
331511	Iron Foundries
331514	Steel Foundries
33152	Non-Ferrous Metal Foundries
331523	Non-Ferrous Die-Casting Foundries
331529	Non-Ferrous Foundries (except Die-Casting)

332 Fabricated Metal Product Mfg.

3321	Forging & Stamping
33211	Forging & Stamping
332113	Forging
332118	Stamping
3322	Cutlery & Hand Tool Mfg.
33221	Cutlery & Hand Tool Mfg.
332210	Cutlery & Hand Tool Mfg.
3323	Architectural & Structural Metals Mfg.
33231	Plate Work & Fabricated Structural Prod. Mfg.
332311	Prefabricated Metal Building & Component Mfg.
332314	Concrete Reinforcing Bar Mfg.
332319	Other Plate Work & Structural Product Mfg.
33232	Ornamental & Architectural Metal Product Mfg
332321	Metal Window & Door Mfg.
332329	Other Ornamental & Arch. Metal Prod. Mfg.
3324	Boiler, Tank & Shipping Container Mfg.
33241	Power Boiler & Heat Exchanger Mfg.
332410	Power Boiler & Heat Exchanger Mfg.
33242	Metal Tank (Heavy Gauge) Mfg.
332420	Metal Tank (Heavy Gauge) Mfg.
33243	Metal Can, Box & Other Metal Container Mfg.
332431	Metal Can Mfg.

332439	Other Metal Container Mfg.
3325	Hardware Mfg.
33251	Hardware Mfg.
332510	Hardware Mfg.
3326	Spring & Wire Product Mfg.
33261	Spring & Wire Product Mfg.
332611	Spring (Heavy Gauge) Mfg.
332619	Other Fabricated Wire Product Mfg.
3327	Machine Shops, Turned Product & Related Mfg.
33271	Machine Shops
332710	Machine Shops
33272	Turned Product & Screw, Nut & Bolt Mfg.
332720	Turned Product & Screw, Nut & Bolt Mfg.
3328	Coating, Engraving & Heat Treating Activities
33281	Coating, Engraving & Heat Treating Activities
332810	Coating, Engraving & Heat Treating Activities
3329	Other Fabricated Metal Product Mfg.
33291	Metal Valve Mfg.
332910	Metal Valve Mfg.
33299	All Other Fabricated Metal Product Mfg.
332991	Ball & Roller Bearing Mfg.
332999	All Other Misc. Fabricated Metal Product Mfg.

333 Machinery Mfg.

3331	Agr., Construction & Mining Machinery Mfg.
33311	Agricultural Implement Mfg.
333110	Agricultural Implement Mfg.
33312	Construction Machinery Mfg.
333120	Construction Machinery Mfg.
33313	Mining & Oil & Gas Field Machinery Mfg.
333130	Mining & Oil & Gas Field Machinery Mfg.
3332	Industrial Machinery Mfg.
33321	Sawmill & Woodworking Machinery Mfg.
333210	Sawmill & Woodworking Machinery Mfg.
33322	Rubber & Plastics Industry Machinery Mfg.
333220	Rubber & Plastics Industry Machinery Mfg.
33329	Other Industrial Machinery Mfg.
333291	Paper Industry Machinery Mfg.
333299	All Other Industrial Machinery Mfg.

3333	Commercial & Service Industry Machinery Mfg.		334290	Other Communications Equipment Mfg.
33331	Commercial & Service Industry Machinery Mfg.		3343	Audio & Video Equipment Mfg.
333310	Commercial & Service Industry Machinery Mfg.		33431	Audio & Video Equipment Mfg.
			334310	Audio & Video Equipment Mfg.
3334	Ventilation, Heating, AC & Refrig. Eqp. Mfg		3344	Semiconductor & Electronic Component Mfg.
33341	Ventilation, Heating, AC & Refrig. Eqp. Mfg		33441	Semiconductor & Electronic Component Mfg.
333413	Fan & Blower & Air Purification Eqp. Mfg.		334410	Semiconductor & Electronic Component Mfg.
333416	Heating & Commercial Refrigeration Eqp. Mfg		3345	Instruments Mfg.
3335	Metalworking Machinery Mfg.		33451	Instruments Mfg.
33351	Metalworking Machinery Mfg.		334511	Navigational & Guidance Instruments Mfg.
333511	Industrial Mould Mfg.		334512	Measuring, Medical & Controlling Devices Mfg.
333519	Other Metalworking Machinery Mfg.		3346	Mfg. & Reproducing Magnetic & Optical Media
3336	Engine, Turbine & Power Transmission Mfg.		33461	Mfg. & Reproducing Magnetic & Optical Media
33361	Engine, Turbine & Power Transmission Mfg.		334610	Mfg. & Reproducing Magnetic & Optical Media
333611	Turbine & Turbine Generator Set Unit Mfg.			
333619	Other Engine & Power Transmission Eqp. Mfg.		**335**	**Electric Equipment, Appliance & Component Mfg**
3339	Other General-Purpose Machinery Mfg.		3351	Electric Lighting Equipment Mfg.
33391	Pump & Compressor Mfg.		33511	Electric Lamp Bulb & Parts Mfg.
333910	Pump & Compressor Mfg.		335110	Electric Lamp Bulb & Parts Mfg.
33392	Material Handling Equipment Mfg.		33512	Lighting Fixture Mfg.
333920	Material Handling Equipment Mfg.		335120	Lighting Fixture Mfg.
33399	All Other General-Purpose Machinery Mfg.		3352	Household Appliance Mfg.
333990	All Other General-Purpose Machinery Mfg.		33521	Small Electrical Appliance Mfg.
			335210	Small Electrical Appliance Mfg.
			33522	Major Appliance Mfg.
334	**Computer & Electronic Product Mfg.**		335223	Major Kitchen Appliance Mfg.
			335229	Other Major Appliance Mfg.
3341	Computer & Peripheral Equipment Mfg.		3353	Electrical Equipment Mfg.
			33531	Electrical Equipment Mfg.
33411	Computer & Peripheral Equipment Mfg.		335311	Transformer (exc. Electronic) Mfg.
			335312	Motor & Generator Mfg.
334110	Computer & Peripheral Equipment Mfg.		335315	Switchgear, Relay & Industrial Control Mfg.
3342	Communications Equipment Mfg.		3359	Other Electrical Equipment & Component Mfg.
33421	Telephone Apparatus Mfg.			
334210	Telephone Apparatus Mfg.		33591	Battery Mfg.
33422	Broadcasting & Wireless Communication Mfg.		335910	Battery Mfg.
			33592	Communication & Energy Wire & Cable Mfg.
334220	Broadcasting & Wireless Communication Mfg.		335920	Communication & Energy Wire & Cable Mfg.
33429	Other Communications Equipment Mfg.		33593	Wiring Device Mfg.
			335930	Wiring Device Mfg.

33599	All Other Electrical Eqp. & Component Mfg.
335990	All Other Electrical Eqp. & Component Mfg.

336   **Transportation Equipment Mfg.**

3361	Motor Vehicle Mfg.
33611	Automobile & Light-Duty Motor Vehicle Mfg.
336110	Automobile & Light-Duty Motor Vehicle Mfg.
33612	Heavy-Duty Truck Mfg.
336120	Heavy-Duty Truck Mfg.
3362	Motor Vehicle Body & Trailer Mfg.
33621	Motor Vehicle Body & Trailer Mfg.
336211	Motor Vehicle Body Mfg.
336212	Truck Trailer Mfg.
336215	Motor Home, Travel Trailer & Camper Mfg.
3363	Motor Vehicle Parts Mfg.
33631	Motor Vehicle Gasoline Engine & Parts Mfg.
336310	Motor Vehicle Gasoline Engine & Parts Mfg.
33632	MV Electrical & Electronic Equipment Mfg.
336320	MV Electrical & Electronic Equipment Mfg.
33633	MV Steering & Suspension Components Mfg.
336330	MV Steering & Suspension Components Mfg.
33634	Motor Vehicle Brake System Mfg.
336340	Motor Vehicle Brake System Mfg.
33635	MV Transmission & Power Train Parts Mfg.
336350	MV Transmission & Power Train Parts Mfg.
33636	Motor Vehicle Seating & Interior Trim Mfg.
336360	Motor Vehicle Seating & Interior Trim Mfg.
33637	Motor Vehicle Metal Stamping
336370	Motor Vehicle Metal Stamping
33639	Other Motor Vehicle Parts Mfg.
336390	Other Motor Vehicle Parts Mfg.
3364	Aerospace Product & Parts Mfg.
33641	Aerospace Product & Parts Mfg.
336410	Aerospace Product & Parts Mfg.
3365	Railroad Rolling Stock Mfg.
33651	Railroad Rolling Stock Mfg.
336510	Railroad Rolling Stock Mfg.
3366	Ship & Boat Building
33661	Ship & Boat Building

336611	Ship Building & Repairing
336612	Boat Building
3369	Other Transportation Equipment Mfg.
33699	Other Transportation Equipment Mfg.
336990	Other Transportation Equipment Mfg.

337   **Furniture & Related Product Mfg.**

3371	Household & Inst. Furniture & Cabinet Mfg.
33711	Wood Kitchen Cabinet & Counter Top Mfg.
337110	Wood Kitchen Cabinet & Counter Top Mfg.
33712	Household & Institutional Furniture Mfg.
337121	Upholstered Household Furniture Mfg.
337123	Other Wood Household Furniture Mfg.
337126	All Other Household Furniture Mfg.
337127	Institutional Furniture Mfg.
3372	Office Furniture (including Fixtures) Mfg.
33721	Office Furniture (including Fixtures) Mfg.
337213	Wood Office Furniture Mfg.
337214	Office Furniture (exc. Wood) Mfg.
337215	Showcase, Partition, Shelving & Locker Mfg.
3379	Other Furniture-Related Product Mfg.
33791	Mattress Mfg.
337910	Mattress Mfg.
33792	Blind & Shade Mfg.
337920	Blind & Shade Mfg.

339   **Miscellaneous Mfg.**

3391	Medical Equipment & Supplies Mfg.
33911	Medical Equipment & Supplies Mfg.
339110	Medical Equipment & Supplies Mfg.
3399	Other Miscellaneous Mfg.
33991	Jewellery & Silverware Mfg.
339910	Jewellery & Silverware Mfg.
33992	Sporting & Athletic Goods Mfg.
339920	Sporting & Athletic Goods Mfg.
33993	Doll, Toy & Game Mfg.
339930	Doll, Toy & Game Mfg.
33994	Office Supplies (exc. Paper) Mfg.
339940	Office Supplies (exc. Paper) Mfg.
33995	Sign Mfg.
339950	Sign Mfg.

33999	All Other Miscellaneous Mfg.
339990	All Other Miscellaneous Mfg.

41   Wholesale Trade

411   Farm Product Whl.

4111	Farm Product Whl.
41111	Live Animal Whl.
411110	Live Animal Whl.
41112	Oilseed & Grain Whl.
411120	Oilseed & Grain Whl.
41113	Nursery Stock & Plant Whl.
411130	Nursery Stock & Plant Whl.
41119	Other Farm Product Whl.
411190	Other Farm Product Whl.

412   Petroleum Product Whl.

4121	Petroleum Product Whl.
41211	Petroleum Product Whl.
412110	Petroleum Product Whl.

413   Food, Beverage & Tobacco Whl.

4131	Food Whl.
41311	General-Line Food Whl.
413110	General-Line Food Whl.
41312	Dairy & Milk Products Whl.
413120	Dairy & Milk Products Whl.
41313	Poultry & Egg Whl.
413130	Poultry & Egg Whl.
41314	Fish & Seafood Product Whl.
413140	Fish & Seafood Product Whl.
41315	Fresh Fruit & Vegetable Whl.
413150	Fresh Fruit & Vegetable Whl.
41316	Red Meat & Meat Product Whl.
413160	Red Meat & Meat Product Whl.
41319	Other Specialty-Line Food Whl.
413190	Other Specialty-Line Food Whl.
4132	Beverage Whl.
41321	Non-Alcoholic Beverage Whl.
413210	Non-Alcoholic Beverage Whl.
41322	Alcoholic Beverage Whl.
413220	Alcoholic Beverage Whl.
4133	Cigarette & Tobacco Product Whl.
41331	Cigarette & Tobacco Product Whl.
413310	Cigarette & Tobacco Product Whl.

414   Personal & Household Goods Whl.

4141	Textile, Clothing & Footwear Whl.
41411	Clothing & Clothing Accessories Whl.
414110	Clothing & Clothing Accessories Whl.
41412	Footwear Whl.
414120	Footwear Whl.

41413	Piece Goods, Notions & Other Dry Goods Whl.
414130	Piece Goods, Notions & Other Dry Goods Whl.
4142	Home Entertainment Eqp. & Hhld. Appl. Whl.
41421	Home Entertainment Equipment Whl.
414210	Home Entertainment Equipment Whl.
41422	Household Appliance Whl.
414220	Household Appliance Whl.
4143	Home Furnishings Whl.
41431	China, Glassware, Crockery & Pottery Whl.
414310	China, Glassware, Crockery & Pottery Whl.
41432	Floor Covering Whl.
414320	Floor Covering Whl.
41433	Linen & Other Textile Furnishings Whl.
414330	Linen & Other Textile Furnishings Whl.
41439	Other Home Furnishings Whl.
414390	Other Home Furnishings Whl.
4144	Personal Goods Whl.
41441	Jewellery & Watch Whl.
414410	Jewellery & Watch Whl.
41442	Book, Periodical & Newspaper Whl.
414420	Book, Periodical & Newspaper Whl.
41443	Photographic Equipment & Supplies Whl.
414430	Photographic Equipment & Supplies Whl.
41444	Sound Recording Whl.
414440	Sound Recording Whl.
41445	Video Cassette Whl.
414450	Video Cassette Whl.
41446	Toy & Hobby Goods Whl.
414460	Toy & Hobby Goods Whl.
41447	Amusement & Sporting Goods Whl.
414470	Amusement & Sporting Goods Whl.
4145	Pharmaceuticals, Toiletries & Related Whl.
41451	Pharmaceuticals & Pharmacy Supplies Whl.
414510	Pharmaceuticals & Pharmacy Supplies Whl.
41452	Toiletries, Cosmetics & Sundries Whl.
414520	Toiletries, Cosmetics & Sundries Whl.

415   Motor Vehicle & Parts Whl.

4151	Motor Vehicle Whl.

41511	New & Used Automobile & Light-Duty Truck Whl.
415110	New & Used Automobile & Light-Duty Truck Whl.
41512	Truck, Truck Tractor & Bus Whl.
415120	Truck, Truck Tractor & Bus Whl.
41519	Recreational & Other Motor Vehicles Whl.
415190	Recreational & Other Motor Vehicles Whl.
4152	New Motor Vehicle Parts & Accessories Whl.
41521	Tire Whl.
415210	Tire Whl.
41529	Other New Motor Vehicle Parts & Access. Whl.
415290	Other New Motor Vehicle Parts & Access. Whl.
4153	Used Motor Vehicle Parts & Accessories Whl.
41531	Used Motor Vehicle Parts & Accessories Whl.
415310	Used Motor Vehicle Parts & Accessories Whl.

416   **Building Material & Supplies Whl.**

4161	Electrical, Plumbing, Heating & AC Eqp. Whl.
41611	Elect. Wiring & Construction Supplies Whl.
416110	Elect. Wiring & Construction Supplies Whl.
41612	Plumbing, Heating & AC Eqp. & Supplies Whl.
416120	Plumbing, Heating & AC Eqp. & Supplies Whl.
4162	Metal Service Centres
41621	Metal Service Centres
416210	Metal Service Centres
4163	Lumber & Other Building Supplies Whl.
41631	General-Line Building Supplies Whl.
416310	General-Line Building Supplies Whl.
41632	Lumber, Plywood & Millwork Whl.
416320	Lumber, Plywood & Millwork Whl.
41633	Hardware Whl.
416330	Hardware Whl.
41634	Paint, Glass & Wallpaper Whl.
416340	Paint, Glass & Wallpaper Whl.
41639	Other Specialty-Line Building Supplies Whl.
416390	Other Specialty-Line Building Supplies Whl.

417   **Machinery, Equipment & Supplies Whl.**

4171	Farm, Lawn & Garden Machinery & Eqp. Whl.
41711	Farm, Lawn & Garden Machinery & Eqp. Whl.
417110	Farm, Lawn & Garden Machinery & Eqp. Whl.
4172	Construction, Forestry & Ind'l Machinery Whl.
41721	Construction & Forestry Mach. & Eqp. Whl.
417210	Construction & Forestry Mach. & Eqp. Whl.
41722	Mining & Oil & Gas Well Mach. & Eqp. Whl.
417220	Mining & Oil & Gas Well Mach. & Eqp. Whl.
41723	Industrial Machinery, Eqp. & Supplies Whl.
417230	Industrial Machinery, Eqp. & Supplies Whl.
4173	Computer & Communications Equipment Whl.
41731	Computer, Computer Peripheral & Software Whl.
417310	Computer, Computer Peripheral & Software Whl.
41732	Electr. Comp. Navig. & Com. Eqp. & Supp. Whl.
417320	Electr. Comp. Navig. & Com. Eqp. & Supp. Whl.
4179	Other Machinery, Equipment & Supplies Whl.
41791	Office & Store Machinery & Equipment Whl.
417910	Office & Store Machinery & Equipment Whl.
41792	Service Est. Machinery, Eqp. & Supplies Whl.
417920	Service Est. Machinery, Eqp. & Supplies Whl.
41793	Professional Machinery, Eqp. & Supplies Whl.
417930	Professional Machinery, Eqp. & Supplies Whl.
41799	All Other Machinery, Eqp. & Supplies Whl.
417990	All Other Machinery, Eqp. & Supplies Whl.

418	**Miscellaneous Whl.**
4181	Recyclable Material Whl.
41811	Recyclable Metal Whl.
418110	Recyclable Metal Whl.
41812	Recyclable Paper & Paperboard Whl.
418120	Recyclable Paper & Paperboard Whl.
41819	Other Recyclable Material Whl.
418190	Other Recyclable Material Whl.
4182	Paper & Disposable Plastic Product Whl.
41821	Stationery & Office Supplies Whl.
418210	Stationery & Office Supplies Whl.
41822	Other Paper & Disposable Plastic Product Whl.
418220	Other Paper & Disposable Plastic Product Whl.
4183	Agricultural Supplies Whl.
41831	Agricultural Feed Whl.
418310	Agricultural Feed Whl.
41832	Seed Whl.
418320	Seed Whl.
41839	Agr. Chemical & Other Farm Supplies Whl.
418390	Agr. Chemical & Other Farm Supplies Whl.
4184	Chemical (exc. Agr.) & Allied Product Whl.
41841	Chemical (exc. Agr.) & Allied Product Whl.
418410	Chemical (exc. Agr.) & Allied Product Whl.
4189	Other Misc. Whl.
41891	Log & Wood Chip Whl.
418910	Log & Wood Chip Whl.
41892	Mineral, Ore & Precious Metal Whl.
418920	Mineral, Ore & Precious Metal Whl.
41893	Second-Hand Goods (exc. Mach. & Auto) Whl.
418930	Second-Hand Goods (exc. Mach. & Auto) Whl.
41899	All Other Whl.
418990	All Other Whl.
419	**Wholesale Electronic Markets Agents & Brokers**
4191	Wholesale Electronic Markets Agents & Brokers
41911	Business-to-Business Electronic Markets
419110	Business-to-Business Electronic Markets
41912	Wholesale Trade Agents & Brokers

419120	Wholesale Trade Agents & Brokers
44-45	**Retail Trade**
441	**Motor Vehicle & Parts Dealers**
4411	Automobile Dealers
44111	New Car Dealers
441110	New Car Dealers
44112	Used Car Dealers
441120	Used Car Dealers
4412	Other Motor Vehicle Dealers
44121	Recreational Vehicle Dealers
441210	Recreational Vehicle Dealers
44122	Motorcycle, Boat & Other MV Dealers
441220	Motorcycle, Boat & Other MV Dealers
4413	Automotive Parts, Accessories & Tire Stores
44131	Automotive Parts & Accessories Stores
441310	Automotive Parts & Accessories Stores
44132	Tire Dealers
441320	Tire Dealers
442	**Furniture & Home Furnishings Stores**
4421	Furniture Stores
44211	Furniture Stores
442110	Furniture Stores
4422	Home Furnishings Stores
44221	Floor Covering Stores
442210	Floor Covering Stores
44229	Other Home Furnishings Stores
442291	Window Treatment Stores
442292	Print & Picture Frame Stores
442298	All Other Home Furnishings Stores
443	**Electronics & Appliance Stores**
4431	Electronics & Appliance Stores
44311	Appliance, TV & Other Electronics Stores
443110	Appliance, TV & Other Electronics Stores
44312	Computer & Software Stores
443120	Computer & Software Stores
44313	Camera & Photographic Supplies Stores
443130	Camera & Photographic Supplies Stores

444	**Building Material & Garden Equipment Dealers**
4441	Building Material & Supplies Dealers
44411	Home Centres
444110	Home Centres
44412	Paint & Wallpaper Stores
444120	Paint & Wallpaper Stores
44413	Hardware Stores
444130	Hardware Stores
44419	Other Building Material Dealers
444190	Other Building Material Dealers
4442	Lawn & Garden Equipment & Supplies Stores
44421	Outdoor Power Equipment Stores
444210	Outdoor Power Equipment Stores
44422	Nursery & Garden Centres
444220	Nursery & Garden Centres

445	**Food & Beverage Stores**
4451	Grocery Stores
44511	Grocery (exc. Convenience) Stores
445110	Grocery (exc. Convenience) Stores
44512	Convenience Stores
445120	Convenience Stores
4452	Specialty Food Stores
44521	Meat Markets
445210	Meat Markets
44522	Fish & Seafood Markets
445220	Fish & Seafood Markets
44523	Fruit & Vegetable Markets
445230	Fruit & Vegetable Markets
44529	Other Specialty Food Stores
445291	Baked Goods Stores
445292	Confectionery & Nut Stores
445299	All Other Specialty Food Stores
4453	Beer, Wine & Liquor Stores
44531	Beer, Wine & Liquor Stores
445310	Beer, Wine & Liquor Stores

446	**Health & Personal Care Stores**
4461	Health & Personal Care Stores
44611	Pharmacies & Drug Stores
446110	Pharmacies & Drug Stores
44612	Cosmetics, Beauty Supplies & Perfume Stores
446120	Cosmetics, Beauty Supplies & Perfume Stores
44613	Optical Goods Stores
446130	Optical Goods Stores
44619	Other Health & Personal Care Stores
446191	Food (Health) Supplement Stores

446199	All Other Health & Personal Care Stores

447	**Gasoline Stations**
4471	Gasoline Stations
44711	Gasoline Stations with Convenience Stores
447110	Gasoline Stations with Convenience Stores
44719	Other Gasoline Stations
447190	Other Gasoline Stations

448	**Clothing & Clothing Accessories Stores**
4481	Clothing Stores
44811	Men's Clothing Stores
448110	Men's Clothing Stores
44812	Women's Clothing Stores
448120	Women's Clothing Stores
44813	Children's & Infants' Clothing Stores
448130	Children's & Infants' Clothing Stores
44814	Family Clothing Stores
448140	Family Clothing Stores
44815	Clothing Accessories Stores
448150	Clothing Accessories Stores
44819	Other Clothing Stores
448191	Fur Stores
448199	All Other Clothing Stores
4482	Shoe Stores
44821	Shoe Stores
448210	Shoe Stores
4483	Jewellery, Luggage & Leather Goods Stores
44831	Jewellery Stores
448310	Jewellery Stores
44832	Luggage & Leather Goods Stores
448320	Luggage & Leather Goods Stores

451	**Sporting Goods, Hobby, Book & Music Stores**
4511	Sport, Hobby & Musical Instrument Stores
45111	Sporting Goods Stores
451110	Sporting Goods Stores
45112	Hobby, Toy & Game Stores
451120	Hobby, Toy & Game Stores
45113	Sewing, Needlework & Piece Goods Stores
451130	Sewing, Needlework & Piece Goods Stores
45114	Musical Instrument & Supplies Stores
451140	Musical Instrument & Supplies Stores
4512	Book, Periodical & Music Stores

45121	Book Stores & News Dealers
451210	Book Stores & News Dealers
45122	Pre-Recorded Tape, CD & Record Stores
451220	Pre-Recorded Tape, CD & Record Stores

452   General Merchandise Stores

4521	Department Stores
45211	Department Stores
452110	Department Stores
4529	Other General Merchandise Stores
45291	Warehouse Clubs & Superstores
452910	Warehouse Clubs & Superstores
45299	All Other General Merchandise Stores
452991	Home & Auto Supplies Stores
452999	All Other Misc. General Merchandise Stores

453   Misc. Store Retailers

4531	Florists
45311	Florists
453110	Florists
4532	Office Supply, Stationery & Gift Stores
45321	Office Supplies & Stationery Stores
453210	Office Supplies & Stationery Stores
45322	Gift, Novelty & Souvenir Stores
453220	Gift, Novelty & Souvenir Stores
4533	Used Merchandise Stores
45331	Used Merchandise Stores
453310	Used Merchandise Stores
4539	Other Misc. Store Retailers
45391	Pet & Pet Supplies Stores
453910	Pet & Pet Supplies Stores
45392	Art Dealers
453920	Art Dealers
45393	Mobile Home Dealers
453930	Mobile Home Dealers
45399	All Other Misc. Store Retailers
453992	Beer & Wine-Making Supplies Stores
453999	All Other Misc. Store Retailers, n.e.c.

454   Non-Store Retailers

4541	Electronic Shopping & Mail-Order Houses
45411	Electronic Shopping & Mail-Order Houses
454111	Internet Shopping
454112	Electronic Auctions
454113	Mail-Order Houses
4542	Vending Machine Operators
45421	Vending Machine Operators

454210	Vending Machine Operators
4543	Direct Selling Establishments
45431	Fuel Dealers
454311	Heating Oil Dealers
454312	Liquefied Petroleum Gas Dealers
454319	Other Fuel Dealers
45439	Other Direct Selling Establishments
454390	Other Direct Selling Establishments

48-49   Transportation & Warehousing

481   Air Transportation

4811	Scheduled Air Transportation
48111	Scheduled Air Transportation
481110	Scheduled Air Transportation
4812	Non-Scheduled Air Transportation
48121	Non-Scheduled Air Transportation
481214	Non-Scheduled Chartered Air Transportation
481215	Non-Scheduled Specialty Flying Services

482   Rail Transportation

4821	Rail Transportation
48211	Rail Transportation
482112	Short-Haul Freight Rail Transportation
482113	Mainline Freight Rail Transportation
482114	Passenger Rail Transportation

483   Water Transportation

4831	Deep Water Transportation
48311	Deep Water Transportation
483115	Deep Water Transportation, exc. by Ferries
483116	Deep Water Transportation, by Ferries
4832	Inland Water Transportation
48321	Inland Water Transportation
483213	Inland Water Transportation, exc. by Ferries
483214	Inland Water Transportation, by Ferries

484   Truck Transportation

4841	General Freight Trucking
48411	General Freight Trucking, Local
484110	General Freight Trucking, Local
48412	General Freight Trucking, Long Distance

484121	General Trucking, Long Distance, Truck-Load
484122	General Trucking, Long Distance, LTL
4842	Specialized Freight Trucking
48421	Used Household & Office Goods Moving
484210	Used Household & Office Goods Moving
48422	Specialized Freight Trucking, Local
484221	Bulk Liquids Trucking, Local
484222	Dry Bulk Materials Trucking, Local
484223	Forest Products Trucking, Local
484229	Other Specialized Freight Trucking, Local
48423	Specialized Freight Trucking, Long Distance
484231	Bulk Liquids Trucking, Long Distance
484232	Dry Bulk Materials Trucking, Long Distance
484233	Forest Products Trucking, Long Distance
484239	Other Specialized Trucking, Long Distance

485	**Transit & Ground Passenger Transportation**
4851	Urban Transit Systems
48511	Urban Transit Systems
485110	Urban Transit Systems
4852	Interurban & Rural Bus Transportation
48521	Interurban & Rural Bus Transportation
485210	Interurban & Rural Bus Transportation
4853	Taxi & Limousine Service
48531	Taxi Service
485310	Taxi Service
48532	Limousine Service
485320	Limousine Service
4854	School & Employee Bus Transportation
48541	School & Employee Bus Transportation
485410	School & Employee Bus Transportation
4855	Charter Bus Industry
48551	Charter Bus Industry
485510	Charter Bus Industry
4859	Other Transit & Ground Passenger Transport
48599	Other Transit & Ground Passenger Transport

485990	Other Transit & Ground Passenger Transport

486	**Pipeline Transportation**
4861	Pipeline Transportation of Crude Oil
48611	Pipeline Transportation of Crude Oil
486110	Pipeline Transportation of Crude Oil
4862	Pipeline Transportation of Natural Gas
48621	Pipeline Transportation of Natural Gas
486210	Pipeline Transportation of Natural Gas
4869	Other Pipeline Transportation
48691	Pipeline Transport of Refined Petroleum Prod.
486910	Pipeline Transport of Refined Petroleum Prod.
48699	All Other Pipeline Transportation
486990	All Other Pipeline Transportation

487	**Scenic & Sightseeing Transportation**
4871	Scenic & Sightseeing Transportation, Land
48711	Scenic & Sightseeing Transportation, Land
487110	Scenic & Sightseeing Transportation, Land
4872	Scenic & Sightseeing Transportation, Water
48721	Scenic & Sightseeing Transportation, Water
487210	Scenic & Sightseeing Transportation, Water
4879	Scenic & Sightseeing Transportation, Other
48799	Scenic & Sightseeing Transportation, Other
487990	Scenic & Sightseeing Transportation, Other

488	**Support Activities for Transportation**
4881	Support Activities for Air Transportation
48811	Airport Operations
488111	Air Traffic Control
488119	Other Airport Operations
48819	Other Support Activities for Air Transport
488190	Other Support Activities for Air Transport

4882	Support Activities for Rail Transportation
48821	Support Activities for Rail Transportation
488210	Support Activities for Rail Transportation
4883	Support Activities for Water Transportation
48831	Port & Harbour Operations
488310	Port & Harbour Operations
48832	Marine Cargo Handling
488320	Marine Cargo Handling
48833	Navigational Services to Shipping
488331	Marine Salvage Services
488332	Ship Piloting Services
488339	Other Navigational Services to Shipping
48839	Other Support Activities for Water Transport
488390	Other Support Activities for Water Transport
4884	Support Activities for Road Transportation
48841	Motor Vehicle Towing
488410	Motor Vehicle Towing
48849	Other Support Activities for Road Transport
488490	Other Support Activities for Road Transport
4885	Freight Transportation Arrangement
48851	Freight Transportation Arrangement
488511	Marine Shipping Agencies
488519	Other Freight Transportation Arrangement
4889	Other Support Activities for Transportation
48899	Other Support Activities for Transportation
488990	Other Support Activities for Transportation

491 Postal Service

4911	Postal Service
49111	Postal Service
491110	Postal Service

492 Couriers & Messengers

4921	Couriers
49211	Couriers
492110	Couriers
4922	Local Messengers & Local Delivery
49221	Local Messengers & Local Delivery
492210	Local Messengers & Local Delivery

493 Warehousing & Storage

4931	Warehousing & Storage
49311	General Warehousing & Storage
493110	General Warehousing & Storage
49312	Refrigerated Warehousing & Storage
493120	Refrigerated Warehousing & Storage
49313	Farm Product Warehousing & Storage
493130	Farm Product Warehousing & Storage
49319	Other Warehousing & Storage
493190	Other Warehousing & Storage

51 Information & Cultural Industries

511 Publishing Industries (exc. Internet)

5111	Newspaper & Other Publishers
51111	Newspaper Publishers
511110	Newspaper Publishers
51112	Periodical Publishers
511120	Periodical Publishers
51113	Book Publishers
511130	Book Publishers
51114	Directory Publishers
511140	Directory Publishers
51119	Other Publishers
511190	Other Publishers
5112	Software Publishers
51121	Software Publishers
511210	Software Publishers

512 Motion Picture & Sound Recording Industries

5121	Motion Picture & Video Industries
51211	Motion Picture & Video Production
512110	Motion Picture & Video Production
51212	Motion Picture & Video Distribution
512120	Motion Picture & Video Distribution
51213	Motion Picture & Video Exhibition
512130	Motion Picture & Video Exhibition
51219	Post-Prod. & Oth. Motion Picture & Video Ind.
512190	Post-Prod. & Oth. Motion Picture & Video Ind.
5122	Sound Recording Industries
51221	Record Production
512210	Record Production
51222	Integrated Record Production/Distribution
512220	Integrated Record Production/Distribution
51223	Music Publishers

512230	Music Publishers
51224	Sound Recording Studios
512240	Sound Recording Studios
51229	Other Sound Recording Industries
512290	Other Sound Recording Industries

515   Broadcasting (except Internet)

5151	Radio & Television Broadcasting
51511	Radio Broadcasting
515110	Radio Broadcasting
51512	Television Broadcasting
515120	Television Broadcasting
5152	Pay & Specialty Television
51521	Pay & Specialty Television
515210	Pay & Specialty Television

517   Telecommunications

5171	Wired Telecommunications Carriers
51711	Wired Telecommunications Carriers
517111	Wired Telecom. Carriers (exc. Cable)
517112	Cable & Other Program Distribution
5172	Wireless Telecom. Carriers (exc. Satellite)
51721	Wireless Telecom. Carriers (exc. Satellite)
517210	Wireless Telecom. Carriers (exc. Satellite)
5174	Satellite Telecommunications
51741	Satellite Telecommunications
517410	Satellite Telecommunications
5179	Other Telecommunications
51791	Other Telecommunications
517910	Other Telecommunications

518   Data Processing, Hosting, & Related Service

5182	Data Processing, Hosting, & Related Service
51821	Data Processing, Hosting, & Related Service
518210	Data Processing, Hosting, & Related Service

519   Other Information Services

5191	Other Information Services
51911	News Syndicates
519110	News Syndicates
51912	Libraries & Archives
519121	Libraries
519122	Archives
51913	Internet Pub. & Brdcst. & Web Search Portals

519130	Internet Pub. & Brdcst. & Web Search Portals
51919	All Other Information Services
519190	All Other Information Services

52   Finance & Insurance

521   Monetary Authorities - Central Bank

5211	Monetary Authorities - Central Bank
52111	Monetary Authorities - Central Bank
521110	Monetary Authorities - Central Bank

522   Credit Intermediation & Related Activities

5221	Depository Credit Intermediation
52211	Banking
522111	Personal & Commercial Banking Industry
522112	Corporate & Institutional Banking Industry
52213	Local Credit Unions
522130	Local Credit Unions
52219	Other Depository Credit Intermediation
522190	Other Depository Credit Intermediation
5222	Non-Depository Credit Intermediation
52221	Credit Card Issuing
522210	Credit Card Issuing
52222	Sales Financing
522220	Sales Financing
52229	Other Non-Depository Credit Intermediation
522291	Consumer Lending
522299	All Other Non-Depository Credit Intermed.
5223	Activities Related to Credit Intermediation
52231	Mortgage & Other Loan Brokers
522310	Mortgage & Other Loan Brokers
52232	Fin. Transactions Process. & Related Act.
522321	Central Credit Unions
522329	Other Fin. Transac. Process. & Related Act.
52239	Other Activities Related to Credit Intermed.
522390	Other Activities Related to Credit Intermed.

523	**Securities, Commodity Contracts & Related**
5231	Securities & Commodity Contracts Intermed.
52311	Investment Banking & Securities Dealing
523110	Investment Banking & Securities Dealing
52312	Securities Brokerage
523120	Securities Brokerage
52313	Commodity Contracts Dealing
523130	Commodity Contracts Dealing
52314	Commodity Contracts Brokerage
523140	Commodity Contracts Brokerage
5232	Securities & Commodity Exchanges
52321	Securities & Commodity Exchanges
523210	Securities & Commodity Exchanges
5239	Other Financial Investment Activities
52391	Miscellaneous Intermediation
523910	Miscellaneous Intermediation
52392	Portfolio Management
523920	Portfolio Management
52393	Investment Advice
523930	Investment Advice
52399	All Other Financial Investment Activities
523990	All Other Financial Investment Activities

524	**Insurance Carriers & Related Activities**
5241	Insurance Carriers
52411	Direct Life, Health & Medical Insurance
524111	Direct Individual Life, etc., Insurance
524112	Direct Group Life, etc., Insurance Carriers
52412	Direct Insurance (exc. Life, Health, etc.)
524121	Direct General Property & Casualty Insurance
524122	Direct, Private, Automobile Insurance
524123	Direct, Public, Automobile Insurance
524124	Direct Property Insurance Carriers
524125	Direct Liability Insurance Carriers
524129	Other Direct Insurance (exc. Life, etc.)
52413	Reinsurance Carriers
524131	Life Reinsurance Carriers
524132	Accident & Sickness Reinsurance Carriers
524133	Automobile Reinsurance Carriers
524134	Property Reinsurance Carriers

524135	Liability Reinsurance Carriers
524139	General & Other Reinsurance Carriers
5242	Agencies, Brokerages & Other Insurance Act.
52421	Insurance Agencies & Brokerages
524210	Insurance Agencies & Brokerages
52429	Other Insurance Related Activities
524291	Claims Adjusters
524299	All Other Insurance Related Activities

526	**Funds & Other Financial Vehicles**
5261	Pension Funds
52611	Pension Funds
526111	Trusteed Pension Funds
526112	Non-Trusteed Pension Funds
5269	Other Funds & Financial Vehicles
52691	Open-End Investment Funds
526911	Equity Funds - Canadian
526912	Equity Funds - Foreign
526913	Mortgage Funds
526914	Money Market Funds
526915	Bond & Income / Dividend Funds - Canadian
526916	Bond & Income / Dividend Funds - Foreign
526917	Balanced Funds / Asset Allocation Funds
526919	Other Open-Ended Funds
52693	Segregated (exc. Pension) Funds
526930	Segregated (exc. Pension) Funds
52698	All Other Funds & Financial Vehicles
526981	Securitization Vehicles
526989	All Other Misc. Funds & Financial Vehicles

53	**Real Estate & Rental & Leasing**
531	**Real Estate**
5311	Lessors of Real Estate
53111	Lessors of Residential Buildings & Dwellings
531111	Lessors of Res. Buildings (exc. Soc. Housing)
531112	Lessors of Social Housing Projects
53112	Lessors - Non-Res. Buildings (exc. Mini-Ware)
531120	Lessors - Non-Res. Buildings (exc. Mini-Ware)
53113	Self-Storage Mini-Warehouses
531130	Self-Storage Mini-Warehouses
53119	Lessors of Other Real Estate Property

531190	Lessors of Other Real Estate Property
5312	Offices of Real Estate Agents & Brokers
53121	Offices of Real Estate Agents & Brokers
531211	Real Estate Agents
531212	Offices of Real Estate Brokers
5313	Activities Related to Real Estate
53131	Real Estate Property Managers
531310	Real Estate Property Managers
53132	Offices of Real Estate Appraisers
531320	Offices of Real Estate Appraisers
53139	Other Activities Related to Real Estate
531390	Other Activities Related to Real Estate

532   Rental & Leasing Services

5321	Automotive Equipment Rental & Leasing
53211	Passenger Car Rental & Leasing
532111	Passenger Car Rental
532112	Passenger Car Leasing
53212	Truck, Utility Trailer & RV Rental & Leasing
532120	Truck, Utility Trailer & RV Rental & Leasing
5322	Consumer Goods Rental
53221	Consumer Electronics & Appliance Rental
532210	Consumer Electronics & Appliance Rental
53222	Formal Wear & Costume Rental
532220	Formal Wear & Costume Rental
53223	Video Tape & Disc Rental
532230	Video Tape & Disc Rental
53229	Other Consumer Goods Rental
532290	Other Consumer Goods Rental
5323	General Rental Centres
53231	General Rental Centres
532310	General Rental Centres
5324	Commercial & Ind'l Machinery Rental & Leasing
53241	Construction, etc., Mach. Rental & Leasing
532410	Construction, etc., Mach. Rental & Leasing
53242	Office Machinery & Equipment Rental & Leasing
532420	Office Machinery & Equipment Rental & Leasing
53249	Other Commercial & Ind'l Mach. Rental/Leasing
532490	Other Commercial & Ind'l Mach. Rental/Leasing

533   Lessors of Non-Financial Intangible Assets

5331	Lessors of Non-Financial Intangible Assets
53311	Lessors of Non-Financial Intangible Assets
533110	Lessors of Non-Financial Intangible Assets

54   Professional, Scientific & Technical Services

541   Professional, Scientific & Technical Services

5411	Legal Services
54111	Offices of Lawyers
541110	Offices of Lawyers
54112	Offices of Notaries
541120	Offices of Notaries
54119	Other Legal Services
541190	Other Legal Services
5412	Accounting, Tax Prep. & Bookkeeping Services
54121	Accounting, Tax Prep. & Bookkeeping Services
541212	Offices of Accountants
541213	Tax Preparation Services
541215	Bookkeeping, Payroll & Related Services
5413	Architectural, Engineering & Related Services
54131	Architectural Services
541310	Architectural Services
54132	Landscape Architectural Services
541320	Landscape Architectural Services
54133	Engineering Services
541330	Engineering Services
54134	Drafting Services
541340	Drafting Services
54135	Building Inspection Services
541350	Building Inspection Services
54136	Geophysical Surveying & Mapping Services
541360	Geophysical Surveying & Mapping Services
54137	Surveying & Mapping (exc. Geophysical) Serv.
541370	Surveying & Mapping (exc. Geophysical) Serv.
54138	Testing Laboratories
541380	Testing Laboratories
5414	Specialized Design Services

54141	Interior Design Services
541410	Interior Design Services
54142	Industrial Design Services
541420	Industrial Design Services
54143	Graphic Design Services
541430	Graphic Design Services
54149	Other Specialized Design Services
541490	Other Specialized Design Services
5415	Computer Systems Design & Related Services
54151	Computer Systems Design & Related Services
541510	Computer Systems Design & Related Services
5416	Mgmt., Scientific & Tech. Consulting Serv.
54161	Management Consulting Services
541611	Administrative & Gen. Mgmt. Consulting Serv.
541612	Human Resources Consulting Services
541619	Other Management Consulting Services
54162	Environmental Consulting Services
541620	Environmental Consulting Services
54169	Other Scientific & Technical Consulting Serv.
541690	Other Scientific & Technical Consulting Serv.
5417	Scientific R&D Services
54171	R&D in the Physical, Eng. & Life Sciences
541710	R&D in the Physical, Eng. & Life Sciences
54172	R&D in the Social Sciences & Humanities
541720	R&D in the Social Sciences & Humanities
5418	Advertising & Related Services
54181	Advertising Agencies
541810	Advertising Agencies
54182	Public Relations Services
541820	Public Relations Services
54183	Media Buying Agencies
541830	Media Buying Agencies
54184	Media Representatives
541840	Media Representatives
54185	Display Advertising
541850	Display Advertising
54186	Direct Mail Advertising
541860	Direct Mail Advertising
54187	Advertising Material Distribution Services
541870	Advertising Material Distribution Services

54189	Other Services Related to Advertising
541891	Specialty Advertising Distributors
541899	All Other Services Related to Advertising
5419	Other Prof., Scientific & Technical Services
54191	Market Research & Public Opinion Polling
541910	Market Research & Public Opinion Polling
54192	Photographic Services
541920	Photographic Services
54193	Translation & Interpretation Services
541930	Translation & Interpretation Services
54194	Veterinary Services
541940	Veterinary Services
54199	All Other Prof., Scientific & Tech. Services
541990	All Other Prof., Scientific & Tech. Services

55 Management of Companies & Enterprises

551	**Management of Companies & Enterprises**
5511	Management of Companies & Enterprises
55111	Management of Companies & Enterprises
551113	Holding Companies
551114	Head Offices

56 Admin., Support, Waste Mgmt. & Remed. Serv.

561	**Administrative & Support Services**
5611	Office Administrative Services
56111	Office Administrative Services
561110	Office Administrative Services
5612	Facilities Support Services
56121	Facilities Support Services
561210	Facilities Support Services
5613	Employment Services
56131	Employ. Placement Agency & Exec. Search Serv.
561310	Employ. Placement Agency & Exec. Search Serv.
56132	Temporary Help Services
561320	Temporary Help Services
56133	Professional Employer Organizations
561330	Professional Employer Organizations
5614	Business Support Services

56141	Document Preparation Services
561410	Document Preparation Services
56142	Telephone Call Centres
561420	Telephone Call Centres
56143	Business Service Centres
561430	Business Service Centres
56144	Collection Agencies
561440	Collection Agencies
56145	Credit Bureaus
561450	Credit Bureaus
56149	Other Business Support Services
561490	Other Business Support Services
5615	Travel Arrangement & Reservation Services
56151	Travel Agencies
561510	Travel Agencies
56152	Tour Operators
561520	Tour Operators
56159	Other Travel Arrangement & Reservation
561590	Other Travel Arrangement & Reservation
5616	Investigation & Security Services
56161	Investigation, Guard & Armoured Car Services
561611	Investigation Services
561612	Security Guard & Patrol Services
561613	Armoured Car Services
56162	Security Systems Services
561621	Security Systems Services (exc. Locksmiths)
561622	Locksmiths
5617	Services to Buildings & Dwellings
56171	Exterminating & Pest Control Services
561710	Exterminating & Pest Control Services
56172	Janitorial Services
561721	Window Cleaning Services
561722	Janitorial Services (exc. Window Cleaning)
56173	Landscaping Services
561730	Landscaping Services
56174	Carpet & Upholstery Cleaning Services
561740	Carpet & Upholstery Cleaning Services
56179	Other Services to Buildings & Dwellings
561791	Duct & Chimney Cleaning Services
561799	All Other Services to Buildings & Dwellings
5619	Other Support Services
56191	Packaging & Labelling Services
561910	Packaging & Labelling Services

56192	Convention & Trade Show Organizers
561920	Convention & Trade Show Organizers
56199	All Other Support Services
561990	All Other Support Services
562	**Waste Management & Remediation Services**
5621	Waste Collection
56211	Waste Collection
562110	Waste Collection
5622	Waste Treatment & Disposal
56221	Waste Treatment & Disposal
562210	Waste Treatment & Disposal
5629	Remediation & Other Waste Mgmt. Services
56291	Remediation Services
562910	Remediation Services
56292	Material Recovery Facilities
562920	Material Recovery Facilities
56299	All Other Waste Management Services
562990	All Other Waste Management Services

61	**Educational Services**
611	**Educational Services**
6111	Elementary & Secondary Schools
61111	Elementary & Secondary Schools
611110	Elementary & Secondary Schools
6112	Community Colleges & C.E.G.E.P.s
61121	Community Colleges & C.E.G.E.P.s
611210	Community Colleges & C.E.G.E.P.s
6113	Universities
61131	Universities
611310	Universities
6114	Business Schools & Computer & Mgmt. Training
61141	Business & Secretarial Schools
611410	Business & Secretarial Schools
61142	Computer Training
611420	Computer Training
61143	Professional & Mgmt. Development Training
611430	Professional & Mgmt. Development Training
6115	Technical & Trade Schools
61151	Technical & Trade Schools
611510	Technical & Trade Schools
6116	Other Schools & Instruction
61161	Fine Arts Schools

611610	Fine Arts Schools		6219	Other Ambulatory Health Care Services
61162	Athletic Instruction		62191	Ambulance Services
611620	Athletic Instruction		621911	Ambulance (exc. Air Ambulance) Services
61163	Language Schools			
611630	Language Schools		621912	Air Ambulance Services
61169	All Other Schools & Instruction		62199	All Other Ambulatory Health Care Services
611690	All Other Schools & Instruction			
6117	Educational Support Services		621990	All Other Ambulatory Health Care Services
61171	Educational Support Services			
611710	Educational Support Services			

62 Health Care & Social Assistance

621 Ambulatory Health Care Services

6211	Offices of Physicians
62111	Offices of Physicians
621110	Offices of Physicians
6212	Offices of Dentists
62121	Offices of Dentists
621210	Offices of Dentists
6213	Offices of Other Health Practitioners
62131	Offices of Chiropractors
621310	Offices of Chiropractors
62132	Offices of Optometrists
621320	Offices of Optometrists
62133	Mental Health Practitioners (exc. Physicians)
621330	Mental Health Practitioners (exc. Physicians)
62134	Physical & Speech Therapists & Audiologists
621340	Physical & Speech Therapists & Audiologists
62139	Offices of All Other Health Practitioners
621390	Offices of All Other Health Practitioners
6214	Out-Patient Care Centres
62141	Family Planning Centres
621410	Family Planning Centres
62142	Out-Patient Mental Health, etc., Centres
621420	Out-Patient Mental Health, etc., Centres
62149	Other Out-Patient Care Centres
621494	Community Health Centres
621499	All Other Out-Patient Care Centres
6215	Medical & Diagnostic Laboratories
62151	Medical & Diagnostic Laboratories
621510	Medical & Diagnostic Laboratories
6216	Home Health Care Services
62161	Home Health Care Services
621610	Home Health Care Services

622 Hospitals

6221	General Medical & Surgical Hospitals
62211	General Medical & Surgical Hospitals
622111	General (exc. Paediatric) Hospitals
622112	Paediatric Hospitals
6222	Psychiatric & Substance Abuse Hospitals
62221	Psychiatric & Substance Abuse Hospitals
622210	Psychiatric & Substance Abuse Hospitals
6223	Specialty (exc. Psych., etc.) Hospitals
62231	Specialty (exc. Psych., etc.) Hospitals
622310	Specialty (exc. Psych., etc.) Hospitals

623 Nursing & Residential Care Facilities

6231	Nursing Care Facilities
62311	Nursing Care Facilities
623110	Nursing Care Facilities
6232	Res. Developmental Handicap, etc., Facilities
62321	Residential Developmental Handicap Facilities
623210	Residential Developmental Handicap Facilities
62322	Res. Mental Health & Substance Abuse Fac.
623221	Residential Substance Abuse Facilities
623222	Homes for the Psychiatrically Disabled
6233	Community Care Facilities for the Elderly
62331	Community Care Facilities for the Elderly
623310	Community Care Facilities for the Elderly
6239	Other Residential Care Facilities
62399	Other Residential Care Facilities
623991	Transition Homes for Women

623992	Homes for Emotionally Disturbed Children
623993	Homes for the Physically Handicapped/Disabled
623999	All Other Residential Care Facilities

624 Social Assistance

6241	Individual & Family Services
62411	Child & Youth Services
624110	Child & Youth Services
62412	Services for the Elderly & Disabled Persons
624120	Services for the Elderly & Disabled Persons
62419	Other Individual & Family Services
624190	Other Individual & Family Services
6242	Community Food & Housing & Emerg., etc. Serv.
62421	Community Food Services
624210	Community Food Services
62422	Community Housing Services
624220	Community Housing Services
62423	Emergency & Other Relief Services
624230	Emergency & Other Relief Services
6243	Vocational Rehabilitation Services
62431	Vocational Rehabilitation Services
624310	Vocational Rehabilitation Services
6244	Child Day-Care Services
62441	Child Day-Care Services
624410	Child Day-Care Services

71 Arts, Entertainment & Recreation

711 Performing Arts, Spectator Sports & Related

7111	Performing Arts Companies
71111	Theatre Companies & Dinner Theatres
711111	Theatre (exc. Musical) Companies
711112	Musical Theatre & Opera Companies
71112	Dance Companies
711120	Dance Companies
71113	Musical Groups & Artists
711130	Musical Groups & Artists
71119	Other Performing Arts Companies
711190	Other Performing Arts Companies
7112	Spectator Sports
71121	Spectator Sports
711211	Sports Teams & Clubs
711213	Horse Race Tracks
711218	Other Spectator Sports

7113	Promoters of Performing Arts, Sports, etc.
71131	Promoters of Arts, Sports, etc. with Fac.
711311	Live Theatres & Other Presenters with Fac.
711319	Sports Stadiums & Other Presenters with Fac.
71132	Promoters of Arts, Sports, etc. w/o Fac.
711321	Performing Arts Promoters w/o Fac.
711322	Festivals w/o Facilities
711329	Sports & Other Presenters w/o Facilities
7114	Agents & Managers for Public Figures
71141	Agents & Managers for Public Figures
711410	Agents & Managers for Public Figures
7115	Independent Artists, Writers & Performers
71151	Independent Artists, Writers & Performers
711511	Independent Artists, Visual Arts
711512	Independent Actors, Comedians & Performers
711513	Independent Writers & Authors

712 Heritage Institutions

7121	Heritage Institutions
71211	Museums
712111	Non-Commercial Art Museums & Galleries
712115	History & Science Museums
712119	Other Museums
71212	Historic & Heritage Sites
712120	Historic & Heritage Sites
71213	Zoos & Botanical Gardens
712130	Zoos & Botanical Gardens
71219	Nature Parks & Other Similar Institutions
712190	Nature Parks & Other Similar Institutions

713 Amusement, Gambling & Recreation Industries

7131	Amusement Parks & Arcades
71311	Amusement & Theme Parks
713110	Amusement & Theme Parks
71312	Amusement Arcades
713120	Amusement Arcades
7132	Gambling Industries

71321	Casinos (exc. Casino Hotels)
713210	Casinos (exc. Casino Hotels)
71329	Other Gambling Industries
713291	Lotteries
713299	All Other Gambling Industries
7139	Other Amusement & Recreation Industries
71391	Golf Courses & Country Clubs
713910	Golf Courses & Country Clubs
71392	Skiing Facilities
713920	Skiing Facilities
71393	Marinas
713930	Marinas
71394	Fitness & Recreational Sports Centres
713940	Fitness & Recreational Sports Centres
71395	Bowling Centres
713950	Bowling Centres
71399	All Other Amusement & Recreation Industries
713990	All Other Amusement & Recreation Industries

72 Accommodation & Food Services

721 Accommodation Services

7211	Traveller Accommodation
72111	Hotels (exc. Casino Hotels) & Motels
721111	Hotels
721112	Motor Hotels
721113	Resorts
721114	Motels
72112	Casino Hotels
721120	Casino Hotels
72119	Other Traveller Accommodation
721191	Bed & Breakfast
721192	Housekeeping Cottages & Cabins
721198	All Other Traveller Accommodation
7212	RV Parks & Recreational Camps
72121	RV Parks & Recreational Camps
721211	RV Parks & Campgrounds
721212	Hunting & Fishing Camps
721213	Rec. (exc. Hunting & Fishing) & Vac. Camps
7213	Rooming & Boarding Houses
72131	Rooming & Boarding Houses
721310	Rooming & Boarding Houses

722 Food Services & Drinking Places

7221	Full-Service Restaurants
72211	Full-Service Restaurants
722110	Full-Service Restaurants
7222	Limited-Service Eating Places
72221	Limited-Service Eating Places
722210	Limited-Service Eating Places
7223	Special Food Services
72231	Food Service Contractors
722310	Food Service Contractors
72232	Caterers
722320	Caterers
72233	Mobile Caterers
722330	Mobile Caterers
7224	Drinking Places (Alcoholic Beverages)
72241	Drinking Places (Alcoholic Beverages)
722410	Drinking Places (Alcoholic Beverages)

81 Other Services (exc. Public Administration)

811 Repair & Maintenance

8111	Automotive R&M
81111	Automotive Mechanical & Electrical R&M
811111	General Automotive Repair
811112	Automotive Exhaust System Repair
811119	Other Automotive Mechanical & Electrical R&M
81112	Auto. Body, Paint, Interior & Glass Repair
811121	Automotive Body, Paint & Interior R&M
811122	Automotive Glass Replacement Shops
81119	Other Automotive R&M
811192	Car Washes
811199	All Other Automotive R&M
8112	Electronic & Precision Equipment R&M
81121	Electronic & Precision Equipment R&M
811210	Electronic & Precision Equipment R&M
8113	Commercial & Ind'l Mach. & Eqp. R&M
81131	Commercial & Ind'l Mach. & Eqp. R&M
811310	Commercial & Ind'l Mach. & Eqp. R&M
8114	Personal & Household Goods R&M
81141	Home & Garden Equipment & Appliance R&M
811411	Home & Garden Equipment R&M
811412	Appliance R&M
81142	Reupholstery & Furniture Repair
811420	Reupholstery & Furniture Repair

81143	Footwear & Leather Goods Repair
811430	Footwear & Leather Goods Repair
81149	Other Personal & Household Goods R&M
811490	Other Personal & Household Goods R&M

812   **Personal & Laundry Services**

8121	Personal Care Services
81211	Hair Care & Esthetic Services
812114	Barber Shops
812115	Beauty Salons
812116	Unisex Hair Salons
81219	Other Personal Care Services
812190	Other Personal Care Services
8122	Funeral Services
81221	Funeral Homes
812210	Funeral Homes
81222	Cemeteries & Crematoria
812220	Cemeteries & Crematoria
8123	Dry Cleaning & Laundry Services
81231	Coin-Operated Laundries & Dry Cleaners
812310	Coin-Operated Laundries & Dry Cleaners
81232	Dry Cleaning & Laundry Serv. (exc. Coin-Op.)
812320	Dry Cleaning & Laundry Serv. (exc. Coin-Op.)
81233	Linen & Uniform Supply
812330	Linen & Uniform Supply
8129	Other Personal Services
81291	Pet Care (exc. Veterinary) Services
812910	Pet Care (exc. Veterinary) Services
81292	Photo Finishing Services
812921	Photo Finishing Laboratories (exc. One-Hour)
812922	One-Hour Photo Finishing
81293	Parking Lots & Garages
812930	Parking Lots & Garages
81299	All Other Personal Services
812990	All Other Personal Services

813   **Relig., Grant-Making, Civic & Similar Orgs.**

8131	Religious Organizations
81311	Religious Organizations
813110	Religious Organizations
8132	Grant-Making & Giving Services
81321	Grant-Making & Giving Services
813210	Grant-Making & Giving Services
8133	Social Advocacy Organizations
81331	Social Advocacy Organizations
813310	Social Advocacy Organizations

8134	Civic & Social Organizations
81341	Civic & Social Organizations
813410	Civic & Social Organizations
8139	Business, Prof., Labour & Other Member. Orgs.
81391	Business Associations
813910	Business Associations
81392	Professional Organizations
813920	Professional Organizations
81393	Labour Organizations
813930	Labour Organizations
81394	Political Organizations
813940	Political Organizations
81399	Other Membership Organizations
813990	Other Membership Organizations

814   **Private Households**

8141	Private Households
81411	Private Households
814110	Private Households

91   Public Administration

911   **Federal Government Public Administration**

9111	Defence Services
91111	Defence Services
911110	Defence Services
9112	Federal Protective Services
91121	Federal Courts of Law
911210	Federal Courts of Law
91122	Federal Correctional Services
911220	Federal Correctional Services
91123	Federal Police Services
911230	Federal Police Services
91124	Federal Regulatory Services
911240	Federal Regulatory Services
91129	Other Federal Protective Services
911290	Other Federal Protective Services
9113	Federal Labour, Employment & Immig. Serv.
91131	Federal Labour & Employment Services
911310	Federal Labour & Employment Services
91132	Immigration Services
911320	Immigration Services
91139	Other Fed. Labour, Employ. & Immig. Serv.
911390	Other Fed. Labour, Employ. & Immig. Serv.
9114	Foreign Affairs & International Assistance

91141	Foreign Affairs		**913**	**Municipal Public Administration**
911410	Foreign Affairs			
91142	International Assistance		9131	Municipal Protective Services
911420	International Assistance		91311	Municipal Courts of Law
9119	Other Fed. Government Public Administration		913110	Municipal Courts of Law
			91312	Municipal Correctional Services
91191	Other Fed. Government Public Administration		913120	Municipal Correctional Services
			91313	Municipal Police Services
911910	Other Fed. Government Public Administration		913130	Municipal Police Services
			91314	Municipal Fire-Fighting Services
			913140	Municipal Fire-Fighting Services
912	**Prov. & Territorial Public Administration**		91315	Municipal Regulatory Services
			913150	Municipal Regulatory Services
9121	Provincial Protective Services		91319	Other Municipal Protective Services
91211	Provincial Courts of Law		913190	Other Municipal Protective Services
912110	Provincial Courts of Law		9139	Other Municipal Public Administration
91212	Provincial Correctional Services			
912120	Provincial Correctional Services		91391	Other Municipal Public Administration
91213	Provincial Police Services			
912130	Provincial Police Services		913910	Other Municipal Public Administration
91214	Provincial Fire-Fighting Services			
912140	Provincial Fire-Fighting Services			
91215	Provincial Regulatory Services		**914**	**Aboriginal Public Administration**
912150	Provincial Regulatory Services			
91219	Other Provincial Protective Services		9141	Aboriginal Public Administration
912190	Other Provincial Protective Services		91411	Aboriginal Public Administration
9122	Provincial Labour & Employment Services		914110	Aboriginal Public Administration
91221	Provincial Labour & Employment Services		**919**	**Extra-Territorial Public Administration**
912210	Provincial Labour & Employment Services			
9129	Other Prov. & Terr. Public Administration		9191	Extra-Territorial Public Administration
91291	Other Prov. & Terr. Public Administration		91911	Extra-Territorial Public Administration
912910	Other Prov. & Terr. Public Administration		919110	Extra-Territorial Public Administration

Alphabetical Index

Alphabetical Index

The Index is a list of activity descriptions, arranged in alphabetical order, with the NAICS Canada code to which each activity belongs.

For users, who wish to code businesses to NAICS Canada, coding tools with more extensive reference lists of activities are available. Enquiries should be addressed to:

Statistics Canada
Standards Division
Jean Talon Bldg., 12th Floor
170 Tunney's Pasture Driveway
Ottawa (Ontario)
K1A OT6
Tel.: 613-951-8576
Fax: 613-951-8578
E-mail: standards@statcan.ca
Website: www.statcan.ca

9

91313   911 emergency services

A

561722   Abattoir cleaning
311611   Abattoirs
91411   Aboriginal administration, public
33911   Abrasive points, wheels and disks, dental, manufacturing
32791   Abrasive products, manufacturing
212323   Abrasive sand mining
41723   Abrasives, wholesale
23731   Abutment construction
315299   Academic caps and gowns, cut and sewn from purchased fabric
61111   Academies, elementary or secondary
32519   Accelerators (i.e., basic synthetic chemicals), manufacturing
52222   Acceptance companies
517111   Access-dependent VoIP services providers, facilities based, except wireless and cable
81331   Accident prevention association
721211   Accommodation services, camping grounds and trailer parks
721198   Accommodation services, guest houses and tourist homes
721111   Accommodation services, hotel
721114   Accommodation services, motel
721192   Accommodation services, tourist courts and cabins
541212   Accountant, professional
81392   Accountants' associations
541212   Accounting services, professional
56144   Accounts collection agencies
33591   Accumulator batteries and parts, manufacturing
32521   Acetal resins, manufacturing
32522   Acetate fibres and filaments, manufacturing
32519   Acetates, not specified elsewhere by process, manufacturing
32519   Acetic acid, manufacturing
33242   Acetylene cylinders, manufacturing
32512   Acetylene, manufacturing
32541   Acetylsalicylic acid, manufacturing
213118   Acidizing wells, on a contract basis
311511   Acidophilus milk, manufacturing
32519   Acids, fatty (e.g., margaric, oleic, stearic), manufacturing
32519   Acids, organic, not specified elsewhere by process, manufacturing

54133   Acoustical engineering consulting services
23831   Acoustical foam, sound barrier, installation
32521   Acrylate rubber, manufacturing
326114   Acrylic film and unlaminated sheet, manufacturing
32521   Acrylic resins, manufacturing
32521   Acrylonitrile-butadiene-styrene (ABS) resins, manufacturing
212398   Actinolite mine
325999   Activated carbon and charcoal, manufacturing
325999   Activated clays, earths and other mineral products, manufacturing
711512   Actors, independent
711512   Actresses, independent
541612   Actuarial consulting services
33399   Actuators, fluid power, manufacturing
62139   Acupuncturists' offices
32511   Acyclic hydrocarbons (except acetylene), made from refined petroleum or natural gas liquids
62221   Addiction hospitals
33331   Adding machines, electronic, manufacturing
33331   Adding machines, manufacturing
23622   Additions, alterations and renovations, commercial and institutional buildings, by general contractors
23622   Additions, alterations and renovations, commercial and institutional buildings, by operative builders
23622   Additions, alterations and renovations, hotels and motels
23621   Additions, alterations and renovations, industrial buildings
23622   Additions, alterations and renovations, industrial warehouses
23611   Additions, alterations and renovations, residential buildings
23611   Additions, alterations and renovations, residential buildings, by operative builders
325999   Additive preparations for gasoline (e.g., anti-knock preparations, detergents, gum inhibitors), manufacturing
56149   Address bar coding services
51114   Address list compilers (except exclusively on Internet)
323119   Address lists, printing without publishing
32222   Adhesive tape (except medical), made from purchased materials
33911   Adhesive tape, medical, manufacturing

32552	Adhesives (except asphalt, dental, gypsum-based), manufacturing
32519	Adipic acid, manufacturing
91121	Administrative courts, federal government
91211	Administrative courts, provincial government
541611	Administrative management consultants
56111	Administrative management services
62411	Adoption services
91291	Adult and recreational education programs, provincial government
62412	Adult day-care centres
54181	Advertising agencies
54181	Advertising consultants (agencies)
54186	Advertising mailing services (i.e., preparing advertising material, such as coupons, flyers or samples, for mailing or other direct distribution)
54187	Advertising material (e.g., circulars, samples), direct distribution services
323119	Advertising material (e.g., coupons, flyers), printing without publishing
54184	Advertising media representatives, offices of
51112	Advertising periodicals, publishing (except exclusively on Internet)
54184	Advertising representatives, media, independent
54184	Advertising representatives, television or radio, independent
54185	Advertising services, indoor or outdoor display
541891	Advertising specialty distribution services (creating and organizing the production of specialty advertising products)
81331	Advocacy groups
481215	Aerial advertising, using general purpose aircraft
48799	Aerial cable cars, sightseeing
481215	Aerial crop dusting, using general purpose aircraft
54192	Aerial photography services (i.e., photographers specializing in aerial photography, except map making)
54137	Aerial surveying (except geophysical), using specialized equipment
48799	Aerial tramways, sightseeing or scenic
33392	Aerial work platforms, manufacturing
71394	Aerobic dance centres
61162	Aerobic dance instructors, independent
334511	Aeronautical systems and instruments, manufacturing

325999	Aerosol can filling, on a job order or contract basis
332431	Aerosol cans, manufacturing
325999	Aerosol packaging services
33291	Aerosol valves, metal, manufacturing
32562	After-shave preparations, manufacturing
32541	Agar culture media, manufacturing
32541	Agar-agar grinding, manufacturing
212398	Agate mining
62331	Aged nursing home
526989	Agency fund
41912	Agents and brokers, wholesale trade
71141	Agents or managers for artists
71141	Agents or managers for authors
71141	Agents or managers for celebrities
71141	Agents or managers for entertainers
71141	Agents or managers for public figures
71141	Agents or managers for sports figures
488511	Agents, shipping (marine)
71141	Agents, theatrical talent
33312	Aggregate spreaders, manufacturing
41639	Aggregate, wholesale
41722	Agitators, crushers and classifiers, mine, wholesale
41722	Agitators, crushers and classifiers, mine, wholesale and repair
41839	Agricultural chemical dusts and sprays, wholesale
54169	Agricultural consulting (technical) services
452999	Agricultural co-op stores (i.e., general stores, not primarily food)
91191	Agricultural extension services, federal government
711322	Agricultural fair promoters, without facilities
33221	Agricultural handtools (e.g., hay forks, hoes, rakes, spades), non-powered, manufacturing
41711	Agricultural implement, wholesale
41711	Agricultural implement, wholesale and repair
32741	Agricultural lime, manufacturing
212315	Agricultural limestone, ground
41839	Agricultural limestone, wholesale
53249	Agricultural machinery and equipment rental
81131	Agricultural machinery and equipment repair and maintenance
41711	Agricultural machinery and equipment, wholesale
41711	Agricultural machinery and equipment, wholesale and repair

51112 Agricultural magazines and periodicals, publishing (except exclusively on Internet)

11511 Agricultural product sterilization service

484229 Agricultural products trucking, local

53119 Agricultural property rental

44422 Agricultural supplies stores selling primarily to other business but also selling to household consumers

41912 Agricultural supplies, wholesale agents and brokers

91291 Agriculture and forestry programs, provincial government

54171 Agriculture research and development laboratories

61121 Agriculture schools (non-university)

54169 Agrology consulting services

54169 Agronomy consulting services

62411 Aid to families with dependent children (AFDC)

33639 Air bag assemblies, manufacturing

481214 Air cargo carriers (except air courier), non-scheduled

48111 Air cargo carriers (except air courier), scheduled

332439 Air cargo containers, light gauge metal, manufacturing

488519 Air cargo customs clearances, service

33391 Air compressors, manufacturing

41639 Air ducts, sheet metal, wholesale

488119 Air freight handling at airports

48111 Air freight transportation service, scheduled

32561 Air fresheners, manufacturing

48111 Air passenger carriers, scheduled

481214 Air passenger charter transportation service

333413 Air purification equipment, stationary, manufacturing

333413 Air scrubbing systems, manufacturing

711329 Air show promoters, without facilities

23822 Air system balancing and testing, contractors

481215 Air taxi services

334511 Air traffic control radar systems and equipment, manufacturing

488111 Air traffic control services

91191 Air transport program, federal government

333413 Air washers (i.e., scrubbers), manufacturing

32512 Air, liquid, manufacturing

48721 Airboats (i.e., swamp buggies) operation

811412 Air-conditioner repair, self-contained units (except automotive)

41422 Air-conditioners, electric, window-type, wholesale

33639 Air-conditioners, motor vehicle, manufacturing

333416 Air-conditioning and warm air heating combination units, manufacturing

333416 Air-conditioning compressors (except motor vehicle), manufacturing

333416 Air-conditioning condensers and condensing units, manufacturing

333416 Air-conditioning equipment (except motor vehicle), manufacturing

41612 Air-conditioning equipment (except window type units), wholesale

44131 Air-conditioning equipment, automobile, sale and installation, retail

811119 Air-conditioning installation and repair, motor vehicle

44311 Air-conditioning room units, self-contained, retail

23822 Air-conditioning systems, installation or repair

333416 Air-conditioning units (e.g., window, travel trailer, motor home), manufacturing

41799 Aircraft and aeronautical equipment (except electronic), wholesale and repair

41799 Aircraft and parts, wholesale

33641 Aircraft assemblies, subassemblies and parts, manufacturing

33641 Aircraft conversions (i.e., major modifications to systems or equipment)

44122 Aircraft dealers, retail

81121 Aircraft electrical equipment repair (except radio)

334512 Aircraft engine instruments, manufacturing

33641 Aircraft engines and engine parts (except carburetors, pistons, piston rings, valves), manufacturing

41799 Aircraft engines and engine parts, wholesale

48819 Aircraft ferrying service

81121 Aircraft flight instrument repair (except electrical)

41211 Aircraft fuelling services, wholesale

33641 Aircraft fuselage, wing, tail and similar assemblies, manufacturing

332311 Aircraft hangars, pre-engineered, metal, manufacturing

33251 Aircraft hardware, metal, manufacturing

48819	Aircraft inspection service
41799	Aircraft instruments, electric, wholesale
524129	Aircraft insurance
561722	Aircraft janitorial services
33632	Aircraft lighting fixtures, manufacturing
33392	Aircraft loading hoists, manufacturing
48819	Aircraft maintenance service (except factory conversions and overhauls)
488119	Aircraft parking service
33641	Aircraft rebuilding (i.e., restoration to original design specifications)
33636	Aircraft seats, manufacturing
48819	Aircraft servicing and repairing (except factory conversions and overhauls)
48819	Aircraft servicing, at airports
48819	Aircraft testing services
32621	Aircraft tires, manufacturing
48819	Aircraft upholstery repair
33641	Aircraft, manufacturing
41799	Aircraft, wholesale
41799	Aircraft, wholesale and repair
334511	Airframe equipment instruments, manufacturing
56159	Airline reservation offices
56159	Airline ticket offices
33993	Airplane models, toy and hobby, manufacturing
53241	Airplane rental and leasing
488119	Airport baggage handling
23622	Airport building construction
488119	Airport cargo handling services
488119	Airport hangar rental
48599	Airport limousine service, scheduled
488119	Airport operations
23731	Airport runway construction, general contractors
23821	Airport runway lighting contractors
488119	Airport runway maintenance service
488119	Airport, civil, operation and maintenance
334511	Airspeed instruments (aeronautical), manufacturing
212395	Alabaster (gypsum) mining
41732	Alarm and signal systems and devices, electronic (except household smoke detectors), wholesale
41732	Alarm and signal systems and devices, electronic (except household smoke detectors), wholesale and repair
41611	Alarm signal systems, wholesale
561621	Alarm system monitoring
33429	Alarm systems and equipment, manufacturing
561621	Alarm systems sale, combined with installation, maintenance or monitoring

323119	Albums (e.g., photo, scrap), manufacturing
41821	Albums (photo) and scrapbooks, wholesale
32519	Alcohol, ethyl (ethanol), non-potable, manufacturing
41841	Alcohol, industrial, wholesale
32519	Alcohol, methyl (methanol), manufacturing
62419	Alcoholic and drug addiction self-help organizations
91215	Alcoholic beverage control boards, provincial government
31214	Alcoholic beverages (except brandy), distilling
41322	Alcoholic beverages, wholesale
41912	Alcoholic beverages, wholesale agents and brokers
32519	Aldehydes, manufacturing
31212	Ale, brewing
11194	Alfalfa hay farming
41831	Alfalfa, wholesale
11251	Algae and seaweed farming
32522	Alginate fibres, manufacturing
32519	Alginates (e.g., calcium, potassium, sodium), manufacturing
33331	Alignment equipment, motor vehicle wheel, manufacturing
32411	Aliphatic (i.e., acyclic) chemicals, made in petroleum refineries
41841	Alkalies, wholesale
33591	Alkaline batteries, manufacturing
325181	Alkalis, manufacturing
32521	Alkyd resins, manufacturing
32411	Alkylates, made in petroleum refineries
44122	All terrain vehicles (ATV's), retail
41519	All terrain vehicles (ATVs), wholesale
41519	All terrain vehicles (ATVs), wholesale and repair
33142	Alloying purchased copper
33149	Alloying purchased non-ferrous metals (except aluminum, copper)
33149	Alloying purchased precious metals
33699	All-terrain vehicles (ATVs), wheeled or tracked, manufacturing
323119	Almanacs, printing without publishing
51113	Almanacs, publishing (except exclusively on Internet)
71392	Alpine skiing facilities
337127	Altars (except stone and concrete), manufacturing
23713	Alternative energy (e.g., geothermal, ocean wave, solar and wind) structure construction

33632	Alternators and generators, for internal combustion engines, manufacturing
331313	Alumina (aluminum oxide), refining from bauxite
32712	Aluminous refractory cement, manufacturing
331317	Aluminum alloys, made from purchased metals
41621	Aluminum and aluminum alloy, primary forms and basic shapes, wholesale
41621	Aluminum bars, rods, ingots, sheets, pipes, plates, wholesale
331317	Aluminum basic shapes (e.g., bar, ingot, rod, sheet), made from purchased aluminum
331313	Aluminum basic shapes (e.g., bar, ingot, rod, sheet), made in primary aluminum plants
331317	Aluminum billet, made from purchased aluminum
332431	Aluminum cans, manufacturing
325189	Aluminum compounds, not specified elsewhere by process, manufacturing
44419	Aluminum doors and screens, retail
32222	Aluminum foil bags, made from purchased foil
32222	Aluminum foil laminates, made from purchased foil
331317	Aluminum foil, made by flat rolling purchased aluminum
332113	Aluminum forgings, unfinished, made from purchased aluminum
331529	Aluminum foundries (except die-castings)
332999	Aluminum freezer foil, made from purchased foil
331313	Aluminum ingot and other primary production shapes, made in primary aluminum plants
331317	Aluminum ingot, made from purchased aluminum
212299	Aluminum ore mining
23621	Aluminum plant construction, general contractors
23817	Aluminum siding, installation
331317	Aluminum wire and cable, made from purchased aluminum
331313	Aluminum, producing from bauxite or alumina
331317	Aluminum, recovering from scrap or dross
81341	Alumni associations
325189	Alums (e.g., aluminum ammonium sulphate, aluminum potassium sulphate), manufacturing
212398	Alunite mining
41732	Amateur radio communications equipment, wholesale
91191	Amateur sports program, federal government
711211	Amateur sports teams, spectator sports
212398	Amblygonite mining
621911	Ambulance service, road
621912	Ambulance services, air
336211	Ambulances, assembling on purchased chassis
212398	Amethyst mining
32521	Amino resins, manufacturing
41841	Ammonia (except fertilizer material), wholesale
325313	Ammonia (i.e., anhydrous or ammonium hydroxyde), manufacturing
32561	Ammonia, household type, manufacturing
325189	Ammonium chloride, manufacturing
325189	Ammonium compounds, not specified elsewhere by process, manufacturing
325313	Ammonium nitrate, manufacturing
325313	Ammonium phosphates, manufacturing
325313	Ammonium sulphate, manufacturing
41447	Ammunition and firearms, sporting, wholesale
332999	Ammunition, manufacturing
212394	Amosite, milled fibre, mining
32541	Amphetamines, uncompounded, manufacturing
33431	Amplifiers (e.g., auto, home, musical instrument, public address), manufacturing
41421	Amplifiers, speakers and related sound equipment, wholesale
41447	Amusement and sporting goods, wholesale
41912	Amusement and sporting goods, wholesale agents and brokers
71312	Amusement arcades
71312	Amusement device (except gambling) parlours, coin-operated
41799	Amusement park equipment, wholesale
41799	Amusement park equipment, wholesale and repair
71311	Amusement parks (i.e., theme parks, water parks)
71399	Amusement rides, concession operators
32541	Analgesic preparations, manufacturing
33411	Analog computers, manufacturing

41793	Analytical instruments (e.g., photometers, spectrographs, chromatographic), wholesale
23799	Anchored earth retention contractors
212326	Andalusite mining
62111	Anesthesiologists, offices of
32541	Anesthetic preparations, manufacturing
32541	Anesthetics, uncompounded, manufacturing
41621	Angles, rods and bars, steel, wholesale
212395	Anhydrite mining
325313	Anhydrous ammonia, manufacturing
311515	Anhydrous butterfat, manufacturing
81391	Animal breeders association
71213	Animal exhibits, live
311611	Animal fats (except poultry and small game), produced in slaughtering plants
311614	Animal fats, rendering
311515	Animal feed, dry milk products for, manufacturing
311119	Animal feed, prepared (except dogs and cats), manufacturing
311614	Animal feed, processing dead stock or carrion for
311611	Animal feed, slaughtering animals (except poultry and small game) for
31311	Animal fibre yarn, spooling, twisting or winding purchased yarn
45391	Animal foods, pet, retail
41119	Animal hair, wholesale
54194	Animal hospitals
311614	Animal oil, rendering
11521	Animal pedigree service
91129	Animal quarantine service, federal government
81331	Animal rights organizations
71213	Animal safari park
11521	Animal semen collection, production and storage services
23622	Animal shelter and clinic construction
81291	Animal shelters
112991	Animal specialty combination farm
11421	Animal trapping, wild, for zoo or game farm
33699	Animal-drawn vehicles and parts, manufacturing
51211	Animated film production
31511	Anklets, hosiery or socks, knitting
41621	Anode metal, wholesale
41422	Answering machines, telephone, wholesale
56142	Answering services, telephone
44311	Antenna stores, household, retail
238299	Antennas, household, installation and service
33422	Antennas, satellite, manufacturing
33422	Antennas, transmitting and communications, manufacturing
212114	Anthracite mining
32541	Antibacterial preparations, manufacturing
32541	Antibiotics (including veterinary), manufacturing
325999	Antifreeze preparations, manufacturing
32541	Antihistamine preparations, manufacturing
32513	Antimony based pigments, manufacturing
212299	Antimony ore mining
33141	Antimony smelting and primary refining
32562	Anti-perspirants, personal, manufacturing
81331	Antipoverty advocacy organizations
811121	Antique and classic automobile restoration
44112	Antique autos, retail
81142	Antique furniture repair and restoration
45331	Antique home furnishings, retail
45331	Antiques, retail
325999	Anti-scaling compounds, manufacturing
32541	Antiseptic preparations, manufacturing
41451	Antiseptic preparations, wholesale
23611	Apartment building, construction
212398	Apatite mining
11291	Apiaries
212326	Aplite mining
44611	Apothecaries, retail
44815	Apparel accessory stores, retail
31599	Apparel findings and trimmings, made from purchased fabric
81232	Apparel pressing service, for the trade
41413	Apparel trimmings, wholesale
41912	Apparel, wholesale agents and brokers
44812	Apparel, women's, retail
91211	Appeal courts, provincial government
41321	Apple cider (less than 2.5% alcohol), wholesale
11133	Apple orchards
41633	Appliance hardware, wholesale
53221	Appliance rental and leasing
44311	Appliance, radio, television and stereo stores, retail
44211	Appliances and furniture, household, retail (primarily furniture)
41422	Appliances, beauty care, electric, wholesale
33521	Appliances, small electrical, manufacturing

45331	Appliances, used, retail
51821	Application hosting
54151	Application software programming services, custom
31499	Appliquéing on textile products (except clothing)
31499	Appliquéing, on clothing owned by others
323119	Appointment books and refills, manufacturing
524291	Appraisal of damaged cars, by independent adjusters
53132	Appraisal services, real estate
54199	Appraising services (except insurance or real estate)
31599	Aprons, household, made from purchased fabric
31599	Aprons, work (except rubberized and plastics), made from purchased fabric
11251	Aquaculture, animal, freshwater
11251	Aquaculture, animal, salt water
11251	Aquaponics
71213	Aquariums
327215	Aquariums, made from purchased glass
23711	Aqueduct construction, general contractors
54199	Arbitration and conciliation service, non-government
91131	Arbitration services, federal government
91221	Arbitration services, provincial government
71213	Arboreta
56173	Arborist services
33512	Arc lighting fixtures, manufacturing
71312	Arcades, amusement
71212	Archaeological sites (i.e., public display)
54172	Archeological research and development services
54172	Archeological sites, excavations
45111	Archery equipment, retail
71399	Archery ranges
321215	Arches, glued-laminated or pre-engineered wood, manufacturing
54131	Architects (except landscape), offices of
81392	Architects' associations
41793	Architects' equipment and supplies, wholesale
41793	Architects' equipment and supplies, wholesale and repair
54132	Architects, landscape, offices of
32733	Architectural block, concrete (e.g., fluted, screen, split, slump, ground face), manufacturing

32551	Architectural coatings (i.e., paint), manufacturing
54131	Architectural design services (except landscape)
332329	Architectural metal work, manufacturing
41621	Architectural metal work, wholesale
453999	Architectural supplies, retail
32739	Architectural wall panels, precast concrete, manufacturing
519122	Archives
33399	Arc-welding equipment, manufacturing
711319	Arena operators, promoting events
23622	Arena, construction
212316	Argillite, dimension, quarrying
32512	Argon, manufacturing
335312	Armature rewinding, remanufacturing
335312	Armatures, manufacturing
91111	Armed services
561613	Armoured car services
33699	Armoured military vehicles and parts (except tanks), manufacturing
32511	Aromatic cyclic hydrocarbons, made from refined petroleum or natural gas liquids
48899	Arrangement of carpools and vanpools
325189	Arsenic compounds, not specified elsewhere by process, manufacturing
41439	Art and decorative ware, household, wholesale
81399	Art councils
45392	Art dealers, retail
712111	Art galleries (except retail)
32742	Art goods (e.g., gypsum, plaster of Paris), manufacturing
712111	Art museums
51119	Art prints, publishing (except exclusively on Internet)
711511	Art restorers, independent
61161	Art schools (except commercial)
54143	Art studios, commercial
323119	Art works, printing (except screen) without publishing
323113	Art works, screen printing without publishing
45322	Artcraft, retail
33999	Artificial Christmas trees, manufacturing
32791	Artificial corundum, manufacturing
32522	Artificial fibres and filaments, manufacturing
33999	Artificial flower arrangements, assembling from purchased components
41899	Artificial flowers, wholesale

446199	Artificial limb stores, retail
41793	Artificial limbs, wholesale
23899	Artificial turf, installation
41793	Artist equipment and supplies, wholesale
41793	Artist equipment and supplies, wholesale and repair
711511	Artists (except commercial, medical and musical), independent
33994	Artists' supplies (except paper), manufacturing
453999	Artists' supplies, retail
54143	Artists, graphic, independent
54143	Artists, independent medical
711322	Arts (except film) festival organizers, without facilities
711322	Arts (except film) festival promoters, without facilities
61161	Arts and crafts school
91191	Arts and cultural programs, federal government
711311	Arts events organizers, with facilities
711321	Arts events organizers, without facilities (except festivals)
711311	Arts festival promoters, with facilities
711321	Arts presenters, without facilities (except festivals)
212394	Asbestos mining
56291	Asbestos removal contractors
56211	Ashes, collection
56221	Ashes, collection and disposal of
327214	Ashtrays, glass, made in glass-making plants
32711	Ashtrays, pottery, manufacturing
111219	Asparagus farming
32411	Asphalt and asphaltic materials, made in petroleum refineries
44221	Asphalt flooring, installation combined with selling
41721	Asphalt mixing and laying machinery, wholesale
41721	Asphalt mixing and laying machinery, wholesale and repair
322121	Asphalt paper, made in paper mills
23731	Asphalt paving (e.g., roads, public sidewalks, streets), contractors
324121	Asphalt paving blocks, made from purchased asphaltic materials
324121	Asphalt paving mixtures, made from purchased asphaltic materials
32411	Asphalt paving mixtures, made in petroleum refineries
23816	Asphalt roof shingles, installation
324122	Asphalt roofing coatings, made from purchased asphaltic materials
41639	Asphalt roofing materials, wholesale
324122	Asphalt saturated mats and felts, made from purchased asphaltic materials and paper
324122	Asphalt shingles, made from purchased asphaltic materials
324122	Asphalt siding, made from purchased asphaltic materials
54138	Assaying services
337127	Assembly hall furniture, manufacturing
33635	Assembly line rebuilding of automotive, truck and bus transmissions
333519	Assembly machines (e.g., rotary transfer, in-line transfer), manufacturing
23621	Assembly plant construction
33611	Assembly plants, passenger car and light duty motor vehicles, on chassis of own manufacture
32561	Assistants, textile and leather finishing, manufacturing
81391	Association for truckers
81331	Associations for retired persons, advocacy
81299	Astrologers, own account
711218	Athletes, independent, amateur
711218	Athletes, independent, professional (i.e., participating in sporting events)
33992	Athletic and sporting goods (except clothing, firearms and ammunition), manufacturing
41447	Athletic and sporting goods, wholesale
81341	Athletic associations
448199	Athletic clothing (except uniforms), retail
31519	Athletic clothing, men's and boys', made in knitting mills
41411	Athletic clothing, wholesale
31519	Athletic clothing, women's and girls', made in knitting mills
71394	Athletic clubs, physical fitness facilities
23622	Athletic courts, indoor, construction
23799	Athletic field construction, general contractors
44821	Athletic footwear, retail
41412	Athletic footwear, wholesale
31621	Athletic shoes, manufacturing
31511	Athletic socks, knitting
315299	Athletic uniforms, cut and sewn from purchased fabric
323119	Atlases, printing without publishing
51113	Atlases, publishing (except exclusively on Internet)
238299	ATM (automated teller machine) installation
522329	ATM network providers

33411	ATM's (automatic teller machines), manufacturing
91191	Atomic Energy Commission (except inspection and defence)
31699	Attaché cases, all materials, manufacturing
33311	Attachments for powered lawn and garden equipment, manufacturing
333413	Attic fans, manufacturing
54111	Attorneys, private practice
454112	Auction, Internet retailing
56199	Auctioneering service, on a commission or fee basis, not done on own facilities (except currency and tobacco)
453999	Auctioneering, with own facilities, open to the general public, retail
41511	Auctioneers, automobile, with own facilities, not open to the general public
41119	Auctioneers, tobacco, wholesale
41711	Auctioning farm machinery, from own facilities
41111	Auctioning livestock, with own facilities
51224	Audio recording post-production services
41421	Audio system sales, wholesale
33461	Audio tape, blank, manufacturing
51229	Audio taping of meetings or conferences
62134	Audiologists, offices of
91191	Auditor General's office, federal government
53112	Auditorium rental or leasing
91291	Auditor's office, provincial government
541619	Auditors, freight rate
711513	Authors, independent
452991	Auto and home supplies, retail
41529	Auto body shop supplies, wholesale
811192	Auto detail shop
41633	Auto mechanics' tools, wholesale
238299	Automated and revolving door installation
238299	Automated and revolving doors, installation
522329	Automated clearing houses, bank or cheque (except central bank)
238299	Automated teller machine installation
51821	Automatic data processing, computer services
334512	Automatic environmental controls and regulators (e.g., heating, air-conditioning, refrigeration), manufacturing
238299	Automatic gate (e.g., garage, parking lot), installation

333519	Automatic screw machines, manufacturing
33411	Automatic teller machines (ATM), manufacturing
44131	Automobile accessory dealers, retail
41511	Automobile auctioneers, with own facilities, not open to the general public
453999	Automobile auctioneers, with own facilities, open to the general public, retail
336211	Automobile bodies, passenger car, manufacturing
484239	Automobile carrier, trucking, long-distance
484229	Automobile carriers, local
56159	Automobile clubs, road and travel services
49319	Automobile dead storage
48899	Automobile delivery service (drive-away)
61169	Automobile driving instruction
41799	Automobile engine testing equipment, electrical, wholesale
41413	Automobile fabrics, wholesale
33251	Automobile hardware, metal, manufacturing
33392	Automobile hoists (i.e., tow truck, wrecker), manufacturing
54142	Automobile industrial design services
33392	Automobile lifts (i.e., service station and garage type), manufacturing
81293	Automobile parking lots
41531	Automobile parts, used, wholesale
32561	Automobile polishes and cleaners, manufacturing
54138	Automobile proving and testing ground
711218	Automobile race tracks, operation of
711218	Automobile racing teams
524133	Automobile reinsurance carriers
48532	Automobile rental with driver (except taxicab)
56149	Automobile repossession services
52222	Automobile sales finance company
41799	Automobile service station equipment, wholesale
56192	Automobile shows, flower shows and home shows, promoters of
332611	Automobile suspension springs, manufacturing
41521	Automobile tires and tubes, wholesale
336212	Automobile transporter trailers, multi-car, manufacturing
33636	Automobile trimmings, textile, manufacturing
811192	Automobile washing and polishing

48532	Automobiles for hire with driver (except taxicab)
33611	Automobiles, assembling on chassis of own manufacture
41511	Automobiles, new and used, wholesale
44111	Automobiles, new, retail
44112	Automobiles, used, retail
41912	Automobiles, wholesale agents and brokers
44131	Automotive accessories and parts, second-hand, retail store
41529	Automotive accessories, new, wholesale
41529	Automotive air-conditioners, new, wholesale
811119	Automotive brake repairing
41529	Automotive chemicals, wholesale
41529	Automotive engines, new, wholesale
332113	Automotive forgings, unfinished, made from purchased metal
811122	Automotive glass replacement and repair service
33632	Automotive harness and ignition wiring sets, manufacturing
532112	Automotive leasing
33632	Automotive lighting fixtures, manufacturing
33637	Automotive metal stampings (e.g., body parts, fenders, hub caps, tops, trim), manufacturing
44131	Automotive parts and accessories stores selling primarily to other businesses but open to the public
41529	Automotive parts, new, wholesale
81121	Automotive radio repair shops
811111	Automotive repair shops, general
811119	Automotive springs, rebuilding and repair
811121	Automotive upholstery and trim shops
41811	Automotive wrecking for scrap, wholesale
33633	Automotive, truck and bus steering assemblies and parts, manufacturing
33633	Automotive, truck and bus suspension assemblies and parts (except springs), manufacturing
71213	Aviaries (bird exhibit)
112999	Aviaries (e.g., raising parakeet, canary, and love birds)
488119	Aviation club providing primarily flying field services to general public
71399	Aviation club, recreation
481215	Aviation clubs, providing air transportation services to the general public

32411	Aviation fuels, made in petroleum refineries
23819	Awning installation
81149	Awning repair shops
41639	Awnings (except canvas), wholesale
31491	Awnings and canopies, outdoor, made from purchased fabrics
326198	Awnings, rigid plastic or fibreglass, manufacturing
33221	Axes, manufacturing
33635	Axle assemblies, differential and rear, automotive, truck and bus, manufacturing
32592	Azides explosive materials, manufacturing
32513	Azine dyes, manufacturing
32513	Azo dyes, manufacturing
32519	Azobenzene, manufacturing

B

41911	B2B electronic auctions
41911	B2B wholesale electronic markets
33993	Baby carriages or strollers, manufacturing
31142	Baby foods (including meats), canning
41319	Baby foods, canned, wholesale
311515	Baby formula, fresh, processed and bottled, manufacturing
337126	Baby seats for automobiles, manufacturing
56131	Babysitter, registries
81411	Babysitting (private households employing babysitters in their home)
81411	Baby-sitting in the child's home
33312	Backhoes, manufacturing
45111	Backpacking, hiking and mountaineering equipment, retail
311614	Bacon, slab and sliced, made from purchased meat
311611	Bacon, slab and sliced, produced in slaughtering plants
32541	Bacterial vaccines, manufacturing
62151	Bacteriological laboratories, diagnostic
41451	Bacteriological medicines, wholesale
54171	Bacteriological research and development laboratories
31499	Badges, fabric, manufacturing
332999	Badges, metal, manufacturing
326198	Badges, plastics, manufacturing
445291	Bagel stores, without baking on the premises, retail
311814	Bagels, made in commercial bakeries

32222	Bags (except plastics only), made by laminating or coating combinations of purchased foil, paper and plastics
31324	Bags and bagging fabrics, made in knitting mills
32222	Bags, coated paper, made from purchased paper
32222	Bags, foil, made from purchased foil
32222	Bags, multiwall, made from purchased uncoated paper
41822	Bags, paper and disposable plastics, wholesale
41822	Bags, paper and plastic, wholesale
31491	Bags, plastic, made from purchased woven plastics
326111	Bags, plastics film, single or multi-wall, manufacturing
31499	Bags, sleeping, manufacturing
31491	Bags, textile, made from purchased woven or knitted materials
32222	Bags, uncoated paper, made from purchased paper
81299	Bail bonding services
54119	Bailiff services
213118	Bailing wells, on a contract basis
45111	Bait and tackle shops, retail
114114	Bait catching, inland
41111	Bait, live, wholesale
31142	Baked beans, canning
311811	Bakeries with baking from flour on the premises, for retail sale but not immediate consumption
445291	Bakeries without baking on the premises, retail
333299	Bakery machinery and equipment, manufacturing
41723	Bakery machinery, equipment and supplies, wholesale
41723	Bakery machinery, equipment and supplies, wholesale and repair
311821	Bakery products, dry (e.g., biscuits, cookies, crackers), manufacturing
311814	Bakery products, frozen (e.g., cakes, doughnuts, pastries), made in commercial bakeries
311814	Bakery products, partially cooked, not frozen, made in commercial bakeries
41319	Bakery products, wholesale
31199	Baking powder, manufacturing
526917	Balanced funds / Asset allocation funds
33399	Balances and scales, laboratory type, manufacturing
33331	Balancing equipment, motor vehicle wheel, manufacturing
23819	Balconies, metal, installation
23812	Balconies, precast, concrete, installation
33311	Balers, farm (e.g., hay, straw, cotton), manufacturing
41812	Baling and grading waste paper
332991	Ball bearings and parts (including mounted), manufacturing
212326	Ball clay mining
33633	Ball joints, motor vehicle, manufacturing
33994	Ball point pens, manufacturing
41722	Ball, rod and pebble mill machinery, wholesale
71112	Ballet companies
71112	Ballet productions, live
61161	Ballet schools
45322	Balloon shops, retail
81299	Balloon-o-gram, service
326198	Balloons, plastics, manufacturing
32629	Balloons, rubber, manufacturing
71399	Ballrooms
33993	Balls, rubber (except athletic equipment), manufacturing
11321	Balsam needles, gathering of
41439	Bamboo furniture, wholesale
33792	Bamboo shades and blinds, manufacturing
41315	Banana ripening for the trade, wholesale
33911	Bandages and dressings, surgical and orthopedic, manufacturing
41452	Bandages, dressings and gauzes, wholesale
71113	Bands, musical
33321	Bandsaws, woodworking type, manufacturing
522112	Bank branches, chartered, providing corporate and institutional banking services
522111	Bank branches, chartered, providing personal and commercial banking services
524129	Bank deposit insurance
551113	Bank holding companies
323119	Bank notes, printing
52111	Bank of Canada
81391	Bankers' association
61151	Banking schools (training in banking)
52311	Banking, investment
54199	Bankruptcy trustees
52219	Banks, private (i.e., unincorporated)
453999	Banner shops, retail
31499	Banners, made from purchased fabric
53112	Banquet halls or rooms, without own catering staff, rental

72232	Banquet halls, with own catering staff, doing outside catering
81392	Bar associations
33411	Bar code scanners, manufacturing
41792	Bar furniture, wholesale
41621	Bar joists, fabricated, wholesale
331317	Bar, made from purchased aluminum
335229	Barbecues, gas, manufacturing
331222	Barbed and twisted wire, made in wire drawing plants
332619	Barbed wire, made from purchased wire
335229	Barbeque grills (charcoal), manufacturing
812116	Barber and beauty shops, combined
41792	Barber shop equipment and supplies, wholesale
812114	Barber shops
61151	Barbering schools
32541	Barbiturate preparations, manufacturing
32541	Barbiturates, uncompounded, manufacturing
53241	Bareboat (vessel) chartering
332319	Barge sections, prefabricated, metal, manufacturing
483115	Barge transport service, coastal
336611	Barges, building
325189	Barium compounds, not specified elsewhere by process, manufacturing
212398	Barium ore mining
113311	Barking mill
11321	Barks, gathering of
11119	Barley farming
41711	Barn machinery and equipment (including elevating), wholesale
41711	Barn machinery and equipment (including elevating), wholesale and repair
41793	Barometers, wholesale
32192	Barrels, wood, coopered, manufacturing
54111	Barrister and solicitor, private practice
72241	Bars (i.e., drinking places), alcoholic beverage
33111	Bars, iron or steel, made in steel mills
41621	Bars, rods and angles, steel, wholesale
56199	Bartering services
32513	Barytes based pigments, manufacturing
212316	Basalt, crushed and broken stone, quarrying
212316	Basalt, dimension, quarrying
56121	Base facilities management and support
31599	Baseball caps, manufacturing
711211	Baseball clubs, professional or semi-professional
71399	Baseball clubs, recreational

33992	Baseball equipment, manufacturing
45111	Baseball equipment, retail
315299	Baseball uniforms, cut and sewn from purchased fabric
41612	Baseboard heaters, electric, non-portable, wholesale
333416	Baseboard heating units, manufacturing
321919	Baseboards, floor, wood, manufacturing
91111	Bases, military
711211	Basketball clubs, professional or semi-professional
71399	Basketball clubs, recreational
33992	Basketball equipment, manufacturing
315299	Basketball uniforms, cut and sewn from purchased fabric
41439	Baskets, boxes, cans and bags, household, wholesale
332619	Baskets, metal, made from purchased wire
41899	Baskets, reed, rattan, willow and wood, wholesale
32192	Baskets, wood (e.g., round stave, veneer), manufacturing
442298	Bath boutique
81219	Bath houses
31499	Bath mats and bath sets, made from purchased carpet
31411	Bath mats and bath sets, made in carpet mills
41433	Bath mats and bathroom sets, wholesale
41452	Bath oils and salts, wholesale
32562	Bath salts, manufacturing
23839	Bath tub refinishing, contractors
23839	Bath tub refinishing, on site
41612	Bath tubs and sinks, wholesale
71399	Bathing beaches
31519	Bathing suits, made in knitting mills
315229	Bathing suits, men's and boys', cut and sewn from purchased fabric
315239	Bathing suits, women's, misses' and girls', cut and sewn from purchased fabric
31519	Bathrobes, made in knitting mills
32711	Bathroom accessories, vitreous china and earthenware, manufacturing
326198	Bathroom and toilet accessories, plastics, manufacturing
326191	Bathroom fixtures, plastics, manufacturing
23822	Bathroom plumbing fixtures and sanitary ware, installation
33399	Bathroom scales, manufacturing
33711	Bathroom vanities, wood, manufacturing
326191	Bathtubs, plastics, manufacturing

31331	Batik work (hand painting on textile fabrics)
41529	Batteries, automotive, new, wholesale
33591	Batteries, primary, dry or wet, manufacturing
41723	Batteries, storage, industrial, wholesale
33591	Batteries, storage, manufacturing
311822	Batters, prepared, made from purchased flour
33599	Battery chargers, manufacturing
44131	Battery dealers, automobile, retail
33399	Battery-powered, hand held power tools, manufacturing
71212	Battlefields
31499	Batts and batting (except nonwoven fabrics), manufacturing
53229	Beach chairs and accessories, rental
56299	Beach maintenance and cleaning services
71399	Beaches, bathing
31519	Beachwear, made in knitting mills
448199	Beachwear, men's and boys', retail
41411	Beachwear, wholesale
41411	Beachwear, women's and misses', wholesale
31311	Beaming wool yarn
31311	Beaming yarn
321215	Beams, glued-laminated or pre-engineered wood, manufacturing
49313	Bean cleaning and warehousing
11113	Bean farming (field crop)
111219	Bean farms (except dry beans)
111219	Bean growing, snap (wax and green)
31142	Beans, baked, canning
41112	Beans, dry, wholesale
33631	Bearings (e.g., camshaft, crankshaft, connecting rod), automotive and truck gasoline engine, manufacturing
332991	Bearings, ball and roller, manufacturing
333619	Bearings, plain (except internal combustion engines), manufacturing
41723	Bearings, wholesale
321999	Bearings, wood, manufacturing
812115	Beauticians
41422	Beauty care appliances, electric, wholesale
41792	Beauty parlour equipment and supplies, wholesale
41792	Beauty parlour equipment and supplies, wholesale and repair
812115	Beauty parlours
41452	Beauty preparations, wholesale
812115	Beauty shops or salons
44612	Beauty supplies retail
44612	Beauty supplies stores selling primarily to other businesses but also selling to household consumers
721191	Bed and breakfast, accommodations
41433	Bed coverings, wholesale
442298	Bedding (sheets, blankets, spreads and pillows), retail
111421	Bedding plants, nursery grown
44422	Bedding plants, retail
41433	Bedding, wholesale
41439	Bedroom furniture, wholesale
337123	Bedroom furniture, wood, manufacturing
41793	Beds, hospital, wholesale
337126	Beds, household, metal, manufacturing
31412	Bedspreads and bed sets, made from purchased fabric
31324	Bedspreads and bed sets, made in knitting mills
311611	Beef carcasses, half-carcasses, primal and sub-primal cuts, produced in slaughtering plants
11211	Beef cattle feedlots
11211	Beef cattle ranching
311614	Beef, primal and sub-primal cuts, made from purchased meat
11291	Beekeeping
41839	Beekeeping supplies, wholesale
51721	Beeper (radio pager) communications carriers
333416	Beer cooling and dispensing equipment, manufacturing
72241	Beer gardens
72241	Beer parlours
44531	Beer stores, retail
31212	Beer, brewing
41322	Beers, wholesale
41111	Bees, wholesale
31131	Beet sugar refining
111999	Beet, sugar, farming
54172	Behavioural research and development services
33392	Belt conveyor systems, manufacturing
482112	Belt line railways
31699	Belting for machinery, leather, manufacturing
41723	Belting, hose and packing, industrial, wholesale
31499	Belting, made from purchased fabric
32622	Belting, rubber (e.g., conveyor, elevator, transmission), manufacturing
31599	Belts, apparel (e.g., fabric, leather, vinyl), made from purchased material
44815	Belts, apparel, custom, retail

337127	Benches, public buildings, manufacturing
333519	Bending and forming machines, metalworking, manufacturing
541612	Benefit consulting services
212326	Bentonite mining
32519	Benzaldehyde, manufacturing
32511	Benzene, made from refined petroleum or natural gas liquids
32411	Benzene, made in petroleum refineries
11133	Berry farming
33141	Beryllium smelting and primary refining
81391	Better business bureaus
31193	Beverage bases, manufacturing
41321	Beverage concentrates, wholesale
445299	Beverages, soft drink, retail
61169	Bible schools (except degree-granting)
81311	Bible societies
45111	Bicycle and bicycle parts dealers (except motorized), retail
33632	Bicycle light fixtures, manufacturing
49221	Bicycle messenger and delivery service
33391	Bicycle pumps, manufacturing
53229	Bicycle rental
41447	Bicycle tires and tubes, wholesale
41447	Bicycles (except motorized), wholesale
33699	Bicycles and parts, manufacturing
81149	Bicycles, repairing (without retail sales of new equipment)
62411	Big Brother services
62411	Big Sister services
54185	Billboard display advertising services
54185	Billboard display agency
31699	Billfolds, all materials, manufacturing
71399	Billiard parlours
33992	Billiard, pool and snooker equipment, manufacturing
541215	Billing and bookkeeping services
541215	Billing services
31499	Binder and baler twine, manufacturing
32312	Binderies (i.e., bookbinding shops)
323119	Binders, looseleaf, manufacturing
333299	Bindery machinery, manufacturing
31499	Binding carpets and rugs for the trade
31499	Bindings, bias, made from purchased fabric
713299	Bingo parlours
81121	Binoculars and other optical goods repair
33331	Binoculars, manufacturing
41793	Binoculars, wholesale
332439	Bins (e.g., grain and feed storage), light gauge metal, manufacturing
62151	Biological laboratories (not manufacturing facility)

41451	Biological medicines, wholesale
54138	Biological testing (except clinical and veterinary)
54171	Biotechnology research and development laboratories
112999	Bird (song and pet) raising
311119	Bird food, prepared, manufacturing
56171	Bird proofing
71219	Bird sanctuaries
32629	Birth control devices (i.e., diaphragms, prophylactics), rubber, manufacturing
32541	Birth control pills, manufacturing
311822	Biscuit mixes and doughs, made from purchased flour
311814	Biscuits, bread-type, made in commercial bakeries
311821	Biscuits, dry, manufacturing
33141	Bismuth smelting and primary refining
112999	Bison production
333519	Bits and knives, for metalworking lathes, planers and shapers, manufacturing
333519	Bits, drill, metalworking, manufacturing
33221	Bits, edge tools, woodworking, manufacturing
33312	Bits, rock drill, construction and surface mining type, manufacturing
33313	Bits, rock drill, oil and gas field type, manufacturing
33313	Bits, rock drill, underground mining type, manufacturing
211114	Bitumen production, extraction by mining
211114	Bitumen production, in-situ extraction
212114	Bituminous coal washeries
212114	Bituminous coal, mining
211114	Bituminous sand and oil shale digging
212398	Black lead mine
32513	Black pigments (except carbon, bone and lamp black), manufacturing
33994	Blackboards, framed, manufacturing
33221	Blades, saw, all types, manufacturing
33461	Blank tapes, audio and video, manufacturing
323119	Blankbooks and refills, manufacturing
41821	Blankbooks, wholesale
31412	Blankets (except electric), made from purchased fabrics or felts
31321	Blankets and bedspreads, made in weaving mills
33521	Blankets, electric, manufacturing
327214	Blanks for electric light bulbs, glass, made in glass-making plants

327215	Blanks, ophthalmic lens and optical glass, made from purchased glass
327214	Blanks, ophthalmic lens and optical glass, made in glass-making plants
31141	Blast freezing, on a contract basis
33111	Blast furnaces
23621	Blast furnaces, construction
23891	Blast hole drilling (except mining)
32592	Blasting accessories (e.g., blasting caps, fuses, ignitors, squibbs), manufacturing
32592	Blasting powders, manufacturing
23891	Blasting, building demolition
23839	Bleachers, installation
32561	Bleaches, formulated for household use, manufacturing
41841	Bleaches, wholesale
325189	Bleaching agents, inorganic, manufacturing
32519	Bleaching agents, organic, manufacturing
41841	Bleaching compounds, wholesale
31331	Bleaching textile fibres, thread, yarn or fabrics
31331	Bleaching textile products (including clothing)
212231	Blende (zinc) mining
33521	Blenders, food, electric, manufacturing
31214	Blending distilled beverages (except brandy)
311225	Blending purchased fats and oils
31213	Blending wines
33792	Blinds, venetian, manufacturing
33792	Blinds, vertical, manufacturing
41439	Blinds, window, wholesale
56191	Blister packaging services
33392	Block and tackle, manufacturing
31211	Block ice, manufacturing
23814	Blocklaying
324121	Blocks, asphalt paving, made from purchased asphaltic materials
32733	Blocks, concrete and cinder, manufacturing
327214	Blocks, glass, made in glass-making plants
62199	Blood banks
32541	Blood derivatives, manufacturing
62199	Blood donor stations
32541	Blood glucose test kits, manufacturing
33911	Blood transfusion equipment, manufacturing
41621	Blooms, billets, slabs and other semi-finished shapes, wholesale
315232	Blouses, women's, misses' and girls', cut and sewn from purchased fabric
33322	Blow moulding machinery for plastics, manufacturing
23831	Blown-in insulation (e.g., vermiculite, cellulose), installation
54134	Blueprint drafting services
56143	Blueprinting services
212316	Bluestone, dimension, quarrying
11221	Boar raising, domestic
45112	Board games (amusement), retail
41446	Board games, wholesale
81391	Board of trade
32742	Board, gypsum, manufacturing
72131	Boarding houses
81291	Boarding kennel service, pet
61111	Boarding schools, elementary or secondary
48721	Boat charters, pleasure
44122	Boat dealers, retail
54133	Boat engineering designing services
484229	Boat hauling, by truck, local
23899	Boat lift installation
33392	Boat lifts, manufacturing
53229	Boat rental, pleasure
332319	Boat sections, prefabricated, metal, manufacturing
336215	Boat transporter trailers, single-unit, manufacturing
71393	Boating clubs (i.e., operating marinas)
336612	Boats (i.e., suitable or intended personal use), manufacturing
48721	Boats, fishing charter, operation
326198	Boats, inflatable plastics, manufacturing
41799	Boats, pleasure (e.g., canoes, motorboats, sailboats), wholesale
41799	Boats, pleasure (e.g., canoes, motorboats, sailboats), wholesale and repair
81232	Bobtailers, laundry and dry cleaning
41519	Bodies, automotive, wholesale
44815	Body belts, leather, retail
71394	Body building studios, physical fitness
41452	Body care preparations, wholesale
41529	Body compounds, automotive, wholesale
446191	Body enhancing supplements, retail
561612	Body guard services
31519	Body stockings, made in knitting mills
238299	Boiler and pipe, insulation of, contractors
23822	Boiler chipping, cleaning and scaling
238299	Boiler covering
524129	Boiler insurance
81131	Boiler, power, repair shops (except manufacturing)
41612	Boilers (e.g., heating, hot water, power, steam), wholesale

333416	Boilers, heating, manufacturing
41723	Boilers, power (industrial), wholesale
33241	Boilers, power, manufacturing
41891	Bolts and logs, wholesale
33272	Bolts, metal, manufacturing
326198	Bolts, nuts and rivets, plastics, manufacturing
41633	Bolts, nuts, rivets, screws and other fasteners, wholesale
113311	Bolts, wooden, cutting
526915	Bond and income / Dividend funds, Canadian
526916	Bond and income / Dividend funds, foreign
49312	Bonded cold storage warehousing
49311	Bonded warehouse, general merchandise
325189	Bone black, manufacturing
33999	Bone novelties, manufacturing
454113	Book club, mail order
32312	Book gilding, bronzing, edging, deckling, embossing and gold stamping, for the trade
32222	Book paper, coated, made from purchased paper
32312	Book repairing
45121	Book stores
45331	Book stores, second-hand, retail
41912	Book, periodical and newspaper, wholesale agents and brokers
41893	Book, second-hand, wholesale
333299	Bookbinding machinery, manufacturing
32312	Bookbinding, without printing
337214	Bookcases, office (except wood), manufacturing
337213	Bookcases, wood office, manufacturing
337123	Bookcases, wood, household, manufacturing
711321	Booking agencies, theatrical (except motion picture)
541215	Bookkeepers, offices of
541215	Bookkeeping services
713299	Bookmakers
519121	Bookmobiles
41442	Books and pamphlets, wholesale
51113	Books, all formats, printing and publishing combined
51113	Books, all formats, publishing (except exclusively on Internet)
323119	Books, printing without publishing
323116	Books, sales, manifold, printing
113311	Booming, bunching, rafting, driving logs
81341	Booster clubs
48611	Booster pumping station, oil transport
41792	Boot and shoe cut stock and findings, wholesale
31699	Boot and shoe cut stock, leather, manufacturing
31699	Boot and shoe findings, all materials, manufacturing
81143	Boot and shoe repair shop
333299	Boot making and repairing machinery, manufacturing
81299	Bootblack parlours
44821	Boots and shoes, retail
31621	Boots, manufacturing
212398	Borax mining
213117	Boring test holes for non-metallic minerals mining (except fuels), on contract basis
325189	Boron compounds, not specified elsewhere by process, manufacturing
41723	Bort, wholesale
71213	Botanical gardens
54171	Botany research and development laboratories
326198	Bottle caps and lids, plastics, manufacturing
332118	Bottle caps and tops, metal, stamping
56199	Bottle exchange
33399	Bottle washers, packaging machinery, manufacturing
41322	Bottled wines and liquors, wholesale
327214	Bottles (i.e., bottling, canning, packaging), made in glass-making plants
41723	Bottles, glass or plastic, wholesale
32616	Bottles, plastics, manufacturing
32629	Bottles, rubber, manufacturing
332439	Bottles, vacuum, manufacturing
41819	Bottles, waste, wholesale
41312	Bottling (not pasteurizing) fresh milk and cream
31211	Bottling flavoured water
33399	Bottling machinery (e.g., washing, sterilizing, filling, capping, labelling), manufacturing
31142	Bouillon, canning
31142	Bouillon, made in dehydration plants
71395	Bowling alleys
71395	Bowling centres
45111	Bowling equipment and supplies, retail
71399	Bowling leagues or teams, recreational
81149	Bowling pins, refinishing or repair
321999	Bowls, wood, turned and shaped, manufacturing
31499	Bows, made from purchased fabrics
31199	Box lunches, for sale off premises, manufacturing

32192	Box shook, manufacturing
41439	Box springs and mattresses, wholesale
33791	Box springs, assembled, manufacturing
32213	Boxboard paperboard stock, manufacturing
311611	Boxed meat (except poultry and small game), produced in slaughtering plants
311614	Boxed meat (except poultry), made by assembly-line cutting of purchased meat
711218	Boxers, independent, professional
322219	Boxes (except corrugated), set-up (i.e., not shipped flat), made from purchased paperboard
322211	Boxes, corrugated, made from purchased paper or paperboard
322212	Boxes, folding (except corrugated), made from purchased paperboard
332439	Boxes, light gauge metal, manufacturing
41822	Boxes, paperboard and disposable plastics, wholesale
322219	Boxes, sanitary food (except folding), made from purchased paper or paperboard
322211	Boxes, shipping, laminated, made from purchased paper or paperboard
322211	Boxes, solid fibre, made from purchased paper or paperboard
336211	Boxes, truck (e.g., dump, cargo, utility, van), assembled on purchased chassis
32192	Boxes, wood, manufacturing
71399	Boxing clubs, recreational
711329	Boxing event promoters, without facilities
721213	Boys' camps
623999	Boys' towns
332619	Brackets, made from purchased wire
332619	Brads, metal, made from purchased wire
41413	Braided material, piece goods, wholesale
333299	Braiding machinery, textile, manufacturing
31322	Braiding narrow fabrics
33634	Brake cylinders, master and wheel, automotive, truck and bus, manufacturing
33634	Brake drums, automotive, truck and bus, manufacturing
33634	Brake shoe relining, on a factory basis
333619	Brakes (except motor vehicle and electromagnetic industrial controls), manufacturing

311211	Bran, shorts and other products of milling grain (except rice)
53311	Brand-name owners
31213	Brandy, distilling
337126	Brass furniture, manufacturing
32561	Brass polishes, manufacturing
33142	Brass products, made by rolling, drawing, extruding or alloying purchased metal
72241	Brasseries (beer gardens)
315231	Brassieres, cut and sewn from purchased fabric
33281	Brazing (i.e., hardening) metals and metal products, for the trade
311822	Bread and bread-type roll mixes, made from purchased flour
311814	Bread and bread-type rolls, made in commercial bakeries
333299	Bread slicing machinery, manufacturing
31123	Breakfast cereals made in flour mills
31123	Breakfast cereals, manufacturing
41319	Breakfast cereals, wholesale
212114	Breaking, washing, grading, bituminous coal (contract)
212115	Breaking, washing, grading, subbituminous coal
23799	Breakwater construction, general contractors
11521	Breeding services, livestock
11521	Breeding services, pet and small animal
11521	Breeding services, poultry
72241	Brew pub
31212	Breweries
333299	Brewery machinery, manufacturing
32712	Brick (i.e., common face, glazed, vitrified, hollow), clay, manufacturing
44419	Brick and tile dealers, retail
23899	Brick driveway contractors
23899	Brick pavers (e.g., driveways, patios and sidewalks), installation
32712	Brick, clay refractory, manufacturing
327214	Brick, glass, made in glass-making plants
32712	Brick, nonclay (e.g., chrome, magnesite, silica) refractory, manufacturing
41639	Brick, tile, cement, wholesale
23814	Bricklaying, contractors
32799	Bricks and blocks, sand-lime, manufacturing
32733	Bricks, concrete, manufacturing
448199	Bridal shops (except custom dressmakers), retail
33399	Bridge and gate lifting machinery, manufacturing
23731	Bridge approaches, construction

71399	Bridge clubs, recreational
23731	Bridge decking construction
332319	Bridge sections, prefabricated, metal, manufacturing
23731	Bridge, construction
48849	Bridge, tunnel and highway operation
23832	Bridges and structures, painting
33911	Bridges, custom made in dental laboratories
31699	Briefcases, all materials, manufacturing
212398	Brimstone mining
31142	Brining of fruits and vegetables
32519	Briquettes, charcoal, manufacturing
32419	Briquettes, petroleum, made from refined petroleum
333519	Broaching machines, metalworking, manufacturing
33422	Broadcast equipment (including studio), for radio and television, manufacturing
54191	Broadcast media rating services
51512	Broadcasting networks, television
23622	Broadcasting stations, construction
51511	Broadcasting stations, radio
51512	Broadcasting stations, television
31321	Broad-woven (more than 30 cm/12 in. wide) fabrics (except rugs, tire fabrics), weaving
41413	Broad-woven fabrics, wholesale
11232	Broiler chicken farming
52314	Brokerages, commodity contract
52231	Brokerages, loan
52231	Brokerages, mortgage
52312	Brokerages, stock
531212	Brokers of manufactured homes, on site
52314	Brokers, commodity contracts, offices
488519	Brokers, customs
531212	Brokers, real estate
52312	Brokers, securities
488519	Brokers, shipping
33142	Bronze products, made by rolling, drawing, extruding or alloying purchased metal
321999	Broom handles, manufacturing
453999	Brooms and brushes, retail
41899	Brooms, brushes and mops, wholesale
33999	Brooms, manufacturing
212116	Brown coal mining
212326	Brucite mining
56211	Brush removal
33994	Brushes, artists', manufacturing
33999	Brushes, household and industrial, manufacturing
41899	Brushes, industrial, wholesale
33392	Buckets, elevators or conveyors, manufacturing
33312	Buckets, excavating (e.g., clamshell, concrete, dragline, drag scraper, shovel), manufacturing
32192	Buckets, wood, manufacturing
33999	Buckles and buckle parts, manufacturing
332999	Buckles, shoe, metal, manufacturing
11119	Buckwheat farming
72232	Buffet catering, social
333519	Buffing and polishing machines, metalworking, manufacturing
32791	Buffing and polishing wheels, abrasive and nonabrasive, manufacturing
33281	Buffing metals and metal products, for the trade
33251	Builders' hardware, metal, manufacturing
44413	Builders' hardware, retail
41633	Builders' hardware, wholesale
23821	Building automation systems, contractors
561722	Building cleaning, janitorial services
23611	Building construction, residential
23891	Building demolition
561799	Building exterior cleaning services (except sandblasting and window cleaning)
23839	Building fixtures and fittings (except mechanical equipment), installation
23813	Building framing (except structural steel)
54135	Building inspection services
23831	Building insulation contractors
23721	Building lot subdividing, land development
326198	Building materials (e.g., fascia, panels, siding, soffits), plastics, manufacturing
45331	Building materials, used, retail
213118	Building oil and gas well foundations on site, on a contract basis
322121	Building paper stock, manufacturing
212314	Building stone, granite, rough, mining
212315	Building stone, limestone, rough, mining
41639	Building stone, wholesale
33592	Building wire and cable, electric, insulated, manufacturing
54131	Buildings and structures, architectural design
332311	Buildings, pre-engineered, metal, manufacturing
321992	Buildings, prefabricated or pre-cut, wood frame, manufacturing
332311	Buildings, prefabricated, metal (except portable), manufacturing

332311	Buildings, prefabricated, metal, manufacturing
44311	Built-in vacuum systems, retail
23835	Built-in wood cabinets constructed on site
41832	Bulbs, flower and field, wholesale
484221	Bulk liquid trucking service, local
484231	Bulk liquids trucking, long-distance
33242	Bulk storage tanks, heavy gauge steel, manufacturing
41211	Bulk tank station, wholesale
23799	Bulkhead wall construction
53241	Bulldozer rental and leasing (without operator)
33312	Bulldozers, manufacturing
33994	Bulletin boards, of metal, manufacturing
41411	Bulletproof vests, wholesale
326193	Bumper components, motor vehicle, plastics, manufacturing
33639	Bumpers and bumperettes, assembled, automotive, truck and bus, manufacturing
321999	Bungs, wood, manufacturing
311814	Buns, bread-type (e.g., hamburger, hot dog), made in commercial bakeries
561621	Burglar alarm sale, combined with installation, maintenance or monitoring
524124	Burglary and theft insurance
33999	Burial caskets, manufacturing
711111	Burlesque companies
212326	Burley mining
31331	Burling and mending fabrics, for the trade
333416	Burners, heating, manufacturing
33281	Burning metals and metal products, for the trade
31699	Burnt leather goods, manufacturing
321999	Burnt wood articles, manufacturing
81321	Bursaries (scholarship trusts), management of
54185	Bus and subway card advertising services
41611	Bus bars and trolley ducts, wholesale
54185	Bus card advertising services
48551	Bus charter service
48521	Bus line operation, intercity
48521	Bus line operation, interurban
48511	Bus line operation, local
48541	Bus operation, school
53212	Bus rental, without driver
48511	Bus service, urban and suburban
23622	Bus shelter construction
332311	Bus shelters, metal frame, manufacturing

48849	Bus terminal operation, independent
56159	Bus ticket offices
811192	Bus washing
33612	Buses, passenger (except trackless trolley), assembling on chassis of own manufacture
48711	Buses, sightseeing, local, operation
41512	Buses, wholesale
41512	Buses, wholesale and repair
23622	Bush depots and camps, construction
333619	Bushings, plain (except internal combustion engine), manufacturing
81391	Business associations
51114	Business directory, publishing (except exclusively on Internet)
51114	Business directory, publishing and printing combined
323119	Business forms (except manifold), printing without publishing
323116	Business forms, manifold, printing
41821	Business forms, wholesale
32223	Business machine paper, cut sheet, made from purchased paper
53242	Business machines, rental (except computers)
41791	Business machines, wholesale
41791	Business machines, wholesale and repair
56111	Business management services
54172	Business research and development services
61141	Business schools (non-university)
56143	Business service centre
541611	Business start-up consulting services
81341	Businessmen's clubs, civic and social
41911	Business-to-business electronic markets, wholesale trade
32521	Butadiene rubber (i.e., polybutadiene), manufacturing
32511	Butadiene, made from refined petroleum or natural gas liquids
32511	Butane, made from refined petroleum or natural gas liquids
44521	Butcher shops, retail
311515	Butter, creamery and whey, manufacturing
311515	Butter, manufacturing
311911	Butter, peanut, manufacturing
41312	Butter, wholesale
311511	Buttermilk, manufacturing
333299	Buttonhole and eyelet machinery, manufacturing
31521	Buttonholing and button covering, on clothing owned by others
33999	Buttons, apparel, manufacturing

41413	Buttons, wholesale
32521	Butyl rubber, manufacturing
32511	Butylene (butene), made from refined petroleum or natural gas liquids

C

61121	C.E.G.E.P. (collège d'enseignement général et professionnel)
33612	Cab and chassis assemblies, heavy-duty trucks, manufacturing
33611	Cab and chassis assemblies, light trucks and vans, manufacturing
48531	Cab service (i.e., taxi)
72241	Cabarets (night clubs)
334511	Cabin environment indicators, transmitters and sensors, manufacturing
23835	Cabinet work performed at the construction site
337126	Cabinets (free standing), metal, manufacturing
44419	Cabinets, kitchen (to be installed), retail
337126	Cabinets, kitchen, free standing, metal or plastic, manufacturing
337214	Cabinets, office (except wood), manufacturing
337123	Cabinets, sewing machine, wood, manufacturing
337123	Cabinets, wood household (e.g., radio, television, stereo, sewing machine), manufacturing
337213	Cabinets, wood office, manufacturing
41621	Cable and rope, wire, steel, wholesale
51521	Cable broadcasting networks
48511	Cable cars operation, commuter
48799	Cable cars, scenic and sightseeing
51521	Cable program broadcasting
517112	Cable program distribution operator
23899	Cable splicing service, non-electrical, contractors
23821	Cable splicing, electrical, contractors
23821	Cable television hookup, contractors
51521	Cable television network
517112	Cable television providers
33422	Cable television transmission and receiving equipment, manufacturing
331222	Cable, iron or steel, insulated or armoured, made in wire drawing plants
332619	Cable, non-insulated wire, made from purchased wire
517112	Cablevision services
33311	Cabs for agricultural machinery, manufacturing
33312	Cabs for construction machinery, manufacturing

33392	Cabs for industrial trucks and tractors, manufacturing
48711	Cabs, horse drawn, sightseeing
31132	Cacao beans, shelling, roasting and grinding
54151	CAD/CAM systems services
54137	Cadastral surveying services
33141	Cadmium smelting and primary refining
54151	CAE (computer-aided engineering) systems services
337127	Cafeteria furniture, manufacturing
41792	Cafeteria furniture, wholesale
72231	Cafeterias, industrial
72221	Cafeterias, public
45391	Cages for pet animals, retail
332619	Cages, made from purchased wire
522321	Caisses populaires, federation, league or regional (i.e., central clearing house services)
23799	Caissons (i.e., marine or pneumatic structures), construction
453999	Cake decorating supplies, retail
311822	Cake mixes, made from purchased flour
212231	Calamine mining
212315	Calcareous tufa, dimension, quarrying
32419	Calcining petroleum coke from refined petroleum
32741	Calcium hydroxide (i.e., hydrated lime), manufacturing
325189	Calcium hypochlorite, manufacturing
325189	Calcium inorganic compounds, not specified elsewhere by process, manufacturing
212315	Calcium limestone, crude, mining
32519	Calcium organic compounds, not specified elsewhere by process, manufacturing
32741	Calcium oxide (i.e., quicklime), manufacturing
33331	Calculators, manufacturing
48711	Calèche service, sightseeing
323119	Calendars, printing without publishing
51119	Calendars, publishing (except exclusively on Internet)
33322	Calendering machinery for plastics, manufacturing
333299	Calendering machinery for textiles, manufacturing
31331	Calendering textile fabrics or textile products (including clothing)
54138	Calibration and certification testing services
33431	Camcorders, manufacturing

33322	Camelback (i.e., retreading material) machinery, manufacturing
32621	Camelback (i.e., retreading materials), manufacturing
33331	Camera lenses, manufacturing
44313	Camera shops, photographic, retail
33331	Cameras (except television, video and digital), manufacturing
41443	Cameras, equipment and supplies, wholesale
72131	Camp, residential, for farm or other workers
721213	Camp, vacation, boys' or girls'
81394	Campaign organizations, political
41519	Campers, motor vehicle, wholesale
41519	Campers, motor vehicle, wholesale and repair
721211	Campground
45111	Camping equipment (except tent trailers), retail
41447	Camping equipment, wholesale
336215	Camping trailers and chassis, manufacturing
721211	Campsites for transients
333519	Can forming machines, metalworking, manufacturing
332431	Can lids and ends, metal, manufacturing
33521	Can openers, electric, domestic, manufacturing
48831	Canal locks, operating
48831	Canal maintenance (except dredging)
48831	Canal operations
483213	Canal transportation
11119	Canary seed farming
62231	Cancer hospital
54171	Cancer research laboratories
31134	Candied fruits and fruit peel, manufacturing
453999	Candle shops, retail
33999	Candles, manufacturing
31134	Candy (except chocolate), manufacturing
31134	Candy bars (except chocolate), manufacturing
31132	Candy bars, chocolate (including chocolate-covered), made from cacao beans
31133	Candy bars, chocolate (including chocolate-covered), made from purchased chocolate
31134	Candy stores (except chocolate), candy made on the premises, not for immediate consumption

31133	Candy stores, chocolate candy made on the premises, not for immediate consumption
445292	Candy stores, retail
31132	Candy, chocolate, made from cacao beans
31133	Candy, chocolate, made from purchased chocolate
41319	Candy, wholesale
337126	Cane chairs, manufacturing
31131	Cane sugar refining
33999	Canes (except orthopedic), manufacturing
41319	Canned foods, wholesale
311611	Canned meats (except poultry and small game), produced in slaughtering plants
311911	Canned nuts, manufacturing
31171	Canning fish, crustaceans and molluscs
31142	Canning fruits and vegetables
33399	Canning machinery, manufacturing
311614	Canning meat (except poultry, small game, pet food, baby food), from purchased meat
311615	Canning poultry (except baby and pet food)
31142	Canning soups (except seafood)
71399	Canoe and kayak clubs, recreational
336612	Canoes and kayaks, manufacturing
336612	Canoes, manufacturing
11112	Canola (rapeseed) farming
311224	Canola oil, cake and meal, made in crushing mills
41723	Cans for fruits and vegetables, wholesale
322219	Cans, fibre (i.e., fibre body, ends of any material), made from purchased paperboard
332431	Cans, metal (e.g., food, beverage, aerosol), manufacturing
111219	Cantaloup farms
31491	Canvas products, made from purchased canvas or canvas substitutes
45439	Canvassers (door-to-door), headquarters for retail sale of merchandise
33599	Capacitors (except electronic), fixed and variable, manufacturing
33441	Capacitors, electronic, fixed and variable, manufacturing
41732	Capacitors, electronic, wholesale
315299	Capes, waterproof (e.g., plastics, rubber, similar materials), cut and sewn from purchased fabric
11232	Capon farming

23711	Capping of water wells
33399	Capping, sealing and lidding packaging machinery, manufacturing
32519	Caprolactam, manufacturing
31599	Caps and hats (except fur, leather), made from purchased fabric
336215	Caps for pickup trucks, manufacturing
32592	Caps, blasting and detonating, manufacturing
31519	Caps, made in knitting mills
41411	Caps, women's and children's, wholesale
532111	Car rental agency
56159	Car rental reservations
336212	Car transporter trailers, multi-car, manufacturing
811192	Car washes, self-service or automatic
33331	Car washing machinery, manufacturing
325189	Carbides (e.g., boron, calcium, silicon, tungsten), manufacturing
41621	Carbon and alloy steels, primary forms and structural shapes, wholesale
325189	Carbon black, manufacturing
41841	Carbon black, wholesale
32512	Carbon dioxide, manufacturing
325189	Carbon inorganic compounds, not specified elsewhere by process, manufacturing
32519	Carbon organic compounds, not specified elsewhere by process, manufacturing
33994	Carbon paper, manufacturing
41821	Carbon paper, wholesale
33599	Carbon specialties for electrical use, manufacturing
32519	Carbon tetrachloride, manufacturing
325999	Carbon, activated, manufacturing
41321	Carbonated beverages, wholesale
31211	Carbonated soda, manufacturing
31211	Carbonated soft drinks, manufacturing
31331	Carbonizing textile fibres
33631	Carburetors, all types, manufacturing
713299	Card rooms (e.g. poker rooms)
337126	Card table and chair sets, metal, manufacturing
32213	Cardboard stock, manufacturing
32222	Cardboard, laminated or surface coated, made from purchased paperboard
32541	Cardiac preparations, manufacturing
31331	Carding textile fibres
62111	Cardiologists' offices
323119	Cards (e.g., business, greeting, playing, postcards, trading), printing without publishing
322299	Cards, die-cut (except office supplies), made from purchased paper or paperboard
32223	Cards, die-cut office supply (e.g., index, library, time recording), made from purchased paper or paperboard
48111	Cargo carriers, air, scheduled
488331	Cargo salvaging, marine
48839	Cargo surveyors, marine
48849	Cargo surveyors, truck transportation
481214	Cargo transportation, air, charter service
48839	Cargo, checkers, marine
33331	Carnival and amusement park rides, manufacturing
33331	Carnival and amusement park shooting gallery machinery, manufacturing
41799	Carnival equipment, wholesale
71119	Carnivals, travelling show
212291	Carnotite mining
33392	Carousel conveyors (e.g., luggage), manufacturing
33221	Carpenters' handtools (except saws), non-powered, manufacturing
44413	Carpenters' tools, retail
41633	Carpenters' tools, wholesale
23835	Carpentry work (except framing)
41432	Carpet and carpet supplies, wholesale
56174	Carpet and furniture cleaning on location, services
31311	Carpet and rug yarn, spinning
56174	Carpet cleaning services
23833	Carpet installation and repair
31323	Carpet paddings, nonwoven, manufacturing
44221	Carpet stores, retail
33331	Carpet sweepers, mechanical, manufacturing
31499	Carpets and rugs, made from purchased fabric
31411	Carpets and rugs, made from textile materials
31411	Carpets, rugs and mats, of textile materials, weaving or knitting
41432	Carpets, wholesale
48599	Carpool operation
33699	Carriages, horse-drawn, manufacturing
31199	Carrots, fresh (i.e., cut, peeled, polished or sliced), manufacturing
336211	Cars in kit form, manufacturing
33313	Cars, mining, manufacturing
54137	Cartographic surveying services
33399	Carton filling machines, manufacturing
322299	Cartons, egg, moulded pulp, manufacturing

322212	Cartons, folding (except milk), made from purchased paperboard
322219	Cartons, milk, made from purchased paper or paperboard
33399	Cartridge (i.e., powder) hand held power-driven tools, manufacturing
332999	Cartridges, ammunition, manufacturing
33392	Carts for moving goods (e.g., laundry, industrial), manufacturing
33699	Carts, horse-drawn, manufacturing
33311	Carts, lawn and garden type, manufacturing
45322	Carvings and artcraft, retail
41792	Carwash equipment and supplies, wholesale
32223	Cash register tapes, made from purchased paper
33331	Cash registers (except point-of-sale terminals), manufacturing
33331	Cash registers, electronic, manufacturing
326121	Casings, sausage, plastics, manufacturing
23622	Casino construction
72112	Casino hotels
71321	Casinos (except casino hotels)
33999	Caskets (burial), metal and wood, manufacturing
41792	Caskets, burial, wholesale
41421	Cassette player, recorder, portable, wholesale
45122	Cassettes and tapes, pre-recorded (audio), retail
41444	Cassettes or tapes, music, wholesale
56131	Casting agencies, motion picture or video
56131	Casting agencies, theatrical
56131	Casting bureau, motion picture or video
56131	Casting bureaus, theatrical
331529	Castings (except die-castings), aluminum, unfinished, manufacturing
331529	Castings (except die-castings), copper, unfinished, manufacturing
331529	Castings (except die-castings), non-ferrous metals, unfinished, manufacturing
41621	Castings and forgings, iron and steel products, wholesale
331511	Castings, unfinished, iron (e.g. ductile, grey, malleable, semisteel), manufacturing
331511	Castings, unfinished, semisteel, manufacturing
331514	Castings, unfinished, steel, manufacturing
311111	Cat food, made from purchased meat and poultry
325999	Cat litter (clay based), manufacturing
454113	Catalog (order taking) offices of mail order houses, retail
452999	Catalogue sales showrooms (except mail order), retail
51119	Catalogues (i.e., mail order, store and merchandise), publishing (except exclusively on Internet)
323119	Catalogues of collections (e.g., museum), printing without publishing
323119	Catalogues, printing without publishing
33639	Catalytic converters, engine exhaust, automotive, truck and bus, manufacturing
56299	Catch basin cleaning services
32739	Catch basin covers, concrete, manufacturing
72231	Caterers, industrial
72231	Catering food service, industrial
72232	Catering for dining room and banquets
33911	Catheters, manufacturing
41732	Cathode ray picture tubes, wholesale
23819	Cathodic protection, installation
112999	Cats, domestic, raising
11521	Cattle dehorning service
41111	Cattle drovers (dealer)
11211	Cattle feedlot operations
11521	Cattle registration service
32552	Caulking compounds (except gypsum-based), manufacturing
33221	Caulking guns, non-powered, manufacturing
41639	Caulking materials, wholesale
23731	Causeway, construction
325181	Caustic potash (i.e., potassium hydroxide), manufacturing
325181	Caustic soda (i.e., sodium hydroxide), manufacturing
41841	Caustic soda, wholesale
71219	Caverns
33422	CB (citizens' band) radios, manufacturing
33411	CD-ROM drives, manufacturing
561799	Cedar (exterior) cleaning, preserving and repairing
337123	Cedar chests, manufacturing
23831	Ceiling tiles, installation
23839	Ceilings, metal, erection and repair, contractors
711512	Celebrity spokesperson, independent
212398	Celestite concentrate, mining
32222	Cellophane adhesive tape, made from purchased materials

32522	Cellophane film or sheet, manufacturing
23713	Cellular phone towers, construction
44311	Cellular plans and/or phone stores (authorized agents)
51721	Cellular telephone services
41732	Cellular telephone, wholesale
33422	Cellular telephones, manufacturing
32522	Cellulosic fibres and filaments, manufacturing
32522	Cellulosic staple fibres, manufacturing
32731	Cement (e.g., hydraulic, masonry, portland, pozzolana), manufacturing
23814	Cement block laying
23811	Cement finishing
41723	Cement making machinery, wholesale
23621	Cement plants, construction
212315	Cement rock, quarrying
41639	Cement, brick, tile, wholesale
32742	Cement, Keene's (i.e., tiling plaster), manufacturing
32712	Cement, refractory, manufacturing
32552	Cement, rubber, manufacturing
213118	Cementing oil and gas well casings, on a contract basis
324122	Cements, asphalt roofing, made from purchased asphaltic materials
81222	Cemetery
56173	Cemetery plot care services
23822	Central air-conditioning equipment, installation
23822	Central cooling equipment and piping, installation
23822	Central heating equipment and piping, installation
33331	Central vacuuming systems, commercial type, manufacturing
32732	Central-mixed concrete, manufacturing
519122	Centres for documentation (i.e., archives)
33391	Centrifugal pumps, manufacturing
32541	Cephalosporin, uncompounded, manufacturing
32513	Ceramic colours, manufacturing
41639	Ceramic construction materials (except refractory), wholesale
41793	Ceramic equipment, greenware and supplies, wholesale
41431	Ceramic goods, household, wholesale
45112	Ceramic greenware and supplies, retail
32711	Ceramic insulators, manufacturing
32712	Ceramic tile, floor and wall, manufacturing
23834	Ceramic tile, installation
41639	Ceramic wall and floor tile, wholesale

45112	Ceramics supplies, retail
45322	Ceramics, handicraft, retail
45322	Ceramics, retail
311211	Cereal grain flour, manufacturing
54171	Cerebral palsy research laboratories
323119	Certificates (e.g., bond, stock), printing without publishing
541212	Certified accountants' offices
52393	Certified financial planner services, customized, fees paid by clients
212231	Cerusite mining
325189	Cesium and cesium compounds, not specified elsewhere by process, manufacturing
56299	Cesspool cleaning services
23891	Cesspool construction, contractors
23899	Chain link fences, installing
332619	Chain link fencing and fence gates, made from purchased wire
331222	Chain link fencing, iron or steel, made in wire drawing plants
33399	Chain saws, hand held power-driven, manufacturing
332619	Chain, made from purchased wire
41633	Chain, metal, wholesale
332619	Chain, welded, made from purchased wire
333619	Chains, power transmission, manufacturing
33221	Chainsaw blades, manufacturing
41633	Chainsaws, wholesale
337121	Chairs, household, upholstered, manufacturing
337127	Chairs, hydraulic, barber and beauty shop, manufacturing
337214	Chairs, office (except wood), manufacturing
337127	Chairs, portable folding, manufacturing
337123	Chairs, wood household (except upholstered), manufacturing
337213	Chairs, wood office, manufacturing
212233	Chalcocite mining
212233	Chalcopyrite mining
33994	Chalk (e.g., carpenters', blackboard, marking, artists', tailors'), manufacturing
212315	Chalk mine or quarry
212315	Chalk, ground or otherwise treated, mining
71113	Chamber music groups
81391	Chambers of commerce
31213	Champagne-method sparkling wines, manufacturing
91121	Chancery courts
33512	Chandeliers, manufacturing

33331	Change making machines, manufacturing
32519	Charcoal (except activated), manufacturing
325999	Charcoal, activated, manufacturing
41899	Charcoal, wholesale
81321	Charitable trusts, awarding grants
61169	Charm schools
48721	Charter fishing boats
48721	Charter yachts, with crew
53241	Chartering of commercial boats without operator
483115	Chartering vessels with crew, deep sea, coastal and Great Lakes
483213	Chartering vessels with crew, inland waters (except Great Lakes)
33281	Chasing metals and metal products (except printing plates), for the trade
33611	Chassis, automobile, light truck and sport utility, manufacturing
33612	Chassis, heavy truck, with or without cabs, manufacturing
56131	Chauffeur registries
81299	Check room service
311515	Cheese (except cottage cheese), manufacturing
311919	Cheese curls and puffs, manufacturing
333299	Cheese processing machinery, manufacturing
311515	Cheese spreads, manufacturing
445299	Cheese stores, retail
311511	Cheese, cottage, manufacturing
311515	Cheese, imitation or substitute, manufacturing
311515	Cheese, natural (except cottage cheese), manufacturing
311515	Cheese, processed, manufacturing
41312	Cheese, wholesale
31194	Cheese-based salad dressings, manufacturing
41413	Cheesecloth, woven, wholesale
212315	Chemical and metallurgical stone, limestone, crude, mining
212316	Chemical and metallurgical stone, marble, rough, mining
54133	Chemical engineering services
41839	Chemical fertilizers, wholesale
31331	Chemical finishing (e.g., for fire, mildew, water resistance) of textile fabrics, for the trade
41723	Chemical industries machinery, equipment and supplies, wholesale
41723	Chemical industries machinery, equipment and supplies, wholesale and repair

33271	Chemical milling job shops
333519	Chemical milling machines, metalworking, manufacturing
333299	Chemical processing machinery and equipment, manufacturing
54171	Chemical research and development laboratories
326191	Chemical toilets, plastics, manufacturing
322112	Chemical wood pulp, manufacturing
213118	Chemically treating wells, on a contract basis
41912	Chemicals (except agricultural), wholesale agents and brokers
41529	Chemicals, automotive, wholesale
41841	Chemicals, industrial and household, wholesale
41443	Chemicals, photographic, wholesale
323116	Cheque books and refills, printing
52239	Cheque cashing services
522329	Cheque clearing services (except central bank)
522329	Cheque validation services
33993	Chessmen and chessboards, manufacturing
337121	Chesterfields, manufacturing
337123	Chests, cedar, manufacturing
332999	Chests, fire or burglary resistive, metal, manufacturing
31134	Chewing gum, manufacturing
41331	Chewing tobacco, wholesale
11234	Chick hatchery service
33311	Chicken brooders, manufacturing
11231	Chicken egg farming
311615	Chicken processing, fresh, frozen, canned or cooked (except baby or pet food)
41313	Chickens, dressed, wholesale
311615	Chickens, slaughtering and dressing
62441	Child care centres
61171	Child guidance centre, vocational
62411	Child support services
62199	Childbirth preparation classes
62411	Children's aid services
44821	Children's and infants' shoes, retail
31521	Children's clothing contractors
44813	Children's clothing stores, retail
41411	Children's clothing, wholesale
31621	Children's footwear (except orthopedic extension shoes), manufacturing
622112	Children's hospitals
623999	Children's villages
23822	Chilled water systems, installation
33599	Chimes, electric, manufacturing
561791	Chimney cleaning services

561791	Chimney sweep services
23811	Chimneys, concrete, construction
45331	China and crockery, household, used retail
442298	China and glassware stores
81149	China firing and decorating to individual order
32711	China tableware, vitreous, manufacturing
41912	China, glassware, crockery and pottery, wholesale agents and brokers
41431	Chinaware, household, wholesale
11293	Chinchilla production
72221	Chinese take out restaurant
72233	Chip wagon
32222	Chipboard, laminated or surface-coated, made from purchased paperboard
333291	Chippers (e.g., logs), stationary, manufacturing
33312	Chippers, portable commercial (e.g., brush, limb and log), manufacturing
321111	Chipping logs (except in the forest)
113311	Chipping logs (in the forest)
62139	Chiropodists' offices
62131	Chiropractic services
81392	Chiropractors' associations
62131	Chiropractors, offices and clinics of
33221	Chisels, manufacturing
325189	Chlorine compounds, not specified elsewhere by process, manufacturing
325181	Chlorine, manufacturing
41841	Chlorine, wholesale
32521	Chloroprene rubber, manufacturing
31132	Chocolate (e.g., coatings, instant, liquor, syrup), made from cacao beans
31133	Chocolate (e.g., coatings, instant, liquor, syrup), made from purchased chocolate
31132	Chocolate bars, made from cacao beans
31133	Chocolate bars, made from purchased chocolate
31132	Chocolate confectionery, made from cacao beans
31133	Chocolate confectionery, made from purchased chocolate
311511	Chocolate milk, manufacturing
31133	Chocolate-covered granola bars, made from purchased chocolate
71113	Choirs
33441	Chokes for electronic circuitry, manufacturing
711512	Choreographers, independent
31171	Chowders, fish and seafood, canning
31171	Chowders, fish and seafood, frozen, manufacturing
31171	Chowders, fish and seafood, manufacturing
81311	Christian Science lecturers
62139	Christian Science practitioners' offices
113311	Christmas tree cutting
111421	Christmas tree farming
33512	Christmas tree lighting sets, electric, manufacturing
33999	Christmas tree ornaments (except electrical and glass), manufacturing
327214	Christmas tree ornaments, glass, made in glass-making plants
33999	Christmas trees, artificial, manufacturing
32513	Chrome pigments (i.e., chrome green, chrome orange, chrome yellow), manufacturing
212299	Chromite mining
212299	Chromite ore milling
325189	Chromium compounds, not specified elsewhere by process, manufacturing
212299	Chromium ore mining
33141	Chromium smelting and primary refining
62231	Chronic disease hospitals
212394	Chrysotile fibre, milling
238299	Church bells and tower clocks, installation
337127	Church furniture, manufacturing
41793	Church pews, wholesale
41899	Church supplies (except silverware and plated ware), wholesale
453999	Church supplies, retail
81311	Churches
31194	Cider vinegar, manufacturing
31213	Cider, alcoholic, manufacturing
31194	Cider, non-alcoholic, manufacturing
453999	Cigar stores and stands, retail
33999	Cigarette holders, manufacturing
333299	Cigarette making machinery, manufacturing
322299	Cigarette paper, made from purchased paper
31222	Cigarette tobacco, prepared, manufacturing
31222	Cigarettes, manufacturing
41331	Cigars, cigarettes and cut tobacco, wholesale
31222	Cigars, manufacturing
32733	Cinder (i.e., clinker) block, concrete, manufacturing
51213	Cinemas
23622	Cinemas, construction
519122	Cinematheques (film library)

333299	Circuit board making machinery, manufacturing
33441	Circuit boards, printed, bare, manufacturing
335315	Circuit breakers, power, manufacturing
41611	Circuit breakers, wholesale
54187	Circular and handbill direct distribution services
33399	Circular saws, hand held power driven, manufacturing
33321	Circular saws, woodworking, stationary, manufacturing
519121	Circulating libraries
71119	Circuses
41732	Citizens' band radios, wholesale
41732	Citizens' band radios, wholesale and repair
91139	Citizenship registration services, federal government
32519	Citrates, not specified elsewhere by process, manufacturing
41723	Citrus processing machinery, wholesale
91391	City and town councils
48511	City bus service
91311	City courts
54132	City planning services (except engineers)
91315	City solicitor
81341	Civic associations
91111	Civil defence services
54133	Civil engineering services
81331	Civil liberties groups
91191	Civil rights commissions, federal government
91191	Civil service commissions, federal government
114113	Clams, digging of
71112	Classical dance companies
321991	Classroom buildings, manufactured portables, manufacturing
32711	Clay and ceramic statuary, manufacturing
32712	Clay brick, manufacturing
212326	Clay pits
33994	Clay, modelling, manufacturing
333299	Clayworking and tempering machinery, manufacturing
81233	Clean room apparel supply service
32561	Cleaners, household type (e.g., oven, toilet bowl, window), manufacturing
32561	Cleaning and polishing preparations, manufacturing
81131	Cleaning and reglazing of baking pans
561799	Cleaning building exteriors (except sand blasting and window cleaning)
41841	Cleaning compounds and preparations, wholesale
81131	Cleaning grease and air filters, service of
23899	Cleaning new buildings interior after construction
48821	Cleaning of freight cars
561722	Cleaning of homes
561722	Cleaning offices
213118	Cleaning out (e.g., bailing out, steam and swabbing) oil and gas wells, on a contract basis
11521	Cleaning poultry houses
11511	Cleaning service, grain
561722	Cleaning shopping centres
561799	Cleaning swimming pools
41841	Cleansers, soaps, detergents, wholesale
522329	Clearing house associations (i.e., bank or cheque)
52399	Clearinghouses (i.e., commodities or securities)
315299	Clerical vestments, cut and sewn from purchased fabric
62132	Clinics of optometrists
33221	Clippers for animal use, non-powered, manufacturing
33221	Clippers, fingernail and toenail, manufacturing
33221	Clippers, hair, for human use, non-powered, manufacturing
33431	Clock radios, manufacturing
44831	Clocks and watches, retail
334512	Clocks, assembling
41422	Clocks, electric, wholesale
41441	Clocks, mechanical, wholesale
51219	Closed captioning service, film or tape
56149	Closed captioning services, real-time (i.e., simultaneous)
517112	Closed circuit television (CCTV) services
33422	Closed circuit television equipment, manufacturing
23839	Closet organizer system installation
332118	Closures, metal, stamping
41822	Closures, paper and disposable plastics, wholesale
326198	Closures, plastics, manufacturing
32791	Cloth (e.g., aluminum oxide, emery, garnet, silicon carbide), abrasive-coated, manufacturing
56199	Cloth, cutting to length, bolting, or winding for textile distributors
332619	Cloth, woven wire, made from purchased wire
335229	Clothes dryers, domestic, manufacturing

326198	Clothes hangers, plastics, manufacturing
321999	Clothes hangers, wood, manufacturing
326198	Clothes pins, plastics, manufacturing
321999	Clothes-drying frames, wood, manufacturing
321999	Clothespins, wood, manufacturing
323113	Clothing (e.g., caps, T-shirts), screen printing
41411	Clothing accessories, wholesale
41411	Clothing accessories, women's, misses' and children's, wholesale
41893	Clothing and furnishings, second hand, wholesale
31521	Clothing contractors, cut-and-sew operations, on materials owned by others
31521	Clothing contractors, men's and boys' clothing
31521	Clothing contractors, women's, girls' and infants' clothing
54149	Clothing design services
41413	Clothing fasteners, wholesale
44811	Clothing stores, men's and boys', retail
45331	Clothing stores, second-hand, retail
315292	Clothing, fur, manufacturing
315292	Clothing, leather or sheepskin-lined, manufacturing
41411	Clothing, men's and boys', wholesale
53222	Clothing, rental of
315299	Clothing, waterproof, cut and sewn from purchased fabric
32561	Cloths, dusting and polishing, chemically treated, manufacturing
11194	Clover hay farming
33635	Clutch assemblies, automotive, truck and bus, manufacturing
33635	Clutch assemblies, automotive, truck and bus, rebuilding
333619	Clutches (except motor vehicle and electromagnetic industrial controls), manufacturing
41899	Coal and coke dealers, wholesale
33313	Coal breakers, cutters and pulverizers, manufacturing
41912	Coal brokers, wholesale
454319	Coal dealers, retail
211113	Coal gasification at the mine site
212114	Coal mining, bituminous
48699	Coal pipeline transport service
211113	Coal pyrolysis at the mine site
32419	Coal tar crudes, produced in coke ovens
32519	Coal tar distillates, manufacturing
324121	Coal tar paving materials, made from purchased coal tar
41841	Coal tar products, primary and intermediate, wholesale
32521	Coal tar resins, manufacturing
483115	Coastal shipping
332619	Coat hangers, made from purchased wire
32222	Coated and treated paper products, made from purchased paper
32222	Coated board, made from purchased paperboard
322121	Coated paper, made in paper mills
32213	Coated, laminated or treated paperboard, made in paperboard mills
33281	Coating metals and metal products, for the trade
33281	Coating products of metal combined with other materials, for the trade
32222	Coating purchased paper for non-packaging applications (except photosensitive paper)
32222	Coating purchased paper for packaging applications
315292	Coats (including tailored), leather or sheepskin-lined, manufacturing
315292	Coats, fur, manufacturing
315239	Coats, non-tailored service apparel (e.g., laboratory, mechanics', medical), women's, misses' and girls', cut and sewn from purchased fabric
315234	Coats, tailored (except fur, leather), women's, misses' and girls', cut and sewn from purchased fabric
33142	Coaxial cable, made in copper wire drawing plants
33592	Coaxial cable, non-ferrous, manufacturing
41611	Coaxial cable, wholesale
325189	Cobalt compounds, not specified elsewhere by process, manufacturing
212299	Cobalt ore dressing and beneficiating
212299	Cobalt ore milling
212299	Cobalt ore mining
33141	Cobalt smelting and primary refining
81143	Cobblers, own account
33291	Cocks, drain, plumbing, manufacturing
72241	Cocktail lounges
31132	Cocoa (e.g., instant, mix, powdered), made from cacao beans
41119	Cocoa beans, wholesale
31133	Cocoa powder drink, made from purchased chocolate
31199	Coconut, desiccated and shredded, manufacturing
31171	Cod liver oil extraction (crude)

33399	Coding, dating and imprinting packaging machinery, manufacturing
31192	Coffee extracts, manufacturing
31192	Coffee flavourings and syrups (i.e., made from coffee), manufacturing
33331	Coffee makers, commercial type, manufacturing
33521	Coffee makers, household, electric, manufacturing
31192	Coffee roasting
333299	Coffee roasting and grinding machinery (i.e., food manufacturing type), manufacturing
72221	Coffee shops (without food services)
445299	Coffee stores, retail
31192	Coffee substitutes, manufacturing
337123	Coffee tables, wood, manufacturing
31192	Coffee, blended, manufacturing
31211	Coffee, iced, manufacturing
31192	Coffee, instant and freeze-dried, manufacturing
41319	Coffee, wholesale
23799	Cofferdams, construction
33999	Coffins, wood or metal, manufacturing
48711	Cog railways, scenic and sightseeing, operation
23713	Co-generation plant construction
54172	Cognitive research and development services
332611	Coil springs, heavy gauge, manufacturing
332619	Coil springs, light gauge (except clock and watch), made from purchased wire
333519	Coil winding and cutting machinery, metalworking, manufacturing
335312	Coils, for motors and generators, manufacturing
33632	Coils, ignition, internal combustion engine, manufacturing
453999	Coin and stamp dealing, retail
81299	Coin operated photo machine, operators
56199	Coin pick-up services, from parking meters
33999	Coin-operated amusement machine (except juke boxes), manufacturing
33999	Coin-operated gambling machines, manufacturing
41792	Coin-operated game machines, wholesale
81231	Coin-operated laundry and dry cleaning service
45421	Coin-operated machines selling merchandise, retail

33999	Coin-operated photograph machines, manufacturing
81299	Coin-operated service machine operation (i.e., scales, shoe shine, lockers, blood pressure)
41441	Coins, wholesale
32419	Coke oven products (e.g., coke, gases, tars), made in coke oven establishments
32419	Coke ovens
32411	Coke, petroleum, made in petroleum refineries
332113	Cold forgings, unfinished, made from purchased metal
32541	Cold remedies, manufacturing
33111	Cold rolled steel shapes (e.g., bar, plate, rod, sheet, strip), made in steel mills
333519	Cold rolling mill machinery, metalworking, manufacturing
53113	Cold storage locker rental (self storage)
49312	Cold storage locker service (except self storage)
331221	Cold-rolled steel shapes (e.g., bar, plate, rod, sheet, strip), made from purchased steel
31199	Cole slaw, fresh, manufacturing
212398	Colemanite mining
31199	Coleslaw, fresh, manufacturing
332439	Collapsible tubes (e.g., toothpaste, glue), light gauge metal, manufacturing
81232	Collecting and distributing agents, laundry and dry cleaning
56144	Collecting delinquent accounts services
56144	Collection agency
453999	Collectors' coins, retail
81299	College clearinghouses
61121	College of applied arts and sciences
61161	College of art
61121	College of fisheries
61121	College of general and vocational education
61121	College of trades and technology
61131	Colleges (except junior)
61111	Collegiate institutes, elementary or secondary
212114	Colliery, bituminous coal
212116	Colliery, lignite coal
212115	Colliery, subbituminous coal
811121	Collision repair, motor vehicle
32562	Colognes, manufacturing
81219	Colour consultants
32513	Colour lakes and toners (i.e., organic pigments), manufacturing
32513	Colour pigments, inorganic (except bone, carbon and lamp black), manufacturing

32513	Colour pigments, organic (except animal black, bone black), manufacturing
32312	Colour separation services, for the printing trade
51119	Colouring books, publishing (except exclusively on Internet)
33281	Colouring metals and metal products, for the trade
31194	Colourings, natural food, manufacturing
41634	Colours and pigments, wholesale
33994	Colours, artists', manufacturing
212299	Columbite mining
212299	Columbium ores mining
48511	Combination bus, subway, and trolley system
111999	Combination field crop farming
112991	Combination livestock farming
11233	Combination turkey farm, meat and eggs
41631	Combinations of lumber and building materials, wholesale
454113	Combined Internet and mail order sales
33311	Combines, harvester-threshers, manufacturing
41711	Combines, wholesale
31331	Combing textile fibres
11511	Combining service, agricultural crop
326198	Combs, plastics, manufacturing
32629	Combs, rubber, manufacturing
54133	Combustion and heating engineering consultants
711512	Comedians, independent
711111	Comedy troupes
81299	Comfort station operation
31412	Comforters, made from purchased fabric
323119	Comic books, printing without publishing
51112	Comic books, publishing (except exclusively on Internet)
51112	Comic books, publishing and printing combined
53112	Commercial and industrial buildings, operators of
61151	Commercial art schools
54143	Commercial art services
54143	Commercial artists, independent
41791	Commercial cooling and refrigeration equipment and supplies, wholesale
41791	Commercial cooling and refrigeration equipment and supplies, wholesale and repair
56145	Commercial credit reporting bureaus
53249	Commercial equipment rental (except coin-operated)
114114	Commercial fishing, inland
114113	Commercial fishing, salt water
54143	Commercial illustrators, independent
11293	Commercial mink ranch
54192	Commercial photography services
23822	Commercial refrigeration systems, installation
61141	Commercial schools (non-university)
41821	Commercial stationers (not printers), wholesale
48849	Commercial vehicle safety inspection, without repairs
51211	Commercials, television, production
238299	Commercial-type door installation
72231	Commissary restaurants
41912	Commission agency, general, wholesale
41912	Commission salesman, representing several products of companies
91191	Commissioner of Official Languages, federal government
52321	Commodity contract exchanges
52313	Commodity contract trading companies (i.e., acting as a principal in dealing commodities to investors)
52313	Commodity contracts dealing (i.e., acting as a principal in dealing commodities to investors)
52314	Commodity contracts floor brokers
52314	Commodity contracts options brokers
41732	Communication equipment, electronic, wholesale
41732	Communication equipment, electronic, wholesale and repair
334512	Communication signal testing apparatus, manufacturing
23713	Communication towers, construction
54143	Communication, design consultants
91191	Communications policy planning, federal government
81331	Community action advocacy groups
81341	Community association
61121	Community colleges
91391	Community development agencies, local government
711322	Community festivals, without facilities
621494	Community health centres, out-patient
91391	Community health programs, local government
62422	Community housing services
62421	Community meals, social services
712119	Community museums
62431	Community service employment training programs

91391	Community social service programs, local government
91291	Community social service programs, provincial government
711111	Community theatres
335312	Commutators, electric motor, manufacturing
48111	Commuter air carriers, scheduled
48511	Commuter bus operation
48511	Commuter rail operation
41444	Compact disc (CD's), music, wholesale
33431	Compact disc players (e.g., automotive, household-type), manufacturing
33461	Compact discs, pre-recorded audio, mass-reproducing
33461	Compact discs, recordable or re-writable, blank, manufacturing
72231	Company cafeteria
334511	Compasses, gyroscopic and magnetic (except portable), manufacturing
541612	Compensation consulting services
311119	Complete feed, livestock, manufacturing
322219	Composite cans (i.e., foil-fibre and other combinations), made from purchased paperboard
56221	Compost dumps
325314	Compost, manufacturing
41841	Compound catalysts, industrial, wholesale
325991	Compounding plastics resins from recycled materials
221119	Compressed air electric power generation
41841	Compressed and liquefied gases (except petroleum gases), wholesale
33322	Compression moulding machinery for plastics, manufacturing
23712	Compressor, metering and pumping stations, gas and oil, construction
41723	Compressors and vacuum pumps, wholesale
41723	Compressors and vacuum pumps, wholesale and repair
41612	Compressors, air-conditioning, wholesale
33391	Compressors, general purpose air and gas, manufacturing
33639	Compressors, motor vehicle air-conditioning, manufacturing
333416	Compressors, refrigeration and air-conditioning (except motor vehicle), manufacturing
23821	Computer and network cable installation
454113	Computer and peripheral equipment, mail order, retail
41912	Computer and related machinery and equipment, wholesale agents and brokers
54151	Computer consulting services
54151	Computer disaster recovery services
81341	Computer enthusiasts' clubs
44312	Computer equipment and supplies sales, retail
54151	Computer facilities management services
23833	Computer flooring installation
323116	Computer forms, manifold or continuous (except paper simply lined), printing
44312	Computer hardware and software, retail
54151	Computer hardware consulting services
51821	Computer input preparation services
61142	Computer operator training
53242	Computer peripheral equipment, rental and leasing
325999	Computer printer toner cartridges, manufacturing
51821	Computer processing
51821	Computer processing services
54151	Computer programming services, custom
54151	Computer programs or systems software development, custom
61151	Computer repair training
54171	Computer research and development laboratories
54151	Computer software consulting services
44312	Computer software games stores
54151	Computer software programming services, custom
51121	Computer software publishing (including designing and developing), packaged
44312	Computer software stores, retail
54151	Computer software systems analysis and design, custom
61142	Computer software training
51121	Computer software, all formats, packaged, publishers
41731	Computer software, packaged, wholesale
54151	Computer systems analysis and design services
54151	Computer systems design consulting services
54151	Computer systems integrators
33411	Computer terminals, manufacturing
41731	Computer terminals, wholesale

51821	Computer time, rental
51821	Computer time-sharing services
56141	Computer word processing
54151	Computer-aided design (CAD) systems services
54151	Computer-aided engineering (CAE) systems services
334512	Computerized axial tomography (CT/CAT) scanners, manufacturing
41911	Computers and peripheral equipment, business to business (B2B) electronic markets, wholesale
41731	Computers and peripheral equipment, wholesale
41731	Computers and peripheral equipment, wholesale and repair
33411	Computers, manufacturing
31193	Concentrates, drink (except frozen fruit juice), manufacturing
31193	Concentrates, flavouring (except coffee-based), manufacturing
31141	Concentrates, frozen fruit and vegetable juice, manufacturing
71113	Concert artists, independent
711321	Concert booking agencies
53112	Concert hall operation, real estate operation
711311	Concert halls, promoting events
711311	Concert organizers, with facilities
711321	Concert promoters, without facilities
91131	Conciliation and mediation services, federal government
325999	Concrete additive preparations (e.g., curing, hardening), manufacturing
41841	Concrete additives, wholesale
44419	Concrete and cinder block dealers, retail
41639	Concrete and cinder block, wholesale
32732	Concrete batch plants (including temporary)
32733	Concrete blocks, bricks and pipe, precast, manufacturing
23891	Concrete breaking and cutting for demolition
41639	Concrete building products, wholesale
41792	Concrete burial vaults and boxes, wholesale
23839	Concrete coating, glazing or sealing
33312	Concrete finishing machinery, manufacturing
23811	Concrete footing and foundation contractors
41621	Concrete forms, steel, wholesale
32739	Concrete furniture (e.g., benches, tables), manufacturing

33312	Concrete gunning equipment, manufacturing
33312	Concrete mixing machinery, portable, manufacturing
41721	Concrete mixing plant machinery, wholesale
41721	Concrete mixing plant machinery, wholesale and repair
41639	Concrete mixtures, wholesale
23731	Concrete paving (i.e., highways, roads, streets, public sidewalks)
32739	Concrete products, precast (except block, brick, pipe), manufacturing
23812	Concrete products, structural precast or prestressed, installation
23811	Concrete pumping (placement)
23812	Concrete reinforcement placement, contractors
332314	Concrete reinforcing bar assemblies, manufacturing
41621	Concrete reinforcing bars, wholesale
332619	Concrete reinforcing mesh, made from purchased wire
23811	Concrete resurfacing
32739	Concrete tanks, manufacturing
23899	Concrete work, private driveways, sidewalks and parking areas, contractors
32799	Concrete, dry mixture, manufacturing
211113	Condensate, cycle, natural gas production
311515	Condensed, evaporated or powdered milk, manufacturing
41732	Condensers, electronic, wholesale
33241	Condensers, steam, manufacturing
41612	Condensing units, air-conditioning, wholesale
52222	Conditional sales finance companies
53131	Condominium management
81399	Condominium owners' associations
56159	Condominium time share exchange services
23611	Condominiums, multifamily, construction, by general contractors
32629	Condoms, manufacturing
711512	Conductors, orchestra, independent
41639	Conduit and pipe, concrete, wholesale
41611	Conduit electric wire and cable, wholesale
32712	Conduit, vitrified clay, manufacturing
33593	Conduits and fittings, electrical, manufacturing
41611	Conduits and raceways, wholesale
11321	Cone gathering service

322219	Cones (e.g., winding yarn, string, ribbons, cloth), fibre, made from purchased paperboard
31131	Confectioners' sugar, manufacturing
44512	Confectionery stores, convenience
31132	Confectionery, chocolate, made from cacao beans
31134	Confectionery, non-chocolate, manufacturing
41319	Confectionery, wholesale
41912	Confectionery, wholesale agents and brokers
322299	Confetti, made from purchased paper
212326	Conglomerate mine or quarry
33593	Connectors and terminals for electrical devices, manufacturing
33441	Connectors, electronic (e.g., coaxial, cylindrical, printed circuit, rack, panel), manufacturing
41732	Connectors, electronic, wholesale
81331	Conservation advocacy groups
91191	Conservation and stabilization agencies, federal government
71219	Conservation areas
91191	Conservation authority, federal government
81321	Conservation foundation
71213	Conservatories, botanical
61161	Conservatory of music (except degree-granting)
61131	Conservatory of music, degree granting
81394	Constituency associations, political party
32552	Construction adhesives (except asphalt, gypsum-based), manufacturing
41912	Construction and forestry machinery and equipment, wholesale agents and brokers
81391	Construction association
23899	Construction elevator, erection and dismantling
54133	Construction engineering services
23891	Construction equipment (except crane) rental with operator
61151	Construction equipment operation schools
53241	Construction equipment, heavy, rental and leasing (without operator)
81131	Construction machinery and equipment, repair
41721	Construction machinery and equipment, wholesale
41721	Construction machinery and equipment, wholesale and repair
33312	Construction machinery, manufacturing

53241	Construction machinery, rental (without operator)
23622	Construction management, commercial and institutional buildings
23799	Construction management, dams
23731	Construction management, highway, road, street and bridge
23621	Construction management, industrial buildings and structures
23799	Construction management, marine structures
23799	Construction management, mass transit
23799	Construction management, miscellaneous heavy and civil engineering construction
23712	Construction management, oil and gas pipelines and related structures
23712	Construction management, oil refineries and petrochemical complexes
23799	Construction management, outdoor recreation facilities
23713	Construction management, power and communication lines and related structures
23611	Construction management, residential buildings
23799	Construction management, tunnels
23711	Construction management, water and sewage treatment plants
23711	Construction management, water and sewer lines and related structures
41611	Construction materials, electrical, interior and exterior, wholesale
484222	Construction rubble, hauling, local
321991	Construction site buildings, manufactured portables, manufacturing
33312	Construction tractors and attachments, manufacturing
91141	Consular service, federal government
91911	Consular service, foreign government in Canada
54194	Consulting and visiting services, veterinary
54133	Consulting engineering services
54141	Consulting services and consultants, interior design
541612	Consulting services, labour relations
541612	Consulting services, personnel management
91191	Consumer and corporate affairs, federal government
91291	Consumer and corporate affairs, provincial government
81299	Consumer buying service
54199	Consumer credit counselling services

56145	Consumer credit reporting bureaus
44311	Consumer electronic equipment stores, retail
32541	Contact lens solutions, manufacturing
33911	Contact lenses, manufacturing
44613	Contact lenses, retail
41793	Contact lenses, wholesale
48821	Container loading or unloading service, railroad
32192	Container parts (shook) ready for assembly, manufacturing
48411	Container trucking service, local
484121	Container trucking service, long-distance, truck-load
32213	Containers (e.g., boxes), made in paperboard mills
32192	Containers (e.g., fruit baskets, boxes), made from veneer made in the same establishment
327215	Containers for packaging, bottling and canning, made from purchased glass
327214	Containers for packaging, bottling and canning, made in glass-making plants
332439	Containers, air cargo, light gauge metal, manufacturing
322211	Containers, corrugated and solid fibreboard, made from purchased paper or paperboard
332999	Containers, foil (except bags), made from purchased foil
322219	Containers, food, sanitary (except folding), made from purchased paper or paperboard
41822	Containers, paper and disposable plastics, wholesale
326198	Containers, plastics (except foam, bottles and bags), manufacturing
32192	Containers, wood, manufacturing
56291	Contaminated site, remediation
71112	Contemporary dance companies
32541	Contraceptive preparations, manufacturing
213118	Contract battery operators
48411	Contract bulk mail, truck transportation, local
484121	Contract bulk mail, truck transportation, long-distance
213117	Contract diamond drilling, metallic minerals
113312	Contract logging
56199	Contract meter reading service, water
335315	Control panels, electric power distribution, manufacturing
334512	Controllers for process variables (e.g., electric, electronic, mechanical, pneumatic operation), manufacturing
41723	Controlling instruments and accessories, wholesale
41723	Controlling instruments and accessories, wholesale and repair
62311	Convalescent homes
62231	Convalescent hospitals
61111	Convent schools, elementary or secondary
56159	Convention and visitors bureaus
56159	Convention bureaus
53112	Convention facilities, rental only
56192	Convention promoters
56192	Convention services
81311	Convents (except schools)
337121	Convertible sofas, manufacturing
33639	Convertible tops, for automobiles, manufacturing
32622	Conveyor belts, rubber, manufacturing
33392	Conveyor systems, general industrial type, manufacturing
41723	Conveyor systems, wholesale
33392	Conveyors, farm type, manufacturing
561613	Convoy guard services
41316	Cooked meats (except canned), wholesale
311822	Cookie dough, made from purchased flour
311821	Cookies, manufacturing
33331	Cooking equipment, commercial type, manufacturing
41792	Cooking equipment, commercial, wholesale
311221	Cooking oil, made by wet-milling corn
311225	Cooking oil, made from purchased fats and oils
311224	Cooking oil, made in oilseed crushing mills
61151	Cooking school
33221	Cooking utensils, fabricated metal, manufacturing
327214	Cooking ware (e.g., pots, baking pans), made in glass-making plants
32711	Cooking ware, china, earthenware, pottery or stoneware, manufacturing
41322	Coolers (2.5% or greater alcohol content), wholesale
332439	Coolers and ice chests (except foam plastics), manufacturing
326198	Coolers or ice chests, plastics (except foam), manufacturing
32614	Coolers or ice chests, polystyrene foam, manufacturing

41791	Coolers, beverage and drinking water, mechanical, wholesale
41791	Coolers, beverage and drinking water, mechanical, wholesale and repair
333416	Coolers, refrigeration, manufacturing
333416	Coolers, water, manufacturing
23822	Cooling towers, installation
333416	Cooling towers, manufacturing
32192	Cooperage stock (e.g., heading, hoops, staves), manufacturing
32192	Cooperage, manufacturing
53131	Cooperative apartment manager
32712	Coping, wall, clay, manufacturing
33142	Copper alloys (e.g., brass, bronze), made from purchased metals and copper-based alloys
33141	Copper alloys, made in primary copper smelting and refining mills
33142	Copper and copper alloy shapes (e.g., bar, ingot, rod, sheet), made from purchased metal or scrap
41621	Copper and copper alloy, primary forms and basic shapes, wholesale
41621	Copper architectural and structural metal products, wholesale
32513	Copper based pigments, manufacturing
325189	Copper compounds, not specified elsewhere by process, manufacturing
331523	Copper die-casting foundries
332113	Copper forgings, unfinished, made from purchased copper
212233	Copper ore dressing and beneficiating
212233	Copper ore grinding
212233	Copper ore milling
212233	Copper ore, mining
33142	Copper powder, paste and flakes, made from purchased copper
33142	Copper products, made by rolling, drawing, extruding or alloying purchased metal
33142	Copper refining, secondary (i.e., from purchased metal or scrap)
33142	Copper rolling, drawing and extruding
23816	Copper roofing, installation
33141	Copper shapes (e.g., bar, billet, ingot, plate, sheet), made in primary copper smelting and refining mills
41621	Copper sheets, plates, bars, rods, pipes, wholesale
33141	Copper smelting and primary refining
325189	Copper sulphate, manufacturing
212233	Copper-zinc ore mining
56143	Copy centres
56143	Copy shops
31499	Cord (except tire, wire), manufacturing
31499	Cord for reinforcing rubber tires, industrial belting and fuel cells, manufacturing
33399	Corded (i.e., electric-powered), hand held power tools, manufacturing
31214	Cordials, alcoholic, manufacturing
33421	Cordless telephones (except cellular), manufacturing
31322	Cords and braids, narrow woven, manufacturing
41899	Cordwood, wholesale
322219	Cores, fibre (i.e., fibre body, ends of any material), made from purchased paperboard
321999	Cork products (except gaskets), manufacturing
41899	Cork, wholesale
31123	Corn breakfast foods, manufacturing
311919	Corn chips and related corn snacks, manufacturing
31134	Corn confections (i.e., candy-coated), manufacturing
11115	Corn farming (except sweet corn)
311211	Corn flour, manufacturing
11115	Corn for fodder, growing
11115	Corn for popping, growing
31199	Corn for popping, manufacturing
11115	Corn for silage, growing
311221	Corn gluten feed, manufacturing
311221	Corn gluten meal, manufacturing
311221	Corn oil, crude and refined, made by wet-milling corn
33521	Corn poppers, electric, manufacturing
333299	Corn popping machinery (i.e., food manufacturing type), manufacturing
311221	Corn starch, manufacturing
311221	Corn sweeteners (e.g., dextrose, fructose, glucose), made by wet-milling corn
311221	Corn syrup, made by wet-milling corn
31199	Corn syrups, made from purchased sweeteners
111219	Corn, sweet, growing
311614	Corned meats, made from purchased meat
212326	Cornwall stone mining
522112	Corporate and institutional banking services
56121	Correctional facilities, privately operated
91212	Correctional school, provincial government
91122	Correctional services, federal government

61151	Correspondence school (except elementary and secondary levels)
41822	Corrugated and solid fibre boxes, wholesale
322211	Corrugated and solid fibreboard pads, made from purchased paper or paperboard
322211	Corrugated boxes, made from purchased paper or paperboard
32213	Corrugated boxes, made in paperboard mills
23816	Corrugated metal roofing, installation
322211	Corrugated paper, made from purchased paper or paperboard
32213	Corrugating medium, manufacturing
32541	Cortisone, uncompounded, manufacturing
212398	Corundum mining
32562	Cosmetic creams, lotions and oils, manufacturing
56191	Cosmetic kits, assembling and packaging
45439	Cosmetics, house-to-house or party-plan selling, retail
41452	Cosmetics, wholesale
61151	Cosmetology schools
44815	Costume accessories (e.g., handbags, costume jewellery, gloves), retail
54149	Costume design services (except independent designers)
711512	Costume designers, theatrical, independent
33991	Costume jewellery (including imitation stones and pearls), manufacturing
44815	Costume jewellery stores, retail
315299	Costumes (e.g., lodge, masquerade, theatrical), cut and sewn from purchased fabric
311511	Cottage cheese, manufacturing
23611	Cottages, construction
41639	Cottages, prefabricated, wholesale
321992	Cottages, prefabricated, wood frame, manufacturing
33272	Cotter pins, metal, manufacturing
33911	Cotton and cotton balls, absorbent, manufacturing
31499	Cotton batting (except nonwoven batting), manufacturing
11192	Cotton farming
31311	Cotton spun yarn, manufacturing
31134	Cough drops (except medicated), manufacturing
32541	Cough medicines, manufacturing
91191	Councils of economic advisers
54111	Counsellors at law, private practice

41639	Counter tops and kitchen cabinets, wholesale
33711	Counter tops, wood, manufacturing
333416	Counters and display cases, refrigerated, manufacturing
23839	Countertop and cabinet, metal (except residential-type), installation
71391	Country clubs
71113	Country music groups
91211	County courts
333619	Couplings, mechanical power transmission, manufacturing
54186	Coupon and sample packages, development of
54187	Coupon direct distribution services
56199	Coupon redemption service (clearinghouses)
49211	Courier operation of Post Office
49211	Courier service
91121	Court of appeal, federal government
91211	Court of law, provincial government
61141	Court reporting schools
56149	Court reporting services
91311	Court, municipal government
91121	Courts of customs and patent appeals
91211	Courts, civil law, provincial government
91211	Courts, criminal law, provincial government
315239	Coveralls, work, women's, misses' and girls', cut and sewn from purchased fabric
11113	Cowpea farming, dry
114113	Crabs, catching of
311821	Crackers (e.g., graham, soda), manufacturing
333519	Cradle assemblies machinery (i.e., wire making equipment), manufacturing
45112	Craft kits and supplies, retail
41446	Craft kits, wholesale
11133	Cranberry bogs
53241	Crane rental and leasing (without operator)
23899	Crane rental with operator
33312	Cranes, construction type, manufacturing
41721	Cranes, construction, wholesale
33392	Cranes, industrial truck, manufacturing
41723	Cranes, industrial, wholesale
33392	Cranes, overhead travelling, manufacturing
325999	Crankcase additive preparations, manufacturing
33631	Crankshaft assemblies, automotive and truck gasoline engine, manufacturing
32192	Crates, wood, manufacturing

48899	Crating goods for shipping
41721	Crawler tractors, construction, wholesale
41721	Crawler tractors, construction, wholesale and repair
33994	Crayons, manufacturing
333299	Cream separators (except farm type), manufacturing
33311	Cream separators, farm type, manufacturing
311515	Cream, dried and powdered, manufacturing
11212	Cream, fluid, raw, producing
311511	Cream, manufacturing
311511	Cream, sour, manufacturing
311515	Creamery butter, manufacturing
323119	Credit and identification card imprinting, embossing and encoding
326198	Credit and identification card stock, plastics, manufacturing
56145	Credit bureaus and agencies
52221	Credit card companies
522329	Credit card processing services
56145	Credit investigation services
56145	Credit rating services
54199	Credit repair services
522321	Credit unions, central, regional or league (i.e., central clearing house services)
52213	Credit unions, local
33399	Cremating ovens, manufacturing
81222	Crematoria
32519	Creosote, made by distillation of coal tar
32519	Creosote, made by distillation of wood tar
321114	Creosoting of wood
322299	Crepe paper, made from purchased paper
32519	Cresols, made by distillation of coal tar
32519	Cresylic acids, made from refined petroleum or natural gas
337123	Cribs, wood, manufacturing
91191	Criminal justice statistics centres, federal government
62419	Crisis intervention centres
31311	Crochet spun yarns (e.g., cotton, man-made fibre, silk, wool), made from purchased fibre
212394	Crocidolite, milled fibre, mining
311814	Croissants, baking, made in commercial bakeries
111999	Crop and animal combination farming (primarily crop)
112991	Crop and animal farming, combination (primarily animal)
111999	Crop and livestock combination farm (primarily crop)
112991	Crop and livestock farming, combination (primarily livestock)
33311	Crop driers, farm type, manufacturing
111999	Crop farms, general
11511	Crop harvesting service
41711	Crop preparation machinery (e.g., cleaning, drying, conditioning), wholesale
11511	Crop spraying service, with or without fertilizing
71392	Cross country skiing facilities
311814	Croutons and bread crumbs, made in commercial bakeries
332118	Crowns (e.g., bottle, can), metal, stamping
41723	Crowns and closures, metal, wholesale
33441	CRT (cathode ray tubes), manufacturing
48611	Crude oil pipeline service
211113	Crude oil, conventional production, mining
211113	Crude oil, conventional, secondary recovering
211113	Crude oil, conventional, waterflood recovering
32411	Crude oil, refining
41211	Crude oil, wholesale
33632	Cruise control mechanisms, electronic, automotive, truck and bus, manufacturing
56159	Cruise ship ticket offices
71321	Cruises, gambling
11531	Cruising timber
41639	Crushed stone, wholesale
41723	Crushing machinery and equipment, industrial, wholesale
33313	Crushing machinery, stationary, manufacturing
41721	Crushing, pulverizing and screening machinery for construction, wholesale
11251	Crustacean farming
41314	Crustaceans and molluscs, wholesale
334512	CT/CAT (computerized axial tomography), scanners, manufacturing
335315	Cubicles (i.e., electric switchboard equipment), manufacturing
212114	Culm bank recovery, anthracite (except on a contract basis)
315239	Culottes, women's, misses', and girls', cut and sewn from purchased fabric
41711	Cultivators, seeders, spreaders, farm, wholesale
91291	Cultural affairs programs, provincial government

91191	Culture and arts support programs, federal
32541	Culture media, manufacturing
326191	Cultured marble plumbing fixtures, manufacturing
326198	Cultured marble products (except plumbing fixtures), manufacturing
11251	Cultured pearl production
32733	Culvert pipe, concrete, manufacturing
23731	Culverts (highway, road and street) construction
32511	Cumene, made from refined petroleum or natural gas liquids
212233	Cuprite ore mining
322299	Cups, moulded pulp, manufacturing
41822	Cups, paper and disposable plastics, wholesale
326198	Cups, plastics (except foam), manufacturing
23899	Curbs and gutters, concrete, residential, installation
23731	Curbs and street gutters, highway, road and street, construction
311515	Curds, cheese, manufacturing
41316	Cured meat (except canned), wholesale
311614	Cured meats (e.g., brined, dried, salted), made from purchased meat
31171	Curing fish and seafood
45322	Curio shops, retail
41899	Curios, wholesale
71399	Curling clubs
71399	Curling rinks
33331	Currency counting machinery, manufacturing
61171	Curriculum development, educational
33792	Curtain rods, poles and fixtures, manufacturing
23819	Curtain wall (except glass and precast concrete) installation, contractors
23815	Curtain wall, glass, installation
23812	Curtain wall, precast concrete, installation
442291	Curtains and draperies, household, new, retail
31412	Curtains and draperies, window, made from purchased fabrics
31324	Curtains, made in knitting mills
41433	Curtains, wholesale
32615	Cushion blocks, foam plastics (except polystyrene), manufacturing
31412	Cushions (except carpet or spring), made from purchased fabrics
41433	Cushions and pillows, wholesale
33636	Cushions, motor vehicle, manufacturing
337121	Cushions, spring, manufacturing

31152	Custard, frozen, manufacturing
561722	Custodial services
325991	Custom compounding of purchased resins
442292	Custom framing, mounting, and laminating pictures, retail store
44831	Custom jewellery, retail
811112	Custom made exhaust systems, installation
44821	Custom made orthopaedic shoes, retail
41632	Custom millwork and woodwork, wholesale
442292	Custom picture frame, retail store
332118	Custom roll forming of metal products
311611	Custom slaughtering (except poultry and small game)
315222	Custom tailors, men's and boys'
337213	Custom-designed office interiors (i.e., furniture, architectural woodwork and fixtures), manufacturing
541619	Customer services management consulting services
488519	Customs brokers
541619	Customs consulting services
91191	Customs tariff, federal government
81149	Cutlery sharpening (without retail sales of new equipment)
442298	Cutlery stores, retail
33221	Cutlery, base metal plated with precious metal, manufacturing
41792	Cutlery, commercial and industrial, wholesale
41439	Cutlery, household, wholesale
33221	Cutlery, non-precious metal, manufacturing
33991	Cutlery, precious metal (except plated), manufacturing
33221	Cutters, glass, manufacturing
213118	Cutting casings, tubes and rods, oil field
113311	Cutting cordwood, in the forest
33221	Cutting dies (except metal cutting), manufacturing
333519	Cutting dies, metalworking, manufacturing
23891	Cutting of rights-of-way contractor
32419	Cutting oils, made from refined petroleum
212326	Cyanite mining
32511	Cyclic aromatic hydrocarbons, made from refined petroleum or natural gas liquids
32411	Cyclic aromatic hydrocarbons, made in petroleum refineries
32519	Cyclic crudes, made by distillation of coal tar

32519	Cycloterpenes, manufacturing
33631	Cylinder heads, automotive and truck gasoline engine, manufacturing
33399	Cylinders, fluid power, manufacturing
33242	Cylinders, pressure, manufacturing

D

11212	Dairy cows and milk, producing
41711	Dairy farm machinery and equipment, wholesale
11212	Dairy farming
11211	Dairy heifer replacement production
311515	Dairy products (except fluid milk)
41319	Dairy products, canned or dried, wholesale
41312	Dairy products, processed (except canned), wholesale
41912	Dairy products, wholesale agents and brokers
311511	Dairy, fluid milk
23799	Dam construction, general contractors
71113	Dance bands
71112	Dance companies
711311	Dance festival promoters, with facilities
711322	Dance festival promoters, without facilities
71399	Dance halls
61161	Dance instruction
61161	Dance studios and schools
41443	Dark room apparatus, wholesale
51821	Data entry services
54151	Data processing facilities management services
51821	Data processing services
51821	Data processing, computer services
51114	Database publishing (except exclusively on Internet)
81299	Dating service
62412	Day care centres, adult and handicapped
81219	Day spa
62441	Day-care centres, child
56211	Dead stock removal services
44111	Dealers in automobiles, new, retail
44112	Dealers in automobiles, used, retail
56144	Debt collection services
333519	Deburring machines, metalworking, manufacturing
32711	Decalcomania on china and glass, for the trade
45322	Decorations, seasonal and holiday, retail
41634	Decorative wall coverings, wholesale
41439	Decorative window accessories, wholesale

54141	Decorators, interior, consulting service
483115	Deep water transportation of freight (except by ferries)
483115	Deep water transportation of passengers (except by ferries)
112999	Deer farming
91111	Defence research board, federal government
91111	Defence services, federal government
325999	Degreasing preparations for machinery parts, manufacturing
61131	Degree-granting institutions
333416	Dehumidifiers (except portable), manufacturing
311515	Dehydrated milk, manufacturing
31142	Dehydrating fruits and vegetables
325999	Deicing preparations, manufacturing
322112	De-inking recovered paper
41611	Demand meters, wholesale
54172	Demographic research and development services
23891	Demolishing buildings and structures
541899	Demonstration services, merchandise
41452	Dental care preparations, wholesale
33911	Dental chairs, manufacturing
62121	Dental clinic
33911	Dental equipment and instruments, manufacturing
41793	Dental equipment and supplies, wholesale
41793	Dental equipment and supplies, wholesale and repair
81392	Dental examining board (national)
32562	Dental floss, manufacturing
33911	Dental furniture, manufacturing
33911	Dental glues and cements, manufacturing
62139	Dental hygienists, offices of
33911	Dental laboratories
62151	Dental laboratory, analysis and diagnostic
54171	Dental research and development laboratories
62121	Dental surgeons, offices of
33911	Dental wax, manufacturing
32561	Dentifrices, manufacturing
61131	Dentistry schools
81392	Dentists' associations
62121	Dentists, offices and clinics of
33911	Denture materials, manufacturing
33911	Dentures, custom made in dental laboratories
62139	Denturists' offices
561722	Deodorant servicing of rest rooms

32561	Deodorants (except personal), manufacturing
41841	Deodorants (except personal), wholesale
32562	Deodorants, personal, manufacturing
45211	Department stores, retail
32562	Depilatory preparations, manufacturing
33281	Depolishing metals and metal products, for the trade
91132	Deportation services
524129	Deposit or share insurance
522111	Deposit-accepting mortgage companies (except co-operative)
52219	Deposit-accepting mortgage companies, co-operative
41451	Dermatological medicines, wholesale
62111	Dermatologists, offices of
33313	Derricks, oil and gas field type, manufacturing
41723	Derricks, wholesale
54151	Design and system analysis, computer services (software)
54141	Designers, interior, offices of
41821	Desk accessories, office supply, wholesale
41791	Desk calculators (including electric and electronic), wholesale
33512	Desk lamps, manufacturing
41793	Desks (including school), wholesale
337214	Desks, office (except wood), manufacturing
337213	Desks, wood office, manufacturing
56141	Desktop publishing services
31152	Desserts, frozen (except bakery), manufacturing
311814	Desserts, frozen bakery, manufacturing
31199	Desserts, ready-to-mix, manufacturing
561611	Detective agencies
91122	Detention centres, federal government
91312	Detention centres, municipal/local
91212	Detention centres, provincial government
32561	Detergents (e.g., dishwashing, industrial, laundry), manufacturing
41841	Detergents, wholesale
32592	Detonators (except ammunition), manufacturing
41841	Detonators and fuses, wholesale
51219	Developing and printing of commercial motion picture film
812921	Developing and printing of films (except for the motion picture industry)
33641	Developing and producing prototypes for aerospace products
41443	Developing apparatus, photographic, wholesale
33331	Developing equipment, photographic film, manufacturing
54171	Development of computer and related technology (hardware)
81331	Developmentally handicap organizations
311221	Dextrose, made by wet-milling corn
212316	Diabase, crushed and broken stone, quarrying
212316	Diabase, quarrying
32541	Diagnostic biological preparations, manufacturing
811199	Diagnostic centres, motor vehicle
334512	Diagnostic equipment, electromedical, manufacturing
41793	Diagnostic equipment, medical, wholesale
334512	Diagnostic equipment, MRI (magnetic resonance imaging), manufacturing
32541	Diagnostic substances, in-vitro, manufacturing
32791	Diamond dressing wheels, manufacturing
212392	Diamond mining
41441	Diamonds (gems), wholesale
41723	Diamonds, industrial, natural and crude, wholesale
41441	Diamonds, jewellery, wholesale
81233	Diaper supply service
31499	Diapers (except disposable), made from purchased fabrics
41411	Diapers (except paper), wholesale
322291	Diapers, disposable, made from purchased paper or textile wadding
322121	Diapers, disposable, made in paper mills
32629	Diaphragms (i.e., birth control devices), rubber, manufacturing
51119	Diaries and time schedulers, publishers (except exclusively on Internet)
212326	Diaspore mining
212398	Diatomaceous earth mining
212398	Diatomite mining
41791	Dictating machines, wholesale
56141	Dictation services
323119	Dictionaries, printing without publishing
51113	Dictionaries, publishing (except exclusively on Internet)
333519	Die-casting machines, metalworking, manufacturing
331523	Die-castings, aluminum, unfinished, manufacturing

331523	Die-castings, non-ferrous metals, unfinished, manufacturing
322299	Die-cut paper products (except office supplies), made from purchased paper or paperboard
32223	Die-cut paper products for office use, made from purchased paper or paperboard
33399	Dielectric industrial heating equipment, manufacturing
33221	Dies, cutting (except metal cutting), manufacturing
333519	Dies, metalworking (except threading), manufacturing
333519	Dies, thread cutting, manufacturing
333619	Diesel and semi-diesel engines, manufacturing
333619	Diesel engine parts, not specified elsewhere by process, manufacturing
811111	Diesel engine repair, automotive
41799	Diesel engines and engine parts, industrial, wholesale
41799	Diesel engines and engine parts, industrial, wholesale and repair
333619	Diesel engines, rebuilding
454319	Diesel fuel, delivered to customers' premises, retail
32411	Diesel fuels, made in petroleum refineries
33651	Diesel-electric locomotives, manufacturing
81219	Diet centres (non-medical)
311515	Dietary drinks, dairy and non-dairy base, manufacturing
41319	Dietary foods, canned, wholesale
445299	Dietary foods, retail
81392	Dieticians' associations
62139	Dieticians, offices of
23822	Diffusers, grilles, air registers, installation
32541	Digestive system preparations, manufacturing
23891	Digging foundations
33411	Digital cameras, manufacturing
33411	Digital computers, manufacturing
323115	Digital printing (e.g., billboards, other large format graphical materials)
323115	Digital printing (e.g., graphics, high resolution)
32541	Digitoxin, uncompounded, manufacturing
23799	Dikes and other flood control structures, construction
321111	Dimension lumber (e.g., 2x4), made from logs or bolts

32799	Dimension stone dressing and manufacturing
32799	Dimension stone for buildings, manufacturing
212314	Dimensional stone, granite, rough, mining
72211	Diner
32629	Dinghies, inflatable rubber, manufacturing
72211	Dining lounge
41439	Dining room furniture, wholesale
337123	Dining room furniture, wood, manufacturing
48721	Dinner cruises
31141	Dinners, frozen (except seafood-based), manufacturing
31171	Dinners, frozen, seafood-based, manufacturing
41319	Dinners, frozen, wholesale
326198	Dinnerware, plastics (except foam), manufacturing
32614	Dinnerware, polystyrene foam, manufacturing
33441	Diodes, solid state (e.g., germanium, silicon), manufacturing
41732	Diodes, wholesale
212314	Diorite, quarrying
32519	Diphenylamine, manufacturing
91141	Diplomatic representation, federal
91141	Diplomatic services, federal government
31194	Dips (except cheese and sour cream-based), manufacturing
311515	Dips, cheese-based, manufacturing
311511	Dips, sour-cream based, manufacturing
33411	Direct access storage devices, manufacturing
32513	Direct dyes, manufacturing
524112	Direct group health insurance carriers
524112	Direct group life and pension insurance carriers
524111	Direct individual health insurance carriers
524111	Direct individual life and pension insurance carriers
524125	Direct liability insurance carriers
54186	Direct mail advertising campaign services
454113	Direct mail marketing operators, retail
45439	Direct personal retailing operators, retail
524122	Direct private, automobile insurance carriers
524121	Direct property and casualty insurance carriers (combination of policies)

33111	Direct reduction of iron ore
454311	Direct sale of heating oil (non-store, delivered to customer's premises)
45439	Direct selling of merchandise (door-to-door), retail
213111	Directional drilling of oil and gas wells, on a contract basis
711512	Director, film and video, independent
323119	Directories, printing without publishing
51114	Directories, publishing (except exclusively on Internet)
54187	Directories, telephone, distribution on a contract or fee basis
51913	Directory publishing, Internet
517112	Direct-to-home (DTH) satellite television service providers
484222	Dirt hauling, truck, local
23891	Dirt moving, for construction
332611	Disc and ring springs, heavy-gauge, manufacturing
711512	Disc jockey, independent
33511	Discharge lamps, high intensity (mercury, sodium, metal halide), manufacturing
72241	Discotheques, alcoholic beverage
45211	Discount department stores
54194	Disease testing services, veterinary
322299	Dishes, made from moulded pulp
41822	Dishes, paper and disposable plastics, wholesale
322219	Dishes, paper, made from purchased paper or paperboard
32711	Dishes, pottery, manufacturing
32561	Dishwasher detergents, manufacturing
335223	Dishwashers, household, electric, manufacturing
41792	Dishwashing equipment, commercial, wholesale
41839	Disinfectants, agricultural, wholesale
32561	Disinfectants, household type and industrial, manufacturing
41841	Disinfectants, wholesale
56171	Disinfecting service
51821	Disk and diskette conversion services
33411	Disk drives, computer, manufacturing
41731	Disk drives, wholesale
33461	Diskettes, blank, manufacturing
45122	Disks, music and video, retail
238299	Dismantling large-scale machinery and equipment
41811	Dismantling machinery for scrap
23891	Dismantling of engineering structures (e.g., oil storage tanks)
41811	Dismantling ships

325181	Disodium carbonate (i.e., soda ash), manufacturing
48531	Dispatch, taxicab, services
44611	Dispensary, retail
33391	Dispensing and measuring pumps (e.g., gasoline), manufacturing
32513	Disperse dyes, manufacturing
54185	Display advertising services
54185	Display card advertising services
337215	Display cases and fixtures (except refrigerated), manufacturing
41791	Display cases and fixtures, for office and store, wholesale
41791	Display cases and fixtures, for office and store, wholesale and repair
333416	Display cases, refrigerated, manufacturing
54185	Display installation services
541899	Display lettering services
56221	Disposal of dead stock, incinerator and combustor
44531	Distilled spirits, retail
41322	Distilled spirits, wholesale
325999	Distilled water, manufacturing
31214	Distilleries
333299	Distillery equipment, beverage, manufacturing
31214	Distilling alcoholic beverages (except brandy)
333299	Distilling apparatus, laboratory type, manufacturing
31213	Distilling brandy
333299	Distilling equipment (except beverage), manufacturing
713291	Distributing lottery tickets
23711	Distribution line, sewer and water, construction
221122	Distribution of electric power
41321	Distribution of water in bottles
335311	Distribution transformers, manufacturing
41611	Distribution transformers, wholesale
33632	Distributors for internal combustion engines, manufacturing
32541	Diuretic preparations, manufacturing
56199	Diving service on a fee or contract basis
23799	Dock and pier construction
48831	Dock, marine, operation
488339	Docking and undocking marine vessel services
62111	Doctors' clinics, general practice
49319	Document storage and warehousing
56141	Document transcription services
311111	Dog and cat food, manufacturing
41831	Dog and cat food, wholesale

311111	Dog food, made from purchased meat and poultry
711329	Dog show promoters, without facilities
322299	Doilies, paper, made from purchased paper
33392	Dollies, industrial, manufacturing
33993	Dolls (including parts and accessories), manufacturing
41446	Dolls, wholesale
212315	Dolomite (limestone), crude, quarrying
32741	Dolomite, dead-burned, manufacturing
212316	Dolomitic marble, crushed and broken stone, quarrying
81411	Domestic service (private households employing cooks, maids)
62311	Domiciliary care with health care
23835	Door and window frames, construction
332321	Door frames and sash, metal, manufacturing
321911	Door frames and sash, wood and covered wood, manufacturing
44413	Door locks and lock sets, retail
33251	Door locks, manufacturing
31411	Door mats, all materials (except entirely of rubber or plastic), manufacturing
326198	Door mats, plastics, manufacturing
33251	Door opening and closing devices (except electrical), manufacturing
33599	Door opening and closing devices, electrical, manufacturing
321911	Door units, prehung, wood and covered wood, manufacturing
326196	Doors and door frames, plastics, manufacturing
41632	Doors and windows, wooden, wholesale
332999	Doors, safe and vault, metal, manufacturing
327215	Doors, unframed glass, made from purchased glass
321911	Doors, wood and covered wood, manufacturing
54187	Door-to-door distribution of advertising material (e.g., circulars, samples)
45439	Door-to-door retailing of merchandise, retail
333299	Dough mixing machinery (i.e., food manufacturing type), manufacturing
311822	Dough, refrigerated or frozen, made from purchased flour
72221	Doughnut shops
311814	Doughnuts, made in commercial bakeries
311211	Doughs, prepared, made in flour mills

23817	Down spout and gutter, installation, contractors
71392	Downhill skiing facilities
81121	Drafting instrument repair
334512	Drafting instruments, manufacturing
41793	Drafting instruments, wholesale
54134	Drafting services
54134	Draftsmen, offices of
711218	Drag strip, operation of
33312	Draglines, crawlers, manufacturing
561799	Drain cleaning services
33291	Drain cocks, plumbing, manufacturing
32561	Drain pipe cleaners, manufacturing
332999	Drain plugs, magnetic, metal, manufacturing
32712	Drain tile, clay, manufacturing
41721	Drainage and tile laying machinery, wholesale
23799	Drainage canals and ditches, construction
23799	Drainage project construction
213119	Draining or pumping of mines, on a contract basis
61161	Drama school
31412	Draperies, made from purchased fabrics or sheet goods
41433	Draperies, wholesale
41413	Drapery material, wholesale
442291	Drapery stores, retail
23839	Drapery track hardware installation
337127	Draughting tables (without attachments), manufacturing
325999	Drawing inks, manufacturing
33111	Drawing iron or steel wire in steel mills
333299	Drawing machinery for textiles, manufacturing
331222	Drawing wire from purchased iron or steel
331222	Drawing wire from purchased iron or steel and fabricating wire products
41721	Dredges and draglines (except ships), wholesale
33312	Dredging machinery, manufacturing
23799	Dredging, canals, channels, waterways and ditches
448199	Dress shops, retail
44813	Dresses, children's, retail
31519	Dresses, hand-knit, manufacturing
31519	Dresses, made in knitting mills
41411	Dresses, wholesale
315233	Dresses, women's, misses' and girls', cut and sewn from purchased fabric
315233	Dressmakers' shops, custom
31142	Dried fruits and vegetables, manufacturing

32551	Driers, paint and varnish, manufacturing
333519	Drill bits, metalworking, manufacturing
33221	Drill bits, woodworking, manufacturing
333519	Drill presses, metalworking, manufacturing
33321	Drill presses, woodworking, manufacturing
23891	Drilled pier (i.e., for building foundations) contractors
23891	Drilled shaft (i.e., drilled building foundations), construction
336611	Drilling and production platforms, floating, oil and gas, building
33313	Drilling equipment, oil and gas field type, manufacturing
33313	Drilling equipment, underground mining type, manufacturing
333519	Drilling machines, metalworking, manufacturing
325999	Drilling mud compounds, conditioners and additives (except bentonites), manufacturing
33313	Drilling rigs, manufacturing
213117	Drilling services for non-metallic minerals mining (except fuels), on a contract basis
213118	Drilling water intake wells, on a contract basis
33399	Drills (except heavy construction, mining type), hand held power-driven, manufacturing
33313	Drills, core, underground mining type, manufacturing
33221	Drills, hand held, non-power, manufacturing
33313	Drills, rock, underground mining type, manufacturing
31199	Drink powder mixes (except chocolate, coffee, milk-based, tea), manufacturing
41612	Drinking fountains, non-refrigerated, wholesale
333416	Drinking fountains, refrigerated, manufacturing
41791	Drinking fountains, refrigerated, wholesale
32711	Drinking fountains, vitreous china, non-refrigerated, manufacturing
72241	Drinking places, alcoholic beverages
31133	Drinks, chocolate instant, made from purchased chocolate
311511	Drinks, chocolate milk, manufacturing
31211	Drinks, fruit (except juice), manufacturing

333619	Drive chains, bicycle and motorcycle, manufacturing
23799	Drive-in movie facility construction
72221	Drive-in restaurants
51213	Drive-in theatres
61169	Driver education, automobile
333619	Drives, high-speed industrial (except hydrostatic), manufacturing
61169	Driving schools, automobile
48899	Driving service (auto and truck delivery)
23831	Drop ceiling installation
31491	Drop cloths, canvas, made from purchased fabric
332113	Drop forgings, unfinished, made from purchased metal
81331	Drug abuse prevention advocacy organizations
62221	Drug addiction rehabilitation hospitals
44611	Drug store
44611	Drug sundries, retail
41452	Druggists' sundries, wholesale
41912	Drugs, wholesale agents and brokers
71113	Drum and bugle corps (e.g., drill teams)
322219	Drums, fibre (i.e., fibre body, ends of any material), made from purchased paperboard
332439	Drums, light gauge metal, manufacturing
41723	Drums, new and reconditioned, wholesale
326198	Drums, plastics (i.e., containers), manufacturing
81331	Drunk driving prevention advocacy organizations
484222	Dry bulk materials trucking (except local garbage hauling without disposal), local
484232	Dry bulk materials trucking, long-distance
81232	Dry cleaning agents, pick-up and delivery services
81232	Dry cleaning plants
41841	Dry cleaning solvents and chemicals, wholesale
11113	Dry field beans, growing
11113	Dry field peas, growing
41413	Dry goods, wholesale
41912	Dry goods, wholesale agents and brokers
23822	Dry heating equipment and controls, installation (except electric baseboard)
32512	Dry ice (i.e., solid carbon dioxide), manufacturing
41841	Dry ice, wholesale

32799	Dry mix concrete, manufacturing
311823	Dry pasta, manufacturing
11113	Dry peas, beans, and lentils, farming
33331	Drycleaning equipment and machinery, manufacturing
41792	Drycleaning plant equipment and supplies, wholesale
41792	Drycleaning plant equipment and supplies, wholesale and repair
32561	Drycleaning preparations, manufacturing
48839	Drydocks, floating, for repairing ships and boats
33331	Dryers, laundry (except household type), manufacturing
31171	Drying fish and seafood
333299	Drying kilns, lumber, manufacturing
333299	Drying machinery for textiles, manufacturing
41639	Drywall and plaster supplies, wholesale
32742	Drywall cement and panels, gypsum-based, manufacturing
23831	Drywall hanging
23831	Drywall, finishing (taping, sanding, stippling)
23831	Drywall, installation
51219	Dubbing sound, motion picture
112399	Duck farming
311615	Ducks, slaughtering and dressing
561791	Duct cleaning services
32222	Duct tape, made from purchased materials
23822	Duct work (e.g., heating, cooling, exhaust, dust collection), installation
332329	Ducts, sheet metal, manufacturing
721213	Dude ranches
31491	Duffel bags, canvas, manufacturing
114113	Dulsing (gathering Irish moss)
238299	Dumb-waiter installation
212326	Dumortierite mining
336212	Dump trailers, manufacturing
336211	Dump truck lifting mechanisms, manufacturing
56211	Dump trucking of non-hazardous construction rubble, with collection or disposal
484222	Dump trucking, local
53242	Duplicating machine rental
41791	Duplicating machines, wholesale
11114	Durum wheat, growing
333413	Dust and fume collecting equipment, manufacturing
31499	Dust cloths, made from purchased fabrics

23822	Dust collecting equipment installation, contractors
41612	Dust collecting equipment, wholesale
33311	Dusters, farm type, manufacturing
32561	Dusting cloths, chemically treated, manufacturing
44531	Duty free liquor shops
45322	Duty free shops, gifts
91191	Duty/tax collection on goods, federal government
33411	DVD (digital video disc) drives, computer peripheral equipment, manufacturing
33431	DVD (digital video disc) players, manufacturing
325999	Dye preparations, clothing, household type, manufacturing
32519	Dyeing and tanning extracts, natural, manufacturing
31331	Dyeing clothing
31611	Dyeing furs
31331	Dyeing textile products, for the trade
31331	Dyeing textile raw stock, fibres, thread, yarn or fabrics
32562	Dyes, hair, manufacturing
32513	Dyes, inorganic and synthetic organic, manufacturing
32519	Dyes, natural, manufacturing
41841	Dyestuffs, wholesale
32592	Dynamite, manufacturing

E

81219	Ear piercing service
33911	Ear stoppers (noise protectors), manufacturing
53241	Earth moving equipment rental and leasing (without operator)
23799	Earth retention system construction
212398	Earth, coloured, mine
32711	Earthenware table and kitchen articles, manufacturing
112999	Earthworm hatcheries
41822	Eating utensils, forks, knives, spoons - disposable plastics, wholesale
332329	Eavestrough, sheet metal, manufacturing
23817	Eavestroughing, contractors
41639	Eavestroughing, wholesale
32742	Ecclesiastical statuary, gypsum, manufacturing
32799	Ecclesiastical statuary, stone, manufacturing
91191	Economic and fiscal policy, federal government

54169	Economic consulting services
91191	Economic development agencies, federal government
54172	Economic research and development services
91191	Economic research programs to improve performance and competitiveness, federal government
33221	Edge tools for woodworking (e.g., augers, bits, gimlets, countersinks), non-powered manufacturing
51219	Editing motion picture films or video
56141	Editing service
91191	Education programs for Indians and Eskimos, federal government
54172	Education research and development services
61171	Educational counselling
61171	Educational testing services
81321	Educational trusts, awarding grants
81392	Educators' associations
541619	Efficiency experts
322299	Egg cartons, moulded pulp, manufacturing
11231	Egg farms, chicken
112399	Egg farms, poultry (except chicken and turkey)
11233	Egg farms, turkey
11234	Egg hatcheries, poultry
311823	Egg noodles, dry, manufacturing
31199	Egg substitutes, manufacturing
31214	Eggnog, alcoholic, manufacturing
311515	Eggnog, canned, non-alcoholic, manufacturing
311511	Eggnog, fresh, non-alcoholic, manufacturing
31199	Eggs, processed, manufacturing
41313	Eggs, wholesale
31321	Elastic fabrics, broad-woven, weaving
31322	Elastic thread, yarn and cord, fabric-covered, manufacturing
32521	Elastomers (except synthetic rubber), manufacturing
32521	Elastomers, synthetic rubber, manufacturing
61121	E-learning, Community Colleges and C.E.G.E.P.s
91191	Electoral offices, federal government
91291	Electoral offices, provincial government
41422	Electric appliances, household, wholesale
33111	Electric arc furnace steel mills
33611	Electric automobiles for highway use, manufacturing
33995	Electric backlight signs, manufacturing

33142	Electric cable and wire, copper, made in wire drawing plants
41611	Electric construction material, wholesale
33599	Electric fence chargers, manufacturing
41612	Electric furnaces, wholesale
44311	Electric household appliances, retail
41611	Electric lamps and lighting fixtures, parts and accessories, wholesale
33512	Electric lighting fixtures, manufacturing
335312	Electric motors, manufacturing
221121	Electric power control (e.g., arranging transmission between utilities)
23821	Electric power control panels and outlets, installation
221122	Electric power distribution systems
221119	Electric power generation (except hydro, fossil fuel or nuclear)
221112	Electric power generation, fossil fuel
221111	Electric power generation, hydroelectric
221113	Electric power generation, nuclear
23713	Electric power transmission lines and towers, construction
221121	Electric power transmission systems
81149	Electric razor repair (without retail sales of new equipment)
44311	Electric razor shops, retail
48511	Electric street railway transportation
811411	Electric tool repair
41611	Electric transformers, wholesale
54133	Electrical and electronic engineering services
41611	Electrical construction materials, wholesale
81131	Electrical generating and transmission equipment repair
54136	Electrical geophysical surveying services
32711	Electrical insulators, porcelain, manufacturing
81391	Electrical manufacturers' association
81121	Electrical measuring instrument repair and calibration
48511	Electrical railway operation, commuter
811119	Electrical repair shops, motor vehicle
33995	Electrical signs and advertising displays, manufacturing
44419	Electrical supplies stores selling primarily to other business but also selling to household consumers
44419	Electrical supplies, retail
54138	Electrical testing laboratory
23821	Electrical wiring contractors
41611	Electrical wiring supplies and electrical construction materials, wholesale

41912	Electrical wiring supplies and electrical construction materials, wholesale agents and brokers
23713	Electricity generating plant (except hydroelectric) construction
56199	Electricity meter reading service, contract
333519	Electro-chemical milling machines, metalworking, manufacturing
33599	Electrodes, carbon, graphite, manufacturing
33399	Electrodes, welding, manufacturing
335315	Electromagnetic clutches and brakes, manufacturing
54136	Electromagnetic geophysical surveying services
335315	Electromagnets, manufacturing
334512	Electromedical apparatus and instruments, manufacturing
334512	Electromedical diagnostic equipment, manufacturing
41793	Electromedical equipment, wholesale
33111	Electrometallurgical ferro-alloys, manufacturing
334512	Electron tube test equipment, manufacturing
33441	Electron tubes, manufacturing
41732	Electronic aircraft instruments, wholesale
41732	Electronic aircraft instruments, wholesale and repair
41732	Electronic coils and transformers, wholesale
41732	Electronic communications equipment, wholesale
23821	Electronic containment fencing for pets, installation
33632	Electronic control modules, motor vehicle, manufacturing
41731	Electronic controllers, modems and related devices, wholesale
81121	Electronic data processing equipment, maintenance
51114	Electronic database publishing (except exclusively on Internet)
522329	Electronic funds transfer services
334511	Electronic guidance systems and equipment, manufacturing
41732	Electronic navigational equipment and devices, wholesale
41732	Electronic navigational equipment and devices, wholesale and repair
32312	Electronic prepress services for the printing trade

54171	Electronic research and development laboratories
33632	Electronic sensors (e.g., air bag, brake, fuel, exhaust), manufacturing
33993	Electronic toys and games, manufacturing
41732	Electronic tubes (e.g., receiving, transmitting, industrial), wholesale
41421	Electronic TV games, wholesale
33281	Electroplating metals and metal products, for the trade
333413	Electrostatic precipitation equipment, manufacturing
32312	Electrotype plate preparation services
61111	Elementary schools
48511	Elevated railway operation
41723	Elevating machinery and equipment (except farm), wholesale
41723	Elevating machinery and equipment (except farm), wholesale and repair
238291	Elevator installation, contractors
33392	Elevators, farm type, manufacturing
33392	Elevators, passenger and freight, manufacturing
41723	Elevators, wholesale
112999	Elk production
325999	Embalming fluids, manufacturing
91141	Embassies, federal government
91911	Embassy, foreign governments in Canada
32312	Embossing plate preparation services
31331	Embossing textile products (including clothing)
31322	Embroideries, Schiffli machine, manufacturing
31499	Embroidering on clothing owned by others
31499	Embroidering on textile products, for the trade
31311	Embroidery spun yarns (e.g., cotton, man-made fibre, silk, wool), made from purchased fibres
62423	Emergency and other relief services
91319	Emergency measures organization services, local government
91219	Emergency measures organizations, provincial government
91129	Emergency planning services, federal government
91219	Emergency program services, provincial
48841	Emergency road service, motor vehicle
811199	Emissions testing service, automotive, without repair
541612	Employee assessment consulting services

48541	Employee bus service
541612	Employee compensation consulting services
56133	Employee leasing service (providing permanent employees paid by supplying company but under the supervision of the hiring company)
81393	Employees' associations, for improvement of wages and working conditions
56131	Employment agencies (except theatrical and motion picture)
56131	Employment agencies, motion picture or video
56131	Employment agencies, radio or television
56131	Employment agencies, theatrical
91221	Employment counselling service, provincial government
56131	Employment placement agencies
56131	Employment registries
91131	Employment services (placement counselling), federal government
112399	Emu farming
32561	Emulsifiers (i.e., surface active agents), manufacturing
32551	Enamel paints, manufacturing
33221	Enamelled metal cooking utensils, manufacturing
33281	Enamelling metals and metal products, for the trade
442298	Enamelware stores, retail
323119	Encyclopedias, printing without publishing
51113	Encyclopedias, publishing (except exclusively on Internet)
51113	Encyclopedias, publishing and printing combined
32541	Endocrine products, uncompounded, manufacturing
54169	Energy consulting services
91291	Energy resources programs, provincial government
331317	Energy wire or cable, made in aluminum wire drawing plants
332113	Engine and turbine forgings, unfinished, made from purchased metal
331511	Engine block castings, iron, unfinished, manufacturing
325999	Engine degreasers, manufacturing
811111	Engine repair, automotive
41799	Engine testing equipment, automobile, electrical, wholesale
54133	Engineering consulting services
54133	Engineering design services

41793	Engineering instruments, equipment and supplies, wholesale
41793	Engineering instruments, equipment and supplies, wholesale and repair
54171	Engineering research and development laboratories
61121	Engineering schools (non-university)
81392	Engineers' associations
54133	Engineers, private practice
41799	Engines (except motor vehicle), wholesale
33641	Engines and engine parts (except carburetors, pistons, piston rings, valves), aircraft, manufacturing
33631	Engines and parts (except diesel), automotive and truck, manufacturing
41799	Engines and turbines, marine, wholesale
333619	Engines, diesel and semi-diesel, manufacturing
333619	Engines, internal combustion (except aircraft and non-diesel automotive), manufacturing
333619	Engines, natural gas or propane (except automotive), manufacturing
33281	Engraving metals and metal products (except printing plates, precious metal jewellery and flatware), for the trade
32312	Engraving printing plates, for the printing trades
33991	Engraving, chasing or etching precious metal flatware
33331	Enlargers, photographic, manufacturing
41443	Enlarging equipment, photographic, wholesale
54171	Entomological research and development laboratories
333291	Envelope making machinery, manufacturing
33331	Envelope stuffing, sealing and addressing machinery, manufacturing
32223	Envelopes (i.e., mailing, stationery), made from any material
41821	Envelopes, paper, wholesale
91191	Environment policy, programs, federal government
81331	Environmental advocacy groups
54162	Environmental consulting services
91291	Environmental control programs, provincial government
23821	Environmental control systems, central, installation
54133	Environmental engineering services
54133	Environmental engineers

54138	Environmental laboratory testing services
56291	Environmental remediation services
54171	Environmental research and development laboratories
32519	Enzyme proteins (i.e., basic synthetic chemicals) (except pharmaceutical use), manufacturing
32541	Enzyme proteins (i.e., basic synthetic chemicals), pharmaceutical use, manufacturing
32552	Epoxy adhesives, manufacturing
23819	Epoxy application, contractors
32521	Epoxy resins, manufacturing
212398	Epsomite, mining
11292	Equines, raising
81391	Equipment distributors' association
41799	Equipment parts for railroads, aircraft, ships and boats, wholesale
41799	Equipment parts for railroads, aircraft, ships and boats, wholesale and repair
23891	Equipment rental with operator (except cranes)
526911	Equity funds, Canadian
526912	Equity funds, foreign
32629	Erasers, rubber, or rubber and abrasive combined, manufacturing
213118	Erecting lease tank, oil and gas field, on a contract basis
54133	Erosion control engineering services
238291	Escalators installation, contractors
33392	Escalators, passenger and freight, manufacturing
81299	Escort service, social
52399	Escrow agencies (except real estate)
53139	Escrow agents, real estate
325999	Essential oils, natural, manufacturing
32519	Essential oils, synthetic, manufacturing
41841	Essential oils, wholesale
522111	Establishments of chartered banks providing personal and commercial banking services
522111	Establishments of trust companies providing personal and commercial banking services
54199	Estate assessment (i.e., appraisal) services
81411	Estates, private employing domestic personnel
32519	Esters, not specified elsewhere by process, manufacturing
81219	Estheticians, services (i.e., hair removal)
33281	Etching metals and metal products (except printing plates, precious metal jewellery and flatware), for the trade

32511	Ethane, made from refined petroleum or natural gas liquids
32519	Ethanol (ethyl alcohol), non-potable, made by the wet-mill process
41451	Ethical drugs, wholesale
81341	Ethnic associations
711322	Ethnic festival promoters, without facilities
32519	Ethyl alcohol (ethanol), non-potable, manufacturing
31214	Ethyl alcohol, potable, manufacturing
32511	Ethylbenzene, made from refined petroleum or natural gas liquids
32511	Ethylene (ethene), made from refined petroleum or natural gas liquids
32519	Ethylene dichloride (dichloroethane), manufacturing
32519	Ethylene glycol, manufacturing
32519	Ethylene oxide, manufacturing
32411	Ethylene, made in petroleum refineries
32521	Ethylene-propylene rubber, manufacturing
32521	Ethylene-vinyl acetate resins, manufacturing
53132	Evaluation services (real estate)
311515	Evaporated milk, manufacturing
333416	Evaporative condensers (i.e., heat transfer equipment), manufacturing
23891	Excavating contractors
41721	Excavating machinery and equipment, wholesale
41721	Excavating machinery and equipment, wholesale and repair
213118	Excavating slush pits and cellars, on a contract basis
23891	Excavating, earthmoving or land clearing, agricultural
23891	Excavating, earthmoving or land clearing, mining (except mine site overburden removal)
23891	Excavating, earthmoving, or land clearing contractors
321999	Excelsior (e.g., pads, wrappers), wood, manufacturing
52399	Exchange clearinghouses, commodity or security
33241	Exchangers, heat, manufacturing
52321	Exchanges, commodity contract
52321	Exchanges, securities
91121	Exchequer court
48721	Excursion boat operation
56111	Executive management services
56131	Executive placement consulting services
56131	Executive search consulting services

53229	Exercise (physical fitness) equipment rental
45111	Exercise and fitness equipment, retail
32223	Exercise books and pads, made from purchased paper
71394	Exercise centres
33992	Exercising machines, manufacturing
41612	Exhaust and air-moving equipment, wholesale
333413	Exhaust fans, industrial and commercial type, manufacturing
811112	Exhaust system repair and replacement shops
33639	Exhaust systems and parts, automotive, truck and bus, manufacturing
32615	Expanded plastics (except polystyrene) products, manufacturing
32614	Expanded polystyrene products, manufacturing
41841	Explosives, all kinds (except ammunition and fireworks), wholesale
32592	Explosives, manufacturing
91191	Export development programs, federal government
62311	Extended care facilities
62231	Extended care hospitals
23831	Exterior insulation finish systems, installation
32532	Exterminating chemical products (e.g., fungicides, insecticides, pesticides), manufacturing
56171	Extermination services
91141	External affairs services, federal government
91142	External aid services, federal government
31192	Extracts, essences and preparations, coffee, manufacturing
31192	Extracts, essences and preparations, tea, manufacturing
31194	Extracts, food (except coffee, meat), manufacturing
32519	Extracts, natural dyeing and tanning, manufacturing
33322	Extruding machinery for plastics and rubber, manufacturing
333299	Extruding machinery, textile, manufacturing
32541	Eye and ear preparations, manufacturing
62199	Eye bank
32562	Eye make-up (e.g., eye shadow, eyebrow pencils, mascara), manufacturing

33911	Eyeglass frames and parts, manufacturing
33911	Eyeglasses, lenses and frames, manufacturing
44613	Eyeglasses, spectacles and frames, retail
41793	Eyeglasses, wholesale

F

11113	Faba beans, growing
32561	Fabric softeners, manufacturing
23831	Fabric wall systems, noise insulating, installation
41413	Fabric, textile, wholesale
45113	Fabric, upholstery, retail
332319	Fabricated bar joists, manufacturing
332319	Fabricated metal plate work, manufacturing
23839	Fabricating metal cabinets or countertops on site
31321	Fabrics (except rugs, tire fabrics), broad-woven, weaving
31499	Fabrics for reinforcing rubber tires, industrial belting and fuel cells, manufacturing
31321	Fabrics, broad-woven, natural hard fibres (e.g., linen, jute, hemp, ramie), weaving
31324	Fabrics, lace, made in lace mills
31324	Fabrics, made in knitting mills
31322	Fabrics, narrow woven (i.e., 30 cm/12 in. or less in width), weaving
31323	Fabrics, nonwoven, manufacturing
332619	Fabrics, woven wire, made from purchased wire
32562	Face creams (e.g., cleansing, moisturizing), manufacturing
33593	Face plates (wiring devices), manufacturing
41822	Facial tissue paper, wholesale
322291	Facial tissues, made from purchased paper
322121	Facial tissues, made in paper mills
56121	Facilities management (except computers)
54151	Facilities management services, computer
56121	Facilities support services (except computer)
54151	Facilities support services, computer
517111	Facilities-based competitive service providers
517111	Facilities-based telecommunication carrier, except wireless and cable operators

33421	Facsimile equipment, stand-alone, manufacturing
41791	Facsimile machinery, sales and service, wholesale
23621	Factories, construction
522299	Factoring companies
337127	Factory furniture (e.g., stools, work benches, tool stands, cabinets), manufacturing
711319	Fair organizers, agricultural, with facilities
711322	Fair, agricultural, promoters, without facilities
81311	Faith healers, religious organization
23819	False work construction
44814	Family clothing stores, retail
41411	Family clothing wholesale
91211	Family courts
71312	Family fun centres
62411	Family location services
62111	Family physicians, general practice
62141	Family planning counselling services
72211	Family restaurant
44821	Family shoe store, retail
91291	Family welfare programs, provincial government
32622	Fan belts, rubber or plastics, manufacturing
41422	Fans, electric, domestic, wholesale
33521	Fans, household, electric (except attic fans), manufacturing
333413	Fans, industrial and commercial type, manufacturing
41723	Fans, industrial, wholesale
41111	Farm animals, live, wholesale
23622	Farm buildings (except dwellings), construction
332311	Farm buildings, prefabricated, metal, manufacturing
81391	Farm bureaus
33392	Farm conveyors, manufacturing
23799	Farm drainage tile installation
33392	Farm elevators, manufacturing
53249	Farm equipment rental or leasing
11511	Farm labour contractors
41711	Farm machinery and equipment, wholesale
41912	Farm machinery and equipment, wholesale agents and brokers
41711	Farm machinery and equipment, wholesale and repair
11511	Farm management service (crop production)
11511	Farm produce packing service

11511	Farm product sorting, grading or packing service (for the grower)
49313	Farm product warehousing and storage, other than cold storage
484229	Farm products hauling, local
33242	Farm storage tanks, heavy gauge metal, manufacturing
33311	Farm tractors and attachments, manufacturing
33311	Farm wagons, manufacturing
11212	Farm, dairy
11242	Farm, goat
11233	Farm, turkey
54171	Farms, experimental
11521	Farriers
11221	Farrow to finish hog farm
23817	Fascia and soffit, metal and plastic, installation
54149	Fashion design services
54149	Fashion designer, service of
72221	Fast food concession
72221	Fast food restaurants
41633	Fasteners, hardware, wholesale
311225	Fats and oils, made from purchased fats and oils
311224	Fats and oils, made in oilseed crushing mills
311614	Fats, animal, rendering
32519	Fatty acid esters and amines, manufacturing
32519	Fatty acids (e.g., margaric, oleic, stearic), manufacturing
32519	Fatty alcohols, manufacturing
33291	Faucets, plumbing, manufacturing
33999	Feathers, preparing for use in clothing and textile products
41119	Feathers, unprocessed, wholesale
51911	Feature syndicate
91191	Federal Communications Commission
91122	Federal correctional services
91121	Federal court of law
91132	Federal immigration services
91123	Federal police services
91124	Federal regulatory services, general
91191	Federal-provincial relations, federal government
81321	Federated charities organizations
81391	Federation of agriculture
81393	Federation of labour
41831	Feed additives, animal, wholesale
11119	Feed grain farms
41831	Feed grains, wholesale
33311	Feed grinders (i.e., crushers and mixers), farm type, manufacturing
311119	Feed premixes, animal (except dogs and cats), manufacturing

33311	Feed processing equipment, farm type, manufacturing
311119	Feed supplements, animal (except cat and dog), manufacturing
311111	Feed supplements, dog and cat, manufacturing
311614	Feed, animal, processing dead stock or carrion for
311611	Feed, animal, slaughtering animals (except poultry and small game) for
311221	Feed, corn gluten, manufacturing
311119	Feed, prepared for animals (except dogs and cats), manufacturing
311119	Feed, specialty (e.g., for mice, guinea pig, mink), manufacturing
11211	Feedlot, beef cattle
11241	Feedlots, lamb
41831	Feeds, animal, wholesale
212326	Feldspar mining
113311	Felling trees (logging)
33994	Felt tip markers, manufacturing
31323	Felts, nonwoven, manufacturing
41639	Fence and accessories, wire, wholesale
332329	Fences and gates (except wire), metal, manufacturing
41639	Fencing and accessories, wire, wholesale
332619	Fencing and fence gates, made from purchased wire
44419	Fencing dealers, retail
23899	Fencing for highway, installation
321999	Fencing, prefabricated sections, wood, manufacturing
321999	Fencing, wood (except rough pickets, poles and rails), manufacturing
41632	Fencing, wood, wholesale
212299	Ferberite mining
33242	Fermentation tanks, heavy gauge metal, manufacturing
32513	Ferric oxide pigments, manufacturing
483116	Ferries, operating on coastal waters
483214	Ferries, operating on rivers or inland lakes (except Great Lakes)
483116	Ferries, operating on the Great Lakes
33111	Ferro-alloys, manufacturing
41621	Ferroalloys, wholesale
41912	Ferrous and non-ferrous metal ores and concentrates, combined, wholesale agents and brokers
41912	Ferrous and non-ferrous metals, combination, wholesale agents and brokers
332113	Ferrous forgings, unfinished, made from purchased iron or steel
41892	Ferrous ores and concentrates, wholesale
41839	Fertilizer and fertilizer materials, wholesale
11511	Fertilizer application service
325313	Fertilizer materials, nitrogenous and phosphatic, manufacturing
325314	Fertilizers, mixed, made in plants not manufacturing fertilizer materials
325313	Fertilizers, mixed, made in plants producing nitrogenous or phosphatic fertilizer materials
325313	Fertilizers, natural organic (except compost), manufacturing
33311	Fertilizing machinery, farm type, manufacturing
711322	Festival of arts (except film) promoters, without facilities
51213	Festivals, film, with or without facilities
322219	Fibre cans and drums (i.e., fibre body, ends of any material), made from purchased paperboard
41822	Fibre cans and drums, wholesale
33441	Fibre optic connectors, manufacturing
322219	Fibre spools, reels and blocks, made from purchased paperboard
322219	Fibre tubes, made from purchased paperboard
321216	Fibreboard, manufacturing
326193	Fibreglass automobile body skins, manufacturing
336612	Fibreglass boats, building
31322	Fibreglass fabric, narrow woven (i.e., 30 cm/12 in. or less in width), weaving
41639	Fibreglass insulation materials, wholesale
32799	Fibreglass insulation products, manufacturing
23821	Fibre-optic cable (except transmission lines), installation
23713	Fibre-optic cable transmission lines, construction
33592	Fibre-optic cable, made from purchased strand (data transmission), manufacturing
32522	Fibres and filaments, artificial, manufacturing
32522	Fibres and filaments, cellulosic, manufacturing and texturizing
32522	Fibres and filaments, synthetic, manufacturing
41119	Fibres, vegetable, wholesale
323119	Fiction books, printing without publishing

51113	Fiction books, publishing (except exclusively on Internet)
51113	Fiction books, publishing and printing combined
41442	Fiction books, wholesale
524129	Fidelity insurance
52399	Fiduciary agencies (except real estate)
111999	Field crop combination farm (except grain and oil seeds)
41832	Field crop seeds, wholesale
11113	Field pea (dry) growing
23814	Field stone, installation
336211	Fifth wheel assemblies, manufacturing
711218	Figure skaters, independent
32522	Filament yarn, man-made, manufacturing
33511	Filaments, for electric lamps, manufacturing
32223	File folders (e.g., accordion, expanding, hanging, manila), made from purchased paper or paperboard
41821	File folders, tabs and accessories, wholesale
33221	Files and rasps, hand held, manufacturing
337214	Filing boxes, cabinets and cases, office (except wood), manufacturing
337213	Filing boxes, cabinets and cases, wood office, manufacturing
212323	Fill dirt pits
32551	Fillers, wood (e.g., dry, liquid, paste), manufacturing
41799	Filling station equipment, wholesale
31199	Fillings, cake or pie (except fruit, meat, vegetable), manufacturing
44313	Film and photographic supplies, retail
51219	Film and video transfer service
519122	Film archives
54138	Film badge testing services
56131	Film casting bureau
41443	Film developing and finishing equipment, wholesale
51212	Film distribution agencies
51219	Film or tape closed captioning
812921	Film processing (except for the motion picture industry), laboratories
51219	Film processing laboratories, motion picture
41443	Film, photographic, wholesale
326114	Film, plastics, manufacturing
326114	Film, plastics, packaging, manufacturing
325999	Film, sensitized (e.g., camera, motion picture, X-ray), manufacturing
51211	Films, motion picture production

32711	Filtering media, pottery, manufacturing
33639	Filters (e.g., air, engine oil, fuel), internal combustion engine, manufacturing
333413	Filters, furnace, manufacturing
33399	Filters, industrial and general line (except for warm air furnaces and internal combustion engines), manufacturing
322299	Filters, paper, made from purchased paper
23711	Filtration plant, construction
22131	Filtration plant, water, municipal
212323	Filtration sand mining
91191	Financial affairs, federal government
52393	Financial investment advice services, customized, fees paid by clients
53241	Financial leasing of construction, mining and forestry machinery
51112	Financial magazines and periodicals, publishing (except exclusively on Internet)
51112	Financial magazines and periodicals, publishing and printing combined
541611	Financial management consulting services (except investment advice)
52393	Financial planning services, customized, fees paid by clients
522329	Financial transactions processing (except central bank)
61161	Fine arts schools
41411	Fine or dress clothing, men's and boys', wholesale
322121	Fine paper stock, manufacturing
41822	Fine papers (except stationery), wholesale
72211	Fine-dining restaurants
11251	Finfish farming
11251	Finfish hatcheries
321215	Finger jointed lumber, manufacturing
11251	Fingerlings (hatchery fish), raising, fisheries service
561611	Fingerprint services
31411	Finishing (e.g., dyeing) rugs and carpets
32561	Finishing agents, textile and leather, manufacturing
31331	Finishing clothing
23831	Finishing drywall contractors
333299	Finishing machinery, textile, manufacturing
31331	Finishing purchased fabrics
31331	Finishing textile fabrics
561621	Fire alarm sale, combined with installation, maintenance or monitoring
23821	Fire alarm systems, installation
23611	Fire and flood damage clean-up

23611	Fire and flood restoration of single-family houses, by general contractors
524124	Fire and theft insurance
32712	Fire brick, clay refractories, manufacturing
212326	Fire clay mining
91314	Fire department, local government
33429	Fire detection and alarm systems, manufacturing
332329	Fire escapes, metal, manufacturing
325999	Fire extinguisher chemical preparations, manufacturing
41841	Fire extinguisher preparations, wholesale
33999	Fire extinguishers, portable, manufacturing
81131	Fire extinguishers, servicing
33291	Fire hydrant valves, manufacturing
33291	Fire hydrants, complete, manufacturing
524124	Fire insurance underwriters
54138	Fire Insurance Underwriters' Laboratories
91314	Fire investigating service, local government
91214	Fire investigation service, provincial government
91214	Fire marshals office, provincial government
91214	Fire prevention programs, provincial government
325999	Fire retardant chemical preparations, manufacturing
23822	Fire sprinkler systems, installation
61151	Fire training school
45111	Firearms and ammunition, retail
41447	Firearms and ammunition, wholesale
332999	Firearms, manufacturing
41799	Fire-fighting equipment, wholesale
41799	Fire-fighting equipment, wholesale and repair
213118	Fire-fighting service, other than forestry or public
91214	Fire-fighting services, provincial government
33399	Fire-fighting sprinklers, automatic systems, manufacturing
33612	Fire-fighting trucks (e.g., ladder, pumper), assembling on chassis of own manufacture
336211	Fire-fighting trucks (e.g., ladder, pumper), assembling on purchased chassis
442298	Fireplace accessories, retail

332999	Fireplace fixtures and equipment, manufacturing
333416	Fireplace inserts (i.e., heat directing), manufacturing
23822	Fireplace installations (except masonry)
333416	Fireplace logs, gas, manufacturing
32419	Fireplace logs, made from refined petroleum or coal
442298	Fireplace stores, retail
23822	Fireplace, natural gas, installation
41612	Fireplaces, metal, wholesale
23833	Fireproof flooring construction, contractors
23819	Fireproofing buildings, contractors
33637	Firewall, motor vehicle, metal, stamping
454319	Firewood dealers, retail
71399	Fireworks display service
325999	Fireworks, manufacturing
453999	Fireworks, retail
41446	Fireworks, wholesale
33911	First-aid equipment and supplies, manufacturing
41452	First-aid supplies, wholesale
72221	Fish and chips, take-out
31171	Fish and marine animal oils, manufacturing
31171	Fish and seafood chowder, canning
41912	Fish and seafood, wholesale agents and brokers
333299	Fish and shellfish processing machinery, manufacturing
31171	Fish egg bait, canning
11251	Fish farming
334511	Fish finders (i.e., sonar), manufacturing
31171	Fish freezing (e.g., blocks, fillets, ready-to-serve products)
32541	Fish liver oils, medicinal, uncompounded, manufacturing
44522	Fish markets, retail
31171	Fish meal, manufacturing
41899	Fish oil, wholesale
45391	Fish tanks (for pets), retail
31171	Fish, canned and cured, manufacturing
41314	Fish, cured, wholesale
31171	Fish, curing, drying, pickling, salting and smoking
31171	Fish, fresh or frozen, manufacturing
41314	Fish, fresh, wholesale
41314	Fish, frozen (except packaged), wholesale
41111	Fish, live, wholesale
41111	Fish, tropical, wholesale
54171	Fisheries research and development laboratories

91291	Fisheries support programs, provincial government
91129	Fishery inspection and protection services
91129	Fishery patrol service
336612	Fishing boats (i.e., suitable or intended personal use), building
336611	Fishing boats, commercial, building
721212	Fishing camps
71399	Fishing guide services
31499	Fishing line, natural or man-made fibres, manufacturing
31499	Fishing nets and seines, made in cordage or twine mills
71399	Fishing piers, operation of
33992	Fishing tackle, manufacturing
114113	Fishing, salt water
71394	Fitness centres
45111	Fitness equipment, retail
41447	Fitness equipment, wholesale
326122	Fittings and unions, rigid plastics pipe, manufacturing
488119	Fixed base operations
51741	Fixed-to-mobile satellite services
33512	Fixtures, electric lighting, manufacturing
337215	Fixtures, office and store, manufacturing
41612	Fixtures, plumbing, wholesale
41791	Fixtures, refrigerated, wholesale
453999	Flag shops, retail
48849	Flagging service (i.e., traffic control)
321999	Flagpoles, wood, manufacturing
31499	Flags, textile (e.g., banners, bunting, emblems, pennants), made from purchased fabrics
212316	Flagstone mining
81233	Flame and heat resistant clothing supply service
33291	Flanges and flange unions, pipe, metal, manufacturing
325999	Flares, manufacturing
23817	Flashing, metal, installation
33591	Flashlight batteries, manufacturing
33512	Flashlights, manufacturing
41611	Flashlights, wholesale
484239	Flat bed trucking, long-distance
327214	Flat glass (e.g., float, plate), made in glass-making plants
41634	Flat glass, wholesale
33411	Flat panel displays (i.e., complete units), computer peripheral equipment, manufacturing
332611	Flat springs, heavy gauge, manufacturing
332619	Flat springs, light gauge (except clock and watch), made from purchased wire
336212	Flatbed trailers, commercial, manufacturing
484229	Flat-bed trucking, local
531111	Flats or apartments, operators
33221	Flatware (cutlery), base metal plated with precious metal, manufacturing
33221	Flatware (cutlery), non-precious metal, manufacturing
44831	Flatware and hollow ware, precious metal, retail
33991	Flatware, precious metal (except plated), manufacturing
31193	Flavouring concentrates (except coffee-based), manufacturing
41319	Flavouring extract (except for fountain use), wholesale
31194	Flavouring extracts (except coffee), manufacturing
32519	Flavouring materials (i.e., basic synthetic chemicals such as coumarin), manufacturing
31193	Flavouring pastes, powders and syrups, for soft drinks, manufacturing
11112	Flaxseed farming
53112	Flea market space renting
332999	Flexible metal hose and tubing, manufacturing
32222	Flexible packaging sheet materials (except foil-paper laminates), made by coating or laminating purchased paper
32222	Flexible packaging sheet materials, made by laminating purchased foil
32312	Flexographic plate preparation services
323119	Flexographic printing (except manifold business forms, textile fabrics), without publishing
333299	Flexographic printing presses, manufacturing
334511	Flight and navigation sensors, transmitters and displays, manufacturing
33331	Flight simulators, manufacturing
31171	Floating factory ships, seafood-processing
41722	Floating roof seals for oil and gas storage tanks, wholesale
41722	Floating roof seals for oil and gas storage tanks, wholesale and repair
56199	Floats, decoration of
54149	Floats, design services
31331	Flock printing of textile fabrics
23799	Flood control project construction
41841	Floor cleaning compounds, wholesale

44221	Floor covering store selling primarily to other businesses but also selling to household consumers
41911	Floor coverings, carpets, rugs and other, business to business (B2B) electronic markets, wholesale
41432	Floor coverings, carpets, rugs and other, wholesale
326198	Floor coverings, resilient, manufacturing
31411	Floor coverings, textile, weaving or knitting
41912	Floor coverings, wholesale agents and brokers
33512	Floor lamps, residential, manufacturing
23833	Floor laying, scraping, finishing, and refinishing, contractors
32629	Floor mats (e.g., bath, door), rubber, manufacturing
33637	Floor pans, motor vehicle, metal, stamping
32561	Floor polishes and waxes, manufacturing
32739	Floor slabs, precast concrete, manufacturing
23833	Floor tile and sheets, composition, installation
44221	Floor tile and sheets, installation combined with selling
44221	Floor tile stores, retail (except ceramic tiles only and hardwood flooring only)
32712	Floor tile, ceramic, manufacturing
41432	Floor tiles (except ceramic), wholesale
326198	Floor tiles (i.e., linoleum, rubber, vinyl), manufacturing
332329	Flooring, open steel (i.e., grating), manufacturing
332329	Flooring, sheet metal, manufacturing
321919	Flooring, wood, manufacturing
41632	Flooring, wooden, wholesale
33461	Floppy disks, blank, manufacturing
56142	Floral wire service
45311	Florist shops, retail
322299	Florists' pots, moulded pulp, manufacturing
41722	Flotation machinery, ore dressing, wholesale
31491	Flour bags, made from purchased woven or knitted materials
333299	Flour mill machinery, manufacturing
311211	Flour mills, cereal grain (except rice, breakfast cereal and feed mills)
311822	Flour mixes (e.g., biscuit, cake, doughnut, pancake), made from purchased flour
311211	Flour mixes (e.g., pancake, cake, biscuit, doughnut), made in flour mills
311822	Flour, blended or self-rising, made from purchased flour
311211	Flour, cereal grain (except rice), made in flour mills
311214	Flour, malt, manufacturing
311214	Flour, rice, manufacturing
311211	Flour, vegetable and fruit, manufacturing
321999	Flour, wood, manufacturing
41832	Flower and field bulbs, wholesale
111422	Flower bulb growing, greenhouse
111422	Flower growing, greenhouse
111422	Flower nursery
326198	Flower pots, plastics, manufacturing
32711	Flower pots, red earthenware, manufacturing
111422	Flower seed production
41832	Flower seeds, bulk and packaged, wholesale
41113	Flowers and florists' supplies, wholesale
33999	Flowers, artificial (except glass or plastic), manufacturing
41899	Flowers, artificial, wholesale
45311	Flowers, fresh, retail
32712	Flue lining, clay, manufacturing
11212	Fluid cream, raw, producing
311511	Fluid milk substitutes, manufacturing
311511	Fluid milk, processing
33399	Fluid power actuators, manufacturing
33291	Fluid power aircraft sub-assemblies, manufacturing
33399	Fluid power cylinders, manufacturing
33291	Fluid power hose assemblies, manufacturing
33399	Fluid power motors, manufacturing
33399	Fluid power pumps, manufacturing
33291	Fluid power valves and hose fittings, manufacturing
332329	Flumes, sheet metal, manufacturing
32513	Fluorescent dyes, manufacturing
33512	Fluorescent lighting fixtures, manufacturing
33511	Fluorescent tubes, manufacturing
325189	Fluorine, manufacturing
32512	Fluorocarbon gases, manufacturing
32521	Fluoro-polymer resins, manufacturing
212398	Fluorspar mining
326191	Flush tanks, plastics, manufacturing
212315	Flux stone, limestone, crude, mining
325999	Fluxes (e.g., brazing, galvanizing, soldering, welding), manufacturing
41839	Fly and animal sprays, wholesale

54187	Flyer direct distribution services
488119	Flying fields operation
61151	Flying school, civilian
33631	Flywheels and ring gears, automotive and truck gasoline engine, manufacturing
41822	Foam plastic food trays, wholesale
33791	Foam plastic mattress, manufacturing
32615	Foam plastics products (except polystyrene), manufacturing
32614	Foam polystyrene products, manufacturing
33791	Foam rubber mattress, manufacturing
41899	Foam rubber, wholesale
32222	Foil bags, made from purchased foil
332999	Foil containers (except bags), made from purchased metal foil
32222	Foil laminates, made from purchased foil
32222	Foil sheet, laminating purchased, for packaging applications
331317	Foil, aluminum, made by flat rolling purchased aluminum
33142	Foil, copper and copper alloy, made by rolling purchased metal or scrap
332999	Foil, made from purchased foil
56191	Folding and refolding service, textiles and apparel
322212	Folding boxes (except corrugated), made from purchased paperboard
322211	Folding boxes, corrugated, made from purchased paper or paperboard
322212	Folding containers (except corrugated), made from purchased paperboard
41822	Folding paperboard boxes, wholesale
71112	Folk dance companies
446191	Food (i.e., health) supplements, retail
91142	Food aid programs, federal government
62421	Food banks
72221	Food bars
333299	Food choppers, grinders, mixers and slicers (i.e., food manufacturing type), manufacturing
32513	Food colouring, synthetic, manufacturing
31194	Food colourings, natural, manufacturing
32615	Food containers, foam plastics (except polystyrene), manufacturing
322299	Food containers, made from moulded pulp
32614	Food containers, polystyrene foam, manufacturing
322219	Food containers, sanitary (except folding), made from purchased paper or paperboard
322212	Food containers, sanitary, folding, made from purchased paperboard
72221	Food court
111419	Food crops (except mushrooms) grown under cover
49221	Food delivery, for restaurants
44511	Food freezer plan, groceries (except direct sellers)
33521	Food grinders, choppers and slicers, electric, domestic, manufacturing
44511	Food markets, retail
33399	Food packaging machinery, manufacturing
41439	Food preparation and storage utensils, household, wholesale
41723	Food product manufacturing machinery, wholesale
54171	Food research and development laboratories
44511	Food store, groceries, retail
54138	Food testing laboratory
322299	Food trays, moulded pulp, manufacturing
41792	Food warming equipment, commercial, wholesale
41792	Food warming equipment, commercial, wholesale and repair
31199	Food, prepared, perishable, packaged for individual resale
72221	Food, take-out services
41912	Food, wholesale agents and brokers
711211	Football clubs, professional or semi-professional
71399	Football clubs, recreational
33992	Football equipment, manufacturing
23811	Footings and foundation contractor
31621	Footwear (except orthopedic extension shoes), manufacturing
326198	Footwear parts (e.g., heels, soles), plastics, manufacturing
32629	Footwear parts (e.g., heels, soles, soling strips), rubber, manufacturing
44821	Footwear stores, retail
41412	Footwear, wholesale
41912	Footwear, wholesale agents and brokers
11194	Forage crops (except corn for grain), farming
52313	Foreign currency exchange dealing (i.e., acting as a principal in dealing commodities to investors)
52313	Foreign currency exchange services (i.e., selling to the public)

91142	Foreign economic and social development services, federal government
91911	Foreign government service, office in Canada
54138	Forensic laboratories (except medical)
11531	Forest fire fighting services
11321	Forest nurseries
484223	Forest products trucking, local
484233	Forest products trucking, long-distance
61121	Forest technology schools
41721	Forestry equipment, wholesale
41721	Forestry equipment, wholesale and repair
11311	Forestry farms
81131	Forestry machinery and equipment repair
54171	Forestry research and development laboratories
61151	Forestry school
333519	Forging machinery and hammers, manufacturing
41621	Forgings and castings, iron and steel products, wholesale
332113	Forgings, ferrous, unfinished, made from purchased iron or steel
33111	Forgings, iron or steel, made in steel mills
332113	Forgings, non-ferrous, unfinished, made from purchased non-ferrous metal
41721	Fork lift trucks for logs, wholesale
41721	Fork lift trucks for logs, wholesale and repair
33392	Forklift trucks, manufacturing
33221	Forks, handtools (e.g., garden, hay, manure, stone), manufacturing
53222	Formal wear rental
32519	Formaldehyde, manufacturing
333519	Forming machines, metalworking, manufacturing
323116	Forms, business, manifold, printing
81299	Fortune tellers
23891	Foundation drilling contractors
526989	Foundation funds
448199	Foundation garments, retail
41411	Foundation garments, women's and misses', wholesale
315231	Foundation garments, women's, misses' and girls', cut and sewn from purchased fabric
32562	Foundations (i.e., make-up), manufacturing
23811	Foundations of buildings, poured concrete, contractors
23813	Foundations, building, of wood, contractors
331529	Foundries, aluminum (except die-castings)
331523	Foundries, die-casting, non-ferrous metals
331511	Foundries, iron (i.e., ductile, grey, malleable, semisteel)
331529	Foundries, non-ferrous metal (except die-castings)
331514	Foundries, steel
333511	Foundry casting moulds, manufacturing
325999	Foundry core oil, wash and wax, manufacturing
81131	Foundry machinery and equipment repair
41723	Foundry machinery and equipment, wholesale
212323	Foundry sand mining
33994	Fountain pens, manufacturing
333416	Fountains, refrigerated drinking, manufacturing
333291	Fourdrinier machinery, manufacturing
332619	Fourdrinier wire cloth, made from purchased wire
326198	Fourdrinier wires, plastics, manufacturing
11293	Fox production
211113	Fractionating natural gas liquids
811121	Frame repair shops, automotive
41439	Frames and pictures, wholesale
321911	Frames, door and window, wood, manufacturing
41632	Frames, door and window, wooden, wholesale
33999	Frames, mirror and picture, all materials, manufacturing
41793	Frames, ophthalmic, wholesale
23813	Framing contractor
53311	Franchises, selling or licensing
81341	Fraternal associations or lodges, social or civic
81341	Fraternal lodges
81341	Fraternal organization
72131	Fraternity residential houses
711513	Freelance journalist
31192	Freeze-dried coffee, manufacturing
31142	Freeze-drying fruits and vegetables
44521	Freezer provisioners (meat only), retail store
335223	Freezers, household, manufacturing
44311	Freezers, household, retail
333416	Freezers, laboratory type, manufacturing

31171	Freezing fish (e.g., blocks, fillets, ready-to-serve products)
48821	Freight car cleaning service
488519	Freight forwarding service
48899	Freight packing and crating
482113	Freight railway, mainline
482112	Freight railway, short-haul
541619	Freight rate consulting services
81391	Freight shippers' association
481214	Freight transportation, air, charter service
484229	Freight transportation, using animal-drawn vehicle
31141	French fries, frozen, pre-cooked, manufacturing
72233	French fries, mobile
31141	French toast, frozen, manufacturing
23831	Fresco work (i.e., decorative plaster finishing) contractors
41314	Fresh fish, wholesale
41912	Fresh fruits and vegetables, wholesale agents and brokers
62411	Friendship and counselling offered to young people
62419	Friendship centre
32551	Frit, manufacturing
11251	Frog production, farm raising
114114	Frogs, catching of (not raised on farms)
811119	Front end alignment shops, motor vehicle
41721	Front-end loaders, wholesale
41721	Front-end loaders, wholesale and repair
311814	Frozen bakery products, manufacturing
311814	Frozen bread and bread-type rolls, made in commercial bakeries
41312	Frozen dairy products, wholesale
31152	Frozen desserts (except bakery), manufacturing
31141	Frozen dinners (except seafood-based), manufacturing
311822	Frozen doughs, made from purchased flour
31141	Frozen food entrées (except seafood-based), manufacturing
41319	Frozen foods, packaged, wholesale
31141	Frozen fruit and vegetable processing
31141	Frozen fruits, fruit juices and vegetables, manufacturing
41316	Frozen meat (except packaged), wholesale
311611	Frozen meat and meat products (except poultry and small game), produced in slaughtering plants
311614	Frozen meats (except poultry, small game, pet food and baby food), made from purchased meat
41912	Frozen packaged food, wholesale agents and brokers
31141	Frozen pot pies, manufacturing
31171	Frozen seafood products, manufacturing
31141	Frozen side dishes (except seafood-based), manufacturing
31141	Frozen soups (except seafood), manufacturing
311221	Fructose, made by wet-milling corn
111993	Fruit and vegetable farming, combination
44523	Fruit and vegetable stores, retail
31213	Fruit brandy, distilling
41319	Fruit concentrates and syrups, fountain, wholesale
32192	Fruit containers (e.g., baskets, boxes, crates), wood, manufacturing
31211	Fruit drinks (except juice), manufacturing
31194	Fruit extracts (except coffee), manufacturing
11133	Fruit farming
311211	Fruit flour, meal and powders, manufacturing
31141	Fruit juice concentrates, frozen, manufacturing
31142	Fruit juices, canning
31142	Fruit juices, fresh, manufacturing
41319	Fruit juices, wholesale
11133	Fruit orchard operating
31134	Fruit peel products (e.g., candied, glazed, crystallized), manufacturing
31152	Fruit pops, frozen, manufacturing
41319	Fruit preparations, wholesale
11511	Fruit sorting, grading and packing service
45439	Fruit stand (temporary), road side, retail
31193	Fruit syrups, flavouring, manufacturing
111421	Fruit trees, nursery stock, growing
31142	Fruit, brining
31142	Fruit, canning
31142	Fruit, dehydrating (except sun drying)
41315	Fruit, fresh, cleaning, sorting and repackaging, on contract for wholesalers
31142	Fruit, pickling
31134	Fruits (e.g., candied, glazed, crystallized), manufacturing
41315	Fruits, fresh, wholesale
31141	Fruits, frozen, manufacturing
33521	Fry pans, electric, manufacturing

11232	Fryer chickens, raising
31134	Fudge (except chocolate), manufacturing
31132	Fudge, chocolate, made from cacao beans
31133	Fudge, chocolate, made from purchased chocolate
41529	Fuel additives, wholesale
32419	Fuel briquettes or boulets, made from refined petroleum
33399	Fuel cell-powered, hand held power tools, manufacturing
33599	Fuel cells, electrochemical generators, manufacturing
811119	Fuel injection service
33631	Fuel injection systems and parts, automotive and truck gasoline engine, manufacturing
454311	Fuel oil dealers, retail
41211	Fuel oil dealers, wholesale
32411	Fuel oils, made in petroleum refineries
325189	Fuel propellants, solid inorganic, not specified elsewhere by process, manufacturing
32519	Fuel propellants, solid organic, not specified elsewhere by process, manufacturing
33632	Fuel pumps, electric, automotive, truck and bus, manufacturing
33631	Fuel pumps, mechanical, automotive and truck gasoline engine, manufacturing
811119	Fuel system conversion, automotive
811119	Fuel system repair, motor vehicle
41899	Fuel, coal and coke, wholesale
113311	Fuelwood cutting
41899	Fuelwood, wholesale
212326	Fuller's earth mining
32799	Fuller's earth, processing beyond beneficiating
54181	Full-service advertising agency
72211	Full-service restaurants
41839	Fumigants, wholesale
56171	Fumigation service
56149	Fundraising service, on a contract or fee basis, for charitable organizations
81221	Funeral directors
81391	Funeral directors' association
41792	Funeral equipment and morticians' goods, wholesale
81221	Funeral home services
81221	Funeral parlours
32532	Fungicides, manufacturing
41839	Fungicides, wholesale
448191	Fur apparel made to custom order, retail

315292	Fur clothing (e.g., capes, coats, hats, jackets, neckpieces), manufacturing
31521	Fur clothing, cut and sewn from materials owned by others
41411	Fur clothing, wholesale
31611	Fur dressing and dyeing
11293	Fur farming
81232	Fur garments, cleaning, repairing and storage
31599	Fur mittens, manufacturing
448191	Fur shops, retail
49312	Fur storage service for the trade
11293	Fur-bearing animal production
11293	Fur-bearing animal skins (ranch raised), undressed, producing
23822	Furnace conversion from one fuel to another
333413	Furnace filters, manufacturing
23822	Furnace humidifiers and filters, installation
23822	Furnace installations and repairs
41612	Furnaces and heaters, wholesale
33399	Furnaces and ovens for drying and redrying, industrial process, manufacturing
33399	Furnaces, industrial process, manufacturing
333416	Furnaces, manufacturing
72131	Furnished rooms, rental of
41411	Furnishings (except shoes), women's, girls' and infants', wholesale
41439	Furnishings, household, wholesale
44413	Furniture and cabinet fittings, retail
41633	Furniture and cabinet hardware and fittings, wholesale
56174	Furniture and carpet cleaning on location, services
41791	Furniture and fixtures, office and store, wholesale
41791	Furniture and fixtures, office and store, wholesale and repair
41893	Furniture and fixtures, second hand, wholesale
54142	Furniture design services
321919	Furniture dimension stock, unfinished wood, manufacturing
337215	Furniture frames, manufacturing
33251	Furniture hardware, metal, manufacturing
48421	Furniture moving, used
337215	Furniture parts and components, manufacturing
32561	Furniture polishes and waxes, manufacturing
81142	Furniture refinishing and repair shops

81142	Furniture repairing, cleaning, redecorating and remodelling shops
81142	Furniture reupholstering
332619	Furniture springs, unassembled, made from purchased wire
49319	Furniture storage (without local trucking)
49319	Furniture storage service (used uncrated), household (without trucking)
45331	Furniture stores, second-hand, retail
81142	Furniture stripping and refinishing
327215	Furniture tops, glass (e.g., bevelled, cut, polished), made from purchased glass
32739	Furniture, concrete (e.g., benches, tables), manufacturing
32799	Furniture, cut stone (i.e., benches, tables, church), manufacturing
33911	Furniture, hospital (e.g., hospital beds, operating room furniture), manufacturing
337126	Furniture, household, glass, manufacturing
337126	Furniture, household, metal, manufacturing
41439	Furniture, household, office, restaurant and public building, wholesale
337126	Furniture, household, plastics (including fibreglass), manufacturing
337126	Furniture, household, rattan, reed, malacca, fibre, willow and wicker, manufacturing
81142	Furniture, household, repair shop
337121	Furniture, household, upholstered, manufacturing
41439	Furniture, household, wholesale
337127	Furniture, institutional, church, public building, manufacturing
337127	Furniture, laboratory (e.g., cabinets, benches, tables, stools), manufacturing
337214	Furniture, office (except wood), manufacturing
48421	Furniture, used, household, moving of
337123	Furniture, wood household, made to individual order
337123	Furniture, wood household, porch, lawn, garden and beach, manufacturing
337123	Furniture, wood household, unassembled or knock-down, manufacturing
337123	Furniture, wood household, unfinished, manufacturing
337213	Furniture, wood office, padded, upholstered or plain, manufacturing
41411	Furs, dressed, wholesale

335315	Fuse mountings, electric power, manufacturing
41611	Fuses and accessories, wholesale
32592	Fuses, detonating and safety, manufacturing
335315	Fuses, electric, manufacturing
52321	Futures commodity contract exchanges
52313	Futures commodity contracts dealing (i.e., acting as a principal in dealing commodities to investors)

G

212316	Gabbro, crushed and broken stone, quarrying
212316	Gabbro, quarrying
23799	Gabion installations
212231	Galena mining
712111	Galleries, art (except retail)
71399	Galleries, shooting
333519	Galvanizing machinery, manufacturing
33281	Galvanizing metals and metal products, for the trade
71321	Gambling cruises
91291	Game and inland fish agencies, provincial government
11293	Game farm (fur-bearing animals)
41792	Game machines, coin-operated, wholesale
311615	Game, small, slaughtering and dressing
33993	Games (except amusement park and playground), manufacturing
33999	Games, coin-operated, manufacturing
51121	Games, computer software, packaged, publishers
41421	Games, video, wholesale
212317	Ganister, quarrying
238299	Garage door, industrial type, installation
23835	Garage door, wooden, installation
332321	Garage doors, metal, manufacturing
23835	Garage doors, residential type, installation
44419	Garage doors, retail (wood)
321911	Garage doors, wood, manufacturing
41799	Garage equipment, wholesale
41799	Garage equipment, wholesale and repair
811111	Garages, general automotive repair and service
56211	Garbage collection
56221	Garbage collection and disposal service
326198	Garbage containers (except bags), plastics, manufacturing
23621	Garbage disposal plants, construction

335229	Garbage disposal units, household, manufacturing
56221	Garbage disposal, incinerator and combustor
56221	Garbage disposal, landfill
44311	Garbage disposers, electric, retail
56221	Garbage dump operation
332439	Garbage or trash cans, light gauge metal, manufacturing
56211	Garbage pick-up
33612	Garbage trucks, assembling on chassis of own manufacture
44421	Garden and lawn tractor stores selling primarily to other businesses but open to the general public
44421	Garden and lawn tractor stores, retail
41711	Garden and lawn tractors, wholesale
41711	Garden and lawn tractors, wholesale and repair
44422	Garden centre, retail, flowers and plants
53229	Garden equipment rental
337123	Garden furniture, wood, manufacturing
33221	Garden handtools, non-powered, manufacturing
32622	Garden hose, rubber or plastics, manufacturing
56173	Garden maintenance services
54132	Garden planning services
32711	Garden pottery, manufacturing
332311	Garden sheds, prefabricated, metal, manufacturing
44422	Garden supplies and tools, retail
71213	Garden, zoological or botanical
332619	Garment hangers, made from purchased wire
81149	Garment repair
31499	Garnetting of textile waste and rags
41612	Gas and oil heating equipment, wholesale
811412	Gas appliance repair service
41612	Gas appliances and supplies, wholesale
335229	Gas barbecues, manufacturing
213118	Gas compressing (natural gas) at the fields, on a contract basis
41793	Gas detecting equipment and supplies, wholesale
44311	Gas household appliance stores, retail
33512	Gas lighting fixtures, manufacturing
41899	Gas lighting fixtures, wholesale
23712	Gas mains, construction
56199	Gas meter reading service, contract
333416	Gas space heaters, manufacturing
33242	Gas storage tanks, heavy gauge metal, manufacturing

333611	Gas turbine generator set units, manufacturing
333611	Gas turbines (except aircraft type), manufacturing
33291	Gas valves, industrial type, manufacturing
213111	Gas well drilling, on a contract basis
213118	Gas well surveying, contract services (except seismographic)
211113	Gas well, natural
22121	Gas, natural, distribution
48621	Gas, natural, pipeline operation
41841	Gases, compressed and liquefied (except liquefied petroleum gas), wholesale
32512	Gases, industrial (i.e., compressed, liquefied, solid), manufacturing
33999	Gaskets, manufacturing
41723	Gaskets, wholesale
33631	Gasoline engine parts, automotive and truck, manufacturing
333619	Gasoline engines (except aircraft and automotive), manufacturing
33631	Gasoline engines, automotive and truck, manufacturing
33391	Gasoline measuring and dispensing pumps, manufacturing
48691	Gasoline pipeline transport service
44719	Gasoline service stations
44711	Gasoline station with convenience store
32411	Gasoline, made in petroleum refineries
41211	Gasoline, wholesale
33399	Gasoline-powered, hand held power tools, manufacturing
33399	Gate and bridge lifting machinery, manufacturing
41639	Gates and accessories, wire, wholesale
332329	Gates, metal (except wire), manufacturing
11321	Gathering of forest products (e.g., gums, barks, seeds)
11321	Gathering of wild mushrooms and truffles
33911	Gauze, surgical, made from purchased fabric
333519	Gear cutting and finishing machines, metalworking, manufacturing
33221	Gear pullers, handtools, manufacturing
333619	Gearmotors (i.e., power transmission equipment), manufacturing
33635	Gears (i.e., crown, pinion, spider), automotive, truck and bus, manufacturing

333619	Gears, power transmission (except motor vehicle and aircraft), manufacturing
112399	Geese farming
311615	Geese slaughtering and dressing
41313	Geese, dressed, wholesale
325999	Gelatin capsules, empty, manufacturing
31199	Gelatin dessert preparations, manufacturing
41319	Gelatin, edible, wholesale
212398	Gem stone mining
44831	Gem stones, rough, retail
41441	Gem stones, wholesale
81299	Genealogical investigation service
91191	General economics statistics agencies, federal government
91291	General economics statistics agencies, provincial
48411	General freight trucking, local
484122	General freight trucking, long-distance, less than truck-load
484121	General freight trucking, long-distance, truck-load
52421	General insurance agency
52421	General insurance broker
56132	General labour contractors (personnel suppliers)
41912	General line building material, wholesale agents and brokers
41912	General line of food, wholesale agents and brokers
41912	General line of merchandise, wholesale agents and brokers
541611	General management consulting services
622111	General medical and surgical hospitals
53231	General rental centres
452999	General store (not primarily food)
48411	General trucking, local
49311	General warehousing and storage
23799	Generating station, construction (hydro)
221112	Generation of electricity using fossil fuels
333611	Generator sets, turbine (e.g., steam, gas, hydraulic), manufacturing
44421	Generators, electric, portable, retail
41611	Generators, electrical, wholesale
54171	Genetics research and development laboratories
54137	Geographic Information System (GIS), base mapping services
54133	Geological engineering services
54136	Geological surveying services
54171	Geology research and development laboratories

54133	Geophysical engineering services
54136	Geophysical surveying for non metallic minerals, services
54137	Geospatial mapping services
54138	Geotechnical testing laboratory
221119	Geothermal electric power generation
62231	Geriatric hospitals
33141	Germanium smelting and primary refining
45322	Gift shops, retail
45322	Gift wrap supplies, retail
32222	Gift wrap, laminated, made from purchased paper
41899	Gifts and novelties, wholesale
45322	Gifts, novelties and souvenirs, retail
212398	Gilsonite mining
111999	Ginseng farming, except greenhouse grown
11321	Ginseng, gathering of
32739	Girders and beams, prestressed concrete, manufacturing
332319	Girders for bridges and buildings, fabricated metal, manufacturing
31519	Girdles and other foundation garments, made in knitting mills
315231	Girdles, women's, misses' and girls', cut and sewn from purchased fabric
81341	Girl guiding organization
721213	Girls' camps
32541	Glandular derivatives, uncompounded, manufacturing
32541	Glandular medicinal preparations, manufacturing
327215	Glass blanks for electric light bulbs, made from purchased glass
23814	Glass block laying
327214	Glass blocks and bricks, made in glass-making plants
23815	Glass cladding installation
31322	Glass fabric, narrow woven (i.e., 30 cm/12 in. or less in width), weaving
31321	Glass fabrics, broad-woven, weaving
32551	Glass frit, manufacturing
23815	Glass installation (except automotive), contractors
327215	Glass packaging containers, made from purchased glass
327214	Glass packaging containers, made in glass-making plants
23815	Glass partitions, installation
327214	Glass products (except packaging containers), made in glass-making plants
327215	Glass products, made from purchased glass

41819   Glass scrap, wholesale
44419   Glass stores, retail
23815   Glass tinting, construction
31499   Glass tire cord and tire cord fabrics, manufacturing
23814   Glass unit (i.e., glass block) masonry
327214 Glass yarn, made in glass-making plants
41529   Glass, automobile, wholesale
327215 Glass, automotive, made from purchased glass
327214 Glass, automotive, made in glass-making plants
41634   Glass, float and plate, wholesale
327214 Glass, plate, made in glass-making plants
323113 Glass, screen printing, for the trade
333299 Glass-making machinery (e.g., blowing, moulding, forming), manufacturing
45331   Glassware and china, used, retail
327215 Glassware for industrial, scientific and technical use, made from purchased glass
327214 Glassware for industrial, scientific and technical use, made in glass-making plants
327215 Glassware for lighting fixtures, made from purchased glass
327214 Glassware for lighting fixtures, made in glass-making plants
442298 Glassware stores, retail
327215 Glassware, cut and engraved, made from purchased glass
41899   Glassware, novelty, wholesale
212398 Glauber's salt, mining
32551   Glaziers' putty, manufacturing
23815   Glazing work, contractors
48799   Glider rides operations
51113   Globe covers (maps), publishing (except exclusively on Internet)
323119 Globe covers and maps, printing without publishing
31599   Glove linings (except fur), manufacturing
33911   Gloves (e.g., surgeons', electricians', household), rubber, manufacturing
31599   Gloves and mittens (except athletic, metal, rubber), made from purchased fabric
31519   Gloves, knit, made in knitting mills
33992   Gloves, sport and athletic (e.g., boxing, baseball, racquetball, handball), manufacturing
41411   Gloves, women's, misses' and children's, wholesale

311221 Glucose, made by wet-milling corn
32552   Glue (except dental), manufacturing
33911   Glue, dental, manufacturing
41841   Glue, wholesale
321215 Glued-laminated timber (glulam), manufacturing
311221 Gluten feed, flour and meal, made by wet-milling corn
311221 Gluten, manufacturing
32541   Glycosides, uncompounded, manufacturing
212314 Gneiss, quarrying
11242   Goat farming
11242   Goat's milk, raw fluid, producing
33699   Go-carts (except children's), manufacturing
41519   Go-carts, wholesale
41519   Go-carts, wholesale and repair
32222   Gold and silver foil laminates, made from purchased foil
21222   Gold bullion production at mine site
33149   Gold foil and leaf, made by rolling purchased metal or scrap
332999 Gold foil and leaf, made from purchased foil
21222   Gold mine, hydraulic
21222   Gold ore mining
41892   Gold ore, wholesale
21222   Gold quartz ore mining
33149   Gold rolling and drawing, purchased metal or scrap
33141   Gold smelting and primary refining
21222   Gold, gravity concentrating
71391   Golf and country clubs
33699   Golf carts, powered, manufacturing
44122   Golf carts, powered, retail
41799   Golf carts, self-propelled, wholesale
71391   Golf clubs, membership
23799   Golf course construction, general contractors
54132   Golf course design services
71391   Golf courses (except miniature), public
71399   Golf courses, miniature
71399   Golf driving ranges
33992   Golf equipment, manufacturing
45111   Golf goods and equipment, retail
71399   Golf practice ranges
31621   Golf shoes, manufacturing
711218 Golfers, independent, professional (i.e., participating in sporting events)
48799   Gondola (cablecar), sightseeing, operations
52311   Government bond underwriters
524123 Government owned automobile insurance carriers

91191	Governor General's office	33311	Grass mowing equipment (except lawn and garden), manufacturing
315299	Gowns, hospital, surgical and patient, cut and sewn from purchased fabric	111999	Grass seed farming
33422	GPS (global positioning system) equipment, manufacturing	484222	Gravel hauling, local
		212323	Gravel pit
33312	Grader attachments, elevating, manufacturing	41639	Gravel, wholesale
		453999	Gravestones, finished, retail
33312	Graders, road, manufacturing	54136	Gravimetric surveying services, geophysical
41721	Graders, wholesale		
41721	Graders, wholesale and repair	32312	Gravure plates and cylinders preparation services
41812	Grading and baling waste paper, wholesale	323119	Gravure printing (except manifold business forms, textile fabrics), without publishing
23731	Grading for highways, roads, streets and airport runways		
56199	Grading lumber services	333299	Gravure printing presses, manufacturing
33311	Grading, cleaning and sorting machinery, farm type, manufacturing	31199	Gravy (except dry mix), manufacturing
		31194	Gravy mixes, dry, manufacturing
23891	Grading, construction site	41899	Greases, animal and vegetable, wholesale
311821	Graham wafers, manufacturing		
31214	Grain alcohol, beverage purposes, manufacturing	32411	Greases, lubricating, made in petroleum refineries
11115	Grain corn farming	32419	Greases, petroleum lubricating, made from refined petroleum
49313	Grain elevators (storage only)		
52321	Grain exchanges	325999	Greases, synthetic lubricating, manufacturing
11114	Grain farming, wheat		
11119	Grain farms (except wheat, rice, corn and soybeans)	483115	Great Lakes and St. Lawrence Seaway transportation (except by ferries)
484232	Grain hauling, long-distance	111419	Greenhouse tomatoes, growing
48821	Grain levelling and trimming service, in railroad cars	111419	Greenhouses for growing food crops
		111422	Greenhouses, growing of floral products
41112	Grain merchant, wholesale		
311211	Grain mills (except rice, breakfast cereal and animal feed)	332311	Greenhouses, prefabricated, metal, manufacturing
		212398	Greensand mining
311119	Grain mills, animal feed	212314	Greenstone, dimension, quarrying
311214	Grain mills, rice	45322	Greeting card shops, retail
311221	Grain starches, manufacturing	323119	Greeting cards (e.g., birthday, holiday, sympathy), printing without publishing
332311	Grain storage buildings, metal, manufacturing		
		51119	Greeting cards, publishing (except exclusively on Internet)
484222	Grain trucking, local		
41112	Grain, wholesale	41821	Greeting cards, wholesale
41912	Grain, wholesale agents and brokers	332999	Grenades, hand or projectile, manufacturing
212314	Granite quarry		
212314	Granite, crushed and broken stone, quarrying	331511	Grey iron foundries
		332329	Grillwork, ornamental metal, manufacturing
31134	Granola bars and clusters (except chocolate-coated), manufacturing		
		32541	Grinding and milling botanicals (i.e., for medicinal use)
81321	Grant-making foundation		
31131	Granulated sugar, manufacturing	331511	Grinding balls, cast iron, manufacturing
33322	Granulating and pelletizing machinery for plastics, manufacturing	41621	Grinding balls, cast or forged, wholesale
		32791	Grinding balls, ceramic, manufacturing
31213	Grape growing and making wine	41819	Grinding into flakes used plastic milk jugs and similar plastic containers
11132	Grapefruit groves and farms		
11133	Grapes (vineyards)		
54143	Graphic arts and related design		
54143	Graphic design services		

333519	Grinding machines, metalworking, manufacturing
32419	Grinding oils, petroleum, made from refined petroleum
212317	Grits, crushed and broken stone mining
41911	Groceries, general line, business to business (B2B) electronic markets, wholesale
41311	Groceries, general line, wholesale
32222	Grocers' bags and sacks, made from purchased uncoated paper
44511	Grocery stores, with or without fresh meat, retail
61151	Ground training service for air crew
322121	Groundwood paper, coated, made in paper mills
322122	Groundwood paper, uncoated, made in paper mills
322111	Groundwood pulp, manufacturing
623999	Group foster homes
62121	Group practice, general dentist
62111	Group practice, osteopaths
62111	Group practice, physicians
81391	Growers' association
561612	Guard dog services
81291	Guard dog training
561612	Guard service
23731	Guardrail construction on highways
81291	Guide dog training
71399	Guide services (i.e., fishing, hunting, tourist)
33641	Guided missile and space vehicle engines, manufacturing
33641	Guided missiles and space vehicles, manufacturing
33641	Guided missiles, complete, assembling
33399	Guides, for hand held woodworking tool, manufacturing
323119	Guides, street map, printing without publishing
51113	Guides, street, publishing and printing combined
323119	Guides, travel books, printing without publishing
112399	Guinea fowl, raising
11321	Gum (i.e., forest product) gathering
32519	Gum and wood chemicals, manufacturing
41841	Gum and wood chemicals, wholesale
31134	Gum, chewing, manufacturing
41822	Gummed kraft paper, wholesale
32222	Gummed paper products (e.g., labels, sheets, tapes), made from purchased paper
23811	Gunite work on construction projects
32592	Gunpowder, manufacturing
33221	Guns, caulking, non-powered, manufacturing
332999	Guns, manufacturing
81149	Gunsmith shops (without retail sales of new equipment)
33911	Gut sutures, surgical, manufacturing
561799	Gutter cleaning services
23817	Gutter installation, contractors
326198	Gutters and down spouts, plastics, manufacturing
332118	Gutters and down spouts, sheet metal, roll formed, manufacturing
23817	Gutters, seamless roof, formed and installed on-site
33992	Gymnasium and playground equipment, manufacturing
45111	Gymnasium equipment, retail
41447	Gymnasium equipment, wholesale
71394	Gymnasiums
61162	Gymnastics instruction
212395	Gypsite mining
32742	Gypsum building products, manufacturing
23831	Gypsum wallboard, installation
334511	Gyroscopes, manufacturing

H

44811	Haberdashery stores, retail
41452	Hair care products, wholesale
33521	Hair clippers for human use, electric, manufacturing
33221	Hair clippers, for human or animal use, non-powered, manufacturing
44311	Hair driers, household, retail
33999	Hair nets, made from purchased netting
33999	Hair pieces (e.g., wigs, toupees, wiglets), manufacturing
32562	Hair preparations (e.g., conditioners, dyes, rinses, shampoos), manufacturing
81219	Hair removal (i.e., by electrolysis)
81219	Hair replacement service
33521	Hair styling equipment, domestic, electric, manufacturing
812114	Hair stylists, men's
812115	Hair stylists, women's
81219	Hair weaving service
31331	Hair, animal (except horse), preparation (e.g., dressing, heckling, teasing, willowing)
623999	Halfway homes for delinquents and offenders
315299	Halloween costumes, cut and sewn from purchased fabric

53112	Halls, reception, rental
33511	Halogen bulbs, manufacturing
32519	Halogenated hydrocarbon (except aromatics) derivatives, manufacturing
311615	Ham, poultry, manufacturing
311614	Ham, preserved (except poultry), made from purchased meat
72221	Hamburger stand
332113	Hammer forgings, unfinished, made from purchased metal
33221	Hammers, handtools, manufacturing
33312	Hammers, pneumatic, hand-operated, manufacturing
311611	Hams (except poultry), produced in slaughtering plants
327215	Hand blowing purchased glass
33221	Hand held edge tools, non-powered, manufacturing
31324	Hand knitting
81232	Hand laundries
33221	Hand saws, all non-powered types, manufacturing
32561	Hand soaps (e.g., hard, liquid, soft), manufacturing
33994	Hand stamps, stencils and brands, manufacturing
33221	Hand tools, metal blade (e.g., putty knives, scrapers, screwdrivers), non-powered, manufacturing
33399	Hand tools, power-driven, manufacturing
31321	Hand weaving fabrics (more than 30 cm/12 in.) in width
31322	Hand weaving narrow fabrics (i.e., 30 cm/12 in. or less in width)
44815	Handbags and pocketbooks, retail
41411	Handbags and pocketbooks, wholesale
31699	Handbags, manufacturing
54187	Handbill and circular direct distribution services
33411	Hand-held computer (e.g., PDA's), manufacturing
48599	Handicapped transportation services
62431	Handicapped workshop
41446	Handicraft and hobbycraft kits, wholesale
33993	Handicraft supplies, manufacturing
45322	Handicraft, retail
61161	Handicrafts school
31599	Handkerchiefs (except paper), made from purchased fabric
321999	Handles (e.g., broom, brush, mop, hand tool), wood, manufacturing
41633	Handtools (except automotive and machinists' precision), wholesale
44413	Handtools, retail
54199	Handwriting analysis services
23622	Handyman construction services, commercial and institutional buildings
23621	Handyman construction services, industrial buildings
23611	Handyman construction services, residential buildings
488119	Hangar operation
23622	Hangars, aeroplane, construction
321999	Hangers, garment, wood, manufacturing
23799	Harbour construction, general contractors
483214	Harbour ferry service
488339	Harbour navigational operations
48831	Harbour operation
48721	Harbour sightseeing tours
41322	Hard cider, wholesale
33911	Hard hats manufacturing
32629	Hard rubber products, not specified elsewhere by process, manufacturing
321216	Hardboard, manufacturing
326198	Hardware (except motor vehicle), plastics, manufacturing
41633	Hardware purchasing, packaging and selling to retailers
44413	Hardware stores, retail
33251	Hardware, metal, manufacturing
326193	Hardware, plastics, motor vehicle, manufacturing
41633	Hardware, wholesale
41912	Hardware, wholesale agents and brokers
23833	Hardwood flooring, installation
44221	Hardwood flooring, installation combined with selling
711213	Harness drivers
711213	Harness race tracks
81143	Harness repair
31699	Harnesses and harness parts, leather, manufacturing
41711	Harrows, ploughs and tillers, farm and garden, wholesale
33311	Harvesting machinery and equipment, manufacturing
41711	Harvesting machinery and equipment, wholesale
11511	Harvesting service, agricultural crop and plant
81232	Hat cleaning and blocking
112391	Hatchery service and poultry production
33221	Hatchets, manufacturing

31599	Hats (except fur, leather), made from purchased fabric
44815	Hats and caps, retail
315292	Hats, fur, manufacturing
322299	Hats, made from purchased paper
31519	Hats, made in knitting mills
41411	Hats, women's, misses' and girls', wholesale
41831	Hay and fodder, wholesale
11194	Hay farming
311119	Hay, cubed, manufacturing
41711	Haying machinery, wholesale
33311	Haying machines, manufacturing
484239	Hazardous materials trucking using specialized equipment, long-distance
56211	Hazardous waste collection
56221	Hazardous waste material treatment and disposal sites
551114	Head offices
337123	Headboards, wood, manufacturing
91191	Health and medical care programs, federal government
446199	Health appliance stores
446199	Health appliance stores selling primarily to other businesses but also selling to household consumers
81321	Health awareness fundraising organization
81392	Health care standards agencies
71394	Health club, physical fitness
41319	Health food, wholesale
524299	Health insurance coverage consulting service
33511	Health lamps, infra-red and ultra-violet-radiation, manufacturing
81392	Health professionals' associations
91291	Health programs, provincial government
524132	Health reinsurance underwriters
54171	Health research and development laboratories
81321	Health research fundraising organization
721111	Health spas (i.e., physical fitness facilities) with hotel accommodations
71394	Health spas (without lodging), physical fitness
71394	Health studio, physical fitness
33591	Hearing aid batteries, manufacturing
334512	Hearing aids, electronic, manufacturing
446199	Hearing aids, retail
41793	Hearing aids, wholesale
621499	Hearing testing service
48532	Hearse rental with driver
532111	Hearse rental, without drivers

532111	Hearses and limousines, rental without drivers
41723	Heat exchange equipment, industrial, wholesale
41723	Heat exchange equipment, industrial, wholesale and repair
33241	Heat exchangers, manufacturing
333416	Heat pumps, manufacturing
41612	Heat pumps, wholesale
33281	Heat treating metals and metal products, for the trade
33399	Heat treating ovens, industrial process type, manufacturing
333416	Heaters, space (except portable electric), manufacturing
333416	Heaters, swimming pool, electric, manufacturing
333416	Heaters, swimming pool, manufacturing
333416	Heating and air-conditioning combination units, manufacturing
41612	Heating and cooking equipment, non-electric, wholesale
23822	Heating contractors
333416	Heating equipment, forced air, manufacturing
333416	Heating equipment, hot water (except hot water heaters), manufacturing
32411	Heating oils, made in petroleum refineries
22133	Heating plant
333416	Heating units, baseboard, manufacturing
23822	Heating, ventilation and air-conditioning (HVAC) contractors
211114	Heavy crude oil extracting
23832	Heavy machinery painting
211114	Heavy oil in place, solution gas drive recovering
211114	Heavy oil, thermal in situ recovering
33612	Heavy trucks, assembling on chassis of own manufacture
325189	Heavy water (i.e., deuterium oxide), manufacturing
811411	Hedge and lawn trimmers, repair service (without retail sales of new equipment)
33221	Hedge shears and trimmers, non-electric, manufacturing
44421	Hedge trimmers, power, retail
33311	Hedge trimmers, powered, manufacturing
32629	Heels, shoe, rubber, manufacturing
332611	Helical springs, heavy gauge, manufacturing

332619	Helical springs, light gauge, made from purchased wire
48111	Helicopter carriers, passenger, scheduled
48799	Helicopter rides, scenic and sightseeing
33641	Helicopters, manufacturing
32512	Helium, manufacturing
56132	Help supply service
41451	Hematinic medicines, wholesale
32541	Hematology in-vivo diagnostic substances, manufacturing
32541	Hematology products (except diagnostic substances), manufacturing
31311	Hemp bags and ropes, made in spinning mills
32511	Heptane, made from refined petroleum or natural gas liquids
32511	Heptene, made from refined petroleum or natural gas liquids
111419	Herb farming, grown under cover
32541	Herb grinding and milling (i.e., for medicinal use)
31192	Herbal tea, manufacturing
62139	Herbalists, private practice
32532	Herbicides, manufacturing
41839	Herbicides, wholesale
54194	Herd inspecting and testing services, veterinary
711322	Heritage festivals promoters, without facilities
71212	Heritage villages
23835	Hermetically sealed glass for window units, installation
23815	Hermetically sealed window units, commercial type, installation
332321	Hermetically sealed window units, metal frame, manufacturing
32519	Heterocyclic chemicals, not specified elsewhere by process, manufacturing
32511	Hexane, made from refined petroleum or natural gas liquids
311221	HFCS (high fructose corn syrup), manufacturing
311611	Hides and skins, produced in slaughtering plants
41119	Hides and skins, raw, wholesale
31611	Hides, tanning, currying, dressing and finishing
61111	High schools
23611	High-rise apartments, construction, by general contractors
91291	Highway and transport programs, provincial government
23731	Highway grading

332329	Highway guardrails, sheet metal, manufacturing
23821	Highway lighting and electrical signal construction, contractors
23731	Highway line painting
33612	Highway maintenance motor vehicles (e.g., road oilers, sanders), assembling on chassis of own manufacture
33612	Highway tractors (i.e., for semi-trailers), assembling on chassis of own manufacture
23821	Highway, street and bridge lighting systems and electrical signal installation
41633	Hinges and butts, wholesale
33251	Hinges, metal, manufacturing
71212	Historic sites
81341	Historical clubs
71212	Historical forts
32541	HIV test kits, manufacturing
45112	Hobby kits, model, retail
41446	Hobbycraft kits, wholesale
711211	Hockey clubs, professional or semi-professional
71399	Hockey clubs, recreational
33992	Hockey equipment (e.g., pants, pads, shinguards), manufacturing
45111	Hockey equipment, retail
61162	Hockey schools
711218	Hockey scouts, independent
33221	Hoes, garden and masons' handtools, manufacturing
33311	Hog feeding and watering equipment, manufacturing
11221	Hog feedlot
11221	Hog raising
238299	Hoisting and placement (only) of large-scale apparatus
41723	Hoisting machinery and equipment, wholesale (except construction and forestry)
33392	Hoists, manufacturing
551113	Holding management companies
33331	Hole punches (except hand operated), office type, manufacturing
33994	Hole punches, hand operated, manufacturing
62139	Holistic medicine, practitioners' offices
44831	Holloware, precious metal, retail
41441	Hollowware, table, sterling and silverplate, wholesale
111422	Holly growing
452991	Home and auto supply stores
23821	Home automation system installation
23611	Home builders, operative
62412	Home care of elderly

44411	Home centre (building supplies)
41731	Home computers, wholesale
41731	Home computers, wholesale and repair
41912	Home electronics, wholesale agents and brokers
442298	Home furnishing stores
62161	Home health care services
53229	Home health equipment, rental
454311	Home heating oil dealer, retail
23611	Home improvement (e.g., additions, remodelling, renovations), single-family, by operative builders
54135	Home inspection services
41443	Home movie cameras, equipment and supplies, wholesale
62161	Home nursing services (except own-account-private practice)
62161	Home physiotherapy services (except own-account-private practice)
45439	Home provisioners, frozen food service, direct seller, retail
44311	Home security equipment, retail
33431	Home stereo systems, manufacturing
33431	Home theatre audio and video equipment, manufacturing
23821	Home theatre installation
53223	Home video movie rental
62412	Home-maker services
61151	Homemaking school
623221	Homes for alcoholics
623991	Homes for battered women
623999	Homes for children in need of protection
623221	Homes for drug addicts
623992	Homes for emotionally disturbed children
623999	Homes for single mothers
62331	Homes for the aged
623993	Homes for the blind
623993	Homes for the deaf
623993	Homes for the deaf or blind
62321	Homes for the developmentally handicapped
623222	Homes for the mentally disabled
623222	Homes for the mentally handicapped
623993	Homes for the physically disabled
623993	Homes for the physically handicapped
336215	Homes, motor, self-contained, assembling on purchased chassis
333299	Homogenizing machinery, food, manufacturing
11291	Honey and beeswax production
31199	Honey processing
11291	Honey, natural, unprocessed, producing
41319	Honey, processed, wholesale
445299	Honey, retail
333519	Honing and lapping machines, metalworking, manufacturing
33272	Hook and eye latches, manufacturing
33272	Hooks (i.e., general purpose fasteners), metal, manufacturing
111999	Hop, growing
23799	Horizontal drilling (e.g., cable, pipeline, sewer installation)
41451	Hormonal medicines, wholesale
32541	Hormone in-vitro diagnostic substances, manufacturing
32541	Hormones and derivatives, uncompounded, manufacturing
311611	Horse meat, produced in slaughtering plants
711213	Horse race tracks, operation of
11292	Horse ranching
711319	Horse show promoters, with facilities
711329	Horse show promoters, without facilities
71399	Horseback riding, recreational
48711	Horse-drawn carriages, sightseeing
31194	Horseradish, prepared sauce, manufacturing
11521	Horses, boarding (except racehorses)
711213	Horses, race, owners of
711213	Horses, racing stables
11521	Horseshoeing
54171	Horticulture research and development
33291	Hose and tube assemblies, fluid power (i.e., hydraulic and pneumatic), manufacturing
33272	Hose clamps, metal, manufacturing
33291	Hose nozzles and couplings, manufacturing
41723	Hose, belting and packing, industrial, wholesale
332999	Hose, flexible metal, manufacturing
32622	Hose, reinforced, made from purchased plastics
32622	Hose, reinforced, made from purchased rubber
32622	Hose, rubberized fabric, manufacturing
31331	Hosiery dyeing and finishing
333299	Hosiery machinery, manufacturing
31511	Hosiery mill
44815	Hosiery stores, retail
41411	Hosiery, women's, misses' and children's, wholesale
81392	Hospital administrators' associations
91291	Hospital and medical insurance plans, provincial government
81391	Hospital associations

41793	Hospital equipment and supplies, wholesale
41793	Hospital equipment and supplies, wholesale and repair
62221	Hospital for emotionally disturbed children
33911	Hospital furniture (e.g., hospital beds, operating room furniture), manufacturing
54194	Hospitals, animal
622111	Hospitals, general medical and surgical
62231	Hospitals, specialty (except psychiatric)
48799	Hot air balloon rides
33281	Hot dip galvanizing metals and metal products, for the trade
72221	Hot dog stands
311614	Hot dogs (except poultry), made from purchased meat
311615	Hot dogs, poultry, manufacturing
332113	Hot forgings, unfinished, made from purchased metal
326191	Hot tubs, plastics or fibreglass, manufacturing
32629	Hot water bottles, rubber, manufacturing
41612	Hot water heaters, oil and gas, wholesale
41792	Hotel and restaurant equipment and supplies, wholesale
41792	Hotel and restaurant equipment and supplies, wholesale and repair
337127	Hotel furniture, manufacturing
721111	Hotel lodging services (except apartment hotel)
721111	Hotel management services (i.e., providing management and operating staff to run hotel)
56111	Hotel management, operating staff not furnished (except complete operations of client business)
56159	Hotel reservation services
23622	Hotel, construction
721111	Hotels (except casino hotels) with integrated health spa facilities
721111	Hotels (except residential)
33111	Hot-rolled iron and steel products, made in steel mills
331221	Hot-rolling purchased steel
453999	Hot-tubs and whirlpools, retail
23611	House construction
23611	House construction, by merchant builders
23891	House demolishing contractors
23891	House moving, contractors

484229	House moving, local (i.e., transportation only)
484239	House moving, long distance (i.e., transportation only)
23832	House painting, contractors
81299	House sitting services
45393	House trailer dealers, retail
336612	Houseboats, building
31519	Housecoats, made in knitting mills
44311	Household appliance stores, electric or gas, retail
41911	Household appliance, business to business (B2B) electronic markets, wholesale
41912	Household appliances and home electronics, wholesale agents and brokers
811412	Household appliances repair service (without retail sales of new equipment)
811412	Household appliances, repair
41911	Household china and glassware, business to business (B2B) electronic markets, wholesale
41431	Household china and glassware, wholesale
41431	Household crockery and pottery, wholesale
41912	Household furnishings, wholesale agents and brokers
337126	Household furniture (except wooden and upholstered), manufacturing
44211	Household furniture and appliances, retail (primarily furniture)
53229	Household furniture rental
44211	Household furniture stores
41439	Household furniture, wholesale
41912	Household furniture, wholesale agents and brokers
49319	Household goods, warehousing and storage (without trucking)
41433	Household linens, wholesale
81411	Household, private employing domestic personnel
561722	Housekeeping (i.e., cleaning service)
721192	Housekeeping cottages and cabins
321992	Houses, prefabricated (except mobile homes), wood frame, manufacturing
321991	Houses, prefabricated mobile homes, manufacturing
45439	House-to-house selling of coffee, soda, beer, bottled water, or other products, retail
442298	Housewares stores, retail
45439	Housewares, house-to-house, telephone or party plan selling, retail

53131	Housing authorities, operating (managers)
531112	Housing for low income elderly
91191	Housing programs, federal government
91391	Housing programs, local government
91291	Housing programs, provincial government
48721	Hovercraft operation (sightseeing)
45439	Hucksters, retail
334511	HUD (heads-up display) systems, aeronautical, manufacturing
212299	Huebnerite mining
11511	Hulling and shelling of nuts
712115	Human history museums
541612	Human resource consulting services
81331	Human rights advocacy organizations
91191	Human Rights Commission, federal government
91291	Human Rights Commission, provincial government
81331	Humane society (advocacy group)
81291	Humane society (animal shelters)
54172	Humanities research and development services
41612	Humidifiers and dehumidifiers (except portable), wholesale
41422	Humidifiers and dehumidifiers, portable, wholesale
33521	Humidifiers, electric, portable, manufacturing
333416	Humidifying equipment (except portable), manufacturing
334512	Humidistats (e.g., duct, skeleton, wall), manufacturing
71399	Hunting and fishing clubs, recreational
11421	Hunting and trapping, wild animals for furs (except seals)
721212	Hunting camps
11421	Hunting carried on as a business enterprise
315229	Hunting coats and vests, men's and boys', cut and sewn from purchased fabric
45111	Hunting equipment, retail
71399	Hunting guide services
11421	Hunting preserves, operation of
23822	HVAC (heating, ventilation and air-conditioning) contractors
331511	Hydrants, unfinished iron castings, manufacturing
32741	Hydrated lime (i.e., calcium hydroxide), manufacturing
33291	Hydraulic aircraft sub-assemblies, manufacturing
32731	Hydraulic cement, manufacturing
33399	Hydraulic cylinders, fluid power, manufacturing
32411	Hydraulic fluids, made in petroleum refineries
32419	Hydraulic fluids, petroleum, made from refined petroleum
325999	Hydraulic fluids, synthetic, manufacturing
32622	Hydraulic hose (without fittings), rubber or plastics, manufacturing
33291	Hydraulic hose fittings, fluid power, manufacturing
33399	Hydraulic pumps, fluid power, manufacturing
33291	Hydraulic valves, fluid power, manufacturing
325189	Hydrazine, manufacturing
325189	Hydrochloric acid, manufacturing
23891	Hydrodemolition (i.e., demolition with pressurized water), contractor
23799	Hydroelectric generating stations, construction
221111	Hydroelectric power generation
336611	Hydrofoil vessels, building and repairing in shipyards
336612	Hydrofoil vessels, recreational type, manufacturing
325189	Hydrogen peroxide, manufacturing
32512	Hydrogen, manufacturing
311225	Hydrogenating purchased oils
54137	Hydrographic mapping services
54169	Hydrology consulting services
23822	Hydronic heating systems, installation
334512	Hydronic limit, pressure and temperature controls, manufacturing
111419	Hydroponic crops, grown under cover
54138	Hydrostatic testing laboratories
212395	Hydrous calcium sulphate (gypsum) mining
212398	Hydrous sodium sulphate (Glauber's salt), mining
41452	Hygiene products, oral, wholesale
33911	Hypodermic needles and syringes, manufacturing

I

31211	Ice (except dry ice), manufacturing
23817	Ice apron, roof, installation
332439	Ice chests and coolers (except foam plastics), manufacturing
32615	Ice chests or coolers, foam plastics (except polystyrene), manufacturing
326198	Ice chests or coolers, plastics (except foam), manufacturing

32614	Ice chests or coolers, polystyrene foam, manufacturing
445299	Ice cream (i.e., packaged) stores, retail
41312	Ice cream and ices, wholesale
311821	Ice cream cones and wafers, manufacturing
311515	Ice cream mix, manufacturing
72221	Ice cream parlour
31152	Ice cream specialties, manufacturing
31152	Ice cream, manufacturing
41312	Ice cream, wholesale
45439	Ice dealers, retail, door-to-door
711211	Ice hockey clubs, professional or semiprofessional
333416	Ice making machinery, manufacturing
41791	Ice making machines, wholesale
41791	Ice making machines, wholesale and repair
31152	Ice milk specialties, manufacturing
31152	Ice milk, manufacturing
23799	Ice rink (except indoor) construction
23622	Ice rink, indoor, construction
33992	Ice skates, manufacturing
71119	Ice skating companies (except theatrical)
71394	Ice skating rinks
71119	Ice skating shows (except theatrical)
32512	Ice, dry (i.e., solid carbon dioxide), manufacturing
41899	Ice, manufactured or natural, wholesale
31211	Iced tea, manufacturing
212398	Iceland spar (i.e., optical grade calcite), mining
31152	Ices, flavoured sherbets, manufacturing
326198	Identification card stock, plastics, manufacturing
334512	Ignition controls for gas appliances and furnaces, automatic, manufacturing
33632	Ignition points and condensers, for internal combustion engines, manufacturing
811119	Ignition service, automotive
33632	Ignition wiring harness, for internal combustion engines, manufacturing
321215	I-joists, wood, manufacturing
54143	Illustrators, commercial
212299	Ilmenite ore mining
21221	Ilmenite, hematite, ore, mining
32312	Imagesetting services, pre-press
41441	Imitation stones and pearls, jewellery, wholesale
31222	Imitation tobacco cigarettes, manufacturing
54119	Immigration consultant
91132	Immigration services, federal

33399	Impact wrenches, hand held power-driven, manufacturing
41322	Importers of wines and spirits for embassies
41119	Importers, raw wool, wholesale
41912	Import-export agents and brokers, wholesale trade
31332	Impregnating and coating of fabrics
33511	Incandescent filament lamp bulbs, complete, manufacturing
33512	Incandescent lighting fixtures, manufacturing
325999	Incense, manufacturing
238299	Incinerator installation, small, contractors
56221	Incinerator operation
33399	Incinerators, industrial process type, manufacturing
541213	Income tax return preparation services without accounting, auditing, or bookkeeping services
33331	Incoming mail handling equipment (e.g., opening, sorting, scanning), manufacturing
33311	Incubators, poultry, manufacturing
517111	Incumbent local exchange carriers (ILECs)
61162	Independent sports instructors
32223	Index and other die-cut cards, made from purchased cardboard
91191	Indian affairs program, federal government
91411	Indian band or tribe council
41723	Indicating instruments and accessories, wholesale
54185	Indoor display advertising services
71312	Indoor play areas
33399	Induction heating equipment, industrial process type, manufacturing
33441	Inductors, electronic component type (e.g., chokes, coils, transformers), manufacturing
81391	Industrial associations
23621	Industrial building construction, general contractors
41841	Industrial chemicals, wholesale
54142	Industrial design consulting services
54142	Industrial design services
54132	Industrial development planning service (i.e., urban planning)
33991	Industrial diamonds, cut and polished, manufacturing
335312	Industrial electrical motor rebuilding
54133	Industrial engineering services

81131	Industrial equipment and machinery, repair and maintenance
41723	Industrial equipment, wholesale
41723	Industrial furnaces, kilns and ovens, wholesale and repair
41841	Industrial gases, wholesale
23621	Industrial incinerator construction, general contractors
81393	Industrial labour unions
81233	Industrial launderers
53249	Industrial machinery and equipment, rental and leasing
41912	Industrial machinery and equipment, wholesale agents and brokers
41723	Industrial machinery, equipment and supplies, wholesale
41723	Industrial machinery, equipment and supplies, wholesale and repair
333511	Industrial moulds (except steel ingots), manufacturing
53119	Industrial park developing and operating
56132	Industrial personnel services (personnel suppliers)
334512	Industrial process control instruments, manufacturing
23822	Industrial process piping installation
91131	Industrial relations services, federal government
91221	Industrial relations services, provincial government
54171	Industrial research and development laboratories (except testing)
41793	Industrial safety devices (e.g., first-aid kits, face and eye masks), wholesale
212323	Industrial sand mining
33399	Industrial scales, manufacturing
61151	Industrial school, government (except corrective or reform school)
91212	Industrial school, provincial government (reform school)
41723	Industrial sewing thread, wholesale
54138	Industrial testing laboratories
33392	Industrial truck cranes, manufacturing
53249	Industrial truck rental and leasing
33392	Industrial trucks and tractors (plant and warehouse), manufacturing
41413	Industrial yarn, wholesale
31142	Infant and junior food, canning
44813	Infants and toddlers clothing, retail
31123	Infants' cereals, dry, manufacturing
315291	Infants' clothing, cut and sewn from purchased fabric
41411	Infants' clothing, wholesale

31621	Infant's footwear (except orthopedic extension shoes), manufacturing
311515	Infants' formulas, manufacturing
44813	Infants' wear stores, retail
32629	Inflatable rubber rafts (non-recreative), manufacturing
32629	Inflatable rubber swimming pool rafts and similar flotation devices, manufacturing
51791	Information access services, on-line
54151	Information management system design services, computer
33399	Infrared ovens, industrial process type, manufacturing
331317	Ingot, made by rolling purchased aluminum
33111	Ingot, made in steel mills
331313	Ingot, primary aluminum, manufacturing
41621	Ingots (except precious), wholesale
41621	Ingots, non-ferrous metals, wholesale
325999	Inhibitors (e.g., corrosion, oxidation, polymerization), manufacturing
33322	Injection moulding machinery for plastics, manufacturing
81121	Ink jet cartridges, recycling (i.e., cleaning and re-filling)
41821	Ink, paste and solvent, office supply, wholesale
41723	Ink, printer's, wholesale
33994	Inked ribbons, manufacturing
41821	Inked ribbons, wholesale
32591	Inkjet cartridges, manufacturing
32591	Inkjet inks, manufacturing
325999	Inks, drawing, stamp pad and writing, manufacturing
32591	Inks, printing, manufacturing
114114	Inland fishing, freshwater
32621	Inner tubes, manufacturing
721111	Inns, furnishing food and lodging
32513	Inorganic pigments (except bone, carbon and lamp black), manufacturing
51821	Input preparation services, computer
41611	Insect control devices, electric, wholesale
44422	Insecticides and weed killers, retail
32532	Insecticides, manufacturing
41839	Insecticides, wholesale
114113	Inshore fishing, salt water
48849	Inspection or weighing service, truck transportation
31192	Instant coffee, manufacturing
31192	Instant tea, manufacturing
61121	Institute of marine technology, post-secondary

23622	Institutional buildings, construction
51211	Instructional film production
51211	Instructional video production
33632	Instrument control panels (i.e., assembling purchased gauges), automotive, truck and bus, manufacturing
334512	Instrument panels, assembling using gauges made in the same establishment
335315	Instrument relays, all types, manufacturing
335311	Instrument transformers (except portable), manufacturing
334512	Instruments for industrial process control, manufacturing
334512	Instruments for measuring electrical quantities, manufacturing
334511	Instruments, aeronautical, manufacturing
334512	Instruments, laboratory analysis type, manufacturing
41793	Instruments, professional, wholesale
332321	Insulated windows, hermetically sealed, metal frame, manufacturing
41611	Insulated wire and cable, annunciator, building and power, wholesale
33592	Insulated wire and cable, made from purchased wire
32799	Insulating batts, fills or blankets, fibreglass, manufacturing
322299	Insulating batts, fills or blankets, made from purchased paper
327215	Insulating glass, sealed units, made from purchased glass
327214	Insulating glass, sealed units, made in glass-making plants
325999	Insulating oils, manufacturing
32615	Insulation and cushioning, foam plastics (except polystyrene), manufacturing
32614	Insulation and cushioning, polystyrene foam, manufacturing
321216	Insulation board, cellular fibre or hard pressed wood, manufacturing
41639	Insulation materials, wholesale
238299	Insulation of pipes and boilers, contractors
23831	Insulation work contractors
32799	Insulation, mineral wool, manufacturing
32711	Insulators, electrical porcelain, manufacturing
41611	Insulators, electrical, wholesale
32541	Insulin preparations, manufacturing
32541	Insulin, uncompounded, manufacturing

524299	Insurance advisory services
52421	Insurance agents and brokers
81391	Insurance association
524291	Insurance claim adjusters
524299	Insurance consultants
524299	Insurance educational services
524299	Insurance information bureaus
524299	Insurance inspection and investigation (except claims investigation), services
524299	Insurance professional standards services
524299	Insurance rate making services
323119	Intaglio printing
33441	Integrated microcircuits, manufacturing
56291	Integrated mine reclamation services
33441	Integrated optical circuits (IOC), manufacturing
51222	Integrated record production and distribution
53311	Intellectual property holders, except copyright
48521	Intercity bus line operation
33429	Intercom systems and equipment, manufacturing
81121	Intercommunication equipment, commercial, repair
41732	Intercommunication equipment, electronic, wholesale
81121	Intercommunication equipment, household type, repair
23821	Intercommunication systems, installation
33241	Intercooler shells, manufacturing
54141	Interior decorating consulting service
54141	Interior design services
62311	Intermediate care facilities
333619	Internal combustion engines (except aircraft and non-diesel automotive), manufacturing
33631	Internal combustion gasoline engines, automotive and truck, manufacturing
91141	International agency representation, federal
91142	International development assistance, federal government
91141	International exchange services (scientific, academic), federal government
91911	International Monetary Fund, office in Canada
51913	Internet book publishing
51913	Internet broadcasting
51913	Internet entertainment sites
51913	Internet game sites
51913	Internet newspaper publishing

54151	Internet page design services, custom
51913	Internet periodical publishing
517112	Internet service providers (ISPs), cable
517111	Internet service providers (ISPs), facilities-based (except cable)
51913	Internet software publishing
54193	Interpreting services
71112	Interpretive dance companies
91291	Interprovincial relations, provincial government
48521	Interurban bus line operation
482114	Interurban passenger railways
53229	Invalid supplies rental and leasing, consumer
53311	Inventors, self-employed
56199	Inventory computing service
541619	Inventory planning and control management consulting services
56199	Inventory taking service
31131	Invert sugar, manufacturing
561611	Investigation services (except credit)
52393	Investment advice counselling services, customized, fees paid by clients
52311	Investment banking
331529	Investment castings, non-ferrous metals, unfinished, manufacturing
331514	Investment castings, steel, unfinished, manufacturing
52391	Investment clubs
551113	Investment holding companies (except banks)
32541	In-vitro diagnostic substances, manufacturing
32541	In-vivo diagnostic substances, manufacturing
325189	Iodine, crude or resublimed, manufacturing
32521	Ion exchange resins, manufacturing
32521	Ionomer resins, manufacturing
33141	Iridium smelting and primary refining
21221	Iron agglomerate and pellet production
41621	Iron and steel in primary forms and shapes, wholesale
41912	Iron and steel primary forms and structural shapes, agents and brokers
41811	Iron and steel scrap, wholesale
41621	Iron and steel wire, wholesale
41621	Iron and steel, rough cast, wholesale
32513	Iron based pigments, manufacturing
331221	Iron basic shapes (except pipe, tube or wire), made from purchased iron
325189	Iron compounds, not specified elsewhere by process, manufacturing
332113	Iron forgings, unfinished, made from purchased iron

331511	Iron foundries
21221	Iron ore dressing (beneficiation) plants
21221	Iron ore milling
213117	Iron ore mine diamond drilling, contract services
21221	Iron ore mining
33111	Iron ore recovery from open hearth slag
33111	Iron, pig, manufacturing
332999	Ironing boards, metal, manufacturing
334512	Irradiation equipment, manufacturing
11511	Irradiation of fruits and vegetables
41711	Irrigation equipment, wholesale
41711	Irrigation equipment, wholesale and repair
22131	Irrigation system operation
32511	Isobutene, made from refined petroleum or natural gas liquids
32521	Isobutylene polymer resins, manufacturing
32519	Isocyanates, manufacturing
32511	Isoprene, made from refined petroleum or natural gas liquids
32519	Isopropyl alcohol, manufacturing
325189	Isotopes, radioactive, manufacturing
51791	ISPs, independent
51791	ISPs, resale

J

315292	Jackets, leather (except welders') or sheepskin-lined, manufacturing
315222	Jackets, tailored (except fur, leather, sheepskin-lined), men's and boys', cut and sewn from purchased fabric
315234	Jackets, tailored (except fur, leather, sheepskin-lined), women's, misses' and girls', cut and sewn from purchased fabric
33312	Jackhammers, manufacturing
33221	Jacks (except hydraulic and pneumatic), manufacturing
33221	Jacks (screw and ratchet), motor vehicle, manufacturing
33399	Jacks, hydraulic and pneumatic, manufacturing
56121	Jails, privately operated
91212	Jails, provincial government
31142	Jam, manufacturing
41319	Jams, jellies and marmalades, wholesale
41792	Janitorial machinery and equipment, wholesale
561722	Janitorial services
41792	Janitors' supplies, wholesale
32629	Jar rings, rubber, manufacturing
71112	Jazz dance companies

71113	Jazz music groups
44814	Jeans stores, retail
315227	Jeans, men's and boys', cut and sewn from purchased fabric
315239	Jeans, women's, misses' and girls', cut and sewn from purchased fabric
31142	Jelly and jam, manufacturing
31199	Jelly powders, manufacturing
31519	Jerseys, made in knitting mills
32411	Jet fuels, made in petroleum refineries
23799	Jetty construction, general contractors
33991	Jewellers' findings, manufacturing
41441	Jewellers' findings, precious metal, wholesale
33221	Jewellers' handtools, non-powered, manufacturing
33991	Jewellery and silverware, metal embossing for the trade
41912	Jewellery and watch, wholesale agents and brokers
54149	Jewellery design services
81149	Jewellery engraving service
33991	Jewellery engraving, chasing or etching for the trade
33991	Jewellery polishing for the trade, manufacturing
81149	Jewellery repair service (without retail sales of new equipment)
44831	Jewellery store
33991	Jewellery, made of precious metal or precious or semiprecious stones, manufacturing
44831	Jewellery, precious stones and precious metals (including custom made), retail
41441	Jewellery, wholesale
33399	Jig saws, hand held power driven, manufacturing
114113	Jigging (fishing), salt water
333519	Jigs (e.g., inspection, gauging, checking), manufacturing
333519	Jigs and fixtures, for use with machine tools, manufacturing
41723	Jigs, wholesale
323119	Job printing, lithographic (except quick)
323119	Job printing, offset (except quick)
323113	Job printing, screen (except on textile fabrics)
711213	Jockeys, horse racing
31519	Jogging suits, made in knitting mills
315239	Jogging suits, women's, misses' and girls', cut and sewn from purchased fabric
32552	Joint compounds (except gypsum-based), manufacturing

32742	Joint compounds, gypsum-based, manufacturing
33321	Jointers, woodworking, manufacturing
333619	Joints, universal (except motor vehicle and aircraft), manufacturing
33635	Joints, universal, automotive, truck and bus, manufacturing
32739	Joists, girders and beams, prestressed concrete, manufacturing
332319	Joists, open web steel, long-span series, manufacturing
332329	Joists, sheet metal, manufacturing
45322	Joke shops
711513	Journalists, print, independent
711512	Journalists, radio and television, independent
323119	Journals and magazines, trade, printing without publishing
323119	Journals, scholarly, printing without publishing
33411	Joystick devices, manufacturing
61162	Judo and jiu-jitsu instruction
332439	Jugs, vacuum, light gauge metal, manufacturing
333299	Juice extractors, fruit and vegetable (i.e., food manufacturing type), manufacturing
31152	Juice pops, frozen, manufacturing
31142	Juice, fruit or vegetable, canned, manufacturing
31142	Juice, fruit or vegetable, fresh, manufacturing
71399	Juke box concession operators, in facilities operated by others
33593	Junction boxes and covers, electrical, manufacturing
81391	Junior Chambers of Commerce
41319	Junior foods, canned, wholesale
41413	Jute fabrics, piece goods, wholesale
623999	Juvenile correctional homes
91311	Juvenile courts
51112	Juvenile magazines and periodicals, publishing (except exclusively on Internet)

K

212326	Kaolin mining
32799	Kaolin, processing beyond beneficiating
33431	Karaoke machines, manufacturing
61162	Karate school
32742	Keene's cement, manufacturing
81291	Kennels, pet boarding
212398	Kernite mining
33512	Kerosene lamps, manufacturing
32411	Kerosene, made in petroleum refineries

31142	Ketchup, manufacturing
32519	Ketone compounds, not specified elsewhere by process, manufacturing
33251	Key blanks, manufacturing
31699	Key cases (except metal), manufacturing
33411	Keyboards, computer peripheral equipment, manufacturing
33632	Keyless entry systems, automotive, truck and bus, manufacturing
621499	Kidney dialysis centres
321999	Kiln drying of lumber
32712	Kiln furniture, clay, manufacturing
33399	Kilns (except cement, chemical, wood), manufacturing
333299	Kilns (i.e., cement, wood, chemical), manufacturing
61111	Kindergartens
336211	Kit car bodies, manufacturing
56191	Kit packaging services
41422	Kitchen appliances (e.g., toasters, kettles, ironers), electric, wholesale
33711	Kitchen cabinets (except free standing), wood, manufacturing
23835	Kitchen cabinets and counters, prefabricated wood, installation only
33711	Kitchen cabinets and counters, prefabricated wood, manufacturing and installation combined
41639	Kitchen cabinets, built in, wholesale
33221	Kitchen cutlery, base metal plated with precious metal, manufacturing
33221	Kitchen cutlery, non-precious metal, manufacturing
337123	Kitchen furniture, wood, manufacturing
33221	Kitchen utensils (e.g., colanders, garlic presses, ice cream scoops, spatulas), fabricated metal, manufacturing
33221	Kitchen utensils (except cutting type), fabricated metal, manufacturing
41792	Kitchen utensils, commercial, wholesale
41439	Kitchen utensils, household, wholesale
326198	Kitchen utensils, plastic, manufacturing
44311	Kitchens, complete (sinks, cabinets), retail
321999	Kitchenware (e.g., utensils, rolling pins), wood, manufacturing
442298	Kitchenware stores, retail
32711	Kitchenware, china, earthenware, pottery or stoneware, manufacturing
33993	Kites, manufacturing
33221	Knife blades, manufacturing
31331	Knit fabrics, dyeing or finishing
41411	Knit wear, wholesale
31311	Knitting and crochet thread, manufacturing

31324	Knitting fabric
31511	Knitting hosiery and socks
333299	Knitting machinery, manufacturing
31311	Knitting yarn (e.g., cotton, man-made fibre, silk, wool), made in spinning mills
45113	Knitting yarn and accessories, retail
41413	Knitting yarns, wholesale
33221	Knives (e.g., hunting, pocket, table non-precious, table precious plated), manufacturing
333519	Knives and bits, for metalworking lathes, planers and shapers, manufacturing
33521	Knives, electric, domestic, manufacturing
33221	Knives, machine (except metal cutting), manufacturing
322121	Kraft paper stock, manufacturing
212326	Kyanite mining

L

33399	Labelling (i.e., packaging machinery), manufacturing
56191	Labelling services
32222	Labels, gummed, made from purchased paper
323119	Labels, printing on a job-order basis
31322	Labels, weaving
41413	Labels, woven, wholesale
54138	Laboratories, product testing
334512	Laboratory analytical instruments (except optical), manufacturing
112999	Laboratory animal production (e.g., rats, mice, and guinea pigs)
33399	Laboratory furnaces, manufacturing
337127	Laboratory furniture (e.g., cabinets, benches, tables, stools), manufacturing
41793	Laboratory instruments and apparatus, wholesale
41793	Laboratory instruments and apparatus, wholesale and repair
334512	Laboratory standards testing equipment (e.g., capacitance, electrical resistance, inductance), manufacturing
54138	Laboratory testing service (except clinical and veterinary)
33399	Laboratory type equipment (e.g., furnaces, balances, centifruges), manufacturing
54138	Laboratory, food testing
56133	Labour leasing services (providing permanent employees paid by supplying company but under the supervision of the hiring company)

56132	Labour pools (except farm labour)
541612	Labour relation consulting services
91131	Labour relations board, federal government
81393	Labour unions
41413	Lace fabrics, wholesale
31499	Lace, burnt-out, manufacturing
31324	Lace, manufacturing
31322	Laces (e.g., shoe), textile, manufacturing
33281	Lacquering metals and metal products, for the trade
32551	Lacquers, manufacturing
41634	Lacquers, wholesale
311515	Lactose, manufacturing
321919	Ladder rounds or rungs, hardwood, manufacturing
332999	Ladders, portable, metal, manufacturing
41633	Ladders, wholesale
321999	Ladders, wood, manufacturing
44812	Ladies clothing, retail
44821	Ladies' shoes, retail
31212	Lager, brewing
23711	Lagoons, sewage treatment construction
483213	Lake (except Great Lakes) transportation (except ferries)
32513	Lakes (i.e., organic pigments), manufacturing
311611	Lamb carcasses, half-carcasses, primal and sub-primal cuts, produced in slaughtering plants
11241	Lamb raising
311614	Lamb, primal and sub-primal cuts, made from purchased meat
327215	Laminated glass, made from purchased glass
32613	Laminated plastics plate, rod and sheet, manufacturing
321215	Laminated veneer lumber (LVL), manufacturing
32222	Laminating purchased foil sheets for flexible packaging applications
32222	Laminating purchased paper for non-packaging applications
32222	Laminating purchased paper for packaging applications
32222	Laminating purchased paperboard
31332	Laminating purchased textile fabrics
325189	Lamp black, manufacturing
332329	Lamp posts, metal, manufacturing
33512	Lamp shades (except glass, plastic), manufacturing
327215	Lamp shades, made from purchased glass
326198	Lamp shades, plastics, manufacturing
442298	Lamps and lighting fixtures, electric, retail
41611	Lamps, floor, boudoir, desk, wholesale
23721	Land (except cemeteries) subdividers
54119	Land and/or title search, service
23891	Land clearing, contractors
23799	Land drainage contractor
23891	Land levelling, irrigation, contractors
41711	Land preparation machinery, agricultural, wholesale
23721	Land servicing (hydro, sewer and water), land development
23721	Land subdivision and development
61121	Land surveying institutes
54137	Land surveying services (except geophysical)
54132	Land use planning services
56221	Landfill, garbage disposal
54132	Landscape architectural services
56173	Landscape contractors
54132	Landscape planning services
56173	Landscape services
54193	Language interpretation services
54172	Language research and development services
61163	Language schools
54193	Language sign services
54193	Language translation services
41723	Lapidary equipment, wholesale
45112	Lapidary supplies, retail
33991	Lapidary work
311611	Lard, produced in slaughtering plants
41316	Lard, wholesale
333519	Laser boring, drilling and milling machines, metalworking, manufacturing
33399	Laser welding equipment, manufacturing
32629	Latex foam rubber, manufacturing
32551	Latex paints (i.e., water-based), manufacturing
32521	Latex rubber, synthetic, manufacturing
32742	Lath, gypsum, manufacturing
321111	Lath, made from logs or bolts
333519	Lathes, metal cutting, manufacturing
33321	Lathes, woodworking type, manufacturing
81231	Laundromat
81232	Laundry and drycleaning agents
31491	Laundry bags, made from purchased woven or knitted materials
32561	Laundry bleaches, formulated for household use, manufacturing
33392	Laundry carts, manufacturing
33331	Laundry machinery and equipment (except household type), manufacturing

41792	Laundry machinery and equipment, wholesale
41792	Laundry machinery and equipment, wholesale and repair
32561	Laundry soap, chips and powder, manufacturing
41841	Laundry soap, chips and powder, wholesale
326191	Laundry tubs, plastics, manufacturing
41612	Laundry tubs, wholesale
114113	Laver gathering
54111	Law offices
61131	Law schools
811411	Lawn and garden equipment, repair service (without retail sales of new equipment)
33221	Lawn and garden handtools, non-powered, manufacturing
33311	Lawn and garden machinery (e.g., hedge trimmers, lawn mowers, tractors), powered, manufacturing
44422	Lawn and garden ornaments, retail
44422	Lawn and garden supplies, retail
44421	Lawn blower/vacuum, retail
71399	Lawn bowling clubs
41839	Lawn care chemical products, wholesale
56173	Lawn care services
41439	Lawn furniture, wholesale
33311	Lawn mowers (except agricultural type), powered, manufacturing
33221	Lawn mowers, non-powered, manufacturing
56173	Lawn seeding services
56173	Lawn spraying services
23822	Lawn sprinkler system installation, contractors
54111	Lawyers, private practice
32541	Laxative preparations, manufacturing
326121	Lay flat tubing, plastics, manufacturing
54141	Layouts-office, factory (designers, interior)
33441	LCD (liquid crystal display) unit screens, manufacturing
212291	Leaching of uranium or radium ore at mine site
41621	Lead and zinc fabricated basic products, wholesale
23839	Lead lining walls for x-ray room, contractor
212231	Lead ore milling
212231	Lead ore mining
56291	Lead paint removal contractors
32513	Lead pigments, manufacturing
41621	Lead primary forms and basic shapes, wholesale
33149	Lead rolling, drawing or extruding, purchased metal or scrap
33141	Lead smelting and primary refining
212231	Lead, zinc, ore, beneficiating
212231	Lead-zinc ore milling
212231	Lead-zinc ore mining
332611	Leaf springs, manufacturing
31221	Leaf tobacco processing and aging
332999	Leaf, metal, manufacturing
81392	Learned societies
54172	Learning disability research and development services
53112	Leasing non-residential buildings
51821	Leasing of computer time
53249	Leasing of industrial machinery and equipment
52222	Leasing, in combination with sales financing
448199	Leather (including suede) clothing stores
41899	Leather and cut stock, wholesale
41411	Leather and sheep-lined clothing, women's and children's, wholesale
315292	Leather clothing (e.g., capes, coats, hats, jackets), manufacturing
31699	Leather cut stock, boot and shoe, manufacturing
32561	Leather finishing assistants, manufacturing
31621	Leather footwear, manufacturing
31599	Leather gloves and mittens (except athletic), manufacturing
41899	Leather goods (except footwear), wholesale
81143	Leather goods repair shops
31699	Leather goods, small personal (e.g., coin purses, eyeglass cases, key cases), manufacturing
31611	Leather tanning, currying and finishing
333299	Leather working machinery, manufacturing
31332	Leather, artificial, made from purchased fabric
31611	Leather, manufacturing
32222	Leatherboard (i.e., paperboard-based), made from purchased paperboard
315292	Leatherette clothing, manufacturing
311225	Lecithin, made from purchased oils
711512	Lecturers, independent
33441	LED's (light emitting diodes), manufacturing
31511	Leg warmers, manufacturing
54111	Legal aid services
91911	Legation services, foreign government in Canada

91291	Legislative assemblies, provincial government	33911	Life preservers, inflatable, manufacturing
11113	Legume (forage) farming	326198	Life rafts, inflatable plastics, manufacturing
11132	Lemon groves and farms	32629	Life rafts, inflatable rubber, manufacturing
519121	Lending libraries	524131	Life reinsurance
327215	Lens blanks, optical and ophthalmic, made from purchased glass	54171	Life sciences research and development laboratories
327214	Lens blanks, optical and ophthalmic, made in glass-making plants	56132	Lifeguard supply service
326198	Lens blanks, optical and ophthalmic, plastics, manufacturing	33911	Lifejackets, plastics, manufacturing
		41723	Lift trucks, wholesale
33911	Lens grinding, ophthalmic (except in retail stores)	33511	Light bulbs and tubes, electric, manufacturing
44613	Lens grinding, ophthalmic, in retail stores	41611	Light bulbs, electric, wholesale
33331	Lens polishing (except ophthalmic)	33331	Light meters, photographic, manufacturing
33331	Lenses (except ophthalmic), manufacturing	23799	Light rail system construction
		48511	Light rail systems
326193	Lenses, plastics, motor vehicle, manufacturing	325999	Lighter fluids (e.g., charcoal, cigarette), manufacturing
11113	Lentils farming, dry	48839	Lighter operation services
31519	Leotards, made in knitting mills	33999	Lighters, cigar and cigarette (except precious metal and motor vehicle), manufacturing
315239	Leotards, women's, misses' and girls', cut and sewn from purchased fabric		
212398	Lepidolite mining	41899	Lighters, cigar and cigarette, wholesale
53119	Lessors of railroad property	48831	Lighthouse operation
33331	Letter folding, stuffing and sealing machines, manufacturing	33512	Lighting fixtures, manufacturing
		41611	Lighting fixtures, residential, commercial and industrial, wholesale
453999	Lettering and designing of monuments, retail	33632	Lighting fixtures, vehicular, manufacturing
541899	Lettering services, door and window		
32312	Letterpress plate preparation services	561799	Lighting maintenance service (i.e., bulb and fuse replacement and cleaning)
323119	Letterpress printing		
333299	Letterpress printing presses, manufacturing	23821	Lighting systems, electric, installation
		711512	Lighting technicians, theatrical, independent
33995	Letters and numerals (except wood and paper), for signs, manufacturing	238299	Lightning rods and conductors, installation
32223	Letters, die-cut, made from purchased cardboard	32521	Lignin plastics, manufacturing
		212116	Lignite mining
111219	Lettuce farming	11132	Lime groves and farms
23799	Levee construction, general contractors	11511	Lime spreading service, agricultural
33221	Levels, carpenters', manufacturing	32741	Lime, manufacturing
524135	Liability reinsurance carriers	212315	Limestone quarry
519121	Libraries (except motion picture and video tape stock footage)	41639	Limestone, wholesale
		72221	Limited-service restaurant
51219	Libraries, motion picture film, stock footage	72221	Limited-service restaurant, licensed
		21221	Limonite mining
51219	Libraries, video tape, stock footage	48532	Limousine rental with driver
91291	License plate issuer (government office), provincial government	532111	Limousine rental, without driver
		48532	Limousine service (except scheduled)
332118	Lids, jar, metal, stamping	48599	Limousine service to airports or stations, scheduled
561611	Lie detection service		
91291	Lieutenant-Governor's office, provincial government		

811121	Limousine, produced by custom conversion
33121	Line pipe for oil or gas, made from purchased steel
56173	Line slash (rights-of-way) maintenance
31321	Linen fabrics, broad-woven, weaving
41413	Linen piece goods, woven, wholesale
442298	Linen shops, retail
81233	Linen supply service
41911	Linen, drapery and other textile furnishings, business to business (B2B) electronic markets, wholesale
41912	Linens, draperies and other textile furnishings, wholesale agents and brokers
32712	Liner brick and plates, vitrified clay, manufacturing
448199	Lingerie stores, retail
41411	Lingerie, wholesale
315231	Lingerie, women's, misses' and girls', cut and sewn from purchased fabric
31599	Linings (e.g., coat, dress, millinery, necktie, suit), made from purchased fabric
41432	Linoleum floor covering, wholesale
326198	Linoleum floor coverings, manufacturing
44221	Linoleum, installation combined with selling
11112	Linseed (flaxseed), growing
311224	Linseed oil, cake and meal, made in crushing mills
311225	Linseed oil, made from purchased oils
41841	Linseed oil, wholesale
32739	Lintels, concrete, manufacturing
32562	Lipsticks, manufacturing
48899	Liquefaction and regasification of natural gas for purposes of transport at mine site
33242	Liquefied petroleum gas (LPG) cylinders, manufacturing
454312	Liquefied petroleum gas (LPG), delivered to customers' premises, retail
22121	Liquefied petroleum gas (LPG), distribution through mains
211113	Liquefied petroleum gases (LPG) natural
32411	Liquefied petroleum gases (LPG), made in petroleum refineries
41211	Liquefied petroleum gases, wholesale
31214	Liqueurs, manufacturing
484221	Liquid petroleum products trucking, local
484231	Liquid petroleum products trucking, long-distance
41819	Liquid waste recovery (collection only)
49221	Liquor delivery services (dial-a-bottle)
44531	Liquor stores, retail
41322	Liquor, wholesale
31214	Liquor-based coolers, manufacturing
31214	Liquors, distilling and blending (except brandy)
53139	Listing service, real estate
71141	Literary agents
32513	Litharge, manufacturing
325189	Lithium compounds, not specified elsewhere by process, manufacturing
212398	Lithium mineral mining
32312	Lithographic plate preparation services
323119	Lithographic printing (except manifold business forms, quick printing, textile fabrics), without publishing
333299	Lithographic printing presses, manufacturing
32513	Lithopone, manufacturing
711311	Live arts centres, promoting events
41111	Live bait, wholesale
711311	Live theatres, promoting events
81411	Live-in babysitter
81411	Live-in housekeeper
112991	Livestock and animal specialty farms, general
112991	Livestock and poultry combination farm
41111	Livestock auctioning, with own facilities
54169	Livestock breeding consulting services
11521	Livestock breeding services
112991	Livestock combination farm
112991	Livestock combination feedlots
332329	Livestock corrals, cattle holders and stalls, metal, manufacturing
48899	Livestock feeding station service, livestock in transit
41831	Livestock feeds, prepared, wholesale
311119	Livestock feeds, supplements, concentrates and premixes, manufacturing
484239	Livestock hauling, long-distance
484229	Livestock trucking, local
41111	Livestock, wholesale
41912	Livestock, wholesale agents and brokers
337123	Living room furniture, wood, manufacturing
112999	Llama production
33441	Loaded computer boards, manufacturing
33312	Loaders, shovel, manufacturing
48821	Loading and unloading rail freight cars
48832	Loading and unloading ships or boats

488119	Loading service, aircraft
52231	Loan brokers' or agents' (i.e., independent) offices
54182	Lobbyists, offices of
31171	Lobster cannery
114113	Lobster catching
41314	Lobsters, fresh or frozen (except frozen packaged), wholesale
48511	Local and suburban transit systems, mixed mode
33421	Local area network (LAN) communication equipment (e.g., bridges, gateways, routers), manufacturing
54151	Local area network (LAN) systems integrators
48511	Local bus service
49221	Local delivery service, small parcels
81394	Local political organization
517111	Local telephone carrier, except wireless and cable operators
48411	Local trucking service, general freight
23799	Lock and waterway construction, general contractors
337215	Lockers (except refrigerated), manufacturing
33251	Locks (except coin-operated and time), manufacturing
41633	Locks and related materials, wholesale
41792	Locksmith equipment and supplies, wholesale
561622	Locksmith services
561622	Locksmith services, with or without sales of locking devices, safes, and security vaults
33632	Locomotive and railroad car light fixtures, manufacturing
333619	Locomotive diesel engines, manufacturing
48821	Locomotives and railroad cars, repair
33651	Locomotives, manufacturing
41799	Locomotives, wholesale
72131	Lodging houses operated by organizations for members only
72131	Lodging houses, private
321992	Log cabins, prefabricated wood, manufacturing
113311	Log cutting (forest trees)
113311	Log grading, scaling, sorting
11531	Log hauling in the bush (i.e., within the logging limits)
23611	Log home, construction
483115	Log rafting and towing, coastal
483213	Log rafting and towing, inland waters (except Great Lakes)

484223	Log trucking, local (i.e., to the mill)
484233	Log trucking, long-distance
113312	Logging contractor (felling, cutting, bucking)
54133	Logging engineering services
41721	Logging machinery and equipment, wholesale
41721	Logging machinery and equipment, wholesale and repair
482112	Logging railways
336212	Logging trailers, manufacturing
541619	Logistics management consulting services
41891	Logs and bolts, wholesale
41912	Logs and wood chips, wholesale agents and brokers
51791	Long distance telecommunication resellers (except satellite)
517111	Long-distance telephone carrier, facilities-based
51791	Long-distance telephone resellers (except satellite)
51741	Long-distance telephone, satellite-communications carriers
48832	Longshoremen service
333299	Looms, textile, manufacturing
323119	Looseleaf binders and devices, manufacturing
41821	Looseleaf binders, wholesale
32223	Looseleaf fillers and paper, made from purchased paper
322121	Looseleaf fillers and paper, made in paper mills
713291	Lotteries, operation of
713291	Lottery control boards (i.e., operating lottery)
713291	Lottery ticket sales agent (except retail stores)
713291	Lottery ticket vendors (except retail stores)
23816	Low slope roofing installation
23816	Low slope roofing installation (cold or hot apply)
23821	Low voltage electrical work
33392	Lowering devices, burial, manufacturing
32411	Lubricating oils and greases, made in petroleum refineries
32419	Lubricating oils and greases, petroleum, made from refined petroleum
325999	Lubricating oils and greases, synthetic, manufacturing
41211	Lubricating oils and greases, wholesale
811199	Lubrication services, motor vehicles
44832	Luggage and leather good stores, retail

44832	Luggage and travelling cases, retail
41633	Luggage and trunk fittings, wholesale
33251	Luggage hardware, metal, manufacturing
31499	Luggage linings, manufacturing
33639	Luggage racks, car top, manufacturing
81143	Luggage repair shop
31699	Luggage, all materials, manufacturing
41899	Luggage, wholesale
321111	Lumber (i.e., rough, dressed), made from logs or bolts
44419	Lumber and planing mill product dealers, retail
41632	Lumber and planing mill products, wholesale
333299	Lumber drying kilns, manufacturing
49319	Lumber terminals, storage
321919	Lumber, dimension, made by resawing purchased lumber
321111	Lumber, hardwood dimension (e.g., 2x4), made from logs or bolts
321999	Lumber, kiln drying
321215	Lumber, parallel strand, manufacturing
41912	Lumber, plywood and millwork, wholesale agents and brokers
41632	Lumber, rough or dressed, wholesale
321111	Lumber, softwood dimension (e.g., 2x4), made from logs or bolts
321114	Lumber, treating with creosote or other preservatives
72233	Lunch wagon
311614	Luncheon meat (except poultry), made from purchased meat
311611	Luncheon meat (except poultry), produced in slaughtering plants
311615	Luncheon meat, poultry, manufacturing

M

311823	Macaroni, dry, manufacturing
33221	Machine knives (except metal cutting), manufacturing
238299	Machine rigging, contractors
33271	Machine shops
33271	Machine shops providing custom and repair services
333519	Machine tool attachments and accessories, manufacturing
41723	Machine tools and accessories, wholesale
333519	Machine tools, metal forming, manufacturing
333519	Machine tools, rebuilding
524129	Machinery and equipment insurance

41723	Machinery and equipment, industrial (except farm and electrical), wholesale
41799	Machinery, equipment and parts for railroad locomotives, aircraft, ships and boats, wholesale
41791	Machines, commercial (except electronic computers), wholesale
41791	Machines, office, wholesale
33271	Machining composite materials parts
33271	Machining plastic parts
33221	Machinists' precision measuring tools (except optical), manufacturing
45112	Macramé supplies, retail
54184	Magazine advertising representatives, independent
51112	Magazine publishers, all formats, publishing (except exclusively on Internet)
45439	Magazine subscription sales (except mail order), retail
45121	Magazines and newspapers, retail
323119	Magazines and periodicals, printing without publishing
454113	Magazines, mail order, retail
51112	Magazines, publishing (except exclusively on Internet)
51112	Magazines, publishing and printing combined
41442	Magazines, wholesale
71119	Magic shows
711512	Magicians, independent
32712	Magnesia refractory cement, manufacturing
212326	Magnesite mining
325189	Magnesium compounds, not specified elsewhere by process, manufacturing
212299	Magnesium ore mining
33149	Magnesium rolling, drawing or extruding, purchased metal or scrap
33141	Magnesium smelting and primary refining
212398	Magnesium sulphate mine
33592	Magnet wire, insulated, manufacturing
334512	Magnetic resonance imaging (MRI) devices, manufacturing
33461	Magnetic tapes, cassettes and disks, blank, manufacturing
21221	Magnetite ore mining
32711	Magnets, permanent, ceramic or ferrite, manufacturing
33911	Magnifiers, vision correcting type, manufacturing
33911	Magnifying glasses, manufacturing
561722	Maid cleaning services
56131	Maid registries

56143	Mail box centres, private
56149	Mail consolidation services
49111	Mail delivery, private (except air)
41791	Mail handling machines, wholesale
41791	Mail handling machines, wholesale and repair
454113	Mail order houses, retail
454113	Mail order offices of department stores, retail
49111	Mail service, contract
322219	Mailing cases and tubes, paper fibre (i.e., fibre body, ends of any material), made from purchased paperboard
51114	Mailing list compilers (except exclusively on Internet)
33411	Mainframe computers, manufacturing
81121	Maintenance and repair of computers and related equipment
48831	Maintenance of piers, docks, wharves
56173	Maintenance of plants and shrubs in buildings
56173	Maintenance of rights-of-way (i.e., controlling vegetation)
48821	Maintenance of rights-of-way and structures, railway
32562	Make-up (i.e., cosmetics), manufacturing
31194	Malt extract, manufacturing
311214	Malt, manufacturing
41319	Malt, wholesale
517112	Managed VoIP services providers, cable
71141	Management agencies for artists, entertainers and other public figures
54151	Management information systems design consulting services
551113	Management offices, subsidiary
56111	Management service, operating staff not furnished (except complete operations of client business)
53131	Managers of commercial real estate
53131	Managers of residential real estate
71141	Managers, artists
71141	Managers, entertainers
71141	Managers, sports figures
56111	Managing office of dentist, general
56111	Managing office of dentist, specialist
56111	Managing office of doctors
56111	Managing office of physicians and surgeons
325189	Manganese dioxide, manufacturing
212299	Manganese ore dressing and beneficiating
212299	Manganese ore mining
21221	Manganiferous ore valued for iron content, mining

212299	Manganite mining
331511	Manhole covers, cast iron, manufacturing
812115	Manicure and pedicure salons
323116	Manifold business forms, printing
41821	Manifold business forms, wholesale
33631	Manifolds (i.e., intake and exhaust), automotive and truck gasoline engine, manufacturing
31321	Man-made fabrics, broad-woven, weaving
31322	Man-made fibre fabric, narrow woven (i.e., 30 cm/12 in. or less in width), weaving
32522	Man-made fibres and filaments, manufacturing
41841	Man-made fibres, wholesale
541899	Mannequin decorating services
41791	Mannequins, wholesale
91221	Manpower employer services, provincial government
56132	Manpower pools
91131	Manpower program, federal (job placement)
23834	Mantel work (stone) installation
23834	Mantel, marble or stone, installation
321919	Mantels, wood, manufacturing
33512	Mantles, incandescent, manufacturing
81391	Manufacturers' associations
41723	Manufacturing industry machinery and equipment, wholesale
41723	Manufacturing industry machinery and equipment, wholesale and repair
541619	Manufacturing operations improvement consulting services
111994	Maple products production, central facility
111994	Maple sap, gathering of
111994	Maple sugar bush, operating
111994	Maple syrup and products production
54137	Mapmaking (except geophysical) services
323119	Maps, printing without publishing
51113	Maps, publishing (except exclusively on Internet)
41442	Maps, wholesale
41639	Marble building stone, wholesale
212316	Marble quarry
23834	Marble, granite and slate work (interior), contractors
311225	Margarine (including imitation), made from purchased fats and oils
311221	Margarine and other corn oils, made by wet-milling corn

311224	Margarine, cooking oil and similar oil and fat products, made in oilseed crushing mills
311225	Margarine-butter blend, made from purchased fats and oils
71393	Marinas
41633	Marine and rigging hardware, wholesale
48839	Marine cargo checkers
48832	Marine cargo handling
23799	Marine construction, general contractors
61121	Marine engineering school, post-secondary
54133	Marine engineering services
31171	Marine fats, oils and meal, manufacturing
33251	Marine hardware, metal, manufacturing
524129	Marine insurance
33241	Marine power boilers, manufacturing
114114	Marine products harvesting, freshwater
114113	Marine products harvesting, salt water
41799	Marine propulsion machinery and equipment, wholesale
488331	Marine salvaging service
44719	Marine service stations, retail
488511	Marine shipping agency
44122	Marine supply dealers, retail
54199	Marine surveyor (i.e., ship appraisal) services
48839	Marine surveyors, cargo
488339	Marine vessel traffic reporting
41811	Marine wrecking, ships for scrap
33994	Marker boards (i.e., whiteboards), manufacturing
54191	Market analysis or research services
111219	Market gardening
111419	Market gardening, greenhouse
41821	Marking devices, pens and pencils, wholesale
31142	Marmalade, manufacturing
62419	Marriage (family) counselling services
81299	Marriage bureau
31134	Marshmallows, manufacturing
61162	Martial arts clubs
32222	Masking tape, made from purchased paper
41639	Masonry bricks, blocks, tile and stone, builders' supply, wholesale
32731	Masonry cement, manufacturing
23814	Masonry pointing, cleaning or caulking
33221	Masons' handtools, manufacturing
41639	Masons' materials, wholesale
33461	Mass reproduction of pre-packaged software

23799	Mass transit, construction
81219	Massage parlours
81233	Mat and rug launders
325999	Matches and match books, manufacturing
41723	Materials handling equipment, wholesale and repair
53249	Materials handling machinery and equipment, rental
541619	Materials management consulting services
23621	Materials recovery facilities, construction
56292	Materials recovery facility (i.e., sorting recyclable materials)
62231	Maternity hospitals
44812	Maternity shops, retail
54171	Mathematics research and development services
332619	Mats and matting, made from purchased wire
31411	Mats and matting, made from textile materials
32629	Mats and matting, rubber, manufacturing
81149	Mattress renovating and repair shops (without retail sales of new equipment)
332619	Mattress springs and spring units, made from purchased wire
44211	Mattress stores (including custom made), retail
41439	Mattresses and box springs, wholesale
33791	Mattresses and springs, manufacturing
326198	Mattresses, air, plastics, manufacturing
32629	Mattresses, air, rubber, manufacturing
81222	Mausoleum
31194	Mayonnaise, manufacturing
91391	Mayor's office
33633	McPherson struts, manufacturing
321216	MDF (medium density fibreboard), manufacturing
62421	Meal delivery programs
311221	Meal, corn oil, made by wet-milling corn
62421	Meals on wheels, social services
41793	Measuring and measuring-controlling instruments, professional, wholesale
41611	Measuring and testing equipment, electrical (except automotive), wholesale
33221	Measuring tools, machinists' (except optical), manufacturing
311614	Meat and bone meal, and tankage, processed in rendering plants

41912	Meat and meat products, wholesale agents and brokers
31142	Meat bouillon, made in dehydration plants
311614	Meat canning (except poultry, small game, pet food, baby food), from purchased meat
311615	Meat canning, poultry (except baby and pet food)
41316	Meat carcasses, wholesale
311614	Meat curing, drying, salting, smoking or pickling, made from purchased meat
44521	Meat market, retail (store)
41316	Meat preparations (except canned), wholesale
311615	Meat products (e.g., hot dogs, luncheon meats, sausages), made from a combination of poultry and other meats
31142	Meat, baby food, canning
311611	Meat, cured or smoked (except poultry and small game), produced in slaughtering plants
311611	Meat, fresh, chilled or frozen (except poultry and small game), produced in slaughtering plants
41316	Meats, fresh, wholesale
41319	Meats, packaged frozen, wholesale
41723	Mechanical and power transmission equipment, wholesale
41723	Mechanical and power transmission equipment, wholesale and repair
54133	Mechanical engineering services
238299	Mechanical equipment insulation
31331	Mechanical finishing of clothing
32629	Mechanical rubber goods (i.e, extruded, lathe-cut, moulded), manufacturing
54138	Mechanical testing, laboratories
322111	Mechanical wood pulp, manufacturing
33392	Mechanics' creepers, manufacturing
33221	Mechanics' handtools, non-powered, manufacturing
33331	Mechanisms for coin-operated machines, manufacturing
33991	Medals, precious or semi-precious metal, manufacturing
54184	Media advertising representatives, independent
54184	Media advertising representatives, offices of
54183	Media buying agencies
54184	Media representatives, independent
91131	Mediation and conciliation services, federal
91221	Mediation and conciliation services, provincial government

33911	Medical and related instruments, apparatus and equipment (except electro-medical), manufacturing
81392	Medical associations
53249	Medical equipment rental and leasing, commercial and industrial
81121	Medical equipment repair, electrical
334512	Medical equipment, ultrasonic, manufacturing
41452	Medical glass, wholesale
54143	Medical illustration services
524299	Medical insurance claims, processing of, contract or fee basis
62151	Medical laboratories (clinical)
62111	Medical offices, specialist, physicians and surgeons
62111	Medical pathologists' offices
62151	Medical pathology laboratories
54192	Medical photography services
334512	Medical radiation therapy equipment, manufacturing
54171	Medical research and development laboratories
61131	Medical schools
41793	Medical, surgical, hospital equipment, wholesale
32541	Medicinal chemicals, uncompounded, manufacturing
41452	Medicinal herbs, non-prescription, wholesale
41451	Medicinals and botanicals, wholesale
321216	Medium density fibreboard (MDF), manufacturing
212398	Meerschaum mining or quarrying
53112	Meeting hall operating
32521	Melamine resins, manufacturing
111219	Melon farming
81341	Membership associations, civic or social
721111	Membership hotel
81222	Memorial gardens (i.e., burial place)
33441	Memory boards, manufacturing
33441	Memory chips, semiconductor, manufacturing
81131	Mending service, fish net
41411	Men's and boys' clothing and furnishings, wholesale
31519	Mens' and boys suits and jackets, made in knitting mills
41411	Men's clothing and furnishings, wholesale
44811	Men's clothing stores
41912	Men's clothing, wholesale agents and brokers
31621	Men's footwear (except orthopedic extension shoes), manufacturing

812114	Men's hair stylist shop
62221	Mental hospitals
56145	Mercantile credit reporting bureaus
31331	Mercerizing textile fibres and fabrics
454111	Merchandise retailing via Internet
41792	Merchandising machines, automatic, wholesale
41792	Merchandising machines, automatic, wholesale and repair
45421	Merchandising, automatic (sale of products through vending machines), retail
23611	Merchant builders (i.e., building on own land, for sale), residential
81391	Merchants' associations
325189	Mercury compounds, not specified elsewhere by process, manufacturing
212299	Mercury ore mining
41621	Mercury, wholesale
332619	Mesh, made from purchased wire
331317	Mesh, wire, made in aluminum wire drawing plants
56142	Message service, telephone answering
49211	Messenger service, courier
41912	Metal and metal products (except ores), wholesale agents and brokers
41639	Metal buildings, wholesale
333299	Metal casting machinery, manufacturing
41892	Metal concentrates and ores (ferrous), wholesale
333519	Metal cutting machine tools, manufacturing
333519	Metal forming machine tools, manufacturing
213117	Metal mining, prospect drilling for, on a contract basis
333511	Metal moulds (e.g., for working plastics, rubber, glass), manufacturing
23839	Metal partitions (e.g., office, washroom), installation
32561	Metal polishes (i.e., tarnish removers), manufacturing
41639	Metal siding and roofing materials, wholesale
332118	Metal stampings (except automotive, cans, coins), unfinished, manufacturing
23812	Metal storage tank erection
41811	Metal waste and scrap, wholesale
41841	Metal working compounds, wholesale
41634	Metallic paints, wholesale
32513	Metallic pigments, inorganic, manufacturing
31332	Metallizing textile fabrics
54138	Metallurgical testing laboratories
53249	Metalworking machinery and equipment rental
41723	Metalworking machinery, wholesale
81121	Meteorological instrument repair
334512	Meteorological instruments, manufacturing
54199	Meteorological services
56199	Meter reading services, contract
335315	Metering panels, electric, manufacturing
334512	Meters (except electrical and industrial process control), manufacturing
334512	Meters, electrical (i.e, graphic recording, panelboard, pocket, portable), manufacturing
334512	Meters, industrial process control type, manufacturing
32519	Methanol (methyl alcohol), natural, manufacturing
32519	Methanol (methyl alcohol), synthetic, manufacturing
32519	Methyl alcohol (methanol), natural, manufacturing
32519	Methyl alcohol (methanol), synthetic, manufacturing
212398	Mica mining
32799	Mica products, manufacturing
311119	Micro and macro premixes, livestock, manufacturing
33411	Microcomputers, manufacturing
33441	Microcontroller chips, manufacturing
33331	Microfiche equipment (e.g., cameras, projectors, readers), manufacturing
33331	Microfilm equipment (e.g., cameras, projectors, readers), manufacturing
41791	Microfilm equipment and supplies, wholesale
51821	Microfilm recording and imaging service
33431	Microphones, manufacturing
33441	Microprocessor chips, manufacturing
81121	Microscopes, repair
23799	Microtunneling contractors
337123	Microwave cabinets, free standing, wood, manufacturing
51791	Microwave communications resellers
33331	Microwave ovens, commercial type, manufacturing
41422	Microwave ovens, household, wholesale
23713	Microwave relay towers, construction
62139	Midwives' offices
31331	Mildew proofing textile fabrics and products

61111	Military academies, elementary or secondary
33699	Military armoured vehicles, manufacturing
91111	Military bases and camps
91111	Military defence services
622111	Military hospital
72241	Military messes (npf)
91111	Military messes (pf)
712115	Military museums
61131	Military training schools (university-degree granting)
445299	Milk and other dairy products specialty stores
32222	Milk carton board stock, made from purchased paperboard
32213	Milk carton board, made in paperboard mills
322219	Milk cartons, made from purchased paper or paperboard
484221	Milk hauling, local
311511	Milk processing (e.g., bottling, homogenizing, pasteurizing, vitaminizing)
333299	Milk processing machinery (i.e., food manufacturing type), manufacturing
11242	Milk production, goat farm
41723	Milk products manufacturing machinery and equipment, wholesale
311511	Milk substitutes, manufacturing
311511	Milk, acidophilus, manufacturing
311515	Milk, concentrated, condensed, dried, evaporated or powdered, manufacturing
311511	Milk, fluid (except canned), manufacturing
11212	Milk, fluid, raw, producing
41312	Milk, processed, wholesale
41119	Milk, raw, wholesale
311515	Milk, UHT (ultra-high temperature), manufacturing
311511	Milk-based drinks (except dietary), manufacturing
311515	Milk-based drinks, dietary, manufacturing
33311	Milking machines, manufacturing
11119	Millet, growing
44815	Millinery stores, retail
41413	Millinery supplies, wholesale
31599	Millinery, made from purchased fabric
41411	Millinery, wholesale
333519	Milling machines, metalworking, manufacturing
23835	Millwork installation
41632	Millwork products, wholesale

11119	Milo farming
23621	Mine loading and discharge station, construction
113311	Mine timbers, cutting
41321	Mineral and spring waters, wholesale
33313	Mineral beneficiating machinery, manufacturing
41722	Mineral beneficiation machinery, wholesale
41722	Mineral beneficiation machinery, wholesale and repair
311119	Mineral feed supplements for animals (except dogs and cats), manufacturing
311111	Mineral feed supplements, dog and cat, manufacturing
91291	Mineral resources programs, provincial government
445299	Mineral water, retail
31211	Mineral waters, purifying and bottling
32799	Mineral wool insulation materials, manufacturing
41639	Mineral wool insulation materials, wholesale
32799	Mineral wool products (e.g., board, insulation, tile), manufacturing
71399	Miniature golf courses
33411	Minicomputers, manufacturing
33111	Mini-mills, steel
81391	Mining associations
33313	Mining cars, manufacturing
212233	Mining copper bearing ores
54133	Mining engineering services
212395	Mining gypsum
212231	Mining lead-zinc bearing ores
33651	Mining locomotives and parts, manufacturing
53241	Mining machinery and equipment, rental
81131	Mining machinery and equipment, repair
41912	Mining machinery and equipment, wholesale agents and brokers
41722	Mining machinery, wholesale
41722	Mining machinery, wholesale and repair
212299	Mining molybdenum bearing ores
53119	Mining property leasing
33313	Mining, underground, machinery, manufacturing
33611	Mini-vans, assembling on chassis of own manufacture
53113	Miniwarehouse rental or leasing
11293	Mink production
111999	Mint farming, except greenhouse grown
33991	Minting of coins
41439	Mirrors (except automotive), wholesale

327215	Mirrors, framed or unframed, made from purchased glass
442298	Mirrors, retail
561611	Missing person tracing service
91141	Missions established in foreign countries, federal government
81311	Missions, religious organization
33221	Mitre boxes, manufacturing
31214	Mixed drinks, alcoholic, manufacturing
11112	Mixed oilseeds (except Soybean), farming
111219	Mixed vegetables growing
311822	Mixes, flour (e.g., biscuit, cake, doughnut, pancake), made from purchased flour
325314	Mixing purchased fertilizer materials
321991	Mobile buildings for commercial use, manufacturing
72233	Mobile canteens, service
56174	Mobile cleaning, carpets and rugs
51721	Mobile data services
45393	Mobile home dealers, retail
53119	Mobile home park operating
23899	Mobile home set-up contractor
23899	Mobile home site set up and tie down, contractors
53119	Mobile home sites, operators of
484229	Mobile home towing service, local
484239	Mobile home towing service, long-distance
321991	Mobile homes, manufacturing
41899	Mobile homes, wholesale
51721	Mobile Internet service
51721	Mobile messaging service (text, picture, video)
51721	Mobile telephone communications carriers
51791	Mobile virtual network operators (MVNO)
811192	Mobile wash unit (trucks, autos)
33993	Model kits, manufacturing
56131	Model registries
56132	Model supply services
71141	Modelling agents
33994	Modelling clay, manufacturing
54142	Modelling services (for scale models)
711512	Models, independent
33421	Modems, carrier equipment, manufacturing
33441	Modems, personal computer, manufacturing
41732	Modems, wholesale
71112	Modern dance companies
321992	Modular buildings, prefabricated, wood frame, manufacturing

23839	Modular furniture system attachment and installation
337214	Modular furniture systems, office (except wood), manufacturing
337213	Modular furniture systems, wood office, manufacturing
23611	Modular housing assembly and installation on site, construction
11242	Mohair farming
31131	Molasses, manufacturing
11251	Mollusk production, farm raising
331317	Molten aluminum, made from purchased aluminum
212299	Molybdenum ore mining
81311	Monasteries (except schools)
212299	Monazite mining
526914	Money market funds
52239	Money order issuance services
33411	Monitors, computer peripheral equipment, manufacturing
23799	Monorail construction
33392	Monorail systems (except passenger), manufacturing
48511	Monorail transport, urban
48711	Monorails, scenic and sightseeing
212316	Monumental and ornamental stone, marble, rough, mining
41899	Monuments and grave markers, wholesale
32739	Monuments and tombstones, concrete, manufacturing
32799	Monuments and tombstones, cut stone (except finishing or lettering to order only), manufacturing
33999	Mops, floor and dust, manufacturing
32561	Mordants, manufacturing
32712	Mortars, refractory, manufacturing
52231	Mortgage brokerages
52231	Mortgage brokers' or agents' (i.e., independent) offices
526913	Mortgage funds
526989	Mortgage investment funds
41792	Morticians' goods, wholesale
81221	Mortuaries
33441	MOS (metal oxide silicon) devices, manufacturing
32712	Mosaic tile, ceramic, manufacturing
11321	Moss, gathering of
337127	Motel furniture, manufacturing
56111	Motel management, operating staff not furnished (except complete operations of client business)
721114	Motel, accommodation services
51219	Motion picture (or video) editing services

51219	Motion picture and video post-production services
51211	Motion picture and video production
56131	Motion picture casting bureau
54169	Motion picture consulting services
711512	Motion picture directors, independent
51212	Motion picture distributing
53249	Motion picture equipment rental
51213	Motion picture exhibition
51213	Motion picture exhibitors for airlines
51212	Motion picture film distributors
51219	Motion picture film library, stock footage
51219	Motion picture film processing, editing and titling
325999	Motion picture film, manufacturing
51219	Motion picture laboratories
51219	Motion picture or video titling or sub-titling
711512	Motion picture producers, independent
51211	Motion picture production
51211	Motion picture production and distribution
51219	Motion picture production special effects, post-production
51219	Motion picture stock footage, film libraries
41792	Motion picture studio and theatre equipment, wholesale
41792	Motion picture studio and theatre equipment, wholesale and repair
51211	Motion picture studios, producing motion pictures
51213	Motion picture theatres, drive-ins
51213	Motion picture theatres, indoor
44122	Motor bicycles, retail
48521	Motor coach operation, interurban and rural
41512	Motor coaches, wholesale
721112	Motor court
484122	Motor freight carrier, general, long-distance, less-than-truckload
484121	Motor freight carrier, general, long-distance, truckload
44121	Motor home dealers, retail
53212	Motor home rental
336215	Motor homes, self-contained, assembling on purchased chassis
33612	Motor homes, self-contained, mounted on heavy truck chassis of own manufacture
33611	Motor homes, self-contained, mounted on light duty truck chassis of own manufacture
41519	Motor homes, wholesale
41519	Motor homes, wholesale and repair
721112	Motor hotel
325999	Motor oils, synthetic, manufacturing
81131	Motor repair, electric
41519	Motor scooters, wholesale
41519	Motor scooters, wholesale and repair
56159	Motor travel clubs
33399	Motor truck scales, manufacturing
811111	Motor vehicle (except motorcycle), general repair service
33639	Motor vehicle air-conditioning systems and compressors, manufacturing
32622	Motor vehicle belts and hoses, rubber or plastics, manufacturing
44112	Motor vehicle dealers, used, retail
41531	Motor vehicle dismantling
811199	Motor vehicle emissions testing, without repairs
811112	Motor vehicle exhaust systems replacement service
238299	Motor vehicle garage and service station mechanical equipment (e.g., gasoline pumps, hoists), installation
811122	Motor vehicle glass replacement service
33251	Motor vehicle hardware, metal, manufacturing
33636	Motor vehicle interior systems (e.g., headliners, panels, seats, trim), manufacturing
56199	Motor vehicle licences, issuer, private franchise
91291	Motor vehicle license bureau, provincial government
33637	Motor vehicle metal stampings (e.g., body parts, fenders, hub caps, tops, trim), manufacturing
326193	Motor vehicle mouldings and extrusions, plastics, manufacturing
41529	Motor vehicle parts and accessories, new, wholesale
33636	Motor vehicle seats, manufacturing
41529	Motor vehicle sound systems, new, wholesale
811119	Motor vehicle suspension shops
41521	Motor vehicle tires and tubes, wholesale
32621	Motor vehicle tires, manufacturing
48841	Motor vehicle towing service
33636	Motor vehicle trimmings, fabric, manufacturing
41912	Motor vehicles (except automobiles, trucks and buses), wholesale agents and brokers
811411	Motor, outboard, repairs
41799	Motorboats, wholesale
44122	Motorcycle dealers, retail

711218	Motorcycle race track operation
711218	Motorcycle racing teams
81149	Motorcycle repair service
53229	Motorcycles and motor-scooters, rental and leasing
33699	Motorcycles and parts, manufacturing
41519	Motorcycles, wholesale
41519	Motorcycles, wholesale and repair
335312	Motors, electric (except starting motors), manufacturing
33399	Motors, fluid power, manufacturing
333619	Motors, outboard, manufacturing
33632	Motors, starter, for internal combustion engines, manufacturing
322299	Moulded pulp products (e.g., egg cartons, food containers, food trays), manufacturing
41822	Moulded pulp products, wholesale
332321	Moulding and trim (except motor vehicle), metal, manufacturing
23835	Moulding or trim, wood or plastic, installation
41632	Moulding, wooden, wholesale
33637	Mouldings and trim, motor vehicle, metal, stamping
321919	Mouldings, wood, manufacturing
333511	Moulds (except steel ingots), industrial, manufacturing
331511	Moulds for casting steel ingots, manufacturing
333511	Moulds for forming materials (e.g., plastics, rubber, glass), manufacturing
333511	Moulds for metal casting (except steel ingots), manufacturing
331511	Moulds, steel ingot, industrial, manufacturing
56191	Mounting merchandise on cards
33411	Mouse devices, computer peripheral equipment, manufacturing
31499	Mouse pads (textile material laminated to a foam backing), manufacturing
41445	Movies, video, wholesale
238291	Moving sidewalks, installation and repair
48421	Moving used goods, office or institutional
334512	MRI (magnetic resonance imaging) medical diagnostic equipment, manufacturing
32552	Mucilage adhesives, manufacturing
23811	Mud-jacking contractors
811112	Muffler replacement shop
33639	Mufflers and resonators, automotive, truck and bus, manufacturing
11292	Mule production

517112	Multichannel multipoint distribution services (MMDS)
23611	Multifamily building construction, by general contractors
33461	Multimedia products, pre-recorded, mass-reproducing
53139	Multiple listing services, real estate
517112	Multipoint distribution systems (MDS)
32222	Multiwall shipping sacks, made from purchased uncoated paper
91291	Municipal affairs, provincial government
91391	Municipal board/council
91312	Municipal correctional services
91311	Municipal courts
91314	Municipal fire-fighting services
91313	Municipal police services
91315	Municipal regulatory services, general
212396	Muriate of potash, mining
212398	Muscovite mining
712111	Museums, art
111411	Mushroom cellars
111411	Mushroom farming
111411	Mushroom houses
111411	Mushroom spawn, production of
519122	Music archives
711512	Music arrangers, independent
51223	Music books (i.e., bound sheet music), publishing
51223	Music books (i.e., bound sheet music), publishing and printing combined
323119	Music books, printing without publishing
33999	Music boxes, manufacturing
51223	Music copyright buying and licensing
711311	Music festival promoters, with facilities
711322	Music festival promoters, without facilities
71113	Music productions, live (except musical theatre production)
61161	Music teachers, own account
51211	Music video production
51223	Music, publishing
51223	Music, publishing and printing combined
323119	Music, sheet, printing without publishing
71113	Musical artists, independent
71113	Musical groups
45114	Musical instrument amplifying equipment, retail
31699	Musical instrument cases, all materials, manufacturing
53229	Musical instrument rental
45114	Musical instrument stores, retail

81149	Musical instruments repairing and tuning (without retail sales of new equipment)
41899	Musical instruments, accessories and supplies, wholesale
33999	Musical instruments, manufacturing
45331	Musical instruments, used, retail
711112	Musical theatre companies
71113	Musicians, independent
11293	Muskrat farm
114113	Mussel fishing
11112	Mustard seed farming
31194	Mustard, prepared, manufacturing
522291	Mutual benefit associations (loan association)
52392	Mutual fund management companies

N

32562	Nail polish removers, manufacturing
32562	Nail polishes, manufacturing
812115	Nail salons
321215	Nailed-laminated lumber beams, manufacturing
332619	Nails, brads and staples, made from purchased wire
331222	Nails, iron or steel, made in wire drawing plants
331317	Nails, made in aluminum wire drawing plants
33149	Nails, made in non-ferrous (except aluminum, copper) wire drawing plants
325999	Napalm, manufacturing
32519	Naphtha, made by distillation of coal tar
32411	Naphtha, made in petroleum refineries
32519	Naphthalene, made by distillation of coal tar
32519	Naphthalene, made from refined petroleum or natural gas
32511	Naphthalene, made from refined petroleum or natural gas liquids
32411	Naphthalene, made in petroleum refineries
31412	Napkins, made from purchased fabrics
322291	Napkins, sanitary, made from purchased paper stock
31331	Napping textile fabrics
31322	Narrow fabrics (i.e., 30 cm/12 in. or less in width), weaving
41413	Narrow fabrics, wholesale
91291	National Assembly, provincial government
71219	National parks
91191	National science foundation

32731	Natural (i.e., calcined earth) cement, manufacturing
22121	Natural gas brokers
211113	Natural gas cleaning plant
22121	Natural gas distribution
22121	Natural gas distribution systems
41722	Natural gas field production equipment, wholesale
211113	Natural gas from oil shale or sand
211113	Natural gas liquids production
211113	Natural gas liquids recovering, mining
48691	Natural gas liquids, pipeline transport service
48621	Natural gas pipeline service
23822	Natural gas piping, installation
23712	Natural gas processing plants, construction
211113	Natural gas pumping, mining
49319	Natural gas storage
211113	Natural gas washing and scrubbing, mining
31321	Natural hard fibre fabrics (e.g., linen, jute, hemp, ramie), broad-woven, weaving
91191	Natural resource conservation programs, federal government
81331	Natural resource preservation organizations
211113	Natural sour gas processing, mining
71219	Natural wonders, tourist attractions
31211	Naturally carbonated water, purifying and bottling
71219	Nature centres
71219	Nature parks
71219	Nature reserves
62139	Naturopaths' offices
81121	Nautical and navigational instrument, repair
334511	Nautical systems and instruments, manufacturing
91111	Naval base
32519	Naval stores, gum or wood, manufacturing
61151	Navigation and fisheries school
41732	Navigational equipment and devices, electronic, wholesale
41732	Navigational equipment and devices, electronic, wholesale and repair
334511	Navigational instruments, electronic, manufacturing
334511	Navigational instruments, manufacturing
31519	Neckties, made in knitting mills
44815	Neckwear, apparel, retail
31599	Neckwear, made from purchased fabric

41411	Neckwear, women's, misses' and children's, wholesale
332991	Needle roller bearings, manufacturing
33999	Needles and pins, sewing, manufacturing
45113	Needlework stores, retail
62419	Neighbourhood centres
81331	Neighbourhood development advocacy groups
62421	Neighbourhood meal services
72241	Neighbourhood pub ·
33995	Neon signs, manufacturing
41792	Neon signs, wholesale
32512	Neon, manufacturing
32521	Neoprene, manufacturing
212326	Nepheline syenite quarrying
31324	Netting, made in knitting mills
332619	Netting, woven wire, made from purchased wire
41912	New and rebuilt auto parts, wholesale agents and brokers
541619	New product development consulting services
51911	News agencies
51919	News clipping service
711513	News correspondents, independent
51911	News feature syndicates
51911	News picture gathering and distributing service
51911	News reporting service
51911	News syndicates
51911	News ticker service
51112	Newsletters, all formats, publishing (except exclusively on Internet)
54184	Newspaper advertising representatives, independent
45121	Newspaper and magazine stores, retail
711513	Newspaper columnists, independent
45439	Newspaper distributor, newspaper boy, retail
51911	Newspaper feature syndicate
323119	Newspapers, printing without publishing
51111	Newspapers, publishing (except exclusively on Internet)
51913	Newspapers, publishing (exclusively on Internet)
51111	Newspapers, publishing and printing
41442	Newspapers, wholesale
322122	Newsprint mills
322122	Newsprint stock, manufacturing
41822	Newsprint, wholesale
41912	Newsprint, wholesale agents and brokers

33149	Nickel and nickel alloy bar, sheet, strip and tubing, made from purchased metal or scrap
41621	Nickel and nickel alloy, primary forms and basic shapes, wholesale
33591	Nickel cadmium storage batteries, manufacturing
331529	Nickel castings (except die-castings), unfinished, manufacturing
325189	Nickel compounds, not specified elsewhere by process, manufacturing
331523	Nickel die-castings, unfinished, manufacturing
212232	Nickel ore dressing and beneficiating
212232	Nickel ore milling
212232	Nickel ore mining
33149	Nickel rolling, drawing and extruding, purchased metal or scrap
33141	Nickel smelting and primary refining
212232	Nickel-copper ore mining
32541	Nicotine and derivatives (i.e., basic chemicals), manufacturing
32532	Nicotine insecticides, manufacturing
72241	Night clubs
315231	Nightgowns, women's, misses' and girls', cut and sewn from purchased fabric
31519	Nightwear, made in knitting mills
33141	Niobium smelting and primary refining
32629	Nipples and teething rings, rubber, manufacturing
32519	Nitrated hydrocarbon derivatives, manufacturing
325313	Nitric acid, manufacturing
32521	Nitrile rubber, manufacturing
32521	Nitrocellulose (i.e., pyroxylin) resins, manufacturing
32512	Nitrogen, manufacturing
325313	Nitrogenous fertilizer materials, manufacturing
325314	Nitrogenous fertilizers, made by mixing purchased materials
32592	Nitroglycerin explosive materials, manufacturing
32519	Nitrosated hydrocarbon derivatives, manufacturing
32512	Nitrous oxide, manufacturing
54138	Non destructive testing services
31212	Non-alcoholic beer, brewing
41912	Non-alcoholic beverages, wholesale agents and brokers
31213	Non-alcoholic wine, manufacturing
311515	Non-dairy creamers, dry, manufacturing

311511	Non-dairy creamers, liquid, manufacturing
32511	Nonene, made from refined petroleum or natural gas liquids
51791	Non-facilities based ISPs
33149	Non-ferrous alloys (except aluminum, copper), made from purchased metals
33141	Non-ferrous alloys, made in primary smelting and refining mills (except aluminum)
33149	Non-ferrous metal (except aluminum, copper) powder, paste and flakes, made from purchased metals
331529	Non-ferrous metal castings (except die-castings), manufacturing
331523	Non-ferrous metal die-casting foundries
33141	Non-ferrous metals (except aluminum), smelting and primary refining
41811	Non-ferrous metals scrap, wholesale
41892	Non-ferrous ores and concentrates, wholesale
323119	Nonfiction books, printing without publishing
51113	Non-fiction books, publishing (except exclusively on Internet)
51113	Non-fiction books, publishing and printing combined
53112	Non-residential buildings, operators
48411	Non-specialized freight transport, local
524139	Non-specialized reinsurance carriers
45439	Non-store retailing, direct sales (door-to-door), retail
315229	Non-tailored coats and jackets, men's and boys' (e.g., ski suits, windbreakers), manufacturing
31323	Nonwoven fabrics, manufacturing
31323	Nonwoven felts, manufacturing
311823	Noodles, dry, manufacturing
54119	Notaries public, private practice (outside Québec)
54112	Notary services (Québec)
45113	Notions, sewing thread and needles, retail
41413	Notions, wholesale
33999	Novelties, not specified elsewhere by process, manufacturing
322299	Novelties, paper, manufacturing
41899	Novelties, wholesale
45322	Novelty merchandise, retail
33291	Nuclear application valves, manufacturing
221113	Nuclear electric power generation
54169	Nuclear energy consulting services
325189	Nuclear fuel scrap reprocessing
325189	Nuclear fuels, inorganic, manufacturing
32541	Nuclear medicine (e.g., radioactive isotopes) preparations, manufacturing
23713	Nuclear power plants, construction
334512	Nuclear radiation detection instruments, manufacturing
33241	Nuclear reactor control rod drive mechanisms, manufacturing
33241	Nuclear reactor steam supply systems, manufacturing
33241	Nuclear reactors, manufacturing
332319	Nuclear shielding, fabricated metal plate, manufacturing
33242	Nuclear waste casks, heavy gauge metal, manufacturing
23799	Nuclear waste disposal site construction
721213	Nudist camps
333519	Numerically controlled metal cutting machine tools, manufacturing
453999	Numismatic supplies, retail
11321	Nurseries for reforestation
111421	Nursery (tree and plant)
44422	Nursery and garden centres selling primarily to other businesses but also selling to household consumers
111421	Nursery plant stock, growing
62441	Nursery school
41911	Nursery stock and plant, business to business (B2B) electronic markets, wholesale
111421	Nursery stock, growing of
44422	Nursery stock, seeds and bulbs, retail
41113	Nursery stock, wholesale
61151	Nurses' aides' school
81392	Nurses' associations
56131	Nurses' registries
61151	Nurses' schools, practical
62139	Nurses, registered and practical, offices of (except home health care services)
61151	Nursing assistants' school
62311	Nursing homes
62231	Nursing stations
445292	Nut shops, retail
32541	Nutraceuticals, botanical based, manufacturing
446191	Nutrition supplements, retail
62139	Nutritionists, offices of
41319	Nuts and seeds, edible, processed, wholesale
41119	Nuts and seeds, unshelled, wholesale
326198	Nuts, bolts and rivets, plastics, manufacturing
41633	Nuts, bolts, rivets, screws and other fasteners, wholesale
31132	Nuts, chocolate-covered, made from cacao beans

31133	Nuts, chocolate-covered, made from purchased chocolate
31134	Nuts, covered (except chocolate covered), manufacturing
311911	Nuts, kernels and seeds, roasting and processing
33272	Nuts, metal, manufacturing
311911	Nuts, salted, roasted, cooked or canned, manufacturing
32522	Nylon fibres and filaments, manufacturing
32521	Nylon resins, manufacturing
31511	Nylons, sheer, women's, misses' and girls' full-length and knee-length, knitting

O

11119	Oat farming
81291	Obedience training services, pet
71399	Observation tower operation
54171	Observatories, astronomical
62111	Obstetricians' offices
315239	Occupational clothing, women's, misses' and girls', cut and sewn from purchased fabric
54169	Occupational health and safety consulting services
91124	Occupational safety and health standards services, federal government
91215	Occupational safety and health standards services, provincial government
62134	Occupational therapists, offices of
54137	Oceanic surveying (except geophysical) services
54136	Oceanic surveying, geophysical
54171	Oceanographic research and development laboratories
212398	Ocher mining
62419	Offender rehabilitation agencies
62419	Offender self-help organizations
33699	Off-highway tracked vehicles (except construction), manufacturing
33312	Off-highway trucks, manufacturing
56111	Office administration services
45321	Office and school supplies (except furniture), retail
41912	Office and store machinery and equipment, wholesale agents and brokers
54151	Office automation, computer systems integration
53112	Office building rental or leasing
23622	Office buildings and complexes, construction

81142	Office chair reupholstering and upholstery repair
561722	Office cleaning service
337214	Office furniture (except wood), manufacturing
48421	Office furniture moving, used
53242	Office furniture rental
44211	Office furniture store selling primarily to other businesses but also selling to household consumers
41791	Office furniture, wholesale
41791	Office furniture, wholesale and repair
337213	Office furniture, wood, padded, upholstered, or plain, manufacturing
56132	Office help supply service
41791	Office machines and equipment (except electronic data processing equipment), wholesale
41791	Office machines and equipment (except electronic data processing equipment), wholesale and repair
56111	Office management services
54133	Office of engineers
32223	Office paper (e.g., computer printer, photocopy, plain paper), cut sheet, made from purchased paper
322121	Office paper (e.g., computer printer, photocopy, plain paper), made in paper mills
56132	Office personnel services (personnel suppliers)
41821	Office supplies (except furniture, machines), wholesale
45321	Office supplies stores selling primarily to other businesses but also selling to household consumers
32223	Office supplies, die-cut, made from purchased paper or paperboard
91291	Official languages office, provincial government
32312	Offset plate preparation services
323119	Offset printing (except manifold business forms, quick printing, textile fabrics), without publishing
333299	Offset printing presses, manufacturing
713299	Off-track betting parlours
32411	Oil (i.e., petroleum) refineries
325999	Oil additive preparations, manufacturing
41529	Oil additives, wholesale
23712	Oil and gas field distribution line construction
33313	Oil and gas field drilling machinery and equipment (except offshore floating platforms), manufacturing

41612	Oil and gas heating equipment, wholesale
53119	Oil and gas rights, leasing (if lessors)
49319	Oil and gasoline storage caverns (for hire)
53241	Oil field equipment rental and leasing
54136	Oil gas field seismographic surveys
45392	Oil paintings, original and prints, retail
33631	Oil pumps, mechanical, automotive and truck gasoline engine, manufacturing
41722	Oil refining machinery and equipment, wholesale
41722	Oil refining machinery and equipment, wholesale and repair
52391	Oil royalty dealing (i.e., acting as principals)
53311	Oil royalty holders
211114	Oil sand mining
11119	Oil seed and grain farming, combination
56291	Oil spill cleanup
33242	Oil storage tanks, heavy gauge metal, manufacturing
33391	Oil well and oil field pumps, manufacturing
213111	Oil well drilling, on contract basis
213118	Oil well logging, on a contract basis
41722	Oil well machinery and equipment, wholesale
41722	Oil well machinery and equipment, wholesale and repair
41722	Oil well supply houses, wholesale
311614	Oil, animal, rendering
311221	Oil, corn, crude and refined, made by wet-milling corn
31171	Oil, fish and marine animal, manufacturing
311224	Oil, vegetable, made in oilseed crushing mills
41819	Oil, waste, wholesale
32551	Oil-based paints, manufacturing
32551	Oil-based stains, manufacturing
31332	Oiling (i.e., waterproofing) purchased textiles and clothing
325999	Oils (e.g., cutting, lubricating), synthetic, manufacturing
32411	Oils (e.g., fuel, lubricating and illuminating), made in petroleum refineries
41899	Oils and greases, animal or vegetable, wholesale
311225	Oils, cooking, made from purchased fats and oils
325999	Oils, essential, manufacturing
32519	Oils, made by distillation of coal tar
32561	Oils, soluble (i.e., textile finishing assistants), manufacturing
32541	Oils, vegetable and animal, medicinal, uncompounded, manufacturing
32519	Oils, wood, made by distillation of wood
333299	Oilseed crushing and extracting machinery, manufacturing
311224	Oilseed crushing mills
41112	Oilseeds, wholesale
91191	Old age security program, federal government
62331	Old folks home
62331	Old soldiers' homes
32511	Olefins (alkenes), made from refined petroleum or natural gas liquids
32519	Oleic acid (red oil), manufacturing
325189	Oleum (i.e., fuming sulphuric acid), manufacturing
311224	Olive oil, made in crushing mills
212326	Olivine (nongem) mining
91291	Ombudsman's office, provincial government
81392	Ontario College of Pharmacy (licensing bureau)
212316	Onyx marble, crushed and broken stone, quarrying
212316	Onyx marble, dimension-quarrying
711112	Opera companies
541619	Operations research consulting services
23621	Operative builders (i.e., building on own land, for sale), industrial buildings
23611	Operative builders (i.e., building on own land, for sale), residential
53119	Operators of "permanent" trailer sites
531111	Operators of apartment buildings
53112	Operators of commercial and industrial buildings
33911	Ophthalmic instruments and apparatus (except laser surgery), manufacturing
62111	Ophthalmologists' offices
54191	Opinion research services
32541	Opium and opium derivatives (i.e., basic chemicals), manufacturing
327215	Optical fibres, strands, bundles and cables, unsheathed, made from purchased glass
327214	Optical fibres, strands, bundles and cables, unsheathed, made in glass-making plants
41793	Optical goods (except cameras), wholesale
41793	Optical goods (except cameras), wholesale and repair
44613	Optical goods stores, retail

33411	Optical readers and scanners, manufacturing
33461	Optical recording media, blank, manufacturing
51821	Optical scanning data services
44613	Opticians, retail
33441	Optoelectronic devices, manufacturing
41793	Optometric equipment and supplies, wholesale
81392	Optometrists' associations
62132	Optometrists, offices and clinics of
32541	Oral contraceptive preparations, manufacturing
11131	Orange groves and farms
41839	Orchard care chemicals, wholesale
11511	Orchard fruit picking, hand
71113	Orchestras
454113	Order taking offices of mail order houses, retail
332999	Ordnance, military, manufacturing
33313	Ore crushing, washing, screening and loading machinery, manufacturing
41722	Ore dressing machinery, wholesale
41722	Ore dressing machinery, wholesale and repair
23621	Ore milling and metal processing plants, construction
41841	Organic chemicals, synthetic, wholesale
32513	Organic pigments, dyes, lakes and toners, manufacturing
541612	Organization development consulting services
32519	Organo-inorganic compounds, manufacturing
321217	Oriented strandboard (OSB), manufacturing
32742	Ornamental and architectural plaster work (e.g., columns, mantels, mouldings), manufacturing
41621	Ornamental iron and steel products, wholesale
23819	Ornamental metal work, installation, contractors
332329	Ornamental metal work, manufacturing
111421	Ornamental plant growing
41113	Ornamental plants and flowers, wholesale
111421	Ornamental shrubs, nursery grown
321919	Ornamental woodwork (e.g., cornices, mantels), manufacturing
32739	Ornaments, concrete lawn and garden, manufacturing
623999	Orphanages
33911	Orthodontic appliances, custom made in dental laboratories
62121	Orthodontists, offices of
446199	Orthopaedic aids, retail
41793	Orthopaedic equipment and supplies, wholesale
446199	Orthopedic and artificial limb stores, retail
33911	Orthopedic devices and materials, manufacturing
33911	Orthopedic extension shoes, manufacturing
31621	Orthopedic shoes (except extension shoes), men's, manufacturing
321217	OSB (oriented strandboard), manufacturing
334512	Oscilloscopes, manufacturing
62111	Osteopaths' offices
621499	Osteoporosis centres
41793	Ostomy supplies, wholesale
112399	Ostrich farming
526919	Other open-ended funds
114113	Otter trawling
44122	Outboard motor dealers, retail
333619	Outboard motors, manufacturing
41799	Outboard motors, wholesale
41799	Outboard motors, wholesale and repair
71399	Outdoor adventure operations (e.g., white water rafting), without accommodation
721213	Outdoor adventure retreats (with accommodation)
54185	Outdoor display advertising services
44211	Outdoor furniture, household, retail
23799	Outdoor recreation facilities, construction
23899	Outdoor residential-type swimming pool construction
51213	Outdoor theatres, motion pictures
31519	Outerwear, made in knitting mills
41411	Outerwear, men's and boys', wholesale
41411	Outerwear, women's, children's, and infants', wholesale
41899	Outfitter (ship chandler)
721212	Outfitters (fishing and hunting)
33593	Outlet boxes (electric wiring devices), manufacturing
33593	Outlet receptacles, electrical, manufacturing
62142	Outpatient mental health clinics
62142	Outpatient treatment clinics for alcoholism and drug addiction
62419	Outreach programs
32561	Oven cleaners, manufacturing
333299	Ovens, bakery, manufacturing
33331	Ovens, commercial type, manufacturing

33399	Ovens, industrial process type, manufacturing
81233	Overall supply service
213119	Overburden removal, mines, on a contract basis
315234	Overcoats (except fur, leather), women's, misses' and girls', cut and sewn from purchased fabric
315222	Overcoats, tailored, men's and boys', cut and sewn from purchased fabric
33392	Overhead conveyors, manufacturing
238299	Overhead door installation, commercial
23835	Overhead door installation, residential
33331	Overhead projectors (except computer peripherals), manufacturing
33411	Overhead projectors, computer peripheral-type, manufacturing
33392	Overhead travelling cranes, manufacturing
41412	Overshoes, wholesale
32519	Oxalates (e.g., ammonium oxalate, ethyl oxalate, sodium oxalate), manufacturing
32519	Oxalic acid, manufacturing
446199	Oxygen tent sales and medical gas supplying, retail store
32512	Oxygen, manufacturing
72221	Oyster bar
114113	Oyster fishing
11251	Oyster production, farm raising
41314	Oysters, fresh or frozen (except frozen packaged), wholesale
212398	Ozokerite mining

P

71399	Pack trains (i.e., trail riding)
54142	Package design (industrial) services
56191	Packaging and labelling service (not packing and crating for transportation)
326114	Packaging film, plastics, single or multi-web, manufacturing
33399	Packaging machinery, manufacturing
56191	Packaging services (except crating for transportation)
32615	Packaging, foam plastics (except polystyrene), manufacturing
326198	Packaging, plastics (e.g., blister, bubble), manufacturing
48899	Packing and crating service, transportable goods
41315	Packing house, fruit, fresh, wholesale
41723	Packing machinery and equipment, wholesale

41723	Packing machinery and equipment, wholesale and repair
31499	Padding and wadding (except nonwoven fabric), manufacturing
31323	Padding and wadding, nonwoven fabric, manufacturing
321999	Paddles, wood, manufacturing
31412	Pads and protectors (e.g., ironing board, mattress, table), made from purchased fabrics or felts
322211	Pads, corrugated and solid fibreboard, made from purchased paper or paperboard
32223	Pads, desk, made from purchased paper
622112	Paediatric hospitals
62111	Paediatricians' offices
33422	Pagers, manufacturing
51721	Paging services
811121	Paint and body shops, motor vehicle
44412	Paint and paint supply stores, retail
32551	Paint and varnish removers, manufacturing
44412	Paint and wallpaper store selling primarily to businesses but also selling to household consumers
23832	Paint and wallpaper stripping (removal), contractors
33399	Paint baking and drying ovens, manufacturing
332431	Paint cans, metal, manufacturing
41634	Paint materials and supplies, wholesale
41723	Paint spray equipment, industrial, wholesale
33399	Paint spray guns, pneumatic, hand held power-driven, manufacturing
33391	Paint sprayers (i.e., compressor and spray gun units), manufacturing
32551	Paint thinner and reducer preparations, manufacturing
41634	Paint, glass and wallpaper, wholesale
41912	Paint, glass and wallpaper, wholesale agents and brokers
32551	Paintbrush cleaners, manufacturing
45112	Paint-by-number sets, retail
711511	Painters (i.e., artists), independent
53249	Painting equipment rental
23731	Painting lines on highways
33281	Painting metals and metal products, for the trade
23731	Painting traffic lanes or parking lots
23816	Painting, spraying or coating of roofs
32551	Paints (except artists'), manufacturing
33994	Paints, artists', manufacturing
32551	Paints, emulsion (i.e., latex paint), manufacturing

32551	Paints, oil and alkyd vehicle, manufacturing
41634	Paints, wholesale
33994	Palettes, artists', manufacturing
212299	Palladium ore mining
33392	Pallet movers, manufacturing
322211	Pallets, corrugated and solid fibre, made from purchased paper or paperboard
332999	Pallets, metal, manufacturing
32192	Pallets, wood or wood and metal combination, manufacturing
81299	Palm readers
32312	Pamphlets and magazines, binding without printing
323119	Pamphlets, printing without publishing
311822	Pancake mixes, made from purchased flour
337213	Panel furniture systems, wood office, manufacturing
23831	Panel or rigid board insulation, installing
41611	Panelboards, electrical distribution, wholesale
23835	Panelling installation
321992	Panels for prefabricated wood buildings, manufacturing
321211	Panels, hardwood plywood, manufacturing
23839	Panels, metal, installation
41632	Panels, plywood, overlaid or prefinished, wholesale
332311	Panels, prefabricated, metal building, manufacturing
321212	Panels, softwood plywood, manufacturing
31519	Panties, made in knitting mills
315292	Pants, leather, manufacturing
31519	Pants, outerwear, made in knitting mills
315229	Pants, washable service type, men's and boys', cut and sewn from purchased fabric
315239	Pants, women's, misses' and girls', cut and sewn from purchased fabric
315234	Pantsuits, women's, misses' and girls', cut and sewn from purchased fabric
31511	Panty hose, manufacturing
32791	Paper (e.g., aluminum oxide, emery, garnet, silicon carbide) abrasive-coated, manufacturing
322121	Paper (except newsprint and uncoated groundwood) mills
322121	Paper (except newsprint and uncoated groundwood) products, made in paper mills

322121	Paper (except newsprint and uncoated groundwood) stock for conversion into paper products, manufacturing
322121	Paper (except newsprint and uncoated groundwood), coated, laminated or treated, made in paper mills
322121	Paper (except newsprint and uncoated groundwood), manufacturing
41912	Paper and paper products, wholesale agents and brokers
333291	Paper and paperboard coating and finishing machinery, manufacturing
333291	Paper and paperboard converting machinery, manufacturing
333291	Paper and paperboard corrugating machinery, manufacturing
333291	Paper and paperboard cutting and folding machinery, manufacturing
333291	Paper and paperboard die-cutting and stamping machinery, manufacturing
333291	Paper bag making machinery, manufacturing
32222	Paper bags, coated, made from purchased paper
32222	Paper bags, uncoated, made from purchased paper
212326	Paper clay mining
331222	Paper clips, iron or steel, made in wire drawing plants
332619	Paper clips, made from purchased wire
41822	Paper cups, dishes, napkins, towels and patterns, wholesale
322219	Paper cups, made from purchased paper or paperboard
322219	Paper dishes (e.g., cups, plates), made from purchased paper or paperboard
315233	Paper dresses, women's, misses' and girls', cut and sewn from purchased fabric
31322	Paper fabric, narrow woven (i.e., 30 cm/12 in. or less in width), weaving
81131	Paper making machinery repair
333291	Paper making machinery, manufacturing
41723	Paper manufacturing machinery, wholesale
322291	Paper napkins (i.e., table), made from purchased paper
322299	Paper novelties, manufacturing
32223	Paper office supplies, made from purchased paper
322219	Paper plates, made from purchased paper or paperboard

322299	Paper products (except office supplies), die-cut, from purchased paper or paperboard
32223	Paper products, die-cut office supplies, made from purchased paper or paperboard
333291	Paper stock preparation machinery, manufacturing
31311	Paper yarn, manufacturing
33994	Paper, carbon, manufacturing
32222	Paper, coated (except photographic and carbon), made from purchased paper
322211	Paper, corrugated, made from purchased paper or paperboard
32222	Paper, laminated, made from purchased paper
322122	Paper, newsprint, manufacturing
325999	Paper, photographic sensitized, manufacturing
32222	Paper, sensitized (except photographic), made from purchased paper
322122	Paper, uncoated groundwood, manufacturing
41822	Paperboard and products (except office supplies), wholesale
322299	Paperboard backs for blister or skin packages, made from purchased paper or paperboard
333291	Paperboard box making machinery, manufacturing
333291	Paperboard making machinery, manufacturing
32213	Paperboard mills
32213	Paperboard products (e.g., containers), made in paperboard mills
32222	Paperboard, pasted, lined, laminated or surface coated, made from purchased paperboard
31499	Parachutes, manufacturing
32511	Paraffins (alkanes), made from refined petroleum or natural gas liquids
54119	Paralegal services
321215	Parallel strand lumber (PSL), manufacturing
48599	Paratransit transportation services
49211	Parcel delivery, private (except air)
49211	Parcel express service, courier
33399	Parcel post scales, manufacturing
62419	Parenting services
81341	Parent-teachers associations
71311	Park, amusement (i.e., theme parks, water parks)
81293	Parking garages
23899	Parking lot and driveway, asphalt resurfacing

81293	Parking services, valet
91391	Parks and recreation commission, municipal government
91291	Parks commission, provincial government
71219	Parks, nature
71213	Parks, wild animal
91191	Parliament, federal government
61111	Parochial schools, elementary or secondary
91212	Parole offices, provincial
91122	Parole services, federal government
321919	Parquet flooring, hardwood (assembled), manufacturing
321216	Particle board, manufacturing
322211	Partitions, corrugated and solid fibre, made from purchased paper or paperboard
337215	Partitions, freestanding, prefabricated, manufacturing
332619	Partitions, made from purchased wire
337215	Partitions, prefabricated (modular or free-standing), manufacturing
41791	Partitions, wholesale
44121	Parts for recreational vehicles, retail
45439	Party plan merchandising, retail
81299	Party planning service
53229	Party supplies rental and leasing
453999	Party supplies store, retail
48111	Passenger air transportation, scheduled
532112	Passenger car leasing (except finance leasing), without drivers
532111	Passenger car rental, without driver
48511	Passenger transit systems, mixed mode
48511	Passenger transit systems, urban and suburban
482114	Passenger transportation services, railway
481214	Passenger transportation, air charter service
54192	Passport photography services
91141	Passport services
31199	Pasta mixes, made from purchased dried ingredients
311823	Pasta mixes, made in dry pasta plants
311823	Pasta, dry, manufacturing
31199	Pasta, fresh, manufacturing
31142	Pasta-based products, canning
33149	Paste, non-ferrous metal (except aluminum, copper), made from purchased metals
32552	Pastes, adhesive, manufacturing
333299	Pasteurizing equipment (i.e., food manufacturing type), manufacturing

311814	Pastries (e.g., Danish, French), made in commercial bakeries
311822	Pastries, uncooked, made from purchased flour
41319	Pastries, wholesale
311822	Pastry mixes, prepared, made from purchased flour
445291	Pastry shops, without baking on the premises, retail
41319	Pastry, quick-frozen, packaged, wholesale
54119	Patent agent services (i.e., patent filing and searching services)
54111	Patent attorneys, private practice
54199	Patent broker services (i.e., patent marketing services)
53311	Patent buying and licensing
53311	Patent holders
32541	Patent medicine preparations, manufacturing
44611	Patent medicines, retail
41451	Patent medicines, wholesale
41793	Patient monitoring equipment, wholesale
32733	Patio blocks, concrete, manufacturing
23899	Patio construction
23899	Patio construction, concrete, contractors
41439	Patio furniture, wholesale
561612	Patrol services, security
54199	Patrolling (i.e., visual inspection) of electric transmission or gas lines
332999	Patterns (except shoe), industrial, manufacturing
323119	Patterns and plans, printing without publishing
41413	Patterns, clothing, wholesale
41822	Patterns, paper, wholesale
23731	Pavement, highways, roads, streets, bridges or airport runways, construction
23899	Pavers, brick (e.g., driveways, patios and sidewalks), installation
23899	Paving (asphalt), residential driveways and commercial parking lots
324121	Paving blocks and mixtures, made from purchased asphaltic materials
32733	Paving blocks, concrete, manufacturing
32712	Paving brick, clay, manufacturing
41639	Paving mixtures, wholesale
522299	Pawnbrokers
51521	Pay television
541215	Payroll processing services
33421	PBX (private branch exchange) equipment, manufacturing
11113	Pea farming (field crop)

81331	Peace advocacy groups
11133	Peach orchards and farms
311911	Peanut butter blended with jelly, manufacturing
311911	Peanut butter, manufacturing
111999	Peanut farming
311224	Peanut oil, cake and meal, made in crushing mills
32513	Pearl essence pigment, synthetic, manufacturing
81149	Pearl restringing, for the trade
11251	Pearls, cultured, production of
33991	Pearls, drilling, sawing, or peeling of, manufacturing
41112	Peas, dry, wholesale
212397	Peat bog
212397	Peat mining
212397	Peat moss digging or harvesting
212397	Peat moss harvesting, extraction, cutting
32799	Peat pots, manufacturing
212397	Peat, fuel, mining
113311	Peeler logs, cutting
81392	Peer review boards
33994	Pen refills and cartridges, manufacturing
33994	Pencil leads, manufacturing
33994	Pencil sharpeners, manufacturing
33994	Pencils, lead and mechanical, manufacturing
32561	Penetrants, manufacturing
32541	Penicillin preparations, manufacturing
32541	Penicillin, uncompounded, manufacturing
91212	Penitentiaries, provincial government
91122	Penitentiary services, federal government
33994	Pens and pen parts (e.g., fountain, stylographic, ballpoint), manufacturing
33994	Pens, manufacturing
524299	Pension and retirement plan consultants
52392	Pension funds, management
526112	Pension funds, not trusteed
32511	Pentane, made from refined petroleum or natural gas liquids
32511	Pentene, made from refined petroleum or natural gas liquids
31194	Pepper (i.e., spice), manufacturing
111219	Pepper farming (e.g., bell, chilli, green, hot, red, sweet)
213118	Perforating well casings, on a contract basis
711311	Performing arts centres, promoting events

91191	Performing arts program, federal government
61161	Performing arts schools
44612	Perfume and cosmetics, retail
32519	Perfume materials (i.e., basic synthetic chemicals such as terpineol), manufacturing
41452	Perfumes and fragrances, wholesale
32562	Perfumes, manufacturing
51112	Periodicals, all formats, publishing and printing combined
323119	Periodicals, printing without publishing
51112	Periodicals, publishing (except exclusively on Internet)
62121	Periodontists, offices of
44312	Peripheral equipment, computer stores, retail
41731	Peripheral equipment, computer, wholesale
212398	Perlite mining
331529	Permanent mould castings, non-ferrous metals, unfinished, manufacturing
32562	Permanent wave preparations, manufacturing
23813	Permanent wood foundations, installation
325189	Peroxides, inorganic, manufacturing
32519	Peroxides, organic, manufacturing
44311	Personal care appliance store
41422	Personal care appliances (e.g., hair dryers, razors, toothbrushes), electric, wholesale
62311	Personal care homes
51721	Personal communication services (PCS) (i.e., communications carriers)
33441	Personal computer modems, manufacturing
44312	Personal computers sales and service
33411	Personal computers, manufacturing
522291	Personal credit institutions
61169	Personal development courses
551113	Personal holding companies (except banks)
52399	Personal investment trusts, administration by trust companies
44815	Personal leather goods, retail
522291	Personal loan companies
51721	Personal mobile communications services
561612	Personal protection services
33911	Personal safety devices, not specified elsewhere, manufacturing
81299	Personal shopping service
33699	Personal watercraft, manufacturing
81392	Personnel management associations
541612	Personnel management consulting services
56132	Personnel pool services (personnel suppliers)
56171	Pest control services
11531	Pest control services, forestry
41839	Pesticides, agricultural, wholesale
32532	Pesticides, manufacturing
334512	PET (positron emission tomography) scanners, manufacturing
45391	Pet animal care equipment and supplies, retail
112999	Pet animal, raising
45391	Pet animals, retail
41111	Pet animals, wholesale
11521	Pet breeding services
81291	Pet care (except veterinary), service
81222	Pet cemeteries
311119	Pet food (except dogs and cats), manufacturing
45391	Pet food stores, retail
311111	Pet food, dog and cat, manufacturing
41831	Pet food, wholesale
81291	Pet grooming services
54194	Pet hospitals
45391	Pet shops, retail
81291	Pet sitting services
41899	Pet supplies (except pet food), wholesale
81291	Pet training services
32411	Petrochemical feedstocks, made in petroleum refineries
32511	Petrochemicals, made from refined petroleum or natural gas liquids
32411	Petrochemicals, made in petroleum refineries
211113	Petroleum (oil) well, crude, conventional
41211	Petroleum bulk station, wholesale
54133	Petroleum engineering services
32419	Petroleum jelly, made from refined petroleum
32411	Petroleum jelly, made in petroleum refineries
41911	Petroleum product, business to business (B2B) electronic markets, wholesale
41722	Petroleum production machinery and equipment, wholesale
41722	Petroleum production machinery and equipment, wholesale and repair
211113	Petroleum production, crude, conventional
32411	Petroleum refineries
23712	Petroleum refineries, construction

333299	Petroleum refining machinery, manufacturing
32419	Petroleum waxes, made from refined petroleum
211114	Petroleum, from shale or sand, production
71213	Petting zoos
33991	Pewter ware, manufacturing
32541	Pharmaceutical preparations (e.g., capsules, liniments, ointments, tablets), manufacturing
41451	Pharmaceutical preparations, wholesale
44611	Pharmaceuticals, retail
44611	Pharmacies, retail
81392	Pharmacists' associations
112399	Pheasant farming
32519	Phenol, manufacturing
32521	Phenolic resins, manufacturing
81321	Philanthropic trusts, awarding grants
453999	Philatelic supplies, retail
45331	Phonograph and phonograph record stores, second-hand, retail
41444	Phonograph records, wholesale
41792	Phonographs, coin-operated, wholesale
212398	Phosphate rock mining
325313	Phosphatic fertilizer materials, manufacturing
325314	Phosphatic fertilizers, made by mixing purchased materials
325313	Phosphoric acid, manufacturing
325189	Phosphorus compounds, not specified elsewhere by process, manufacturing
323119	Photo albums and refills, manufacturing
711511	Photo journalist, independent
32312	Photocomposition services, for the printing trades
41791	Photocopy machines, wholesale
41791	Photocopy machines, wholesale and repair
33331	Photocopying machines, manufacturing
32312	Photoengraving plate preparation services
41443	Photofinishing equipment, wholesale
812921	Photofinishing services (except one-hour)
812922	Photofinishing services, one-hour
54137	Photogrammetric mapping services
812921	Photograph developing, printing and enlarging services (except one-hour)
322299	Photograph folders, mats and mounts, manufacturing
33511	Photographic bulbs, lamps and cubes, manufacturing
44313	Photographic camera parts and accessories, retail

41443	Photographic cameras, projectors, equipment and supplies, wholesale
325999	Photographic chemicals, manufacturing
41443	Photographic chemicals, wholesale
41912	Photographic equipment and supplies, wholesale agents and brokers
33331	Photographic equipment, coin operated, manufacturing
81121	Photographic equipment, repairing
44313	Photographic equipment, retail
44313	Photographic film and plates (unexposed), retail
41443	Photographic film and plates, wholesale
33331	Photographic film developing equipment, manufacturing
325999	Photographic film, cloth, paper and plate, sensitized, manufacturing
812921	Photographic laboratories (except for the motion picture industry)
33331	Photographic lenses, manufacturing
519122	Photographic libraries, archives
41443	Photographic paper and cloth, wholesale
44313	Photographic supply stores, retail
326114	Photographic, micrographic and X-ray plastics sheet and film (except sensitized), manufacturing
54192	Photography studios
325999	Photomasks, manufacturing
33441	Photonic integrated circuits (PIC), manufacturing
81299	Phrenologists
32519	Phthalic anhydride, manufacturing
541619	Physical distribution consulting services
621499	Physical examination service (except by physicians)
71394	Physical fitness centres
71394	Physical fitness studio
334512	Physical properties testing and inspection equipment, manufacturing
54171	Physical science research and development laboratories
41793	Physicians' equipment and supplies, wholesale
41793	Physicians' equipment and supplies, wholesale and repair
62111	Physicians' offices, general practice
54169	Physics consulting services
62134	Physiotherapists' offices, private practice
33999	Pianos, manufacturing
45114	Pianos, retail
113311	Pickets and paling, round or split, cutting

333519	Picklers and pickling machinery, metalworking, manufacturing
31142	Pickles, manufacturing
41319	Pickles, preserves, jellies, jams and sauces, wholesale
31142	Pickling fruits and vegetables
33221	Picks (i.e., hand tools), manufacturing
33611	Pick-up trucks, light duty, assembling on chassis of own manufacture
71399	Picnic grounds
442292	Picture frames, retail
45392	Pictures and art objects, retail
311822	Pie crust shells, uncooked, made from purchased flour
41413	Piece goods, textile, wholesale
71311	Piers, amusement
48831	Piers, docks and wharves, maintenance
48831	Piers, docks and wharves, operation
311814	Pies, dessert type (except ice cream), manufacturing
41621	Pig and other primary iron, wholesale
11221	Pig farming
33111	Pig iron, manufacturing
33992	Pigeons, clay (targets), manufacturing
32513	Pigments (except animal black, bone black), organic, manufacturing
32513	Pigments (except bone, carbon and lamp black), inorganic, manufacturing
41634	Pigments and colours, wholesale
23891	Pile driving, contractors
23799	Pile driving, marine
31324	Pile fabrics, weft knit, made in knitting mills
321114	Piles, foundation and marine construction, treating
23891	Piling (i.e., bored, cast-in-place, drilled), building foundation, contractors
113311	Piling, wood, untreated, cutting
31412	Pillow cases, made from purchased fabrics
48849	Pilot car services (i.e., wide load warning service)
488332	Piloting service, water transport
71312	Pinball arcades
33999	Pinball machines, coin-operated, manufacturing
32519	Pinene, manufacturing
212326	Pinite mining
71212	Pioneer villages
33121	Pipe (e.g., heavy riveted, lock joint, seamless, welded), made from purchased iron or steel
331511	Pipe and fittings, cast iron (e.g., soil, pressure), manufacturing

332999	Pipe and pipe fittings, made from purchased metal pipe
333519	Pipe and tube rolling mill machinery, metalworking, manufacturing
332999	Pipe couplings, made from purchased metal pipe
333519	Pipe cutting and threading machines, metalworking, manufacturing
332999	Pipe fabricating (e.g., bending, cutting, threading), of purchased metal pipe
332999	Pipe fittings, made from purchased metal pipe
326122	Pipe fittings, rigid plastics, manufacturing
332329	Pipe railings, metal, manufacturing
32552	Pipe sealing compounds, manufacturing
31222	Pipe tobacco, prepared, manufacturing
41331	Pipe tobacco, wholesale
331317	Pipe, aluminum, made from purchased aluminum
32733	Pipe, concrete, manufacturing
33142	Pipe, copper and copper alloy, made from purchased metal or scrap
32629	Pipe, hard rubber, manufacturing
33111	Pipe, iron or steel, made in steel mills
326122	Pipe, rigid plastics, manufacturing
332329	Pipe, sheet metal, manufacturing
23799	Pipe-jacking contractors
54199	Pipeline and power line inspection (i.e., visual inspection) services
23712	Pipeline rehabilitation contractors
48899	Pipeline terminal facilities independently operated
48691	Pipeline transport service, gasoline
48621	Pipeline transport service, natural gas
48691	Pipeline transport service, natural gas liquids
48611	Pipeline transport, crude oil
23712	Pipeline wrapping construction contractors
48691	Pipelines transport service, refined petroleum products
23712	Pipelines, oil and gas, construction
453999	Pipes and smokers' supplies, retail
41621	Pipes and tubes, metal, wholesale
33999	Pipes, smoker's, manufacturing
332999	Pistols (except toy), manufacturing
33631	Pistons and piston rings, manufacturing
41723	Pistons and valves, industrial, wholesale
32519	Pitch, made by distillation of coal tar
32519	Pitch, wood, manufacturing
212291	Pitchblende mining
113311	Pitprops, wooden, untreated, cutting

32541	Pituitary gland derivatives, uncompounded, manufacturing
311822	Pizza doughs, made from purchased flour
72221	Pizza take out store
31199	Pizza, fresh, manufacturing
31141	Pizza, frozen, manufacturing
72221	Pizzerias, take-out, food service
56131	Placement services, casting bureaus
56131	Placement services, employment agency
81311	Places of worship
33312	Planers, bituminous, manufacturing
33321	Planers, woodworking type, stationary, manufacturing
33221	Planes, hand held, non-powered, manufacturing
712119	Planetariums
41632	Planing mill products, wholesale
321919	Planing mills (i.e., dressing purchased rough lumber)
321919	Planing purchased lumber
62141	Planned parenthood
32532	Plant growth regulators, manufacturing
111421	Plant nursery
11511	Planting crops
41711	Planting machinery and equipment, wholesale
33311	Planting machines, farm type, manufacturing
45311	Plants and cut flowers, retail
33399	Plasma welding equipment, manufacturing
621499	Plasmapheresis centres
41639	Plaster and drywall supplies, wholesale
32742	Plaster of Paris, manufacturing
32742	Plaster, gypsum, manufacturing
23831	Plastering (i.e., ornamental, plain), contractors
41723	Plastic and rubber industries machinery, equipment and supplies, wholesale
811121	Plastic bumpers (auto), repair and installation
212326	Plastic fire clay mining
41412	Plastic footwear, wholesale
62111	Plastic surgeons' offices
326196	Plastic window and door manufacturing
32551	Plastic wood fillers, manufacturing
32519	Plasticizers (i.e., basic synthetic chemicals), manufacturing
41841	Plasticizers and stabilizers, wholesale
325999	Plasticizers, preparations, manufacturing

32521	Plastics and synthetic resins, regenerating, precipitating and coagulating
41841	Plastics basic shapes, wholesale
326193	Plastics extrusions and mouldings, for making automobile parts, manufacturing
326114	Plastics film and unlaminated sheet, manufacturing
326111	Plastics film bags, single or multi-wall, manufactured and printed in the same establishment
326111	Plastics film bags, single or multi-wall, manufacturing
41899	Plastics foam, wholesale
41841	Plastics materials, wholesale
325991	Plastics resins, compounding from recycled materials
325991	Plastics resins, custom compounding of purchased
41841	Plastics resins, wholesale
41841	Plastics sheet and rods, wholesale
33322	Plastics working machinery, manufacturing
32552	Plastics-based adhesives, manufacturing
32613	Plate, laminated plastics, manufacturing
41621	Plate, sheet and strip, steel, wholesale
33221	Plated (with precious metal) cutlery, manufacturing
33221	Plated (with precious metal) flatware (cutlery), manufacturing
32312	Platemaking, for the printing trades
322299	Plates, moulded pulp, manufacturing
33281	Plating metals and metal products, for the trade
33141	Platinum smelting and primary refining
23799	Playground construction
45111	Playground equipment, retail
41799	Playground equipment, wholesale
323119	Playing cards, printing without publishing
711513	Playwrights, independent
53229	Pleasure boats rental
721113	Pleasure resort (summer hotel)
31499	Pleating and hemstitching of made-up textile articles (except clothing)
33221	Pliers, hand tool, manufacturing
11511	Ploughing service, agricultural
33311	Ploughs, farm type, manufacturing
41711	Ploughs, harrows and tillers, farm and garden, wholesale
41711	Ploughs, harrows and tillers, farm and garden, wholesale and repair
23822	Plumbers

41612	Plumbers' brass goods, fittings and valves, wholesale
41633	Plumbers' tools and equipment, wholesale
41612	Plumbing and heating equipment and supplies, wholesale
33291	Plumbing and heating inline valves (e.g., check, cut-off, stop), manufacturing
33291	Plumbing fittings and couplings (e.g., compression fittings, metal unions, metal elbows), manufacturing
33291	Plumbing fixture fittings and trim, all materials, manufacturing
326191	Plumbing fixtures (e.g., shower stalls, toilets, urinals), plastics or fibreglass, manufacturing
23822	Plumbing fixtures, installation
332999	Plumbing fixtures, metal, manufacturing
32711	Plumbing fixtures, vitreous china, manufacturing
44419	Plumbing supplies stores selling primarily to other businesses but also selling to household consumers
44419	Plumbing supplies, retail
41612	Plumbing supplies, wholesale
41912	Plumbing, heating and air-conditioning equipment, wholesale agents and brokers
321211	Plywood mills, hardwood
321212	Plywood mills, softwood
321114	Plywood, treating with creosote or other preservatives
41632	Plywood, wholesale
81131	Pneumatic controls, oil field equipment, repair
33399	Pneumatic cylinders, fluid power, manufacturing
33291	Pneumatic hose fittings, fluid power, manufacturing
32622	Pneumatic hose, without fittings, rubber or plastic, manufacturing
33399	Pneumatic pumps, fluid power, manufacturing
33392	Pneumatic tube conveyors, manufacturing
33291	Pneumatic valves, fluid power, manufacturing
33399	Pneumatic, hand held power tools, manufacturing
41442	Pocket books, wholesale
62139	Podiatrists, offices and clinics of
337215	Point of purchase display racks, wire, manufacturing

33411	Pointing devices, computer peripheral equipment, manufacturing
33411	Point-of-sale (POS) terminals, manufacturing
33593	Pole line hardware, manufacturing
41611	Pole line hardware, wholesale
321999	Poles (e.g., clothesline, flag, tent), wood, manufacturing
113311	Poles and pilings, wooden, untreated, cutting
41891	Poles and pilings, wooden, untreated, wholesale
32739	Poles, concrete, manufacturing
113311	Poles, wood, untreated, cutting
91313	Police force, municipal
91213	Police forces, provincial government
61151	Police schools
32561	Polishes (e.g., automobile, furniture, metal, shoe), manufacturing
41841	Polishes (e.g., furniture, automobile, metal, shoe), wholesale
333519	Polishing and buffing machines, metalworking, manufacturing
33281	Polishing metals and metal products, for the trade
81142	Polishing of furniture
32561	Polishing preparations, manufacturing
41841	Polishing preparations, wholesale
32791	Polishing wheels, manufacturing
81394	Political Action Committees (PACs)
81394	Political campaign organizations
711511	Political cartoonists, independent
54182	Political consultants, offices of
54191	Political opinion polling services
81394	Political organizations and clubs
81394	Political parties
54138	Pollution testing service (except automotive emissions testing)
31519	Polo shirts, made in knitting mills
32521	Polyamide resins, manufacturing
32522	Polyester fibres and filaments, manufacturing
326114	Polyester film and unlaminated sheet, manufacturing
32521	Polyester resins, manufacturing
326114	Polyethylene film and unlaminated sheet, manufacturing
32521	Polyethylene resins, manufacturing
32521	Polyethylene rubber, manufacturing
32522	Polyethylene terephathalate (PET) fibres and filaments, manufacturing
32521	Polyethylene terephathalate (PET) resins, manufacturing
561611	Polygraph service
32521	Polyisobutylene resins, manufacturing

32521	Polyisobutylene rubber, manufacturing
32522	Polyolefin fibres and filaments, manufacturing
326114	Polypropylene film and unlaminated sheet, manufacturing
32521	Polypropylene resins, manufacturing
32614	Polystyrene foam packaging, manufacturing
23831	Polystyrene insulating, installation
32521	Polystyrene resins, manufacturing
32521	Polysulfide rubber, manufacturing
32551	Polyurethane coatings, manufacturing
32615	Polyurethane foam products, manufacturing
32521	Polyurethane resins, manufacturing
32521	Polyvinyl alcohol resins, manufacturing
32521	Polyvinyl chloride (PVC) resins, manufacturing
32521	Polyvinyl resins, manufacturing
315299	Ponchos and similar waterproof raincoats, cut and sewn from purchased fabric
45111	Pool and billiard table stores, retail
33992	Pool balls, cues, cue tips and tables, manufacturing
71399	Pool halls
31211	Pop, soda, manufacturing
31199	Popcorn (except popped), manufacturing
31134	Popcorn balls and other candy-covered popcorn products, manufacturing
445292	Popcorn stands, retail
311919	Popcorn, popped (except candy-covered), manufacturing
31152	Pops, dessert, frozen (i.e., flavoured ice, fruit, pudding and gelatin), manufacturing
71113	Popular music groups
32711	Porcelain parts, electrical and electronic devices, moulded, manufacturing
32711	Porcelain, chemical, manufacturing
31142	Pork and beans, canning
311611	Pork carcasses, half-carcasses, primal and sub-primal cuts, produced in slaughtering plants
311919	Pork rinds, manufacturing
311614	Pork, primal and sub-primal cuts, made from purchased meat
23799	Port facilities construction
48831	Port facilities operation
332311	Portable buildings, prefabricated, metal, manufacturing
33312	Portable crushing, pulverizing and screening machinery, manufacturing
326191	Portable toilets, plastics, manufacturing

81131	Portable welding shop (mobile)
81299	Porter service
31212	Porter, brewing
31699	Portfolios, manufacturing
32731	Portland cement, manufacturing
54192	Portrait photographers
54192	Portrait photography services
54192	Portrait photography studios
41899	Portrait, wholesale
23813	Post frame contractors
49111	Post Office operations
33331	Postage meters, manufacturing
323119	Postage stamps, printing without publishing
337215	Postal service lock boxes, manufacturing
49111	Postal service on a contract basis
323119	Postcards, printing without publishing
54185	Poster advertising services
442292	Posters and prints, retail
323119	Posters, printing (except quick, digital) without publishing
323113	Posters, screen printing without publishing
32312	Postpress services (e.g., bevelling, binding, bronzing, edging, foil stamping), on printed products
51219	Post-production facilities
32739	Posts, concrete, manufacturing
41891	Posts, logs, hewn ties and poles, wholesale
113311	Posts, wood, hewn, round or split, producing
61121	Post-secondary or non-university educational
51219	Post-synchronization, sound dubbing
212396	Potash mining and/or beneficiating
212396	Potash screening and pulverizing, mining
325314	Potassic fertilizers, made by mixing purchased materials
325181	Potassium carbonate, manufacturing
212396	Potassium chloride (i.e., potash), mining and/or beneficiating
325181	Potassium hydroxide (i.e., caustic potash), manufacturing
325189	Potassium inorganic compounds, not specified elsewhere by process, manufacturing
32519	Potassium organic compounds, not specified elsewhere by process, manufacturing
325189	Potassium salts, manufacturing
325189	Potassium sulphate, manufacturing
49313	Potato cellars

311919	Potato chips, manufacturing
111211	Potato farming
111211	Potato farms, sweet
31199	Potato mixes, made from purchased dried ingredients
31142	Potato products (e.g., flakes, granules), dehydrating
311221	Potato starch, manufacturing
31142	Potatoes, canning
31199	Potatoes, fresh (i.e., cut, peeled, polished or sliced), manufacturing
33999	Potpourri, manufacturing
33242	Pots (e.g., annealing, melting, smelting), heavy gauge metal, manufacturing
32711	Pottery products, manufacturing
442298	Pottery stores, retail
41431	Pottery, household, wholesale
325314	Potting soil, manufacturing
311615	Poultry (e.g., canned, cooked, fresh, frozen) processing (except baby or pet food)
112391	Poultry and egg farm
41911	Poultry and egg, business to business (B2B) electronic markets, wholesale
41912	Poultry and eggs, wholesale agents and brokers
11521	Poultry breeding services
33311	Poultry brooders, feeders and waterers, manufacturing
112391	Poultry combination farming
44521	Poultry dealers, retail
41711	Poultry equipment, wholesale
311614	Poultry fat, rendering
41831	Poultry feeds, prepared, wholesale
311119	Poultry feeds, supplements, concentrates and premixes, manufacturing
11234	Poultry hatchery
112391	Poultry production and hatchery service
41313	Poultry products, wholesale
311615	Poultry slaughtering, dressing and packing
41313	Poultry, dressed, wholesale
41319	Poultry, packaged frozen, wholesale
32562	Powder (e.g., baby, body, face, talcum, toilet), manufacturing
33281	Powder coating metals and metal products, for the trade
333519	Powder metallurgy forming presses, manufacturing
332118	Powder metallurgy products, manufactured on a job or order basis
33142	Powder, made from purchased copper

33149	Powder, non-ferrous metal (except aluminum, copper), made from purchased metals
33399	Powder-actuated hand held power tools, manufacturing
31199	Powdered drink mixes (except chocolate, coffee, milk-based, tea), manufacturing
311515	Powdered milk, manufacturing
31199	Powders, baking, manufacturing
33241	Power boilers, manufacturing
238299	Power boilers, purchased, erection
33592	Power cables, electric, manufacturing
33599	Power capacitors, manufacturing
561799	Power cleaning paved areas (except streets)
44413	Power driven hand tools, retail
41633	Power handtools, wholesale
41723	Power house equipment (except electrical), wholesale
41723	Power house equipment (except electrical), wholesale and repair
41611	Power house equipment, electrical, wholesale
81232	Power laundries (except coin operated)
81232	Power laundry and dry cleaning plants
41723	Power plant machinery, wholesale
41723	Power plant machinery, wholesale and repair
33633	Power steering pumps, manufacturing
33633	Power steering pumps, rebuilding on a factory basis
335315	Power switching equipment, manufacturing
811411	Power tools, repair (without retail sales of new equipment)
335311	Power transformers, manufacturing
41611	Power transmission equipment, electric, wholesale
41723	Power transmission equipment, mechanical, wholesale
561799	Power washing building exteriors
56173	Power, communication and pipe lines, maintenance of rights of way
23891	Power, communication and pipe lines, rights of way clearance (except maintenance)
33399	Power-driven hand tools, manufacturing
212398	Pozzolana (volcanic ash), mining
114114	Prairie jigging, fishing
32733	Precast concrete blocks and bricks, manufacturing
32733	Precast concrete pipe, manufacturing

32739	Precast concrete products (except block, brick, pipe), manufacturing
33281	Precious metal plating of metals and metal products, for the trade
41892	Precious metals and alloys, primary forms and basic shapes, wholesale
33141	Precious metals smelting and primary refining
212398	Precious stones mining
33991	Precious stones, cutting and polishing
81121	Precision instrument repair
41723	Precision tools, machinists', wholesale
332311	Pre-engineered metal buildings, manufacturing
332311	Prefabricated buildings, metal, manufacturing
41639	Prefabricated buildings, wholesale
41639	Prefabricated cottages, wholesale
23835	Prefabricated door and window installation
41639	Prefabricated homes, wholesale
44419	Prefabricated house and building dealers, retail
23835	Prefabricated kitchen and bath cabinet, residential-type, installation
321992	Prefabricated wood buildings, manufacturing
23813	Prefabricated wood trusses and other building wood-frame components, installation
321215	Prefabricated wood trusses, manufacturing
32541	Pregnancy test kits, manufacturing
11292	Pregnant mares' urine (pmu), producing
62441	Pre-kindergarten (except when part of elementary school system)
62441	Pre-kindergarten care services (except when part of elementary school system)
212114	Preparation plants, bituminous coal
61111	Preparatory schools, elementary or secondary
31199	Prepared meals, perishable, packaged for individual resale
31331	Preparing textile fibres for spinning
32312	Prepress printing services (e.g., colour separation, imagesetting, photocomposition, typesetting)
51222	Pre-recorded audio tapes and compact discs, integrated manufacture, release and distribution
33461	Pre-recorded magnetic audio tapes and cassettes, mass-reproducing
62441	Preschool centres (except when part of elementary school system)

44613	Prescription eyeglasses and contact lenses made on the premises, retail
41451	Prescription medicines, wholesale
711311	Presenters, arts events, with their own facilities
31142	Preserves, jams and jellies, manufacturing
31331	Preshrinking textile fabrics and clothing
56149	Presorting mail services
332113	Press forgings, unfinished, made from purchased metal
51911	Press service (news syndicate)
41822	Pressed and moulded pulp goods, wholesale
333519	Presses (e.g., punching, shearing, stamping), metal forming, manufacturing
333299	Presses (i.e., food manufacturing type), manufacturing
33321	Presses for making composite wood (e.g., hardboard, fibreboard, plywood, particleboard), manufacturing
333519	Presses, drill, metal cutting, manufacturing
333299	Presses, printing (except textile printing machinery), manufacturing
33331	Pressing machines (except household type), manufacturing
33635	Pressure and clutch plate assemblies, automotive, truck and bus, manufacturing
33291	Pressure control valves (except fluid power), industrial type, manufacturing
33291	Pressure control valves, fluid power, manufacturing
33221	Pressure cookers, household type, manufacturing
32222	Pressure sensitive paper and tape (except medical), made from purchased materials
41821	Pressure sensitive tape, wholesale
321114	Pressure treated plywood, made from purchased plywood
23812	Pre-stressed concrete beams, slabs or other components, installation
32733	Prestressed concrete pipe, manufacturing
32739	Prestressed concrete products (except block, brick, pipe), manufacturing
445291	Pretzel stores and stands, without baking on the premises, retail
311919	Pretzels (except soft), manufacturing
311814	Pretzels, soft, made in commercial bakeries

41621	Primary forms and basic shapes, non-ferrous metal, wholesale
33141	Primary refining of non-ferrous metals (except aluminum)
61111	Primary schools
331313	Primary smelting of aluminum
91191	Prime Minister's office, federal government
32551	Primers, paint, manufacturing
323115	Print shops, digital
323113	Print shops, screen (except on textile fabrics)
33441	Printed circuit boards, bare (i.e., without mounted electronic components), manufacturing
33441	Printed circuit laminates, manufacturing
31331	Printed fabrics, made from purchased fabric
33411	Printers, computer, manufacturing
41723	Printing and lithographing industries machinery, wholesale
41723	Printing and lithographing industries machinery, wholesale and repair
32591	Printing inks, manufacturing
333299	Printing machinery for textiles, manufacturing
323116	Printing manifold business forms
323113	Printing on clothing (e.g., caps, T-shirts)
31331	Printing on narrow fabrics
31331	Printing on textile fabrics
323113	Printing on textile products (e.g., napkins, placemats, towels), own account
41822	Printing paper, wholesale
333299	Printing plate engraving machinery, manufacturing
32312	Printing plate preparation services
32312	Printing postpress services (e.g., bevelling, binding, bronzing, edging, foil stamping)
32312	Printing prepress services (e.g., colour separation, imagesetting, photocomposition, typesetting)
333299	Printing presses (except textile printing machinery), manufacturing
81131	Printing trade machinery repair
41723	Printing trades machinery and equipment, wholesale
323119	Printing, books, without publishing
323115	Printing, digital (e.g., billboards, other large format graphical materials)
323115	Printing, digital (e.g., graphics, high resolution)
323119	Printing, flexographic (except manifold business forms, textile fabrics)
323119	Printing, gravure (except manifold business forms, textile fabrics), without publishing
323119	Printing, letterpress (except manifold business forms, textile fabrics)
323119	Printing, lithographic (except manifold business forms, quick, textile fabrics)
323119	Printing, offset (except manifold business forms, quick, textile fabrics)
323114	Printing, quick (except photocopy service)
323113	Printing, screen (except on textile fabrics)
23622	Prison construction
33421	Private branch exchange (PBX) equipment, manufacturing
561611	Private detectives services
23821	Private driveway or parking area lighting contractors
721111	Private hotels
81411	Private households employing domestic personnel
561611	Private investigation services
56143	Private mail box rental centres
56143	Private mail centres
61111	Private schools, elementary or secondary
91191	Privy Council office
91211	Probate courts
212398	Probertite mining
23822	Process piping, installation
54119	Process server
311515	Processed cheese, manufacturing
41443	Processing and finishing equipment, photographic, wholesale
212393	Processing of salt at the mine site
41912	Produce brokers, wholesale
56191	Product sterilization and packaging service
54138	Product testing services
711111	Production of live theatrical entertainment
51221	Production of master recordings, exclusive of distribution
54137	Production of topographic materials and maps
541619	Production planning and control consulting services
541619	Productivity improvement consulting services
61143	Professional and management development training
81392	Professional associations

51113	Professional books, publishing (except exclusively on Internet)
56133	Professional employer organizations
41912	Professional machinery and equipment, wholesale agents and brokers
41793	Professional machinery, equipment and supplies, wholesale
41793	Professional machinery, equipment and supplies, wholesale and repair
51112	Professional magazines and periodicals, publishing and printing combined
711211	Professional or semi-professional sports clubs
61131	Professional schools (e.g., dental, engineering, law, medical)
61162	Professional sports instructors for golf, skiing, swimming
81392	Professional standards review boards
32613	Profile shapes (e.g., plate, rod, sheet), laminated plastics, manufacturing
326121	Profile shapes (e.g., rod, tube), non-rigid plastics, manufacturing
32614	Profile shapes, polystyrene foam, manufacturing
54151	Programming services, computer, custom
51211	Programs producing, television
323119	Programs, for sporting events, printing without publishing
41443	Projection equipment (e.g., motion picture, slide), photographic, wholesale
33331	Projection screens (i.e., motion picture, slide, overhead), manufacturing
711311	Promoters of arts events, with facilities
711319	Promoters of sports events, with facilities
711329	Promoters, sports events, without facilities
56141	Proofreading service
211113	Propane (natural) production
454312	Propane dealer, retail
454312	Propane gas sales and distribution, retail
32411	Propane gases, made in petroleum refineries
33641	Propellers, aircraft, manufacturing
332999	Propellers, ship and boat, machined, manufacturing
524124	Property damage insurance
53131	Property management, non residential
81399	Property owners' association
524134	Property reinsurance carriers
32629	Prophylactics, rubber, manufacturing
41451	Proprietary (patent) medicines, wholesale

44611	Proprietary medicines, retail
32511	Propylene (propene), made from refined petroleum or natural gas liquids
32521	Propylene resins, manufacturing
213117	Prospect drilling for metal mining, on a contract basis
213117	Prospect drilling for non-metallic minerals (except fuels), on contract basis
33911	Prosthetic devices, manufacturing
62121	Prosthodontists, offices of
33911	Protective industrial clothing, manufacturing
32522	Protein fibres and filaments, manufacturing
32521	Protein plastics, manufacturing
91212	Provincial correctional services
91211	Provincial courts of law
71219	Provincial parks
91213	Provincial police services
91291	Provincial-federal fiscal relations, provincial government
91291	Provincial-federal relations, provincial government
334511	Proximity warning (i.e., collision avoidance) equipment, manufacturing
212299	Psilomelane mining
62221	Psychiatric hospitals
62133	Psychiatric social workers, offices of
62111	Psychiatrists' offices
81299	Psychic services
81392	Psychologists' associations
62133	Psychologists' offices
54172	Psychology research and development services
62133	Psychotherapists (except M.D.), offices of
541212	Public accountants, offices of
41732	Public address equipment, wholesale
53249	Public address system rental
33431	Public address systems and equipment, manufacturing
51512	Public broadcasting television
337127	Public building furniture, manufacturing
41439	Public building furniture, wholesale
621494	Public health clinics
91291	Public health service programs, provincial government
81331	Public interest groups (e.g., environment, conservation, human rights, wildlife)
519121	Public libraries
54191	Public opinion polling services
54191	Public opinion research services
54182	Public relations agencies

54182	Public relations services
54182	Public relations, consultants, offices of
81331	Public safety advocacy groups
91191	Public Service Commission, federal government
91291	Public Service Commission, provincial government
91191	Public Service Staff Relations Board, federal government
81341	Public speaking improvement clubs
61169	Public speaking schools
56149	Public stenography services
49311	Public storage (except self storage)
91291	Public utility commissions, provincial government
53119	Public utility property, lessors of
23622	Public warehouse construction
91291	Public welfare assistance programs, provincial government
91191	Public works programs, federal government
54184	Publishers' advertising representatives, independent
51114	Publishers, database (except exclusively on Internet)
51111	Publishers, newspaper (except exclusively on Internet)
51111	Publishers, newspaper, combined with printing
51121	Publishers, packaged computer software, all formats
51112	Publishers, periodicals, all formats (except exclusively on Internet)
51221	Publishing and reproducing audio materials in integrated facilities
51223	Publishing music
51113	Publishing, books (except exclusively on Internet)
51113	Publishing, maps, street guides and atlases (except exclusively on Internet)
51913	Publishing, maps, street guides and atlases (exclusively on Internet)
72241	Pubs
41319	Puddings, dessert, wholesale
333619	Pulleys, power transmission, manufacturing
322122	Pulp and newsprint (including uncoated groundwood) combined, manufacturing
322121	Pulp and paper (except newsprint and uncoated groundwood) combined, manufacturing
41723	Pulp and paper industry machinery, wholesale

32213	Pulp and paperboard combined, manufacturing
333291	Pulp making machinery, manufacturing
322112	Pulp mills, chemical, not making paper or paperboard
322111	Pulp mills, mechanical or semi-chemical, not making paper or paperboard
322299	Pulp products, moulded, manufacturing
333291	Pulp washers and thickeners, manufacturing
113312	Pulpwood cutting, on contract
113311	Pulpwood logs, cutting
484223	Pulpwood trucking, local (i.e., to the mill)
41891	Pulpwood, wholesale
11113	Pulses, dry, growing
41723	Pulverizing machinery and equipment, industrial, wholesale
212398	Pumicite mining
213118	Pumping of oil and gas wells, on a contract basis
23711	Pumping stations, water, construction
41723	Pumps and pumping equipment, wholesale
41612	Pumps, electrical (except industrial), wholesale
33399	Pumps, fluid power, manufacturing
33391	Pumps, industrial and commercial type, general purpose, manufacturing
33391	Pumps, measuring and dispensing (e.g., gasoline), manufacturing
41799	Pumps, measuring and dispensing, gasoline and oil, wholesale
33391	Pumps, oil well and oil field, manufacturing
33391	Pumps, sump or water, residential type, manufacturing
333519	Punching machines, metalworking, manufacturing
711111	Puppet theatres
41912	Purchasing agents, wholesale trade
91291	Purchasing services, provincial government
31699	Purses (except precious metal), manufacturing
44815	Purses and bags, leather, retail
41411	Purses, women's and misses', wholesale
33221	Putty knives, manufacturing
32551	Putty, glaziers', manufacturing
32552	Putty, plumbers', manufacturing
45112	Puzzles (game), retail
41446	Puzzles, wholesale
31519	Pyjamas, made in knitting mills

315221	Pyjamas, men's and boys', cut and sewn from purchased fabric
315231	Pyjamas, women's, misses' and girls', cut and sewn from purchased fabric
212398	Pyrites mining
32519	Pyroligneous acids, manufacturing
212299	Pyrolusite mining
212398	Pyrophyllite mining
325999	Pyrotechnics (e.g., flares, flashlight bombs, signals), manufacturing

Q

112399	Quail farming
33313	Quarrying machinery and equipment, manufacturing
41721	Quarrying machinery and equipment, wholesale
33637	Quarter panels, motor vehicle, metal, stamping
212398	Quartz crystal mining (pure)
212317	Quartzite, crushed and broken stone, quarrying
212317	Quartzite, quarrying
31141	Quick freezing of fruit and vegetables
32741	Quicklime (i.e., calcium oxide), manufacturing
212299	Quicksilver (mercury) ore mining
45113	Quilting materials and supplies, retail
31499	Quilting of textiles
31412	Quilts, made from purchased materials
52399	Quotation services, securities

R

11293	Rabbit raising
311615	Rabbits, slaughtering and dressing
711218	Race car drivers and owners
33699	Race cars, manufacturing
711218	Race horse trainers
711213	Race horse training
332991	Races, ball or roller bearing, manufacturing
51119	Racing forms, publishing (except exclusively on Internet)
711213	Racing stables, horse, operation of
33633	Rack and pinion steering assemblies, rebuilding on factory basis
33992	Rackets and frames, sports (e.g., tennis, badminton, squash, racquetball, lacrosse), manufacturing
33639	Racks (e.g., bicycle, luggage, ski, tire), automotive, truck and bus, manufacturing
332619	Racks, household type, made from purchased wire

71394	Racquetball clubs
334511	Radar detectors, manufacturing
41732	Radar equipment, wholesale
51791	Radar station operation
91111	Radar stations, defence
334511	Radar systems and equipment, manufacturing
23822	Radiant floor heating equipment, installation
334512	Radiation detection and monitoring instruments, manufacturing
81233	Radiation protective garments supply service
33911	Radiation shielding aprons, gloves and sheeting, manufacturing
54138	Radiation testing services
325999	Radiator additive preparations, manufacturing
32622	Radiator and heater hoses, rubber, manufacturing
811119	Radiator repair shops, motor vehicle
333416	Radiators (except motor vehicle, portable electric), manufacturing
33639	Radiators and cores, automotive, truck and bus, manufacturing
41612	Radiators, heating equipment, wholesale
54184	Radio advertising representatives, independent
23622	Radio and television broadcast studio construction
61151	Radio and television broadcasting schools
332319	Radio and television tower sections, fabricated structural metal, manufacturing
488339	Radio beacon service, ship navigation
51511	Radio broadcasting network services
51511	Radio broadcasting stations
41732	Radio communications equipment, wholesale
41732	Radio communications equipment, wholesale and repair
51721	Radio paging communications carriers
41732	Radio receiving and transmitting tubes, wholesale
33431	Radio receiving sets, manufacturing
56141	Radio transcription service
325189	Radioactive elements, manufacturing
32541	Radioactive in-vivo diagnostic substances, manufacturing
325189	Radioactive isotopes, manufacturing
212291	Radioactive ore mining
41451	Radioactive pharmaceutical isotopes, wholesale

56221	Radioactive waste disposal service
54138	Radiographic testing services
62111	Radiologists' offices
41529	Radios and tape decks, motor vehicle, new, wholesale
41421	Radios, household-type, wholesale
212291	Radium bearing ore milling
212291	Radium ore mining
23899	Radon mitigation contractors
54138	Radon testing services
41819	Rags, paper, rubber and bottles (scrap), wholesale
33651	Rail laying and tamping equipment, manufacturing
48511	Rail transportation, commuter
332329	Railings, metal, manufacturing
48821	Railroad car repair (except factory rebuilding of rolling stock)
33651	Railroad cars, self-propelled, manufacturing
41799	Railroad equipment and supplies, wholesale
41799	Railroad equipment and supplies, wholesale and repair
41799	Railroad locomotive machinery and equipment parts, wholesale
53119	Railroad property, lessor of
48821	Railroad switching services
48821	Railroad terminals, independent operation
56159	Railroad ticket offices
321114	Railroad ties (i.e., bridge, cross, switch), wood, treating
113311	Railroad ties, hewn, cutting
33651	Railroad track equipment (e.g., rail layers, ballast distributors), manufacturing
48511	Railroads, commuter operation
48711	Railroads, scenic and sightseeing, local
41621	Rails and accessories, metal, wholesale
332319	Railway bridge sections, prefabricated metal, manufacturing
53241	Railway car leasing (except financial)
23799	Railway construction (track, roadbed, trestles, signals, interlockers)
48821	Railway maintenance services (i.e., rights-of-way, structures)
482112	Railway transportation, freight, short-haul
482112	Railways, belt line
482113	Railways, freight, mainline
482112	Railways, freight, short-haul
482112	Railways, logging
482114	Railways, passenger (except urban transit and scenic and sightseeing)

448199	Raincoat stores, retail
31332	Raincoats, oiling (i.e., waterproofing)
315299	Raincoats, waterproof (except infants'), cut and sewn from purchased fabric
11221	Raising hogs
11241	Raising sheep
31142	Raisins, made in dehydration plants
33221	Rakes, non-powered hand tool, manufacturing
33441	RAM (random access memory) chips, manufacturing
41612	Ranges (except electric), wholesale
33331	Ranges, commercial type, manufacturing
44311	Ranges, gas and electric, retail
41612	Ranges, stoves and furnaces (except electric), wholesale
62419	Rape crisis centres
311224	Rapeseed oil, made in crushing mills
33651	Rapid transit cars and equipment, manufacturing
45331	Rare book stores
325189	Rare earth compounds, not specified elsewhere by process, manufacturing
212299	Rare-earths ore mining
33221	Ratchets, non-powered, manufacturing
337126	Rattan furniture, manufacturing
41119	Raw leaf tobacco, wholesale
41119	Raw sugar, wholesale
32522	Rayon fibres and filaments, manufacturing
41413	Rayon piece goods, wholesale
33221	Razor blades, manufacturing
33221	Razors (except electric), manufacturing
41452	Razors and blades, non-electric, wholesale
33521	Razors, electric, manufacturing
33241	Reactors, nuclear, manufacturing
81311	Reading rooms, promoting a religion
32732	Ready-mixed concrete manufacturing and distribution
31123	Ready-to-serve breakfast cereal foods, manufacturing
53139	Real estate advisory services
531212	Real estate agencies
81391	Real estate boards
531212	Real estate brokers
53112	Real Estate Investment Trusts (REIT's), operating non-residential buildings (except mini-warehouses)
53119	Real Estate Investment Trusts (REIT's), operating real estate other than buildings

531111	Real Estate Investment Trusts (REIT's), operating residential buildings, except social housing
53113	Real Estate Investment Trusts (REIT's), operating self-storage mini-warehouses
53131	Real estate management
531212	Real estate sales and brokerage services
61151	Real estate schools
54119	Real estate title searching and consulting
23721	Real property (except cemeteries) subdivision
56149	Real time closed captioning (i.e., simultaneous)
531212	Realtor
531212	Realty company
332314	Rebar (deformed steel bars for concrete reinforcement), manufacturing
332314	Rebar (i.e., concrete reinforcing bar), manufacturing
23812	Rebars (deformed steel bars for concrete reinforcement), installation
33631	Rebuilding automotive and truck gasoline engines
333519	Rebuilding machine tools, metal cutting types
333519	Rebuilding machine tools, metal forming types
33632	Rebuilding motor vehicle electrical equipment (e.g., alternators, generators and distributors)
335312	Rebuilding motors, electric, other than automotive
32621	Rebuilding tires
41723	Recapping machinery, for tires, wholesale
54199	Receivership services
41611	Receptacles, electrical, wholesale
33111	Reclaiming iron and steel scrap from slag
32629	Reclaiming rubber from waste or scrap
337121	Reclining chairs, household, upholstered, manufacturing
81131	Reconditioning metal drums and shipping containers
454113	Record clubs, mail order, retail
711512	Record producers, independent
51221	Record production (except independent record producers), without duplication or distribution
51222	Record production and distribution combined
51221	Record production companies (producing only)
51229	Recording of books on tape or disc (except publishing)
51229	Recording seminars and conferences, audio
51224	Recording studios (except integrated record company)
51224	Recording studios, operating on a contract or fee basis
45122	Records and tapes retail
541611	Records management consulting services
53229	Recreation and sports equipment rental
23799	Recreation areas (open space), construction
721213	Recreation camps (except fishing and hunting camps)
91191	Recreation policy and planning, federal government
91391	Recreation programs, municipal administration
721113	Recreational hotels
71399	Recreational sports teams and leagues
53212	Recreational trailer rental
44121	Recreational vehicle dealers, retail
23799	Recreational vehicle park construction
721211	Recreational vehicle parks
336215	Recreational vehicles (RV), self-contained, manufacturing
41519	Recreational vehicles, wholesale
41519	Recreational vehicles, wholesale and repair
33599	Rectifiers (electrical apparatus), manufacturing
33441	Rectifiers, electronic component-type, manufacturing
41732	Rectifiers, electronic, wholesale
56211	Recyclable material, collection
41812	Recyclable paper, wholesale
41812	Recyclable paperboard, wholesale
41912	Recycled materials (except auto parts), wholesale agents and brokers
81121	Recycling (i.e., cleaning and re-filling) ink jet cartridges
32419	Recycling (i.e., re-refining) used motor oils
32561	Recycling drycleaning fluids
41819	Recycling empty bottles
322112	Recycling paper (i.e., making pulp from waste and scrap paper)
325999	Recycling services for degreasing solvents (e.g., engine, machine part)
41911	Red meat and meat product, fresh, business to business (B2B) electronic markets, wholesale

213111	Redrilling oil and gas wells, on a contract basis
333619	Reducers, speed, manufacturing
322219	Reels, fibre, made from purchased paperboard
321999	Reels, wood, manufacturing
519121	Reference libraries
48691	Refined petroleum products, pipeline transport service
41211	Refined petroleum products, wholesale
32411	Refineries, petroleum
33142	Refining copper, secondary (i.e., of purchased metal or scrap)
212393	Refining salt at the mine site
81142	Refinish office furniture
81142	Refinishing furniture
11531	Reforestation services
91212	Reformatories, provincial government
334512	Refractometers, manufacturing
32712	Refractories (e.g., block, brick, mortar, tile), manufacturing
32712	Refractory cement and mortar, manufacturing
72221	Refreshment stands
333416	Refrigerated counters and display cases, manufacturing
484229	Refrigerated products trucking, local
484239	Refrigerated products trucking, long-distance
49312	Refrigerated warehousing
41791	Refrigeration and cooling equipment and supplies, commercial, wholesale
333416	Refrigeration compressors, manufacturing
334512	Refrigeration controls, residential and commercial type, manufacturing
333416	Refrigeration equipment, industrial and commercial type, manufacturing
41529	Refrigeration units, motor vehicle, sales and service
333416	Refrigeration units, truck type, manufacturing
811412	Refrigerator repair service, electric (without retail sales of new equipment)
44311	Refrigerators and related electric and gas appliances, retail
41422	Refrigerators, electric, domestic, wholesale
41612	Refrigerators, gas, domestic, wholesale
335223	Refrigerators, household, manufacturing
62419	Refugee services
91132	Refugee settlement, federal government
56221	Refuse collection and disposal service
56211	Refuse collection service
23621	Refuse disposal plants, construction
56221	Refuse disposal, incinerator and combustor
56221	Refuse disposal, landfill
91391	Regional board/council, local government
621494	Regional health services centre
91191	Regional industrial development programs, federal government
541212	Registered industrial accountants' offices
62139	Registered nurses' offices
56131	Registries, employment (e.g., maid, nurses, teachers)
56131	Registries, nurses'
91124	Regulation and inspection of agricultural products
91215	Regulatory services, general, provincial government
62142	Rehabilitation clinics, out-patient
62431	Rehabilitation counselling and training, vocational
62221	Rehabilitation hospitals, drug addiction and alcoholism
91212	Rehabilitation services, provincial government (correctional)
41621	Reinforcement mesh, wire, wholesale
332619	Reinforcing mesh, concrete, made from purchased wire
23812	Reinforcing rods, bars, mesh and cage, installation
41621	Reinforcing rods, steel, wholesale
23812	Reinforcing steel contractors
524132	Reinsurance carriers, accident and health
524131	Reinsurance carriers, life
335315	Relays, electrical, manufacturing
41611	Relays, wholesale
323119	Religious books, printing without publishing
51113	Religious books, publishers (except exclusively on Internet)
51113	Religious books, publishing and printing combined
453999	Religious goods stores (except books), retail
51112	Religious magazines and periodicals, publisher (except exclusively on Internet)
81311	Religious organizations
41899	Religious supplies, wholesale
31142	Relishes, canning
45113	Remnant stores, retail
23611	Remodelling and renovating single-family houses

33429	Remote control units (e.g., garage door, television) manufacturing
311614	Rendering plants
23611	Renovation, residential, general contractor
91215	Rent control agencies, provincial government
53139	Rental accommodation referral service
53249	Rental agency, theatrical equipment (except costumes)
56299	Rental and pumping of portable toilets
53249	Rental and sales of public address systems
53242	Rental of business machines (not manufacturing)
53222	Rental of clothing or costumes
51821	Rental of computer time
53221	Rental of consumer audio-visual equipment (including rent-to-own)
53229	Rental of dishes, silverware, tables and banquet accessories
53231	Rental of floor waxing and sanding machines
53229	Rental of golf carts
53249	Rental of industrial machinery and equipment
53241	Rental of oil field equipment (without operator)
53241	Rental of scaffolding (including mobile platforms)
53231	Rental of tools, consumer
53212	Rental of trailers
484229	Rental of truck, with driver
53242	Rental service, computer
53231	Rent-all centres
53241	Rentals, heavy machinery and equipment (except construction with operator)
56299	Renting of portable toilets
53212	Renting travel, camping, or recreational trailers
541611	Reorganization consulting service
81121	Repair and maintenance of computers and related equipment
41521	Repair materials, tire and tube, wholesale
811411	Repair motors for boats (without retail sales of new equipment)
81131	Repair of electrical switchgear and control equipment
81121	Repair of electronic equipment
81131	Repair of industrial furnaces
81121	Repair of industrial process control equipment
81131	Repair of machine tools

81131	Repair of machinery for food, beverage and tobacco processing
81121	Repair of motion picture studio equipment
81131	Repair of non-domestic cooling and refrigeration equipment
81131	Repair of paperboard making machinery
81131	Repair of pumps and compressors (except for refrigeration)
81131	Repair of rubber or plastic industry machinery
81131	Repair of taps and valves
81131	Repair of textile, apparel and leather production machinery
811111	Repair shops, automotive, general
32312	Repairing books
81142	Repairing furniture (without retail sales of new equipment)
81149	Repairing golf clubs (without retail sales of new equipment)
23731	Repairing highways, roads, streets, bridges or airport runways
81149	Repairing horse-drawn wagon
81131	Repairing pallets (except wooden)
711111	Repertory or stock companies, theatrical
41732	Replacement parts, electronic, wholesale
711513	Reporters, independent
56149	Repossession services
56143	Reprographic services
71213	Reptile exhibits, live
54151	Requirements analysis, computer hardware
311225	Re-refining purchased fats and oils
32419	Re-refining used petroleum lubricating oils
54171	Research and development laboratories or services, engineering
54171	Research and development laboratories or services, life sciences
54171	Research and development laboratories or services, physical sciences
51791	Resellers, long-distance telephone communications (except satellite)
51791	Resellers, microwave communications
51741	Resellers, satellite telecommunications
51791	Resellers, telephone communications (except satellite)
51791	Reselling dial-up or broadband ISP services
56159	Reservation service (e.g., airline, car rental, hotel, restaurant)
23711	Reservoir construction, general contractors

72131	Residence, college (if separate establishment from college)
561722	Residential cleaning services
72131	Residential clubs
531111	Residential hotels, operators of
23611	Residential house construction
326198	Resilient floor coverings (e.g., sheet, tile), manufacturing
44221	Resilient floor tiles or sheets (e.g., linoleum, rubber, vinyl), installation combined with selling
32521	Resins, plastics (except custom compounding purchased resins), manufacturing
41841	Resins, plastics, wholesale
41841	Resins, synthetic (except rubber), wholesale
33399	Resistance welding and cutting equipment, manufacturing
33441	Resistors, electronic, manufacturing
41732	Resistors, electronic, wholesale
721113	Resort hotel
721113	Resort management services (i.e., providing management and operating staff to run resort)
721113	Resorts with integrated health spa facilities
33911	Respiratory protection equipment, personal, manufacturing
621499	Respiratory therapy clinics
561722	Rest room cleaning services
81299	Rest room operation
41792	Restaurant and hotel equipment, wholesale
41792	Restaurant and hotel equipment, wholesale and repair
81391	Restaurant association
337127	Restaurant furniture, manufacturing
561722	Restaurant kitchen cleaning services
61151	Restaurant operation schools
23622	Restaurants, construction
81142	Restoration and repair of antique furniture
81149	Restoration and repair of antiques (except furniture and automobiles)
81149	Restringing tennis rackets (without retail sales of new equipment)
56141	Resume writing service
23833	Resurfacing hardwood floors
23731	Resurfacing highways, roads, streets, bridges or airport runways
45311	Retail florists
44521	Retail meat market
33399	Retail scales (e.g., butcher, delicatessen, produce), manufacturing

44821	Retail shoe store
81391	Retailers' associations
44419	Retailers of ceramic floor and wall tiles
44132	Retailing and repairing tires
23814	Retaining wall construction, block, stone, or brick, contractors
23799	Retaining walls, anchored (e.g., with piles, soil nails, tieback anchors), construction
23811	Retaining walls, poured concrete, construction
325999	Retarders (e.g., flameproofing agents, mildewing agents), manufacturing
81341	Retirement associations, social
32621	Retreading materials, tire, manufacturing
32621	Retreading tires
81311	Retreat houses, religious
91191	Revenue ministry, federal government
91291	Revenue ministry, provincial government
23799	Revetment construction
332999	Revolvers, manufacturing
238299	Revolving doors, installation, contractors
33141	Rhenium smelting and primary refining
212299	Rhodium mining
212299	Rhodochrosite mining
33994	Ribbons, inked (e.g., typewriter, adding machine, cash register), manufacturing
31322	Ribbons, made in narrow woven fabric mills
31323	Ribbons, made in nonwoven fabric mills
11116	Rice (except wild rice) farming
311214	Rice brans, flour and meal, manufacturing
31123	Rice breakfast foods, manufacturing
311214	Rice cleaning and polishing
311214	Rice malt, manufacturing
311214	Rice milling
31199	Rice mixes, made from purchased dried ingredients
311214	Rice mixes, made in rice mills
311221	Rice starch, manufacturing
41319	Rice, polished, wholesale
41112	Rice, unpolished, wholesale
61162	Riding academies and schools
448199	Riding apparel stores, retail
81394	Riding association, political party
71399	Riding clubs, recreational
45111	Riding goods and equipment, retail
71399	Riding stables (except racing)
332999	Rifles (except toy), manufacturing
238299	Rigging large-scale equipment
23891	Rights of way, cutting (except maintenance)

56173	Rights of way, cutting, maintenance
336612	Rigid hull inflatable boats
33991	Rings, jewellery, manufacturing
33631	Rings, piston, manufacturing
71394	Rinks, ice or roller skating
212316	Riprap (except limestone and granite), quarrying
483213	River freight transportation (except using the St. Lawrence Seaway)
483213	River passenger transportation (except ferries)
71399	River rafting, recreational
71321	Riverboat casinos
33272	Rivets, metal, manufacturing
711111	Road companies, theatrical
41721	Road construction and maintenance machinery, wholesale
41721	Road construction and maintenance machinery, wholesale and repair
311911	Roasted nuts and seeds, manufacturing
31192	Roasting coffee
41411	Robes and gowns, women's and children's, wholesale
33312	Rock crushing machinery, portable, manufacturing
33313	Rock crushing machinery, stationary, manufacturing
33313	Rock drill bits, oil and gas field type, manufacturing
33313	Rock drill bits, underground mining type, manufacturing
41721	Rock drilling machinery and equipment, wholesale
71113	Rock music groups
23799	Rock removal, underwater, contractor
212393	Rock salt mining
212393	Rock salt processing at the mine site
33637	Rocker panels, motor vehicle, metal, stamping
33641	Rockets (guided missiles), space and military, complete, manufacturing
32613	Rod, laminated plastics, manufacturing
331317	Rod, made from purchased aluminum
32532	Rodenticides, manufacturing
41839	Rodenticides, wholesale
53229	Rodeo animal rental
711319	Rodeo promoters, with facilities
711329	Rodeo promoters, without facilities
41621	Rods, bars and angles, steel, wholesale
31171	Roe, fish, processing
332118	Roll forming of metal products
331221	Rolled steel products, made from purchased steel
332991	Roller bearings, manufacturing

711211	Roller hockey clubs, professional or semi-professional
33992	Roller skates, manufacturing
71394	Roller skating rinks
333519	Rolling mill machinery and equipment, metalworking, manufacturing
331511	Rolling mill rolls, iron, manufacturing
331514	Rolling mill rolls, steel, manufacturing
33149	Rolling, drawing and extruding purchased non-ferrous metal (except aluminum, copper)
32223	Rolls (e.g., adding machine, calculator, cash register), made from purchased paper
81311	Roman Catholic church
23816	Roof membrane, installation
321215	Roof trusses, wood, manufacturing
32629	Roofing (i.e., single-ply rubber membrane), manufacturing
324122	Roofing felts, made from purchased asphaltic materials
44419	Roofing material dealers, retail
41639	Roofing materials, dealers (except wooden)
41632	Roofing materials, wood, wholesale
32712	Roofing tile, clay, manufacturing
32739	Roofing tile, concrete, manufacturing
72131	Rooming houses
31499	Rope (except wire rope), manufacturing
41899	Rope, binder twine and string, wholesale
41621	Rope, wire (except insulated), wholesale
332619	Rope, wire, made from purchased wire
111421	Rose bushes, growing
32521	Rosin (i.e., modified resins), manufacturing
32519	Rosin, made by distillation of pine gum or pine wood
113311	Rossing mill
323119	Rotogravure printing
32312	Rotogravure printing plates and cylinders preparation services
32562	Rouge, cosmetic, manufacturing
41891	Roundwood, wholesale
33399	Routers, hand held power-driven, manufacturing
71399	Rowing clubs, recreational
91123	Royal Canadian Mounted Police
41723	Rubber and plastic industries machinery, equipment and supplies, wholesale
32629	Rubber bands, manufacturing
32552	Rubber cement, manufacturing
212326	Rubber clay mining
238299	Rubber doors, installation

41412	Rubber footwear, wholesale
32629	Rubber goods, mechanical (i.e, extruded, lathe-cut, moulded), manufacturing
325999	Rubber processing preparations (e.g., accelerators, stabilizers), manufacturing
33994	Rubber stamps, manufacturing
31322	Rubber thread and yarns, fabric-covered, manufacturing
41819	Rubber waste, wholesale
33322	Rubber working machinery, manufacturing
32521	Rubber, synthetic, manufacturing
31332	Rubberizing fabrics and clothing
56211	Rubbish collection
484239	Rubbish hauling without collection, long-distance
81149	Rug and carpet repair only
41841	Rug cleaning compounds, wholesale
32561	Rug cleaning preparations, manufacturing
56174	Rug cleaning services
45112	Rug hooking supplies, retail
44221	Rug stores, retail
33221	Rulers, metal, manufacturing
31214	Rum, manufacturing
31621	Running shoes, manufacturing
48521	Rural bus service (except school bus)
49111	Rural mail carrier service
325999	Rust preventative preparations, manufacturing
33281	Rust proofing metals and metal products, for the trade
32561	Rust removers, manufacturing
41841	Rustproofing chemicals, wholesale
23832	Rustproofing contractor, buildings and structures (except automotive)
811199	Rustproofing service, automotive
111219	Rutabaga farming
212299	Ruthenium ore mining
11119	Rye, growing

S

32222	Sacks, multiwall, made from purchased uncoated paper
81143	Saddlery repair
41899	Saddlery, wholesale
31699	Saddles and parts, leather, manufacturing
332999	Safe deposit boxes and chests, metal, manufacturing
332999	Safe doors and linings, metal, manufacturing
332999	Safes, metal, manufacturing

33911	Safety appliances and equipment, personal, manufacturing
33911	Safety clothing, manufacturing
54169	Safety consulting services
327215	Safety glass (including motor vehicle), made from purchased glass
327214	Safety glass (including motor vehicle), made in glass-making plants
23899	Safety net systems, erecting and dismantling
33999	Safety pins, manufacturing
33291	Safety valves, industrial type, manufacturing
11112	Safflower farming
33992	Sailboards, manufacturing
41799	Sailboat, wholesale
71393	Sailing clubs (i.e., operating marinas)
71399	Sailing clubs, without marinas
41447	Sails and tents, wholesale
325181	Sal soda (i.e., washing soda), manufacturing
31142	Salad dressing mixes, dry, made in dehydration plants
31194	Salad dressing mixes, dry, manufacturing
31194	Salad dressings, manufacturing
31199	Salads, fresh or refrigerated, manufacturing
311614	Salami, made from purchased meat
531211	Sales agents, real estate
323116	Sales books, manifold, printing
52222	Sales finance companies
541619	Sales management consulting services
44419	Sales of aluminum doors and installation
453992	Sales of beer making supplies and use of brewing equipment
54181	Sales promotion campaign services
91291	Sales tax collection, provincial government
32541	Salicylic acid, medicinal, uncompounded, manufacturing
31171	Salmon cannery
72241	Saloons (drinking places)
31142	Salsa, canning
212393	Salt brining (deposit extraction)
212393	Salt mining, common
212393	Salt refining at the mine site
31194	Salt, substitute, manufacturing
41841	Salts, industrial, wholesale
54186	Sample and coupon packages, development of
54187	Sample direct distribution services
32312	Samples and displays mounting
54191	Sampling services, statistical

23832	Sand blasting and painting (non-masonry surfaces)
23899	Sand blasting building exteriors
331529	Sand castings, non-ferrous metals, unfinished, manufacturing
484222	Sand hauling, local
212323	Sand pit or quarry
41639	Sand, gravel and cement, builders' supply, wholesale
211114	Sand, oil, mining
33281	Sandblasting metals and metal products, for the trade
33399	Sanders, hand held power-driven, manufacturing
33321	Sanding machines, woodworking type, stationary, manufacturing
333291	Sandpaper making machinery, manufacturing
32791	Sandpaper, manufacturing
212317	Sandstone quarry
72221	Sandwich shop
31194	Sandwich spreads, manufacturing
31199	Sandwiches, fresh (i.e., assembled and packaged for the wholesale market), manufacturing
41319	Sandwiches, wholesale
322219	Sanitary food containers (except folding), made from purchased paper or paperboard
322212	Sanitary food containers, folding, made from purchased paperboard
56221	Sanitary landfill operation
322291	Sanitary napkins and tampons, made from purchased paper
322121	Sanitary paper products, made in paper mills
41822	Sanitary paper products, wholesale
322121	Sanitary paper stock (e.g., for making towels, serviettes, tampons), manufacturing
322291	Sanitary products, made from purchased sanitary paper stock
41452	Sanitary products, personal, wholesale
23711	Sanitary sewers, construction
332999	Sanitary ware (e.g., bathtubs, lavatories, sinks), metal, manufacturing
41612	Sanitary ware, wholesale
54162	Sanitation consulting services
41841	Sanitation preparations, wholesale
41632	Sash, door, planing mill products, wholesale
51741	Satellite communication service
51741	Satellite communications carriers
51791	Satellite earth stations facilities operators

44311	Satellite ground station receivers, retail
812921	Satellite photographs, processing
51511	Satellite radio networks
23713	Satellite receiving stations, construction
51741	Satellite service resellers
51791	Satellite telemetry operation on a contract or fee basis
51721	Satellite telephone services
51521	Satellite television networks
517112	Satellite television operators
51791	Satellite terminal stations
51791	Satellite tracking stations
31142	Sauce mixes, dry, made in dehydration plants
31194	Sauce mixes, dry, manufacturing
31194	Sauces (except tomato-based, gravy), manufacturing
31142	Sauces, tomato-based, canning
31142	Sauerkraut, manufacturing
41612	Sauna equipment, wholesale
81219	Saunas
326121	Sausage casings, plastics, manufacturing
41316	Sausage casings, wholesale
311614	Sausages and similar cased products, made from purchased meat
311611	Sausages and similar products, produced in slaughtering plants
33221	Saw blades, all types, manufacturing
321111	Sawdust and shavings, made from logs or bolts (i.e., in a sawmill)
41899	Sawdust, wholesale
333519	Sawing machines, metalworking, manufacturing
113311	Sawlogs, cutting
41723	Sawmill and woodworking machinery, equipment and supplies, wholesale
33321	Sawmill equipment, manufacturing
53249	Sawmill machinery rental service
321111	Sawmills
33321	Saws, bench and table, power, woodworking type, manufacturing
33399	Saws, hand held power driven, manufacturing
33221	Saws, hand, non-powered, manufacturing
333519	Saws, metal cutting (except hand held), manufacturing
41721	Scaffolding, dismantable, wholesale
23899	Scaffolds, erecting and dismantling
41791	Scales, wholesale
81219	Scalp treatment service
41411	Scarves and neckwear, women's, misses' and children's, wholesale
31599	Scarves, made from purchased fabric

31519 Scarves, made in knitting mills

48711 Scenic and sightseeing bus transportation, local

48711 Scenic railroad, local, operation

323119 Schedules (e.g., radio, television, transportation), printing without publishing

212299 Scheelite ore mining

31322 Schiffli machine embroideries, manufacturing

51112 Scholarly journals, publishing (except exclusively on Internet)

81321 Scholarship trusts

51112 Scholastic magazines and periodicals, publishing and printing combined

61111 School boards, elementary and secondary

323119 School books, printing without publishing

48541 School bus operator

48541 School bus service

336211 School buses, assembling on purchased chassis

41512 School buses, wholesale

41512 School buses, wholesale and repair

72231 School cafeteria service

41793 School classroom equipment and supplies (except stationery), wholesale

41793 School classroom equipment and supplies (except stationery), wholesale and repair

337127 School furniture, manufacturing

61151 School of cooking

54192 School photography (i.e., portrait photography) services

41821 School supplies (except furniture and fixtures), wholesale

51113 School textbooks, publishing (except exclusively on Internet)

51113 School textbooks, publishing and printing combined

61161 School, arts and crafts

61111 School, elementary

61151 School, hairdressing and beauty culture

61151 School, trade post-secondary

61162 Schools and camps, sports instructional

61111 Schools for the physically handicapped (elementary and secondary)

61161 Schools of the dance (ballroom and popular)

712115 Science and technology museums

41446 Science kits or sets, wholesale

81121 Scientific instrument, repair

41793 Scientific instruments and apparatus, wholesale

41793 Scientific instruments and apparatus, wholesale and repair

81392 Scientist membership associations

33221 Scissors, non-powered, manufacturing

33221 Scoops, metal, hand (except kitchen), manufacturing

33995 Scoreboards, electric, manufacturing

212398 Scoria mining

31331 Scouring and combing textile fibres

32561 Scouring cleansers (e.g., pastes, powders), manufacturing

41841 Scouring cleansers, wholesale

81341 Scouting organization

331317 Scrap and dross aluminum, refining into ingot

323119 Scrapbooks and refills, manufacturing

33312 Scrapers, construction type, manufacturing

323113 Screen printing (except on textile fabrics)

323113 Screen printing on clothing, for the trade

323113 Screen printing paper documents (e.g., pictures, large-format banners), without publishing

323113 Screen printing T-shirts, for the trade

32591 Screen process inks, manufacturing

41723 Screening machinery and equipment, industrial, wholesale

212397 Screening peat

332619 Screening, woven, made from purchased wire

32312 Screens for printing, preparation services

33331 Screens, projection (i.e., motion picture, slide, overhead), manufacturing

33399 Screwdrivers and nut drivers, hand held power driven, manufacturing

33221 Screwdrivers, non-powered, manufacturing

33272 Screws, metal, manufacturing

711513 Script writers, independent

23822 Scrubbers (i.e., for air-purification) installation

61162 Scuba and skin diving instruction

711511 Sculptors, independent

61161 Sculpture teachers, own account

114113 Sea worm gathering

31171 Seafood and seafood products, canning

31171 Seafood and seafood products, curing

31171 Seafood and seafood products, fresh prepared, manufacturing

31171 Seafood and seafood products, frozen, manufacturing

31171	Seafood dinners (e.g., fish and chips), frozen, manufacturing
44522	Seafood markets, retail
41314	Seafood, dressed, wholesale
31171	Seafood, fresh, chilled or frozen, manufacturing
41314	Seafood, frozen (except packaged), wholesale
41319	Seafood, packaged frozen, wholesale
114113	Seal hunting
41841	Sealants, wholesale
33511	Sealed beam lamps, manufacturing
32552	Sealing compounds for pipe threads and joints, manufacturing
41723	Seals, gaskets and packing, wholesale
33399	Seam welding equipment, manufacturing
33512	Searchlights, manufacturing
721113	Seasonal hotel
56173	Seasonal property maintenance services (i.e., snow ploughing in winter, landscaping during other seasons)
31194	Seasoning salt, manufacturing
33636	Seat belts, motor vehicle and aircraft, manufacturing
811121	Seat cover and auto upholstery shop
32615	Seat cushions, foam plastics (except polystyrene), manufacturing
33636	Seating for buses, railway cars and aircraft, manufacturing
48831	Seaway operation
114113	Seaweed gathering (uncultivated)
31171	Seaweed processing (e.g., dulse)
111419	Seaweed, grown under cover
41893	Second hand goods (except machinery and motor vehicles), wholesale
522299	Secondary market financing (i.e, buying, pooling and repackaging loans for sale to others)
33149	Secondary refining (i.e, of purchased metal and scrap), precious metals
61111	Secondary schools
45331	Second-hand book store, retail
41912	Second-hand goods (except machinery and auto parts), wholesale agents and brokers
45331	Second-hand merchandise, retail
61141	Secretarial schools
56141	Secretarial service
332311	Sections for prefabricated metal buildings (except portable), manufacturing
52311	Securities distributing (i.e., acting as a principal in dealing securities to investors)
52321	Securities exchanges
52311	Securities originating (i.e., acting as a principal in dealing new securities to investors)
91124	Securities regulation commissions
52399	Securities transfer agencies
52311	Securities underwriters
526981	Securitization vehicles (fund)
23821	Security and fire systems, installation only
561612	Security patrol service
561621	Security system sale, combined with installation, maintenance or monitoring
32541	Sedative preparations, manufacturing
212397	Sedge peat mining
23799	Sediment control system construction
212315	Sedimentary rock quarry
31491	Seed bags, made from purchased woven or knitted materials
111211	Seed potatoes, growing
54138	Seed testing laboratories
11511	Seeding crops
56173	Seeding lawns
41832	Seeds (e.g., field, garden, flower), wholesale
44422	Seeds, bulbs, and nursery stock, retail
41832	Seeds, farm and garden, wholesale
311911	Seeds, snack (e.g., canned, cooked, roasted, salted), manufacturing
41912	Seeds, wholesale agents and brokers
52693	Segregated funds (except pension), of life insurance carriers
526112	Segregated pension funds, of life insurance carriers
54136	Seismic drilling
54136	Seismic geophysical surveying services
212395	Selenite mining
325189	Selenium compounds, not specified elsewhere by process, manufacturing
33141	Selenium smelting and primary refining
62419	Self-help action group
623999	Self-help group homes for persons with social or personal problems
44719	Self-serve gasoline stations
81231	Self-service laundry and dry cleaning
41119	Semen, bovine, wholesale
212115	Semibituminous coal mining
322111	Semi-chemical wood pulp, manufacturing
33441	Semiconductor devices, manufacturing
41732	Semiconductor devices, wholesale
333299	Semiconductor making machinery, manufacturing
333619	Semi-diesel engines, manufacturing
212398	Semiprecious stones mining

711211	Semiprofessional sports clubs
91191	Senate
62412	Senior citizen centres
48599	Senior citizen transportation service
81341	Senior citizens' club
56299	Septic tank cleaning services
56299	Septic tank pumping services
41639	Septic tanks (except concrete), wholesale
23891	Septic tanks and weeping tile, installation
33242	Septic tanks, heavy gauge metal, manufacturing
51821	Service bureaus, computer
41792	Service industries machinery and equipment, wholesale
41912	Service machinery and equipment, wholesale agents and brokers
44719	Service station (gasoline, lubricating oils and greases), retail
561722	Service station cleaning and degreasing service
41799	Service station equipment and supplies, wholesale
41799	Service station equipment and supplies, wholesale and repair
23721	Servicing of raw land for subsequent sale
213118	Servicing oil and gas wells, on a contract basis
322291	Serviettes, paper, made from purchased paper
54149	Set design, theatrical (except independent)
711512	Set designers, independent
54119	Settlement offices, real estate
322219	Set-up (i.e., not shipped flat) boxes (except corrugated), made from purchased paperboard
322211	Set-up boxes, corrugated, made from purchased paper or paperboard
23711	Sewage collection and disposal line construction
23711	Sewage treatment and disposal plants, construction
33331	Sewage treatment equipment, manufacturing
22132	Sewage treatment plant operation
56299	Sewer and storm basin cleanout services
56299	Sewer cleaning and rodding services
32712	Sewer pipe and fittings, clay, manufacturing
331511	Sewer pipe, cast iron, manufacturing
32733	Sewer pipe, concrete, manufacturing
22132	Sewer system, operation

811412	Sewing machine repair shops (without retail sales of new equipment)
44311	Sewing machine stores, retail
333299	Sewing machines (including household type), manufacturing
333299	Sewing machines and attachments, household, manufacturing
333299	Sewing machines and attachments, industrial, manufacturing
41422	Sewing machines, electric, domestic, wholesale
41723	Sewing machines, industrial, wholesale
41723	Sewing machines, industrial, wholesale and repair
45113	Sewing supplies, retail
31311	Sewing thread, manufacturing
31491	Shades, outdoor, made from purchased fabrics
321112	Shakes (i.e., hand split shingles), manufacturing
212326	Shale quarry
211114	Shale, oil, mining
41452	Shampoo, hair, wholesale
32562	Shampoos and conditioners, hair, manufacturing
41632	Shaped or turned wood products, wholesale
81149	Sharpening saws, lawn mowers, knives and scissors (without retail sales of new equipment)
32562	Shaving preparations (e.g., creams, gels, lotions, powders), manufacturing
31599	Shawls, made from purchased fabric
31519	Shawls, made in knitting mills
33221	Shears, non-powered, manufacturing
23813	Sheathing (house, building, structure), wood, construction
11521	Sheep dipping and shearing
11241	Sheep farming
33311	Sheep shears, powered, manufacturing
315292	Sheepskin linings, manufacturing
32614	Sheet (i.e., board), polystyrene foam insulation, manufacturing
41639	Sheet metal roofing materials, wholesale
23816	Sheet metal roofing, installation
332329	Sheet metal work (except stamped), manufacturing
323119	Sheet music, printing without publishing
51223	Sheet music, publishing
51223	Sheet music, publishing and printing combined
45114	Sheet music, retail
41899	Sheet music, wholesale
41621	Sheet piling, steel, wholesale

331317	Sheet, aluminum, made by flat rolling purchased aluminum
32613	Sheet, laminated plastics, manufacturing
326114	Sheet, plastics, unlaminated, manufacturing
31412	Sheets and pillow cases, made from purchased fabrics
31321	Sheets and pillow cases, made in broad-woven fabric mills
41621	Sheets, galvanized or other coated, wholesale
41621	Sheets, metal, wholesale
41633	Shelf hardware, wholesale
33999	Shell novelties, manufacturing
32551	Shellac, manufacturing
41634	Shellacs, wholesale
114114	Shellfish digging, freshwater
11251	Shellfish, farming
114113	Shellfish, fishing, salt water
62431	Sheltered workshops
23839	Shelving, metal, constructed on site
337215	Shelving, office and store, manufacturing
41791	Shelving, office and store, wholesale
332619	Shelving, wire, made from purchased wire
23835	Shelving, wood, constructed on site
31152	Sherbets, manufacturing
321112	Shingle mills, wood
41639	Shingles (except wood), wholesale
41632	Shingles and shakes, wooden, wholesale
324122	Shingles, made from purchased asphaltic materials
41899	Ship chandlers, wholesale
33392	Ship cranes and derricks, manufacturing
56131	Ship crew agencies
56131	Ship crew registries
48832	Ship hold cleaning
488332	Ship piloting service
48839	Ship repair and maintenance, not in a shipyard
336611	Ship repair, done in a shipyard
488331	Ship salvaging
48839	Ship scaling services
332319	Ship sections, prefabricated metal, manufacturing
488519	Shipping agents, freight forwarding
31491	Shipping bags, made from purchased woven or knitted materials
332439	Shipping barrels, drums, kegs and pails, light gauge metal, manufacturing
32192	Shipping cases and drums, wood, wirebound, manufacturing
23799	Shipping channel construction
81131	Shipping container (cargo) repair service
322211	Shipping containers, made from purchased paperboard
32615	Shipping pads and shaped cushioning, foam plastics (except polystyrene), manufacturing
32614	Shipping pads and shaped cushioning, polystyrene foam, manufacturing
41822	Shipping supplies, paper and disposable plastics (e.g., cartons, gummed tapes), wholesale
336611	Ships (i.e., not suitable or intended for personal use), manufacturing
31171	Ships, floating seafood-processing factory
41799	Ships, wholesale
41799	Ships, wholesale and repair
51721	Ship-to-shore broadcasting communications carriers
336611	Shipyard (i.e., facility capable of building ships)
315226	Shirts, outerwear (except washable service type), men's and boys', cut and sewn from purchased fabric
31519	Shirts, outerwear, men's and boys', made in knitting mills
315232	Shirts, outerwear, women's, misses' and girls', cut and sewn from purchased fabric
31519	Shirts, underwear, made in knitting mills
33633	Shock absorbers, automotive, truck and bus, manufacturing
322212	Shoe boxes, folding, made from purchased paperboard
322219	Shoe boxes, set-up, made from purchased paperboard
54149	Shoe design services
333299	Shoe making and repairing machinery, manufacturing
326198	Shoe parts (e.g., heels, soles), plastics, manufacturing
32561	Shoe polishes and cleaners, manufacturing
41792	Shoe repair equipment and supplies, wholesale
81143	Shoe repair shops
31621	Shoes, manufacturing
33911	Shoes, orthopedic extension, manufacturing
41412	Shoes, wholesale

81299	Shoeshine service
71399	Shooting clubs, recreational
71399	Shooting ranges
23622	Shopping centres and complexes, construction
53112	Shopping centres, property operation only
23622	Shopping mall construction
81299	Shopping service
23899	Shoring, construction
311225	Shortening, made from purchased fats and oils
311224	Shortening, made in oilseed crushing mills
315229	Shorts (e.g., Bermuda, Jamaica, gym), men's and boys', cut and sewn from purchased fabric
315239	Shorts, outerwear, women's, misses' and girls', cut and sewn from purchased fabric
31519	Shorts, underwear, men's and boys', made in knitting mills
23811	Shotcrete contractors
332999	Shotguns, manufacturing
213118	Shot-hole drilling service, oil and gas field, on a contract basis
31599	Shoulder pads (e.g., coats, suits), made from purchased fabric
41413	Shoulder pads, wholesale
33312	Shovel loaders, manufacturing
41791	Show cases, refrigerated, wholesale
337215	Showcases (except refrigerated), manufacturing
31412	Shower and bath curtains, all materials, made from purchased fabrics or sheet goods
332999	Shower rods, metal, manufacturing
326191	Shower stalls, plastics or fibreglass, manufacturing
212397	Shredding peat mining
41819	Shredding rubber tires for rubber and metal content
114113	Shrimp fishing
81311	Shrines, religious
56191	Shrink wrapping services
31331	Shrinking textile fabrics and products (including clothing)
33461	Shrink-wrapped computer software, mass-reproducing
111421	Shrub nursery, ornamental, growing
44422	Shrubs and trees, ornamental, retail (except nurseries)
31171	Shucking and packing fresh shellfish
332321	Shutters, door and window, metal, manufacturing
321911	Shutters, door and window, wood and covered wood, manufacturing
23819	Shutters, installation
48599	Shuttle services (except employee bus)
23817	Siding (aluminum, steel, asbestos, cement, plastic, hardboard), installation
23817	Siding, contractors (installation and repair)
321111	Siding, dressed lumber, manufacturing
324122	Siding, made from purchased asphaltic materials
41639	Siding, metal, wholesale
326198	Siding, plastics, manufacturing
23812	Siding, precast concrete, installation
332329	Siding, sheet metal, manufacturing
41632	Siding, wood, wholesale
212398	Sienna mining
333299	Sieves and screening equipment, chemical processing type, manufacturing
333299	Sieves and screening equipment, food manufacturing type, manufacturing
33399	Sieves and screening equipment, general industrial type, manufacturing
48721	Sightseeing boat operation
48799	Sightseeing helicopter operations
48711	Sightseeing services, human-drawn vehicle
23731	Sign erection (i.e., highway, street) contractors
23731	Sign erection, highway, road, street and bridge
54193	Sign language services
541899	Sign painting and lettering services
41732	Signal systems and alarm devices, electronic (except household smoke detection), wholesale
41611	Signalling equipment, electrical, wholesale
323119	Signs and notices, paper, printing (except quick, digital) without publishing
33995	Signs and signboards, non-electric, of wood, manufacturing
23899	Signs on buildings, erection
41792	Signs, electrical, wholesale
212323	Silica sand, mining
32791	Silicon carbide abrasives, manufacturing
33441	Silicon waveguides, manufacturing
32519	Silicone (except resins), manufacturing
32521	Silicone resins, manufacturing
32521	Silicone rubber, manufacturing
41413	Silk piece goods, wholesale
54143	Silk screen design service

333299	Silk screen machinery for textiles, manufacturing
41119	Silk, raw, wholesale
212326	Sillimanite mining
332311	Silos, prefabricated metal, manufacturing
332311	Silos, prefabricated, metal, manufacturing and installation
21222	Silver bullion, produced at mine site
325189	Silver compounds, not specified elsewhere by process, manufacturing
21222	Silver ore milling
41892	Silver ore, wholesale
21222	Silver ores mining
32561	Silver polishes, manufacturing
333299	Silver recovery equipment, electrolytic, manufacturing
33149	Silver rolling, drawing or extruding, purchased metal or scrap
33141	Silver smelting and primary refining
44831	Silverware and plated ware, retail
41441	Silverware and plated ware, wholesale
81149	Silverware-cleaning, repairing and replating
326191	Sinks, plastics, manufacturing
32711	Sinks, vitreous china, manufacturing
21221	Sintering iron ore produced at the mine
56291	Site remediation
54162	Site remediation consulting services
541611	Site selection consulting services
31621	Skate boots, without blades or wheels, manufacturing
81149	Skate sharpening
33992	Skates, ice (boots and blades assembled), manufacturing
33992	Skates, roller (boots and wheels assembled), manufacturing
61162	Skating instruction, ice or roller
71394	Skating rinks, ice or roller
711511	Sketch artists, independent
54132	Ski area planning services
33992	Ski boots, manufacturing
53229	Ski equipment rental
71392	Ski lift and tow operation
721113	Ski lodges and resorts
315229	Ski pants, men's and boys', cut and sewn from purchased fabric
71392	Ski resorts, without accommodations
315239	Ski suits, jackets and pants, women's, misses' and girls', cut and sewn from purchased fabric
31519	Ski suits, made in knitting mills
315229	Ski suits, men's and boys', cut and sewn from purchased fabric
23799	Ski tow erection, general contractors
32192	Skids and pallets, wood or wood and metal combination, manufacturing
45111	Skiing equipment, retail
61162	Skiing instruction
56191	Skin blister packaging services
45111	Skin diving and scuba equipment, retail
41119	Skins, raw, wholesale
561611	Skip tracers services
315234	Skirts (except leather, tennis), women's, misses' and girls', cut and sewn from purchased fabric
33992	Skis, manufacturing
481215	Sky writing, using general purpose aircraft
23816	Skylights, installation
332321	Skylights, metal frame, manufacturing
31519	Slacks, made in knitting mills
315239	Slacks, women's, misses' and girls', cut and sewn from purchased fabric
23814	Slate (i.e., exterior work), contractors
41639	Slate and slate products, wholesale
212316	Slate, quarrying
311611	Slaughterhouses (except poultry and small game)
31499	Sleeping bags, manufacturing
721111	Sleeping car operation, contract service
721111	Sleeping car services not operated by railway company
41411	Sleepwear, men's and boys', wholesale
41411	Sleepwear, women's, misses' and children's, wholesale
333299	Slicing machinery (i.e., food manufacturing type), manufacturing
212326	Slip clay mining
41412	Slippers (footwear), wholesale
31621	Slippers, manufacturing
315231	Slips, women's, misses' and girls', cut and sewn from purchased fabric
713299	Slot machines parlours
56221	Sludge disposal sites
48699	Slurry pipeline transport service
213118	Slush pits and cellars, excavation of, on a contract basis
11521	Small animal breeding services
54194	Small animal veterinary services
332999	Small arms (e.g., revolvers), manufacturing
91291	Small business support programs, provincial government
91211	Small claims court provincial government
111993	Small fruit and vegetable farming, combination
11133	Small fruit farming
311615	Small game, slaughtering and dressing

811411	Small gas engines, repair (without retail sales of new equipment)
11119	Small grains (except wheat), growing
41723	Smelting machinery and equipment, wholesale
33141	Smelting of non-ferrous metals (except aluminum), primary
33399	Smelting ovens, manufacturing
33242	Smelting pots and retorts, manufacturing
212231	Smithsonite mining
41422	Smoke detectors, household, wholesale
33429	Smoke detectors, manufacturing
44311	Smoke detectors, retail
453999	Smoke shop
41899	Smokers' supplies, wholesale
72233	Snack truck operation
811411	Snow- and leaf-blower, repair service (without retail sales of new equipment)
48849	Snow clearing, highways and bridges, road transport service
321111	Snow fence lath, made from logs or bolts
333416	Snow making machinery, manufacturing
23821	Snow melting cable, electric, installation
23822	Snow melting systems (hot water or glycol), installation
561799	Snow ploughing services, parking lots and driveways, not combined with any other service
48849	Snow removal, highway
31519	Snow suits, made in knitting mills
315229	Snow suits, men's and boys', cut and sewn from purchased fabric
44421	Snowblowers and lawn-mowers, retail
33311	Snowblowers and throwers, residential type, manufacturing
41529	Snowmobile engines, wholesale
484229	Snowmobile operation, freight
711218	Snowmobile race track operation
711218	Snowmobile racing teams
315229	Snowmobile suits, men's and boys', cut and sewn from purchased fabric
33699	Snowmobiles and parts, manufacturing
44122	Snowmobiles, retail
41519	Snowmobiles, wholesale
41519	Snowmobiles, wholesale and repair
33312	Snowplough attachments (except lawn and garden type), manufacturing
33992	Snowshoes, manufacturing
315239	Snowsuits, women's, misses' and girls', cut and sewn from purchased fabric
41331	Snuff (powdered tobacco), wholesale
31222	Snuff, manufacturing

41452	Soap, toilet, wholesale
332999	Soap-impregnated steel wool pads, manufacturing
32561	Soaps (e.g., bar, chip, powder), manufacturing
711211	Soccer clubs, professional or semi-professional
71399	Soccer clubs, recreational
45111	Soccer equipment, retail
72232	Social catering services (weddings, parties)
91191	Social development services, federal government
531112	Social housing projects, operators of
81341	Social organization, civic and fraternal
54172	Social science research and development services
81331	Social service advocacy organizations
81392	Social workers' associations
54172	Sociological research and development services
33221	Sockets and socket sets, manufacturing
31511	Socks, knitting
56173	Sod laying services
44422	Sod, retail
325181	Soda ash (i.e., disodium carbonate), manufacturing
212398	Soda ash mining
311821	Soda crackers, manufacturing
333416	Soda fountain cooling and dispensing equipment, manufacturing
41792	Soda fountain fixtures (except refrigerated), wholesale
41791	Soda fountain fixtures, refrigerated, wholesale
31193	Soda fountain syrups, manufacturing
31211	Soda, carbonated, manufacturing
325181	Sodium bicarbonate (i.e., baking soda), manufacturing
325181	Sodium carbonate (i.e., soda ash), manufacturing
325189	Sodium chlorate, manufacturing
32541	Sodium chloride pharmaceutical preparations, manufacturing
212398	Sodium compounds, natural (except common salt) mining
325181	Sodium hydroxide (i.e., caustic soda), manufacturing
325189	Sodium hypochlorite, manufacturing
325189	Sodium inorganic compounds, not specified elsewhere by process, manufacturing
32519	Sodium organic compounds, not specified elsewhere by process, manufacturing

325189	Sodium phosphate, manufacturing
325189	Sodium silicate, manufacturing
325189	Sodium sulphate, manufacturing
337121	Sofas (including sofa beds), manufacturing
31193	Soft drink concentrates (i.e., syrup), manufacturing
31211	Soft drinks, manufacturing
41321	Soft drinks, wholesale
45111	Softball equipment, retail
54151	Software installation services
54151	Software programming, custom
54151	Software systems analysis and design, custom
321919	Softwood flooring, manufacturing
32532	Soil conditioning preparations, manufacturing
11511	Soil preparation service
334512	Soil testing and analysis instruments, manufacturing
54138	Soil testing services
33441	Solar cells, manufacturing
221119	Solar electric power generation
333416	Solar energy heating equipment, manufacturing
41612	Solar heating panels and equipment, wholesale
23816	Solar reflecting coatings, application onto roofs
33399	Soldering equipment (except hand held), manufacturing
33221	Soldering guns and irons, hand held (including electric), manufacturing
33291	Solenoid valves (except fluid power), industrial type, manufacturing
33291	Solenoid valves, fluid power, manufacturing
41792	Soles, shoe, wholesale
322211	Solid fibre boxes, made from purchased paper or paperboard
71113	Soloists, musical, independent
325999	Solvents recovery service, on a contract or fee basis
41732	Sonar equipment, wholesale
41732	Sonar equipment, wholesale and repair
334511	Sonar systems and equipment, manufacturing
711513	Song writers, independent
51223	Songs, publishing
51223	Songs, publishing and printing combined
72131	Sorority residential houses
56292	Sorting, cleaning, and baling of commingled recyclable materials (except hazardous)
53249	Sound and lighting equipment rental
51219	Sound dubbing service, motion picture
23821	Sound equipment installation
41639	Sound proofing materials, wholesale
51224	Sound recording studio
51222	Sound recordings, integrated production, reproduction, release and distribution
41421	Sound systems, domestic, wholesale
41529	Sound systems, motor vehicle, new, wholesale
44131	Sound systems, motor vehicle, retail
23831	Soundproofing contractors
62421	Soup kitchen
31199	Soup mixes, dry, made from purchased dry ingredients
31142	Soup mixes, made in dehydration plants
31171	Soup, fish and seafood, canning
31171	Soup, fish and seafood, frozen, manufacturing
31142	Soups (except seafood), canning
31141	Soups, frozen (except seafood), manufacturing
41319	Soups, wholesale
311511	Sour cream, manufacturing
45322	Souvenirs, retail
31194	Soy sauce, manufacturing
11111	Soya bean (soybean) farming
311224	Soybean crushing mills
311224	Soybean oil, cake and meal, made in crushing mills
11111	Soybeans (soya beans), growing
41112	Soybeans, wholesale
333416	Space heaters (except portable electric), manufacturing
33521	Space heaters, portable, electric, manufacturing
91191	Space research and development, federal government
33422	Space satellites, communications equipment, manufacturing
334511	Space vehicle guidance systems and equipment, manufacturing
33641	Space vehicle propulsion units, manufacturing
33641	Space vehicles parts, manufacturing
31142	Spaghetti sauce, canning
311823	Spaghetti, dry, manufacturing
32711	Spark plug insulators, porcelain, manufacturing
33632	Spark plugs, for internal combustion engines, manufacturing
31213	Sparkling wines, manufacturing
71394	Spas, fitness (without lodging)

33431	Speaker systems, manufacturing
71141	Speakers' bureaus, agents or managers
711512	Speakers, independent
51219	Special effects for motion picture, post production
48599	Special needs passenger transportation service
81299	Special occasion greeting service
336211	Special purpose highway vehicle (e.g., fire-fighting vehicles) bodies, manufacturing
33612	Special purpose highway vehicles (e.g., firefighting vehicles), assembling on chassis of own manufacture
336211	Special purpose highway vehicles (e.g., fire-fighting vehicles), assembling on purchased chassis
541891	Specialty advertising distribution services (creating and organizing the production of specialty advertising products)
51521	Specialty cable television (e.g., music, sports, news) networks
481215	Specialty flying services, using general purpose aircraft
44613	Spectacle and eyeglass accessories, retail
23839	Spectator seating installation, contractors
23622	Speculative builders (i.e., building on own land, for sale), commercial and institutional buildings
54193	Speech interpretation services, language
62134	Speech pathologists, offices of
62134	Speech therapy clinics
333619	Speed changers (i.e., power transmission equipment), manufacturing
61169	Speed reading courses
333619	Speed reducers (i.e., power transmission equipment), manufacturing
44131	Speed shops, retail
334511	Speed, pitch and roll navigational instruments and systems, manufacturing
711218	Speedway operation
62199	Sperm banks
212231	Sphalerite ore mining
445299	Spice and herb stores, retail
31194	Spice grinding and blending
41319	Spices, wholesale
33111	Spiegeleisen ferro-alloys, manufacturing
333299	Spindles for textile machinery, manufacturing

31311	Spinning carpet and rug yarns from purchased fibre
333519	Spinning machines, metalworking, manufacturing
333299	Spinning machines, textile, manufacturing
332118	Spinning unfinished metal products
31311	Spinning yarns from purchased fibre
33911	Splints, manufacturing
326198	Sponges, plastics, manufacturing
332999	Sponges, scouring, metal, manufacturing
41899	Sponges, wholesale
31331	Sponging textile fabrics
31331	Sponging textiles for tailors and dressmakers
31311	Spooling yarn
333299	Spools for textile machinery, manufacturing
322219	Spools, fibre, made from purchased paperboard
33221	Spoons, table, base metal plated with precious metal, manufacturing
33221	Spoons, table, non-precious metal, manufacturing
81399	Sport leagues
33611	Sport utility vehicles assembling on chassis of own manufacture
53229	Sporting goods rental
45111	Sporting goods, equipment and supplies, retail
41447	Sporting goods, wholesale
71141	Sports agents
53229	Sports and recreation equipment rental
448199	Sports apparel stores, retail
711319	Sports arenas, promoting events
315229	Sports clothing (except team uniforms), non-tailored, men's and boys', cut and sewn from purchased fabric
315299	Sports clothing, team uniforms, cut and sewn from purchased fabric
71394	Sports clubs, physical fitness facilities
711319	Sports event promoters, with facilities
711329	Sports events organizers, without facilities
23799	Sports fields and facilities, construction
712119	Sports hall of fame
61162	Sports instructors, independent
61162	Sports instructors, professional (e.g., golf, skiing, swimming)
711218	Sports professionals, independent (i.e., participating in sporting events)
711319	Sports stadiums, promoting events
71399	Sports teams and leagues, recreational or youth

711211	Sports teams, professional or semi-professional
56159	Sports ticket offices
711218	Sports trainers, independent
41411	Sportswear, women's and children's, wholesale
32561	Spot removers (except laundry presoaks), manufacturing
33311	Sprayers and dusters, farm type, manufacturing
41711	Sprayers and dusters, farm, wholesale
33391	Sprayers, manually-pumped units, general purpose type, manufacturing
311515	Spreads, cheese, manufacturing
337121	Spring cushions, manufacturing
33272	Spring washers, metal, manufacturing
31211	Spring waters, purifying and bottling
11114	Spring wheat, growing
333519	Spring winding and forming machines, metalworking, manufacturing
332619	Springs and spring units (except clock and watch), light gauge, made from purchased wire
33791	Springs, assembled, bed and box, manufacturing
41621	Springs, general purpose, steel, wholesale
332611	Springs, heavy-gauge, manufacturing
332619	Springs, precision (except clock and watch), manufacturing
33399	Sprinkler systems, automatic fire, manufacturing
23822	Sprinkler systems, lawn and garden, installation
41612	Sprinkler systems, wholesale
333619	Sprockets, power transmission equipment, manufacturing
112399	Squab farming
71394	Squash clubs
41841	Stabilizers and plasticizers, wholesale
33641	Stabilizers, aircraft, manufacturing
325999	Stabilizers, chemical preparations, manufacturing
711213	Stables, horse racing
41723	Stackers, industrial, wholesale
53112	Stadium operating
711319	Stadiums, promoting events
56133	Staff leasing services (providing permanent employees paid by supplying company but under the supervision of the hiring company)
711512	Stage sets, erecting and dismantling
327215	Stained glass and stained glass products, made from purchased glass
327214	Stained glass and stained glass products, made in glass-making plants
23815	Stained glass, installation
41621	Stainless steel fabricated products, wholesale
32551	Stains (except biological), manufacturing
32513	Stains, biological, manufacturing
321919	Stair railings, wood, manufacturing
32629	Stair treads, rubber, manufacturing
332329	Stairs, metal, manufacturing
23812	Stairs, precast concrete, installation
321919	Stairs, prefabricated wood, manufacturing
32739	Stairs, steps and landings, prefabricated concrete, manufacturing
41632	Stairs, wooden, wholesale
33392	Stairways, moving, manufacturing
23835	Stairways, wood, installation
321919	Stairwork (e.g., newel posts, railings, staircases, stairs), wood, manufacturing
321999	Stakes, surveyors', wood, manufacturing
453999	Stamp collection sets, retail
33994	Stamping devices, hand operated, manufacturing
333519	Stamping machines, metalworking, manufacturing
33637	Stamping metal, motor vehicle body parts
332118	Stampings (except automotive, cans, coins), metal, unfinished, manufacturing
41899	Stamps, for collectors, wholesale
33994	Stamps, hand (e.g., time, date, postmark, cancelling, shoe and textile marking), manufacturing
81392	Standards review committees, professional
337215	Stands, merchandise display, manufacturing
337215	Stands, merchandise display, wire, manufacturing
33399	Staplers and nailers, hand held power-driven, manufacturing
33994	Staplers, office, manufacturing
331222	Staples, iron or steel, made in wire drawing plants
332619	Staples, wire, made from purchased wire
32552	Starch glues, manufacturing
311221	Starches (except laundry), manufacturing
32561	Starches, laundry, manufacturing
11231	Started pullet farms

91141	State and official visits, organization of, federal government
41912	Stationery and office supplies, wholesale agents and brokers
41821	Stationery and stationery supplies, wholesale
32213	Stationery products, made in paperboard mills
45321	Stationery retail
32223	Stationery, made from purchased paper
323119	Stationery, printing (except quick) on a job-order basis
32711	Statuary, clay and ceramic, manufacturing
32799	Statuary, marble, manufacturing
41899	Statuary, wholesale
23899	Statues, erection
561799	Steam cleaning of building exteriors
41612	Steam fittings, heating equipment, wholesale
22133	Steam generation plant
48711	Steam train excursions, local
33291	Steam traps, industrial type, manufacturing
311614	Stearin, animal, rendering
331221	Steel basic shapes (except pipe, tube or wire), made from purchased steel
332431	Steel cans, manufacturing
332113	Steel forgings, unfinished, made from purchased steel
331514	Steel foundries
23813	Steel framing (except structural) contractors
33111	Steel mills
33121	Steel pipe and tubing, made from purchased steel
33111	Steel products (e.g., bar, plate, rod, sheet, structural shapes), made in steel mills
32791	Steel shot abrasives, manufacturing
41621	Steel strapping, wholesale
41621	Steel tubing, wholesale
332999	Steel wool, manufacturing
33111	Steel, manufacturing
23816	Steep slope roofing installation
23899	Steeplejack work
32591	Stencil inks, manufacturing
56141	Stenographic services (except court or stenographic reporting)
56149	Stenography services, public
56149	Stenotype reporting services
332999	Stepladders, metal, manufacturing
81121	Stereo equipment, repair service
44311	Stereo equipment, retail

41839	Sterilizing compounds and disinfectants, agricultural, wholesale
32541	Steroids, uncompounded, manufacturing
48832	Stevedoring service
33992	Sticks, sports (e.g., hockey, lacrosse), manufacturing
323119	Stock and bond certificates, printing without publishing
52312	Stock brokers, offices
711218	Stock car race track operation
711218	Stock car racing teams
52321	Stock exchanges
51219	Stock footage, film libraries
52321	Stock or commodities options exchanges
711111	Stock or repertory companies, theatrical
51919	Stock photo agencies
31511	Stockings, manufacturing
23834	Stone flooring, installation
212315	Stone quarrying, limestone
31331	Stone washing textile fabrics and clothing, for the trade
41639	Stone, building, wholesale
41639	Stone, crushed or broken, wholesale
32799	Stone, cut products (e.g., blocks, statuary), manufacturing
41441	Stones, precious, wholesale
212326	Stoneware clay mining
337126	Stools, household (except wood), manufacturing
337214	Stools, rotating, office (except wood), manufacturing
62199	Stop smoking clinic
41439	Storage and food preparation utensils, household, wholesale
335312	Storage battery chargers, engine generator type, manufacturing
33411	Storage devices, computer, manufacturing
49319	Storage of natural gas
32739	Storage tanks, concrete, manufacturing
33242	Storage tanks, heavy gauge metal, manufacturing
23712	Storage tanks, natural gas or oil, construction
54185	Store display advertising services
41791	Store equipment (except furniture), wholesale
23819	Store front frames, metal, installation
337127	Store furniture, manufacturing
23711	Storm sewers, construction
31212	Stout, brewing
33331	Stoves, commercial type, manufacturing

335223	Stoves, domestic, electric or non-electric, manufacturing
41422	Stoves, electric, domestic, wholesale
33392	Straddle carriers, mobile, manufacturing
321217	Strandboard, oriented, manufacturing
332619	Stranded wire, uninsulated, made from purchased wire
541611	Strategic planning consulting services
11133	Strawberries, growing
322219	Straws, drinking, made from purchased paper or paperboard
48849	Street cleaning service
51113	Street guide, publishers (except exclusively on Internet)
33512	Street lighting equipment, manufacturing
41611	Street lighting equipment, wholesale
48511	Street railway operation
72233	Street vendors, food
23799	Streetcar line construction
33612	Street-cleaning motor vehicles (e.g., street flushers, sprinklers, sweepers), assembling on chassis of own manufacture
23899	Streets, interlocking brick (i.e., not mortared), installation
71394	Strength development centres
336211	Stretch limousines, assembling on purchased chassis
31499	String, manufacturing
212114	Strip mining, bituminous coal (except on a contract basis)
33142	Strip, copper and copper alloy, made from purchased metal or scrap
33111	Strip, galvanized iron or steel, made in steel mills
33111	Strip, iron or steel, made in steel mills
213119	Stripping services, coal and lignite, on a contract basis
212398	Strontianite mining
325189	Strontium compounds, not specified elsewhere by process, manufacturing
41639	Structural assemblies, prefabricated, wood, wholesale
32712	Structural clay tile, manufacturing
41621	Structural shapes and plates, wholesale
331317	Structural shapes, made from purchased aluminum
23812	Structural steel erection, contractors
321215	Structural wood members, prefabricated (e.g., arches, trusses, I-joists and parallel chord ceilings), manufacturing

32799	Stucco and stucco products, manufacturing
41639	Stucco, wholesale
11521	Stud services, farm animal
23813	Stud walls, wood or steel, installation
61171	Student exchange programs
81341	Students' associations
53249	Studio property rental for motion picture film production
54143	Studios, commercial art
332329	Studs, sheet metal, manufacturing
33993	Stuffed toys (including animals), manufacturing
32521	Styrene resins, manufacturing
32511	Styrene, made from refined petroleum or natural gas liquids
23831	Styrofoam insulating, installation
212115	Subbituminous coal mining
23721	Subdividing and servicing land owned by others
51521	Subscription television, network
33651	Subway cars, manufacturing
23799	Subway construction
23799	Subway construction, general contractors
31331	Sueding textile fabrics
111999	Sugar beet farming
11193	Sugar cane farming
325999	Sugar substitutes (i.e., synthetic sweeteners blended with other ingredients), made from purchased synthetic sweeteners
31131	Sugar, manufacturing
41319	Sugar, refined, wholesale
62419	Suicide crisis centre
31699	Suitcases, all materials, manufacturing
31519	Suits, made in knitting mills
41411	Suits, men's and boys', wholesale
315239	Suits, non-tailored (e.g., jogging, snow, warm-up), women's, misses' and girls', cut and sewn from purchased fabric
315222	Suits, tailored, men's and boys', cut and sewn from purchased fabric
315234	Suits, tailored, women's, misses' and girls', cut and sewn from purchased fabric
32541	Sulpha drugs, uncompounded, manufacturing
325189	Sulphides and sulphites, manufacturing
32519	Sulphonated derivatives, manufacturing
325189	Sulphur and sulphur compounds, not specified elsewhere by process, manufacturing
325189	Sulphur dioxide, manufacturing

212398	Sulphur, ground or otherwise treated
325189	Sulphur, recovering or refining (except from sour natural gas)
41841	Sulphur, wholesale
31142	Sulphured fruit and vegetables, manufacturing
325189	Sulphuric acid, manufacturing
41841	Sulphuric acid, wholesale
721213	Summer camps (except day and sports instructional)
71399	Summer day camp
711111	Summer theatres (except theatre-dinner)
23822	Sump pump installation and servicing, contractors
33391	Sump pumps, residential type, manufacturing
11112	Sunflower farming
311224	Sunflower seed oil, cake and meal, made in crushing mills
33911	Sunglasses, manufacturing
32562	Sunscreen lotions and oils, manufacturing
32562	Suntan lotions and oils, manufacturing
33111	Superalloys, iron or steel, made in steel mills
33149	Superalloys, non-ferrous based, made from purchased metals or scrap
44511	Supermarkets, grocery, retail
325313	Superphosphates, manufacturing
45291	Superstores (i.e. food and general merchandise), retail
483115	Supply vessels to drilling rigs
33911	Supports, orthopedic (e.g., abdominal, ankle, arch, kneecap), manufacturing
91121	Supreme Court of Canada
32561	Surface active agents, manufacturing
41841	Surface active agents, wholesale
33312	Surface mining machinery (except drilling), manufacturing
23731	Surfacing highways, roads, streets, bridges or airport runways
62111	Surgeons, offices of
54194	Surgeons, veterinary, offices of
11511	Surgery on orchard trees and vines
54194	Surgery services, veterinary
41793	Surgical and medical instruments, wholesale
33911	Surgical bandages (including medicated), manufacturing
81121	Surgical instrument repair
334512	Surgical support systems (e.g., heart-lung machines) (except iron lungs), manufacturing
23821	Surveillance systems, installation only

81121	Surveying instrument repair
334512	Surveying instruments, manufacturing
54137	Surveying services (except geophysical)
48839	Surveyors, marine cargo
61169	Survival schools
23831	Suspended ceilings, installation
31599	Suspenders, made from purchased fabric
33911	Sutures, manufacturing
213118	Swabbing wells, on a contract basis
48721	Swamp buggy operations
315232	Sweat shirts, women's, misses' and girls', cut and sewn from purchased fabric
315239	Sweat suits and pants, women's, misses' and girls', cut and sewn from purchased fabric
31519	Sweat suits, made in knitting mills
31519	Sweaters, knitting on a contract basis
31519	Sweaters, made in knitting mills
315229	Sweaters, men's and boys', cut and sewn from purchased fabric
315239	Sweaters, women's, misses' and girls', cut and sewn from purchased fabric
41721	Sweepers and snow removal equipment, wholesale
41721	Sweepers and snow removal equipment, wholesale and repair
111219	Sweet corn farming
111211	Sweet potato farming
31199	Sweetening syrups (except pure maple), made from purchased sweeteners
61162	Swimming instruction
325999	Swimming pool chemical preparations, manufacturing
561799	Swimming pool cleaning and maintenance service
23622	Swimming pool construction (indoor)
23899	Swimming pool construction (residential)
326198	Swimming pool covers and liners, plastic, manufacturing
333416	Swimming pool heaters, manufacturing
23899	Swimming pool screen enclosures, construction
71394	Swimming pools
41447	Swimming pools and equipment, wholesale
23799	Swimming pools, outdoor nonresidential-type, construction
33992	Swimming pools, prefabricated, manufacturing
453999	Swimming pools, retail
31519	Swimsuits, made in knitting mills

315239	Swimsuits, women's, misses' and girls', cut and sewn from purchased fabric
448199	Swimwear stores, retail
112991	Swine and poultry combination farms
11221	Swine farm
11221	Swine farrow to finish (farming)
311119	Swine feeds, supplements, concentrates and premixes, manufacturing
33593	Switch boxes, electric, manufacturing
335315	Switchboards and parts, power, manufacturing
41611	Switchboards, electrical distribution, wholesale
33593	Switches for electric wiring (e.g., snap, tumbler, pressure, pushbutton), manufacturing
335315	Switches, electric power (except snap, push button, tumbler and solenoid), manufacturing
41611	Switchgear and protective equipment, electrical, wholesale
335315	Switchgear and switchgear accessories, manufacturing
33421	Switching equipment, telephone, manufacturing
48821	Switching services, railroad
212314	Syenite (except nepheline), quarrying
71113	Symphony orchestras
81311	Synagogues
52391	Syndicates, investment
51911	Syndicates, news
31134	Synthetic chocolate, manufacturing
22121	Synthetic gas distribution
32521	Synthetic rubber (i.e., vulcanizable elastomers), manufacturing
41841	Synthetic rubber, wholesale
32799	Synthetic stones, for gem stones and industrial use, manufacturing
32519	Synthetic sweeteners (i.e., sweetening agents), manufacturing
33911	Syringes, hypodermic, manufacturing
31193	Syrup, beverage, manufacturing
31132	Syrup, chocolate, made from cacao beans
31133	Syrup, chocolate, made from purchased chocolate
311221	Syrup, corn, made by wet-milling
31193	Syrup, flavouring (except coffee-based), manufacturing
31131	Syrup, sugar, manufacturing
31199	Syrups, table, artificially flavoured, manufacturing
54151	Systems analysis and design, computer services (software)
54151	Systems analysis and design, computer software
54151	Systems engineering (system integration)
54151	Systems integration, computer

T

442298	Table and floor lamps, retail
32711	Table articles, earthenware, manufacturing
32711	Table articles, vitreous china, manufacturing
33221	Table cutlery, base metal plated with precious metal, manufacturing
33221	Table cutlery, non-precious metal, manufacturing
33991	Table cutlery, precious metal (except plated), manufacturing
41441	Table flatware and hollowware, sterling and silverplate, wholesale
33991	Table flatware, precious metal (except plated), manufacturing
33512	Table lamps, manufacturing
41433	Table linens, wholesale
33711	Table or counter tops (e.g., kitchen, bathroom, bar), plastic laminated, manufacturing
31194	Table salt, manufacturing
31412	Tablecloths (except paper), made from purchased materials
322291	Tablecloths, paper, made from purchased paper
337214	Tables, office (except wood), manufacturing
32223	Tablets and pads, made from purchased newsprint
41431	Tableware, ceramic, wholesale
326198	Tableware, plastics (except foam), manufacturing
321999	Tableware, wood, manufacturing
21221	Taconite mining
33641	Tail assemblies and parts (empennage), aircraft, manufacturing
41792	Tailors' supplies, wholesale
72221	Take-out restaurant
212398	Talc mining
32562	Talcum powders, manufacturing
71141	Talent agencies
541215	Talent payment services
32519	Tall oil (except skimmings), manufacturing
311614	Tallow, produced in rendering plants
311611	Tallow, produced in slaughtering plants

322291	Tampons, sanitary, made from purchased paper
23899	Tank lining contractors
31519	Tank tops, men's and boys', made in knitting mills
315232	Tank tops, outerwear, women's, misses' and girls', cut and sewn from purchased fabric
31519	Tank tops, women's and girls', made in knitting mills
336212	Tank trailers, liquid and dry bulk, manufacturing
41612	Tanks and bowls, toilet, wholesale
41799	Tanks and tank components, wholesale
32711	Tanks, flush, vitreous china, manufacturing
33242	Tanks, heavy gauge metal, manufacturing
33699	Tanks, military (including factory rebuilding), manufacturing
81131	Tanks, repairing (heavy gauge)
326198	Tanks, storage, plastic or fibreglass, manufacturing
31611	Tanneries, leather, manufacturing
333299	Tannery machinery, manufacturing
32519	Tannic acid (i.e., tannins), manufacturing
32519	Tanning extracts and materials, natural, manufacturing
81219	Tanning salon
212299	Tantalum ore dressing and beneficiating
212299	Tantalum ore mining
33141	Tantalum smelting and primary refining
71112	Tap dance companies
51212	Tape distribution for television
33221	Tape measures, metal, manufacturing
56199	Tape slitting for the trade (i.e., cutting plastic, leather, other materials into widths)
33411	Tape storage units (e.g., drives, backups), computer peripheral equipment, manufacturing
51219	Tape transfer service
33911	Tape, medical adhesive, manufacturing
32223	Tapes (e.g., adding machine, calculator, cash register), made from purchased paper
32222	Tapes (e.g., cellophane, masking, pressure sensitive), gummed, made from purchased paper or other materials
45122	Tapes and cassettes, pre-recorded (audio), retail
41444	Tapes or cassettes, music, wholesale
33461	Tapes, magnetic recording (i.e., audio, data, video), blank, manufacturing
31332	Tapes, varnished and coated (except magnetic), made from purchased fabric
41445	Tapes, video, recorded, wholesale
41433	Tapestries, household furnishings, wholesale
23831	Taping and finishing drywall, contractors
324121	Tar and asphalt paving mixtures, made from purchased asphaltic materials
32519	Tar and tar oils, made by distillation of wood
324122	Tar paper, made from purchased asphaltic materials and paper
324122	Tar roofing cements and coating, made from purchased asphaltic materials
211114	Tar sand mining for oil extraction
32419	Tar, made in coke ovens
541619	Tariff consulting services
31491	Tarpaulins, made from purchased fabrics
23731	Tarring roads
81219	Tattoo parlours
72241	Taverns
56144	Tax collection services on a contract or fee basis
91391	Tax collection, local administration
541213	Tax return preparation services (without accounting, auditing, or bookkeeping services)
91191	Taxation, federal government
54185	Taxicab card advertising services
48531	Taxicab fleet owners
48531	Taxicab operation
48531	Taxicab owner-operator
48531	Taxicab service
711511	Taxidermists, independent
41899	Taxidermy supplies, wholesale
81331	Taxpayers advocacy organizations
445299	Tea and coffee, retail
31192	Tea blending
31192	Tea, herbal, manufacturing
31211	Tea, iced, manufacturing
41319	Tea, wholesale
81392	Teacher associations (except bargaining)
61121	Teachers' colleges
56131	Teachers' registries
33331	Teaching machines (e.g., flight simulators), manufacturing
41793	Teaching machines (except computers), electronic, wholesale
315299	Team athletic uniforms, cut and sewn from purchased fabric
31331	Teaseling textile fabrics

51113	Technical books, publishing (except exclusively on Internet)
51913	Technical books, publishing (exclusively on Internet)
61121	Technical institute, post-secondary
51112	Technical magazines and periodicals, publishing (except exclusively on Internet)
323119	Technical manuals and papers (books), printing without publishing
61121	Technical school, post-secondary non-university
448199	Tee shirts, custom printed, retail
33312	Teeth, bucket and scarifier, manufacturing
33911	Teeth, custom made in dental laboratories
33281	Teflon (TM) coating metals and metal products, for the trade
51791	Telecommunication resellers (except satellite)
51721	Telecommunications carriers, cellular telephone
541619	Telecommunications management consulting services
56142	Telemarketing bureaus
56142	Telemarketing service on a contract or fee basis
51791	Telemetry and tracking system operation on a contract or fee basis
113311	Telephone and telegraph poles, logging
33441	Telephone and telegraph transformers, electronic component type, manufacturing
23821	Telephone and telephone equipment installation, contractors
33421	Telephone answering machines, manufacturing
56142	Telephone answering services
56142	Telephone call centre
33421	Telephone carrier line equipment, manufacturing
33421	Telephone carrier switching equipment, manufacturing
51741	Telephone communications carriers, satellite
51791	Telephone communications resellers (except satellite)
517111	Telephone companies
62419	Telephone counselling service
323119	Telephone directories, printing without publishing
51114	Telephone directories, publishing (except exclusively on Internet)

51114	Telephone directories, publishing and printing combined
54187	Telephone directory distribution services, door-to-door
41732	Telephone equipment and apparatus, wholesale
41732	Telephone equipment and apparatus, wholesale and repair
23713	Telephone line stringing
56142	Telephone message service
45439	Telephone selling of merchandise (retailing by home solicitation)
56142	Telephone solicitation service on a contract or fee basis
44311	Telephone stores, retail
33592	Telephone wire and cable, insulated, manufacturing
51919	Telephone-based information services
51919	Telephone-based recorded information services
33421	Telephones (except cellular telephones), manufacturing
51219	Teleproduction services
33431	Television (TV) sets, manufacturing
54184	Television advertising representatives, independent
51512	Television broadcasting network services
51512	Television broadcasting stations
51211	Television commercial production
56131	Television employment agencies
51112	Television guides, publishing (except exclusively on Internet)
517112	Television operation, closed circuit
711512	Television producers, independent
53221	Television rental and leasing
81121	Television repair shops
41421	Television sets, wholesale
51211	Television show production
51212	Television show syndicators
23622	Television station construction
51219	Television tape services (e.g., editing, transfers)
454113	Television, mail order (home shopping), retail
44311	Television, radio and stereo stores
44311	Television, radio, stereo and appliances stores
33141	Tellurium smelting and primary refining
81331	Temperance organizations
334512	Temperature controls, automatic, residential and commercial type, manufacturing

334512	Temperature instruments (except glass and bimetal thermometers), industrial process type, manufacturing
33281	Tempering metals and metal products, for the trade
81311	Temples, religious
56132	Temporary employment services
81331	Tenant advocacy associations
81399	Tenant associations (except advocacy)
71394	Tennis clubs
23799	Tennis court construction (outdoor), general contractors
23622	Tennis courts, indoor, construction
41447	Tennis equipment and supplies, wholesale
33992	Tennis equipment, manufacturing
711218	Tennis professionals, independent (i.e., participating in sporting events)
81149	Tennis rackets restringing
31519	Tennis shirts, men's and boys', made in knitting mills
334512	TENS (transcutaneous electrical nerve stimulators), manufacturing
81149	Tent repair shops (without retail sales of new equipment)
31491	Tents, made from purchased fabrics
33411	Terminals, computer, manufacturing
56171	Termite control services
41621	Terneplate, wholesale
32739	Terrazzo products, precast (except block, brick and pipe), manufacturing
23834	Terrazzo, pouring, setting and finishing
213117	Test drilling for metal mining, on a contract basis
213117	Test drilling for non-metallic minerals mining (except fuels), on a contract basis
41611	Testing and measuring equipment, electrical (except automotive), wholesale
54194	Testing laboratories, veterinary
54138	Testing laboratory (except medical or dental)
33399	Testing, weighing and inspecting packaging machinery, manufacturing
32541	Tetracycline, uncompounded, manufacturing
323119	Textbooks, printing without publishing
41442	Textbooks, wholesale
31321	Textile broad-woven fabrics mills
41841	Textile chemicals, wholesale
56199	Textile cutting service
54149	Textile design services
32561	Textile finishing assistants, manufacturing

333299	Textile finishing machinery (e.g., bleaching, dyeing, mercerizing), manufacturing
56191	Textile folding and packaging services
41723	Textile machinery and equipment, wholesale
53249	Textile machinery rental or leasing
333299	Textile making machinery (except sewing machines), manufacturing
31322	Textile mills, narrow woven fabric
45113	Textile piece goods, retail
41413	Textile piece goods, wholesale
333299	Textile printing machinery, manufacturing
31321	Textile products (except clothing), made in broad fabric weaving mills
31322	Textile products (except clothing), made in narrow woven fabric mills
31331	Textile products finishing
322219	Textile reels and bobbins, fibre, made from purchased paperboard
32561	Textile scouring agents, manufacturing
31499	Textile waste, processing
41819	Textile waste, wholesale
333299	Texturizing machinery for textiles, manufacturing
31311	Texturizing purchased monofilament yarn
213118	Thawing and cleaning wellheads in oil fields
61161	Theatre arts school
711111	Theatre companies
41792	Theatre equipment and supplies (including projection equipment), wholesale
41792	Theatre equipment and supplies (including projection equipment), wholesale and repair
711311	Theatre festival promoters, with facilities
337127	Theatre furniture, manufacturing
711311	Theatre operators, promoting events
711111	Theatre production agencies
41792	Theatre projection equipment, wholesale
41792	Theatre seats, wholesale
711112	Theatre, musical
51213	Theatres, motion picture, drive-in
51213	Theatres, motion picture, indoor
711111	Theatrical and other staged entertainment services
711321	Theatrical booking agencies (except motion picture)
711111	Theatrical companies, amateur
53222	Theatrical costume rental

56131	Theatrical employment agencies
53249	Theatrical equipment (except costumes), rental
711111	Theatrical production, live
711321	Theatrical promoters, without facilities
711111	Theatrical road companies
71141	Theatrical talent agents
56159	Theatrical ticket agencies
56159	Theatrical ticket offices
71311	Theme parks, amusement
61131	Theological colleges or seminary (degree-granting)
41793	Therapeutic beds, wholesale
41793	Therapy equipment, wholesale
212114	Thermal coal, bituminous, mining
32614	Thermal insulation, polystyrene foam, manufacturing
23713	Thermal power plants, construction
54138	Thermal testing, laboratories
334512	Thermocouples, manufacturing
33399	Thermoform, blister and skin packaging machinery, manufacturing
33322	Thermoforming machinery for plastics, manufacturing
322111	Thermo-mechanical wood pulp (TMP), manufacturing
41793	Thermometers, wholesale
32521	Thermoplastic resins and plastics materials, manufacturing
32521	Thermosetting plastics resins, manufacturing
32521	Thermosetting vulcanizable elastomers, manufacturing
334512	Thermostats (e.g., air-conditioning, appliance, comfort heating, refrigeration), manufacturing
33639	Thermostats, automotive, truck and bus, manufacturing
332999	Thimbles, wire rope, manufacturing
11511	Thinning of crops, mechanical and chemical
212299	Thorium ore mining
711213	Thoroughbred race tracks
31331	Thread bleaching, dyeing and finishing
333299	Thread making machinery, manufacturing
31311	Thread mills
31322	Thread, elastic, fabric-covered, manufacturing
32629	Thread, rubber (except fabric covered), manufacturing
41413	Thread, wholesale
41723	Threading tools, wholesale
11511	Threshing service, agricultural crop and plant

32522	Throwing cellulosic yarn, made in the same establishment
32522	Throwing non-cellulosic yarn, made in the same establishment
31311	Throwing purchased man-made fibres and yarns
31311	Throwing, twisting and winding purchased yarn
32532	Tick powder or spray, manufacturing
56159	Ticket agencies, amusement (except theatrical)
56159	Ticket agencies, sports
56159	Ticket agencies, theatrical
56159	Ticket agencies, transportation
56159	Ticket offices for foreign cruise ship companies
56159	Ticket sales agency
221119	Tidal electric power generation
113311	Tie bolts, cutting
33633	Tie rods, tie rod ends and assemblies, manufacturing
44815	Tie shops, retail
32739	Ties, concrete railroad, manufacturing
31519	Ties, made in knitting mills
113311	Ties, railroad, hewn, producing
321111	Ties, railroad, made from logs or bolts
31511	Tights, knitting
44419	Tile and brick dealers, retail
41432	Tile carpets, wholesale
333299	Tile making machinery (except kilns), manufacturing
32799	Tile, acoustical, mineral wool, manufacturing
32712	Tile, ceramic wall and floor, manufacturing
41639	Tile, clay or other ceramic (except refractory), wholesale
32712	Tile, clay refractory, manufacturing
32712	Tile, clay, structural, manufacturing
32712	Tile, roofing and drain, clay, manufacturing
32712	Tile, sewer, clay, manufacturing
326198	Tiles, floor (i.e., linoleum, vinyl, rubber), manufacturing
33311	Tillers, lawn and garden type, manufacturing
41631	Timber and building materials, combinations of, wholesale
41912	Timber brokers, wholesale
11311	Timber crop operations
11531	Timber cruising
113312	Timber cutting, on contract
41891	Timber products, rough, wholesale
23799	Timber removal underwater, general contractors

11311	Timber tracts operations
484223	Timber trucking, local (i.e., to the mill)
11531	Timber valuation
321111	Timber, made from logs or bolts
321215	Timber, structural, glued-laminated or pre-engineered wood, manufacturing
113311	Timbers, mine, hewn, producing
113311	Timbers, round mine, cutting
323119	Time planners/organizers and refills, manufacturing
56159	Time share exchange services
23611	Time-share condominiums, construction, by operative builders
33631	Timing gears and chains, automotive and truck gasoline engine, manufacturing
41793	Timing instruments, wholesale
325189	Tin compounds, not specified elsewhere by process, manufacturing
212299	Tin ore mining
41621	Tin plate, wholesale
33149	Tin rolling, drawing or extruding, purchased metal or scrap
33141	Tin smelting and primary refining
33221	Tinners' snips, manufacturing
32562	Tints, dyes and rinses, hair, manufacturing
41633	Tinware, wholesale
332619	Tire chains, made from purchased wire
31499	Tire cord and fabric, of all materials, manufacturing
33322	Tire making machinery, manufacturing
33322	Tire recapping machinery, manufacturing
811199	Tire repairing
32621	Tire retreading, recapping or rebuilding
33322	Tire shredding machinery, manufacturing
44132	Tire stores selling primarily to other businesses but also selling to household consumers
33291	Tire valves and parts, manufacturing
32621	Tires (e.g., pneumatic, semi-pneumatic, solid rubber), manufacturing
44132	Tires (new or used), retail
41521	Tires and tubes, wholesale
41521	Tires, used (except scrap), wholesale
41912	Tires, wholesale agents and brokers
322121	Tissue paper stock, manufacturing
41822	Tissue paper, toilet and facial, wholesale
32513	Titanium based pigments, manufacturing
325189	Titanium dioxide, manufacturing
332113	Titanium forgings, unfinished, made from purchased titanium
212299	Titanium ore mining
33141	Titanium smelting and primary refining
54119	Title abstract companies, real estate
54119	Title search companies, real estate
51219	Titling of motion picture film or video
32592	TNT (trinitrotoluene), manufacturing
33521	Toasters, electric (including sandwich toasters), manufacturing
41119	Tobacco auctioning, wholesale
11191	Tobacco farming
31221	Tobacco leaf processing and aging
333299	Tobacco processing machinery (except farm type), manufacturing
31222	Tobacco products (e.g., chewing, smoking, snuff), manufacturing
41912	Tobacco products, wholesale agents and brokers
31221	Tobacco stemming and redrying
453999	Tobacco stores and stands
49313	Tobacco warehousing, storage
111999	Tobacco, corn and beans growing, combination
41331	Tobacco, cured or processed, wholesale
44813	Toddlers clothing, retail
31134	Toffee, manufacturing
31199	Tofu (i.e., bean curd) (except frozen desserts), manufacturing
31152	Tofu frozen desserts, manufacturing
33272	Toggle bolts, metal, manufacturing
32561	Toilet bowl cleaners, manufacturing
326191	Toilet fixtures, plastics, manufacturing
32711	Toilet fixtures, vitreous china, manufacturing
322291	Toilet paper, made from purchased paper
32562	Toilet preparations (e.g., cosmetics, deodorants, perfumes), manufacturing
44612	Toilet preparations, retail
41452	Toilet waters and colognes, wholesale
41452	Toiletries, wholesale
56299	Toilets, portable, rental, leasing and pumping
32511	Toluene, made from refined petroleum or natural gas liquids
32411	Toluene, made in petroleum refineries
32519	Toluidines, manufacturing
31142	Tomato juice, manufacturing
31142	Tomato paste, manufacturing
453999	Tombstones, retail
41899	Tombstones, wholesale
325999	Toner cartridges, manufacturing
325999	Toner cartridges, rebuilding
32513	Toners (except electrostatic, photographic), manufacturing

325999	Toners (i.e., for photocopiers, laser printers and similar electrostatic printing devices), manufacturing
325999	Toners (i.e., photographic), manufacturing
321919	Tongue and groove lumber, made by resawing purchased lumber
332439	Tool boxes, light gauge metal, manufacturing
321999	Tool handles, turned and shaped wood, manufacturing
333519	Tools and accessories for machine tools, manufacturing
41633	Tools, carpenters', mechanics', plumbers' and other trades, wholesale
33221	Tools, garden, hand held, non-powered, manufacturing
33399	Tools, hand held power-driven, manufacturing
33221	Tools, hand held, metal blade (e.g., putty knives, scrapers, screwdrivers), non-powered, manufacturing
33221	Tools, hand held, non-powered (except kitchen type), manufacturing
41723	Tools, machinists' precision, wholesale
33221	Tools, woodworking edge (e.g., augers, bits, countersinks), manufacturing
33999	Tooth brushes (except electric), manufacturing
41452	Toothbrushes (except electric), wholesale
41452	Toothpaste, wholesale
32561	Toothpastes, gels and tooth powders, manufacturing
321999	Toothpicks, wood, manufacturing
41899	Top soil or potting soil, wholesale
212326	Topaz (nongem) mining
33635	Torque converters, automotive, truck and bus, manufacturing
332611	Torsion bars (i.e., springs), manufacturing
311919	Tortilla chips, manufacturing
31183	Tortillas, manufacturing
334512	Totalizing fluid meters, manufacturing
56152	Tour operators
91291	Tourism development programs, provincial government
91191	Tourism promotion programs, federal government
721192	Tourist cabins, accommodations
721213	Tourist camp
721211	Tourist camping park
721211	Tourist camps (campground)
721192	Tourist courts, accommodations
71399	Tourist guide services
721198	Tourist homes, accommodations
56159	Tourist information bureaus
91391	Tourist information, local government
311614	Tourtière meat pies, frozen, made from purchased meat
81233	Towel supply service
32562	Towelettes, premoistened, manufacturing
31412	Towels and washcloths, made from purchased fabrics
31324	Towels and washcloths, made in knitting mills
322291	Towels, paper, made from purchased paper
23713	Towers, power distribution and communication, construction
48841	Towing service, motor vehicle
54132	Town planners, offices of
56291	Toxic material abatement services
32541	Toxoids (e.g., diphtheria, tetanus), manufacturing
45112	Toy and game stores, retail
53229	Toy library (i.e., renting toys)
45112	Toy vehicles, children's, retail
41912	Toys and hobby goods, wholesale agents and brokers
33993	Toys, electric (including parts), manufacturing
41446	Toys, wholesale
45111	Track and field equipment, retail
484229	Tracked vehicle freight transportation, local
48711	Tracked vehicle, passenger, sightseeing operation
51791	Tracking missiles by telemetry and photography on a contract basis
41721	Tracklaying equipment, wholesale
41721	Tracklaying equipment, wholesale and repair
53212	Tractor rental (truck), without drivers
41711	Tractors (farm), new or used, wholesale
41711	Tractors (farm), new or used, wholesale and repair
33312	Tractors and attachments, construction type, manufacturing
33311	Tractors and attachments, farm type, manufacturing
33311	Tractors and attachments, lawn and garden type, manufacturing
41721	Tractors, construction, wholesale
41721	Tractors, construction, wholesale and repair
33312	Tractors, crawler, manufacturing
33392	Tractors, industrial, manufacturing
41723	Tractors, industrial, wholesale

41723	Tractors, industrial, wholesale and repair
33612	Tractors, truck, for highway use, assembled on chassis of own manufacture
81391	Trade associations
32312	Trade binding services
56192	Trade fairs promoters
51112	Trade magazines and periodicals, publishing (except exclusively on Internet)
61151	Trade school post-secondary
23839	Trade show exhibit installation and dismantling
56192	Trade show promoters
81393	Trade unions
53311	Trademark holders
53311	Trademark lessors
53311	Trademark owners
54133	Traffic consultants, engineering services
23821	Traffic signal installation
33429	Traffic signals, manufacturing
45393	Trailer, house, dealers, retail
41519	Trailers for passenger automobiles, wholesale
41519	Trailers for passenger automobiles, wholesale and repair
41519	Trailers for trucks, new and used, wholesale
41519	Trailers for trucks, new and used, wholesale and repair
41723	Trailers, industrial, wholesale
41912	Trailers, wholesale agents and brokers
11521	Training horses (except racehorses)
81291	Training of pets, service
711213	Training race horses
48511	Tramway operation, commuter
48711	Tramways (except aerial), scenic and sightseeing
32541	Tranquilizers preparations, manufacturing
33635	Transaxles, automotive, truck and bus, manufacturing
56141	Transcription services
48411	Transfer (trucking) service, general freight, local
23713	Transformer stations and substations, electric power, construction
41611	Transformers, electric, wholesale
33441	Transformers, electronic component type, manufacturing
33441	Transistors, manufacturing
41732	Transistors, wholesale
48511	Transit system, operation of

623991	Transition homes for women (except short stay)
32732	Transit-mixed concrete, manufacturing
54193	Translation services
32622	Transmission belts, rubber, manufacturing
32419	Transmission fluids, petroleum, made from refined petroleum
325999	Transmission fluids, synthetic, manufacturing
221121	Transmission of electric power
811119	Transmission repair and replacement, motor vehicle
332319	Transmission towers and masts, prefabricated, manufacturing
33635	Transmissions and parts, automotive, truck and bus, manufacturing
41732	Transmitters, wholesale
91291	Transportation and communications, provincial government
488519	Transportation brokers
41799	Transportation equipment and supplies (except motor vehicles), wholesale
41799	Transportation equipment and supplies (except motor vehicles), wholesale and repair
41723	Transportation equipment industries, machinery, equipment and supplies, wholesale
33636	Transportation equipment seating, manufacturing
561613	Transportation guard service
484229	Transporting automobiles and other motor vehicles, local
484229	Transporting mobile homes, local
11421	Trapping
11421	Trapping fur-bearing animals for furs
332619	Traps, animal and fish, made from purchased wire
71399	Trapshooting facilities, recreational
33331	Trash and garbage compactors, commercial type, manufacturing
56211	Trash collection
56151	Travel agencies
323119	Travel guide books, printing without publishing
51113	Travel guide books, publishing (except exclusively on Internet)
51113	Travel guide books, publishing and printing combined
56152	Travel tour operators
56152	Travel tour services, tour operators
721211	Travel trailer parks
41519	Travel trailers (e.g., tent trailers), wholesale

41519	Travel trailers (e.g., tent trailers), wholesale and repair
336215	Travel trailers, recreational, manufacturing
44121	Travel trailers, retail
52239	Travellers' cheque issuance services
212315	Travertine, quarrying
322299	Trays, moulded pulp, manufacturing
32621	Tread rubber (i.e., camelback), manufacturing
91191	Treasury board secretariat, federal government
81233	Treated mops, dust cloths and tool covers, supply service
23816	Treating roofs (by spraying, painting or coating)
321114	Treating wood products with creosote or other preservatives
113311	Tree felling, bucking, cutting
111993	Tree fruit and vegetable farming, combination
11133	Tree fruit farming
33312	Tree harvesting equipment, manufacturing
11133	Tree nut groves and farms
311225	Tree nut oils (e.g., tung, walnut), made from purchased oils
311224	Tree nut oils (e.g., tung, walnut), made in crushing mills
56173	Tree removal services
11321	Tree seeds gathering
56173	Tree surgery service
33999	Trees and plants, artificial, manufacturing
41113	Trees, bushes and plants, wholesale
23891	Trenching, construction site
23799	Trenching, underwater
45111	Tricycles and parts, retail
33699	Tricycles, adults', metal, manufacturing
33993	Tricycles, children's toy, manufacturing
33699	Tricycles, children's, metal, manufacturing
332321	Trim, metal, manufacturing
326193	Trim, motor vehicle, plastic mouldings and extrusions, manufacturing
41639	Trim, sheet metal, wholesale
33221	Trimmers, hedge, non-electric, manufacturing
315292	Trimmings, fur, manufacturing
31322	Trimmings, made in narrow fabric weaving mills
32592	Trinitrotoluene (TNT), manufacturing
48511	Trolley operation, commuter
48711	Trolley operation, scenic and sightseeing
212398	Trona mining
33991	Trophies, precious metal (except plated), manufacturing
332999	Trophies, precious plated metal, manufacturing
321999	Trophy bases, wood, manufacturing
453999	Trophy shops, retail
111422	Tropical foliage and green plants, greenhouse grown
213111	Troubleshooting, natural gas and oil well
31519	Trousers, made in knitting mills
315227	Trousers, men's and boys', cut and sewn from purchased fabric
336211	Truck bodies and cabs, manufacturing
336215	Truck campers (i.e., slide-in campers), manufacturing
61151	Truck driving schools
111219	Truck farming
48849	Truck loading and unloading service
811121	Truck or trailer body repair
53212	Truck rental (except industrial), without drivers
44719	Truck stops
41521	Truck tires and tubes, wholesale
33612	Truck tractors for highway use, assembling on chassis of own manufacture
41512	Truck tractors, road, wholesale
41512	Truck tractors, road, wholesale and repair
48411	Truck transport service, general freight, local
48899	Truck transportation brokers
811192	Truck washing
48849	Truck weighing station operation
484231	Trucking bulk liquid, long-distance
48421	Trucking service, used goods, household, office or institutional
48849	Trucking terminals, independent, with or without maintenance facilities
484229	Trucking, agricultural products, local
484229	Trucking, automobiles, local
484239	Trucking, automobiles, long-distance
48411	Trucking, general freight, local
484122	Trucking, general freight, long-distance, less than truckload
484121	Trucking, general freight, long-distance, truckload
484239	Trucking, hazardous materials, using specialized equipment, long-distance
484239	Trucking, refrigerated, long-distance
41512	Trucks and buses, wholesale
41912	Trucks and buses, wholesale agents and brokers

41512	Trucks and buses, wholesale and repair
33612	Trucks, heavy (except off-highway), assembling on chassis of own manufacture
33392	Trucks, industrial (plant and warehouse), manufacturing
33611	Trucks, light duty, assembling on chassis of own manufacture
33312	Trucks, off-highway, manufacturing
111419	Truffles farming, grown under cover
44832	Trunks, storage or travel, retail
321215	Trusses, wood, roof or floor, manufacturing
52399	Trust companies, nondepository
522112	Trust company branches, chartered, providing corporate and institutional banking services
522111	Trust company branches, chartered, providing personal and commercial banking services
526111	Trusteed pension funds
54199	Trustees, bankruptcy
52399	Trusts administration
52399	Trusts administration, personal investment
81321	Trusts, charitable, awarding grants
81321	Trusts, educational, awarding grants
81321	Trusts, religious, awarding grants
31519	T-shirts, men's and boys', made in knitting mills
315226	T-shirts, outerwear, men's and boys', cut and sewn from purchased fabric
315232	T-shirts, outerwear, women's, misses' and girls', cut and sewn from purchased fabric
315231	T-shirts, underwear, women's, misses' and girls', cut and sewn from purchased fabric
31519	T-shirts, women's and girls', made in knitting mills
32561	Tub and tile cleaning preparations, manufacturing
33121	Tube (e.g., heavy riveted, lock joint, seamless, welded), made from purchased iron or steel
333519	Tube rolling mill machinery, metalworking, manufacturing
33111	Tube, iron or steel, made in steel mills
326121	Tube, non-rigid plastics, manufacturing
62231	Tuberculosis hospital
41732	Tubes, electronic (e.g., receiving, transmitting, industrial), wholesale
322219	Tubes, fibre, made from purchased paperboard
32621	Tubes, inner, manufacturing
332999	Tubes, made from purchased metal pipe
33142	Tubing, copper and copper alloy, made from purchased metal or scrap
332999	Tubing, flexible metal, manufacturing
33149	Tubing, made from purchased non-ferrous (except aluminum, copper) metal or scrap
41621	Tubing, metal, wholesale
32629	Tubing, rubber, manufacturing
23814	Tuck pointing, contractors
333299	Tufting machinery for textiles, manufacturing
488339	Tugboat service, harbour operations
325189	Tungsten compounds, not specified elsewhere by process, manufacturing
212299	Tungsten ore dressing and beneficiating
212299	Tungsten ore mining
33141	Tungsten smelting and primary refining
81149	Tuning of pianos and organs (without retail sales of new equipment)
23821	Tunnel lighting contractors
332319	Tunnel lining, fabricated metal plate, manufacturing
23799	Tunnel, construction
213119	Tunnelling, coal and lignite mining, on a contract basis
31599	Tuques, made from purchased fabric
31519	Tuques, made in knitting mills
333611	Turbine generator set units, manufacturing
333611	Turbines (except aircraft type), manufacturing
111421	Turf (sod) farming
56173	Turf installation (except artificial)
23899	Turf, artificial, installation
11233	Turkey egg production
11233	Turkey farming
41313	Turkeys, dressed, wholesale
311615	Turkeys, slaughtering and dressing
81219	Turkish baths
41632	Turned or shaped wood products, wholesale
41634	Turpentine and resin, wholesale
32519	Turpentine, made by distillation of pine gum or pine wood
212398	Turquoise mining
11251	Turtle and other animal aquaculture
114113	Turtle fishing
61169	Tutors, private
315222	Tuxedos, cut and sewn from purchased fabric
33431	TV (television) sets, manufacturing
31499	Twine (except paper), manufacturing
51721	Two-way paging communications carriers

44311	Two-way radios, home or auto, retail
32312	Typesetting (i.e., computer-controlled, hand, machine), for the printing trade
333299	Typesetting machinery, manufacturing
81121	Typewriters and desk calculators, repair service
41791	Typewriters, wholesale
56141	Typing services
212291	Tyuyamunite mining

U

311515	UHT (ultra-high temperature) milk, manufacturing
212398	Ulexite mining
33599	Ultrasonic cleaning equipment (except medical and dental), manufacturing
33911	Ultrasonic dental equipment, manufacturing
33911	Ultrasonic medical cleaning equipment, manufacturing
33399	Ultrasonic welding equipment, manufacturing
212398	Umber mining
44815	Umbrella stores, retail
33999	Umbrellas, manufacturing
322122	Uncoated groundwood paper mills
324122	Undercoating for motor vehicles, made from purchased asphaltic materials
811199	Undercoating service, automotive
23713	Underground cable (e.g., cable television, electricity, and telephone) laying
33313	Underground mining machinery, manufacturing
23891	Underground tank (except hazardous material) removal
32615	Underlay, carpet and rug, foam plastics (except polystyrene), manufacturing
23899	Underpinning, construction
81221	Undertakers
336612	Underwater ROV (remotely operated vehicle), manufacturing
315221	Underwear, men's and boys', cut and sewn from purchased fabric
31519	Underwear, men's and boys', made in knitting mills
41411	Underwear, men's and boys', wholesale
31519	Underwear, women's and girls', made in knitting mills
41411	Underwear, women's, misses' and children's, wholesale
315231	Underwear, women's, misses' and girls', cut and sewn from purchased fabric

52311	Underwriters, securities
31599	Uniform hats and caps (except protective head gear), made from purchased fabric
315299	Uniform shirts, team athletic, cut and sewn from purchased fabric
81233	Uniform supply service
448199	Uniforms and work clothing, retail
41411	Uniforms and work clothing, wholesale
315222	Uniforms, dress (e.g., fire fighter, military, police), men's and boys', cut and sewn from purchased fabric
315234	Uniforms, dress, tailored (e.g., firefighter, military, police), women's and misses', cut and sewn from purchased fabric
41411	Uniforms, men's and boys', wholesale
315229	Uniforms, non-tailored, washable service type, men's, cut and sewn from purchased fabric
315299	Uniforms, team athletic, cut and sewn from purchased fabric
315239	Uniforms, washable service apparel (e.g., maids', nurses', waitresses'), women's, misses' and girls', made from purchased fabric
41411	Uniforms, women's and children's, wholesale
81393	Union organizations
526989	Union trust funds
44814	Unisex clothing stores, retail
41411	Unisex clothing, wholesale
812116	Unisex hair stylist shops
333416	Unit heaters (except portable, electric), manufacturing
323116	Unit set forms (e.g., manifold credit card slips), printing
81321	United fund councils
333619	Universal joints (except motor vehicle and aircraft), manufacturing
33641	Universal joints, aircraft, manufacturing
33635	Universal joints, automotive, truck and bus, manufacturing
61131	Universities
311814	Unleavened bread, made in commercial bakeries
48832	Unloading ships or boats
41792	Upholsterers' equipment and supplies, wholesale
56174	Upholstery cleaning services
45113	Upholstery fabric, retail
41792	Upholstery filling and padding, wholesale
31499	Upholstery filling, textile (except nonwoven fabric), manufacturing

81142	Upholstery repair
332619	Upholstery springs and spring units, made from purchased wire
332113	Upset forgings, unfinished, made from purchased metal
212291	Uraninite (pitchblende) mining
325189	Uranium compounds, not specified elsewhere by process, manufacturing
212291	Uranium ore milling
325189	Uranium oxide, manufacturing
33141	Uranium smelting and primary refining
325189	Uranium, enriched, manufacturing
48511	Urban and suburban passenger transit system operation
48511	Urban and suburban transit systems, mixed mode
91391	Urban community council
91313	Urban community police force
54132	Urban planning services
32521	Urea resins, manufacturing
325313	Urea, manufacturing
32521	Urethane rubber, manufacturing
326191	Urinals, plastics, manufacturing
62111	Urologists, offices of
41912	Used (recycled) auto parts, wholesale agents and brokers
45331	Used appliances, household, retail
44112	Used automobiles, retail
44131	Used automotive parts, retail
41511	Used cars, wholesale
48421	Used uncrated goods, moving and storage
33221	Utensils, kitchen (e.g., spatulas, ice cream scoops, garlic presses, colanders), fabricated metal, manufacturing
321999	Utensils, wood, manufacturing
332311	Utility buildings, prefabricated, metal, manufacturing
23713	Utility line (e.g., communication and electric power), construction
23711	Utility line (i.e., sewer and water), construction
53212	Utility trailer rental
336215	Utility trailers, manufacturing
44122	Utility trailers, retail

V

721213	Vacation camps (except hunting and fishing camps)
526989	Vacation funds for employees
32541	Vaccines (i.e., bacterial, virus), manufacturing
332439	Vacuum bottles and jugs, manufacturing

332439	Vacuum bottles, light gauge metal, manufacturing
33634	Vacuum brake boosters, automotive, truck and bus, manufacturing
44311	Vacuum cleaner stores, retail
41422	Vacuum cleaners, electric, domestic, wholesale
41422	Vacuum cleaners, household, wholesale
33331	Vacuum cleaners, industrial and commercial type, manufacturing
238299	Vacuum cleaning systems, built-in, contractors
33391	Vacuum pumps (except laboratory), manufacturing
41723	Vacuum pumps and compressors, wholesale
33242	Vacuum tanks, heavy gauge metal, manufacturing
33441	Vacuum tubes, manufacturing
81293	Valet parking services
81232	Valet service, cleaning and pressing clothing
41723	Valves and fittings (except plumbers'), wholesale
41612	Valves and fittings, plumbers', wholesale
33631	Valves, engine, intake and exhaust, manufacturing
33291	Valves, for water works and municipal water systems, manufacturing
33291	Valves, hydraulic and pneumatic, fluid power, manufacturing
33291	Valves, industrial type (e.g., gate, globe, check, pop safety, relief), manufacturing
33291	Valves, inline plumbing and heating (e.g., check, cut-off, stop), manufacturing
48421	Van lines, moving and storage service
212291	Vanadium ore mining
33711	Vanities, bathroom, wood, manufacturing
31699	Vanity cases, leather, manufacturing
337123	Vanity dressers, manufacturing
48599	Vanpool operation
33611	Vans, commercial and passenger, light duty, assembling on chassis of own manufacture
44512	Variety and convenience store
311611	Variety meats (i.e., edible organs), produced in slaughtering plants
452999	Variety stores, retail
32551	Varnish removers, manufacturing
32551	Varnishes, manufacturing
41634	Varnishes, stains, lacquers and shellacs, wholesale

33281	Varnishing metals and metal products, for the trade
31332	Varnishing textile fabrics and clothing
32711	Vases, pottery (e.g., china, earthenware and stoneware), manufacturing
33242	Vats, heavy gauge metal, manufacturing
332439	Vats, light gauge metal, manufacturing
711111	Vaudeville companies
41791	Vaults and safes, wholesale
41791	Vaults and safes, wholesale and repair
32622	V-belts, plastics, manufacturing
32622	V-belts, rubber, manufacturing
33431	VCR (video cassette recorders), manufacturing
311611	Veal carcasses, half-carcasses, primal and sub-primal cuts, produced in slaughtering plants
311614	Veal, primal and sub-primal cuts, made from purchased meat
32541	Vegetable alkaloids (e.g., caffeine, codeine, morphine, nicotine), basic chemicals, manufacturing
44523	Vegetable and fruit stands, retail
41119	Vegetable and fruit, crude, unprocessed, wholesale
111219	Vegetable bedding plants, growing of
41831	Vegetable cake and meal, wholesale
311225	Vegetable cooking and table oils, made from purchased oils
111219	Vegetable crops, growing
111219	Vegetable farming (except field crops)
111419	Vegetable farming, grown under cover
311211	Vegetable flour, manufacturing
31141	Vegetable juice concentrates, frozen, manufacturing
31142	Vegetable juices, canning
333299	Vegetable oil processing machinery, manufacturing
311224	Vegetable oils, made in oilseed crushing mills
41315	Vegetable packing shed, wholesale
111219	Vegetable seed growing
41832	Vegetable seeds, bulk and packaged, wholesale
311221	Vegetable starches, manufacturing
44523	Vegetables and fruit, fresh, retail store
31142	Vegetables, brining
31142	Vegetables, canning
31142	Vegetables, dehydrating
31199	Vegetables, fresh (i.e., cut, peeled, polished or sliced), manufacturing
41315	Vegetables, fresh, wholesale
31141	Vegetables, frozen, manufacturing
31142	Vegetables, pickling
31142	Vegetables, sulphured, manufacturing

238299	Vehicle lifts, installation
33993	Vehicles (except bicycles), children's, manufacturing
41447	Vehicles, children's, wholesale
41519	Vehicles, recreational and special purpose, wholesale
33632	Vehicular lighting fixtures, manufacturing
45421	Vending machine merchandise, non-store, retail
33331	Vending machines, manufacturing
53249	Vending machines, rental only
41792	Vending machines, wholesale
41792	Vending machines, wholesale and repair
33321	Veneer and plywood forming machinery, manufacturing
333299	Veneer drying machinery, manufacturing
113311	Veneer logs, logging
321211	Veneer mills, hardwood
321212	Veneer mills, softwood
32192	Veneer, manufacturing and converting into containers (e.g., fruit baskets, boxes)
41632	Veneer, wholesale
442291	Venetian blind shops, retail
33792	Venetian blinds (wood), manufacturing
23839	Ventilated wire shelving (i.e., closet organizing-type) installation
561791	Ventilating ducts, cleaning services
41612	Ventilating equipment and supplies, wholesale
333413	Ventilating fans, industrial and commercial type, manufacturing
52391	Venture capital companies
212398	Vermiculite mining
32799	Vermiculite, exfoliated, manufacturing
33792	Vertical blinds, manufacturing
442291	Vertical blinds, retail
315292	Vests, leather, fur or sheepskin-lined, manufacturing
91191	Veterans' benefits program, federal government
622111	Veterans' hospital
81331	Veterans' rights associations
41793	Veterinarians' equipment and supplies, wholesale
54194	Veterinarians, offices of
54194	Veterinary clinics
32541	Veterinary medicinal preparations, manufacturing
54194	Veterinary practices
54171	Veterinary research and development laboratories

54194	Veterinary testing laboratories
41722	Vibrating and screening equipment, mine, wholesale
23839	Vibration isolation contractor
54138	Vibration testing services
51821	Video and audio streaming services
519122	Video archives
44311	Video camera stores, retail
33431	Video cameras, household-type, manufacturing
33431	Video cassette recorders (VCR), manufacturing
53223	Video cassette rental
33461	Video cassettes, blank, manufacturing
33461	Video cassettes, pre-recorded, mass-reproducing
51219	Video conversion services (i.e., between formats)
41421	Video disc players, wholesale
53223	Video disk rental to the general public
71312	Video game arcades (except gambling machines)
33461	Video game software cartridges, mass-reproducing
54192	Video photography services, portrait
51219	Video post-production services
51211	Video production
51212	Video productions, distributing
53221	Video recorder and player rental and leasing
41421	Video recorder, domestic, wholesale
44311	Video recorders, retail
53223	Video rental
45122	Video tape stores, retail
33461	Video tapes, blank, manufacturing
41445	Video tapes, recorded, wholesale
54192	Video taping services for special events
54192	Video taping services for weddings
31194	Vinegar, manufacturing
11511	Vineyard cultivation services
11133	Vineyards
32519	Vinyl acetate (except resins), manufacturing
326114	Vinyl and vinyl copolymer film and unlaminated sheet, manufacturing
32519	Vinyl chloride (chloroethylene), manufacturing
23833	Vinyl floor tile and sheet installation, contractors
32521	Vinyl resins, manufacturing
23817	Vinyl siding, soffit and fascia, installation
326196	Vinyl window and door manufacturing
32521	Vinylidene resins, manufacturing

33221	Vises (except machine attachments), manufacturing
337213	Visible record equipment (e.g., filing cabinets, boxes), wood, manufacturing
91132	Visitor admissions (tourists and temporary)
56159	Visitor bureaus
56159	Visitor information centres
33636	Visor assemblies, motor vehicle, manufacturing
71113	Vocalist, independent
61151	Vocational apprenticeship training
61171	Vocational counselling (except rehabilitation)
61151	Vocational institute post-secondary
62431	Vocational rehabilitation services
31214	Vodka, manufacturing
56142	Voice mail box services
51791	VoIP services, access-independent (non-managed)
212316	Volcanic rock, quarrying
41611	Voltage regulators (except motor vehicle), wholesale
81321	Voluntary health organization
91314	Volunteer fire-fighter
33331	Voting machines, manufacturing
51741	VSAT (very small aperture terminal) services
322219	Vulcanized fibre products, made from purchased paperboard
33322	Vulcanizing machinery, manufacturing

W

333299	Wafer processing equipment, semiconductor, manufacturing
321217	Waferboard, manufacturing
33441	Wafers (i.e., semiconductor devices), manufacturing
33699	Wagons, horse-drawn, manufacturing
56142	Wake up call services
33392	Walkways, moving, manufacturing
23831	Wall cavities and attic space, insulating
23832	Wall covering or removal contractors
41634	Wall coverings (e.g., fabric, plastic), wholesale
41439	Wall decorations, household, wholesale
32712	Wall tile, ceramic, manufacturing
32742	Wallboard, gypsum, manufacturing
41632	Wallboard, wooden, wholesale
44412	Wallcovering stores, retail
31699	Wallets (except metal), manufacturing
44815	Wallets and billfolds, leather, retail
321999	Wall-mounted hat and coat racks, wood, manufacturing

23832	Wallpaper stripping (removal)
32222	Wallpaper, made from purchased paper or other materials
41634	Wallpaper, wholesale
311224	Walnut oil (except artists' materials), made in crushing mills
53222	Wardrobe rental for motion picture film production
23622	Warehouse (e.g., commercial, industrial, manufacturing, public or private) construction
41723	Warehouse trucks and supplies, wholesale
41723	Warehouse trucks and supplies, wholesale and repair
81391	Warehousing association
49319	Warehousing service, furniture and household goods (except used uncrated goods)
49311	Warehousing, general
53113	Warehousing, self-storage
41612	Warm air heating and cooling equipment, wholesale
31519	Warm-up suits, made in knitting mills
41413	Warp knit fabrics, wholesale
333299	Warping machinery, manufacturing
315229	Washable service apparel (e.g., barbers', hospital, professional), men's and boys', cut and sewn from purchased fabric
315239	Washable service apparel (e.g., maids', nurses', waitresses'), women's, misses' and girls', cut and sewn from purchased fabric
212114	Washeries, anthracite
53221	Washers and dryers, rental
33272	Washers, metal, manufacturing
41422	Washing machines, electric, domestic, wholesale
335229	Washing machines, household (including coin-operated), manufacturing
33331	Washing machines, laundry (except household type), manufacturing
561722	Washroom sanitation service
56211	Waste collection
56211	Waste collection, solid
56221	Waste disposal, hazardous
56221	Waste disposal, solid, incinerator and combustor
56221	Waste disposal, solid, landfill
41819	Waste oil collection
41819	Waste rags, wholesale
56292	Waste recovery facility
56221	Waste treatment, hazardous
31499	Waste, textile, processing of
322219	Wastebaskets, fibre, made from purchased paperboard
327215	Watch crystals, made from purchased glass
326198	Watch crystals, plastics, manufacturing
81149	Watch repair service (without retail sales of new equipment)
44831	Watches and clocks, retail
334512	Watches and parts (except crystals), manufacturing
41441	Watches, wholesale
22131	Water collection, treatment and distribution systems
453999	Water conditioning equipment, retail
56199	Water conditioning service
333416	Water coolers, manufacturing
32541	Water decontamination or purification tablets, manufacturing
23711	Water desalination plant construction
22131	Water distribution for irrigation
22131	Water filtration plant, operation
23822	Water heater installation
41612	Water heaters, electric, wholesale
335229	Water heaters, household (including non-electric), manufacturing
213118	Water intake well drilling, on a contract basis
23711	Water main line construction, general contractors
23711	Water mains and hydrants, construction
56199	Water meter reading service, contract
41612	Water meters, wholesale
71311	Water parks, amusement
48699	Water pipelines (long distance) without water treatment activities
33331	Water purification equipment, manufacturing
334512	Water quality monitoring and control systems, manufacturing
32551	Water repellent coatings for wood, concrete and masonry, manufacturing
45439	Water selling, home distribution, retail
71399	Water slides, operation of
23822	Water softeners, installation
41612	Water softeners, wholesale
56199	Water softening and conditioning services
41792	Water softening equipment, commercial, wholesale
33331	Water softening equipment, manufacturing
41792	Water sterilization equipment, wholesale
23822	Water system balancing and testing, contractors

33242	Water tanks, heavy gauge metal, manufacturing
483213	Water taxi service, inland waterways
325999	Water treatment chemical preparations, manufacturing
33331	Water treatment equipment, manufacturing
23711	Water treatment plant construction
333611	Water turbines, manufacturing
23711	Water well drilling (except water intake wells in oil and gas fields)
33313	Water well drilling machinery, manufacturing
23711	Water well pumps and well piping systems, installation
31211	Water, artificially carbonated, manufacturing
325999	Water, distilled, manufacturing
31211	Water, naturally carbonated, purifying and bottling
31211	Water, purifying and bottling
44211	Waterbeds-retail
44122	Watercraft, retail
48831	Waterfront terminal operation
111219	Watermelon farming
41412	Waterproof footwear, wholesale
31332	Waterproofing clothing
31332	Waterproofing fabrics, for the trade
71394	Wave pools
33999	Wax figures (i.e., manikins), manufacturing
712119	Wax museums
32222	Waxed paper, made from purchased paper
32419	Waxes, petroleum, made from refined petroleum
32411	Waxes, petroleum, made in petroleum refineries
32561	Waxes, polishing (e.g., floor, furniture), manufacturing
41841	Waxes, wholesale
811192	Waxing and polishing, automotive
31332	Waxing fabrics and clothing
11221	Weanling (feeder) pigs, raising
33699	Weapons, self-propelled, manufacturing
54199	Weather forecasting services
332321	Weather strip, metal, manufacturing
23839	Weatherstripping installation
31499	Weatherstripping made from purchased textiles
32629	Weatherstripping, rubber, manufacturing
31321	Weaving and finishing of broad-woven fabrics (except rugs, tire fabric)

31321	Weaving broad-woven fabrics (except rugs, tire fabric)
31321	Weaving broad-woven felts
333299	Weaving machinery, manufacturing
31322	Weaving narrow fabrics
51821	Web hosting
54151	Web page developing
51913	Web search portals
54192	Wedding and portrait photography services
81299	Wedding chapels (except churches)
81299	Wedding planning services
56173	Weed control and fertilizing services (except for crops)
41413	Weft knit fabrics, wholesale
71394	Weight training centres
81219	Weight-reduction centres (non-medical)
311611	Weiners, sausages, luncheon meats and other prepared meat products (except poultry), produced in slaughtering plants
311614	Weiners, sausages, luncheon meats and other processed meat products (except poultry and small game), made from purchased meat
56159	Welcome centres
541899	Welcoming services (i.e., advertising services)
23819	Welding contractors, operating at site of construction
41723	Welding electrodes and wire, wholesale
33399	Welding electrodes, manufacturing
33399	Welding equipment, manufacturing
53249	Welding equipment, rental
81131	Welding equipment, repair and maintenance
41723	Welding machinery and equipment, wholesale
41723	Welding machinery and equipment, wholesale and repair
81131	Welding repair services (except construction)
33399	Welding wire or rod (i.e., coated or cored), manufacturing
332319	Weldments, manufacturing
213118	Well foundation building, at oil and gas wells, on a contract basis
213118	Well pumping, oil and gas, on a contract basis
211113	Well, natural gas
213118	Wells, cleaning out, bailing, swabbing, oil field
44814	Western wear retail
311221	Wet-milling corn and other vegetables
32561	Wetting agents, manufacturing

48721	Whale watching excursions
23799	Wharves, construction
41912	Wheat brokers, wholesale
11114	Wheat farming
11114	Wheat, spring, winter and durum, growing
41112	Wheat, wholesale
33637	Wheel centres and trim, motor vehicle, metal, stamping
334511	Wheel position indicators and transmitters, aircraft, manufacturing
33392	Wheelbarrows, manufacturing
33911	Wheelchairs, manufacturing
33639	Wheels (i.e., rims), automotive, truck and bus, manufacturing
32791	Wheels, abrasive, manufacturing
41529	Wheels, motor vehicle, new, wholesale
32791	Wheels, polishing and grinding, manufacturing
311515	Whey butter, manufacturing
311515	Whey, condensed, dried, evaporated and powdered, manufacturing
311515	Whey, raw, liquid, manufacturing
311515	Whipped topping, dry mix, manufacturing
311511	Whipped toppings (except frozen or dry mix), manufacturing
311511	Whipping cream, manufacturing
49319	Whisky warehousing
31214	Whisky, manufacturing
32513	White extender pigments (e.g., barytes, blanc fixé, whiting), manufacturing
71399	White water rafting, recreational
56152	Wholesale tour operators
81391	Wholesalers' associations
41899	Wholesalers of coal and coke
337126	Wicker and reed furniture, manufacturing
33421	Wide area network communications equipment (e.g., bridges, gateways, routers), manufacturing
41899	Wigs and hairpieces, wholesale
33999	Wigs, wiglets, toupees, hair pieces, manufacturing
11321	Wild berry picking
112999	Wild boar, raising
11321	Wild rice gathering
11119	Wild rice, farming
721213	Wilderness camps (except hunting and fishing camps)
91291	Wildlife conservation programs, provincial government
81331	Wildlife preservation advocacy organizations
71219	Wildlife sanctuaries

212231	Willemite mining
33392	Winches, manufacturing
221119	Wind electric power generation
23713	Wind energy equipment, construction
41711	Wind machines (frost protection equipment), wholesale
41711	Wind machines (frost protection equipment), wholesale and repair
333611	Wind powered turbine-generator sets, manufacturing
315229	Windbreakers (except leather), men's and boys', cut and sewn from purchased fabric
315239	Windbreakers (except leather), women's, misses' and girls', cut and sewn from purchased fabric
315292	Windbreakers, leather, men's and boys', manufacturing
31311	Winding, spooling, beaming and rewinding purchased yarn
33311	Windmills, farm type, manufacturing
326196	Window and door manufacturing, plastic or fibreglass
32561	Window cleaning preparations, manufacturing
561721	Window cleaning services
541899	Window dressing or trimming services
321911	Window frames and sash, wood and covered wood, manufacturing
332619	Window screening, made from purchased wire
332321	Window screens, metal frame, manufacturing
81149	Window shade repair shops (without retail sales of new equipment)
23839	Window shades and blinds installation, contractors
41439	Window shades and blinds, wholesale
32613	Window sheeting, laminated plastics, manufacturing
326114	Window sheeting, unlaminated plastics, manufacturing
811122	Window tinting, automotive
321911	Window units, wood and covered wood, manufacturing
41639	Windows and doors (except wooden), wholesale
326196	Windows and window frames, plastics, manufacturing
33639	Windshield wiper blades and refills, manufacturing
33632	Windshield wiper systems, automotive, truck and bus, manufacturing
326198	Windshields, plastics, manufacturing

31213	Wine (grape, berry or other fruit), manufacturing
41911	Wine and spirits, business to business (B2B) electronic markets, wholesale
41322	Wine coolers, alcoholic, wholesale
31213	Wine coolers, manufacturing
453992	Wine making supplies, retail
44531	Wine stores, retail
31213	Wineries
41322	Wines, wholesale
33641	Wing assemblies and parts, aircraft, manufacturing
11114	Winter wheat, growing
333299	Wire and cable insulating machinery, manufacturing
331317	Wire cloth, made in aluminum wire drawing plants
337215	Wire display racks, manufacturing
333519	Wire drawing machines, metalworking, manufacturing
41639	Wire fences, gates and accessories, wholesale
331222	Wire garment hangers, iron or steel, made in wire drawing plants
332619	Wire mesh, concrete reinforcing, made from purchased wire
33111	Wire products, iron or steel, made in steel mills
331222	Wire products, iron or steel, made in wire drawing plants
331317	Wire products, made in aluminum wire drawing plants
33142	Wire products, made in copper wire drawing plants
41621	Wire rods, wholesale
33392	Wire rope hoists, manufacturing
331317	Wire screening, made in aluminum wire drawing plants
41621	Wire screening, wholesale
51911	Wire services, news
331317	Wire, aluminum, made in wire drawing plants
331317	Wire, armoured, made in aluminum wire drawing plants
331317	Wire, bare, made in aluminum wire drawing plants
33142	Wire, copper and copper alloy, made in wire drawing plants
331221	Wire, flat, rolled strip, made from purchased iron or steel
331317	Wire, insulated, made in aluminum wire drawing plants
41611	Wire, insulated, wholesale

331222	Wire, iron or steel (e.g., armoured, bare or insulated), made in wire drawing plants
331222	Wire, iron or steel, electric, made in wire drawing plants
33149	Wire, non-ferrous metal (except aluminum, copper), made in wire drawing plants
517112	Wireless cable television operators
51721	Wireless data communications carriers
51721	Wireless telephone communications carriers
51721	Wireless video service
41611	Wiring devices and related electrical supplies, wholesale
33632	Wiring harness and ignition sets, for internal combustion engines, manufacturing
212398	Withrite mining or quarrying
212299	Wolframite mining
41912	Women's and children outerwear, wholesale agents and brokers
41411	Women's clothing wholesale
44812	Women's clothing, stores
31621	Women's footwear (except orthopedic extension shoes), manufacturing
812115	Women's hair stylist shop
113311	Wood chips produced in the forest
321111	Wood chips, made in sawmills
41891	Wood chips, wholesale
454319	Wood dealers, fuel, retail
32519	Wood distillates, manufacturing
321911	Wood door frames and sash, manufacturing
333299	Wood drying kilns, manufacturing
32551	Wood fillers, manufacturing
23833	Wood floor finishing (e.g., coating, sanding)
44221	Wood flooring, installation combined with selling
321919	Wood flooring, manufacturing
23813	Wood frame components, installation
32519	Wood oils, manufacturing
56199	Wood piling
321114	Wood products, treating with creosote or other preservatives
322112	Wood pulp, chemical, manufacturing
322111	Wood pulp, mechanical or semi-chemical, manufacturing
41899	Wood pulp, wholesale
23817	Wood siding, installation
41632	Wood siding, wholesale
321919	Wood squares, unfinished blanks, manufacturing
32551	Wood stains, manufacturing

41841	Wood treating preparations, wholesale
321911	Wood window frames and sash, manufacturing
442298	Woodburning stoves, retail
321919	Woodwork, interior and ornamental (e.g., windows, doors, sash, mantels), manufacturing
41723	Woodworking and sawmill, machinery, equipment and supplies, wholesale
53249	Woodworking machinery and equipment rental
33321	Woodworking machines (except hand-held), manufacturing
49313	Wool and mohair warehousing
31322	Wool fabric, narrow woven (i.e., 30 cm/12 in. or less in width), weaving
31321	Wool fabrics, broad-woven, weaving
31321	Wool felts, broad-woven, weaving
11241	Wool production, farming
31311	Wool yarn, spinning
41119	Wool, raw, wholesale
31194	Worcestershire sauce, manufacturing
56141	Word processing service
31621	Work boots and shoes, manufacturing
81233	Work clothing supply services, industrial
31599	Work gloves, leather, manufacturing
91124	Work safety and health program administration, federal government
315229	Work shirts, men's and boys', cut and sewn from purchased fabric
72131	Workers' camp or hostel (at work site)
524129	Workmen's compensation, insurance
81331	World peace and understanding advocacy groups
11421	Worm gathering
112999	Worm production
41111	Worms, wholesale
48841	Wrecker service (towing), motor vehicle
41811	Wreckers, auto, wholesale
33221	Wrenches, hand tools, non-powered, manufacturing
711329	Wrestling event promoters, without facilities
711319	Wrestling promoters, with facilities
711513	Writers, independent
325999	Writing inks, manufacturing
32223	Writing paper, cut sheet, made from purchased paper
337126	Wrought iron furniture, manufacturing
212299	Wulfenite mining
212398	Wurtzilite mining

X

334512	X-ray apparatus and tubes (e.g., control, industrial, medical, research), manufacturing
325999	X-ray films and plates, sensitized, manufacturing
54138	X-ray inspection service
62151	X-ray laboratories, medical
41793	X-ray machines and related equipment and supplies, wholesale
32511	Xylene, made from refined petroleum or natural gas liquids
32411	Xylene, made in petroleum refineries

Y

71393	Yacht clubs (i.e., operating marinas)
71399	Yacht clubs, without marinas
41799	Yacht sales, wholesale
53229	Yachts rental
336612	Yachts, building, not done in shipyards
111211	Yam farming
45113	Yard goods (textile fabric), retail
41413	Yard goods, textile, wholesale
113312	Yarding, timber, on contract
41413	Yarn and thread, wholesale
31331	Yarn bleaching, dyeing and finishing
31311	Yarn spinning mills
333299	Yarn texturizing machinery, manufacturing
31322	Yarn, elastic, fabric-covered, manufacturing
327214	Yarn, fibreglass, made in glass-making plants
32522	Yarn, monofilament, man-made, manufacturing
32522	Yarn, monofilament, man-made, manufacturing and texturizing
31311	Yarn, throwing, twisting and winding of purchased yarn
51119	Yearbooks (i.e., high school, college, university), publishing (except exclusively on Internet)
31199	Yeast, manufacturing
311511	Yogurt (except frozen), manufacturing
31152	Yogurt, frozen, manufacturing
41312	Yogurt, wholesale
62411	Youth centres
721198	Youth hostels, accommodations
62411	Youth self-help organizations
71399	Youths sports leagues or teams
212291	Yttrium ore mining

Z

32513	Zinc based pigments, manufacturing

325189	Zinc compounds, not specified elsewhere by process, manufacturing		33999	Zippers (i.e., slide fasteners), manufacturing
212231	Zinc ore, mining		41413	Zippers, wholesale
41892	Zinc ore, wholesale		212299	Zirconium ore mining
325189	Zinc oxide, manufacturing		33141	Zirconium smelting and primary refining
33149	Zinc rolling, drawing and extruding, purchased metal or scrap		71213	Zoological gardens
33141	Zinc smelting and primary refining		71213	Zoos
31322	Zipper tape, weaving			